Cases, Problems, and Materials on
BANKRUPTCY

Cases, Problems, and Materials on
BANKRUPTCY

Douglas G. Baird
Professor of Law
University of Chicago

Thomas H. Jackson
Professor of Law
Stanford University

Little, Brown and Company
Boston   **Toronto**

Library of Congress Catalog Card No. 84-82546

ISBN 0-316-07677-5

MV

Published simultaneously in Canada
by Little, Brown & Company (Canada) Limited

PRINTED IN THE UNITED STATES OF AMERICA

To Our Parents

SUMMARY OF CONTENTS

TABLE OF CONTENTS

Chapter 3
ASSESSING THE CLAIMS AGAINST
THE ESTATE 123

Chapter 4
DEFINING THE BASIC ESTATE 171

Chapter 5
THE POWERS OF THE TRUSTEE TO ENHANCE THE ESTATE   219

Chapter 6
TRUSTEE AVOIDING POWERS DIRECTED AT THE "OPT OUT" PROBLEM   **279**

Chapter 7
PRESERVING THE ESTATE 361

Chapter 8
CONCLUDING THE CASE: PAYOUT (PRIORITIES)   **547**

Chapter 9

BANKRUPTCY ALTERNATIVES TO LIQUIDATION: REORGANIZATIONS UNDER CHAPTER 11

Chapter 10
BANKRUPTCY'S "FRESH START" POLICY
FOR INDIVIDUALS   729

Chapter 12
BANKRUPTCY ALTERNATIVES TO
LIQUIDATION: "WAGE-EARNER'S" PLANS
UNDER CHAPTER 13   907

Chapter 13
JURISDICTION AND PROCEDURES OF
BANKRUPTCY COURTS   941

Chapter 14
STATE LAW COLLECTIVE PROCEEDINGS   997

PREFACE

Bankruptcy law has come of age. The passage of the Bankruptcy Reform Act of 1978 — the first major overhaul of our nation's bankruptcy law in 40 years — paralleled a major rise in the importance of bankruptcy law and the prestige of its practitioners. Bankruptcy law not only is the vehicle through which literally hundreds of thousands of individuals receive a "new opportunity in life and a clear field for future effort, unhampered by the pressure and discouragement of preexisting debt,"* but it also has become a major feature in the life cycle of some of our largest and most preeminent business firms — corporations such as Braniff, Manville, and Wickes. Its importance, moreover, seems now to be largely independent of growth and recession cycles, as the bankruptcy of numerous computer firms in the healthy "high-tech" industry attests. This upsurge in interest is a mixed blessing. As bankruptcy law becomes more visible, special interest lobbying is more likely, and tinkering with the statute may become more frequent. The changes made by the Bankruptcy Amendments and Federal Judgeship Act of 1984, many of which respond more to the desires of particular groups than to uniform bankruptcy principles, amply attest to that.

We began this book with the conviction that bankruptcy law had not received the scrutiny that the old staples of the curriculum such as contracts and torts had. The function of a law school is to impart a basic sense of both how the law operates and what principles underlie it, yet the principles of bankruptcy law remained largely unexplored, in part because bankruptcy law was often buried in a course on general creditor remedies. We discovered that it was not sufficient to select principal cases and to develop problems that explore the intricacies of the statute. We found it necessary to write extensive notes that lay bare transactions and draw connections between cases and between various sections of the Bankruptcy Code. The result is a text that is somewhat longer than is typically used in a one semester course, but it is, we hope, a text that illuminates rather than confounds, and one that shows bankruptcy law to be as rich and as challenging a body of doctrine as any in the curriculum. The number of

---

* Local Loan Co. v. Hunt, 292 U.S. 234, 245 (1934).

principal cases, moreover, is easily manageable, and we find that most of the material can be covered in a one semester, three hour course.

The first chapter of the book focuses on the enduring themes of bankruptcy, as well as orients the student to the world of individual creditor remedies against which bankruptcy operates. Thereafter, the materials are grouped into two distinct parts. Because we think the issues are conceptually distinct, we have attempted to separate out questions that essentially involve battles among competing claimants against a particular pool of assets from questions that concern what bankruptcy can (and can't) do for debtors who are individuals in pursuit of a "fresh start." For that reason, the focus of Chapters 2 through 9 is principally on reorganizing firms. Even though most of that material is equally applicable to liquidating businesses and to individual debtors, the issues are most vivid in the context of the corporate battle to survive. It is important, moreover, to see that the question of what happens to a corporation in bankruptcy is generally a question of who — creditors, shareholders, workers, or consumers, to name a few — has what rights to the corporate assets, and not a question of the rights of a corporate debtor (a fictitious legal entity) against its creditors. The benefits and costs of bankruptcy to individuals who use it so as to gain a fresh start are the subject of Chapters 10 through 12, and the focus is, accordingly, quite different. There, the question is much more one of what the individual debtor gets to keep from his existing creditors and why. The book closes with a look at the distinct jurisdictional provisions of bankruptcy law and with a look at state-law alternatives to the bankruptcy process.

We have found that bankruptcy law provides an intellectually exciting subject, and one on which far too little work has been done. While we have no illusions that these materials are the final word on an immensely complicated and interesting subject, we hope they will stimulate others to interest in and debate over the issues that we have found so engaging.

D.G.B.
T.H.J.

April 1985

ACKNOWLEDGMENTS

These materials have benefitted from innumerable discussions with many other academics, practitioners, and students. There is no adequate way we can thank all of them for their input. We would, however, like to thank our research assistants Timothy Moore (Stanford J.D. '85), David Crowley (Chicago J.D. '86), and Barbara St. Clair (Chicago J.D. '86) for their valuable help and Carroll Rudy for her hours of work in preparing these materials for classroom use and for publication.

We express our thanks to authors and publishers for permission to reprint portions of the following copyrighted material.

Clark, The Duties of the Corporate Debtor to Its Creditors, 90 Harv. L. Rev. 505 (1977). Copyright © 1977 by The Harvard Law Review Association. Reprinted by permission of the author and The Harvard Law Review Association.

Clark, The Interdisciplinary Study of Legal Evolution, 90 Yale L.J. 1238 (1981). Reprinted by permission of the author, The Yale Law Journal Company, and Fred B. Rothman & Company.

Coogan, Confirmation of a Plan Under the Bankruptcy Code, 32 Case W. L. Rev. 301 (1982). Copyright © 1984 by Matthew Bender & Co., Inc. and reprinted with permission from UCC Secured Transactions.

Countryman, Executory Contracts in Bankruptcy, 57 Minn. L. Rev. 439 (1973).

Countryman, The Uses of State Law in Bankruptcy Cases (Part I), 47 N.Y.U. L. Rev. 407, 438, 450–452, 158–461, 473–474 (1972).

Eisenberg, Bankruptcy Law in Perspective, 28 U.C.L.A. L. Rev. 953 (1981). Originally published in 28 U.C.L.A. L. Rev. 953. Copyright © 1981, The Regents of the University of California. All rights reserved.

Jackson, Bankruptcy, Non-Bankruptcy Entitlements, and the Creditors' Bargain, 91 Yale L.J. 857 (1982). Reprinted by permission of the author, The Yale Law Journal Company, and Fred B. Rothman & Company.

Jackson, Translating Assets and Liabilities to the Bankruptcy Forum, 14 J. Legal Studies 73 (1985).

Landers, A Unified Approach to Parent, Subsidiary, and Affiliate

Questions in Bankruptcy, 42 U. Chi. L. Rev. 589 (1975). Reprinted by permission of the author and the University of Chicago Law Review.

Landers, Another Word on Parents, Subsidiaries and Affiliates in Bankruptcy, 43 U. Chi. L. Rev. 527 (1976). Reprinted by permission of the author and the University of Chicago Law Review.

McCoid, Bankruptcy, Preferences and Efficiency: An Expression of Doubt, 67 Va. L. Rev. 249, 264–265 (1981). Reprinted by permission of the author, the Virginia Law Review Association, and Fred B. Rothman & Company.

Note, Substantive Consolidations in Bankruptcy: A Flow-of-Assets Approach, 65 Calif. L. Rev. 720 (1977). Reprinted by permission of the author, the California Law Review, and Fred B. Rothman & Company.

Posner, The Rights of Creditors of Affiliated Corporations, 43 U. Chi. L. Rev. 499 (1976). Reprinted by permission of the author and the University of Chicago Law Review.

EDITORS' NOTE ON CITATIONS
AND CONVENTIONS

Bankruptcy Code sections are cited by section number only (e.g., §544(a)). The Bankruptcy Code is usually referred to as "the Bankruptcy Code," while the Bankruptcy Act of 1898 is referred to as "the 1898 Act" or "the old Act." Since a number of the cases discuss the Bankruptcy Code prior to the 1984 Amendments, we have noted by footnote when a statutory section cited in a principal case has been renumbered or where a statutory section quoted in a principal case has been reworded, whether or not those changes would have been important to the issues being decided. Ellipses have been used to indicate deletion of material, whether portions of sentences or paragraphs. The original footnote numbering is retained. References to "the legislative history" without more refer to the 1977 House Report, H.R. Rep. No. 595, 95th Cong., 1st Sess., the 1978 Senate Report, S. Rep. 989, 95th Cong., 2d Sess., or the floor statements (in lieu of a conference report) of Senator DeConcinni and Representative Edwards, 124 Cong. Rec. H11,089 et seq.; S17,406 et. seq. (1978). Because access to statutes other than the Bankruptcy Code is sometimes necessary, we recommend that instructors assign "Commercial and Debtor-Creditor Law: Selected Statutes" (D. Baird, T. Eisenberg and T. Jackson, eds.). In addition to including all statutory material needed for teaching most courses on commercial law, it has been designed to complement the coverage of this book.

Cases, Problems, and Materials on
BANKRUPTCY

Chapter 1
DEBT AND DEBT COLLECTION

A. INDIVIDUAL DEBT COLLECTION PROCEDURES

1. *Extensions of Credit and Bankruptcy Rules*

Many extensions of credit help both debtor and creditor. A firm borrows to develop and market a new product. The profits enable the firm to repay the loan and still leave it with more than it would have had if the loan had never been made. The creditor recovers the principal with interest. Of course, to say that extensions of credit often promote the interests of debtor and creditor is not to say that they always do. People made poor decisions, and sometimes even well-calculated plans turn out badly. A necessary corollary of a contract-based credit economy, however, is that people must be free to make poor decisions as well as good ones, and they should for the most part suffer the consequences of their decisions. Legal rules, of course, have a role to play in ensuring that borrowers are protected from overreaching creditors and that relevant information is made available. Nevertheless, the willingness of individuals and firms alike to make loans depends on their degree of confidence that, as long as they stay within the bounds of well-defined legal rules, they will be repaid. Commerce as we know it can thrive only if the obligation of the debtor is legally enforceable: If a debtor does not pay what it owes, a creditor must be able to call upon the state for help. Without legal rules, contracting with others would be enormously difficult. See Kronman, Contract Law and the State of Nature, 1 Yale J. Law Econ. & Organ. — (1985).

In a world where people need to obtain — or give — credit many times, borrowers may be as concerned about their reputations as the threat of legal coercion. See R. Axelrod, The Evolution of Cooperation (1984); Macauley, Non-Contractual Relations in Business: A Preliminary Study, 28 Am. Soc. Rev. 55 (1963). Nonetheless, legal rules governing the collection of debts are in the background of every credit transaction. Much turns

1

on how well crafted those rules are. If they are cumbersome and ineffective, creditors will be more reluctant to lend and debtors will find it harder and more expensive to borrow. On the other hand, if these rules allow for creditors to behave in a way that is arbitrary and capricious, people as well as firms will be less likely to borrow, and creditors and borrowers alike will be worse off.

The rules governing debt collection, like legal rules generally, have both a procedural and a substantive component. These rules in the first instance tell creditors *how* to enforce their claims against their debtor. As a general matter, unless a creditor has taken a security interest — that is, unless it has contracted for collateral to support the loan — a creditor typically has to sue its debtor. If the creditor prevails in the lawsuit and "reduces its claim to judgment," as it is typically called, the creditor may call upon the clerk of the court and others (such as the sheriff) to enforce the judgment. Enforcement of the judgment may involve foreclosing on real property, physically seizing (or "levying upon") personal property, or requiring some third party (such as an employer) to pay part of what it owes the debtor directly to the creditor. This last procedure is usually called garnishment. As we explore in the next note, the procedures that are used vary from one jurisdiction to another, although their basic contours are the same.

But these rules also demarcate the substantive rights of creditors and debtors. In most states, for example, a creditor can lay claim only to a percentage of a worker's wages, and a creditor cannot look to certain types of other property (such as spendthrift trusts, clothes, or tools of trade) to satisfy obligations owed that creditor. In the case of a general partnership, creditors can look to the assets of individual partners, but in the case of a corporation, creditors can usually reach only the assets of the corporation itself, and not the assets of those who own shares of stock in the corporation.

This book focuses on the special set of rules governing debt collection that comes into play when a bankruptcy petition is filed. A bankruptcy petition can be filed either by a group of creditors or by the debtor. Once this petition is filed, the substantive and procedural rules of debt collection change. The questions that will be constantly before us are why we need this second set of rules and how we can justify the procedural and substantive differences between the rights of creditors and debtors before and after the filing of a bankruptcy petition.

The most prominent feature of our bankruptcy law is probably the discharge it offers individuals. It is a truism that bankruptcy aids the "honest but unfortunate" debtor. If an individual files a bankruptcy petition, that individual usually has the right to be free of past obligations and enjoy a "fresh start" unencumbered by past misfortune. But this substantive right, which individual debtors enjoy only inside of bankruptcy, explains little of the complexity of the current Bankruptcy Code, much of which arises from the problems caused by sorting out rights among creditors. Corporations, unlike individuals, already have limited liability under state law. Shareholders of a corporation in financial trouble can dissolve the corporation under state law and start a new one without ever filing a bankruptcy petition. In nearly all cases, creditors cannot reach assets that shareholders have not contributed to the corporation. The issue when a corporation is in bankruptcy is not how much of the assets the creditors of the corporation will receive. (If the corporation owes more that it has, the creditors are entitled to everything the corporation — as opposed to its shareholders — own, although, as we will see in Chapter 9, they can contractually waive a part of that in a plan of reorganization under Chapter 11 of the Bankruptcy Code.) The issue is how to divide what there is among the corporation's claimants. Corporations, like individuals, usually have many claimants. Bankruptcy law is complicated precisely because, instead of a single creditor trying to satisfy its claim against a pool of assets, there are many creditors. The questions that concern us most in these first chapters are the procedural ones of how a bankruptcy proceeding is structured, who participates in the process, and how the rights of participants are sorted out. These problems, unlike the question of an individual's "fresh start," cut across all types of bankruptcy cases — from those involving giant corporations to those involving individuals. After those questions have been addressed, we shall turn to the provisions of the Bankruptcy Code that focus on the individual debtor and what it means to give such a debtor a financial fresh start.

To take measure of the Bankruptcy Code, we first need to know how it changes the rules that exist without it. The basic question to ask is how a creditor goes about recovering from an uncooperative debtor when no bankruptcy petition has been filed.

2. Individual Collection of Money Judgments Under State Law

Fundamental to understanding the bankruptcy process is some understanding of individual creditor rights in the absence of bankruptcy. One needs a basic understanding of the essential differences between (a) a general creditor, (b) an execution (or lien or judgment) creditor, and (c) a secured creditor. The materials in this chapter provide an overview of the rights and remedies of these creditors. In reading these materials, two principal questions should be kept in mind. First, what rights does a particular creditor have against a *debtor* or the debtor's property? This question is fundamentally a two-party issue and, as such, is principally governed by general rules of contract law. Bankruptcy has a role to play here, particularly with respect to discharge of individual debtors and associated issues. We shall examine these issues in Chapters 10 through 12. Second, what rights does a particular creditor have against other *creditors* (or other claimants) to the debtor's property? This second issue is generally referred to as a "priority" issue, and it is fundamental to understanding the ordering of individual creditor claims and to many of the rules of bankruptcy. In the sense used here, "priority" means the legal right of a particular creditor to use (i.e., to take over and sell) the debtor's property to satisfy a debt to that creditor before the claims of other creditors are satisfied. The principal priority question, in turn, is: *When* does one creditor gain priority over another as to a particular asset of their common debtor?

We start by examining the rights and remedies of a garden-variety creditor. The details of the debt collection process vary, but the basic steps are relatively constant across time and place. Although we shall examine a fairly simple transaction, most of the following discussion applies equally to larger and more complex arrangements.

Supplier sells suits to local clothing stores on open account. Supplier usually requires these stores to pay it within 30 days. Supplier discovers that one of its customers, Retailer, has not paid for the suits it sent over 40 days before. Supplier will probably start by sending Retailer another bill. If this tactic fails, Supplier will have additional nonjudicial remedies. Supplier can stop any new shipments. It can also plead with Retailer, or, if Supplier is careful, threaten him with lawsuits. Supplier can also discount its claim to a collection agency that will do the same things as Supplier, but perhaps more effectively. (In that case, of course, the inquiry of creditors' remedies has simply been shifted from Supplier to a third party.) Supplier might also put pressure on Retailer by reporting Retailer's name to a creditors' checking bureau, which may adversely affect Retailer's chances of getting credit in the future.

These remedies are not trivial: through them, Supplier may be able to literally destroy Retailer's ability to get credit in the future. But they may not be enough. Retailer may simply be unwilling — or unable — to pay Supplier and all its other creditors in full. Supplier's remaining remedies, then, essentially involve the judicial process. As an unsecured creditor, Supplier is not permitted, without the actual consent of Retailer (or its agent), to go to Retailer's store and take back the suits, or, indeed to take any other property of Retailer (such as shirts or overcoats of roughly equivalent value). Generally speaking, self-help remedies are not available to unsecured creditors. (Secured creditors have slightly greater rights, as we shall examine later in this chapter.)

Supplier's use of the court to make Retailer pay it will ultimately involve the court's assistance in the two distinct issues we have already set out: property and priority. The first issue concerns the assistance the court will give Supplier to gain access to Retailer's property. This is an aspect of rights between Supplier and Retailer — a part of Supplier's "property" rights. Second, the judicial process can also help Supplier prevail against Retailer's other creditors. It can, in other words, establish Supplier's "priority" right. Retailer may have delayed paying Supplier because Retailer is in financial trouble. Retailer may be behind in its obligations to many others in addition to Supplier. If Retailer is insolvent — that is, if Retailer's liabilities to all its creditors exceed Retailer's assets — some of Retailer's creditors will not be paid. Supplier's "priority right" marks Supplier's place in line; it determines Supplier's right to be paid in relation to the rights of other creditors and will establish whether Supplier will be paid in full, in part, or perhaps not at all.

Priority right

To establish either its property right or its priority right, Supplier must follow an established set of procedures. The remedies that are available to Supplier can be roughly divided into two sorts: remedies available at the start of a lawsuit and those that become available following the successful conclusion of a lawsuit.

a.   Pre-Judgment Remedies

At the early stages of its lawsuit, before Supplier has proven its case, Supplier may be able to take advantage of a "pre-judgment" or "provisional" remedy. These pre-judgment or provisional remedies vary from one jurisdiction to another, but they come in two principal varieties: attachment and garnishment. An attachment, even if used only for jurisdictional purposes, gives Supplier a *res* — specific items of property — from which Supplier's claim, once reduced to judgment, can be satisfied. Many jurisdictions limit the class of creditors that can use attachment (for example, to creditors whose claims arise out of contract) and also the *grounds* for attachment (such as establishing that the debtor is likely to hide assets during the pendency of the lawsuit). A number of statutory restrictions limit prejudgment remedies. Moreover, a series of Supreme Court cases in the early 1970s placed significant limits on the ability of an unsecured creditor to "attach" or "garnish" property of its debtor as a pre-judgment remedy without first having some sort of notice and hearing before a judicial officer. See North Georgia Finishing, Inc. v. Di-Chem, Inc., 419 U.S. 601 (1975); Mitchell v. W.T. Grant Co., 416 U.S. 600 (1974); Fuentes v. Shevin, 407 U.S. 67 (1972). Most states have amended their statutory procedures to take account of these constitutional requirements.

a Attachment

If Supplier meets all the tests for attachment, the court will issue a "writ of attachment," addressed to the sheriff, commanding the sheriff to "levy attachment" on the property described in the writ. (The term "levy attachment" simply describes how the sheriff obtains possession of the property; we examine the actual process of obtaining possession of property in somewhat greater detail when looking at post-judgment remedies.) The fact that the sheriff has levied on the property pursuant to Supplier's writ of attachment does not mean that Supplier may keep the property; Supplier might (for example) not win its lawsuit. Supplier must still obtain a judgment and then pursue its post-judgment remedies (although this will be simpler, due to the previous attachment). Until Supplier has obtained a judgment and has taken the prescribed additional steps, its attachment is "inchoate." But this does not mean the attachment is without consequence. By virtue of the attachment, Supplier has taken the property out of the hands of Retailer, who might otherwise have abused or hidden it.

The attachment, moreover, gives Supplier a set of rights against other potential third-party claimants to the property. In particular, Supplier's attachment will protect it — give it "priority" over — other unsecured creditors of Retailer, even if they prosecute their claims to judgment first and follow their post-judgment remedies first, as long as they did not get an attachment on the property in question before Supplier. It also protects Supplier's interest if the property is subsequently used as collateral for a loan or if it is sold. Except in a few cases, once the attachment has been properly completed through levy by the sheriff — and sometimes even before then — any transferee will take subject to Supplier's interest.

These rights can be summarized by saying that Supplier's attachment gives it a "lien" — or actually an "attachment lien." (As we shall soon see, there are many different types of liens.) Supplier's attachment lien on personal property will also make Supplier a "lien creditor" within the meaning of the Uniform Commercial Code, a term of significance when evaluating Supplier's rights relative to those of a secured creditor.

b.   Post-Judgment Remedies

We now jump from the beginning of the lawsuit to the end. In examining post-judgment remedies, it is simpler if we assume that no pre-judgment remedy (such as attachment) was available, or that one was not obtained. In order to proceed against Retailer's property, Supplier must first win its lawsuit. There may be a contested proceeding before a judge or jury. If Retailer does not appear at all, Supplier may obtain a default judgment. (This happens most commonly in consumer finance transactions.) Assuming Supplier wins its lawsuit, the court will issue a "judgment." Judgments normally take a form resembling the following:

> It is ordered and adjudged that Plaintiff recover $500 from Defendant and that Plaintiff have execution therefor.

Liens on Real Property. The judgment is "docketed," which means it is recorded on a "judgment roll." A judgment is a lien (called, not suprisingly, a "judgment lien") on a debtor's real property in all states except Kentucky, Maine, Massachusetts, Michigan, New Hampshire, Rhode Island, and Vermont. States are split on whether the judgment lien arises when the judgment is rendered or docketed. In three states —

Alabama, Georgia, and Mississippi—the judgment lien extends to personal property. See generally S. Riesenfeld, Creditors' Remedies and Debtors' Protection 94-175 (3d ed. 1979). In many of the states that provide that a lien on real property arises only on docketing, the docketing must be in the county where the property is located—so a judgment rendered in one county must be docketed in all other counties in which the debtor has real property in order for it to cover that property. Once a judgment has been entered, however, docketing is a ministerial act (at least, within the jurisdiction of the court issuing the judgment).

The term "lien" covers a number of quite different things. A judgment lien does essentially the same thing as an attachment lien. A judgment lien usually does not give the creditor a right to immediate possession of the property. Often, a judgment lien merely encumbers the property in the creditor's favor—it establishes the creditor's place in line and fixes rights against third parties (transferees from the debtor as well as competing creditors). What the lien gives Supplier is a *right* to go after the property, and priority over all those who acquire later liens or who acquire the property after the lien arises. In some states, the judgment lien will ordinarily be enforced by levy and sale under a writ of execution. This levy creates yet another kind of lien, which is generally called an "execution lien." The execution lien will relate back to the date of the judgment lien for purposes of establishing priority. In other states, a foreclosure action is required. In some states, a levy may not be necessary and the creditor may simply obtain an order of sale.

In most jurisdictions in which a judgment or its docketing gives rise to a lien on real property, the lien even reaches property the debtor acquires after the judgment. There is a conflict of authority as to the relative priority of several judgment liens held by different creditors on after-acquired property. To illustrate, in year 1, *A* obtains a judgment against Debtor and dockets his judgment in Cook County; in year 2, *B* obtains a judgment against Debtor and she also dockets her judgment in Cook County. In year 3, Debtor purchases real property in Cook County. Does *A*'s judgment lien on the real property acquired by Debtor in year 3 have priority over *B*'s judgment lien on the same property? Some courts would rule that priority was governed by the order of docketing. A majority of courts, however, that order priorities by the date of docketing with respect to existing property, would find that *A* and *B*'s judgments attach simultaneously to after-acquired property, and thus the liens are of equal standing.

Liens on Personal Property. In order to reach Retailer's personal property, such as the suits it sold it, Supplier would, in virtually every jurisdiction, have to do more than simply ensure that its judgment was entered on the docket roll. The docketing of the judgment gives Supplier only the right to obtain a "writ of execution" from the clerk of the court. A writ of execution is essentially a collection device, which will be issued as a matter of course. As with the writ of attachment, it is addressed to the sheriff, and directs the sheriff to seize and (unlike a writ of attachment) sell sufficient property of Retailer to pay the judgment entered in Supplier's favor. The writ of execution gives the sheriff a stated period of time in which to levy upon the property — usually 60 or 90 days — at the end of which the writ expires, and a new one must be issued.

The levy by the sheriff on personal property creates an "execution lien." The priority right of Supplier, therefore, would normally date from the time of the levy. In some states, however, once the levy is obtained, priority is dated back to the time the writ of execution was issued, or perhaps from the time that the writ of execution was delivered to the sheriff. In those states in which a levy is necessary to establish a lien for real property as well as personal property, notice must be given the debtor and the person in possession, if that is someone else. To put third parties on notice, a copy of the execution lien must also be recorded in the appropriate land office.

Unlike a levy on real property, a levy on tangible personal property requires that the sheriff take possession of the property, or deprive the debtor or any lessee of use of the property — by removing a crucial component from a machine or by padlocking the warehouse in which goods are stored, for example. Differences in the nature of the property leads to different procedures. Land is not going to go anywhere, but chattels may. As for personal property in the hands of a third party that is not capable of delivery, the levy must be by notice. If the personal property involved is intangible, such as a debt owed by someone else to the debtor, the levy involves a "garnishment," which also requires notice to the person who owes the debt. Garnishment is used to reach an individual's wages. Every employer is a debtor of its employees to the extent they have done work for which they have not been paid.

In levying, the sheriff faces a dilemma. On the one hand, if the sheriff takes the wrong property — property that belongs to someone other than Retailer — the true owner can not only recover its property, it can also sue the sheriff for conversion. On the other hand, if the sheriff is too cautious, and does not levy on enough property to satisfy Supplier's claim, Supplier can sue the sheriff for the difference. The sheriff, however, is usually able to insist on an indemnification bond from the creditor before seizing the debtor's property.

After the property has been taken, a sale will be held. Such sales are usually heavily regulated to protect the debtor and junior creditors. For example, in some states, the property must be appraised, and cannot be sold for less than a stated percentage of the appraised value, which is then called the "upset" price. The modern tendency has been to expand the debtor-protective devices surrounding the sale. Although the sale is run by the sheriff (and unlike a judicial sale is not actually overseen by the court awarding the judgment), a court may undo the sale for sufficient cause, such as fraud. Insufficient price alone, however, is generally not enough. Any surplus proceeds resulting from the sale (after the payment of expenses and the judgment under which the property was seized and sold) are returned to the debtor. Purchasers of the property usually take free of the judgment/execution lien.

As a practical matter, sheriff's sales bring less than sales of comparable goods would bring in a traditional market. Used goods (which goods seized from a debtor typically are) usually sell at a sizable discount. Moreover, goods sold at a sheriff's sale come without any warranty. And, unlike an entrepreneur who depends upon profits from sales for a livelihood, the sheriff has no incentive to invest a lot of energy in selling the goods for the best possible price. The creditor has an incentive to ensure only that the goods are sold for enough to repay him what is owed. Creating legal rules that make the sheriff or the creditor behave the same way as an owner would in selling property has proved very difficult.

The problems that follow focus on selected provisions of the New York Civil Practice Law and Rules (CPLR), Article 52 (Enforcement of Money Judgments), which are contained in Selected Commercial and Debtor-Creditor Statutes (D. Baird, T. Eisenberg, and T. Jackson eds.). These problems should give you a sense of post-judgment collection remedies available to a creditor under one state's law. Though the problems may turn on narrow questions of New York law, they make plain at least two basic features of state collection law that are of great significance to the jurisprudence of bankruptcy in sorting out rights among creditors. First, state collection law is a "race of diligence" or, expressed from a different viewpoint, a species of "grab law." In general, creditors who are quickest to exercise their rights against a debtor obtain "priority" in the debtor's assets against other parties who claim similar rights. Second, creditors may obtain "liens" by judicial process in specific property of a debtor in order to secure their position before the ultimate satisfaction of their judgments.

PROBLEMS

1.1 *Levy Upon Personal Property.* Creditor sued Debtor for breach of contract in the appropriate court in New York. After a jury verdict for Creditor, the court entered judgment against Debtor on September 1 for $60,000. Debtor refuses to pay that judgment voluntarily.

a. On September 1, the day Creditor obtained her judgment against Debtor, the judgment was duly docketed by the clerk of the court. On September 2, Debtor sold her color television for $250 to her friend, Buyer-1, who knew of the judgment. On September 3, Creditor's lawyer went over to the clerk's office, and on the basis of the judgment asked for and received a document called an "execution." See CPLR §5230. On

September 4, Debtor sold five cases of Bordeaux wine for $500 to Buyer-2, who also knew of the judgment. On September 5, Creditor's lawyer brought the execution over to Sheriff, the sheriff of the county, and gave it to him. On September 6, Debtor sold her automobile for $1,400 to Buyer-3, who knew of the judgment. On September 8, Creditor's lawyer and Sheriff drove over to Debtor's house, where Debtor and her three friends happened to be sitting in the front yard discussing a tennis game. The automobile was parked in front, and the recently sold television and wine were in the trunk. Following the directions of Creditor's lawyer, Sheriff served each of the four with a copy of the execution, and then stepped into the car and drove it away. Read CPRL §5232. After giving a proper "public notice" of a sale of the television, wine, and car, Sheriff sold these items at a public auction on September 28 for the net amounts of $100, $50, and $1,500, to three purchasers. On September 29, he began wondering what rights Creditor, Debtor, and Buyer-1, -2, and -3 had in the $1,650 proceeds that he held. Vaguely alarmed, Sheriff consulted his attorney. What advice should Sheriff be given? See CPLR §§5202, 5234(a).

   b. CPLR §5202 deliberately does not use the word "lien" in describing a judgment creditor's rights in the debtor's personal property subject to an execution. In many states, the sheriff's "levying" upon property — that is, seizure of it under a writ of execution (or, in the case of property not readily seized and carried away, e.g., a pin-setting machine in a bowling alley, dismantling of the property, appointing a custodian for it, or service of the writ upon its possessor) — gives rise at that moment to a "lien" in favor of the judgment creditor on whose behalf the execution was issued. Subject to various constraints, the lien gives the creditor an interest in the property superior to that of subsequent purchasers, judgment creditors, secured parties, statutory lienors, and the like. Under prior New York law, it was said that delivery of the writ of execution to the sheriff (as opposed to actual levy) created a kind of "lien," though good faith purchasers before actual levy and without notice of the execution's issuance were still protected. Might this still be said today? The next problem shows why this question has more than semantic importance.

   1.2 *Levy Upon Personal Property: Execution Creditor Versus Execution Creditor.* Neighbor is keeping in his basement, for Debtor, Debtor's not-readily-removable model train installation, which is worth $2,000. On September 14, Creditor-1 obtains a money judgment in the amount of $1,500 against Debtor. On September 15, Creditor-2 gets a money judgment in the amount of $1,600 against Debtor. On September 16, Creditor-2 obtains an execution from the clerk of the court and delivers it to Sheriff. On September 17, Creditor-1 obtains an execution from the clerk of the court and delivers it to Sheriff. On September 18, Sheriff serves a copy of Creditor-1's execution on Neighbor. On September 19, she serves a copy of Creditor-2's execution on Neighbor. After the train installation is sold at an execution sale, who, as between Creditor-1 and Creditor-2, has priority in the proceeds? See CPLR §§5202, 5232, 5234(b).

1.3 *Income Execution (Wage Garnishment and the Like).* **a.** Debtor is employed as a management consultant by Consulting Firm, at an annual gross salary of $35,000. Creditor obtains a judgment against Debtor for $40,000. Creditor wants to know how it might go about "garnishing" Debtor's wages, how much it can garnish, and whether it will obtain anything comparable to a lien by using a garnishment-type procedure. Read CPLR §§5231 and 5205.

b. Creditor also wants to know if there is some way of garnishing, or otherwise getting at, Debtor's large collection of vintage wine in the hands of Warehouse Company, as well as Debtor's checking account. Read CPLR §5232.

1.4 *Enforcement Against Real Property.* Creditor obtains a judgment against Debtor for $50,000. After the judgment is docketed in the county clerk's office, what are Creditor's rights in Debtor's residence? Look at CPLR §5203. In what major respects does it differ from CPLR §5202? Regardless of what a superficial reading of CPLR §5203 might suggest, liens on real estate are not always "automatic," and a judgment may be enforced against real estate despite the judgment creditor's never having had a lien on the property. Look again at CPLR §5230(b), and notice that an execution may direct the sheriffs "of one or more counties of the state" to satisfy the judgment out of the "real and personal" property of the debtor. Thus, for example, if Creditor's judgment were obtained and docketed in *A* County, but Debtor's residence was located in nearby *B* County, Creditor could obtain an execution directed to the sheriff of *B* County, and could share in the proceeds of a subsequent sheriff's sale of the residence *without* docketing a transcript of Creditor's judgment with the clerk of *B* County or filing a notice of levy there. CPLR §5236. But, as CPLR §5203 makes clear, unless Creditor had either docketed a transcript of the judgment with the clerk of *B* County, or filed a notice of levy, Creditor would not have obtained a *lien.* Consequently, the rights of some third party might intervene between the time of levy and the time of sale and be superior to those of Creditor if it neglected to record the required public notice of its interest in the *B* County clerk's records. (These rules preserve the reliability of public real estate records.)

How might Creditor's rights in Debtor's residence be enforced? Look at CPLR §5236. Several points should be noted about the provisions concerning sale of real property. First, the judgment debtor is not given a right of redemption (as under prior New York law). Second, there is no requirement that execution be levied first against personal property. Third, if two judgment creditors of a debtor have their judgments docketed at different times with the county clerk, the judgment first docketed will usually have priority even if an execution on the later-docketed judgment is first issued and levied upon. CPLR §5236(c) makes it encumbent upon the creditor whose judgment is first levied upon to furnish the sheriff a list of other judgment creditors of the debtor, who is then required to notify the other judgment creditors before the sale. The notice gives them the chance to issue execution on their own judgments and thereby to secure their priorities in the sale proceeds under CPLR §5236(e) and (g). Contrast the priority rules governing creditors seeking satisfaction out of the personal property of a debtor: Priority depends on the order of delivery of the executions to the sheriff, CPLR §5234(b). Why is this rule chosen, rather than one establishing priorities in the order in which the sheriff actually levies pursuant to the various executions?

3.   Exemptions for Individuals

In considering creditor remedies, we have been focusing on what may be considered to be "involuntary" remedies — remedies available to a creditor against a recalcitrant debtor. It is important to note that when the debtor is an individual, such involuntary remedies are not available against all of the debtor's property. In every state, some items of property held by an individual are exempt from the process of creditors. These exemptions come from two sources. First, all states have a list of property that is exempt from execution. Second, in most states, some property that is not explicitly on such a list is nonetheless not available for execution at the behest of a creditor, because it is defined as property that is not assignable. We shall see both kinds of exempt property when looking at the next problem. Moreover, one also needs to be aware that certain kinds of property may be exempt because of federal law. The Consumer Credit Protection Act, 15 U.S.C. §1601, for example, limits the extent to which any one creditor may garnish wages of an individual. See id., §303(a), 15 U.S.C. §1673(a) (garnishment of aggregate disposable earnings limited to the lesser of 25 percent or the amount by which the debtor's disposable earnings for a week exceed 30 times the federal minimum hourly wage). In addition, certain types of federal payments, such as Social Security payments, are not assignable and, accordingly, are exempt from creditor execution. See 42 U.S.C. §407.

Although every state has exemption laws, their content, as with creditor collection laws in general, varies from one state to another. Not only do states differ with respect to the sorts of property they exempt, but some are strikingly more generous to debtors than others. A number of exemption laws were passed decades ago, when our country was far more agrarian and when a dollar bought far more. The next problem addresses New York's exemption scheme.

PROBLEM

1.5 *Property Subject to Enforcement.* Creditor brought an action against Debtor for breach of contract in the appropriate court in New York. After a jury verdict for Creditor, the court entered judgment against Debtor in the amount of $60,000. Debtor owns the following: (1) a "homesteaded" residence worth $80,000 but subject to a recorded mortgage securing a $60,000 loan from First Bank; (2) an automobile owned free and clear, worth $1,500; (3) sofas, chairs, and miscellaneous household furniture worth $3,000; (4) a stereo worth $1,200; (5) a television worth $260; (6) three pedigreed Siamese cats worth $300 each, together with 500 eight ounce cans of specially made cat food; (7) a life insurance policy on which she is the insured and her parents are the beneficiaries, in the face amount of $50,000 and with a cash surrender value of $7,000; (8) a checking account with Second Bank, having a balance of $543; (9) a pending tort action for assault against Tortfeasor, who allegedly punched Debtor in the nose, causing $1,000 in actual damages and $40,000 in pain and suffering; (10) 100 shares (worth a total of $5,000) in Mutual Fund; and (11) a warehouse receipt issued by Warehouse Company and indicating that Warehouse Company is storing 50 cases of special cat food for her. Debtor is not married.

Creditor wants to know which of the listed assets can be reached to satisfy its judgment and which are exempt. Read CPLR §§5201, 5205, 5206. (We shall examine exemptions more closely, in Chapter 11, in connection with §522 of the Bankruptcy Code.) Creditor also wants to know, in the case of assets (7) through (11), the proper person upon whom the service of legal process should be made, or against whom the sheriff should proceed. See CPLR §5201(c); compare Problems 1.1 and 1.3.

4. Consensual Security Interests

To this point, we have principally been examining the ways in which a creditor can "grab" property from an uncooperative debtor. In addition, as we have seen, these remedies sort out priority rights among all creditors who are interested in "grabbing" assets. A creditor, however, can acquire a priority right by other means. A debtor and creditor may agree, consensually, that a creditor may take property of the debtor in the event the debtor defaults on its obligations. In other words, a debtor, at the time of the loan, may give its creditor a contingent interest in property the debtor owns that will ripen only if the debtor defaults. Such contingent property rights are called "security interests." If real estate is involved, the state law of mortgages governs the property right of the creditor against the debtor and its priority right against third parties. Article 9 of the Uniform Commercial Code (UCC), as enacted in a particular jurisdiction, governs the cases in which the collateral is personal property.

Of course, all extensions of credit involve a contingent right, upon default, to take possession of the debtor's property if the debtor should fail to pay, and a host of state collection laws — such as those we have just examined — is concerned with how a creditor goes about the process of reducing a claim to judgment and then "executing" (or "levying") on property to satisfy the judgment. A secured creditor may have two additional rights against the debtor that are not enjoyed by unsecured creditors. First, property exempt from execution by unsecured creditors generally is available as collateral for a debt. State v. Avco Financial Service of New York, Inc., 50 N.Y.2d 383, 429 N.Y.S.2d 181, 406 N.E.2d 1075 (1980) explains this difference in treatment:

> It is well recognized, however, that simply because the law exempts such property from levy and sale upon execution by a judgment creditor does not mean that the exemption statute was intended to serve the far more paternalistic function of restricting the freedom of debtors to dispose of these possessions as they wish. . . . No statute precludes exempt property from being sold; nor is there any which expressly interdicts the less drastic step of encumbering such property. So, for example, while contractual waivers of a debtor's statutory exemptions are usually held to be void . . . , the law has not forbidden a debtor to execute a mortgage upon the property so protected and thus create a lien which may be foreclosed despite the property's exempt status.

Second, in the case of security interests in personal property — although almost never in the case of real property — the secured creditor has the right, after default, to take specific property of a debtor without first going to court (or obtaining the debtor's consent). The importance of this right in distinguishing secured from unsecured creditors can be overstated, however, because UCC §9-503 generally allows "self-help" repossession, as it is called, only if it can be accomplished without "breach of the peace." In practice, a secured creditor can repossess without the assistance of a court only when the debtor does not *affirmatively* object. A secured creditor may be able to repossess a car if the debtor parks in the street, but not if it is kept in a garage. See, e.g., Deavers v. Standridge, 144 Ga. App. 673, 242 S.E.2d 331 (1978); Stone Machinery Co. v. Kessler, 1 Wash. App. 750, 463 P.2d 651 (1970).

The principal advantage of security interests, therefore, is the favorable set of rights in the debtor's property, relative to the rights of other creditors, that they give the secured creditor, from the moment the security interest is created. These rights are generally referred to as "priority" rights, and they order a creditor's right of access to the property interest represented by its security interest, relative to the competing claims of third parties.

When and how these rights are established is the subject of real estate mortgage law and Article 9 of the Uniform Commercial Code. Real estate systems generally order claims to a particular piece of real property according to the time that such claims are noted by a recording in the real estate files. But there are several types of statutorily designed recording systems. The three principal real property recording systems are "notice," "race-notice," and "race" statutes.

Under a "notice" statute, a subsequent purchaser of an interest in realty who does not have actual or constructive knowledge of an existing property claim of a prior purchaser at the time of its purchase, prevails over the prior purchaser, unless the prior purchaser had previously recorded its interest in the recording system in a proper fashion, thereby providing "record notice." In a notice system, a recording by the prior purchaser before a subsequent purchase will defeat the claim of the subsequent purchaser. In addition, if the subsequent purchaser has knowledge or constructive notice of the existence of the prior purchaser's interest, that will give the prior purchaser priority, even if the prior purchaser fails to record evidence of its interest. But if the subsequent purchaser acquires its interest without such knowledge or constructive notice, and if the prior purchaser has not yet recorded, the subsequent purchaser will prevail, whether or not either of the two parties ever records.

Under a "race-notice" statute, a subsequent purchaser, if it does not have knowledge or constructive notice of the claim of a prior purchaser at the time it enters into a purchase transaction, will prevail if, but only if, it records the notice of its claim first. Thus, up to the time of the subsequent purchase transaction, notice and race-notice statutes are identical in their treatment of knowledge: The subsequent purchaser may prevail only if it does not have actual or constructive knowledge of the prior purchaser's interest at the time of its purchase transaction. The two statutory schemes diverge only in the post-transaction period. While the notice statute treats events occurring after that transaction as irrelevant for purposes of determining the priority as between these two purchasers, the race-notice statute imposes an additional "race," the outcome of which turns upon which party records first.

Under a "race" statute, knowledge gained outside the filing system is irrelevant. The first party to record wins, irrespective of the state of knowledge of either party. Pure race systems are quite rare in real estate systems, but they do form the basis of the Article 9 system for security interests in personal property.

One of our concerns is the set of rules that determine when a person with a security interest is entitled to priority over other creditors of the debtor, or creditors of the debtor who have acquired a judicial lien. You

should direct your attention to UCC §§9-201 and 9-301 and the following
case.

UNITED STATES SHOE CORP. v.
CUDMORE-NEIBER SHOE CO.
419 F. Supp. 135 (D.S.D. 1976)

BOGUE, District Judge. . . .
On June 30, 1968 Defendant Cudmore-Neiber Shoe Company, Inc.
sold a business known as "The Bootery" to Defendant Merlyn Pugh.
Cudmore-Neiber and Pugh executed a security agreement in conjunction
with the sale. Under the security agreement the business which was the
object of the sale became the collateral for an installment purchase contract. Specifically, Pugh granted Cudmore-Neiber a security interest in the
business, including its inventory, accounts receivable, fixtures, furniture,
air conditioner, canopy and good will. A security interest in after-acquired
collateral was also granted. The security agreement specifically gave the
seller, Cudmore-Neiber Shoe Company, the rights of a secured creditor
under the Uniform Commercial Code upon default. These rights include
the right of self-help repossession. . . . A financing statement as to the
collateral in the security agreement was filed in the county of the debtor's
(Pugh) residence on May 29, 1973. . . . A financing statement was properly filed in the Secretary of State's office June 17, 1975.
On May 29, 1973 Cudmore-Neiber retook the business from Pugh
after a default. On that day, Pugh executed a release of any claims against
Cudmore-Neiber which he may have under their sales and security agreement.
While Pugh was operating "The Bootery" he obtained merchandise
from Plaintiff United States Shoe Company. He allegedly still owes Plaintiff in excess of $10,000.00 for some of the merchandise he acquired from
the Plaintiff. Plaintiff did not obtain any security agreement from Defendant Pugh. This action is brought to recover the amount owed Plaintiff by
Pugh. As to Defendant Cudmore-Neiber, Plaintiff claims that the repossession of "The Bootery" was a bulk sale and that the requirements of the
Bulk Sales Act were not complied with. Plaintiff further claims that, as an
unperfected secured creditor as of May 29, 1973, Cudmore-Neiber had
no right to self-help repossession. Finally, Plaintiff claims that the repossession was in effect an assignment for the benefit of creditors accomplished without the double bond required by S.D.C.L. §54-9-11. . . .
Generally speaking, a security agreement becomes enforceable
when . . . [t]he debtor has signed a security agreement which contains a
description of the collateral . . . [UCC §9-203 (1962)]. In this case, Pugh
had, as noted above, signed an agreement which granted Cudmore-Neiber
a security interest in "The Bootery" and, inter alia, its inventory, accounts

receivable and fixtures. Value was given by Cudmore-Neiber in the extension of credit to Pugh. . . .

Pugh received possessory rights in the collateral. Thus the security agreement attached under [UCC §9-204 (1962)]. Cudmore-Neiber thus became a secured creditor, although it did not perfect its security interest until May 29, 1973 at the earliest. (The May 29, 1973 filing arguably constituted perfection of Cudmore-Neiber's security interest in fixtures. . . . The security interest in the remaining collateral was perfected with the filing of June 17, 1975 in the Secretary of State's office, although the May 29, 1973 repossession may have constituted perfection of at least some of the collateral. . . .) However, this Court need not, and does not, decide whether or when Cudmore-Neiber became a perfected secured creditor. Plaintiff has no claim to the status of a secured creditor, and may therefore be properly characterized as a general creditor. Thus the general question presented concerns the right of an unperfected secured creditor to repossess collateral, and the effect of such a repossession upon the rights of a general creditor.

[UCC §9-201 (1962)] provides in relevant part as follows:

> Except as otherwise provided by this title a security agreement is effective according to its terms between the parties, against purchasers of the collateral *and against creditors.* (Emphasis added.)

It should be noted at this point that the above-quoted [section] does not draw a distinction between a perfected and an unperfected security interest. If Plaintiff is to prevail against Cudmore-Neiber on the ground that Cudmore-Neiber had not perfected its security interest, then Plaintiff must, under the above-quoted statute, point to some provision in Article 9 of the Uniform Commercial Code which would work as an exception to [§9-201].

[UCC §9-301 (1962)] contains several exceptions to the general rule of [§9-201] that an unperfected security agreement is effective as against creditors. The only exception in [§9-301] that is arguably relevant in this case is found in [§9-301(1)(b)], which gives "[a] person who becomes a lien creditor without knowledge of the security interest and before it is perfected . . ." priority over an unperfected security interest. However, Plaintiff in this case is merely a general creditor and has not ". . . acquired a lien on the property involved by attachment, levy or the like . . ." [UCC §9-301(3)]. Contrary to Plaintiff's contention advanced at oral argument, the mere filing of the instant lawsuit does not elevate Plaintiff to the status of a lien creditor.

In short, Plaintiff as a general creditor cannot prevail simply because Cudmore-Neiber had not perfected its security interest. The numerous cases cited by Plaintiff in support of this theory are simply inapposite.

[Most of these cases] stand for the proposition that an unperfected secured creditor does not prevail against a Trustee in Bankruptcy who is vested with such powers as those given a lien creditor without knowledge of secured interests. Swift & Company v. Jamestown National Bank, 426 F.2d 1099 (8th Cir. 1970) holds on the facts there that an unperfected security interest is not good as against a subsequent purchaser. Plaintiff in this case has unavoidably encountered the general rule contained in [UCC §9-201 (1962)] that a security interest, even though unperfected, is generally valid as against general creditors. . . . [A discussion of the effect of bulk sales law is omitted.]

Finally, Plaintiff argues that the repossession was an assignment for the benefit of creditors accomplished without the bond required by S.D.C.L. §54-9-11. The repossession does not, either in form or substance, even approach a transfer in trust for the benefit of creditors. This argument is thus without merit.

For the foregoing reasons this Court concludes that there is no genuine issue as to any material fact and that Cudmore-Neiber is entitled to judgment as a matter of law. Accordingly, this Court will grant Cudmore-Neiber's Motion to Dismiss, treated as a Motion for Summary Judgment. . . .

NOTE ON ARTICLE 9 SECURITY INTERESTS AND LIEN CREDITORS

Under the 1972 version of Article 9 of the Uniform Commercial Code, which is currently in force in over 40 jurisdictions, a security interest is *enforceable* upon *attachment.* A security interest attaches under §9-203(1) when:

> (a) the collateral is in the possession of the secured party pursuant to agreement, or the debtor has signed a security agreement which contains a description of the collateral and in addition, when the security interest covers crops growing or to be grown or timber to be cut, a description of the land concerned; and
> (b) value has been given; and
> (c) the debtor has rights in the collateral.

A secured creditor cannot assert priority against other property claimants until its interest is *perfected.* An interest is perfected under Article 9 "when it has attached and when all of the applicable steps required for perfection have been taken." §9-303. The "applicable steps required for perfection" vary somewhat for particular types of secured transactions. Nothing, for example, is required to be done to perfect a purchase money security interest (§9-107) in consumer goods (§9-109(1)). Certain types of collateral, moreover, may have special rules for perfection — the most common of which are automobiles and similar motor vehicles, where most states, in most instances, require a notation of the security interest on the certificate of title as a condition of perfection. §9-302(3)(b); Uniform Motor Vehicle Certificate of Title Statute. In most cases, however, the additional steps necessary for perfection are either possession of the collateral by the secured party or its agent or the filing of a "financing statement" in the proper office (or offices). §§9-302(1), 9-304, 9-305.

The details of taking and perfecting a security interest in personal property are many and cannot be examined here. But in order to understand bankruptcy law, it is necessary that you be familiar in a general way with the basic Article 9 rules governing priorities between a secured party and other creditors, particularly a "lien creditor." United States Shoe Co. v. Cudmore-Neiber Shoe Co. sets forth the rule governing conflicts between *unperfected* secured creditors and *general* creditors. UCC §9-301 contains the basic rule governing conflicts between Article 9 security interests and lien creditors. This is an important conflict for purposes of bankruptcy law. The following problems require you to focus on that section.

PROBLEMS

1.6 Debtor buys a drill press from Seller in 1983. Debtor borrows $50,000 from Bank on an unsecured basis to pay for it. In 1984, Debtor borrows an additional $50,000 from Finance Company and grants it a security interest in the drill press and signs a written security agreement. Finance Company never files a financing statement. In 1985, Bank sues Debtor. Before Bank reduces its claim to judgment, Finance Company takes possession of the machine. Can Bank argue that Finance Company's exercise of self-help repossession, although permitted by Article 9, violated its rights?

In answering this problem, you should attempt to analyze it by addressing a series of subissues first. Does Finance Company have an unperfected security interest in the machine? Did it perfect its security interest by repossessing the machine? What were the rights of Bank before the time that Finance Company repossessed the machine? What were the rights of Bank after the time that Finance Company repossessed the machine? See Comment 3 to UCC §9-301.

1.7 On the same facts as above, Bank reduces its claim to judgment on January 1. The writ of execution is issued by the clerk of the court on January 3. It is delivered to the sheriff on January 5. On January 7, the sheriff attempts to seize the drill press. Who has superior rights to the press if Finance Company repossesses the drill press on January 2? January 4? January 6?

In answering this problem, you must date events carefully. When did

Bank become a lien creditor? Was it before Finance Company's security interest became perfected? Where do you look to determine what a "lien creditor" is? Does the definition in UCC §9-301(3) help? When does a lien created by "attachment, levy or the like" become effective? The answer to when an execution lien becomes effective, as we have seen, may vary from one jurisdiction to another. Does UCC §9-301(3) adopt each of these state's timing rules, or does it override these rules by specifying "attachment, levy or the like"?

1.8 Would your analysis of Problems 1.6 and 1.7 change if Debtor never signed a written security agreement? When did the steps necessary for attachment take place? Did the security interest ever attach? See §9-203(1). What, then, about perfection, §9-303?

1.9 Bank made an unsecured loan to Debtor of $50,000 in 1983. In 1984, Finance Company lent Debtor $50,000 and took a security interest in all of Debtor's inventory, then existing or thereafter acquired. Debtor signed a written security agreement and Finance Company made a proper Article 9 filing in the same year. Debtor defaulted on both loans in 1985. Bank sued and reduced its claim to judgment. The clerk issued a writ of execution and it was delivered to the sheriff. Debtor then acquired a new shipment of inventory. Can Finance Company contend that its interest takes priority both as to the old and the new inventory? Does it matter whether an execution lien becomes effective under state law at the time that the writ is delivered to the sheriff?

1.10 On January 1, Seller delivered a large drill press to Debtor. Seller retained a security interest in the press until Debtor paid for it in full. A general creditor reduced its claim to judgment and levied on the drill press on January 8 by having the sheriff remove a key operating part (giving the creditor an execution lien under applicable state law). Seller filed a proper financing statement on January 9. Who has superior rights to the goods? (Ignore any rights that the Seller may enjoy under UCC §2-702.) See UCC §§1-201(37), 9-107(a), 9-301(1)(b), 9-301(2). Would it have mattered if, instead of filing, Seller repossessed the goods on January 9?

B. INTRODUCTION TO THE BANKRUPTCY PROCESS

To this point, we have addressed, in the most general fashion, the ways in which creditors can enforce obligations their debtor owes them. These issues, we have seen, involve not only questions of how to sort out rights as between a debtor and a creditor but, also, how to order rights among creditors themselves. We shall now turn to the origins and purposes of bankruptcy law. A crucial question we need to face is why and to what extent the debt collection devices we have just examined are not sufficient, and how the world would change if there were no bankruptcy system to supplement individual creditor remedies.

1. The History of Bankruptcy Law

a. Continental and English Origins

Bankruptcy law can be traced back to the days of Roman law. Its name is derived from statutes of Italian city-states that called it "banca rupta," after a medieval custom of breaking the bench of a banker or tradesman who absconded with property of his creditors. Treiman, Acts of Bankruptcy: A Medieval Concept in Modern Bankruptcy Law, 52 Harv. L. Rev. 189 (1938). It was transplanted to England in 1542, when Parliament enacted an "Act Against Such Persons As Do Make Bankrupt," 34 and 35 Henry VIII ch. 4 (1542). The early English bankruptcy statutes, which were limited to debtors of an ill-defined (but expanding) "merchant" class, and which provided solely for involuntary petitions, were viciously punitive from the perspective of the debtor. They tried to prevent the debtor from secreting assets, and they offered no discharge or relief.

What these first English statutes governing bankruptcy did do was give a merchant's creditors rights as a group that they did not enjoy as individuals. These statutes were triggered by "acts" of bankruptcy that suggested that conduct, not financial embarrassment, was the gist of the offense. These acts were considered to be ways by which a debtor unjustly kept creditors at bay. England's first bankruptcy statute reached acts of flight "to parts unknown" (the relevance of which is obvious) and the practice of "keeping house" (where a debtor would stay at home, immune from forcible intrusion under the English view that a "man's home is his castle"). The second bankruptcy statute, 13 Eliz. ch. 7 (1571) (passed in the same year as the first fraudulent conveyance statute), added three additional acts: taking oneself to "sanctuary"; making an alienation in fraud of creditors; and voluntarily procuring one's own arrest (usually on a fictitious claim by a friend) so as to prevent one's creditors from attacking one's property. (While under a writ of capias ad satisfaciendum, no other process could be sued out against that person's property.) See generally Treiman, Escaping the Creditor in the Middle Ages, 43 L.Q. Rev. 230 (1927).

If a merchant committed a specified act of bankruptcy, creditors could petition the Lord Chancellor to appoint a commission that had the power to gather the debtor's assets together and sell them. The commissioners would then distribute the proceeds "to every of the said creditors a portion, rate and rate like, according to the quantity of his or their debts." 13 Eliz. ch. 7, III (1571). If creditors were not paid off in full, "then the said creditor or creditors, and every of them, shall and may have their remedy for the recovery and levying of the residue of their said debts or duties . . . in like manner and form as they should and might have had before the making of this act." Id. at X.

There are several things to note about these early English bankruptcy statutes. Early bankruptcy laws did not help or protect unlucky debtors; they gave creditors of merchants another method of collecting debts in addition to those they already had. Moreover, the new remedy was a collective one. Although an individual creditor did not lose the right to sue the merchant debtor at some later time (because there was no discharge), each creditor had to share the debtor's existing assets with every other creditor. Essential elements of these early English bankruptcy statutes, then, were the sequestration of the merchant's assets and the imposition of restraint on creditors, to ensure that a creditor did not seek repayment in full at the expense of other creditors. Acts of bankruptcy (the concept of which disappeared from our bankruptcy statutes only in 1979) were limited largely to acts that kept creditors from enforcing their rights through conventional lawsuits. As a practical matter, in the absence of the collective bankruptcy remedy, creditors might not have any other means of reaching their debtor's assets. Nevertheless, cases could arise in which an individual creditor fared worse under the bankruptcy statute. A creditor who might have been able to recover in full if left to pursue individual remedies would have to share whatever the debtor had with all the other creditors.

In English bankruptcy law, the notion of discharge was a century and a half in coming and, when it did come, it came largely to reward cooperation rather than to assist the unlucky. Parliament first gave merchants a discharge from their debts in the Statute of 4 Anne ch. 17 (1705). The discharge in bankruptcy, however, began as only one half of a procedural device that enabled creditors to gather more information about a debtor's assets. The preamble to the statute read: "[w]hereas many persons have and do daily become bankrupt, not so much by reason of losses and unavoidable misfortunes, as to the intent to defraud and hinder their creditors of their just debts and duties to them due and owing; for the prevention thereof, be it enacted . . .." The 1705 statute went on to provide that anyone declared a bankrupt must submit to an examination before the bankruptcy commissioners. Creditors could hope to be repaid only if the merchant-debtor helped them locate assets. The drafters of the Statute of 4 Anne sought to give debtors an incentive to disclose. The statute provided that a debtor who conformed to the act and revealed everything would be able to keep 5 percent of whatever assets were gathered together and would be discharged from all prebankruptcy obligations. At the same time, however, the statute also provided that an uncooperative debtor would "suffer as a felon without the benefit of clergy" — an eighteenth century term of art for the death penalty. During the eighteenth century merchants who did not respond to the bankruptcy commissioners or who concealed their assets from them were in fact convicted and executed on occasion. Alexander Thompson was an embroiderer who, in 1756, owed his creditors more than two hundred pounds. He did not respond to a notice to appear before a bankruptcy commission. Thompson claimed that he had no knowledge of the notice because he had been in the north of Scotland when it was made. That defense failed. He was found guilty, sentenced to die, and later executed. 1756 Old Bailey Session Papers vol. 2, at 85. In 1761, John Perrot was executed for trying to hide some bank notes from his creditors after being adjudicated a bankrupt. 1761 Old Bailey Session Papers vol. 8, at 394.

The discharge in early English bankruptcy law should be seen in this light. Bankruptcy law applied only to debtors who were merchants (although the definition encompassed more people as time passed), and the discharge given merchants began as an element of a debt collection device that included capital punishment. The death penalty was the stick; the discharge was the carrot. They were part of the same package. The discharge for merchant debtors began not as a substantive right, but as a procedural device to facilitate the gathering of information about the debtor's assets. See generally Cohen, The History of Imprisonment for Debt and Its Relation to the Development of Discharge in Bankruptcy, 3 J. Legal Hist. 153 (1982). Early English bankruptcy proceedings could be started only by creditors; the voluntary bankruptcy petition was unknown. The characteristic of bankruptcy law that remained constant throughout the eighteenth century was that it was a collective remedy that enabled creditors to gather together and then divide among themselves assets of a common merchant debtor. Early bankruptcy statutes were entirely procedural. The beneficiaries of the statutes were preexisting creditors, and their rights were modified in bankruptcy only to take account of the fact that the proceedings were collective and that a debtor would not have enough assets to pay creditors everything they were owed.

b.   *Bankruptcy Law in American History*

When the Constitutional Convention met in Philadelphia in 1787, Charles Pinckney proposed that Congress have the power to establish uniform laws upon the subject of bankruptcies. The lone delegate who voted against the proposal feared that giving Congress the power to pass bankruptcy laws would permit Congress to punish bankruptcies by death, as had been done in England. The response to this objection was not that bankruptcy laws were debtor protection measures, but rather that there was little danger of abuse. 2 Farrand, The Records of the Federal Convention of 1787, at 489 (1911). In the Federalist Papers, James Madison discussed the Bankruptcy Clause:

The power of establishing uniform laws of bankruptcy is so intimately connected with the regulation of commerce, and will prevent so many frauds
where the parties or their property may lie or be removed into different
States, that the expediency of it seems not likely to be drawn into question.

Federalist Papers, No. 42, at 277-278. Madison seems to have thought
bankruptcy law an appropriate subject for federal legislation because disputes were likely to involve parties and property in multiple jurisdictions
and, in the absence of federal legislation, debtors would find it easy to
escape from creditors merely by crossing a state line. Because bankruptcy
law was viewed as essentially procedural, its role in the eyes of those who
argued for and against its inclusion in the Constitution had little to do with
protecting unlucky debtors.

Congress passed the first bankruptcy act in 1800 (2 Stat. 19) and it was
repealed in 1803. This statute was much like its English counterparts at
that time. District judges instead of the Lord Chancellor appointed bankruptcy commissioners. As in England, the statute applied only to debtors
who were merchants or to others in commerce, such as bankers, brokers,
underwriters, and marine insurers. There were no voluntary petitions,
and a bankruptcy proceeding could begin only after a debtor had committed a specified act of bankruptcy (such as concealing goods so that creditors
could not levy on them). Debtors could obtain a discharge, but only if
two-thirds of the creditors in number and value consented to it. §36, at 2
Stat. 31.

The Bankruptcy Act of 1800, like its English antecedents, was designed to enable creditors to collect the assets of an insolvent merchant. A
constant feature of bankruptcy law in this country, as in England, has been
that after the enactment of a new bankruptcy reform, creditors have been
quick to find that the rights provided debtors were subject to widespread
abuse and the remedies provided creditors were unwieldy and ineffective.
Under the Bankruptcy Act of 1800, creditors found that they rarely recovered more than a few cents on the dollar. Most of the debtors in bankruptcy had long since become hopelessly insolvent. They were frequently
already in debtors' prison, and they rarely had any assets. The Bankruptcy
Act of 1800 did not allow debtors to file a bankruptcy petition. Indeed, a
creditor could begin a proceeding only if a debtor had committed an act of
bankruptcy. Nevertheless, a debtor could persuade a sympathetic creditor
to file a petition on his behalf. Among the beneficiaries of the 1800 Act was
Robert Morris, a signer of the Declaration of Independence who, until he
used the bankruptcy act, had spent nearly three years in jail. See C. Warren, Bankruptcy Law in United States History 19-21 (1935).

Between 1803 and 1841, there was no federal bankruptcy legislation
in this country at all. Bankruptcy law, however, was not what unlucky
debtors wanted. It was still primarily a creditor remedy that applied only to
merchants. During the eighteenth century, a variety of state laws had

emerged to protect debtors, including those who were not merchants, from their creditors. These were called insolvency acts. They enabled debtors to gain release from prison; some even offered debtors a discharge. These laws grew out of a practice in England where nonmerchant debtors could initiate proceedings under an insolvency law whereby they could obtain a release from prison, but not a discharge of debts, on surrendering their property to their creditors. Many states had insolvency laws, and some still do. After 1789, however, states could no longer pass insolvency statutes with retroactive application because of the Contracts Clause, Sturges v. Crowninshield, 17 U.S. (4 Wheat.) 122 (1819), and they could not discharge debtors from obligations owed nonresident creditors, Ogden v. Saunders, 25 U.S. (12 Wheat.) 213 (1827). In addition, while the *unexercised* power of the federal government was held not to preclude the operation of these state laws even though they granted the debtor a discharge, id., the question was decided to the contrary once Congress enacted a bankruptcy statute. See International Shoe Co. v. Pinkus, 278 U.S. 261 (1929), discussed infra page 1012.

Until 1841, insolvency acts, rather than a bankruptcy law, offered debtors a means of discharging their debts. The two were thought distinct. The insolvency acts protected debtors in the first instance, while a bankruptcy statute protected creditors. The Bankruptcy Act of 1800 expressly provided that it did not preempt state insolvency acts as they applied to those, such as nonmerchants, who were not covered by the act. It also provided that even merchants could still rely on these acts if creditors did not start a bankruptcy proceeding within three months of a debtor's imprisonment for debt. §61, at 2 Stat. 36.

The Bankruptcy Act of 1841, 5 Stat. 440, was the first piece of federal bankruptcy legislation that explicitly combined the function of providing creditors a forum for sorting out claims to their debtor's assets and providing relief to debtors generally. It permitted voluntary petitions, was no longer restricted to merchants (although it excluded corporations), and provided for discharge, unless a majority in number and value of the creditors filed a written dissent, §4. (It did not, however, recognize the exemptions that debtors frequently enjoyed under state law, such as those that protected homesteads.) Much of the impetus for this came from changing views of the benefits of bankruptcy. Most businesses of the time could not incorporate, and lawmakers thought it important that merchants who were simply unlucky should not face imprisonment and should be able to free themselves from past debt.

The focus of the Bankruptcy Act of 1841, then, was distinct. Relief of debtors was the paramount concern. Northern Whigs wanted to rescue victims of the Panic of 1837 and its aftermath. Indeed, Henry Clay proposed that provisions for involuntary bankruptcy in the proposed legislation be stricken altogether on the grounds that existing remedies under state law were more effective. Daniel Webster admitted his "leading object to be to relieve those who are at present bankrupt, hopeless bankrupts, and who cannot be discharged or set free but by a bankrupt act passed by Congress." C. Warren, Bankruptcy Law in United States History 63, 67 (1935). Those who opposed the statute argued that a statute designed primarily to protect debtors was an "insolvency" act, not a "bankruptcy" act and hence beyond the power of Congress, which could enact laws only on the subject of bankruptcies.

The Bankruptcy Act of 1841 was repealed after only 18 months. There was little political pressure against its repeal after the many victims of the depression of the late 1830s had taken advantage of its provisions for voluntary petitions and discharge. Like the Bankruptcy Act of 1800, the statute proved unexpectedly favorable to debtors. Creditors rarely received more than a few cents on the dollar. The procedures proved to be very expensive. Moreover, creditors found that they lost the job of controlling and monitoring the debtor's behavior to a less skilled and less informed judge. Few cases brought under the statute were involuntary.

There was little pressure for another bankruptcy statute until just before the Civil War. It was a time of relative prosperity, and states passed additional insolvency statutes to protect debtors. Some statutes might, for example, stay the rights of creditors to foreclose upon property and prevent forced sales unless the property was sold for at least a specified fraction of its appraised value. Although these stay and appraisal statutes were often of doubtful constitutionality, C. Warren, Bankruptcy Law in United States History 89-90 (1935), debtors enjoyed the benefit of these statutes while their validity was being litigated. Often the crisis that precipitated the statute disappeared by the time the Supreme Court found it unconstitutional.

Congress passed another bankruptcy act in 1867 (14 Stat. 517). For the first time, corporations were permitted to take advantage of the bankruptcy laws. Unlike the Bankruptcy Act of 1841, property exempt from creditor's claims under state law was similarly exempt under federal bankruptcy law. This act also quickly became unpopular. Northern creditors had urged passage of the act because they believed that it would enable them to collect debts southerners owed them, but along with other creditors they quickly became disenchanted with the statute. As with the Bankruptcy Act of 1841, their objections went as much to the costly, lengthy, and ineffective procedures of the act as to its generosity to debtors. Bankruptcy proceedings seemed interminable and when they ended there were rarely any assets for creditors. As early as 1873, commentators observed that the law was "perplexing, cumbersome, annoying, and expensive," C. Warren, Bankruptcy Law in United States History 113 (1935). In 1874, several amendments were made to this statute, generally in the direction of increased liberality for debtors. In terms of our story, one of the most important of these amendments provided for compositions among creditors, §17, at 18 Stat 182. A debtor could propose to pay creditors a certain percentage of their claims, and all the debtor's creditors would be bound if two-thirds in number and one-half in value of all the creditors of the debtor agreed to the proposal. The Bankruptcy Act of 1867 was repealed in 1878.

Another bankruptcy statute was passed in 1898. Like its predecessors, the financial swings in the decade before led to its passage. The Bankruptcy Act of 1898 was, however, the first that showed any staying power. It survived, albeit with substantial amendments, until 1979, and it ushered in the modern period where bankruptcy legislation seems a fixed part of our society. The Bankruptcy Act of 1898 accommodated both the creditors' desire for an effective means of gathering and selling the assets of their debtor and the interest insolvent individuals had in securing a discharge for past indebtedness. The Bankruptcy Act of 1898 essentially provided a discharge for nearly all obligations of individual debtors (who were still called "bankrupts") who were willing to cooperate with their creditors.

By the time the Bankruptcy Act of 1898 was passed, the difference between merchant debtors and others had once again become important. Although the discharge right might have been important for merchants in the last part of the eighteenth century, it became increasingly less important. Entrepreneurs could limit their liability by incorporating. A person who took advantage of state corporation law no longer needed bankruptcy law to protect against financial reverses. If one corporation failed, it could be dissolved under state law and another started. Bankruptcy law as it affected merchants was once again largely a collective procedure that creditors could invoke. By contrast, for most others, the Bankruptcy Act of 1898 completely replaced insolvency acts as their safe harbor in the event of financial distress. In such cases of financially distressed individuals, the Bankruptcy Act of 1898 offered creditors very little, especially if they were relying on the debtor's future wages for repayment.

Bankruptcy law became closely linked with the idea of a discharge for individuals. Most bankruptcy cases under the Bankruptcy Act of 1898 involved individual debtors who were hopelessly in debt and had no assets other than those exempt from levy under state law or their potential future income, which bankruptcy's discharge provisions now protected. These cases, however, could be handled summarily, and had little to do with sorting out the rights of various creditors. The complexities of the Bankruptcy Act of 1898 had little to do with its discharge provisions but rather with its rules governing creditors. The most important amendments to the Bankruptcy Act of 1898, in particular the Chandler Act of 1938, were primarily aimed at the problems raised by insolvent corporations. The value of an on-going firm saddled with large debts arising from past misfortunes could not be preserved, it was thought, if all the assets were sold for cash. The fear was that a quick, piecemeal sale of the assets would realize only a fraction of their true value and would leave creditors in a worse position than if they exchanged their claims against the debtor for an interest in a reconstituted firm. Devices such as the equity receivership began to develop in the nineteenth century to deal with business "reorganizations." See, e.g., Northern Pacific Ry. v. Boyd, 228 U.S. 432 (1913). By the 1930s, these provisions were borrowed, modified, and placed in bankruptcy law, where the ideas associated with restructuring an ongoing business assumed substantial importance, even in the portions of bankruptcy law not technically thought of as specifically addressed to business reorganizations.

Preserving the going-concern value of a business was thought to benefit both the creditors and the economy generally. Creditors ultimately recover more of what they had lent, and everyone benefits by having a business survive that produces needed goods and employs workers who might be unable to find work elsewhere if the firm closed. Nevertheless, the track record of the bankruptcy courts was poor. Many firms that entered bankruptcy proceedings did not even survive long enough for a bankruptcy court to complete its effort to revive them. Even when a firm passed through a bankruptcy reorganization, it often failed within a few years. Creditors of such a firm would receive much less than if the firm had been liquidated or sold as a unit to a third party upon entry into bankruptcy. These creditors argued that in practice many reorganizations had more to do with enabling managers to keep their jobs and shareholders to enjoy a second chance — at their creditors' expense — than with preserving going-concern values for the benefit of the common weal. Creditors also complained that even in a straight liquidation many of the assets of the debtor went to the trustee in bankruptcy and the trustee's lawyers and friends.

One of the perceived vices of the Bankruptcy Act of 1867 was the scope of its jurisdictional provisions and the power it gave federal judges to rule on issues that state courts usually decided. As a result, the jurisdictional provisions of the Bankruptcy Act of 1898 were more modest. As the act evolved, a district judge would appoint a referee in bankruptcy to administer the debtor's assets and resolve disputes between the debtor and those creditors who had actually or constructively consented to the referee's jurisdiction. The trustee in bankruptcy, who represented the interests of the general creditors, would have to resort to state court or federal district court if the trustee wanted to gather other assets.

c.   The Bankruptcy Code

A new Bankruptcy Code was passed by Congress in 1978 as part of the Bankruptcy Reform Act of 1978 and became effective in 1979. It codified many of the judicial developments in bankruptcy law and consolidated the provisions governing corporate reorganizations. In addition, it created a new bankruptcy court and gave new bankruptcy judges greatly expanded powers, including the right to issue writs of habeas corpus, the power to conduct jury trials, and the power to issue writs of execution. These judges were to be nominated by the President and confirmed by the Senate for 14-year terms. It was expected that the most capable of the existing bankruptcy judges would be appointed to these new positions.

In Northern Pipeline Construction Corp. v. Marathon Pipe Line Co., 458 U.S. 50 (1982), the Supreme Court struck down the jurisdictional provisions of the Bankruptcy Reform Act of 1978 on the grounds that bankruptcy judges exercised "judicial power" within the meaning of Article III of the Constitution and therefore had to have life tenure. For two years after *Marathon*, bankruptcy judges continued much as before, although they were nominally under the supervision of the District Courts. The arrangement was justified by an emergency rule promulgated in each judicial circuit whose validity was at least questionable, although the federal courts of appeals consistently upheld the rule based on what they perceived to be jurisdictional provisions that survived *Marathon*.

In 1984 Congress passed a statute, the Bankruptcy Amendments and Federal Judgeship Act of 1984, to cure the jurisdictional defect of the 1978 Act that the Court found in *Marathon*. Largely because of lobbying by the Chief Justice and other federal judges, bankruptcy judges were not granted life tenure. Although their powers were more fragmented than in the 1978 legislation — splitting jurisdiction with district courts and, in some instances, with state courts — it is not clear that these judges do not also exercise "judicial power" in deciding some "core" jurisdictional issues. The new legislation also contained a farrago of substantive amendments to the Bankruptcy Code in response to the lobbying of interest groups ranging from labor unions to grain farmers and fishermen to consumer lenders to shopping center financers.

d. Summary

The history of bankruptcy legislation in this country, as well as in England, contains two rather distinct stories. First, it has shown the gradual rise of the individual's right to discharge past indebtedness and obtain a financial fresh start. The concept of limited liability has been extended from merchants to the population at large. This was cut back somewhat for the first time in 1984 because of perceived abuses under the 1978 Bankruptcy Code and intense lobbying by consumer lenders. Nevertheless, the basic principle that individuals are entitled to a fresh start has become uncontroversial. The second story has nothing to do with discharge. Instead it has to do with the use of bankruptcy as a collective device for creditors. While applicable to individual debtors as well, this has had its greatest impact in the area of businesses, first with merchants, and later with corporations and other forms of business enterprises. It shows how bankruptcy has responded to the interests of creditors, their debtors, and the large social problems of business failures.

2. Bankruptcy Law and the Interests of Creditors and Debtors

Most of the procedural and substantive provisions of bankruptcy law apply whether the debtor is an individual worker or a giant corporation. While special rules in Chapter 13 of the Bankruptcy Code govern a special form of bankruptcy for individuals only, and while certain other rules relating to discharge and exemptions are generally applicable only to individuals, most of the provisions of the Bankruptcy Code are indifferent to the *type* of debtor in bankruptcy. While we will focus on the special rules governing individual debtors in Chapters 10, 11, and 12 of this book, most of our focus until then will be on the creditors and their relation to the debtor, whether the debtor is an individual, a partnership, or a corporation. Given this focus, we need to recognize the basic questions we should raise:

1. Does bankruptcy law serve the interests of creditors? Bankruptcy began as a device to assist creditors that became available when the debtor had engaged in conduct that made conventional means of enforcing obligations impractical. Should bankruptcy law still be considered a device that assists creditors? What kind of help does it offer that creditors cannot enjoy by pursuing individual remedies under state law?
2. Does bankruptcy law serve the interests of the debtor? The owners of a corporation, the shareholders, already enjoy limited liability under state law. Should they enjoy any additional rights in a bankruptcy proceeding? Should they, or other debtors, be able to trump property or contract rights that they could not have outside of bankruptcy?
3. Does bankruptcy law serve a wider societal interest distinct from the interests of the creditors or debtor? Should a bankruptcy proceeding strive to keep a business (whether a corporation or sole proprietorship) intact, quite apart from the interests of those with rights to it, because of the value of the business to the society at large, given, for example, the jobs it provides? Is it sensible to have this concern in bankruptcy proceedings if it is not relevant to the dissolution or liquidation of business outside of bankruptcy?
4. Given that bankruptcy law imposes a different set of procedural and substantive rules, what sorts of constraints should be placed on its use?

5. How well does the current Bankruptcy Code carry out its purposes? Once we understand why we have a Bankruptcy Code, we need to ask how successfully the drafters implemented their concerns. Is this statute, unlike all the previous ones, free of unnecessarily wasteful and time-consuming procedures? Does it provide opportunities for undesirable advantage-taking by interested parties?

In the note that follows, we focus on the features of bankruptcy law that seem designed to advance the interests of creditors.

NOTE ON BANKRUPTCY AND THE PROBLEM OF THE COMMON POOL

We can often explain phenomena that appear different by appealing to a single principle. Newton taught us that gravity explains both why an object falls toward the earth when it is released and why the earth orbits the sun. Problems that the legal system must address may also appear different, yet reflect the same basic concern. One of the most basic and pervasive problems is that of the common pool. Imagine a small lake filled with fish. If a single individual owned the lake, that individual would limit the amount of fishing that was done. The owner would check the desire to consume or sell fish now, in order to ensure that sufficient fish were left to reproduce and maintain the population for future years.

The story might be quite different if no one person owned the lake. If a group of diverse, self-interested individuals were free to fish, each might try to catch as many fish as possible without considering the future. Although everyone would benefit if the total amount of fishing were limited, everyone would also realize that self-imposed limits on fishing would not ensure that a supply of fish would remain. Each individual might well think that any restraint practiced today would simply benefit other fishers without doing anything to ensure there would be fish in the future. Self-interest would dictate that everyone catch fish without restraint, despite the interest of the group as a whole in preserving the resource for the future. In the absence of any mechanism for restraining others, no one has an incentive to practice restraint.

There is a more general point to be drawn from this example: Market economies are premised on the notion that individuals acting in their own self-interest can make everyone better off. But self-interest does not always produce the best result. Situations frequently arise when an individual's incentives run counter to the interests of the group as a whole. Many legal rules are designed to induce individuals to act in the group's interest, despite the individual's incentive to do otherwise if left alone. The common pool problem permeates the law of oil and gas, insurance, corporations, and eminent domain, as well as labor law. An idea to consider is whether, when thinking about creditors, bankruptcy law should not also be considered a response to the common pool problem.

In the absence of any bankruptcy law (or other type of collective proceeding), an individual creditor is free to seek repayment on its own. It need not pay attention to other creditors and has no way of controlling their actions. These are the rules that we saw in the first part of this chapter. If a debtor is solvent and there are sufficient assets to satisfy everyone, the creditors are like fishers in a large lake or ocean: Their actions collectively are not significant enough to deplete and endanger the common pool. No creditor has an incentive to act precipitously, because it knows its loan will be repaid, even if its claim is the last to be honored.

The picture changes, however, when the debtor has too few assets to satisfy its creditors. If the debtor is insolvent, each creditor has an incentive to act quickly. General creditors have an incentive to reduce their claims to judgment and levy on the debtor's property. Secured creditors may exercise their rights to repossess collateral. Assets may be sold off for far less than if a single individual or entity had controlled their disposition. Such individual action by creditors may destroy the value of the debtor's business as a going concern. If the creditors had acted collectively, they might have been able to sell the business intact to a third party and split the proceeds among themselves. They might even have taken over the business themselves and run it for their common benefit. Collective action, of course, is no guarantee that all the creditors will be paid, but where one person acts on behalf of the group and individual creditors are restrained from pursuing their self-interest, it may be more likely that the creditors will derive the most benefit possible from the existing assets. Outside of a collective proceeding, each creditor has an incentive to watch the actions of other creditors to ensure that it does not lose out to them. Such monitoring may be costly, yet, because all do it, the monitoring may not improve anyone's chances of being repaid. Each creditor may stay in the same place on the treadmill.

One of the principal justifications of any bankruptcy law may be that it encourages creditors and others with rights to a debtor's assets to act as a sole owner of the assets would act. After a point, individual actions of creditors can become wasteful or even self-destructive. A secured creditor who repossesses a drill press may force a debtor to shut down its entire operation. Once the debtor shuts down its factory, its entire business may fall apart. If the debtor cannot produce goods, it cannot sell them. If it cannot sell them, it will have no income. Without income, the debtor cannot pay off existing debts. The rules of bankruptcy law try to counteract these effects. When a bankruptcy petition is filed, all creditors are stayed from pursuing individual remedies. Those who grabbed assets from the debtor shortly before the petition was filed in anticipation of the collective proceeding must give them back. The debtor's business may continue to run as its affairs are sorted out and the claims of pre-petition creditors are satisfied. Just as a legal rule can force fishers to act as if a lake were owned by a single individual (such as a rule limiting the catch of each fisher), bankruptcy law in large measure simply requires many diverse creditors to act as one. And, because of the presence of bankruptcy law, each creditor may have to spend less to ensure that it isn't left behind in any ensuing race.

Like all justifications, this one is subject to a number of qualifications. To say that a common pool problem exists — that the self-interested actions of individual creditors run counter to the interest of the group — is not to say that individual behavior is entirely self-interested or that legal rules can solve all collective action problems. A legal rule may not be able to prevent littering in a remote wilderness, yet in such cases there might not be a collective action problem. Their self-interest to the contrary notwithstanding, hikers in a remote wilderness, to which they will never return, frequently will not leave any trash behind them, even though they do not stand to gain from their own care. Everyone is tempted to free-ride on everyone else's efforts to clean up litter, yet in practice many people do not succumb to this temptation. In reality, we often observe people behaving in a cooperative fashion over time. See R. Axelrod, The Evolution of Cooperation (1984).

Similarly, creditors do not always rush to seize a debtor's assets whenever the debtor seems to be in financial trouble. First, creditors sometimes recognize the need for self-restraint. Moreover, unlike hikers or fishers, there may be only a few creditors (or only a few large creditors) of any single debtor, and they may be able to surmount the common pool problem by negotiating with one another without a compulsory collective proceeding. These negotiations (or "workouts," as they are called) are common. The restructuring of Chrysler Corporation's debt in the early 1980s is only one of many prominent examples (although the federal government may have aided negotiations both by dangling out a guarantee "carrot" and by using subtle forms of persuasion among recalcitrant creditors as a "stick"). Yet it remains true that creditors may have less incentive to cooperate when a debtor is failing than they do when there are greater prospects of repeated dealings with a debtor. R. Axelrod, supra.

A question one must ask (and one that we face squarely in the next chapter) is whether a collective proceeding is necessary under the facts of any particular case. It is possible that the rules specifying when a bankruptcy petition may be filed prevent a collective proceeding from happening until it is too late to save the debtor's assets from the self-interested actions of various creditors. But another possibility is that the collective proceeding will begin too soon. Forcing all the creditors to refrain from individual actions (many of which have the effect of monitoring the debtor and preventing it from misbehaving) brings its own costs.

As a second qualification, this justification of bankruptcy law —

encouraging creditors to work together—explains only its procedural component. As we have already noted, legal rules governing debt collection both tell creditors how to enforce their debtor's obligations and prescribe the substantive limitations on their rights, as against both their debtor and other creditors. The need for bankruptcy law to respond to a common pool problem may explain why the procedures provided by state law for enforcing security interests and judgments need to be changed, but not why the relative value of the creditors' rights under state law should be changed. If a creditor cannot satisfy its claims out of a debtor's pension fund before bankruptcy starts, nothing about having a collective procedure to promote the interests of the creditors as a group explains why the creditor should be able to look to the fund in bankruptcy. Similarly, if a creditor has priority over other creditors outside bankruptcy, nothing about settling all claims in a single forum suggests that the value of that priority should not be respected in bankruptcy as well.

A question to which we shall return often is whether bankruptcy law, at least when it is not dealing with an individual's right to a fresh start, should ever alter the value of the substantive rights creditors have outside of bankruptcy. For example, why should Congress limit the rights of a secured creditor in bankruptcy, but not elsewhere? If we oppose granting secured creditors special treatment in bankruptcy, why should we want them to receive special treatment outside of bankruptcy? In answering this question, we should keep in mind that business failures and bankruptcy proceedings do not go hand in hand. Most businesses fail without a bankruptcy petition ever being filed, and the debts of many firms are restructured without bankruptcy. Should the decision whether to force creditors and others with rights to the debtor's assets to enter a collective proceeding be colored by anything other than whether collective action offers greater advantages than does individual action?

For general discussions of the common pool problem, see Friedman, The Economics of the Common Pool: Property Rights in Exhaustible Resources, 18 U.C.L.A. L. Rev. 855 (1971); Sweeney, Tollison, and Willett, Market Failure, the Common Pool Problem, and Ocean Resource Exploitation, 17 J.L. & Econ. 179 (1974). Much related work has been done under the rubric of game theory, see R. Axelrod, The Evolution of Cooperation (1984); M. Shubik, Game Theory in the Social Sciences (1982); A. Rapoport and A. Chammah, Prisoner's Dilemma (1965); R. Hardin, Collective Action (1982).

For discussions of the purposes of bankruptcy law, see Jackson, Bankruptcy, Non-Bankruptcy Entitlements, and the Creditors' Bargain, 91 Yale L.J. 857 (1982); Baird and Jackson, Corporate Reorganizations and the Treatment of Diverse Ownership Interests: A Comment on Adequate Protection of Secured Creditors in Bankruptcy, 51 U. Chi. L. Rev. 97 (1984); Eisenberg, Bankruptcy Law in Perspective, 28 U.C.L.A. L. Rev. 953 (1981). See also Report of the Commission on Bankruptcy Laws of the

United States, Part I, Chapter 3 (A Philosophical Basis for a Federal
Bankruptcy Act) 61-83 (1973), H.R. Doc. No. 93-137, Part I, 93d Cong.,
1st Sess.; Shuchman, An Attempt at a "Philosophy of Bankruptcy," 21
U.C.L.A. L. Rev. 403 (1973); Bulow and Shoven, The Bankruptcy Decision, 9 Bell. J. Econ. 437 (1978). For a discussion of the relationship
between individual remedies and a bankruptcy proceeding that views individual remedies as essentially aiding in enforcing the creditor's right to
payment and bankruptcy proceedings as principally protective of debtors,
see LoPucki, A General Theory of the Dynamics of the State Remedies/
Bankruptcy System, 1982 Wis. L. Rev. 311.

Even if we assume for a moment that bankruptcy law should be largely
if not exclusively procedural, many problems remain. The distinctions
between a creditor's procedural rights under state law and its substantive
rights may be elusive. In the case that follows the Supreme Court observes
that in the absence of any specific bankruptcy policy, rights that creditors
have under state law should be preserved. Is the Court, however, sensitive
to the changes in the procedural rights of the parties that are necessary just
by virtue of a bankruptcy proceeding being a collective proceeding?

BUTNER v. UNITED STATES
440 U.S. 48 (1979)

JUSTICE STEVENS delivered the opinion of the Court.

A dispute between a bankruptcy trustee and a second mortgagee over
the right to the rents collected during the period between the mortgagor's
bankruptcy and the foreclosure sale of the mortgaged property gave rise
to the question we granted certiorari to decide. . . . That question is
whether the right to such rents is determined by a federal rule of equity or
by the law of the State where the property is located.

On May 14, 1973, Golden Enterprises, Inc. (Golden), filed a petition
for an arrangement under Chapter XI of the Bankruptcy Act. 11 U.S.C.
§§701-799. In those proceedings, the bankruptcy judge approved a plan
consolidating various liens on North Carolina real estate owned by
Golden. As a result, petitioner acquired a second mortgage securing an
indebtedness of $360,000. Petitioner did not, however, receive any ex-
press security interest in the rents earned by the property.

On April 18, 1974, the bankruptcy judge granted Golden's motion to
appoint an agent to collect the rents and to apply them as directed by the
court. The order of appointment provided that the money should be
applied to tax obligations, payments of the first mortgage, fire insurance
premiums, and interest and principal on the second mortgage. There is no
dispute about the collections or payments made pursuant to that order.

The arrangement plan was never confirmed. On February 14, 1975, Golden was adjudicated a bankrupt, and the trustee in bankruptcy was appointed. At that time both the first and second mortgages were in default. The trustee was ordered to collect and retain all rents "to the end that the same may be applied under this or different or further orders of [the bankruptcy] [c]ourt." . . .

After various alternatives were considered, and after the District Court refused to confirm a first sale, the properties were ultimately sold to petitioner on November 12, 1975, for $174,000. That price was paid by reducing the estate's indebtedness to petitioner from $360,000 to $186,000.

As of the date of sale, a fund of $162,971.32 had been accumulated by the trustee pursuant to the February 14 court order that he collect and retain all rents. On December 1, 1975, petitioner filed a motion claiming a security interest in this fund and seeking to have it applied to the balance of the second mortgage indebtedness. The bankruptcy judge denied the motion, holding that the $186,000 balance due to petitioner should be treated as a general unsecured claim.

The District Court reversed. It recognized that under North Carolina law, a mortgagor is deemed the owner of the land subject to the mortgage and is entitled to rents and profits, even after default, so long as he retains possession. But the court viewed the appointment of an agent to collect rents during the arrangement proceedings as tantamount to the appointment of a receiver. This appointment, the court concluded, satisfied the state-law requirement of a change of possession giving the mortgagee an interest in the rents; no further action after the adjudication in bankruptcy was required to secure or preserve this interest.

The Court of Appeals reversed and reinstated the disposition of the bankruptcy judge. Golden Enterprises, Inc. v. United States, 566 F.2d 1207. The court acknowledged that the agent appointed to collect rents before the bankruptcy was equivalent to a state-court receivership, but held that the adjudication terminated that relationship. Because petitioner had made no request *during the bankruptcy* for a sequestration of rents or for the appointment of a receiver, petitioner had not, in the court's view, taken the kind of action North Carolina law required to give the mortgagee a security interest in the rents collected after the bankruptcy adjudication. One judge dissented, adopting the position of the District Court. Id, at 1211.

I

We did not grant certiorari to decide whether the Court of Appeals correctly applied North Carolina law. Our concern is with the proper interpretation of the federal statutes governing the administration of bankrupt estates. Specifically, it is our purpose to resolve a conflict between the

Third and Seventh Circuits on the one hand, and the Second, Fourth, Sixth, Eighth, and Ninth Circuits on the other, concerning the proper approach to a dispute of this kind.

The courts in the latter group regard the question whether a security interest in property extends to rents and profits derived from the property as one that should be resolved by reference to state law. In a few States, sometimes referred to as "title States," the mortgagee is automatically entitled to possession of the property, and to a secured interest in the rents.[3] In most States, the mortgagee's right to rents is dependent upon his taking actual or constructive possession of the property by means of a foreclosure, the appointment of a receiver for his benefit, or some similar legal proceeding. Because the applicable law varies from State to State, the results in federal bankruptcy proceedings will also vary under the approach taken by most of the Circuits.

The Third and Seventh Circuits have adopted a federal rule of equity that affords the mortgagee a secured interest in the rents even if state law would not recognize any such interest until after foreclosure. Those courts reason that since the bankruptcy court has the power to deprive the mortgagee of his state-law remedy, equity requires that the right to rents not be dependent on state-court action that may be precluded by federal law.[6] Under this approach, no affirmative steps are required by the mortgagee — in state or federal court — to acquire or maintain a right to the rents.

Mortgagee's rights

3. In some title States, the mortgagee's right to rents and profits may be exercised even prior to default . . . ; in all events, the right at least attaches upon default. . . .

North Carolina has been classified as a "title" State, Comment, The Mortgagee's Right to Rents After Default, 50 Yale L.J. 1424, 1425 n.6 (1941), although it does not adhere to this theory in its purest form. Under its case law, a mortgagee is entitled to possession of the mortgaged property upon default, and need not await actual foreclosure. Such possession might be secured either with the consent of the mortgagor or by an action in ejectment. But so long as the mortgagor does remain in possession, even after default, he — not the mortgagee — appears to be entitled to the rents and profits. See . . . Kistler v. Development Co., 205 N.C. 755, 757, 172 S.E. 413, 414 (1934) ("In the absence of a stipulation to the contrary a mortgagor of real property who is permitted to retain possession is entitled to the rents and profits. Credle v. Ayers, 126 N.C. 11. As between the mortgagor and the mortgagee equity makes the mortgage a charge upon the rents and profits when the mortgagor is insolvent and the security is inadequate . . . but the prevailing rule is that a mortgagee is not entitled to rents until entry is made or a suit for foreclosure is begun").

6. See, e.g., Central Hanover Bank & Trust Co. v. Philadelphia & Reading Coal & Iron Co., 99 F.2d 642, 645 (C.A.3 1938):

It is settled in this circuit that in a bankruptcy proceeding a mortgage creditor is entitled without prior demand to the net income of the mortgaged property from the date of adjudication if it is needed to pay the amount due him. . . . This is because the bankruptcy proceeding has taken from the Debtor the possession of his property and in so doing has deprived the mortgage creditor of his ordinary remedy to reach the property mortgaged and its income. It, therefore, follows upon equitable principles, as Judge Woolley pointed out in Bindseil v. Liberty Trust Co., supra, . . . "that after insolvency has taken the debtor's property out of his hands, its income or product belongs to the lien creditor, who has thus become its virtual owner; and that such income or product issuing from mortgaged property, should not be diverted from the mortgage creditor who has a lien to general creditors who have no lien."

II

for ▷   We agree with the majority view.

The constitutional authority of Congress to establish "uniform Laws on the subject of Bankruptcies throughout the United States" would clearly encompass a federal statute defining the mortgagee's interest in the rents and profits earned by property in a bankrupt estate. But Congress has not chosen to exercise its power to fashion any such rule. The Bankruptcy Act does include provisions invalidating certain security interests as fraudulent, or as improper preferences over general creditors. Apart from these provisions, however, Congress has generally left the determination of property rights in the assets of a bankrupt's estate to state law.[9]

Property interests are created and defined by state law. Unless some federal interest requires a different result, there is no reason why such interests should be analyzed differently simply because an interested party is involved in a bankruptcy proceeding. Uniform treatment of property interests by both state and federal courts within a State serves to reduce uncertainty, to discourage forum shopping, and to prevent a party from receiving "a windfall merely by reason of the happenstance of bankruptcy." Lewis v. Manufacturers National Bank, 364 U.S. 603, 609. The justifications for application of state law are not limited to ownership interests; they apply with equal force to security interests, including the interest of a mortgagee in rents earned by mortgaged property.

The minority of courts which have rejected state law have not done so because of any congressional command, or because their approach serves any identifiable federal interest. Rather, they have adopted a uniform federal approach to the question of the mortgagee's interest in rents and profits because of their perception of the demands of equity. The equity powers of bankruptcy court play an important part in the administration of bankrupt estates in countless situations in which the judge is required to deal with particular, individualized problems. But undefined considerations of equity provide no basis for adoption of a uniform federal rule affording mortgagees an automatic interest in the rents as soon as the mortgagor is declared bankrupt.

---

9. "The Federal Constitution, Article I, §8, gives Congress the power to establish uniform laws on the subject of bankruptcy throughout the United States. In view of this grant of authority to the Congress it has been settled from an early date that state laws to the extent that they conflict with the laws of Congress, enacted under its constitutional authority, on the subject of bankruptcies are suspended. While this is true, state laws are thus suspended only to the extent of actual conflict with the system provided by the Bankruptcy Act of Congress. Sturges v. Crowninshield, 4 Wheat. 122; Ogden v. Saunders, 12 Wheat. 213.

"Notwithstanding this requirement as to uniformity the bankruptcy acts of Congress may recognize the laws of the State in certain particulars, although such recognition may lead to different results in different States. For example, the Bankruptcy Act recognizes and enforces the laws of the States affecting dower, exemptions, the validity of mortgages, priorities of payment and the like. Such recognition in the application of state laws does not affect the constitutionality of the Bankruptcy Act, although in these particulars the operation of the act is not alike in all the States." Stellwagen v. Clum, 245 U.S. 605, 613.

In support of their rule, the Third and Seventh Circuits have emphasized that while the mortgagee may pursue various state-law remedies prior to bankruptcy, the adjudication leaves the mortgagee "only such remedies as may be found in a court of bankruptcy in the equitable administration of the bankrupt's assets." Bindseil v. Liberty Trust Co., 248 F. 112, 114 (C.A.3 1917). It does not follow, however, that "equitable administration" requires that all mortgagees be afforded an automatic security interest in rents and profits when state law would deny such an automatic benefit and require the mortgagee to take some affirmative action before his rights are recognized. What does follow is that the federal bankruptcy court should take whatever steps are necessary to ensure that the mortgagee is afforded in federal bankruptcy court the same protection he would have under state law if no bankruptcy had ensued. This is the majority view, which we adopt today.

holding for Δ

The rule of the Third and Seventh Circuits, at least in some circumstances, affords the mortgagee rights that are not his as a matter of state law. The rule we adopt avoids this inequity because it looks to state law to define the security interest of the mortgagee. At the same time, our decision avoids the opposite inequity of depriving a mortgagee of his state-law security interest when bankruptcy intervenes. For while it is argued that bankruptcy may impair or delay the mortgagee's exercise of his right to foreclosure, and thus his acquisition of a security interest in rents according to the law of many States, a bankruptcy judge familiar with local practice should be able to avoid this potential loss by sequestering rents or authorizing immediate state-law foreclosures. Even though a federal judge may temporarily delay entry of such an order, the loss of rents to the mortgagee normally should be no greater than if he had been proceeding in a state court: for if there is a reason that persuades a federal judge to delay, presumably the same reason would also persuade a state judge to withhold foreclosure temporarily. The essential point is that in a properly administered scheme in which the basic federal rule is that state law governs, the primary reason why any holder of a mortgage may fail to collect rent immediately after default must stem from state law.

III

Recognizing that the bankruptcy frustrated petitioner's right to take possession of the mortgaged property and thereby to establish his right to rents as a matter of North Carolina law, the Court of Appeals assumed that a request to the bankruptcy judge for sequestration of rents, for the appointment of a receiver, or for permission to proceed with a state-court foreclosure would have satisfied the state-law requirement. Since none of these steps was taken during the bankruptcy, the Court of Appeals held that petitioner had no right to the rents.

The dissenting judge in the Court of Appeals, as well as the District

Judge, felt that the action taken during the arrangement proceedings, coupled with informal requests for abandonment of the property during the bankruptcy, was sufficient to comply with North Carolina law. Neither of these judges, however, based his analysis on the federal rule followed in the Third and Seventh Circuits. They merely disagreed with the majority about the requirements of North Carolina law.

In this Court the parties have argued the state-law question at great length, each stressing different aspects of the record. We decline to review the state-law question. The federal judges who deal regularly with questions of state law in their respective districts and circuits are in a better position than we to determine how local courts would dispose of comparable issues.

The judgment is affirmed.

for A

NOTE ON *BUTNER* AND RIGHTS UNDER STATE LAW IN BANKRUPTCY

Butner represents one of the first attempts by the Supreme Court to articulate when it would adopt a state rule in bankruptcy and when it would fashion a federal rule in a situation where the bankruptcy statute was silent.

The principal issue in *Butner* is who gets the rents accumulated in the period *after* the adjudication of bankruptcy and *before* the sale of the parcels to the secured party. The two potential claimants are the second mortgagee (presumably, the first mortgagee has been paid off) and the trustee, as representative of the unsecured creditors. The history of Golden Enterprises' bankruptcy calls for a bit of an explanation. Golden first filed for a Chapter XI arrangement under the 1898 Act. (A Chapter XI arrangement was the less formal of two reorganization chapters under the 1898 Act.) As was often the case, the enterprise failed once again despite the effort to resuscitate it, and several years later Golden went into straight liquidation under Chapter VII. In Chapter VII of the 1898 Act, as in Chapter 7 of the 1978 Code, a debtor's assets are sold for cash to one or more third parties, and the proceeds are divided among creditors.

The primary assets of Golden's estate were certain parcels of commercial real estate. During the pendency of the proceedings, the parcels generated substantial rents. Under North Carolina law, as the Supreme Court describes it, the mortgagor (i.e., Golden) was entitled to the rents as long as it remained in possession. During the arrangement proceeding, Golden asked for an agent to collect rents, and this agent collected rents during the Chapter XI proceeding, and continued to do so after the adjudication of bankruptcy (i.e., after the start of the Chapter VII case). It is that post-adjudication-in-bankruptcy period that is in issue in *Butner*.

The case may be thought of as deciding two issues, although one of them is decided *sub silentio*. The first issue, which is really an issue precedent to the one the Supreme Court addresses, is: Why should the security interest (mortgage) even apply to those rents? They are, or may be thought to be, *post-petition* assets, and bankruptcy usually is thought of as cutting off pre-petition claimants by leaving them with pre-petition assets. Why is either the mortgagee or the trustee claiming these rents? What, if anything, justifies this "exception" to the freeing up of post-petition assets? One way to answer this question is to note the nature of many types of property. When the asset is real estate, for example, does it make any sense to try to allocate the value of the asset pre-petition and post-petition? Isn't the value of real estate today simply a discounted calculation of the "rents" it can generate in the future? Isn't this, indeed, true of all property owned by a corporation? (The Bankruptcy Code codifies this idea. Section 541(a)(6) brings into the "estate" of the debtor in bankruptcy proceeds, rents, and the like, and §552 extends pre-petition security interests to cover such proceeds, rents, and the like, if allowed under applicable nonbankruptcy law and the security agreement.)

The second issue, and the one the Court addresses, is: Which rule (state or federal) should be followed in defining how the secured party may realize on these post-bankruptcy rents? The Court offers three interests that, it asserts, support a conclusion that state law should be followed: Such a rule (1) reduces uncertainty; (2) discourages forum shopping; and (3) prevents a party from "receiving a windfall" merely by reason of the happenstance of bankruptcy. Consider each of these three justifications. How persuasive are they? How much guidance do they give you as to when a court should deviate from a state rule? Do they also give guidance as to the type of statutes that should be drafted in bankruptcy? Does the court persuade you that "undefined considerations of equity" should not be given much play?

The ultimate disposition of the case was a remand, the Supreme Court stating "[w]e decline to review the state-law question." Is it clear that the ultimate issue *is* a state law issue? Has the Court confused substance (where bankruptcy takes its cue from nonbankruptcy rules) with procedure (which bankruptcy sometimes must supplant)? Put another way, isn't the question one of what would serve as a good surrogate, in the bankruptcy court, for state-law procedures that now *couldn't* be followed, because of the intervention of bankruptcy? Doesn't *that* issue have federal overtones?

3. Overview of a Bankruptcy Proceeding

In this section, we present the story of a typical firm that fails and ends up in a bankruptcy proceeding. The case is entirely fictional, although we shall encounter many of the same basic features in actual cases throughout the rest of this book. This overview is designed to give you a perspective on the workings of the Bankruptcy Code as applied to creditors, so that when we examine its particulars in detail in Chapters 2 through 9, you will have some sense of the larger picture. Of course, not all of the details these materials cover later will be touched on here, and those that are will be done in cursory fashion. "Fresh start" rules applicable to debtors who are individuals are also not covered in this overview.

Firm was incorporated by Founder in the 1920s. It made metal parts. Some of these parts were standard, such as nuts and bolts, that could be manufactured without any specific buyer in mind. Others were custom designed, such as parts that an electric motor manufacturer might need to build its machines. In 1985, shares of Firm were in the hands of thirty different children, grandchildren, and great-grandchildren of Founder. President, the president of Firm, is the grandson of Founder, and he owns 20 percent of the stock in his own name. Firm owes Bank $5 million. It borrowed the money in the early 1970s to refurbish its plant and acquire new computer-driven machines that were supposed to be far more efficient than the ones Firm had been using. Bank supported its loan with a security interest in all of Firm's real property and equipment. When its financial troubles began in the late 1970s, Firm obtained a credit line of $1 million (subsequently raised to $3 million) from Finance Company. Finance Company took a security interest in Firm's inventory and accounts receivable. In addition, Finance Company required President to guarantee Firm's obligations and to grant Finance Company a mortgage on his home.

Early in 1985, Firm started dragging out payments to its suppliers. Instead of being paid within 10 days, most were kept waiting for six weeks or more. To pay trade creditors even enough to continue shipments, President decided that Firm had to skip a property tax installment payment to City. In March, the trade creditors were owed $2 million, Finance Company was owed $3 million, Bank $5 million, and City $500,000. Firm's real property and equipment is worth at most $4 million. Its other assets, including inventory and accounts receivable, are worth at most $2.5 million.

President began a series of talks with Bank, Finance Company, and the trade creditors. He asked Bank to reschedule payments of principal on its loan, Finance Company to increase its credit line, and trade creditors to continue to sell goods on open account. These talks went nowhere. Just before City was ready to file a property tax lien against Firm, Firm filed a Chapter 11 petition under §301 of the Bankruptcy Code. If Firm had not filed the petition, three or more of its creditors could have begun either a Chapter 11 or a Chapter 7 proceeding, through filing an involuntary petition, if they had unsecured claims, not contingent as to liability or the subject of a bona fide dispute, that totaled more than $5,000. §303(b). If the creditors had filed a Chapter 7 petition, Firm might have been able to convert it into a Chapter 11 petition (§706(b)), but it could not have dismissed the petition, unless it could show that it was generally paying its debts as they became due (§303(h)), or that such dismissal would be in the best interests of both Firm and its creditors (§305).

Unlike a Chapter 7 proceeding, a Chapter 11 proceeding envisions keeping Firm intact as a going concern. (Under Chapter 11, a "debtor in possession" has the same powers as a trustee in bankruptcy, including the right to run the business. §1107.) Whether in Chapter 7 or Chapter 11, however, the filing of the petition itself puts a stop to all efforts by pre-petition creditors to collect pre-petition debts. §362. Even if Firm is in default on its obligations under the security agreements, Bank and Finance Company cannot repossess their collateral without permission from the bankruptcy court. City can no longer file its property tax lien. The trade creditors cannot demand payment on their past obligations. Strictly speaking, Firm is unable even to pay its employees for work done before the filing of the petition. As a practical matter, however, Firm, if it wishes to continue as a going concern, is likely to meet its payroll obligations. Other creditors of Firm would not object, especially if continuing to operate the business seemed a good idea to the creditors and the workers threatened to strike if they were not paid.

Firm cannot use any of its cash collateral without court approval because of Finance Company's security interest. §363. It may, however, be able to persuade Finance Company to extend it a credit line similar to the one that existed before the filing of the petition, in return for giving Finance Company a security interest in all accounts receivable that arise after the petition was filed. §364. Finance Company may be particularly concerned about keeping Firm intact, because the inventory and accounts receivable of a firm in piecemeal liquidation are oftentimes worth only a fraction of what they would be if the firm were kept alive as a going concern. If it is in Chapter 11, Firm can also sell assets in the ordinary course of business and, with the approval of the bankruptcy judge, sell assets outside the ordinary course of its business. §363.

Bank has the right to go to court and insist that, unless it is given its collateral, its security interest in Firm's real property and equipment be "adequately protected." §§361, 362. Firm and Bank will probably dispute the amount of protection the Bankruptcy Code requires. Firm will argue that it simply must ensure that the real estate and equipment will still be worth $4 million when the Chapter 11 proceeding ends. Bank will argue that, because it has a right under state law to $4 million as of the time the petition was filed (which is almost certainly a default under the security agreement), it is entitled to protection for the equivalent of that amount — $4 million *and* the interest that would run on a loan of that amount during the course of the bankruptcy proceeding. This legal question has not been definitively resolved.

If Firm has entered into an unfavorable collective bargaining agreement with its workers, it may try to repudiate that agreement, although Congress enacted legislation in 1984 attempting to impose some restraint on its ability to do so. If it has a favorable supply contract or a favorable lease, Firm may be able to cure its past defaults and reinstate the contract or lease. §365. It may have the choice of insisting that the seller or lessor continue its performance, or assigning the favorable contract to someone else for cash. Id.

The bankruptcy process has two elements. If Firm is to be kept intact as a going concern, a mechanism must be provided to ensure that its operations continue. This involves what we have just discussed in a general way. In addition, the bankruptcy process must provide a means of sorting out the rights of competing claimants. Part of this process is deciding who has claims against the assets under §§501 and 502. Bank, Finance Company, and the trade creditors certainly do, as well as City. But there are likely to be other claimants as well. For example, Firm may have liabilities to a pension fund it has joined. Moreover, buyers of its metal parts may have contract actions against it, and ultimate users or bystanders may have tort actions. Finally, President has a claim against Firm because of his contingent obligation to pay Finance Company if Firm is unable to do so. These claimants not only need to be identified, but their priority rights against each other must also be identified. Secured creditors, for example, will have a right to get paid first out of their collateral. §§506, 725. And there may be rankings among unsecured creditors. §507. Unsecured creditors, in turn, have the right to be paid before equity interests. §726. President's claim is special because of the problems of double-counting. See §§502(e); 509.

Firm's assets must be identified and assembled. §§541-543. These assets include tangible and intangible property (for example, causes of action Firm has against others), and perhaps some assets previously transferred by Firm. If, as seems almost certain, Firm was "insolvent" (§101(29)) during the 90-day period before the bankruptcy petition, transfers made to creditors during that period may be voidable (§547). Whether such transfers are voidable will depend on a lot of factors; perhaps the most important for this example is whether the payments were made in the ordinary course of business. §547(c)(2). Bank would probably not have to return any payments of principal (and perhaps interest as well) made during the 90-day period. Trade creditors, who generally are unsecured, however, might be required to return any payments made to them during the 90-day period on account of prior deliveries if the accounts were backlogged, because it may be possible for the trustee to show the payments were made outside the ordinary course of Firm's business. §547(c)(2). Moreover, assets that Firm conveyed for less than reasonably equivalent value or fair consideration while it was insolvent during the year (and perhaps more) before the filing of the petition may also be set aside. §548; see also §544(b).

Unlike a Chapter 7 proceeding, where a trustee is charged with assembling assets, selling (or otherwise disposing) of them, and distributing the

proceeds in a specified manner, Chapter 11 is substantially more complicated. A Chapter 11 reorganization can be thought of principally as a
framework for bargaining among parties, where the statute provides various rights and limitations. For six months after the petition is filed, the
debtor in possession generally has the exclusive right to propose what is
known as a plan of reorganization. §1121. A plan will divide creditors into
classes (§§1122, 1123) and propose to give each class a certain amount of
cash or an interest in the reorganized company. If Bank's original loan was
at a favorable interest rate, Firm may want to reinstate it through a process
known as "nonimpairment." §1124. If Bank's interest is unimpaired, the
plan may contemplate curing past defaults and continue payments on the
old schedule. The plan might also propose making a series of cash payments to Finance Company. Alternatively, Finance Company might be
willing to accept on a long-term basis an arrangement similar to the financing arrangement it arranged with Firm to enable it to continue operations.
The plan would have to provide for payment to City, which has a right to
be paid before general creditors. §507(a)(7)(B). Trade creditors might be
given stock in the reorganized company. The smaller creditors might be
paid all or a fraction of their claims in cash. The shareholders (such as
President) might be offered a small percentage of the new shares of common stock. (All this represents, of course, one of many possibilities.)

But the plan must meet certain degrees of either creditor acceptance
or statutory minimums. Creditors are allowed to accept the plan both by
class and individually. If the interests of a class of creditors is not impaired
by the plan of reorganization (as Bank's interest would probably be if past
defaults were cured), that class and each of its members will be deemed to
have accepted the plan. §1126(f). Apart from nonimpairment, however,
there are two levels of protection for creditors. Individual creditors can
veto a plan they do not agree with if they can show that they will receive less
in the reorganization than in a straight liquidation under Chapter 7.
§1129(a)(7). This is often called the "best interests of creditors" test.
Applying this test, however, is often difficult. If the trade creditors are
paid with shares of the reorganized company and a trade creditor objects,
for example, it would be difficult to determine whether trade creditors are
receiving more than they would in a straight liquidation because there is no
market for the stock that the reorganized corporation issues.

Even if this test is met, the *class* of creditors (unless unimpaired) can
block a plan if they vote against it by requisite amount (§1126), *unless* the
judge finds that the plan either pays that class, in present value terms, in
full, *or* finds that no junior class (such as equity) has received anything.
§1129(b). This is often called the "absolute priority rule." In the plan
proposed by Firm, if the common stockholders were to retain anything,
the creditors must approve the plan by class-wide vote or be shown to
receive payment in full. Because both override of an individual creditor's
objection and override of a class's objection involves imprecise valuation

questions, a bankruptcy judge has wide discretion to approve (or "cram down," as it is usually called) plans over the objections of creditors.

In reading the cases and materials that follow in the next eight chapters, it is important to bear in mind that the usefulness of a bankruptcy law cannot be measured by the mere fact that virtually all the players suffer economic loss, any more than medical science can be judged by the existence of death and disease. Firms that fail are an inevitable feature of our economy. Just as successful and innovative firms prosper, badly managed firms suffer. In medicine the central concern — minimizing disease and prolonging life — is not hard to identify, at least in principle. The central concern of bankruptcy, however, is harder to define and far more controversial. Bankruptcy law is in some measure simply a vehicle by which creditors can enforce obligations owed them more effectively than permitted by individual remedies that exist under state law or by bargaining among creditors. Whether, in the case of corporate debtors (or, indeed, individual debtors apart from the fresh start), it can or should be anything more is perhaps the most important question of bankruptcy policy.

Chapter 2
COMMENCEMENT OF THE
BANKRUPTCY CASE

A. INTRODUCTION

A bankruptcy proceeding affects the rights of creditors and debtor alike. Creditors are stayed from exercising their individual remedies. A debtor is freed from the constraints imposed by the wide variety of monitoring devices that its creditors might employ outside of bankruptcy. On the other hand, creditors gain some kinds of control over the debtor (and over competing creditors) that would be unavailable for many of them except in bankruptcy. A bankruptcy judge supervises many decisions the debtor once made for itself (such as whether to borrow money or to sell assets) subject only, perhaps, to limited creditor contractual constraints. The debtor might or might not find these new constraints more burdensome than the ones outside of bankruptcy, just as the creditors might or might not prefer them. The debtor or the creditors must balance the advantages of this new freedom (or control) against the costs of the bankruptcy proceeding itself. These costs include not merely the fees of the trustee and the trustee's lawyers, §§326-331, but also the costs a debtor might incur when others learn of the filing.

As a practical matter, the filing of a bankruptcy petition itself may hurt the debtor and all its creditors by reducing the value of the debtor's business. The debtor may have trouble finding buyers. Potential buyers may fear that the debtor will not be around to honor its warranties (a problem a durable goods manufacturer, such as an automobile manufacturer, might find more vexing than a restaurant chain or a manufacturer of consumables). Managers or entrepreneurs may be less willing to join the business and learn firm-specific skills. The debtor may also find it harder to collect money it is owed. Its debtors may assert set-off rights or they may simply think their reputations will suffer little if they fail to pay a firm in bankruptcy. Note that bankruptcy rules do not themselves directly cause these harms. A business may experience financial trouble and suffer similar losses without ever using bankruptcy. But the filing of a bankruptcy petition conveys information to customers, suppliers, and others. In the early 1980s, Chrysler Corporation was in financial trouble whether or not it used bankruptcy. But most feel that its problems with buyers would have been greatly exacerbated had it filed for bankruptcy, largely because of the informational content of that filing. Both Chrysler and its creditors, then, had a strong incentive to negotiate a deal without using bankruptcy. The strategic threat of bankruptcy was there nonetheless.

The filing of a bankruptcy petition may ultimately benefit both creditors and their debtor (or its shareholders or managers); indeed, as we suggested in Chapter 1, this possibility may justify the basic existence of the bankruptcy process (insofar as it is concerned with issues other than an individual's right to a financial fresh start). But using the bankruptcy process might help only some of them. A bankruptcy proceeding can work to the advantage of everyone, or it can work to the advantage only of the debtor, a single creditor, or one group of creditors, while making everyone else worse off. Hence we cannot decide who should be able to begin a bankruptcy proceeding until we know why a bankruptcy proceeding exists and who is supposed to benefit from it. It is this question that underlies the materials in this chapter and suggests why the Bankruptcy Code has restrictions on its use. In addressing this question, however, we are not merely asking whether the Bankruptcy Code is well crafted. In its present form, bankruptcy law contains many flexible standards rather than clear-cut rules. A bankruptcy judge cannot effectively interpret the flexible language in our Bankruptcy Code without a firm sense of the purposes a bankruptcy proceeding is supposed to serve.

For example, there is no clear statutory answer to the question of whether an Illinois Land Trust — the debtor in the first case in this chapter — is a "person" within the meaning of the Bankruptcy Code and thus can become the debtor in a bankruptcy proceeding. To answer this question, one needs to know something about the attributes of an Illinois Land Trust as well as something about what ends a bankruptcy proceeding is supposed to serve. Unless one knows the answer to these questions, one has no way of knowing exactly how the word "person" (which excludes "trusts" but which, through incorporation of the word "corporation," includes "business trusts") should be interpreted and hence whether an Illinois Land Trust belongs in bankruptcy or not.

A return to the history of bankruptcy law illustrates this point. As we observed in Chapter 1, bankruptcy law in the sixteenth century was simply a collection remedy that became available to the creditors of a merchant debtor when the merchant did something to defeat their other remedies. Creditors could invoke bankruptcy law, for example, when the debtor took sanctuary or stayed within his house, preventing creditors from completing service of process and hence preventing them from reducing their claims to judgment. The purpose of the law was to supplement other remedies that were available both before and after the bankruptcy proceeding commenced.

Deciding whether a bankruptcy proceeding was proper ought to have been a straightforward enterprise. First, the enumerated acts of bankruptcy provided rules that were relatively easy to apply — a debtor either had taken sanctuary (by going to a specified precinct where the King's writ could not enter) or had not. Even if it were difficult to decide whether the debtor had in fact committed an act of bankruptcy, the approach was clear: In construing whether one of the specified acts of bankruptcy described the debtor's actions, one would bear in mind that a bankruptcy proceeding should be triggered when the debtor had behaved in a way that defeated the ordinary debt collection remedies available to creditors. The other question was somewhat more troublesome: Was the debtor a merchant? Even though this category gradually expanded over time, the idea behind it was reasonably clear.

Under modern bankruptcy law, the approach is far less clear. There is no simple benchmark by which we can judge the propriety of a bankruptcy proceeding in a particular case. Bankruptcy is no longer simply a creditor remedy available when other collection devices are unavailing. The notion of a voluntary bankruptcy proceeding is inconsistent with the idea that bankruptcy law enables creditors to defeat a debtor's efforts to avoid a day of reckoning. By filing a petition, the debtor is in effect demanding a day of reckoning. One major purpose of present bankruptcy law is to stop individual creditors from successfully employing other collection devices and entering into a counterproductive race to the debtor's assets, but it is not its only purpose. In the case of debtors who are individuals, there is, of course, the provisions for a discharge that explain many uses of the bankruptcy process. But even in the case of debtors who are not individuals, there are many more voluntary than involuntary petitions. In certain circumstances, as we will see in Chapter 7 of this book, collective bargaining agreements can be rejected in bankruptcy under conditions where they could not be rejected outside of bankruptcy. This, along with many other explicit bankruptcy rule changes, and procedural changes as well, create strategic opportunities. Should these opportunities be freely available, or only if certain other underlying "bankruptcy-specific" problems are first found to exist?

In this chapter, we are concerned with when and under what circumstances a bankruptcy proceeding should take place. In an ideal world, this question would be unimportant. If a bankruptcy system were perfectly designed so that it accommodated the interests it was trying to serve (such as preventing a race to assets among creditors) and did nothing else, we would not have to worry about whether a case was properly commenced. No one would have an incentive to start a bankruptcy proceeding unless it were necessary to serve those goals. If someone mistakenly started the proceeding, a few costs might be incurred, but the party who began the proceeding could be forced to bear them. In any event the proceeding would not enable any parties to gain an improper advantage. Our bankruptcy law, however, like any law in a world in which facts and motives are complex and full information is usually not available, is imperfect in trying to sort out proper and improper cases. Parties can gain advantages over others by resorting to bankruptcy, even if enjoying such advantages has nothing to do with the purposes of bankruptcy law. Therefore, we have to ask *when* it is appropriate to have a bankruptcy proceeding and how to devise statutory rules that implement that policy. This question, in turn, can be broken down into several parts:

1. Who should be eligible for a bankruptcy proceeding?
2. When should a debtor be allowed to start a bankruptcy proceeding (a "voluntary" petition)?
3. When should creditors be able to bring a bankruptcy proceeding (an "involuntary" petition) and defeat a debtor's efforts to dismiss it?
4. When should a bankruptcy judge dismiss a bankruptcy case, notwithstanding compliance with the technical tests for commencement of a bankruptcy case and notwithstanding the wishes of at least some of the creditors or the debtor?

A useful way of approaching any bankruptcy problem, or indeed any commercial law problem, is to try to understand it from the perspective of the parties. The motivations of a party who files a bankruptcy petition may not be dispositive of whether the petition is appropriate, but it may tell us what the relevant stakes are. A recent case illustrates this point.

In June 1984, Franklin Computer Corp. filed a bankruptcy petition. Franklin was a maker of personal computers, and its stock was closely held by present and former managers and their families. It had sales of $71 million in the previous year. Franklin's troubles might be traced to a copyright infringement suit brought against it by Apple Computer, whose machine Franklin had imitated. Franklin settled the suit by agreeing to pay $2.5 million to Apple, but the costs of the suit and the uncertainties it caused allegedly threw the firm off track. Franklin sought to turn its fortunes around with a new computer, but, according to what Franklin said when it filed for bankruptcy, it had trouble delivering the product to its dealers because of a parts shortage. Its delivery difficulties led to a decline in orders. It trimmed its work force from over 400 to 100. Still unable to produce its new computer in sufficient numbers, however, Franklin filed a bankruptcy petition. In conjunction with that filing, Franklin claimed to have assets of $33.9 million and liabilities of $22.8 million. Creditors included a bank that was owed almost $5 million and that had a security interest in Franklin's property. The largest unsecured creditors included suppliers of components to Franklin, Apple Computer, which was still owed $650,000 from its settlement, and Franklin's lawyers, who were owed $450,000. The chairman of Franklin said that Franklin was forced into bankruptcy because declining revenue could not meet operating costs. Wall St. J., June 25, 1984, at 4.

Should Franklin Computer have been in a bankruptcy proceeding? In addressing this question from the perspective of June of 1984, it is profitable to break the inquiry down into parts. As we do so, we will run across many questions of substance and procedure that we cannot address in detail until later chapters. Still, it is important to raise them now, for many of the *basic* issues can be addressed in this chapter.

Should a corporation ever be allowed to file a bankruptcy petition? Why are the state laws that sort out the rights of a corporation's creditors and shareholders not sufficient? Why should Franklin, or indeed any other corporation in difficulty, not be able to restructure its affairs by an agreement among all of its creditors? Why should Franklin not be forced to rely on whatever stay the state provides for the dissolution of corporations?

If we assume that it is appropriate for corporations in general to file bankruptcy petitions under some circumstances, is it appropriate for Franklin to do so under these circumstances? Is the chairman's explanation of the filing plausible? If Franklin's assets were in fact worth $33.9 million, and its liabilities were $22.8 million, does it need bankruptcy? If Franklin has a net worth of some $11.1 million, shouldn't Franklin be able to meet its operating costs by borrowing an additional $10 million or so? Why couldn't the shareholders lend the firm $10 million or sell their shares to someone who could? Did Franklin file for bankruptcy merely to try to preserve the $11.1 million for its shareholders, which might be jeopardized if the firm continued to operate without the protection of bankruptcy's automatic stay? Does or should the automatic stay have this effect?

How reliable are Franklin's numbers when one is trying to decide what to do with the firm? What are the assets and liabilities behind those numbers? If the numbers come from an accounting balance sheet, they may represent historical costs. Do they reflect the value of Franklin as a going concern? Or might Franklin, even though solvent, have been worth more by dissolving than by continuing? Even if Franklin's figures reflected its value as a going concern in June of 1984, who determined that value? Franklin's managers or shareholders may be incurable optimists (because they, like many of us, underestimate risks or because it is to their advantage to delay Franklin's liquidation). Franklin's managers may have been unrealistic to think the new computer would save the company and that they faced only a cash flow problem. But even if they are not overly optimistic or unrealistic, Franklin might have difficulty persuading existing shareholders or potential investors that its assets exceeded its liabilities by over $11 million. For example, allegedly one of the most valuable assets Franklin had was its new computer. The value of the computer depends upon much that was unclear as of June of 1984 (such as whether Franklin's rivals will introduce new models or cut their prices). It is also possible that the shareholders would not all agree to sell their stock, or that loan covenants will prevent Franklin from easily incurring additional debt. Franklin, for example, probably could not grant a new creditor a security interest in its assets superior to the bank's. It may be worth noting that, later in 1984, Franklin announced that it intended to liquidate its assets, turning over all proceeds to the company's creditors, and then dissolve. This decision was taken, when no buyer for the company as a whole materialized while Franklin was in bankruptcy. Wall St. J., Nov. 2, 1984, at 50. In January 1985, Franklin proposed to continue operations and pay creditors between 15 and 24 cents on the dollar and offered them 16 percent of the reorganized company's stock. A cash infusion of several million dollars from another entity would facilitate the reorganization. Wall St. J., Jan. 8, 1985, at 7.

Why would the directors and officers of Franklin want to file a bankruptcy petition? A bankruptcy petition gives the firm "breathing space" in the sense that its obligation to pay its existing creditors interest and principal is suspended (although it will still need to get ongoing supplies and perhaps credit). Nevertheless, as we will see, all the creditors are entitled to be paid in full and to have interest on their loans run (although only at the legal rate) from the filing of the petition before the shareholders are entitled to anything. Is it possible that in practice bankruptcy law advances the interests of junior claimants (such as shareholders) at the expense of those who are more senior (such as general creditors or secured creditors)? If it does so, is that a permissible reason for Franklin to be in bankruptcy?

Is bankruptcy appropriate because it keeps the firm intact notwithstanding a cash flow problem? But how often will there be a cash flow problem when there is not a good chance that the firm is in fact insolvent (in the sense of its liabilities, at fair valuation, exceeding its assets, at fair valuation)? Does not the existence of a cash flow problem necessarily mean that the debtor is having trouble borrowing money or raising capital from old or new sources? Is a cash flow problem usually a symptom of a more serious problem? In any event, why should the managers or directors have the *power* to begin a bankruptcy case (but no *obligation* to bring it)? The managers and directors of a corporation are, in some respects at least, the fiduciaries of the shareholders. In the absence of a legal obligation, they would have a duty to bring the petition only if it were in the shareholders' interest. Whether it was in the creditors' interest or would preserve a going concern and thus save jobs would be irrelevant to their fiduciary duties (although not perhaps to their contractual duties or practical realities).

If the firm were not insolvent, shareholders might have some interest in preventing a race to assets that a debtor's inability to meet present or future obligations may precipitate. They are entitled to the difference between the firm's assets and liabilities. In the typical case, however, a firm that files a bankruptcy petition eventually is shown to have liabilities in excess of assets. (If a firm is in fact solvent (and if the creditors believe it), there may not be a race to assets in the first place.) In some cases, the debtor's insolvency is clear from the start. In such a case, the filing of the petition can, in theory, only make shareholders worse off. Once a bankruptcy proceeding begins, the value of the firm is measured and rights are divided accordingly. If liabilities exceed assets at the moment, the shareholders will receive nothing, even though there had been a chance that, if the firm continued to operate as before, its fortunes might have changed and at some later day of reckoning assets would have exceeded liabilities. But this is in theory. In practice, bankruptcy proceedings take time. This time, plus some powers in bankruptcy, may work to the advantage of the shareholders. For, without bankruptcy, if the firm was going to have to release information disclosing its insolvency or potential insolvency, creditors might predictably start to grab assets. In those cases, a bankruptcy proceeding may in fact keep a firm's operating assets together as a going concern or otherwise delay its demise, and may explain why a voluntary petition would be filed.

If Franklin Computer is in fact insolvent, is there any reason to believe that it will act in the interests of the creditors or in anyone's interest but its own (and that of its owners)? If one thinks that bankruptcy is intended largely to give creditors protection from a race to the debtor's assets, why should the firm have a right to file a petition? Will there not always be some danger that it will file for some other reason? Is the case different if Franklin is in fact solvent?

What if Franklin did not file a bankruptcy petition? Should any creditor be entitled to file a petition? Should it matter whether one is a secured creditor (such as bank) or an involuntary creditor (such as Apple)? Should it take more than one creditor to file? Should a creditor whose claim is not matured, or is disputed, or is contingent, be entitled to file a petition? Should the petitioning creditor be required to hold a claim of some particular size? If so, should the minimum size be different for a firm that has income of $100,000 a year and one that has income of $100 million a year? Should corporate debtors be treated differently than individuals?

What must a debtor show to dismiss a bankruptcy petition brought by its creditors? Should it be enough to show (as Franklin claimed) that its assets exceeded liabilities? Would the existence of a cash flow problem be enough to force a debtor into a bankruptcy proceeding involuntarily? These questions are all addressed by §§301-305 and by the materials in this chapter.

B. ELIGIBILITY FOR BANKRUPTCY

We start with a case that raises the question of whether an entity generically known as an Illinois Land Trust can file a petition in bankruptcy. An Illinois Land Trust is a form of property ownership. Under it, real property is held in trust, generally for the purpose of allowing the beneficiaries to remain unknown. The land trust device also serves to convert real property into personal property. Owning personal property might have tax advantages, and personal property may be easier to transfer. Unlike an ordinary trust, such as one wealthy parents may set up for their children, the "beneficiaries" retain full right of control, although these beneficial owners frequently turn the day-to-day management of the property over to a managing agent. Typically, the only creditor of an Illinois Land Trust is a bank that makes a nonrecourse secured loan. When a general creditor of the trust does exist (such as a tort victim), the creditor can reach the trust property directly. Such a creditor can also reach the beneficiaries of the trust but must employ a court proceeding to discover who they are. An Illinois Land Trust is, as its name indicates, a form of real property owner-ship used widely in Illinois, particularly by those who own low income rental housing on the south side of Chicago.

In approaching this case, one should be aware of an array of sections of the Bankruptcy Code and related terminology. Section 101(12) defines "debtor" as the "person . . . concerning which a case under this title has been commenced." The basic section governing eligibility for the Bank-ruptcy Code is §109, but because it tells you that only a "person" or a "municipality" can be a debtor under the Bankruptcy Code, it leads you to the definition of "person" in §101(33), which, in turn, leads you to the definition of "corporation" in §101(8). This case also raises policy ques-tions, the principal one of which concerns those to whom the bankruptcy process should be made available. How well does the court mesh the statutory questions with the policy questions?

IN RE TREASURE ISLAND LAND TRUST
2 Bankr. 332 (Bankr. M.D. Fla. 1980)

George L. PROCTOR, Bankruptcy Judge.

The petition in this cause was filed in the name of Treasure Island Land Trust (the "Trust") on November 28, 1979. On November 30, 1979, R.E. Carrigan, Jr., and Lester E. Larson (the "Movants"), secured creditors, moved to dismiss the petition on the basis that the Trust is not entitled to be a debtor under the Bankruptcy Code. A hearing on the motion was held on January 9, 1980.

The Trust was created by contractual document entitled "Land Trust Agreement," dated March 26, 1971, between the trustee and var-ious named beneficiaries. There have been certain modifications to the contract, but none that change the nature of the agreement or that are otherwise pertinent to the arguments here.

Section 109(a) of the Bankruptcy Code (the "Code") (11 U.S.C. Sec-tion 109) states that "only a person that resides in the United States, or has a domicile, a place of business, or property in the United States, or a municipality, may be a debtor under this title." Section 109(d) then states that "[o]nly a person that may be a debtor under chapter 7 of this title, except a stockbroker or a commodity broker, and a railroad may be a debtor under chapter 11 of this title." Section 101(30) of the Code* defines "person" to include individuals, partnerships, and corporations. Section 101(8)(A)(v) defines "corporation" to include business trusts.

Under prior law, section 1(8) of the Bankruptcy Act defined "corporation" substantially the same as section 101(8) of the Code, with the exception that the new Code includes all business trusts, while section 1(8) of the old Bankruptcy Act only included "any business conducted by a trustee or trustees wherein beneficial interest or ownership is evidenced by certificate or other written instrument." This last requirement had been strictly construed by the courts. See, e.g., Associated Cemetery Management, Inc. v. Barnes, 268 F.2d 97 (8th Cir. 1959); Walker v. Federal Land Bank of Columbia, 468 F. Supp. 831 (M.D. Fla. 1979). In eliminating the requirement of written instruments, Congress has presumably made it possible for a broader variety of trusts to obtain relief in the bankruptcy courts. . . . It is under such a broader definition that the Trust seeks to qualify as a debtor.

A

In two excellently written memoranda, the debtor contends that it is a business trust. In their also able briefs, movants point to the language in the trust instrument specifically stating that the Trust is not a business trust. Debtors invoke the maxim of "substance over form," and urge the Court to look at the true nature of the Trust.

The debtor asserts that it is an "Illinois Land Trust" organized under the laws of Illinois. As a base of argument, it cites Ill. Ann. Stat. ch. 29, sec. 8.31 to show that the definition of a land trust under Illinois law is consistent with the general characteristics of a business trust. However, nowhere in the trust instrument is the debtor identified as an "Illinois Land Trust" or does even the word "Illinois" appear. To the contrary, paragraph 19 of the instrument states in its entirety: "FLORIDA LAW GOVERNS CONSTRUCTION: this Agreement shall be construed in accordance with the Laws of the State of Florida." Thus, the law of Illinois is of no weight in the construction of the instrument. "Illinois Land Trust" is a generic label, not a statement of legal existence.

The focus then shifts from the definition of a land trust under Illinois law to the question of whether this particular trust has the characteristics of a business trust.

The basic distinction between business trusts and nonbusiness trusts is

---

* Renumbered as §101(33) in the 1984 Code — Eds.

that business trusts are created for the purpose of carrying on some kind of business or commercial activity for profit; the object of a nonbusiness trust is to protect and preserve the trust res. The powers granted in a traditional trust are incidental to the principal purpose of holding and conserving particular property, whereas the powers within a business trust are central to its purpose. It is the business trust's similarity to a corporation that permits it to be a debtor in bankruptcy.

The debtor points to, and the Court notes, that the Trust shares several characteristics with a corporation. The Trust was not created by a grant of a settlor, but was formed through the voluntary association of unrelated persons and subscriptions sold through a prospectus. The "beneficial interests" are very much like shares in that they are equal in value, held by a large number of people in varying amounts, and are transferrable. However, the interests are not reified in written instruments.

The trust instrument itself rejects any construction of it as a business trust. Paragraph 5 states, in its entirety:

5. OBJECTS AND PURPOSES OF TRUST:
The objects and purposes of this Trust shall be to hold title to the trust property and to protect and conserve it until its sale or other disposition or liquidation. The TRUSTEE shall not manage or operate the trust property nor undertake any other activity not strictly necessary to the attainment of the objects and purposes stated herein; *nor shall the TRUSTEE transact business of any kind* with respect to the trust property within the meaning of Chapter 609 of the Florida Statutes, or any other law; *nor shall this agreement be deemed to be, or create or evidence the existence of a corporation* de facto or de jure, *or a Massachusetts Trust,* or any other type of *business trust,* or an association in the nature of a corporation, or a co-partnership or joint venture by or between the TRUSTEE and the BENEFICIARIES, or by or between the BENEFICIARIES. (emphasis added)

The debtor urges the Court to look beyond the terminology of the instrument at what it insists are the economic realities of the situation.

In its brief, the debtor claims that the Trust was created to enable the participants to carry on a business and divide the gains and that the Trust in fact operates as a business enterprise. Support for this contention is based on a ruling in the United States District Court for the Middle District of Florida that the Trust's sale of subscriptions to purchasers constitutes a sale of securities under applicable securities law, SEC v. Hermil, Inc., Case No. 71-141-Orl-Civ-Y. Sale of securities, debtor asserts, is a clear indicium of a business purpose.

Were there nothing else before it, the Court might find this argument persuasive. However, not only is the debtor unable to point to any business activity in which it was actively engaged, the Court is faced with continuous conduct and assertions to the contrary.

In August, 1979, the trustee of Treasure Island Land Trust filed a motion in the SEC v. Hermil case to clarify her position as trustee. The ruling she sought, and which she obtained, was that the collection of assessments was necessary to preserve and protect assets and properties of the Trust. No mention was made of carrying on a business enterprise.

In its schedules and statement of affairs filed in this Chapter 11 proceeding, in response to question 1b, "In what business are you engaged?," the debtor answered, "Purchase of land and holding for resale at a profit." The Court notes that the debtor lists no trade creditors or other debts that customarily result from the conduct of business; the unsecured creditors are principally the accountants and the lawyers.

As the debtor suggests, the Court cannot close its eyes to the economic realities of the situation. The Trust sought, at all costs, to avoid the registration requirements of the securities laws. Now that its form has proven inadequate for its intended purposes, the debtor seeks to abandon it and escape its consequences altogether.

On the one hand, it can be argued that the creators of the trust were free to select the form and language, and that by gambling as to its future construction they assumed whatever risks may ultimately befall them. On the other hand, the debtor might claim that it is being whipsawed, being called a business for securities regulation purposes but not for bankruptcy purposes. Having run afoul of the securities laws, should the debtor be permitted to turn the SEC's arguments to its own advantage? Or should an estoppel theory prevail, binding the debtor to its own representations?

This is an equitable problem which can only be answered by equitable considerations. Equity embraces consistency. It is clear that, in its own view, Treasure Island Land Trust became a business trust on or about November 29, 1979, the day after it filed its petition. It had not registered with the State of Florida as a business trust as required by ch. 609, Florida Statutes. The debtor correctly points out that by virtue of the Supremacy Clause of the United States Constitution, Article VI, this failure to register cannot affect its eligibility for relief under the bankruptcy laws. However, it does give a reading of the Trust's intent. The debtor argues that failure to comply with the registration requirement cannot affect the legal existence or nature of the Trust. It draws an analogy to the provisions of Florida foreign corporation law. If a foreign corporation fails to comply with applicable registration requirements, its contracts, deeds, mortgages, security interests, liens or other acts are nonetheless valid. The corporation is only precluded from maintaining an action, suit, or proceeding in a state court until it complies with the statutory requirements. Fla. Stat. sec. 607.354. A failure to comply with registration requirements does not, however, deprive a foreign corporation of its existence as a legal entity. If the Court may continue the analogy, much as an unregistered corporation is precluded from the state courts, the existence and validity of the Trust are not here in issue, merely its right to seek relief in the bankruptcy court.

In what might otherwise be a close question, the debtor's course of conduct since its inception causes the Court to refuse to permit the debtor to baldly deny the language of the trust instrument. Treasure Island Land Trust does not qualify as a business trust within the meaning of Section 101(8)(A)(v).

B

If the trust is not a corporation, the next inquiry is to whether it can otherwise be a debtor. The definition of "person" in sec. 101(30) states that "'person' *includes* individual, partnership, and corporation, but does not include governmental unit." (emphasis added) Because the definition is nonexclusive, one could argue that a trust might qualify as some other category of debtor.

Under the old Chapter XII of the Bankruptcy Act, debtors eligible for relief were limited to persons other than corporations. Sec. 406(6). Debtors seeking relief under that Chapter thus sought to avoid corporate status. Massachusetts trusts were included in the definition of corporation in Section 1(8) of the Act. The question, then, was whether a simple land trust, not a natural person and not a corporation could otherwise be a "person."

In Walker v. Federal Land Bank of Columbia, supra, this Court held that a land trust was not a person within the meaning of Chapter XII. This conclusion has been reached by other courts as well. See, e.g., Cantor v. Wilbraham and Monson Academy, 609 F.2d 32 (1st Cir. 1979); Associated Cemetery Management, Inc. v. Barnes, supra; In re Associated Developers Trust, 2 B.C.D. 903, 9 C.B.C. 434 (D. Mass. 1976 Bky).

Far more problematic is the holding in Mayo v. Barnett Bank of Pensacola, 448 F. Supp. 250 (N.D. Fla. 1978). There, the court ruled that an Illinois Land Trust was not a corporation and thus was eligible for relief under Chapter XII. The case is troubling for both sides. The debtor here styles itself an Illinois Land Trust, yet seeks relief as a corporation. The movants can take heart in the rationale of *Mayo*, but cannot approve of the result. This court chooses to avoid the implications of *Mayo*, whatever those implications may be, on three grounds:

1. Treasure Island Land Trust is factually distinguishable, in that the *Mayo* trust was an Illinois Land Trust "undoubtedly set up for business purposes." 17 C.B.C. at 9.
2. The decision was not within this District. See *Walker*, 20 C.B.C. at 687.
3. The case was decided under Chapter XII, not Chapter 11.

This last reason, that Chapter XII decisions are inapplicable here, has been advanced by the debtor to escape the rule of the *Walker* case. Yet the debtor has been unable to point to, and the Court is unable to find, anything in the legislative history of the Bankruptcy Reform Act that indicates that Congress intended to expand the category of debtors eligible for relief to include simple trusts. Pub. L. 95-598 was entitled the Bankruptcy *Reform* Act. If the plain meaning of the statute does not contradict the old law, and if no intention to alter the Bankruptcy Act can be divined from the legislative materials, this court must assume that there has been no change. Any trust, business or nonbusiness, may be an entity under 11 U.S.C. sec. 101(14), but not every entity can be a debtor. . . .

In view of the foregoing discussion, the court shall enter an order granting the motion to dismiss.

NOTE

See also In re Dolton Lodge Trust No. 35188, 22 Bankr. 918 (Bankr. N.D. Ill. 1982) (same result; noting that the filing "is apparently seeking to shield the beneficiaries, the real parties in interest, from liability" and that the land trust "has no real creditors other than the mortgage holder and no employees"); In re Old Second Natl. Bank of Aurora, 7 Bankr. 37 (Bankr. N.D. Ill. 1980) (same result); In re Cohen, 4 Bankr. 201 (Bankr. S.D. Fla. 1980) (same result).

NOTE ON *TREASURE ISLAND LAND TRUST* AND THE EXCLUSION OF ENTITIES

The narrow statutory issue in *Treasure Island Land Trust* is whether the trust that was in issue falls within the definitional scope of the term "debtor" for purposes of the Bankruptcy Code. Section 101(12) tells us that a "debtor" is the "person . . . concerning which a case under this title has been commenced." Section 109(a) tells us that only a "person" or a "municipality" may be a debtor under the Bankruptcy Code. (Municipalities are governed by the special rules of Chapter 9, and may be ignored for present purposes.) "Person," in turn, is defined in §101(33) as including "individual, partnership, and corporation." Neither "individual" nor "partnership" is defined further, which suggests that one must rely on nonbankruptcy definitions of these terms to flesh them out. No one was contending, however, that Treasure Island Land Trust was either an individual or a partnership. If it is permitted to proceed as a debtor under the Bankruptcy Code, therefore, Treasure Island Land Trust must either fit in the category of "corporation" *or,* fitting into none of the listed categories, nonetheless be picked up as a "person" since the definition uses the word "includes" and hence is not limited to the enumerated categories.

As for the corporation category, §101(8) defines "corporation" as including a list of entities. One of the types of entities that is not listed, but clearly is implied, is the group of businesses that meet the general state law definition of a corporation. Presumably, the Bankruptcy Code defines "corporation," but not "individual" or "partnership," in order to pick up certain entities that may not be corporations as defined by applicable state laws, but that have the *attributes* of corporations that make a bankruptcy proceeding appropriate. The definition, accordingly, includes "unincorporated compan[ies]" (but presumably *not* unincorporated companies that are individuals or partnerships). Should Treasure Island Land Trust fit here? The term "corporation" also includes an "association having a power or privilege that a private corporation, but not an individual or partnership, possesses." While this makes reference to *a* power or privilege, presumably among many, what powers or privileges, other than limited liability, are included here? Does Treasure Island Land Trust fit here? The term "corporation" also includes "business trust[s]," and a fair amount of attention is directed at that portion of the definition in the *Treasure Island Land Trust* case.

In deciding what is and what is not a "business trust," one other definition seems important. That is the definition of "entity" in §101(14), which is defined as including "person, estate, trust, and governmental unit." The Senate Report, in discussing the definition of person, states that it "does not include an estate or a trust, which are included only in the definition of 'entity.' . . ."

If the legislative history can be taken at face value, then, it suggests that general "trusts" are excluded from the coverage of the Bankruptcy Code, but that "business trusts" are included. In Federal Home Loan Mortgage Corp. v. Wynn, 29 Bankr. 679 (Bankr. D.N.J. 1983), however, the bankruptcy judge stated that "[i]t clearly seems to be the intent of the 1978 Bankruptcy Code to allow a trust to commence a voluntary case. . . . Section 301 allows a voluntary case to be commenced by 'an entity.' Section 101(14) of the code defines 'entity' to include a 'trust.' Thus, it was contemplated that a trust could seek the protection of the Bankruptcy Code. . . ." The problem with this approach is that it ignores §109, the section that specifies *which* entities can be debtors. The only entities covered there are "persons" and "municipalities." *Wynn* is a warning that a little knowledge may be a dangerous thing; you must be able to relate various sections of the Bankruptcy Code to each other, and finding one relevant section may not exhaust your inquiry.

Definitions, however, can take us only so far; here, we seem to reach the point that a "trust" is excluded from bankruptcy but that a "business trust" is not. How do we go any further? Should one resort to nonbankruptcy law? For example, many taxing statutes include certain business trusts within their definition of a corporation, and specify what attributes will qualify a trust as a business trust for these purposes. See, e.g., 26 U.S.C. §7701; Cal. Rev. & Taxation Code §23038; see also Morrissey v.

Commissioner of Internal Revenue, 296 U.S. 344, 359 (1935) (listing six relevant attributes). Are these persuasive? Helpful? Or are bankruptcy purposes so different from taxation purposes that these tax labels are of no help in deciding on relevant attributes for bankruptcy purposes?

In deciding whether Treasure Island Land Trust is an excluded "trust" or an included "business trust," perhaps one should ask why regular "trusts" are excluded from the scope of the Bankruptcy Code. *Treasure Island Land Trust* suggests that traditional trusts conserve property and do not carry on a "business" — their object "is to protect and preserve the trust res" — whereas "business trusts are created for the purpose of carrying on some kind of business or commercial activity for profit." Does this adequately explain why an Illinois Land Trust is not a business trust? Doesn't anyone owning real property try to conserve its value? Would it matter if Treasure Island Land Trust were holding undeveloped land for development? An apartment building? According to the case, the trust instrument says that the Trust was designed to hold property and protect and conserve it until sale or other disposition. Isn't that a business? Aren't the owners of the Treasure Island Land Trust, just like owners of a business, trying to make money? What other conceivable purpose could have brought together a "large number" of "unrelated persons" who purchased transferrable "certificates of beneficial ownership"? The Florida statute under which the Treasure Island Land Trust was organized entitled the beneficial owners to "manage, operate, rent, and sell" the trust property. Does this make it a business trust? Or must we draw a distinction between "investments" and other forms of businesses? Can such a line be drawn with any certainty? Consider the following, from In re Maidman, 668 F.2d 682 (2d Cir. 1982), a case under the 1898 Act, which disagreed with the line of cases holding Illinois Land Trusts to be outside the scope of Chapter XII of the 1898 Act. The Second Circuit reasoned as follows:

> Chapter XII is open to non-corporate debtors who can file a voluntary bankruptcy petition. . . . Any "person," with exceptions not here relevant, may file a voluntary petition, §4(a), 11 U.S.C. §22(a). Person is defined in §1(23), 11 U.S.C. §1(23), as follows:
>
>> (23) "Persons" shall include corporations, except where otherwise specified, and officers, partnerships, and women. . . .
>
> Because this definition uses the words "shall include," rather than the words "shall mean," which appear in other definitions, the Supreme Court read this language "to expand not to restrict" the meaning of "person." American Surety Co. of New York v. Marotta, 287 U.S. 513, 517, 53 S. Ct. 260, 261, 77 L. Ed. 466, 469 (1933). . . . We believe that, although land trusts are not expressly mentioned as "persons," the statute should not be read to exclude them. As the statute provides no further specific indication as to the meaning of the word "person," we should give weight to the general purposes of the Bankruptcy Act. Bankruptcy legislation has two purposes:

debtor relief . . . and equity among creditors. . . . The first purpose is
clearly served by permitting Land Trust No. 2 to operate in bankruptcy
court. Even in liquidation proceedings, the Act allows the debtor or his
trustee to proceed without harassment. . . . Compass [a creditor] has tried
to deprive the debtor of possession and control of the hotels through state
court litigation; even in bankruptcy proceedings, Compass has objected to
the debtor's efforts to lease an unproductive wing of the Barcelona
Hotel. . . .

The second purpose of the Act, equity among creditors, is served best
by allowing Land Trust No. 2 to proceed under the Act because the Act
gives the debtor or trustee power to recover preferences and fraudulent
conveyances . . . beyond the powers available in state courts. . . .

Permitting land trusts access to bankruptcy courts will also further efficient administration of the Bankruptcy Act. As the law now stands, the
individual beneficiaries of a land trust may protect the business by filing as
individuals under Chapter XII. . . . But this means either that one beneficiary's Chapter XII shields all beneficiaries by protecting the land trust or
that all beneficiaries become necessary parties for the restructuring of the
land trust's debts in Chapter XII. It makes more sense to allow the land trust
as an entity to proceed under the Act.

Are there any other reasons why traditional trusts might be excluded
from bankruptcy? Normally, the assets of traditional trusts are not reachable directly by the creditors of the trustee. See Restatement (Second) of
Trusts §266. Does this suggest that trusts *cannot* be "insolvent," and the
reason for excluding them, therefore, may be to keep out of the bankruptcy arena what are likely to be essentially fights between the beneficiaries and the trustee? Or does this overstate the invulnerability of trust
assets from creditor claims, and hence the need for traditional trusts to be
excluded from bankruptcy? Trust assets are reachable by the trustee, in an
action for indemnity, after the trustee has been sued by creditors. Additionally, trust assets can be reached directly by creditors when actions
against the trustee will not be sufficient, when the settlor of the trust
manifested an intention to allow direct proceedings, or where the trustee
and beneficiaries contract to that effect, Restatement (Second) of Trusts
§267.

But when the debtor is a traditional trust, how great is the chance of a
destructive race to its assets even in the unusual case in which a trust has
multiple creditors (as might arise when the settlor of the trust wants the
corpus to be leveraged)? In such a case, are not the assets typically shares of
stock, not a firm with a going-concern value that would be lost if creditors
simply levied on the assets? If there is no danger that a business will be torn
apart, so that assets lose their value, and if rights to the assets under state
law are sufficiently clear, why do we need a collective proceeding to sort
them out? Might traditional trusts, then, be excluded from bankruptcy on
the ground that they so rarely need its protections that it is best, all around,
simply to exclude all traditional trusts?

Assuming we can articulate why traditional trusts are excluded, what do we do with Treasure Island Land Trust? Is an Illinois Land Trust different from an investment trust in any relevant respect? For purposes of bankruptcy law, was Treasure Island Land Trust more like the typical investment trust or a business? Does Treasure Island Land Trust need the protection of bankruptcy laws? Is it insolvent? Or is this just a fight among beneficiaries? Can any clue be garnered from the opinion? Is *Treasure Island Land Trust* conceivably a different case than *Dolton Lodge*, discussed in note 1 supra, where the court explicitly noted that Dolton Lodge had only one creditor? Even if they are different, should a court decide inclusion on a case-by-case basis?

Now that Treasure Island Land Trust has been denied access to bankruptcy proceedings, what happens? Could Treasure Island Land Trust now transfer its property (by merger or otherwise) into a newly formed corporation, and then have that corporation file for bankruptcy? See In re Northwest Recreational Activities, Inc., 4 Bankr. 36 (Bankr. N.D. Ga. 1980) (permissible to form a corporation immediately before bankruptcy, if not for impermissible purpose); see also In re Dutch Flat Investment Co., 6 Bankr. 470 (Bankr. N.D. Cal. 1980). Could the *trustee* of Treasure Island Land Trust, as legal owner of the trust's property, file under the Bankruptcy Code, as trustee? See Cantor v. Wilbraham and Monson Academy, 609 F.2d 32 (1st Cir. 1979) (trustee of Illinois Land Trust is not eligible for Chapter XII of the 1898 Act in her personal capacity, as a natural person "owning" real estate); compare Federal Home Loan Mortgage Corp. v. Wynn, 29 Bankr. 679 (Bankr. D.N.J. 1983) with In re Kirby, 9 Bankr. 901 (Bankr. E.D. Pa. 1981). What about the beneficiaries? See *In re Maidman,* discussed above.

In answering these questions, it might be useful to ask why Treasure Island Land Trust wanted a bankruptcy proceeding and why the creditors resisted. Did the managers wish to delay securities actions from being brought against them? Were they seeking a means of restructuring the "business" now that the apparent reason for structuring it as a land trust (avoiding the securities laws) did not apply? Is the court correct in forcing creditors of Treasure Island Land Trust, as well as the land trust itself, to be bound by the characterization in the trust documents? Could one argue that bankruptcy law should be concerned with the attributes of the entity, not characterizations that the parties may have once given it or the characterizations that would be made by state law? Should the eligibility of Treasure Island Land Trust for bankruptcy turn on whether it is being sought by the trust itself (which is responsible in some sense for the characterization in the trust documents) or by the creditors (who might not be)? Should your view of the case change if the Treasure Island Land Trust's creditors had filed an involuntary petition and Treasure Island Land Trust resisted on the ground that it was not an entity that could be in bankruptcy? But can the §109 definition of who can be in bankruptcy depend on who brings the petition?

PROBLEMS

2.1 Tru Block Concrete Products is a liquidating trust. It is in the "business" of liquidating its predecessor, a corporation of the same name that manufactured and sold concrete blocks. Tru Block was created to liquidate the predecessor corporation under a Shareholders' Agreement executed immediately after a two-year period during which the predecessor corporation was attempting, under an agreement among its creditors, to sell its property to satisfy Tru Block's obligations. During the pendency of that creditors' agreement, the creditors agreed not to foreclose on any liens or security interests or otherwise attempt to collect their claims. At the conclusion of the two years, Tru Block, a liquidating trust, was formed to dispose of the remaining real property valued at $1.4 million. Shortly thereafter, Tru Block filed a petition in bankruptcy. Is a liquidating trust a proper debtor? (Under state law, a liquidating trust operates in the same manner as a dissolving corporation.) In considering this question, does it matter that a liquidating trust is not an association for purposes of the Internal Revenue Code if its sole or principal objective is the liquidation of a trust or estate? Treasury Reg. §301.7701-4. Does it matter that state law includes the liquidation of corporations as "doing business" for purposes of taxation? That the shareholders of the corporation could reconvey the property to the predecessor corporation and dissolve the trust? See In re Tru Block Concrete Products, Inc., 27 Bankr. 486 (Bankr. S.D. Cal. 1983).

2.2 Labor, a labor union consisting of freight dockmen, has recently had a large lawsuit filed against it for damages caused during an allegedly illegal strike. Labor wants to know if it can file a petition in bankruptcy. If so, under what part of the definition of "person" will it fit? See Highway & City Freight Drivers, Dockmen and Helpers, Local Union No. 600 v. Gordon Transports, Inc., 576 F.2d 1285 (8th Cir. 1978) (case arising under the old Act).

2.3 Debtor is hopelessly insolvent and files a petition in bankruptcy. Three weeks later, Debtor dies. May her estate be administered in the bankruptcy proceeding? See Bankruptcy Rule 1016. If Debtor had died before filing a petition, may her estate file a petition in bankruptcy? See §101(33); In re Brown's Estate, 16 Bankr. 128 (Bankr. D.D.C. 1981).

2.4 Debtor, who has a job in San Diego, resides and is domiciled in Mexico. Is he capable of being a "debtor" in a bankruptcy proceeding brought in the United States? See §109(a). Would it matter if he keeps a suitcase of clothes at a friend's house? What if he keeps a car at that friend's house? What if he has a right to get paid for the past two weeks of work?

2.5 Debtor is a corporation formed under Canadian law and headquartered in Toronto. Most of its manufacturing operations are in Toronto, although it has an assembly plant and some executive offices in Cleveland. May debtor file a petition in bankruptcy in the United States? See §109(a).

NOTE ON OTHER LIMITS ON VOLUNTARY BANKRUPTCY PETITIONS

Not everyone who is a "person" residing in the United States can be a debtor under the Bankruptcy Code. Each chapter governing a particular type of bankruptcy proceeding (Chapters 7, 11, and 13 — Chapter 9, dealing with municipal bankruptcies, is outside the subject of these materials) has its own set of restrictions on what sorts of persons may be debtors under that chapter. Chapter 7, the basic "liquidation" chapter, cannot be used by "railroads," domestic or foreign insurance companies, banks, savings banks, savings and loan associations, credit unions, and the like. See §109(b). Railroads, defined in §101(36), are excluded because they are picked up by special provisions in Chapter 11. This is, in large part, a vestige of history. Railroad reorganizations originally had a totally separate set of rules (Section 77 of the 1898 Act) that, indeed, preceded the concept of corporate reorganizations in bankruptcy (provisions governing them were first added to the 1898 Act as Section 77B). This focus on railroad reorganizations stemmed from the view that, at least during the first part of the twentieth century, railroads were too important to allow them to liquidate and die. Although many of the reasons for these special rules are attenuated today, the Bankruptcy Code continues this tradition, at least in part, by providing a special set of rules for railroads, §§1161-1174. These rules are located in a separate part of the "reorganization" chapter — Chapter 11 — although they now permit a railroad to liquidate in those proceedings.

Insurance companies, banks, and similar institutions, unlike railroads, are *completely* excluded from being debtors under the Bankruptcy Code. This exclusion is based principally on the notion that these bodies are heavily regulated by states, and federal bankruptcy law should not interfere with such regulation. See legislative history to §109. The exclusion of such entities reflects a codification of what was called the "state classification test," under which courts excluded entities from bankruptcy relief using the following guidelines: (1) whether the entity was extensively regulated by well-organized state or federal departments; (2) whether the entity was subject to express statutory procedures for nonbankruptcy liquidation; and (3) whether the nature of the entity's business was public or quasi-public and involved interests other than those of the creditors. See In re First American Bank & Trust Co., 540 F.2d 343 (8th Cir. 1976); Sims v. Fidelity Assurance Assn., 129 F.2d 442 (4th Cir. 1942). While it is true that state laws govern matters such as the liquidation of insurance companies, it is quite another thing to suggest that these laws are developed to any significant extent. Many are skeletal, incomplete, and not fleshed out with a developed body of administrative or case law. It seems likely that state procedures will borrow heavily from the provisions of, and experience under, the Bankruptcy Code.

To what extent does §109 *replace* an inquiry into state attributes? In re

Cash Currency Exchange, Inc., 37 Bankr. 617 (N.D. Ill. 1984), dealt with the question of whether currency exchanges were excluded from bankruptcy because, by analogy at least to §109(b)(2), they performed financial services and were regulated by the state. The district court, using the state classification test, held that currency exchanges were proper debtors in a bankruptcy case. The court noted that currency exchanges were not defined as banking institutions, and that they "possess very different and more limited powers under the Currency Exchange Act than banks and banking institutions possess under the Illinois Banking Act" (such as the prohibition on a currency exchange receiving deposits). And while the currency exchanges in question had all been placed under administrative receiverships pursuant to the Illinois Community Currency Exchanges Act a week before they filed their petitions in bankruptcy, the district court noted that "the statutory liquidation provisions governing currency exchanges are more meager and limited than the comprehensive liquidation provisions governing banks and banking institutions." *Currency Exchange* also noted that the categories of §109(b) were narrow, and that currency exchanges were not listed there.

Chapter 11 — the "reorganization" chapter, which we will look at later — is limited to persons entitled to use Chapter 7 (not just corporations or other business entities, see In re Gregory, 39 Bankr. 405 (Bankr. M.D. Tenn. 1984); but cf. In re Ponn Realty Trust, 4 Bankr. 226 (Bankr. D. Mass. 1980)), except that, as noted above, it picks up railroads (in its special set of railroad reorganization rules), §109(d). Stockbrokers and commodity brokers, however, are excluded from using Chapter 11, for the same reason that railroads are included: Chapter 7 has special rules governing the liquidation of stockbrokers and commodity brokers, §§741-752 and §§761-766. These rules are designed to govern the treatment of customer accounts. The legislative history suggests that stockbrokers and commodity brokers are not allowed to use Chapter 11 because "their complexity would make reorganization very difficult at best and unintelligible at worst."

Chapter 13, finally, is limited to individuals, and then only to certain individuals. §109(e). Chapter 13 — the chapter for what are often described as "wage-earner plans" — provides a mechanism for individuals to pay off a portion of debts through future income instead of through a turn-over of existing assets. We will defer looking at the Chapter 13 eligibility rules until later, infra page 908. The presence of Chapter 13, however, has led to a partial restriction on the use of Chapter 7 by individuals. The 1984 amendments to the Bankruptcy Code now permit a court to dismiss a Chapter 7 case filed by a consumer if the court finds that the granting of relief "would be a substantial abuse of the provisions of this chapter" — such as perhaps where the debtor could pay more to his creditors through the use of Chapter 13. See §707(b); In re Bryant, 12 B.D.C. 565 (Bankr. W.N.C. 1984).

PROBLEM

2.6 Debtor is a "Health Maintenance Organization." As such, it offers health-related services to members through a variety of physicians, for a yearly fee that covers most charges. Debtor is regulated, inter alia, by the Oregon Insurance Commissioner pursuant to Oregon Revised Statutes 750.055 and Chapter 734, and by the Federal Department of Health and Human Services under 42 U.S.C. §300e-11. May Debtor file a petition in bankruptcy? *See* §109(b)(2); In re Portland Metro Health, Inc., 15 Bankr. 102 (Bankr. D. Or. 1981). In considering this problem, what factors are relevant? *regulation, necessary services*

C.   COMMENCEMENT OF A VOLUNTARY CASE

NOTE ON FILING A VOLUNTARY PETITION IN BANKRUPTCY

Procedure to file

Assuming the debtor is a "proper" debtor for the chapter of the Bankruptcy Code to be used (§109), the commencement by the debtor of the bankruptcy case is simple: The debtor files a petition with the proper bankruptcy court (§301) accompanied by the proper fee. The schedule of fees is set out in 28 U.S.C. §1930(a) ($60 for cases commenced under Chapters 7 or 13; $200 ($500 for railroads) for cases commenced under Chapter 11; $300 for cases commenced under Chapter 9), which an individual may pay in installments. Constitutional challenges by individuals to the "restriction" on access to the bankruptcy system (and hence to their discharge) imposed by the fee requirement have been rejected. United States v. Kras, 409 U.S. 434 (1973) (noting that discharge is a legislatively created right and that, historically, bankruptcy systems did not include a right of discharge). Once the petition is filed, §301 states that the case "is commenced" and that "[t]he commencement of a voluntary case . . . constitutes an order for relief. . . . " (Certain provisions of the Bankruptcy Code are triggered by commencement of a case; certain others by the entry of an order for relief.)

Who is required to authorize the petition in bankruptcy? May a partnership file a voluntary petition in bankruptcy with less than the unanimous consent of the general partners? *yes* See §303(b)(3). Who authorizes a corporation to file a petition in bankruptcy? May an officer of the corporation? Or must the board of directors authorize the filing? See In re Great Northwest Development Co., 28 Bankr. 141 (Bankr. E.D. Mich. 1983); In re American International Industries, 10 Bankr. 695 (Bankr. S.D. Fla. 1981). In the petition of Itel Corporation, which follows, we are told that "the filing of this petition on behalf of the corporation has been authorized by resolution of the Board of Directors." Is it clear that Board authorization is sufficient? For example, the California Corporations Code requires a vote of the shareholders on certain major transactions involving the corporation, such as the sale of substantially all assets, Cal. Corp. Code. §1001, and, in most cases, on dissolution, id., §1900. Does this mean that shareholders of a California corporation must approve the filing of a voluntary petition? In considering that question, does bankruptcy law follow state law in what the attributes of "consent" for a voluntary petition are? What if the state statute were silent, but the corporation's certificate of incorporation required shareholder approval? What if the state law (or the certificate) required a supermajority vote? In considering these questions, should bankruptcy law care *what* limits are placed by state law on a corporation's ability to use bankruptcy voluntarily, since corporations can always dissolve under state law and are subject to involuntary petitions?

The following is an example of a petition filed in bankruptcy by a major corporation under Chapter 11, the reorganization chapter.

UNITED STATES BANKRUPTCY COURT
NORTHERN DISTRICT OF CALIFORNIA

In re
 	
ITEL CORPORATION, a
Delaware corporation,
doing business as per
Attachment I hereto
 	
Debtor
	CASE NO.
	VOLUNTARY PETITION
	  UNDER CHAPTER 11 OF
	  THE BANKRUPTCY
	  CODE
	
	Employer I.D. No.
	94-1658138

    1. Petitioner's post office address is One Embarcadero Center, San Francisco, California 94111.

    2. Petitioner has had its principal place of business within this district for the preceding 180 days.

    3. Petitioner is qualified to file this petition and is entitled to the benefits of title 11, United States Code, as a voluntary debtor.

4. Petitioner intends to file a Plan pursuant to Chapter 11, title 11, United States Code.

5. Accompanying this petition and marked as Exhibits "A" and "B" hereto are lists of petitioner's creditors and their addresses.

WHEREFORE, petitioner prays for relief in accordance with Chapter 11 of title 11, United States Code.

DATED: January 19, 1981

Herman L. Glatt/s
————————————————
Herman L. Glatt,
Member of Stutman, Treister
& Glatt
Attorney for Debtor and
Debtor-In-Possession

DECLARATION

I, James H. Maloon, Chairman of the Board, Chief Executive Officer, and President of the corporation named as petitioner in the foregoing petition, certify under penalty of perjury that the foregoing is true and correct, and that the filing of this petition on behalf of the corporation has been authorized by resolution of the Board of Directors of Itel Corporation.

EXECUTED at San Francisco, California, on January 19, 1981.

James H. Maloon/s
————————————————
James H. Maloon

D. COMMENCEMENT OF AN INVOLUNTARY CASE

The question of when creditors can put a debtor into bankruptcy proceedings under the Bankruptcy Code is the subject of "involuntary" petitions. Section 303 of the Bankruptcy Code is the principal section governing involuntary petitions. It contains both procedural and substantive requirements that we will have to examine. In scanning it for the first time, however, you will note that there are some entities for whom voluntary bankruptcy is possible, but involuntary bankruptcy is not: "farmers" and corporations that are not "moneyed, business, or commercial." _non-profit_

Why does the Bankruptcy Code exclude farmers and charitable corporations from the scope of involuntary petitions in bankruptcy? The legislative history to §303 attempts to justify the exclusion of farmers from involuntary bankruptcies (and extends that rationale to charitable corporations):

> Farmers . . . are excepted because of the cyclical nature of their business. One drought year or one year of low prices, as a result of which a farmer is temporarily unable to pay his creditors, should not subject him to involuntary bankruptcy. Eleemosynary institutions . . . likewise are exempt from involuntary bankruptcy.

Is extending the rationale to charitable organizations sensible? Do their fortunes rise and fall the same way as those of farmers do? Does the distinction make sense even as applied to farmers? If a farmer is solvent, but unable to pay his bills, why shouldn't the farmer be able to borrow additional funds? Is the inability to do so evidence that there may be more than a cash flow problem? Even if it does not, how different is a farmer from businesses generally? Don't most businesses — from the automobile industry to the tourism industry — go through good times and bad? Should creditors be able to bring an involuntary petition against a debtor whose assets exceed its liabilities, merely because it cannot pay its bills as they become due? Section 303 contains restrictions on involuntary petitions against any kind of debtor. Why are these restrictions not sufficient for farmers and charitable corporations as well?

Perhaps as important, how exactly does a debtor in economic distress benefit if it is insulated from an involuntary petition? Even if bankruptcy were simply a creditor remedy, it does not follow that the benefits creditors receive come at the debtor's expense. By denying a farmer's creditors the right to file an involuntary petition, are we not forcing them to rely on self-help and other state law remedies? Are these remedies less threatening than an involuntary bankruptcy proceeding? Will they simply force the farmer to file a voluntary petition? If so, can we maintain the distinction between voluntary and involuntary petitions? Do we want to?

PROBLEM

2.7 Debtor, a real estate broker in Santa Monica, holds an investment in an egg ranch corporation. Last year he received slightly over 80 percent of his income from that investment. May Debtor resist the filing of an involuntary petition against him on the ground that he is a farmer? See §101(17) and (18). Would it matter if Debtor's investment gave him a 5 percent equity interest in the egg ranch? A 55 percent equity interest?

1. General Limits on Involuntary Petitions

Are there reasons to think that particular creditors will file an involuntary petition when it is not in the interest of the debtor and the creditors as a whole? How great is the danger that one creditor will push a debtor into bankruptcy, because it seems to that creditor's individual advantage, even if the costs of bankruptcy make it less desirable to the creditors as a group? Just as shareholders will not necessarily act in the collective interest of all claimants, isn't it equally the case that a particular group of creditors may not accurately reflect the interests of all claimants?

Moreover, as we will see, sometimes bankruptcy changes non-bankruptcy rules — an issue we first examined in connection with Butner v. United States. In these situations, certain creditors may seek access to the bankruptcy process in order to take advantage of this rule change. For example, bankruptcy accelerates the time the debtor must pay the principal on the loans it has taken. A lender who has a long-term loan at a below-market rate may have an incentive to trigger this automatic acceleration, so that it can get its money out and reinvest it in a venture at a higher interest rate. This lender, accordingly, may seek bankruptcy for its debtor even if a bankruptcy proceeding is not in the best interests of the creditors as a group.

An ability to file an involuntary petition is sometimes desirable because the debtor's (or shareholders' or managers') interests are not necessarily in perfect harmony with those of its creditors. Nevertheless, individual creditors also have interests that run counter to the collective interests of the creditors (or the shareholders). Indeed, as we explored in Chapter 1, bankruptcy is needed in large part because of the divergence of interests among the individual creditors. The question, then, becomes one of how to sort between "good" involuntary petitions and "bad" ones. Some schemes — such as those involving majority votes by creditors — seem unpromising, both because of the costs of identifying all the creditors and the time it would take.

The Bankruptcy Code does the sorting in two distinct ways. It focuses (1) on the *type* of creditor that can involuntarily subject an entity to bankruptcy, and (2) on which substantive events allow creditors to use bankruptcy at all. We will look at each in turn. We start by examining the types of creditors that can file involuntary petitions in bankruptcy. You should look at the requirements of §§303(b), 101(9), and 101(4) carefully and do the following problems.

PROBLEMS

2.8 Creditors *A*, *B*, and *C*, each with an undisputed, noncontingent claim, file an involuntary petition in bankruptcy against Debtor. Each creditor has a security interest in certain of Debtor's collateral. The amount of each claim, and the value of each creditor's security, is as follows:

Creditor	Claim	Security
A	$4,000	$5,000
B	75,000	75,000
C	6,000	1,000

[handwritten annotations:]
85,000 − 80,000 = 5,000
see §303 (b)(1)
can file invol. b/c ≥ 5,000
value of lien = 4,000. Can't get more than claim
85,000   81,000 (80,000 in claims)

Can these three creditors commence an involuntary case against Debtor? *yes*
See §303(b)(1). Can one simply add up the claims and security? Is there any reason why Creditor *A*'s over-collateralization should affect the ability of the three creditors to place Debtor into bankruptcy? *no* On the other hand, is there any reason why Creditors *A* and *B* should count as petitioning creditors at all, given that they are fully collateralized? What guidance does the statute give in addressing each of these questions? To the extent the statute is ambiguous, what policy arguments do you think should be persuasive?

2.9 Creditor *A* holds an undisputed, noncontingent claim against Debtor for $2,000, as does Creditor *B*. Creditor *C* holds an undisputed, noncontingent $3,000 claim against Debtor that is secured by collateral worth slightly more than $3,000. Creditors *A*, *B*, and *C* file an involuntary petition against Debtor. After they file, Creditor *D*, who holds a $5,000 undisputed, noncontingent claim against Debtor, secured by collateral worth $1,000, joins the petition. Is the petition proper? *yes* See §303(c). Does §506(a) have any bearing on the workings of §303?

2.10 Creditors *A*, *B*, and *C* hold unsecured, noncontingent, undisputed claims against Debtor for $5,000. Creditors *B* and *C* are wholly owned subsidiaries of Creditor *A*. Can Creditors *A*, *B*, and *C* put Debtor into bankruptcy? See In re Gibraltor Amusements, 291 F.2d 22 (2d Cir.), cert. denied, 368 U.S. 925 (1961).

2.11 Debtor has 18 creditors with claims that aggregate $467. Debtor also owes Bank $40,000 on an unsecured claim. Can Debtor avoid an involuntary bankruptcy petition by keeping the 18 creditors with small claims content, so that none of them will join with Bank in an involuntary bankruptcy petition? Compare Denham v. Shellman Grain Elevator, 444 F.2d 1376 (5th Cir. 1971) with In re Rassi, 701 F.2d 627 (7th Cir. 1983);

In re Okamoto, 491 F.2d 496 (9th Cir. 1974). Does Bank have any need for a bankruptcy proceeding in this case? Why? Conversely, if Debtor pays Bank its claim in full, and ignores the 18 other creditors, can they put Debtor into bankruptcy? (As we shall explore in Chapter 6, these creditors, if they could file a petition, may be able to set aside the transfer to Bank as a preference.)

2.12 Debtor has 15 creditors. Five of them are bondholders under a common bond indenture. Three of them have received a transfer from the Debtor that would be avoidable by the trustee in bankruptcy as a preference. Two of them are joint payees under a promissory note of debtor. How many creditors are needed to file an involuntary petition against Debtor? See §303(b)(1) and (2); see also In re McMeekin, 18 Bankr. 177 (Bankr. D. Mass. 1982). Why does §303(b)(2) exclude insiders and persons who have received voidable transfers when counting for fewer than 12 creditors? May an insider or a creditor who has received a voidable transfer nonetheless count as a petitioning creditor? Under §303(b)(1)? Under §303(b)(2)? In re Kriedler Import Corp., 4 Bankr. 256 (Bankr. D. Md. 1980), reasoned as follows:

> Section 303(b)(2) requires that no such claimant could be counted to determine whether there are fewer than twelve total creditors. However, Section 303(b)(1) refers merely to "three or more entities" without the exclusions of Section 303(b)(2). Under former Bankruptcy Act, case law developed the policy that although a creditor with a voidable preference may have had a provable claim, that creditor was only qualified to join in the involuntary petition if he surrendered his preference at some time prior to adjudication. . . .
>
> The Court finds that neither the new code nor its legislative history requires a departure from the case law existing under the Act with respect to the disqualification of creditors in receipt of voidable preferences.

Under the former Bankruptcy Act, however, surrender of the preference solved a jurisdictional problem of where the preference action would otherwise have to be brought. The Bankruptcy Code abolished that problem. Given that, is it clear that the Bankruptcy Code intended to follow pre-Code law respecting whether holders of preferential transfers could join involuntary petitions? See In re Kenval Marketing Corp., 38 Bankr. 241 (Bankr. E.D. Pa. 1984) (disagreeing with *Kreidler*); cf. In re United Kitchen Associates, 33 Bankr. 214 (Bankr. W.D. La. 1983) (employees).

2.13 Creditor A has three claims against Debtor, each for $5,000. No other existing creditor of Debtor wishes to join Creditor A in an involuntary petition against Debtor. Thereupon, Creditor A transfers one of his three claims to Creditor B, and one of his three claims to Creditor C. Creditors A, B, and C, subsequently file an involuntary petition against Debtor. Is this valid? See Bankruptcy Rule 1003(c); legislative history to §303.

2.   *Contingent and Disputed Claims*

Section 303(b) requires that the creditors filing an involuntary petition hold claims that are not contingent and that are not the subject of a bona fide dispute. If you examine §101(4), you will note that contingency is one of a number of categories the Bankruptcy Code uses to describe claims. Disputed claims form another category. In interpreting §303, one of the principal difficulties is defining exactly which claims are contingent or disputed and which are not. In looking at this inquiry, you might want to keep in mind the question of why §303(b) focuses exclusively on contingency and dispute. Is there anything special about these categories that make separate treatment desirable? Are there any problems in excluding them?

Consider contingency first. Start by looking at §101(4) and by trying to decide what *is* a "contingent" claim. If a debtor promised to pay a creditor by a particular time, that time has passed, and the creditor has reduced its claim to judgment, the claim is not contingent (nor would it be unliquidated, unmatured, or — in a legal sense — disputed any more). The only remaining steps (a levy on the debtor's assets and subsequent sale) would, if carried out, extinguish the debtor-creditor relationship entirely. Nor would a claim be contingent merely because the time for payment had not come: There is no question that the debtor owes the money. There is no contingency (other than the passage of time) upon which the debtor's obligation turns. When passage of time is the only matter at issue, the debt is "unmatured" within the meaning of §104, but is not "contingent."

Consider a more complicated case. A debtor warrants that the goods it sells will work as promised. What kind of claim does a buyer have if the goods fail prior to the time the bankruptcy petition is filed? Unlike the claim of a garden-variety creditor who lends money, the amount of the buyer's claim is not certain. It is entitled to damages as a result of the seller's breach, but the extent of those damages must be resolved by a court. In such a case, however, even though the size of the obligation has not been established, its existence is not subject to any future event. The debt is not "liquidated," but does not sound as though it is contingent. A court must find that there has been a breach of warranty and the amount of damages, but this is only gathering information and making a judgment about an event that has already occurred. The uncertainties of the outcome of a lawsuit, accordingly, should not be considered a "contingency" within §101(4). Is this claim the subject of a "bona fide dispute"? Passing for the moment the question of what bona fide means in this context, the claim would be disputed if the debtor denies that there was a breach of warranty. But what if the debtor acknowledges that there was a breach of warranty, but asserts the damages were $100, instead of the $10,000 the buyer was claiming? In that case, the claim is unliquidated; is it also the subject of a bona fide dispute? In deciding that question, can you articulate *why* claims that are the subject of a bona fide dispute are excluded for purposes of §303(b)?

Consider the following. Pedestrian alleges that Debtor struck her with his car. Debtor admits that he ran over Pedestrian, but asserts that he is not liable to Pedestrian because he was not negligent. This claim sounds as though it is disputed. Is it, however, also contingent? Should one conclude that the claim is not "contingent" because Debtor's liability turns entirely on events that have already happened. Either Debtor was negligent or he was not. No future event is going to affect Debtor's liability. But is it possible for Debtor to argue that his liability is still contingent upon some future event (a court or jury deciding that he is in fact negligent)? Is this case any different than the previous one, involving a warranty claim?

A bankruptcy judge in In re All Media Properties, 5 Bankr. 126, 133 (Bankr. S.D. Tex. 1980), aff'd, 646 F.2d 193 (5th Cir. 1981), answered yes, noting:

> [I]n the case of the classic contingent liability of a guarantor of a promissory note executed by a third party, both the creditor and guarantor knew there would be liability only if the principal maker defaulted. No obligation arises until such default. In the case of a tort claim for negligence, the parties at the time of the alleged negligent act would be presumed to have contemplated that the alleged tort feasor would be liable only if it were so established by a competent tribunal. Such a tort claim is contingent as to liability until a final judgment is entered fixing the rights of the parties. On the other hand, in the ordinary debt arising from, for example, a sale of merchandise, the parties to the transaction would not at that time view the obligation as contingent. Subsequent events might lead to a dispute as to liability because of, for example, defective merchandise, but that would merely serve to render the debt a disputed one but would not make it a contingent one. A legal obligation arose at the time of the sale, although the obligation can possibly be avoided. Such a claim is disputed, but it is not contingent. A claim is contingent as to liability if the debtor's legal duty to pay does not come into existence until triggered by the occurrence of a future event and such future occurrence was within the actual or presumed contemplation of the parties at the time the original relationship of the parties was created.

How well does the court distinguish between contingent tort claims and noncontingent, but disputed, contract claims? If the right of the victim of the tort is "contingent" upon a court finding the debtor negligent, why is the right of a buyer of defective goods not also "contingent" upon a court finding the debtor's performance deficient? Why is court action a "future event" in one case, but not in the other? What if the dispute was not bona fide? Is the claim still contingent (because the court hasn't actually resolved it yet), and hence not usable for purposes of §303(b)?

What if Debtor manufactured a carcinogenic chemical until two years ago and exposed millions of people to it? Assume that under applicable nonbankruptcy law, Debtor is liable to anyone who develops cancer from the chemical, but though it is certain that thousands will develop cancer eventually, no one has it yet. Are those who have been exposed to the chemical (only some of whom will develop cancer as a result of Debtor's conduct) "creditors" within the meaning of §101(9)? Or does their "claim" arise only if and when they contract cancer? Can the exposed population argue that they are "creditors" whose right to payment is "contingent" upon a future event (succumbing to cancer)? Could these creditors go further and argue that their claims are not even contingent and that they ought to have the right to bring an involuntary petition against Debtor? In support of this last point, note that even though it is not certain that any one of them will develop cancer, they have already been exposed to the chemical, and whether or not they have a claim against the Debtor depends simply on the passage of time. Is this, then, the same as a warranty claim that a court has not yet adjudicated? If different, why is it different? Are these claims the subject of a bona fide dispute? What if Debtor acknowledges that some 10,000 individuals will eventually develop the disease from products it manufactured, but no one individual can be identified yet with certainty? Can one exposed to the carcinogenic chemical file a claim? Is that claim one that is in bona fide dispute? Is it contingent? Would your reaction change if Debtor, although acknowledging that it manufactured the chemical and that it causes disease, denies liability on the ground that it was not negligent? What if Debtor had, in the past, consistently raised and lost on that negligence issue?

Consider another case. Debtor leases the store from which it runs its small retailing operation from Landlord. The lease is for a five-year term, and neither party has an option to cancel. At the time the petition is filed, one year into the lease, Debtor is current on its rental payments. Can Landlord join other creditors in an involuntary petition? The court in In re Kreidler Import Corp., 4 Bankr. 256 (Bankr. D. Md. 1980), held that because no rent was due and owing, the landlord in that case had no right to payment as required by the definition of "claim" in §101(4). Is this conclusion correct? A bank that lends money remains a creditor within the meaning of §101(4) even if the debtor is not behind on any of the installment payments. An existing right to payment is not necessary. In our example, Debtor is in fact obliged to pay Landlord for its use of the store for the rest of the lease term. Doesn't Debtor's promise to pay Landlord rent make Landlord a "creditor" holding a "claim," §101(9), (4)?

On the other hand, one can argue that Landlord cannot join the petition because its claim is "contingent." Although Debtor has promised to pay Landlord rent, Debtor's obligation will not arise simply through the passage of time. Debtor's obligation to pay rent exists only as long as Landlord lives up to its end of the bargain. If the store burns down or becomes uninhabitable, or if Landlord fails to live up to its end of the deal in other respects, Debtor may not have to pay rent. Because it depends upon future events (Landlord honoring its promises), isn't Debtor's obligation "contingent" as well as "unmatured"?

If a claim is disputed, how should the bankruptcy judge decide at the start of the case whether the claim is the subject of a bona fide dispute? How great a showing must someone filing a bankruptcy petition make? Before the addition of the "bona fide dispute" test in 1984 (before then, §303(b) excluded only contingent claims), Judge Friendly held, in In re B.D. International Discount Corp, 701 F.2d 1071, 1077 (2d Cir. 1983):

> In order to qualify a claim as a basis for seeking involuntary bankruptcy, a claimant need not make out a case warranting summary judgment although in fact [the plaintiff] came close to this. It is sufficient to establish, as [the plaintiff] did here, that there are good grounds for the claim and that no defenses have been asserted in [substantial] form. Whether less may suffice we need not decide.

See also In re Curtis, 38 Bankr. 364 (Bankr. N.D. Okla. 1983) (would-be petitioners are required "to make at least some minimal showing of evidentiary basis for their claims"); In re Tampa Chain Co., 35 Bankr. 568 (Bankr. S.D.N.Y. 1983) ("if the debtor's defenses to a claim of a petitioning creditor are not clear and require adjudication of either substantial factual or legal questions, the creditors should be recognized as qualified to join in the bringing of an involuntary petition"). Does the addition of the bona fide dispute language change this standard? How?

In looking at the requirements of §303(b), how does one value a claim (for purposes, say, of the $5,000 requirement)? If a creditor's claim is for $100,000, but the amount of the claim is disputed (the debtor asserting it is worth only $500) or the claim is denied entirely (the debtor asserting its value is zero), how should it be valued for purposes of §303(b)? If the debtor denies the claim entirely, and one concludes that this denial is bona fide, presumably the claim does not count at all for purposes of §303(b). But what of the $100,000 claim that the debtor says should be $500? Is the entire claim excluded for purposes of §303(b) (assuming the disagreement is bona fide)? Or is only that portion of it above $500 "disputed," so the $500 claim should still count? That is to say, should this claim — an unliquidated one — be bifurcated into two parts: a $500 claim that is not disputed, and a $99,500 claim that is the subject of a bona fide dispute? What if there is a counterclaim asserted by the debtor? In re Kreidler Import Corp., 4 Bankr. 256 (Bankr. D. Md. 1980), held that a bona fide counterclaim extinguished the claim for purposes of §303(b). But why is this so? Does a claim that is offset make it contingent as to liability? Is the claim itself disputed, or only the ultimate amount that has to be paid (because of the offset right)? Should a claim subject to an offset to be treated, not as disputed, but as a secured claim for purposes of §303(b)? See §§506; 553; In re Moses, infra page 147.

Rather than focusing on whether the entity filing a petition has a noncontingent and undisputed claim, should the bankruptcy judge rely on his power to dismiss the petition under §303(h) if Debtor was paying its debts as they became due? How separate should these two inquiries — that under §303(b) and that under §303(h) — be? In considering that, don't we return to the question of why "contingent" and "disputed" claims are excluded from §303(b) if "unliquidated" and "unmatured" claims are not? Are they excluded because the role of §303(b) is so rough-and-cut that it isn't worth passing beyond the facial validity of a claim? If so, how much inquiry should there be into the bona fides of a dispute? If your answer is "very little," does the debtor's ability to dispute claims give the debtor too much power? We will return to these questions in addressing §303(h).

PROBLEMS

2.14 Supplier sells electronic components to Debtor. In 1983, Supplier loaned Debtor $10,000 to help Debtor through a financial downturn. Supplier took an interest in all Debtor's equipment, securing the loan and all other obligations Debtor subsequently owed it. In 1984, Supplier shipped $12,000 worth of goods to Debtor. Debtor did not pay supplier for the shipment on schedule. It alleged the components were defective and worth just a few hundred dollars. Debtor's equipment is worth $10,000. Can supplier bring an involuntary petition against Debtor if two trade creditors who are each owed $100 joins it? No

2.15 Debtor has more than 12 creditors. Creditors A and B, each holding a $10,000 liquidated, unsecured claim, file an involuntary petition against Debtor. After the petition is filed, Creditor C joins the petition. Creditor C claims it is owed $15,000. Debtor, however, disputes that claim, and asserts it owes Creditor C nothing. Assume that Debtor's dispute is bona fide. May Creditor C's claim count? No Compare §303(c) with §303(b). Would your answer be any different if Debtor acknowledges Creditor C's claim, but asserts a $20,000 counterclaim? Yes

3. The Substantive Requirements of §303(h)

Even though the requirements of §303(b) have been met, §303(h) imposes a substantive limitation on the use of involuntary petitions as well. That section requires, in the case of an involuntary petition opposed by the debtor (involuntary petitions cannot be opposed by other creditors, §303(d)), a showing *either* that "the debtor is generally not paying such debtor's debts as such debts become due unless such debts that [sic] are the subject of a bona fide dispute" *or* that "within 120 days before the date of the filing of the petition, a custodian, other than a trustee, receiver, or agent appointed or authorized to take charge of less than substantially all of the property of the debtor for the purpose of enforcing a lien against such property, was appointed or took possession." Why do these require-ments exist? Why should the creditors' access to bankruptcy's collective proceeding be limited in any way, once the procedural requirements of §303(b) have been met? Is it due to a fear that the bankruptcy process will be abused (to harass debtors or whatever)? If so, how would a debtor be harassed? Even assuming that creditors should be restrained from filing petitions against debtors, are the tests of §303(h) appropriate? Would a system of penalties for wrongful filings be more appropriate? Cf. §303(e), (i).   *to hard to manage*

In 1980, out of a total of over 330,000 bankruptcy petitions, less than 1,400 — or less than one-half of one percent — were involuntary. This percentage is virtually identical with the percentage under the 1898 Act. See Administrative Office of the U.S. Courts, Tables of Bankruptcy Sta-tistics A-2, A-4 (1978); Federal Judicial Workload Statistics for 1980. One reason for this low percentage is that the vast majority of bankruptcy petitions filed are so-called no asset cases — individuals with few or no nonexempt assets who go through bankruptcy in order to get a discharge and whose creditors get little or nothing from the process. Undoubtedly another reason is that the line between "voluntary" and "involuntary" is hazy. A debtor hounded and harassed by its creditors may file a voluntary petition, perhaps in response to a threat that, if it does not, the creditors will file an involuntary petition or dismember its assets. Are there other reasons for the minuscule percentage? Consider these questions in light of the following excerpt, summarizing the procedures under the 1898 Act and proposing changes, Report of the Commission on the Bankruptcy Laws of the United States, Part I, at 14-15 (1973):

> The Commission has encountered a generally prevalent opinion in the business community that a major factor explaining the smallness of distribu-tions in business bankruptcies is the delay in the institution of proceedings for liquidation until assets are largely depleted. Debtors are reluctant to file voluntary petitions until after the situation has become hopeless, and credi-tors are obliged to allege and prove the commission of one of six acts of bankruptcy. For most of these acts the petitioner must be able to establish that the debtor was insolvent at the time the act was committed. Insolvency is defined in the Act as insufficiency of the debtor's property at a fair valuation to pay his debts. It is frequently difficult for a debtor's creditors to establish this fact, and the debtor is entitled to jury trial of the issue of whether he committed an act of bankruptcy. . . .
>
> In order to make the Bankruptcy Act more effective as an instrumental-ity for relief at the instance of creditors, the Commission recommends that:
>
> (1) The concept of "an act of bankruptcy" be abolished and the debtor be made amenable to involuntary proceedings when he has ceased to pay his debts or will be generally unable to pay his current liabilities.

(2) A debtor be protected against the risks of ill-founded petitions by requiring the court to hold a hearing immediately after the filing of an involuntary petition to determine whether the relief sought is in the best interests of the debtor and its creditors.

(3) A general assignment or general receivership continue to be a basis for involuntary proceedings without regard to whether the debtor was insolvent or unable to pay his debts at the time of the filing of the petition, on the premise that such a disposition or proceeding contemplates a liquidation and that creditors be able to require it to be conducted subject to the safeguards provided by the Bankruptcy Act.

(4) There be no jury trial of any issue raised on an involuntary petition.

(5) A creditor or creditors who have aggregate claims of $2,500 be able to file an involuntary petition for liquidation of the debtor, and one or more creditors having claims of $10,000 or more be able to file a petition seeking reorganization of the debtor. . . .

(8) The exclusion of corporations other than those that are moneyed, business or commercial from amenability to involuntary proceedings be eliminated.

Section 303(h)(2) permits the filing of an involuntary bankruptcy petition, if within 120 days of the filing "a custodian . . . was appointed or took possession." See §101(10). (This does not include a lien enforcement proceeding against "less than substantially all of the property of the debtor.") The legislative history to §303 supports this test as follows:

> If a custodian of all or substantially all of the property of the debtor has been appointed, this paragraph creates an irrebuttable presumption that the debtor is unable to pay its debts as they mature. Moreover, once a proceeding to liquidate assets has been commenced, the debtor's creditors have an absolute right to have the liquidation (or reorganization) proceed in the bankruptcy court and under the bankruptcy laws with all of the appropriate creditor and debtor protections that those laws provide. Ninety days [120 days as enacted] gives creditors ample time in which to seek bankruptcy liquidation after the appointment of a custodian.

This policy obviously reflects the concern that a nonbankruptcy "workout" may attempt to treat some creditors inequitably or may encounter a hold-out creditor. (We will examine nonbankruptcy collective procedures in Chapter 14.) It is this provision, perhaps more than any other, that ensures that out-of-bankruptcy workouts will not deviate too substantially from the bankruptcy order of entitlements. Why, however, is there a 120-day limit in this test? Negotiations may still be proceeding at the end of 120 days and some creditors may still feel pressured or attempt to take advantage of others after that time. Should the three-creditor requirement of §303(b)(1) be called off in the case of an (h)(2) involuntary petition? What types of events does §303(h)(2) apply to?

To the extent there has been litigation over involuntary petitions

under the Bankruptcy Code, most of it has involved
response to this litigation, in 1984 Congress modifie
adding (with questionable grammar) "unless such debt
ject of a bona fide dispute." That section tests for what
"cash flow" insolvency, which involves the "inability" c
debts as they become due. (Under the 1898 Act, this kin
known as "insolvency in the equity sense.") Rather than focusing on *actual*
inability to pay, however, §303(h)(1) simply asks whether such debts have
been paid. But the Bankruptcy Code uses a different "insolvency" test for
other purposes, such as determining whether a transfer is preferential.
Section 101(29) defines "insolvent" with reference to a financial condition
such that the sum of debts is greater than all the property of the debtor, at a
fair valuation, excluding property that may be exempted under §522 and
property fraudulently conveyed. (Under the 1898 Act, this kind of insolvency was known as "insolvency in the bankruptcy sense.") Section
101(29), therefore, expresses a form of what is known as "balance sheet"
insolvency, except that "fair valuation" does not rely on historical cost, or
other accounting formalities.

Why does the Bankruptcy Code use equity insolvency — §303(h)(1)
— instead of bankruptcy (or balance sheet) insolvency — §101(29) — in
deciding whether a debtor can be placed involuntarily into bankruptcy? If
a debtor can keep up current payments on debts by selling off its assets,
should creditors be able to call on the collective asset disbursement process? Cf. Rostow & Cutler, Competing Systems of Corporate Reorganization: Chapters X and XI of the Bankruptcy Act, 48 Yale L.J. 1334 (1939).
The 1898 Act relied more heavily on a balance sheet test: Section 3(a)
required the showing of one of six "acts" of bankruptcy, three of which
incorporated a balance sheet test of insolvency. Is a balance sheet test less
desirable for purposes of deciding on the propriety of involuntary petitions than the current test of §303(h)(1), because of difficult valuation
issues associated with a balance sheet test? Are those valuation problems
too intractable to require a decision regarding them at the *start* of a bankruptcy case (even if they might, as we will see, require such a decision later
in the process)? Should "balance sheet" insolvency be offered as a third
alternative justification for an order of relief against debtors under §303?

One can justify using the balance sheet insolvency test if one believes
that a major purpose of bankruptcy law is to prevent a destructive race to
the debtor's assets by the creditors. (Creditors will typically engage in such
a race only if they believe the debtor has too few assets to satisfy all of its
creditors.) But will some other test serve much the same purpose at lower
cost? Is a debtor who fails to pay its debts as they become due likely not to
have enough assets to satisfy its creditors? Are most debtors who claim to
have "cash-flow" problems really insolvent in the balance sheet sense? Are
there many debtors who can pay their debts when due, but who do not
have enough to pay all of their existing creditors whose claims will ripen

entually? In such a case, mightn't the two collapse? That is, if the creditors discover that the debtor is in fact insolvent in the balance sheet sense,
mightn't they call in their loans, *producing* insolvency in the equity sense?

PROBLEMS

2.16 Debtor owns a building worth $100,000. He owes a group of
creditors $60,000 because of a loan they made him several years before.
Debtor has also guaranteed a $90,000 loan Finance Company made to his
son. Is Debtor "insolvent" within the meaning of §101(29)? Assume there
is a good chance that Finance Company will call on the guarantee. Assume
further, however, that if Debtor honors the guarantee, he will probably be
able to recover much of what he pays out by virtue of his rights of indemnification and subrogation. Is this inquiry too difficult, given that resolving
the question of Debtor's insolvency only determines whether a bankruptcy
proceeding is appropriate? Much of a bankruptcy proceeding is consumed
with ascertaining the debtor's assets and liabilities. Would it be unwieldy to
make the major question faced by a bankruptcy court the same question
the court must answer before it can proceed?

2.17 Debtor owes Bank $1 million, which it has promised to repay in
the form of a balloon payment of $1 million plus accrued interest in five
years. It owes its ten other creditors a total of $100,000, all of which
represents short-term trade credit. Debtor's business is now worth
$90,000. Debtor is current on all of its obligations. Should Bank be able to
bring an involuntary bankruptcy petition against Debtor? Note that if
Bank cannot, the other creditors in all likelihood will be paid most of what
they are owed and Bank will receive nothing. Moreover, all the creditors
will have an incentive to try to obtain payment earlier than planned out of
fear that otherwise they will not be paid in full. Could Bank have protected
itself by inserting an acceleration clause in its loan agreement? (A clause,
for example, that was triggered if debtor's sales fell below a certain level or
its obligations to other creditors rose above a certain level.) If Bank could
accelerate Debtor's obligation, wouldn't Debtor be unable to pay and
hence unable to dismiss the petition under §303(h)? But what if, instead of
Bank, the creditors were tort victims whose causes of action had not yet
ripened under state law? Should they be able to bring a bankruptcy petition? If they cannot, other creditors may be paid in full and leave no assets
for them. See Roe, Bankruptcy and Mass Tort, 84 Colum. L. Rev. 846
(1984).

2.18 If one assumes that the balance sheet insolvency test is too complex to use at the start of a bankruptcy case, how much easier to apply is the
"generally not paying debts as they become due" test? In re R.N. Salem
Corp., infra, raises this question. What does "generally" mean? The Senate Bill, S. 2266, had cast the test as follows: Creditors can put a debtor

involuntarily into bankruptcy "if the debtor is generally unable to pay or has failed to pay a major portion of his debts as such debts become due." Is this the same test? What if Debtor pays a $10,000 debt, but ignores its remaining claims, all little ones of about $50?

Debtor has 11 creditors, all with debts due and owing. Ten of them have claims for $50; one has a past-due claim for $10,000. Debtor pays the ten little ones (recall Problem 2.11), but does not pay the creditor to whom it owes $10,000. Is Debtor "generally" paying debts as they become due? In re Luftek, Inc., 6 Bankr. 539 (Bankr. E.D.N.Y. 1980), suggests that "both the number and amount of unpaid claims should be considered in determining whether non-payment of debt is the alleged debtor's regular course of conduct." See also In re North County Chrysler-Plymouth, 13 Bankr. 393 (Bankr. W.D. Mo. 1981) ("no evidence to show that these creditors and the amounts owed are de minimis in comparison to the debts which have been paid."). Does the failure to pay a single debt in a timely fashion satisfy §303(h)(1)? See In re Goldsmith, 30 Bankr. 956 (Bankr. E.D.N.Y. 1983) (not paying one creditor, even a large one, not enough); In re Blaine Richards & Co., 16 Bankr. 362 (Bankr. E.D.N.Y. 1982). Should it be enough? Are state remedies inadequate at this point? Does it matter who the petitioning creditors are? Is bankruptcy appropriate if the dispute is essentially between a debtor and a single creditor?

NOTE ON *COVEY* AND THE PROBLEM OF DISPUTED DEBTS

One of the announced reasons for using the equity insolvency test in §303(h)(1) was "[t]he existence or nonexistence of this ground should be more easily determined" than that of balance sheet insolvency, Commission on the Bankruptcy Laws of the United States, 93rd Cong., 1st Sess., H.R. Doc. No. 137, Part II, p. 75 (1973). As originally passed in 1978, §303(h)(1) did not contain the qualifier regarding bona fide disputes. Substantial litigation soon erupted over the question of when a debtor was "generally" paying its debts as they became due. By 1983, Judge Friendly commented "that if Congress thought it had provided a test that would lead to quick and sure determinations, it was badly misadvised and should consider returning to the drawing board," In re B.D. International Discount Corp., 701 F.2d 1071, 1076 (2d Cir. 1983).

The problem arose out of the following. Creditors would allege that a number of debts were not being paid as they became due. The debtor would deny that it owed these debts, or at least would dispute the amount of them. Courts feared that to take the creditors' claims at face value might make it too easy to "fabricate" a petition against a debtor who did not belong in bankruptcy but was simply being harassed by its creditors. In re All Media Properties, 5 Bankr. 126, 144 (Bankr. S.D. Tex. 1980), aff'd,

646 F.2d 193 (5th Cir. 1981). On the other hand, courts feared that to exclude from the "generally" paying standard *any* debt that the debtor disputed might give the debtor unwarranted freedom to defeat justified involuntary petitions. But, if neither of those "all-or-nothing" approaches appeared satisfactory to the judges, an intermediate approach had problems of its own. As described by In re Covey, 650 F.2d 877 (7th Cir. 1981): "an important goal of the new Bankruptcy Code is to ensure prompt resolution of the question of whether a debtor is generally paying its debts in an initial proceeding, reserving the litigation of specific disputes and defenses for subsequent proceedings. . . . Creditors are entitled to a prompt resolution of the 'generally paying debts' question in order to prevent wasting of assets and in order to ensure that they receive all of their rights to the debtor's property. . . ."

Covey became the leading case on how to deal with disputed claims for purposes of §303(h)(1). The Coveys ran a car dealership in Illinois that lasted from 1978 to November 1979, when they suspended the operations of the dealership. In January 1980, Chrysler Credit Corporation, Chrysler Corporation, and Anderson Dodge, Inc. (the lessor of the space where the car dealership was), filed an involuntary petition against the Coveys. The three creditors alleged trade debts in excess of $100,000; the Coveys disputed all but $500 of that. How should the §303(h)(1) standard be resolved? *Covey* set down a three-part test that largely, although not entirely, put a thumb on the scales on the side of the petitioning creditors:

Because the Code is silent as to the calculation of disputed debts, and because there are solid policy reasons in support of both creditors' and debtors' interests, we conclude that there cannot be any absolute rule that disputed debts either should or should not be considered with regard to the "generally paying debts" standard. Rather, we conclude that the bankruptcy courts should initially examine the dispute and, under certain circumstances, should then balance the interests of creditors and debtors with regard to the Code's specific goals of prompt resolution of the initial involuntary bankruptcy determination.

First, bankruptcy courts must initially examine the nature of the dispute claimed. If the debtor merely has a colorable dispute as to the *amount* of a claim, there is no reason why the debt should be excluded in the determination of the "generally paying debts" standard. . . .

Second, if the debtor disputes the entire claim, then the bankruptcy courts must consider the complexity of the litigation required. If the debtor's dispute of the entire debt will require substantial litigation of either legal or factual issues, that litigation should occur later. . . . Thus, the debtor's argument must be clearly persuasive. If the dispute will require substantial litigation, or if the "substantial litigation" question itself will itself require substantial litigation, there is no reason to reach the "dispute" issue initially. The disputed debt, then, should be counted in the determination of "generally paying debts."

Third, if the debtor's dispute of the entire claim will not require substantial litigation, bankruptcy courts should then carefully balance . . .
creditors' interests against the debtor's interest. This balancing process will
require a precise analysis of the danger to creditors' interests from some
delay in the litigation of the bankruptcy determination against the danger of
harm to a debtor by unfairly forcing a debtor holding a legitimate dispute of
an entire claim into involuntary bankruptcy.

If the debtor's interests in avoiding the involuntary bankruptcy outweigh the creditors' interests in a more rapid decision, then the bankruptcy
courts should reach the "dispute" issue. . . . But if the bankruptcy courts
determine that the creditors' interests in a rapid decision outweigh the
debtor's interest in litigating the dispute, the bankruptcy courts should not
reach the merits of the dispute; the disputed debts should be considered
regarding the "generally paying debts" standard.

Where the scales seem equally balanced, because the new Code emphasizes prompt resolution of the involuntary bankruptcy question without litigation of specific disputes, we conclude that the bankruptcy courts should
not exclude the disputed debts from the "generally paying debts" calculation.

Covey instantly became the recognized standard, see, e.g., In re Doc Edi-
son's Video Emporium, 38 Bankr. 398 (Bankr. N.D. Ill. 1984); In re
Hudson, 28 Bankr. 876 (Bankr. E.D. Tenn. 1983); In re Bokum Resource
Corp., 26 Bankr. 615 (D.N.M. 1982), although some judges had misgiv-
ings about the test. Among them was Judge Friendly, who commented on
this issue in In re B.D. International Discount Corp., 701 F.2d 1071, 1077
(2d Cir. 1983) as follows.

In Covey the late Judge Sprecher developed an intricate balancing formula, designed to afford a rule of decision in all cases, with respect to the
inclusion of disputed debts in the "generally not paying debts" determination. Apart from the question whether the treacherously simple statutory
language will support so elaborate a gloss, we think it a bit early in the day to
essay a "guideline" opinion on the subject. As Justice Harlan said . . . such
opinions "suffer the danger of pitfalls that usually go with judging in a
vacuum. However carefully written, they are apt in their application to carry
unintended consequences which once accomplished are not always easy to
repair." We prefer to see some more cases before we decide whether to
accept Covey.

The Ninth Circuit, in agreeing with Judge Friendly and believing that the
"Covey rule appears to lean too heavily toward favoring creditors', as op-
posed to debtors', interests," noted in In re Dill, 731 F.2d 629, 632 (9th
Cir. 1984):

Inclusion of disputed debts in the §303(h)(1) generally not paying debts
calculation involves difficult policy evaluations with little legislative guid-

ance. In the absence of a preferable formulation, the rule to be applied by the Bankruptcy Court on remand is to balance the interests of the creditors against those of the debtor. Case law is developing along this line. . . .

In balancing the interests herein, the Bankruptcy Court should consider any underlying policies of bankruptcy law which may be implicated in these facts.

The Ninth Circuit went on to observe that the debtor might have made preferential transfers that a trustee in bankruptcy would be able to set aside and then distribute to the petitioning creditors and that this "would argue strongly in favor of inclusion of the disputed claims in the generally not paying debts calculation." Is this a policy that a bankruptcy judge should take into account? To characterize a transfer as a voidable preference under §547, as we will examine in detail in Chapter 6, a judge must find, inter alia, that the debtor was insolvent in the sense of liabilities exceeding assets when the transfer was made. (A judge might be able to take advantage of the usual presumption for preference purposes that a debtor is insolvent within 90 days before the filing of the petition, §547(f), but should a judge be able to rely on this provision in deciding whether the petition was properly filed? Moreover, some voidable transfers can take place more than 90 days before the filing of the petition, when that presumption is no longer applicable.) Isn't §303(h) designed to avoid an inquiry, at the very start of a bankruptcy case, into whether the debtor is insolvent?

In 1984, Congress modified both §303(b) and §303(h) to exclude claims that were the subject of a bona fide dispute. How much, if at all, does this change the *Covey* test? How does one decide whether a dispute is bona fide? Is the difference from *Covey* two-fold? First, if the entire debt is not disputed, does one only include, for purposes of §303(h)(1), the undisputed amount? (This is a solution Congress has adopted outside of bankruptcy for purposes of disputes under consumer credit purchases, see Consumer Credit Protection Act §161; Truth in Lending Regulation Z §226.13(d)(1).) Second, if the dispute is complex, does the change mean that the claim will be *excluded* (instead of possibly included)?

Does this give too much power to a debtor who wants to avoid involuntary petitions? That is to say, is it too easy under the revised test for a debtor to dispute claims in a way that will pass the "bona fide" test simply because, at the start of a case, judges will not want to resolve the merits of disputes? In light of that, how should the bona fide test be resolved? In *Covey*, for example, the court thought that the disputes with two of the three petitioning creditors would "require complex factual investigations." Does this mean that the claims are the subject of a bona fide dispute? In deciding that, what would you do with *Covey*'s observation that "the Coveys' disputes seem to represent strategic gamesmanship. The Coveys are not just disputing some of their business debts . . . , [they] are disputing 99½ percent of their business debts." Does this mean that, notwithstanding the "complex factual investigations" required to resolve the disputes, they are not bona fide disputes? Finally, is it improper, at the §303(h) stage, to take account, as *Covey* did, of the fact that "the Coveys had voluntarily closed their dealership. There was no ongoing business to be harmed by the stigma of an involuntary bankruptcy"?

PROBLEM

2.19 Supplier has shipped a new part for Debtor's printing press. Debtor promised to pay $10,000 for it. Before Debtor paid for the part, the printing press broke and was seriously damaged. Debtor now alleges that the part was defective and caused the damage, which Debtor estimates will cost $10,000 to repair. Debtor is not otherwise in financial difficulty, and it refuses to pay Supplier $10,000 and then litigate the question of how much Supplier owes it in damages. See §2-717. Should Supplier be able to threaten a bankruptcy petition? What if Debtor were in financial difficulty, but none of its other creditors (who number less than 12) favor a bankruptcy proceeding? If the only person who wants the bankruptcy process to commence wants it for a nonbankruptcy reason (to be able to defuse a bargaining technique that buyers commonly use against sellers), should there be one? Can one take all these issues into account in the deciding whether Debtor is "generally paying debts as they become due unless such debts that are the subject of a bona fide dispute"? Should the judge examine whether a collective bankruptcy proceeding advances the interests of the parties? Or does such an inquiry take a judge too far beyond §303(h), which was intended to provide a substantive test that would be easy to apply? (See, in connection with this question, §305, which we examine infra, page 97.) Should a bankruptcy judge examine the costs of an erroneous decision? Should the judge ask what will happen to Supplier if the petition is dismissed and it turns out that Debtor in fact owed Supplier the full $10,000 (and hence was not, at the time the petition was filed, paying debts that were due)? Should the judge also ask what would happen if the proceeding continues and Debtor is found not to owe Supplier anything because of the damages it had suffered (and thus was paying its debts as they became due)? How does one weigh two interests? In the event that a judge properly dismisses the bankruptcy proceeding, how much harm has Debtor suffered? In answering that, would you want to know the nature of Debtor's business? Do subsections 303(e) and (i) take these into account adequately?

The next case, which was decided prior to the 1984 Amendments, takes issue with the *Covey* standard. In reading the case, consider how

close Judge Spiegel's approach would adhere to the new standard in
§303(h)(1), which excludes claims that are the subject of a bona fide dispute. Is his analysis still viable? Or has it been supplanted by another form
of analysis? If so, how would this case be approached under the new standard? (Note also that the court's discussion of §303(b) would be substantially different in light of the exclusion, in 1984, of claims that are the
subject of a bona fide dispute.)

IN RE R.N. SALEM CORP.
29 Bankr. 424 (S.D. Ohio 1983)

SPIEGEL, District Judge.

Petitioners, Glass City Spring Corp., Telectron, Inc., and Wayne-Dalton Corp. (Wayne-Dalton), commenced this case on August 20, 1982 by
filing an involuntary petition under Chapter 7 of the Bankruptcy Code, 11
U.S.C. §303, against R.N. Salem Corporation (Salem Corp.). Salem Corp.
answered, denying the petitioners were qualified to file the involuntary
petition and denying that it was not generally paying its debts as they came
due. Following an evidentiary hearing, the Bankruptcy Court, 23 B.R.
452, held that the petitioners were qualified to file the involuntary petition, 11 U.S.C. §303(b)(1), but that they had failed to prove that Salem
Corp. was generally not paying its debts as they came due, 11 U.S.C.
§303(h)(1). Accordingly, the Bankruptcy Court dismissed the involuntary
petition.

Wayne-Dalton brings this appeal arguing that the Bankruptcy Court
applied the improper legal standard in excluding a disputed debt prior to
making the 303(h)(1) determination that the debtor was generally paying
its debts as they came due. . . .

INTRODUCTION

Salem Corp. is in the business of selling automatic garage doors. Wayne-
Dalton, a manufacturer of garage doors, has been supplying Salem with
doors on a consignment basis since 1977. Wayne-Dalton would ship goods
to Salem's warehouse. Each month the Wayne-Dalton representative
would take inventory at the warehouse; that inventory became the basis
for Wayne-Dalton's billing of Salem Corp. Payment was due thirty days
after the end of the month. In early 1982 Salem Corp. was put on a C.O.D.
basis.

Testimony at the evidentiary hearing established that as of the date of
the hearing Salem Corp. had an unpaid balance with petitioning creditor
Telectron of something in excess of $6,700.00, but also that in April, 1982
Telectron had agreed with Salem upon a payment schedule of $1,000.00

per month. Salem had made payments pursuant to this agreement in June, July, and August.

The second petitioning creditor, Glass City Spring Corp., testified that on the date the petition was filed it was owed $516.60 by the debtor. This debt was based upon two invoices, one payable August 20, 1982 and the other, August 27, 1982. The first of these invoices was paid September 3, 1982. A check on account of the second invoice was sent, but returned because it was improperly addressed; the envelope with that check was post-marked August 22, 1982. Payment was tendered to Glass a few days before and again at the hearing. The Bankruptcy Judge specifically found that both Telectron and Glass City joined in the petition upon the solicitation of Wayne-Dalton.

To establish that Salem Corp. was not paying its debts as they came due, Wayne-Dalton called an expert witness, Edward L. Cromer, Jr., a partner in the accounting firm of Price Waterhouse retained by the petitioning creditors to review Salem Corp.'s financial records. Price Waterhouse examined the aging of the Salem Corp.'s accounts payable for June, July and August, 1982. Based upon this study, Mr. Cromer testified that ninety percent of debtor's accounts payable were past due and that Salem Corp. was not paying its debts as they came due. Upon cross-examination, Mr. Cromer stated that when the study upon which he based his opinion was done, he was unaware that any of the debts were disputed or of any payment schedule agreements other than those reflected by the invoices.

The Price Waterhouse analysis of Salem Corp.'s accounts payable . . . reveals a total accounts payable of $397,996.96, $364,047.13 of which was owed to Wayne-Dalton. Of the amount owed to Wayne-Dalton, $340,038.61 was overdue. Of the $33,949.83 owed to other creditors, $15,561.16 was overdue ($13,838.95 of this amount had been due for more than ninety days).

R.N. Salem, president of the debtor corporation, then testified on behalf of the corporation. A large part of his testimony consisted of describing the disputes about the amount owed to Wayne-Dalton. These disputes, which date back to 1978, revolve around the amount of credits due to Salem from Wayne-Dalton for returned or defective goods. In addition, Mr. Salem asserted that he had a claim in an unspecified amount against Wayne-Dalton pursuant to an alleged oral exclusive dealership agreement. The Bankruptcy Judge concluded that there were "genuine areas of dispute about the claim and this is the reason it is not being paid." He also pointed out that "Salem testified that without any question, some amount was owed by debtor to Wayne-Dalton" . . .

Mr. Salem also testified that Wayne-Dalton held a secured interest in Salem Corp.'s inventory, machinery, equipment, and accounts receivable which he valued at $288,000.00 total. Wayne-Dalton also holds a second mortgage on real estate belonging to Mr. Salem personally in addition to Mr. Salem's personal guarantee of the corporation's obligation to Wayne-

Dalton. Mr. Salem testified that the value of the second mortgage is
$310,000.00 and that his net worth is $600,000.00.

The Bankruptcy Judge found first that the petitioning creditors had
met their burden under section 303(b)(1) of demonstrating that their
claims aggregated at least $5,000.00 more than the value of any liens
securing these claims. He then addressed the question of whether the
petitioning creditors had demonstrated, as required by section 303(h)(1),
that Salem Corp. was not generally paying its debts as they came due. He
found that there was a genuine dispute about the overage account payable
to Wayne-Dalton and, therefore, excluded the Wayne-Dalton arrearage
from the determination. Judge Perlman stated:

> It would simply not make sense to do otherwise. The provision at §303(h)(1)
> is intended to be a test of insolvency, and where a debt is not being paid for
> demonstrably other reasons than insolvency, the test is not met. See also In
> re All Media Properties, 2 C.B.C.2d 449, 469-470, 5 B.R. 126 (B.J.S.D. Tex.
> 1980). P. 8, Bankruptcy Court opinion.

He added that Cromer's testimony that Salem was not generally paying its
debts as they became due was based on the total accounts payable, not on
the accounts payable excluding amounts owed to Wayne-Dalton.

The Bankruptcy Court then stated that the record alone, independent of Mr. Cromer's testimony, did not satisfy the "generally not paying"
standard. He compared the approximately $14,000.00 in accounts pay-
able older than ninety days to creditors other than Wayne-Dalton and the
approximately $16,000.00 in total past due accounts payable to creditors
other than Wayne-Dalton with the almost $400,000.00 in total accounts
payable including amounts owed to Wayne-Dalton. Judge Perlman concluded that:

> [t]his evidence alone, undistinguished as to number and amount of creditors,
> as well as uninformative about the comparative relationship to current ac-
> counts, cannot show compliance with the test of §303(h)(1). . . .

Finally, the Court addressed the creditors' reliance on Matter of
Covey, 650 F.2d 877 (7th Cir. 1981), which states that whether a disputed
claim should be included in the "generally not paying" calculation should
be decided on a case-by-case basis. The Court wrote that it had applied
such a test here and further that *Covey* was distinguishable because that
debtor, unlike Salem Corp., had ceased to do business.

The issue on appeal is how the Bankruptcy Court should treat debts
disputed by the debtor for the purposes of deciding whether "the debtor is
generally not paying such debtor's debts as such debts become due." 11
U.S.C. §303(h)(1). . . .

. . . It is obvious from the language of the Bankruptcy Code as well as
the case law that the right to be a petitioning creditor does not depend on

the existence of an undisputed claim. Section 303(b)(1) gives the right to initiate involuntary proceedings to any holder of a claim so long as the claim is not contingent as to liability. Claim is defined in section 101(4)(A) as the "right to payment whether or not . . . disputed." . . .

That the Code does not bar holders of disputed claims from being petitioning creditors is evidence of Congressional intent that "even holders of disputed claims should be able to seek a determination of whether a debtor is generally not paying its debts as they become due." In re All Media Properties, Inc., 5 B.R. 126 (Bkrtcy. Tex. 1980), aff'd (on the basis of the Bankruptcy Court's opinion) 646 F.2d 193 (5th Cir. 1981). However, once the holder of the disputed claim exercises its right to file the involuntary petition and the debtor timely challenges the petition, the Bankruptcy Court must determine, after trial, whether the debtor is generally not paying its debts as they become due. 11 U.S.C. §303(h)(1). . . .

Where a debt is disputed, the section 303(h)(1) determination is obviously a two-step process. First, the Bankruptcy Court must determine whether or not a particular disputed debt should be included in the calculation. Having decided which disputed debts, if any, should be included, the Court must then decide whether the debtor is generally paying its debts as they come due. . . .

The leading case on the treatment of disputed debts in making the "generally not paying" determination of section 303(h)(1) is Matter of Covey. . . . In that case the Court concluded that given the Code's silence on this issue and the strong policy arguments in support of both creditors' and debtors' interests, an absolute rule either excluding or including such debts would not be appropriate. The Court then developed a three-part test for determining whether disputed debts should be included. . . .

. . . Although not necessary to its conclusion that all three challenged debts should be included, the Covey Court concluded that the creditors' interest outweighed those of the debtors. Two factors weighing against the debtor were that the debtor had voluntarily closed its business and that it was disputing 99½ percent of its business debt. . . .

Appellant here insists that Covey governs and that an analysis of the facts as found by the Bankruptcy Court and supported by the record on appeal requires that the disputed debt to Wayne-Dalton be included. First, appellant argues that the dispute goes to the amount — not the existence of the claim — and, therefore, the debt should be included. Second, even if the dispute did go to the existence of the claim, the parties agree that substantial litigation would be required to resolve the dispute and, therefore under Covey the disputed debt should be included. Finally, even if substantial litigation were not required, the creditors' interest in a speedy resolution outweighs the debtors' interest in not being forced into bankruptcy and thus, according to appellant, the debt should be included. Appellant also points out that Covey requires that if the debtor's interest is greater than that of the creditor then the Bankruptcy Court should reach the 'dispute' issue. If the debtor does establish that the entire debt is barred or otherwise invalid, then the disputed debt should be excluded. 650 F.2d at 883.

In summary, appellant argues that *Covey* requires either that the disputed debt be included or that the Bankruptcy Court decide the merits of the dispute.

We agree with appellant that a strict application of *Covey* would require the inclusion of the debt. However, we are not bound by *Covey*. Our own Court of Appeals has not addressed the particular issue. Accordingly, we reject a strict application of *Covey*. We find that a balancing analysis which weighs the interests of the creditors against those of the debtor the proper approach in determining whether a disputed debt should be included.

It seems fairly clear that application of the *Covey* test will generally result in the inclusion of disputed debts. We find the result harsh, for we do not believe a debtor should have to pay legitimately disputed debts to avoid bankruptcy. See In re All Media Properties, Inc., 5 B.R. 126, 144 (Bkrtcy. Tex. 1980). Furthermore, a rigid application of *Covey* may enable creditors to use the involuntary petition as a collection device where debts are disputed, a strategy which if widely employed would paralyze bankruptcy courts. Congress intended the Bankruptcy Code as a shield for debtors, not a sword for creditors.

On the other hand, it is equally apparent that it was not the intention of Congress that a debtor be able to avoid bankruptcy by merely disputing the existence or amount of a claim. Furthermore, creditors are entitled to a speedy determination so that if the debtor is generally not paying its debts the creditors' rights can be protected and the debtor can be prevented from wasting creditors' assets. . . .

The resulting tension between the rights of the debtor and those of the creditor is inherent in the Bankruptcy Code. We thus agree with the *Covey* Court that an absolute rule either including or excluding disputed debts is inappropriate. 650 F.2d at 882. However, we find the *Covey* test overly favorable to creditors and conclude it should be used as a guideline only. In our view, the essential question requires the Court to weigh the creditors' interest against those of the debtor. In other words, the first two steps of the *Covey* analysis should be utilized in the balancing process — not precede, and in many cases perhaps preclude — the balancing analysis. . . .

The *Covey* Court and the . . . courts adopting that approach refer to the creditors' interest in a speedy determination as a factor weighing in favor of inclusion of disputed debts. Too much weight should not be accorded this interest. The creditor's interest in speedy determination is protected insofar as it can file an involuntary petition even though the claim is disputed. 11 U.S.C. §303(b)(1). Once the petition is filed, it is up to the Court to be sure that the "not generally paying" determination is made expeditiously. The Bankruptcy Code gives the creditor a right to a speedy determination of the "not generally paying" determination only. The creditors bear the burden of establishing that the debtor is generally not paying its debts in order to trigger the additional protections of the Bankruptcy Code. If the creditor is unsuccessful in meeting this burden, then he has no right to a speedy determination of anything.

The Bankruptcy Court here stated that it was excluding the disputed debt, but did not explain its rationale for doing so other than to state it "would simply not make sense" to include it. It also stated that "where a debt is not being paid for demonstrably other reasons than insolvency" the generally not paying test has not been met. The reasons why a debt is not being paid, however, are irrelevant to the section 303(h)(1) calculation. The statutory language is clear that the only factor to be considered is that of payment. However, the reasons why a debt is disputed may well bear on the threshold question of whether a disputed debt is to be included. Once that decision is made then the fact-finder can address the generally not paying issue.

Although the Court stated it had used *Covey's* case-by-case approach, it clearly did not adopt *Covey's* three-step analysis. Neither did it enumerate the factors upon which it relied in deciding that the Wayne-Dalton debt should be excluded.

However, the record before us is sufficiently developed that we may conduct the balancing analysis which in the future the Bankruptcy Court should engage in. Because we conclude that Salem's interests in not being forced into involuntary bankruptcy outweigh those of the creditors, we find that the Bankruptcy Court properly excluded the Wayne-Dalton debt prior to making the generally not paying determination.

First, as noted earlier, the creditors' interest in a speedy determination was satisfied by the filing of the involuntary petition. Second, Wayne-Dalton holds a security interest in the debtor's inventory and equipment which it can enforce in state court if it feels itself insecure. It also holds a security interest in the personal real estate of the debtor corporation's major shareholder, Mr. Salem. Although a security interest in property that would not be included in the bankrupt's estate does not make the secured party a secured creditor for purposes of the bankruptcy, we do find it a factor to be included in the balancing equation. In other words, Wayne-Dalton is not without other remedies if the involuntary petition is dismissed. In open court counsel for Wayne-Dalton stated that it did not seek its remedy in state court because that remedy would take far more time and afford it far less protection than the remedies available from the Bankruptcy Court. That may well be true, but alone is not sufficient to justify including the disputed debt for purposes of forcing Salem Corp. into involuntary bankruptcy. Moreover, the debtor has not voluntarily terminated its business, unlike the debtor[] in *Covey* . . . , nor does it apparently intend to. . . . Accordingly Salem Corp. has a greater interest in avoiding the stigma of involuntary bankruptcy than did those three debtors.

Wayne-Dalton insists that section 303(i), which permits the Bankruptcy Court to award costs, attorney's fees, and proximate damages, plus punitive damages if a petition is filed in bad faith, where the involuntary petition is dismissed other than upon the consent of all petitioners and the debtor, adequately protects the interest of the debtor and that, therefore disputed debts that meet the *Covey* test should be included. We disagree. Money damages are an inadequate remedy for the harm done to an ongoing business by an involuntary petition.

Having concluded that the debtor's interests in this case outweigh those of Wayne-Dalton and, therefore, that the disputed debt should be excluded, we find ourselves in agreement with the Bankruptcy Court's conclusion although not with its process. In the future, we anticipate the Bankruptcy Court will do this balancing analysis on the record so that the district court will know the basis for the Court's decision to exclude or include a disputed debt.

THE GENERALLY NOT PAYING CALCULATION

The next step is to review the Bankruptcy Court's conclusion that the debtor was generally paying its debts as they came due. Although we would have preferred some amplification of its reasoning, we do not find the Bankruptcy Court's determination clearly erroneous. Accordingly, we affirm.

The language of 303(h)(1) is not very helpful in establishing what Congress intended by "generally not paying its debts as such debts come due." Despite the Committee on the Judiciary's observation that this equity insolvency test would be easy to apply, Notes of the Committee on the Judiciary, Senate Report No. 95-989 (1978), experience has proved otherwise. . . .

The Bankruptcy Court here stated that figures "undistinguished as to number and amount of creditors, as well as uninformative about their comparative relationship to current accounts, cannot show compliance with the test of §303(h)(1)." We agree with the standard expressed, but are not totally persuaded that the evidence presented by the creditors was as "undistinguished" and "uninformative" as the Court believed. In addition, the Bankruptcy Court reached its conclusion by comparing the somewhat less than $16,000.00 of overdue accounts with the Wayne-Dalton debt excluded against the total amount of current and overdue debt — *including* the Wayne-Dalton account — of almost $400,000.00. We agree with appellant that the Court has thus weighed apples against apples and oranges. The better procedure would be to compare the overage non-Wayne-Dalton accounts against the total non-Wayne-Dalton accounts (or approximately $14,000.00 against approximately $34,000.00. . . .

If we were considering this question de novo, we might decide that the creditors had met the 303(h)(1) test and find that the debtor was not generally paying its debts as they came due. Our role as a reviewing court, however, is limited and we must not disturb the facts as found by the Bankruptcy Court unless they are clearly erroneous.

We do not believe that the 303(h)(1) standard involves merely comparing percentages. Instead we agree with the standard apparently utilized by the Court here and clearly enunciated by the Bankruptcy Court in *All Media*:

> [T]he court believes that generally not paying debts includes regularly missing a significant number of payments to creditors or regularly missing payments which are significant in amount in relation to the size of the debtor's operation. Where the debtor has few creditors the number which will be significant will be fewer than where the debtor has a large number of [creditors]. Also, the amount of the debts not being paid is important. If the amounts of missed payments are not substantial in comparison to the magnitude of the debtor's operation, involuntary relief would be improper. 5 B.R. at 143.

These are determinations which can best be made by the Bankruptcy Court as the trier of fact. In the future, we would expect that the Bankruptcy Court would state both the standard it is utilizing and the facts upon which it bases its conclusion. However, because we conclude on this record that the Wayne-Dalton debt should have been excluded and because we cannot find the Court's subsequent determination that the debtor was generally paying his debts clearly erroneous, we cannot substitute our judgment for that of the Bankruptcy Court.

Accordingly, the decision of the Bankruptcy Court to dismiss the involuntary petition is affirmed.

So ordered.

NOTE

In *R.N. Salem*, the business had not closed. The business might have been in financial difficulty, but can R.N. Salem's president argue that Wayne-Dalton should not be able to bring a bankruptcy proceeding because it has nothing to gain by doing so? If the president's figures can be believed, Wayne-Dalton has nothing to gain in bankruptcy because outside of bankruptcy it is fully protected by its security interest and by its second mortgage on the president's real property. Why can't R.N. Salem make the following argument: R.N. Salem and Wayne-Dalton have a dispute, and like all businessmen they have to negotiate. R.N. Salem is bargaining from a position of strength because Wayne-Dalton is owed money and it must take the initiative. This bargaining, R.N. Salem might argue, is part of everyday life. Wayne-Dalton should not be able to circumvent it and use bankruptcy as an individual collection device, especially not in a case in which it will be paid in full in any event. If Wayne-Dalton can throw R.N. Salem into bankruptcy, why wouldn't any large company be able to throw a small company into bankruptcy?

But does this argument take account of all the facts? Is Wayne-Dalton actually fully protected? Can R.N. Salem's valuation of the inventory be trusted? Isn't the relevant value from the perspective of Wayne-Dalton the amount the goods would be worth in its hands if it exercised its default rights? How sure can we be that the second mortgage on the president's property would be worth $310,000?

Does the court in *R.N. Salem* think that if a claim is disputed, it should not be calculated at all in determining whether a debtor is paying its debts as they become due? The court thought that R.N. Salem's obligation to Wayne-Dalton should not be taken into account at all, and that instead one should compare the $16,000 overdue to other creditors against the total of $34,000 that these other creditors were owed. How can it therefore affirm the bankruptcy court, which, in deciding that Wayne-Dalton was generally paying its debts, compared the $16,000 amount overdue to the other creditors against the amounts due both Wayne-Dalton and the other creditors? In the absence of any special finding that R.N. Salem *would* have been generally paying its debts as they became due when $16,000 of the $34,000 it owed was overdue, how can the district court defer to the bankruptcy court's fact-finding?

PROBLEMS

2.20 Debtor has assets of $10,000 and trade creditors who are owed $5,000. There are fewer than 12 creditors. Supplier claims it is owed $20,000; Debtor asserts it owes Supplier only $10,000. Debtor is current on all claims with its trade creditors, and Supplier has a security interest in all of Debtor's assets. Is a bankruptcy proceeding appropriate in a case such as this? Can Supplier bring an involuntary petition against Debtor? Assuming Supplier can (or assuming one of the trade creditors brings the petition), is Debtor generally paying its debts as they become due under the standard of §303(h)(1)?

2.21 Debtor and Creditor entered into a contract whereby Debtor was to manufacture for Creditor three specialized computerized test machines, to assist Creditor in opening its new business. Debtor was three months late in delivering these machines. Creditor sues Debtor for breach of contract, claiming that it was damaged by the delay, and that it is entitled to lost profits during the delay. Creditor's complaint asks for $200,000 in lost profits. Debtor is in default on several other debts, for which it owes some $15,000. Debtor has kept current on various other debts, and has paid over $100,000 during the past month on such debts. May Debtor be put involuntarily into bankruptcy? Under the 1898 Act, §59b, an unliquidated claim "shall not be counted . . . if the court determines that the claim . . . cannot be readily determined or estimated to be sufficient . . . to aggregate $500, without unduly delaying the decision upon the adjudication." See In re Coldiron and Peeples Oil Co., 356 F.2d 266 (9th Cir. 1966). How is this issue now to be resolved? Cf. §506(c).

E. DISMISSALS OF PETITIONS THAT COMPLY WITH FORMAL REQUIREMENTS FOR COMMENCEMENT

NOTE ON DISMISSALS OF PETITIONS

A debtor, as we have seen, has to pass no hurdles at all under §301 before a petition it files is deemed to commence a case. Creditors, as we have also seen, have to pass several hurdles before they can commence a case against a debtor, expressed principally in the requirements of §303(b) and (h). In either situation, should any subjective elements be at issue? In other words, should it matter, for purposes of allowing a bankruptcy case to proceed, what the motives of the debtor or creditors are? In the classic case where the debtor is insolvent, in the sense of having liabilities exceeding assets, the need for a collective bankruptcy proceeding is usually apparent (at least if there are more than a small number of creditors). In those cases, is an inquiry into motive ever necessary or productive? And what of the situation in which the debtor does not seem to be insolvent? Is this clearly an *improper* case for bankruptcy, or may there still be occasions where the advantages of a collective proceeding would make bankruptcy desirable? To what extent should motive be examined where the debtor appears solvent?

The issue may not be the same for involuntary petitions as it is for voluntary petitions. In the case of involuntary petitions, have the §303 tests done the necessary sorting, or is there still something to be gained (considering the costs) from an inquiry into subjective motive or circumstances? Should §303's tests, in other words, be deemed necessary but not sufficient conditions for bringing an involuntary petition?

Is motive less important in the case of voluntary petitions? Is this, in any event, the policy enunciated by §301? Whether or not one should actually engage in inquiries into motive, and without even asking whether we can truly distinguish "voluntary" from "involuntary" petitions, isn't it clear at some level that debtors — like creditors — have reasons for resorting to bankruptcy other than those motivated by the problems that bankruptcy is designed to solve? Consider the case of Tinti Construction Company. Tinti, a corporation wholly owned by two brothers, was in the business of constructing single-family homes. In mid-1982, Tinti (as a member of a construction association) entered into a two-year collective bargaining agreement with Carpenters' Union. Because of a construction slump commencing in 1981, Tinti started suffering large losses. Tinti had also lost a number of recent bids to construction companies that had not signed the union contract. According to the court, if Tinti did not get out from under its union contract, it "will almost certainly fail, and its 8 to 12 employees will be out of a job." Tinti, however, bought most supplies on a cash basis, and had never borrowed extensively, except in the form of equity infusions from the shareholders. Again, according to the court, Tinti had "no outstanding claims other than those of the Union for contributions to employee benefit plans and unpaid wage differentials."

Notwithstanding that Tinti had, effectively, only one creditor and no apparent need for a collective proceeding, it filed for bankruptcy. Why? As we will see throughout this book, the Bankruptcy Code changes a number of nonbankruptcy rules. One of the rules it has been construed as changing is the rule regarding "breach" of a collective bargaining agreement. Under certain circumstances, debtors in bankruptcy can "reject" collective bargaining agreements under §365. See §1113 (added in 1984) and the Note on Labor Law Contracts in Bankruptcy, infra page 474. Under the tests that were in existence prior to 1984, Tinti seemed to be able to reject the collective bargaining agreement. But in In re Tinti Construction Co., 29 Bankr. 971 (Bankr. E.D. Wis. 1983), the court saw an issue precedent: Did Tinti belong in bankruptcy at all? The court concluded no: It was improper to resort to bankruptcy *solely* to gain access to this rule change. (The issue came up in the context of rejection of the contract, so the result was denial of the rejection, not dismissal of the petition.) It was, in other words, improper to resort to bankruptcy to save a business (by resorting to a rule available only in bankruptcy), when there was no collective bankruptcy function to be served (because of the absence of multiple creditors). But see In re Waldron, 36 Bankr. 633 (Bankr. S.D. Fla. 1984) (proper to use bankruptcy solely to avoid an option to purchase real property granted by debtors); cf. In re Cordova, 34 Bankr. 70 (Bankr. D.N.M. 1983) (single-creditor involuntary bankruptcy proper because bankruptcy process could sell ongoing business better and sheriff ill-equipped to do so).

Isn't it fair to say that Tinti's problem was caused by a nonbankruptcy rule (the inability to unilaterally reject collective bargaining agreements) that was unrelated to the reasons for a system of bankruptcy law in the first place? If that is so, isn't the result in *Tinti Construction Co.* correct? That is to say, if any company was entitled to use bankruptcy for no purpose other than to gain access to a rule change (such as one permitting rejection of collective bargaining agreements), there would have been no point to put the rule change in the Bankruptcy Code in the first place, as opposed to enacting it generally. (Note that Tinti could now dissolve under state law, but this would probably not accomplish the same goal as bankruptcy — getting "out from under" the collective bargaining agreement. The labor law doctrine of "successor enterprise" would likely bind a construction company that the brothers subsequently formed to the union contract.)

Whether or not you agree with the particular result, *Tinti Construction Co.* illustrates the basic point: Debtors may file a petition in bankruptcy for a number of reasons. The next two cases explore the question of the propriety of petitions — first in the context of a voluntary petition and then in the context of an involuntary petition. The first case raises the general policy issues sought to be addressed by §305. You should ask how successfully the court identifies those policies and whether the policies themselves are sensible. The second case requires you to attempt to determine motives where, depending on one's reading of the facts, the situation might involve an entity that needs bankruptcy. Lurking in both cases is a common approach you should focus on: first, whether the petition complies with §303; second, whether it should be dismissed under §305. In examining these cases, consider the relationship between §303 and §305, and under what circumstances a creditor's petition should be dismissed because it is in the best interest of the debtor or other creditors.

IN RE COLONIAL FORD
24 Bankr. 1014 (Bankr. D. Utah 1982)

Ralph R. Mabey, Bankruptcy Judge.

INTRODUCTION AND BACKGROUND

The Bankruptcy Code contains several provisions which promote the private, cooperative, negotiated rebuilding of financially distressed debtors. One of these measures, 11 U.S.C. Section 305(a)(1), is the subject of inquiry in this case. The facts relevant to this inquiry, briefly summarized, are as follows.

In January, 1977, Colonial Ford, Inc., the debtor, ceased operation as an automobile dealership. Since May, 1975, it has been embroiled in litigation with Ford Motor Company, Ford Motor Credit Company, the United States Small Business Administration, and other creditors. This litigation embraces three lawsuits, one of which has journeyed to the Tenth Circuit Court of Appeals and back and resulted in a judgment for $2,897,125 in favor of Ford Credit and against Colonial. Execution on this judgment and liquidation of the former dealership site, which Colonial continues to hold and lease to others, was enjoined by the district court pending resolution of these cases.

In July, 1981, Colonial and its creditors settled their differences. The agreement, in essence, accomplished two objectives. First, with the exception of a single cross-claim, it concluded all three lawsuits. Second, creditors reduced their claims and gave Colonial nine months to sell or refinance the dealership site; if this did not occur, a decree of foreclosure would be entered. Creditors, in other words, were willing to take less in exchange for an end to the litigation and swifter realization on their claims.[2]

Colonial was unable to sell or refinance the property and filed a petition under Chapter 11 on March 30, 1982. Ford Credit filed a motion to abstain pursuant to Section 305(a)(1) on June 1. . . .

THE POLICY OF ENCOURAGING WORKOUTS

Section 305(a)(1) reflects a policy, embodied in several sections of the Code, which favors "workouts": private, negotiated adjustments of creditor-company relations. Congress designed the Code, in large measure, to encourage workouts in the first instance, with refuge in bankruptcy as a last resort. As noted in the legislative history: "Most business arrangements, that is, extensions or compositions (reduction) of debts, occur out-of-court. The out-of-court procedure, sometimes known as a common law composition, is quick and inexpensive. However, it requires near universal agreement of the business's creditors, and is limited in the relief it can provide for an overextended business. When an out-of-court arrangement is inadequate to rehabilitate a business, the bankruptcy laws provide an alternative. An arrangement or reorganization accomplished under the Bankruptcy Act binds nonconsenting creditors, and permits more substantial restructuring of a debtor's finances than does an out-of-court work-out." H.R. Rep. No. 95-595, 95th Cong., 1st Sess. 220 (1977), U.S. Code Cong. & Admin. News 1978, pp. 5787, 6179-6180. The reasons for blessing the workout are at least threefold.

First, the workout is expeditious. Debtors and creditors, unbridled by bankruptcy, enjoy a flexibility conducive to speed. By contrast, the "bankruptcy machinery [of] today," may be "a very time-consuming and hydra-headed kind of delaying structure" which "frequently works to the detriment of creditors." Hearings on S. 2266 and H.R. 8200 Before the Subcomm. on Improvements in Judicial Machinery of the Senate Comm.

---

2. These reductions, with other concessions, were substantial. Ford Credit, for example, held a judgment for $2,897,125. An injunction barring execution, however, had prevented collection from the fall of 1976 until the settlement in 1981. The settlement reduced the judgment to $1,250,000, provided a moratorium on interest for all but $50,000 of this amount, and postponed foreclosure another nine months. All but three creditors, by default or acquiescence, are dealt with in the settlement. One of these, Ken Rothey, is counsel to and an officer of Colonial. He holds an attorneys lien on the unsettled cross-claim. The others, LeGrande Belnap and Doris Belnap, shareholders of Colonial, have a claim for wages.

on the Judiciary, 95th Cong., 1st Sess. 599 (1977). Indeed, it has been noted, apropos the settlement in this case, that "delay. . . . is the most costly element in any bankruptcy proceeding and particularly in a business reorganization. The same amount of money received by the senior creditors 4 years from now is worth probably less than half of what would be an amount of money received today. In other words, if [a creditor] can anticipate, after this elaborate procedure, [that he] will receive $1 million, then he would be well-advised and usually is anxious to take $500,000 today because it's worth more to him. He has to consider the investment value and the ravages of inflation. This is worth more than the prospect of getting $1 million 4 years from now." Id. at 490. Many provisions in the Code were fashioned in response to this testimony and as inducements to alacrity in reorganization, including the expansive jurisdiction of the court, the opportunity for creditors to file plans, and modification of the absolute priority rule, to name three. The assist to workouts complements these features of the Code.

Second, workouts are economic. Economy, of course, is improved through expedition, as noted above. But the workout is economic because it avoids the superstructure of reorganization: trustees, committees, and their professional representatives. These and other costs of administration push junior interests "under water," and because they must be paid at confirmation, diminish prospects for a plan. Moreover, bankruptcy may shipwreck relationships necessary to keep a business afloat. Customers are reluctant to deal with the manufacturer who may not survive to honor the warranty of his product or with the lessor who cannot guarantee the habitability of his premises. The cost of overcoming this reluctance, through marketing campaigns and the like, may be high. Sales will be difficult; prices may be low. Suppliers may dwindle. Costs of credit may increase. "[W]hen word of financial difficulty spreads, the debtor's own debtors often decline to pay as they would have in the ordinary course, suddenly reporting that the dresses were the wrong size, were the wrong color, or were not ordered." Coogan, Broude and Glatt, "Comments on Some Reorganization Provisions of the Pending Bankruptcy Bills," 30 Bus. Law. 1149, 1155 (1975). Likewise, "accounts receivable can deteriorate to an unbelievable extent as soon as word gets around that the debtor is headed for the cemetery." Hearings on H.R. 31 and H.R. 32 Before the Subcomm. on Civil and Constitutional Rights of the House Comm. on the Judiciary, 94th Cong., 1st Sess., Ser. 27, pt. 1, at 483 (1975). These circumstances, among others, handcuff a debtor doing business in Chapter 11.

Third, the workout is sensible. Workouts contemplate, indeed depend upon, participation from all parties in interest, good faith, conciliation, and candor. The alternative is litigation and its bedfellows — bluff, pettifoggery, and strife. Moreover, the parties who are "on-site," and prepared by education or experience, are more able than a judge, ill-equipped in resources and training, to rescue a beleaguered corporation. "The courtroom," after all, "is not a boardroom. The judge is not a business consultant." In re Curlew Valley Associates, 14 B.R. 506, 511 (Bkrtcy. D. Utah 1981). The problems of insolvency, for the most part, are matters for extra-judicial resolution, calling for "business not legal judgment." Id.

With these advantages in mind, the authors of the Code encouraged workouts in at least two ways.

First, the Code, "[l]ike a 'fleet-in-being' . . . may be a force towards mutual accommodation," and as such, sets parameters for negotiations preceding a workout. Hearings on H.R. 31 and H.R. 32 Before the Subcomm. on Civil and Constitutional Rights of the House Comm. on the Judiciary, 94th Cong., 1st Sess., Ser. 27, pt. 1, at 396 (1975). . . .

Second, the Code, in several specific respects, contemplates that workouts will be a prelude to, yet consummated in, bankruptcy. . . . Indeed, incentives to use "prepackaged plans" are "written all through the new Act." They lead to a "revolving door" in and out of Chapter 11. Aaron, "The Bankruptcy Reform Act of 1978: The Full-Employment-for-Lawyers Bill: Part V: Business Reorganization," 1982 Utah L. Rev. 1, 38.

SECTION 305(a)(1) AND THE POLICY OF ENCOURAGING WORKOUTS

Thus, the Code encourages workouts outside, or concluded inside, Chapter 11. Encouragement on both fronts is necessary because dissent from a workout may assume a variety of shapes. Creditors who would otherwise pursue their rights under state law are kept in tow because preferences may be undone following a petition in bankruptcy. Others may be bound, assuming a consensus in number and amount, through confirmation of a plan. What, however, of the maverick who threatens prematurely to disrupt out-of-court negotiations by an involuntary petition, or the party, creditor or debtor, who has "buyer's remorse" and seeks a recapitulation of the settlement in bankruptcy? This form of dissent is the target of Section 305(a)(1) which provides:

> (a) The Court, after notice and a hearing, may dismiss a case under this title, or may suspend all proceedings in a case under this title, at any time if—
> (1) The interests of creditors and the debtor would be better served by such dismissal or suspension.

Section 305(a)(1) evolved from Section 4-208(a) of the Commission proposal which permitted dismissal of an involuntary, but not a voluntary, petition which was not in the "best interests of the debtor and its creditors." The Commission relaxed the standards for involuntary bankruptcy

in the belief that early, albeit involuntary, relief against marginal enterprises would increase dividends available to creditors. Section 4-208(a) was
the counterweight to this reform, safeguarding against the precipitate or
malicious involuntary petition.[8]

Congress realized, however, at some point in the study and revision of
the Commission bill, that abuse could occur in connection with voluntary
as well as involuntary petitions. Hence, it rewrote Section 4-208(a) and
moved it to Section 305(a)(1). Moreover, it added Section 305(c) which
makes any decision under Section 305(a)(1) nonappealable. This measure
insulates the workout from time-consuming and expensive litigation and
thus underscores the role of Section 305(a)(1) in furthering out-of-court
solutions to the rehabilitation of debtors.

APPLICATION OF SECTION 305(a)(1) IN THIS CASE

Colonial questions the applicability of Section 305(a)(1) in voluntary cases,
and whether dismissal, under the circumstances of this case, "better
serves" the interests of creditors and the debtor.[11]

THE APPLICABILITY OF SECTION 305(a)(1)
IN VOLUNTARY CASES

Section 305(a)(1) applies in any case, voluntary or involuntary,
"under this title." This is consistent with the evolution of the statute, noted

8. The notes to the Commission proposal observed: "Subdivision (a) recognizes that
involuntary relief has been facilitated under the proposed Act. This has been done to allow
creditors to force timely proceedings and to encourage voluntary proceedings while there is
still a possibility of rehabilitation or before all assets are dissipated. It is also hoped that
litigation will be avoided and expenses thereby saved. On the other hand, the need for
protection of a business debtor from the devastating impact of the mere filing of an involuntary petition is recognized. This section supplies safeguards that are not found in the present
Act, except as indirectly provided, both to debtors that should and those that should not be in
proceedings, by technical niceties and the expense of litigation. The judge is given broad
discretion to dismiss a case after hearing. The case may be dismissed even though the
requirements of §4-205(c)(1) or (2) are met. This is necessary since a debtor may temporarily
be unable to pay debts or one creditor might properly force a liquidation that would harm
creditors. The judge can best deal with these difficult cases, given adequate discretion. It is
anticipated that Rules of Bankruptcy Procedure will treat the filing of the petition like the
situation where there has been the issuance of a temporary restraining order and establish
procedures similar to those found in Rule 65 of the Federal Rules of Civil Procedure. The
petitioner must furnish a bond, if required by the court, indemnifying the debtor for damages allowed pursuant to §4-210(f) if the case is dismissed." Report of the Commission on the
Bankruptcy Laws of the United States, H. Doc. No. 93-137, pt. II, at 78 (1973).

11. Colonial also argues that abstention is inappropriate because its composition occurred in federal not state court. Some cases have suggested that Section 305(a)(1) may be
invoked only where insolvency proceedings have been initiated in a nonfederal forum. . . .
This proposition, however, draws no support from the statute, and is contradicted by the
legislative history, which far from centering on a particular forum, states a preference for
settlements "worked out by creditors and the debtor *out-of-court*." H.R. Rep. No. 95-595,
supra at 325, U.S. Code Cong. & Admin. News, p. 6281. (Emphasis supplied.)

above, beginning as a bylaw in Section 4-208(a), and moving to general applicability in Chapter 3 of the Code. Moreover, this reading is consistent with the policy to encourage workouts. It would be anomalous to protect workouts from involuntary petitions while leaving them vulnerable to voluntary petitions. Creditors would be protected from the renegades in their number who sought involuntarily to commit a debtor to bankruptcy, but they would have no similar check against debtors who compose their debts with the promise that matters will be left out of court and then stage an ambush in Chapter 11.

WHETHER THE INTERESTS OF CREDITORS AND THE DEBTOR ARE BETTER SERVED BY DISMISSAL

Section 305(a)(1) permits dismissal where it will "better serve" the interests of creditors and debtors. The statute affords no guidance in defining the "interests" to be considered, nor does it delineate criteria for determining when parties will be better served in or out of bankruptcy. Given the policies underlying Section 305(a)(1), however, the standards for dismissal may include speed, economy, and freedom from litigation. Other considerations may be fairness, priorities in distribution, capacity for dealing with frauds and preferences, and the importance of a discharge to the debtor. . . . Not all of these factors will be involved, nor will they assume equal importance, in every case. Hence, Congress intended the court to exercise considerable discretion in sifting and weighing grounds for dismissal under Section 305(a)(1).[14]

14. It could be argued that a court should be more cautious where an involuntary case is brought under 11 U.S.C. Section 303(h)(2) which provides for the entry of an order for relief if "within 120 days before the date of the filing of the petition, a custodian, other than a trustee, receiver, or agent appointed or authorized to take charge of less than substantially all of the property of the debtor for the purpose of enforcing a lien against such property, was appointed or took possession." The legislative history observes that "once a proceeding to liquidate assets has been commenced, the debtor's creditors have an *absolute right* to have the liquidation (or reorganization) proceed in the bankruptcy court and under bankruptcy laws with all of the appropriate creditor and debtor protections that those laws provide." H.R. Rep. No. 95-595, *supra* at 323-324, U.S. Code Cong. & Admin. News, p. 6280 (emphasis supplied). The Commission bill, according to one observer, did not permit abstention from an involuntary case "where there has been a general assignment for the benefit of creditors or where a receiver, trustee, or a liquidating agent has been appointed to take charge of the debtor's property. Apparently, the Commission believes that in such a case, a liquidation was contemplated, and that creditors should be able to obtain the safeguards available under the Bankruptcy Act." Cook, Involuntary Bankruptcy and the Proposed Bankruptcy Act of 1973: Reform at Last, [20 N.Y.L. F. 97] at 117-118. The observer concludes that this is "sound" but "not convincing," since even in these cases, given certain facts, dismissal may be appropriate. *Id.* at 118. The Code may adopt these views, permitting dismissal under Section 305(a)(1) in a case involving Section 303(h)(2), but only in exceptional circumstances.
[Footnote moved.— EDS.]

THE INTERESTS OF CREDITORS

In this case, the interests of creditors are better served by dismissal. They agreed to a workout because it ended the litigation, and although they compromised their claims, the present value of the amounts to be realized at payout or foreclosure exceeded what they might have gained over time. This was not a workout where debt is rolled over with an eye to recovery, while recognizing the possibility of bankruptcy. Nor was it a workout where a deal was struck prepetition to be confirmed under the auspices of Chapter 11. Here the out-of-court composition was comprehensive, including virtually all creditors and the debtor. It was also final. A business which had lain dormant for years was not to be revived without the elimination of prior debt and the infusion of fresh capital.[15]

THE INTERESTS OF COLONIAL

Colonial argues that its interests are better served in Chapter 11; otherwise it would not have filed a petition. This argument, however, may be astigmatic for at least two reasons.

First, it ignores the question of who is the debtor for purposes of Section 305(a)(1). If the case is in Chapter 11, for example, the debtor will be a debtor in possession, and hence the trustee or fiduciary for the estate. The interests of the debtor, under these circumstances, are coincidental with the interests of creditors. Indeed, no debtor is an island, self-existent apart from its creditors who supply the capital, goods, and services necessary to his survival. This idea finds expression, not only in the construct of a debtor in possession, but also at common law where insolvent entities became funds managed in trust for the benefit of creditors. From this standpoint, the interests of creditors receive double weight under Section 305(a)(1), once from a partisan and again from a fiducial perspective. In any event, the corporate debtor will be a complex of constituencies, including not only creditors but also a board of directors, management, and shareholders. These parties may be divided on some issues; even when united, their views may change from circumstance to circumstance, or from time to time. To say, with Colonial, that the debtor speaks with one voice on all occasions, and that its interests are circumscribed in the management's act of filing a petition, is oversimple.

Second, it overlooks the benefits which debtors in general may derive from out-of-court workouts and which Colonial in particular obtained in this settlement. The choice to settle out of court rather than to file for

---

15. Indeed, Ford Credit, in reliance upon the settlement, has made payments of $50,000 in attorneys fees to Colonial, and $85,000 in property taxes to its shareholder. Colonial has not offered to refund these monies or otherwise unscramble performance under the agreement.

reorganization, more often that not, will be enlightened. Management eager for asylum in bankruptcy may pause if faced with displacement by a trustee. Shareholders likewise must reckon with the prospect of a creditor's plan, wresting control of the business and eliminating their interest. Moreover, their equity, already thin or nonexistent, may not survive the burden of administrative debt. Debtors, as well as creditors, are familiar with the old saw that a "good" liquidation out of court is better than a "bad" reorganization in Chapter 11. Since the odds are stacked against obtaining confirmation of a plan,[18] and in light of the probability of conversion to Chapter 7, debtors may be well-advised, where their creditors are cooperative, to forego the dislocations and trauma, the depressed markets, the higher cost of money, and other disadvantages of bankruptcy, and work out an arrangement, even if it contemplates an eventual liquidation.

Colonial (or its shareholder, if she is the debtor) garnered these general benefits and two additional bonuses from its settlement. (1) Mrs. Belnap, by paying the SBA, may assume its right of redemption upon foreclosure of the property. This assumption, if exercised, is free and clear of any claim by Colonial or its creditors. This option . . . might be unavailable to her in Chapter 11. (2) Colonial may have grown weary of the protracted litigation, and realizing that it had reached a point of diminishing returns in court, sought disentanglement from its adversaries through the settlement. Colonial now seeks to keep the benefits of this compact, the reduction in debt, and avoid its burdens, the foreclosure, but this may not be done. An accord, with no satisfaction, releases parties from any duty to honor the compromise, and returns them to the status quo ante. The petition, therefore, may have revived the litigation in district court, with the risks and imponderables which prompted settlement in the first instance. There is no assurance that changing forums and prolonging the fight for another 7 years will produce a better bargain for Colonial.

These reasons motivated Colonial to make an agreement with its creditors which composed the debt and provided for sale, refinancing, or foreclosure of the property. The alternative of bankruptcy was available then, as now, and entered the calculus of decisionmaking, but was rejected in favor of the settlement. Colonial asserts, however, that reorganization better serves its interests at present. Attempting to divine the interests of Colonial, given this doublemindedness, is problematical. But even if full credit is given to its present protestations, these do not counterbalance the reasons for avoiding bankruptcy. Even assuming that the protestations and the reasons have equal weight, the policy of encouraging out-of-court

18. Statistics are sparse. In this district, however, 261 petitions under Chapter 11 had been filed and were pending for over 6 months as of September 30, 1982. Of these, 43 or 16 percent had achieved confirmation. R. Wily, Estate Administrator's Report of Chapter 11 Cases iii (United States Bankruptcy Court, District of Utah, Third Quarter, 1982).

workouts, embodied in Section 305(a)(1), dictates that the interests of Colonial are "better served" by the settlement than by a petition in Chapter 11.

CONCLUSION

The Code encourages out-of-court workouts. Section 305(a)(1) is one of several instruments useful in achieving this goal. Because an order of dismissal under Section 305(a)(1) is nonreviewable, the statute should be invoked sparingly. Indeed, Section 305(a)(1) permits "suspension" as well as dismissal of a case, suggesting the possibility that efforts toward settlement may proceed on more than one front at the same time. Where, however, the workout is comprehensive, and designed to end, not perpetuate, the creditor-company relations, dismissal under Section 305(a)(1) is appropriate. One "reorganization," under these circumstances, is enough. Section 305(a)(1) precludes an encore, thereby furthering the policies of expedition, economy, and good sense.

NOTE ON *COLONIAL FORD* AND NONBANKRUPTCY WORK-OUTS

In some sense is not *Colonial Ford* like *Tinti?* Although there is more than one creditor in this case, effectively all the creditors have reached an agreement with one another. A major purpose of bankruptcy law—resolving conflicts among creditors—is not implicated here, because there are no conflicts among creditors. They all participated in the workout and they all agree that it is in their interest to stay out of bankruptcy. Given that creditors are unanimous on the course of action that is in their interest, can we not therefore ask if bankruptcy would be appropriate in this case if there were in fact only one creditor? Would the debtor have any right in such a case to insist upon bankruptcy? Is the debtor's desire to delay the exercise of the creditor's default rights (either by going into bankruptcy or by staying out of it) a legitimate one? Cases that raise §305 issues frequently arise because while a creditor's individual remedy and its collective remedy are both slow and costly, they are not equally slow and costly. Creditors have an incentive to choose the faster one and the debtor the slower one, regardless of which one is in the interests of all as a group. These differences between bankruptcy procedure and nonbankruptcy procedure may have nothing to do with the policy of having bankruptcy in the first instance. How should this problem be taken into account by the drafters of a bankruptcy law? How should it be taken into account by the judges who must interpret the Bankruptcy Code?

How should *Colonial Ford* have been resolved, however, if one of the creditors who had signed the work-out agreement had second thoughts? Put another way, can creditors effectively waive their right to use the bankruptcy process, at least against a corporation? (As we shall learn later, debtors who are individuals cannot — although the reasons for that have to do with discharge policy. It is unclear whether a corporate debtor's contractual waiver of its right to file a voluntary petition would be enforced, although the Second Circuit recently stated, in dicta, that such waivers "generally" were not enforceable, while holding, in the case before it, that a corporation had effectively waived it by stipulating that the Small Business Administration would be its receiver. United States v. Royal Business Funds Corp., 724 F.2d 12 (2d Cir. 1983).) Moreover, how would we treat the case if most of the creditors did not favor the bankruptcy process and most of them had signed the work-out agreement, but some new creditors had entered the picture who were not signatories to that agreement? Wouldn't the problem in this case be not merely one of weighing the interests of creditors against the debtor, but also of weighing the interests of one creditor against another? How would the court in *Colonial Ford* apply its analysis to that case?

IN RE WIN-SUM SPORTS
14 Bankr. 389 (Bankr. D. Conn. 1981)

Robert L. KRECHEVSKY, Bankruptcy Judge.

On March 9, 1981, an involuntary Chapter 11 petition was filed pursuant to 11 U.S.C. §303(h)(1) against Win-Sum Sports, Inc. (Win-Sum) by three petitioning creditors — Nordica/RNC, Inc., Rossignol Ski Co., and Salomon/North America, Inc. An accompanying application for an immediate appointment of an interim trustee was denied. Win-Sum moved to dismiss the involuntary petition and to disqualify the petitioner's attorney on grounds of conflict of interest. When both motions were denied, Win-Sum attempted an appeal of the ruling concerning disqualification of the attorney but its application for leave to appeal was denied by the district court on April 29, 1981. Win-Sum then filed an answer generally denying the essential allegations of the petition and pleaded as a special defense that the petitioners are "estopped from claiming that the debtor is in default". Win-Sum also filed a motion to dismiss alleging that the involuntary petition had not been brought by the real party in interest pursuant to F.R.C.P. 17(a) (B.R. 717) because the petition was filed at the request of Arthur W. Benson, Jr., a Win-Sum stockholder. This motion was denied on May 26, 1981. After extensive discovery by both sides which required rulings by the court on several occasions, the trial commenced on July 28, 1981 and ended on August 13, 1981. During these hearings, Win-Sum filed a motion to dismiss the case pursuant to 11 U.S.C. §305(a)(1) on grounds that "the interest of creditors and the debtor would be better served by such dismissal. . . ." At the conclusion of the trial, the parties agreed that the court would rule on both the §303 involuntary petition and the §305 motion to dismiss based on the entire record by taking judicial notice of all prior proceedings.

BACKGROUND

Win-Sum, the alleged debtor, is a corporation operating a retail sporting goods store. Prior to the time of its incorporation in March, 1979, the same business had been conducted for a number of years as a partnership by William Paluska, Jr. and Benson. Upon incorporation, each partner became a 50 percent shareholder of the corporation, with Benson being elected a director and president, and Paluska becoming vice-president, secretary and treasurer as well as a director. Benson resigned his offices as president and director sometime later in 1979, however, and never regained these positions. Due to a lack of snow, the winter of 1979-1980 was a disastrous one for winter sports in New England. Win-Sum experienced financial difficulties at this time and became unable to pay its suppliers as their invoices fell due during 1980. The winter season of 1980-1981 was only marginally better and unpaid bills accumulated. During this same period, Paluska and Benson were negotiating for Benson to buy out Paluska's share of the business. The terms of the buy out included repayment of Paluska's loans of $60,000.00 to the corporation and payment of $30,000.00 for his shares of stock. A contract of sale was entered into in April, 1980, under which Paluska received a payment of $20,000.00 on his loans to the corporation. Benson furnished the funds for this payment to Win-Sum which, in turn, issued its check to Paluska.

Prior to September, 1980, either Paluska, or Paluska together with Benson, operated the store. During the period from September, 1980 to February, 1981, however, Benson was the sole manager of the business because Paluska, by agreement with Benson, left the store although he continued to draw his salary. When the buy out negotiations finally broke down early in February, 1981, Benson retained Attorney Christopher Noble. On February 20, 1981, Attorney Noble, who had no prior connection with Win-Sum, filed a voluntary chapter 11 petition on behalf of Win-Sum in this court. After trial, the petition was dismissed on March 3, 1981 as not having been properly authorized by officers or directors of the corporation. Six days later, on March 9, 1981, Attorney Noble, on behalf of the three petitioning creditors, filed the present involuntary petition. Benson, testifying on behalf of the petitioning creditors, stated that while the business normally had a monthly arrearage of $30,000.00 of supplier debts and $18,000.00 of other unpaid expenses, Win-Sum had incurred about $75,000.00 of overdue debts on March 9, 1981. Two of the three petitioning creditors testified that neither of them would have brought the involuntary petition had not each received a written indemnity agreement from Benson. This agreement provided that Benson would bear all costs of bringing the petition, including attorney's fees, and would hold these creditors harmless from any loss or damage should the petition be dismissed. As the result of the filing of the first voluntary petition, Win-Sum's bank, The Vernon National Bank, set off approximately $12,500.00 in funds which Win-Sum had on deposit in its checking account, thereby causing approximately $9,000.00 in checks drawn by Win-Sum to be dishonored. Prior to the filing of the involuntary petition, Win-Sum was negotiating for another loan from The Vernon National Bank, the proceeds of which were to be used to make payments to trade creditors. The filing of the involuntary petition apparently aborted the loan. At the time of the trial on the involuntary petition, except for the three petitioners' debts, Win-Sum had paid or made acceptable arrangements to pay all debts claimed by the petitioners as past due on March 9, 1981. This was accomplished through a $20,000.00 loan from the Manchester Community Bank, secured by Win-Sum's merchandise inventory and Paluska's personal assets. Paluska obtained additional cash for Win-Sum's account by conducting several markdown inventory clearance sales.

DISCUSSION

I

Under §303(h)(1), the petitioners in an involuntary case bear the burden of proving that an alleged debtor is "generally not paying such debtor's debts as such debts become due". This test, the equity insolvency test, represents the most significant departure from prior law concerning grounds for involuntary bankruptcy. . . . While Congress did not make explicit what "generally not paying" under §303(h)(1) means, courts have considered such factors as the number of creditors an alleged debtor has and the amount of debts not being paid in construing the "generally not paying" standard. Since the standard is a flexible one, all circumstances surrounding the payment practices of the alleged debtor should be explored throughly. As one court has stated:

> The new test for involuntary petitions was adopted not to restrict and limit the involuntary process but was included to allow more flexibility. . . . [T]he court believes that generally not paying debts includes regularly missing a significant number of payments which are significant in amount in relation to the size of the debtor's operation. Where the debtor has few creditors the number which will be significant will be fewer than where the debtor has a large number of creditors. Also, the amount of debts not being

paid is important. If the amounts of missed payments are not substantial in comparison to the magnitude of the debtor's operation, involuntary relief would be improper.

In re All Media Properties, Inc., 5 B.R. 126, 142-143, 6 B.C.D. 586, 593-94 (Bkrtcy. S.D. Tex. 1980). . . .

For purposes of granting or denying relief under §303(h)(1), the alleged debtor's payment activity must be examined at the time of the filing of the petition. . . . While post-petition payments of delinquent accounts may be material in some circumstances to the issue of whether relief should be granted under §303(h)(1), post-petition payments ordinarily indicate a last ditch effort on the part of the alleged debtor to avoid bankruptcy proceedings. . . . Of course, post-petition payments to creditors may be germane to other issues in a particular proceeding.

Win-Sum contends that the petitioning creditors are estopped from claiming that Win-Sum is not generally paying its debts. Win-Sum bases its argument on the relationship between the petitioning creditors and Benson, and particularly refers to Benson's agreement to indemnify the petitioners from any losses resulting from the dismissal of the involuntary petition and for attorney's fees. Win-Sum argues that the indemnity agreement induced the filing of the bankruptcy petition and this estops the petitioners from bringing this involuntary proceeding. In support of its position, Win-Sum cites four cases under the Bankruptcy Act of 1898 which hold that creditors who induce an act of bankruptcy later claimed to require an adjudication in an involuntary proceeding are precluded from being petitioning creditors. . . . The petitioning creditors in the present case do not stand on the same footing, however. The Bankruptcy Code has eliminated the traditional "acts of bankruptcy" as a basis for involuntary relief and substituted, with one other ground, the "generally not paying such debtor's debts as such debts become due" standard. §303(h)(1). Notwithstanding Benson's indemnity agreement, the petitioning creditors had the burden of showing that Win-Sum was generally unable to meet its obligations as they fell due. Hence, unlike the cases cited by Win-Sum, the petitioning creditors have not participated in inducing any ground for the granting of relief in an involuntary case.

Win-Sum further argues that involuntary relief should be denied because the petitioning creditors never pressed for payment of these debts nor sent any notices of delinquency. Consequently, Win-Sum says, the debts owed to the petitioning creditors were not "due" within the meaning of §303(h)(1). Win-Sum's argument on this point is not well taken. A debt is no less due because a creditor has seen fit for a time to forebear in collecting it. The Bankruptcy Code does not obligate a creditor to press a debtor for payment of the creditor's own debt as an antecedent condition to filing an involuntary petition. To hold otherwise could unnecessarily chill bona fide attempts on the part of creditors to aid a financially troubled debtor. Further, §303(b) refers to the commencement of an involuntary case by the filing of a petition by three entities, each of which is the "holder of a claim." "Claim" is defined in 11 U.S.C. §101(4) as a "right to payment, whether or not such right is . . . matured, unmatured. . . ." Thus, even if these three creditors' claims were not "due" as alleged by Win-Sum, such fact would not prohibit them from being petitioners.

At the time of the filing of the involuntary petition on March 9, 1981, Win-Sum had twenty-six past due accounts payable over $50.00. In total, Win-Sum owed $74,436.57 to these twenty-six creditors, double its normal indebtedness. Most of the debts were three months old; some of the oldest were past due for over a year. Rossignol and Nordica were owed $4,457.02 and $2,623.40, respectively, most of which had been due for ninety days. Salomon/NA was owed $8,915.54, the greater part of which had been due for 150 days. Benson further testified to receiving dunning phone calls from some unnamed creditors concerning their past due debts. Considering both the number of debts past due, their amounts, and the usual payment methods of Win-Sum, I conclude that the petitioning creditors have met their burden of proving that Win-Sum was not generally paying its debts on March 9, 1981 as those debts became due.

II

Win-Sum contends that if the court finds that the basis for an involuntary case is established, the court should dismiss the case pursuant to §305(a)(1) because the interests of Win-Sum and its creditors would be better served by such a dismissal. Section 305(a)(1) of the Bankruptcy Code is new. Legislative history states that the section is designed to allow out-of-court insolvency arrangements to continue if those arrangements are in the best interests of all concerned and the petition is filed by "recalcitrant creditors".

> This section recognizes that there are cases in which it would be appropriate for the court to decline jurisdiction. Abstention under this section, however, is of jurisdiction over the entire case. . . . The court may dismiss or suspend under the first paragraph, for example, if an arrangement is being worked out by the creditors and the debtor out of court, there is no prejudice to the rights of creditors in that arrangement, and an insolvency case has been commenced by a few recalcitrant creditors to provide a basis for future threats to extract full payment.

House Report No. 95-595, 95th Cong., 1st Sess. (1977) 325; Senate Report No. 95-989, 95th Cong., 2d Sess. (1978) 35, U.S. Code Cong. & Admin. News 1978, p. 6281. Since a dismissal pursuant to §305(a) is not reviewable by appeal or otherwise, this court will not grant such a dismissal lightly.

I believe that for abstention purposes pursuant to §305(a)(1), the Win-Sum postpetition payments and the motivation of the petitioners become pertinent and significant. Paluska testified that Win-Sum became current on many of its old accounts payable after the filing of the present petition. It obtained a $20,000.00 loan from The Manchester Community Bank, the proceeds of which were used to pay trade creditors, and made arrangements with other creditors for extensions of time to pay their debts. Moreover, the appearing petitioning creditors admitted at trial that they would not have retained Benson's attorney and filed the petition but for the indemnity agreement received from Benson. Nordica and Rossignol credit managers readily acknowledged that they never demanded payment of their debts from Win-Sum prior to bringing the involuntary petition, that they never advised Win-Sum they were dissatisfied with the payment schedule in effect, and that their normal credit practices would have been first to call Win-Sum to discuss an alternate payment arrangement if they were dissatisfied. In fact, Nordica and Rossignol acknowledged receiving a total of $17,623.40 and $5,267.01, respectively, on past due accounts from Win-Sum within sixty days of the filing of the voluntary petition. The Rossignol credit manager called Win-Sum an "excellent account" and he stated he was satisfied with the periodic payments being received from Win-Sum until Benson filed the voluntary petition in February, 1981. The brief filed on behalf of the petitioning creditors states that they refused to accept further paydown on their debts immediately prior to March 9, 1981 when offered by Win-Sum because it "would have been an obvious preference." This is a curious assertion in view of their previous acceptance of monies, and there is certainly nothing improper or illegal in creditors accepting payments on their debts. The involuntary petition does not seek to liquidate Win-Sum with immediate distribution of its assets to creditors. Rather, it seeks to have Win-Sum continue to operate, but under a trustee to displace Paluska as management. The indemnity agreement signed by Benson, without which there would have been no petitioning creditors and which put Benson's own business into bankruptcy, suggests the real purpose of these proceedings. The court is convinced that Benson is seeking to use the bankruptcy court as an alternate approach to state court procedures to resolve intra-company management and stockholder problems. The court concludes that Benson and the petitioning creditors are comparable to the "recalcitrant" creditor described in the legislative history of §305(a)(1).

A contention of the petitioners made in their brief, which gives the court pause in considering dismissal of the case, is that the payment of $20,000.00 to Paluska in April, 1980, is a preference, and it is in the best interests of creditors, therefore, not to dismiss the case. However, even assuming that Win-Sum was insolvent in April, 1980, and that Paluska had reason to know this, Benson merely substituted himself as a creditor of the corporation for the $20,000.00 which he caused the corporation to pay

Paluska. It is obvious that Benson put $20,000.00 into the corporation in order to pay Paluska and that Benson would not otherwise have provided these monies. Under such circumstances, there was no diminution of the estate, and no preference to be set aside. . . .

In view of all that has been said, the petition against this alleged debtor is dismissed pursuant to §305(a)(1), as the court finds the interests of Win-Sum and its creditors will be better served by such dismissal. It is so ordered.

NOTES

1. In re Luftek, Inc., 6 Bankr. 539 (Bankr. E.D.N.Y. 1980), involved Luftek, a wholly-owned subsidiary of East Coast Erektors & Fabrikators, Inc., with the same president. Luftek was in the business of heavy construction of environmental smoke stacks. Luftek had virtually no assets, and its books and records were consolidated with East Coast's. East Coast and Luftek maintained a file "which, as a general rule, contained approximately 100 unpaid bills." Krautz, the president, "would periodically select some of these bills for payment while the others remained unpaid." A motion to dismiss an involuntary petition was granted, the court reasoning as follows:

> In support of that motion, the alleged debtor points to the fact that many of its creditors have consented to its motion, that it would lose a substantial amount of its receivables if it is forced out of business as a result of bankruptcy liquidation, that the petition was joined by the subsidiary of one of its competitors, and that it has entered into a commitment for a loan which would enable it to privately reorganize its debts and pay its creditors in full. . . .
>
> . . . These facts indicate that the petition was filed by a group of recalcitrant creditors.
>
> Clearly, the interests of creditors would be better served by dismissal. There is no dispute that administration expenses would consume the meager assets of this debtor in the event that bankruptcy liquidation takes place. It also appears that Luftek's unsecured creditors have claims in excess of $700,000.00, which would be discharged without payment of any dividends. In contrast, the alleged debtor has shown its willingness to pay these creditors in full by entering into a loan commitment; the loan would be secured by the personal assets of the debtor's President. . . . With or without the loan commitment, it is apparent that the best interests of creditors and the debtor would be better served by dismissal under section 305(a).

2. In a §303 hearing, the court in In re Sago Palms Joint Venture, 27 Bankr. 33 (Bankr. S.D. Fla. 1982), was confronted with a case where the debtor conceded that the §303 statutory requirements had been met, but where the debtor argued "that this court has discretion to deny relief and

that it should do so where both the secured and unsecured creditors could receive full and complete relief through the State court in a pending foreclosure proceeding and that the debtor hopes to work its way out of its present difficulties, but that it cannot do so under the stigma of a bankruptcy proceeding." The court, disagreeing with In re Arker, 6 Bankr. 632 (Bankr. E.D.N.Y. 1980), held that §303 was unambiguous, and left no room for discretion:

> The petitioning creditors, if they carry their burden of proof as they have here, are entitled to an order for relief, the appointment of a trustee, a creditors' meeting, the examination of the debtor under oath and the opportunity to recover fraudulent and preferential transfers. The relief may, and frequently does, produce assets available for distribution to the creditors.

The court viewed that conclusion as reinforced by §303(i)'s provision for the award of costs in the case of dismissal. Do you agree? Is this case consistent with §305? Would you now advise the debtor to move for dismissal under §305? If so, what factors should guide the bankruptcy judge's discretion there?

NOTE ON *WIN-SUM SPORTS*

Should Win-Sum Sports be in bankruptcy? Perhaps it is best to approach this question by asking what appears to be the best argument for asserting that Win-Sum Sports needs the protection of the bankruptcy laws, as well as what appears to be the best argument for asserting that Win-Sum Sports should not be in bankruptcy.

Win-Sum Sports is clearly in some financial difficulty, due, according to the court at least, principally to the winters of 1979-80 and 1980-81. As a result, Win-Sum Sports has had some problem paying its bills. Does this suggest that Win-Sum Sports needs bankruptcy? What are Win-Sum Sports' assets? Who are its creditors? Aren't its principal creditors likely to be ski suppliers? Isn't it likely that, given the past winters, Win-Sum Sports' financial position might be similar to that of a lot of other sporting goods stores in the Northeast? Mightn't this be a case where Win-Sum Sports' liabilities appear to exceed its assets, but that, because of the seasonal fluctuations in business, things will probably get better soon? In that case, can we say that Win-Sum Sports is insolvent? Isn't it also likely that the creditors will forbear from pushing their collection efforts, because they need retail outlets when the next good winter comes along?

Still, if the creditors *want* to put Win-Sum Sports into bankruptcy, why shouldn't that be their choice? By doing so, can't they assure themselves, in a way that they otherwise cannot, of equal treatment? Moreover, to the extent they need retail outlets down the line, bankruptcy does not mean that Win-Sum Sports must go out of business. It can be reorganized or sold as a going concern. The result of this may well be that these creditors will end up owning Win-Sum Sports. But what is so terrible about that? Is it that the creditors are "unfairly" cashing out the owners at the bottom of a cycle? But isn't it the case that if this is indeed a cyclical business, and business is expected to pick up, that expected improvement will also be reflected in the value of the business as a going concern? Doesn't this, in turn, mean that it is possible that its assets, as a going concern, will exceed the liabilities? In that case, there will be something left over for the current owners. Isn't this exactly how things should work out?

Is there, however, another way to view this case? Can this be viewed as a dispute between Paluska and Benson where Benson is using bankruptcy to try to squeeze Paluska out of the picture? If so, isn't it really a state-law issue, where the appropriate vehicle for resolving it is the state corporate remedy of involuntary dissolution? If so, then use of §305 to dismiss the case would seem to be an appropriate vehicle. But even assuming this view of the case, what is so terrible about allowing bankruptcy to be used? What will Benson accomplish by dragging Win-Sum through bankruptcy? He can, of course, dissolve Win-Sum Sports in bankruptcy, but does he gain anything over state procedures that way? Perhaps he has a deal with the creditors that can be implemented in a plan of reorganization. See In re Toy and Sport Warehouse, Inc., 37 Bankr. 141 (Bankr. S.D.N.Y. 1984) (possibly such a case).

May there not be a grain of truth to both of these views of the case? Isn't it possible that there is both a shareholder squabble *and* a desire among some of the creditors to have a collective proceeding? How does one sort between these goals? Perhaps, as the court suggests, the creditors do not really care about the bankruptcy proceeding, but what if three or four of them wanted it? What should the court then do? How much justice, in other words, can we accomplish by a fact-specific inquiry in a case where there may in fact be mixed motives? Should it be enough to show that the enterprise would be insolvent, if it were broken up on a piecemeal basis, and that at least three creditors really want a collective proceeding? Under that view, is the case nonetheless correct, because even *that* showing has not been made by the creditors?

PROBLEMS

2.22 Debtor is a corporation, among whose assets is a piece of real estate in Orange County. Debtor is in default on a large secured loan on that property to Bank. Bank has threatened foreclosure actions against the property. Debtor thereupon sets up Subsidiary, a subsidiary corporation, and transfers the piece of real estate to Subsidiary. A week later, Subsidiary files a petition for reorganization under Chapter 11 of the Bankruptcy Code (a move that, as we will examine in Chapter 7 of this book, starts the automatic stay of §362, which will prevent Bank from taking any action against the real estate until the termination of the case or the lifting of the stay). Should this petition be dismissed under §305? What factors should be considered in making that determination? Compare In re Spenard Ventures, 18 Bankr. 164 (Bankr. D. Alaska 1982) with In re Sacramento Metropolitan Real Estate Investors, 28 Bankr. 228 (Bankr. E.D. Cal. 1983); In re Avan, Inc., 25 Bankr. 121 (Bankr. D. Or. 1982); In re Dutch Flat Investment Co., 6 Bankr. 1134 (Bankr. N.D. Cal. 1980).

2.23 Tarletz was President of a retail ski clothing and ski equipment rental business in Colorado known as Keyport Summit, Inc. Tarletz guaranteed obligations of Keyport to a number of creditors. Due to a poor snowpack during the winter of 1980-81, Keyport became unable to pay its suppliers, and filed for bankruptcy in the spring of 1981. Keyport is in the process of liquidating its business in bankruptcy. Three creditors, rather than waiting for the receipt of proceeds from that liquidation, and then suing Tarletz for the difference, brought suit against Tarletz on the personal guarantees. Finding that it would be over one year before that suit would come to trial, the three creditors filed an involuntary petition against Tarletz. On these guarantees, Tarletz is liable for some $60,000. Tarletz has other unpaid debts amounting to about $50,000, all of which are current. Tarletz has assets amounting to over $350,000. Has an involuntary petition been properly filed against Tarletz under §303? If it has, should the court dismiss the case under §305? In deciding this, does the motive of the creditors matter? Does the speed in which the bankruptcy case can be wound up matter? What if it will take almost a year to wind up the bankruptcy case? See In re Tarletz, 27 Bankr. 787 (Bankr. D. Colo. 1983).

In the following case, a debtor has filed a voluntary Chapter 11 petition and some of its creditors seek to dismiss the petition on the grounds that it was not filed in good faith. In concluding that a bankruptcy proceeding is appropriate, the court relies upon §1112. To what extent are the issues raised the same as those that should be considered under §305? As those raised by involuntary petitions?

IN RE JOHNS-MANVILLE CORP.
36 Bankr. 727 (Bankr. S.D.N.Y. 1984)

Burton R. LIFLAND, Bankruptcy Judge. . . .
Whether an industrial enterprise in the United States is highly successful is often gauged by its "membership" in what has come to be known as the "Fortune 500." Having attained this measure of financial achievement, Johns-Manville Corp. and its affiliated companies (collectively referred to as "Manville") were deemed a paradigm of success in corporate America by the financial community. Thus, Manville's filing for protec-

tion under Chapter 11 of Title 11 of the United States Code ("the Code or
the Bankruptcy Code") on August 26, 1982 ("the filing date") was greeted
with great surprise and consternation on the part of some of its creditors
and other corporations that were being sued along with Manville for
injuries caused by asbestos exposure. As discussed at length herein, Manville submits that the sole factor necessitating its filing is the mammoth
problem of uncontrolled proliferation of asbestos health suits brought
against it because of its substantial use for many years of products containing asbestos which injured those who came into contact with the dust of
this lethal substance. According to Manville, this current problem of approximately 16,000 lawsuits pending as of the filing date is compounded
by the crushing economic burden to be suffered by Manville over the next
20-30 years by the filing of an even more staggering number of suits by
those who had been exposed but who will not manifest the asbestos-related
diseases until some time during this future period ("the future asbestos
claimants"). Indeed, approximately 6,000 asbestos health claims are estimated to have arisen in only the first 16 months since the filing date. This
burden is further compounded by the insurance industry's general dis-
avowal of liability to Manville on policies written for this very purpose.
Indeed, the issue of coverage has been pending for years before a state
court in California. . . .

It is the propriety of the filing by Manville which is the subject of the
instant decision. Four separate motions to dismiss the petition pursuant to
Section 1112(b) of the Code have been lodged before this Court. . . .

. . . Preliminarily, it must be stated that there is no question that
Manville is eligible to be a debtor under the Code's statutory requirements. . . .

Moreover, it should also be noted that neither Section 109 nor any
other provision relating to voluntary petitions by companies contains any
insolvency requirement. . . .

Accordingly, it is abundantly clear that Manville has met all of the
threshold eligibility requirements for filing a voluntary petition under the
Code. This Court will now turn to the issue of whether any of the movants
have demonstrated sufficient "cause" pursuant to Code Section 1112(b)
to warrant the dismissal of Manville's petition. . . .

In determining whether to dismiss under Code Section 1112(b), a
court is not necessarily required to consider whether the debtor has filed in
"good faith" because that is not a specified predicate under the Code for
filing. Rather, according to Code Section 1129(a)(3), good faith emerges
as a requirement for the confirmation of a plan. The filing of a Chapter 11
case creates an estate for the benefit of all creditors and equity holders of
the debtor wherein all constituencies may voice their interests and bargain
for their best possible treatment. See In re UNR Industries, Inc., 725 F.2d
1111 (7th Cir.1984) where . . . the Seventh Circuit in dicta declared in
the context of an asbestos-predicated bankruptcy, that the UNR which

emerges from bankruptcy is synonymously "the creditors who will own UNR at the conclusion of the reorganization." . . . It is thus logical that the good faith of the debtor be deemed a predicate primarily for emergence out of a Chapter 11 case. It is after confirmation of a concrete and immutable reorganization plan that creditors are foreclosed from advancing their distinct and parochial interests in the debtor's estate.

A "principal goal" of the Bankruptcy Code is to provide "open access" to the "bankruptcy process." Report of the Commission on the Bankruptcy Laws of the United States, H.R. Doc. No. 137, Part II, 93rd Cong., 1st Sess. 75, 79 (1973); H.R. Rep. No. 595, 95th Cong., 1st Sess. 220 (1977). The rationale behind this "open access" policy is to provide access to bankruptcy relief which is as "open" as "access to the credit economy." Id. at 75. Thus, Congress intended that "there should be no legal barrier to voluntary petitions." Id. Another major goal of the Code, that of "rehabilitation of debtors," requires that relief for debtors must be "timely." Id. at 79. Congress declared that it is essential to both the "open access" and "rehabilitation" goals that

> [i]nitiating relief should not be a death knell. The process should encourage resort to it, by debtors and creditors, that cuts short the dissipation of assets and the accumulation of debts. Belated commencement of a case may kill an opportunity for reorganization or arrangement.

Id. at 75.

Accordingly, the drafters of the Code envisioned that a financially beleaguered debtor with real debt and real creditors should not be required to wait until the economic situation is beyond repair in order to file a reorganization petition. The "Congressional purpose" in enacting the Code was to encourage resort to the bankruptcy process. Id. This philosophy not only comports with the elimination of an insolvency requirement, but also is a corollary of the key aim of Chapter 11 of the Code, that of avoidance of liquidation. The drafters of the Code announced this goal, declaring that reorganization is more efficient than liquidation because "assets that are used for production in the industry for which they were designed are more valuable than those same assets sold for scrap." H.R. Rep. No. 95-989, U.S. Cong. & Ad. News at 6179, cited in In re Ponn Realty Trust, 4 B.R. 226, 230 (Bkrtcy. D. Mass. 1980). Moreover, reorganization also fosters the goals of preservation of jobs in the threatened entity. . . .

In the instant case, not only would liquidation be wasteful and inefficient in destroying the utility of valuable assets of the companies as well as jobs, but, more importantly, liquidation would preclude just compensation of some present asbestos victims and all future asbestos claimants. This unassailable reality represents all the more reason for this Court to adhere to this basic potential, liquidation avoidance aim of Chapter 11 and

for Manville

deny the motions to dismiss. Manville must not be required to wait until its economic picture has deteriorated beyond salvation to file for reorganization. . . .

[N]one of the justifications for declaring an abuse of the jurisdiction of the bankruptcy court . . . are present in the *Manville* case. In *Manville*, it is undeniable that there has been no sham or hoax perpetrated on the Court in that Manville is a real business with real creditors in pressing need of economic reorganization. Indeed, the Asbestos Committee has belied its own contention that Manville has no debt and no real creditors by quantifying a benchmark settlement demand approaching one billion dollars for compensation of approximately 15,500 prepetition asbestos claimants, during the course of negotiations pitched toward achieving a consensual plan. This huge asserted liability does not even take into account the estimated 6,000 new asbestos health claims which have arisen in only the first 16 months since the filing date. The number of post-filing claims increases each day as "future claims back into the present." *See* Brief of Equity Holders Committee in Opposition to Motions to Dismiss the Petition.

Moreover, asbestos related property damage claims present another substantial contingent and unliquidated liability. Prior to the filing date, various schools initiated litigation seeking compensatory and punitive damages from, *inter alia,* Manville for their unknowing use of asbestos-containing products in ceilings, walls, structural members, piping, ductwork and boilers in school buildings. . . .

. . . Manville's liability for compensatory, if not punitive, damages to school authorities is not hypothetical, but real and massive debt. A range of $500 million to $1.4 billion is the total projected amount of Manville's real debt to the school creditors.

In addition, claims of $425 million of liquidated commercial debt have been filed in this proceeding. The filing also triggered the acceleration of more than $275 million in unsecured public and institutional debt which had not been due prior to the filing. Upon a dismissal of this petition, Manville may be liable in the amount of all of the above-described real debts, plus interest. Manville's present holdings of cash and liquid assets would be insufficient to pay these obligations and, as noted above, its insurance carriers have repeatedly expressed their unwillingness to contribute to the payment of this debt. Thus, upon dismissal, Manville would become a target for economic dismemberment, liquidation, and chaos, which would benefit no one except the few winners of the race to the courthouse. The economic reality of Manville's highly precarious financial position due to massive debt sustains its eligibility and candidacy for reorganization. . . .

In sum, Manville is a financially besieged enterprise in desperate need of reorganization of its crushing real debt, both present and future. The reorganization provisions of the Code were drafted with the aim of liquidation avoidance by great access to Chapter 11. Accordingly, Manville's filing does not abuse the jurisdictional integrity of this Court. . . . [We should await] the determination of Manville's good faith until it is considered under Code Section 1129(a)(3) as a prerequisite to confirmation or as a part of the cadre of motions before me which are scheduled to be heard subsequently. In this case, all creditors and equity holders of Manville have vigorously espoused their positions by means of committee or party in interest representation. This representation has protected their interests throughout the course of the past long and arduous 16 months. Now, with an anticipated appointment of a representative for all future claimants, ... all interests will be more fully put forward and protected. The Code provides a forum in which these diverse and conflicting interests can be harmonized. The . . . motion to dismiss is thus denied in its entirety. *holding*

for Manville

NOTE ON THE GOOD FAITH
OF MANVILLE'S PETITION

What were the motivations of those who filed the bankruptcy petition on behalf of Manville? Is a bankruptcy proceeding in the interests of the shareholders of the firm? If the bankruptcy proceeding has the effect of accelerating all of Manville's obligations (including its obligations to victims of asbestosis) and if these obligations exceed Manville's assets, as Manville alleges, the shareholders of Manville have, if push comes to shove, no right to any of these assets. If the firm had stayed out of bankruptcy, it might have been able to continue paying dividends for a while longer. Did the officers and directors of Manville act contrary to the interests of the shareholders? (In considering that, it might be worthwhile noting that the payment of dividends to shareholders of an insolvent corporation are probably fraudulent conveyances (see Uniform Fraudulent Conveyance Act §4) and probably also violate the corporations laws of most states. See, e.g., Cal. Corp. Code §501.) One, of course, cannot make that determination in a vacuum and, as we will see when examining the corporate reorganization provisions in Chapter 9 of this book, shareholders of even an insolvent corporation have a number of procedural rights that, in practice, will mean that a portion of the firm's value will be left with them. But even so, why play this form of brinkmanship with the shareholders' future? In considering an answer to that, consider what would have happened had Manville *not* filed a bankruptcy petition and attempted to continue "business as usual." Had Manville not filed its bankruptcy petition when it did, it is likely that its accountants would have required it to disclose that it faced some $2-5 billion in future asbestos-related tort claims—a figure substantially in excess of anything Manville had previously publicly estimated. Upon the release of such information, what shape would Manville have been in had it not filed the petition?

Would a bankruptcy proceeding be in the interests of the shareholders as well even if Manville's assets exceeded its liabilities, if bankruptcy provided a cheap way of resolving many tort claims? But is bankruptcy appropriate if its procedures are simply cheaper and not because of a danger that there would be a race to the debtor's assets caused by the fact that there were more claims than assets? Could it be that the directors and managers of Manville filed the petition because they thought the rights of the creditors, including the rights of the future victims of asbestosis, would be undervalued in the bankruptcy process, thereby leaving more for the shareholders?

In the opinion you just read, the court takes account of Manville's huge potential tort liabilities. Are these liabilities "claims" that have arisen before the filing of the petition? If they are not, and if the future victims are therefore not "creditors" (see §101(9)) does one need to take their interests into account at all? If one does not need to take their interests into account, should Manville be in bankruptcy? A buyer of Manville or its assets *would* take account of its future tort liabilities if it was required to assume them (as the doctrine of successor liability makes likely). Is it therefore appropriate or even possible for a bankruptcy judge to ignore them? We pursue the questions of what a "claim" is and who "creditors" are in the next chapter and will return to this precise question there.

Chapter 3
ASSESSING THE CLAIMS
AGAINST THE ESTATE

A. INTRODUCTION

The basic bankruptcy process works by assembling a debtor's assets and dividing them among its claimants in a specified order. In this chapter we examine how the rights of creditors and other claimants are measured in a bankruptcy proceeding. In the next chapter, we study the problem of determining what assets a debtor has and which ones are available to satisfy creditors' claims in bankruptcy. As we shall see, the questions of what a creditor claims and what the debtor has frequently arise at the same time. For example, if one decides that an asset belongs to a bailor instead of to the debtor, one fixes both the rights of a particular person (the bailor) and the assets that are available to the debtor's general creditors. One can say either that the property in question is "property of the estate," but that the bailor has priority to it, or that the property is the bailor's in the first place. We can make distinctions between ownership of an asset outright and an interest in a debtor's property that takes priority over others, but for purposes of bankruptcy, different ownership labels may have similar consequences.

For the moment, however, we look at the first crucial structural block to the bankruptcy process: deciding who the claimants are that share in the bankruptcy estate. This question has several components. First, we need to *identify* these claimants: Does someone have a right to participate at all? Second, we must determine how to fix the *amount* of each such claimant's claim: Is the claim for $10 or for $10,000? A third, critically important, factor is the *order* in which claimants "admitted" to the bankruptcy process are entitled to satisfy themselves: Does a claimant with a $10,000 claim get paid in full, ahead of others, or does it share pro rata with others, receiving ten cents on the dollar? See Jackson, Translating Assets and Liabilities to the Bankruptcy Forum, 14 J. Legal Studies 73 (1985). By the conclusion

123

of this chapter and the next, the general framework for analyzing these issues will be set out, although a detailed study of priorities (largely among unsecured creditors) is deferred to Chapter 8.

A useful way to begin the process of sorting out claims against a debtor's assets might be to ask who would be entitled to what if the debtor had gone out of business on the date of the bankruptcy petition. The reason for starting with nonbankruptcy law to identify claimants is simple: Bankruptcy law seems an odd place to generate new, federal causes of action. The rights of an individual would, in that case, turn on whether conditions were otherwise ripe for a bankruptcy proceeding. We should bear in mind the danger of linking financial distress with a bankruptcy proceeding. Most firms fail without a bankruptcy petition ever being filed. Moreover, as the Supreme Court suggested in *Butner*, supra page 95, confining a cause of action to a bankruptcy proceeding creates strategic incentives to use the bankruptcy process for individual gain, without regard to its underlying purposes.

A bankruptcy proceeding should start by deciding whether a particular claimant has a right to reach the debtor's assets. If, for example, a competitor claims that it was injured by the debtor's allegations that its product was inferior to the debtor's, the law of torts, not bankruptcy law, should determine whether the competitor has a cause of action. If the debtor is liable because the relevant state recognizes the tort of commercial disparagement and the competitor can satisfy all of its elements, the competitor should hold a "claim" cognizable in bankruptcy. If, however, the competitor cannot prove all the required elements, or if state law does not provide a cause of action because, for example, the state has chosen to promote comparative advertising, the competitor should have no greater rights in bankruptcy than outside it, and accordingly should not share in debtor's assets. In such an instance, nonbankruptcy law would provide the attributes that allow us to conclude that the competitor, at least insofar as this alleged claim is concerned, is not a claimant for purposes of bankruptcy.

In asking what a claimant's rights would have been under nonbankruptcy law, however, we must bear two things in mind. First, we have to look to substance rather than form. What matters is whether someone could have levied on the debtor's property, not whether state law characterizes that right as a "claim" or as something else. Second, we must remember that nonbankruptcy law can form only a baseline. In order to make a collective bankruptcy proceeding effective, it may be necessary to modify rights existing under state law, such as by respecting the value of a claimant's rights, rather than the specific rights themselves.

Sections 501 and 502 are the principal sections providing guidance on participating as a claimant in bankruptcy. Sections 101(4) and 101(9) are also crucial, as they define "claim" and "creditor." Finally, you should look at §506(a) and §1111(a), the latter provision being applicable in

Chapter 11 cases only. Section 501 states simply that a creditor may file a proof of claim and an equity holder may file a proof of interest. As the proof-of-claim form below suggests, such a filing is not difficult.

UNITED STATES BANKRUPTCY COURT
for the Northern District of California

IN RE: Case No.
                                        PROOF OF CLAIM
                                        OF _____
                                                  (Name of claimant)
                                        FOR $ _____
                                        [ ] Unsecured   [ ] Priority   [ ] Secured

1. [If claimant is an individual claiming for himself] The undersigned, who is the claimant herein, resides at* _____
_____

[If claimant is a partnership claiming through a member] The undersigned, who resides at* _____
a partnership, is a member of _____ composed of the undersigned and _____
of* _____ and doing business at*
_____ and is authorized to make this proof of claim on behalf of the partnership.

[If claimant is a corporation through an authorized officer] The undersigned, who resides at* _____ is
the _____ of _____ a corporation organized under the laws of _____
and doing business at* _____ and is authorized to make this proof of claim on behalf of the corporation.

[If claim is made by agent] The undersigned, who resides at*
_____ is the agent of
_____ of*
_____, and is authorized to make this proof of claim on behalf of the claimant.

2. The debtor was, at the time of the filing of the petition initiating this case, and still is indebted [or liable] to this claimant, in the sum of $ _____

3. The consideration for this debt [or ground of liability] is as follows: _____
_____

* State post office address

4. [If the claim is founded on writing] The writing on which this claim is founded (or a duplicate thereof) is attached hereto [or cannot be attached for the reason set forth in the statement attached hereto].

5. [If appropriate] This claim is founded on an open account, which became [or will become] due on _____, as shown by the itemized statement attached hereto. Unless it is attached hereto or its absence is explained in an attached statement, no note or other negotiable instrument has been received for the account or any part of it.

6. No judgment has been rendered on the claim except _____

_____

7. The amount of all payments on this claim has been credited and deducted for the purpose of making this proof of claim.

8. This claim is not subject to any setoff or counterclaim except

_____

_____

9. No security interest is held for this claim except _____

_____

[If security interest in property of the debtor is claimed] The undersigned claims the security interest under the writing referred to in paragraph 4 hereof [or under a separate writing which (or a duplicate of which) is attached hereto, or under a separate writing which cannot be attached hereto for the reason set forth in the statement attached hereto]. Evidence of perfection of such security interest is also attached hereto.

10. This claim is a general unsecured claim, except to the extent that the security interest, if any, described in paragraph 9 is sufficient to satisfy the claim. [If priority is claimed, state the amount and basis thereof _____]

Dated: Signed: _____

                          _____
                          (Print or Type Name)

                          Title: _____

                          Claimant: _____

Penalty for Presenting Fraudulent Claim. Fine of not more than $5,000 or imprisonment for not more than 5 years or both—Title 18. U.S.C., §152.

NOTE ON THE MECHANICS OF §§501 AND 502

Bankruptcy Rule 3002(c) provides that:

In a chapter 7 liquidation or chapter 13 individual's debt adjustment case, a proof of claim shall be filed within 90 days after the first date set for the meeting of creditors called pursuant to §341(a) of the Code, except as follows:

(1) On motion of the United States, a state, or subdivision thereof before the expiration of such period and for cause shown, the court may extend the time for filing of a claim by the United States, a state, or subdivision thereof.

(2) In the interest of justice and if it will not unduly delay the administration of the case, the court may extend the time for filing a proof of claim by an infant or incompetent person or the representative of either.

(3) A claim which arises in favor of a person or becomes allowable as a result of a judgment may be filed within 30 days after the judgment becomes final if the judgment is for the recovery of money or property from that person or denies or avoids the person's interest in property. . . .

(4) A claim arising from the rejection of an executory contract of the debtor may be filed within the time as the court may direct.

Section 501 does not require a claimant to file a claim. If it is not filed by the claimant, another party — guarantor, debtor, or trustee — may file the claim. (In Chapter 11, appearance of a claim on the debtor's schedules is deemed equivalent to filing. Therefore, it is not necessary to file, unless the claim appears scheduled as disputed, contingent, or unliquidated — or the creditor disagrees with the way the claim is scheduled, §1111(a).)

Why would someone not file a claim, other than due to sheer ignorance? Two categories of claimants might decide not to file: the holder of a nondischargeable claim and a secured creditor with a lien that may "pass through" the bankruptcy proceeding (an issue we will explore in Chapter 10). But in both these cases, there is no affirmative reason not to file and try to gain at least something in the bankruptcy proceeding itself. Under the 1898 Act, however, another reason existed why one might not file a claim. If a creditor had received a voidable preference, but also had a claim remaining, that creditor might have wanted to stay out of the bankruptcy proceeding because of the limited jurisdiction of the bankruptcy courts. Under the 1898 Act, if the creditor did not file a claim in the bankruptcy proceeding, the trustee, in order to recover the preference, was required to pursue the creditor in state court. But this reason does not apply today. Under the Bankruptcy Code, the trustee can sue a creditor in a federal forum to recover the preference, whether or not the creditor "consents" to that jurisdiction, 28 U.S.C. §§157, 1334. So, even though §502(d) preserves the notion that a claim won't be allowed unless any preference is first surrendered, the reasons for that requirement have essentially evaporated.

Once a claim is filed, the next step is to have it "allowed." The requirements for this process are set forth in §502, and vary in some respects from the procedures under the 1898 Act. Under the 1898 Act, a claimant first had to show that the claim was "provable"; that is to say, the claimant had to show that the claim was noncontingent enough and clear enough in amount that a definite value could be placed on it. If the claim were too contingent, then under §57d, it was not provable. A consequence of this is the claim did not participate in the bankruptcy case, but neither was it dischargeable. This history is recounted in Kuehner v. Irving Trust Co., infra page 160. Once the claim was shown to be provable, the creditor had to prove it by liquidating it, if feasible. After the claim was proved, it had to be allowed.

Section 502 of the Bankruptcy Code eliminates the concept of provability. The other two steps, however, still exist: The claim must be liquidated and the claim must be allowed. Claims are deemed allowed unless some party in interest objects. Upon an objection, §502(b)—and perhaps §502(c)—comes into play (although the court can lift the stay on the creditor's pursuit of the claim outside the bankruptcy forum, to allow the claim to be liquidated by normal nonbankruptcy channels). Assuming the court is going to liquidate the claim itself, §502 requires the court to determine the value of a disputed, unliquidated, or contingent claim. Once the amount of the claim has been fixed, the court must decide if any or all of that amount falls into one of the subsection (b) categories that preclude allowance.

This process will be examined in a bit more detail in the materials that follow. We start, however, with two cases that raise the question of what constitutes a "claim."

B.   DEFINITION OF A "CLAIM"

IN RE VILLARIE
648 F.2d 810 (2d Cir. 1981)

Per Curiam.

A member of the New York City Employees' Retirement System (NYCERS or the Retirement System) contributes to his annuity savings fund by authorizing NYCERS to deduct an actuarially determined amount from his weekly paycheck. Membership in this organization entitles a City employee to obtain a loan from the Retirement System, but the amount of the allowance cannot exceed fifty percent of the employee's previous contributions to the fund. In effect, this disbursement is an advance against the member's future retirement benefits. Nonetheless, the New York City Administrative Code requires a member to repay the loan, with interest, through payroll deductions in excess of the member's ordinary contribution.[1] If a member fails to replenish the fund before he retires, his benefits are reduced by the amount of the outstanding balance. Similarly, if a member resigns from his employment with the City, the unpaid amount is deducted from the sum he was due to receive from the Retirement System.

In January 1980, Dennis Villarie, an employee of the New York City Sanitation Department, borrowed $670 from the annuity fund. When interest charges and his previous withdrawals were added to this amount, Villarie's obligations totalled $2776.76. Since this sum equalled one-half of his previous contributions to the fund, he could not secure further advances from NYCERS. The Retirement System proceeded to recoup this amount by increasing the deductions from Villarie's weekly compensation to $16.87 for 182 weeks. Six weeks later, however, Villarie and his wife, Gail Ann, filed a joint petition in bankruptcy, thereby automatically staying these recoupments. See 11 U.S.C. §362. The Villaries listed NYCERS as a secured creditor in their petition and included the advance they had received from the fund in the schedule of obligations they intended to repay.

Shortly thereafter, NYCERS commenced the instant proceeding pursuant to 11 U.S.C. §105 for a declaration that the advance was not a "debt" under the Bankruptcy Code, 11 U.S.C. §§101-1330, and therefore could not be discharged in bankruptcy. NYCERS also requested an order allowing it to resume deducting $16.87 from Villarie's paychecks. Bankruptcy Judge Radoyevich, to NYCERS's surprise, ruled that the advance was a debt and was therefore discharged. He ordered that NYCERS not deduct any extra amounts from Villarie's wages, and decreed that the actuarial equivalent of the unpaid balance of the loan would be deducted from any benefits Villarie would otherwise have received from the fund. NYCERS asked Judge Pratt to review this decision, which he thereafter affirmed. This appeal followed.

It was well settled under the old Bankruptcy Act that two analogous transactions failed to give rise to a debtor-creditor relationship: an annui-

---

1. Section B3-28.0 of the Administrative Code of the City of New York provides, in pertinent part:

> The amount so borrowed, together with interest on any unpaid balance thereof shall be repaid to the retirement system in equal installments by deduction from the compensation of the member at the time the compensation is paid. . . .

Subdivision c of this section provides further that:

> the additional deductions required to repay the loan shall be made, and the interest paid on the loan shall be credited to the proper funds of the retirement system. The actuarial equivalent of any unpaid balance of a loan at the time any benefit may become payable shall be deducted from the benefit otherwise payable. . . .

tant's withdrawal from the savings account of his annuity fund, . . . and an insured's advance from the reserve fund of his insurance policy. . . . The Act's definition of "provable debt" did not encompass such situations, because in both instances the acquirer had merely borrowed back his own money; he was not liable to the lender for repayment. The lender's only remedy was to deduct the unpaid portion of the amount advanced from any benefits the borrower was to receive.

The 1978 Bankruptcy Code abandons the concept of "provability," substituting instead new definitions of "claim" and "debt." A claim is a right to payment. . . ." 11 U.S.C. §101(4)(A). A debt is simply "liability on a claim." Id. at §101(11). The two concepts are thus coterminous. The Notes of the Committee on the Judiciary, Sen. Rep. No. 95-989, reprinted in 11 U.S.C.A. §101, at 36 (1979), summarize the Code's treatment of advances on life insurance policies:

> the loan is not a claim (it is not a right to repayment) that the [insurance] company can assert against the estate; nor is the debtor's obligation a debt (a liability on a claim) that will be discharged under proposed 11 U.S.C. 523 or 524.

Nevertheless, Judge Radoyevich determined that the Code required a different result in the case of a loan from the NYCERS annuity fund. He interpreted §B3-28.0 of the NYC Administrative Code to require Villarie to repay the money he had borrowed. Judge Radoyevich reasoned, therefore, that this provision established a "claim" in NYCERS's favor and that this transaction did create a "debt" that was dischargeable in bankruptcy.

The error in this syllogism was in the Bankruptcy Judge's interpretation of the Administrative Code. Notwithstanding §B3.28.0's multiple use of the word "shall," *see* note 1, supra, this provision merely directs NYCERS to deduct additional sums from a member's paycheck. It does not give NYCERS the right to sue a member for the amount of the advance. Indeed, should a member retire or resign from the City's employ, NYCERS would merely offset the amount borrowed against his future benefits. In the language of 11 U.S.C. §502(b), this "claim is unenforceable against the debtor. . . ." Therefore, it cannot give rise to a debt that can be discharged in bankruptcy.

Accordingly, the order below is reversed. NYCERS may deduct from Villarie's weekly compensation an amount sufficient to recoup the advance.

NOTE ON *VILLARIE*

Is *Villarie* convincing? Is the Retirement System unable to participate in the distribution of the bankruptcy estate? Should the conclusion that the advance is not a "debt" also mean that the Retirement System can continue to make deductions from future paychecks? See In re Carpenter, 23 Bankr. 318 (Bankr. D.N.J. 1982) ("While the loan may not be a 'debt' or a 'claim' giving rise to a debtor-creditor relationship, the clear fact is that by allowing the deductions to continue, the Court would be granting the Retirement System the right to exercise control over the debtor's future wages").

In thinking about this case, it is, as usual, important to try to grasp what is at stake. The issue being raised in *Villarie* is whether the right to "repayment" of the amount "borrowed" from Villarie's retirement fund constitutes a "claim" within the meaning of the Bankruptcy Code. As long as Villarie continues to work for New York City, the repayment will be automatic (by virtue of payroll deductions). But if Vallarie leaves the City's employ, the repayment stops and, instead, the "actuarial equivalent of any unpaid balance of a loan . . . shall be deducted from the benefit otherwise payable."

Why is it important to determine whether or not this is a claim? Consider the following. Assume that Villarie has $5,000 in his retirement fund. Villarie then borrows $2,500 — the maximum allowable. If Villarie were to retire at that time, he would get a pension based on contributions of $2,500, not $5,000. That is the effect of footnote 1 of *Villarie.*

If, however, Villarie borrows the $2,500, and then, before retirement or repayment, files a petition in bankruptcy, what is the result of treating the repayment "obligation" as a claim? The Retirement System, at first glance (although we will have to return to this point), would seem to be an unsecured creditor in bankruptcy. If Villarie's unsecured creditors are receiving ten cents for each dollar of their claims, the Retirement System, if it is the holder of an unsecured claim, will receive $250. What will Villarie then receive from the Retirement System? Won't he have a pension fund worth $5,000, not $2,500? This $5,000 will then either go to his creditors as a group (or to Villarie himself, if he can shelter this as exempt property). Isn't the effect of treating the Retirement System as a claimant and then paying it in bankruptcy at the rate of ten cents on the dollar, equivalent to allowing Villarie to cancel the debt by paying only $250? Doesn't Villarie's retirement fund go up by $2,500 upon a payment of $250? Isn't it a transfer of $2,250 from the Retirement System to Villarie (or his creditors as a group)?

If this is the proper scenario, then the crux of the case is clear. The Retirement System is attempting to keep the repayment "obligation" from being deemed a "claim" to prevent Villarie from escaping from his promise to repay. It seems to argue, in essence, that Villarie's pension fund is simply like a savings account. When he withdraws money from a savings account, the balance goes down; when he puts money back in, it goes up. If Villarie had a $5,000 savings account at Bank and withdrew $2,500 before bankruptcy, Villarie would have only a $2,500 savings account. Bank would have no right to go after Villarie for the $2,500 he withdrew and, more important, Villarie would have no right to claim $5,000 from the

Issue in Villar[ie] p. 128

savings account. Under this view, attempting to fit this into the rubric of a "claim" is simply wrong because the Retirement System's position is no different than Bank's.

Assuming that is the Retirement System's argument, are there any weaknesses in it? Is Villarie's pension fund in fact like a savings account? Is Villarie equally free in deciding whether he wants to replace the $2,500 he borrowed from the Retirement System? Note that the Retirement System charges interest on withdrawn money. Does this decisively distinguish it from the bank account case? Or is it simply a reflection that Villarie, if he repays the money, will be deemed to have gained an accrual of retirement benefits during the time of withdrawal? From the Retirement System's perspective, is the loan to Villarie any different from its other investments?

The Retirement System's desire to escape being classified as a "creditor" holding a "claim," however, may depend on the scenario we have just examined being true — and a key factor is the assumption that the Retirement System would be the holder of an unsecured claim. Is there another way, however, to view this case? Isn't the transaction in *Villarie* just like a nonrecourse loan, secured by Villarie's retirement benefits? (Does it matter that retirement benefits ordinarily cannot be used as collateral for a loan?) As we will see explicitly in Chapter 8, but an important point to make now, a secured creditor will be paid, in bankruptcy, ahead of unsecured creditors. See §725. (This is one of the reasons why determining what is a "claim" and what is "property of the estate" bear a symbiotic relationship.) Consider another situation. Villarie wants to buy a house. He borrows $100,000 from Bank and gives it a mortgage on the house. The loan (as is true by statute in a number of states) is nonrecourse. If Villarie fails to repay it, Bank can foreclose on the house, but cannot otherwise go after Villarie or his remaining assets. If the house is worth enough to pay Bank in full, Bank will come out whole irrespective of bankruptcy, but if Bank falls short, there is nothing it can do. If, before repayment of the house loan, Villarie filed for bankruptcy, would Bank's nonrecourse right to repayment be considered a "claim" in bankruptcy? The answer is almost surely yes. What else could it be? Is there anything different about the Retirement System's rights?

Is not the appropriate course in *Villarie* and other cases to examine the attributes of the claim under state law? Do the relevant attributes in this case suggest any reason for treating the Retirement System differently from other claimants with garnishment or recoupment rights against the debtor? If not, it seems to follow that the Retirement System should have been considered a "creditor" holding a "claim" in the bankruptcy proceeding whose relative value (analogous to a secured claim) would be respected. The nonbankruptcy attributes of the System's position would, for example, have suggested that rights were superior to that of unsecured creditors, as the Retirement System was effectively a secured creditor (by having a right to offset borrowed amounts against one of Villarie's assets

—his pension fund). If this reasoning were followed, the Retirement System would eventually be repaid in full, because bankruptcy either would allow it to exercise its offset right or would otherwise respect the value of those rights as a secured claim. See §§542; 553.

The last paragraph of the opinion suggests why this issue may be of more than semantic importance and raises several other questions. The court concludes that the Retirement System may continue to deduct "repayments" from Villarie's paychecks. This would not be the case had the court determined the amount borrowed was a claim. Garnishing post-bankruptcy wages would be an attempt to collect on a debt that was treated—and discharged—in bankruptcy. §524(a). The interest of the Retirement System, however, was treated differently on the ground that it was not a "claim." This leaves, however, two questions that we shall examine later: First, do the deductions violate the automatic stay of §362? Second, can Villarie get out from under this repayment obligation (other than by quitting his job) by rejecting it as an executory contract under §365? Even if he does reject the contract, however, he may lose his retirement benefits. The benefits of and limits on assumption and rejection of executory contracts under §365 are issues we shall study in Chapter 7 of this book.

PROBLEMS

3.1 Debtor files a petition in bankruptcy on January 1. On February 1, Debtor negligently drives his car into Bystander's house. May Bystander file a claim in Debtor's bankruptcy? See §502(b) and compare §502(f), (g), (h), and (i). Even if Bystander cannot file a claim, he may still be paid. The way in which Bystander is paid may depend on whether Debtor is an individual or a corporation, and whether the expense is viewed as an "administrative expense" under §503(b). We return to this problem in connection with Reading Co. v. Brown, infra page 553.

3.2 Manville Corp. is a large diversified manufacturer of materials for the construction industry. From 1930 to 1970, Manville manufactured a number of asbestos products. Certain asbestos-related diseases occur among workers who have handled asbestos, although oftentimes these diseases do not manifest themselves until 30 or 40 years after exposure. In 1982, Manville filed a petition in bankruptcy, at a time when some 16,000 asbestos-related suits were pending against it. What procedures should be adopted for determining the claims of the plaintiffs in those lawsuits? At the time of filing, Manville also estimated that some 30,000 other persons who handled asbestos products manufactured by Manville prior to 1970 would discover, in the future, that they had asbestos-related diseases. May these people file "claims" in Manville's bankruptcy? Look carefully at the definition of "claim" in §101(4) and "creditor" in §101(9). Does it matter if state law has said (in the context of suits over the tolling of the statute of limitations) that an asbestos victim has no "claim," for purposes of the limitations statute, until he knows, or has reason to know, he has the disease? If these people have "claims" cognizable in bankruptcy, how should those claims be determined? How binding would the bankruptcy court's determination of those claims be if, after the close of the bankruptcy case, an asbestos victim filed suit and claimed he was not notified when a claims determination proceeding took place in the bankruptcy?

NOTE ON UNMANIFESTED TORT INJURIES IN BANKRUPTCY

The issues raised in Problem 3.2 have been the subject of much popular, academic, and judicial interest. For a sampling of the academic writing, see Schwartz, Products Liability, Corporate Structure and Bankruptcy: The Unknowable Risk Relationship, 14 J. Legal Studies — (1985); Roe, Bankruptcy and Mass Tort, 84 Colum. L. Rev. 846 (1984); Note, Mass Tort Claims and the Corporate Tortfeasor: Bankruptcy Reorganization and Legislative Compensation Versus the Common-Law Tort System, 61 Tex. L. Rev. 1297 (1983); Note, The Manville Bankruptcy: Treating Mass Tort Claims in Chapter 11 Proceedings, 96 Harv. L. Rev. 1121 (1983).

In In re UNR Industries, 29 Bankr. 741 (N.D. Ill. 1983), appeal dismissed, 725 F.2d 1111 (7th Cir. 1984), Judge Hart refused to appoint a representative to file claims on behalf of individuals who might develop asbestosis from past exposure to products manufactured and sold by UNR, reasoning:

> The debtors contend that the putative claimants are holders of contingent claims. Three principles determine the question presented here:
>
> 1. A claim of which a bankruptcy court may take cognizance must be one that is recognized by state or federal law. . . . The asbestos claims and rights all arise under state law.
> 2. The existence of a claim turns on when it arose. . . . In the case of a claim sounding in tort, it is not the wrongful or negligent act which gives rise to the claim. Instead, no claim arises until the plaintiff suffers an injury. . . .
> 3. The claim of an asbestos plaintiff (including a putative claimant) does not arise under state law until the plaintiff knows or should have known about the injury. . . .
>
> Therefore, under the definition imposed in the debtors' Application, the putative claimants — who have been exposed to asbestos some time in their lives but do not now have or do not know that they have an asbestos-related disease — have no claims under state law, and therefore do not have

claims cognizable under the Code. Further, by the debtors' own definition the claims of the putative claimants will not have arisen either "at the time of or before the order for relief," 11 U.S.C. §101(9), since a putative claimant is one who does not know that he has an asbestos-related disease.

The Code provision for the possibility of the evaluation and discharge of a *contingent* claim does not change the definition of "claim." It is not true that any conceivable claim is contingent. The contingency must be one that arises out of the prior contractual relationship of the claimant and the debtor. A tort claim does not meet this requirement. Instead, a tort action brought against a debtor is covered by other definitions: it is a "right to payment [not yet] reduced to judgment [which is] unliquidated [and] disputed. . . ." 11 U.S.C. §101(4)(A).

Judge Hart read the legislative history to §101(9), which discusses guarantors and sureties as holding a contingent claim as confirmatory of this analysis: "This seems strong evidence that the term 'contingent' was intended to apply to situations arising from prior contractual relationships." (You might recall at this point the similar comment in *All Media Properties,* discussed supra page 75.) Some other cases have agreed with Judge Hart that contingent tort claims are not "claims" within the meaning of the Bankruptcy Code. See In re Amatex Corp., 30 Bankr. 309 (Bankr. E.D. Pa. 1983), aff'd on opinion below, 37 Bankr. 613 (E.D. Pa. 1983) (unknown, future, asbestos claimants do not hold "claims" as defined by §101(4), because "no cause of action for asbestos related injuries arises until the symptoms have appeared."); In re Gladding Corp., 20 Bankr. 566, 568 (Bankr. D. Mass. 1982) (old Act case concluding "a mere possibility of a [tort] claim of unknown origin, in an unknown amount, and which only might arise, if at all, at some unknown time" not cognizable in bankruptcy.)

On appeal in the *UNR* case, Judge Posner, writing for the Seventh Circuit, did not reach the merits on the ground that Judge Hart's order in which he refused to appoint a representative was not "final" within the meaning of 28 U.S.C. §1291 and hence was not appealable, 725 F.2d at 1118:

[F]or an order to be appealable . . . its consequences for the appellant must be irreversible by subsequent proceedings. . . . There is nothing irreversible, at least so far as the potential asbestosis plaintiffs themselves are concerned, about the district court's order refusing to appoint someone to represent them. Any such victim is free to file a claim with the district court, and if the claim is denied to appeal the denial to sue as a final decision. And he can if he wants try to file a claim on behalf not only of himself but of others who have been exposed to asbestos sold by UNR but have not yet developed a diagnosable case of asbestosis. The judicial process will benefit from waiting for an actual claim to be filed. When that happens the district court — and, if it dismisses the claim and the dismissal is appealed, the court of appeals — will have before it a concrete claim and not merely speculation

about potential claimants. This will create a more informative context for
deciding whether the interests of potential victims of asbestosis can be dealt
with—whether one-by-one or in gross—in this bankruptcy proceeding.

Judge Posner, however, went on to suggest what his own views of the
cognizability of asbestosis claims might be if the issue were before him, 725
F.2d at 1119-1120:

> The practical difficulties of identifying, giving constitutionally adequate no-
> tice to, and attempting to estimate the damages of the thousands upon
> thousands of people who have been exposed to asbestos sold by UNR but
> have not yet developed asbestosis are formidable, and possibly insurmount
> able. Yet if any of them have already suffered a tort there would be no basis
> we can think of for not letting them file claims in this bankruptcy proceed-
> ing. And some, at least, probably have suffered a tort. The states differ on
> whether a cause of action in an asbestosis case accrues upon inhala-
> tion . . . or not until there is palpable disease . . . or the disease is discov-
> ered. . . . Even in a "discovery" state the cause of action may "exist" before
> it "accrues"—that is, before the statute of limitations on bringing it begins
> to run. . . . These states postpone the date of accrual of the cause of action
> not in order to prevent the early filing of claims but in order to lift the bar of
> the statute of limitations to later filings. Since there is "medical evidence that
> the body incurs microscopic injury as asbestos fibers become lodged in the
> lungs and as the surrounding tissue reacts to the fibers thereafter," Keene
> Corp. v. Insurance Co. of North America, 667 F.2d 1034, 1042 (D.C. Cir.
> 1981), and since no particular amount of injury is necessary to create tort
> liability, courts in these states might hold that a tort claim arises as soon as
> asbestos fibers are inhaled, however much time the victim might have for
> bringing suit. In any event, some at least of the many thousands of workers
> who have been exposed to asbestos sold by UNR must have been exposed in
> states such as Indiana and New York where the cause of action accrues upon
> inhalation, and their claims against the bankrupt estate—accrued tort
> claims—would appear uncontroversially to be provable in bankrutpcy.
>   Even in states where exposed workers are not injured in a tort sense till
> the disease manifests itself, and therefore do not have an accrued tort claim
> in any sense, and even assuming that an unaccrued tort claim cannot be a
> "claim" within the meaning of 11 U.S.C. §101(4)(A) . . . , a bankruptcy
> court's equitable powers . . . just might be broad enough to enable the
> court to make provision for future asbestosis claims against the bankrupt
> when it approved the final plan of reorganization. The date on which a
> person exposed to asbestos happens to develop a diagnosable case of asbes-
> tosis is arbitrary. Could it not be argued therefore that a bankruptcy court
> can and should use its equitable powers, which traditionally "have been
> invoked to the end that . . . substance will not give way to form, that tech-
> nical considerations will not prevent substantial justice from being done"
> [Pepper v. Litton, 308 U.S. 295, 305 (1939)] (especially, perhaps, in a reor-
> ganization case, see In re Michigan Brewing Co., 24 F. Supp. 430 (W.D.

Mich.1938)), to prevent the liquidation or discharge of the bankrupt before provision is made for such persons? And more than arbitrariness is involved. If future claims cannot be discharged before they ripen, UNR may not be able to emerge from bankruptcy with reasonable prospects for continued existence as a going concern. In that event, and assuming that UNR's going-concern value would exceed its liquidation value, both UNR (which is to say the creditors who will own UNR at the conclusion of the reorganization) and future plaintiffs would be made worse off, and UNR's current creditors would not necessarily be made better off, by the court's failure to act along the lines proposed by UNR. . . .

Fortunately we need not decide these difficult and far-reaching questions here; their very difficulty, and far-reaching nature, are reasons for our refusing to decide them prematurely through a permissive interpretation of 28 U.S.C. §1291. We merely point out that they are substantial questions which the district court did not finally decide when it turned down the application to appoint a representative and on which the district court in any event does not have the final say.

In the case that follows, the court addresses problems similar to the ones posed in the *UNR* litigation, but does not explicitly reach the issue of whether potential victims of asbestosis have claims that are cognizable in bankruptcy. But you might question whether the court's discussion would be consistent with any holding other than one that deemed them to be "creditors" holding "claims" in bankruptcy. Is the court consistent in its intimation on this issue? Compare, for example, footnote 1 with footnote 6. What bankruptcy policy requires New York to have the same statute of limitation rules as does, say, Illinois, as Judge Lifland suggests in footnote 4?

IN RE JOHNS-MANVILLE CORP.
36 Bankr. 743 (Bankr. S.D.N.Y. 1984)

Burton R. LIFLAND, Bankruptcy Judge.

INTRODUCTION AND ISSUE PRESENTED

Keene Corp. has put before this Court a motion to appoint a legal representative for asbestos-exposed future claimants in the Manville reorganization case. It is abundantly clear that the Manville reorganization will have to be accountable to future asbestos claimants whose compelling interest must be safeguarded in order to leave a residue of assets sufficient to accommodate a meaningful resolution of the Manville asbestos-related health problem. The term "future asbestos claimants" is defined for these purposes to include all persons and entities who, on or before August 26,

1982, came into contact with asbestos or asbestos-containing products mined, fabricated, manufactured, supplied or sold by Manville and who have not yet filed claims against Manville for personal injuries or property damage. These claimants may be unaware of their entitlement to recourse against Manville due to the latency period of many years characterizing manifestation of all asbestos related diseases. . . .

From the inception of this case, it has been obvious to all concerned that the very purpose of the initiation of these proceedings is to deal in some fashion with claimants exposed to the ravages of asbestos dust who have not as of the filing date manifested symptoms of asbestos disease. Indeed, but for this continually evolving albeit amorphous constituency, it is clear that an otherwise economically robust Manville would not have commenced these reorganization proceedings. . . . It should also be noted that there are suggestions in the vast record before this Court that Manville is not as economically sound as reputed. . . . It is the spectre of proliferating, overburdening litigation to be commenced in the next 20-30 years, which litigation would be beyond the company's ability to manage, control, and pay for, which has prompted this filing. . . .

Accordingly, a resolution of the interests of future claimants is a central focus of these reorganization proceedings. Any plan emerging from this case which ignores these claimants would serve the interests of neither the debtor nor any of its other creditor constituencies in that the central short and long-term economic drain on the debtor would not have been eliminated. Manville might indeed be forced to file again and again if this eventuated. Each filing would leave attenuated assets available to deal with interests of emerging future claimants. Manville could also be forced into liquidation. The liquidation of this substantial corporation would be economically inefficient in not only leaving many asbestos claimants uncompensated, but also in eliminating needed jobs and the productivity emanating from an ongoing concern. It fosters the key aims of Chapter 11 to avoid liquidation at all reasonable costs. . . .

Section 1109(b) of the Code, 11 U.S.C. §1109(b), makes clear that any "party in interest" may appear and be heard in a Chapter 11 case. It provides:

> Any party in interest, including the debtor, the trustee, a creditors' committee, an equity security holders' committee, an equity holder, or any indenture trustee, may raise and may appear and be heard on any issue in a case under this chapter.

. . . While the precise contours of Code Section 1109(b) have yet to be fixed, they are certainly broad enough to embrace the interests of future claimants as affected parties. Future claimants are undeniably parties in interest to these reorganization proceedings pursuant to the broad, flexible definition of that term enunciated by the foregoing authorities. The drafting of "party in interest" as an elastic concept was designed for just this kind of situation. As detailed above, future claimants are indeed the central focus of the entire reorganization. Any plan not dealing with their interests precludes a meaningful and effective reorganization and thus inures to the detriment of the reorganization body politic. Any meaningful plan will either provide funding for future claimants directly or provide for the continuation of some form of responsive, ongoing entity post-confirmation, from which to glean assets with which to pay them. If they are denied standing as parties in interest, they will be denied all opportunity either to help design the ship that sails away from these reorganization proceedings with their cargo on board or to assert their interests during a pre-launching distribution. . . . Thus, because none of the existing committees of unsecured creditors and present asbestos claimants represents this key group, a separate and distinct representative for these parties in interest must be established so that these claimants have a role in the formulation of such a plan. This is especially so given that any plan of reorganization must necessarily balance the rights and needs of prepetition creditors against the anticipated rights and needs of postpetition creditors with Manville's purportedly limited assets and further economic prospects apportioned accordingly. . . .

Another basis for this Court's holding that the future claimants are a wholly cognizable constituency as parties in interest under Section 1109(b) is that the vast majority of courts considering the issue have held that mere exposure to asbestos triggers insurance coverage. . . .

It follows logically that if exposure triggers a sufficient interest on the part of future claimants to warrant insurance coverage, then this same exposure should a fortiori justify a declaration that they are parties in interest to be impacted by these proceedings. As background, it should be noted that the controversy regarding the appropriate trigger for insurance coverage is part of the major litigation which Manville and other asbestos defendants are embroiled in with their insurance carriers. These carriers, approximately 25 in number who wrote approximately 100 policies for Manville, have by and large refused to provide defense and indemnity to Manville in asbestos cases. Manville asserts that its inability to look to at least $600 million in insurance coverage is a major factor in its decision to seek Chapter 11 relief. . . .

A major argument advanced in In re Amatex Corp., 30 B.R. 309 (Bkrtcy. E.D. Pa. 1983), Adopted No. 6011. (E.D. Pa. filed Nov. 9, 1983), where the court held that future claims are not cognizable in bankruptcy was that courts in most states date the statute of limitations from the point of manifestation. . . . This fact, however, does not vitiate the status of future claimants as parties in interest to this bankruptcy. Unlike the trigger of insurance coverage at the point of exposure, the fixation of a statute of limitations is totally unrelated to the status of future claimants as parties in interest.[4] . . .

First, it should be noted that not all states date the statute of limitations from point of manifestation. New York and Indiana law have been construed to date their asbestos inhalation actions for statute of limitations purposes not from the point of manifestation of disease, but rather from the point of exposure or inhalation of the toxic substance. . . .

Second, that a majority of jurisdictions date the statute of limitations from the point of manifestation of the disease should not have the unintended effect of barring those who have not as yet manifested disease from asserting their status as parties in interest in this bankruptcy proceeding. This is because the policy reasons underlying the fixation by each state of a point from which to date a limitations statute are wholly different from those governing a bankruptcy court's finding that those who have not yet manifested symptoms of the disease are parties in interest in the case. . . .

Thus, the fixation of the point from which to date a statute of limitations includes an assessment of the general need for repose against the need for redress of injury. In contrast, the assessment of whether future claimants are parties in interest is an ad hoc determination of the potential detriment to these parties which nonrepresentation would work.

In any event, the factors militating in favor of declaring future claimants parties in interest are more akin to those factors which prompted a majority of courts to hold that exposure is an appropriate trigger to insurance coverage than to those considered in fashioning an appropriate statute of limitations. . . .

[I]t is unnecessary for this Court to face the dischargeability issue at this time in order to decide whether these claimants are parties in interest.

4. Along these lines, it is clear (at least in the Manville case) that state-created statutes of limitation, which differ widely from state to state, if applied as a bar to recovery must yield to one nationwide uniform standard for claims allowability in bankruptcy. Otherwise, future claimants, who are parties in interest in this reorganization, in a state like New York, which dates the statute for asbestos claims from point of exposure, would be barred from asserting their claims, while future claimants in states like Virginia or Wisconsin, which date these claims as of various points of manifestation, could assert such claims. . . . Because a significant number of future claimants would be so barred without this uniform measure, this reorganization cannot ultimately succeed without such measure embodied in any reorganization plan. Although bankruptcy courts have looked to state law for guidance in, *e.g.*, determining the enforceability of a claim . . . bankruptcy courts are federal courts with original and exclusive jurisdiction over bankruptcy cases under Article I of the United States Constitution and are thus not inalienably bound to enforce state law. . . . In so exercising its discretion, a bankruptcy court is not vitiating state created rights, but rather is determining their enforceability. . . .

Accordingly, there is great justification for a bankruptcy court to authorize a uniform standard specifying some form of disease manifestation as the point of health claim allowability. This will avoid the unfairly inconsistent results which would otherwise eventuate in applying multitudinous statutes of limitations to like claims.

This Court believes it is imperative that such a nationwide standard declare that for purposes of allowability, a claim accrues, measured in some form from the point of discovery or manifestation of the disease in conformity with the great weight of authority favoring this position and the logic contained therein. . . .

In fact, this Court may never be faced with deciding the dischargeability issue since Manville's currently proposed nonconsensual plan intends to treat future claims as nondischargeable. This plan impacts on future claimants only in a de facto manner in shaping the claims estimation process and the residue Manville entity that will emerge post-confirmation. That is not to say that during the course of these proceedings a plan confronting dischargeability of future claims will never be filed. Or, this group may be considered as a distinct, cognizable, certifiable class in light of the *Agent Orange* opinion dealing with mass exposure to a toxic substance. . . .

In any event, the concept of "party in interest" is an elastic and broad one designed to give a Court great latitude to insure fair representation of all constituencies impacted in any significant way by a Chapter 11 case.

In contrast, the concept of dischargeability of claims cognizable in the reorganization may require a showing that due process has been achieved in binding unknown putative claimants to a plan of which they may or may not have had notice. Thus, Judge Hart's pronouncement that the contingent claims of future asbestos claimants are not cognizable in bankruptcy for dischargeability purposes because they are grounded in tort instead of contract law, whether correct or incorrect,[6] is not binding on this Court's

---

6. It is the view of this Court that the declarations by Judges Hart and King that these future claims are nondischargeable in bankruptcy are based on superannuated and considerably narrow notions of what constitutes a claim dischargeable in bankruptcy. These notions are at odds with the expanded definition of "claim" contained in Section 101(4) of the Code. In enacting the Bankruptcy Code, Congress specifically intended to afford the broadest possible scope to the definition of "claim" so as to enable Chapter 11 to provide pervasive and comprehensive relief to debtors. The legislative history of Section 101(4) explains:

The effect of the definition [of claim] is a significant departure from present law [under the former Bankruptcy Act]. Under present law, "claim" is not defined in straight bankruptcy. Instead it is simply used, along with the concept of provability in section 63 of the Bankruptcy Act, to limit the kinds of obligations that are payable in a bankruptcy case. The term is defined in the debtor rehabilitation chapters of [the Bankruptcy Code] far more broadly. *The definition in paragraph (4) adopts an even broader definition of claim. . . . The definition is any right to payment, whether or not reduced to judgment, liquidated, unliquidated, fixed, contingent, matured, unmatured, disputed, undisputed, legal, equitable, secured, or unsecured. . . .* The definition also includes as a claim an equitable right to performance that does not give rise to a right to payment. *By this broadest possible definition, and by the use of the term throughout the title 11, especially in subchapter I of chapter 5, the bill [Bankruptcy Code] contemplates that all legal obligations of the debtor, no matter how remote or contingent, will be able to be dealt with in the bankruptcy case. It permits the broadest possible relief in the bankruptcy court.*

House Report. No. 95-595 to accompany H.R. 8200 95th Cong. 1st Sess. 309 (1977), pp. 308-314, U.S. Code Cong. & Admin. News 1978, pp. 5787, 6265-6271 (emphasis supplied).

In this reorganization case, that a vast group of future claimants will exist is a statistical certainty, with projections differing only as to the precise quantity and size of these claims. These claims were and remain the *raison d'etre* for the filing here. Accordingly, the *Amatex* and *UNR* Court refusal to declare future claims cognizable in bankruptcy not only ignores the reality of their existence and importance, but also runs contrary to Congress' intention in drafting Code Section 101(4) that all obligations of the debtor should be dealt with in a Chapter 11 case. . . .

Furthermore, under the Bankruptcy Code, if state law notions so narrow the definition of a "claim" as to frustrate the stated objective of providing the debtor the broadest possible

determination of whether these claimants are parties in interest. He declares: "The Court is not unaware that in refusing to approve of a procedure by which the rights of putative claimants would be adjudicated and cut off, the putative claimants may wind up with judgments against corporations left with only one asset: a corporate charter." In re UNR, 29 B.R. at 748. Thus, even Judge Hart recognizes the probability of significant detriment which future claimants will suffer if not provided for either directly within the reorganization itself or indirectly, by restructuring the company in such a way as to provide more than a mere corporate charter with which to pay these claims. . . .

It is thus the unprecedented, extraordinary nature of these proceed-

---

relief, state law must yield to an overriding federal construction. Cf. Chicago Board of Trade v. Johnson, 264 U.S. 1, 10, 44 S. Ct. 232, 234, 68 L. Ed. 533 (1924) (property rights are generally regulated by state law, but "when the language of Congress indicates a policy requiring a broader construction of the [bankruptcy] statute than the state decisions would give it, federal courts cannot be precluded by them"). . . .

Moreover, the problem of sufficient notice of the impact of these proceedings on these putative claimants alluded to by the lower courts in UNR and Amatex, and raised by some of the movants herein, while difficult in the extreme, is a logistical one which can be handled by resort to innumerable media tools now available in our electronically aware society for use by the representative of future claimants. . . .

The First Circuit in In re DCA Development Corp., 489 F.2d 43, 46 (1st Cir. 1973), declared that under the Act, the notice requirements simply required "such notice and an opportunity for a hearing as is reasonable and appropriate in each particular case". With reference to the Supreme Court's landmark decision in Mullane v. Central Hanover Bank & Trust Co., 339 U.S. 306, 313-314, 70 S. Ct. 652, 656-657, 94 L. Ed. 865 (1950), the First Circuit in DCA continued: "The court in each case must balance the individual's interest in adequate protection against the overall interest of efficient, final resolution of claims". DCA, 489 F.2d at 46. The DCA court also stated that "even where formal notice to affected parties is omitted or is insufficient, informal or constructive notice which provides them with the same opportunity for a fair hearing can satisfy the procedural requirements of the Bankruptcy Act." Id. at 47. See also In re GAC Corp., 681 F.2d 1295 (11th Cir. 1982), where the Eleventh Circuit held that a mailing to approximately 280,000, potential claimants and a publication of the order suffice as adequate notice comporting with due process requirements. The GAC Court so held, citing Mullane, supra, and declaring that adequate notice is that which is reasonably calculated under all the circumstances to afford interested parties an opportunity to be heard. Id. at 1300.

These cases demonstrate that the bankruptcy court must balance the need for individual notice against the need for moving forward to facilitate a reorganization plan. Under the Code, this elastic concept of notice would seem to remain unchanged because the court is given discretion in establishing the time within which proofs of claim must be filed as well as the form of notice informing creditors of the proceeding. See Rules of Bankruptcy Procedure 3003(c)(3); Code Section 342.

In light of these cases, the burden of solving the logistical problem of notice in the Manville case does not outweigh the burden on all constituencies should this essential constituency be denied its rightful consideration in these proceedings. Should future claimants be denied all consideration, it is likely that the petition would be dismissed and the debtor would be forced to liquidate to the detriment of the asbestos victims. This is especially so given the intense publicity surrounding every aspect of Manville's filing which potentially has already gone and will continue to go a long way toward giving notice to putative claimants. Also, since notice is an elastic concept, nothing would prevent this Court from requiring supplemental publications and/or mailings at a later date should it appear that the number of claims filed differs markedly from statistical projections. . . .

holding

ings that mandates a declaration that these claimants are parties in interest under Code Section 1109(b) in need of a legal representative to act independently and impartially where appropriate in the case. The participation of such a representative is especially important to the development of any plan, consensual or otherwise, which will include the formulation of claims estimation procedures. Such appointment is also grounded on the Court's pervasive equitable powers emanating from Section 1481 of Title 28, U.S. Code and Section 105(a) of the Bankruptcy Code. These equitable powers are vested in this Court specifically to enable it to respond to extraordinary problems in estate administration consistent with the statutory goals of Chapter 11 of Title 11 U.S.C. . . .

The concept of the appointment of some kind [of] representative for parties in interest whose identities are yet unknown is not unprecedented. The power to appoint such a representative is inherent in every court. . . .

[W]here circumstances warrant, courts readily use their equitable powers to protect the substantive rights of persons similarly situated who are not before the court.

The instant case presents an even stronger legal basis for the appointment of some kind representative in that there is present here the statutory basis of Code Section 1109(b) regarding parties in interest. . . .

NOTE ON BANKRUPTCY AND CONTINGENT TORT CLAIMS

Johns-Manville Corp., along with the other "mass tort" cases in bankruptcy, raises an important question about the role of and limits on bankruptcy. Assume Debtor is a manufacturing corporation. It has just received a report that it has, at best present guess, outstanding "liabilities" with a present value of $4 billion. Some of these liabilities might arise out of obligations to banks and others with security interests, but it will be simpler for the moment if we assume that there are no secured creditors. Some of these liabilities almost certainly are to trade creditors, and some may arise out of obligations to workers. But a fair number of them arise out of potential liabilities to people who will become entitled to sue Debtor for something it manufactured in the past, such as asbestos insulation.

Debtor also has received a report that its assets are worth something like one and one half billion dollars if sold off piece by piece, and about two billion dollars if kept together in the current business (which is now manufacturing nontoxic products). This latter figure, of course, means that investors would not pay more than two billion dollars for the right to capture Debtor's future income stream, even if there were *no* claims against Debtor's assets.

Under these assumptions, should tort claims of individuals that Debtor injured in the past, but that do not yet know they are injured, be cognizable in bankruptcy, as "claims"? If they are, they will be included in the bankruptcy pool (as Judge Posner and Judge Lifland noted, a matter of no small complexity itself), and their claims will be discharged (subject to a constitutional question of proper notice, again, as those judges noted, a matter of no small complexity). But if they are not included, they will receive nothing in the bankruptcy distribution, and their claims will not be discharged.

Are these "claims" within the meaning of §101(4)? Note one thing about these claims: They arise out of Debtor's past. They are not like future tort claims, where the seeds have not even been planted. For example, if Debtor were to go out of business today and completely disappear, Debtor's delivery trucks would not run over anyone six months or a year from now. (Whoever buys the delivery trucks might run over someone, but that would not give rise to a claim against Debtor.) With respect to those sorts of accidents, if Debtor were to stop business today, no torts would happen, and there would be no "claim" to worry about. But that is not true with respect to the asbestos "claims" against Debtor. If Debtor stopped business today, those people would still be injured. Debtor has already taken the actions that may cause the injury. The chain of events has occurred, and only the identity of the victims remains unknown, because of the substantial "gestation" period for the injury to manifest itself.

Looking at §101(4), are these potential asbestos claims "claims" for purposes of bankruptcy? They certainly are unliquidated, and they may also be contingent, disputed, and unmatured, but all those sorts of uncertainties are explicitly covered by §101(4). As a statutory matter, isn't it clear that these are "claims"? In *UNR Industries,* however, Judge Hart focused not on whether the asbestosis victims had "claims," but rather on whether claims had arisen at the time of the filing of the petition within the meaning of §101(9). Judge Hart assumed that because state law determined *whether* potential victims had claims, state law also determined *when* those claims arose for purposes of the bankruptcy proceeding.

Assume that Judge Hart was correct in asserting that those exposed to asbestos fibers have a cause of action only when they develop symptoms of asbestosis (a conclusion that Judge Posner seems to reject and Judge Lifland seems to support in footnote 4 and to reject in footnote 6). Does it follow that state law should control the question of whether a claim has "arisen"? Even if Judge Hart was correct in asserting that the language covering "contingent" claims applies only to guarantors, does this not undercut the conclusion that state law governs the question of *when* a claim arises? A guarantor who has not been called upon to honor his guarantee does not have a cause of action against the debtor at the time the petition is filed, yet the guarantor almost certainly has a claim that has arisen before the filing of the petition under the Bankruptcy Code. Assuming that a tort claim is not contingent under the Bankruptcy Code, why should state law govern when it arises, when state law does not control when a contractual claim arises?

Why should state-law procedural rules as to when a lawsuit may be brought (many of which postpone the time a cause of action arises simply to overcome statute of limitations problems) control in bankruptcy? What is the consequence of concluding that tort victims' potential assertions of liabilities are not "claims"? As we have noted, at least part of the result is that they do not participate in the division of assets and that their claims are not discharged. As a policy matter, is this a sensible result?

Consider this by examining Debtor's options, apart from bankruptcy. Debtor could, of course, continue on a "business as usual" basis. But as its financial position became known, its "existing" (i.e., known) creditors would scramble to get paid in full — the "grab" race we examined in Chapter 1. Ultimately, Debtor would be stripped of its assets, and the fastest creditors would get $1.5 billion dollars, leaving nothing for the others (or more probably, as the race occurred, someone would force Debtor into bankruptcy). Note that this process could culminate in a de facto "discharge" of the liability to the "future" tort victims, because, after being stripped of all its assets, Debtor could simply dissolve under state law, and the state-law corporate doctrine of limited liability for share-holders would ensure that the "future" tort claimants had no one to sue. (The state-law tort doctrine of successor liability would probably not apply in the case of a piecemeal break-up of Debtor.)

If Debtor sees this event coming, it can take action now. Wholly apart from bankruptcy, Debtor can dissolve under state law and sell off its assets one by one. This will convert Debtor into a company holding $1.5 billion of cash. This cash will be distributed to the claimants in some prescribed fashion, depending on state law. Either all the assets will go to "existing" claimants, or some of the money will have to be set aside (as a matter of state dissolution law) for these "future" tort claimants.

Both these solutions, however, result in an aggregate of $1.5 billion for the creditors as a group; in a sense, the creditors taken as a whole lose a half billion dollars in a piecemeal liquidation. It is in the collective interest of the creditors to keep the company together, as a going concern. If Debtor's assets can be sold, as a unit, free and clear of liabilities, for example, the creditors could share in $2 billion of cash, instead of $1.5 billion. Should there be a mechanism that keeps Debtor's assets together as a going concern and allows the $2 billion to be preserved? Isn't this collec-tivizing of creditors precisely one of the goals of bankruptcy? Can this goal be accomplished other than through bankruptcy? Under the tort doctrine of successor liability, it is unlikely that Debtor can be sold as a going concern outside of bankruptcy, free of its liabilities. Similarly, if Judge

Hart's opinion in *UNR Industries* is followed, that is effectively the result of any sale or reorganization in bankruptcy — the resulting entity continues with its "past" tort liability.

If Debtor has nonmanifested tort claims that will not be discharged with a present value of $2 billion, no one will pay anything for Debtor as a going concern, except to the extent that investors think they can benefit — through dividends, for example, or through the imposition of a new capital structure that will give them superior or pro rata treatment — before the asbestos claims manifest themselves and are asserted. To simplify things, assume that the investors believe they can gain $1 billion before claims are asserted. This means that Debtor can be sold, with the asbestos claims, for about $1 billion. Is this an asset deployment we should favor? On its face, it is, *if* one assumes that the investors value the going concern at $2 billion *and* expect the assets to stay together despite the probable scenario. (But is this assumption plausible?) All the general creditors receive 50 cents on the dollar. The "existing" claimants receive $1 billion from the sale of the assets, and the asbestos claimants should later be able to get (in present value terms) $1 billion from Debtor in its new form. That totals $2 billion. The shareholders receive nothing.

But is this necessarily the end of the matter? *If* the definition of "claim" in bankruptcy excludes the unasserted asbestos claims, can't the existing creditors liquidate Debtor on a piecemeal basis, in bankruptcy, and gain $1.5 billion, which they (because they are the only holders of "claims" in bankruptcy) do not have to share with the unasserted asbestos claims? The present creditors will recover 75 cents on the dollar, while the asbestosis victims who have not contracted the disease receive nothing. But it is not simply that the present creditors gain and the victims lose. The creditors as a group are worse off, because they recover only $1.5 billion instead of $2 billion.

Don't the "existing" creditors have an incentive to reach this result notwithstanding that it uses assets in a way that the creditors as a group would not favor? (Note one irony of this: The unasserted tort claimants will *want* to be included as "claimants" in the bankruptcy process, as long as they do not know who they are. Once they know who they are — and become "present" claimants — they will have an incentive to keep other unasserted claimants out, because that means more assets for those who know who they are, and hence have "claims" cognizable in bankruptcy.) Therefore, isn't the best solution, from the viewpoint of the claimants as a group, to *include* the unasserted tort claimants in the bankruptcy process (so they share in the assets, but have their claims discharged), and then to sell the assets for $2 billion, free of the claims? Is this a solution towards which bankruptcy policy should be directed? To what extent can one apply the conclusions one draws from this example to a case such as *Manville*, in which the opportunities for strategic gamesmanship abound and the facts are clouded with uncertainty?

Note that this analysis takes as a given the rights existing under non-bankruptcy law. It assumes, for example, that victims of asbestosis should be compensated by Debtor if, but only if, it is obliged to compensate these victims under nonbankruptcy law.

C. ALLOWING AND ESTIMATING CLAIMS

Assuming a claim meets the tests of §101(4), has arisen under §101(9), and has been asserted through the filing of a proof of claim form, it still must be "allowed." How is a claim allowed? In what amounts? Consider these questions in light of the next two cases and the problems.

IN RE MOSES
9 Bankr. 370 (Bankr. N.D. Ga. 1981)

A. D. KAHN, Bankruptcy Judge.

The debtor, Frances Burdett Moses, filed a petition pursuant to Chapter 13 of the Bankruptcy Reform Act of 1978 (11 U.S.C. §101 et seq.) (the "Code"). Liberty Loan Corporation ("LLC") filed a proof of claim and the debtor objected on two grounds: (1) the loan violated Georgia law and the debtor was entitled to a penalty; and, (2) the loan violated the Truth in Lending Act (15 U.S.C. §1601 et seq.) ("TIL") and the debtor was entitled to set off the $1,000 penalty prescribed by the Act. Household Finance Corporation of Georgia ("HFC") also filed a proof of claim and the debtor raised objections similar to those raised in response to the claim of LLC. . . .

Each creditor responded to the debtor's objections. LLC generally denied the basis of the debtor's objections. HFC answered and asserted that its claim was based on a judgment and not violative of Georgia law. HFC also raised certain affirmative defenses to the debtor's TIL objections, including the statute of limitations, res judicata, and estoppel.

Debtor Moses then moved for summary judgment in each case, contending that (1) a debtor may raise a TIL claim defensively in a Chapter 13 proceeding to reduce a creditor's proof of claim, and (2) that debtor's TIL claim was not barred even though the statute of limitations had run. The foregoing issues of law are common to the TIL dispute between the debtor and each creditor and will be considered first. Other issues, including those objections based on Georgia law, will be addressed subsequently.

First, it is helpful to examine the nature of the debtor's TIL objection to the proofs of claim.

Although debtor Moses did not explicitly state it in the briefs, the TIL objection she asserts is a claim for the penalty to which a borrower in a loan transaction is entitled when a lender fails to comply with the Truth in Lending Act. See 15 U.S.C. §1640(a). Such noncompliance by a lender does *not* result in the invalidation of the underlying loan. Actual damages might also be available to debtor Moses, but they have not been sought. See 15 U.S.C. §1640(a).

Importantly, there is no dispute that debtor Moses' TIL claim is now being asserted *after* the running of the applicable statute of limitations, and, under ordinary circumstances, is barred. See 15 U.S.C. §1640(e). In an effort to overcome the bar of the statute, debtor Moses has attempted to classify her objection as a recoupment (a counterclaim which arises from the same transaction as the main claim), and she has asserted that a recoupment is "never barred by the statute of limitations so long as the main action itself is timely," citing Bull v. U.S., 295 U.S. 247, 262, 55 S. Ct. 695, 79 L. Ed. 1421 (1935).

Debtor Moses initially raised the TIL objections in response to the filing of proofs of claim by both HFC and LLC. See 11 U.S.C. §502. Therefore, this court is called on to interpret Section 502 of the Code and determine the procedural and substantive rights of the parties accorded by that provision of law.

I. Can Debtor Moses Raise a TIL Objection to Reduce a Creditor's Proof of Claim in a Section 502(b) Determination under the Bankruptcy Code?

There is no question that the bankruptcy court has the power to adjudicate TIL claims that arise out of loan transactions which form the underlying basis for proofs of claims filed by creditors in a Chapter 13 proceeding. . . .

The question of the *procedural* route for deciding questions that arise under nonbankruptcy law but are subject to the jurisdiction of the bankruptcy court, such as the instant TIL claims, is not answered specifically by the Code. Under former law the power of the bankruptcy court, which was more restricted in its jurisdiction, was inextricably linked to summary proceedings. Since the jurisdiction of the bankruptcy court has expanded under the Code, it is necessary to reexamine the procedures that enable parties to exercise their substantive rights, whether those rights arise under the Code, or other federal, or state law.

The Code specifies the procedures to be followed in allowability determinations. When an objection to a proof of claim is filed, it becomes the duty of the bankruptcy judge to make a determination of the allowability of a claim "after notice and a hearing." 11 U.S.C. §502(b).

The meaning of the phrase "after notice and a hearing" is fully delineated elsewhere in the Code. Section 102(1) of the Code states:

"after notice and a hearing," or a similar phrase —

(A) *means after such notice as is appropriate in the particular circumstances, and such opportunity for a hearing as is appropriate in the particular circumstances;* but

(B) authorizes an act without an actual hearing if such notice is given properly and if

      (i) such a hearing is not requested timely by a party in interest; or

      (ii) there is insufficient time for a hearing to be commenced before such act must be done, and the court authorizes such act; . . . (emphasis added)

11 U.S.C. §102(1).

Although "notice and a hearing" in Section 502(b) might seem to imply that a hearing is required in each instance, Section 102(1) makes it clear that a hearing is not statutorily required, but only that parties are given an *opportunity* for a hearing and may have a hearing if it is so requested. As the legislative history of Section 102(1) states, "If a provision of title II (sic) authorizes an act to be taken 'after notice and a hearing' this means that if appropriate notice is given and no party to whom such notice is sent timely requests a hearing, then the act sought to be taken may be taken without an actual hearing." 95 Cong. Rec. H11090 (Sept. 28, 1978), Bkr-L Ed §81:3.

The overall importance of the "after notice and a hearing" requirement in the bankruptcy process is highlighted in the House Report:

> The concept is central to the bill and to the separation of the administrative and judicial functions of bankruptcy judges. The phrase means after such notice as is appropriate in the particular circumstances . . . and such opportunity for a hearing as is appropriate in the particular circumstances. Thus, a hearing will not be necessary in every instance. If there is no objection to the proposed action, the action may go ahead without court action. This is a significant change from present law, which requires the affirmative approval of the bankruptcy judge for almost every action. The change will permit the bankruptcy judge to stay removed from the administration of the bankruptcy or reorganization case, and to become involved only when there is a dispute about a proposed action, that is, only when there is an objection. The phrase "such opportunity for a hearing as is appropriate in the particular circumstances" is designed to permit the Rules and the courts to expedite or dispense with hearings when speed is essential.

H.R. Rep. No. 95-595, 95th Cong., 1st Sess. 315 (1977), U.S. Code Cong. & Admin. News 1978, pp. 5787, 6272.

The need for ease in the administration of estates and the desire for judicial economy while assuring just results was effectuated in the statutory procedures governing the allowability of claims. Section 502(a) of the Code promotes the administration of estates by providing that claims are allowed unless an objection is entered. 11 U.S.C. §502(a). If an objection is entered, the allowability of the claim becomes a question for determination by the bankruptcy judge. The setting for this determination may be as elaborate as the parties require, i.e., one or more of the parties may request a hearing. If no hearing is requested the bankruptcy court may proceed to determine the allowability question without the hearing.

Heretofore the considerations in the allowability determination have not been discussed. Section 502(b) describes certain substantive issues that may be raised in an allowability determination. See 11 U.S.C. §502(b)(1)-502(b)(9).*

The parties, in determining whether to request a hearing, should be mindful of these limitations. Thus, the *substantive* limitations on allowability mesh with the *procedures* defined by the Code, and ideally both function to facilitate the administration of estates.

 For example, if a creditor filed a proof of claim with appropriate documentation, and the trustee objected on the basis of Section 502(b)(2) (unmatured interest), the court is mandated to determine the allowability of the claim. The court decides this question after giving notice and an opportunity for a hearing. The creditor may request a hearing if there is a real dispute concerning the inclusion of unmatured interest in the claim, but if there is no such dispute, the creditor may decide to waive the hearing, and permit the court to determine allowability without same.

In the case sub judice debtor Moses entered her TIL objections pursuant to Section 502(b)(1) of the Code, which states in part:

> the court, after notice and a hearing, shall determine the amount of such claim . . . , and shall allow such claim in such amount, except to the extent that—
> (1) such claim is unenforceable against the debtor, under any agreement or applicable law. . . .

11 U.S.C. §502(b)(1).

Debtor Moses' TIL claim for penalties is *not* encompassed by §502(b)(1). The legislative history of Section 502(b)(1) explains the nature of a claim that is "unenforceable against the debtor." Id. Unenforceable claims include those that are usurious, unconscionable, or unenforceable because of a failure of consideration. H.R. Rep. No. 95-595, 95th Cong., 1st Sess. 352-354 (1977). Even if a borrower seeks actual damages under TIL in addition to a penalty, such violations do not render the underlying loan transactions *unenforceable* against the debtor. Debtor Moses' reliance on §502(b)(1) is simply misplaced. Furthermore, the TIL objection cannot properly be founded on the remaining enumerations of Section 502(b). . . .

The question here presented is the mode of procedure when an "objection" is raised that does not come within the substantive limitations set

---

* In 1984, one part of §502(b) was deleted. Under current law, the cite would be §502(b)(1)-(8).—Eds.

forth in Section 502(b). Such an objection includes the TIL objection raised by debtor Moses.

There are several considerations involved. The right of a creditor to have the allowability of his claim determined in an expeditious manner is a primary concern. . . . If determinations regarding the allowance of claims are limited in scope to the bases for disallowance that are enumerated in Section 502(b), the allowance of claims would be facilitated.

A more basic consideration is the obvious fact that Congress substantially changed bankruptcy law with the enactment of the Code. The bankruptcy court has tremendously expanded jurisdiction. Additionally, Section 502(b) far more specifically addresses and outlines the considerations in the allowance of claims than did prior law.[3]

A TIL claim is a *separate cause of action,* whether the claimant seeks damages or the penalty. Such a claim is an independent cause of action and can be instituted regardless of the status of the underlying loan. The presence of the enumerations in Section 502(b) of the Code may well indicate that Congress did not intend TIL claims to be adjudicated in an allowability determination made in a notice and hearing context.

Finally, Rule 7001 of the Suggested Interim Bankruptcy Rules states:

> A proceeding before a bankruptcy judge for legal, equitable, or declaratory relief which arises under nonbankruptcy law is an *adversary* proceeding governed by Part VII of the Bankruptcy Rules. (emphasis added)

Rule 7001 thus provides the procedure for claims that fall within the jurisdiction of the bankruptcy court but are *not* subject to determination in a hearing on the allowability of claims. Thus, debtors wishing to assert TIL claims must file a complaint in bankruptcy court in order to have their TIL claims heard.

Common factual issues may arise in allowability settings and TIL actions, but this does not lead to the conclusion that the TIL claim should properly be adjudicated in a 502(b) hearing, as substantial rights of the parties are protected by more formal adversary proceedings. However, in some cases the interests of justice may require the consolidation *for trial* of factual issues that are common to allowability determinations and adversary proceedings.

Therefore, this court concludes, based on the foregoing considerations, that a 502(b) hearing is not the proper procedural context for asserting TIL claims that debtor Moses may have in this case, and that if debtor Moses wishes to pursue a TIL remedy, the proper procedure is the filing of a complaint in this or other court of competent jurisdiction.

---

3. Section 2(a)(2) of the Bankruptcy Act of 1898, as amended, provided that courts of bankruptcy could "allow claims, disallow claims, reconsider allowed or disallowed claims, and allow or disallow them against bankrupt estates; . . ."

Accordingly, it is unnecessary for this court to address any other TIL issues. . . .

NOTE

Is the court persuasive in holding that it needs to limit the determinations regarding the allowance of claims to the bases set forth in §502(b)? What purpose is served by postponing the inquiry into whether the debtor has a setoff right? See also 28 U.S.C. §157(a).

PROBLEMS

3.3 Bank has loaned Debtor $1,000,000 to be repaid in ten annual installments of $100,000, plus accrued interest at the rate of 14 percent per year on the unpaid amount. The first payment comes due at the end of this year. Debtor files a petition in bankruptcy. For what amount should Bank file a claim? See New York v. Saper, 336 U.S. 328 (1949) ("More than forty years ago, Mr. Justice Holmes wrote for this Court that the rule stopping interest at bankruptcy had then been followed for more than a century and a half. He said the rule was not a matter of legislative command or statutory construction but, rather, a fundamental principle of the English bankruptcy system which we copied. Sexton v. Dreyfus, 219 U.S. 339, 344"). Would it matter if the contractual interest rate were 5 percent instead of 14 percent? The legislative history to §502 notes:

> Section 502(b) . . . contains two principles of present law. First, interest stops accruing at the date of the filing of the petition, because any claim for unmatured interest is disallowed under this paragraph. Second, bankruptcy operates as the acceleration of the principal amount of all claims against the debtor. One unarticulated reason for this is that the discounting factor for claims after the commencement of the case is equivalent to contractual interest rate on the claim. Thus, this paragraph does not cause disallowance of claims that have not been discounted to present value because of the irrebuttable presumption that the discounting rate and the contractual interest rate (even a zero interest rate) are equivalent.

3.4 Seller has sold Debtor a machine for $100,000, to be paid in five annual installments of $20,000 "without interest." Prior to the time the first installment is due, Debtor files a petition in bankruptcy. For what amount should Seller file a claim? Does your conclusion in Problem 3.3 still apply?

3.5 Creditor holds a zero coupon debenture Debtor issued. Debtor borrowed $500,000 from Creditor in 1980, and promised to pay Creditor

$1,000,000 in 1990. Debtor files a bankruptcy petition in 1985. For what amount should Creditor file a claim? Does your conclusion in Problem 3.3 still hold? The following observations were made in the legislative history:

> Interest disallowed under this paragraph includes postpetition interest that is not yet due and payable, and any portion of prepaid interest that represents an original discounting of the claim, yet that would not have been earned on the date of bankruptcy. For example, a claim on a $1,000 note issued the day before bankruptcy would only be allowed to the extent of the cash actually advanced. If the original discount was 10 percent, so that the cash advanced was only $900, then notwithstanding the face amount of [the] note, only $900 would be allowed. If $900 was advanced under the note some time before bankruptcy, the interest component of the note would have to be prorated and disallowed to the extent it was for interest after the commencement of the case.

Is this consistent with the policy behind the legislative history quoted in Problem 3.3?

3.6 Chrysler Credit Corp. had loaned the Coveys, who ran a car dealership, money based on a capital loan and a floor plan arrangement. When the Coveys defaulted, Chrysler Credit repossessed the inventory of automobiles and sold them. After crediting the proceeds from these sales to the Coveys, Chrysler Credit claimed the Coveys still owe $90,000. The Coveys file a petition in bankruptcy. Chrysler Credit files a claim for $90,000. The Coveys assert that the claim is invalid because Chrysler Credit failed to give them proper notice of the sale under UCC §9-504, and that this failure bars a deficiency judgment under UCC §9-507 (one of several views expressed by the courts as to the effect of an improper notice). In what amount should Crysler Credit Corp.'s claim be allowed? See §502(b)(1).

3.7 Chrysler Corporation delivered parts and accessories to the Coveys for their car dealership. The Coveys file for bankruptcy. Chrysler Corporation files a claim for $25,000, attaching a computer print-out of its shipment and payment records. The Coveys dispute this amount, asserting that they owe Chrysler Corporation only $10,000 and that, furthermore, some of the parts were defective so that they have a $5,000 claim against Chrysler Corporation. In what amount should Chrysler Corporation's claim be allowed? See UCC §2-717.

Assuming that disputes over the amount of a claim must be resolved, how is this accomplished? One way, of course, is simply to allow the claims to be determined by ordinary nonbankruptcy channels, a procedure that usually is available under the Bankruptcy Code if the bankruptcy judge decides to lift the automatic stay of §362 for such purposes. (An exception exists in 28 U.S.C. §157(b)(5) for personal injury tort and wrongful death claims—such as asbestosis claims in Manville's bankruptcy case—that must be tried in district court, see Chapter 13, page 962.) But non-bankruptcy procedures may be slow and cumbersome. It may also not be worth the fixed costs of determining such suits by ordinary means, when the resulting claim may only be paid ten cents on the dollar. For these reasons, it may be in the interests of the creditors to have special bankruptcy procedures that are more streamlined. See Jackson, Translating Assets and Liabilities to the Bankruptcy Forum, 14 J. Legal Studies 73 (1985).

Section 502 provides for such procedures. Section 502(b) specifies that, if an objection is made, "the court, after notice and hearing, shall determine the amount of such claim . . . as of the date of the filing of the petition." See §102(1) (definition of "after notice and a hearing"). Section 502(c) provides an alternative way of determining a claim "for purpose of allowance under this section" if determination under §502(b) would unduly delay the administration of the bankruptcy case. What limits on the §502(b) or §502(c) procedure are imposed by the Bankruptcy Code? By other law? To what extent, for example, can creditors insist on a jury trial? See 28 U.S.C. §1411, discussed infra page 963. See Note, Procedures for Estimating Contingent or Unliquidated Claims in Bankruptcy, 35 Stan. L. Rev. 153 (1982).

PROBLEMS

3.8 *A* Corp. has filed a lawsuit against Debtor, alleging antitrust violations in Debtor's manufacture and distribution of a microprocessor from 1975 through 1983. Some discovery has commenced, but counsel estimate that approximately 12 more months of discovery are required before the case is ready for trial, and trial will take approximately six months. Appeals will consume another year or two. Debtor, at this point, files a petition in bankruptcy. Does *A* Corp. have a proper claim? If so, how should *A* Corp.'s claim be allowed? Should the bankruptcy court allow the case to proceed in state or federal court, decide it itself, or adopt some other procedure?

3.9 Debtor is a paint manufacturer. Approximately 200 products liability lawsuits are pending against it in various state and federal courts. None of them involve personal injury or wrongful death claims. Debtor files a petition in bankruptcy. If each of the plaintiffs in these products liability lawsuits files a claim in the bankruptcy proceeding, should the claims be allowed, and if so, in what fashion? (28 U.S.C. §157(b)(5) may be applicable to this problem, see infra page 962.)

BITTNER v. BORNE CHEMICAL CO.
691 F.2d 134 (3d Cir. 1982)

GIBBONS, Circuit Judge.

Stockholders of The Rolfite Company appeal from the judgment of the district court, affirming the decision of the bankruptcy court to assign a zero value to their claims in the reorganization proceedings of Borne Chemical Company, Inc. (Borne) under Chapter 11 of the Bankruptcy Code (Code), 11 U.S.C. §§1-151326 (Supp. IV 1981). [W]e affirm.

dist, ct.
& B. ct.
for Δ

I

Prior to filing its voluntary petition under Chapter 11 of the Code, Borne commenced a state court action against Rolfite for the alleged pirating of trade secrets and proprietary information from Borne. The Rolfite Company filed a counterclaim, alleging, inter alia, that Borne had tortiously interfered with a proposed merger between Rolfite and the Quaker Chemical Corporation (Quaker) by unilaterally terminating a contract to manufacture Rolfite products and by bringing its suit. Sometime after Borne filed its Chapter 11 petition, the Rolfite stockholders sought relief from the automatic stay so that the state court proceedings might be continued. Borne then filed a motion to disallow temporarily the Rolfite claims until they were finally liquidated in the state court. The bankruptcy court lifted the automatic stay but also granted Borne's motion to disallow temporarily the claims, extending the time within which such claims could be filed and allowed if they should be eventually liquidated.

Upon denial of their motion to stay the hearing on confirmation of Borne's reorganization plan, the Rolfite stockholders appealed to the district court, which vacated the temporary disallowance order and directed the bankruptcy court to hold an estimation hearing. The parties agreed to establish guidelines for the submission of evidence at the hearing, and, in accordance with this agreement, the bankruptcy court relied on the parties' choice of relevant pleadings and other documents related to the state court litigation, and on briefs and oral argument. After weighing the evidence, the court assigned a zero value to the Rolfite claims and reinstated its earlier order to disallow temporarily the claims until such time as they might be liquidated in the state court, in effect requiring a waiver of discharge of the Rolfite claims from Borne. Upon appeal, the district court affirmed.

II

Section 502(c) of the Code provides: There shall be estimated for purposes of allowance under this section—

(1) any contingent or unliquidated claim, fixing or liquidation of which, as the case may be, would unduly delay the closing of the case. . . .*

The Code, the Rules of Bankruptcy Procedure, 11 U.S.C. app. (1977), and the Suggested Interim Bankruptcy Rules, 11 U.S.C.A. (1982), are silent as to the manner in which contingent or unliquidated claims are to be estimated. Despite the lack of express direction on the matter, we are persuaded that Congress intended the procedure to be undertaken initially by the bankruptcy judges, using whatever method is best suited to the particular contingencies at issue. The principal consideration must be an accommodation to the underlying purposes of the Code. It is conceivable that in rare and unusual cases arbitration or even a jury trial on all or some of the issues may be necessary to obtain a reasonably accurate evaluation of the claims. . . . Such methods, however, usually will run counter to the efficient administration of the bankrupt's estate and where there is sufficient evidence on which to base a reasonable estimate of the claim, the bankruptcy judge should determine the value. In so doing, the court is bound by the legal rules which may govern the ultimate value of the claim. For example, when the claim is based on an alleged breach of contract, the court must estimate its worth in accordance with accepted contract law. . . . However, there are no other limitations on the court's authority to evaluate the claim save those general principles which should inform all decisions made pursuant to the Code.

In reviewing the method by which a bankruptcy court has ascertained the value of a claim under section 502(c)(1), an appellate court may only reverse if the bankruptcy court has abused its discretion. That standard of review is narrow. The appellate court must defer to the congressional intent to accord wide latitude to the decisions of the tribunal in question. Section 502(c)(1) of the Code embodies Congress' determination that the bankruptcy courts are better equipped to evaluate the evidence supporting a particular claim within the context of a particular bankruptcy proceeding. . . .

According to the Rolfite stockholders, the estimate which section 502(c)(1) requires is the present value of the probability that appellants will be successful in their state court action. Thus, if the bankruptcy court should determine as of this date that the Rolfite stockholders' case is not supported by a preponderance or 51 percent of the evidence but merely by 40 percent, they apparently would be entitled to have 40 percent of their claims allowed during the reorganization proceedings, subject to modification if and when the claims are liquidated in state court. The Rolfite stockholders contend that instead of estimating their claims in this manner, the bankruptcy court assessed the ultimate merits and, believing that

_____
* Reworded slightly in 1984.— Eds.

they could not establish their case by a preponderance of the evidence, valued the claims at zero.

We note first that the bankruptcy court did not explicitly draw the distinction that the Rolfite stockholders make. Assuming however that the bankruptcy court did estimate their claims according to their ultimate merits rather than the present value of the probability that they would succeed in their state court action, we cannot find that such a valuation method is an abuse of the discretion conferred by section 502(c)(1).

The validity of this estimation must be determined in light of the policy underlying reorganization proceedings. In Chapter 11 of the Code, Congress addressed the complex issues which are raised when a corporation faces mounting financial problems.

> The modern corporation is a complex and multi-faceted entity. Most corporations do not have a significant market share of the lines of business in which they compete. The success, and even the survival, of a corporation in contemporary markets depends on three elements: First, the ability to attract and hold skilled management; second, the ability to obtain credit; and third, the corporation's ability to project to the public an image of vitality. . . .
>
> One cannot overemphasize the advantages of speed and simplicity to both creditors and debtors. Chapter XI allows a debtor to negotiate a plan outside of court and, having reached a settlement with a majority in number and amount of each class of creditors, permits the debtor to bind all unsecured creditors to the terms of the arrangement. From the perspective of creditors, early confirmation of a plan of arrangement: first, generally reduces administrative expenses which have priority over the claims of unsecured creditors; second, permits creditors to receive prompt distributions on their claims with respect to which interest does not accrue after the filing date; and third, increases the ultimate recovery on creditor claims by minimizing the adverse effect on the business which often accompanies efforts to operate an enterprise under the protection of the Bankruptcy Act.

124 Cong. Rec. H11101-H11102 (daily ed. Sept. 28, 1978) (statement of Rep. D. Edwards of California, floor manager for bankruptcy legislation in the House of Representatives). Thus, in order to realize the goals of Chapter 11, a reorganization must be accomplished quickly and efficiently.

If the bankruptcy court estimated the value of the Rolfite stockholders' claims according to the ultimate merits of their state court action, such a valuation method is not inconsistent with the principles which imbue Chapter 11. Those claims are contingent[5] and unliquidated. According to the bankruptcy court's findings of fact, the Rolfite stock-

---

5. The Rolfite stockholders assert that the claims are not contingent since they are not dependent on some future event which may never occur. In as much as the very existence of the claims in the reorganization proceeding is dependent on a favorable decision by the state court, the Rolfite stockholders are clearly mistaken.

holders' chances of ultimately succeeding in the state court action are uncertain at best. Yet, if the court had valued the Rolfite stockholders' claims according to the present probability of success, the Rolfite stockholders might well have acquired a significant, if not controlling, voice in the reorganization proceedings. The interests of those creditors with liquidated claims would have been subject to the Rolfite interests, despite the fact that the state court might ultimately decide against those interests after the reorganization. The bankruptcy court may well have decided that such a situation would at best unduly complicate the reorganization proceedings and at worst undermine Borne's attempts to rehabilitate its business and preserve its assets for the benefit of its creditors and employees. By valuing the ultimate merits of the Rolfite stockholders' claims at zero, and temporarily disallowing them until the final resolution of the state action, the bankruptcy court avoided the possibility of a protracted and inequitable reorganization proceeding while ensuring that Borne will be responsible to pay a dividend on the claims in the event that the state court decides in the Rolfite stockholders' favor.[8] Such a solution is consistent with the Chapter 11 concerns of speed and simplicity but does not deprive the Rolfite stockholders of the right to recover on their contingent claims against Borne.[9]

for Δ

III

Π

The Rolfite stockholders further contend that, regardless of the method which the bankruptcy court used to value their claims, the court based its estimation on incorrect findings of fact. Rule 810 of the Rules of Bankruptcy Procedure permits an appellate court to overturn a bankruptcy referee's findings of fact only when they are clearly erroneous. . . . A bankruptcy court may not, however, mask its interpretation of the law as findings of fact. In determining the legal merits of a case on which claims such as those of the Rolfite stockholders are based, the bankruptcy court

---

8. While the "equitable considerations" referred to by the bankruptcy court could have properly influenced the method of evaluation of the claims chosen by the court, they would not have permitted the court to evaluate as zero claims which in fact have a higher value under the method of evaluation chosen by the bankruptcy court. But because we find that the bankruptcy court did not err in its evaluation of the claims, the error, if any, in the court's references to "equitable considerations" as buttressing its decision would not affect the outcome.

9. The Rolfite stockholders apparently contend that in barring them from voting on the reorganization plan, the bankruptcy court deprived them of a property right without due process of law. Congress has given the bankruptcy courts broad discretion to estimate a claim pursuant to section 502(c)(1). As classic economic regulation, the federal bankruptcy laws need only be supportable on a rational basis to survive substantive due process challenges. . . . A bankruptcy court's discretion to treat a contingent, unliquidated claim as did the court here is undoubtedly rationally related to the legitimate governmental interests expressed in Chapter 11.

should be guided by the applicable state law. The determination of such law is of course subject to plenary review. . . .

The Rolfite stockholders argue that in assessing the merits of its state court action for the purpose of evaluating their claims against Borne, the bankruptcy court erred both in finding the facts and in applying the law. In reviewing the record according to the standards we have just described, we cannot agree. . . .

The court's ultimate finding of fact — that the Rolfite stockholders' claims in the reorganization proceeding were worth zero — must also be upheld since it too is not clearly erroneous. The subsidiary findings of the court plainly indicated that the Rolfite counterclaim in the state action lacked legal merit. Faced with only the remote possibility that the state court would find otherwise, the bankruptcy court correctly valued the claims at zero. On the basis of the court's subsidiary findings, such an estimation was consistent both with the claims' present value and with the court's assessment of the ultimate merits.

IV

The judgment appealed from will be affirmed.

NOTE ON *BITTNER* AND ESTIMATING CLAIMS

Section 502(c) states that the bankruptcy court may estimate claims "for purpose of allowance." *Bittner*, however, suggests that the estimation may be for substantially more than simple allowance. Indeed, if no other determination is later made (and the Bankruptcy Code provides for none), the "estimated" claim becomes the basis for payment and discharge. In that context, is §502(c) a proper vehicle for handling disputes? How rigorously should §502(c) be applied? In re Nova Real Estate Investment Trust, 23 Bankr. 62 (Bankr. E.D. Va. 1982), suggests one possible solution that may be available some (but not all) of the time: Estimate pursuant to §502(c), but allow the claim to be liquidated in the ordinary manner in state (or federal) court. If the regular court acts in time (i.e., determines the amount of the claim), the claim will be readjusted, §502(j). If the regular court does not act promptly, then the claim survives bankruptcy. Is this solution optimal? Doesn't it create somewhat of a disincentive to continue with the state court proceeding, assuming that general creditors in bankruptcy will recover only a few cents on the dollar?

Should the court have valued the claims of the Rolfite stockholders below their present probability of success? The court is concerned that too much voice will be given to someone who may not have a claim at all, but isn't that already taken into account in an estimate of the probability of success? What will happen if the Chapter 11 proceeding comes to an end before the state litigation ends, and the shareholders win their lawsuit? Does the "waiver of discharge" ordered by the bankruptcy court have the effect of entitling the shareholders to be paid by the reorganized debtor in full? Would such a result make sense?

PROBLEM

3.10 Consider the facts of Problem 3.2. If it were decided that the asbestos victims had "claims" cognizable in bankruptcy, how should the claims be determined? Presumably, the provisions of 28 U.S.C. §157(b)(5) apply and require that they "be tried in the district court." Do the provisions of §502(b) and (c) apply, or does the word "tried" call them off? Assuming they can be used, under either §502(b) or (c), what is the proper manner in which to proceed with respect to claims that are not yet asserted, and may not be known? 28 U.S.C. §1411 might require a jury trial for all cases commenced after July 1984. How would this work? Does it override §502(c)? In considering this question, does it matter whether or not the *pool* of likely victims is reasonably contained and ascertainable (for example, from records of workers in manufacturing plants that handled asbestos)? Does insurance provide an analogy? An investment pool?

Consider the exceptions to the allowance of claims in §502(b). (Several of them have already been examined.) How sensible are these exceptions — in particular, the exceptions of (b)(6) and (b)(7)?

KUEHNER v. IRVING TRUST CO.
299 U.S. 445 (1937)

Justice ROBERTS delivered the opinion of the Court.

In this case we are concerned with that portion of subsection (b)(10) of §77B of the Bankruptcy Act which limits the claim of a landlord for indemnity under a covenant in a lease to an amount not to exceed three years' rent.

The questions are: (1) Is the claim so limited in all events and for all purposes or is the surplus over the specified amount, though subordinated to the claims of other creditors, to have priority over the interests of stockholders or to be reserved as a liability of the reorganized corporation? (2) If the claim is limited in all events to the named amount, is the provision obnoxious to the Fifth Amendment of the Constitution?

The petitioners leased real estate to United Cigar Stores Company in 1926 for a term expiring in 1946. August 29, 1932, the company was adjudicated a voluntary bankrupt. November 14, 1932, the trustee rejected the lease and abandoned the premises. The following day the petitioners reëntered and terminated the leasehold in accordance with the provisions of the lease which contained a covenant by the lessee to indemnify them against all loss of rent from such termination. Immediately upon adoption of §77B the bankrupt filed its petition for reorganization thereunder, which was approved by the court.

The petitioners presented a proof of claim, measuring the injury resulting from the termination of the leasehold by the difference between the rental value and the value of the rent reserved for the remainder of the term. They prayed that the amount claimed be ranked on a parity with other provable debts to the extent of three years' rent and, as to the balance, be subordinated to other provable debts but awarded priority over the claims or interests of the debtor's stockholders. The trustee asked that the allowance be in an amount limited as provided by the statute. . . .

The uncontroverted testimony is that the fair rental value for the balance of the term is $111,545.36. The future instalments of rent to the end of the term aggregate $199,237.66. A special master recommended that the petitioners' claim be allowed and liquidated at the amount of the difference between present rental value and present value of the rent reserved. He found that the sum so ascertained would be not less than the equivalent of three years' rent and recommended allowance of the claim on a parity with provable debts to the extent of three years' rent,—$44,377.55,—and the reservation of all questions as to the balance until the time for classification of creditors and consideration of a reorganization plan. The District Court confirmed the master's report save that it decided the claim as allowed should represent the extent of claimants' right to participate in the proceedings. Cross appeals were taken to the Circuit Court of Appeals, which held . . . that §77B required limitation of allowance to a sum not in excess of the three years' rent mentioned in the statute and that such limitation does not take petitioners' property without due process of law in violation of the Fifth Amendment. . . .

. . . The relevant provision, so far as applicable to petitioners' claim is:

> The claim of a landlord . . . for . . . indemnity under a covenant contained in such lease shall be treated as a claim ranking on a parity with debts which would be provable under section 63 (a) of this Act, but shall be limited to an amount not to exceed the rent, without acceleration, reserved by said lease for the three years next succeeding . . . the date of reëntry of the landlord, . . .

The legislative history of this provision, and the successive alterations of its wording in both houses of Congress and in conference, to which we are referred, cannot affect its interpretation, since the language of the act as adopted is clear. . . . We agree . . . with the Circuit Court of Appeals that if, upon liquidation by deduction of present rental value from the present value of rent reserved, the difference exceeds the amount of the total rent for the three years succeeding the landlord's reëntry, the claim may be allowed only for that amount. . . .

Is the enactment in excess of the power to legislate on the subject of bankruptcies, conferred upon Congress by Art. I, §8, of the Constitution? Congress evidently considered the limitation imposed on claims of this class necessary or advantageous to a successful reorganization and its judgment is conclusive upon us, if the enactment is within its power.

The petitioners concede Congress has power to exclude contingent claims from proof and allowance so long as the obligations they represent are not extinguished by the statute. They refer, however, to the statement in Louisville Joint Stock Land Bank v. Radford, 295 U.S. 555, that Congress has never attempted to supply a bankrupt with capital to engage in business at the expense of his creditors, as persuasive that a statute cannot discharge a bankrupt's assets from liability for his debts but can only discharge the bankrupt from encumbrances on his future exertions. This principle, they assert, the statute violates. The short answer is that the object of bankruptcy laws is the equitable distribution of the debtor's assets amongst his creditors; and the validity of the challenged provision must be tested by its appropriateness to that end. Congress, in determining what such an equitable distribution demands, is free to establish standards of provability and measures of allowance regardless of the claimant's ability to maintain an action in a court or the measure of his recovery in such an action if maintainable. The contested provision is within the power of Congress. The exercise of the power is, nevertheless, subject to the commands of the Fifth Amendment.

Does the Act offend the due process guaranty by destruction of rights conferred by the petitioners' contract? They affirm that it does, not merely by impairing those rights but by a direct taking pro tanto of all remedies for their enforcement and, to that extent, of the contract itself. Conceding they have no lien upon, or property right in, the debtor's assets, such as was the subject of decision in Louisville Joint Stock Land Bank v. Radford, supra, they maintain that the Fifth Amendment assures them some effective procedure for the enforcement of the obligation of their contract; that the debtor's assets are a trust fund for creditors which cannot be invaded for the benefit of stockholders. As pointed out in the case last cited there is, as respects the exertion of the bankruptcy power, a significant difference between a property interest and a contract, since the Constitution does not forbid impairment of the obligation of the latter. The equitable distribution of the bankrupt's assets, or the equitable adjustment of creditors' claims in respect of those assets, by way of reorganization, may therefore be regulated by a bankruptcy law which impairs the obligation of the debtor's contracts. Indeed every bankruptcy act avowedly works such impairment. While, therefore, the Fifth Amendment forbids the destruction of a contract it does not prohibit bankruptcy legislation affecting the creditor's remedy for its enforcement against the debtor's assets, or the measure of the creditor's participation therein, if the statutory provisions are consonant with a fair, reasonable, and equitable distribution of those assets. The law under consideration recognizes the petitioners' claim and permits it to share in the consideration to be distributed in reorganization. The question is whether the remedy is circumscribed in so unreasonable and arbitrary a way as to deny due process.

Bankruptcy originated as a seizure of the debtor's assets for equitable distribution amongst creditors. It was akin to a taking in execution. The concept was subsequently broadened to embrace the discharge of the embarrassed debtor from antecedent debts and to make the process available at his instance as well as at that of his creditors. Claims not provable, since they did not participate in the avails of the bankrupt's assets, were not discharged but remained recoverable by action against the discharged bankrupt. The object of §77B was to extend the system to permit and facilitate the reorganization of certain types of insolvent or embarrassed business corporations. The theory of the legislation is that the extension will serve the interests of the public, the creditors, and the shareholders.

If the bankruptcy act was to be broadened to embrace reorganization of corporate debtors the wisdom of relieving them of continuing liability for rent or under contracts of indemnity was apparent. And if the landlords' claims were to be discharged in the reorganization they must be admitted to participation on an equitable basis with other claims in shaping the reorganization and in distribution of that which is to go to creditors pursuant to any plan adopted. The section therefore made such claims provable. Its legislative history attests the diverse views entertained in Congress as to the amount for which a claim should be allowed. Only after mature deliberation was the limit set at the amount fixed in the act. The reasonableness of the limitation is to be determined in the light of all circumstances Congress might properly consider.

In City Bank Farmers Trust Co. v. Irving Trust Co., [299 U.S. 433], the peculiar and unfortunate status of landlords' claims under the Bankruptcy Act of 1898 is described. The tenant's bankruptcy removed all his assets from the reach of the landlord and left, as the latter's only remedy, suits against an empty corporate shell or a destitute individual. In framing the reorganization statute Congress obviously attempted to award landlords an equitable share in the debtor's assets as, in justice, it was bound to do since the purpose was to discharge the debtor from liability to future suits based upon the lease. It is incorrect to say that Congress took away all remedy under the lease. On the contrary, it gave a new and more certain remedy for a limited amount, in lieu of an old remedy inefficient and uncertain in its result. This is certainly not the taking of the landlord's property without due process.

But we are told that if Congress determined to admit landlords' claims to a share in debtors' assets it was bound by the Fifth Amendment not to be arbitrary in the allotment of such share or to discriminate between landlords and other creditors and between individual landlords. We cannot pronounce the limit set upon petitioners' claim arbitrary or unreasonable. It is well known that leases of business properties, particularly retail business properties, commonly run for long terms. The longer the term the greater the uncertainty as to the loss entailed by abrogation of the lease. Testimony as to present rental value partakes largely of the character of prophesy and, although that value is the cardinal factor in the measure of damages for which petitioners contend, it is obvious that, since the landlord is not bound to relet the premises for the unexpired term of the lease, that factor may have little real bearing upon the realities of the case. And, in any event, the possibility of the landlord's using the premises for his own purposes, their sale, their condemnation for public use, or their loss by foreclosure, renders an estimate of present rental value highly uncertain. Add to this the fact that bankruptcies multiply in hard times, and that estimates of rental value are made upon the basis of what a new tenant will pay in an era of economic depression, and the estimate becomes even more unreliable. Whatever courts, in the absence of a statutory formula, might feel compelled to adopt as the measure of damage in such a case, we cannot hold that Congress could not reasonably find that an award of the full difference between rental value and rent reserved for the remainder of the term smacks too much of speculation and that a uniform limit upon landlords' claims will, in the long run, be fair to them, to other creditors, and to the debtor.

The petitioners insist that the amount to which the claim must be limited has no reasonable relation to the facts; that a sum equal to three times the annual rent can have no relation to the probable loss by the ending of the leasehold. But the rent reserved, broadly speaking, has some relationship to the value of the property and the value of a lease thereon. What the statute does, is to assure at least three full years' rent to a landlord whose possible loss may exceed that amount, evidently upon the theory that with such an allowance the landlord stands a reasonable chance of restoring himself to as good a position as if the lease had not been terminated.

The petitioners say that by limiting their claim they are put upon a different basis from other creditors. A sufficient ground for the distinction is that petitioners get back their property. In other words, they have lost merely a bargain for the use of real estate, whereas merchandise creditors, lenders, and others, recover in specie none of the property or money which passed from them to the debtor.

Finally, it is said that the statute is whimsical and arbitrary in that the limit fixed upon landlords' claims necessarily represents a varying proportion of the actual loss of individual landlords and that this is discrimination of the most obvious sort. If, however, the statute does not deal unfairly with the petitioners it does not lie in their mouths to object because someone else perchance will receive a larger proportion of his ultimate loss as the same is ascertained years hence than will the petitioners. Congress, not unreasonably, felt that it was necessary, in the interest of expedition of proof and allowance of landlords' claims, which had never theretofore been permitted to share in a bankrupt debtor's assets, to fix a reasonable limit upon such claims. Naturally the amount fixed cannot bear the same relation to the ultimate loss or damage in every case. But it does not follow that, for this reason, all effort at uniformity of treatment of a peculiar class of claims, difficult of liquidation, is doomed to condemnation. All the arguments which petitioners submit would equally apply to any general and uniform formula for the limitation of such claims which the Congress might adopt. We are unable to say that that which Congress did select so discriminates between individual claimants to the detriment of the petitioners as to render it unconstitutional as to them.

The judgment is affirmed.

for A, not π landlord

NOTE

Look at §502(b)(6) and (b)(7). What kinds of claims do they apply to? In re Vic Snyder, Inc., 23 Bankr. 185 (Bankr. E.D. Pa. 1982), in deciding a case under (b)(7), concluded that (b)(7) applied only to claims arising from a rejection of an employment contract in bankruptcy. If the claim arose from a pre-bankruptcy termination of the contract, (b)(7), according to the court, did not limit the claim. Is there any support for this distinction in the statute?

NOTE ON *KUEHNER*

Justice Roberts notes the substantial uncertainties surrounding estimates of rental values far into the future. He suggests that the "longer the term the greater the uncertainty as to the loss" and that "an award of the full difference between rental value and rent reserved for the remainder of the term smacks too much of speculation." Is that convincing? Is there any reason to think that this uncertainty, even assuming it exists, is systematically going to *benefit* the landlord? Even if it did, is bankruptcy a proper occasion to redress a nonbankruptcy result that favors landlords relative to other claimants?

In discussing the unreliability of estimates of future rentals, Justice Roberts discusses, in passing, the issue of condemnation. Does that, however, support his position? Say that this lease was condemned, because the government needed the building. Wouldn't the Fifth Amendment require the government to pay "just compensation"? Could Congress, in that case, pass a statute saying "we only have to pay three years' worth of rent, in case damages from condemnation exceed that"? Is *Kuehner* any different in principle? The constitutional issue, of course, may be distinct, especially in the case of prospective legislation. *Kuehner* discusses the concept of provability, and the difficulties landlords had before the amendments in even asserting a claim in bankruptcy at all. To what extent can it be argued that the change involved in *Kuehner* is actually favorable to the landlords? As a matter of constitutional law, should this make a difference? As a matter of bankruptcy policy?

NOTE ON OLDDEN v. TONTO REALTY CORP.

In Oldden v. Tonto Realty Corp., 143 F.2d 916 (2d Cir. 1944), a breach of a lease of real property gave rise to damages calculated at approximately $40,000. A limitation similar to that existing in the Bankruptcy Act at the time of *Kuehner,* however, provided that a claim "for damages . . . shall in no event be allowed in an amount exceeding the rent reserved by the lease, without acceleration, for the year next succeeding the date of the surrender of the premises to the landlord or the date of reentry of the landlord, whichever first occurs. . . ." Under that provision, damages were calculated to be approximately $26,000. The landlord, however, also had security worth approximately $3,000. The issue in *Oldden* was whether the landlord could apply the security against the unallowed portion of the claim — that is, whether the landlord could take the $3,000, and then file a claim for $26,000, or whether he had to subtract the $3,000 from his $26,000 claim, leaving him with a claim of $23,000.

The issue was posed in a particularly acute fashion, for secured claims were not provable under the 1898 Act: Creditors filed only for the unsecured portion of the claim. Did this mean that the limitation in the Act dealt only with the unsecured claim? Judge Clark held no:

> In the light of this history [most of which is recounted in *Kuehner*] and purpose of the statutory provision and its clearly expressed intent, we should construe it so as to give it full force and effect, and not allow it to be nullified by crafty draftsmanship in particular leases. . . . Nor should a landlord obtain an advantage beyond that usually accorded under the statute merely because he has been shrewd or economically powerful enough to have obtained a substantial deposit as security. The contrary result would mean that a landlord with security would be able to exceed the statutory limit by as much as the security he holds, and that landlords would receive different treatment in bankruptcy proceedings, depending upon the existence and size of the security in their possession.

dissent ↓

Judge Frank dissented, finding it "difficult . . . to believe that Congress has become so collectivist-minded, so opposed to the common characteristics of our profit system, that it intended that a landlord should not (to quote my colleagues) 'obtain an advantage merely because he has been shrewd or economically powerful enough to have obtained a substantial deposit as security.'" Instead, Judge Frank thought the issue was whether Congress intended landlords who get security "to be treated differently from other secured creditors." "Under §57, sub. h, if a landlord is wholly secured, he, like any other secured creditor, has no provable claim. He has one only if he is partially unsecured. With respect to his unsecured balance, he is, I think, in precisely the same position as a landlord without any security."

How would the issue of *Oldden* be resolved under the Bankruptcy Code? See §502(a), (b)(6); 506(a); see also legislative history to §502.

PROBLEMS

3.11 In 1985, Debtor leases Blackacre from Landlord for $40,000 a year for 30 years. The Great Depression of 1994 comes, and Debtor files a petition in bankruptcy. There are 21 years remaining in the lease. At this time, Landlord is able to lease Blackacre to another tenant for 21 years at only $20,000 a year. Debtor's trustee rejects the lease. How large is Landlord's allowed claim? Would your answer change if the facts were otherwise the same, but there were only 10 years left on the lease? What if there were only 5 years left? Note that in determining Landlord's actual damages, we have to discount the difference between the rent under the lease and the market rent to present value. (The damages are $20,000 each year, but the damages for 5 years are less than $100,000 because money received later is always worth less than money received now.) On the other hand, discounting plays no role in determining the cap on damages imposed by §502(b)(6).

3.12 Same facts as Problem 3.11, except assume that the lease was set at $40,000 a year for the first 15 years and at $60,000 a year for the last 15 years. Thus, in 1994, there are six years remaining on the lease at $40,000 a year and 15 years at $60,000 a year. How should the claim now be determined?

3.13 Debtor arranges for Creditor to buy land, build a structure on it, and lease the improved property to Debtor for ten years. The cost of the land and structure is $1 million. The annual rent is set at $110,000 (assume expenses and taxes will be paid by Debtor during the lease). This rental will net Creditor $1,100,000 over the term of the lease. At the end of the lease, Debtor has the right to buy the property for $100,000. Assume Debtor files for bankruptcy one year into the lease and plans to disaffirm the lease

(an event, as will be explored in Chapter 7 of this book, giving rise to a
pre-petition claim for damages by Creditor). Because of unforeseen developments, the market value of the leased property has fallen from
$1,000,000 to $300,000, and the property's current rental value is
$30,000 a year. If this lease is viewed as a true lease, what is Creditor's
allowed claim? If the arrangement, however, is classified either as a loan
secured by the property, or as an installment sale with security, what would
be the measure of damages?

3.14 Boeing leases a 747 jumbo jet to Debtor for $1,500,000 a year on
a 20-year lease. Two years into the lease, Debtor defaults and Boeing
repossesses the jet. Debtor files a petition in bankruptcy. Due to the depressed state of the airline industry, 747 jumbo jets currently can be leased
for $500,000 a year. Boeing files a claim for $18,000,000 in Debtor's
bankruptcy. What will Boeing's allowed claim be?

NOTE ON THE RELATIONSHIP BETWEEN
CLAIMS AND ASSETS

In this chapter, we have examined a creditor's claim against a debtor
independent of what assets the debtor has. The nature of a creditor's
claim, however, may to some degree turn on what assets a debtor owns and
the extent of his ownership rights. Nonbankruptcy law sometimes provides a particular claimant with a prior right to some or all of the assets of
the debtor. This claimant may be a holder of a consensual security interest,
execution lien, statutory lien, or any one of a number of other interests
that permit the holder to claim some or all of the debtor's assets before
other claims to those assets. Because nonbankruptcy law raises this issue in
many forms, characterizing the priority of a particular claim in bankruptcy
requires an understanding of the nature of the nonbankruptcy right.

An individual's right to specific performance against a debtor who has
defaulted illustrates the problem. Debtor has contracted to sell her Chagall
painting to Collector for $10,000, and to sell her drill press to Firm for
$10,000. Under applicable state law, Collector has a right upon breach to
specific performance, while Firm's right is limited, as with ordinary contract creditors, to monetary damages only. Collector and Firm both pay
Debtor $10,000 and then Debtor files for bankruptcy. Firm's claim is that
of an unsecured creditor, either in restitution (to recover its $10,000) or in
expectancy, for breach of contract. (In the absence of a contract-market
differential, the claim will again be for $10,000.) If, in Debtor's bank-
ruptcy, the unsecured creditors are getting paid ten cents on the dollar,
Firm will receive $1,000.

Does Collector's right to specific performance justify treating him
differently from Firm in bankruptcy? Can one separate his claim against
Debtor from Debtor's right to keep an asset (the particular painting)?

Should Creditor recover the painting or should all the creditors share it? The right to specific performance of certain contracts is usually justified on the ground that it protects the party enjoying that right from the undercompensation that would result if the claim were viewed as one that could be satisfied by monetary damages. See Kronman, Specific Performance, 45 U. Chi. L. Rev. 351 (1978). But does this rationale justify giving Collector $10,000 (in cash or in kind), while leaving Firm only $1,000?

What seems important is not the label that state law applies to Collector's right (for example, whether it deems Collector to have a "property right" in the painting that is now in Debtor's hands), but rather the attributes of that right under state law. An examination of state law is likely to reveal that, considered against the claims of other creditors (instead of against Debtor), the value of the right to specific performance, on the eve of bankruptcy, was nowhere near 100 cents on the dollar. See Cal. Civ. Code §3440; but cf. Proyectos Electronicos, S.A. v. Alper, 37 Bankr. 931 (Bankr. E.D. Pa. 1983). The relevant question for fixing relative values is how state law would measure Collector's rights against those of an execution creditor whose rights arose before the filing of a bankruptcy petition. It is not how state law would treat Collector against Debtor. See Jackson, Translating Assets and Liabilities to the Bankruptcy Forum, 14 J. Legal Studies 73 (1985).

Chapter 4
DEFINING THE BASIC ESTATE

A. INTRODUCTION

A bankruptcy proceeding requires both fixing the value of the claims of the creditors and assembling the assets of the debtor. For the most part, this second task is fairly straightforward. The assembled assets of the debtor form what is called an "estate." Under §541, this estate is comprised of all "legal or equitable interests of the debtor in property as of the commencement of the case." Thus, if Debtor is a retail store, its inventory, its equipment, and the store itself (assuming that Debtor owns it) are property of the estate. If Debtor leases property, the bankruptcy estate consists only of Debtor's interest in the property, namely, its right to use the property during the duration of the leasehold. The estate also includes intangible property, such as accounts receivable or the patents, trade secrets, or copyrights that Debtor holds. As a first approximation, in the case of a corporate debtor, property of the estate is simply any right the debtor enjoys that enhances the debtor's value.

Determining a debtor's property rights is often difficult. There are some easy cases. A debtor does not own property of which it is merely the bailee. Creditors of a dry cleaner, for example, cannot lay claim to all the suits being cleaned at the time of the bankruptcy petition. Nor can general creditors assert a right to property to the extent that it is subject to a properly perfected security interest. The security interest is itself a property interest giving a particular creditor rights superior to the debtor and its other creditors. In many cases, however, it is difficult to determine exactly what property general creditors can look to. A disagreement may arise between the debtor and its creditors, or between an entity claiming the property and all other claimants of the debtor. If the entity raising the property claim wins, it will enjoy the full value of the asset; if it loses, the asset will enter the general pool of assets made available for the claimants as a group. If a debtor, for example, holds a seat on a stock exchange, the rules of the exchange may prohibit outright transfer or condition transfer on payment of debts to specific creditors (such as other members of the exchange). We must ask whether and to what extent the seat is an asset of the estate. Is the prohibition on transfer one that bankruptcy law should respect? Should bankruptcy law allow specified creditors to be paid before others? These questions are inherent in determinations of what is and is not property of the estate; a point we raised in the discussion of specific performance rights at the end of the last chapter.

This view of property of the estate needs several qualifications. First, it applies only in the case of corporations. The most valuable asset individuals have is usually their future income from labor, and this asset is not part of the bankruptcy estate (§541(a)(6)) at least to the extent it can be traced to labor and not to capital. In re Fitzsimmons, 725 F.2d 1208 (9th Cir. 1984). A bankruptcy proceeding gives individuals the discharge right that shareholders of corporations already enjoy under state law. To give substance to the individual's entitlement to a "fresh start" free of past indebtedness, one must draw a distinction between future income and present assets. Much of the case law about property of the estate concerns drawing this line. A typical case might involve retirement benefits an employee has a vested right to receive, but that the employee cannot now enjoy.

A related, but distinct, issue concerns property an individual debtor owns at the time of the petition, but is nevertheless thought necessary for his fresh start. For example, one might allow an individual to keep, in addition to his future income stream, the clothes on his back and the tools of his trade. As the Bankruptcy Code is structured, however, such property, unlike future income, is deemed property of the estate under §541. Another Code section, §522, distinguishes between property of the estate that creditors may enjoy and property of the estate that the debtor is allowed to keep. In this chapter, we begin by discussing the history of §541, then problems concerning property of the estate that can arise in the case of individual debtors. We shall return to these questions in greater detail in Chapters 10 and 11. They relate more to the question of the individual's right to a fresh start than they do to any process whereby assets are gathered for distribution among creditors, our current focus. In the rest of this chapter we examine the general problem of identifying assets of the debtor that creditors in bankruptcy can look to for the purpose of satisfying obligations owed them.

NOTE ON THE BACKGROUND TO §541

The 1898 Act in §70a identified the property to which the trustee would be vested with "title." While complicated, that provision was based on an overriding concept that "property which is held to be exempt" never passed to the trustee. The principal operative provision of §70a was subsection (5), which stated that the trustee took title "to all of the following kinds of property wherever located . . . (5) property, including rights of action, which prior to the filing of the petition [the bankrupt] could by any means have transferred or which might have been levied upon and sold under judicial process against him, or otherwise seized, impounded, or sequestered. . . ." Thus, apart from the question of exempt property, the relevant focus was on property that could have been *transferred* by any means before the filing of the petition.

By the time the new Bankruptcy Code was drafted, there were substantial doubts about the 1898 Act's approach to identifying what was property of the bankruptcy estate. The Report of the Commission on the Bankruptcy Laws of the United States, H.R. Doc. 93-137, 93rd Cong., 1st Sess., pt. 1, at 194 (1973), endorsed the following analysis, Countryman, The Use of State Law in Bankruptcy Cases (Part I), 47 N.Y.U.L. Rev. 407, 473-474 (1972):

> On balance, there is little to justify the distinctions made in sections 70a(5) and (6) among: (1) types of property which vest in the trustee regardless of transferability or vulnerability to creditors' process; (2) those which vest only if subject to creditors' process; and (3) those which vest if either transferable or subject to creditors' process. The results are far from uniform and very often are the products of archaic state rules harking back to the days when causes of action and other nonpossessory interests were generally regarded as nontransferable or to equally archaic state statutes governing attachment, garnishment and execution. Even where the state law may be said to reflect some special concern for debtors, such concern is so haphazard that it should not be embodied in what is supposed to be a uniform bankruptcy law.
>
> It would be preferable to replace sections 70a(5) and (6) with a single provision giving the trustee title, as of the date of bankruptcy, to all nonexempt property of the bankrupt, whether or not transferable or subject to judicial process at the time of bankruptcy, except insurance, damages, or other awards representing compensation for loss of the bankrupt's postbankruptcy earnings or loss of postbankruptcy support for the bankrupt's dependants. . . . If the trustee then finds that there is no effective way he can sell and assign a particular type of property without delaying the closing of the estate he can abandon it. (Or, alternatively, the Bankruptcy Act could authorize the trustees to make an effective transfer of property nontransferable under nonbankruptcy law.) To the extent that it is thought, as a matter of federal bankruptcy policy, that certain amounts or types of property should be saved to aid in the bankrupt's rehabilitation, that is a matter for a separate, federal bankruptcy exemption policy. It should not be a reason for cluttering up section 70a with references to nonuniform state law on transferability and the reach of judicial process.

Section 541 of the Bankruptcy Code, in contrast to §70a of the 1898

Act, starts out with a sweeping claim that the estate "is comprised of . . . all legal or equitable interests of the debtor in property as of the commencement of the case. . . ." As under §70a, it is still necessary to know what "property" is, so one can decide whether the debtor has a legal or equitable interest in it. But, unlike §70a, there is no reference to excluding exempt property, and no reference to transferability.

The House Report on the bill that became the Bankruptcy Code states, H.R. Rep. No. 595, 95th Cong., 1st Sess. 175-176, 368 (1977):

> The bill makes significant changes in what constitutes property of the estate. Current law is a complicated melange of references to State law, and does little to further the bankruptcy policy of distribution of the debtor's property to his creditors in satisfaction of his debts. . . .
>
> The bill determines what is property of the estate by a simple reference to what interests in property the debtor has at the commencement of the case. This includes all interests, such as interests in real or personal property, tangible and intangible property, choses in action, causes of action, rights such as copyrights, trade-marks, patents, and processes, contingent interests and future interests, whether or not transferable by the debtor. . . .
>
> These changes will bring anything of value that the debtors have into the estate. The exemption section will permit an individual debtor to take out of the estate that property that is necessary for a fresh start and for the support of himself and his dependents. . . .
>
> Paragraph (1) . . . includes all property of the debtor, even that needed for a fresh start. After the property comes into the estate, then the debtor is permitted to exempt it under proposed 11 U.S.C. §522, and the court will have jurisdiction to determine what property may be exempted and what remains as property of the estate. . . .

Were there other ways to deal with the confusing guidance thought to exist in §70a? Why is it important to have nationwide uniformity in defining what assets are included in the bankruptcy estate? Does §541 even accomplish that? Because the attributes of property are still determined by state law, can §541 achieve this kind of uniformity? Does §541(a)'s broad reach introduce new problems? Consider these questions in looking at the cases and problems that follow. First, however, focus carefully on §541. The section requires you to focus on *interests* in *property*—not just on property itself—and to do so at the commencement of the case, not some earlier or later point (except as provided in §541(a)(5) and (6)). In addition to the basic definition in §541(a)(1), you should note the additional refinements in (a)(2) through (a)(7), as well as the limitations expressed in §541(b), (c), and (d). Since "interests" in property come into the estate, property that others (such as secured creditors) may eventually receive nonetheless becomes part of the estate—at least to the extent of the debtor's "interests" in that property.

NOTE ON INDIVIDUAL DEBTORS AND PROPERTY OF THE ESTATE

One of the most valuable assets an individual has is the ability to earn income in the future. Lenders make many loans to individuals on the promise of future incomes. Recent graduates of law or medical school may have few assets other than the promise of future earnings. Indeed, if one excludes their future earnings, many are insolvent in the sense that their liabilities vastly exceed their assets. Nevertheless, there may be reasons why creditors should not be able to count on an individual's future earnings. We shall explore the bankruptcy discharge and some of its contours more closely in Chapter 10. We shall discuss, for example, the wisdom of excluding federally-backed educational loans or tort judgments against drunk drivers from the bankruptcy discharge, and the powers of a bankruptcy judge, under the 1984 Amendments to the Bankruptcy Code, to dismiss a case under Chapter 7 (and hence deny the debtor a discharge in exchange for existing assets) if the debtor is an individual who primarily has consumer debts and if granting relief would be a "substantial abuse" of the bankruptcy process, §707(b). (The individual may still file under Chapter 13, but the contours of the relief provided by that chapter, as we will examine later in these materials, are substantially different.)

The fresh start policy seems to allow a debtor to start over again from scratch. It permits the debtor to gain future income subject to the claims of only future creditors, not existing ones. An exact division of present from future is impossible to achieve, as debtors never enter the post-bankruptcy period completely free of assets from their prior existence. Nonetheless, one fruitful line might be drawn here. Bankruptcy is a form of financial "death" for the individual in question. If a debtor, knowing he was to die tomorrow, attempted to gather together all assets today, we would find three rough categories of assets. The first category would consist of assets that are reachable today by creditors of the debtor, such as computers, sailboats, and bonds. The second category would consist of assets that are reachable today by neither the debtor nor his creditors. These would have value to the debtor if he lived, but the value would disappear if the debtor (and others) knew that he would die tomorrow. Human capital is in this category, as are its particular manifestations, such as law or medical degrees. Also in this category are special forms of nonbankruptcy property rights, such as spendthrift trusts. Finally, the third category would consist of assets that the debtor can reach today but that will be unavailable to his creditors unless and until the debtor first "cashes in" on them. This category includes traditional exempt property as well as certain types of rights, such as Keogh retirement plans or IRA accounts, and a variety of miscellaneous rights, such as a spouse's right of election against a will.

The first category of property — that reachable today by creditors —

should be property of the estate under almost any view. There is no particular reason to have a bankruptcy proceeding in which creditors have fewer assests available to them than under nonbankruptcy law, unless some assets, not exempt under state law, are necessary for the fresh start. The second category of property is likewise relatively easy to handle, once one assumes a fresh start policy. These are assets available to debtor and creditors alike only if the debtor continues to live. In this respect, the core of the fresh start policy seems to dictate that these are assets that should belong to the debtor, and his future creditors as and when they "mature" under nonbankruptcy law. As such, they are "future" assets that should not be considered property of the estate.

The third category of property is the most difficult to assess. Creditors cannot reach this form of property by their own actions, but the debtor can. Once the debtor has reached the property, creditors may reach it as well. Here, as elsewhere in bankruptcy law, the crucial task is focusing not on the label that state law applies (such as whether state law deems the asset "exempt" property or a "spendthrift trust"), but rather on the relevant *attributes* that state law attaches to this property. The relevant attribute here seems to be that the property in question, like future wages or spendthrift trusts, is not property that the creditors can reach directly.

The questions of what things of value are not "property of the estate," and what property of the estate is exempt from creditors' claims, are related to the bankruptcy discharge and to each other. A lawyer's license to practice law has great value, but it is not something that creditors can enjoy. One could justify the exclusion on the grounds that a debtor who no longer had the right to practice his trade was not being given a "fresh start." The easier justification, however, may be that the license is not "property of the estate" because it is not an asset that creditors can levy upon outside of bankruptcy. If creditors cannot look to the asset under nonbankruptcy law, there may be no reason they should be able to do so inside of bankruptcy, quite apart from the debtor's need for a fresh start. Nonbankruptcy law may sometimes insulate these assets from creditor's claims because they are surrogates for future wages, as is the case with Keogh retirement funds, e.g., In re Goff, 706 F.2d 574 (5th Cir. 1983), or army retirement funds, e.g., In re Harter, 10 Bankr. 272 (Bankr. N.D. Ind. 1981); In re Haynes, 679 F.2d 718 (7th Cir. 1982). States may have also tried to implement some nonbankruptcy policy, as in the case of a spouse's right of election against a will. See In re McCourt, 12 Bankr. 587 (Bankr. S.D.N.Y. 1981). But the important factor may not be so much why states choose to protect certain assets from creditors' claims, but that they in fact choose to do so and that this state policy affects creditors both in and out of bankruptcy as well as inside. States have proven remarkably resistant to expanding the scope of a debtor's exemptions. There accordingly seems no reason to expect states to permit too many of a debtor's assets to be reachable by him, yet shielded from his creditors.

One can argue that making property exempt only in bankruptcy is unnecessary. The policies that lead states to exempt property are not fundamentally different in bankruptcy, and it may create potentially perverse incentives to have two different kinds of exempt property depending upon whether the debtor is in bankruptcy. On the other hand, one can argue that the "fresh start" in bankruptcy has no counterpart in state law and hence that a separate set of exemptions is appropriate. This justification, however, does not explain why individual states should be able to choose between federal exemptions and their own.

Providing states with an election introduces additional problems of defining what is property of the estate. If certain property, such as pension fund rights, is listed as exempt under §522(d), one might infer that such rights were necessarily property of the estate under §541, quite apart from whether they were subject to levy by creditors outside of bankruptcy. This might not seem to be a distinction that matters. (A debtor would enjoy the pension either because it was not property of the estate or because it was exempt.) But the federal exemption for certain pension funds is limited to an amount reasonably necessary for the support of the debtor, and in the majority of states that have not adopted the federal exemptions, rights under pension funds are not listed as exempt property. In these states, deciding whether pension rights are property of the estate determines whether creditors can reach them. See Eisenberg, Bankruptcy Law in Perspective, 28 U.C.L.A. L. Rev. 953, 972-973 n.60 (1981).

PROBLEMS

4.1 Debtor attended medical school, graduated, and set up practice. Debtor has both a medical degree and a license to practice medicine. When debtor was divorced, the divorce court held that the medical degree and license to practice were "property," and subject to "equitable distribution" in the divorce. The divorce court concluded that the license and medical degree had a "current value" of $300,000, and awarded Debtor's wife 20 percent or $60,000 thereof, payable in semi-annual installments over the next six years. Debtor then files for bankruptcy. Are his medical degree and license to practice property of the estate under §541? See In re Lynn, 18 Bankr. 501 (Bankr. D. Conn. 1982).

4.2 Debtor's spouse of 20 years dies in January. Under the will that she wrote 15 years before, the spouse leaves everything she has to her father. Under state law, Debtor may, if he files the appropriate document within six months of his wife's death, elect to take one-third of his wife's estate, notwithstanding the will. Debtor files a bankruptcy petition in April. Should the trustee be able to compel Debtor to exercise his right to a nonbarrable share of his wife's estate? See In re McCourt, 12 Bankr. 587

(Bankr. S.D.N.Y. 1981), infra page 839. Should it make any difference if the wife changed her will moments before she died so that her property would go to her father rather than her husband's many creditors?

4.3 Debtor was the victim of an automobile accident. At the time he filed his bankruptcy petition, he had filed suit against Tortfeasor, but the case had not yet come to trial. Is Debtor's claim against Tortfeasor "property of the estate"? Can the trustee compel Debtor to pursue the lawsuit? Is it relevant that the cause of action would survive, even if Debtor were to die suddenly? Is it relevant that, outside of bankruptcy, creditors would be unable to compel the debtor to take any action against Tortfeasor or to garnish Tortfeasor's contingent obligation to Debtor? See Tignor v. Parkinson, 729 F.2d 977 (4th Cir. 1984).

B. THE ROLE OF STATE LAW IN DEFINING PROPERTY RIGHTS

The issue of what constitutes property of the estate often turns not on whether the estate or an individual debtor gets to enjoy the property, but rather on whether someone else has a right superior to the debtor's or any creditor's. For example, a person may claim that an asset in debtor's possession really is not the debtor's, because, for example, it is on lease, on a bailment, or held in trust. Concluding that a third party is the "owner" of a piece of property, or that the debtor and everyone else takes the property subject to the third party's rights, may not really be very much different than a conclusion that the asset is property of the estate, but that the person — perhaps a secured creditor — has the first crack at it in the bankruptcy proceeding. Indeed, bankruptcy treats them the same. (This is the result of §725's directive that the trustee dispose of property that others claim an interest in, before a general distribution of assets of the estate to the creditors under §726. See H.R. Rep. No. 595 ("The purpose of this section is to give the court appropriate authority to ensure that collateral or its proceeds is returned to the proper secured creditor, that consigned or bailed goods are returned to the consignor or bailor and so on."))

Although issues as to who gets what property in what order are examined in Chapter 8 in connection with the subject of priorities, that subject is usually a treatment of an ordering among unsecured creditors — people who have not been able to assert (successfully) a competing property claim to the asset in question. We now focus on the question from the perspective of competing property claimants, and ask when state law property rights or claims should be respected in bankruptcy. This is not merely a priority issue, for sometimes the distinctions make other differences as well. For example, while the automatic stay applies both to property *of* the estate and to property in the *possession of* the estate, §362(a)(3), certain rights of the trustee to use property apply only to property *of* the estate, see, e.g., §363(b) and (c); §542.

The question we are exploring here is the extent to which state law is allowed to determine property of the estate, although inevitably the inquiry will shade over into whether a particular party is able to defeat the trustee with respect to a particular asset. This returns us, in part at least, to the discussion we began with *Butner* in Chapter 1.

IN RE GUNDER
8 Bankr. 390 (Bankr. S.D. Ohio 1980)

Fed. law controls over state law

R. J. SIDMAN, Bankruptcy Judge.

This matter is before the Court on the merits of a Motion to Recover Repossessed Automobile filed by the debtors. The matter was tried to the Court on its merits and was submitted for decision.

The debtors have a Chapter 13 proceeding pending before this Court. . . . The debtors filed their petition on July 14, 1980 and listed BancOhio National Bank (BancOhio) as a creditor secured in a 1978 Plymouth Horizon which had been repossessed before the filing. BancOhio filed its proof of claim on August 22, 1980, attaching a certificate of title to the 1978 Plymouth Horizon which reflected John Gunder, the father of the debtor Kevin Gunder, as the owner of the vehicle. BancOhio filed its claim as unsecured.

The present motion under consideration is the attempt of the debtors *to be determined* to assert an interest in the 1978 Plymouth sufficient to cause its return to their possession for use in executing the terms of their proposed plan. A threshold question to be addressed by the Court concerns the objection raised by BancOhio to the introduction of any evidence tending to dispute the ownership of the car except as reflected on the title. Section 4505.04 of the Ohio Revised Code provides:

> No person acquiring a motor vehicle from the owner thereof, whether such owner is manufacturer, importer, dealer, or otherwise, shall acquire any right, title, claim, or interest in or to said motor vehicle until such person has had issued to him a certificate of title to said motor vehicle, or delivered to him a manufacturer's or importer's certificate for it. . . . No court in any case at law or in equity shall recognize the right, title, claim, or interest of any person in or to any motor vehicle sold or disposed of, or mortgaged or encumbered, unless evidenced:
>
> (A) By a certificate of title or a manufacturer's or importer's certificate issued in accordance with sections 4505.01 to 4505.19, inclusive, of the Revised Code.
> (B) By admission in the pleadings or stipulation of the parties. §4505.04, O.R.C.

This statute sets out a conclusive presumption of ownership based upon a notation on the face of the certificate of title to the automobile. . . . To the extent 4505.04 O.R.C. states a rule of evidence or sets forth a matter of procedure, this statute has no effect in a federal bankruptcy court. Rules 101 and 1101(a) & (b) of the Federal Rules of Evidence, Rule 13-1 of the Rules of Bankruptcy Procedure, and §405(d) of the Bankruptcy Reform Act of 1978 (P.L. 95-598). It has been said, however, that a conclusive presumption is not merely a rule of evidence or a procedural guide, but rather that, in effect, it is a rule of substantive law. . . . In the area of bankruptcy law, the United States Constitution has expressly granted power to the federal government to make uniform laws regarding bankruptcy. . . . In such an area, where power has expressly been granted to the federal government, any state statute which conflicts with that federal law will have to yield to the federal rule of law. . . . A state has no power to make or enforce any law which conflicts with the federal bankruptcy laws. Furthermore, decisions of state courts defining property rights do not bind the federal bankruptcy courts when those decisions are contrary to the policy and proper construction of the bankruptcy laws. Board of Trade of the City of Chicago v. Johnson (In Re Henderson), 264 U.S. 1, 44 S. Ct. 232, 68 L. Ed. 533 (1923). The policy of the Bankruptcy Code, as reflected in 11 U.S.C. §541, is to provide for an estate consisting of all legal and equitable property interests of the debtors. Section 4505.04 of the Ohio Revised Code cannot be applied in this proceeding to the extent that it purports to deny to the bankruptcy court the right to hear evidence pertaining to any interest which the debtors may have in the 1978 Plymouth. A clear intent of the Bankruptcy Reform Act of 1978 was to minimize, if not eliminate, the vagaries of state law upon the administration and application of the bankruptcy law. With the recognition of certain limited areas of exception (for example, the matter of exemptions under §523), this intent should be implemented by a restrained deference to state law on matters raised in a bankruptcy case. In the present case, this Court holds that the state statute (§4504.04, O.R.C.) on the presumption of ownership will not be applied.

Section 541 of the Bankruptcy Reform Act of 1978 (11 U.S.C. §541) has eliminated the concept of title as it relates to the inclusion of property as property of the estate. . . . All legal and equitable interests in property are included. Moreover, federal law will determine what property becomes property of the estate. State law, to the extent it does not conflict with the policy or spirit of the bankruptcy laws, will then be used to determine the type or extent of the interest which the debtor possesses. Property of the estate is generously defined under federal law and does not exclude novel interests. Segal v. Rochelle, 382 U.S. 375, 86 S. Ct. 511, 15 L. Ed. 2d 428 (1966) (construing §70a of the Bankruptcy Act of 1898, the predecessor in part to 11 U.S.C. §541). Important recognition is often given to interests which are not necessarily considered relevant in state law allocation of title. . . .

This Court finds that the 1978 Plymouth automobile is property of the debtors' estate. Although the interest of the debtors in the vehicle is not a legal interest under applicable state law, a literal interpretation of that state law is not appropriate where certain intervening events have occurred. Other courts, when faced with intervening situations, have recognized equitable rights in persons not shown on the certificate of title. . . .

This Court, therefore, concludes that Kevin and Andrea Gunder *holding* have an equitable interest in the 1978 Plymouth which subjects the disposition of the vehicle to the jurisdiction of the bankruptcy court. The Court notes that it was established by uncontested testimony at the hearing on this matter that the car had been placed in Kevin Gunder's father's name so that a fleet discount price and fleet insurance could be obtained by John Gunder as part of an insurance package covering other vehicles which he owns. The cost to the debtors was thus lower than the debtors, as minors, could obtain were the car titled in their names. Kevin Gunder then testified that his father had co-signed with him and his wife on the note to BancOhio, but that inquiries and notices from the bank had always been sent to Kevin Gunder (at least one demand letter, however, was also sent to John Gunder). Furthermore, the payment book issued by BancOhio was in the name of Kevin and Andrea Gunder, and no payments had ever been made directly by John Gunder.

Having concluded that Kevin and Andrea Gunder have an equitable interest in the 1978 Plymouth, the Court must next determine the nature and extent of that interest under state law. Ohio Revised Code §1309.49 *Issue* states in relevant part:

> §1309.49 (UCC 9-506) Debtor's right to redeem collateral.
> At any time before the secured party has disposed of collateral . . . , the debtor or any other secured party may, unless otherwise agreed to in writing after default redeem the collateral by tendering fulfillment of all obligations secured by the collateral as well as the expenses reasonably incurred by the secured party in retaking, holding, and preparing the collateral for disposition, in arranging for the sale.

Based upon O.R.C. §1309.49, the interest which remained in the Gunders (as debtors under the state statute) at the time of the filing of their Chapter 13 petition is a right to redeem the automobile by tendering fulfillment of all obligations secured by the collateral plus any reasonable expenses incurred by the bank in the repossession and storage of the car. "Tendering fulfillment" of all obligations can be interpreted as requiring an offer of payment of all obligations due and performance of all obligations which are matured. See Official Comment to O.R.C. §1309.49. The question then becomes what obligations are due.

[The remainder of this discussion, and the court's discussion of adequate protection, are omitted. We shall examine §§542 and 543, infra.]

NOTE ON *GUNDER* AND PROPERTY
OF THE ESTATE

The procedural context in which this case arises is a bit unusual. Here, the *debtors* are asserting that the property is property of the estate. Why would a debtor ever want something included as property of the estate? We will look, in examining United States v. Whiting Pools and §542 in Chapter 7 of this book, at the issue of when a debtor can get property back from a secured party who is in possession of the collateral following repossession, but for present purposes it is enough to know that a debtor can retrieve the property and use it only if, but for the repossession, it would have been property of the estate.

The basic question in the case is whether state law should govern what is property of the estate. The issue arises because Ohio, like many states, has a statute providing that "[n]o person acquiring a motor vehicle from the owner thereof . . . shall acquire any right, title, claim, or interest in or to said motor vehicle until such person has had issued to him a certificate of title to said motor vehicle. . . ." Doesn't this statute conclusively establish that the automobile belongs to the father—and has belonged to him since it was purchased (so there is no question of a preference)? Or at least shouldn't that matter be resolved by state law? See, e.g., In re Sommer, 28 Bankr. 95 (Bankr. D. Colo. 1983) (certificate of title, under Colorado law, only prima facie evidence of facts; actual facts show that father—who had filed for bankruptcy—was holding automobile for son, who was actual owner; therefore, automobile not property of father's estate).

The court in *Gunder* finds that state law is not controlling, apparently on the ground that it would conflict with bankruptcy law. Why? Can such an assertion be made without examining how the issue would be resolved under state law outside of bankruptcy? Consider that question by thinking of this case as one involving a liquidation under Chapter 7 of the Bankruptcy Code. Could the creditors of the debtors get the automobile in satisfaction of their claims? To answer that, we should ask whether the automobile was of some value to those creditors outside of bankruptcy, under state law. Could they levy on it? Could they get a security interest in it, granted by the debtors? Could the debtors even sell the car? If the answer to these questions is no (because of the statute's conclusive presumption that the father owns the automobile), is there any policy reason for §541 to override those state-law determinations, and consider this automobile property of the estate?

If the father filed for bankruptcy, are his creditors entitled to the automobile? Would we have to resolve that question by looking to state law? Is that conclusion of any relevance? If the father's creditors could get the automobile outside of bankruptcy, shouldn't they also be able to get it inside of bankruptcy? If both father and son file bankruptcy petitions, should the creditors of both share the car or should the father's creditors take precedence? If state law is dispositive of the rights of the father's creditors, why should it not also be dispositive of the rights of the son's creditors? Should bankruptcy law "peek" at the result under state law and reject it only if it disadvantaged the debtor or his creditors? Or should bankruptcy law reject state law only when it seems likely that the state is trying to develop a special rule that applies only in a federal bankruptcy proceeding, not across the board? Is it even necessary to worry about states developing such rules?

What bankruptcy policy exists for overriding the state statute? Assume that, under state law, the automobile in *Gunder* is considered to be the father's and, under such law, only his creditors can reach it. If the son has been paying off the automobile loan, how should that be treated? Have these payments violated the rights of the creditors? Every time the children made a payment on the loan, they have pushed assets — cash — out of their estate, and hence have reduced the amount the creditors were entitled to receive. Should this give the children's creditors a right against the father (if not against the automobile itself)? Or should this be viewed as if such loan repayments by the children were really equivalent to rental payments to the father, for use of the automobile? Should it matter whether the bank can go against the children (who signed the note along with the father)? This means that the bank will have a claim against the children's estate in bankruptcy. Should it mean that the asset is property of the estate as well? Does that depend on who *ultimately* is liable for the automobile? Consider whether the concerns these questions raise about the creditors' rights are not peculiar to bankruptcy law and hence should be resolved under state law, such as its fraudulent conveyance statute.

What if the automobile were owned by Hertz, rented to the children for a week, and, in the middle of that week, the children filed for bankruptcy? Is the automobile "property of the estate"? The answer clearly seems to be no. As we will see, however, §362 will stay any efforts by Hertz to get the automobile back without court permission. But ultimately Hertz has the right to get the car back. See §725.

PROBLEM

4.4 Manufacturer has delivered goods to Debtor, a retail dealer, on consignment. Under state law, a consignment is a form of handling the distribution and sale of merchandise, where the seller (usually a manufacturer) delivers ("consigns") goods to an agent ("consignee") for the purpose of sale to a third party, often at a specified price. Under state law, one of the attributes of a consignment is that the consignor retains title to the goods until they are sold by the consignee. When the goods are sold, title passes directly from the consignor to the buyer. Section 2-326(2) and (3) of the Uniform Commercial Code, however, subjects the goods to the claims of the consignee's creditors while they are in its possession, unless one of the enumerated steps of §2-326(3) — such as noting the consignor's interest in the Article 9 files — is taken. Manufacturer has taken none of these steps against Debtor. Debtor files for bankruptcy. Manufacturer asserts that the goods are not property of the estate under §541, since under state law title remained in Manufacturer. Evaluate that contention. See In re Brusich & St. Pedro Jewelers, 28 Bankr. 545 (Bankr. E.D. Pa. 1983).

The next case raises the question of whether certain special attributes of particular types of "property" should affect the determination of whether an asset should be deemed to be property of the estate for purposes of §541. *Swift Aire* discusses special attributes of letters of credit, a form of legal relationship that raises several bankruptcy issues. To resolve the property of the estate issues in *Swift Aire*, it is necessary to understand the law governing letters of credit. The note following *Swift Aire* discusses the attributes of letters of credit in a bit more detail. The kind of issue in *Swift Aire* arises most clearly in a Chapter 11 reorganization. For a number of purposes (principally rejecting collective bargaining agreements in bankruptcy), courts have talked about the "debtor" in a reorganization proceeding — often referred to as the "debtor in possession" (because usually no trustee is appointed) — as being a "different" entity than it was when it filed the petition in bankruptcy, although the Supreme Court has recently questioned the use of this mode of analysis, see NLRB v. Bildisco & Bildisco, discussed infra page 475. One important question, which *Swift Aire* raises, is whether this conceptual division of the debtor into a pre- and a post-petition entity should make any difference for purposes of resolving questions about property of the estate.

Issue

Colin v. Trustee of Swift

IN RE SWIFT AIRE LINES
30 Bankr. 490 (9th Cir. Bankr. App. 1983)

VOLINN, Bankruptcy Judge.

I. FACTS

Prior to filing bankruptcy on September 18, 1981, Swift Aire Lines, Inc., operated a commercial airline service. Business operations were financed primarily through Wells Fargo Bank.

In November, 1980, appellant, Justin Colin, purchased an 80 percent stock ownership interest in the debtor for $1,775,000. Colin also agreed in a separate investment agreement dated November 19, 1980, to contribute an additional $775,000 to Swift by loan or purchase of stock. The additional contribution was to be made "in the event that either Wells Fargo Bank, N.A. . . . or the Board of Directors of Swift determines in good faith, that such funds are required by Swift for the continuing operation of its business. . . ." Colin was to deliver to Swift a bank letter of credit in the amount of $775,000 to secure payment of the additional contribution to the debtor, in the event such payment was required.

Colin applied for a letter of credit from appellant, Crocker National Bank. On January 19, 1981, Crocker issued an irrevocable letter of credit for $775,000 with Swift as beneficiary. The Board of Directors of Swift and Wells Fargo[1] were each given the power to draw on the letter of credit.

Colin also signed and sent a letter dated January 20, 1981, to an officer of Wells Fargo stating that Colin agreed that the debtor could draw on the Crocker letter of credit even if Swift filed a petition under any chapter of bankruptcy, and that the provisions of 11 U.S.C. §365(e)(2)(B) were waived and would not be asserted by Colin in any attempt by Swift to draw on the letter of credit.

As a condition to Swift or Wells Fargo being able to draw on it, the Crocker letter of credit required a statement that Wells Fargo or Swift had demanded payment of the additional contribution and that such amount remained unpaid for a period of five days. On September 15, 1981, Wells Fargo made formal demand on Colin to make the additional contribution to the debtor.

Prior to expiration of the five days, on September 18, 1981, Swift filed a petition under 11 U.S.C. Chapter 7. Three days later, the appellee, David Y. Farmer was appointed interim trustee.

On October 6, 1981, the trustee presented certain documents to Crocker in an attempt to draw against the letter of credit. The documents included the following:

1) A draft to Crocker to pay to the order of the trustee for the debtor the amount of $775,000.

2) A letter from the trustee to Crocker demanding payment of the draft pursuant to the letter of credit.

3) A letter from the trustee to Crocker stating that Wells Fargo had requested "that a drawing be made" under the letter of credit.

4) A letter from Wells Fargo to Crocker requesting that $775,000 be drawn under the letter of credit. The letter stated that Colin failed to pay said amount within five days after demand and that the funds were necessary for continued operation of the business of the debtor.

5) A letter from Wells Fargo to the trustee with the same content as document 4) above.

6) A copy of the agreement which required Colin to make the additional contribution and provide the letter of credit.

7) A copy of the letter from Colin to Wells Fargo waiving Swift's bankruptcy as a defense to payment under the letter of credit.

1. The Board of Directors, being controlled by Colin, might have been reluctant to draw on the letter of credit. As a result, Wells Fargo as the principal lender of the debtor desired an independent right to draw on the letter of credit on Swift's behalf. . . .

8) A copy of the letter whereby Wells Fargo made demand on Colin to make the original contribution.

9) A copy of the notice of the trustee's appointment and a copy of the trustee's oath.

On October 7, 1981, Crocker refused to honor the documents submitted by the trustee. The reasons were as follows:

1) The draft was not drawn by the beneficiary of the letter of credit and was not payable at sight, as required by the letter of credit.

2) The letter of credit required a statement from Wells Fargo which must be manually signed by the beneficiary and followed by the designation "Corporate Secretary, Swift Aire Lines, Inc." This requirement was not met.

3) The letter of credit required a statement from Wells Fargo that the "funds are required by Swift Aire Lines, Inc. for the continued operation of its business . . ." Crocker contended that this statement was false at the time the documents were presented and, therefore, such presentment was defective.

4) The trustee did not have the power to draw under the letter of credit. 11 U.S.C. §365(c) was cited as an example.[2]

On October 19, 1981, the trustee filed a complaint against Crocker in the bankruptcy court for wrongful refusal to honor the letter of credit.

On March 25, 1982, the trial court filed its memorandum of decision stating that the trustee had filed the necessary documents to draw against the letter of credit and that there was no fraud by the trustee. On April 7, 1982, the court entered a corresponding money judgment against Crocker in favor of the trustee for $775,000 principal plus interest and costs. Crocker and Colin appeal this judgment.

II. PROCEDURAL RULINGS

[Omitted.]

III. SUMMARY JUDGMENT

LETTERS OF CREDIT

Generally three parties are involved with a letter of credit: the applicant or customer, the issuer, and the beneficiary. Normally, the applicant

---

2. This was presumably a reference to 11 U.S.C. §365(c)(2) which prevents assumption of an executory contract for a financial accommodation to or for the benefit of the debtor.

engages the issuer to pay a sum of money to the beneficiary when the beneficiary tenders certain documents, specified in the letter of credit, to the issuer. Letters of credit are used primarily to insure or support an underlying agreement by the applicant to pay money to the beneficiary. Nevertheless, the issuer's obligation to pay the beneficiary is not dependent on the underlying agreement between the applicant and the beneficiary. The issuer is only concerned with the documents tendered. If the issuer considers that the tendered documents appear on their face to not be in accordance with the terms and conditions of the letter of credit, the issuer must determine on the basis of the *documents alone* that compliance has not been effected. Uniform Customs and Practices for Documentary Credits, International Chamber of Commerce, Publication No. 290 (1974 rev. ed.)[4] When the necessary documents are tendered by the beneficiary to the issuer, the issuer is obligated to pay the beneficiary.[5]

Thus, in normal commercial settings, the beneficiary will prevail in an action for wrongful dishonor of documents tendered against a letter of credit only if such documents strictly comply with the terms of the letter of credit. . . . Crocker argues that the trial court erred as a matter of law in concluding that the documents tendered by the trustee strictly complied with the terms of the letter of credit. . . .

TRUSTEE AS BENEFICIARY AND POWER TO SIGN IN LIEU OF CORPORATE SECRETARY

A

There were two alternative means of drawing on the subject letter of credit. The first alternative required a statement from Swift that the additional contribution funds which Colin had agreed to pay remained unpaid five days following demand by Swift and that the Board of Directors of Swift has determined that such funds are required for the continued operation of the business. Such statement not appearing in the record, only the second alternative remained whereby the trustee might meet the requirements for drawing on the letter of credit.

The second alternative required a statement from Swift that Wells Fargo requested that a drawing of the additional contribution be made under the investment agreement. This statement was to be signed by the corporate secretary of Swift. This alternative also required a statement from Wells Fargo that the additional contribution which Colin had agreed to pay under the investment agreement remained unpaid five days following demand by Wells Fargo, and that Wells Fargo had determined that the funds were necessary for continued operation of Swift's business.

---

4. The letter of credit was made subject to these standards.
5. See California Commercial Code §5114.

B

Upon the filing of a bankruptcy petition under Chapter 7, the debtor's estate became the successor to certain legal and equitable property interests of Swift. The trustee became the representative of the estate with the power to deal with its property for the benefit [of] the estate. The bankruptcy estate of Swift is, represented by the trustee, a new legal entity distinct from the debtor Swift Aire Lines, Inc. E.g., 11 U.S.C. §§323, 363, 541, 704, and 721.

Swift's officers and directors have no power or authority to deal with the estate, its assets or its affairs. The trustee, only, is empowered to dispose of business assets, and when appropriate authority is obtained, to operate the business. By filing bankruptcy, Swift has made it impossible for Wells Fargo or Swift to draw against the letter of credit. Since there is no longer a corporate secretary able to act for the debtor, the statement required by the letter of credit cannot be signed by the designated individual.

The trial court has determined that the trustee is entitled to draw on the letter of credit because: 1) Bankruptcy law controls over applicable conflicting state law, and 2) that Crocker's refusal to recognize the trustee as legal successor and beneficiary on the letter of credit would only elevate form over substance, citing American Bell International v. Islamic Republic of Iran, 474 F. Supp. 420, 424 (S.D.N.Y. 1979).

We are unable to perceive the conflict of law alluded to by the court below. Assuming the letter of credit became property of the estate, the Bankruptcy Code did not give the trustee the power to automatically enforce payment thereunder if state law requiring strict compliance of tender documents would dictate otherwise.

The trial court's determination that Crocker's refusal to recognize the trustee as beneficiary would only elevate form over substance, is at odds with the doctrine of strict compliance. *American Bell* is clearly distinguishable from the case at bar and turns on principles of international law. In that case, presentation of a document from the Imperial Government of Iran, Ministry of War was required to draw against a letter of credit. Demand on the letter of credit was made after the Imperial Government was overthrown by the Islamic Republic of Iran, the actual presentation of documents being made by and in the name of the Islamic Republic. In allowing demand against the letter of credit, the court held that:

> American courts have traditionally viewed contract rights as vesting not in any particular government but in the state of which that government is an agent. 174 F. Supp. at 423.

In the domestic arena, American courts have traditionally viewed such rights under this type of transaction to vest in the named beneficiary alone.

Pursuant to the principle of strict compliance, the trustee failed to, and was precluded from, presenting documents conforming to the requirements of the letter of credit. As a result, Crocker's dishonor of the trustee's demand to draw on the letter of credit was justified. . . .

for TT

EXECUTORY CONTRACT/FINANCIAL ACCOMMODATION

[Omitted. See Chapter 7.]

IV. CONCLUSION

Pursuant to the doctrine of strict compliance and the inability of the trustee to assume the letter of credit, we reverse the decisions of the court below denying Crocker's motion for summary judgment and granting the trustee's motion for partial summary judgment. The case is remanded to the trial court to enter judgment consistent with this Opinion.

holding *see p. 190*

NOTES

1. Had *Swift Aire* filed a petition to reorganize under Chapter 11, would the case have come out the same? If the letter of credit had been issued to an individual, instead of to a corporation, would the filing of a petition in bankruptcy by that individual have produced the same result?

2. Does the rationale of *Swift Aire* apply to other types of property? We will look at one particular type of property when examining executory contracts and unexpired leases under §365 in Chapter 7 of this book. (Indeed, in a portion of the opinion omitted above, which we will discuss in Chapter 7, *Swift Aire* looked at the letter of credit as a form of executory contract.) Could other forms of property rights be limited by adding a provision conditioning access to that property right upon the existence of a writing signed by an officer of the debtor? If the debtor files for bankruptcy, does the property right disappear? Is that conclusion consistent with §541(c)(1)? If not, is there anything in the nature of the beneficiary's rights under a letter of credit requiring treatment different from other property rights? The following note discusses the attributes of letters of credit and the issues in *Swift Aire* in more detail.

NOTE ON *SWIFT AIRE* AND LETTERS OF CREDIT IN BANKRUPTCY

Letters of credit can be issued by anyone. The principal source of letters of credit, however, are banks, which issue them instead of guarantees. The parties to a letter-of-credit transaction are the "issuer" (the bank or other party that issues the letter), the "customer," who asks the bank to issue a letter of credit to "back up" its payment obligation, and the "beneficiary," who is entitled to draw on the letter of credit. It is thus a tripartite arrangement, with an underlying transaction between customer and beneficiary, a contract between customer and issuer, and a legal obligation upon issuance of the letter of credit between bank and beneficiary. (This legal obligation cannot be characterized as a contractual obligation or anything other than a "letter-of-credit obligation." It is an elementary relationship that cannot be broken down any further, and the nature of the relationship is the subject of a distinct body of law.)

The linchpin of the letter-of-credit transaction is the unique legal relationship between the bank and the beneficiary. Unlike a guarantor, the bank is primarily liable whenever the beneficiary presents a draft and documents that conform to the letter. (These documents, as is usually the case in what is called a "standby" letter of credit, may amount to nothing more than a letter, signed by an officer of the beneficiary, reciting a right to be paid because, for example, of a default in performance owed to the beneficiary by the customer on a contract between them.) Unlike its counterpart in a third-party beneficiary contract, the bank may not invoke the defenses its customer might have on the underlying contract. Moreover, the status of a beneficiary of a letter of credit is radically different from that of a payee of a check, who has no right to compel payment from the drawee bank. In the letter-of-credit transaction, the beneficiary does have the right to compel payment, and once the letter of credit is issued, the customer is powerless to stop payment in the absence of fraud. This difference exists because a letter of credit, unlike a negotiable instrument such as a check, is a binding and irrevocable obligation of the bank itself, not of the customer who procured it. The legal relationship between bank and beneficiary is governed by special principles which, like the law merchant in an earlier era, are nearly uniform throughout the world. See generally Baird, Standby Letters of Credit in Bankruptcy, 49 U. Chi. L. Rev. 130, 133-137 (1982).

The question in _Swift Aire_ was whether the trustee in bankruptcy could draw on a letter of credit naming the debtor as beneficiary. The court held no, seeing an irreconcilable conflict between allowing the trustee to do so and letter of credit policy. The nature of the conflict grew out of the court's view that a liquidating debtor under Chapter 7 of the Bankruptcy Code was a "new entity" from the pre-bankruptcy debtor, who could not enforce the letter of credit given that applicable law on letters of credit prohibited any assignment of the right to draw.

Considering the debtor in bankruptcy as a new entity, however, is merely creating a label. What matters are the attributes of a debtor in bankruptcy and of one outside of bankruptcy, and whether they are sufficiently different in some relevant respect to justify denying a debtor in bankruptcy rights that one outside of bankruptcy would have. Letters of credit may be drawn upon by presenting documents that comply exactly with those required by the letter of credit. In *Swift Aire*, the letter of credit called for a statement signed by the corporate secretary of Swift Aire. Presumably that requirement — unlike, for example, one calling for the signature of "John Smith, as corporate secretary" — would be satisfied by the signature of whomever happened to be Swift Aire's corporate secretary at the time of the draw. The letter of credit, for example, probably could have been drawn on by the corporate secretary in a state-law dissolution of Swift Aire. The appropriate question in bankruptcy may be whether the powers of the trustee have the same attributes as a successor outside of bankruptcy who could have drawn on the letter of credit. Does the trustee in bankruptcy here look like a surrogate for the officers of Swift Aire? If so, then the best way to allow bankruptcy law to mirror state law might be to allow the bankruptcy trustee to draw on the letter of credit. The court's perceived "conflict" between bankruptcy and nonbankruptcy law may have been of its own making.

Many bankruptcy cases involve businesses that will continue. In many Chapter 11 cases, the only thing that changes with the filing of the petition is the owners of the shares of stock. The old managers remain as debtors in possession and no trustee is appointed. The firm carries on its old business more or less as usual. The old shareholders, however, are cashed out, and the old creditors now enjoy the equity interest in the enterprise. If all that has really happened is a change in equity ownership, why should the debtor's right to draw on the letter of credit be limited? This may not thwart letter of credit policy; rather, it may simply approximate the non-bankruptcy consequences of the actual changes that have taken place in the enterprise.

The hard case we need to consider arises when the letter of credit requires the signature of the corporate secretary, but expressly provides that a bankruptcy trustee's signature would be insufficient. Must bankruptcy law respect this restriction or is this a situation explicitly covered by §541(c)(1)? It provides that an interest of the debtor in property (such as a letter of credit) becomes property of the estate notwithstanding any provision "that is conditioned on . . . the commencement of a case under this title . . . and that effects or gives an option to effect a forfeiture, modification, or termination of the debtor's interest in the property."

The troublesome feature of *Swift Aire* may be one that is adequately handled by nonbankruptcy law. To draw on the letter of credit, Swift Aire had to present a document certifying that cash was necessary for its ongoing business. But, as best we can tell, Swift Aire had ceased operations and would never operate again. Under nonbankruptcy law, however, there is an exception to the general rule that the issuer of the letter of credit must honor it when the documents comply. In most jurisdictions, a bank may be enjoined from honoring the letter of credit if the documents presented are fraudulent. See, e.g., Sztejn v. Schroder Banking Corp., 177 Misc. 719, 722, 31 N.Y.S.2d 631, 634-635 (Sup. Ct. 1941); UCC §5-114(2). Can one argue that the trustee's ability to draw on the letter of credit should turn on this doctrine rather than some independent bankruptcy rule?

A debtor and his general creditors do not always enjoy all of the proceeds from the sale of an asset. Sometimes one or more third parties have a superior right to a part or all of these proceeds. A recurring question is whether the right of some to payment before others should be respected in bankruptcy. The issue is often litigated because the continuation or transfer of a state privilege or license is conditioned on making certain payments on specified debts. The classic discussion of the problem is contained in the following case, in which the question was whether bankruptcy courts should recognize the rule that a seat on the Chicago Board of Trade could be sold only after debts to members of the Board were paid in full.

CHICAGO BOARD OF TRADE v. JOHNSON
264 U.S. 1 (1924)

Chief Justice TAFT delivered the opinion of the Court.

We have brought this cause before us by certiorari to review the action of the Circuit Court of Appeals of the Seventh Circuit in affirming, upon petition to review, a decree of the District Court for the Northern District of Illinois, in a summary proceeding dealing with the membership of a bankrupt in the Chicago Board of Trade. The District Court, finding that the membership was property and under the rules of the Board passed to the trustee in bankruptcy free of all claims of the members, ordered that it be held for transfer and sale for the benefit of the general creditors. . . .

Wilson F. Henderson, the bankrupt, a citizen of Chicago, was admitted to membership in the Board of Trade in 1899, and for many months prior to March 1, 1919, was president and one of the principal stockholders in a corporation known as Lipsey and Company, and actively engaged in making contracts on its behalf for present and future delivery of grain on the Board of Trade. In March, 1919, Lipsey and Company became insolvent and ceased to transact business, being then indebted to thirty or more members of the Exchange on its contracts in an aggregate amount of more than $60,000. A corporation is not admitted to membership of the Board, but under the rules it may do business on the Exchange if two of its executive officers, substantial stockholders, are members in good standing and give its name as principal in their contracts. The rules further provide that, if the corporation is accepted as a party to a contract and fails to comply with any of its obligations under the rules, its officers, as members, are subject to the same discipline as if they had failed to comply with an obligation of their own.

Any male person of good character and credit and of legal age, after his name has been duly posted for ten days, may be admitted to membership in the Board of Trade by ten votes of the Board of Directors, provided that three votes are not cast against him and that he pays an initiation fee of $25,000, or presents "an unimpaired or unforfeited membership, duly transferred," and signs "an agreement to abide by the Rules, Regulations and By-Laws of the Association." The rules further provide that a member, if he has paid all assessments and has no outstanding claims held against him by members, and the membership is not in any way impaired or forfeited, may, upon payment of a fee of $250, transfer his membership to any person eligible to membership approved by the Board, after ten days posting, both of the proposed transfer and of the name of substitute.

No rule exists giving to the Board of Trade or its members the right to compel sale or other disposition of memberships to pay debts. The only right of one member against another, in securing payment of an obligation, is to prevent the transfer of the membership of the debtor member by filing objection to such transfer with the Directors.

The membership of Henderson was worth $10,500 on January 24, 1920, when the petition in bankruptcy was filed against him. All assessments then due had been paid and the membership was not in any way impaired and forfeited. On May 1, 1919, Henderson had posted on the bulletin of the Exchange a notice and application for a transfer of his membership. Within ten days, two objections were filed, one of them on account of a debt due from Lipsey and Company. The objections were withdrawn, however, in December, 1919. On January 29, 1920, however, five days after the petition in bankruptcy was filed, members, creditors of Lipsey and Company on its defaulted contracts signed by Henderson, lodged with the Directors objections to the transfer. These objectors were respondents in the District Court and are petitioners here.

Under par. a, §70 of the bankrupt law of July 1, 1898, c. 541, 30 Stat. 565, the trustee takes the title of the bankrupt (3) to "powers which he might have exercised for his own benefit," and (5) to "property which prior to the filing of the petition he could by any means have transferred or which might have been levied upon and sold under judicial process against him." Petitioners insist that the membership is not property within (5). The Supreme Court of Illinois, from which State this Board of Trade derives its charter, has held, in Barclay v. Smith, 107, Ill. 349, that the membership is not property or subject to judicial sale, basing its conclusion on the ground that it can not be acquired except upon a vote of ten Directors, and can not be transferred to another unless the transfer is approved by the same vote, and that it can not be subjected to the payment of debts of the holder by legal proceedings. It is not possible to reconcile

Barclay v. Smith with the decisions of this Court. In Hyde v. Woods, 94 U.S. 523, the bankrupt was a member of the San Francisco Stock and Exchange Board, a voluntary association with an elective membership, and with a right in each member to sell his seat subject to an election, by the Directors, of the vendee as a member. This Court held the membership to be an incorporeal right and property which would pass to the trustee of the bankrupt, subject to the rules of the Board, which required first the payment of all debts due to the members. In Sparhawk v. Yerkes, 142 U.S. 1, the conclusion in Hyde v. Woods was reaffirmed in respect of seats in the Stock Exchanges of New York and Philadelphia, which were then voluntary unincorporated associations, with the same provision as to membership and preference for the debts of member creditors. In Page v. Edmunds, 187 U.S. 596, the question was whether a seat of a bankrupt in the Philadelphia Stock Exchange was property passing to the trustee under subdivision 5 of §70 of the Bankrupt Act. In that association, no member could sell his seat if he had unsettled claims on the Exchange. In case of insolvency, the seat could be sold, and the proceeds distributed to the member creditors. The Supreme Court of Pennsylvania had held, just as in this case the Supreme Court of Illinois has held, that such membership was not property, and could not be seized in execution for debts of its holder. Thompson v. Adams, 93 Pa. St. 55; Pancoast v. Gowen, 93 Pa. St. 66. These were the cases relied on by the Supreme Court of Illinois to sustain its view. Referring to the Pennsylvania decisions in Page v. Edmunds (p. 603), this Court said:

> It is not certain whether the learned court intended to say that the seat was not property at all, or not property because it could not be seized in execution for debts. If the former, we cannot concur. The facts of this case demonstrate the contrary. If the latter, it does not affect the pending controversy. The power of the appellant to transfer it was sufficient to vest it in his trustee.

The Court thus held that the question was to be determined by reference to the language of the Bankrupt Act and that the seat was property "which prior to the filing of the petition he [the bankrupt] could by any means have transferred." It declined to limit the definition of property under subdivision (5) to such as the state courts might hold could be seized in execution by judicial process. Subdivision (3), vesting in the trustee title to powers which the bankrupt might exercise for his own benefit, manifests a purpose to make the assets of the estate broadly inclusive. By a construction not unduly strained, subdivision (3) might be held to include a power to transfer a seat on the Exchange, subject to its rules, if it were necessary. . . .

Congress derives its power to enact a bankrupt law from the Federal Constitution, and the construction of it is a federal question. Of course, where the bankrupt law deals with property rights which are regulated by the state law, the federal courts in bankruptcy will follow the state courts; but when the language of Congress indicates a policy requiring a broader construction of the statute than the state decisions would give it, federal courts can not be concluded by them. Board of Trade v. Weston, 243 Fed. 332.

Counsel for petitioners urges that the *Hyde, Sparhawk* and *Page* cases differ from the one before us, in that the rules of the associations there under consideration provided specifically for a sale of the seat and a preferred distribution of the proceeds to the creditor members, whereas here there is no sale provided for at all, at the instance of the Board or its members who are creditors. Their only protection is in the power to prevent a transfer as long as the member's obligations to them are unperformed. We do not think this makes a real difference in the character of the property which the member has in his seat. He can transfer it or sell it subject to a right of his creditors to prevent his transfer or sale till he settles with them, a right in some respects similar to the typical lien of the common law, defined as "a right in one man to retain that which is in his possession belonging to another, till certain demands of him the person in possession are satisfied." Hammonds v. Barclay, 2 East 235. Peck v. Jenness, 7 How. 612, 620. The right of the objecting creditor members differs, however, from the common law lien, in that the latter, to exist and be effective, must deprive the owner of possession and enjoyment, whereas the former is consistent with possession and personal enjoyment by the owner, and only interferes with, and prevents, alienation. . . .

. . . The District Court ordered the transfer and sale of the seat free from all the claims and objections of the petitioners. The view of the court was that, because Henderson had duly posted his intention to transfer in May, 1919, and all the objections of creditor members then filed against such transfer had been settled or withdrawn before the petition in bankruptcy was filed against him, the right of the member creditors to object to the transfer had been lost. [The Supreme Court's reasons for disagreeing with this reading of the Board's rules are omitted.]

Nor is there any weight to the argument that, as the preference claims of petitioners were not asserted until after bankruptcy proceedings were begun, the transfer to the trustee was rendered free from their objection. Such a claim was negatived in Hyde v. Woods, supra. The preference of the member creditors is not created after bankruptcy. The lien, if it can be called such, is inherent in the property in its creation, and it can be asserted at any time before actual transfer. Indeed, the danger of bankruptcy of the member is perhaps the chief reason, and a legitimate one, for creating the lien.

We think, therefore, that the District Court and the Circuit Court of Appeals erred on the merits of the case. The claims of the petitioners amount to more than sixty thousand dollars, and these must be satisfied before the trustee can realize anything on the transfer of the seat for the general estate. . . .

NOTE ON CHICAGO BOARD OF TRADE v. JOHNSON

In *Chicago Board of Trade,* exactly what is property of the estate? In light of *Butner v. United States,* supra page 35, was it proper for the Court to reject the interpretation placed on a seat by the Illinois Supreme Court in *Barclay v. Smith?* We will later consider, in connection with §365, what limitations may be placed on the assignment of contracts in bankruptcy, but §541(c)(1) does not allow such limitations to keep property out of the estate in the first place. For now, consider Professor Countryman's comment on *Chicago Board of Trade:* "But, while what is 'property' was a question of federal bankruptcy law, the attributes of that property were still determined by state law and . . . the trustee won a Pyrrhic victory." Countryman, The Use of State Law in Bankruptcy Cases, Part I, 17 N.Y.U. L. Rev. 407, 438 (1972).

Chicago Board of Trade reminds us that when we speak of whether something has value, we have to identify: *value to whom?* In this case, the Court's holding is that membership on the Board of Trade has value to Henderson's creditors, but that this value is subject to the superior claims of those creditors who also are members of the Board of Trade.

But is there another issue lurking in *Chicago Board of Trade?* In the case as it existed, Henderson had already put the seat up for sale. But what if he had not? Illinois had said that the seat was not "property," but behind that label was a statement of attributes. According to the Illinois courts, creditors could not levy on this membership, nor could they force its sale. Under such circumstances, should the trustee be able to sell the seat if Henderson objects? We will examine that question in Chapter 11 of this book, since it principally involves a question of debtors who are individuals.

Assume, however, that the debtor in *Chicago Board of Trade* was a corporation. If creditors could not force sale of the seat outside of bankruptcy, should the trustee be able to force its sale inside of bankruptcy? Isn't it proper to view the trustee as manager of the corporation in bankruptcy, and, thus, the decision to sell it as effectively being made by the debtor?

What if the rule of the Board of Trade was that the seat could not be assigned at all? Would that rule be respected in bankruptcy? Under the old Act, the answer would seem to be that, because it was not assignable, the seat was not property of the estate. Does anything change in looking at §541(c)(1)? Is §541(c)(2) relevant? With such a rule, in a dissolution of the corporation outside of bankruptcy, wouldn't the membership be without value to the creditors? Should the answer be any different because the debtor is liquidating in bankruptcy? What if the debtor was reorganizing in bankruptcy? Would the same result follow? Do *Chicago Board of Trade* and *Swift Aire* ultimately raise similar issues?

In the materials we have so far examined in this Chapter, we have been focusing on how to distinguish state law directives: When will bankruptcy law respect a state determination that someone else should "win," in the sense of having first "dibs" to some assets? The inquiry can be focused in terms of "ownership" or "trust," on the one hand, or "lien," "security interest," or "priority," on the other. The issue is whether the estate should have the right to the asset for the benefit of the creditors as a group, or whether one particular creditor should be able to exclude the others from sharing in the asset (at least until its claim is satisfied). Do we have a guiding principle to help us decide when state law should be followed and when it should be overridden? Consider this question in light of the following material, which revolves around the Ninth Circuit's attempt to grapple with these issues over the last two decades.

NOTE ON ELLIOTT v. BUMB AND TRUST TRACING

Elliott v. Bumb, 356 F.2d 749 (9th Cir.), cert. denied, 385 U.S. 829 (1966), involved a statute providing that an issuer of money orders (called, in the statute, the "agent") held the proceeds of money orders in trust for the benefit of the person in whose name the money order was issued (called the "licensee"). The statute further provided that if the agent commingled the proceeds with its own assets, "all assets of such agent shall be impressed with a trust in favor of . . . the licensee in the amount equal to the aggregate funds received or which should have been received by the agent from such sale." The statute also provided that the trust would remain until the amount due to the licensee was paid in full. The Ninth Circuit held that, insofar as the funds were identifiable, they were properly held in trust, and hence immune from the claims of the agent's creditors in bankruptcy, because "[a]lthough one may become bankrupt, property which is held by him in trust belongs to the beneficiaries of the trust." The Ninth Circuit, however, invalidated in bankruptcy any trust extending to the general assets of the issuer of the money orders. The court, after noting that this would "relieve check and money order principals from the burden of tracing commingled funds," concluded that:

> Giving effect to the provisions of [the statute] . . . would open the door to state creation of priorities in favor of various classes of creditors by labeling such priorities as "trusts." This would tend to thwart or obstruct the scheme of federal bankruptcy.

Elliott v. Bumb, 356 F.2d, at 754-755. In re Telemart Enterprises, 524 F.2d 761 (9th Cir. 1975), had this to say about the *Elliott* distinction:

> Under state law, the issuer of the money order accepted payment only in the capacity of a trustee; he never held absolute ownership of the funds. We respected the state's definition of the issuer's relationship to those paid-in funds. On the other hand, we disregarded the state's attempt to impose a

"trust" on funds whose ownership had vested previously in the issuer. Regardless of the state's terminology, the effect of the statute was to give one class of creditors — purchasers of money orders — priority in the distribution of the bankrupt issuer's general assets.

Has *Elliott* focused on the right question? Does bankruptcy law have a policy against certain forms of tracing rules? All state-created entitlements act in favor of some group of creditors, but bankruptcy law recognizes them nonetheless. Isn't the relevant inquiry whether the state statute applied only in bankruptcy? *Elliott* never gets around to that issue; can its opinion be justified in absence of that issue? At that time, the Bankruptcy Act of 1898 contained a provision invalidating, as against the trustee, statutory liens "on personal property not accompanied by possession of, or by levy upon or by sequestration or distraint of, such property." §67(c)(2). Does this provision help explain the distinction drawn in Elliott v. Bumb? (The statute appeared to validate the trust outside of bankruptcy, by stating that an amount equal to the trust funds "shall not be subject to attachment, levy of execution or sequestration, by order of court. . . ." The actual effect of this provision, however, was unexplored.)

In re Independence Land Title Corp., 18 Bankr. 673 (Bankr. N.D. Ill. 1982) discussed the limits of trust law in bankruptcy as follows:

> [T]he extent to which Staub can identify and trace any money from the original escrow account into the trustee's fund is the extent to which Staub can claim the identified and traceable funds as his own, to the exclusion of all other creditors. However, to the extent that Staub cannot identify and trace the trustee's funds as proceeds of the original escrow account, Staub only has the rights of a general unsecured creditor. Numerous cases have held that when a trustee possesses funds which the debtor once held as trustee or agent, the person claiming such funds is a general unsecured creditor to the extent he cannot identify or trace the funds in the trustee's hands back to the original trust or escrow account.

See also In re Casco Electric Corp., 28 Bankr. 191 (Bankr. E.D.N.Y.) aff'd, 35 Bankr. 731 (E.D.N.Y. 1983); In re Treiling, 21 Bankr. 940 (Bankr. E.D.N.Y. 1982).

Pursue this inquiry further. Could state law adopt a method of tracing commingled funds, such as a lowest intermediate balance method for tracing into a deposit account? (Under this approach, if one can identify how much trust money goes *into* a deposit account, then one presumes that withdrawals from that account are made first from nontrust money, and only after nontrust money is exhausted, from trust money. The process can repeat itself. See Restatement (Second) of Trusts §202.) See In re Martin, 25 Bankr. 25 (Bankr. N.D. Tex. 1982) (yes). If a state could adopt such a tracing method and have it enforced in bankruptcy, why can't it simply impress all of the debtor's assets with a "trust" for the amount of the money coming in? Isn't this simply another, equally fictional, form of "tracing"? See Elliott v. Bumb, and consider the following excerpt, from the legislative history to §541, discussing the applicability of trust tracing rules to the Internal Revenue Service's location of withheld taxes:

> The courts should permit the use of reasonable assumptions under which the Internal Revenue Service, and other tax authorities, can demonstrate that amounts of withheld taxes are still in the possession of the debtor at the commencement of the case. For example, where the debtor had commingled that amount of withheld taxes in his general checking account, it might be reasonable to assume that any remaining amounts in that account on the commencement of the case are the withheld taxes. In addition, Congress may consider future amendments to the Internal Revenue Code making clear that amounts of withheld taxes are held by the debtor in a trust relationship and, consequently, that such amounts are not property of the estate.

PROBLEM

4.5 Debtor incurs a $3,000 medical bill from Hospital for a recent illness. Debtor submits a reimbursement bill to her insurance company, and the insurance company sends her a check for $2,500. The Debtor then files for bankruptcy, not yet having paid Hospital. May Hospital assert that it is entitled to the $2,500 from the insurance company? See legislative history to §541. Does it matter whether or not the check has been deposited in Debtor's bank account? Whether Debtor's bank account has $2,500 in it at the time of bankruptcy? see p. 197

NOTE ON *TELEMART ENTERPRISES* AND TYPES OF PROPERTY INTERESTS

A recurrent issue in bankruptcy is how one distinguishes between property of the debtor at the time of bankruptcy (which is property of the estate) and property of another. In such cases, a particular claimant is attempting to use a state-law definition of property to get "its" asset back. If the claimant loses that argument, it then must file a claim, generally as an unsecured creditor, in the bankruptcy proceeding, where it will share in the general assets of the estate along with other unsecured creditors.

In examining this issue, the question is often posed as one asking the extent to which bankruptcy law should follow state law determinations of property rights. That is, for example, how the issue was framed in *Gunder*.

In re Telemart Enterprises, 524 F.2d 761 (9th Cir. 1975), discussed three categories of state-property rights that have different bankruptcy attributes: (1) true statutory liens; (2) "spurious" statutory liens; and (3) state priorities. Generally, *Telemart* noted, true statutory liens are "valid" in bankruptcy (i.e., the holder's property right will be respected in bankruptcy, and that holder may exercise it in full), whereas the other two categories — "spurious" statutory liens and state priorities — were not to be recognized in bankruptcy.

Distinguishing between these categories, then, may be important. According to *Telemart*, a state-created priority is a specification, by the state, of who gets paid first out of the *general* assets of the estate in bankruptcy. The court suggested that such a rule would "derogate from the rights of general creditors" by attempting "to direct the disposition of assets to which the bankrupt had received a nondefeasible title." Consider, however, this rationale. Is the state attempting to direct the disposition of title in bankruptcy more here than with respect to other sorts of property rights? This question is examined in some detail in the material that follows.

As for a spurious statutory lien, *Telemart* stated that such liens were really nothing more than disguised state-created priorities. Because of the drafting history of the 1898 Act, state-created priorities were first disallowed in 1938; states then renamed what once had been called priorities as "liens." Section 67c of the 1898 Act attempted to disallow this by invalidating "every statutory lien which first becomes effective upon the insolvency of the debtor, or upon distribution or liquidation of his property" as well as "every statutory lien which is not perfected or enforceable at the date of bankruptcy against one acquiring the rights of a bona fide purchaser from the debtor on that date." (This provision is now in §545.) Spurious liens were considered bad, therefore, because they had no operative consequence outside of bankruptcy — they did not look like true liens at all. Either they were effective only in bankruptcy *or*, unlike true liens, they were not effective against purchasers. So, the conclusion was: This is really just another attempt to provide for who receives what from the general assets of the estate — and hence is like a priority. It makes sense to invalidate such spurious liens *if* one is already invalidating state-created priorities. The question that remains, of course, is why one invalidates state-created priorities.

This leaves a third category of property rights — "true" statutory liens — that *Telemart* suggested were valid in bankruptcy. The difference between true and spurious statutory liens, essentially, is that true statutory liens are effective whether or not an insolvency proceeding (such as bankruptcy) has begun. The "principle" that *Telemart* seems to enunciate is that state interests cannot discriminate against bankruptcy. Instead, a state must show that it is serious about the property rights it grants by making them general rights, before it will be allowed to override bankruptcy's policy to treat like claims alike.

What is the force of this principle, however? The excerpt that follows addresses that question.

JACKSON, BANKRUPTCY, NON-BANKRUPTCY ENTITLEMENTS, AND THE CREDITORS' BARGAIN
91 Yale L.J. 857, 901-906 (1982)

Beginning in the late 1930's, changes made to the Bankruptcy Act of 1898 have consistently moved in the direction of refusing to recognize attempts by a state to elevate the claims of any one type of claimant in bankruptcy through the device of either a state-created priority[204] or a statutory lien effective only in bankruptcy (or a similar non-bankruptcy occurrence).[205] These attempts by a state were felt to contradict, in a fundamental way, the notion that "equality is equity." Initiation of a bankruptcy proceeding is not, under this view, a reason for calling forth a different set of allocative entitlements by any creditor or class of creditors than existed outside of bankruptcy. The refusal to recognize a state's attempt to influence directly bankruptcy's allocation rules has raised few, if any, eyebrows. Indeed, the opposite has occurred: the purported application of the . . . principle has sometimes struck down state-created entitlements that, instead of suffering from the "bankruptcy only" problems of state-created priorities or bankruptcy statutory liens,[206] appeared to be all but indistinguishable from ordinary non-bankruptcy entitlements.

What, if anything, is wrong with state-created priorities and bankruptcy statutory liens? . . . First, is there any justification at all for a state's attempt to prefer a given type of creditor in bankruptcy? Second, if there is a justification for such an attempt, is there any reason to believe that the use of state-created priorities and bankruptcy statutory liens is not a proper way to implement those desired preferences?

Several reasons, other than simply political expedience or special interest group pressure, may explain a state's desire to provide a level of protection to certain types of claimants, instead of leaving the issue to the area of consensual security interests. First, non-consensual claimants, such

---

204. "Priorities are to be distinguished from property rights. . . . The priority creditor . . . has no property right, merely a statutory advantage to be given effect on distribution." J. MacLachlan, [Bankruptcy 145 (1956)]. . . .

205. The 1938 legislation, which dropped the bankruptcy priority for state-created priorities, also expressly validated state-created statutory liens, but declared that they would be paid after administration and wage priorities. Chandler Act, ch. 575, §67c, 52 Stat. 877 (1938). In 1952, an amendment struck down all statutory liens that attached to personal property and were not accompanied by "possession, levy, sequestration or distraint." Act of July 7, 1952, ch. 579, 66 Stat. 420. When this test proved unsatisfactory, Congress amended §67c of the Bankruptcy Act of 1898 to strike down statutory liens that became "effective upon the insolvency of the debtor, or upon distribution or liquidation of his property, or upon execution against his property levied at the instance of one other than the lienor" or were not "perfected or enforceable at the date of bankruptcy against one acquiring the rights of a bona fide purchaser from the debtor on that date. . . ." 11 U.S.C. §107c(1)(B) (1975) (repealed prospectively, effective October 1, 1979). . . .

206. Hereinafter, statutory liens effective only in bankruptcy will be referred to as "bankruptcy statutory liens," to distinguish them from statutory liens of a normal sort, which have a recognized existence and validity in and out of bankruptcy.

as tort creditors, pose special problems to which application of a consensual model seems largely inapplicable. Should a state believe that a certain level of deterrence is desirable to protect against certain behavior, a system of priority entitlements to "victims" of that behavior may help the state achieve that goal, at least with respect to some types of torts.[210] By giving non-consensual tort claimants priority over general unsecured creditors, those general creditors (whose chance of repayment has been made more risky than under a proportional payment scheme) will have an increased incentive to monitor the debtor to reduce the likelihood of such torts occurring in the first place.[211] Second, a state may have reason to believe that, with respect to a particular class of claimants, there is systematic advantage-taking of them by other creditors, because of an informational disparity or other reasons. Intervention by a state, in giving this class of claimants priority entitlements, may be a way of addressing a form of market inefficiency. Finally, the state is itself likely to be a claimant (often-times, as in its taxing capacity, a non-consensual one), in which case the level of priority it provides is a part of the cost calculus it has decided on in setting its rates (whether tax rates or otherwise).

There may be inefficient interferences by a state as well, due to politically-motivated causes. But the relevant point is that state interventions may sometimes be efficient or otherwise justified and, in any event, are generally recognized in bankruptcy. The bankruptcy law upholds state-created entitlements unless the entitlement is directed specifically at the bankruptcy process.[215] Unless there is some reason to believe that inefficiently motivated instances of state interference are more common with respect to state-created priorities or bankruptcy statutory liens than with respect to other forms of state-created entitlements, inquiry into the validity of an entitlement should first be directed at the *form* of the intervention. The relevant inquiry is whether there is anything particularly undesirable about state-created priorities or bankruptcy statutory liens that justifies the blanket prohibition against them in the bankruptcy process and that distinguishes them from other forms of non-bankruptcy entitlements.

State-created priorities and bankruptcy statutory liens attempt to direct allocative entitlements in bankruptcy, but in this respect they are

210. Cf. Posner, The Rights of Creditors of Affiliated Corporations, 43 U. Chi. L. Rev. 499, 506 (1976) (discussing involuntary extensions of credit in negotiation-based model). To be sure, insurance may also serve some of these goals. But it is unlikely that insurance will be able to curb that behavior as well as a priority rule. Therefore, even if one were to have an insurance scheme, one might nonetheless want to have a priority scheme as well.

211. The issue of priority among creditors that is raised by a state-created priority or bankruptcy statutory lien does not deal directly with incentives to have the debtor behave in a socially desirable fashion. Equity-holders come after creditors, whether or not a state-created priority is created or recognized. (Indirectly, of course, there are incentives arising from monitoring and the cost of credit.) Direct incentives are created by such things as removing the discharge right with respect to certain debts. . . .

215. See Bankruptcy Code §545 (distinguishing between valid and invalid statutory liens); 124 Cong. Rec. H11,114 (Sept. 28, 1978).

indistinguishable from other types of non-bankruptcy entitlements routinely recognized in bankruptcy. The difficulty with state-created priorities and bankruptcy statutory liens is that they suffer from [a] "bankruptcy incentive" problem[].

. . . Since the rules of the bankruptcy process set the minimum level of entitlements against which non-bankruptcy "workouts" must be evaluated, a creditor enjoying a state-created priority effective only in bankruptcy will demand to be treated similarly outside of bankruptcy as well. A creditor with such a priority might push for initiation of the bankruptcy process when it is not in the aggregate interests of the creditors to do so. But because a creditor with a state-created priority does not necessarily have that priority right outside of the bankruptcy process, he must negotiate with the other creditors in order to receive that preferential treatment. These negotiations, because they are likely to involve a number of unsecured creditors, may involve free-rider problems that will not only make negotiations costly but also may lead ultimately to an inefficient use of the bankruptcy process. . . . Refusing to recognize state-created priorities and bankruptcy statutory liens simply requires a state that wishes to give someone a "priority" to do so by means of an entitlement that is good in and out of bankruptcy. . . .

[B]ankruptcy law's obsession with formulating a rule on the subject may have done more harm than good. For while the prohibition on state-created entitlements good only in bankruptcy may occasionally strike down an aberrant state statute designed to create an irrational form of entitlement, the presence of the federal rule has, meanwhile, led to substantial confusion in its application. For if an entitlement is enforceable both in and out of bankruptcy, there is no reason, stemming from the justifications underlying condemnation of state-created priorities or bankruptcy statutory liens, to refuse recognition of the entitlement. The failure to recognize this simple point has led to a variety of confusing and ill-considered decisions by appellate courts. The rule against state-created priorities and bankruptcy statutory liens, if correctly understood, may be harmless and even occasionally beneficial. But since the reasons for the rule are misperceived, the resulting misapplications may engender more uncertainty than continuation of the rule is worth.

NOTE ON STATUTORY TRUSTS

Characterizations may matter, as cases such as Elliott v. Bumb and In re Telemart Enterprises suggest. Selby v. Ford Motor Co., 590 F.2d 642 (6th Cir. 1979), presents a common example. That case dealt with a Michigan statute providing for a "trust fund" for the benefit of the owner and subcontractors on construction projects. The statute provided:

the building contract fund paid by any person to a contractor . . . shall be considered by this act to be a trust fund, for the benefit of the person making the payment, contractors, laborers, subcontractors or materialmen, and the contractor . . . shall be considered the trustee of all such funds so paid to him for building construction purposes.

In *Selby,* Ford had hired Debtor to do construction work. Debtor, in turn, hired subcontractors. When the work was finished, Ford owed $350,000 to Debtor and Debtor, in turn, owed most of that to the various subcontractors. Ford, by agreement with Debtor, paid the subcontractors directly and those amounts were deducted from Ford's obligations to Debtor. (Because the payments were made before bankruptcy, the actual issue in the case involved one of preferences. But the underlying question was whether the money was Debtor's or the subcontractors. The issue would be the same if Debtor had filed for bankruptcy before Ford made the payments.) The question is really one of the priority of the subcontractors to the money, although it can be phrased in terms of whether the money is Debtor's or someone else's — whether, in short, it is property of the estate or not. The issue comes up because of the Michigan statute. Should this statute be recognized in bankruptcy? *Selby* had the following analysis:

> Conceptually, the Michigan builders trust fund statute can be viewed in any one of three ways: (1) as imposing a traditional trust on the contractor's funds for the benefit of subcontractors, laborers and materialmen; or (2) as creating a security arrangement in the nature of a statutory lien; or (3) as creating no security or other interest recognizable under the Bankruptcy Act.
>
> Viewed as a traditional trust, the beneficial interests in the trust fund would not be the "property" of the bankrupt contractor or his estate in bankruptcy. The subcontractors would own the beneficial title to the trust, and the contractor would simply hold legal title to the funds as trustee. . . .
>
> A statutory lien, on the other hand, is not effective against the claims of the trustee in bankruptcy unless it is perfected prior to the filing of the petition in bankruptcy. . . . Statutory trusts, however, arise automatically. No notice or filing is required, and perfection is beside the point. . . .
>
> Although there is authority to the contrary with respect to statutory tax trusts, the few cases on the question characterize other statutory trusts as traditional trusts for purposes of bankruptcy. Commentators have criticized this result, however. They say that statutory trusts should be treated as statutory liens because statutory trusts function as a security device, and "the application of a national bankruptcy statute to legal interests diversely defined" by the states requires classification "on the basis of function rather than nomenclature." But no cases have adopted this approach, and this criticism overlooks the traditional role of the states in creating and defining the underlying property interests and commercial arrangements to which the Bankruptcy Act applies.

Is this convincing? In light of cases such as *Elliott,* how would the statute have fared if Ford had made a payment of $350,000 to Debtor shortly before bankruptcy? Would it depend on whether the money could be traced? If so, is that because of state law or bankruptcy law?

In the cases that follow, the Ninth Circuit addresses the issue raised in *Chicago Board of Trade* in a series of cases involving the transfer of liquor licenses.

IN RE LESLIE
520 F.2d 761 (9th Cir. 1975)

DUNIWAY, Circuit Judge.

Twelve creditors of Leslie, the bankrupt, appeal from the district court's affirmance of an order of the referee in bankruptcy directing that certain proceeds from the sale of the bankrupt's liquor business be turned over to trustee of the bankrupt estate. We affirm.

The facts are not in dispute. In March, 1971, the bankrupt executed an agreement to sell his California on-sale liquor license and related business assets to one Daniels for $25,000. In April, 1971, as required by §§24073-24074 of the California Business and Professions Code, an escrow was opened in which Daniels deposited the consideration. In August, 1971, the state Alcoholic Beverage Control Department (ABC) approved the sale. On September 9, 1971, Leslie filed his petition in bankruptcy.

Sections 24073-24074 provide that transfer of a licensed liquor business must be approved by ABC and that before the filing of the transfer application the transferee must deposit in an escrow the consideration for both the license itself and the other business assets. Upon ABC approval, the license and other assets pass to the transferee and the escrow holder distributes the proceeds to the seller and his creditors following a specified procedure. If the proceeds are insufficient to pay all of the creditors' claims, they are distributed in accordance with a priority scheme delineated in §24074.

The appellant-creditors claim that they are entitled to share the funds remaining in the escrow by virtue of the sixth priority. Priority Sixth reads:

> Sixth, to the payment of claims for goods sold and delivered to the transferor for resale at his licensed premises and the payment of claims for services rendered, performed, or supplied in connection with the operation of the licensed business.

Other general creditors are relegated to priority Seventh.

Appellants are wrong. Upon Leslie's bankruptcy, title to the proceeds in question passed to the trustee under §70(a)(5) of the Bankruptcy Act, 11 U.S.C. §110(a)(5), for distribution in accordance with the priorities enumerated in §64 of the Act, 11 U.S.C. §104, with any remainder to be divided pro rata among the bankrupt's general creditors. Conflicting priorities established by state law must yield upon the intervention of bankruptcy to superior federal law. See Elliott v. Bumb, 9 Cir., 1966, 356 F.2d 749, 754-755. . . . Section 24074 creates statutory priorities, not statutory liens. See Grover Escrow Corp. v. Gole, 1969, 71 Cal. 2d 61, 65, 77 Cal. Rptr. 21, 23, 453 P.2d 461, 463 [characterizing §24074 as establishing a mandatory and exclusive system of priorities].

The cases relied on by appellants are inapposite. In United States v. State of California, 9 Cir., 1960, 281 F.2d 726, we held that ABC could validly condition transfer of a bankrupt's liquor license on payment of delinquent state taxes, even though the license was subject to a paramount federal tax lien and the transferee was the purchaser at an auction held to satisfy the lien. The panel observed that the issue in the case was not the supremacy of the federal tax lien over the claim for state taxes, but the nature of property to which the lien attached:

> Here the license existed because the state had issued it. If the licensee acquired something of value, it was because the state had bestowed it upon him. Whatever value the license, as property, may have had to a purchaser depended upon its transferability. If it was transferable, it was because the state had made it so. If the state had seen fit to impose conditions upon issuance or upon transfer of property *it has wholly created*, that is the state's prerogative *so long as its demands are not arbitrary or discriminatory*. Id., 281 F.2d at 728 (emphasis added).

The case at bar is different in two respects. First, not only the proceeds from the bankrupt's liquor license, but the proceeds from his other business assets are involved here. While §24074 is applicable to the latter proceeds, . . . the rationale of *State of California* is not, because the property sold is not state created. Second, as to transfer of the license itself, the condition imposed by §24074 on which appellants rely, *viz.*, the sixth priority for distribution of the escrow funds, does not seek to benefit the state, but a particular group of creditors. Precisely such attempts by the states to prefer favored groups of creditors led to the Chandler Act's elimination of state created priorities from the Bankruptcy Act in 1938. . . .

Thus, while a state, as the creator of a liquor license, may validly impose conditions on its transferability for the state's own benefit, it may not, consistently with paramount federal law, impose conditions which discriminate in favor of particular classes of creditors.

Board of Trade v. Johnson, 1924, 264 U.S. 1, 44 S. Ct. 232, 68 L. Ed. 533, and Hyde v. Woods, 1877, 94 U.S. 523, 24 L. Ed. 264, are also distinguishable. Each held that a trading exchange could validly condition transfer of a bankrupt member's seat on payment of debts owed to other members of the exchange, who collectively constituted the exchange and thus had created the seats. As in the *State of California* case, the property involved in each case was only that created solely by the creditor(s), and the conditions on transfer were imposed solely for the benefit of the seat's creator(s).

Appellant's suggestion that title to the escrow funds did not pass to the trustee under §70(a)(5) is also wrong. That section provides that the trustee is vested by operation of law with title to "property . . . to which prior to the filing of the petition he [the bankrupt] could by any means have transferred or which might have been levied upon and sold under judicial process against him, or otherwise seized, impounded, or sequestered. . . ." Under §24074 title to the funds in escrow after ABC approval of the transfer was in the transferor, Leslie, subject to the claims of bona fide creditors. If the transferor disputes any claim, the creditor must attach the funds and institute judicial proceedings. Clearly, therefore, the escrow funds are "property . . . which . . . might have been levied upon and sold under judicial process . . . or otherwise seized, impounded or sequestered. . . ."

Affirmed.

NOTE

The Ninth Circuit states that "section 24074 creates statutory priorities, not statutory liens." Why should that characterization make any difference? Is the characterization, in any case, correct? The Ninth Circuit cites Grover Escrow Corp. v. Gole in support of that statement. The statement from *Grover Escrow Corp.* follows. Does it support the Ninth Circuit's view?

> The precise issue is whether that section [24074] precludes a creditor from establishing priority over the escrowed proceeds of such a transaction by attachment or garnishment. We conclude that section 24074 represents a mandatory and exclusive scheme for payment of creditors of liquor license transferors, giving creditors who comply with that section priority over those who employ any form of levy on the proceeds.

Would *Leslie* have been decided differently if the court in *Grover Escrow Corp.* had used "a lien" instead of "priority" in the last sentence? Should this choice of words in a nonbankruptcy context matter? Shouldn't what matters be the substantive result — that complying creditors trump those who later levy?

NOTE ON *PROFESSIONAL BAR* AND
PETITE AUBERGE VILLAGE

One year after *Leslie,* in In re Professional Bar Co., 537 F.2d 338 (9th
Cir. 1976), the Ninth Circuit confronted the question of whether the State
of California could keep money paid it as a condition of transferring
on-sale liquor licenses. The trustee asserted, on behalf of certain wage
claimants, that the state had to return the money because, under bankruptcy law, these wage claims had priority over those of general creditors.
(We shall examine the subject of bankruptcy priorities in Chapter 8.)
Under Cal. Bus. & Prof. Code §24049 as it existed at that time, the Department of Alcoholic Beverage Control could refuse to transfer a liquor
license as long as certain state taxes remaind delinquent. In light of that
statute, the Ninth Circuit held for the state, asserting that "the problem is
not so much one of priority of claims as one of defining the nature of the
bankrupt's property to which the claims attach." It went on to elaborate as
follows:

> Our conclusion that Section 24049 is not in conflict with the law of
> bankruptcy is compatible with our prior holdings that conflicting priorities
> established by state law must yield to federal supremacy upon the interven-
> tion of bankruptcy. See, e.g., Elliott v. Bumb, 356 F.2d 749 (9th Cir. 1966).
> Because the state creates and controls its liquor licenses, the terms of any
> transfer of a license necessarily remain the prerogative of the state. If the
> state chooses to create conditions which make the transfer value of a license a
> net value after the state's claims are satisfied, that residual value is all that the
> trustee may look to.
>   We agree with the district court that the state is entitled to its exactions,
> but it is federal and not state law that must be applied to determine the
> distribution of the estate as diminished. *In re Leslie.* . . . Although Cal. Bus.
> and Prof. Code §24074 . . . establishes a system of priorities among credi-
> tors in the transfer of a state liquor license, federal rather than California law
> must be applied in deciding priority when the net proceeds in issue have
> become available to the trustee.

Is this case consistent with *Leslie*? Is *Professional Bar* correct to suggest
that "the problem is not so much one of priority of claims as one of
defining the nature of the bankrupt's property"? Isn't the state just making
sure that it gets paid first? Should the issue be any different if the state were
ensuring that another creditor would be paid first? Isn't that what the state
was doing in *Leslie*? Does *Leslie's* focus on who created the property present
a defensible *bankruptcy* distinction?

Five years later, the issue returned to the Ninth Circuit. In re Petite
Auberge Village, Inc., 650 F.2d 192 (9th Cir. 1981), held that California
could not exact tax penalties and post-bankruptcy petition interest as a
condition of the transfer of a liquor license. The Ninth Circuit observed

that §57j of the 1898 Act barred states from recovering tax penalties from the estate of a bankrupt (under the Bankruptcy Code, see §726(a)(4)) and that interest on a debt stops when the bankruptcy petition is filed (under the Bankruptcy Code, see §502(b)(2)). Accepting arguendo California's argument that tax penalties and post-petition interest are part of a delinquent "tax," the Ninth Circuit held that they are not recoverable under section 24049 as a part of the state's right to define the nature of state-created property rights: "California's definition of 'tax' would not necessarily be applied in federal bankruptcy proceedings." Quoting from Chicago Board of Trade v. Johnson, the Ninth Circuit concluded that the state law must yield here, since "[a]llowing the state to recover tax penalties conflicts with the language of the act . . . and with the 'broad aim of the Act to provide for the conservation of the estates of insolvents to the end that there may be as equitable a distribution of assets as is consistent with the type of claims involved.'" Does this adequately distinguish *Professional Bar*?

In 1983, the Ninth Circuit had an occasion to bring this series of cases together. That case follows. How successful is it?

IN RE ANCHORAGE INTERNATIONAL INN
718 F.2d 1446 (9th Cir. 1983)

FLETCHER, Circuit Judge.

This appeal is from the bankruptcy court's ruling (affirmed by the district court) that the provisions of an Alaska statute requiring payment of creditors of a liquor establishment before transfer of a liquor license are preempted by federal bankruptcy law. We have jurisdiction under 11 U.S.C. §47(a) (1976) (repealed 1978) and reverse.

I

On March 28, 1979, Anchorage International Inn, Inc. (Inn), the owner of an Alaska liquor license, was adjudicated a bankrupt. Prior to bankruptcy, the Inn had incurred two substantial debts arising out of the operation of a tavern connected to the Inn: (1) approximately $20,000 in taxes and employee withholding contributions due the State of Alaska, Department of Labor; and (2) approximately $143,000 in employee benefit contributions owed to the Alaska Hotel and Restaurant Employees Health & Welfare Trust and Pension Trust (Trust Funds).

During the bankruptcy proceedings, the trustee of the Inn arranged and secured the bankruptcy court's approval of the sale of the assets of the Inn, contingent upon approval of the transfer of the liquor license by the

Alaska Alcoholic Beverage Control Board (ABC Board). Under Alaska law, the ABC Board has sole authority to issue and transfer liquor licenses; no license may be transferred without ABC Board approval. The Alaska statute requires that approval of a transfer be denied if

> (4) The transferor has not paid all debts or taxes arising from the conduct of the business licensed under [the] title [governing alcoholic beverages] *unless* (A) *he gives security* for the payment of the debts or taxes *satisfactory to the creditors* or taxing authority.

Alaska Stat. §04.11.360(4)(A) (1982) (emphasis added).

Relying on section 04.11.360(4)(A), the ABC Board initially denied the trustee's request for a license transfer because no arrangement had been made to pay the creditors of the liquor-related portion of the business. In order to facilitate sale of the assets of the Inn on the favorable terms arranged, the Trust Funds, the State, and the trustee entered into a stipulation under which the trustee promised to hold the proceeds from the sale of the license pending a judicial determination of their proper distribution. This stipulation constituted "security . . . satisfactory to the creditors" as required under section 04.11.360(4)(A), permitting the ABC Board to approve transfer of the license to the purchaser. The proceeds are presently held by the trustee, to abide the result of this appeal.

On December 31, 1981, the bankruptcy court ordered that the $20,000 in state tax and contribution claims be paid first from the license sale proceeds, but denied any preferred right to payments from the sale proceeds to other liquor-related creditors of the debtor, including the Trust Funds. The court concluded that, because the license had been created by the State of Alaska, the Alaska statute did not conflict with federal law insofar as the statute required payment of state tax claims prior to transfer of the license.

As to the claims of the Trust Funds, however, the court ruled that the requirement of section 04.11.360(4) "that all general debts of the business be paid before a license may be transferred . . . interfere[s] with the Bankruptcy Act's priority distribution scheme." The court concluded that under the Supremacy Clause, the Alaska statute "may not be enforced where the transferor has initiated bankruptcy proceedings." The court ruled that application of the statute "in bankruptcy situations would frustrate the Bankruptcy Act's purpose of providing an equitable distribution of the bankrupt's non-exempt property to all creditors of the same class" and "would also frustrate the purpose of Congress to establish unified federal priorities."

The district court affirmed the bankruptcy court's decision. The Trust Funds timely took this further appeal. The trustee has not cross-appealed from the decision in favor of the State of Alaska.

II

Appellants challenge the judgment below asserting that the Alaska statute does *not* "establish priorities" in contravention of the general system of priorities pertaining to unsecured claims against the bankrupt estate. Rather, they argue, section 04.11.360(4) simply establishes in effect a lien on one asset of the bankrupt (the liquor license), in favor of those creditors whose claims arose out of the use of the license. This "lien," like any encumbrance, reduces the value of the asset and diminishes what is available for distribution in accordance with the general priority scheme of the federal bankruptcy law. But, liens are not void in bankruptcy simply because they favor secured creditors at the expense of general creditors.

The trustee, in defense of the judgment, argues that the state cannot substitute its distribution scheme for that established under the Bankruptcy Act. According to the trustee, permitting payment of the claims related to the liquor business prior to payment of other claims would unconstitutionally frustrate the "primary" objective of the Bankruptcy Act: to provide for an equitable distribution of assets among all creditors. . . . She decries the notion of permitting some creditors of the bankrupt (e.g., persons earning wages in the operation of the tavern) to be paid ahead of other creditors (e.g., bedding manufacturers). She relies on In re Leslie, 520 F.2d 761 (9th Cir. 1975).

A

As a preliminary matter, we must determine whether the Alaska statute gives the creditors of the licensed business a claim against the liquor license superior to that of other creditors of the bankrupt or whether it seeks simply to regulate license transfers without providing priority to the creditors of the liquor business. If the Alaska statute does not create a priority, the Trust Funds would have no superior right in bankruptcy to payment from the license sale proceeds. We would stop our analysis there.

The creditor of an owner of an Alaska liquor license, unlike the holder of a security interest or a mechanic's lien, cannot enforce the lien by self-help or by execution on the license. . . . Nevertheless, the creditor's interest in the license is an encumbrance superior to the rights of others. The Alaska statute assures the liquor-related creditor that the sale of the license will not occur until his debt is paid or security satisfactory to him is provided. Other creditors whose debts are not related to the licensed business receive no similar assurances. Under Alaska law, the creditors of the liquor business do have a superior right to payment from the license sale proceeds.[2]

2. The determination of the bankruptcy court that the proceeds of the sale of the liquor license must be used first to pay taxes and contributions owed to the State of Alaska before distribution to general creditors accords precisely with this conclusion. The State of Alaska

Although the lien interest created by Alaska Stat. §04.11.360(4) differs in form from other more typical creditor-protection devices such as a security interest or a materialman's lien, all serve the same function. Regardless of its label, each encourages the extension of credit by providing that, upon the occurrence of certain conditions, the creditor has a priority right to payment from a particular asset.

B

Ordinarily, an asset subject to a lien such as the license in this case passes into the hands of the trustee on the date of filing subject to the lien. In this case, however, the bankruptcy court concluded that, since the Alaska statute "creates statutory priorities, not statutory liens or encumbrances on property," the license passed into the estate unencumbered except for the taxes due the State of Alaska. This was error.

For its rationale, the bankruptcy court relied heavily on In re Leslie, in which we stated in broad terms that "[c]onflicting priorities established by state law must yield upon the intervention of bankruptcy to superior federal law" and ruled that a California statute regulating the transfer of California liquor licenses "creates statutory priorities, not statutory liens." 520 F.2d 761, 762 (9th Cir. 1975). We directed that the proceeds of the sale of a liquor business (the assets of which included a liquor license) be paid according to the distribution scheme for general unsecured claims established by the Bankruptcy Act and *not* according to the California statutory scheme for allocation for proceeds among creditors when a California liquor business is sold. Id. See also In re Professional Bar Co., 537 F.2d 339, 340 (9th Cir. 1976).

Although *Leslie* and this case seem similar, there are significant differences. In *Leslie,* at the time the petition in bankruptcy was filed, the liquor license (as well as the related business assets of the debtor) had already been sold and the proceeds placed in an escrow account. . . .

Under California law, consent to the sale of the license by the liquor-related creditors is not required. Thus, what the trustee received in *Leslie* was the cash proceeds from a sale of a liquor business, not a license transferable only on the approval of creditors. Since, at the time of filing, creditors of the debtor were free to attach or levy against the proceeds, . . . the *Leslie* court correctly concluded that the trustee took unencumbered title to the proceeds, . . . *see* 11 U.S.C. §110(a)(5).

The California statute differs from the Alaska statute in two other regards. The California statute attempted to determine priorities in the

---

had no ordinary statutory tax lien nor any judicial lien on the license, and in fact could not have obtained one. See Alaska Stat. §09.35.087 (1973). Implicit in the holding below therefore was a determination that it is section 04.11.360(4) that creates for certain creditors of the licensed business, i.e., the State of Alaska, a right to the proceeds of the sale of the license superior to that of other creditors.

distribution of the proceeds of the sale not only of the liquor license but also of all other assets of the licensed business. See . . . Cal. Bus. & Prof. Code §24074 (West Supp. 1975). The statute further specified the order of distribution among all claims against the debtor, regardless of whether the particular claim was related to the liquor business. See . . . Cal. Bus. & Prof. Code §24074.

By contrast, the Alaska statute establishes priority for one particular group of creditors in one specific asset. See Alaska Stat. §04.11.360(4). Moreover, the creditors of the license holder can prevent the sale of the license unless the license transferor provides security "satisfactory to the creditors." Id. In this case, the ABC Board initially refused to allow the license to be sold and finally did so only after the creditors had agreed that the proceeds of the license sale were "satisfactory" security.

Given the significant differences in scope and effect between the California and Alaska statutes, we do not find the holding in *Leslie* controlling.[3] See In re Professional Bar Co., 537 F.2d 339, 340 (9th Cir. 1976) (creditor that state authorizes to prevent license transfer has valid pre-

---

3. Certain suggestively broad language in *Leslie* might be misread to the effect that state law can *never* alter the order of distribution to creditors prescribed by the bankruptcy statutes. Such a proposition, not necessary to the decision presented by the peculiar California statute at issue in *Leslie,* does not comport with the general principles of federal bankruptcy law. State law often vests some creditors with special rights, sometimes called "liens" or "security interests," that enable certain creditors to collect ahead of general creditors in bankruptcy. The inherent purpose of *any* such lien or encumbrance is to give the holder of the lien a position superior to other creditors in a particular asset.

What is essential in determining whether a prior right to proceeds of an asset is valid in bankruptcy is not whether it has been labeled as a "lien" by the state statute, but whether it has any purpose or effect independent of bankruptcy. See 11 U.S.C. §107(c)(1)(A) (1976); Jackson, Bankruptcy and the Creditors' Bargain, 91 Yale L.J. 857, 905-906 (1982). As Professor Jackson states, when a state-created entitlement is enforceable inside *and* outside bankruptcy, "there is no reason stemming from the justifications underlying condemnation of state-created priorities . . . to refuse recognition of the entitlement" in the bankruptcy situation. Id. The problem with the dictum in *Leslie* that would strike down all state-created entitlements is that it "misperceive[s] the nature of the inquiry," since "[a]ll state-created entitlements act in favor of some group of creditors, but bankruptcy law generally recognizes them nonetheless." Id. at 906 n. 228.

The Ninth Circuit recognized as much a year after *Leslie* in In re Professional Bar Co., 537 F.2d 339 (9th Cir. 1976). There, the court evaluated the contention of general creditors of an estate, one asset of which was a California liquor license, that a California statute requiring payment of California tax claims prior to license transfer was invalid since it overrode the priority federal bankruptcy law gave to wage claimants over tax claimants. 537 F.2d at 340. The court, upholding the priority of the tax claims, responded:

This [notion of the supremacy of the federal distribution scheme] is true as a general principle. In this case, however, the problem is not so much one of priority of claims as one of defining the nature of the bankrupt's property to which the claims attach. . . . California has placed a limitation on the value of a state liquor license by authorizing the Department of Alcoholic Beverage Control to refuse to transfer a state-created liquor license so long as certain state taxes remain delinquent. The bankrupt estate, insofar as it includes liquor licenses, has only the limited value of the licenses encumbered as they may be by the terms of the statutes which create the licenses and provide the conditions of their transfer. It is to that limited value that any claims against the estate attach.

ferred right in bankruptcy). Nothing in *Leslie* compels us to strike down the
Alaska statute simply because it attempts to give certain creditors a preferred right in a particular asset.[4]

We recognize, of course, that Congress has the authority to make
uniform laws governing the subject of bankruptcies, see U.S. Const. art. I,
§8, cl. 4, and, pursuant to that authority, might invalidate in bankruptcy
any or all pre-bankruptcy entitlements encumbering the debtor's assets.
But Congress has not done so. The mechanic's lien and the security interest under the Uniform Commercial Code are but two examples of interests
in particular property, created pursuant to state statutes, that are fully
respected by the general bankruptcy law. The trustee's contention that
states cannot allow some creditors to receive more of the proceeds of the
sale of a bankrupt's assets than others receive is thus incorrect. No statutory bankruptcy policy forbids a state from giving one creditor a greater
right to payment of his claim from a given asset than that conferred on
another.[5]

Perez v. Campbell, 402 U.S. 637, 649, 91 S. Ct. 1704, 1711, 29 L. Ed.
2d 233 (1971), which holds that a state statute is invalid if it "stands as an
obstacle to the accomplishment and execution of the full purposes and
objectives of Congress," does not contradict our conclusion. In *Perez*, an
Arizona statute, which conditioned the issuance of a driver's license to a
discharged debtor on the payment of pre-bankruptcy debts, was held to be
preempted. Id. at 652, 91 S. Ct. at 1712. The Arizona statute directly

---

Id. at 340 (citations deleted). By so holding, the court in *Professional Bar* failed to follow the
broad principle for which *Leslie* could perhaps be read, that simply because a state-related
entitlement is not denominated a lien and looks less like a lien than other creditor-protection
devices, the entitlement is invalid in bankruptcy.

4. Neither of the two cases relied on by the *Leslie* court in support of the proposition that
state-created priorities must yield to "superior federal law" actually hold anything of the sort.
In the first, the court simply struck down a statutory lien on the basis of a then applicable
bankruptcy act provision invalidating all nonpossessory, unexecuted statutory liens, a provision that was completely revised in 1966 and is no longer in effect. See Elliott v. Bumb, 356
F.2d 749, 755 (9th Cir. 1966); 11 U.S.C. §107(c)(a) (1964) (repealed 1966). In the second,
the preferred interest was invalid in bankruptcy, because it came into effect only upon the
debtor's insolvency. See In re Crosstown Motors, Inc., 272 F.2d 224, 226-227 (7th Cir.
1959); 11 U.S.C. §107(c)(1)(A).

5. In re Petite Auberge Village, Inc., 650 F.2d 192 (9th Cir. 1981), in which the court
denied California's claim of a superior right to the proceeds of the sale of a liquor license for
post-petition interest and tax penalties, does not compel a contrary result. The court explicitly denied the former claim on the ground that "interest on a debt stops when the bankruptcy petition is filed," id. at 194, and the latter on the basis of the bankruptcy law's strong
policy against enforcing penalties unrelated to pecuniary loss since such claims penalize
creditors *not* delinquent taxpayers, id. at 194, 196.

. . . The court did state in passing that the liquor license was an "asset[ ] of the estate
even before the sale of the license" and hence its proceeds, as "part of the bankrupt's
estate . . . could not be used to pay tax penalties and post-petition interest." 630 F.2d at
195. The court did not, however, gainsay the general rule of bankruptcy that where a
pre-bankruptcy entitlement encumbers an asset, only the residual value of the asset passes
into the estate. In fact, this was precisely the basis on which *Petite Auberge* acknowledged the
prior right of the state to payment of its taxes. See id. at 194.

conflicted with the discharge provisions of federal bankruptcy law. Id. at 648, 652, 91 S. Ct. at 1710, 1713.

Here, by contrast, the Alaska statute does not conflict with the federal distribution scheme because there is no general federal policy against state-created liens that favor one class of creditors over others. Section 04.11.360(4) does not, as the bankruptcy court concluded, frustrate the Act's "purpose of providing an equitable distribution of a bankrupt's non-exempt property to all creditors of the same class." Creditors who hold prior rights under the Alaska statute are simply not in the "same class" as other creditors.

C

Since federal bankruptcy law does override state-created priorities that apply only in the event of bankruptcy, we must examine the statute to determine whether it in fact has force and effect independent of the bankruptcy proceeding.[7] See 11 U.S.C. §107(c)(1)(A). We conclude that the creditors' rights created by the Alaska statute exist independent of the debtor's insolvency and accordingly should be recognized by the trustee.[8]

Regardless of when a license holder seeks to transfer an Alaska liquor license, all liquor-related claims must be paid first. See C.Y., Inc. v. Brown, 574 P.2d 1274, 1277 (Alaska 1978). The transfer caused by the trustee's need to liquidate the assets of the estate is not different from any other transfer in or outside of bankruptcy. Under Alaska law, the encumbrance has its full restrictive effect on the transfer of the underlying security (the liquor license) regardless of whether the transferor is or is not insolvent or undergoing a general distribution or liquidation of his property. The Alaska statute is not a bankruptcy distribution scheme in disguise.

Therefore, we hold that the Trust Funds have a prior right to the proceeds of the license sale to the extent of claims arising from the conduct of the licensed business.[9]

---

7. Section 67c(1)(A) of the Bankruptcy Act, 11 U.S.C. §107(c)(1)(A) (1976), states:

(c)(1) The following liens shall be invalid against the trustee:
    (A) every statutory lien which first becomes effective upon the insolvency of the debtor, or upon distribution or liquidation of his property levied at the instance of one other than the lienor.

The legislative history indicates that "distribution . . . of his property" means a "general distribution" of all of the debtor's property and not the transfer of a "particular asset." See S. Rep. No. 1159, 89th Cong., 2d Sess. 2, 7, reprinted in 1966 U.S. Code Cong. & Admin. News 2456, 2457, 2461; . . .

8. The prior right to payment from the proceeds of sale of the Alaska license constitutes a "statutory lien" within the ambit of §67c(1) of the Bankruptcy Act. 11 U.S.C. §1(29a) (1976) ("[s]tatutory lien shall mean a lien arising solely by force of statute upon specified circumstances or conditions").

9. Neither of two other provisions of the Bankruptcy Act governing statutory liens operates to invalidate the rights of the liquor-related claimants, considered as "statutory liens." Section 67c(1)(B) invalidates a lien only if it is "not enforceable" against a bona fide

III

We reverse the district court's ruling that the Bankruptcy Act preempts Alaska Stat. §04.11.360(4) conditioning the transfer of an Alaska liquor license on the payment of debts arising from the conduct of the licensed business. We conclude that the proceeds of the sale of the license are to be used first to pay debts related to the licensed business. We therefore remand for a determination of what portion of the $143,000 owed the Trust Funds arose from the "conduct of the business licensed."

Reversed and remanded.

NOTE

In re Farmers Markets, Inc., 36 Bankr. 829 (Bankr. E.D. Calif. 1984), distinguished *Anchorage International Inn* on the ground that it involved the 1898 Act and "the Code greatly expanded the definition of property of the estate and reduced the reliance upon state law," pointing specifically to §541(c)(1)(A). Do you agree that the Bankruptcy Code mandates a different result?

C. CUT-OFF OF POST-PETITION RIGHTS AND INTERESTS

Section 552 of the Bankruptcy Code deals with the effect of a security interest on assets acquired by either the debtor or the estate after the filing of a bankruptcy petition. If a secured creditor has a perfected security interest in after-acquired inventory and proceeds, a reorganizing debtor may have both. Section 552 describes the effect of the security interest on those post-petition inventory and proceeds. The following excerpt describes §552.

H.R. REP. NO. 95-595
95th Cong., 1st Sess. 376-377 (1977)

Under the Uniform Commercial Code, Article 9, creditors may take security interests in after-acquired property. This section governs the effect of such a prepetition security interest in postpetition property. It

---

purchaser from the debtor on the date of bankruptcy. 11 U.S.C. §107(c)(1)(B) (1976). Since under Alaska law a person attempting to purchase the license cannot do so without the liquor-related creditors' consent, see Alaska Stat. §04.11.360(4), the "lien" *is* enforceable against any purchaser, bona fide or not. Section 67c(1)(C) applies only to rent liens. See 11 U.S.C. §107(c)(1)(C) (1976).

applies to all security interests as defined in section 101 of the bankruptcy code, not only to UCC security interests.

As a general rule, if a security agreement is entered into before the case, then property that the estate acquires is not subject to the security interest created by the security agreement. Subsection (b) provides the only exception. If the security agreement extends to proceeds, product, offspring, rents, or profits of property that the debtor had before the commencement of the case, then the proceeds, etc., continue to be subject to the security interest, except to the extent that the estate acquired the proceeds to the prejudice of other creditors holding unsecured claims. "Extends to" as used here would include an automatically arising security interest in proceeds, as permitted under the 1972 version of the Uniform Commercial Code, as well as an interest in proceeds specifically designated, as required under the 1962 Code or similar statutes covering property not covered by the Code. "Prejudice" is not intended to be a broad term here, but is designed to cover the situation where the estate expends funds that result in an increase in the value of collateral. The exception is to cover the situation where raw materials, for example, are converted into inventory, or inventory into accounts, at some expense to the estate, thus depleting the fund available for general unsecured creditors. The term "proceeds" is not limited to the technical definition of the term in the UCC, but covers any property into which property subject to the security interest is converted.

PROBLEM

4.6 Debtor borrows $50,000 from Bank. Bank takes a security interest in Debtor's accounts receivable. Its only account receivable is the promise of Buyer to pay it $5,000 a month in return for the goods Debtor sends it each month. On January 1, Debtor files a petition for reorganization under Chapter 11. On January 29, Debtor ships its goods to Buyer. On January 30, Buyer pays Debtor $5,000 in cash. Debtor wants to use this money to pay its workers and suppliers. Bank asserts that it has a security interest in the $5,000 and that, at a minimum, its interest must be adequately protected under §362 (which we will look at in detail in Chapter 7). Must the interest of Bank be adequately protected? See UCC §9-106; In re Stein, 19 Bankr. 458 (Bankr. E.D. Pa. 1982).

Chapter 5
THE POWERS OF THE TRUSTEE TO ENHANCE THE ESTATE

In this chapter and the three that follow, we will be concerned with how the property of the estate should be divided among those with claims against it. We begin by examining the right of general creditors in most cases to be paid pro rata according to the amount of their allowed claims and the right of the trustee to succeed to the power of actual creditors, and thus set aside transactions, such as fraudulent conveyances, that actual creditors could set aside under nonbankruptcy law. The principles we examine in this chapter apply even if bankruptcy proceedings occurred suddenly and were over in an instant. But because they do not appear out of nowhere and vanish as quickly, it is not sufficient to have the trustee step into the shoes of existing creditors and divide property of the estate according to the value of each creditor's entitlement under nonbankruptcy law. The trustee must also have powers to ensure that creditors did not obtain unilateral advantages for themselves before the bankruptcy petition was filed or during the proceeding. These powers are the focus of Chapters 6 and 7. Exceptions to the rule that general creditors share pro rata are the subject of Chapter 8.

A. THE TRUSTEE AS IDEAL LIEN CREDITOR (§544(a))

NOTE ON THE TRUSTEE AS A HYPOTHETICAL LIEN CREDITOR

Section 544(a) of the Bankruptcy Code is the successor to §70c of the Bankruptcy Act of 1898 — the so-called strong-arm clause. It gives the trustee the rights of a fictional (or hypothetical) contract creditor with a judicial lien or execution lien on any property in which the debtor may claim an interest. With respect to real property, it also confers on the trustee the rights of a bona fide purchaser. Because the trustee has these powers, we are provided with a measuring rod, so to speak, for determining who prevails in a contest between the trustee and adverse claimants. If an imaginary creditor (or purchaser) with the characteristics of a §544(a) creditor (or purchaser) would prevail against the adverse interest, the trustee wins. Not only does the trustee win, but §544(a) goes on to say that the trustee may "avoid" the interest, making the unlucky claimant an unsecured creditor for purposes of bankruptcy. And, as we will see in Problem 5.6, §551 will allow the trustee to preserve the transfer "for the benefit of the estate."

Through this power, the trustee can strike down some interests in property acquired outside of bankruptcy. The effect of this is to shift the value of the "avoided" transfer from the transferee to the bankruptcy estate, leaving the transferee worse off and the estate (i.e., generally the unsecured creditors) better off. This power exists whenever the transfer was *avoidable* by the *type* of creditor (or purchaser) specified in §544(a). It is, therefore, necessary to become accustomed to two things: The trustee's rights are being measured by those of a third party, and this particular third party is a hypothetical one.

What is the justification for giving the trustee the powers of a hypothetical lien creditor? Consider the most common illustration of the trustee's lien creditor power: the trustee's ability to avoid, under §544(a), security interests that are not yet perfected. Outside of bankruptcy, an unperfected secured creditor has rights superior to those of a general creditor. See UCC §§9-201; 9-301. A secured creditor who has never filed a financing statement is free to repossess collateral from its defaulting debtor, even if the debtor has borrowed, on an unsecured basis, from many others. In bankruptcy, however, the trustee will be able to set aside the security interest and sell the property for the benefit of the general creditors. Is there any justification for this rule, which appears to give general creditors more in bankruptcy than they had outside of it?

The difference between a perfected and an unperfected secured creditor is principally that the perfected secured creditor has given public notice to others that it may claim a property interest in the debtor's assets. The difference, in other words, rests on an act designed to cure an ostensible ownership problem created by the secured party's assertion of an interest in property that appears to be owned by the debtor. Yet, this act is "required" mainly for the benefit of other property claimants, because unperfected secured creditors still prevail over those who have no security interest at all. In order to prevail over an unperfected security interest, a creditor must obtain a property right (such as a security interest or an execution lien) in its own right, and it must do so before the other security interest is perfected. See UCC §9-301.

A. The Trustee as Ideal Lien Creditor (§544(a))

Imagine the rights of all the creditors relative to one anotl, instant before the bankruptcy petition was filed. Because of the dict UCC §9-301, the holder of an unperfected security interest is entitl prevail over the claim of an unsecured creditor, if the "race" were to at that moment. Given that, it is not at all illogical to ask why the trustee should have the power to strike down, on behalf of the unsecured creditors, an unperfected security interest that none of them could defeat at that time.

But it may be somewhat misleading to describe the respective positions of the parties at the moment before bankruptcy in this way. Although the unperfected secured party would certainly be entitled to prevail over the unsecured party *if* no further action were taken, the more relevant point is that neither party has taken the step that assures ultimate victory. The general creditor has not yet reduced its claim to judgment and had a sheriff levy on the property, but the unperfected secured creditor has not yet filed or exercised its right to repossess its collateral. Until the secured creditor takes one of these steps, we cannot say that it will in fact prevail against any particular general creditor.

In a one-on-one race, it may be possible to predict, with a fair degree of confidence, ultimate victory for the secured creditor, because the secured creditor's remaining steps are likely to be somewhat easier than those of any individual unsecured creditor. But a secured creditor whose interest is unperfected may not know it. The secured creditor may be unaware that it filed the financing statement improperly or that a filing that was once proper has become improper (as might happen if the debtor or the collateral has moved). The secured creditor may lose the race with a general creditor because it erroneously believes it has already won it.

Moreover, most debtors have a number of unsecured creditors, and the relevant comparison is not one-on-one, but the secured creditor against the pool of unsecured creditors. If any of the unsecured creditors obtains a lien or takes (and perfects) a security interest first, the unperfected secured creditor will lose. Looking at the pool of unsecured creditors, some of whom may be close to judgment or attachment, an unperfected secured creditor may be in substantial danger of being defeated. This makes the relevant race, for predictive purposes, more of a dead heat.

Because neither the unperfected secured creditor nor any of its unsecured counterparts has in fact taken the ultimate step assuring priority before the bankruptcy commenced, their positions in the collective proceeding seem comparable. In "avoiding" the unperfected interest of the secured party by asserting the rights of a hypothetical lien creditor, the trustee does not bring victory in the race to the unsecured creditors; rather, he assures a tie. An unperfected secured creditor whose interest is struck down in bankruptcy is treated as an unsecured creditor, and hence entitled to a pro rata share of the debtor's assets as are any general creditors. This respects the relative *value* of the creditors' rights the moment before bankruptcy begins.

The trustee's hypothetical lien creditor power, then, exists to assure all creditors that parties actually equal in any hypothetical race outside of bankruptcy, at the moment of bankruptcy, will be treated as equals once the collective proceeding commences. Yet this rationale may also indicate the limits on that avoiding power. The trustee cannot set aside a security interest simply because an uncured (but curable) ostensible ownership problem exists. The trustee prevails because state law has decided that such an ostensible ownership problem makes an interest vulnerable to a lien creditor. Even in the case of Article 9 security interests, state law generally has not chosen to protect general creditors (the parties whose interests the trustee protects) from this kind of ostensible ownership of property by the debtor. The trustee's power as a hypothetical lien creditor seems to rest on nonbankruptcy entitlements, for it measures, by the yardstick of rights existing the moment before bankruptcy, the value of the relative rights of competing claimants to the debtor's property. If those rights are fixed outside of bankruptcy, nothing in the collectivizing nature of bankruptcy calls for their value to be reallocated.

For a discussion of these questions in greater detail, see Jackson, Avoiding Powers in Bankruptcy, 36 Stan. L. Rev. 725, 732-736 (1984).

PROBLEM

5.1 Debtor has two assets — a $50,000 machine and an undeveloped piece of real estate worth $100,000. Debtor has borrowed $20,000 from Bank and has given Bank a security interest in all of its property. Bank fails to file a UCC-1 form in the Article 9 filing system or note its interest in the relevant real estate records. Debtor also owes general creditors $150,000. Debtor files a bankruptcy petition. The trustee raises $150,000 from the sale of Debtor's assets. How are the proceeds to be divided among the creditors?

NOTE ON §544(a)(3)

Section 544(a)(3) of the Bankruptcy Code permits the trustee to avoid any transfer of the debtor's property that would be "voidable" by "a bona fide purchaser of real property, other than fixtures, from the debtor, against whom applicable law permits such transfer to be perfected, that obtains the status of a bona fide purchaser and has perfected such transfer at the time of the commencement of the case, whether or not such a purchaser exists." The difference in the powers of a trustee against holders of security interests in real and personal property in bankruptcy stems from a difference in their rights outside of bankruptcy. In a number of states, many unrecorded interests in real property, while disfavored, are still effective against nonconsensual claimants, such as holders of judgment liens. They are, however, not effective against consensual claimants, such as subsequent purchasers of interests in the property who, because of an earlier party's failure to record, had no constructive notice of that earlier party's interest.

The argument for giving the trustee the rights of a bona fide purchaser of real estate runs as follows: Property interests that create ostensible ownership problems that have not been cured before the filing of the bankruptcy petition are "bad" and, hence, deserve to be struck down, even though substantive law outside of bankruptcy did not consider these interests sufficiently "bad" to justify giving general creditors priority (or even parity). Because a number of states protected purchasers, but not holders of liens, against unrecorded real estate interests, the trustee should be given the power of a bona fide purchaser of real property in order to achieve the same result that a lien creditor power gave the trustee against personal property. See generally In re Great Plains Western Ranch Co., 38 Bankr. 899 (Bankr. C.D. Cal. 1984) ("[t]he strong-arm clause may be read as relying on the principle of ostensible ownership—the principle that . . . what the creditor sees ought to be what the creditor gets.").

Section 544, in short, gives the trustee the same status relative to all secured creditors, notwithstanding the different rights each has outside of bankruptcy. Is there a bankruptcy reason for making the trustee's rights turn on a curable, but uncured, ostensible ownership problem? Can one fault §544(a)(3) for ignoring that state law treats real property differently from personal property, and that these differences are reflected in the priority rights between unsecured creditors and unrecorded holders of real estate interests? In states that have a bona fide purchaser rule, unsecured creditors are unable, outside of bankruptcy, to defeat the holder of an unrecorded real estate interest, at least without themselves first becoming purchasers. To become a purchaser, however, one must extend *new* credit to the debtor and obtain, to the extent of that new credit, an interest in the real estate. Put another way, the moment before bankruptcy, an unsecured creditor in those jurisdictions has no way (because neither taking a mortgage nor obtaining a judgment lien is sufficient) to defeat, for the benefit of its existing claims, the rights of a holder of an unrecorded interest in the debtor's real estate. This race, unlike the race between the unsecured creditors and the holder of an unperfected Article 9 security interest, arguably is over *before* the bankruptcy process begins. See Jackson, Avoiding Powers in Bankruptcy, 36 Stan. L. Rev. 725, 736-741 (1984).

The principal benefit of §544(a) is the ability it gives the trustee to avoid unrecorded real estate mortgages, unperfected security interests, and other forms of property claims where the notice requirements have not been met. The mechanics of §544(a) are explored in the next case.

IN RE HARMS
7 Bankr. 398 (Bankr. D. Colo. 1980)

Glen E. KELLER, Jr., Bankruptcy Judge.

This matter is before the Court upon the motion of Jane Frist to withdraw and exclude property from the bankrupt estate. Ms. Frist was formerly the wife of Arnold Harms, who filed a petition in this Court on July 31, 1980, seeking relief under Chapter 11 of the Bankruptcy Code (11 U.S.C. §1101, et seq.). Ms. Frist contends that prior to her ex-husband's petition in bankruptcy, her interest in certain real property and limited partnerships was set aside to her by order of the Denver District Court in a dissolution proceeding between the parties. It follows, she claims, that this property was not owned by Mr. Harms on the date of the petition and title did not pass to the estate under 11 U.S.C. §541.

Mr. Harms filed the dissolution proceeding on July 1, 1976. A master was then appointed. He determined that all marital property should be divided equally between the parties and recommended an "in kind" division of the real properties, together with an equitable division of the proceeds from the sale of the family residence to even out the value of the distribution. The master found it impossible to assign a value to Mr. Harms' interest in the limited partnerships. He suggested that a receiver be appointed to liquidate these interests. These recommendations were in large measure adopted by the District Court in an order dated March 30, 1979.

On February 1, 1980, the family residence at 345 Franklin Street was ordered listed for sale. At that time, the Court specifically found that "as of May 9th, 1978, each party owned 50 percent of the partnership interests and each were subjected to fifty percent of the liability." These interests were ordered sold at public auction 90 days after the appointment of a broker if private sale was not accomplished. Upon the sale of the partnership interests, the proceeds were to be divided equally. Before distribution of the real properties and the sale of the limited partnerships, Mr. Harms filed a petition pursuant to Chapter 11 in this Court, effectively staying any further action in the state court proceeding.

Under the Bankruptcy Reform Act of 1978, upon the filing of a petition, an estate is created, comprised, inter alia, of all legal or equitable interests of the debtor in property as of the commencement of the case. 11 U.S.C. §541. The representative of the estate is the trustee. 11 U.S.C. §323. . . . [T]he trustee is given certain specific powers which he can use in marshalling the assets of the debtor. Those powers include those of a hypothetical lien creditor and a hypothetical bona fide purchaser of real property from the debtor. 11 U.S.C. §544. . . .

In light of the above, the issue for purposes of this motion is as follows: On the day the petition in bankruptcy was filed, would a judicial lien creditor of Mr. Harms or a bona fide purchaser of real property from Mr. Harms have rights superior to Ms. Frist with respect to the real property and partnership interests in question? The answer to this question is a matter of state law. . . .

The Colorado Supreme Court has held that upon the commencement of a dissolution proceeding, a wife has a vested interest in the marital property. When the court divides the marital property, the transaction "resembles a division of property between co-owners rather than a conveyance by the husband for the release of an independent obligation owed by him to the wife. . . ." In re Questions Submitted by the United States District Court, Imel v. United States, 184 Colo. 1, 517 P.2d 1331 (Colo. 1974). In other words, upon the commencement of a dissolution proceeding, the wife has an interest in the marital property in the nature of a co-owner, rather than as a mere creditor of her husband. In the *Imel* case, the court also said:

> Upon and after the filing of the action, the rights of the wife are analogous to those of a wife who can establish a resulting trust, irrespective of a divorce action, in the property of her husband. We use this analogy because we are not saying that after the filing of the divorce action it is necessary for both spouses to enter into the conveyance of property held in the name of one only. Upon the filing of the action the court may protect this vested interest of the wife pending the division order, even though the property to be transferred to her has not yet been determined. 517 P.2d at 1335.

In the case at hand, not only had a dissolution action been filed, thus creating vested rights in Ms. Frist, but the state court on February 1 entered its division order specifically setting aside to the Movant certain real properties or the proceeds from the sale thereof and specifically finding her to be the owner of 50 percent of the partnership interests.

Whether Ms. Frist's rights in real property are superior to the bankruptcy trustee's depends on whether she has an interest of record. Colorado law provides that a bona fide purchaser of realty who records his interest will cut off the rights of a previous transferee who fails to record. . . . The bankruptcy trustee is given all the powers of a bona fide purchaser from the debtor who perfects his claim. Thus, Ms. Frist cannot prevail unless her interest was recorded in the appropriate counties prior to the filing of the bankruptcy. She took no action to record any interests in marital real property that derived from the dissolution proceeding and orders entered therein. A wife may, upon the commencement of a dissolution action, file a lis pendens, which will operate as notice to all of the wife's claims. . . . Furthermore, the Colorado recording statute leaves little doubt that court decrees affecting title to real property may be recorded. . . . Failure to record one's decreed interest can result in its being rendered worthless if a subsequent bona fide purchaser records first. The *Imel* case does not affect this rule. Whatever interest a wife has in her husband's property upon the filing of a dissolution proceeding is still subject to the requirements of Colorado's recording laws. Hence, if the wife does not record, the ex-husband's trustee may acquire superior rights.

The limited partnership interests present a different problem for analysis. In Colorado, the interest of a limited partner in the partnership is personal property. . . . A lien upon personalty can be judicially acquired either by prejudgment attachment under Rule 102 C.R.C.P. or by levy and execution. In the latter case, the lien arises at the time the writ of execution is delivered to the appropriate authority. . . . There would appear to be little doubt that shares in a limited partnership are subject to attachment, levy, and execution in Colorado. The "non-exempt property" of a debtor may be attached, and it appears undisputed that shares of stock in a corporation may be so seized. . . . Would a levying creditor have priority over Ms. Frist in the partnership interests? The answer to this question in the Tenth Circuit appears to be yes. In Panton v. Lee, 261 F.2d 183 (10th Cir. 1958), an Oklahoma divorce decree gave the wife judgment for one-half of all property, including money, acquired by the husband during the marriage. Subsequently, the husband filed a petition in bankruptcy. The court held that the trustee's rights were superior to the wife in both the real and personal property involved. The court emphasized that on the date of bankruptcy, the property was in the name and possession of the husband and that the divorce decree gave the wife no lien thereon. The same is true here. Title to the limited partnerships stands to this day in the name of Mr. Harms. So far as the Court can discern, Ms. Frist never acquired possession thereof. The decree of the state court regarding the fifty-fifty ownership of the partnership shares was necessarily somewhat general in terms due to the difficulty of valuing those assets. It gave the wife no lien or title which would be superior to a levying creditor of Mr. Harms.

The *Imel* case does not change this result. At its most concrete, *Imel* states that upon the filing of a dissolution, the wife has all the rights of one who can establish a resulting trust in the property of her husband. To the extent this is so, Ms. Frist had only an equitable interest in the marital property standing in Mr. Harms' name. It is settled law that mere equities will be cut off by judicial lien creditors of the legal title holder of property. . . . This analysis would also apply to any proceeds of the sale of the "Tweedy" property that were in the possession of Mr. Harms at the time of the bankruptcy petition.

The powers of the bankruptcy trustee under the Code are extensive. He is clothed with all the rights that the law gives to creditors of the debtor to recover property in satisfaction of their claims, whether or not such creditors actually exist. There is perhaps even more justice in the trustee's vigorous assertion of his legal rights in the context of a Chapter 11 reorganization, wherein, if successful, the debtor can be expected to deal with his creditors in a more meaningful way than upon mere liquidation. In denying the motion of Debtor's ex-wife, she is not being condemned to see her rights against Mr. Harms made worthless. Her interests can easily be asserted in the context of the reorganization proceeding. Now, therefore, it is Ordered that the motion of the wife to exclude property is denied.

NOTE ON THE IRRELEVANCE OF KNOWLEDGE

Section 544(a) is often said to give the trustee the rights of an "ideal" lien creditor or purchaser. The trustee enjoys his rights "without regard to any knowledge of the trustee or of any creditor." Thus, to the extent that knowledge plays any role in priorities outside of bankruptcy, the trustee's position is not affected by any knowledge that he or any creditor might have. (Under the 1972 revisions of Article 9 of the Uniform Commercial Code, knowledge is not relevant to determining priorities between the holder of an unperfected Article 9 security interest and a lien creditor. Compare §9-301(1)(b) (1972) with §9-301(1)(b) (1962). Real estate systems may or may not give a role to knowledge in determining priorities, as was described in Chapter 1.) Knowledge by the *trustee* properly is irrelevant because he simply acts as a collection agent. Is it so clear, however, that it is also inappropriate to ignore knowledge of particular creditors despite what nonbankruptcy law says? Doesn't this reallocate entitlements in bankruptcy? Can you articulate a bankruptcy-related reason for this, such as, for example, the costs of proving knowledge in bankruptcy?

As we shall learn in Chapter 9 of this book, when a firm attempts to reorganize under Chapter 11 of the Bankruptcy Code, the existing management usually continues to run the day-to-day operations of the firm and a trustee is not appointed. The debtor in possession (as the old managers are called), however, has the same duties and powers as the trustee. §1107. Can the debtor in possession assert the rights of a hypothetical lien creditor or bona fide purchaser for value, or is it bound by whatever knowledge it has? In In re Hartman Paving, — F.2d — (4th Cir. 1984), the court found that a debtor in possession was limited by whatever knowledge it had:

> When Hartman filed for bankruptcy . . . he became a debtor in possession under §1107(a) and was entitled to avoid any obligations that would have been voidable by a subsequent bona fide purchaser for value or lien creditor under West Virginia law. *Tavenner*—the controlling West Virginia precedent—states in part that a deed [executed the way it was in the present case] will not be valid against subsequent bona fide purchasers for value. Thus Hartman argued below, and now contends on appeal, that as debtor-in-possession he was entitled under §544(a) to avoid the deed of trust and treat Pyne as an unsecured creditor.
>
> We are not persuaded by Hartman's argument because it ignores a critical part of the *Tavenner* holding. *Tavenner* stands for the proposition that

an improperly acknowledged deed is only void against subsequent bona fide purchasers for value who take without actual notice. . . . This rule makes considerable practical sense, for one who purchases with actual notice, even if a subsequent purchaser, is not subject to the same dangers of fraud as a subsequent purchaser who is dependent solely on record notice. To treat both the same simply because each is a subsequent purchaser would elevate form over substance. . . .

. . . *Tavenner* was concerned primarily with protecting against danger of fraud. Because Hartman had actual notice, he cannot now claim that the improper acknowledgement caused him injury. To read West Virginia law as the district court did, therefore, permits Hartman to turn a legal "fiction" found in §544(a) to unfair personal gain. In short, the lower court's interpretation of *Tavenner* turns West Virginia law on its head.

Hartman was a party to the transaction and consequently had actual notice of the conveyance. Thus although Hartman is entitled to claim the powers of a subsequent purchaser for value under §544(a), those powers, as properly defined under local law, do not permit him to void the deed because — simply stated — Hartman is not the type of subsequent purchaser that Tavenner was designed to protect.

How can there be "unfair personal gain" under the facts of this case? Hartman is a corporate debtor, and if, as is likely, the corporation is insolvent, the shareholders will have no right to share in the assets of the firm and will take only if everyone, including the unperfected secured creditor, is paid in full or agrees to split the assets with the shareholders. Is there any doubt that the general creditors of Hartman Paving would have prevailed if a trustee had been appointed, regardless of the actual knowledge of whoever happened to be made trustee? The trustee is the agent of the general creditors. It is *their* knowledge that is relevant. Why should the analysis change if it is the debtor in possession who represents their interests? Why isn't their knowledge still what is relevant? Should the decision of whether to appoint a trustee turn on the knowledge of the debtor in possession and of the trustee or on the comparative advantage one might have over the other in managing the firm's assets? Note that under Chapter 7 a trustee must be appointed. If there were a liquidation under Chapter 7 in *Hartman,* the transfer would have been set aside for the benefit of the creditors. Is there any reason to have a different result simply because the filing was under Chapter 11?

How absolute is this protection given the trustee? Consider the following problems.

PROBLEMS

5.2 Debtor purchases an office building on June 1, after borrowing $250,000 from Bank for this purpose. Debtor gives Bank a mortgage on the building to secure the loan, but Bank fails to record the mortgage. On

September 1, Debtor files a petition in bankruptcy. May the trustee "avoid" Bank's mortgage? Review the discussion of types of recording systems on page 15. In a number of states (such as California), the recording acts do not protect judgment or execution lien creditors. In such jurisdictions, in order to avoid a transaction like this one, the trustee must be using his powers of a bona fide purchaser under §544(a)(3).

5.3 Debtor borrows $100,000 from Finance Company on January 1, and grants Finance Company a security interest in its accounts receivable. Finance Company fails to file a financing statement in the proper office. On March 1, Debtor files a petition in bankruptcy. May the trustee avoid Finance Company's security interest? See §544(a)(1); U.C.C. §9-301(1)(b) and (3). Note carefully the language of the two sections just cited: is "subordinate to" the same as "voidable by"?

5.4 Same facts as Problem 5.3, except Finance Company makes a proper filing in the proper office on February 28. May the trustee avoid Finance Company's security interest under §544(a)(1)?

5.5 Same facts as Problem 5.3, except Finance Company makes a proper filing in the secretary of state's office on January 1. Because of the state involved, however, Finance Company also was required to make a filing in the office of the county recorder, and failed to do so (see UCC §9-401(1)(c), third alternative). May the trustee avoid Finance Company's security interest? See §544(a); UCC §§9-401(2); 9-301(1)(b).

5.6 Same facts as Problem 5.5. Debtor, on February 1, also borrowed $10,000 from Credit Union. Credit Union filed proper financing statements in all relevant locations. Credit Union, however, knows of Finance Company's loan and security interest, because it had checked in the secretary of state's office. As a result, Finance Company's security interest is effective against Credit Union under the doctrine of UCC §9-401(2). If the collateral is worth $80,000, in what order will Finance Company, Credit Union, and the general creditors get paid in bankruptcy?

To analyze this problem, it might be useful to analyze the result if Credit Union did not know of Finance Company's interest. What would happen outside of bankruptcy? Does anything in the Bankruptcy Code change this result? Does §551 allow the trustee to prevail over Credit Union, or does it simply give him the power to step into Finance Company's shoes and assert in bankruptcy whatever rights Finance Company could assert against Credit Union outside of bankruptcy? How does Credit Union's knowledge change the result? What happens outside of bankruptcy? Does any bankruptcy rule provide further guidance?

5.7 Debtor contracts to buy a machine from Seller on January 1 on an installment sale, Debtor paying $10,000 down, and agreeing to pay $10,000 a month for each of the next 24 months. Seller retains title to the machine until Debtor has paid for it in full and thus has a security interest under UCC §1-201(37). On January 10, the machine is delivered to Debtor's plant. On January 15, Debtor files a petition in bankruptcy. On

January 16, Seller files a financing statement in the proper office. May the trustee in bankruptcy avoid Seller's security interest in the machine under §544(a)? See §546(b); UCC §§9-107(a); 9-301(2). (Does Seller's action violate the automatic stay of §362? See §362(b)(3).)

5.8 Purchaser bought a condominium in 1984. He moved in later that year. Purchaser, however, never recorded his interest. In July 1985, Seller filed a bankruptcy petition. Seller's trustee asserts that his rights to the condominium are superior to Purchaser's because of Purchaser's failure to record the transfer. Under state law, clear and open possession of real property generally constitutes constructive notice to subsequent purchasers of the rights of the party in possession. Such possession, even in the absence of recording, obliges any prospective subsequent purchaser to inquire into the possessor's claimed interest in that property. Is the trustee bound by such a rule?

Can the trustee argue that any notice which might be imputed to the trustee from possession is irrelevant because the rights of the trustee are independent of his knowledge or the knowledge of any creditor? Or should one conclude that the trustee's rights should be no greater than the right of a bona fide purchaser, who would lose a priority contest to a buyer in possession, regardless of his actual knowledge? Courts have generally concluded that constructive notice is imputed to the trustee in such cases. See McCannon v. Marston, 679 F.2d 13 (3d Cir. 1982); In re Morse, 30 Bankr. 52 (1st Cir. Bankr. App. 1983); In re Gurs, 27 Bankr. 163 (9th Cir. Bankr. App. 1983); In re Hardway Restaurant, Inc., 31 Bankr. 322 (Bankr. S.D.N.Y. 1983); In re Fitzpatrick, 29 Bankr. 701 (Bankr. W.D. Wis. 1983).

NOTE ON THE EVOLUTION OF §544(a) AND THE TIMING OF HYPOTHETICAL EVENTS

Section 544(a) dates voidability questions from the time of the "commencement of the case," using that date to examine the powers of a creditor who, somewhat unrealistically, both extends credit to the debtor on that date and simultaneously obtains a judicial lien on the debtor's property, §544(a)(1).

Is this the proper date for measuring the trustee's powers? This issue came up under the predecessor to §544(a). Under §70c(3) of the Bankruptcy Act of 1898, the trustee was given, as of the date of bankruptcy, the rights and powers of:

> a creditor who upon the date of bankruptcy obtained a lien by legal or equitable proceedings upon all property . . . upon which a creditor of the bankrupt upon a simple contract could have obtained such a lien, whether or not such a creditor exists.

This language, although more awkward in its syntax, may seem similar to that of §544(a): One needs to imagine that a creditor has levied on the property of the debtor on the date of bankruptcy. Then, if that imaginary levy would have established rights in the property, those rights are taken over by the trustee.

The language of §70c(3), however, gave rise to one important ambiguity: When does one imagine the (hypothetical) *credit* being extended? The issue was first raised by Constance v. Harvey, 215 F.2d 571 (2d Cir. 1954), cert. denied, 348 U.S. 913 (1955). At the time of Constance v. Harvey, a New York statute allowed a gap creditor to prevail over the secured creditor. (A "gap" creditor was one who advanced credit to a debtor in the interval between the time a secured creditor took a security interest in the debtor's property and the time the secured creditor properly filed a notice of its security interest.) This gap creditor would prevail even though it did not obtain a judicial lien until after the secured party had filed the notice of its interest. (Indeed, under the famous rule of Karst v. Gane, 136 N.Y. 316, 32 N.E. 1073 (1893), creditors would be protected from the claim of a secured creditor who delayed filing notice of its interest even if they had extended their credit before the "gap" in question: "[A]ntecedent creditors may be lulled into security, and forbear the collection of their debts at maturity, by the apparent unencumbered possession and ownership by the debtor of property covered by an undisclosed mortgage.")

In Constance v. Harvey, the secured party delayed for ten months before finally filing the documents necessary to perfect his security interest, but the record failed to show either the date of the debtor's bankruptcy petition or whether any of the debtor's creditors had become creditors before the delayed filing (thus allowing them to fit either in the "gap" or under the rule of Karst v. Gane). The Second Circuit first decided that it did not possess enough information to apply either §70c or §70e, and remanded for further findings. On petition for rehearing, however, the Second Circuit, on its own motion, decided that the security interest was invalid under §70c. The court stated:

> the provisions of §230 of the N.Y. Lien Law . . . , as construed by the New York Courts, mak[e] unrecorded chattel mortgages void as to *simple contract creditors* becoming such, without notice, prior to actual recording . . . in contrast to the provisions of §65 of the N.Y. Personal Property law . . . making unrecorded *conditional sales contracts* void as to creditors, without notice, who have acquired *liens* on the goods prior to recording of the contract. Since an existing creditor without notice of the chattel mortgage, could have obtained a lien at the time of the filing of the petition in bankruptcy, and since under §70, sub. c of the Bankruptcy Act the Trustee was entitled to be put in the position of an "ideal" hypothetical creditor . . . we think his position must prevail over that of the mortgagee-appellant. (Emphasis in original.)

In light of the facts, what precisely is the holding of Constance v. Harvey? Section 70c of the Bankruptcy Act of 1898 prescribed when the trustee takes his hypothetical status as a *lien* creditor (the date of bankruptcy); Constance v. Harvey decided when the trustee obtains his status as a *creditor*—that is, the date at which he hypothetically advances credit.

Is Constance v. Harvey a correct reading of §70c? A compelling one? Lewis v. Manufacturers Natl. Bank, 364 U.S. 603 (1961), said no. *Lewis* involved essentially the same facts as Constance v. Harvey. Justice Douglas stated that the statutory words "the rights . . . of a creditor then holding a lien" refer to "the date of bankruptcy," not "an anterior point of time." He continued:

> This construction seems to us to fit the scheme of the Act. . . . The construction of §70c which petitioner urges would give the trustee power to set aside transactions which no creditor could void and which injured no creditor. That construction would enrich unsecured creditors at the expense of secured creditors, creating a windfall merely by reason of the happenstance of bankruptcy.
>
> It is true that in some instances the trustee has rights which existing creditors may not have. [Justice Douglas discusses several, such as the preference power.]
>
> Congress in striking a balance between secured and unsecured creditors has provided for specific periods of repose beyond which transactions of the bankrupt prior to bankruptcy may no longer be upset—except and unless existing creditors can set them aside. Yet if we construe §70c as petitioner does, there would be no period of repose.

Is this persuasive? Justice Harlan, who, while he was on the Second Circuit, was the author of Constance v. Harvey, wrote: "I think it appropriate to say that I have long since come to the view that [Constance v. Harvey] was ill-considered. I welcome this opportunity to join in setting the matter right."

But does Justice Douglas suggest why the line between hypothetical and real powers needs to be drawn where he draws it? At least a part of the point of a section such as §70c (or §544(a)) seems to be that it gives the trustee powers to set aside transactions that no actual creditor could set aside. Isn't the real question how extensively should the rights of secured creditors, as against unsecured creditors, be protected? You will want to consider the facts of *Lewis* when we examine §544(b) and Moore v. Bay, and ask what the outcome would be if there had been one actual "gap" creditor.

Is the construction given to §70c in *Lewis,* and carried forward in §544(a), justified on the grounds of the type of agreement the creditors would have negotiated for themselves had they been able? Should the trustee's hypothetical powers, in other words, reflect (at least abstractly) the real powers enjoyed by the creditors? Is that what Justice Douglas had in mind when he focused on whether actual creditors were hurt?

Is the emphasis on whether actual creditors are hurt correct as a matter of policy? Shortly after *Lewis,* the Ninth Circuit decided Pacific Finance Corp. v. Edwards, 304 F.2d 224 (9th Cir. 1962). In *Pacific Finance,* a Washington statute provided that a conditional sales contract (a form of a security interest) remaining unrecorded for more than ten days was unenforceable against subsequent creditors, even creditors who came into existence after the "gap." Is the security interest arising out of a conditional sales contract, not recorded until after the ten-day grace period, avoidable by the trustee in bankruptcy under §70c? The Ninth Circuit, discussing *Lewis* extensively, held no. The court noted that all of the debtor's creditors were creditors as to whom the conditional sales contract was effective: There were no subsequent creditors. The court reasoned:

> Under its plain language, §70, sub. c applies only where there is property . . . "upon which a creditor of the bankrupt could have obtained a lien by legal or equitable proceedings at the date of bankruptcy. . . ." We believe that the word "creditor" in the foregoing quoted language means an *actual* creditor. . . . The clause "whether or not such a creditor actually exists" refers only to a "creditor then holding a lien thereon." Under our construction of §70, sub. c the Trustee is empowered to exercise the powers given him even if no actual creditor has obtained a lien, but he cannot do so if no actual creditor could have obtained a lien. . . .
>
> In the instant case, as in the *Lewis* case, there was no actual creditor of the bankrupt who extended credit after [the date of the conditional sales contract] and prior to the date of bankruptcy. There was no creditor of the bankrupt who was injured. . . .
>
> . . . We find nothing . . . indicating an intent on the part of Congress to penalize the security holder by giving to the trustee the status of a hypothetical creditor holding a lien at the date of bankruptcy in instances where there existed no actual creditor who could have obtained a lien on the property of the bankrupt by legal or equitable proceedings at such date. . . .
>
> . . . In our view, §70, sub. c grants to the Trustee the status of a lien creditor whenever an actual creditor exists who could have become a lien creditor but did not do so.

Is this reasoning persuasive? Consistent with *Lewis?* How would the case come out under §544(a)? To what extent does §544(a) depart from the reasoning of *Lewis?* Are those departures sensible?

The wording of this "strong-arm" power, now in §544(a), is not the only thing that has changed. The trustee's powers, even under this strong-arm provision, rest ultimately on the powers of a lien creditor under state law, which can also change, as it has since the time of these cases. Even if Constance v. Harvey had been codified in the Bankruptcy Code, therefore, it would not have been a major threat to security interests arising under Article 9 of the Uniform Commercial Code. For, unless a court posited not only a creditor, but a *lien* creditor, arising on or before the "gap," Article 9 forecloses use of a section drafted like §70c, as interpreted by Constance v. Harvey. Section 9-301(1)(b) of the Uniform Commercial Code subordinates an unperfected security interest to "a person who becomes a *lien* creditor before the security interest is perfected" (emphasis supplied). Will the same result follow, however, with respect to a "true" consignor who files late? See UCC §§1-201(37); 2-326(2), (3); 9-114.

B.   THE TRUSTEE AS SUCCESSOR TO CREDITOR CLAIMS (§544(b))

Section 544(b) allows the trustee to "inherit" the rights of *existing unsecured creditors* of the debtor, so that if any one of them could set aside a transaction, the trustee takes over that power and may use it for the benefit of the unsecured creditors generally. To use §544(b), the trustee must find a real, existing creditor of a particular type — one with an *allowable* and *unsecured* claim. The trustee must also both identify the actual creditor and the basis on which that creditor could avoid the transfer in question. This, then, is a *particularized* test: Unlike §544(a), it is not a constant standard (i.e., a lien creditor) operating at a constant point in time (i.e., the date of the commencement of a bankruptcy case).

PROBLEM

5.9 M.I.I. Corp. entered into an agreement with Goldco, a limited partnership, for ownership and operation of a hotel in Riverside, California. Goldco has three general partners. M.I.I. files a petition in Chapter 11. The trustee of M.I.I. brings a suit against M.I.I., Goldco, and its three general partners, seeking, on an alter ego theory, to disregard M.I.I.'s corporate existence and establish defendants' personal liability for all of M.I.I.'s debts. Assuming the trustee can make out a case for application of the alter ego doctrine under state law, may the trustee pursue the action? The trustee argues that "he represents the corporate creditors and that by virtue of section [544(b)] he has the rights of a creditor and can therefore maintain this action on behalf of the creditors." As the judge hearing that argument, how do you rule? See Stodd v. Goldberger, 73 Cal. App. 3d 827, 141 Cal. Rptr. 67 (4th Dist. 1977).

It is §544(b) that gives the trustee access to state fraudulent conveyance laws, state bulk sales statutes, and comparable nonbankruptcy rights of unsecured creditors against property transfers that occurred prior to bankruptcy. The scope of §544(b), however, cannot be understood without recognizing the impact of Moore v. Bay. The lower court opinion in that case follows.

IN RE SASSARD & KIMBALL, INC.
45 F.2d 449 (9th Cir. 1930)

NORCROSS, District Judge.

This is an appeal from an order made by the court below reversing a ruling of the referee in bankruptcy holding a certain chattel mortgage void as to all creditors.

The facts are stipulated, and those material are as follows: At all times important to be considered in this case Sassard & Kimball, Inc., was a corporation engaged in the business of a merchant selling automobiles, automobile parts and accessories. On the 31st day of December, 1929, the corporation filed a voluntary petition in bankruptcy, and on the same date appellant was appointed receiver for the estate of the bankrupt, and upon qualifying, took into his possession all property claimed to be a part of the estate, including that covered by a certain chattel mortgage in question. On November 23, 1928, the bankrupt executed a chattel mortgage as security for the payment of a certain promissory note for $10,000, payable thirty days after date to the assignor of appellee. The mortgage was acknowledged of date November 30, 1928, the affidavit of good faith was executed December 5, 1928, and the instrument filed for record and recorded by the county recorder of Los Angeles county on December 19, 1928. The chattel mortgage covered a certain Studebaker service car, a Ford roadster, the furniture, showroom, and shop equipment of the bankrupt. Prior to the execution or filing of the mortgage, no notice of intention to mortgage the stock in trade, fixtures, and equipment belonging to the mortgagor was recorded in accordance with the provisions of section 3440 of the Civil Code of California. In relation to the mortgage, the proceeding presents three classes of creditors of the bankrupt: (1) Those existing at the date of the mortgage; (2) those who became such between the date of the mortgage and its recordation; (3) those so becoming subsequent to the recording of the mortgage.

Section 3440 of the Civil Code of California provides that a chattel mortgage "will be conclusively presumed to be fraudulent and void as against the existing creditors . . . unless at least seven days before the consummation of such . . . mortgage, the . . . mortgagor . . . shall record in the office of the county recorder . . . a notice of said intended . . . mortgage," setting out the particulars of its proposed effect and purpose.

It is clear that the mortgage, by reason of the provisions of the statute, is void as to creditors of the first class, and it is conceded it is also void as to those of the second class. As held by decisions of the Supreme Court of California, the mortgage would be valid as against creditors of the third class. . . .

It is the contention of appellant that, under section 70e of the Bankruptcy Act of 1898 (11 USCA §110(e)), the mortgage in question, being void as to one creditor or class of creditors, is void in toto at the suit of the trustee.

Section 70e of the Bankruptcy Act reads: "The trustee may avoid any transfer by the bankrupt of his property which any creditor of such bankrupt might have avoided, and may recover the property so transferred, or its value, from the person to whom it was transferred, unless he was a bona fide holder for value prior to the date of the adjudication. Such property may be recovered or its value collected from whoever may have received it, except a bona fide holder for value. For the purpose of such recovery any court of bankruptcy as defined in this title, and any State court which would have had jurisdiction if bankruptcy had not intervened, shall have concurrent jurisdiction."

There is no express language in this section which specifically gives to any unsecured creditor of a bankrupt any greater rights or any secured creditor any less right than he had before adjudication in bankruptcy. The rights of a trustee in bankruptcy to "avoid any transfer" are no greater than those of a creditor or particular class of creditors. It is clear, we think, that a trustee in bankruptcy is limited in his control and disposition of the estate of the bankrupt to the rights of creditors as such rights existed and could be enforced under the state law prior to the time proceedings in bankruptcy were instituted. This is not a case of an ordinary transfer of property in whole or in part in fraud of creditors, but a case of a transfer made void by statute only as to a specific class of creditors. In National Bank v. Moore, 247 F. 913, 919, this court said: "The trustee in the interest of the general creditors may therefore contest any claim of lien that a judgment creditor might contest if bankruptcy had not intervened."

In the case at bar, only judgment creditors of the first or second class specified could have successfully contested the mortgage had not bankruptcy intervened.

We quote with approval the following from the memorandum opinion of Judge Killits filed in the court below: "In 1910, the Bankruptcy Act was amended to make clear the position of the Trustee. It seems to have been the theory of the Referee that the effect of this amendment, which gave the Trustee the status of an execution creditor, so far affected the status of the creditors of each of the three classes, as against the mortgage, as to place them all on the same level of superiority. In this we are very clear that the Referee was wrong. There is nothing whatever in the cause for, or the language of the amendment of 1910 to produce such a result. The Trustee indeed represents all creditors, but only as their respective interests in the property under administration were fixed by local law when the bankruptcy proceedings intervened, and it is his duty to administer and distribute accordingly as he finds at that time liens or inferiorities of respective creditors were established. If at that time any creditors had no inchoate right under existing state laws to reduce his claim to judgment and thereby establish a lien by execution superior to an existing and recorded mortgage, he is bound in distribution to recognize the latter's superior position. It is said, as a settled law in federal courts, that there is so much of local nature entering into chattel mortgages that federal courts accept as decisive the state law fixing the priority of such encumbrance. . . ."

The order is affirmed.

NOTES

1. The court quotes a portion of §3440, Civil Code of the State of California, as it existed at the time of the mortgage involved in the case. A fuller version of that section provides as follows:

> Every transfer of personal property, other than a thing in action, or a ship or cargo at sea or in a foreign port and every lien thereon, other than a mortgage, when allowed by law, and a contract of bottomry or respondentia, is conclusively presumed if made by a person having at the time the possession or control of the property, and not accompanied by an immediate delivery, and followed by an actual and continued change of possession of the things transferred, to be fraudulent, and therefore void, against those who are his creditors while he remains in possession, and the successors in interest of such creditors, and against any persons on whom his estate devolves in trust for the benefit of others than himself, and against purchasers or encumbrancers in good faith subsequent to the transfer. . . . Provided, also, . . . that the sale, transfer, assignment or mortgage of the fixtures or store equipment of a . . . garage owner . . . or retail or wholesale merchant, will be conclusively presumed to be fraudulent and void as against the existing creditors of the vendor, transferor, assignor or mortgagor, unless at least seven days before the consummation of such sale, transfer, assignment or mortgage, the vendor, transferor, assignor or mortgagor or the intended vendee, transferee, assignee, or mortgagee, shall record in the office of the county recorder in the county or counties in which said . . . fixtures or equipment are situated a notice of said intended sale, transfer, assignment or mortgage, stating the name and address of the intended vendor, transferor, assignor or mortgagor, and the name and address of the intended vendee, transferee, assignee or mortgagee, and a general statement of the character of the merchandise or property intended to be sold, assigned, transferred or mortgaged, and the date when and the place where the purchase price or consideration, if any there be, is to be paid.

2. Section 2957 of the Civil Code of the State of California, at the relevant time, read as follows:

> A mortgage of personal property is void as against creditors of the mortgagor and subsequent purchasers and encumbrancers of the property in good faith and for value, unless:
>   1. It is accompanied by the affidavit of all the parties thereto that it is made in good faith and without any design to hinder, delay, or defraud creditors;
>   2. It is acknowledged or proved, certified, and recorded in like manner as grants of real property.

Moore v. Bay follows. It is reprinted in full.

MOORE v. BAY
284 U.S. 4 (1931)

Justice HOLMES delivered the opinion of the Court.

The bankrupt executed a mortgage of automobiles, furniture, show room and shop equipment that is admitted to be bad as against creditors who were such at the date of the mortgage and those who became such between the date of the mortgage and that on which it was recorded, there having been a failure to observe the requirements of the Civil Code of California, §3440. The question raised is whether the mortgage is void also as against those who gave the bankrupt credit at a later date, after the mortgage was on record. The Circuit Court of Appeals affirmed an order of the District Judge giving the mortgage priority over the last creditors. Whether the Court was right must be decided by the Bankruptcy Act since it is superior to all state laws upon the subject. Globe Bank v. Martin, 236 U.S. 288, 298.

The trustee in bankruptcy gets the title to all property which has been transferred by the bankrupt in fraud of creditors, or which prior to the petition he could by any means have transferred, or which might have been levied upon and sold under judicial process against him. Act of July 1, 1898, c. 541, §70; U.S. Code, Title 11, §110. By §67, Code, Title 11, §107(a), claims which for want of record or for other reasons would not have been valid liens as against the claims of the creditors of the bankrupt shall not be liens against his estate. The rights of the trustee by subrogation are to be enforced for the benefit of the estate. The Circuit Courts of Appeals seem generally to agree, as the language of the Bankruptcy Act appears to us to imply very plainly, that what thus is recovered for the benefit of the estate is to be distributed in "dividends of an equal percentum on all allowed claims, except such as have priority or are secured." Bankruptcy Act, §65, Code, Title 11, §105. In re Kohler, 159 F. 871.

Mullen v. Warner, 11 F.2d 62. Campbell v. Dalbey, 23 F.2d 229. Cohen v. Schultz, 43 F.2d 340. Globe Bank v. Martin, 236 U.S. 288, 305.

Decree reversed.

NOTES

1. "Subsection (b) [of §544] is derived from current section 70e. It gives the trustee the rights of actual unsecured creditors under applicable law to void transfers. It follows Moore v. Bay, 284 U.S. 4 (1931), and overrules those cases that hold section 70e gives the trustee the rights of secured creditors." H.R. Rep. No. 595, 95th Cong. 1st Sess. 370 (1977).

2. What is the holding of Moore v. Bay? Justice Holmes noted that the "rights of the trustee by subrogation are to be enforced for the benefit of the estate." Is Moore v. Bay consistent with the concept of subrogation? Of the cases Justice Holmes cites, only Campbell v. Dalbey, 23 F.2d 229, 230 (5th Cir. 1927), suggests that the trustee can set aside the entire transaction, and it is cited following the statement that "what thus is recovered for the benefit of the estate is to be distributed in 'dividends of an equal percentum on all allowed claims, except such as have priority or are secured.'" Two other cases cited in the same place by Justice Holmes, moreover, quite clearly deal only with the question of distribution, not the scope of the trustee's avoiding powers. *Globe Bank,* the one Supreme Court case cited by Justice Holmes, discusses only the distributional question. For a discussion of Moore v. Bay, see Kennedy, The Trustee in Bankruptcy as a Secured Creditor Under the Uniform Commercial Code, 65 Mich. L. Rev. 1419, 1421 (1967). In any event, why should rights derived from one creditor be used for the benefit of the estate, instead of that one creditor? These issues are explored in the next note.

NOTE ON MOORE v. BAY AND §544(b)

Two issues were raised before the Ninth Circuit in *Sassard.* The first issue involved the question of the *extent* to which the trustee could avoid the chattel mortgage. The second issue, which normally would arise only if the first issue were decided so as to limit the trustee's power to avoid such mortgages, asked: *Who benefits* from the trustee's avoiding the mortgage? For example, assume that the chattel mortgage was for $10,000, on property worth at least that amount. Apart from the claim secured by that chattel mortgage, the debtor, at the time it filed for bankruptcy, had unsecured claims against it amounting to $100,000. Of these unsecured claims, $3,000 arose prior to the time the chattel mortgage came into existence, and another $2,000 arose during the "gap" between the time the chattel mortgage was taken and the time it was recorded. The remaining $95,000 arose after the recording of the chattel mortgage.

The Ninth Circuit was clear about its resolution of the first issue: The chattel mortgage could be avoided by the trustee only to the extent of $5,000—the amount by which it could have been avoided outside of bankruptcy by the earlier and "gap" unsecured creditors. On the second issue, however, the opinion of the Ninth Circuit was not clear. The opinion has been read as saying that the trustee takes this $5,000 "recovered," and holds it for the benefit of *all* unsecured creditors (the $100,000 of original unsecured creditors plus, presumably, the $5,000 debt originally covered by the chattel mortgage.) The Ninth Circuit, however, may have in fact reached the opposite conclusion, as had some courts before it. Its opinion can be read as holding that the nonbankruptcy result provided by state law is to be followed in full. If state law were the basis for determining rights in bankruptcy, then the $5,000 avoided by the trustee should be preserved for the benefit of the earlier and gap unsecured creditors, but not the subsequent creditors. Under this reading, which a review of the record suggests is far more plausible, relative nonbankruptcy rights are preserved among the unsecured creditors. The record is discussed in Jackson, Avoiding Powers in Bankruptcy, 36 Stan. L. Rev. 725, 742-750 (1984).

If the latter interpretation were actually the Ninth Circuit's holding in *Sassard,* then one could read the Supreme Court's reversal (and Justice Holmes' cryptic opinion) in Moore v. Bay, as overturning the Ninth Circuit only on that second issue—holding, in other words, that the $5,000 avoided was to be taken "for the benefit of the estate." Justice Holmes, in short, may have held exactly what many critics of Moore v. Bay argue he should have held—that the chattel mortgage was to be set aside for the benefit of all creditors only to the extent of the interest of the actual "gap" creditor. The conventional reading of Moore v. Bay, however, is that the Supreme Court held that the chattel mortgage could be avoided entirely, and the $10,000 so recovered was an asset of the estate to be shared by all unsecured creditors. See In re Plonta, 311 F.2d 44 (6th Cir. 1962); City of New York v. Rassner, 127 F.2d 703, 707 (2d Cir. 1942); Kennedy, The Trustee in Bankruptcy as a Secured Creditor Under the Uniform Commercial Code, 65 Mich. L. Rev. 1419 (1967). As such, it has been excoriated by one of the principal drafters of the 1938 amendments to the Bankruptcy Act. Consider the following, J. MacLachlan, Handbook of the Law of Bankruptcy 330-331 (1956):

> The scope of section 70e [the predecessor to §544(b)] is, however, clouded by one of the most glaring misconstructions to be encountered in the history of Anglo-American law. The result must be attributed in large part to the fact that the decision was made on reversing a judgment of the Circuit Court of Appeals without the benefit of argument on the part of respondent. Mr. Justice Holmes, then over 90 years old, stated the facts in

two sentences and the procedure below in one, and the law in five more. The opinion thoroughly concealed the critical point of the case. An examination of the record leads to the conclusion that the Court did not grasp the point and did not understand the effect of its decision. The Court said: "The bankrupt executed a mortgage of automobiles, furniture, showroom, and shop equipment that is admitted to be bad as against creditors who were such at the date of the mortgage and those who became such between the date of the mortgage and that on which it was recorded, there having been a failure to observe the requirements of . . . §3440. . . . The question raised is whether the mortgage is void also as against those who gave the bankrupt credit at a later date, after the mortgage was on record." This is a serious misstatement. The record shows that there were two questions, but this was not a proper statement of either. The questions were: (1) whether the trustee in bankruptcy could appropriate all the mortgaged property or whether his right to attack it was measured by the claims of creditors who could attack it. (2) Assuming that his recovery was the more limited one (as all previous cases had assumed), was his recovery to inure only to the direct benefit of the creditors who could attack or did it become a general asset of the estate?

While the reading that MacLachlan attacks has generated widespread criticism of Moore v. Bay, is it not troubling that either reading upsets rights that had already been fixed outside of bankruptcy? Is rearranging rights in either fashion consistent with any bankruptcy policy? Doesn't Moore v. Bay under either reading upset nonbankruptcy rights in bankruptcy for the benefit of some creditors, but not for the collective benefit of the creditors as a group?

The difference in the two ways of interpreting Moore v. Bay seems to be the group that is being harmed. If—to continue with our example from above—the opinion in Moore v. Bay simply took the $5,000 and distributed it among the unsecured creditors as a group (the reading seemingly favored by most commentators), the costs imposed, compared with nonbankruptcy rights, would be on the earlier and gap unsecured creditors, not on the holder of the chattel mortgage. The group of creditors thereby harmed, however, seems entirely blameless under any theory of entitlements. The holder of the chattel mortgage, who created the ostensible ownership problem in the first place, ironically might wind up in a slightly better position in bankruptcy than he would be otherwise. Outside of bankruptcy, he would lose $5,000 to the actual gap creditors. Inside, he would participate, pro rata, in the $5,000 the trustee avoids under §544(b).

Even if the trustee could set aside only part of the secured creditor's interest when there was a gap creditor, it seems wrong, as a matter of bankruptcy policy, to allow an asset—a right to avoid a property interest—to be taken from a particular unsecured creditor, or group of creditors (such as gap creditors), to be made generally available to unsecured creditors as a class. The harm is imposed on different parties and may differ in amount than if Moore v. Bay is interpreted as traditionally understood, but the nature of the harm is no different in principle. It leads, moreover, to the same result: The creation of incentives to resort to bankruptcy, not for collective benefit of all interested parties, but for reasons of individual advantage-taking. Such rules seem imprudent, especially in the absence of reason to reject the nonbankruptcy rule. Does such a reason exist?

PROBLEMS

5.10 Debtor owns a machine worth $20,000. Debtor has borrowed $10,000 from Bank, secured by this machine. Debtor has also borrowed small amounts of money from each of Creditors 1, 2, and 3 on an unsecured basis. The sequence of these events is as follows:

June 1:   Loan of $10 by Creditor 1
July 1:   Loan of $10,000 from Bank; security interest granted
August 1:   Loan of $20 by Creditor 2
September 1:   Bank files financing statement in proper office
October 1:   Loan of $30 by Creditor 3

Debtor defaults against all concerned on November 1.

a. What are the rights of Bank and Creditors 1, 2, and 3 outside of bankruptcy? For purposes of answering this question, assume that each of Creditors 1, 2, and 3 levy on the property during November pursuant to an execution lien. Analyze this as if each levied first: i.e., Creditor 1 versus Bank, Creditor 2 versus Bank, and Creditor 3 versus Bank.

1. What are their rights with respect to the equipment under the California statutes quoted following *Sassard & Kimball*, supra?

2. Under UCC §9-301(1)(b)?

b. Assume that no creditor takes any individual action during November, and that Debtor files for bankruptcy on December 1.

1. To what extent can the trustee in bankruptcy avoid Bank's security interest under §544(b) if the relevant state statutory scheme is that of the California statutes quoted following *Sassard & Kimball*, supra? See In re Plonta, 311 F.2d 44 (6th Cir. 1962) (conditional sale interest of seller, "being invalid under the Michigan statute as to [an] interim creditor . . . , was null and void as against the Trustee." The amount of credit extended to [the debtor] "is immaterial"); Mercantile Trust Co. v. Kahn, 203 F.2d 449 (8th Cir. 1953).

2. To what extent can the trustee in bankruptcy avoid Bank's security interest under §544(b) if the relevant state statutory scheme is that of Article 9 of the Uniform Commercial Code? See UCC §§9-201; 9-301(1)(b).

5.11 Consider the facts of Lewis v. Manufacturer's Natl. Bank, supra page 232. Had one gap creditor existed, how would the case have come out, given Moore v. Bay? Would that result have been consistent with Justice Douglas' explanation in the case? If the facts of *Lewis* were to arise today, under Article 9 of the Uniform Commercial Code, how would the case come out if one gap creditor had existed? See UCC §9-301. Would it matter if there existed a creditor who had acquired a lien during the gap? See legislative history to §544, quoted above, note 1 after Moore v. Bay.

5.12 Debtor runs a small grocery store. She owes $100,000 to an assortment of trade creditors. She sells her store to Buyer for $250,000 without telling the trade creditors. $50,000 is paid in cash and $200,000 is in the form of a promissory note payable in a year's time. Two months later, Debtor commits a tort and becomes liable for an additional $200,000. Debtor has no assets beyond the $50,000 cash and the $200,000 note receivable. She files a bankruptcy petition. To what extent can the trustee set aside the sale of the grocery store to Buyer? To what extent can he keep the money Buyer has paid and enforce the $200,000 promissory note?

Article 6 of the Uniform Commercial Code, governing "bulk sales," provides that most transfers "in bulk and not in the ordinary course of the transferor's business of a major part of the materials, supplies, merchandise or other inventory" by an enterprise "whose principal business is the sale of merchandise from stock," (§6-102) are "ineffective against any creditor of the transferor" (§6-104) unless, inter alia, the transferee gives notice, pursuant to §6-107, to the transferor's creditors at least ten days before the transferee "takes possession of the goods or pays for them." §6-105. Noncomplying transfers are subject to attack for six months from the date the transferee takes possession of the goods. §6-111. (The six months is subject to extension if the transfer has been concealed.) Bulk transfers of equipment are also covered by Article 6 if, but only if, that transfer is made in connection with a bulk transfer of inventory. §6-102(2).

Article 6, therefore, places burdens on the transferee in a situation where the transferor appears to be "cashing out" of its existing business. The burden placed on the transferee is that of notifying the transferor's creditors. In this way, those creditors can take steps to protect their rights, having been notified that their debtor has just converted its assets into a more liquid (and concealable) form. See §6-101, comment.

Article 6 provides, in §6-109, that

> The creditors of the transferor mentioned in this Article are those holding claims based on transactions or events occurring before the bulk transfer, but creditors who become such after notice to creditors is given (Sections 6-105 and 6-107) are not entitled to notice.

See In re Verco Industries, 10 Bankr. 347 (9th Cir. Bankr. App. 1981), rev'd in part, 704 F.2d 1134 (9th Cir. 1983). See also In re Curtina

International, 34 U.C.C. Rep. 1311 (Bankr. S.D.N.Y. 1982) (in bulk sale where transferee acted in good faith and gave a reasonably equivalent value, "it would be inequitable to allow the trustee to retain a portion of the proceeds held by him that are traceable to the [transferee's] payment for the debtor's wafer inventory and, nevertheless, require the [transferee] to pay in full for the inventory a second time"; "the [transferee's] liability should be limited to the value of any unrecovered or unaccounted for proceeds").

As these problems indicate, the retention of Moore v. Bay is far less important in a world where the governing priority rule is UCC §9-301 than it would have been in the world of Constance v. Harvey, Karst v. Gane, and Moore v. Bay.

NOTE ON STATE PREFERENCE SECTIONS AND §544(b)

Assume that Debtor, who has owed Creditor some $50,000 on an unsecured basis, pays Creditor in full on April 10. On August 1, Debtor files for bankruptcy. As we shall see in Chapter 6, the payment cannot be reached under §547, the Bankruptcy Code's preference section, because the payment was made more than 90 days before the commencement of the bankruptcy case. But what if Debtor resides in a state that provides by statute that any transfer made by a debtor on account of an antecedent debt within four months before the commencement of proceedings in insolvency shall "inure to the benefit of all creditors" of the debtor? Can the trustee use §544(b) in conjunction with the statute to reach the payment? Copter, Inc. v. Gladwin Leasing, 725 F.2d 37 (3d Cir. 1984), held no, construing the state statute as applying only to state insolvency proceedings. But what if the state statute were construed otherwise? The district court, 28 Bankr. 665, held that the statute could not be used, because it was preempted by §547. In considering whether this is correct, note that although the Bankruptcy Code contains its own fraudulent conveyance section, §548, §544(b) is routinely used to give trustees access to state fraudulent conveyance laws and their longer reach-back provisions. See, e.g., In re Porter, 37 Bankr. 56 (Bankr. E.D. Va. 1984). Is §544(b) improperly used there as well, or is there some difference between a state preference section and a state fraudulent conveyance section? While full exploration of this question must be deferred until you examine the materials on fraudulent conveyances and preferences later in this chapter and in the next, it might be worth noting now that preferences generally are not avoidable except in connection with a collective proceeding, whereas fraudulent conveyances are voidable whether or not a proceeding has commenced. Fraudulent conveyances are considered general wrongs by the debtor against creditors whereas preferences are considered wrongs by creditors who thereby attempt to "opt out" of an impending collective proceeding. Given that, might there not be good reason to look to state law to determine what activities are considered to be wrongs against creditors, but *not* to look to state law to determine what actions are considered by the state to be wrongs *against a collective proceeding*? With respect to the latter issue, isn't that a question to be determined by bankruptcy law? Do *Butner*, supra page 35, and the discussion there of substance and procedure, assist at all in resolving this? Would it make any difference if a state insolvency proceeding (such as an assignment for the benefit of creditors) had been commenced and *then* a bankruptcy case were commenced, under §303(h)(2)? See In re Kenval Marketing Corp., 40 Bankr. 445 (Bankr. E.D. Pa. 1984).

C. FRAUDULENT CONVEYANCES

INTRODUCTORY NOTE

In 1571, Parliament passed a statute making illegal and void any transfer made for the purpose of delaying, hindering, or defrauding creditors. This law, commonly known as the Statute of 13 Elizabeth, was intended to curb what was thought to be a widespread abuse. Until the seventeenth century there were certain sanctuaries in England into which the King's writ could not enter. A sanctuary was not merely the interior of a church, but certain precincts defined by custom or royal grant. Debtors could take sanctuary in one of these precincts, live in relative comfort, and be immune from execution by their creditors. It was thought that debtors commonly removed themselves to one of these precincts only after selling their property to friends and relatives for a trivial sum, with the tacit understanding that they would reclaim their property when the dust settled and their creditors gave up or compromised their claims. The Statute of 13 Elizabeth limited this practice. Because half of the property deemed to be fraudulently conveyed was forfeited to the Crown, the statute was also in part a revenue measure. See G. Glenn, Fraudulent Conveyances and Preferences §§61-61e (rev. ed. 1940).

The basic prohibition of this statute has survived unchanged for over four centuries. A debtor cannot manipulate his affairs in such a way that he shortchanges his creditors and pockets the difference. Those who collude with a debtor in these transactions are not protected either. An individual creditor who discovers its debtor's assets have been fraudulently conveyed can reduce its claim to judgment and simply have the sheriff levy on the property wherever it now lies (as long as it is not in the hands of a bona fide purchaser for value). The difficulty that courts and legislators have faced for more than five hundred years has been trying to define what kinds of transactions delay, hinder, or defraud creditors and what kinds do not.

An insolvent debtor who pays off one creditor but not another does not make a fraudulent conveyance. Such a transfer does in fact "delay" and "hinder" those creditors who remain unpaid. The debtor has received nothing for making the transfer, and the remaining creditors are less likely to be paid in full. But merely preferring one creditor over another cannot render a transaction voidable by the unpaid creditors. As long as no collective proceeding has been commenced, each creditor must look after its own interests. If Debtor owes $100 to each of A and B and has a piece of property worth $100, the creditor that will be paid is the one who acts the swiftest. If A recovers $100, it makes no sense to treat the transaction as a fraudulent conveyance and allow B to levy on it. When no legal rule forces creditors to cooperate or share the debtor's assets among themselves, there is no reason to protect A or B. Making simple preferences fraudulent conveyances would not keep one creditor from being paid at the other's expense; it would only shift the benefit to the creditor who acted second, rather than the one who acted first. A simple preference improves the position of some creditors, but it does not make the debtor better off. The hallmark of a fraudulent conveyance is a benefit to the debtor.

It is nevertheless difficult under any set of facts to determine whether a transaction is in fact an ordinary business deal, a simple preference, or an effort to manipulate one's affairs to thwart creditors. From very early on, common law judges developed per se rules, known as "badges of fraud," that would allow them to treat a transaction as a fraudulent conveyance, even though there was no specific evidence of a debtor's effort to profit at its creditors' expense. For example, common law judges assumed that an insolvent debtor who sold property, but retained possession of it without any special reason (such as a need to complete unfinished goods) was up to no good.

In addition to cases of presumed fraudulent intent, the law was also used to reach other transactions thought to be objectionable to creditors, such as gifts by insolvents, irrespective of intent. We cannot assume that a debtor is trying to shortchange creditors if it pays off one creditor without more (such as entering a side deal that allows it to keep possession of the property it purports to transfer). But the number of cases in which an insolvent debtor otherwise gives away something for nothing in which his creditors would not object is sufficiently small that we can treat such transfers as fraudulent conveyances.

The reach of the fraudulent conveyance laws is quite substantial and presents a constant worry to lawyers who plan garden variety commercial transactions, such as guarantees among related corporations or leveraged buy-outs. An individual who owns all his assets outright bears all the losses and enjoys all the benefits from any transaction he enters into. As soon as he borrows money or otherwise obtains credit, however, his incentives become skewed. He enjoys all the residual benefits but, given the limited liability of corporations and the availability of a discharge in bankruptcy, he does not bear all the losses. All who have creditors have an incentive to take risks that are not in the interests of the creditors or the creditors and debtor collectively. Fraudulent conveyance law can be understood as a partial response to the incentives for advantage-taking that exist whenever a debtor-creditor relationship arises. The fundamental problem to be addressed in studying the law of fraudulent conveyances is determining how much advantage-taking it controls.

In virtually every American jurisdiction, the Statute of 13 Elizabeth has been either recognized as part of the common law or enacted in more or less similar terms. In 1919, the National Conference of Commissioners on Uniform State Laws proposed the Uniform Fraudulent Conveyance Act (UFCA), drafted principally by Professor Williston. The statute, with some minor variations, has been enacted in about one-half the states. See 7A Unif. Laws Ann. 16 (Supp. 1980). Drafting of a new Uniform Fraudulent Transfer Act is now underway.

Creditors can set aside, under the UFCA or comparable state statutes, transfers that a debtor makes with an actual intent to delay, hinder, or defraud them as well as transfers by insolvent debtors that bring too little in return. If a debtor conveys an expensive computer to his sister (as a gift or for a nominal amount) and then disappears for parts unknown, the creditors can set aside the transfer and levy on the asset, even though the computer is now in the possession of the sister. UFCA §9(1)(b). A transfer is also a fraudulent conveyance, under this provision, if the computer is sold to a bona fide purchaser for fair consideration, as long as the debtor has the requisite fraudulent intent (such as to convert assets to cash and hide them). The difference in this case (and it is a substantial one) is that the creditors, under UFCA §9(2), have no power to retrieve the property from the hands of the purchaser.

Litigation over fraudulent conveyances usually focuses on the rule that requires only a transfer for less than fair consideration while the debtor is insolvent without a showing of actual intent to delay, hinder, or defraud. It is important, however, to remember not merely that a fraudulent conveyance can exist even if there is fair consideration, but also that the rule is best thought of as a surrogate for striking down transactions thought to be objectionable to creditors. When we ask whether a case at the margin should be treated as a fraudulent conveyance, we should remember that we allow creditors to set aside transfers made for less than adequate consideration while they are insolvent not because such transfers are always bad in themselves, but because so many of these transfers would be deemed objectionable by creditors that we do not think it worth the cost of an actual inquiry in any individual case.

CLARK, THE DUTIES OF THE CORPORATE
DEBTOR TO ITS CREDITORS
90 Harv. L. Rev. 505, 506-517 (1977)

The law of fraudulent conveyances, of which the Uniform Fraudulent Conveyance Act (UFCA) is the principal but not exclusive embodiment, allows creditors to set aside certain transfers by debtors. Fraudulent conveyance law has a broad applicability, restricted neither to conveyances — since virtually all transfers of property, and, under the UFCA and under the Bankruptcy Act, the incurrence of obligations, are covered — nor to fraud — since unfair transfers made without deceptive intent are included. Court opinions involving allegedly fraudulent transfers have not infrequently sounded muddled and uncertain notes because of a failure to discriminate among the various distinct ideals that this body of law seeks to implement. Although more than one of these distinct ideals are usually involved in actual cases, what these ideals are, and how closely they are related to the ideal underlying the law of preferential transfers, can be seen through an examination of four simple situations.

1. Debtor grants Friend a mortgage on his small factory in return for a loan of $160,000, which Friend actually makes to Debtor. Debtor, wishing to discourage unpaid trade creditors having $30,000 of claims from litigating them to judgment and seeking execution against the factory, prevails upon Friend to have the recorded mortgage recite that it secures a debt for $200,000, which equals the well-known market value of the factory.[12] The trade creditors' attorneys search the real estate records, discover and give credence to the false mortgage, and, knowing that Debtor has few assets other than the factory, become discouraged and cease pursuing Debtor.

Here, then, is a case of Ur-Fraud, that primeval fraud on creditors than which no greater can be thought. The transfer of the mortgage interest to Friend was known to be false, was intended to thwart legitimate creditors, and actually did so. The keynote of the evil is the *actual deception* or falsehood practiced on the trade creditors to their detriment. By hypothesis, Friend gave full and fair consideration for the extent of the mortgage interest that he could enforce against Debtor. Further, the mortgage interest that he obtained did not actually render Debtor incapable of satisfying the remaining creditors. The ideal offended is simply that of Truth: in connection with transfers of property rights to others, a debtor is forbidden to tell lies to his creditors that will lead to the nonsatisfaction of their claims.

---

12. In order to protect himself from possible double-crossing on the part of Friend, Debtor has Friend sign a secret affidavit stating that as of the date after the recording he is owed only $160,000 by Debtor, and the promissory note given by Debtor is in only this amount. Given the affidavit and the note, Friend's recovery would be limited to the $160,000 in any legal action.

2. Debtor has reached the point where $100,000 of her debts are due and payable, and her entire assets have a fair market value of the same dollar amount. Thinking that she would prefer that her husband and sister rather than her creditors get the benefits of her assets, she makes a deed of gift of all her possessions to those two fortunate relatives, and immediately delivers full and exclusive actual possession of the property to them, relinquishing any use or benefit from the transferred property. She makes no secret of the transaction or of her intentions: she reports the deed of gift in every conceivable recording office, and mails a copy by certified mail to each and every creditor, together with a detailed and psychologically accurate account of her motivations, purposes, and feelings toward her creditors. In this case, Debtor has made a transfer which would clearly be voidable since it was made without fair and full consideration and she was insolvent immediately after the transfer.

The ideal offended by Debtor in the above example is not that of truthful conduct toward creditors. Debtor has been completely open with her creditors and has never tried to deceive them, unless one wants to overstretch the notion of fraud by saying that, when she originally borrowed from her creditors, she "implicitly" promised to satisfy her legal obligations before her moral obligations and personal allegiances, that she has now failed to fulfill this promise, and that the failure is conclusive evidence that the promise was falsely and deceptively given. Instead, it is much simpler, and intellectually more honest, to recognize that another ideal is served by fraudulent conveyance law. The ideal can be captured by a cliche: be just before you are generous.[16] The debtor has a moral duty[17] in transferring his property to give *primacy* to so-called legal obligations, which are usually the legitimate, conventional claims of standard contract and tort creditors, as opposed to the interests of self, family, friends, shareholders, and shrewder or more powerful bargaining parties. I will somewhat hesitantly refer to this as the normative ideal of Respect.

3. Pierce is indebted to Twyne for $400 and to *C* for $200. Pierce's

---

16. More specifically, this statement can be unpacked into a small family of commandments: Always act so that you can fulfill your legal obligations after any of the following: 1) transferring property to satisfy moral obligations and personal allegiances; 2) making inadvertent or coerced transfers for less than full value; and 3) retaining property for your personal benefit or, in the corporate context, transferring it to your shareholders. Considerations of human dignity, as evidenced by the exemptions available in bankruptcy proceedings, now obviously limit the third commandment.

17. I describe the duties inherent in fraudulent conveyance law as "moral" for at least two reasons. First, they are standards of right and wrong in debtor-creditor relationships, both commercial and personal, that have endured over many centuries and have governed extremely common transactions. The relation between debtors and creditors is as old as civilization, is only slightly less significant than relationships among family members, social classes, and races, has always occupied a substantial portion of the resources of legal systems, and has always been regulated in the commercial context by attitudes and emotions of a decidedly moral sort. Second, these duties are, I think, not really perceived as *imposed* by the statutes and cases which reflect them—as are many modern legal obligations—but are perceived to be a part of normative custom.

nonexempt assets are worth only $300. Suppose that Pierce, simply because Twyne is the first to ask that he do so and because he dislikes *C*, and for no other reason, transfers all of his property to Twyne. Suppose, contrary to the apparent facts in a similar, well-known case,[20] that Pierce makes the transfer openly and with much publicity and fanfare, so that no deception of any sort is practiced on *C*, and that Pierce does not intend to and never does get a kickback of part of the transferred property or its use or any other kind of benefit from Twyne. Assume also that Twyne's claim is a completely valid, unobjectionable, due and payable, legal obligation of the most conventional sort.

Pierce's transfer to Twyne does not run afoul of the normative ideals of Truth and Respect toward creditors because Pierce has fully and truthfully described the transaction and has given primacy to his legal obligations. It is, however, objectionable for a debtor to satisfy the claims of just one creditor at a time when he lacks sufficient assets to meet his other legitimate and conventional legal obligations. A preferential payment of this sort hinders pro tanto the interest of all the other creditors. In such a situation, a debtor should deal equally with all his creditors. I will dub this principle the ideal of Evenhandedness toward creditors, with the understanding that in using this term the connotation is of equality of treatment of legal obligations in connection with liquidation proceedings.[21] Evenhandedness, in its fullest expression, has two aspects. Whenever a debtor is or is about to become insolvent and thus unable to satisfy all his creditors in full, the debtor should refrain from preferring one creditor over another. Similarly, in such cases creditors should refrain from seeking such a preference. In either instance, transfers resulting in better than equal treatment on the eve of liquidation proceedings should be undone—and may actually be undone in bankruptcy proceedings as voidable preferential transfers.

4. Debtor, who owns 250 shares of stock, sold those shares to her husband for full value in illiquid assets. She was not insolvent at the time of the sale but the stock had been her only liquid asset and as a result of the transaction she had no assets which creditors could easily reach. She made the transfer for the purpose of hindering her creditors but did not deceive them. This transaction would be avoided under the open-ended language

---

20. Twyne's Case, 3 Coke 80b, 76 Eng. Rep. 809 (Star Chamber 1601).

21. The ideal of Evenhandedness is not always adopted, especially in piecemeal liquidations, when individual creditors separately levy upon and exhaust the debtor's property, as opposed to collective liquidations such as dissolution and winding up under state corporate law, straight bankruptcy proceedings under federal law, liquidating receiverships, and assignments for the benefit of creditors. The ideal is, however, sometimes enforced, as among creditors of the same class, in proceedings looking toward reorganization rather than liquidation of the distressed debtor—for instance, in reorganizations under Chapter X of the Bankruptcy Act, 11 U.S.C. §§101-276 (1970).

of the UFCA, which covers transactions made with actual intent to hinder or delay creditors.[23]

Although the debtor intends and accomplishes a transfer leading to a hindering of her creditors, this case does not strictly offend the ideals of Truth, Respect or Evenhandedness as developed above. The scheme involves no actual deception, for she has truthfully informed all her creditors of the transaction. Moreover, the transfer of the shares is not for less than their fair value, nor does the transfer leave the debtor insolvent, so the transfer does not violate the ideal of Respect. Finally, the scheme results in no preference of any preexisting creditor over the others. Hence, one could say that there may be transactions which are not offensive of the above ideals in their normal applications, but which are yet fraudulent conveyances because they violate the more general expression of the ideal of which all three of the subsumed ideals are specifications. The general ideal might be described as that of Nonhindrance of the enforcement of valid legal obligations against oneself, in connection with transfers of one's property.

In summary, then, fraudulent conveyance law embodies a general ideal, in connection with a debtor's transfers of property rights and incurrences of new obligations, of Nonhindrance of creditors. This vague ideal is made operational through the effectuation of the more specific ideals of Truth, Respect, and Evenhandedness as well as a general, residual prohibition of conduct which hinders creditors in attempting to satisfy their claims.

Thus far, Evenhandedness has been conceived of as one of three particular duties derived from the general duty of Nonhindrance, because a violation of the duty of Evenhandedness operates to hinder the nonpreferred creditors. It is also possible, however, to view Evenhandedness as a policy independent of, and on a par with, a general ideal of Nonhindrance, and this aspect of the policy has led to its development as a separate topic. While like the other two ideals Evenhandedness specifies the moral duties of a debtor to his creditor, Evenhandedness is also the ideal behind what is referred to as the law of voidable preferences and many cases assume or state explicitly that a preference is not a fraudulent conveyance. However, the fact situations in many fraudulent conveyance cases suggest that those cases might have been treated equally as well as instances of voidable preferences.

For example, one of the great ironies of legal history is that *Twyne's Case,* which is widely regarded as the fountainhead of the modern Anglo-American law of fraudulent conveyances, does not, as presented in the reports, clearly involve anything more than a preference. The transaction

---

23. This hypothetical is based on the facts in Klein v. Rossi, 251 F. Supp. 1 (E.D.N.Y. 1966).

offended the ideal of Evenhandedness, which was not then an ideal that the common law of individual collection efforts respected, but it is not clear that it offended the ideals of Truth and Respect in any relevant way. The facts, which are roughly similar to those in the third example discussed above, do appear to include the circumstance that Pierce's transfer to Twyne was secret. But why a transaction which would be a mere nonvoidable preference if done openly should become a voidable fraudulent conveyance because done secretly is not at all clear, either from the report of the case or in logic. Perhaps the secrecy led C to pursue his collection efforts longer than he would have had he known of the preference, and thus to waste money. This possibility, it seems, could have been covered quite adequately by letting C recover the pointless expenses, rather than condemning the whole transfer to Twyne as a criminal act. It might conceivably be that the key to the case was that Pierce was satisfying some moral obligation to Twyne, for the report is full of apparently irrelevant remarks concerning that theme. More likely, and supported by inferences from the report,[30] is the hypothesis that Pierce violated the ideal of Truth because he did not really transfer the entire amount of his property, but under a kickback arrangement with Twyne (who was apparently too slow of foot at that point to win his race against C via the use of judicial process) kept the use and benefit of certain property. Pierce was to keep some of his assets, though insolvent; Twyne was to obtain a larger percentage of his claim than if he resorted to legitimate collection procedures; and both were to defraud C in his collection efforts by pretending that Pierce no longer had any assets. The case may actually be understandable, then, as a case similar to the first example above, which involved actual, detrimental deception.

Despite their essential kinship, the fact that fraudulent conveyances and voidable preferences have emerged as distinct legal doctrines has significant consequences. While both fraudulent conveyances and preferences are voidable in bankruptcy, preferences can be avoided only by the bankruptcy trustee while fraudulent conveyances are voidable under state

---

30. "[N]otwithstanding that [the deed of gift of all Pierce's goods and chattels to Twyne, in satisfaction of his debt] Pierce continued in possession of the said goods, and some of them he sold; and he shore the sheep, and marked them with his own mark. . . ." 76 Eng. Rep. at 811. "The donor continued in possession, and used them as his own; and by reason thereof he traded and trafficked with others, and defrauded and deceived them." 76 Eng. Rep. at 812-813. "[N]otwithstanding here was a true debt due to Twyne, and a good consideration of the gift, yet it was not within the proviso of the said Act of 13, Eliz. . . . it is not bona fide, for no gift shall be deemed to be bona fide within the said proviso which is accompanied with any trust . . . [and] continuance of the possession in the donor, is a sign of trust." 76 Eng. Rep. at 814.

Twyne's case is, of course, the fountainhead of doctrines of fraudulent retention of possession, the ultimate development of which was to plague the development of the law governing security interests in personal property left in the debtor's possession. Indeed, a good number of the fraudulent conveyance cases decided under the "actual fraud" rubric involve transfers of property without a change of possession. . . .

law at the behest of individual creditors.[33] Similarly, whereas preferences must have occurred within four months before the filing of the bankruptcy petition in order to be voidable, fraudulent conveyances which took place one year or possibly more before filing may be set aside. And the lists of technical requirements concerning the two branches of law could be differentiated at point after point.[36]

Perhaps the key to the existence of the two great, "separate" branches of the law concerning the debtor's moral duties to his creditors is that the ideal of Evenhandedness has never been considered as important to the functioning of the commercial system, which constitutes the essence of our culture, as the ideals of Truth and Respect. Evenhandedness, therefore, has been relegated in part to a separate doctrinal category, where it can be diluted and adjusted by limited implementing rules, without affecting the other two ideals. This strategy is reflected in such tired, and not entirely accurate or meaningful, saws as the one that there is nothing morally or legally "wrong" with giving or seeking a preference, though fraudulent conveyances should not be counselled by the debtor's or the creditors' attorneys.[37] It is also reflected, of course, in the enormous number of exceptions made to the principle of equal treatment of creditors in bankruptcy — exceptions ranging from security interests through statutory priorities to contractual and other forms of subordination among creditors.

The ideals of Nonhindrance, including the special evolution of Evenhandedness in the voidable preference doctrine, have been presented above in a rather tidy and purified form. In actual implementation, the ideals are often balanced against other objectives of the legal system, especially that of fairness toward the debtor's transferee. . . .

---

33. Indeed, in the area of piecemeal liquidation of insolvent estates, state law not only allows debtors to give creditors preferred treatment but permits creditors to seek to obtain it forcibly, by selfconsciously rejecting the principle of equal treatment in favor of the "grab" principle: the guiding notion is that diligence in the use of individual coercive collective procedures should be rewarded, so that the swiftest of wing — he who, or it which, first gets a judicial lien — should be first satisfied. See, e.g., Cal. Civ. Code Ann. §3432 (1970).

36. An antecedent debt equal to the value of the transferred property can be fair consideration for fraudulent conveyance purposes; a transfer can be a preference only when it is given for or on account of an antecedent debt. A fraudulent conveyance may be voidable, at least in part, despite the transferee's complete good faith; a preference is voidable under §60b only if the preferee had, at the time of the transfer, reasonable cause to believe that the debtor was insolvent. Transfers may sometimes be voidable fraudulent conveyances even when the transferor is not afterwards insolvent; a preference can only be made by an insolvent debtor. Different definitions of "insolvency" govern the two contexts. Fraudulent conveyance rules apply to transfers made and obligations incurred; preference rules obviously apply only to transfers.

37. As the Supreme Court put it, "The Statute recognizes the difference between the intent to defraud and the intent to prefer, and also the difference between a fraudulent and a preferential conveyance. One is inherently and always vicious; the other innocent and valid, except when made in violation of the express provisions of a statute. One is malum per se and the other malum prohibitum, — and then only to the extent that it is forbidden." Van Iderstine v. National Discount Co., 227 U.S. 575, 582 (1913).

In addition, the legal system, in implementing the ideals of Nonhindrance, has had to go beyond the fraudulent conveyance doctrine, embedding Nonhindrance principles in other branches of the law. In theory, the norms of Nonhindrance could be effectuated through three radically different modes. First, the ideals could be expressed as a system of transactional rules; decision of cases under the rules would necessitate examination of specific transactions and proof of a violation of an ideal in each transaction. Fraudulent conveyance law fits this mode. The second mode of implementation is the gestalt approach: when transactions are complex or involve elements that are not normally covered under the transactional mode, this approach would permit a court to apply a remedy, albeit a crude one, to correct a pattern of fraudulent transfers or obligations that may reasonably be inferred. . . . Finally, the ideals could be embodied in a system of preventive rules. . . .

NOTE ON THE JUSTIFICATION FOR §548

The trustee can use state fraudulent conveyance statutes to the same extent that a lien creditor whose interest arose at the time of the filing of the petition could. In addition, the trustee under §544(b) succeeds to the power of actual creditors to set aside fraudulent conveyances. The essence of the fraudulent conveyance — a bad act whereby the debtor thwarts its creditors — exists independently of whether the debtor is in a collective proceeding. The filing of a bankruptcy petition does not seem to make any of the debtor's previous transfers more or less fraudulent. If the basic purpose of bankruptcy law is to preserve in bankruptcy the substantive rights of creditors, one might expect that the trustee's power to set aside transfers as fraudulent conveyances would be identical to the power of actual creditors (or a hypothetical lien creditor at the time of the filing of the petition) outside of bankruptcy. Nevertheless, §548 of the Bankruptcy Code gives the trustee a special power to set aside fraudulent conveyances.

How can one justify giving the trustee a special substantive right in bankruptcy to set aside certain transfers as fraudulent conveyances? A possible justification may stem from the fact that a transfer that occurs before the petition was filed may not be one that a lien creditor who came into existence upon the filing of the petition could set aside. (Section 7 of the UFCA applies explicitly to past or future creditors, but §4 does not.) The trustee would then have to find an actual creditor into whose shoes he could step under §544(b) in order to set aside such a transfer. Locating such a creditor may not be worth the cost, if explicitly giving the trustee a substantive right would produce nearly the same result in most cases. (This justification, of course, rests on the soundness of §544(b) and its incorporation of Moore v. Bay.)

Section 548 should be read carefully and compared with the Uniform

Fraudulent Conveyance Act. Even though it uses different language (such as "reasonably equivalent value" instead of "fair consideration") and there are substantive differences (compare UFCA §9 with Bankruptcy Code §548(c)), the reach of §548 is more or less parallel to applicable state fraudulent conveyance statutes. Arguably, the trustee should assert rights that already exist under state law rather than a special substantive power under §548, yet, as a practical matter, most transfers the trustee seeks to set aside under §548 could also be set aside under §544(b).

PROBLEMS

5.13 Debtor runs a business that is worth $500. He also has $500 in cash. Debtor owes, on an unsecured basis, $400 to Creditor A and $400 to Creditor B. He has no other debts. Debtor conveys the business to a good faith buyer for $500, who takes possession of it immediately. Debtor invests his entire fortune ($1000) in an oil and gas venture, which fails within a few months. Can Creditors A and B set aside the sale of the business?

5.14 Instead of selling his business, Debtor gives the business to his sister as a birthday present. His sister takes possession of it. If Debtor hits upon hard times a few months later, can Creditors A and B set the gift aside as a fraudulent conveyance?

5.15 Debtor owns a business worth $1000. Debtor has no other assets, and owes, on an unsecured basis, $600 to Creditor A and $600 to Creditor B. Debtor is behind on his payments to both creditors. Debtor goes to his cousin and sells him his business for $10. Debtor disappears. Creditor A reduces its claim to judgment. Can Creditor A have the sheriff levy on the assets of the business that are now in the hands of Debtor's cousin?

5.16 Debtor sells his business for $1000, its fair market value. The buyer knows nothing about Debtor's $1200 indebtedness to Creditors A and B. Debtor takes the $1000 and disappears. Is the answer to this problem different from Problem 5.15? Is the transfer a fraudulent conveyance? If so, what is the remedy?

NOTE ON THE SCOPE OF FRAUDULENT CONVEYANCE LAW

The scope of fraudulent conveyance law at some level comes — or should come — out of a view of its purposes. We have already seen that this law is designed to control debtor's actions against creditors. Because fraudulent conveyances are "wrongs" by debtors against creditors, they represent the type of behavior we would expect to see creditors prohibit their debtors from engaging in as a condition of lending money. Therefore, fraudulent conveyance law is like a standardized term that the law supplies to fill in the gap left by parties who would want this term, but who cannot afford to bargain for it explicitly. But what is the scope of that set of standardized terms? We have already seen two polar cases. A classic fraudulent conveyance arises when an insolvent debtor gives assets to a relative (with or without the deliberate intent to hinder, delay, or defraud creditors). On the other hand, preferring one creditor to another is deemed to be for fair consideration and hence not a fraudulent conveyance (although it may be a voidable preference in bankruptcy). Such actions are part and parcel of the concept of individual creditor remedies, not the type of behavior that creditors (absent the advent of a collective proceeding) would want to prohibit.

But what about intermediate cases? We have already explored a basic tension between debtors and creditors. After entering into a loan contract (at a particular interest rate), a creditor has an incentive to squeeze further profit from the contract by making the loan *less* risky (so the risk premium represented by the interest rate becomes larger than the risk). At the extreme, this incentive may lead a creditor to opt for a bankruptcy proceeding prematurely: to cash out a loan. On the other hand, however, debtors — and particularly insolvent debtors — have an incentive to string out payments of debts. If a debtor (or its shareholders) would receive nothing if the firm were liquidated today, it (or they) have nothing to lose by delaying and gambling on future success with the creditors' money.

Consider this in the context of an example. Firm has $100 in assets and $100 in liabilities. If Firm were to liquidate today, its creditors would get paid in full and its shareholders would be left with nothing. Firm knows of an investment opportunity, however, which costs $100, and will return $200 if successful, but nothing if unsuccessful. There is a fifty-fifty chance of success or failure. Should Firm make the investment? From the standpoint of its creditors, it should not. If the investment succeeds, they still get no more than $100, but they stand a 50 percent chance of not being paid at all. From the standpoint of Firm's shareholders, however, there is every reason to make the investment. They gain nothing if they do not make it and they stand to gain $100 if they do.

Is making the investment a fraudulent conveyance? Is it made for fair consideration? At one level, it is. The expected value of the investment is $100. But is that the appropriate focus? The investment's expected value, *from the perspective of the creditors,* is only $50. Should "fair consideration" be viewed from the creditor's perspective? What about an "investment" of $100 at a Las Vegas table, where the $100 is put on a number that has a one-in-a-hundred chance of coming up? Putting aside the casino's (and the state's) take, this too has an expected value of $100: a 1 percent chance of making $10,000 and a 99 percent chance of coming up empty-handed. Is *this* fair consideration? Is it a fraudulent conveyance?

Again, we should ask this question by trying to picture what the debtor and its creditors would agree to if they had thought about it at the time debtor borrowed money. Almost all investments convert cash into something riskier. Undoubtedly, however, not every investment a firm makes should be considered a fraudulent conveyance. Does this suggest that fraudulent conveyance law is an inappropriate vehicle to analyze investment decisions such as these — and that "fair consideration" should not be limited to an examination of the values from the creditors' perspective? Or are the other constraints on fraudulent conveyance actions sufficient to protect most investment decisions? Section 7, recall, requires a showing of an intent to hinder, delay, or defraud creditors, while §4 requires a showing of insolvency, either *before* or as a *result* of such transactions. Moreover, fraudulent conveyance actions against the debtor are often futile, and UFCA §§9 and 10 place limits on creditors' ability to recover the assets in the hands of third parties. Do these provide sufficient constraints? Recall, too, that fraudulent conveyance law is only one of a number of devices geared towards controlling debtor misbehavior against creditors.

NOTE ON FRAUDULENT CONVEYANCES AND LEVERAGED BUY-OUTS

In United States v. Gleneagles Investment Co., 565 F. Supp. 556 (M.D. Pa. 1983), the court examined a leveraged buy-out and set it aside as a fraudulent conveyance. The facts of that case were unusual. (One of the participants was Jimmy Hoffa, a Teamster labor leader convicted of jury tampering and later pardoned by President Nixon. Hoffa disappeared mysteriously in the mid-1970s, shortly after the transaction at issue in *Gleneagles.* Although his body was never found, some suspected foul play.) Nevertheless, the basic leveraged buy-out transaction in *Gleneagles* presents a serious fraudulent conveyance problem, that arises whenever there is a leveraged buy-out. In theory, it cannot arise unless the firm was insolvent or in shaky financial condition at the time of the buy-out. Yet one always needs to address it in planning these transactions because a debtor's true financial status is always easier to determine with the benefit of hindsight, and because the reachback period of state fraudulent conveyance law is as long as the relevant statute of limitations.

Firm owes its general creditors $4 million, and has no secured debt. Firm's managers decide to acquire it, and the old shareholders agree to sell their shares for $1 million. The managers put up $200,000 of their own money, and borrow $800,000 from Bank, agreeing to give Bank a security interest in all of Firm's assets to support the loan. The managers proceed to buy all the stock in the shareholders' hands with the money they borrowed from Bank and the cash they put up. When the transaction is over, the managers own 100 percent of the stock, the old shareholders are cashed out, and Firm has $4.8 million in debt. The general creditors come after

Bank's security interest and therefore find that the pool of assets available to satisfy their loans is $800,000 smaller.

It is rare that a transfer (or the incurring of an obligation) is set aside on a showing of an actual intent to hinder, delay, or defraud creditors, at least in transactions that have the appearance of being arms length bargains. Courts nearly always rely on the per se rules discussed earlier that allow them to set aside transactions without engaging in a messy, fact-filled inquiry into the parties' intent.

There are any number of ways to structure the transaction so that the money the managers borrow goes to the Firm and is never actually held by the managers. For example, the transaction could be split into three separate deals: The managers acquire a few shares of Firm's stock; Firm borrows $800,000; and Firm reacquires all the stock in the hands of the nonmanager shareholders. Under this view, it looks like Firm received $800,000 in return for incurring an $800,000 secured obligation. Courts, however, should have no problem linking such transactions, and will not allow the characterization of the transaction by the interested parties to control the rights of third parties. One would therefore start by observing that Firm incurred an obligation (it promised Bank $800,000) and made a transfer (it gave Bank a security interest in all of its property) without getting anything in return (the $800,000 went to the old shareholders).

There are two common rules that might lead to the characterization of this transaction as a fraudulent conveyance. The rule we examined earlier, embodied in §4 of the Uniform Fraudulent Conveyance Act, provides that any transfer made by a debtor without fair consideration while the debtor is insolvent is a fraudulent conveyance. In a more perfect world, a leveraged buy-out would never run afoul of this provision. If the old shareholders and the managers were fully informed (which, of course, they aren't), the price paid for the stock would be the difference between all of Firm's assets and liabilities. If Firm's liabilities exceeded its assets, the managers would not be willing to pay a positive price for that stock.

In a world such as ours in which information is imperfect, however, it may not be clear whether Firm is solvent. Indeed, even if liabilities are greater than assets at fair valuation, the stock might trade for a positive price because of the chance that Firm's assets will prove larger than expected or its liabilities less. (For example, if Firm owed its creditors $100 and its only asset were a lottery ticket having one chance in ten of paying $200 and nine chances in ten of paying nothing, Firm would be insolvent (it has an asset worth $20 and liabilities of $100), but its stock would still trade for $10, because there is a 10 percent chance that all creditors will be paid off and $100 will be left over.) If the managers are mistaken and buy out the shareholders when Firm is insolvent, the leveraged buy-out will be a fraudulent conveyance.

Another rule, embodied in §5 of the Uniform Fraudulent Conveyance Act, may reach the leveraged buy-out, even when the transaction does not render Firm insolvent, but simply leaves it with "an unreasonably small capital." Assume that before the buy-out, Firm has assets of $5 million and liabilities of $4 million (as the purchase price of $1 million suggests). After the transaction, Firm still has assets of $5 million, but now it has liabilities of $4.8 million. A firm that is this highly leveraged is arguably too thinly capitalized.

As a matter of sound practice, lawyers must make certain that a firm acquired in a leveraged buy-out is not insolvent or rendered insolvent, and that managers and others put up enough capital to ensure that the firm is not too thinly capitalized. Lawyers also face obstacles other legal principles impose. (For example, various state corporations codes forbid distributions to shareholders while a firm is insolvent. While such rules do not affect Bank's rights, they might not allow the old shareholders to keep the money received from the transaction.) But an important conceptual question that should be asked is whether a leveraged buy-out in fact presents fraudulent conveyance problems, or falls under a rule that is overbroad as applied to this particular case. A firm that incurs obligations in the course of a buy-out does not seem at all like the Elizabethan deadbeat who sells his sheep to his brother for a pittance.

The question, in other words, is whether a corporate debtor that incurs additional debt in a leveraged buy-out is engaging in a manipulation to profit at its creditors' expense. At one level, the answer to this question is quite straight-forward: This transaction does indeed hinder Firm's general creditors. Before the transaction, there was a $1 million cushion protecting them. Firm could suffer a million dollar loss and the general creditors would still be protected. After the buy-out, if Firm lost only a few hundred thousand dollars, the general creditors would not be repaid in full.

Moreover, Firm's owners (the old and new shareholders) benefit to the same extent that the general creditors are made worse off. Before the transaction, the shareholders invested $1 million to enjoy the profits of a Firm with assets of $5 million. After the transaction, the shareholders have only $200,000 at risk, yet can enjoy almost the same amount of profits. Their investment is of course riskier and additional interest is owed Bank, but a portion of the risks have been passed on to the general creditors. To the extent the general creditors are in a worse position because they have a riskier loan, the beneficiaries must be the shareholders.

A leveraged buy-out, when it leaves a firm insolvent or too thinly capitalized, implicates the principle underlying the Statute of 13 Elizabeth in a way that a preference of one creditor over another does not. But it does not follow that it should be treated as a fraudulent conveyance. A standard that allowed a court to set aside any transaction in which a debtor could be profiting at its creditors expense could threaten to undermine every transaction a firm enters into. Whenever ownership interests are diverse, junior owners have an incentive to increase the riskiness of the investment of the senior owners. They can do this by making the firm more highly leveraged, but they can also do it by each investment decision they make. They may prefer a project with a 10 percent chance of returning $100 and a 90 percent chance of returning $0 to one that has a 100 percent chance of returning $11. A risk neutral sole owner would always prefer the latter.

It is not sensible to give creditors the power to set aside every transaction that makes their investment riskier. If a firm is financially healthy, for example, we assume that all parties would usually agree that the firm's investment decisions should be made by the managers. Therefore, we do not allow creditors control over the management of a firm in the absence of a special agreement. The "off-the-rack" term most investors would prefer would allow discretion to managers over a wide range of issues. Identifying the proper limits of fraudulent conveyance law requires that we identify the conditions under which the usual presumptions do not hold. The rule that treats as fraudulent conveyances all transfers made without fair consideration may reach too many transactions that are more likely to be arms-length business transactions within the range of risks creditors expect when they lend money. Is it possible, however, to create a set of rules that is more sensitive and that does not introduce the kind of litigation that rules such as §4 of the Uniform Fraudulent Conveyance Act are designed to avoid? See Baird and Jackson, Fraudulent Conveyance Law and Its Proper Domain, 38 Vand. L. Rev. — (1985).

In looking at these next several cases, do the courts come to grips with the policies underlying fraudulent conveyance law?

KINDOM URANIUM CORP. v. VANCE
269 F.2d 104 (10th Cir. 1959)

Lewis, Circuit Judge.

The Kindom Uranium Company as appellant complains of the judgment of the District Court of New Mexico wherein a conveyance to the company of certain real estate was declared void as violative of 11 U.S.C.A. §107, sub. d (2)[1] (Sec. 67, sub. d of the Bankruptcy Act) and title to the property was declared vested in appellee as Trustee in Bankruptcy of Edith M. Cole, the bankrupt and transferor. . . .

1. "Every transfer made and every obligation incurred by a debtor within one year prior to the filing of a petition initiating a proceeding under this title by or against him is fraudulent . . . (c) as to then existing and future creditors, if made or incurred without fair consideration by a debtor who intends to incur or believes that he will incur debts beyond his ability to pay as they mature; or (d) as to then existing and future creditors, if made or incurred with actual intent as distinguished from intent presumed in law, to hinder, delay, or defraud either existing or future creditors."

On April 10, 1956, a properly acknowledged quitclaim deed to a residence in Albuquerque, New Mexico, was executed by Edith M. Cole as grantor and, a few days later, delivered to the Kindom Uranium Corporation, the grantee. Thereafter, Mrs. Cole was involved in an automobile accident with one Broadus E. Campbell which, on February 1, 1957, resulted in a judgment against Mrs. Cole for $15,000. During the course of this trial, but before judgment, the deed was recorded at the instance of the president of Kindom. The recordation, undoubtedly, was effectuated for the purpose of establishing a safeguard against the potentiality of a judgment adverse to Mrs. Cole and in excess of her insurance coverage. The potentiality became the fact and Campbell became the unsatisfied judgment creditor of Mrs. Cole in the sum of $5,000. His efforts to collect the judgment, including the suit in state court to set aside the conveyance to Kindom as fraudulent, failed.

On January 3, 1958, Mrs. Cole filed a voluntary petition in bankruptcy.[2] Listed among her debts was the Campbell judgment, $250 as owing the Kindom Corporation, $900 to her brother and some $1,446.55 in miscellaneous obligations.

Pointing out that neither the bankrupt nor the principal creditor, Campbell, could successfully set aside the subject conveyance, appellant contends that the trustee is vested with no greater rights. The position finds comfort in frequent judicial assertion, usually interpreting the omnibus title provision of the Bankruptcy Act, Sec. 70, 11 U.S.C.A. §110c, e, that the rights of the trustee are derived from and limited by those of the bankrupt and creditors existing at the date of bankruptcy. Section 70, however, is but one of "the full arsenal of weapons with which the trustee may attack various transfers, encumbrances or obligations and collect the assets of the estate thereby for equal distribution among creditors." 4 Collier on Bankruptcy, 14 Ed. §70.01, p. 927. The trustee's title to property fraudulently transferred is not derived solely from that of the bankrupt or his creditors but also by virtue of the several positive provisions of the Bankruptcy Act including Sec. 67, sub. d. The trustee's rights are, of course, not absolute; they are for the benefit of all creditors and limited by that concept in particular application. . . .

2. This filing was within one year after the recordation of the deed to Kindom and therefore opens the door to inquiry as to the bona fides of the transfer of the debtor's property to Kindom. Sec. 67, sub. d(5) of the Bankruptcy Act provides:

For the purposes of this subdivision, a transfer shall be deemed to have been made at the time when it became so far perfected that no bona fide purchaser from the debtor could thereafter have acquired any rights in the property so transferred superior to the rights of the transferee therein, but, if such transfer is not so perfected prior to the filing of the petition initiating a proceeding under this title, it shall be deemed to have been made immediately before the filing of such petition.

Innocent purchasers and judgment creditors are protected against unrecorded instruments of this nature under New Mexico law. New Mexico Stats. Ann. 71-2-2, 3.

Such limitations are not bound by the identical bars that may exist against the bankrupt, particular creditors, or, indeed, all creditors. . . .

Mrs. Cole, the bankrupt, at the time of the conveyance, was a stockholder, officer and director of the Kindom Uranium Corporation. The property which she conveyed was her residence in Albuquerque where she lived with her daughter. She accepted telephone calls and received mail at her home for the Kindom Corporation and its president but received no salary for her services. She had outside employment but had had financial burdens for some time. Her debts, she stated, exceeded everything she had and always had since her divorce. Her home was mortgaged. According to her testimony, she began negotiations for the sale of the property to the corporation in November, 1955; her proposal was accepted by the Board of Directors the following month and the company agreed to purchase her equity for a consideration of $3,000, which was to be paid as follows: An antecedent debt for $1,000 was canceled and she was to receive 4,000 shares of the corporate stock having a par value of fifty cents a share. The evidence does not show that the debt was ever carried on the books of the corporation and its origin is in some confusion, the bankrupt testifying to several transactions whereby the company or its president lent her varying amounts over a period of time. Likewise, there is no evidence as to the market value of the stock, although the parties in their various transactions have treated the par value as its true value. The president of the corporation testified that it was agreed that Mrs. Cole was to receive 500 shares every six months by way of compensation for her services as secretary, but that she had waived payment in some instances because of the company's financial difficulties.

Appellant contends that there is no evidence to demonstrate a fraudulent intent on the date of the perfection of transfer, January 23, 1957, to bring this action within the purview of 67, sub. d(2)(d) quoted above. Indeed, the activities of Mrs. Cole with respect to this transfer were completed at a time long prior to bankruptcy and apparently prior to a time when she could have envisaged the accident and lawsuit which resulted in her indebtedness for $5,000 of the $7,000 in obligations which she sought to discharge. It is only through connivance with the transferee that an actual intent to defraud either future or existing creditors could be suspected and such a suspicion is not justified by the record.

However, Section 67, sub. d(2)(c) makes fraudulent as a matter of law a transfer without fair consideration by a debtor who believes that he will incur debts beyond his ability to pay. Since the time of the transfer was during the trial of a claim against her, large in amount as tested by her income, and since she was already indebted to her brother and responsible for supporting herself and her daughter, the deduction is inescapable that at that time she contemplated incurring liabilities which she could not discharge as they matured.

The "fair consideration" necessary to save this transaction from the taint of fraud under Section 67, sub. d(2)(c) is defined in 67, sub. d(1)(e):

> consideration given for the property or obligation of a debtor is 'fair' (1) when, in good faith, in exchange and as a fair equivalent therefor, property is transferred or an antecedent debt is satisfied, or (2) when such property or obligation is received in good faith to secure a present advance or antecedent debt in an amount not disproportionately small as compared with the value of the property or obligation obtained.

This definition is practically a verbatim adoption from the Uniform Fraudulent Conveyance Act, section 3, and hence the cases decided under that act are persuasive in the determination of whether fair consideration was given in the instant case. . . .

As previously mentioned, the existence of the antecedent debt in the present case was evidenced only by confusing, inexact testimony by the parties to the transfer. The value of the stock was never established, except as the parties themselves valued it at its par value. The corporation has not at any time paid a dividend on its capital stock and federal and state income tax returns for the year 1956 show a net operating loss of $2,388.89.

The trial court refused to accept the par value of the stock as evidence that it had any value at all. Under the circumstances, proof of the value of the stock, if any, must be shown by market sales or the financial condition of the company. The company is in the superior position with respect to such proof and must bear the consequences of having failed to produce it. . . . The issue of the giving of a fair consideration is plainly a matter for factual determination and the findings by the trier of the facts who has heard the witnesses should not be set aside unless clearly erroneous. . . . We believe the trial court could well find the transaction to be without substance and consequently fraudulent in law.

Affirmed.

NOTE

Shapiro v. Wilgus, 287 U.S. 348 (1932) involved the following facts. Robinson was a lumber dealer in Philadelphia. "He was unable to pay his debts as they matured, but he believed that he would be able to pay them in full if his creditors were lenient." Most of his creditors were willing to give him time, but two resisted. Robinson thus cast about for a device to allow the business to continue and the two dissident creditors to be held at bay. Pennsylvania law did not permit the appointment of a receiver for a business conducted by an individual, as distinguished from one conducted by a corporation or partnership. The Court observed: "To make such remedies available there was need to take the title out of Robinson and put it somewhere else." He formed a Delaware corporation, Miller Robinson Co., and conveyed to it all of his property, receiving the stock and a covenant by the grantee to assume the payment of the debts. Robinson then, in conjunction with an (apparently lenient) simple contract creditor, brought suit in federal court (diversity), requesting the appointment of a receiver and an injunction on suits. One of the recalcitrant creditors thereupon got a judgment, and applied to the court for leave to levy on the property in the possession of the receiver, alleging that the conveyance from Robinson to the corporation and the ensuing receivership were part of a single scheme to hinder and delay creditors in their lawful suits. The Third Circuit, affirming the denial of the petition by the district court, found that Robinson's aim was to prevent the disruption of his business at the suit of hostile creditors and to cause the assets to be nursed, by the receiver, for the benefit of all concerned. While the Third Circuit approved of this aim, the Supreme Court announced that "there is a misconception of the privileges and liberties vouchsafed to an embarrassed debtor." Justice Cardozo, writing for the Court, stated:

> A conveyance is illegal if made with an intent to defraud the creditors of the grantor, but equally it is illegal if made with an intent to hinder and delay them. Many an embarrassed debtor holds the genuine belief that if suits can be staved off for a season, he will weather a financial storm, and pay his debts in full. . . . The belief, even though well founded, does not clothe him with a privilege to build up obstructions that will hold his creditors at bay. . . . Tested by [the Uniform Fraudulent Conveyance Act], this conveyance may not stand.

What section of the UFCA is being applied by the Court? Does this case meet the tests of the UFCA? See also Reed v. McIntyre, 98 U.S. 507 (1871) (debtor made an assignment for the benefit of creditors while a creditor was suing him and one day before she obtained a judgment. The deed of assignment did not reserve to the debtor any control over, or interest in, the property. Held: no fraudulent conveyance; indeed, it "was the most honest act the party could do"). Is this case consistent with Shapiro v. Wilgus?

NOTE ON *KINDOM URANIUM CORP.*

This case involves §67d of the 1898 Act, which is very similar to §548 of the Bankruptcy Code. Section 67d, like §548, only reached transfers occurring within one year of the filing of the bankruptcy petition. As with preferences under §547, much turns on the date of the transfer and a special definition of "transfer" is used. See §67d(5); §548(d)(1). The debtor Cole must also be insolvent at the time of the transfer, and, again, the statutory section must be examined carefully. See §548(a)(2)(B)(iii).

If Cole had filed for bankruptcy a month later, the trustee would have been unable to use §67d of the 1898 Act, and today would be precluded from using §548. The trustee could, however, attempt to use state fraudulent conveyance law, which often has a longer "reachback" period. California's law, for example, reaches back three years. But to avail oneself of state law under §544(b), one must comply with the requirements of applicable state law. Assume Cole was a resident of a state with a three-year reachback period and the Uniform Fraudulent Conveyance Act. Would the case come out the same? Note particularly the definition of "conveyance." Also, the trustee, to use §544(b), may need to find an actual, unsecured creditor who can set aside the fraudulent conveyance under state law. Will Campbell do?

Should Kindom have lost? What bankruptcy policies do the events in this case violate? Under the facts you are given in the case, is it likely that the debtor was trying to hinder, delay, or defraud creditors? Kindom, to be sure, failed to record the deed until later, but why doesn't that simply make this a preference (i.e., an attempt by the creditor, Kindom, to protect itself in light of an incipient bankruptcy), subjecting Kindom to the risk of a bankruptcy filing by Cole during the preference period (four months under the 1898 Act)? After that preference period has run, is there any additional policy in fraudulent conveyance law that should leave Kindom further at risk? Doesn't the principle behind fraudulent conveyance law focus on actions by a debtor against creditors? What actions did the debtor, Cole, do during the relevant reachback period (other than incur a debt) to run afoul of fraudulent conveyance law?

Is it possible that the debtor may have been trying to defraud her other creditors? Could it be, for example, that Cole and Kindom Uranium conspired together not to record the deed, for the purpose of allowing Cole to obtain false credit? But are such efforts to thwart creditors likely to be at work when a creditor delays recording a deed? Can one argue that the transaction is so unlikely to be a fraudulent conveyance that it should not fall within a rule and that a creditor (or trustee) who wants to set such a transaction aside should have to show actual intent to "hinder, delay, or defraud" at the time the original transaction was set up and Kindom Uranium failed to record? See Jackson, Avoiding Powers in Bankruptcy, 36 Stan. L. Rev. 725, 784-786 (1984).

PROBLEM

5.17 Debtor borrows $100,000 from Finance Company on an unsecured basis in January 1984. The loan is callable on demand. By January 1985, Debtor is insolvent. Finance Company could threaten to call the loan, but that would probably force Debtor to file a petition in bankruptcy and, in a bankruptcy proceeding, Finance Company would realize at most 20 cents on the dollar. Instead, Finance Company persuades Debtor to give it an interest in real estate the Debtor owns that is worth $100,000. Finance Company immediately records its interest in the local real estate records. Debtor eventually files a petition in bankruptcy in May. Can Bank enforce its security interest? Assuming that Bank is not an insider within the meaning of §101(28), the trustee, as we will see in Chapter 6, cannot set aside the transfer as a voidable preference, because the security interest was transferred to Bank outside the 90-day preference period. Is the transfer a fraudulent conveyance? Assume that Debtor did not have the actual intent to defraud its other creditors. Was this a transfer made for less than fair consideration while Debtor was insolvent?

Finance Company will, of course, argue that Debtor transferred a $100,000 security interest to satisfy a $100,000 antecedent debt. Because an antecedent debt is "fair consideration" (to use the language of the UFCA) and "reasonably equivalent value" (to use the language of §548(a)(2)(A) and (d)(2)), the transfer was not a fraudulent conveyance. But can the trustee make the following counterargument: Although the antecedent debt is "value" within the meaning of §548, nothing requires that it be valued at its face amount. In January 1985, Finance Company had a $100,000 promissory note from Debtor, but one has to ask how much the note was worth at that time. Because Debtor could pay its general creditors only 20 cents on the dollar, it follows that this note was worth $20,000. Any security interest transferred to Finance Company on that date in excess of that amount was a fraudulent conveyance and should be set aside, §548(c).

Do you find this argument persuasive? The court in Inland Security Co. v. Estate of Kirshner, 382 F. Supp. 338 (W.D. Mo. 1974), did and affirmed the finding "that the receipt of a secured note is not the fair equivalent of an unsecured indebtedness." Doesn't this logic, however, make any transfer on account of an antecedent debt made by an insolvent debtor within a year of the petition voidable if the creditor was not fully secured at the time of the transfer? Finance Company is benefitting at the expense of the other creditors, for it is being paid off in full, while the others are not. But how would voiding the transaction vindicate the principles underlying fraudulent conveyance law?

Consider the issues previously raised in examining the next case. Is anything involved other than an outright preference (i.e., one creditor ensuring that it does better than other creditors)? As we will see in Chapter 6, this transaction may (because of the guarantee) now run afoul of the longer reachback provision in preference law for "insider preferences."

BULLARD v. ALUMINUM CO. OF AMERICA
468 F.2d 11 (7th Cir. 1972)

William J. CAMPBELL, Senior District Judge.

The defendant Aluminum Company of America (Alcoa) appeals from an order of the district court which granted the motion of the plaintiff, trustee in bankruptcy of the estate of Kritzer Radiant Coils, Inc. (Kritzer Radiant), for summary judgment. The district court held that a transfer of $23,370.60 from the bankrupt to Alcoa was a "fraudulent transfer" under §67d(2)(a) of the Bankruptcy Act. 11 U.S.C. §107d(2)(a). Alcoa raises three contentions on appeal: (1) that the transfer was not fraudulent inasmuch as there was no evidence that Alcoa participated in a scheme to defeat the other creditors of Kritzer Radiant or that the transaction involving the transfer of monies was lacking in good faith; (2) that summary judgment was improperly entered since the pleadings and affidavits raised genuine issues of material fact concerning the intentions and motives of Alcoa; and (3) that the district court erred in failing to hold Alcoa had a right under §67d(6) of the Bankruptcy Act to retain the $23,370.60 as security for repayment of the actual consideration given by Alcoa.

The facts as gleaned from the pleadings, affidavits and from defendant's answers to plaintiff's interrogatories show that on December 1st, 1965, the date of the transfer in question, the bankrupt, Kritzer Radiant, was indebted to Alcoa in the amount of $46,741.20. As of that time 85 percent of the outstanding capital stock of Kritzer Radiant was owned by Bastian Morely Company, Inc. (Bastian Morely) and the remaining 15 percent of the stock was held by Henry Kritzer, Sr. Henry Kritzer at that time also owned 15 percent of the outstanding common stock of Bastian Morely and was a director of that Company. The $46,741.20 debt of Kritzer Radiant, which had been personally guaranteed by Henry Kritzer, had been reduced to a judgment against Kritzer individually and in favor of Alcoa in the Circuit Court of Lake County, Illinois. For a period of time prior to December 1st, 1965, both Kritzer Radiant and Bastian Morely had dealt with Alcoa as a supplier of materials used in manufacturing their products. Bastian Morely was also indebted to Alcoa as of that date in the amount of $11,319.78.

On the critical date of December 1, 1965 an agreement was entered into by and between Kritzer Radiant, Henry Kritzer, Bastian Morely and Alcoa. Pursuant to this agreement, Kritzer Radiant paid to Alcoa $23,370.60 in full satisfaction of the antecedent debt owed Alcoa in the amount of $46,741.20. Additionally, Alcoa released Henry Kritzer from the judgment it had recovered against him in the state court. Finally, Bastian satisfied its debt to Alcoa in the amount of $11,319.78, and ordered from Alcoa additional materials for payment upon receipt. On the date the settlement agreement was executed, Kritzer Radiant was insolvent and there existed creditors of Kritzer Radiant with outstanding claims against it.

The pertinent portion of §67d(2)(a) of the Bankruptcy Act provides as follows:

> (2) Every transfer made and every obligation incurred by a debtor within one year prior to the filing of a petition initiating a proceeding under this Act by or against him is fraudulent (a) as to creditors existing at the time of such transfer or obligation, if made or incurred without fair consideration by a debtor who is or will be thereby rendered insolvent, *without regard to his actual intent;* . . . (11 U.S.C. §107d(2)(a) (Emphasis supplied).)

The definition of fair consideration is furnished in §67d(1)(e) which provides:

> Consideration given for the property or obligation of a debtor is 'fair' (1) when, in *good faith,* in exchange and as a fair equivalent therefor property is transferred or an antecedent debt is satisfied, . . . (11 U.S.C. §107d(1)(e). (Emphasis supplied).)

As the district court indicated in its memorandum opinion, essentially four elements must be present for a transfer to be fraudulent under §67d(2)(a) of the Act:

1. The transfer must occur within one year of the initiation of the bankruptcy proceedings;
2. Creditors of the debtor must exist at the time of the transfer;
3. The debtor must be insolvent at the time of the transfer; and
4. There must be a failure of consideration for the transfer.

The bankruptcy petition here was filed on November 22nd, 1966, clearly within one year of the date of the transfer in question. Creditors of Kritzer Radiant were in existence when the transfer was made. Also there is no serious dispute regarding the insolvency of Kritzer Radiant on the date of the transfer. Alcoa then possessed a financial statement of Kritzer Radiant which reflected a negative net worth. Also, some three weeks prior to the execution of the settlement agreement the defendant wrote its attorneys suggesting that certain precautions be undertaken ". . . should either Bastian Morely or Kritzer Radiant Coils go into bankruptcy within four months of the transaction." While it is true that the defendant denied the allegation of insolvency in its answer, we agree with the district court that since Alcoa did not challenge plaintiff's assertion by counter-affidavit nor make any attempt to demonstrate the inaccessibility of information on this question, the issue of insolvency did not present a fact issue precluding the entry of summary judgment.

Thus, the question becomes, under the undisputed facts as set forth above, whether the transfer from Kritzer Radiant to Alcoa was for "fair consideration." Where the transfer is made to extinguish an antecedent debt, the Bankruptcy Act provides that the consideration given must represent a "fair equivalent" for the antecedent debt and must be given in "good faith." 11 U.S.C. §§107d(1)(e), 107d(2)(a). . . . As the defendant itself recognizes, a transfer lacking in good faith is fraudulent within the meaning of the Bankruptcy Act even though fair equivalent may have been present. And the question of good faith depends under the circumstances on whether the "transaction carries the earmarks of an arms-length bargain." Holahan v. Henderson, D.C., 277 F. Supp. 890, aff'd 394 F.2d 177 (5th Cir. 1969).

Considering all the facts that attended this transaction we agree with the district court that the transfer was fraudulent within the meaning of §67d(2)(a) of the Bankruptcy Act. We find most significant the relationship of the parties to the settlement agreement and the respective allocation of its benefits. Henry Kritzer, the President of the bankrupt as well as a director and stockholder of Bastian Morely, was released entirely and without any consideration on his part from a legally enforceable state court judgment against him. Moreover, Bastian Morely, the principal stockholder of the bankrupt, was permitted to retain its supplier and, for a consideration, extinguished its own antecedent debt to Alcoa. Finally, Alcoa acquired an advantage over the other creditors of the bankrupt at a time when Alcoa was certainly aware of the precarious financial position of Kritzer Radiant. Thus the primary and important benefits of this transaction ran to parties other than the bankrupt. Since transfers made to benefit third parties are not considered as made for "fair" consideration . . . we agree that on these facts, which are not disputed by the defendant, the transfer here was a fraudulent one within the meaning of §67d(2)(a) of the Bankruptcy Act.

Alcoa next contends that summary judgment was improper here since there was a fact question raised by the pleadings and affidavits as to the motives and intentions of Alcoa with respect to this transaction. In this regard Alcoa maintains that the transfer here could not have been fraudulent unless Alcoa participated in scheme to defeat the other creditors of Kritzer Radiant or unless Alcoa acted on bad faith in valuing the properties exchanged. We have been unable to find any support, either statutory or in case law, for this argument. Indeed, the Act itself is to the contrary. A transfer made without "fair consideration," such as the one involved here, represents but one of the several types of fraudulent transfers defined in §67 of the Act. See 11 U.S.C. §107d. A transfer is rendered fraudulent under §67d(2)(a), the section here involved, when made or incurred without fair consideration by a debtor who is or will be thereby rendered insolvent, irrespective of the intent of the parties to the transaction. See 11 U.S.C. §107d(2)(a). . . . The situation that Alcoa refers to, where there is an actual intent to defraud, is specifically covered by §67d(2)(d) of the Act.

Thus, under the section of the Act on which the Trustee proceeded in this case, the motives and intentions of Alcoa are simply immaterial.

Lastly, Alcoa contends that under §67d(6) of the Bankruptcy Act, it may retain the transferred funds as security for payment of its antecedent debt. See 11 U.S.C. §107d(6). Under our long-standing rule that issues not presented to the district court cannot be raised for the first time on appeal, we need not consider this question.

For the reasons given the judgment of the district court is hereby affirmed.

NOTE

Bullard was decided under the fraudulent conveyance provisions of the old Bankruptcy Act. Would the outcome be the same if §548 of the Bankruptcy Code were used?

PROBLEM

5.18 Debtor is a firm that sells money orders to currency exchanges. (Currency exchanges are businesses common in urban neighborhoods. "[They] cash checks for a fee, sell money orders, and often perform other financial services for their customers, such as selling food stamps and acting as collection agents for local utilities." Rubin v. Manufacturers Hanover Trust Co. 661 F.2d 979, 981-982 n.3 (2d Cir. 1981)). In an effort to expand the number of currency exchanges selling its money orders, Debtor guarantees loans that some of the exchanges obtain from local banks and gives these banks a security interest in all of its property. Debtor makes such a guarantee for a $10,000 loan Currency Exchange obtained from Bank in late 1984. In early 1985, Currency Exchange defaults on its obligations to Bank. Bank calls on Debtor's guarantee, and Debtor honors its obligation. Six months later, Debtor files a bankruptcy petition. Can the trustee argue that Debtor's payment to Bank was a fraudulent conveyance?

NOTE ON FRAUDULENT CONVEYANCES AND GUARANTEES

Problem 5.18 requires an analysis of fraudulent conveyance law when the debtor has made guarantees. This problem, however, presents the simple case, because the principal and the guarantor dealt with one another at arm's length. In many litigated cases, the guarantees are between related corporations. As elsewhere, it is useful to begin by positing the easy case. In Problem 5.18, all the events happened within a year of the filing of the petition, hence all the transactions fall within the temporal reach of §548. Let us assume that this transaction was not a §548(a)(1) fraudulent conveyance, because there was no actual intent to delay, hinder, or defraud. Debtor was making a good faith (and presumably reasonable) business decision that the best way to expand was to guarantee the debts of currency exchanges. This deal turned out badly, but so do many business deals, and not all are fraudulent conveyances.

What about §548(a)(2)? There are two questions we must answer: (1) Did Debtor receive less than a reasonably equivalent value in exchange for incurring the obligation under the guarantee and transferring the interest in its property that secured the debt?; and (2) Was Debtor insolvent on the date that the transfer was made and the obligation was incurred? To answer the first question, you have to look at both sides of the ledger: How large was Debtor's obligation in comparison with the benefits it received in return? We might ask whether it was worth $10,000 to Debtor to have Currency Exchange in business and using its money orders. But when Debtor executed the guarantee, did it think that it was giving up $10,000? It did expose itself to the risk of losing $10,000, but this is quite different. If there was a one-in-ten chance of Currency Exchange failing, wouldn't Debtor calculate its cost of issuing the guarantee at $1,000? The axial question seems to be whether Debtor was getting a $1,000 benefit from its guarantee, rather than a $10,000 benefit. Shouldn't the examination after the fact follow the calculus that Debtor would engage in before the fact?

One might be able to show that guaranteeing the obligations of Currency Exchange was a poor idea and really didn't bring Debtor enough business to compensate for the risks it was taking, but as long as the guarantee is part of a plausible business decision, why should it be second-guessed? Do we have, under these assumptions, a debtor trying to shortchange its creditors and pocket the difference? We do have risk-taking, but creditors are always exposed to risk-taking by their debtors.

But suppose there wasn't fair consideration or reasonably equivalent value. Was Debtor insolvent at the time the obligation was incurred or the transfer was made? Let us assume that Debtor was insolvent when the guarantee was called on, but not at the time it issued the guarantee. Here we have a clear answer, at least with respect to the time that the security interest was transferred. Under §548(d), the transfer is deemed made at the time the initial guarantee is signed and a financing statement is filed. When these events happen, no subsequent bona fide purchaser can trump Bank's interest. Is the obligation incurred at the same time? Should the important time be the moment of payout or the moment that Debtor's liability, though contingent, passed out of its control into the hands of others?

What if Currency Exchange had a periodic need for additional cash for a few days (like on payday when everyone comes in to cash large checks)? Debtor discovers it is losing a lot of business because Currency

Exchange has these periodic cash shortages. It closes up shop early and is forced to turn away potential money order customers. Worse, Currency Exchange may stay open for business, but cash checks with the proceeds from the money orders and drag its heels with respect to turning over the proceeds to Debtor. Debtor makes its profit by earning interest on money it receives until the money order it issued is cashed. Debtor therefore arranges for Currency Exchange to be able to draw up to $10,000 from Bank to prevent these occasional cash shortages. Bank gets a guarantee from Debtor. Again it takes a security interest in Debtor's property. Bank has the unlimited right to give up to $10,000 to Currency Exchange. Once Debtor issues the guarantee, it cannot retract it. This deal is different from the first example only in that the actual amount of money Bank has lent can change at any moment. How do we analyze this problem?

Isn't the reasonably equivalent value issue the same? One must assess the probability, at the time Debtor put itself on the hook, that Currency Exchange would default and how much the default would come to. One would then discount its maximum exposure, $10,000, by this probability and come up with a certain amount of money. Then one would ask whether this amount — the cost of issuing the guarantee — was reasonably equal to the benefits (i.e., a better-run currency exchange) Debtor would receive in return.

But when do we measure insolvency? When did Debtor make the transfers or incur the obligations? Let's assume the following dates:

January 1:   Guarantee signed and Bank files and perfects its security interest.

February 1:   Payday. Currency Exchange draws on credit line for $10,000. It returns the money three days later when all the paychecks clear.

May 1:   The money order business turns sour; Debtor is insolvent.

June 1:   Another payday: Currency Exchange draws on the credit line again. But the local factory goes under, and all its employees' paychecks that Currency Exchange honored prove worthless.

June 3:   Currency Exchange files its petition in bankruptcy. Bank draws on the guarantee Debtor made.

June 5:   Debtor files its petition in bankruptcy.

Assume that there is no fair consideration for making the transfer or incurring the obligation, even though it seems to be an arms-length transaction. Is the transaction a fraudulent conveyance? Did Debtor incur an obligation or transfer property while it was insolvent? The answer turns on when the transfer was made or the obligation incurred. Note that under these facts, there are several possible dates: (1) the date Debtor issued the guarantee and Bank perfected its security interest (January 1); (2) the date Currency Exchange drew on the $10,000 credit line for the last time (June 1); or (3) the date Debtor honored the guarantee (June 3).

We have already ruled out the last date in the previous example. We must choose between the first two alternatives. If we pick the date on which Bank actually lent the money, Debtor's obligation turns on only a single contingency — whether Currency Exchange pays the money back. If we pick the date that Debtor signed the guarantee, Debtor's obligation hinges upon two contingencies: (1) whether Currency Exchange borrows the money; and (2) whether Currency Exchange fails to pay it back.

Was the obligation incurred when the guarantee was signed? At that point Debtor's discretion in the transaction disappeared. It was then that the transfer was perfected within the meaning of §548(d). More to the point, nothing seems to happen after the issuing of the initial guarantee that implicates the policies behind the fraudulent conveyance statutes. To be sure, Bank has the power to make the position of Debtor's other creditors more risky, but it is hardly going to use this power manipulatively. Bank can put Debtor's other creditors in a riskier position only by shelling out its own cold, hard cash and taking risks itself. Currency Exchange can make the position of Debtor's creditors riskier by calling on the credit line, but it bargained for this in January. If something is wrong with allowing Currency Exchange to draw upon Debtor's credit whenever it needs money, then it is a defect of the original deal. Therefore, shouldn't the moment we measure Debtor's solvency be the time of the original deal?

Can one go further and argue that the transaction with Bank was not a fraudulent conveyance, regardless of whether Debtor received reasonably equivalent value or fair consideration from Currency Exchange? When Bank calls upon the guarantee, it simply wants repayment of money that it actually extended to Currency Exchange. From its perspective, the principal and its guarantor are like a single entity. It provides fair consideration and reasonably equivalent value for the antecedent debt it undertook on behalf of both Debtor and Currency Exchange. Any flaw in the transaction arises because Debtor provided a benefit to Currency Exchange that the latter did not reciprocate, not because Bank received any special benefit. Making such guarantees potential fraudulent conveyances requires Bank to monitor the affairs of both principal and guarantor, investigate the consideration the principal is providing the guarantor, and determine whether the principal is solvent at whatever the relevant time proves to be. Are parties like Bank well equipped to do any of this? If not, why should we have an intepretation of the fraudulent conveyance laws that obliges them to do so? See Comment, Guarantees and Section 548(a)(2) of the Bankruptcy Code, 52 U. Chi. L. Rev. — (1985).

Problem 5.18 draws upon the facts of Rubin v. Manufacturers Hanover Bank, 661 F.2d 979 (2d Cir. 1981), which was decided under the old Act. The actual case differed in several important respects from the variations presented here. First, most of the currency exchanges (though not all) were related to Debtor. It was therefore much harder to answer the "reasonably equivalent value" question. For the most part, we do not have arms-length transactions and hence cannot be confident that guaranteeing the funds for check cashing really enhanced the money order business. If one person manages two corporations, that person is indifferent whether a transfer from one corporation to another is reciprocated, while the creditors of those corporations are not. Second, in *Rubin,* the guarantors were not on the hook from the moment they put their signatures on the guarantee. The debtor in *Rubin* controlled the amount of the credit line every month. Bank could only lend money to the currency exchanges if Debtor said it could. It was therefore possible to argue that the obligations weren't incurred until Debtor actually authorized the use of the existing credit line. On the other hand, it may be hard to square this approach with the language of the statute governing the timing of the transfer. The security interest is transferred, at the latest, when it becomes perfected under state law. This happens the moment all the steps for attachment take place and the financing statement is filed, quite apart from whether the beneficiary of the guarantee has lent the money or not. (One could, however, focus on the moment the obligation was incurred instead of the time of the transfer.) See Rosenberg, Intercorporate Guaranties and the Law of Fraudulent Conveyances: Lender Beware, 125 U. Pa. L. Rev. 235 (1976); Everdell and Longstreth, Some Special Problems Raised by Debt Financing of Corporations Under Common Control, 17 Bus. Law. 500 (1962).

PROBLEMS

5.19 Parent borrows $100,000 from Bank on January 1, and Subsidiary, a wholly owned subsidiary of Parent with a lot of assets, guarantees the obligation and secures it with a security interest on the assets. On November 1, Parent and Subsidiary both file for bankruptcy. Can Subsidiary's security interest be avoided as a fraudulent conveyance under §548? If Subsidiary had paid Bank on June 1, could the payment be attacked by the trustee as a fraudulent conveyance under §548?

5.20 Subsidiary borrows $100,000 from Bank on January 1, and Parent, who owns Subsidiary and who has a lot of assets, guarantees the obligation and secures it with a security interest in its assets. On November 1, Parent and Subsidiary both file for bankruptcy. Can Parent's security interest be avoided as a fraudulent conveyance under §548? Is this problem any different than the previous one? If Parent had paid Bank on June 1, could the payment be attacked by the trustee as a fraudulent conveyance under §548?

5.21 R-C Boaz, a soft drink bottler, was undergoing a reorganization and change of management at the urging of Royal Crown Cola Company, who refused to add new capital to R-C Boaz unless it undertook such changes. Part of this deal involved the sale to R-C Boaz, by Individual, of his capital stock in R-C Boaz. The purchase price of that stock was fixed at

$115,000, with $35,000 to be paid by R-C Boaz at the closing of the transaction and with the balance to be evidenced by a promissory note. This closing occurred in January 1980 and at that time Individual received a check for $35,000 issued by Royal Crown Bottlers of North Alabama (Bottlers), a wholly owned subsidiary of R-C Boaz. Royal Crown Cola Company thereupon infused "substantial" capital into R-C Boaz.

Despite that infusion, in May 1980, both R-C Boaz and Bottlers filed a petition in bankruptcy. The trustee of Bottlers seeks to recover the payment to Individual as a fraudulent conveyance, on the ground that Bottlers paid Individual $35,000 on an obligation owed by R-C Boaz for R-C Boaz's purchase of its own stock from Individual, and therefore all the consideration from Individual passed to R-C Boaz, not to Bottlers. The trustee asserts he is entitled to recover the $35,000 because it was not transferred for a "reasonably equivalent value." Individual responds that, under *Rubin*, this transfer was for "reasonably equivalent value" because of the identity of interests between the two entities, and because the infusion of cash by Royal Crown Cola Company was contingent, inter alia, on sale of Individual's stock. Evaluate the contentions. See In re Royal Crown Bottlers of North Alabama, 23 Bankr. 28 (Bankr. N.D. Ala. 1982).

5.22 Debtor borrowed $8,000 from Credit Union in December 1977, and used the money to purchase a truck for Son. The truck was registered in Son's name, and Credit Union had a security interest in the truck. Debtor made monthly installment payments of $210 by direct payroll deductions to Credit Union. Debtor, who was insolvent at all relevant times, filed a petition in bankruptcy in February of 1981. The trustee seeks to recover the installments paid during the year prior to Debtor's bankruptcy under §548. The trustee's argument is that Debtor's payments to Credit Union increased the equity in Son's truck, for which Debtor received no consideration. Evaluate this claim. Does Bullard v. Aluminum Co. of America, supra, offer any support for trustee's position? See In re Jamison, 21 Bankr. 380 (Bankr. D. Conn. 1982). Were the last three payments to Credit Union preferential? See Chapter 6.

NOTE ON FORECLOSURE SALES UNDER MORTGAGES AND FRAUDULENT CONVEYANCE LAW

There is one additional problem of great importance under fraudulent conveyance law: To what extent are foreclosure sales under mortgages avoidable as fraudulent conveyances? The issue was first raised by two cases out of the Fifth Circuit, Durrett v. Washington National Insurance Co., 621 F.2d 201 (5th Cir. 1980), and Abramson v. Lakewood Bank and Trust Co., 647 F.2d 547 (5th Cir. 1981). The facts of *Abramson* were typical. The Johnsons borrowed $74,000 from Lakewood in 1975, secured by a deed of trust on 73 acres of land. The deed of trust was promptly recorded. A year later, the Johnsons being unable to pay off the debt to Lakewood, Lakewood held a foreclosure sale pursuant to state statutory procedures, at which Lakewood purchased the property for $65,000. Five months later, the Johnsons filed for bankruptcy. The Fifth Circuit focused on the language of §67d(2) of the 1898 Act, which provided that "[e]very transfer made . . . by a debtor within one year prior to the filing" of a bankruptcy petition "is fraudulent . . . as to creditors existing at the time of such transfer . . . , if made or incurred without fair consideration. . . ." The Fifth Circuit viewed the issue in both *Durrett* and *Abramson* as whether a nonjudicial foreclosure sale constituted a "transfer." "Transfer" was defined in §1(30) of the 1898 Act as:

> the sale and every other and different mode, direct or indirect, of disposing of or of parting with property or with an interest therein or with the possession thereof or of fixing a lien upon property or upon an interest therein, absolutely or conditionally, voluntarily or involuntarily, by or without judicial proceedings, as a conveyance, sale, assignment, payment, pledge, mortgage, lien, encumbrance, gift, security, or otherwise; the retention of a security title to property delivered to a debtor shall be deemed a transfer suffered by such debtor.

The Fifth Circuit held that such a transfer occurred upon the foreclosure sale, noting that although the actual transfer of title was made by the deed of trust at the time of its execution, the debtor retained possession of the property, subject to the mortgagee's power to sell and deliver possession of the property, on default, at a foreclosure sale. Therefore, "[t]he 'transfer' within the contemplation of the Act, was not final until the day of the foreclosure sale. . . ." The only remaining question, as the Fifth Circuit saw it, was whether the sale was made for fair consideration.

The dissent in *Abramson* disagreed that there was a "transfer" at the time of the foreclosure sale, as a foreclosure sale "is not a transfer *by* the debtor, although done in his name pursuant to a power of sale in the mortgage or deed of trust." The dissent also thought that the decisions in *Durrett* and *Abramson* cast "a cloud upon mortgages and trust deeds," with the perverse effect that such decisions "will naturally inhibit a purchaser other than the mortgagee from buying at a foreclosure. This tends to depress further the prices of foreclosure sales. . . ."

The Ninth Circuit followed the dissent in *Abramson*. See In re Madrid, 725 F.2d 1197 (9th Cir. 1984). Two members of the panel thought the transfer took place when the deed was recorded. A third judge concurred on the more narrow ground that §548 only comprehends transfers in which the debtor participates, because in the absence of participation by the debtor there can be no effort on the debtor's part to defraud its creditors, which is the touchstone of a fraudulent conveyance.

"Transfer" was redefined in 1984 and now expressly includes foreclosure of a debtor's equity of redemption, §101(48), although subsequent legislative history indicated that this was not intended to overrule *Madrid*. 130 Cong. Rec. §13771 (daily ed. Oct. 5, 1984). Amendments to the Bankruptcy Code in 1984 also expressly provided that a transfer could be a fraudulent conveyance even if the transfer was made without the help of the debtor. §548(a).

Can one argue that focusing on the meaning of words like "transfer" ignores the more important question of whether the policies of fraudulent conveyance law are in fact implicated? The vice at issue in these cases seems to be that the amount of money raised at foreclosure sales is less than the true market value of the property. Is this a problem that bankruptcy or fraudulent conveyance law ought to be concerned with?

Legislatures have enacted statutes specifically dealing with foreclosure sales. Haven't they implicitly rejected the notion that the debtor's creditors should be able to set aside such sales (perhaps years after the fact) by showing that their debtor turned out to have been insolvent at the time of the sale and the price was inadequate? Is litigation over the adequacy of the price at such a sale worth its rather obvious costs (increased uncertainty and hence lower prices at such sales in the first instance)? Perhaps the easiest way to mesh fraudulent conveyance law and foreclosure sales would be to adopt a per se rule that prices realized at foreclosure sales were for "reasonably equivalent value" or for "fair consideration." This rule has been proposed for the new Uniform Fraudulent Transfer Act, but Congress decided not to add it to the Bankruptcy Code in the 1984 Amendments. Even after the 1984 Amendments, however, courts may be free to adopt the per se rule in interpreting §548. The Bankruptcy Appellate Panel adopted such a rule in In re Madrid, 21 Bankr. 424 (9th Cir. Bankr. App. 1982), aff'd on other grounds, 725 F.2d 1197 (9th Cir. 1984).

PROBLEMS

5.23 Debtor borrows $74,000 from Bank in 1982, secured by a mortgage on 70 acres of land. The mortgage is promptly recorded. In January 1985, when Debtor fails to make three installment payments, Bank forecloses on the property, and it is sold to Buyer for $65,000. In May 1985, Debtor files a petition in bankruptcy. Assume that the bankruptcy court concludes that a fraudulent conveyance has occurred. What rights does the trustee then have against Buyer? Does it matter whether he proceeds under §548 or under state fraudulent conveyance law (via §544(b))? See §548(c); UFCA §9(2).

5.24 Debtor owns Blackacre. Debtor, who wants cash so she can "take the money and run," thereby avoiding her creditors, sells Blackacre to Buyer for $200,000, its fair market value at that time. Buyer has no inkling of Debtor's intentions. Debtor dissipates the $200,000, and six months later is forced into bankruptcy. At that time, Blackacre has a fair market value of $300,000. Is there a fraudulent conveyance? See §548(a)(1); UFCA §7. If there is, can the trustee go after Buyer? Does it matter whether he proceeds under §548 or under state fraudulent conveyance law? See §548(c); UFCA §9(1).

Chapter 6
TRUSTEE AVOIDING POWERS DIRECTED AT THE "OPT OUT" PROBLEM

A. INTRODUCTION

The descent of a healthy firm into insolvency and then bankruptcy is a slow one. Creditors sometimes can see what is coming, and may learn about impending trouble at different times. The creditors that are the first to learn about the debtor's difficulties may try to collect what they are owed before the collective proceeding starts, instead of attempting to begin the proceeding themselves. If a debtor's liabilities exceed its assets, even the best-run collective proceeding cannot give general creditors 100 cents on the dollar. The creditors who know the most and act the swiftest have an incentive to do better for themselves by pursuing individual remedies, even though the creditors as a group may be worse off. We need legal rules to check the temptation creditors have to jump the gun when a bankruptcy proceeding looms on the horizon. The rules that govern the transition from individual to collective creditor remedies are the subject of this chapter.

We look first at the primary transitional rule, the "voidable preference" rule. In their simplest form, preferences are simply transfers that favor one existing creditor over another. Debtor prefers Creditor *A* to Creditor *B* if Debtor pays *A* before *B*. As we saw in the last chapter, favoring *A* over *B* is not a fraudulent conveyance — assuming Debtor is not motivated by an actual desire to hinder, delay, or defraud *B* — because Debtor's antecedent debt to *A* is fair consideration for the transfer. Debtor plans to pay *B* eventually, but would simply prefer to pay *A* first. The strength of this idea was expressed in Shelly v. Boothe, 73 Mo. 74 (1880):

279

[T]he debtor has a clear and undisputed right to prefer one creditor to another, and apply his property to the payment of one set of creditors to the exclusion of other creditors, and when this is done in payment of bona fide debts the transaction will be upheld, although in doing so the act of the debtor had the effect, and it was his intention, to defer or hinder another creditor, who at the time had a suit pending against him. . . .

. . . A debtor may give a preference to a particular creditor or set of creditors by a direct payment or assignment, if he does so in payment of his or their just demands, and not as a mere screen to secure the property to himself. The pendency of another creditor's suit is immaterial, and the transaction is valid though done to defeat that creditor's claim. . . . The right of a debtor to prefer one creditor over another necessarily implies the right of such creditor to accept such preference. While the effect of such preference must, to the extent that it is made, necessarily be to defer or to hinder or delay other creditors, the mere knowledge of the preferred creditor that such will be its effect, and the debtor intended it should have that effect, will not be sufficient to avoid the transaction as to a creditor not preferred. But if . . . the preferred creditor was not acting from an honest purpose . . . , but from a desire to aid the debtor in defeating other creditors, or in covering up his property, . . . he will not be protected, and the sale would be fraudulent as to other creditors, because in such cases the fraud of the debtor becomes the fraud of the preferred creditor because of his participancy therein.

Preferences are generally permitted outside of bankruptcy. Sometimes, the justification is given that one cannot undo a preference at the behest of another creditor without creating a new preference. See, e.g., Smith v. Whitman, 39 N.J. 397, 402, 189 A.2d 15, 18 (1963) ("True, a creditor who collects from an insolvent debtor fares better than other claimants. Yet if the transfer were set aside in favor of another creditor, there would be but a substitution of one preference for another"). Such an explanation, however, is at best only partially correct. A preference could be undone in order to retrieve the asset transferred to one creditor for the benefit of the creditors as a group. Such an action, however, would inevitably be a part of a collective proceeding to gather and disburse assets. It is for this reason that preferences do not seem inherently objectionable outside of bankruptcy (or other collective proceedings), for the idea of preference law is part and parcel of the substitution of collective remedies for individual remedies. Allowing a debtor to prefer one creditor over another is a corollary of the principle that every creditor is left to its own devices to obtain repayment. Any system that prevented preferences would necessarily be a collective one in which creditors could not recover from their debtor without considering the interests of other creditors.

But when there needs to be a collective proceeding, there also needs to be a voidable preference rule to ensure that the proceeding is effective. To be effective, a system of bankruptcy laws must have rules that prevent creditors from grabbing the debtor's assets during the period when a bankruptcy petition is imminent, but before the actual filing. Without such rules, the bankruptcy proceeding may commence after all the debtor's assets have been dispersed among a few speedy creditors. For that reason, the examination of avoiding powers in Chapter 5 was incomplete. It is not enough to freeze the creditors' positions the moment before the petition is filed and evaluate the value of their rights under state law. To enable the collective proceeding to work successfully, one must ensure that, during the period leading up to the filing, none of the creditors deplete the firm's assets by engaging in a last minute "grab" in anticipation of the collective proceeding. See Note, Preferential Transfers and the Value of the Insolvent Firm, 87 Yale L.J. 1449 (1978).

The essence of a collective proceeding such as bankruptcy is ratable distribution among those similarly situated. It substitutes collective procedures for individual actions, in the interests of the creditors as a group. A bankruptcy statute's voidable preference provision embodies the following principle: If a creditor tries to improve its position, after extending credit, in actual anticipation of a bankruptcy proceeding, or if the debtor, at the creditor's behest, tries to improve that creditor's position, in actual anticipation of a bankruptcy proceeding, the creditor must return any advantage so obtained. See Jackson, Avoiding Powers in Bankruptcy, 36 Stan. L. Rev. 725, 765 (1984). But one cannot simply enact this principle into law. Having a perfect fit with an underlying set of policies is not the only goal of statutes. The basic dilemma that faced the drafters of the Bankruptcy Code is one that drafters always face. They can either establish a clear rule that reaches particular transactions or they can lay down a loose standard that repeats the general principle and directs judges to set aside transactions that are at odds with it. The first approach has the virtue of being easy to apply. Its vice is that any clear rule is both under- and overinclusive. The second approach, although more precise in theory, is harder and more costly to apply and allows for more uncertainty, both before the filing of the bankruptcy petition and during the proceeding itself. The transitional provisions of the Bankruptcy Code are a mix of rules and standards.

The purpose of the Bankruptcy Code's preference section was to nullify most of the objectionable transfers (creditors taking special action in anticipation of the collective proceeding) without touching unobjectionable transactions (for example, payments of gas and electricity bills in the ordinary course of business). Although the voidable preference provisions of the Bankruptcy Code are both over- and underinclusive, the question we must ask is whether it is possible to create more refined rules without introducing too many complexities and uncertainties.

B.   PREFERENCES UNDER §547: THE BASIC ELEMENTS

NOTE ON THE RATIONALE FOR PREFERENCE LAW

Voidable preference law tries to prevent creditors from changing their position relative to one another in anticipation of a bankruptcy proceeding. Its purpose is not to prevent creditors from bargaining for priority at the time of the original loan (such as by taking a security interest). In that event, the advantages gained are recognized from the start and paid for (in the form of a lower interest rate). Nor is preference law designed to strike down *all* activity that results in payment for one creditor ahead of another, for such behavior simply restates the idea of individual creditor remedies. Preference law is, instead, concerned with post-loan collection attempts — attempts to opt out of the class of unsecured creditors into a class of paid (or secured) creditors — that are done with an eye towards bankruptcy.

This behavior comes in two main forms, and modern preference law captures both. See Jackson, Avoiding Powers in Bankruptcy, 36 Stan. L. Rev. 725, 760-764 (1984). The first kind of behavior is forbidden by what we may describe as the "anti-last minute grab" policy. Let us imagine that Debtor has assets worth $100 and owes two creditors, Bank and Finance Company, $100 each. Debtor is contemplating declaring bankruptcy. In bankruptcy, each creditor would receive $50. Debtor, in light of the impending bankruptcy, may "prefer" Bank by paying Bank's debt in full, or by granting Bank a security interest in all of its property. Bank, on the other hand, may act directly to "prefer" itself by acquiring a judicial lien. Once the bankruptcy petition is filed, the trustee probably can set aside any of these transactions as a preference, with the result that both Finance Company and Bank will still receive $50 in a bankruptcy proceeding.

Most commentators recognize that the preference section, by striking down "last-minute grabs" designed to benefit existing individual creditors, enables the creditors as a group to gain the advantages of a collective proceeding. Even here, however, one should distinguish "grabs" involving payment or the taking of other tangible property from "grabs" involving the taking of security interests or liens. The former are more directly detrimental to the collectivizing nature of bankruptcy, for they actually remove assets from the firm and hence directly impede its operations.

Another category of behavior is proscribed under what is commonly (and somewhat misleadingly) called modern preference law's "anti-secret lien" policy. Assume in the example above that a year or two before the bankruptcy, Debtor borrowed from Finance Company and gave Finance Company a security interest in all of its personal property. Finance Company, however, neither took possession of Debtor's property nor filed a financing statement until ten days prior to Debtor's bankruptcy petition. But because Finance Company filed its financing statement before Bank got an execution lien, Finance Company would be entitled under Article 9 to be paid ahead of Bank, even though Finance Company was exceedingly slow in perfecting its security interest. As we will see, however, §547(e) of the Bankruptcy Code ignores that outcome by manipulating the time the security interest was transferred when a filing is delayed. Finance Company is deemed to have received a transfer at the moment of filing which the trustee in bankruptcy can avoid because the transfer is on account of an antecedent debt. (A similar manipulation is involved in the definition of "transfer" used in the fraudulent conveyance section, see *Kindom Uranium Corp.*, supra page 260.)

Although few people have ever doubted in principle the value of the anti-last minute grab policy, the anti-secret lien policy is more controversial. Some have argued that an anti-secret lien policy is unrelated to the core notion of preference law. See Morris, Bankruptcy Law Reform: Preferences, Secret Liens and Floating Liens, 54 Minn. L. Rev. 737, 759-761 (1970) ("Such a transaction is not factually a preference and the law of preferences is not the appropriate vehicle for handling secret liens in bankruptcy"). The reason is that the two policies, at first glance, have little to do with one another. The creditor acquired its property right (i.e., the security interest) well before the preference period. Other creditors cannot complain that property was grabbed at the last minute. Their complaint, rather, is that notice of the transaction was not given until the last minute. Giving creditors adequate notice of a property transfer may seem to have little to do with ensuring that creditors do not try to opt out of a collective proceeding.

Despite this difference, the anti-secret lien policy is consistent with the underlying rationale of the preference section, which is to protect the collective proceeding. It is consistent because during the time that the anti-last minute grab policy prevents general creditors from boosting their status to that of a lien creditor, the anti-secret lien policy restricts existing *secured* creditors from improving their position, relative to that of general creditors, by imposing a similar limitation on them. See Jackson, Avoiding Powers in Bankruptcy, 36 Stan. L. Rev. 725, 764 (1984). In many cases, it is not coincidental that a financing statement is filed or the collateral repossessed just before the filing of the petition: The prospect of bankruptcy looming on the horizon forces the secured creditor to reassess its position. If it had not anticipated a collective proceeding, the secured creditor might have done nothing.

NOTE ON THE ELEMENTS OF A PREFERENCE

In §60 of the Bankruptcy Act of 1898, much of the sorting between objectionable and unobjectionable transactions was done using two prerequisites to finding a voidable preference: (1) that the debtor was insolvent when the event under question took place; and (2) that the recipient of the preference "knew or had reason to know" of that insolvency. The subjective "knew or had reason to know" test — probably the most litigated question under the preference provisions of the 1898 Act — was dropped from the Bankruptcy Code in 1978 as a requirement of finding most preferences, but in 1984 Congress insulated from voidable preference attack any transfer made in the ordinary course of business §547(c)(2). The effect of this amendment may be much the same as the reason to know requirement, both in the transactions it saves and the litigation it generates. The debtor's insolvency is still a condition of voidable preference, although the debtor is presumed insolvent during the 90 days before the petition. See §§547(b)(3) and (f); 101(29).

The Bankruptcy Code's general provisions for preferences are contained in §547(b). It empowers the trustee to avoid some "transfers" made for "antecedent debts." If the requirements of §547(b) are not met, there is no voidable preference. If they are met, §547(c) should be consulted to see if a "safe harbor" can be found. The trustee has the burden of showing that the elements of §547(b) have been satisfied; the creditor has the burden of showing that it fits within an exception in §547(c). §547(g). If the trustee avoids a transfer, it is preserved for the benefit of the estate. §551.

Section 547(b) of the Bankruptcy Code contains a number of elements that must be found before a voidable preference can be said to exist. First, there must be a "transfer" of "property of the debtor." "Property of the debtor" must be construed in light of the goals of preference law, as we will see in *A. J. Nichols* and *Gurs*, the next cases. "Transfer" is defined broadly, as meaning "every mode, direct or indirect, absolute or conditional, voluntary or involuntary, of disposing of or parting with property or with an interest in property, including retention of title as a security interest." §101(48). The transfer, moreover, must be "to or for the benefit of a creditor." This, as is discussed in *Church Buildings and Interiors,* infra, picks up transfers to a creditor and transfers that benefit a creditor. The most common example of the latter arises when there is a guarantor. A guarantor is a "creditor" of its principal within the meaning of §101(9), because it has a contingent right to recover from the principal in the event that the guarantee is called on. The guarantor is benefitted when its principal repays the debt, because it no longer has to honor its guarantee.

The transfer must also be "for or on account of an antecedent debt owed by the debtor before the transfer was made." In any transaction in which a voidable preference is a possibility, therefore, one must ask two

questions: (1) When was the debt incurred? (2) When was the transfer *a)*
made? As long as the transfer was made at the same time as the debt was *b)*
incurred or before the debt was incurred, there can be, by definition, no
voidable preference.

For a transfer to be avoidable, it must have been made on or within 90 *3)*
days of the filing of the petition, or within one year of the filing if the
creditor is an "insider." §101(28). The final requirement of a voidable *4)*
preference is that it must make the creditor better off than if no transfer
had been made and the creditor only enjoyed its rights in the bankruptcy
proceeding. The idea behind this requirement is that a creditor cannot be
trying to opt out of the collective proceeding if the transfer brings it no
special advantages.

In the following problems, you should assume insolvency at all relevant times.

PROBLEMS

6.1 Debtor borrowed $1,000 from a friend. The friend did not ask for
any interest, but insisted at the outset that the loan be callable on demand.
Debtor's financial condition deteriorated, although the friend was completely unaware of it. When the friend decided to buy a new stereo, he
called Debtor's loan, and Debtor repaid him the $1,000. Two months
later, Debtor filed a petition in bankruptcy. Can the trustee reclaim the *No,*
$1,000? *not in anticip. of B*

6.2 A large bakery buys great quantities of sugar. On January 1, the
bakery contracts with Debtor to provide it with 100,000 pounds of sugar
on May 1. The bakery pays for the sugar in full on January 1. On May 1,
Debtor delivers the sugar. On July 1, Debtor files a petition in bankruptcy.
Can the trustee force the firm to give back the sugar (or its dollar value
equivalent)? *No* Was there a "transfer" within the 90-day period for or on
account of an antecedent debt, as that term is defined in §101(48)? Cf.
Note on "Property of the Debtor" and §547, infra page 294. (Ignore for
the moment whether any of the exceptions in §547(c) apply.)

6.3 Debtor and Creditor had a contract whereby Creditor promised
to ship Debtor 10,000 widgets a month throughout 1985; Debtor would
pay Creditor $100,000 C.O.D. for each delivery. Shipments were made
and paid for in January and February. On March 10, Debtor and Creditor
agree to cancel the contract. At that time, the market price for widgets is
$13 each. On April 1, Debtor files for bankruptcy. Is there a "transfer" of
"property of the debtor"? *yes* See In re Jermoo's, Inc., 38 Bankr. 197 (Bankr.
W.D. Wisc. 1984). The question is of some importance because, as we will
see in Chapter 7 of this book, if the contract were not cancelled, the trustee
could assume and assign it under §365.

6.4 Father makes a large loan to Firm, a business his son started and of which his son is the president and majority stockholder. A year later, Father becomes uneasy about Firm's fortunes. He asks that his loan be repaid. Firm obliges. Nine months later, Firm files a petition in bankruptcy. Can the trustee force Father to give up the repayment? See §101(28). *Yes if acting as father, No if acting as outside lender*

6.5 Finance Company loans Debtor $50,000. A year later, Debtor defaults. Finance Company, after pursuing other debt collection tactics, sues Debtor, reduces its claim to judgment, and has the sheriff levy on Debtor's property. Later the same day, Debtor files a petition in bankruptcy. Can the trustee argue that Finance Company should return the property it acquired through the judgment, because the levy was a "transfer" on account of an antecedent debt (albeit an involuntary one) to Finance Company from Debtor? *Yes ?*

6.6 Acquiring Firm negotiates the purchase of substantial assets from Target Corporation. To finance that contemplated acquisition, Acquiring Firm arranges with Bank that Bank will advance Acquiring Firm 75 percent of the purchase price of those assets. Bank will take a security interest in those assets. On January 1, Acquiring Firm and Target Corporation sign an Agreement of Sale specifying a number of conditions that must be satisfied before the sale will be consummated. A closing is scheduled for February 1, at which time all conditions are expected to be met. One document to be signed at closing is the security agreement between Bank and Acquiring Firm. The closing proceeds without a hitch. As promised, Bank presents a check to Acquiring Firm for 75 percent of the purchase price of the assets. Is Bank's security interest acquired for an "antecedent debt"? When did Bank extend credit to Acquiring Firm? (Under Article 9, Bank's security interest in the collateral did not become effective until the security agreement was signed.)

The next two cases deal with the requirement that a preferential transfer involve "property of the debtor." Can you define that term, in light of the goals of a preference section?

IN RE A. J. NICHOLS, LTD.
21 Bankr. 612 (Bankr. N.D. Ga. 1982)

ORDER

W. Homer DRAKE, Jr., Bankruptcy Judge.

This case is before the Court on the trustee's Complaint to Avoid a Preferential Transfer. The defendant is a dealer of oriental rugs, who supplied oriental rugs to the debtor on either a "consignment" or "sale or return" basis. . . . On March 6, 1980, the debtor shipped to the defendant forty-six (46) rugs with a consignment wholesale value of $29,505.00. Forty-five (45) of the aforementioned forty-six (46) rugs had previously been shipped by the defendant to the debtor on a consignment basis. A security interest was not taken by the defendant in any of these rugs. On April 11, 1980, A. J. Nichols, Ltd. filed a petition under Chapter 7 of the Bankruptcy Code resulting in the March 6, 1980 transfer falling within the preference period of 11 U.S.C. §547. . . .

The sole question before this Court is whether the return of certain consigned goods within the preference period constitutes a voidable preference under 11 U.S.C. §547(b). . . .

The plaintiff . . . asserts that the transfer in question satisfies each and every provision of §547(b) of the Bankruptcy Code, thus making the transfer a voidable preference. The defendant contends that no property of the debtor was transferred and that the elements set forth in 11 U.S.C. §547(b)(2), (3), and (5) have not been satisfied. The plaintiff has the burden of proof on each of the elements of 11 U.S.C. §547(b).

The threshold requirement of 11 U.S.C. §547(b) is that there must be a transfer of property of the debtor in order for there to be a voidable preference. "Transfer" is defined in 11 U.S.C. §101(40)* as every mode of parting with property or with an interest in property. The term "property of the debtor" is not defined in the Bankruptcy Code, but it has been held that a preference may exist "where property in which a debtor has any interest is transferred out of his estate." In re Lucasa International, 14 B.R. 980, 8 B.C.D. 444, 445 (Bkrtcy. S.D.N.Y. 1981). Ga. Code §§109A-2-326(2) and (3) state that goods delivered primarily for resale, as were the rugs in the instant case, are deemed to be "on sale or return." . . . It is clear that at the time of the transfer of the rugs, since these goods were subject to the claims of the debtor's creditors, some property interest did exist in the debtor concerning said rugs.

The defendant's contention that a distinction exists between the property of the debtor and the estate of the debtor is without merit. There can be no estate prior to the filing of a petition in bankruptcy. The commencement of such a case creates an estate which is made up of all legal or equitable interests of the debtor in property. 11 U.S.C. §541(a)(1). Thus, when one enters bankruptcy, the property of the debtor is the property of the estate.

Moreover, the debtor in this case had more than just a possessory interest in the rugs. These rugs were in the possession of the debtor on a "consignment" or "sale or return" basis. Under Georgia law, goods held on a sale or return basis are subject to the claims of a buyer's creditor while in the buyer's possession. Ga. Code §109A-2-326(2). At the time of the transfer, the rugs were in the debtor's possession, and were subject to the

* Renumbered as §101(48) in 1984. — Eds.

claims of the debtor's creditors. The only exceptions to this rule appear in Ga. Code §109A-2-326(3).

The defendant contends that the arrangement between the debtor and the defendant was a true consignment and not an attempt to retain a security interest or a sale or return. In this case, Ga. Code §109A-9-114 provides that a consignor who has not retained a security interest has an interest in the subject goods which is subordinated to that of a person who would have a perfected security interest in said goods. This section implies that in an instance in which there is a true consignment, the consignor would have priority over an unsecured creditor. The determination of whether the defendant in the instant case has a true consignment is governed by Ga. Code §109A-2-326(3). Ga. Code §100A-2-326(3) provides three exceptions to the general rule that delivery of goods to a person for sale in the ordinary course of business is deemed to be on sale or return even though the agreement (1) purports to reserve title to the person making delivery until payment or resale or (2) uses such words as "on consignment" or "on memorandum." Ga. Code §109-A-2-326.

The first exception contained in Ga. Code §109A-2-326(3) requires compliance with "an applicable law providing for consignor's interest or the like to be evidenced by a sign." Ga. Code §109A-2-326(3)(a). The evidence presented at the trial on March 31, 1982 established that the debtor never posted such signs.

The second exception to Ga. Code §109A-2-326 exists if the consignor can show that the consignee is generally known by his creditors to be substantially engaged in selling the goods of others. Ga. Code §109A-2-326(3)(b). The burden of proof is on the defendant to prove such knowledge by its creditors. The defendant has failed to meet this burden in the case *sub judice*. The evidence before the Court shows that the debtor's creditors did not have actual knowledge that the goods sold by the debtor were on consignment, as required by Ga. Code §109A-1-201(25).

The final exception to Ga. Code §109A-2-326 is that the consignor meet the filing requirements of Article 9 of the Georgia U.C.C. provisions. Ga. Code §109A-2-326(3)(c). There is no dispute that the defendant did not file a financing statement in the instant case.

Therefore, as the above discussion indicates, the defendant has failed to meet any of the requirements of Ga. Code §109A-2-326(3) that would result in the defendant's being deemed a consignor of the rugs which the debtor returned to the defendant. Accordingly, the Court finds that the relationship between the defendant and the debtor is not that of a consignor and consignee, but finds instead that the transaction which the parties entered into was a sale or return as contemplated by Ga. Code §109A-2-326. It follows from this determination that the March 6, 1980 transfer of certain rugs from the debtor to the defendant was a transfer of the debtor's property under 11 U.S.C. §547(b). . . .

Once the threshold requirement of transfer of the debtor's property has been met, the trustee must prove the five elements of 11 U.S.C. §547(b). The first requirement is that the transfer be to or for the benefit of a creditor. 11 U.S.C. §547(b)(1). Under 11 U.S.C. §101(9) a "creditor" is an "entity that has a claim against the debtor that arose at the time of or before the order for relief concerning the debtor." A "claim" is "a right to payment or a right to an equitable remedy." 11 U.S.C. §101(4). The Court finds that prior to the transfer, the defendant, whether a consignor or a seller on a sale or return basis, had a right to either payment for the rugs or the right to an equitable remedy for the return of the rugs. Thus it is clear that the defendant had a claim against the debtor and that the defendant was a creditor within the ambit of §101(9) of the Bankruptcy Code. For this reason, the Court finds that the transfer was to or for the benefit of a creditor. 11 U.S.C. §547(b)(1).

The Court also finds that the transfer was "for or on account of an antecedent debt owed by the debtor before such transfer was made." 11 U.S.C. §547(b)(2). According to 11 U.S.C. §101(11), "debt" means "liability on a claim." Thus, by virtue of the same analysis in which this Court determined the defendant was a creditor of A. J. Nichols, Ltd., the Court finds that the transfer was made on account of a claim owed by the debtor before the transfer was made.

The third requirement to be shown by the plaintiff is that the transfer must be made while the debtor was insolvent. 11 U.S.C. §547(b)(3). Under 11 U.S.C. §547(f), there is a presumption that for ninety days preceding the filing of the debtor's petition, the debtor is insolvent. This places the burden of going forward with the evidence of the debtor's solvency on the defendant. The Court finds that the defendant has failed to overcome the presumption of insolvency. Moreover, the trustee has proven the insolvency of the debtor. The evidence showed that a $50,000 claim against an officer of the debtor, who left in 1979 with $50,000 of the debtor's assets, was scheduled as an asset of the debtor. As the claim was shown to have no prospect of collection, the debtor's schedules are not a fair indication of the debtor's solvency. This Court finds that the debtor was insolvent at the time of the transfer of the property.

It is undisputed by the parties that the property was transferred from the debtor to the defendant within ninety days of the filing of the petition.

Finally, the plaintiff must show that this transfer enabled the creditor to receive more than the creditor would have received if the transfer had not been made and the defendant had received payment of its claim to the extent provided by the provisions of the Bankruptcy Code. 11 U.S.C. §547(b)(5). Because this transfer allowed the defendant to recover the entire amount of his claim and because the defendant did not have a perfected security interest nor a true consignment, the Court finds that the creditor received more than it would have under a Chapter 7 liquidation if this transfer had not been made.

Therefore, for the above-stated reasons, the Court finds that the plaintiff has carried the burden of proof with respect to each element of 11 U.S.C. §547(b) and that the transfer of forty-five (45) rugs from the debtor to the defendant was a voidable preference. Judgment is granted in favor of the plaintiff in the amount of $29,505.00.

It is so ordered.

NOTE

See also In re P.M.R.C. Corp., 39 Bankr. 912 (Bankr. E.D.N.Y. 1984).

NOTE ON CONSIGNMENTS AND SPECIAL PROPERTY INTERESTS

A.J. Nichols concerns a consignment, and asks first if the transaction involves a true consignment. To consider the case, it is important to distinguish between a true consignment and one (called a "security consignment") that the Uniform Commercial Code considers simply a form of security agreement. A security consignment — where the "consignment is intended as security" (UCC §1-201(37)) — is viewed as a disguised secured transaction, so that "the reservation of title thereunder," notwithstanding shipment to the consignee (the buyer), is limited in effect to a reservation of a security interest. The trustee will be able to reach such a transaction, unless the "consignor" (the seller) perfects its interest before the filing of the bankruptcy petition. Delaying perfection of the security interest will cause the acquisition of the interests to be a "transfer" for an "antecedent debt." The consignor's rights remain subject to the rights of a lien creditor claiming through the debtor/consignee, until such time as the consignor takes the steps required to give it priority under UCC §9-301(2).

Distinguishing this from a true consignment requires a little digression into the form of a consignment. Historically, a consignment is designed to allow a seller to retain some control over the terms of distribution and sale of goods. In a typical arrangement, a seller ("consignor") delivers ("consigns") goods to an agent/distributor ("consignee"), to sell to third parties, often at a specified price. The consignor retains title to the goods until they are sold by the consignee. When the goods are sold, title passes directly from the consignor to the ultimate buyer. As noted by Professor Hawkland, "[t]he hallmark of a consignment is agency or bailment. The consignee is not a buyer. The ownership of the goods does not move to or through him." Hawkland, The Proposed Amendments to Article 9 of the UCC — Part 5: Consignments and Equipment Leases, 77 Com. L.J. 108, 108 (1972).

When goods on consignment are sold, the consignee is obligated to account to the consignor for a portion of the sale price. But the consignor assumes the risk of the sale. If the goods are not sold, the consignee returns them without obligation to pay for them. Most consignment arrangements also authorize the consignor to demand return of the goods at any time. Under pre-UCC law, close adherence to these attributes, especially the power of the consignee to return unsold goods without obligation, usually insulated the transaction from the clutches of the trustee in bankruptcy. See, e.g., Liebowitz v. Voiello, 107 F.2d 914 (2d Cir. 1939).

The UCC's treatment of true consignments under §2-326 is hard to divine. Some courts have concluded that a "sale or return" is not the same thing as a consignment. See, e.g., American Natl. Bank of Denver v. First Natl. Bank of Glenwood Springs, 28 Colo. App. 486, 476 P.2d 304 (1970). Under such a reading, UCC §2-326(2) (which makes goods held on a sale or return basis subject to the claims of a buyer's creditors while in the buyer's possession) would not apply directly, but would be made applicable, if at all, through UCC §2-326(3). That subsection provides:

> Where goods are delivered to a person for sale and such person maintains a place of business at which he deals in goods of the kind involved, under a name other than the name of the person making delivery, then with respect to the claims of creditors of the person conducting the business the goods are deemed to be on sale or return. The provisions of this subsection are applicable even though an agreement purports to reserve title to the person making delivery until payment or resale or uses such words as "on consignment" or "on memorandum." However, this subsection is not applicable if the person making delivery
>
> > (a) complies with an applicable law providing for a consignor's interest or the like to be evidenced by a sign, or
> > (b) establishes that the person conducting the business is generally known by his creditors to be substantially engaged in selling the goods of others, or
> > (c) complies with the filing provisions of the Article on Secured Transactions (Article 9).

This suggests that UCC §2-326(2) will be made applicable to most consignments unless one of the three "requirements" is met. Realistically, in most jurisdictions, the only relevant "escape" is that of (3)(c)— compliance with the filing provisions of Article 9. See UCC §9-114.

A question raised in *A.J. Nichols*, however, is the relationship of true consignments to the preference provisions of bankruptcy law. Does anything in UCC §2-326 make the goods delivered to the consignee on a true consignment "property of the debtor"? If not, can §547 find a preference? Or is it sufficient to trigger the applicability of §547 that creditors of the consignee could defeat the consignor before it took the proper notoriety steps under Article 9 or regained possession of the goods? How well does *A.J. Nichols* sort out the competing arguments? Can its reasoning be squared with the reasoning of the court in the next case, dealing with the filing of a lis pendens — an act of notoriety that places people on notice of a competing claim of ownership? Absent that filing, that putative owner's claim is subject to the claim of creditors of the record owner.

TT = Trustee

IN RE GURS
34 Bankr. 755 (9th Cir. Bankr. App. 1983)

ORDER ON MOTION FOR REHEARING . . .

Prior decision

Record title to the real property in question was vested in the debtors. As the holder of the "rights and powers of" a bona fide purchaser under Title 11 U.S.C. (the "Code") §544(a)(3), the Trustee sought to invalidate Appellants' claims that the debtors held the property subject to a constructive or resulting trust. The key feature of our prior determination [at 27 Bankr. 163] was that the Trustee was bound by the notice constructively given by a lis pendens filed by one of the purported equitable owners of the property.

Issue

On the grounds that the issue had not been raised before the trial court, we refused to consider the Trustee's argument that, because the lis pendens was filed less than 90 days prior to the bankruptcy petition, the effect of the lis pendens should be disregarded as a preferential transfer under Bankruptcy Code §547. The Trustee has moved for rehearing on the grounds that the §547 issue was properly presented to the trial court and preserved upon appeal.

holding

§547

TT

Upon reexamination, we agree that the Trustee's §547 argument was presented to the trial court and that we are bound to consider it. However, having now considered the claim, we hold that there is no merit in the Trustee's claim and therefore deny the motion for rehearing.

Section 547 allows the Trustee to recover on behalf of the estate certain prepetition transfers of property which are preferential to transferee-creditors. Apparently the Trustee's theory is that the filing of the lis pendens within the preference period is comparable to the perfection of a security interest on property of the estate or the perfection of a transfer of the debtor's property in satisfaction of an antecedent debt by a creditor.

☆☆

For the purposes of §547 the granting of a security interest in the debtor's property or its outright conveyance is a "transfer" under the broad definition of that term contained in Code §101(41).* Moreover under §547(e)(2) the time of transfer is generally equated with "perfection," or in the case of unperfected interests, with the commencement of the case. Thus, such transfers which are perfected within the preference period or remain unperfected at the commencement of the case are often

_____
* Renumbered as §101(48) in 1984. — EDS.

avoidable. With respect to transfers of interests in real property §547(e)(1) generally equates "perfection" with that time when the transferee's interest could not be defeated by a competing bona fide purchaser from the debtor. Certainly the filing of the lis pendens within the 90 day preference period is an act that "perfects" the Appellants' claim to the property. Moreover that act may well be a "transfer" under §101(41). Finally, it is that act of perfection which we have found may preclude the Trustee from recovering under §544(a)(3). In this sense then, the Appellants have perfected an interest in property which may be a "transfer" within the preference period.

But to suggest that this means an avoidable transfer occurred ignores the elements of the Trustee's case contained in §547:

> Except as provided in subsection (c) of this section, the Trustee may avoid any transfer *of property of the debtor* — . . .
> (2) *for or on account of an antecedent debt* owed by the debtor before such transfer was made. . . .*

Code §547(b) (emphasis added). The filing of this lis pendens cannot be characterized as a transfer of the debtor's property nor can it be characterized as a transfer on account of an antecedent debt. To argue otherwise confuses avoidance of a transfer of an interest in the debtor's property with avoidance of an act that perfects, as against potential bona fide purchasers, a claim of *ownership*. Section 547 permits the avoidance of the former not the latter.

TRANSFER OF PROPERTY OF THE DEBTOR

Under §547 there is an avoidable transfer only if "property of the debtor" is transferred within the preference period. As vigorously argued by Appellants, where a debtor possesses only legal and not equitable interests in property, under §541(d) the equitable interest does not become part of the bankruptcy estate. But, adopting arguendo the Trustee's theory, the thrust of §544(a)(3) is that equitable interests in property not otherwise brought into the estate by §541 may become part of the estate through the operation of that section in conjunction with §551 and §541(a)(4). Thus, in cases such as this, the property is not property of the debtor, unless §§544(a)(3), 551, 541(a)(4) apply. However we have established that those sections do not apply in the face of the lis pendens filed in this case. Yet the only argument in favor of avoidance of the effect of the lis pendens regarding the claim under §544(a)(3) is that it is a "transfer" under §547.

The Trustee's theory depends upon a claim that §547 and §544(a)(3)

---

* Reworded slightly in 1984. — EDS.

operate interactively. Under the Trustee's theory, as a prerequisite to §547's applicability, §544(a)(3) must transform the property equitably owned by Appellants into something belonging to the debtor. But as a prerequisite to operation of §544(a)(3) the argument requires that the effect of the lis pendens under §547 first be negated. The circular logic required to accommodate the Trustee's theory illustrates the error of assuming that §544 and §547 operate interactively. Each is an independent power of the Trustee. The Trustee must exercise his powers separately, and prove the elements of his case under §547 or §544 independently.

ANTECEDENT DEBT

The Trustee's claim under §547 also falters on the requirement that the "transfer" be on account of an antecedent debt. The Appellants' claim is that of an equitable owner, not that of a creditor. The Trustee responds that because of the broad definition of "claim" contained in §101(4), the Appellants' claims of equitable ownership are "liabilities on a claim" which fall under the definition of "debt" contained in §101(11). The Trustee argues that, "[a]lthough a Court might equitably grant them an interest in specific real property, an equally valid remedy under California law would be a judgment for the payment of monetary damages." Appellee's Motion for Rehearing at 11. Although the quoted assertion is arguably correct, the conclusion that the availability of money damages as an alternative remedy to enforcement of a trust transforms the relationship into that of debtor and creditor, is a non sequitur. . . .

Section 547 is not a power to avoid a particular instrument which perfects a claim of ownership such as a lis pendens. It is a power to avoid transfers of property of the debtor on account of antecedent debts. It has no application in this case and accordingly there is no reason for rehearing.

Motion denied.

NOTE ON "PROPERTY OF THE DEBTOR" AND §547

The applicability of §547 is not always clear. Consider, for example, the fo[…] wing problem. Buyer orders goods from Debtor, to be manufactured Debtor. Buyer prepays the $100,000 contract price. Later, during reference period, Debtor ships the goods to Buyer. Is the goods a voidable preference (assuming, as always, that Debtor all relevant times)? Or can Buyer defend a preference action at before the preference period it had obtained a "special st" in the goods being manufactured for it under UCC sulated the later shipment of the goods from attack as a preference? See In re Tennecomp Systems, Inc., 12 Bankr. 729 (Bankr. E.D. Tenn. 1981) (to allow special property interests to insulate a transaction from avoidance under §547 would "enable an insolvent seller by his unilateral act to identify goods or pass title and thus prefer one creditor over another, even though both are in the same class."). Do you agree that both creditors, in such a case, should be viewed as "in the same class"? Would anything change if the contract had called for the passage of title upon identification of the goods to the contract under UCC §2-401?

Individual debtors, as we have discussed briefly in Chapter 4 and will examine in more detail in Chapter 11, have a set of "exemptions" they can use to insulate or remove property from their creditors. If a debtor transfers such property to a creditor in the pre-bankruptcy period, should that transfer be subject to attack under §547? Does it involve "property of the debtor" within the purpose of the preference section? The historical answer has been that such transfers are not voidable preferences. See, e.g., Smith v. Idaho State Bank, Bankr. Rep. (CCH) ¶65,170 (D. Ohio 1973). In the Proposed Bankruptcy Act of 1973, the Commission on Bankruptcy Laws recommended reversing these cases. Report of the Commission on the Bankruptcy Laws of the United States, H.R. Doc. No. 137, 93rd Cong., 1st Sess., Part I, at 204 (1973). It asserted that:

> There is no valid reason supporting the case law that is being overruled; the mere fact that the property used to prefer a creditor may be claimed as exempt does not establish a reason why preference attack is not appropriate. The goals of equality and avoidance of unwise extension of credit would be furthered by allowing preference attack. The only rationale for the cases is that other creditors are not hurt since they are not entitled to expect payment or security from exempt property.

Is the Bankruptcy Commission correct? Should the "only rationale" in support of excluding exempt property from preferential attack be dismissed so lightly? Cf. In re Hale, 15 Bankr. 565 (Bankr. S.D. Ohio 1981). The Bankruptcy Commission's proposal is criticized in Jackson, Avoiding Powers in Bankruptcy, 36 Stan. L. Rev. 725, 767-768 (1984).

NOTE ON INSIDERS

Section 547 contains a special provision for "insiders" that essentially extends the preference period for such persons to one year. The legislative history to §101(28), which defines "insider," suggests that "[a]n insider is one who has a sufficiently close relationship with the debtor that his conduct is made subject to closer scrutiny than those dealing at arms length with the debtor." Presumably the extension is appropriate because the insider is likely to learn of the impending bankruptcy before other creditors, and hence to take protective actions earlier, that might not be caught up in the 90-day preference period. Before the 1984 Amendments, transfers during the extended period for insiders could be attacked as preferential only if the insider-creditor "had reasonable cause to believe the debtor was insolvent at the time of such transfer." This language, however, was dropped in 1984. The materials below explore some of the complications introduced by the extended preference period for insiders.

PROBLEMS

6.7 Bank has a large, revolving credit line with Debtor. The agreement between Bank and Debtor contains a number of covenants, such as net working capital requirements. In addition, the agreement provides that Debtor will not issue any secured debt, make any investment over $100,000, make a distribution to shareholders, merge, or sell assets other than in the ordinary course of business, without first obtaining Bank's permission. Is Bank an insider?

6.8 Same facts as Problem 6.7. Assume Debtor is in default under the terms of the loan agreement. Bank agrees with Debtor not to call in the loan as long as Debtor makes several changes in management and its conduct of business. Bank places a bank officer in Debtor's headquarters to assist Debtor in restructuring its business relationships, and to keep tabs on the business for Bank's benefit. Even if Bank was not an insider under the facts of Problem 6.7, has it become one as a result of its post-default actions?

6.9 Bank loaned Debtor $100,000 on November 1. President, Debtor's president and principal stockholder, pledged stock to secure the debt. On February 1, Debtor repaid the $100,000 loan. On April 1, Debtor files for bankruptcy. May Debtor's trustee recover the payment to Bank as a preference? May the trustee recover, from President, the payment made to Bank? See In re Herman Cantor Corp., 15 Bankr. 747 (Bankr. E.D. Va. 1981). What if Debtor did not file for bankruptcy until June 1? See In re Church Buildings and Interiors, Inc., the next case.

6.10 Bank loans $200,000 to Corporation. Shareholder, a major shareholder of Corporation, guarantees repayment of the loan. Bank has a perfected security interest in most of Corporation's assets, including all Corporation's "rights to the payment of money, now existing or hereafter arising." Shareholder owes $50,000 to Corporation. On January 1, 1983, Shareholder pays to Bank, in reduction of Corporation's loan, the $50,000 he owes to Corporation. On March 1, 1983, Corporation files a petition in bankruptcy. Trustee asserts that, by virtue of the $50,000 payment to Bank, Shareholder has received a preference, because it reduced his obligation as guarantor of Bank's loan. (For now, analyze the question without considering the impact of §509 (subrogation of co-debtors) or §553 (setoff), two sections we will examine later in this book.) See Kapela v. Newman, 649 F.2d 887 (1st Cir. 1981).

IN RE CHURCH BUILDINGS AND INTERIORS, INC.
14 Bankr. 128 (Bankr. W.D. Okla. 1981)

Robert L. BERRY, Bankruptcy Judge.

STATEMENT OF THE CASE

On April 23, 1981, Thad H. Seeley, a judgment creditor of the defendant-debtor CBI and plaintiff herein, filed an involuntary bankruptcy petition against CBI. In his petition Seeley alleged that certain transfers of security interests from CBI to the Republic Bank, codefendant herein, were preferential. On April 24, 1981, Seeley filed a complaint seeking relief from the automatic stay provisions of 11 U.S.C. §362 to allow the continuance of a pending state court garnishment action against Republic Bank. . . .

FACTS

On June 20, 1980, CBI obtained a business loan from the Republic Bank in the amount of $40,000.00. As security for the loan William Vinyard, Secretary of CBI, and Ronald Priddy, Vice President of CBI, served as guarantors. Each of these guarantors had sufficient net worth to satisfy the debt.

On January 22, 1981, the bank released the guarantors in exchange for a security agreement from CBI which granted the bank a security interest in all of CBI's tangible and intangible property including accounts receivable and proceeds therefrom. This security interest was duly perfected in accordance with applicable law on January 26, 1981.

The bank now contends that CBI is in default and claims principal and interest in the amount of $30,043.19 as of March 18, 1981.

LAW

Plaintiff Seeley takes the position that CBI's transfer of a security interest in all of its property to the bank in exchange for the bank's release of the guarantors was preferential and avoidable under the provisions of 11 U.S.C. §547. . . .

Plaintiff contends that all of the elements of [§547(b)] have been met. As to the first element, plaintiff states in his brief, "The transfer must be to or for the benefit of a creditor, and in this instance the creditor was Republic Bank." While this statement is correct insofar as it goes, it must also be remembered that the guarantors were benefited by this transfer since the result of the transfer was their release by the bank. . . . As stated in 4 Collier on Bankruptcy §547.18 (15th ed. 1981):

> A guarantor or surety for the debtor, or an endorser of his notes or checks, will be a creditor under the Code because he will hold a contingent claim against the debtor that becomes fixed when he pays the creditor whose claim he has guaranteed or insured. Consequently, any transfer of property made by a debtor to or for the benefit of an endorser, guarantor or surety, may constitute a preference. Accordingly, any payment made by the debtor-maker to the holder of his notes may be a preference to the endorser, even though the endorser himself is solvent and did not procure the payment.

As to the second element, this Court agrees with Plaintiff's contention that the transfer was made "for or on account of an antecedent debt owed by the debtor before such transfer was made". It is obvious that the security agreement of January 22, 1981, was made on account of the debt incurred on June 20, 1980.

The third element of a preferential transfer requires that the transfer be "made while the debtor was insolvent". In this regard Plaintiff relies heavily on §547(f) which states, "For the purposes of this section, the debtor is presumed to have been insolvent on and during the 90 days immediately preceding the date of the filing of the petition." In connection with this presumption Plaintiff contends that the transfer was made "on or within 90 days before the date of the filing of the petition" as provided by §547(b)(4)(A), which constitutes the fourth element of a preferential transfer when the transfer does not involve an insider.

Plaintiff maintains that the transfer was made within 90 days of the filing of the petition because the transfer was perfected on January 26, 1981 — 87 days before the petition's filing date. 11 U.S.C. §547(e) provides in part:

> (e)(1) For the purposes of this section — . . .
> (B) a transfer of a fixture or property other than real property is perfected when a creditor on a simple contract cannot acquire a judicial lien that is superior to the interest of the transferee.
> (2) For the purposes of this section, except as provided in paragraph (3) of this subsection, a transfer is made —
>> (A) at the time such transfer takes effect between the transferor and the transferee, if such transfer is perfected at, or within 10 days after, such time;

(B) at the time such transfer is perfected, if such transfer is perfected after such 10 days; or

(C) immediately before the date of the filing of the petition, if such transfer is not perfected at the later of—

(i) the commencement of the case; and

(ii) 10 days after such transfer takes effect between the transferor and the transferee.

(3) For the purposes of this section, a transfer is not made until the debtor has acquired rights in the property transferred.

As to the above quoted subsection (c), 9A Am. Jur. 2d, Bankruptcy §542 contains the following comment:

. . . Before it can be determined when the transfer was 'made' it is necessary to determine when a transfer is deemed to be 'perfected.' . . . A transfer of . . . property other than real property is 'perfected' when a creditor on a simple contract cannot acquire a judicial lien that is superior to the interest of the transferee.

It is with these rules established that the Bankruptcy Code provides when a transfer is 'made.' If the transfer was perfected at, or within 10 days after, the time that the transfer took effect between the transferor and the transferee, then the transfer was 'made' at the time it took effect. If the transfer, however, was not perfected until after 10 days, then the transfer was 'made' at the time it was perfected. . . .

In the instant case, the security interest was perfected on January 26, 1981 — well within 10 days of the making of the security agreement on January 22, 1981. It must therefore be concluded that the transfer was 'made' on January 22, 1981 — 91 days before the petition was filed and thus one day prior to the 90-day period of insolvency presumption.

This conclusion, however, does not necessarily negate the possibility of a preferential transfer. As stated previously, the real beneficiaries of this transfer were the debtor's guarantors who were thereby released from their obligations. It is also true that these guarantors were corporate officers of the debtor. Under 11 U.S.C. §101(25), corporate officers are deemed "insiders" of a debtor corporation, and, §547(b)(4)(B) allows avoidance of a preferential transfer for the benefit of a creditor made between 90 days and one year before the petition's filing date where the creditor was an insider who had reasonable cause to believe that the debtor was insolvent at the time of the transfer.*

If this line of reasoning is applied then it might very well be found that a voidable preferential transfer did in fact occur when the security agreement was made. Nevertheless, this Court does not feel that it can properly make such a finding due to the fact that these guarantors, whose rights

---

* In 1984, §101(25) was renumbered as §101(28) and the "reasonable cause to believe" language was deleted. — EDS.

would be substantially affected, were not made a party to these proceedings.

Moreover, this Court does not believe that a determination of whether or not a voidable preference occurred is required to dispose of the matter before it. Assuming, for the sake of argument *without so ruling,* that a preferential transfer did occur, we would then be faced with the issue of whether, and if so from whom, recovery should be allowed.

11 U.S.C. §550 "prescribes the liability of a transferee of an avoided transfer, and enunciates the separation between the concepts of avoiding a transfer and recovering from the transferee." See House Report 95-595, 95th Cong., 1st Sess. (1977), p. 375, U.S. Code Cong. & Admin. News 1978, pp. 5787, 6331.

As to the application of §550, 4 Collier on Bankruptcy §550.02 (15th ed. 1981) contains the following comment:

> The trustee can theoretically recover from both the initial transferee and any secondary transferee of the debtor, as well as from any entity for whose benefit the transfer was made, but his right to do so is limited by sections 550(b) and (c). Of course, the trustee is still entitled only to one satisfaction under section 550(c). . . . In some circumstances, a literal application of section 550(a) would permit the trustee to recover from a party who is innocent of wrongdoing and deserves protection. In such circumstances the bankruptcy court should exercise its discretion to use its equitable powers under section 105(a) and 28 U.S.C. §1481 to prevent an inequitable result. For example . . . *if a transfer is made to a creditor who is not an insider more than 90 days but within one year before bankruptcy and the effect is to preferentially benefit an insider-guarantor, recovery should be restricted to the guarantor and the creditor should be protected.* Otherwise a creditor who does not demand a guarantor can be better off than one who does. (Emphasis added.)

The instant case is precisely that as given in Collier's example. Furthermore, this Court agrees with Collier's treatment thereof and reaches the same equitable result. Therefore, this Court concludes that even if a preferential transfer did occur, no recovery should be had against the defendant Republic Bank. . . .

NOTES

1. See also In re Mercon Industries, 37 Bankr. 549 (Bankr. E.D. Pa. 1984); In re Duccilli Formal Wear, 8 B.C.D. 1180 (Bankr. S.D. Ohio 1982).

2. Consider the facts of Bullard v. Aluminum Co. of America, supra page 267. How would the case have been decided if §547 of the Bankruptcy Code had been in force? Assume no fraudulent conveyance attack is available.

NOTE ON INSIDER PREFERENCES

The fact pattern in *Church Buildings and Interiors* is very common. Bank loans money to Company, which is small or just starting up. In either case, Bank requires, as a condition of the loan, that Shareholder, the major shareholder of Company, guarantee repayment. This additional promise makes Bank's loan safer, and it is a de facto circumvention of the concept of shareholders' limited liability for a corporation's debts. (Bank, and indeed other creditors, may get a lot out of this guarantee, for with Shareholder on the hook, Company will be a little less likely to misbehave.)

The preference question arises when Company continues to make monthly payments on its debt to Bank until it files for bankruptcy. Payments made within 90 days of bankruptcy would be prima facie voidable preferences. We shall see in the next section, however, that Bank will be able to escape a voidable preference attack if it can show that the payment was made in the ordinary course of business according to ordinary business terms. But what about the payments made between 90 days and one year of Company's bankruptcy? Does Bank even have to worry about finding an exception? Bank is not an insider. But Shareholder, who guarantees Bank's loan, is. The language of §547 includes transfers "to or for the benefit of a creditor." Shareholder is the holder of a contingent claim: Every time Company makes a payment to Bank, its contingent liability to Shareholder is reduced. Does this, then, make the transfers to Bank "to or for the benefit of" Shareholder? If so, the extended preference period for insiders applies.

Even if it is a preference, should the trustee be able to recover the payments from Bank? If Bank had not gotten the insider guarantee, these payments would have been fine. Should Bank be in a worse position *because* of the guarantee? *Church Buildings and Interiors* concludes that it should not. But isn't it possible that Bank received those payments like clockwork because Shareholder feared that he otherwise would be liable on the guarantee? If so, this is exactly the sort of activity that should be reached by the preference section. Bear in mind that Bank and Shareholder can fend off a voidable preference attack if they can show that the transfer was made in the ordinary course of business or financial affairs of Debtor, Bank, and Shareholder. §547(c)(2).

In considering this, is there any harm in holding that Bank must return the money? Bank can then go after Shareholder on the guarantee. And Shareholder, after reimbursing Bank, can file a claim against Company for the amount of those payments. As long as Shareholder is solvent, the result of *Church Buildings and Interiors* seems merely to circumvent this process, by reaching directly what would have been reached in any event, indirectly. But what if Shareholder were insolvent? Should the result in *Church Buildings and Interiors* continue to prohibit recovery from Bank?

NOTE ON DELAYED PERFECTION OF SECURITY INTERESTS AND §547(e)

Section 547(e) tells us that a transfer of a security interest is "deemed" to occur when the interest takes effect as between the parties (or, to use the language of Article 9, at the time of "attachment"), provided that the interest is perfected within 10 days of the time it takes effect. If perfection takes place later, the transfer is then deemed to take effect at the time of perfection. The Bankruptcy Code provides that the transfer is deemed to take effect just before the filing of the petition, if the security interest is not perfected by the time the petition is filed or within 10 days of the time the transfer takes effect between the parties. Section 547(e)(3) states that for purposes of §547 a transfer is not made until the debtor has acquired rights in the collateral; we will see the reasons for this last requirement when examining DuBay v. Williams, infra page 322.

The following problems require that you look closely at the provisions of §547(e). Bear in mind the consequences that follow from finding that the transfer, for purposes of §547, did not take place when the security interest became effective between the parties. Once a party has given "value" to the debtor, it may become a creditor and the debtor may owe it a "debt" within the meaning of §101(4) and (11), even if the elements for attachment of the security interest under UCC §9-203 have not yet occurred. If the transfer is found to take place at some later time, there is a potential voidable preference, because the transfer, taking place *after* the debt has been incurred, will be made on account of an *antecedent* debt, thus meeting the requirement of §547(b)(2).

PROBLEMS

6.11 Debtor borrows $1,000 from Bank on January 1, and signs a security agreement giving Bank a mortgage on his building. Bank makes a proper recording in the real estate files on January 9. Debtor files a petition in bankruptcy on February 1. Was there a transfer on account of an antecedent debt? Would the answer change if Bank had recorded on January 15? Would there potentially be a voidable preference within the meaning of §547(b), if Bank recorded its mortgage on January 15 and Debtor filed its petition in bankruptcy on April 5?

6.12 Bank gives Debtor $1,000 on January 1, and Debtor signs a security agreement giving Bank a mortgage on Debtor's building. On January 5, before Bank has recorded the mortgage in the proper real estate files, Debtor files a petition in bankruptcy. Bank comes to you late in the day on January 5, and asks if its security interest will survive a voidable preference attack by the trustee in bankruptcy. If it will not, Bank wants to know what it can do to improve its position, without risking being held in contempt by the bankruptcy judge for violating the automatic stay. See §§547(e)(2)(C); 362(a)(4), (b)(3); 546(b).

6.13 Bank loans Debtor $1,000 on January 1 and Debtor agrees to give Bank a security interest in its machines. Bank makes a proper Article 9 filing on that date. Debtor, however, does not get around to signing the security agreement until January 9. Debtor files a petition in bankruptcy on March 1. Is there a transfer for an antecedent debt within the meaning of §547? Under Article 9, §9-203 provides that

> A security interest is not enforceable against the debtor or third parties with respect to the collateral and does not attach unless:
>
> (a) the collateral is in the possession of the secured party pursuant to agreement, or the debtor has signed a security agreement which contains a description of the collateral . . . ; and
> (b) value has been given; and
> (c) the debtor has rights in the collateral.

When does the transfer take effect between the parties? In other words, when did Bank have an enforceable right to take possession of the machines in the event the Debtor defaulted? When is the transfer perfected? Note that when considering perfection, we are dealing with a term defined by the Bankruptcy Code, not by state law, §547(e). If another creditor had levied on the machine on January 8, would its interest be superior to Bank's? When was the debt incurred? Did the debt arise before the security interest became effective between the parties? Did the debt arise before the transfer was perfected? (Once we find that a transfer was made on account of an antecedent debt and the other requirements of §547(b) have been met, we still need to see if any of the exceptions to §547(b) that are contained in §547(c) apply. We pursue this question below.)

6.14 Elmer Fox & Co. is a certified accounting firm that provided regular accounting services to Rosen Oil Corp. In November 1981, at a time when Rosen Oil was behind in its payments to Elmer Fox by some $20,000, Rosen Oil gave Elmer Fox a note and a security interest on certain oil properties, both to secure past services and for contemplated future services. Subsequently, Elmer Fox performs an additional $20,000 of accounting services, some $15,000 of these during 1982. On April 1, 1982, Rosen Oil files a petition in bankruptcy. Can the trustee avoid any portion of the security interest held by Elmer Fox as a voidable preference? Which portion? See §547(b) and (e). Do you agree with the following analysis, E.F. Corp. v. Smith, 496 F.2d 826 (10th Cir. 1974):

> Elmer Fox was not bound [at the time it received the note and security interest] to perform future accounting services. . . . Value was given when

the services were performed and not until then. Accordingly, there was no relation back to the November transaction and the claim of secured status falls.

When was the transfer made? When was the debt incurred?

NOTE ON §547(b)(5)

An essential element of a voidable preference is that the transfer make the creditor better off than it would have been if the transfer had not been made. If the transfer did not make the creditor better off, it could not have been a last-minute grab by the creditor to improve its position at the expense of the other creditors. But how does one go about determining whether the transfer made the creditor better off? Consider the following problems.

PROBLEMS

6.15 Creditor is owed $10,000. On January 1, Creditor accepts from Debtor a payment of $6,000 in full satisfaction of its unsecured claim. If Debtor were to file for bankruptcy on that date and his assets were distributed immediately, his unsecured creditors would receive 60 cents for every dollar they were owed. Debtor, however, does not file a bankruptcy petition until March 1, and in the interim his financial position took an unexpected turn for the worse. If there were an immediate distribution on March 1, unsecured creditors would receive only 50 cents on the dollar. Debtor attempts to reorganize and fails. When the assets are distributed in November, general creditors receive 30 cents on the dollar. Is the transfer to Creditor in January a voidable preference? What is the proper date for determining whether the transfer enabled Creditor to receive more than it would have in a Chapter 7 liquidation?

If the idea behind the preference provision is to prevent last-minute grabs, the time of the transfer to Creditor would seem to be appropriate for taking stock of Debtor's financial picture. If Creditor received in January no more than it appeared it would be able to get in a bankruptcy proceeding, Creditor would not appear to be gun jumping. (Is that true?) Is it crucial, however, that Creditor gave up its entire claim against Debtor in return for the $6,000? (If it had not, it would be better off than other general creditors. Creditor would benefit if Debtor's fortunes rose, but would bear none of the costs if they fell.)

There has been little case law on this problem. An early Supreme Court case, Palmer Clay Products v. Brown, 297 U.S. 227 (1936), suggests that the relevant test is determined "not by what the situation would have been if the debtor's assets had been liquidated and distributed among his creditors at the time the alleged preferential payment was made, but by the actual effect of the payment as determined when bankruptcy results." Notwithstanding this, a recent Fifth Circuit case suggested that one should consider the situation at the time of transfer. In re Abramson, 715 F.2d 934 (5th Cir. 1983). Even if it were less consistent with the core notion of a voidable preference, can one argue that the Supreme Court's approach is preferable because of the difficult valuation problems associated with the other test?

6.16 Debtor borrows $1,000,000 from Bank for 30 days. At the end of that time, Debtor repays the $1,000,000 and borrows another $1,000,000 from Bank. Thirty days later, Debtor repays Bank in full and immediately files a bankruptcy petition. Debtor is insolvent during the entire period, and the general creditors will recover very little in the bankruptcy proceeding. Trustee moves to recover $2,000,000 from Bank. Trustee argues that Debtor borrowed this amount from Bank and later repaid Bank during the 90 days before the filing of the bankruptcy petition. To what extent should the trustee prevail? Is there any doubt that the second million-dollar payment is voidable? But what about the first? Can Bank argue that the first repayment did not improve its position? If Bank had not been repaid on the first loan, would it have made the second? If not, then how can the first repayment be considered a last-minute grab? Should one engage in these inquiries under the aegis of §547(b)(5), or does one need a specific exception (such as §547(c)(4))? To what extent do the exceptions in §547(c) flesh out what is implicit in (b)(5)? These questions are the focus of the next section of this chapter.

6.17 Creditor loans Debtor $100,000 in January and contemporaneously takes and perfects a security interest in Debtor's printing press. On July 1, Debtor pays Creditor $60,000, reducing Creditor's loan to $40,000. Debtor files for bankruptcy on August 1. At all relevant times, the printing press is worth $70,000. Is the payment to Creditor preferential?

NOTE ON PAYMENTS TO SECURED CREDITORS

Problem 6.17 raises a question as to how to treat payments to secured creditors. Suppose that Bank loaned $100,000 to Debtor in 1981 and, at the time of the loan, took and perfected a security interest in Debtor's building. The building is worth enough so that Bank is fully secured at all relevant times. In January of 1984, Debtor repays Bank's loan. In February of 1984, Debtor files a petition in bankruptcy. May the trustee avoid the payment to Bank as a voidable preference under §547(b)? Is there any evil that the preference section is designed to avoid here? Is Bank getting paid more than it would have been receiving in bankruptcy, had it not been paid off ahead of time? Is there any other evil associated with this payment that the preference section is designed to reach? In any event, what in the language of §547(b) leads you one way or the other? Would it matter if the collateral were worth $60,000 and the Debtor's repayment amounted to only $50,000? Barash v. Public Finance Corp., 658 F.2d 507 (7th Cir. 1981), noted that payments to fully secured creditors were not preferential, as "[p]ayments on secured claims do not diminish the estate, i.e., they do not enable a creditor to receive more than he would under the liquidation provisions of the Code." The court, however, reached a different result with respect to payments to partially secured creditors, reasoning:

> A principal goal of the preference provisions is the assurance of equal distribution among creditors. . . .
>
> For example, if upon liquidation unsecured creditors would be paid 20 percent of their claims . . . , to defeat a trustee's avoidance rights a creditor would have to show only that the payments received during the 90-day period do not exceed 20 percent of the creditor's unsecured claim. This sole comparison, however, does not account for what happens thereafter. If the payments made were less than 20 percent, there would be no preference and the creditor would keep the payments and later also receive a pro-rata share of the balance of his claim. In the final analysis, this would violate the fundamental principle of equal distribution among a class of claims.
>
> Section 547(b)(5) is directed at transfers which *enable* creditors to receive more than they would have received had the estate been liquidated and the disputed transfer not been made. As long as the transfers diminish the bankrupt's estate available for distribution, creditors who are allowed to keep transfers would be enabled to receive more than their share.

Is the following, from In re K. Pritchard Co., 17 Bankr. 508, 509-510 (Bankr. S.D. Ala. 1981), a convincing (if partial) response to *Barash* on this point?

> The example used in *Barash* . . . assumes that (a) the creditor receiving the pre-petition transfer has filed a claim in the proceeding and (b) upon distribution of the estate its prior recovery on the debt would be ignored. Such assumptions cannot be justified. If a creditor had received a pre-petition payment equal to 10 percent of his unsecured debt, but did not file a claim for the balance of his debt, then he would not have received a statutory preferential transfer, considering a 20 percent dividend to other unsecured creditors, because he would not have received "more than such creditor would receive if (A) the case were a case under Chapter 7 of this title, (B) the transfer had not been made and (C) such creditor received payment of such debt to the extent provided by the provisions of this title." Bankruptcy Code, Sec. 547(b)(5).

In assessing this question, would anything turn on whether the collateral were marketable securities instead of a building? If, instead of a cash payment, the collateral were turned over to the creditor in partial satisfaction of the debt (assuming such action were permitted cf. UCC §9-505)?

C.   THE "SAFE HARBORS" OF §547(c)

Not all "transfers" on the eve of bankruptcy, even those technically for or on account of an antecedent debt, are last-minute grabs. Subsection (c) tries to carve out classes of cases in which creditors are not trying to jump ahead in line because a collective proceeding is in the works. In examining this set of safe harbors for transfers otherwise deemed preferential by §547(b), you should ask how successfully they identify transfers that are not in fact last-minute manipulations. It is also important to ask whether the costs the inquiries subsection (c) requires are worth the benefits. In other words, you should ask whether creditors as a group would be better off if the preference rule were less finely tuned (and hence more or fewer transfers were found to be preferential than should have been), but did not require costly inquiries into things such as intent.

Section 547 places the burden of establishing a prima facie case under subsection (b) on the trustee and that of applying an exception under subsection (c) on the creditor. §547(g). We begin with Problem 6.16 from the last section, which was whether a creditor could offset payments to the debtor against payments the debtor makes to it. Even if not implicit in §547(b)(5), this concept makes an explicit appearance in §547(c)(4).

PROBLEMS

6.18 On January 1, Bank loans Debtor $50,000. On February 1, Debtor repays $20,000 to Bank. On March 1, Bank loans Debtor $10,000 more. On April 1, Debtor files for bankruptcy. The trustee asserts that Debtor's $20,000 payment to Bank on February 1 is a voidable preference. Is it? See §547(c)(4).

6.19 On January 1, Bank loans Debtor $50,000. On February 1, Debtor repays $20,000 to Bank. On March 1, Bank loans Debtor $30,000 more. On March 15, Debtor repays Bank $10,000. On April 1, Debtor files for bankruptcy. The trustee asserts that Debtor's February 1 payment of $20,000 and March 15 payment of $10,000 are preferential. Are they?

The following case was decided under the old Bankruptcy Act. How would the case be decided under the Bankruptcy Code? *Fulghum*, which follows *Bernstein*, addresses that question.

BERNSTEIN v. HOME LIFE INSURANCE CO.
25 Bankr. 321 (S.D.N.Y. 1982)

SOFAER, District Judge.

Plaintiff Lawson F. Bernstein, the Trustee in Bankruptcy of Frigitemp Corporation, has sued defendant Home Life Insurance Company to recover an alleged voidable preference paid by Frigitemp to Home Life. Home Life has moved for summary judgment, claiming that payments it received from Frigitemp within four months of Frigitemp's bankruptcy petition were not preferential.

The relevant facts are adequately supported by affidavits and exhibits submitted by both parties and are not meaningfully controverted by plaintiff. In April 1975, Home Life issued a group insurance policy providing major-medical coverage for eligible Frigitemp employees. On September 1, 1977 Frigitemp failed to pay a $75,205.59 premium due for that month. The policy, however, included a 31-day grace period, and Home Life therefore processed Frigitemp employee claims incurred in (i.e. resulting from events occurring during) September 1977. When on October 2, 1977 Frigitemp had still not paid the premium for September, the policy lapsed by its terms and Home Life stopped processing newly incurred Frigitemp employee claims.

In December 1977, Frigitemp and Home Life reached an agreement whereby Home Life would reinstate the policy and process claims incurred in October and November in exchange for a $151,895.85 payment from Frigitemp representing the $75,205.59 premium for September as well as a $76,690.26 premium for October. On December 22, 1977, Home Life received $151,895.85 from Frigitemp and began processing the October and November claims which it had been holding in abeyance. Although at that point the November payment was overdue, and the policy's grace period had once again expired, Home Life appears to have extended the grace period beyond that provided in the policy by processing claims incurred through December 1977. This extension was apparently due to Frigitemp's assurances that further premium payments would be forthcoming and to Home Life's subsequent inability to rescind the extension without substantial confusion when premium payments for November ($77,303.28) and December ($81,180.17) were not paid. See Affidavit of John J. Egan (October 20, 1982), Attachments 4 & 5. In any event, on January 1, 1978 Home Life treated the policy as having once again lapsed.

On March 20, 1978, Frigitemp filed for an arrangement under Chapter [XI] of the 1898 Bankruptcy Act and was authorized to operate as a debtor-in-possession. The Bankruptcy Court specifically permitted Frigitemp to pay "any and all insurance premiums (other than life insurance) that were accrued but not paid prior to the filing of the original petition herein." Pursuant to this provision, Frigitemp and Home Life entered into a second agreement in May 1978 reinstating the policy retroactive to

January 1, 1978 in exchange for a $400,000 premium payment. On July 12, 1978 Home Life paid Frigitemp a premium rebate of $124,246.03, based on a formula in which claims, expenses, and other charges are subtracted from total premiums paid. The policy thereafter remained in effect until May 29, 1979, when Frigitemp entered liquidation proceedings and the policy was permanently terminated.

The Trustee maintains that the December 22, 1977 payment which reinstated the policy following its lapse on October 2, 1977 was a voidable preference. Section 60(a)(1) of the 1898 Bankruptcy Act, 11 U.S.C. §96(a)(1) defines a preference as

> a transfer . . . of any of the property of a debtor to or for the benefit of a creditor for or on account of an antecedent debt, made or suffered by such debtor while insolvent and within four months before the filing by or against him of the petition initiating a proceeding under this Act, the effect of which transfer will be to enable such creditor to obtain a greater percentage of his debt than some other creditor of the same class.

The December 22 payment was made within four months of the March 20, 1978 bankruptcy petition and, for purposes of this motion, Frigitemp's insolvency at the time of payment is assumed.

Home Life denies that the $151,895.85 it received on December 22, 1977 was "for or on account of an antecedent debt." As far as the $76,690.26 attributable to the October premium is concerned, defendant is plainly correct. Home Life stopped processing newly incurred Frigitemp employee claims when the policy lapsed on October 2, 1977. Only after receipt of the December 22 payment did Home Life reinstate the policy and resume processing October claims. The October premium was therefore paid not for an antecedent debt but rather for present consideration in the form of processing and payment on claims arising from October occurrences. At least as far as preferences are concerned, "services rendered followed by payment is [not] equivalent to payment followed by services rendered." In re Mobley, 15 B.R. 573, 575 (Bkrtcy. S.D. Ohio 1981).

The $75,205.59 paid for the September premium presents a more difficult issue. Frigitemp employee claims incurred in September had been and were being processed and paid by Home Life when it received the December 22 payment. Because of the 31-day grace period, the policy remained in effect for September despite the failure to pay the premium for that month. Thus, Frigitemp's December payment of the September premium was for services which Home Life had either rendered or would render regardless of whether the premium was paid. As such, payment of the September premium was "for or on account of an antecedent debt."

A payment for an antecedent debt is not, however, by that fact alone a voidable preference. To be voidable, the payment must also have the effect of enabling the creditor to obtain more than its fair share of the debtor's assets. "The purpose of the law of preferences is to secure an equal distribution of the bankrupt's assets among his creditors of like class. If a transaction, or series of transactions in their entirety, do not interfere with this purpose it does not constitute a voidable preference." Farmers Bank v. Julian, 383 F.2d 314, 327 (8th Cir.), cert. denied, 389 U.S. 1021, 88 S. Ct. 593, 19 L. Ed. 2d 662 (1967). Given the entire series of transactions between Home Life and Frigitemp, Frigitemp's payment of the September premium cannot fairly be viewed as interfering with the goal of an equal distribution of Frigitemp's assets among its creditors.

Although the payment was made primarily to discharge Frigitemp's debt to Home Life for the September coverage, it also caused Home Life retroactively to extend grace-period coverage for November. The price for September coverage, $75,205.59, was less than that for November coverage, $77,303.28. Home Life thus effectively extended new credit in the form of unpaid-for services of greater value than the antecedent debt extinguished by the allegedly preferential payment. As a result, following the December 22 transaction Home Life was in essentially the same position under its Frigitemp policy as before the transaction, i.e., it was owed the premium for one month's worth of processed claims. As for Frigitemp, the $75,205.59 it paid in cash was at least theoretically balanced by the $77,303.28 gain it realized when its employees' November claims were paid.

Section 60(c) of the 1898 Bankruptcy Act, 11 U.S.C. §96(c) specifically provides:

> If a creditor has been preferred, and afterward in good faith gives the debtor further credit without security of any kind for property which becomes a part of the debtor's estate, the amount of such new credit remaining unpaid at the time of the adjudication in bankruptcy may be set off against the amount which would otherwise be recoverable from him.

"Property" in §60(c) may include services which do not result in a traceable, balance-sheet increase in the assets of the debtor. In re Ira Haupt & Co., 424 F.2d 722, 724 (2d Cir. 1970). It is thus not fatal to defendant's case that no specifically identifiable property became part of Frigitemp's estate as a result of the credit extended by Home Life in the form of November coverage. Moreover, even if §60(c) is not exactly applicable, its provisions confirm that the overriding purpose of the preference law is "to require the preferred creditor to surrender only the net amount of the benefit he received in excess of that received by other creditors of his class." Farmers Bank, supra; see In re Thomas W. Garland, Inc., 19 B.R. 920, 924-25 (Bkrtcy. E.D. Mo.1982); In re Fulghum Construction Co., 7 B.R. 629, 646-47 (Bkrtcy. M.D. Tenn.1980). When Frigitemp was adjudicated in bankruptcy on March 20, 1978, the arguably preferential payment Home Life received for the September coverage was more than offset by the unpaid services performed by Home Life as a result of the policy's reinstatement. That Home Life was eventually paid under the Bankruptcy Court's order for the November coverage is irrelevant to the question whether at the time of the bankruptcy petition Home Life had received a voidable preference. It would be anomalous to conclude that, by authorizing payment of certain pre-petition debts, the Bankruptcy Court caused the pre-petition payment of a similar debt to become a voidable preference.

The $124,246.03 premium rebate paid by Home Life to Frigitemp in July 1978 must also be considered in determining whether the December 1977 payment for September coverage enabled Home Life to gain an unfair advantage over Frigitemp's other creditors. Although no provision of the Bankruptcy Act provides specific guidance as to how this rebate should be treated, Home Life plainly made a substantial sum available to Frigitemp as debtor-in-possession and thus to the creditors now represented by the Trustee. Under the policy, unless all premiums have been paid in a given year, Home Life is not obligated to pay any rebate for that year. Alternatively, however, Home Life may simply reduce the rebate by the full amount of any premiums due. In fact, the July rebate was reduced from $143,266.27 to $124,246.03 because of past due premiums of $19,020.24. See Affidavit in Opposition of Patricia I. Avery, Esq. (October 12, 1982), Exhibit J. Therefore, if the September premium had remained unpaid, and Home Life had nevertheless agreed to continue the policy following the April 1978 payment, the rebate would never have been owed to Frigitemp. As demonstrated by the fact that Home Life reduced the July rebate by $19,020.24 in unpaid premiums, Home Life at least would have been entitled further to reduce the rebate by the amount of the September premium. See In re Dynamic Electronics, 120 F. Supp. 126 (S.D.N.Y. 1954); In re Mortman, 36 F. Supp. 897 (E.D.N.Y. 1941).

The trustee's effort to ignore the rebate is in effect an effort to undo a completely performed contract, in which the September and October payments were part of the consideration paid by Frigitemp to entitle it to the rebate. Only by keeping the contract of insurance alive for that entire year, was Frigitemp able to claim its rebate. The trustee cannot now seek to undo a piece of that year's agreed-upon exchanges, thus depriving Home Life of part of the benefits of the bargain it made in making its end-of-the-year payment. The premium surplus that accumulated in Home Life's hands represented an economic cushion that the insurance company was entitled to rely upon as a form of security for the insured's payment of premiums due. To deprive Home Life of this contractual advantage would in no way serve the bankruptcy law's goal of preventing unfair advantage to selected creditors; rather it would unfairly disadvantage Home Life by transforming its premium rebate into a gratuitous donation to the pool of funds available to all creditors.

For the foregoing reasons defendants' motion for summary judgment is hereby granted.

So ordered.

NOTE ON *BERNSTEIN*

It is often useful to break a case down into simpler components. What would *Bernstein* be like if there had been no $400,000 payment in May and no $124,000 rebate in July? In applying §547 we first need to ask whether we get to subsection (c) at all. If there is no preference within the meaning of subsection (b), there is no need to go further. Assuming the transfer took place within 90 days of bankruptcy, was it on account of an anteced-ent debt? The payment for September is on account of an antecedent debt, because it repays Home Life for the "credit" it extended Frigitemp by processing the September claims before being paid for this service. But the October claims seem different. Home Life had not yet extended any credit to Frigitemp (because it had refused to process the claims). The payment for October therefore seems to be on account of a contemporaneous debt. Is the entire payment voidable or just the part attributable to the September payment?

The next question we face is whether the (b)(5) test is satisfied. Does the transfer of some $75,000 attributable to processing the September claims give Home Life more than it would have received in bankruptcy? Frigitemp has a right to a rebate when it overpays premiums. Assuming that it had a right to a rebate of $75,000 at the time of its payment to Home Life, Home Life had a right to offset this sum against Frigitemp's other obligations. Hence, even if Frigitemp did not pay Home Life for the September processing services, Home Life was arguably not any worse off, because it could have obtained the same amount of money with its offset right. See §§553; 506(a).

What if no rebate or the offset right were available? Home Life processed not only the October claims, but also those for November and December. One can argue that no preference exists here at all, because Home Life was effectively providing a new service (processing of addi-tional claims) at the same time it was being paid for it. But should one be able to recharacterize payments after the fact? Should Home Life be able to argue that the transfer was in any event not preferential, because with-out the September payment, it would not have extended further credit to Frigitemp by processing the November and December claims? Should Home Life have to make a factual showing on this point, or should there be a per se rule that a transfer on account of an antecedent debt is not a voidable preference if there is a subsequent extension of credit? Is this the effect of §547(c)(4)? Does (c)(4) imply that Congress meant to exclude a more general standard-based inquiry derived from (b)(5)?

IN RE FULGHUM CONSTRUCTION CORP.
706 F.2d 171 (6th Cir. 1983)

KRUPANSKY, Circuit Judge.

This action joins inquiry into the long-standing judicially evolved application of the "net result rule" as the criteria for determining a preferential transfer as defined in 11 U.S.C. §547 of the Bankruptcy Reform Act of 1978. An involuntary petition in bankruptcy was filed against Fulghum Construction Corporation (Fulghum) whereupon the trustee initiated the instant proceeding to, inter alia, avoid as preferential transfers certain monetary transactions which transpired between Fulghum and its sole shareholder, Ranier & Associates (Ranier), during the one year period immediately preceding the filing of the bankruptcy petition. Both the bankruptcy court and reviewing district court adjudged that application of the net result rule, incorporated into 11 U.S.C. §547(b)(5) as a judicial gloss, foreclosed a finding that the transfers were preferential. See: In re Fulghum Construction Corp., 7 B.R. 629 (Bankr. M.D. Tenn.1980); In re Fulghum Construction Corp., 14 B.R. 293 (M.D. Tenn. 1981). The operative facts, detailed in the lower courts' opinions, disclose that approximately 100 transactions occurred between Ranier and Fulghum during the year immediately preceding the filing of the bankruptcy petition. The aggregate amount of the payments by Ranier to Fulghum exceeded the aggregate amount of the payments tendered by Fulghum to Ranier during this period and the value of the estate was accordingly appreciated.

Preferential transfers which may be avoided by the trustee are defined in 11 U.S.C. §547(b). . . . As is facially evident from this provision, all five enumerated criteria must be satisfied before a trustee may avoid any transfer of property as a preference. . . .

Section 547(b) is proscribed by its own terms to the numerous "defenses" available to creditors which appear in §547(c) and which, if applicable, preclude the trustee from avoiding the §547(b) preferential transfer. Particularly, §547(c)(4) provides:

> (c) The trustee may not avoid under this section a transfer— . . .
> (4) to or for the benefit of a creditor, to the extent that, after such transfer, such creditor gave new value to or for the benefit of the debtor—
>> (A) not secured by an otherwise unavoidable security interest; and
>> (B) on account of which new value the debtor did not make an otherwise unavoidable transfer to or for the benefit of such creditor

Section 547(c)(4) is perhaps most accurately characterized as a "subsequent advance rule". Preferential transfers as defined in §547(b) may not be avoided by the trustee if "*after* such transfer, such creditor gave new value". Id. . . .

In the action sub judice, the district court adjudged, and the parties do not dispute on appeal, that the criteria of §547(b)(1) through (b)(4) have been satisfied. In addressing the application of §547(b)(5) to the facts of the case at bar, however, the district court relied upon its equitable powers to justify its application of the net result with the following rationale:

> [T]his Court must agree with the Bankruptcy Court that two "net result rules" actually exist in bankruptcy law. One, that of section 547(c)(4) and insisted upon by the trustee, is statutory. The other, that applied by the Bankruptcy Court, is nonstatutory, a judicial gloss upon the requirements of section 547(b).

14 B.R. at 303. Applying the net result rule as a condition implicitly incorporated into §547(b)(5) and, correspondingly, a threshold requirement to support a preferential transfer, the district court observed that the net effect of all the transactions between the debtor, Fulghum, and the creditor, Ranier, appreciated the value of the estate and, accordingly, the transfers could not be avoided by the trustee as preferences. Upon concluding that no preferential transfers existed it was unnecessary for the district court to identify the defenses available to the creditor under §547(c).

The net result rule is a judicially created doctrine, predicated upon principles of equity, which evolved shortly after the enactment of the Bankruptcy Act of 1898 to presumably rectify what was judicially perceived to be inequities in bankruptcy law.

. . . As an equitable doctrine its application, of necessity, must "comport to and remain compatible with the prevailing legislative intent". In re Bell, 700 F.2d 1053, 1057 (6th Cir. 1983). . . . Logic dictates that judicial interposition of the net result rule into §547(b)(5) vitiates the congressional intent clearly reflected both on the face of §547 and in the legislative history of the enactment.

Since the net result rule is "broader" in scope than the subsequent advance rule of §547(c)(4), engrafting the former doctrine upon §547(b)(5) as a threshold requirement for the qualifying preference would render the defense incorporated in §547(c)(4) impotent. The broader scope of the net result rule permits its utilization by the creditor irrespective of whether the value furnished by the creditor to the debtor is advanced either before or after the transfer from the debtor to the creditor. Contrawise, the subsequent advance rule of §547(c)(4) is more circumscribed in application and forecloses avoidance of the transfer by the trustee only if the creditor provides additional value *after* the transfer from the debtor to the creditor. A "judicial gloss" which significantly restricts the statutory definition of "preference" and pragmatically emasculates the creditor defense thereto as intended by Congress in §547(c)(4) constitutes nothing less than legislation by judicial decree.

Moreover, judicial interposition of the net result rule into §547(b)(5) finds no sanction in the legislative history of the Bankruptcy Reform Act of 1978. The legislative proceedings attendant to the promulgation of §547(b)(5) are significantly devoid of any allusion to the net result rule. Contrawise, the House Report discussing the subsequent advance rule, §547(c)(4), incorporates concise language reflecting the intent of Congress:

> The fourth exception [§547(c)(4)] codifies the net result rule in section 60c of current law. If the creditor and the debtor have more than one exchange during the 90-day period, the exchanges are *netted out according to the formula in paragraph (4)*. Any new value that the creditor advances must be unsecured in order for it to qualify under this exception. (Emphasis added).

H.R. Rep. No. 95-595, 95th Cong., 1st Sess. 374, reprinted in 1978 U.S. Code Cong. & Ad. News 5787, 6330. The Senate Report is identical. . . . Thus, it would appear that the "net result rule" is an anachronism of §547(c). . . . Congressional metamorphosis has transformed the judicially created net result rule into what may be characterized as a subsequent advance rule and has codified this augmented version into §547(c)(4) rather than §547(b)(5). See also: . . . Report of the Commission on the Bankruptcy Laws of the United States, H. Doc. No. 93-137, 93rd Cong., 1st Sess., Pt. 1, 210-211 (1973) ("A true 'net result' rule would total all payments and all advances and offset the one against the other. This is not allowed under the Commission's recommendation, since the advance to be offset must be subsequent to the preference.")

Section 547(b) deliberately defines a preference as a "transfer", rather than as an aggregate of transfers or netting of transactions between the creditor and debtor, and §547(c) artfully articulates equitable "defenses" whereby the trustee may be foreclosed from avoiding the preference. In particular, §547(c)(4) permits a netting procedure to be applied when the debtor and creditor are both recipients and initiators of transactions. Construed in pari materia, §547(b) and (c) disclose a calculated legislative scheme and intent to implement equitable considerations which the judiciary at the turn of this century adjudged as lacking and responded by evolving the net result rule. This legislative response reflected in the promulgation of §547(b) and particularly §547(c)(4) mirror the congressional version of equitable principles, expressed as the subsequent advance rule, to be incorporated into the 1978 revision of the Bankruptcy Act.

Accordingly, the judgment of the district court dismissing the trustee's complaint to avoid transfers from Fulghum to Ranier as preferential is hereby vacated and this case is remanded for further proceedings consistent with this opinion. . . .

NOTE

In re Wadsworth Building Components, Inc., 711 F.2d 122 (9th Cir. 1983), reached the same conclusion as *Fulghum:*

> Bankruptcy courts have disagreed as to whether the net result rule applies under the new bankruptcy code as it applied under the old act. . . . While there are reasonable arguments about whether the net result rule should be applied under the new Code, it is clear that Congress did not intend the rule to apply. We are bound by that Congressional intent.

The Ninth Circuit also relied on the Bankruptcy Commission's views (quoted in *Fulghum*) on the net result rule. Some of the mechanics of applying §547(c)(4) are treated in In re Isis Foods, Inc., 39 Bankr. 645 (W.D. Mo. 1984).

PROBLEMS

6.20 At 10:00 AM on January 1, Bank makes an unsecured loan to Debtor of $100,000. Later that same day, Bank learns that Debtor is in financial difficulty and demands that Debtor provide collateral, which Debtor does. On February 1, Debtor files for bankruptcy. May the trustee invalidate the security interest? See §547(c)(1); National City Bank v. Hotchkiss, 231 U.S. 50 (1913). Does §547(e) add anything to this? What about §547(c)(4) and the rationale of *Fulghum*? Would the outcome be any different if Bank demanded, and received, repayment of the loan later that same day? What if Bank had committed itself to loan the money and then retracted the commitment on learning of Debtor's difficulties?

6.21 Debtor buys a painting from Seller for $10,000 on January 1, and pays by check. Seller cashes the check on January 2. Debtor files for bankruptcy on February 1. May the trustee go after Seller for the $10,000? What if Seller did not cash the check until January 15? See §547(c)(1); legislative history to §547.

6.22 Debtor borrows $10,000 from Bank on January 1, and promises at that time to give Bank a security interest in all of its assets. On January 1, Bank makes a proper Article 9 filing. Because of Bank's lawyer's forgetfulness, however, Debtor did not actually sign the security agreement until January 2. On March 20, Debtor files a petition in bankruptcy. Is the security interest that Debtor transfers to Bank a voidable preference within the meaning of §547(b) and (e)? (Recall, under UCC §9-203, a security interest does not attach, and is not enforceable, until, inter alia, the debtor has signed a security agreement.) Do any of the exceptions in §547(c) apply? Compare In re Lyon, 35 Bankr. 759 (Bankr. D. Kan. 1982);

In re Burnette, 14 Bankr. 795 (Bankr. E.D. Tenn. 1981) with In re Davis, 22 Bankr. 644 (Bankr. M.D. Ga. 1982).

6.23 Debtor borrows $10,000 from Bank on January 1, and gives Bank, pursuant to written agreement, a security interest in Debtor's machine. Bank files a financing statement on January 9. Debtor files for bankruptcy on March 1. Is there a transfer for an antecedent debt? What if Bank filed on January 12 instead of January 9? Can one argue that even though the transfer is deemed to take place on January 12 under §547(e), the transfer is not a voidable preference because it is a substantially contemporaneous exchange for new value? The court in In re Arnett, 731 F.2d 358 (6th Cir. 1984), held that one could not make such an argument.

6.24 Repairer performs $2,000 of body work on Debtor's automobile, and retains possession of the automobile pending payment by Debtor. Under state law, Repairer has a repairman's lien on the automobile as long as it remains in his possession. On January 1, Repairer releases the automobile to Debtor in exchange for a security interest Debtor grants him in $2,000 worth of bonds. On February 1, Debtor files for bankruptcy. May the trustee avoid the transfer to Repairer of the security interest in the bonds? Is this a substitution of collateral, to which §547(c)(1) applies? Has Repairer contributed new value or is this an "obligation substituted for an existing obligation"? See §547(a)(2).

6.25 Debtor borrows $50,000 from Bank on an unsecured basis. Debtor promises to pay $1,000 a month until the loan is repaid. Debtor makes all of its payments on schedule until Debtor files its petition in bankruptcy two years later. Are the last three payments voidable preferences under §547(b)? Does §547(c)(2) apply? Do the provisions of the exception in §547(c)(2) (requiring, inter alia, that payments be made according to ordinary business terms in the ordinary course of business) ensure that the safe harbor is not abused? Would your decision on whether the transfer was voidable change if it turned out that Bank was the only creditor paid during the entire 90-day period? What if Bank had a guarantee from Debtor's president, secured by a second mortgage on her home? What if Debtor paid the installments only after Bank threatened to call on the guarantee?

Before the 1984 amendments, §547(c)(2) also required that the transfer be "made not later than 45 days after such debt was incurred." This requirement was generally construed as not protecting timely principal payments on installment loans, as the loan was "incurred" when the money was lent and not when the payments were due. Barash v. Public Finance Corp., 658 F.2d 504 (7th Cir. 1981). A different result was reached with respect to the portion of such installment payments that represented interest, on the view that interest obligations were "incurred" on a day-to-day basis. In re Iowa Premium Service Co., 695 F.2d 1109 (8th Cir. en banc 1982). As a result of cases such as these, it was widely felt that (c)(2) failed to protect many transactions that should not have been subject to preference attack. Dropping the requirement that the transfer be within 45 days of when the debt was incurred responded to that concern; does the resulting test, however, leave too much uncertain?

NOTE ON §547(c)(3)

The Uniform Commercial Code has special filing rules for secured parties who take a purchase money security interest in an asset being acquired by their debtor. A purchase money security interest, defined in UCC §9-107, essentially is an interest of a seller of goods or a financing institution that lends money to the debtor to purchase the asset in question. These are commonly referred to as "enabling loans," because they make possible the acquisition of assets that a debtor previously did not own. Special rules governing the priority of purchase money security interests relative to the interests of other secured creditors are set forth in UCC §9-312(3) and (4). More important for our present purposes, however, is the special rule governing conflicts between the holder of a purchase money security interest and a lien creditor.

Under UCC §9-301(2), the rights of a secured party who "files with respect to a purchase money security interest before or within ten days after the debtor receives possession of the collateral," take priority over the rights "of a lien creditor which arise between the time the security interest attaches and the time of filing." This changes the general rule for testing the rights of the holder of a security interest against those of a lien creditor, for generally those disputes are resolved by looking to see if the security interest was perfected when the creditor acquired the lien. Because perfection generally requires attachment plus filing, the effect of UCC §9-301(2) is to grant the holder of a purchase money security interest a grace period against lien creditors extending from the time of attachment until ten days after the debtor receives possession of the collateral. Section 547(c)(3) reflects this special treatment given to holders of purchase money security interests. Section 547(c)(3) contains its own definition of what sorts of security interests will qualify for the protections it affords, and these must be used instead of the one in UCC §9-107.

PROBLEMS

6.26 Debtor borrows $10,000 from Bank on January 1 and gives Bank, as collateral, a security interest in all of Debtor's equipment, including after-acquired equipment. Bank files a financing statement on January 1. On January 1, Debtor has no equipment, but using the money it borrowed from Bank, Debtor buys a drill press on January 9. Debtor files for bankruptcy on March 1. Is there a transfer for an antecedent debt? Can Bank fit within an exception in §547(c)? Would your answer be the same if Debtor borrowed the money on January 1, but did not sign the security agreement until later that day? What if the security agreement was not signed until January 3?

6.27 Debtor borrows $10,000 from Bank on January 1, and signs a security agreement giving Bank a security interest in the drill press it plans to purchase with the $10,000. Debtor buys the drill press on January 3 with that $10,000 and the press is delivered the same day. Bank files its financing statement on January 11. On March 20, Debtor files a petition in bankruptcy. Is Bank's security interest a voidable preference within the meaning of §547(b) and (e)? Do any of the exceptions in §547(c) apply? Would your answer change if the press was not delivered until March 1 and Bank did not file until March 5? March 12? Can §547(c)(1) still be used if (c)(3) does not fit? See In re Vance, 721 F.2d 259 (9th Cir. 1983) (no).

6.28 On January 1, Seller sells Debtor a machine on conditional sale, and marks the machine for delivery. On January 10, the machine is delivered to Debtor. On January 20, Seller files a financing statement covering the machine in the proper office. On March 1, Debtor files a petition in bankruptcy. May the trustee avoid Seller's security interest?

NOTE ON REASSESSING PREFERENCE LAW

The theory of preference law is fairly clear. Yet in practice it cuts, at best, rough justice. Preferential transfers can avoid the grasp of §547 by being outside the preference period, even though they were clearly engaged in with an eye towards an impending bankruptcy. The party that benefits from the preferential transfer may also have persuaded the debtor to postpone filing a bankruptcy petition for 90 days. In addition, the current version of §547(c)(2) invites litigation in many cases over whether the repayment of a creditor was in the ordinary course of business.

Professor McCoid takes a critical view of the operation of existing preference rules in Bankruptcy, Preferences and Efficiency: An Expression of Doubt, 67 Va. L. Rev. 249 (1981). He asserts that preference law "operates through recapture and deterrence," that not much is actually recaptured, and that the deterrent effect of preference law may be greatly exaggerated. The latter point he defends as follows, id., at 264-265:

> The creditor must balance the probability of successfully retaining a preference against the costs of failure. The only sanction for unsuccessful preference behavior is recapture plus payment of interest from the time of the demand for return or from the commencement of proceedings to recover the property. At worst, return of the property simply restores the status quo. Use of the property during the period before demand or during

the proceedings to recover may even yield a net advantage to the creditor. If a creditor may be able to keep the payment and at worst only has to return it, he has every incentive to accept it. . . .

Unsuccessful preference behavior, on the other hand, may entail real costs. If the creditor must incur expenses, such as litigation costs, to acquire the preference, those expenses will be lost if the preference is recaptured. The creditor cannot deduct his cost of acquiring the preference from what must be returned to the trustee. Moreover, to the extent that preference behavior has prevented maximization of the estate, the preferred creditor will lose along with other creditors. The creditor should take such costs into account in determining what action to take.

The chances of success and the costs of failure vary from case to case and from creditor to creditor. Creditor behavior, therefore, can be expected to vary as well. It seems fair to anticipate, however, that a creditor frequently will conclude that the sensible course is to accept the preference, and hope for success. To the extent that this is true, preference law is not an effective deterrent, and achievement of equality and maximum estate value will be limited to the results of recapture. . . .

Thus, it appears that preference law is not a very effective means of achieving equality and maximum estate value. Although some success in achieving these goals must be acknowledged, its value depends on its incidence and costs.

NOTE ON THE FLOATING LIEN

Creditor lends Debtor $100,000, and takes a security interest in Debtor's inventory. Creditor wants Debtor to sell its inventory so Debtor can stay in business and eventually repay the loan. But, as inventory is sold, the collateral securing Creditor's loan will decrease unless Creditor's security interest "floats" to cover the proceeds from selling the inventory and the new inventory Debtor acquires (perhaps with the proceeds from the sale of the old).

As simple as this sounds, much of the history of personal property security interests during the past 150 years has involved the issue of whether and how to allow Creditor to acquire just such an interest. A major innovation of Article 9 was to make it easy for asset-based lenders to take a security interest in collateral that was constantly changing. Article 9 largely rejects both the nineteenth century doctrine that "a man cannot give what he hath not," see Cohen & Gerber, The After-Acquired Property Clause, 87 U. Pa. L. Rev. 635 (1939), and the doctrine of Benedict v. Ratner, 268 U.S. 353 (1925), that required a creditor to maintain control over disposition of collateral and its proceeds in order to have a security interest enforceable against third parties. See also UCC §§9-204; 9-205, Comments 1-4.

If Creditor wants to acquire a security interest in all of Debtor's inventory, now existing and after-acquired, it only need make an Article 9 filing and have Debtor sign a single security agreement giving it an interest in all such inventory. See, e.g., UCC §§9-203(3), 9-204(1), 9-204(3), 9-205, and 9-206(2). (An interest in proceeds will be acquired automatically. See UCC §9-306(2).) Accordingly, the security agreement Debtor signs will probably contain an "after-acquired property clause"—a provision giving Creditor a security interest in inventory now owned or *hereafter acquired*—and a security interest in such after-acquired collateral will arise automatically when Debtor acquires the inventory.

The enactment of Article 9 solved the "problem," as a matter of chattel security law, of effective security interests in inventory and accounts. Outside of a bankruptcy proceeding, Creditor, assuming it is the first to file or perfect, will prevail over all other creditors with interests in Debtor's inventory, unless one of them enables Debtor to acquire specific inventory and takes the steps required to give it the super-priority of a purchase money secured party under UCC §§9-107 and 9-312(3).

Given this resolution under Article 9, the last 20 years has seen the problem shift to the field of bankruptcy law, and bankruptcy challenges to the floating lien began; some of this history is essential to understanding the "solution" that §547(c)(5) offers to the perceived problem. Under the 1898 Act, the cases in which the trustee attacked the floating lien usually involved the following fact pattern. The secured creditor extended credit and acquired a security interest in the debtor's accounts receivable (or inventory) by means of a security agreement with an after-acquired property clause. The security agreement was executed and a financing statement filed more than four months prior to the institution of any bankruptcy proceeding.

While the trustee would not attack the transfer of the security interest itself, he would contend that, under §60 of the 1898 Act, each acquisition by the secured creditor of further collateral within four months of bankruptcy was invalid as a preferential transfer. The trustee's argument generally ran as follows:

(a)   For purposes of §60 of the 1898 Act, a transfer is deemed made when valid as against a subsequent judicial lien creditor. §60a(2).

(b)   An Article 9 security interest satisfies this test only when perfected. UCC §9-301(1)(b).

(c)   Perfection requires attachment. UCC §9-303.

(d)   If the additional steps required for perfection (e.g., filing of a financing statement) occur before the security interest attaches, it is perfected at the time it attaches. UCC §9-303(1).

(e)   Attachment requires, inter alia, that the debtor have rights in the collateral. UCC §9-203.

(f)   A debtor cannot have rights in accounts or items of inventory until they are in existence.

(g)   Thus: (1) attachment occurs at the time the inventory (or accounts) comes into existence; (2) perfection also occurs at such time; (3) the transfer is deemed to have occurred at such time for purposes of §60 of the 1898 Act; and (4) the elements of §60a and b are determined as of the time that the inventory (or accounts) come into existence.

Should this argument prevail? Note that the trustee must use his preference power, because the trustee (as the representative of general creditors who have hypothetically reduced all their claims to judgment on the date the petition is filed) loses to a perfected secured creditor under §544(a). But has there been a transfer to a secured creditor that violates the policies (such as the "anti-secret lien" or the "anti-last minute grab" policies) underlying the preference section? Has a secured creditor tried to improve its position because it anticipated a bankruptcy proceeding?

UCC §9-108 provides that when a secured creditor obtains rights in after-acquired property, "his security interest shall be deemed to be taken for new value and not as security for an antecedent debt if the debtor acquires his rights in such collateral either in the ordinary course of his business or under a contract of purchase made pursuant to the security agreement within a reasonable time after new value is given." Article 9 is a creature of state law and it cannot define the moment of transfer for purposes of federal bankruptcy law. Is the distinction it draws, however, sound in principle? Why should it matter that the debtor acquired its property according to the terms of the security agreement or in the ordinary course of its business?

The following case represents the culmination of the pre-Bankruptcy Code battle between the floating lienor and the trustee in bankruptcy. Is its statutory reading compelling? Is its policy argument compelling?

DuBAY v. WILLIAMS
417 F.2d 1277 (9th Cir. 1969)

HUFSTEDLER, Circuit Judge.
Before us are three appeals from orders of the United States District Court for the District of Oregon adjudicating the claims of three creditors asserting security interests in the net proceeds of accounts receivable of the Portland Newspaper Publishing Co., Inc. (the "Bankrupt"). The three creditors are Rose City Development Company, Inc. ("Rose City"), Robert J. Davis, and R. Anthony DuBay. The Referee disallowed all three claims as preferences under section 60 of the Bankruptcy Act, 11 U.S.C. §96. Petitions for review resulted in orders of the District Court affirming disallowance of the claims of Davis and DuBay reversing disallowance of Rose City's claims,[1] from which orders the parties adversely affected appeal.

1. In re Portland Newspaper Publishing Co. (D. Ore. 1967) 271 F. Supp. 395.

The combined appeals present a chromatic scale of questions relating to the interaction of the provisions of the Uniform Commercial Code concerning security interests in accounts receivable and the preference provisions of the Bankruptcy Act.[2] Each of the creditors claims a security interest, good against the trustee in bankruptcy, in the existing and future balances of the Bankrupt's accounts receivable pursuant to security agreements. . . .

The three creditors were closely involved in the short and turbulent life of the Portland Reporter, a newspaper, and in the operation of its publisher, the Bankrupt, and the Bankrupt's predecessor, the Portland Reporter Publishing Company, Inc. (the "Reporter"). In November 1959 the Portland Stereotypers Union struck Portland's two dailies, the Oregonian and the Oregon Journal. Members of the other local unions refused to cross the Stereotypers' picket lines. The two dailies joined forces and continued publication of their respective papers despite the strike. The affected local unions organized Reporter to employ their idled workers and to compete with the struck dailies. The Reporter was organized early in 1960 to publish the paper, and, concurrently, the unions incorporated Rose City to acquire the physical plant for Reporter. Rose City acquired and converted a warehouse and leased it to Reporter for its publication base. The financial condition of Reporter, precarious from the outset, steadily deteriorated until, in February 1964, the Reporter announced that it would suspend publication. The announcement touched

2. The questions presented are of such novelty and importance that they have received widespread attention and discussion in the law reviews. E.g., Hogan, Games Lawyers Play With the Bankruptcy Preference Challenge to Accounts and Inventory Financing, 53 Cornell L. Rev. 553 (1968); Krause, Kripke and Seligson, The Code and the Bankruptcy Act: Three Views on Preferences and After-Acquired Property, 42 N.Y.U. L. Rev. 278 (1967); Henson, The Interpretation of the Uniform Commercial Code: Article 9 in the Bankruptcy Courts, 22 U. Miami L. Rev. 101 (1967); Henson, The Portland Case, 1 Ga. L. Rev. 257 (1967); Henson, "Proceeds" Under the Uniform Commercial Code, 65 Colum. L. Rev. 232 (1965); Gordon, The Security Interest in Inventory Under Article 9 of the Uniform Commercial Code and the Preference Problem, 62 Colum. L. Rev. 49 (1962); Friedman, The Bankruptcy Preference Challenge to After-Acquired Property Clauses Under the Code, 108 U. Pa. L. Rev. 194 (1959); King, Section 9-108 of the Uniform Commercial Code: Does It Insulate the Security Interest From Attack by a Trustee in Bankruptcy?, 114 U. Pa. L. Rev. 1117 (1966); Kennedy, The Trustee in Bankruptcy Under the Uniform Commercial Code: Some Problems Suggested by Articles 2 and 9, 14 Rut. L. Rev. 518 (1960); Hogan, Future Goods, Floating Liens and Foolish Creditors, 17 Stan. L. Rev. 822 (1965); Viles, The Uniform Commercial Code v. The Bankruptcy Act, 55 Ky. L.J. 636 (1967); Riemer, Bankruptcy—Preference—Conflict Between Section 9-108 of the Uniform Commercial Code and Section 60(a) of Bankruptcy Act, 70 Com. L.J. 63 (1965); Riemer, The After-Acquired Property Clause Revisited, 70 Com. L.J. 334 (1965); Kennedy, The Impact of the Uniform Commercial Code on Insolvency: Article 9, 67 Com. L.J. 113 (1962); Comment, Toward Commercial Reasonableness: An Examination of Some of the Conflicts Between Article 9 of the Uniform Commercial Code and the Bankruptcy Act, 19 Syr. L. Rev. 939 (1968); Recent Developments. Bankruptcy Preferences—Secured Transactions, 65 Mich. L. Rev. 1004 (1967); Comment, After-Acquired Property Security Interests in Bankruptcy: A Substitution of Collateral Defense of the UCC, 77 Yale L.J. 139 (1967); Note, Rosenberg v. Rudnick: An Examination of the Potential Conflict Between the After-Acquired Property Provisions of Article 9 of the U.C.C. and Section 60(a) of the Bankruptcy Act, 15 U.C.L.A. L. Rev. 678 (1968).

the pocketbooks as well as the sentiments of the public, producing contributions of $50,000 and temporary loans of another $50,000, which was enough money to keep the newspaper afloat a few months longer. Robert J. Davis, who had recently become a member of Reporter's board, was so heartened by the public response that he agreed to continue his guaranteed bank loan of $25,000 in Reporter's favor and agreed to finance the paper up to $225,000 by buying stock of a corporation (the Bankrupt) into which Reporter could be merged. Reporter thereafter merged into the Bankrupt. Davis bought $156,000 of the Bankrupt's stock between April and September 1964. The paper's financial rally was fleeting. Infusions of capital were inadequate to withstand the mounting drain of operating losses. On September 27, 1964, the board announced the impending cessation of publication and relieved Davis of further obligation to buy stock. The paper died on September 30, 1964.

On September 28, 1964, Rose City, Davis, and DuBay (who had been a director of Reporter from 1961 to the merger) appointed a representative to collect the accounts receivable which they claimed were subject to their security interests. As of the time of adjudication $107,000 net had been collected from the receivables and was being held by the creditors' trio and the trustee. About two thirds of the collections came from display and classified advertising and the remainder from circulation accounts.

On October 15, 1964, wage claimants filed an involuntary bankruptcy petition against the Bankrupt and four days later it was adjudicated a bankrupt. In addition to the accounts receivable, the assets of the estate amount to about $14,000. Priority claims against the estate total over $54,000, general claims total about $80,000, and the claims here considered are, respectively, for DuBay, $25,000 principal; for Davis, $25,000 principal; and for Rose City, a total of $53,122.26 principal. Davis, DuBay, and Rose City do not here challenge the findings of the Referee that the Bankrupt had been insolvent during the four months prior to October 15, 1964, and that each of them knew or should have known of the insolvency.

THE DUBAY CLAIM

[Omitted.]

THE DAVIS CLAIM

[Omitted.]

THE ROSE CITY CLAIM

Rose City lent Reporter $45,000 on November 16, 1963, and $10,300 on November 22, 1963, for which Reporter executed two promissory notes in Rose City's favor. To secure the loans the parties entered into a security agreement dated November 22, 1963, by which Reporter assigned to Rose City a security interest in all of its accounts receivable "now existing or hereafter arising," other than those accounts assigned to DuBay and Davis. A financing statement was filed on November 26, 1963. The security agreement did not contain any provision for Rose City's policing the accounts.

When Reporter was merged into the Bankrupt, the Bankrupt took over all of the Reporter's assets and assumed Reporter's liabilities. The Bankrupt did not itself enter a security agreement with Rose City and no financing statement was thereafter filed reflecting Reporter's metamorphosis.

On the date of the Bankrupt's adjudication, there was owed $42,822.26 on the $45,000 note and the full amount of the $10,300 note. The Referee held that Rose City's security interest in the accounts receivable did not come into existence until four months prior to bankruptcy and was a voidable preference under section 60. The District Court disagreed with the Referee and held that Rose City's security interest in the Bankrupt's after-acquired accounts receivable did not result in preferential transfers. The trustee appeals from the District Court's order reversing the Referee's order disallowing Rose City's claim.

Before reaching the issues decided by the District Court we dispose of two contentions by the trustee: Rose City did not have a valid security interest because it failed to execute a new security agreement with the Bankrupt after the merger, and it failed to file a new financing statement after the merger. Neither of these contentions was raised before the Referee or the District Court.[6] . . . For the purpose of the appeal we treat the security agreement as if it had been executed by the Bankrupt and the filing as if it had been made after the merger.

Can the trustee set aside as preferential Rose City's security interest in these accounts receivable which arose within four months of bankruptcy? Is there an unavoidable collision between section 60 of the Bankruptcy Act and the floating lien created and protected by article 9 of the Commercial Code (Ore. Rev. Stat. §§79.2040, 79.3020, 79.4020 [UCC §§9-204, 9-302, 9-402])?

Section 60a(1) of the Bankruptcy Act (11 U.S.C. §96a(1)) defines a "preference" as (1) a transfer of any property of the debtor, (2) to or for the benefit of a creditor, (3) for or on account of an antecedent debt, (4) while the debtor is insolvent, (5) within four months of bankruptcy, (6) which enables the creditor to obtain a greater percentage of his debt than some other creditor of the same class. Section 60b permits the trustee to avoid a preference if the creditor had reasonable cause to believe that the

---

6. Counsel representing the trustee on appeal were not counsel below. [Footnote moved because of deletion.— EDS.]

debtor was insolvent at the time of the transfer. The trustee has succeeded in having resolved in his favor all section 60 issues save two: (1) Did the Bankrupt's transfer of a security interest to Rose City occur during the four months preceding bankruptcy? (2) Was the transfer for or on account of an antecedent debt?

The validity of Rose City's floating lien on after-acquired accounts receivable arising prior to the four-month period preceding bankruptcy is unchallenged. Rose City's security agreement complied with the provisions of Oregon Commercial Code section 79.2040(3) (UCC §9-204(3))[7] and its lien was perfected by filing its financing statement in accordance with section 79.4020 of the Code (UCC §9-402).

The trustee contends that any interest Rose City claims in accounts receivable which came into existence within four months before bankruptcy is voidable as a preference because the transfer of such an interest could not have occurred earlier than the date upon which the account arose. The Commercial Code says that the debtor has no rights "[i]n an account until it comes into existence." (Ore. Rev. Stat. §79.2040(2)(d), UCC §9-204(2)(d).) To obtain a right, there must be a transfer to the creditor, and that transfer cannot occur, he says, until the right arose. A transfer occurring during the four months preceding bankruptcy cannot be related back to the filing of a financing statement and thus perfected before the preference period because to do so would violate the federal policy expressed in section 60.

Some ingenious theories have been spun to avoid the result to which the trustee's logic leads.[8] It is unnecessary for us to resort to any of them to reject the trustee's argument. The unarticulated premise is that Congress left to state law the definition of "transfer" and of "perfection," thereby permitting state law to control the impact of preferences. The premise is flawed. Congress itself defined these concepts leaving only some details to be brushed in by state law.

---

7. The Code states that "a security agreement may provide that collateral, whenever acquired, shall secure all obligations covered by the security agreement." The draftsmen's intent was to validate security interests in after-acquired property, including inventory and accounts receivable, and to place such security interests on a par with security interests in property in which the debtor has present rights. Draftsmen's Comments to UCC §9-204.

8. One theory, variously called the "res," "entity," or "Mississippi River" theory, conceives of accounts receivable as a single entity with an identity apart from the individual account components which make up the mass. The reified mass is the thing to which the creditor's lien adheres and which gives the creditor a present interest in all future accounts perfected upon filing a financing statement. Therefore, so long as the financing statement is filed before the four-month period antedating bankruptcy, the transfer is not voidable by the trustee. (E.g., Manchester National Bank v. Roche (1st Cir. 1951) 186 F.2d 827; Rosenberg v. Rudnick (D. Mass. 1967) 262 F. Supp. 635.)

Another theory is labeled the "sophisticated res" theory, which treats the secured creditor as having a continuously perfected security interest in after-acquired accounts as the proceeds of a previous interest in contract rights or general intangibles. The perfected interest adheres to the contract right, and not to the later performance of the right by the transfer of the after-arising account. (Coogan & Bok, The Impact of Article 9 of the Uniform Commercial Code on the Corporate Indenture, 69 Yale L.J. 203 (1959)).

Section 60a(2) of the Bankruptcy Act provides that "a transfer of property . . . shall be deemed to have been made or suffered at the time when it became so far perfected that no subsequent lien upon such property obtainable by legal or equitable proceedings on a simple contract could become superior to the rights of the transferee."

Congress did not state that a "transfer" occurs when a security interest attaches or when state law says a conveyance has been made. Congress provided that a transfer is "deemed" to have been made when it became "so far perfected" that no subsequent lien creditor could achieve priority. "Transfer" for the purpose of section 60a(2) is thus equated with the act by which priority over later creditors is achieved and not with the event which attaches the security interest to a specific account.

We look to state law, therefore, only to decide the point at which Rose City's claim to the future accounts was sufficiently asserted to prevent a subsequent lien creditor from achieving priority over it in those accounts. That time was the date upon which Rose City filed its financing statement. (Grain Merchants of Indiana, Inc. v. Union Bank & Savings Co., Bellevue, Ohio (7th Cir. 1969) 408 F.2d 209.) Because Rose City filed its financing statement long before the four-month period anteceding bankruptcy, its security interest is immune from the trustee's preference challenge.

There is no conflict between this result and the federal policy expressed in section 60 of the Bankruptcy Act. From the inception of section 60 in 1898, through its amendments, including the adoption of the present version in 1950, Congress intended to achieve two aims: (1) to prevent an insistent creditor from harvesting more than his fair share of the insolvent's assets by obtaining transfers from the debtor on the eve of bankruptcy, and (2) to discourage extension of credit to debtors under circumstances which concealed from general creditors the precarious financial condition of the debtor.

The 1898 edition of the statute contained no definition of the time at which a transfer was deemed made for preference purposes. It was completely inadequate to deal with transfers by security instruments, particularly by chattel mortgages with after-acquired property clauses, in which the creditor's interest did not publicly appear until bankruptcy was imminent. Typically the debtor was given all the appearance of unencumbered ownership of his personalty upon the strength of which general creditors unaware of the secured creditor's lien continued to advance credit. Shortly before the insolvent's collapse, the secured creditor would take possession of the liened assets, or otherwise perfect his lien, leaving the other creditors the pickings from a nearly barren estate. Federal courts, applying the "Massachusetts rule" on perfection of liens on after-acquired property, upheld such transfers against the trustee's attacks. (Humphrey v. Tatman (1905) 198 U.S. 91, 25 S. Ct. 567, 49 L. Ed. 956; Thompson v. Fairbanks (1905) 196 U.S. 516, 25 S. Ct. 306, 49 L. Ed. 577; Petition of Post (In re Robert Jenkins Corp.) (1st Cir. 1927) 17 F.2d 555, cert. denied, Levy v. Post (1927) 275 U.S. 527, 48 S. Ct. 20, 72 L. Ed. 407.)

The Chandler Act amendment to section 60, enacted in 1938, was intended to prevent the drain of assets caused by the eve of bankruptcy perfections validated by *Humphrey* and *Thompson* and the equitable lien theories applied by such cases as *Robert Jenkins Corp.* The 1938 version provided that a transfer was deemed made when it became so far perfected under state law that no bona fide purchaser from the debtor could obtain rights in the property superior to those of the secured creditor. The effect of the bona fide purchaser test was to invalidate as preferences legitimate financing transactions, particularly security interests in accounts receivable and inventory which involved none of the evils at which Congress aimed. Congressional response was the enactment of the present lien creditor test found in section 60a(2).

Rose City's floating lien on accounts receivable was easily ascertainable by any creditor who cared to look at the financing statement. After the financing statement was filed, no creditor could reasonably have been misled into believing that Rose City's receivables would provide assets to which he could look to satisfy debts incurred for subsequent extensions of credit. Neither the Bankrupt nor Rose City took any affirmative action to obtain for Rose City a favored position over other creditors of its class during the four months before bankruptcy.

Nothing in the legislative history of section 60a(2) suggests that Congress intended to permit a trustee to upset floating liens on accounts receivable which, as here, were automatically perfected and which involved none of the symptoms of last minute favoritism characterizing true preferences. On the contrary, the history of the section shows that Congress knew how important accounts receivable financing was to the business community, particularly to small-business men, and one of Congress' principal objectives in amending section 60a(2) was to loosen the flow of credit to small-business men whose financing had been seriously impaired by the old bona fide purchaser test.

If we read section 60a(2) the way the trustee asks us to do, we would defeat, not implement, Congress' intent, and we would impair, not promote, the intent of the draftsmen of the Uniform Commercial Code to make security transactions conform to the legitimate needs of commerce, rather than to the common-law lawyer's wish for conceptual nicety.[15]

The validation of Rose City's security interest and the invalidation of

15. The intent of the draftsmen to insulate Rose City's security from preference attack is evidenced by §9-108 of the Uniform Commercial Code (Ore. Rev. Stat. §79.1080). The insulation is in the form of a definition designed to defeat a trustee's claim that subjection of an after-arising account to an antecedent security agreement complying with the Code is a transfer in consideration of an antecedent debt within the meaning of §60a(1). We do not reach the question, hotly contested by the parties, whether the Commercial Code draftsmen were successful in thus defeating a claim of preference. We cite the section simply to indicate the policy of the Commercial Code draftsmen to uphold security interests in after-acquired accounts receivable perfected upon filing a financing statement against a claim of preference by the trustee.

the claimed security interests of DuBay and Davis to which Rose City's security interest had been expressly subordinated raises the questions: (1) Did Rose City and the Bankrupt intend that accounts theretofore assigned to DuBay and Davis would become part of Rose City's security if either or both of the DuBay and Davis security interests were invalid? (2) To what extent, if at all, may the trustee preserve the senior DuBay and Davis claims for the benefit of the estate? Neither of these questions was decided below. The questions were raised before the Referee, but they were not resolved, because the Referee's invalidation of all three claims made the decision of the questions moot. The questions are to be resolved upon ultimate remand to the Referee. . . .

NOTE ON THE POLICIES UNDERLYING UPHOLDING THE FLOATING LIEN

Is it plausible to believe that §60a(2) was designed to *define* "transfer" for all cases, or simply to *postpone* transfers otherwise deemed made under state law? The argument for the latter interpretation ran as follows. As originally drafted, the 1898 Act did not contain §60a(2), and the definition of "transfer" was left entirely to state law. Trustees found themselves unable to set aside security interests kept secret until the creditor made a filing just before the debtor filed its petition. Without a provision attacking delayed filings, the preference section had no operative provision striking down secret liens. The provision deeming when a transfer was made, this argument asserted, was therefore designed to limit, rather than expand, a secured creditor's rights. The statute did not define the moment of transfer, for that was handled by state law. Rather, the effect of §60a(2) was to *delay* a transfer that had already taken place, thereby reaching the secret lien problem. If a transfer between debtor and creditor was ineffective under state law because an essential action had not been taken, nothing in §60a(2), the argument went, would force a bankruptcy court to advance the moment of transfer. The new section ensured that even if steps necessary for enforcing a transfer under state law had taken place, the transfer would not be recognized for purposes of federal bankruptcy law until the creditor's rights were superior to those of a lien creditor. Judge Hufstedler's reading was wrong, this argument concluded, because it used a limitation on the state law definition of "transfer" to supplant it entirely. See generally Countryman, Code Security Interests in Bankruptcy, 75 Com. L.J. 269 (1970).

Is this a persuasive counterargument, based on the language of the statute? If the statutory language is ambiguous, do Judge Hufstedler's policy arguments carry the day in support of her opinion? She identifies two policies of preference law (preventing secret liens and last minute grabs), and finds that neither was implicated in the transaction before her.

Is, however, her linguistic analysis at war with her policy analysis? How would Judge Hufstedler handle a case in which the debtor deliberately took steps to increase the value of its inventory for the benefit of (and perhaps at the behest of) a secured creditor?

In Grain Merchants v. Union Bank & Savings Co., 408 F.2d 209 (7th Cir.), cert. denied, 396 U.S. 827, 90 S. Ct. 75 (1969), the Seventh Circuit offered two theories to support the floating lien, in addition to adopting the theory, later used in *DuBay*, that the transfer is deemed to have been made at the moment of the Article 9 filing. A floating lien, the court suggested, is like the Heraclitean river. See Henson, "Proceeds" Under the Uniform Commercial Code, 65 Colum. L. Rev. 232 (1965); Manchester Natl. Bank v. Roche, 186 F.2d 827 (1st Cir. 1951). The lien exists over all the inventory. The "transfer" to the creditor takes place when the creditor first acquires a perfected interest in the inventory. The security interest continues to be perfected even when the collateral changes. Just as a river retains its identity even though the water in it is constantly changing, the security interest continues in the "inventory" as an entity, even though the elements of that inventory change constantly. The Seventh Circuit asserted that the purpose of making it easy to acquire security interests in inventory was to ensure that such interests could exist even where the creditor had no responsibility for or control over the collateral. It would be inconsistent with such a policy, the Seventh Circuit reasoned, to force the secured creditor to identify which part of the inventory the debtor acquired within four months of the bankruptcy petition and which part it acquired before.

This justification of the "floating lien," however, suffers from two difficulties (over and above the absence of any particular statutory support under the 1898 Act). First, it is inconsistent with the state law definition of "transfer." State law is in fact quite clear that a debtor cannot transfer a present interest in property it has yet to acquire. See UCC §9-203. Second, under this theory some last-minute manipulations (dramatic increases in the amount of inventory) that favor the secured creditor at the general creditors' expense are not voidable preferences, even though it seems they should be.

The court in *Grain Merchants,* however, relied on one further theory —that transfers are nonpreferential when the security interest in new property is merely a substitute for one in old property that the creditor is giving up. This rested on a longstanding exception to §60 of the 1898 Act. See, e.g., Sawyer v. Turpin, 91 U.S. 114, 120-121 (1875). In other applications of the theory, however, it had two limitations: (1) the new collateral must be transferred to the secured party either prior to or contemporaneously with the release of the old, and (2) if the new value was worth more than the old at any time, a preference resulted to the extent of the difference. The Seventh Circuit held, however, that due to UCC §9-205, "it is no longer appropriate to apply strict timing or value rules so long as at all relevant times the total pool of collateral, as here, exceeded the total debt."

NOTE ON THE FLOATING LIEN AND THE BANKRUPTCY CODE

Section 547(e)(3) tries to make impossible the technical argument underlying Judge Hufstedler's opinion in *DuBay* by *postponing* the moment of transfer until the debtor acquires rights in the collateral. If a creditor has a security interest in inventory and the debtor acquires new inventory during the 90-day period, the security interests thereby created (or "attached," to use the language of Article 9) are voidable preferences within the meaning of §547(b) (provided its other requirements, such as the debtor's insolvency, are met). The question we face is whether any of the exceptions in §547(c) apply. Section 547(c)(5) provides that a perfected security interest in "inventory or a receivable or the proceeds of either" is not a voidable preference unless (1) the new security interest improves the position of the secured creditor and (2) that improvement of position is "to the prejudice of other creditors holding unsecured claims." The transfers are not voidable if, when aggregated, they do not reduce the amount the debtor owed the secured creditor that was unsecured when the preference period began to run or when the secured creditor first extended value under the security agreement, whichever was later. Section 547(c)(5) embodies what is known as the two-point net improvement test. Read the section closely and do the following problems.

PROBLEMS

6.29 Debtor decided to open a foreign car dealership in Detroit. He took delivery of 40 cars on January 1. At that time, their market value was $500,000. On the same day, Debtor borrowed $500,000 from Bank to pay for them. Bank gave Debtor a check and Debtor signed a security agreement. Foreign cars did not prove as popular in Detroit as they had elsewhere in the country, so sales were slow. Debtor sold only 5 cars over the next few months. Because he harbored doubts about the wisdom of this venture, Debtor did not acquire any new cars to replace those he sold. On February 1, the cars Debtor had on hand were worth $450,000. Exactly 90 days later, Debtor threw in the towel and filed a petition in bankruptcy. Because of a dramatic decrease in the value of the dollar, the remaining cars increased in value. At the time of the petition they were worth $500,000. Can the trustee set aside any part of Bank's security interest?

6.30 On January 1, Finance Company takes and properly perfects a security interest in Debtor's inventory to support a $20,000 loan made the previous year. On that day, the inventory is worth $15,000, the same value it has had for the previous several months. On February 1, the inventory has a value of $5,000. On March 1, Debtor files a petition in bankruptcy, and the inventory is worth $14,000. To what extent is Finance Company's security interest safe from a voidable preference attack? What was the value of Finance Company's security interest at the later of (1) 90 days before Debtor filed its petition or (2) the time Finance Company extended new value?

6.31 Bank had a perfected Article 9 security interest in Debtor's inventory on January 1. Debtor's inventory turns over completely at least once a month. On January 1, Debtor owes Bank $20,000, and its inventory is worth $15,000. Between January 1 and April 1, the date Debtor files a petition in bankruptcy, Debtor repays Bank $5,000 of what it owes. Over the same period, the amount of inventory it has on hand declines steadily. Thus, on April 1, Debtor owes Bank $15,000 and its inventory is worth $10,000. Can the trustee recover the $5,000 paid to Bank? Can the trustee set aside any part of Bank's security interest?

6.32 Creditor, who is also president of Debtor, has loaned it $100,000, secured by Debtor's inventory. On January 1, Debtor's inventory is worth $120,000. Debtor's business is slowly sinking and, by October 1, its inventory is worth $50,000. Creditor instructs Debtor to build up its inventory. By December 31, the day Debtor files for bankruptcy, Debtor's inventory has increased in value to $100,000. May the trustee avoid any portion of Creditor's security interest as a preference? See §§547(c)(5), (b)(4)(B); 101(28). Is the 90-day period relevant for insiders? Would a one-year period under §547(c)(5) for insiders provide opportunities for advantage taking?

6.33 Debtor is an oil refinery. Bank has a perfected security interest in Debtor's inventory on January 1, securing a $10 million loan. Debtor's supply of fuel turns over completely at least once a month. On January 1, Debtor's inventory consists of 300,000 barrels of oil, each worth $25. Debtor keeps approximately 300,000 barrels of oil on hand through April 1, when it files a petition in bankruptcy. On April 1, each barrel of oil is worth $40 on the spot market. Can the trustee set aside any of Bank's security interest? Can Bank argue that the increase in the inventory's value was the result of market forces, not manipulation favoring Bank at the other creditors' expense, and that therefore the reduction in the amount of unsecured debt was not "to the prejudice of other creditors holding unsecured claims" within the meaning of §547(c)(5)? See In re Nivens, 22 Bankr. 287 (Bankr. N.D. Tex. 1982). What does "prejudice" mean here? Cf. §552, discussed supra page 216.

If this argument works when the increase in value results simply from market forces, can it also work if the inventory is worth more because of the labor Debtor invests (as would happen if newly acquired crude oil were converted into an equal amount of more valuable gasoline and diesel fuel)? Is there, in this case, a "transfer" of "property of the debtor"? What meaning should be given to the concept of "prejudice of other creditors holding unsecured claims"? This language was derived from a suggestion made by Professor Kripke to the Gilmore Committee in 1970, and first appeared in the Proposed Bankruptcy Act of 1973, stating that the increase must be "at the expense of the estate" to be avoidable. As the accompanying Report of the Commission on Bankruptcy Laws stated:

> Improvement in position is alone not enough. The trustee must also establish that the improvement was at the expense of the estate. This is intended partially to meet Professor Kripke's criticism that increase in value of collateral due to, e.g., harvesting crops, completing work in process, sales of inventory, and seasonal fluctuations in value, would [otherwise] constitute improvement in position and be recoverable.

6.34 On January 1, Debtor owes Bank $10,000. Bank has a perfected security interest in all of Debtor's inventory, existing and thereafter acquired. The inventory is then worth $9,000. During January, Debtor sells $5,000 worth of inventory and, instead of restocking, saves the money and pays it to Bank on February 1, leaving Debtor with $4,000 of inventory and a $5,000 debt to Bank. On April 1, Debtor files a petition in bankruptcy. The inventory has completely turned over during that time, and is now worth $5,000. To what extent has Bank received a preference? Is the February 1 payment a preference? Does one restore (hypothetically) *both* the payment and the inventory that was sold to the estate to determine whether and to what extent Bank's position has been improved? What does §547(b)(5) require? Would anything change if Debtor's remaining inventory on April 1 were worth $2,000, not $5,000?

NOTE ON THE TWO-POINT NET IMPROVEMENT TEST

We can view the two-point net improvement test of §547(c)(5) as implementing the preference section's anti-last minute grab policy by way of a presumptive rule. In other words, the "two-point net improvement test" announces the following presumption: Improvements in position by a secured creditor holding an interest in inventory or accounts within the preference period are unusual, and therefore will be presumed to result from a last-minute grab by the secured creditor. That creditor, however, may defeat the presumption by showing that the increase did not result from a last-minute grab — by showing, in the language of the statute, that it did not prejudice other creditors holding unsecured claims. So viewed, a general rule has been substituted for a case-by-case analysis.

But the process that led to §547(c)(5) was not informed by a consensus as to the role of preference law — or even by any clear theory of how preference law should relate to a nonbankruptcy rule such as the "floating lien." This description, therefore, may be more a fortuitous characteristic of the "two-point net improvement test" than an elaboration of the drafting motivations that produced it. Moreover, if creditors can rebut the presumption of a last-minute grab when the collateral increases in value during the preference period, why shouldn't the trustee be able to rebut the presumption that there was no manipulation when the two-point net improvement test is not satisfied? See Jackson, Avoiding Powers in Bankruptcy, 36 Stan. L. Rev. 725, 775 (1984).

Once the mechanics of §547(c)(5) are grasped, the section — at least apart from the prejudice to unsecured creditors language — is not difficult to apply to any particular set of numbers. The problem in applying the section may be to come up with the numbers in the first instance. How does one value the accounts a debtor had 90 days before the filing of a petition? Should the same method be used to calculate the value of the accounts at the time the petition is filed? Or must one recognize, in applying the two-point net improvement test, that the value of accounts may drop dramatically once a petition is filed? (Debtor's account debtors may also be its creditors. They have nothing to gain by putting money into the pot before the dust settles. Moreover, if a Chapter 7 liquidation is in the works, the account debtor may have little sense of loyalty to those that are carving up its supplier. Account debtors may assume they can get away with not paying.) When applying the two-point net improvement test, should one use the value of the inventory as if the debtor were a going concern at both points or the liquidation value of the inventory? Or one value for the first point and the other for the second? In re Lackow Bros., Inc., 19 Bankr. 601 (Bankr. S.D. Fla. 1982), suggested that, where a voidable transfer is at issue, "the 'ongoing concern' value of the inventory and accounts receivable pledged to [the secured party] . . . is the proper valuation standard to apply." Do you agree? What, exactly, is the valuation related to? Can you answer that without asking what good the collateral does a secured party?

D.   THE SCOPE OF §547

The reach of §547 is still not entirely clear. In examining the next case, you should ask whether the drafters of §547 took sufficient account of the danger that by tinkering with the preference section (such as by redefining "transfer" to avoid the statutory reasoning of *DuBay*), they may have obscured its underlying policies. See Eisenberg, Bankruptcy Law in Perspective, 28 U.C.L.A. L. Rev. 953, 963 (1981) (preference policies offer "no justification for the new preference rule unfavorable to accounts receivable and inventory lenders"). As a result, transactions that violate none of the policies of voidable preference doctrine may be struck down by courts that track its language mechanically. For example, the court in In re Diversified World Investments, 12 Bankr. 517 (Bankr. S.D. Tex. 1981), held that an assignment of rents constituted a voidable preference under §547:

> Although not specifically considered by the legislative history, the court believes that §547(e)(3) was intended to bring payments made pursuant to an assignment within the term "transfer." Under §101(40) [now (48)] the term transfer was intended to be "as broad as possible" . . . , and §101(40) clearly includes indirect payments. Furthermore, when §547(e)(3) is read together with §101(40) it appears to the court that the rental payments from [the account debtor] to [the creditor] were indirect transfers made for the benefit of [the debtor] as the rental payments were intended to reduce [the debtor's] indebtedness to [the creditor]. Thus, while indirect, the rental payments were made when [the debtor] obtained a right to receive them and not at the time of the assignment. [The creditor] occupies a position analogous to that of the secured creditor in *Grain Merchants* . . . , with the difference being that the transfer is indirect rather than direct.

Does this result seem correct as a reading of the preference section? As a matter of its policies? Consider the following analysis, from In re E. P. Hayes, Inc., 29 Bankr. 907 (Bankr. D. Conn. 1983):

> . . . Under the trustee's theory, §547(e)(3) turned each payment under the Enfield contract into a discrete transfer unrelated to the date of the assignment since the debtor had no right to these payments until it performed the services for the town. He cites In re Diversified World Investments, Ltd., 12 B.R. 517, 8 B.C.D. 28 (Bkrtcy. S.D. Tex. 1981) in support of this proposition. An examination of the purposes behind the inclusion of §547(e)(3) in the Bankruptcy Code, however, negates the trustee's reasoning.
>
> Section 547(e)(3) was a legislative response to such decisions as DuBay v. Williams, 417 F.2d 1277 (9th Cir. 1969) and Grain Merchants of Indiana, Inc. v. Union Bank & Savings Co., 408 F.2d 209 (7th Cir. 1969). . . . These cases reasoned that since the secured creditor's rights in the after-acquired collateral could not be defeated by a judicial lien levied after perfection, neither could the trustee defeat such rights. The enactment of §547(e)(3) overcomes this result. . . .
>
> Against this background, no basis exists for construing §547(e)(3) as affecting settled law beyond its effect on after-acquired property clauses. . . . [T]he payments received by IHCC under the Enfield contract are not after-acquired property. Section 547(a)(3) acknowledges the continuation of such financing arrangements by defining "receivable", for purposes of the preference section, as a "right to payment, whether or not such right has been earned by performance." This definition is essentially the

same as that of an "account" under the Uniform Commercial Code and includes the former separate concept of a "contract right." The Enfield contract was an existing executory contract when the debtor assigned its rights to payment to IHCC. The debtor's receivable was acquired at the time of contract execution, even though not yet earned by performance. In short, the debtor acquired its rights to the payments from the town on August 30, 1977; these rights were transferred on October 22, 1979 to IHCC; and receipt of the payments by IHCC in April and May, 1982 do not constitute transfers avoidable by the trustee under §547.

Having pondered this problem, consider the following case. Does it correctly interpret §547? Its underlying policies?

IN RE RIDDERVOLD
647 F.2d 342 (2d Cir. 1981)

FRIENDLY, Circuit Judge.

David B. and Susan R. Riddervold filed voluntary petitions in the Bankruptcy Court for the Northern District of New York for relief under Chapter 7 of the Bankruptcy Reform Act of 1978 (the Code) on December 3, 1979. A month later they filed a complaint against four judgment creditors. In a first cause of action, not at issue on this appeal, they sought to cancel judgment liens recorded in the Saratoga County Clerk's office in the aggregate amount of $4,367.45 under §522(f) of the Code to the extent that such liens would impair their equity of some $5,500 in their residence allowed by §522(d)(1). A second cause of action asserted on behalf of David B. Riddervold (hereafter Riddervold) that between September 3 and December 3, 1979, one of the defendants, the Saratoga Hospital, had caused monies to be deducted from his wages by virtue of an income execution served on his employer in the amount of $260; that such monies constituted preferences which Riddervold's trustee could have avoided; that if the trustee had avoided these payments, Riddervold could have exempted them under the blanket exemption of §522(d)(5), to wit, $400 plus any unused amount of the exemption provided in §522(d)(1);* but that the trustee had not attempted and would not attempt to recover the alleged preferences. In its answer Saratoga Hospital prayed for judgment dismissing the second cause of action. Bankruptcy Judge Mahoney granted this prayer. . . .

The Hospital's claim here at issue arose from medical treatment rendered to Susan R. Riddervold in 1976 and 1977. When the Hospital's bill was not paid, at least in full, it obtained a New York state court judgment, in the amount of $1,410.50 against Mr. Riddervold on March 17, 1977,

---

* Section 522(d)(5) was amended in 1984 to place a $3750 cap on the unused exemption under §522(d)(1).— EDS.

which it recorded in the office of the Saratoga County Clerk. On January 17, 1978, it served an "income execution" pursuant to this judgment upon Riddervold's employer, the State of New York, under N.Y.C.P.L.R. §5231. Under this execution the State made two payments aggregating $227 to the Hospital from wages otherwise payable to Riddervold within 90 days of the petition in bankruptcy. Riddervold contends that these payments constituted preferences which his trustee could have avoided under §547 and that since the trustee has not taken and will not take proceedings to that end, Riddervold is entitled to do so under §522(h). The validity of this contention depends on applying the section of the 1978 Code relating to preferences, §547, to the result of the action taken by the Hospital under N.Y.C.P.L.R. §5231.

Section 547 of the 1978 Code completely rewrote §60, the preference section of the Act of 1898 as amended, and removed or altered related material that had previously been dealt with in the lien provision, §67. The key provision for this case is §547(b). This allows the trustee to "avoid any transfer of property of the debtor", to or for the benefit of a creditor, for or on account of an antecedent debt, made while the debtor was insolvent and within specified periods, here 90 days, before the filing of the petition and that enables the creditor to receive more than such creditor would receive if —

(A) the case were a case under chapter 7 of this title;
(B) the transfer had not been made; and
(C) such creditor received payment of such debt to the extent provided by the provisions of this title.

Apparently the Riddervolds' exemptions exceeded their debts so that the Hospital would have received nothing under this test. Section 101(40)* broadly defines "transfer" to include "every mode, direct or indirect, absolute or conditional, voluntary or involuntary, of disposing of or parting with property or with an interest in property, including retention of title as a security interest." . . . Since the income execution was issued on January 17, 1978, it is safe to assume that the steps to and including the levy on the employer occurred long before the 90 days prior to the bankruptcy petition of December 3, 1979. Riddervold has not claimed the contrary.

There is a dearth of authority on the question whether payments by an employer during the crucial period — then four months — to a judgment creditor who had levied on the employer before the beginning of that period under N.Y.C.P.L.R. §5231 and its predecessors, N.Y.C.P.A. §684 and §1391 of the N.Y. Code of Civil Procedure, constituted prefer-

---

* Section 101(40) was amended and became §101(48) under the 1984 Amendments.— EDS.

ences under §60 of the Bankruptcy Act of 1898 if the other requirements of that section were met. Indeed we have been cited to none.[5] . . .

Early in his judicial career Judge L. Hand held in In re Sims, 176 F. 645 (S.D.N.Y. 1910), that moneys withheld from the bankrupt's salary under a levy under §1391 of the New York Code of Civil Procedure more than four months old at the date of the bankruptcy and still in the hands of the sheriff at the date of adjudication belonged to the creditors, whereas post-adjudication earnings of the bankrupt did not. On the former point he reasoned that the execution operated as a "continuing levy". In re Beck, 238 F. 653 (S.D.N.Y. 1915), involved a portion of Beck's salary retained by the city paymaster pursuant to an execution under the same statute also long antedating the bankruptcy. Without referring to In re Sims, supra, and in misplaced reliance on Clarke v. Larremore, 188 U.S. 486, 23 S. Ct. 363, 47 L. Ed. 555 (1903), not a garnishment case, where the judgment, levy and execution all occurred within the four-months period, Judge Hough held that the trustee was entitled to such moneys still in the paymaster's hands as represented retentions during the four-month period. He argued that "there could be no levy upon Beck's salary until there was a salary to levy upon. Therefore the date of levy is coincident with the date of accruing wage." However, he also held that if the debtor did not receive a discharge, amounts retained after the beginning of the four-months period and indeed after the adjudication should be payable to the judgment creditor. Judge Hough's reasoning had scant appeal to Judge Mayer, a judge with great experience in bankruptcy, when he was shortly confronted with a similar problem in In re Wodzicki, 238 F. 571 (S.D.N.Y. 1916). He expressed a preference for Judge Hand's "continuing levy" theory, sought to confine In re Beck to the decision that only the trustee and not the bankrupt could obtain the money in the hands of the city paymaster, and upheld rights of the judgment creditor, as against those of the bankrupt, to moneys in the city paymaster's hands representing collections during the four-months period. However, the contest was simply between the bankrupt and the judgment creditor, no trustee having been appointed. Finally, in In re Prunotto, 51 F.2d 602 (W.D.N.Y. 1931), Judge Knight followed the portion of Judge Hand's In re Sims decision which denied the validity of the execution against post-adjudication wages on the basis that to uphold this would conflict with the provisions of the Bankruptcy Act with respect to discharge.

In principle it does not appear to us that the State's paying $227 to the

---

5. Under §60(b) of the 1898 Act only the trustee could avoid a preference. In view of the accepted learning that "[a] preference is not an act evil in itself but one prohibited by the Bankruptcy Act in the interest of equality of division," Canright v. General Finance Corp., 35 F. Supp. 841, 844 (E.D. Ill. 1940), aff'd, 123 F.2d 98 (7 Cir. 1941), see 4 Collier, Bankruptcy ¶547.01 (15th ed. 1980), it is not clear why the 1978 Code extended the power to avoid preferences to bankrupts. However, it unquestionably did, subject to certain restrictions set forth in §522(g), none of which is applicable here.

hospital during the 90-day period now provided by §547(b)(4)(A) constituted a "transfer of property of the debtor." This is not because Riddervold took no action to cause the payments to be made, since "transfer" is defined to include an involuntary transfer. It is rather because after the sheriff has taken the step described in N.Y.C.P.L.R. §5231(d), the debtor has no property or interest in property subject to the levy which can be transferred. Service of the income execution on the employer in effect works a novation whereby the employer owes 10 percent of the employee's salary not to the employee but to the sheriff for the benefit of the judgment creditor. This view is substantiated by the provision in N.Y.C.P.L.R. §5231(e) that if the employer fails to pay the sheriff, the judgment creditor may sue the employer to recover accrued installments.

It is true that the employer comes under no liability to pay the sheriff until the wages are earned. Indeed the last sentence of N.Y.C.P.L.R. §5231(e) expressly provides for this eventuality of stating that if "employment is terminated by resignation or dismissal . . . , the levy shall thereafter be ineffective." But this does not require us to hold that the portion of the salary subject to the income execution vests in the employee for a fleeting second after it has been earned, when in fact the employer becomes bound at that very time to pay it to the sheriff.

We emphasize that we are here concerned with payments which were not made simply in discharge of a lien but were pursuant to an execution levied many months before the beginning of the 90-day period. Our decision follows the "continuing levy" principle announced by Judge L. Hand and adopted by Judge Mayer under the Act of 1898 scores of years ago.[7] It seems also to conform to the intimations of Clarke v. Larremore, supra, 188 U.S. at 488-490, 23 S. Ct. at 364-365, that when a writ of execution under a valid lien has been fully executed by payment to the execution creditor, a subsequent bankruptcy does not affect the creditor's rights. To be sure, these cases were decided under the Act of 1898 but we find nothing in the language or the policy of the 1978 Code that forbids their continued application.

Affirmed.

NOTE

Many courts have faced the *Riddervold* problem, but there is no clear consensus. The Seventh Circuit, applying Indiana law, reached the same result as Judge Friendly in In re Coppie, 728 F.2d 951 (7th Cir. 1984). For examples of bankruptcy court opinions that have reached a different result, see In re Tabita, 38 Bankr. 511 (Bankr. E.D. Pa. 1984); In re Larson,

---

7. To the extent that our decision runs counter to the views expressed by Judge Hough in In re Beck, supra, we prefer the reasoning of Judges L. Hand and Mayer.

21 Bankr. 264 (Bankr. D. Utah 1982). In both *Coppie* and *Larson,* the courts professed to be letting everything turn on whether a debtor whose wages are garnished retains an interest in them under state law. Should bankruptcy law defer to state law to determine whether the debtor has a property interest in these wages? If it should, could Article 9 be redrafted so that floating liens were not voidable preferences at all, quite apart from the two-point net improvement test?

PROBLEM

6.35 Debtor borrows money from Bank. In order to obtain the loan, Debtor had to persuade Guarantor to endorse, as an accommodation party, the promissory note Debtor gave to Bank. Guarantor, in turn, demanded an interest in Debtor's property to secure Guarantor's contingent obligation to Bank. Ten days before the filing of the petition, Debtor defaulted on its loan to Bank. Bank insisted that Guarantor honor its guarantee. Guarantor paid Bank. Guarantor then exercised its rights under its security agreement with Debtor and took possession of enough of Debtor's property to satisfy Debtor's obligation to reimburse Guarantor. Can the trustee take the property back from Guarantor on the ground that Guarantor's security interest did not come into being until ten days before the filing of the petition and was a transfer on account of Guarantor's already existing obligation to honor its guarantee? Would your analysis change if, instead of using Guarantor, a bank had issued a standby letter of credit? See In re Twist Cap, 1 Bankr. 284 (Bankr. M.D. Fla. 1979); In re Page, 18 Bankr. 713 (D.D.C. 1982); In re M.J. Sales & Distributing Co., 25 Bankr. 608 (Bankr. S.D.N.Y. 1982); Baird, Standby Letters of Credit in Bankruptcy, 49 U. Chi. L. Rev. 130 (1982).

NOTE ON THE DEAN v. DAVIS PROBLEM

Dean v. Davis, 242 U.S. 438 (1917), involved the following facts. Jones obtains $1,600 from Bank through forgery. Bank learns of the forgery. Jones, to avoid criminal prosecution, borrows $1,600 from Dean (his brother-in-law), to pay the Bank debt. Dean takes a security interest in Jones's property at the time of making the loan. The money is paid over to Bank by Dean.

Is there anything wrong with this transaction from the perspective of bankruptcy law? First, is the payment of $1,600 to Bank a preference? Is it paid with property of the debtor? Isn't the $1,600 really Dean's, not Jones's? Is giving Dean a security interest a preference? The debt to Dean is contemporaneous with the granting of the security interest. But don't we have an indirect preference here? This would seem to be the same situation as if Bank assigned its claim against Jones to Dean, and *then* Dean asked for security. Isn't that exactly the same as if Bank had asked for security?

We seem, therefore, to have an indirect preference in the above transaction. (Dean v. Davis, however, held that there was no preference since, at least as §60b then read, "a transfer to a third person is invalid under this section as a preference, only where that person was acting on behalf of the creditor . . . [and here] Dean acted on the debtor's behalf. . . .") Do we also have a fraudulent conveyance, giving the trustee the advantage of a longer "reachback" period? Dean v. Davis held yes:

> But under §67e the basis of invalidity is much broader [than §60b]. It covers every transfer made by the bankrupt "within four months prior to the filing of the petition, with the intent and purpose on his part to hinder, delay, or defraud his creditors, or any of them" "except as to purchasers in good faith and for a present fair consideration." As provided in §67d, only "liens given or accepted in good faith and not in contemplation of or in fraud upon this Act" are unassailable. A transfer, the intent (or obviously necessary effect) of which is to deprive creditors of the benefits sought to be secured by the Bankruptcy Act "hinders, delays or defrauds creditors" within the meaning of §67e. . . . Making a mortgage to secure an advance with which the insolvent debtor intends to pay a preexisting debt does not necessarily imply an intent to hinder, delay or defraud creditors. The mortgage may be made in the expectation that thereby the debtor will extricate himself from a particular difficulty and be enabled to promote the interest of all other creditors by continuing his business. The lender who makes an advance for that purpose with full knowledge of the facts may be acting in perfect "good faith." But where the advance is made to enable the debtor to make a preferential payment with bankruptcy in contemplation, the transaction presents an element upon which fraud may be predicated. The fact that the money advanced is actually used to pay a debt does not necessarily establish good faith. It is a question of fact in each case what the intent was with which the loan was sought and made.

The "rule" of Dean v. Davis was purportedly codified in §67d(3) of the 1898 Act, which reads:

> Every transfer made and every obligation incurred by a debtor who is or will thereby be rendered insolvent, within four months prior to the filing of a petition initiating a proceeding under this Act by or against him is fraudulent, as to then existing and future creditors: (a) if made or incurred in contemplation of the filing of a petition initiating a proceeding under this Act by or against the debtor . . . with intent to use the consideration obtained for such transfer or obligation to enable any creditor of such debtor to obtain a greater percentage of his debt than some other creditor of the same class, and (b) if the transferee or obligee of such transfer or obligation, at the time of such transfer or obligation, knew or believed that the debtor intended to make such use of such consideration. . . .

Simply stated, that section provides that transfers made in contemplation of bankruptcy, even though for fair consideration, for the purpose of obtaining for the debtor the wherewithal to make a preference, are avoidable by the trustee as fraudulent. The provision was often criticized as doing more harm than good, and purportedly was omitted from §548. See J. Trost, et al., The New Federal Bankruptcy Code: Resource Materials 149 (1979). In light of the concept of indirect preferences, is its omission proper?

Was the "rule" of Dean v. Davis in fact omitted? In re American Properties, 14 Bankr. 637 (Bankr. D. Kan. 1981), suggests that "the holding of Dean v. Davis is still reflected in Code §548(a)(1). . . ." The facts of *American Properties,* simplified somewhat, were as follows. American and Coleman Nebraska were subsidiaries of Companies. Coleman Nebraska owed Bank approximately $136,000. Bank thereupon entered into the following arrangement. Bank loaned American the sum of $211,000, secured by a mortgage on American's real property. Of that amount $136,000 was sent to Second Bank, and placed in a joint account of both American and Coleman Nebraska. Coleman Nebraska thereupon repaid its debt of $136,000 to Bank by writing a check on that joint account, and the check was honored by Second Bank. "Through an intercompany bookkeeping entry made at some later date, Coleman Nebraska was shown to owe American" $136,000. American and Coleman Nebraska both filed for bankruptcy within 90 days of that event. The court held that this was a fraudulent conveyance under §548 (in addition to a voidable preference under §547):

> Though there are more parties involved, the purpose of [Bank's] scheme was to pay off an unsecured debt and create a secured debt. In Dean v. Davis one creditor was substituted for another. In the instant case, one debtor was substituted for another, but the results are the same. Certainly the inference of knowledge by the creditor must be very great where the creditor orchestrates a scheme to "pay off" its unsecured claim and substitute a secured claim.

The court's remedy was as follows:

> Viewing the transaction either the way it was orchestrated on paper or in reality, the fact is the bank advanced [$136,000] and received back the same [$136,000]. The [$136,000] portion of the transaction was a "wash," a nullity, a sham. The only portion of the transaction which had any substance to it was the $75,000 advance to American in return for which [Bank] received a mortgage. . . .
>   . . . The Court orders the following: all transfers related to the [$136,000] portion of the transaction are avoided; [Bank] retains the same unsecured claim against Coleman Nebraska in the amount of [$136,000] that it had before this transaction occurred; [Bank] is not required to return

[$136,000] to Coleman Nebraska or the debtors-in-possession because in substance, although a preferential transfer, the transfer was a "wash," a nullity, and a sham; the $75,000 portion of the transfer to American was neither preferential nor fraudulent, and therefore [Bank] has a secured claim against the debtors-in-possession as represented by the mortgage granted by American in the amount of $75,000.

What if American and Coleman Nebraska filed for bankruptcy more than 90 days, but less than one year, after the sequence of events recounted above? Is this problem a fraudulent conveyance or is it simply an indirect preference? Should the "rule" of Dean v. Davis be found in §548, shorn of its preference period limitation?

E. SET-OFFS

Section 553 acts as a complement of §547, as well as a limitation on what otherwise appear to be the trustee's powers under the latter section. Section 553 carries forward the policy of §68 of the 1898 Act, by recognizing the right of "set-off" in certain situations, despite the seemingly preferential nature of such transfers. Section 553 states explicitly that nothing in the Bankruptcy Code, other than itself and the automatic stay provisions of §362, affect the right to a set-off. The effect of this provision is to treat the holder of a set-off right as tantamount to the holder of a security interest, a status that §506 recognizes explicitly.

Section 553 does not create a right of set-off; rather, it generally recognizes set-off rights that exist under nonbankruptcy law. Set-off rights arise under nonbankruptcy law when two parties are mutual debtors and creditors. This can be illustrated by the following. Two businessmen, Smith and Jones, often go to lunch together. They find it convenient for one person to pick up the check for both and then they settle their accounts every several months. Over the course of the year, Smith buys $150 worth of lunches for Jones and Jones buys $200 worth of lunches for Smith. Each party, therefore, owes the other some money.

It is possible to view these two debts as entirely separate items. So viewed, if Smith goes into bankruptcy, his trustee can demand that Jones pay what he owes ($150). But when Jones in turn tries to collect what he is owed ($200), the trustee will tell him to stand in line with everyone else as a general creditor of Smith, to share pro rata with others and receive perhaps only ten cents on the dollar for his claim, or $20. Instead of being owed $50 (the result of netting out the transactions), Jones discovers that he ends up owing $130.

Often, however, state law treats these mutual debts as related, and allows the solvent businessman in our example (Jones) to "self-help" by deducting what the debtor owes him from the amount he owes Smith. If state law recognized a set-off right in such a case, Jones will have a claim for $50 and be paid $5. This is a "set-off" right, and, when it exists under state law, §553 generally recognizes it.

The most frequently discussed set-off right is a bank's right to set-off monies in a deposit account against a debt owing to it. See generally Clark, Bank Exercise of Setoff: Avoiding the Pitfalls, 98 Bank. L.J. 196 (1981). This situation involves the following typical transaction. Bank loans Debtor $100,000, which creates a debt from Debtor to Bank. Debtor has a checking account in Bank that is, ultimately, a debt owing from Bank to Debtor. So, Bank and Debtor are mutual creditors and debtors. When Debtor fails to repay its loan to Bank, Bank is generally entitled, under state law, to "set-off" the monies "in" the checking account against the obligation that Debtor owes Bank.

The recognition of the set-off right itself is not particularly related to the topic of this chapter; what justifies examining it here are the preference-type limitations placed on that right in §553. Why does bankruptcy respect, for the most part, these set-off rights? What limitations does bankruptcy place on set-offs and why? Keep these questions in mind as you read §553, and work through the following cases and problems.

IN RE ALLBRAND APPLIANCE & TELEVISION CO.
16 Bankr. 10 (Bankr. S.D.N.Y. 1980)

Joel LEWITTES, Bankruptcy Judge.

In the underlying adversary proceeding commenced by Allbrand Appliance & Television Co., Inc., a Chapter 11 debtor-in-possession (hereafter referred to either as "Allbrand" or "the debtor"), the debtor seeks the return of moneys allegedly due and owing to it from the defendant, Merdav Trucking Company ("Merdav"), prior to the commencement of this Chapter 11 case. Merdav duly served and filed its answer to the complaint and presently before this Court, for resolution, is Allbrand's motion for summary judgment and Merdav's cross-motion for summary judgment.

A

UNDISPUTED FACTS

Allbrand presently is, and was, at the time it filed its Chapter 11 petition in this Court, engaged in the purchasing and distribution of electrical appliances, television sets, audio equipment and components therefor. It utilized the services of independent truckers both to deliver merchandise to Allbrand's customers and to collect moneys due to Allbrand on its cash-on-delivery ("C.O.D.") sales. Defendant Merdav, for the past seventeen years, acted as an independent trucker performing such services on behalf of Allbrand, but without benefit either of a written or verbal agreement. Nevertheless, it is not disputed by the adversarial parties here that in connection with Merdav's trucking services, Merdav assumed responsibility for the merchandise it undertook to deliver, collected the C.O.D. payments from Allbrand's customers, billed Allbrand weekly for such services, and within a week of delivery, remitted to Allbrand the C.O.D. moneys collected by Merdav.

Merdav is a prepetition creditor of the debtor holding a general unsecured claim for unpaid trucking charges in the approximate sum of $100,000. On the eve of the filing of the Chapter 11 petition in this case, a representative of Allbrand informed Merdav that a petition was about to be filed in this Court. Thereupon, Merdav, prior to the filing, retained the proceeds in its hands from outstanding C.O.D. collections it made on behalf of the debtor, in an approximate amount of $25,000. Merdav has set off that amount against moneys due it for trucking and delivery services. It is this $25,000 (denominated by the debtor both in its complaint in the underlying adversary proceeding and in its instant cross-motion, as the "Fund") which the debtor seeks to recover from Merdav.

B

GENERAL CONTENTIONS OF THE PARTIES

Allbrand asserts that since the "Fund" is "property" of the debtor, as the latter quoted term is statutorily defined in the Bankrutpcy Code,[7] it is entitled to a turnover thereof.[8] Merdav resists the debtor's argument by relying upon the right of setoff recognized by Section 553 of the Bankruptcy Code.

We find, for the reasons about to be recited, that Merdav is entitled to judgment as a matter of law.

C

THE STATUTE INVOLVED

The relevant section of the Bankruptcy Code which controls the result we reach here is Section 553(a). It provides, in pertinent part, as follows:

7. 11 U.S.C. §541(a).
8. 11 U.S.C. §542(a).

. . . this title [11 U.S.C.] does not affect any right of a creditor to offset a mutual debt owing by such creditor to the debtor that arose before the commencement of the case under this title against a claim of such creditor against the debtor that arose before the commencement of the case, except to the extent that— . . . (3) the debt owed to the debtor by such creditor was incurred by such creditor—

    (A) after 90 days before the date of the filing of the petition;

    (B) while the debtor was insolvent; and

    (C) for the purpose of obtaining a right of setoff against the debtor.

D

DISCUSSION

(1) Mutuality of Debts

In accordance with the Code provisions just cited, as under the former Bankruptcy Act,[10] "[a] basic requirement . . . is that the setoff be of 'mutual credits' against 'mutual debts.' "[11]

The debtor, quite naturally, seeking to avoid the setoff here, argues that there is a lack of mutuality of debts since the C.O.D. collections received by Merdav from Allbrand's customers constitute a "Fund" held by Merdav, in effect, in trust for the debtor. If such contention were to be sustained, the debtor would indeed be permitted to avoid the setoff since the liabilities involved would not emanate from "the same right and between the same parties, standing in the same capacity".[12] This follows because there can be no mutuality "when the liability of the one claiming a set off arises from a fiduciary duty or is in the nature of a trust. . . ."[13] In that situation, ". . . the creditor has become not the debtor of his debtor, but the trustee of a specific trust."[14]

Merdav anchors its reliance, in opposition to the debtor's "Fund" or "trust" theory, upon a case strikingly similar to the one at bar.

In the case of In re W & A Bacon Co. ("Bacon")[15] the claimants were in the business of delivering parcels for several stores in Boston, including the bankrupt, Bacon. In connection with C.O.D. deliveries made by the claimants, the claimants collected the sales price due on delivery and returned the moneys collected to the bankrupt.

    10. Former Bankruptcy Act §68, 11 U.S.C. §108 (repealed).

    11. Wolf v. Aero Factors Corp., 126 F. Supp. 872, 883 (S.D.N.Y. 1954) (a case interpreting former Bankruptcy Act §68).

    12. 4 Collier on Bankruptcy ¶553.04[3] at 553.22 (15th ed. 1979).

    13. 4 Collier on Bankruptcy ¶68.04[2.1] at 872-873 (14th ed. 1975) (cited in Matter of Esgro, Inc., 645 F.2d 794, 797 (9th Cir. 1981) [interpreting former §68 of the Bankruptcy Act of 1898]). Compare 4 Collier on Bankruptcy ¶553.04 at 533.26 (15th ed. 1979) (commenting upon the 1978 Bankruptcy Code §553).

    14. Lehigh Valley Coal Sales Co. v. Maguire, 251 F. 581, 582 (7th Cir. 1918).

    15. 261 F. 109 (D. Mass. 1919).

The claimants rendered bills, to the bankrupt, for delivery charges either monthly or semi-monthly. The amounts collected by the claimants, on C.O.D. transactions, were normally paid over to the bankrupt within days after collection. In the instant matter, as in *Bacon*, there was not a written or oral agreement, expressed or implied, between the carriers and bankrupt. Moreover, both the carriers and the bankrupt understood in *Bacon*, as in the case at bar, that the carriers were responsible for all parcels that were to be delivered. It appears, in *Bacon*, that receipts of C.O.D. transactions were deposited by the claimants in their general bank accounts and there was no understanding between the claimants and the bankrupt that such sums be kept in a separate and distinct account for the benefit of the bankrupt.

The *Bacon* court, in allowing the claimants to setoff moneys, in their hands, from C.O.D. collections as against current bills due them from Bacon on account of delivery charges, critically held:

> . . . the fact that one person collected money for, and has in his possession money belonging to, another, does not, without more, establish the relation of trustee and cestui que trust between them.[16]

On the record here, we similarly perceive no basis to find that a trust relationship existed between Merdav and the debtor.

It should, however, be noted that some courts have found a lack of mutuality of debts when a creditor of the debtor is in possession of the debtor's property as a bailee "without color of lien."[17] In such cases the property sought to be setoff remained that of the debtor pending further instructions by the debtor to its bailee. In denying the equitable principles of setoff to such bailee, the courts, in effect, held that such bailee as "a creditor of a bankrupt shall not be permitted to pay himself through the device of setoff by converting the bankrupt's property, particularly at a time when he knows of the bankrupt's insolvency."[18]

Of course, neither in *Bacon*, supra, nor in the case at bar, did the debtor contend that there was a bailment agreement or understanding between it and the carrier with respect to the C.O.D. collection or that such collections were to be segregated or returned by the carrier "in specie." . . .

Quite clearly, the law applicable to the motions now before this Court depends upon the legal relationship between the parties. On the basis of the submissions here, in the absence of a material and genuine issue of fact to the contrary, we conclude that the exceptions to mutuality in cases "where the bankrupt's property is in the possession of the creditor as bailee

16. Id. at 111. . . .
17. In re Lykens Hosiery Mills, 141 F. Supp. 891, 894 (S.D.N.Y. 1956). . . .
18. Brunswick Corporation v. Clements, 424 F.2d 673, 676 (6th Cir. 1970).

or trustee, without color of lien"[22] are not appropriate here. Rather the relationship between the instant parties was simply one of debtor-creditor and the setoff here was based solely upon mutual debts or credits.

(2)　Is Merdav's Setoff Denounced by Bankruptcy Code §553(a)(3)?

It may be recalled that immediately before Allbrand filed its Chapter 11 petition, a representative of Allbrand informed defendant Merdav that the former was about to seek relief, in this Court, for reorganization. In light of that divulgence, the debtor contends, Merdav's retention of the debtor's C.O.D. collections, in the amount of $25,000, was "for the purpose of obtaining a right of setoff against the debtor"[24]—thus excepting such amount from setoff. We find no merit to this contention. The last quoted provision, it has been authoritatively noted, "involves [a] deliberate manipulation by the creditor"[25] to incur a prepetition debt to his debtor for the sole purpose of triggering a setoff. However, even reading the submissions here most favorably to the debtor, we must conclude that Merdav's debts to Allbrand, i.e., the oustanding prepetition C.O.D. collections, were incurred by Merdav in the ordinary course of its business dealings with the debtor. To be sure, those debts were in existence and owed to Allbrand prior to Merdav's retention of the collections. Thus, it is clear that those debts were not incurred for "the purpose of obtaining a right of setoff against the debtor."[27] Accordingly, those debts are not excepted from setoff.

E

CONCLUSION

Although we speak in terms of a right to setoff, that right is discretionary and must be exercised, inter alia, in accordance with principles of equity. With this in mind, it has been contended by some that in rehabilitation and reorganization cases, where a setoff may have a deleterious effect upon the successful outcome of a case, setoff should be denied. But where, as here, no "compelling circumstances" justifying a denial of setoff are discernible, or have been pleaded, setoff is appropriate.

For the reasons set forth earlier, we conclude that Merdav is entitled to summary judgment dismissing Allbrand's complaint seeking a turnover of the C.O.D. collections setoff by Merdav. Allbrand's cross-motion for summary judgment is, in all respects, denied.

Settle order on notice.

22. In re Lykens Hosiery Mills, supra note 17.
24. 11 U.S.C. §553(a)(3), quoted in subsection "C" of this opinion.
25. Weintraub & Resnick, Bankruptcy Law Manual ¶5.10[1] at 5-34 (1980).
27. 11 U.S.C. §553(a)(3).

NOTES

1. Consider the last two paragraphs of the opinion. On what basis might a set-off be denied? Is §553 subject to an overriding principle of equity?

2. Judge Friendly spoke of the set-off right as follows, In re Applied Logic Corp., 576 F.2d 952 (2d Cir. 1978):

> It is true, of course, that "equitable principles govern the exercise of bankruptcy jurisdiction," Bank of Marin v. England, 385 U.S. 99, 103, 87 S. Ct. 274, 277, 17 L. Ed. 2d 197 (1966), and that, as said by the bankruptcy judge, "One of the dominant impulses in bankruptcy is equality among creditors." But we are here concerned with §68a, "the dominant impulse" of which is inequality among creditors. . . . For example, in a case where there are no other assets, §68a allows a creditor who owes the estate the same amount that it owes him to come out whole while other creditors get nothing. The rule allowing setoff, both before and after bankruptcy, is not one that courts are free to ignore when they think application would be "unjust." It is a rule that has been embodied in every bankruptcy act the nation has had, and creditors, particularly banks, have long acted in reliance upon it. . . . Efforts made during the passage of the Chandler Act to render §68a inapplicable even in a limited fashion . . . , namely, when the creditor incurred his indebtedness to the bankrupt under such circumstances that a transfer by the bankrupt to him at the time would constitute a voidable preference and similarly to limit setoff against bank deposits were rejected by Congress. . . .
>
> It is indeed settled law that a bank cannot exercise a setoff against a deposit which is known by it to be dedicated to a special use, e.g., for the sole purpose of meeting payrolls or paying taxes. . . . If in fact such deposits were "made in trust," as some courts have said . . . , the cases could be explained on the simple ground that the situation was not one of "mutual debts or credits," to which alone §68a applies. However, the principle seems to go beyond such cases and to include others where courts say that the bank is "equitably estopped from a setoff." What this really means is that by accepting the deposit for a special purpose the bank has agreed, at least implicitly, that the deposit should not be subject to its claims against the depositor and that it will be held to such agreement.

3. Does the following adequately explain why deposits in bank accounts entitle a bank to a set-off? Katz v. First Natl. Bank of Glen Head, 568 F.2d 964 (2d Cir. 1977):

> It is well settled that deposits in an unrestricted checking account, made in the regular course of business, do not constitute transfers within the meaning of the Bankruptcy Act. . . . The theory of these cases is that a deposit creates a debt owed to the depositor by the bank and does not constitute a parting with property by the depositor. As the court said in [Citizens Natl. Bank of Gastonia v. Lineberger, 45 F.2d 522, 527 (4th Cir.

1930)]: "A deposit in a bank . . . does not deplete the estate of the depositor, but results in substituting for currency, bank notes, checks, drafts, and other bankable items a corresponding credit with the bank, which may be checked against. . . . A deposit of funds differs from a payment in the essential particular that it is withdrawable at the will of the depositor."

All of the courts that have relied on a debtor-creditor relationship between bank and depositor to preclude a finding of transfer have emphasized not only the requirement that the funds be withdrawable at the will of the depositor but also the requirement that the deposits be made in the regular course of business. . . .

. . . In view of the purpose of the inquiry, it does not make sense to consider only the bank's course of business. If the deposits somehow are out of the regular course of the depositor's business, the bank's normal procedures, or the usual course of dealings between the depositor and the bank, then an inference can be drawn that the deposits were not ordinary deposits but served to transfer the depositor's property to the bank.

PROBLEMS

6.36 On August 1, Debtor owes Bank $8,000 under the terms of an unsecured demand note. At that time, Debtor has $5,000 in its account at Bank. On August 25, Debtor deposits $3,000 in the account so that it totals $8,000. On August 28, Bank charges the account for the collection of the note. On August 30, Debtor files a petition in bankruptcy. What are the rights of the trustee under §553(b)? If the Bank had not set-off on August 28, what would the result be (omitting, for the moment, any consideration of the automatic stay)? See *In re Compton*, the next case. Does it matter what Debtor's motives were for the $3,000 deposit? Whether Bank had a hand in it? See §553(a)(3); Freeman, Setoff Under the New Bankruptcy Code: The Effect on Bankers, 97 Banking L.J. 484, 498 (1980); Katz v. First Natl. Bank of Glen Head, supra.

6.37 On August 1, Debtor owes Bank $8,000. Bank has a security interest in Debtor's accounts receivable. At that time, Debtor has $5,000 worth of accounts. On August 25, Debtor sells a painting, and gets another account receivable for $3,000, so Debtor's accounts total $8,000. On August 30, Debtor files a petition in bankruptcy. What may the trustee recover under §547? What accounts for the difference in this problem from Problem 6.36?

6.38 Debtor owes Bank $10,000. Debtor has $1,000 in its checking account at Bank. On January 1, Bank sets-off the $1,000 in Debtor's checking account. On January 2, Debtor files a petition in bankruptcy. May Bank keep the $1,000?

6.39 Debtor owes Bank $10,000. Debtor has $1,000 in its checking account at Bank. On January 1, Debtor writes a check on that account to Bank for $1,000. On January 2, after Bank has paid the check (drawing Debtor's account to $0), Debtor files a petition in bankruptcy. May Bank keep the $1,000?

6.40 Bank loaned Debtor $7,000 to buy an automobile. Installments on the loan were due monthly in the amount of $220. At a time when the debt to Bank is $5,000, and the automobile has a value of $3,000, Debtor files a petition in bankruptcy. The trustee asserts that the last three monthly payments to Bank on its loan were preferential under §547. Debtor's bank account had $1,000 in it 90 days prior to bankruptcy and $1,500 in it on the date Debtor filed for bankruptcy. May the trustee recover the three payments under §547? Recall Note on Payments to Secured Creditors, supra page 305. Can Bank fashion an argument under §553 that will make the payments nonpreferential? See In re McCormick, 5 Bankr. 726 (Bankr. N.D. Ohio 1980).

6.41 Debtor has a deposit account at Bank with $20,000 in it. Bank has loaned Debtor $10,000. On January 1, Bank "purchases" a $10,000 claim against Debtor from Creditor, an unsecured creditor, for $6,000. On January 15, Debtor files a petition in bankruptcy. Does Bank have a set-off right that will be recognized in bankruptcy? For what amount? See §553(a)(2).

6.42 Debtor owes Bank $1,000. Debtor has a deposit account at Bank. On May 3, Debtor has $900 in that account. Debtor withdraws $10 on May 4, $500 on May 5, and $390 on May 6. On July 25, Debtor deposits $500, and Bank sets it off on July 26. What will the trustee be able to recover from Bank if Debtor files a petition in bankruptcy on:

(a) August 1 (90 days from May 3)?
(b) August 2?
(c) August 3?
(d) August 4?

6.43 Debtor has just filed a petition in bankruptcy. Ninety days before this filing, Debtor owes Bank $100,000 on an unsecured loan, and Debtor has a deposit account at Bank with $150,000 in it. Seventy-five days prior to the filing, Debtor withdraws $100,000 from the deposit account, leaving $50,000 in the account. Fifty days before the filing, Debtor pays Bank $70,000 on its debt from a source of funds other than the deposit account. Eleven days before the filing, Debtor withdraws $30,000 from the deposit account, leaving $20,000. Ten days before the filing, Bank sets-off against the account. (At this time, Bank's debt is $30,000, and the amount in the account is $20,000.) What happens in bankruptcy? When was there first an insufficiency? To what extent has the insufficiency been decreased by the date of the petition? How much was offset? How does §553 relate to §547? What is to be done, in analyzing this problem, with the fact that Debtor paid Bank $70,000—a transaction to which §553 does not apply? Should the problem be analyzed as if, instead of paying Bank the $70,000, Debtor placed it in the deposit account?

6.44 Same facts as Problem 6.43, except assume that 90 days before bankruptcy, Debtor's account has $95,000 in it and 75 days before bankruptcy, Debtor withdraws $45,000. Does anything in the result change? Should it?

IN RE COMPTON CORP.
22 Bankr. 276 (Bankr. N.D. Tex. 1982)

John C. FORD, Bankruptcy Judge.

The case at bar presents the narrow question of whether the 90 day improvement of position test found in Code section 553(b), 11 U.S.C. §553(b), applies to a post-petition setoff. . . .

On May 7, 1982, an involuntary Chapter 7 bankruptcy petition was filed against the Gratex Corporation and the Compton Corporation. After a hearing held on May 20, 1982, the Court granted the Debtor's motion to consolidate and convert these proceedings to a voluntary Chapter 11 reorganization proceeding. By order of the Court, the date of filing the petition was then fixed as May 7, 1982.

On June 10, 1982, Exxon Corporation filed a Complaint for Relief from the Automatic Stay asserting a right to setoff mutual pre-petition debts with the Compton Corporation. In response to Exxon's complaint, Compton admits that Exxon has the right to setoff the mutual pre-petition debts and that it has no plan for adequate protection for Exxon's cash collateral. However, Compton argues that a setoff would improve Exxon's position during the 90 days preceding bankruptcy, and that Exxon's recovery should be limited by the amount of that improvement. Exxon contends that section 553(b) applies only to setoffs which occur prior to bankruptcy, and that the 90 day improvement of position test is inapplicable in this case.

The transactions giving rise to the mutual debts result from two contracts between Compton and Exxon. For several years, Exxon has sold crude oil to Compton from offshore leases in Aransas County, Texas pursuant to a Division Order. Compton has sold South Texas Mixed crude oil to Exxon at Pearsall Station, Texas pursuant to a separate contract. The crude oil deliveries under these contracts are made by way of a constant flow of oil which is calculated periodically and billed on a monthly basis. It is impossible to determine the precise flow of oil on any particular day, so the month-end balances are the most useful and feasible way to determine the relative obligations of the parties. These month-end balances are as follows:

	Exxon Deliveries to Compton	Compton Deliveries to Exxon	Section 553(b)(2) Insufficiency
Feb.	$174,175.54	$278,293.94	None
Mar.	263,281.92	172,019.96	$91,261.96
Apr.	344,867.52	271,588.38	—
May 7	378,695.68	288,787.71	89,907.97
			$ 1,353.99

According to the month-end balances, the first date upon which there was an insufficiency was March 31, 1982. This figure is greater than the insufficiency on May 7 by $1,353.99. Therefore, if section 553(b) applies, Exxon's setoff right would be $288,787.71 minus $1,353.99, or $287,433.72. Otherwise, Exxon has the right to setoff $288,787.71.

Additionally, Defendant has paid Plaintiff for all crude oil delivered to Defendant since May 7, 1982. Plaintiff owes $96,255.52 for crude oil delivered by Defendant through the end of May, 1982, which is now due and payable.

CONCLUSIONS OF LAW

In general, setoffs in bankruptcy are allowed to the extent that they are based upon mutual obligations existing between the debtor and a creditor. The rationale for permitting setoffs in bankruptcy is based on a concept of fairness. The creditor should not be forced to disgorge full payment on a debt owed to the debtor in bankruptcy, only to receive in return a minimal dividend on his claim owed to him by the debtor.

The Bankruptcy Reform Act carries into current practice the prevailing pre-Code concept of viewing a setoff claim as a form of security interest recognized under state law. This approach is adopted from commercial practice and is most understandable when analyzing the Code's treatment of setoff of bank deposits. Although retaining much of the pre-Code theory supporting the allowance of setoffs, the Code shifts the analysis of setoff rights from the field of preference law and places the controlling provisions in Bankruptcy Code section 553.

Two forms of direct limitation on setoffs are contained in §553. In §553(a), certain limitations regarding transfers of claims and the accrual of claims during the 90 days preceding filing of the petition are outlined. The second limitation is contained in §553(b) and concerns only the creditor's right to implement the setoff during the 90 days prior to bankruptcy. It provides that pre-petition setoffs may be reduced and recovered by the trustee to the extent that the creditor's position is improved within the 90-day period.

The Bankruptcy Code substantially changed former bankruptcy law by allowing post-petition setoffs. The automatic stay provision contains a section enjoining the post-petition setoff of pre-petition claims except with the approval of the bankruptcy court. See 11 U.S.C. §362(a)(7). By inference, a clear implication exists that a creditor can utilize his setoff remedy prior to bankruptcy without approval of a court. Although stayed by §362(a)(7), a creditor who failed to setoff prior to the commencement of a case does not lose his right to a setoff. . . . Exxon's setoff right still exists, however, it must litigate and receive the opportunity to enforce that right by appearing before the bankruptcy court.

If Exxon had setoff its claim against Compton prior to filing the petition, it is very clear that Code §553(b) would enable a trustee to utilize the improvement of position test to recover the amount by which the claim against the debtor exceeds the debt available for setoff assuming the insufficiency on the date of setoff is less than the insufficiency present on the later of 90 days before the date the petition was filed, or the date on which an insufficiency first arises. This improvement of position test is somewhat analogous to the improvement of position test found in preference law, except that the avoidance provisions of Code §547(c)(5) permits avoidance of a security interest regardless of the creditor's pre-petition actions. Early drafts of the Bankruptcy Code provided that the improvement test be applied to bar setoffs to the extent that there was any improvement in position. A review of the legislative history reveals that the earlier drafts were replaced by a compromise amendment modifying section 553 "to clarify application of a two-point test with respect to setoffs." See 124 Cong. Rec. H11,098 (daily ed. Sept. 28, 1978); and S17,414 (daily ed. Oct. 6, 1978). As enacted, Code §553(b) permits avoidance and recovery only if the setoff is exercised on or before the filing of the petition. . . .

The framers of the Bankruptcy Code sought to provide a structure to review a creditor's self-help right to exercise setoff prior to bankruptcy. In response to the perceived need, the provisions of Code §553(b) were made available to permit the recovery of abusive setoffs which unduly improve the position of one creditor over that of another. In the case at bar, Exxon failed to exercise its right of setoff prior to the filing of the petition. Although not losing that right, Exxon must now proceed in the bankruptcy court by means of a complaint to lift the automatic stay so as to be allowed to exercise its already existing right to offset. By virtue of the availability of court review and the control now vested by the bankruptcy court over the exercise of Exxon's right to setoff, the need for a system of "checks and balances" like that found in §553(b) is simply not present. Although this Court may decide to weigh the improvement of position test when framing the relief to be granted the Plaintiff, it would be sheer folly to fashion a decision allowing Exxon to setoff and then to mechanically require the disgorgement of a portion of that amount in satisfaction of the §553(b) test. It is not necessary to mechanically apply the §553(b) test, insofar as this Court is capable of taking the improvement factor into consideration when making a judgment as to the amount that Exxon may be allowed to setoff its claim. Consequently, in the case at bar, Exxon is to be allowed the right to setoff $288,787.71.

NOTE ON MUTUALITY

Section 553, as we have noted, creates no independent right of set-off, but rather recognizes set-off rights that exist under nonbankruptcy law. Thus, if set-offs are limited under state law, §553 will not provide the creditor with a new right. See In re Haffner, 12 Bankr. 371 (Bankr. M.D. Tenn. 1981) (creditor's right of set-off may not, under state law, be exercised against exempt property). Yet §553 does not recognize all set-off rights that might exist under nonbankruptcy law. Instead, as was discussed in *Allbrand Appliance*, it extends the set-off right only to "a mutual debt owing by such creditor to the debtor that arose before the commencement of the case . . . against a claim of such creditor against the debtor that arose before the commencement of the case." §553(a). This reflects two ideas. The first is that "mutuality" ceases upon the filing of the bankruptcy petition so that, for example, sums deposited in a bank account after filing cannot be setoff against a debtor's pre-bankruptcy indebtedness to the bank. See In re Dartmouth House Nursing Home, 24 Bankr. 256 (Bankr. D. Mass. 1982) (Section 553 "does not address the legality of setting off pre-petition debt against post-petition credit" but "[i]t is well established that the requisite element of mutuality is lacking and the setoff is improper where a creditor applies a credit owed a Chapter 11 debtor to satisfy a pre-filing [creditor] because the debtor and the debtor-in-possession are separate and distinct entities"); In re All-Brite Sign Service Co., 11 Bankr. 409 (Bankr. W.D. Ky. 1981). As such, this requirement simply reflects the cleavage running throughout the Bankruptcy Code, such as in §541, between pre-petition and post-petition events.

Assuming that both sets of debts were pre-petition, however, what justifies the requirement that the debts be "mutual"? Mutuality is generally interpreted as importing the requirement that "the debts must be in the same right and between the same parties, standing in the same capacity." In re Ohio-Erie Corp., 22 Bankr. 340 (Bankr. N.D. Ohio 1982), quoting 4 Collier on Bankruptcy ¶553.04 (15th ed. 1981). Whether this test has been met is not always easy to determine. Consider the following case. Fore Improvement Corp. v. Selig, 278 F.2d 143 (2d Cir. 1960), involved a claim by a landlord for a set-off against his claim for unpaid rent, based on his holding of a security deposit of $1,750 received from the tenant upon execution of the lease. A New York statute provided that any such deposit should remain the money of the tenant and should not be commingled with the landlord's money. Landlord had commingled the deposit. The Second Circuit held that because the statute made the landlord a trustee, no set-off right would be recognized in bankruptcy:

> the right to set-off is determined by the provisions of section 68 of the Bankruptcy Act, notwithstanding the fact that the obligations involved are creatures of state law. And it is clear that the requirement of mutuality in section 68 precludes set-off where the party asserting it holds in trust the funds sought by the trustee in bankruptcy. . . . The rationale of this rule is simply that the liability arising from a fiduciary duty is entirely independent of the debt owing from the bankrupt. . . . There is no mutuality because the indebtedness is "all on the side of" the bankrupt . . . ; the trust *res* is not owing to the bankrupt's estate but rather is owned by it. . . .
>
>   . . . Nor is it of any moment that New York law may permit set-off where the tenant seeks to recover his deposit. As noted above, federal law determines the right, if any, to set-off in an action brought by a trustee in bankruptcy. . . .

Judge Friendly concurred on the basis that there was no indication that "New York law would have allowed the landlord to make a set-off here." But he disagreed that "mutuality" should be decided without reference to state law, absent any overriding bankruptcy policy. He noted that "any allowance of a setoff works a financial advantage, and in that general sense a preference, to the creditor who obtains it; but I cannot think this offends the Bankruptcy Act if the state that created the claims would have permitted a setoff *dehors* insolvency proceedings." Do you agree with Judge Friendly's final point? In considering this, note that mutuality is a requirement imposed by §553. In most cases, where one of the parties is a bailee or fiduciary, that party will not be able to exercise a set-off under state law. That is to say, in most cases, state law requires something akin to mutuality as a condition of a set-off right. But if state law is willing to recognize a right of set-off where mutuality is lacking, what bankruptcy policy is served by denying recognition of that right?

PROBLEM

6.45 Debtor is a corporation engaged in the business of selling audio equipment through various retail stores. Micro manufactures audio equipment, and sells it through various dealers, including Debtor. Under the agreement between Micro and Debtor, Debtor accepts returns by those who buy Micro equipment that prove defective, and provides such consumers with replacement equipment from Debtor's stock. This satisfies Micro's liability to the consumers under its warranty. When a significant quantity of Micro's defective equipment is accumulated by Debtor, it is shipped to Micro for repair, replacement, or credit on future purchases. Micro holds $2,800 worth of this returned audio equipment at the time Debtor files a petition in bankruptcy. Micro asserts that it is entitled to retain the audio equipment as a set-off against a $14,800 debt owed to Micro by Debtor. The trustee asserts that Micro holds the defective merchandise as a bailee, and hence the debts are not "mutual." Evaluate these respective contentions. See In re Brendern Enterprises, 12 Bankr. 458 (Bankr. E.D. Pa. 1981).

NOTE ON RECOUPMENT

What occurs when the offsetting debts arise out of the same transaction? For example, Buyer orders a new drill press from Seller, who warrants that the drill press will drill 1,000 holes per hour. Buyer agrees to pay Seller $10,000 for the drill press one month after delivery. This creates a debt running from Buyer to Seller. The machine is delivered to Buyer, who discovers that the machine can drill only 800 holes per hour, causing

Buyer a $1,000 injury (under standard measures of contract damages). This damage amount is an obligation that Seller owes to Buyer. Each party owes the other some money: Buyer owes Seller $10,000, as the purchase price of the drill press; Seller owes Buyer $1,000, as damages for breach of warranty. UCC §2-717 provides that Buyer may use "self-help," deducting the $1,000 that Seller owes Buyer from the amount Buyer owes Seller. See also UCC §2-718(2).

This transaction looks like the set-off transactions we have been examining. It differs from a typical setoff because the cross-cutting debts arise out of the same transaction. This might become important if the transaction did not fall within §553, because, for example, Seller's position improved within the meaning of §553(b). Several cases have distinguished the case of mutual debts arising out of the same transaction — called "recoupments" — from other set-off cases. In re Yonkers Hamilton Sanitarium, 22 Bankr. 427 (Bankr. S.D.N.Y. 1982), for example, relied on this distinction to reject a trustee's claim to recover some $72,000 in payments made in the 90 days prior to bankruptcy:

> A setoff under Code §553 involves mutual debts or mutual credits between the estate of a debtor and a creditor whereby claims arising out of different transactions or occurrences are offset. . . .
>
> Recoupments, unlike setoffs, do not involve the concept of mutuality of obligations and arise out of the same transaction rather than out of different transactions. As stated in 4 Collier on Bankruptcy, ¶553.03, at 553.12 (15th ed. 1981):
>
>> Recoupment . . . is the setting up of a demand arising from the same transaction as the plaintiff's claim or cause of action, strictly for the purpose of abatement or reduction of such claim . . . the defendant should be entitled to show that because of matters arising out of the transaction sued on, he is not liable in full for the plaintiff's claim. *There is no element of preference here or of an independent claim to be offset, but merely an arrival at a just and proper liability on the main issue, and this would seem permissible without any reference to former Section 68, or to Section 553(a).*

See also Waldschmidt v. CBS, 14 Bankr. 309 (W.D. Tenn. 1981). What is the policy reason for treating recoupments different from set-offs?

F. FURTHER EXTENSIONS OF AND LIMITATIONS ON AVOIDING POWERS

NOTE ON POST-PETITION TRANSFERS AND §549

Section 542(c) carves out a safe-harbor for anyone who, without knowledge that a bankruptcy proceeding has commenced, transfers property of the estate, or pays a debt owing to the debtor, in good faith, to anyone other than the trustee. The section is a codification of *Bank of Marin v. England*, 385 U.S. 99 (1966). *Bank of Marin* involved a bank that honored checks that were drawn before, but presented for payment after, the depositor had filed a petition in bankruptcy. As stated by the Court, the issue was whether the bank "is liable to the trustee for the amount of the checks paid where the bank had no knowledge or notice of the proceeding." In holding that the bank was not liable, the Court stated that it rejected the argument "that the bankrupt's checking accounts are instantly frozen in the absence of knowledge or notice of the bankruptcy on the part of the drawee." Rather, "the act of filing a voluntary petition in bankruptcy" is not "*per se* . . . reasonably calculated to put the bank on notice." Therefore, "the contract between the bank and the drawer remains unaffected by the bankruptcy. . . ." This conclusion is not changed by §70d(5) of the 1898 Act ("no transfer by or in behalf of the bankrupt after the date of bankruptcy shall be valid against the trustee"), for these statutory words cannot be read "with the ease of a computer. There is an overriding consideration that equitable principles govern the exercise of bankruptcy jurisdiction." Justice Harlan dissented: "I fully sympathize with the discomfort of the bank's position, but I cannot escape the impact of what Congress has done."

While §542(c) protects the entity making the payment, no similar provision protects the recipient of the payment. Sections 549 and 550 cover the transferee. Section 549 provides that the trustee may avoid such post-petition transfers. The only exceptions are transfers to good faith purchasers without knowledge of the commencement of the case (or purchasers at judicial sales) of real property located outside the county in which the bankruptcy case was commenced, unless a copy of the petition was filed in that county's real estate office. If the purchase is for fair value, the transfer may not be avoided. If not, the transfer may be avoided, but the transferee has a lien on the property for the amount of the purchase price. Section 550(a) subjects the initial transferee to the trustee's power under §549, but protects transferees to the extent they take "for value, including satisfaction or securing of a present or antecedent debt, in good faith, and without knowledge of the voidability of the transfer avoided." §550(b).

NOTE ON RECLAMATION RIGHTS AND §546

Section 2-702(2) of the Uniform Commercial Code provides:

Where the seller discovers that the buyer has received goods on credit while insolvent he may reclaim the goods upon demand made within ten days after the receipt, but if misrepresentation of solvency has been made to the particular seller in writing within three months before delivery the ten day limitation does not apply. Except as provided in this subsection the seller may not base a right to reclaim goods on the buyer's fraudulent or innocent misrepresentation of solvency or of intent to pay.

Before the enactment of the Bankruptcy Code, the validity of this provision in bankruptcy was challenged on a number of grounds, notably, that it was invalid as a state created priority or statutory lien effective on bankruptcy (or similar event) or because it was subject to the powers of a lien creditor. If state law interpreted UCC §2-702 as giving priority to a lien creditor over this reclamation right, the trustee succeeded to that power under his "strong-arm" power. See In re Kravitz, 278 F.2d 820 (3rd Cir. 1960). Otherwise, the reclaiming seller usually prevailed. See In re Telemart Enterprises, 524 F.2d 761 (9th Cir. 1975); In re PFA Farmers Mkt. Assn., 583 F.2d 992 (8th Cir. 1978); In re Federal's, Inc., 553 F.2d 509 (6th Cir. 1977).

Section 546(c) provides a safe harbor for a reclamation right that meets the requirements of that section — requirements different in some respects from those of UCC §2-702. (For example, §546(c), unlike UCC §2-702, requires that the demand for reclamation be in writing, and §546(c) provides no extended reclamation period for written misrepresentations of solvency.) Section 546(c) also provides that the reclamation right may be denied if the court secures the claim by a lien. Alternatively, the court may grant the seller's claim priority as an administrative expense, provided the seller is not a producer of grain or a United States fisherman.

A number of ambiguities are left by §546(c). The section speaks only of making the "rights and powers of the trustee under sections 544(a), 545, 547, and 549" "subject" to the reclamation right. (Note nothing is said about the automatic stay of §362.) What of a reclamation that complies with UCC §2-702, but does not meet the requirements of §546(c)? Is §546(c) an exclusive provision, or is it simply a nonexclusive safe harbor? Compare In re Deephouse Equipment Co., 22 Bankr. 255 (Bankr. D. Conn. 1982) and In re Contract Interiors, 14 Bankr. 670 (Bankr. E.D. Mich. 1981) (exclusive) with In re A.G.S. Food Systems, 14 Bankr. 27 (Bankr. D.S.C. 1980) (nonexclusive).

The common law "cash sale" doctrine has been codified in UCC §2-507. Comments to the section, plus case law, suggest that a cash seller has at least the equivalent reclamation right under UCC §2-507 as the credit seller does under UCC §2-702. Assuming this is so, what result for the cash seller under §546(c)? In re Koro Corp., 20 Bankr. 241 (1st Cir. Bankr. App. 1982), relying on statements made on the floor of the House and Senate, stated that the section applies equally to the credit and the cash seller. See generally Mann and Phillips, Section 546(c) of the Bankruptcy Reform Act: An Imperfect Resolution of the Conflict Between Reclaiming Seller and the Bankruptcy Trustee, 54 Am. Bankr. L.J. 239, 263-264 (1980).

Chapter 7
PRESERVING THE ESTATE

Bankruptcy proceedings take time. It may not be clear at the start who all the debtor's creditors are or what claims they have. Moreover, only rarely will a debtor's assets be in the form of cash. Months may pass before a buyer for the assets can be found and they can be converted into cash. Equally time consuming may be efforts to reorganize the debtor's capital structure and then to compensate the creditors (and perhaps shareholders) with interests in the new firm according to their nonbankruptcy entitlements. Bankruptcy law should ensure that the passage of time itself does not change the value of various creditors' rights relative to one another. Yet it should have as small an effect as possible on the debtor's relationships with the rest of the world. A debtor who files a bankruptcy petition should receive no special privileges against entities that are not pre-petition creditors. A firm that stays in business must continue to conform its conduct to the dictates of the law, even if doing so makes the survival of the enterprise less likely. A debtor in bankruptcy has, and should have, no more license to pollute the environment or pay less than the minimum wage in violation of the law than it does to sell cocaine. Nor does a debtor in bankruptcy enjoy any special right to make people buy its goods or services, even if increased business is necessary to the survival of the enterprise. An airline that resorts to bankruptcy must entice people to fly on it; a court cannot, and should not, order people to use the debtor to fly.

These twin principles, however, are not always kept separate. It is necessary to resolve the tension between preserving the rights of creditors vis-a-vis one another and allowing the debtor's relations with the rest of the world to continue as before. The relevant statutory provisions are contained for the most part in §§361 to 365 of the Bankruptcy Code. Why should secured creditors (who generally get first dibs on the assets securing their claims) wait to exercise their default rights? What about people other than creditors with whom the debtor has been doing business? What sorts of rights should the debtor have to keep its contracts in place? To keep the value of those contracts? To use property? To borrow money? And how should these issues be decided when the post-bankruptcy lender or supplier is also a pre-bankruptcy creditor? These questions are the focus of this chapter.

A. SCOPE OF THE AUTOMATIC STAY

INTRODUCTORY NOTE

For the collective bankruptcy proceeding to be effective, all efforts by creditors to obtain repayment of their debts must stop, regardless of whether the petition is voluntary or involuntary. If such conduct were not restrained, creditors would continue pursuing individual remedies, even though such individual actions run counter to the basic bankruptcy principle that once the proceeding begins, the creditors' interests are best served if they work together.

This is accomplished through what is known as the "automatic stay." Under §362 of the Bankruptcy Code, the filing of a bankruptcy petition operates as a stay of all efforts to collect a debt from the debtor, to put a lien on its property, or to take any of the other actions set forth in subsection (a). It is tantamount to an injunction. Subsection (c) defines the duration of this stay, but it must be read in conjunction with the procedures for lifting the stay set forth in subsections (d) through (g). We shall examine these procedures after looking at the scope and effect of the automatic stay.

Subsection (b) lists actions that fall outside the scope of the automatic stay, although the legislative history states that "[t]he effect of an exception is not to make the action immune from injunction. The court has ample other powers to stay actions not covered by the automatic stay [such as §105]. . . . By excepting an act or action from the automatic stay, the [statute] simply requires that the trustee move the court into action, rather than requiring the stayed party to request relief from the stay."

Because the stay takes effect upon the filing of the petition, it is "issued" by operation of law rather than by a court. Unlike most other injunctions, there is no hearing and no notice. And apparently there is no geographical limit on the stay, except insofar as actions of Congress are limited in effect to territories of the United States. Section 542, codifying Bank of Marin v. England, 385 U.S. 99 (1966), provides in subsection (c) that an entity (such as a bank) without actual knowledge of the commencement of the case that transfers property of the estate or pays a debt owed the debtor to a third party in good faith will only be liable to the same extent as if no bankruptcy proceeding had commenced. The effect of this rule is to protect people who cash the debtor's checks and other such things without knowing that bankruptcy proceedings have commenced. Section

542(c), however, protects only the transferor and only to the extent that the actions are specified in that section. Sections 549 and 550 deal with the transferee. What if the entity, instead of taking one of the actions enumerated in §546(c), files a lawsuit on a claim, in violation of §362, without knowledge of the bankruptcy petition? No provision of the Bankruptcy Code protects the entity in that event, so the action would appear to violate the automatic stay. Whether a court would impose any penalty, other than the undoing of the action, is, of course, a different question.

Section 362 is designed to keep the estate together, so as to secure the advantages, if any, of a collective proceeding for the debtor and its creditors. These advantages, however, may vary depending on whether the debtor is an individual, a corporation, or a partnership and on what disposition of the assets is most appropriate. The debtor's assets may largely be items such as securities, or the debtor may be liquidating and seeking to dispose of its property on an item-by-item basis. In those cases, the justification for the stay—at least insofar as secured creditors and other property claimants are concerned—may last only as long as it takes to sort out competing rights. On the other hand, the debtor may be a business attempting to reorganize or to keep itself together for sale as an entity to a third party, or an individual pursuing a route (such as Chapter 13) that allows him to keep his assets together. In these cases, because the end goal of the proceeding is not dismemberment of the assets, justifications for the automatic stay are distinct and more compelling.

Many entities may be affected by the automatic stay. Section 362 clearly covers the case of a pre-petition secured creditor. Once a petition is filed, a secured creditor may not perfect its security interest or take any steps to possess the collateral. The section also covers the efforts of a garden variety pre-petition general creditor to acquire a security interest or a judgment lien or to receive cash. Section 362(a), moreover, because it covers "property in the possession of the debtor," covers the attempt of a lessor or a bailor of personal property to regain control of something that it "owns" but that the debtor has possession of at the moment the bankruptcy case commences. The activities reached by the automatic stay include those of a litigant pursuing a lawsuit to establish a claim and may even include those of an entity seeking to extricate itself from a contractual relationship with the debtor. Some issues arise that are not clear-cut. It is not always possible to distinguish between actions taken by a pre-petition creditor who is pulled into the collective proceeding and who is attempting to extricate itself, and actions taken by a third party (including a former creditor) who is free to deal with the debtor or not as it pleases. Then there are questions as to what kinds of acts are forbidden by the automatic stay that are raised by the inclusive categories of §362(a) or the exclusive categories of §362(b).

In the case that follows, both questions arise. In reading it, consider both whether Holland America Insurance performed any act violating the automatic stay, and the extent to which it still has the power to terminate a contract that it could have terminated outside of bankruptcy.

IN RE CAHOKIA DOWNS
5 Bankr. 529 (Bankr. S.D. Ill. 1980)

J. D. TRABUE, Bankruptcy Judge. . . .

1. Cahokia Downs, Inc. is a Delaware Corporation which has operated a race track and owns track facilities on land leased from Cahokia Land Trust.

2. Sportservice, Inc. is the largest creditor of Cahokia Downs and filed an involuntary Chapter 11 on April 2, 1980.

3. Pursuant to the consent of Cahokia Downs, Inc., an order of relief was entered on said petition, and there are at present efforts being made to formulate a plan of arrangement.

4. Sometime in July, 1979, Holland America Insurance Company and Cahokia Downs, Inc. entered into a policy of insurance under policy No. FN 013505, being a standard fire policy with a policy period of July 26, 1979 to July 26, 1980, insuring the race track premises.

5. Sayre & Toso, Inc. is the underwriter of said policy.

6. Logger Insurance Agency, Inc., acting as agent of Cahokia Downs, Inc., obtained the policy of insurance and advanced the full premium payment on behalf of Cahokia Downs, Inc. in the amount of $32,309.

7. Cahokia Downs, Inc. is indebted to Logger Insurance Agency for said premium and also to Mark Twain National Bank on a loan agreement for payment of a portion of the policy premium in the approximate amount of $14,000.

8. The race track operated on a seasonal basis, and for a part of each year is completely shut down except for a custodian and certain employees.

9. On April 11, 1980, without prior consent of this Court and after filing of the petition in this matter, the plaintiff, Sayre & Toso, attempted to cancel the policy of insurance on behalf of the plaintiff, Holland America Insurance Company, pursuant to a clause in the contract allowing Holland America Insurance Company to cancel upon thirty days written notice.

10. Sportservice, Inc., the principal creditor, filed a petition for injunctive relief against the cancellation, and, in that matter, this Court held that, while service had not been perfected, the automatic stay was statutory and applied to the cancellation of the insurance. Pursuant to the prior order of this Court, the plaintiffs have now filed this complaint for request to terminate the automatic stay.

11. The primary differences between the status of the insured property in 1979 and the present time are that in approximately October,

1979, the Illinois Racing Commission denied racing dates for the Spring and Summer of 1980 to the debtor, and the subsequent filing of this Chapter 11 on April 2, 1980.

12. No attempt was made to cancel the insurance policy because of the cancellation of racing dates until April 11, 1980.

13. The maintenance of insurance on the property is essential for the rehabilitation of the debtor and the protection of the creditors.

14. The evidence indicates that the real reason for the attempted cancellation of the insurance was the filing of the bankruptcy proceeding under Chapter 11.

The enactment of the Bankruptcy Code in 1978 greatly enlarged the scope and powers of the Bankruptcy Court. One of the expressed aims of Congress in enacting the Code was to give the Bankruptcy Court sufficient power to enable it to protect the rights of the parties in interest — the debtors and creditors — and, in the case of arrangements, to effect the rehabilitation of the debtor. To that end, Congress enacted [§§105, 362(a), 363(*l*), and 365(a)].

Each of these sections creates very broad powers and is applicable to a debtor under an arrangement as well as the Trustee-in-Bankruptcy. In the instant case, there is no question but that a policy of insurance, especially one in which the premium has been paid, is a valid and binding contract between the insurance company and the insured and would constitute an asset of the bankrupt estate. Furthermore, fire insurance is a necessary protection for both the debtor and its creditors. The cancellation of the insurance would certainly come within the provisions of the automatic stay under §362(a)(3). It is also property which could, within the meaning of §363, be used by the Trustee, and certainly paragraph (*l*) of §363 would be applicable to the cancellation provision in spite of the fact that the provision does not refer to insolvency or the financial condition of the debtor. This is especially true when, as in the instant case, it is quite obvious that the prime reason for the attempted cancellation of the insurance was the bankruptcy.

While the plaintiffs have asserted that their reason for the cancellation of the insurance was the vacancy of the building and the inadequacy of protection, there is, and was, no proof that there was a substantial change in that situation as a result of the bankruptcy. All of the things which the insurance company cited as being indicative of increased risk existed long before the attempted cancellation and the bankruptcy. In fact, a number of them existed and were known to the insurance company at the time of the creation of the original policy. The principal change subsequent to the inception of the policy was the loss of racing dates for the Spring and Summer of 1980, which occurred in October. This was many months before the actual filing of the bankruptcy, and consequently was, or should have been, known by the insurance company. In addition, since only a month remains on the insurance policy, should this Court allow the company to cancel its policy, the rebate and the premium would assuredly be minimal and would, accordingly, cause an increased cost to the debtor's estate in obtaining additional insurance. Therefore, even if additional insurance were available, there is no showing that it would be at a lesser price. It is, of course, understood and not contemplated by this Court that the insurance policy should or could be extended beyond its original term.

. . . In the Matter of R. S. Pinellas Motel Partnership, 2 B.R. 113, 5 BCD 1292, 1 C.B.C. 2nd 349 (Bkrtcy. M.D. Fla. 1979), supports the position of this Court that the new Bankruptcy Code is extremely broad in giving the Bankruptcy Court jurisdiction and broad powers over the contractual relations of a debtor in order to permit the debtor's rehabilitation.

Wherefore, it is ordered that the plaintiffs' petition for termination of the automatic stay be and the same is hereby denied.

NOTE ON *CAHOKIA DOWNS*

In considering a case such as *Cahokia Downs* and deciding whether the action involved in the case violates the policy behind the automatic stay, it may be useful to try to identify not only *what* happened, but *why* it happened.

Is there any reason why Cahokia Downs should have any greater rights to keep insurance in force in bankruptcy than outside? Considered in the abstract, the answer seems to be no. The court infers something similar in suggesting that the insurance company would have no obligation to renew. But if that is so, what is wrong with cancelling the policy pursuant to one of its terms? Holland America was fully paid. Had Holland America anything to gain, strategically, by cancellation? Could it have been responding to anything other than its perception that its risks had increased? Holland America, however, is not the only potentially interested party in the picture. Note that Logger Insurance Agency, the agent, prepaid the insurance premiums and, upon cancellation, would receive a rebate. In light of that, can you argue that the cancellation was like preference activity, designed to make Logger better off than it would be in bankruptcy? If the policy were not cancelled, Logger would be the holder of an unsecured claim. Under this view, the result in *Cahokia Downs* may fit directly into the rationale of the automatic stay, because Logger seems to be trying to opt out of the class of unsecured creditors. Can we be sure, however, that Holland America cancelled to benefit Logger? There may in fact have been an increased risk of fire, given that the race track is not being operated and the debtor may care less what happens to it. If it is responding simply to the added risk of fire, is there any bankruptcy reason not to allow it to cancel? Would holding otherwise force someone (in this case an insurance company) to provide something (insurance) to a debtor at a bargain price simply because it was in bankruptcy? See the discussion of In re

Garnas, infra page 489. But assuming that Holland America ordinarily could terminate if it was not opting out or helping some one else opt out, how do we identify which motive moved Holland America? How should we sort them out in deciding a case such as *Cahokia Downs?* It is a question of how to decide whether an action is legitimate when two plausible stories might be told. Should we presume violation of the automatic stay anytime there is at least the possibility of opt-out behavior, such as possibly was the case with Logger?

PROBLEMS

7.1 On January 1, Manufacturer sells Debtor a machine for $1,000, on an installment sale, and takes a purchase money security interest in that machine. On January 5, the machine is delivered to Debtor. On January 10, Debtor files a petition in bankruptcy. May Manufacturer file a financing statement (an action necessary to perfect its purchase money security interest)? See §§362(b)(3); 546(b); UCC §9-301(2), (3).

7.2 Some time ago, Debtor injured Bystander in an automobile accident. Bystander has been planning to bring a lawsuit. Yesterday, 30 days before the statute of limitations period expires, Debtor filed a petition in bankruptcy. May Bystander commence a lawsuit? See §108(c).

7.3 Debtor manufactures widgets, and has a contract to supply Retailer with 10,000 widgets, for delivery in five monthly installments of 2,000 widgets each. Retailer prepays. Debtor makes the first three deliveries in a timely fashion. The fourth delivery is not made. Prior to the time of the fifth delivery, Debtor files a petition in bankruptcy. The time for the fifth delivery passes. May Retailer take legal action against Debtor without violating the automatic stay? Would it matter if Debtor had made the fourth delivery, and so was only in default on the fifth? Does Debtor's obligation arise pre- or post-petition? See §§362(a)(1); 101(4); 549.

7.4 Bank held a mortgage on Debtor's property. On January 1, pursuant to a state foreclosure action, a foreclosure sale was held, and a deed issued to the purchaser. Under state law, the debtor has a 60-day period after the foreclosure sale to "redeem" the property by paying the purchaser the sale price. Debtor files for bankruptcy on February 1. Is the expiration of the statutory redemption period stayed by §362? Compare Johnson v. First Natl. Bank of Montevideo, 719 F.2d 270 (8th Cir. 1983) (§108(b) controls), with In re St. Amant, 41 Bankr. 156 (Bankr. D. Conn. 1984) (§362(a) controls).

7.5 Recall the facts of Problem 3.1. Can Bystander file a lawsuit against Debtor and seek damages based on Debtor's negligence? See §362(a)(1); cf. §323(b); 28 U.S.C. §959. If Bystander is allowed to file such a lawsuit and wins, may Bystander attach or execute on the property of the estate? See §362(a)(3), (a)(4). On property that Debtor acquires after the commencement of the bankruptcy proceeding? See §362(a)(5). See generally In re York, 13 Bankr. 757 (Bankr. D. Maine 1981).

7.6 Debtor acquires an exclusive right to market Franchisor's products in its geographic area. The franchise agreement provides that Franchisor has the right to terminate its relationship with Debtor and sell the franchise to someone else if Debtor defaults on his obligation to make monthly payments to Franchisor and fails to cure within a period specified in the contract. Franchisor's products become much more popular, making Debtor's franchise worth much more than he paid for it. Debtor proves a poor businessman, however, and in January, Debtor defaults and Franchisor exercises its right to terminate and reassign the franchise to Third Party. Two months later, Debtor files a bankruptcy petition. Trustee moves to set aside the cancellation of the franchise agreement as a voidable preference. He argues that the right to market Franchisor's products was a valuable intangible property right that, if not cancelled before bankruptcy, Debtor could have assumed and assigned under §365. (Assume, for the moment, that this latter assertion is true.) The effect of the "cancellation" of the exclusive marketing agreement was to transfer this property right from Debtor to Franchisor to Third Party. Franchisor was owed money by Debtor and was hence its creditor. The "cancellation" of the franchise took place on account of an antecedent debt within 90 days of the filing of the petition. The cancellation enabled Franchisor to receive more than if Debtor had been able to assume and assign the franchise in bankruptcy and forced Franchisor to stand in line with general creditors for what it was owed.

Is Trustee's argument sound? Has Franchisor engaged in a last-minute grab? Is cancellation of an executory contract a transfer of property in the same way a foreclosure on a debtor's equity of redemption is? Does it fit within the definition of §101(48)? The separate treatment of executory contracts and leases in §365 may suggest that the drafters thought there was a distinction between "property" and "executory contracts," so that the termination of the latter cannot be a "transfer." Can a sound distinction, however, be made between contract rights and property rights? For a case in which a court rejected the argument that cancellation of an executory contract was a transfer (in the context of a fraudulent conveyance attack), see In re Jermoo's, Inc., 38 Bankr. 197 (Bankr. W.D. Wis. 1984).

NOTE ON LIMITATIONS ON THE SCOPE OF THE AUTOMATIC STAY

Limitations on the scope of the automatic stay come from two sources. One is within §362 itself — the exceptions of subsection (b). A second set of potential restrictions come from other bodies of law, and may limit not only the scope of §362, but also the power of the bankruptcy judge under

§105. We start by examining §362(b), and, in particular, the scope of §362(b)(4), perhaps the most widely litigated of the exceptions.

PENN TERRA LTD. v. DEPARTMENT OF ENVIRONMENTAL RESOURCES
733 F.2d 267 (3d Cir. 1984)

GARTH, Circuit Judge.

This case demonstrates the difficulty encountered when two governmental policies — one federal and one state — come into arguable conflict. On the one hand, the federally created bankruptcy policy requires that the assets of a debtor be preserved and protected, so that in time they may be equitably distributed to all creditors without unfair preference. On the other hand, the environmental policies of the Commonwealth of Pennsylvania require those within its jurisdiction to preserve and protect natural resources and to rectify damage to the environment which they have caused. The potential conflict between these two policies is presented in this case, in which the Commonwealth has attempted to force a company which has petitioned in bankruptcy to correct violations of state antipollution laws, even though this action would have the effect of depleting assets which would otherwise be available to repay debts owed to general creditors. . . .

The facts in this case are largely undisputed. Penn Terra Limited was the operator of coal surface mines in Armstrong County in western Pennsylvania. The Commonwealth's Department of Environmental Resources (hereafter "DER") found that Penn Terra was operating its mines in violation of various state environmental protection statutes. In February 1981, DER served Penn Terra with a total of 36 citations, both against the corporation and against Harvey Taylor, the president of Penn Terra, for these violations. . . . Penn Terra apparently never contested that these violations existed. On November 9, 1981, DER and Mr. Taylor entered into a consent order and agreement to rectify these infractions and thus place Penn Terra in compliance with the state statutes. The consent agreement listed the violations, and established a schedule for corrective measures to be taken.[2] Penn Terra, however, apparently did not comply with that schedule.

---

2. As noted in the opinion of the bankruptcy court, In re Penn Terra Ltd., 24 B.R. 427 (Bkrtcy. W.D. Pa. 1982), the violations complained of by DER included: mining of a bonded area, failure to maintain adequate backfilling equipment, failure to maintain adequate erosion and sedimentation controls, failure to pump pitwater accumulations, failure to treat mine drainage properly, storage of top strata over gas lines, and failure to seal a deep mine pit. Id. at 430.

The consent agreement required Penn Terra to complete all backfilling by operating one D-8 bulldozer or its equivalent, and one tractor scraper for eight hours a day, five days a week until reclamation of the mines was completed. Penn Terra was also required to submit

On March 15, 1982, Penn Terra filed a Petition for Bankruptcy under Chapter 7 of the Bankruptcy Code, having previously ceased all operations. In its schedule of assets, Penn Terra listed total property worth $14,000. Of this, $13,500 was designated as "certificates of deposit with DER," which Penn Terra had furnished as bonds for the backfilling operation. The schedule further noted that the cost of reclamation, as required under the consent agreement, would greatly exceed the market and book value of those bonds. The total amount of debts listed was $660,000.

On April 14, 1982, DER brought an equitable action in the Commonwealth Court of Pennsylvania, seeking a preliminary injunction against Penn Terra and Harvey Taylor to correct the violation of the state statutes and to enforce the terms of the consent order. DER apparently did not receive a notice of Penn Terra's bankruptcy petition until April 29, 1982. A hearing was conducted on DER's application in Commonwealth Court on May 24, 1982, as previously scheduled; Harvey Taylor appeared but Penn Terra did not, nor did the Trustee. After taking testimony, The Commonwealth Court granted injunctive relief to DER.

On May 28, 1982, Penn Terra filed a Petition for Contempt in the bankruptcy court against DER and two of its attorneys, Patti J. Saunders and Diana J. Stares, for proceeding with the Commonwealth Court hearing. Penn Terra contended that this proceeding violated the automatic stay provision of 11 U.S.C. §362(a). DER responded that the proceedings and the resulting injunction fell within the exception to the automatic stay which exempts actions by governmental units performed pursuant to the police power of the government. 11 U.S.C. §§362(b)(4)-(5).

The bankruptcy court found that the actions by DER were, in its opinion, actions to enforce a money judgment, which do not fall within the exception to §362(a). The bankruptcy judge opined that, given the "obvious insolvency" of the debtor, DER's pursuit of its action in state court has resulted in the entry of a "meaningless order." Pursuant to that ruling, on June 29, 1982, the bankruptcy court preliminarily enjoined DER from enforcing the Commonwealth Court injunction. On November 4, 1982, the preliminary injunction was made permanent.

On appeal, the district court affirmed the bankruptcy court's injunction. The district court noted that

> [i]n the instant case, although the DER's action was ostensibly undertaken to enforce state environmental laws, the effect of the action, in light of the disparity between the costs and funds available to do the reclamation work,

---

soil erosion and sedimentation control plans, implement those plans upon approval by DER, remove water from all pits, restore and revegetate the original contour, seal a deep mine entry, submit plans for removal of top strata stored over a gas line, and implement these plans upon approval by DER. The agreement provided that failure to restore the mines within the timetable contained in the agreement would require Penn Terra to rebond the entire area. Id.

was to collect a money judgment against Penn Terra; the purpose was not only to enforce a regulation, but to exhaust the debtor's assets.

. . . Appeal to this court ensued. DER argues that the courts below misconstrued the Bankruptcy Code's automatic stay provision by applying it to the Commonwealth of Pennsylvania, and thus it was error to issue an injunction forbidding DER from enforcing the order obtained from the Commonwealth Court. . . .

The crux of this case depends on an interpretation of 11 U.S.C. §362. . . .

The general policy behind this section is to grant complete, immediate, albeit temporary relief to the debtor from creditors, and also to prevent dissipation of the debtor's assets before orderly distribution to creditors can be effected. Indeed, this relief is available even against those claims which in the end are found to be secured and therefore payable in full. Penn Terra claims that this section operates to remove from the Commonwealth the power to enforce its antipollution laws while the automatic stay is in effect.

The statute does clearly intend to limit State action at least to some extent. Section 362(a) provides that the automatic stay shall operate against "all entities." The legislative history is clear that, in general, this was intended to extend to governmental entities as well as private ones:

> With respect to stays issued under other powers, or the application of the automatic stay, to government actions, this section and the other sections mentioned are intended to be an express waiver of sovereign immunity of the Federal Government, *and an assertion of the bankruptcy power over State governments under the supremacy clause notwithstanding a State's sovereign immunity.*

S. Rep. No. 95-989, 95th Cong., 2d Sess. 51, reprinted in 1978 U.S. Code Cong. & Ad. News 5787, 5837; H. Rep. No. 95-595, 95th Cong., 2d Sess. 342, reprinted in 1978 U.S. Code Cong. & Ad. News 5963, 6299 (emphasis added). Indeed, the fact that Congress created an exception to the automatic stay for certain actions by governmental units itself implies that such units are otherwise affected by the stay.

Subsections 362(b)(4) and (5), however, return to the States with one hand some of what was taken away by the other. The purpose of this exception is also explained in the legislative history of the Code:

> Paragraph (4) excepts commencement or continuation of actions and proceedings by governmental units to enforce police or regulatory powers. *Thus, where a government unit is suing a debtor to prevent or stop violation of fraud, environmental protection,* consumer protection, safety, or similar police or regulatory laws, or attempting to fix damages for violation of such law, the action or proceeding is not stayed under the automatic stay.

S. Rep. No. 95-989 at 52, 1978 U.S. Code Cong. & Ad. News at 5787, 5838; H. Rep. No. 95-595 at 343, 1978 U.S. Code Cong. & Ad. News at 6299 (emphasis added).

Subsection 362(b)(5), however, creates a further "exception to the exception," in that actions to enforce money judgments *are* affected by the automatic stay, even if they otherwise were in furtherance of the State's police powers. As the legislative history explains:

> Paragraph (5) makes clear that the exception extends to permit an injunction and enforcement of an injunction, and to permit the entry of a money judgment, but does not extend to permit enforcement of a money judgment. Since the assets of the debtor are in the possession and control of the bankruptcy court, and since they constitute a fund out of which all creditors are entitled to share, enforcement by a government unit of a money judgment would give it preferential treatment to the detriment of all other creditors.

S. Rep. No. 95-989 at 52, 1978 U.S. Code Cong. & Ad. News at 5787, 5838; H. Rep. No. 95-595 at 343, 1978 U.S. Code Cong. & Ad. News at 6299.

Our task is to determine: (1) whether DER's actions come within the police or regulatory power of the state; if so, then it must further be determined (2) whether DER's actions are an attempt to enforce a money judgment. . . .

At its core, interpretation of section 362 involves questions of federal supremacy and pre-emption. It is undisputable that the Commonwealth is normally empowered to regulate the environment, in its role as protector of the public health and welfare, and thus may rightfully compel adherence to environmental standards. Penn Terra claims, however, that in this instance, the federal government has pre-empted that power through the Bankruptcy Code. . . .

Given the general rule that pre-emption is not favored, and the fact that, in restoring power to the States, Congress intentionally used such a broad term as "police and regulatory powers," we find that the exception to the automatic stay provision contained in subsections 362(b)(4)-(5) should itself be construed broadly, and no unnatural efforts be made to limit its scope. The police power of the several States embodies the main bulwark of protection by which they carry out their responsibilities to the People; its abrogation is therefore a serious matter. Congress should not be assumed, therefore, to have been miserly in its refund of that power to the States. Where important state law or general equitable principles protect some public interest, they should not be overridden by federal legislation unless they are inconsistent with explicit congressional intent such that the supremacy clause mandates their supersession. For the same policy reasons, the "exception to the exception" created by subsection

362(b)(5), rendering "enforcement of a money judgment" by a government unit susceptible to the automatic stay, should be construed *narrowly* so as to leave to the States as much of their police power as a fair reading of the statute allows.

There is another reason, specific to this case, why the automatic stay provision should, whenever possible, be read in favor of the States. Concededly, in some individual situations, the exercise of State power, even for the protection of the public health and safety, may run so contrary to the policy of the Bankruptcy Code that it should not be permitted. The statute provides for such exigencies, however. The bankruptcy court, in its discretion, may issue an appropriate injunction, even if the automatic stay is not operative. 11 U.S.C. §105. Congress explicitly took note of this provision when it excepted government regulation from the automatic stay:

> Subsection (b) lists seven exceptions to the automatic stay. The effect of an exception is not to make the action immune from injunction.
>
> The court has ample other powers to stay actions not covered by the automatic stay. Section 105, of the proposed title 11, derived from the Bankruptcy Act §2a(15), grants the power to issue orders necessary or appropriate to carry out the provisions of title 11. The district court and the bankruptcy court as its adjunct have all the traditional injunctive powers of a court of equity [statutory citations omitted]. Stays or injunctions issued under these other sections will not be automatic upon commencement of the case, but will be granted or issued under the usual rules for the issuance of injunctions. By excepting an act or action from the automatic stay, the bill simply requires that the trustee move the court into action, rather than requiring the stayed party to request relief from the stay. There are some actions, enumerated in the exceptions, that generally should not be stayed automatically upon commencement of the case, for reasons of either policy or practicality. Thus, the court will have to determine whether a particular action which may be harming the estate should be stayed.

S. Rep. No. 95-989 at 51, 1978 U.S. Code Cong. & Ad. News at 5787, 5837; H. Rep. No. 95-595 at 342, 1978 U.S. Code Cong. & Ad. News at 5963, 6298.

Therefore, little harm is done to congressional purpose in allowing some latitude in favor of State regulatory powers when interpreting §362(b), since if, in a particular case, that latitude results in an impermissible dilution of federal bankruptcy policy, then the bankruptcy court may always issue an injunction tailored to fit those circumstances. Such an injunction, however, would be based upon traditional equitable standards, and its propriety would also be reviewable on an abuse of discretion standard. The automatic stay, on the other hand, is not discretionary and must remain in effect unless and until the bankruptcy court later grants relief.

We find that the foregoing considerations favoring liberal construction of the exception to the automatic stay provisions found in subsections 365(b)(4)-(5) outweigh the contrary considerations, relied upon by Penn Terra and the bankruptcy court below, favoring a more restrictive construction.[6] . . .

Turning now to the specific issues in this case, it first is clear to us that the actions taken by DER in obtaining and attempting to enforce the Commonwealth Court's injunction falls squarely within Pennsylvania's police and regulatory powers. DER seeks to force Penn Terra to rectify harmful environmental hazards. No more obvious exercise of the State's power to protect the health, safety, and welfare of the public can be imagined. Indeed, both the Senate and the House committee reports on the Bankruptcy Reform Act explicitly acknowledge environmental protection as a part of the State's police power.[7] . . .

Having found that DER's actions constitute an exercise of the Commonwealth's police power, the dispositive issue in this case is whether the Commonwealth Court injunction ordering Penn Terra to perform reclamation work is in fact an attempt to enforce a money judgment. The Bankruptcy Court found that it was, as did the district court. Our analysis suggests otherwise. . . .

At least as a matter of form, it is clear to us that the proceeding initiated by DER in Commonwealth Court was not to enforce a money judgment. Indeed, it could not have resulted even in the mere entry of a money judgment. DER brought its action in equity to compel the performance of certain remedial acts by Penn Terra. It did not seek the payment of compensation to the Commonwealth's coffers, and the injunction actually issued by the Commonwealth Court did not direct such payment. This

6. We recognize that both Rep. Don Edwards, Chairman of the Subcommittee on Civil and Constitutional Rights of the House Judiciary Committee, and Senator Dennis DeConcini, Chairman of the Subcommittee on Improvements in the Judicial Machinery of the Senate Judiciary Committee remarked during the debates on the Bankruptcy Reform Act that "This section is intended to be given a narrow construction in order to permit governmental units to pursue actions to protect the public health and safety and not to apply to actions by a governmental unit to protect a pecuniary interest in the property of the debtor or property of the estate." 1978 U.S. Code Cong. & Ad. News at 6444-6445 (remarks of Rep. Edwards); 1978 U.S. Code Cong. & Ad. News at 6513 (remarks of Sen. DeConcini). Those remarks, however, do no more than state the very problem which we are required to resolve.

7. We also acknowledge that exercise of a State's police powers may, depending on the circumstances, take the form of an execution on a money judgment. For example, if a coal mining company conducted operations in violation of applicable surface reclamation laws, then the assessment and *collection* of a civil penalty to serve as a punishment and deterrence against future violations would be no less an exercise of the police power than if the State had ordered the company to cease operations entirely. See Surface Mining Control and Reclamation Act of 1977, 30 U.S.C. §§1201-1328 (Supp. II 1978) (imposing civil penalties against mine operators who violate provisions of Act). It is important to remember that §362(b)(5), which prohibits governmental units from enforcing money judgments while the automatic stay is in effect, does not *exclude* such enforcement by definition from the meaning of "police power," or imply that when a state seeks to execute a money judgment it is not acting for the public health, safety, or welfare. Section 362(b)(5) is merely an *exception* to the rule that the exercise of police power by a State is not affected by the automatic stay.

proceeding, therefore, could never have resulted in the adjudication of liability for a sum certain, an essential element of a money judgment. Since this action was in form and substance (see discussion infra), not one to obtain a money judgment, it follows that it could not be one to *enforce* the payment of such a judgment.

Penn Terra contends, however, that whatever the appearance in form of DER's suit may have been, it was in substance an action to obtain and enforce a money judgment, and therefore was affected by the automatic stay. We generally agree, of course, that the legislative intent behind subsection 362(b)(5) should not be defeated by artful pleading that depends on form rather than substance. We must therefore determine whether, although not facially resembling an enforcement of a money judgment, DER's action in Commonwealth Court sought to achieve in actuality what a money judgment was traditionally intended to accomplish and more. . . .

. . . [A]n important factor in identifying a proceeding as one to enforce a money judgment is whether the remedy would compensate for *past* wrongful acts resulting in injuries already suffered, or protect against potential *future* harm. Thus, it is unlikely that any action which seeks to prevent culpable conduct *in futuro* will, in normal course, manifest itself as an action for a money judgment, or one to enforce a money judgment. This is consistent with our earlier observations, since a traditional money judgment requires *liquidated* damages, i.e. a sum certain, and one cannot liquidate damages which have not yet been suffered due to conduct not yet committed. Nor can one calculate such a sum with any certainty. Indeed, the very nature of injunctive relief is that it addresses injuries which may not be compensated by money.

The bankruptcy court adopted a totally different functional definition of money judgment, however. In its opinion, it apparently reasoned that a money judgment is anything which costs money to enforce. The court stated:

> Although DER characterizes its action as a governmental action in the exercise of its police or regulatory powers, it seeks a mandatory injunction requiring the debtor's expenditure of funds for the correction of violations. This Court concludes that the mandatory injunction sought by DER requiring the expenditure of funds is in essence the attempted enforcement of a money judgment. As such, it is subject to the automatic stay by virtue of §362(b)(5).

In re Penn Terra Ltd., 24 B.R. 427, 432 (Bkrtcy. W.D. Pa. 1982). The court below drew support from In re Kovacs, 681 F.2d 454 (6th Cir. 1982), vacated and remanded,— U.S. —, 103 S. Ct. 810, 74 L. Ed. 2d 1010 (1983) *(Kovacs I)*. There, as here, the debtor had not complied with various environmental control laws. A state court had ordered him to cease pollution and remove hazardous wastes from the premises. When Kovacs did not comply, the state court appointed a receiver to take possession of the debtor's property and effect a clean-up of the site. The Court of Appeals for the Sixth Circuit found that such action amounted to enforcement of a money judgment and was therefore automatically stayed.

To the extent that it found that a state effort to force a debtor to clean up his waste was in essence a money judgment, *Kovacs* lends support to the bankruptcy court's position.[11] We find, however, that the definition of "money judgment" implied in *Kovacs* and adopted by the bankruptcy court is unduly broad. Were we to find that any order which requires the expenditure of money is a "money judgment," then the exception to section 362 for government police action, which should be construed broadly, would instead be narrowed into virtual nonexistence. Yet we cannot ignore the fundamental fact that, in contemporary times, almost everything costs something. An injunction which does not compel some expenditure or loss of monies may often be an effective nullity.[12]

It appears that, in defining the scope of the exception to the automatic stay, the Bankruptcy Court in this case placed too much weight on the value of preserving the corpus of the debtor's funds and estate under its own exclusive control. Admittedly, that goal is normally central to the statutory scheme of the Bankruptcy Code. As noted at the beginning of

---

11. The Sixth Circuit itself recognizes that the original *Kovacs I* opinion has no authoritative value, since it had been vacated by the Supreme Court. In re Kovacs, 717 F.2d 984, 987 (6th Cir. 1983) (on remand from Supreme Court), cert. granted sub nom. Ohio v. Kovacs,— U.S.—, 104 S. Ct. 1438, 79 L. Ed. 2d 759 (1984) *(Kovacs II)*. [The Supreme Court's opinion in *Kovacs* is reprinted below. See page 744 infra.] *Kovacs II* did not address the issue of a money judgment in the context of a §362 automatic stay. Because of the Supreme Court remand, the Sixth Circuit has not yet been afforded an opportunity to address that issue. See 711 F.2d at 987 n. 5. *Kovacs II* was concerned with whether Kovacs' obligation under the state court order met the statutory definitions of "claim or debt" as set forth in 11 U.S.C. § 101(4) & (11). The State of Ohio contended that the obligation did not qualify as a claim or debt and therefore was not dischargeable in bankruptcy. *Kovacs II* held that Ohio essentially was seeking to obtain a money payment from Kovacs and affirmed Kovacs' discharge. Thus, since different sections of the Bankruptcy Code are at issue which involve different policies and considerations, we are not prepared to declare that our decision is in conflict with *Kovacs II*. Nor are we prepared to predict that the Sixth Circuit, if confronted with the issue that is presented in this case, would hold that the Commonwealth was enforcing a money judgment by requiring compliance with an environmental injunction. We would disagree with such a result if it did so, for the reasons we have expressed in text.

12. The distinction between mandatory and prohibitory injunctions advanced by Penn Terra draws no support from the statute. Had Congress intended to restore to the States only the power to enforce prohibitory injunctions, it could have said so, yet no such distinctions are contained in the statute. Moreover, the distinction itself is misleading. Not all mandatory injunctions cost money to perform, and not all prohibitory injunctions are free from cost.

Moreover, it is sometimes difficult to distinguish between a mandatory injunction and a prohibitory one. An order requiring that Company X cease discharging pollutants into the river could be interpreted as a prohibitory injunction. It might also be perceived as a mandatory injunction because such an injunction would have the effect of forcing the Company to transport the wastes elsewhere. While the terms "mandatory" and "prohibitory" may, in general, be useful terms of art for some purposes, if they are to be used as definitional terms which limit the power of States, then they have little utility.

this opinion, however, in some instances this policy is in inexorable conflict with other, no less salutary, governmental goals. We believe that the resolution of this conflict is contained in the statute itself. In enacting the exceptions to section 362, Congress recognized that in some circumstances, bankruptcy policy must yield to higher priorities. Indeed, if the policy of preservation of the estate is to be invariably paramount, then one could not have exceptions to the rule. Since Congress did provide for exceptions, however, we may assume that the goal of preserving the debtor's estate is not always the dominant goal.

We believe that the inquiry is more properly focused on the nature of the injuries which the challenged remedy is intended to redress — including whether plaintiff seeks compensation for past damages or prevention of future harm — in order to reach the ultimate conclusion as to whether these injuries are traditionally rectified by a money judgment and its enforcement. Here, the Commonwealth Court injunction was, neither in form nor substance, the type of remedy traditionally associated with the conventional money judgment. It was not intended to provide compensation for past injuries. It was not reduceable to a sum certain. No monies were sought by the Commonwealth as a creditor or obligee. The Commonwealth was not seeking a traditional form of damages in tort or contract, and the mere payment of money, without more, even if it could be estimated, could not satisfy the Commonwealth Court's direction to complete the backfilling, to update erosion plans, to seal mine openings, to spread topsoil, and to implement plans for erosion and sedimentation control. Rather, the Commonwealth Court's injunction was meant to prevent future harm to, and to restore, the environment. Indeed, examining the state order, it is clear that erosion control, backfilling, and reseeding were additionally meant to preserve the soil conditions from further deterioration (as well as to rectify a safety hazard).

Absent some other clear indication that these proceedings, although appearing in the guise of a request for equitable relief, are actually aimed toward the enforcement of a money judgment, we decline to equate DER's actions, which are those of a governmental unit enforcing the Commonwealth's police power, with those affected by the automatic stay of Section 362(a). We therefore conclude that the suit brought by DER to compel Penn Terra to remedy environmental hazards was properly brought as an equitable action to prevent future harm, and did not constitute an action to enforce a money judgment. The automatic stay provision of 11 U.S.C. §362 is therefore inapplicable.[14] . . .

14. Given the record before us and the narrow issues addressed by the parties, we decline to speculate upon whether the bankruptcy court could have issued a discretionary injunction under 11 U.S.C. §105 for reasons other than the automatic stay. See In re Penn Terra, 24 B.R. at 433. . . .

NOTE ON TOXIC WASTES AND THE AUTOMATIC STAY

The time a bankruptcy proceeding consumes gives an individual creditor an opportunity to take actions that increase its chances of repayment at the expense of the other creditors. Sections 361 to 365 try to ensure that this doesn't happen. But it is very hard to draw up the right set of rules, given the corollary notion that debtors aren't supposed to get any special breaks concerning their ongoing operations while they are in bankruptcy.

This notion was seen in *Cahokia Downs*, but the problem is more basic. *Penn Terra* suggests the deeper issue: Is there any reason to give firms in bankruptcy a competitive advantage over firms outside of bankruptcy? Should firms in bankruptcy have to play by the same rules as everyone else? Allowing them to play by different rules would distort the decision on how to deploy the assets. If a firm were worth keeping intact only if it could play by different rules, its owners might be led to bankruptcy to keep it intact.

But what does it mean to say that a debtor must play by the same rules as everyone else? This notion is captured by §362(b)(4). That section roughly assures that filing a petition stays only the efforts of creditors to be repaid (and, as we will see later, of parties to a favorable contract from terminating it). It does not stay a government's enforcement of its police or regulatory powers. According to the legislative history:

> where a governmental unit is suing a debtor to prevent or stop violation of fraud, environmental protection, consumer protection, safety or similar police or regulatory laws, or attempting to fix damages for violation of such a law, the action or proceeding is not stayed under the automatic stay.

Having a rule such as §362(b)(4) is serious business. Complying with a variety of health and safety laws may require huge expenditures of funds and result in creditors receiving much less. Those creditors may include victims of fraud and pollution for which the debtor is responsible. The regulations themselves may be profoundly misguided. But these are not fundamentally bankruptcy problems. The best justification for a section such as §362(b)(4) therefore is probably not that the public's health and safety is an important goal that must be balanced against the need to rehabilitate a debtor. It may, instead, be preferable to consider §362(b)(4) as following naturally from the proposition that bankruptcy law is largely procedural and is not designed to change the value of substantive rights.

Consider this point in the following context. Imagine that Debtor runs a plant that emits a minute amount of sulfur dioxide. If Debtor shut down operations and liquidated the firm's assets, Debtor would be worth $100,000. If Debtor can continue running the plant, emitting the sulfur dioxide, it would be worth $150,000—assuming those harmed by the emissions have no effective way of suing Debtor. But the state environmental agency wants to force Debtor to put a $75,000 scrubber on the plant's smokestack. It threatens to go to an administrative judge and force Debtor to stop operating the plant if a scrubber is not installed. The existing creditors as a group, of course, would prefer to delay installation of the scrubber as long as possible (again assuming that those harmed by the sulfur dioxide have no effective way of suing Debtor). Enforcing the regulation will shut Debtor down, because the creditors would then be better off liquidating (where they can receive $100,000) than they would be installing the scrubber and operating (where they gain only $75,000 — the value of the firm ($150,000) minus the cost of the scrubber ($75,000)).

The effect of §362(b)(4) is that Debtor has a choice. It can either stay in business or close up shop. If Debtor wants to keep operating, it must use a scrubber, because everyone else whose plant emits sulfur dioxide has to do so. Whether a firm should remain intact depends in part on the legal rules that govern it. A legal rule may turn a profitable firm into an unprofitable one. In this case where scrubbers are required, Debtor's business as a going concern is worth less than if it is liquidated. That it might be worth twice as much in a different legal universe is completely irrelevant as a matter of *bankruptcy* law. The decision to force firms to install scrubbers or shut down is a choice the legislature has already made, and it has already accepted the possible consequences (fewer firms; cleaner air). In *this* legal universe, Debtor should liquidate.

But is this the case we encountered in *Penn Terra*? Penn Terra has already filed a Chapter 7 bankruptcy petition. It has ceased doing business, and all the trustee is trying to do is close up shop. The case does not involve a regulation affecting Penn Terra's future operations, because Penn Terra has no future. Instead, the state wants Penn Terra to take action to undo past wrongs. Isn't the state really acting like a pre-petition creditor? Shouldn't its actions therefore be stayed? In other words, can one argue that §362(b)(4) does not apply here, because what is at issue has nothing to do with forcing Penn Terra to play by the same rules as everyone else with respect to its ongoing activities, but rather has to do with requiring Penn Terra to pay for something it did in its pre-bankruptcy past? Isn't the state, therefore, a "creditor" holding a "claim"? Does what the state wants fit within the definition of "claim" in §101(4)? We will pursue that inquiry in *Kovacs*, infra page 744.

But even assuming that is so, it isn't necessarily the end of the matter. To say that Pennsylvania is a "creditor," subject in the first instance to the automatic stay, doesn't also mean that it must stand in line with other pre-petition unsecured creditors. There is still another way to view this case. One can argue that the injunction essentially operates as a limitation on Penn Terra's property rights, like the one we saw in Chicago Board of Trade v. Johnson, supra page 192. Under this view, whatever the effect of the automatic stay, the creditors are entitled to Penn Terra's property, but may not take or sell it unless they comply with the injunction. In order

380 Chapter 7. Preserving the Estate

to answer that, one needs to look at nonbankruptcy law. If, outside of bankruptcy, anyone who takes Penn Terra's property (whether by levy or by voluntary sale) must comply with this governmental order, then it seems to have the characteristics of a first priority lien. The trustee succeeds only to what Penn Terra has, and Penn Terra is not free to do anything until it complies with this injunction.

In re Quanta Resources, 739 F.2d 912 (3d Cir. 1984), *cert. granted,* 105 S. Ct.—(1985), provides a good illustration of this approach to the problem. In that case, the trustee asserted the power to abandon, under §554, a waste oil processing and storage facility that contained more than 500,000 gallons of waste oil and other chemicals, including at least 70,000 gallons contaminated with polychlorinated biphenyls (PCBs). The trustee asserted that the requisite expenditures to comply with numerous federal, state, and local laws governing the storage and disposal of PCBs would render the property a burden on the estate, and that the property would be of inconsequential or no value to the estate, thereby meeting the §554 tests for abandonment. New York asserted that abandonment of the property would itself violate state and local law, because it would, in effect, constitute disposal of hazardous wastes. The Third Circuit concluded that if trustees in bankruptcy were permitted to dispose of hazardous wastes under the cloak of the abandonment power, compliance with environmental protection laws would be transformed into governmental cleanup by default and that Congress could not have intended such a radical change in the nature of local and public health and safety regulation. A dissenting opinion criticized the majority opinion on the ground that it failed to reach the critical issue in the case, which was how the trustee could pay for the cost of the cleanup and how it would affect the relative rights of the creditors. The debtor was a corporation with limited liability. It would not be able to meet all of its obligations, regardless of what bankruptcy law said or did. The debtor could clean up the toxic wastes. It could pay off its creditors. It could do some of each. But it could not do everything in full.

Consider the following cases. Debtor has a large quantity of PCBs or other toxic chemicals. Debtor has $100,000 in assets other than chemicals and general creditors with claims of $200,000. The chemicals cannot be sold and it would cost $50,000 to dispose of them. The effect of the court's decision in *Quanta Resources* is that Debtor has an additional obligation of $50,000 by virtue of its ownership of the PCBs. Usually, we think of assets as having a positive or at worst a zero value. But if state law imposes obligations on the owner of certain property and forbids its abandonment without satisfying those obligations, the obligations may in fact be larger than the benefits of ownership. But how are the obligations that Debtor owes state or local governments different from the obligations that Debtor owes its conventional creditors? The obligation gives rise to a property right in Debtor's assets, but to assess the right of the government against others holding property rights, one must determine what priority right the government enjoys in Debtor's assets.

Assume that Debtor is obliged to spend $50,000 to clean up toxic wastes. How is that different from Debtor's obligation in tort to someone who has contracted cancer because of these toxic wastes? (This obligation does not enjoy any special priority.) Is the obligation to clean up toxic wastes like a lien that attaches to all of Debtor's assets? But if it is a lien, how does one measure the priority of it relative to, let us say, Article 9 security interests? It is one thing to say that Debtor has a legal obligation (i.e., to pay $50,000 to effect a clean-up) and quite another to determine how this obligation ranks relative to other obligations that Debtor has. Can the government in a case such as *Quanta Resources* make the argument that the holder of a security interest in the property succeeds to the debtor's obligation to clean up environmental wastes or does such a holder always have the right not to foreclose upon the property?

Do similar questions arise in other contexts? Are these considerations relevant in the following case?

DONOVAN v. TMC INDUSTRIES
20 Bankr. 997 (N.D. Ga. 1982)

Harold L. MURPHY, District Judge. . . .

I

TMC Industries, Ltd. (TMC) is a holding company whose assets include 80 percent of the stock of WWG Industries, Inc. (WWG). WWG is a manufacturer of carpet goods, doing business in Floyd and Gordon Counties, Georgia, and Hamilton County, Tennessee. Commercial Affiliates, Inc. (CAI), a wholly-owned subsidiary of TMC, is WWG's sales and distribution arm.

In February, 1982, Chemical Bank of New York (Chemical), WWG's primary source of credit since 1978, informed WWG that further funding of its operations was not forthcoming. The practical effect of this decision was to cause some WWG payroll checks not to be issued and others to be dishonored. On March 1, 1982, WWG filed a petition for reorganization under Chapter 11 of the Bankruptcy Code, 11 U.S.C. §§301 and 1101 et seq. . . . On March 11, 1982, the Bankruptcy Court approved debtor's application for authority to borrow additional money from Chemical for interim operations in exchange for an additional security interest in favor of Chemical.

Contemporaneous with these events, the Secretary of Labor applied to this Court for an injunction to restrain defendants TMC, WWG and CAI from violating certain provisions of the Fair Labor Standards Act (FLSA), 29 U.S.C. §201 et seq. On March 4, 1982, the Court denied the motion for a temporary restraining order because there was no showing that defendants intended to place the so-called "hot goods" in commerce.

On March 11, 1982, the Secretary filed an amended complaint and the Court heard evidence and argument of counsel on the motion for a preliminary injunction. In an Order issued March 12, 1982, the Court found that TMC, WWG and CAI constituted an enterprise within the meaning of §§3(r) and (s) of the FLSA. 29 U.S.C. §§203(r) and (s). Under authority of §17 of the FLSA (29 U.S.C. §217), the Court enjoined those defendants pursuant to §15(a)(1) of the FLSA (29 U.S.C. §215(a)(1)) from transporting, shipping or delivering any carpet produced by the employees of WWG who were employed in violation of §§6, 7, and 15(a)(2) of the FLSA (29 U.S.C. §§206, 207, and 215(a)(2)).[3]

The combined effect of the Order and bankruptcy proceedings was to cease all operations by WWG and CAI, except for some bookkeeping and inventory. There was no manufacturing or shipping of carpets, nor funds with which to compensate the WWG workers for regular and overtime work. The defendants, the Secretary, and counsel for the creditors' committee conferred, under the auspices of the Court, in an effort to iron out a settlement satisfactory to all concerned. When these talks failed, the Court entered an Order setting forth certain conditions which, if satisfied, would relieve the defendants from the constraints of the injunction and allow them to resume operations. . . .

---

3. 29 U.S.C. §206 provides in part:

(a) Every employer shall pay to each of his employees who in any workweek is engaged in commerce or in the production of goods for commerce, or is employed in an enterprise engaged in commerce or in the production of goods for commerce, wages at the following rates:

(1) not less than $2.65 an hour during the year beginning January 1, 1978, not less than $2.90 an hour during the year beginning January 1, 1979, not less than $3.10 an hour during the year beginning January 1, 1980, and not less than $3.35 an hour after December 31, 1980, except as otherwise provided in this section;

29 U.S.C. §207 provides in part:

(a)(1) Except as otherwise provided in this section, no employer shall employ any of his employees who in any workweek is engaged in commerce or in the production of goods for commerce for a workweek longer than forty hours, unless such employee receives compensation for his employment in excess of the hours above specified at a rate not less than one and one-half times the regular rate at which he is employed; and

29 U.S.C. §215(a)(2) provides:

(a) After the expiration of one hundred and twenty days from June 25, 1938, it shall be unlawful for any person—

(2) to violate any of the provisions of section 206 or section 207 of this title, or any of the provisions of any regulation or order of the Administrator issued under section 214 of this title.

Defendants' basic contention is that the initiation of bankruptcy proceedings prevented this Court from exercising authority to enjoin defendants' shipping of goods. They argue that prohibiting the "hot goods" from entering commerce is tantamount to requiring the payment of back wages and overtime compensation, as those payments to the employees would present the only way to have the injunction lifted. And that course would disrupt the priority scheme of the Bankruptcy Code. Accordingly, the automatic stay prescribed by 11 U.S.C. §362(a)(1) applies.

The Secretary contends that this is not an action to collect wages, but an action to prevent the tainted goods from entering the "channels of competition." The Secretary asks the Court to issue the injunction pursuant to the police and regulatory exception to the automatic stay. 11 U.S.C. §362(b)(4).

The Fair Labor Standards Act was originally enacted in 1938 as the cornerstone of President Roosevelt's effort to protect labor from substandard working conditions. The principal features of the Act establish minimum wages (§206) and maximum hours (§207), and prohibit oppressive child labor (§212). The Act prohibits the shipment or sale of any goods in the production of which any employee was employed in violation of §206 or §207 (§215(a)(1)). This Section also prohibits the violation of the minimum wage and maximum hour provisions (§215(a)(2)). The enforcement scheme is found in §216 and §217 of the Act. First, there is criminal exposure for violating §215 (§216(a)). Second, an action may be brought by individual employees to receive unpaid wages or overtime compensation (§216(b)), or by the Secretary on behalf of employees (§216(c)). An action brought under §216(b) or (c) is a damage action. Third, the Secretary may bring an action for injunctive relief (§217). The Secretary may seek to enjoin any activity proscribed by §215: that is, the sale or transport of goods manufactured by individuals who were not legally compensated (§215(a)(1)), or to restrain the withholding of unpaid wages or overtime compensation (§215(a)(2)).

It bears repeating: this is an action brought under §217 of the Act to enforce §215(a)(1). It is not an action for damages under §216(c); it is not an injunctive action under §217 to restrain the withholding of unpaid wages in violation of §215(a)(2). The Secretary only seeks a Court order enjoining the violation of §215(a)(1), the sale or transportation of goods in the production of which employees were employed in violation of §§206 or 207.

An injunction under §217 is "not to collect a debt but rather to redress a wrong being done to the public good." . . . Even aside from this conceptual underpinning of all §217 actions, this case does not even resemble an action to collect a debt: the complaint does not seek the recovery of any money.

The issue in this case can now be viewed in sharper focus. . . . The Bankruptcy Code generally prohibits the exercise of jurisdiction over the affairs of a debtor in any Court except the Bankruptcy Court. One exception protects the public interest by permitting the government to enforce its police or regulatory power in the appropriate forum. The Fair Labor Standards Act authorizes the Secretary to seek an injunction in U.S. District Court to restrain the shipment of tainted goods. The issue is whether this Court's exercise of jurisdiction over the FLSA suit is authorized by the (b)(4) exception to the automatic stay.

II

The purpose of the automatic stay is to facilitate the orderly administration of the debtor's estate. It provides "a 'defensive' weapon in the limited arsenal of a debtor against the phalanx of creditor efforts." In re Purdy, 16 B.R. 860, 867 (N.D. Gal. 1981).

> The automatic stay is one of the fundamental debtor protections provided by the bankruptcy laws. It gives the debtor a breathing spell from his creditors. It stops all collection efforts, all harassment, and all foreclosure actions. It permits the debtor to attempt a repayment or reorganization plan, or simply to be relieved of the financial pressures that drove him into bankruptcy.

S. Rep. 95-989, 95th Cong., 2nd Sess. 55. . . .

The exception to the automatic stay reflects a concern for the efficacy of the state and federal government's police and regulatory power. Congress concluded that the government's interest in the enforcement of these laws outweighed the debtor's interest in disentangling himself from sundry creditors. Additionally, it would be anomalous to permit the debtor to use the stay to shield his activities which violate state and federal laws.

> The Bankruptcy Court is not a haven for wrongdoers and the policy of the Code is to permit regulatory, police and criminal actions to proceed in spite of §362(a)(1) but to not permit a seizure of property without a bankruptcy Court order.

2 Collier ¶362.05[4] at 362-40 (15th ed. 1981). . . . While the stay is designed to stabilize the status of the assets, the (b)(4) exception permits the government to enforce its laws uniformly without regard to the debtor's position in the bankruptcy court. The legislative history highlights the function of (b)(4):

> Paragraph (4) excepts commencement or continuation of actions and proceedings by governmental units to enforce police or regulatory powers. Thus, where a governmental unit is suing a debtor to prevent or stop viola-

tion of fraud, environmental protection, consumer protection, safety, or similar police or regulatory laws, or attempting to fix damages for violation of such a law, the action or proceeding is not stayed under the automatic stay.

S. Rep. 95-989, 95th Cong., 2d Sess. 55 . . . ; H.R. Rep. No. 595, 95th Cong., 1st Sess. 343. . . . Section 362(b)(4) indicates that the stay under section 362(a)(1) does not apply to affect the commencement or continuation of an action or proceeding by a governmental unit to enforce the governmental unit's police or regulatory power. This Section is intended to be given a narrow construction in order to permit governmental units to pursue actions to protect the public health and safety and not to apply to actions by a governmental unit to protect a pecuniary interest in property of the debtor or property of the estate. Remarks of Rep. Don Edwards, 124 Cong. Rec. H11089 (1978) . . . ; Remarks of Sen. Dennis DeConcini, 124 Cong. Rec. S17406 (1978). . . .

III

Recent cases which have explored the contours of the (b)(4) exception emphasize the distinction between the government acting in its own pecuniary interest (or the pecuniary interest of a favored creditor), and the government acting to enforce police and regulatory laws.

A

Government authorities have been permitted to proceed with a variety of regulatory or police measures despite pendency of bankruptcy proceedings. Commodity Futures Trading Commission v. Incomco, Inc., 649 F.2d 128 (2nd Cir. 1981) (requiring CFTC access to debtor's books and records on trading activity); Securities and Exchange Commission v. First Financial Group of Texas, 645 F.2d 429 (5th Cir. 1981) (S.E.C. obtaining injunction to enjoin debtor's offer of securities; receiver appointed); Matter of Canarico Quarries, Inc., 466 F. Supp. 1333 (D.P.R. 1979) (stay inapplicable to action investigating environmental protection law violations by debtor); Matter of Alessi, 12 B.R. 96 (Bkrtcy. N.D. Ill. 1981) (denying debtor's application for license to race horses not violation of automatic stay); Colonial Tavern Inc. v. Byrne, 420 F. Supp. 44 (D. Mass. 1976) (suspending liquor license); In re Cousins Restaurants, Inc., 11 B.R. 521 (Bkrtcy. W.D.N.Y. 1981) (enforcing zoning ordinance requiring special permit for discos); In re Mansfield Tire and Rubber Co., 660 F.2d 1108 (6th Cir. 1981) (permitting Ohio workmen's compensation proceedings to continue).

Proceedings concerning the employer-employee relation also have been held to come within the (b)(4) exception. See In re D.M. Barber, Inc.,

13 B.R. 962 (Bkrtcy. N.D. Tex. 1981). In National Labor Relations Board v. Evans Plumbing Company, 639 F.2d 291 (5th Cir. 1981), the Fifth Circuit granted the petition for enforcement of the Board's decision ordering the reinstatement of two employees with back pay who were discriminatorily discharged by the debtor. The court concluded that the Board's action was undertaken to enforce the federal law regulating the relationship between employer and employee, i.e., an exercise of police or regulatory power. While the question of whether the Board could *enforce* the back pay award was left unresolved, the *Evans* decision left no doubt about the authority under §362(b)(4) to require employee reinstatement. . . .

B

In the last two years, a number of courts have enforced the stay against the government, holding that the governmental action was not in furtherance of police or regulatory powers, and thus, not sanctioned by (b)(4).

A Missouri statute authorizes the State to apply to state court for appointment as receiver of a bankrupt's grain warehouse. The State is then permitted to operate and liquidate the warehouse. The statute is designed to protect the interest of those who stored grain in the debtor's warehouse. In State of Missouri v. U. S. Bankruptcy Court, 647 F.2d 768 (8th Cir. 1981), the Court of Appeals held that the automatic stay prohibited the State from exercising this statutory power. The Court pointed out that the objective promoted by the statute was the pecuniary interest of the firms which stored grain in the warehouse, and not the public health or welfare; and the statute operated to sanction a direct and irreparable interference with the res under the control of the bankruptcy court. As will be discussed shortly, the injunctive relief granted by this Court was designed to promote public health and welfare, and did not interfere with the debtor's property to the extent that the State of Missouri threatened in the Eighth Circuit case. . . .

Similar considerations prompted the court in In re Dan Hixson Chevrolet Co., 12 B.R. 917 (Bkrtcy. N.D. Tex. 1981) to stay a state proceeding. The Texas Department of Motor Vehicles sought to terminate a dealer's license because of its failure to honor warranty claims and its fraudulent practices. However, a private party instigated the proceedings and . . . the state played a quasi-judicial role. The Court concluded that "where the administrative agency is acting in a quasi-judicial capacity seeking to adjudicate private rights rather than effectuate public policy as defined by regulatory law the (b)(4) exception is inapplicable." Id. at 921. Of course, in the case sub judice the Court is not concerned with the adjudication of private rights. Significantly, the Dan Hixson Chevrolet court distinguished NLRB v. Evans Plumbing Co., supra, noting that although an NLRB proceeding is initiated by an aggrieved party, the Board's adjudicative function is in fact designed to effectuate public policy. 12 B.R. at 922 n.8. The FLSA, like the National Labor Relations Act, does more than fix certain contract terms relating to wages and hours; the act reflects the concern of Congress for the health and safety of every worker in America, a legislative enactment spawned by public policy decisions of unmatched importance.

One other case involves the government's efforts to regulate the relationship between two private parties. In In re Jacobsmeyer, 13 B.R. 298 (Bkrtcy. W.D. Mo. 1981), the Missouri Department of Liquor Control attempted to enforce a state law which limited the amount of credit which a wholesaler could extend to a retailer. The object of the law was to inhibit wholesalers from controlling, through the extension of credit, the liquor retailers. In *Jacobsmeyer*, the retailer who had filed under Chapter XIII was indebted to the wholesaler in excess of the statutory limit. The State sought to enjoin the debtor from purchasing any additional liquor from that wholesaler, arguing that the injunction did not legally obligate the retailer to pay prepetition debts — at least, not in the sense of a money judgment. The retailer, however, insisted that to operate a liquor store he had to purchase beer from that particular wholesaler. The State law, in practical effect, barred the retailer from operating under the auspices of Chapter XIII until that prepetition debt was paid. The Court accepted the retailers argument and prohibited the State from enforcing the liquor law.

The *Jacobsmeyer* case is not easily reconcilable with the Court's holding in this case. In both cases, the State (or federal government) sought an injunction which would effectively preclude a viable reorganization plan. In both cases, the only avenue open to the debtor to dissolve the injunction was to pay a prepetition debt. Indeed, the injunction was granted solely because of the prepetition obligations. While the Court notes the similarity between the *Jacobsmeyer* case and this case, the Court is not persuaded by that bankruptcy court's reasoning in this context. First, there is a substantial difference between a state liquor law which regulates the relationship between retailers and wholesalers and the Fair Labor Standards Act. While there are surely important public welfare concerns which prompted the enactment of the state law, they certainly don't compare with the purposes underlying the FLSA. Second, the FLSA protects not only the employees but also the employer's competitors.

. . . The bankruptcy court could not ensure, in approving the reorganization plan, that this goal of the FLSA would be furthered.

Finally, in this case, it would be inaccurate to describe the means by which defendants could gain relief from the injunction as simply the payment of a prepetition debt. The FLSA imposes a statutory duty on the employer to pay his employees at least a minimum wage. The employer has violated a federal statute, it has not merely breached a private agreement, and it is the enforcement of the statute, not compliance with a private contract that concerns the Secretary.[4] . . .

IV

. . . Defendants' argument is not without force: the Bankruptcy Code has an elaborate priority scheme which is designed to protect the interests of the debtor as well as all creditors. The employees of the debtor have their place in that system. To entertain the Secretary's action is to disrupt this orderly scheme and propel the employees into a super-priority status. Furthermore, the employer argues, the injunction interferes with the debtor's assets, the property of the estate which should be under the exclusive control of the bankruptcy judge and not subject to the chaos generated by conflicting decisions of various forums.

This argument is alluring. However, it ignores the thrust of the (b)(4) exception which was intended to give the government a super-priority, not a priority to proceeds from the estate, but a priority in terms of having access to any proper court to enforce laws which promote public health and welfare. Whether the law is designed to prohibit fraud, prevent pollution, remove safety hazards, or insure domestic tranquility, the government is not stymied by the debtor's petition in the bankruptcy court. The Fair Labor Standards Act is just such a law. . . .

Compliance with the FLSA by one firm protects the workers of competitors. Violation of the minimum wage and overtime compensation provisions threatens the welfare of every worker in that firm as well as the workers in competing companies and related industries. The only means of reducing the impact of violations on an entire industry is to enjoin the shipment of tainted goods. . . .

The concern with the health and welfare for the American worker, and the need to reduce labor strife is at the core of the FLSA. To allow a petition in bankruptcy to preempt the relief available to the Secretary to protect the health and welfare of American workers is unimaginable.

It is important to note that this Court's first decision was to grant the injunction on March 12. Following that decision the attorneys for Chemical Bank, Defendants, and the Labor Department met continuously — at their offices and in chambers — to work out a compromise to permit Defendants to begin operations. The parties had tentatively agreed on a plan, but the agreement was aborted when representatives from an ad hoc

---

4. Thus, the tainted goods would be purged once the employer satisfied the requirements of §§206 and 207, the payment of the minimum wage. Although the parties never raised this matter at the hearings, *it would seem that the payment of the minimum wage, and not actual accrued wages is all that is necessary.* The Court has searched in vain for any authority for the Secretary to seek any more than the payment of the minimum wage and appropriate overtime compensation.

employee group objected. The Court's order of March 19, 1982 was based on the parties' tentative agreement. The conditions set out for lifting the stay should not be construed as a money judgment. Rather, the conditions represent an option available to the debtor to comply with the FLSA and thereby dissolve the injunction.

In order to cleanse the goods of WWG which were produced in violation of the FLSA from the taint resulting from that violation, provision must be made for certain payments to the Secretary. Although the sum required to remove the "taint" of such goods is measured by the unpaid wages[5] of the employees of WWG employed in the production of these goods, the sums provided for herein are not wages but are the sums required to remedy the FLSA violation.

NOTES

1. Joe DeLisi Fruit Co. (DeLisi) was a dealer in wholesale produce, licensed by the Department of Agriculture of the State of Minnesota. As part of the licensing requirements, the license applicant must post a surety bond or, in lieu thereof, a letter of credit, to assure performance of the duties prescribed by statute. DeLisi, to comply, posted an $8,000 letter of credit issued by Bank. One of the prescribed duties is to pay suppliers when due; a breach of that duty gives rise to a claim on the bond. When DeLisi defaulted against several suppliers (Suppliers), they notified the Commissioner of Agriculture. On January 7, 1981, DeLisi filed a petition in bankruptcy under Chapter 11. On March 20, the Commissioner issued an order for a hearing pursuant to the statute, to investigate Suppliers' charges. In re Joe DeLisi Fruit Co., 11 Bankr. 694 (Bankr. D. Minn. 1981), concluded that permitting the Commissioner's proceeding to continue would violate §362(a)(1) and was not protected by §362(b)(4):

> The action is against the debtor. The Department is correct that recovery will be from the letter of credit and not from property of the debtor, at least initially. The stay does more than prevent claims against assets of the debtor. It is to give the debtor a breathing period to organize his or her affairs and a period in which the debtor does not have to defend himself from creditors.
>
> The action by the Department requires that the debtor defend itself from the claims asserted by the Department and the Suppliers. It requires the expenditure of time and money when the debtor should be putting its financial structure in order. . . .
>
> The action by the Commissioner is not to restrain or punish any violation of the statute. It is not to determine licensing requirements or to collect damages from the debtor for violation. The State of Minnesota is not the

5. But see n.4 supra.

complainant. The action is by and for the benefit of the creditors of the debtor. Any recovery will be to their benefit. The statute which [prescribes] this procedure was enacted to provide "financial protection" for a certain class of individuals favored by the state. It was not done to protect the public health, welfare and safety.

2. In re Brada Miller Freight System, Inc., 8 Bankr. 62 (Bankr. N.D. Ala. 1980), concluded as follows:

> Congress evidently intended to vest the Bankruptcy Court with the jurisdiction to enforce rights granted under the National Labor Relations Act and to share the same collaterally with the National Labor Relations Board and other administrative proceedings, even to the point of enjoining or excluding proceedings before such administrative court processes and to the exclusion, in the discretion of the Bankruptcy Court, of the normal administrative processes before the Board.

Do you agree? (The court enjoined all parties "including the Local Unions, the National Labor Relations Board, former employees, present employees, and all creditors" from "in any way, interfering with the operation of the business and its normal flow of traffic.") Consider this injunction in light of In re Crowe & Associates, infra page 397. In considering *Brada Miller,* of what relevance is the following? Section 15 of the National Labor Relations Act, 29 U.S.C. §165, provides:

> Wherever the application of the provisions of section 272 of chapter 10 of the Act entitled "An act to establish a uniform system of bankruptcy throughout the United States," approved July 1, 1898, and Acts amendatory thereof and supplementary thereto (U.S.C. title 11, sec. 672), conflicts with the applicable provisions of this Act, this Act shall prevail: *Provided,* That in any situation where the provisions of this Act cannot be validly enforced, the provisions of such other Acts shall remain in full force and effect.

This section was not amended at the time of the passage of the Bankruptcy Code. What impact should it have? Consider, in this respect, the following excerpt from In re Shippers Interstate Service, 618 F.2d 9 (7th Cir. 1980):

> the fact that Congress did not provide in like manner for the National Labor Relations Act to take precedence over Chapter XI proceedings distinguishes cases which hold that the Labor Board matters are not stayed by Chapter X proceedings. It does not necessarily follow . . . that Board proceedings *are* stayed by Chapter XI proceedings. . . .
> On balance, we agree with [In re] Bel Air [Chateau Hospital, Inc., 611 F.2d 1248 (9th Cir. 1979)] that "[i]f regulatory proceedings threaten the assets of the estate, the decision to issue a stay can then be made on a discretionary basis." . . . But where, as here, it appears that the assets of

the estate are not threatened and the company is being reorganized rather than liquidated, . . . regulatory proceedings of the National Labor Relations Board are not [automatically stayed by the] provisions of [a] bankruptcy rule. This does not preclude imposition of a stay where a proper showing was made that the regulatory proceedings threatened the estate assets or that the bankruptcy or other proceedings would result in the liquidation of the company.

NLRB v. Evans Plumbing Co., 639 F.2d 291 (5th Cir. 1981), discussed in *Donovan,* relying solely on §362(b)(4), held that the NLRB was not subject to the automatic stay, since "the NLRB is a governmental unit" and the "action was undertaken to enforce the federal law regulating the relationship between employer and employee." However, "should it be necessary to enforce [a] judgment for back pay [issued by the NLRB], a different question would be presented," which question the Fifth Circuit left open.

PROBLEMS

7.7 Debtor sues Bank in state court and Bank counterclaims. Debtor wishes to take depositions of Bank's officers and otherwise prepare for trial. Debtor claims, however, that Bank cannot take depositions against its officers, or otherwise prepare itself for trial, as those actions would violate the automatic stay. Evaluate Debtor's position. See In re Bailey, 11 Bankr. 199 (Bankr. E.D. Va. 1981).

7.8 Barnette writes $37,000 worth of bad checks to Auto Auction for the purchase of automobiles. A month later, Barnette files a petition in bankruptcy. A month after that petition was filed, Barnette is indicted by a grand jury for theft by deception in violation of a state criminal statute. A mandatory provision of the statute would require restitution by Barnette to Auto Auction on conviction under the criminal statute, and the making of such restitution would be a condition of probation. Is this action within the scope of §362(b)(1)? May the state court criminal action be enjoined by §105 in any case? Compare Barnette v. Evans, 673 F.2d 1250 (11th Cir. 1982) with In re Reid, 9 Bankr. 830 (Bankr. M.D. Ala. 1981). Do cases such as *Donovan* or *Evans Plumbing* shed any light on how to resolve these cases? If the action is enjoinable, should the result change if the debtor is a corporation, and the criminal action for issuing fraudulent checks is against its president? The past president? See In re Herman Hassinger, Inc., 20 Bankr. 517 (Bankr. E.D. Pa. 1982) (old Act case).

7.9 *A* Corp. is suing *B* Corp. in a complicated securities fraud case. Debtor, a past president of *A* Corp., is called for a deposition by *B* Corp. Debtor has recently filed for bankruptcy. May Debtor refuse to attend the deposition on the ground that the automatic stay is designed to give him a "breathing spell" and allow him to focus his energies exclusively on the bankruptcy? Cf. In re Joe DeLisi Fruit Co., discussed supra.

7.10 Bank loaned money and took a mortgage on Debtor's house, in which Relative lives. Both Debtor and Relative signed the note. Debtor files for reorganization under Chapter 11. Bank wants to bring an action against Relative personally. Debtor argues that an action against Relative would put pressure on Debtor and ultimately might affect the bankruptcy. Is Bank's action against Relative stayed by §362? Could it be stayed under §105? See First Federal Savings & Loan Assn. v. Pettit, 12 Bankr. 147 (E.D. Ark. 1981). Does §1301, a provision that is applicable to Chapter 13 cases but not otherwise, have anything to say about this problem?

IN RE M. FRENVILLE CO.
744 F.2d 332 (3d Cir. 1984)

ADAMS, Circuit Judge. This is an appeal by Avellino & Bienes (A&B) from a ruling by the district court, affirming the judgment of the bankruptcy court, that A&B's action against M. Frenville Co., Inc. and Rudolf Frenville, Sr. was barred by the automatic stay provision of the Bankruptcy Reform Act of 1978 (the Code), 11 U.S.C. §362(a)(1) (1982). The critical issue is whether the automatic stay provision applies to cases in which the acts of the debtor occurred before the filing of the bankruptcy petition yet the cause of action stemming from those acts arose post-petition. For the reasons set forth, we reverse the district court's judgment.

I

The facts of this case are undisputed. A&B is a certified public accounting firm located in New York City. From 1977 to 1979 A&B was engaged by M. Frenville Co., Inc. as an independent auditor and accountant. As part of its duties, A&B prepared certified financial statements of the company for fiscal years 1978 and 1979.

In July 1980, creditors of Frenville filed an involuntary petition for bankruptcy against the company under chapter 7 of the Bankruptcy Reform Act of 1978, 11 U.S.C. §§701 et seq. (1982). In January, 1981, creditors also filed involuntary petitions under chapter 7 of the Code against two principals of the company: Rudolph Frenville, Sr. and Rudolph Frenville, Jr.[1]

The Chase Manhattan Bank, N.A., the Fidelity Bank, Fidelity International Bank and Girard International Bank (the banks) filed suit in the Supreme Court of New York on November 16, 1981 against A&B. The

1. M. Frenville Co., Inc. will be referred to as "Frenville." M. Frenville Co., Inc. and Rudolph Frenville, Sr. collectively will be referred to as the "Frenvilles." Rudolph Frenville, Jr., although involved in the bankruptcy proceedings, is not a party to A&B's proposed action.

complaint alleged that A&B negligently and recklessly prepared the Frenville financial statements, that the statements were false, and that because of their reliance on the statements, the banks had collectively suffered losses in excess of five million dollars.

As a result of the suit by the banks, A&B filed a complaint on January 10, 1983, in the Bankruptcy Court for the District of New Jersey, which was administering the Frenvilles' chapter 7 proceedings. In the bankruptcy court, A&B sought relief from the automatic stay provision of §362(a) in order to include the Frenvilles as third-party defendants in the New York state proceeding. The purpose of the third-party complaint was to obtain indemnification or contribution from the Frenvilles for any loss suffered by A&B as a result of the suit by the banks.

The bankruptcy judge held the automatic stay provision of §362(a) was applicable to A&B's suit because the Frenvilles' liability, if any, resulted from their pre-petition acts. Moreover, the bankruptcy judge refused to grant relief from the automatic stay as provided in §362(d) of the Code. The district court affirmed the bankruptcy judge's order that the automatic stay barred A&B's action for indemnification or contribution.

II

We must decide today whether the automatic stay of §362(a) of the Code is applicable when the debtor's acts which form the basis of a suit occurred pre-petition but the actual cause of action which is being instituted did not arise until after the filing of a bankruptcy petition. . . .

The automatic stay provision of §362(a) is one of the fundamental protections provided to a debtor by the Code. Congress' intent in enacting §362(a) is clear—it wanted to stop collection efforts for all antecedent debts. Congress intended that the debtor obtain a fresh start, free from the immediate financial pressures that caused the debtor to go into bankruptcy. . . .

Yet despite the broad reach of the automatic stay, it is not all encompassing. Section 362(b), for example, provides exemptions from the automatic stay. As a further restriction, the Code requires that the proceeding stayed "was or could have been commenced" before filing or that the proceeding was based on a claim that arose pre-petition. §362(a)(1). . . . Proceedings or claims arising post-petition are not subject to the automatic stay. . . .

Only proceedings that could have been commenced or claims that arose before the filing of the bankruptcy petitions are automatically stayed. It is undisputed that the Frenvilles' acts which ultimately led to A&B's suit for indemnification or contribution occurred in 1978 or 1979, well before the chapter 7 petitions were filed. Section 362(a)(1), however, refers to "proceedings" and "claims" against, not acts done by, the debtor.

Pre-petition acts by a debtor, by themselves, are not sufficient to cause the automatic stay to apply. In most cases, the claim or cause of action will arise simultaneously with the underlying act. But to the extent that the harm is separated from the underlying conduct, at least for purposes of §362(a), Congress has focused on the harm, rather than the act. . . . Thus, unless A&B could have proceeded with its suit before the bankruptcy petitions were filed in July, 1980,[4] or had a claim against the Frenvilles which arose before that date, the automatic stay is inapplicable.

The proceeding which A&B sought to institute was an action for indemnity or contribution in New York state court. According to New York law, a third-party complaint for contribution or indemnity may be commenced at the time the defendant (in the present case A&B) serves his answer in the suit brought by the plaintiff (here, the banks), but not before. . . . In the present situation, A&B could not bring a proceeding for indemnification or contribution until it filed its answer in the suit instituted by the banks on November 16, 1981, some fourteen months after the filing of the bankruptcy petitions. Consequently, A&B's suit cannot be stayed by the "proceeding" language of §362(a)(1).

The applicability of the automatic stay, therefore, depends on whether A&B's claim arose pre-petition. . . .

Congress intended the definition of a claim to be very broad; the legislative history states:

> The definition is any right to payment, whether or not reduced to judgment, liquidated, unliquidated, fixed, contingent, matured, unmatured, disputed, undisputed, legal, equitable, secured or unsecured. . . . By this broadest possible definition and by the use of the term throughout the title 11, especially in subchapter I of chapter 5, the bill contemplates that all legal obligations of the debtor, no matter how remote or contingent, will be able to be dealt with in the bankruptcy case. It permits the broadest possible relief in the bankruptcy court.[6]

At first glance, A&B might be thought to have had an unliquidated, contingent, unmatured and disputed claim pre-petition. While all of these adjectives may describe A&B's cause of action against the Frenvilles, the threshold requirement of a claim must first be met — there must be a "right to payment." §101(4)(A). . . .

Thus we must determine at what point A&B had a "right to payment" for its claim for indemnification or contribution. Of course, if A&B is found liable to the banks, it would have a right to payment from the

4. For convenience, we will refer to the earlier July 1980 petition against Frenville as the filing date for both petitions; nothing of consequence occurred between July 1980 and January 1981.

6. H.R. Rep. No. 595, 95th Cong., 2d Sess. 309, reprinted in 1978 U.S. Code Cong. & Ad. News 5963, 6266; see also S. Rep. No. 989, 95th Cong., 2d Sess. 21-22, reprinted in 1978 U.S. Code Cong. & Ad. News 5785, 5807-5808 (virtually identical statement).

Frenvilles (assuming liability for the moment), albeit a disputed and unliquidated one. The crucial issue, however, is when did A&B's right to payment arise, for the automatic stay provision applies only to claims that arise pre-petition. . . .

The present case is different from one involving an indemnity or surety contract. When parties agree in advance that one party will indemnify the other party in the event of a certain occurrence, there exists a right to payment, albeit contingent, upon the signing of the agreement. . . . Such a surety relationship is the classic case of a contingent right to payment under the Code — the right to payment exists as of the signing of the agreement, but it is dependent on the occurrence of a future event. . . . A&B, however, had no indemnity agreement with the Frenvilles. Accordingly, cases holding that a claim arises upon the signing of an indemnity agreement are inapposite.

We must ascertain when a right to payment for an indemnity or contribution claim arises where there is no specific agreement. Although "claim" is defined by §101(4), the Code does not define when a right to payment arises. Thus, while federal law controls which claims are cognizable under the Code, the threshold question of when a right to payment arises, absent overriding federal law, "is to be determined by reference to state law." Vanston Bondholders Protective Committee v. Green, 329 U.S. 156, 161 (1946). . . .

We look to New York law to ascertain at what point A&B's claim arose. For both separate actions and third-party complaints, a claim for contribution or indemnification does not accrue at the time of the commission of the underlying act, but rather at the time of the payment of the judgment flowing from the act. . . . Although such a claim does not mature until payment is made, the New York Civil Practice Code permits a defendant to institute a third-party claim against a party who may be liable to him for all or part of the plaintiff's claim after service of his answer. N.Y. Civ. Prac. Law §1007 (McKinney 1976). In circumstances similar to the present case, one court stated:

> Technically a claim for indemnity does not arise until the prime obligation to pay has been established. . . . Nevertheless, for the sake of fairness and judicial economy, [N.Y. Civ. Prac. Law §1007] allows third-party actions to be commenced in certain circumstances before they are technically ripe, so that all parties may establish their rights and liabilities in one action. . . . Moreover, there is no justification for permitting a claim of indemnity where the primary action which might be the source of the right to indemnity . . . is not even pending.

Burgundy Basin Inn v. Watkins Glen Grand Prix Corp., 51 A.D.2d 140, 379 N.Y.S.2d 873, 880 (1976 N.Y. App. Div.) (citations omitted).

In the case at bar, A&B had an unmatured, unliquidated, disputed claim when the banks brought suit against it in New York state court. Until the banks instituted suit, however, A&B did not have any claim or cause of action based on indemnity or contribution against the Frenvilles. Since the banks' suit began some fourteen months after the filing of the Frenvilles' involuntary chapter 7 proceedings, A&B's claim, as well as its cause of action, arose post-petition. Although arguably A&B may have had some claim at the time the Frenvilles gave it allegedly false information, it did not have a claim for indemnification or contribution until the banks filed their suit. Thus, by its very terms, the automatic stay provision of §362(a) is inapplicable to A&B's suit.

NOTE ON *FRENVILLE*

As the court in *Frenville* notes, "the Frenvilles' acts which ultimately led to A&B's suit for indemnification or contribution occurred in 1978 or 1979, well before the chapter 7 petitions were filed." Notwithstanding that conclusion, the court holds that the automatic stay provision of §362(a) is inapplicable to the suit by A&B. In part, the court reaches this result by holding that the liability in issue was not a "claim" as defined by §101(4) prior to the filing of the petitions in bankruptcy. Can anything but mischief come from this conclusion, however? You might want to recall at this point the Note on Bankruptcy and Contingent Tort Claims, supra page 750. If M. Frenville Co. were liquidating, its assets, as we will see in detail in Chapter 8 of this book, would be distributed to its "claimants," under §726. If A&B does not hold a pre-petition "claim," what does it have? To say that it is not the holder of a "claim," and hence not a "claimant," does not seem satisfactory, as that means that A&B would receive nothing in a bankruptcy liquidation of the company. On the other hand, it might be possible to say that the claim of A&B, because it arose post-petition, is a post-petition claim. But then, as we will also see in Chapter 8, it is almost certainly an administrative expense claim, entitled to be paid ahead of all pre-petition unsecured claimants in the Chapter 7 liquidation. Is there any reason you can think of why this claim should receive that sort of treatment? Is that any more satisfactory than a conclusion that it should receive nothing?

If not, has *Frenville* lost sight of the forest for the trees? What purpose is served in construing §362(a) — or, indeed, §101(4) — in the way it does? Does *Frenville* have a conception of what these sections are doing? If these sections are not attempting to sort out, as best as possible, those actions that arose out of the debtor's pre-bankruptcy past from those actions that arise after the debtor files for bankruptcy, what *are* they doing? We will return to this issue in examining *Kovacs*, infra page 744.

Are there other limits on the automatic stay or the judge's §105 power? Consider the following case, which deals with the effect of the Norris-LaGuardia Anti-Injunction Act, 29 U.S.C. §101 et seq., on the

scope of those sections. Does the opinion accurately mesh the policies
enunciated by the Bankruptcy Code and Norris-LaGuardia?

IN RE CROWE & ASSOCIATES
713 F.2d 211 (6th Cir. 1983)

Per Curiam.

The question presented by this appeal is whether the district court
properly dissolved the bankruptcy court's permanent injunction against
appellee Bricklayers and Masons Union's strike to collect pre-petition
pension payments. The bankruptcy court 16 B.R. 271, had held the strike
violated §362(a)(6) of the Bankruptcy Reform Act of 1978. We affirm the
district court's 20 B.R. 225, dissolution of the bankruptcy court's permanent injunction.

Plaintiff-appellant, Crowe & Associates, Inc. (Crowe) is a subcontractor on a construction project in Detroit, Michigan. Defendant-appellee,
Bricklayers and Masons Union Local No. 2 of Detroit, Michigan (Union) is
a union whose membership includes bricklayers employed by Crowe. On
September 23, 1981, Crowe filed a voluntary Chapter 11 petition for
relief under the reorganization provisions of the Bankruptcy Reform Act
of 1978. Before filing this petition, Crowe was delinquent in its payments
to various union employee benefit funds. The collective bargaining agreement between Crowe and the Union required payment of these funds.
That agreement specifically provided that the Union could strike if Crowe
failed to make the required payments. On the date it filed its Chapter 11
petition, Crowe owed the Union more than $36,000. The Union de-
manded immediate payment of the amount. Crowe did not make the
payments. The Union ordered its members to leave the job site. Crowe
filed a complaint in the bankruptcy court seeking to enjoin the strike.

Without a hearing, the bankruptcy court issued a permanent injunction against the strike, holding that the strike violated the automatic stay
provisions of the Bankruptcy Code, 11 U.S.C. §362(a)(6). The bankruptcy
court reasoned that the Norris-LaGuardia Act did not bar the issuance of
an injunction because (1) the dispute between Crowe and the Union was
not a labor dispute within the meaning of the Norris-LaGuardia Act, 29
U.S.C. §113(c); and (2) the Norris-LaGuardia Act bars injunctions against
legal strikes not illegal ones. The Union then appealed to the district court.
Judge DeMascio reversed, finding that the bankruptcy court lacked jurisdiction to enjoin the strike. Crowe now appeals from the decision of the
district court. The Union's threat to strike continues so the issue is not
moot.

On appeal, appellant argues that the bankruptcy court, in this case,
had jurisdiction to issue a permanent injunction against appellee's strike
because that strike did not arise from a "labor dispute." Section 4 of the

Norris-LaGuardia Act explicitly withdraws jurisdiction from all courts of
the United States which includes bankruptcy courts, to issue injunctions
against strikes "in any case involving or growing out of a labor dispute." 29
U.S.C. §104. The initial question on appeal, therefore, is whether the
dispute between Crowe and the Union is a "labor dispute" within the
meaning of Norris-LaGuardia.

Section 13(c) of the Act defines "labor dispute" as:

> [a]ny controversy concerning terms or conditions of employment, or con-
> cerning the association or representation of persons in negotiating, fixing,
> maintaining, changing, or seeking to arrange terms or conditions of employ-
> ment, regardless of whether or not the disputants stand in the proximate
> relation of employer and employee.

29 U.S.C. §113(c). In issuing the injunction, the bankruptcy court opined
that Crowe's payments into the employee benefit fund are "terms or
conditions of employment," but held that no "controversy" existed as
Crowe refused to pay its pre-petition debts only because the Bankruptcy
Code would prohibit such payments. The district court reversed, holding
that the relationship between Crowe and the Union amounted to a "controversy" within the scope of the Norris-LaGuardia Act.

On the issue of whether a labor dispute exists, we find that the district
court properly reversed the bankruptcy court. In In re Petrusch, 667 F.2d
297 (2d Cir. 1981), cert. denied, 456 U.S. 974, 102 S. Ct. 2238, 72 L. Ed.
2d 848 (1981), the Second Circuit squarely addressed this issue and decided that employee pension fund benefits constituted "the terms and
conditions of employment" within the meaning of the Norris-LaGuardia
Act. In Petrusch, the debtor in a Chapter 13 proceeding appealed an order
staying the bankruptcy court's injunction of labor union picketing. The
union picketed when the debtor failed to make fringe benefit payments to
the union's health, hospital, pension and retirement funds, pursuant to its
collective bargaining agreement. The Second Circuit found that because
the debtor was obligated by the terms of its collective bargaining agreement to make these payments, such payments were part of the "terms and
conditions of employment." The Union's concern with these "terms and
conditions of employment," therefore, gave rise to a "labor dispute"
within the Norris-LaGuardia Act.

Like the debtor in Petrusch, Crowe failed to make payments to the
employee pension fund. Those payments are a "term" of the collective
bargaining agreement between Crowe and the Union. The collective bargaining agreement embodies "terms and conditions of employment." The
strike controversy arising from those terms of employment, therefore, is a
"labor dispute" within the broad purposes of the Norris-LaGuardia Act,
29 U.S.C. §113(c). In Jacksonville Bulk Terminals v. ILA, 457 U.S. 702,
712, 102 S. Ct. 2673, 2681, 73 L. Ed. 2d 327, 337 (1982), the Supreme

Court stated that "The term labor dispute should be most broadly and liberally construed. The term 'labor dispute' comprehends disputes growing out of labor relations. . . . All such disputes seem to be clearly included." . . . In view of the specific holding in *Petrusch* and the broad purposes of the Norris-LaGuardia Act's anti-injunction provisions, the district court properly held that the controversy between Crowe and the Union is a "labor dispute."

Crowe argues that even if we find that the controversy between Crowe and the Union is a "labor dispute," the bankruptcy court properly enjoined this particular strike because the Union's activity is illegal and because the provisions of the Bankruptcy Code preclude Crowe from meeting the obligations of its collective bargaining agreement.

Section 362(a)(6) of the Bankruptcy Reform Act prohibits any "act to collect, assess, or recover a claim against the debtor that arose before the commencement of the case." The Union's strike in this case is such an "act" designed to collect a pre-commencement debt. Union activity is not among the exceptions to the automatic stay provision enumerated in §362(b). The Union's strike, therefore, is arguably an act violative of §362(a)(6) of the Bankruptcy Reform Act. The Supreme Court has held, however, that the "Norris-LaGuardia Act's ban on federal injunctions is not lifted because the conduct of the Union is unlawful under some other nonlabor statute." Telegraphers v. Chicago & N.W.R. Co., 362 U.S. 330, 80 S. Ct. 761, 4 L. Ed. 2d 774 (1960); citing, Brotherhood of Railroad Trainmen v. Chicago River, 353 U.S. 30, 77 S. Ct. 635, 1 L. Ed. 2d 622 (1957). As the district court concluded, the entire history of the Act suggests that activities must not be enjoined merely because they violate the antitrust laws. In *Telegraphers,* the Supreme Court warned that a holding "that mere unlawfulness under any law is enough to remove the strictures of the Norris-LaGuardia Act would require a modification or abandonment" of the declared congressional purpose and "would run counter to the mandate of the Act." 362 U.S. at 339, 80 S. Ct. at 766. . . .

Section 107(a) of that Act does allow injunctive relief where "unlawful acts have been threatened and will be committed unless restrained or have been committed and will be continued unless restrained." Crowe relies on the case of Scott v. Moore, 680 F.2d 979 (5th Cir. 1982), cert. granted,— U.S. —, 103 S. Ct. 442, 74 L. Ed. 2d 599 for the proposition that the bankruptcy court properly enjoined the Union's "unlawful" strike activity. *Scott,* however, only went so far as to enunciate the well-settled principle that the "anti-injunction provisions of the Norris-LaGuardia Act do not deprive the district court of jurisdiction to enjoin violence." 680 F.2d at 1004. There is no evidence that the Union in the case at bar engaged in violence. The Union's nonviolent strike activity cannot be enjoined merely because it is violative of the Bankruptcy Reform Act. We are unwilling to modify or abandon the declared congressional purpose of the anti-injunction provisions of the Norris-LaGuardia Act. . . .

Neither are we willing to find that the Bankruptcy Reform Act supersedes or provides an exception to those anti-injunction provisions. Crowe argues that the bankruptcy court has such jurisdiction to issue an injunction because Congress intended that the automatic stay provisions in the Bankruptcy Reform Act of 1978 would supersede the anti-injunction provisions of the Norris-LaGuardia Act. This Court must look to the legislative history of the Bankruptcy Reform Act to determine congressional intent. The purpose of the automatic stay is stated in the House Report for the Bankruptcy Reform Act, H.R. Rep. 95-595, 95th Cong., 2d Sess., 340, U.S. Code Cong. & Admin. News 1978, pp. 5787, 6295, 6297:

> The automatic stay is one of the fundamental debtor protections provided by the bankruptcy laws. It gives the debtor a breathing spell from his creditors. It stops all collection efforts, all harassment, and all foreclosure actions. It permits the debtor to attempt a repayment or reorganization plan, or simply to be relieved of the financial pressures that drove him into bankruptcy.
>
> The automatic stay also provides creditor protection. Without it, certain creditors would be able to pursue their own remedies against the debtor's property. Those who acted first would obtain payment of the claims in preference to and to the detriment of other creditors.

The Bankruptcy Reform Act's legislative history does not mention the Norris-LaGuardia Act. . . . The *Petrusch* court concluded that this silence was "self-evident proof that Congress never intended to supersede or transcend [Norris-LaGuardia], since we cannot believe that the Norris-LaGuardia Act was to be superseded sub silentio." 667 F.2d at 300.

We find the reasoning of *Petrusch* persuasive. Congress would not have silently decided to alter its anti-injunction policy. As the district court concluded, "it never occurred to Congress that a conflict could arise between §362(a)(6) and the Norris-LaGuardia Act." Congress' mere adoption of §362(a)(6) in 1978, therefore, does not provide sufficient evidence of a congressional intent to supersede the anti-injunction provisions.

Crowe argues that even if §362(a)(6) does not supersede the anti-injunction provisions, this Court should carve out a specific exception for acts prohibited by that section. In Boys Markets, Inc. v. Retail Clerks, Union Local 770, 398 U.S. 235, 90 S. Ct. 1583, 26 L. Ed. 2d 199 (1970), the Supreme Court held:

> That the unavailability of equitable relief in the arbitration context presents a serious impediment to the congressional policy of favoring the voluntary establishment of a mechanism for the peaceful resolution of labor disputes, that the core purpose of the Norris-LaGuardia Act is not sacrificed by the limited use of equitable remedies to further this important policy, and consequently that the Norris-LaGuardia Act does not bar the granting of injunctive relief in the circumstances of the instant case.

Boys Markets carves out a narrow exception to the anti-injunction provisions of Norris-LaGuardia for the situation in which a collective bargaining contract contains a mandatory grievance adjustment or arbitration procedure. Crowe contends that because the anti-injunction provisions of the Norris-LaGuardia Act are an impediment to the congressional policy of protecting bankrupt debtors from their creditors and because the injunction in this case does not sacrifice the core purpose of the Act, the Court should create another narrow exception for this case. As the *Boys Market* Court emphasized, however, the exception carved out in that case was confined to injunctions against strikes over arbitrable disputes, when an anti-strike provision and a mandatory arbitration clause exist in the parties' collective bargaining agreement. The Supreme Court, in *Jacksonville*,— U.S.—, 102 S. Ct. at 2678, reinforced the narrowness of *Boys Markets* and upheld the vitality of the anti-injunction provisions of the Norris-LaGuardia Act:

> This court has consistently given the anti-injunction provisions of the Norris-LaGuardia Act a broad interpretation, recognizing exceptions only in limited situations where necessary to accommodate the Act to specific federal legislation or paramount congressional policy.

Furthermore, this Circuit in Plain Dealer Publishing Co. v. Cleveland Type, Union No. 53, 520 F.2d 1220 (6th Cir. 1975) established that the:

> employer seeking an injunction has the burden of proving that he comes within the *Boys Market* doctrine. He must provide the Court with an evidentiary basis for making the findings required by that case requisite to the issuance of an injunction.

In order to meet its burden, Crowe must demonstrate that the "unions are in fact engaged in an unlawful work stoppage, that such work stoppage is over a grievance that the parties are contractually bound to arbitrate, and that the collective bargaining agreements contain no-strike clauses, express or implied, which afford a basis for an injunctive order." *Plain Dealer*, 520 F.2d at 1228. Crowe has not met the burden of the *Boys Markets* doctrine. Thus, we are unable to find that the Norris-LaGuardia Act permits injunctions of the Union's strike activity, that the Bankruptcy Reform Act of 1978 supersedes Norris-LaGuardia's anti-injunction provisions, or that a *Boys Markets* exception to those provisions is appropriate.

We recognize that this legal result casts upon Crowe inequities. Even if Crowe desired to make the delinquent payments, the bankruptcy court may not permit it to do so. Crowe might have to liquidate because of a strike concerning demands over which it has no control. But Crowe has no control over many economic forces which affect the outcome of its reorganization. Moreover, the strike is a legitimate weapon, designed to strip the employer of economic control. The labor laws recognize that a strike may drive an employer out of business. See, e.g., *Petrusch*, 667 F.2d at 297. The anti-injunction provisions of the Norris-LaGuardia Act were intended to protect workers in the exercise of organized economic power. In *Chicago River*, 353 U.S. at 39, 77 S. Ct. at 640, the Supreme Court stated that, in enacting Norris-LaGuardia:

> Congress acted to prevent injunctions of the federal courts from upsetting the natural interplay of the competing economic forces of labor and capital.

Mindful of this congressional policy and of the case law in this area, we hold that the district court properly dissolved the bankruptcy court's injunction against the Union's strike activity.

Accordingly, the judgment of the district court is affirmed.

NOTES

1. See Note, The Automatic Stay of the 1978 Bankruptcy Code Versus the Norris-LaGuardia Act: A Bankruptcy Court's Dilemma, 61 Tex. L. Rev. 321 (1982) (arguing that an injunction would be appropriate).

2. In re Tom Powell & Son, Inc., 22 Bankr. 657 (Bankr. W.D. Mo. 1982), offered the following analysis of *Petrusch* and the District Court opinion in *Crowe*. Is it convincing?

> Both In re Petrusch and *Crowe* are distinguishable from the case at bar on the narrow ground that court-ordered injunctions were issued in both, whereas here the question is the impact of a stay mandated by statute and effective upon filing even if the court does nothing. Other distinctions exist. While it is true that this is a labor dispute within the broad definition contained in the Norris-LaGuardia Act, it is also true that the strike was an "act to collect . . . a claim against the debtor that arose before the commencement of the case under this title." Further, the strike was intended to enforce rights growing out of express provisions of the collective bargaining agreement rather than to vindicate rights contained in the Act.
>
> Section 362(b) of the Code provides for exceptions to the automatic stay in situations where Congress balanced the policy underlying the stay against the continuation of certain kinds of procedures, such as a criminal prosecution. Few of those exceptions permit an action for the recovery of a pre-petition debt. None mention Norris-LaGuardia. It may well be that Congress simply did not consider the relationship between the two statutes. . . . Where the activity is intended to collect a debt arising out of contract as opposed to an effort to vindicate statutory rights, outright abdication of jurisdiction seems inappropriate. There should be a balancing of the policy considerations underlying the prohibitions against self-help and preferences contained in the Code against the anti-injunction provisions of the Norris-LaGuardia Act.

How much could the court have relied on its distinction between the case before it and *Petrusch* if it actually decided that the union had violated the automatic stay? Would it not then issue an injunction of some sort?

B.   RELIEF FROM THE AUTOMATIC STAY

The respective strengths of the competing interests in having the automatic stay continue and having it removed are covered in subsections (d) through (g) of §362. These subsections enunciate both a set of *procedures* and a dual set of *substantive* standards for seeking and obtaining relief from the automatic stay.

An action to remove the automatic stay is designed to be brought and heard quickly. See §362(e); see also Bankruptcy Rule 4001(b) ("The stay of any act against property of the estate under §362(a) of the Code expires 30 days after a final hearing is commenced pursuant to §362(e)(2) unless within that time the court denies the motion for relief from the stay"). Courts may, however, be able to circumvent these time restrictions through use of §105, see In re Martin Exploration Co., 731 F.2d 1210 (5th Cir. 1984). Section 362(f) provides for ex parte relief if there would otherwise be irreparable injury.

Section 362(d) sets forth the substantive standards for relief from the automatic stay: Relief (which may be absolute or conditional) *shall* be granted either "for cause, including the lack of adequate protection" or, with respect to actions against *property,* if "the debtor does not have an equity in such property" and if the "property is not necessary to an effective reorganization." Section 361, which provides "illustrations" of adequate protection, deserves careful attention as well. These substantive standards form the principal battleground for determining when the stay should be continued, continued conditionally, or lifted.

1.   *Property That Is Not Necessary for an Effective Reorganization*

Most cases involving relief from the automatic stay involve the issue of whether there is "adequate protection" of the interest in the property while the bankruptcy proceeding is pending. But lack of adequate protection is only one of two grounds specified in §362(d) for gaining relief from the stay. Although we shall spend most of our time on the concept of adequate protection, we start with a case that examines the scope of §362(d)(2). What does it mean to say that property is not necessary for an effective reorganization? Is the secured creditor entitled to relief from the stay as a matter of right any time it can show that the debtor has no equity in the property, unless the debtor is seeking to reorganize itself?

PROBLEMS

7.11 Debtor is a partnership that owns a large townhouse subdivision being developed in Marin County. Bank has a $10 million construction loan on the project. Some of the partners have also loaned the partnership $3 million, and have a second mortgage on the project. The development is worth $12 million. Is Bank entitled to relief from the automatic stay under §362(d)(2)? Compare Stewart v. Gurley, 745 F.2d 1194 (9th Cir. 1984) (debtor's "equity" focuses on residual value after all liens) with In re Certified Mortgage Corp., 25 Bankr. 662 (Bankr. M.D. Fla. 1982) (consider only challenging lien holder and those interests senior to it). What if the partnership is in Chapter 7, and wants to sell the property?

7.12 Bank holds a mortgage on Debtors' house. The mortgage secures a loan of $80,000. A second mortgage has a claim of $10,000. One of the Debtors uses the house as an office. Bank files an action in state court to foreclose on the mortgage. Shortly thereafter, Debtors file a petition in bankruptcy. Debtors propose to sell the house in the bankruptcy. Bank wants relief from the automatic stay to foreclose on the house. The house is worth at least $120,000. Should the court grant relief from the automatic stay? On what grounds? See In re Vincent, 7 Bankr. 866 (Bankr. M.D. Fla. 1980).

IN RE KOOPMANS
22 Bankr. 395 (Bankr. D. Utah 1982)

Ralph R. Mabey, Bankruptcy Judge.

This case asks when property is "necessary to an effective reorganization" under 11 U.S.C. Section 362(d)(2)(B).

Debtors filed a petition under Chapter 11 on February 18, 1981. Plaintiff Empire Enterprises, Inc. (Empire) brought this action for relief from the stay on October 27. The complaint alleged, among other things, that debtors have no equity in the property at issue and no "prospect of rehabilitation."

A preliminary evidentiary hearing was held November 25. The evidence showed that debtors are in the business of buying and managing real property. They own 14 homes which have been converted into apartments and rented. The homes are valued at $973,000. Total debt equals $484,504. Empire holds a lien for $41,000 on one of these homes worth

$60,000. Other debt, however, totalling $62,600, encumbers the home. Hence, debtors have no equity in the home.[2]

No evidence was presented concerning the rehabilitation of debtors. The home, however, earns $226 net income per month,[3] and if sold, would satisfy Empire and some of the junior debt. Moreover, this junior debt encumbers the other property. Reduction in this debt, therefore, would enlarge the equity in the other property.

By its complaint, Empire argued that the debtors have no equity in the home and no prospect of rehabilitation. Debtors have no equity in the home. And since they did not carry their burden of persuasion on the issue of rehabilitation, if this be the standard under Section 362(d)(2)(B), Empire would be entitled to relief from the stay. By resisting the complaint, however, debtors maintained that the standard is not whether they have a prospect of rehabilitation, but whether the property is "necessary to an effective reorganization." The court concurred with debtors and held that property may be "necessary to an effective reorganization" if it is necessary either to an effective rehabilitation or to an effective liquidation. Because the meaning of Section 362(d)(2)(B) is frequently debated in stay litigation in this district, the court files this explanatory opinion.

THE MEANING OF SECTION 362(d)(2)(B)

Section 362(d)(2) requires relief from the stay of an act against property when two conditions are met: (2)(A) "the debtor does not have an equity in such property" and (2)(B) "such property is not necessary to an effective reorganization."

Some courts, taking their cue from Collier, have construed subpart (2)(B) to require relief from the stay when there is no prospect of rehabilitation: "[N]ot every asset will be necessary for an *effective* reorganization. The reference to an 'effective' reorganization should require relief from the stay if there is no reasonable likelihood of reorganization due to creditor dissent or feasibility considerations." 2 Collier on Bankruptcy

---

2. There is a divergence of opinion over what constitutes "equity" within the meaning of Section 362(d)(2)(A). The statute refers to the equity of the debtor which suggests the difference between the value of the property and all encumbrances against it. This is the predominant view. . . . Some, however, see equity as the difference between the value of the property and the lien which is the subject of relief. . . . In this case, the junior lienors on the home have interests in other property of the estate. Through marshaling, this other property may satisfy the junior lienors. Whether these circumstances permit a finding of equity in the home was not argued by the parties and is not decided by the court.

3. The home has 7 apartments. At full occupancy it might generate $950 per month. The average income for September, October, and November was $765. Expenses include $309 to Empire, $200 for utilities, and $30 for maintenance. This means a monthly net income of $226. An officer of Empire testified that the annual net income was $5,000, which means a monthly net income of $416.

¶362.07[2] at 362-49– 362-50 (15th ed. 1981) (emphasis in original). See also id. ¶362.07[3] at 362-51.[4]

This construction, while plausible, may be questioned on several fronts. The language of subpart (2)(B) may bear faint resemblance to a rehabilitation test. The legislative history of subpart (2)(B) appears to reinforce this view, since the genesis and evolution of the statute may evince a concern with the need for property in the business or a plan, not with the rehabilitation of debtors. And while the language and history of subpart (2)(B) may not be conclusive, reading a rehabilitation test into the statute may be anomalous in light of other provisions of the Code.

THE LANGUAGE AND LEGISLATIVE HISTORY OF SECTION 362(d)(2)(B)

. . . Section 362(d)(2)(B) asks whether the property is necessary to an effective reorganization. This language, viewed alone or in tandem with subpart (2)(A), may be different from the rehabilitation test. The former is concerned with whether an asset may be instrumental in the continued operation or ultimate sale of the business. The latter is concerned with whether the business, viewed as a bundle of assets, liabilities, management, markets, and the economy at large, can stay alive. If the business rather than one house were the focus under subpart (2)(B), then net worth of the business rather than equity in the property might be considered under subpart (2)(A).[5] Instead, Section 362(d)(2) is satisfied when the business is under water (even when rehabilitation is hopeless) so long as there is equity in the house.[5a]

4. The leading case may be In the Matter of Terra Mar Associates, 3 B.R. 462 (Bkrtcy. D. Conn. 1980) which held that Section 362(d)(2)(B) required a showing "that there is a reasonable possibility of a successful reorganization within a reasonable time." Id. at 466. Noting that in single asset real estate cases the property may be essential, it nevertheless ruled that " '[i]ndispensability of the property to the debtor's survival and hope of rehabilitation is not enough . . . to justify continuation of the stay when rehabilitation is hopeless.' " Id. The "reasonable possibility" standard does not include a hope " 'that somewhere, someone will fund an arrangement or refinance the mortgage with the plaintiff. This is entirely too slim a reed upon which this court should exercise its discretion and keep the plaintiff at bay while the debtor continues to pray.' " Id. . . .

5. In this case, for example, the schedules show a net worth for the business, although there is no equity in the home.

5a. Under the Act, relief from stay was possible, even where property had equity, if there was no prospect of rehabilitation. See, e.g., In re Empire Steel Co., 228 F. Supp. 316 (D. Utah 1964). But relief from stay was denied, even where property had no equity, if there was a prospect of rehabilitation. See, e.g., In re Yale Express System, Inc., 384 F.2d 990 (2d Cir. 1967). Thus, under the Act, the rehabilitation test, as a criterion for relief from stay, was independent of the question of equity. . . . The necessity test, on the other hand, was associated with the question of equity. . . . It is improbable, in light of this background, that rehabilitation and equity rather than necessity and equity would be coupled in the Code.

Similarly, Section 362(d)(2)(B), by forbidding relief from stay where property has equity, overrules cases such as *Empire Steel* which held that a want of rehabilitation, even with equity, was dispositive. These circumstances are explained, in part, by the provisions for plans of liquidation, discussed below, but they also suggest that there is no place for a rehabilitation test in subpart (2)(B).

The term, "effective reorganization," may not transform subpart (2)(B) into a rehabilitation test. First, "effective" modifies "reorganization," which embraces rehabilitation and liquidation; property may be necessary either to an "effective" rehabilitation or to an "effective" liquidation. But courts which apply the rehabilitation test, because they look to the condition of the business rather than the need for an asset, will give relief from the stay where there is no prospect of rehabilitation, whether or not the asset is necessary for an effective liquidation. Under these circumstances, neither word, "necessary" or "reorganization," may be accorded the breadth intended by Congress.

Second, where Congress meant to employ a rehabilitation test, as in 11 U.S.C. Section 1112(b)(1), it knew how to say so. The negative implication may be that no similar meaning was attached to subpart (2)(B).

Third, the choice of words, "effective reorganization," may be explained by formulations of the necessity test under prior law. This was phrased as "the likely need of the property subject to the lien for a successful reorganization," Kennedy, "The Automatic Stay in Bankruptcy," 11 U. Mich. J.L. Ref. 175, 239 (1978), and whether "the withdrawal of the property by the secured party will materially affect the prospect of a successful arrangement or reorganization," Seidman, The Plight of The Secured Creditors in Chapter XI, 80 Com. L.J. 343, 347 (1975). Thus, the term "effective reorganization," may be a carryover of familiar verbiage employed with and merely incidental to the necessity test under the Act, which held that the property is necessary, because without it, there may be no reorganization.

Moreover, the necessity test, notwithstanding its use of the term, "effective reorganization," was distinct from the rehabilitation test. This distinction continues in subpart (2)(B), but with the modification, noted above, that "reorganization" has an expanded scope; it includes liquidation. Prior law used the rehabilitation test in addition to the necessity test; if they both had meant the same thing, one or the other would have been superfluous. Congress, by focusing on necessity rather than rehabilitation in subpart (2)(B), showed that it intended to recognize and perpetuate, rather than blur, this distinction. Indeed, now that reorganization may mean liquidation, necessity cannot be tied to rehabilitation alone. In light of this distinction, and the new scope for reorganization, it is improbable that the necessity language creates a rehabilitation test in subpart (2)(B).

The legislative history lends some support to this analysis. As proposed, Section 362(d) of H.R. 8200, 95th Cong., 1st Sess. (1977) and Section 362(d) of S. 2266, 95th Cong., 1st Sess. (1977) did not contain a necessity test. The former permitted relief for cause including a lack of adequate protection. The latter allowed relief where debtor had no equity in the property.

The necessity test was the brainchild of insurance industry representatives who testified at hearings on S. 2266. They believed "that the basic concept of Section 362(d) which authorizes the court to lift the automatic stay where the debtor has no equity in the property is sound," but "in order to permit reorganization to go forward *where the property is essential to an ongoing business,* an exception must be provided for such situation." Hearings on S. 2266 and H.R. 8200 Before the Subcomm. on Improvements in Judicial Machinery of the Sen. Comm. on the Judiciary, 95th Cong., 1st Sess. 856 (1977) (emphasis supplied). In their view, "[i]n the case of a piece of real property . . . which is the security for a real estate mortgage *and not part of a business* that should be reorganized for the benefit of all parties in interest, the stay should be lifted." Id. (Emphasis supplied.) They argued that "whatever changes are made to Section 362(d) . . . to accommodate to corporate reorganizations [sic] not affect the real estate mortgage transactions which warrants [sic] different treatment. This can be accomplished by providing in Section 362(d) that relief from the automatic stay is limited to a situation where the debtor has no equity in the property and the property is not necessary to an effective reorganization of the debtor, *and that property shall be deemed not necessary to the reorganization if it is real property on which no business is being conducted by the debtor other than the business of operating the real property and activities incidental thereto.*" Id. at 857. (Emphasis supplied.)

These proposals, including guidelines explaining "necessary to an effective reorganization," were added to Section 362(d), S. 2266, 95th Cong., 2d Sess. (1977) and were elucidated in the Senate Report: Section 362(d) is intended "to reach the single-asset apartment type cases which involve primarily tax-shelter investments and for which the bankruptcy laws have provided a too facile method to relay [sic] conditions, but not the operating shopping center and hotel cases where attempts at reorganization should be permitted." Sen. Rep. No. 95-989, 95th Cong., 2d Sess. 53 (1978), U.S. Code Cong. & Admin. News 1978, pp. 5787, 5839.[10]

As enacted, Section 362(d)(2) dropped the guidelines explaining "necessary to an effective reorganization," but floor leaders commented upon its purpose: Section 362(d)(2) "is intended to solve the problem of real property mortgage foreclosures of property where the bankruptcy

---

10. Section 362(d), as amended, and for purposes of the Senate Report, read as follows: "The court shall grant relief from the stay if the court finds that the debtor has no equity in the property subject to the stay and such property is not necessary to an effective reorganization of the debtor. For the purpose of this subsection (d), property is not necessary to an effective reorganization of the debtor if it is real property on which no business is being conducted by the debtor other than the business of operating the real property and activities incidental thereto. Where the debtor owns two or more properties for which an established business enterprise has been created for the purpose of managing and leasing such properties, however, the court may find that one or more of such properties are essential to the effective reorganization of such real estate management enterprise. Where a request is made to grant relief from the stay with respect to property not necessary to an effective reorganization of the debtor, and the court determines that the debtor has equity in the property, the court shall authorize or order the sale of the property pursuant to Section 363. The hearing of such motion shall take precedence over all matters except older matters of the same character."

petition is filed on the eve of foreclosure. The section is not intended to apply if the business of the debtor is managing or leasing real property, such as a hotel operation, even though the debtor has no equity if the property is necessary to an effective reorganization of the debtor." 124 Cong. Rec. H11,092-11,093 (daily ed., September 28, 1978).

Section 362(d)(2)(B), by its terms and in light of its history, contains a necessity not a rehabilitation test. Congress was concerned with the need for property, according to the type of property and its relation to the business. If lenders were correct in their conclusion that Chapter 11 is inappropriate for certain tax-sheltered, single-asset real estate projects, "[t]his limitation on stays, by its very nature, would not conflict with the goal of debtor rehabilitation." Senate Hearings, supra at 705.

THE REHABILITATION TEST AND OTHER PROVISIONS OF THE CODE

"Relief from the stay cannot be viewed in isolation from the reorganization process," including all remedies, such as dismissal, vouchsafed to creditors, and all options, such as liquidation, available to others under the Code. In re Alyucan Interstate Corp., 12 B.R. 803, 805-806 (Bkrtcy. D. Utah 1981). Congress, of course, was concerned with the circumstances, including a want of rehabilitation, which bear upon a stay of reclamation. It provided for this concern, however, not in Section 362(d)(2)(B), but in Section 1112(b)(1), while preserving the right of parties to propose a plan of liquidation under 11 U.S.C. Section 1123(b)(4).

. . . Sections 362(d)(2)(B) and 1112(b)(1) involve elements and procedures which are tailored to their own purposes. These elements, procedures, and purposes are distinct; their mixture, for example, by making determinations akin to dismissal in stay litigation, may do both theoretical and practical violence to the statutory scheme.

Under Section 362(d)(2)(B) relief is mandatory, whereas under Section 1112(b)(1) dismissal is discretionary, when certain conditions are met. This is because the standards for relief in subpart (2)(B) are definite and easily applied. There is either equity or not. The property is either necessary or not. As between the creditor and the estate there is a bright line for decision. The standards for dismissal, however, are indefinite and difficult to apply. Whether or not rehabilitation is "probable" or even "possible" may be imponderable. How much "delay" and "prejudice" are tolerable is a matter of degree. The "best interests" of creditors and the estate, for better or for worse, must be measured by the length of the chancellor's foot.

For these reasons, relief from stay hearings are held upon request, usually by a single creditor, often early in a case. The hearings are expedited and may be informal. The debtor has the burden of proof on all questions except for the existence of equity. The issues are confined to the creditor and his collateral; thus, notice to all parties in interest is unnecessary. Counterclaims, even those which seek to invalidate liens or reduce claims, and which may affect the value of the estate, are discouraged. Resolution must be swift.

Motions to dismiss, on the other hand, may be brought by any party. The hearings need not be accelerated and may be formal. The movant has the burden of proof. The issues are broad, involving the future of the estate, thus, notice to all or representative parties in interest is necessary. The presentation of views should be many-sided. Indeed, the trustee or creditor committees may investigate the business as a prelude to the hearing. Time and preparation commensurate with the relief sought are expected.

In short, the rehabilitation test must be applied with discretion, not compulsion. It is amenable to ultimate, complex issues such as dismissal, but not to interim, abbreviated contests over the stay. It is workable given the procedures of Section 1112(b)(1), but not of Section 362(d)(2)(B).[17]

17. A further reason for rejecting a rehabilitation test in Section 362(d)(2)(B) is that such a test is impracticable. When a debtor files a petition, he is on the verge of collapse. He may have suffered losses for months. Creditors are foreclosing. Financial aid is a mirage. The forecast required under the rehabilitation test extrapolates from the past. But does the past of any debtor suggest a propitious future? Thus the rule, *circulum in probando*, becomes a self-fulfilling prophecy.

The debtor needs an overhaul using the tools of reorganization. He files because executory contracts may be rejected. Liens may be avoided. Property may be sold. Liabilities may be reduced or the terms of payment altered. If mismanagement is the cause of failure, a trustee may be appointed. Meanwhile, debtor, the trustee, creditor committees, and other parties in interest are bargaining toward a plan. These activities and the times set for their accomplishment are at odds with the rehabilitation test. No one knows whether the debtor can survive until he has done what Chapter 11 affords him occasion to do: clean house and work out a plan. . . .

Creditors might answer that, whether a patient can survive is not known before surgery, but a skillful physician, with reasonable certainty, can diagnose a terminal illness. But business is not an exact science. The rehabilitation test "requires the court to speculate on the probable outcome of a complicated and uncertain process." Kennedy, "The Automatic Stay in Bankruptcy," 11 U. Mich. J.L. Ref. 175, 242 (1978).

Indeed, at several points in the legislative history, creditors questioned the ability of courts to forecast the outcome of cases. They insisted, for example, that Congress strike the concept of an administrative priority as a method of adequate protection on the grounds that "such protection is too uncertain to be meaningful," Sen. Rep. No. 95-989, 95th Cong., 2d Sess. 54 (1978), U.S. Code Cong. & Admin. News 1978, p. 5840, and "in every case there is uncertainty that the estate will have sufficient property to pay administrative expenses in full." 124 Cong. Rec. H11,092 (daily ed., September 28, 1978).

Creditors also insisted that the valuation of collateral be open-ended, that a finding of value for one purpose and at one stage not be binding for other purposes and in other phases of a case, and that mistakes in valuation be remedied with a superpriority. . . .

In short, creditors, aware of the perils of prognostication, and doubting the prescience of courts, were not satisfied with an administrative priority which might not materialize. Likewise aware that the exigencies of litigation and the vagaries of value further clouded this forecast, they insisted upon flexibility in valuation and a "fail-safe" superpriority. But this uncertainty is a double edged sword. Congress did not place the rights of creditors at the mercy of judicial speculation. But neither should the opportunities of others turn on crystal-gazing. . . .

[Footnote moved.— EDS.]

APPLICATION TO THIS PROCEEDING

For the most part, this opinion has discussed what Section 362(d)(B) does not mean. It does not embrace a rehabilitation test. But since most authorities have analyzed subpart (2)(B) according to a rehabilitation test, few have articulated criteria for a necessity test.

A simple, workable test, which is faithful to the language of Section 362(d)(2)(B), and which implements the policy of maximum value for creditors is wanted. Accordingly, property in which the debtor has no equity is necessary to an effective reorganization whenever it is necessary, either in the operation of the business or in a plan, to further the interests of the estate through rehabilitation or liquidation. This test, in large measure, will turn upon the facts of each case. The property may be important to the liquidation of other property, as for example a warehouse or refrigerator which, although overencumbered, may be needed to store inventory or groceries pending sale. The property standing alone may have no equity, but when sold as a package, may bring a better price for other assets, as for example, workings for watches yet to be assembled, or contiguous parcels of real property. Or the property may be sold for the direct benefit of junior lienors and the indirect benefit of unsecured creditors. Indeed, it may have no equity but may deserve the protection of the stay because, in order to continue operations, its value has been appropriated to supply adequate protection for others or pledged to secure postpetition credit.

While further definition must await future cases, the home in this case is necessary to an effective reorganization. It has a net income. These earnings, by servicing the debt or reducing the lien to Empire, may create an equity in the home. They are available to satisfy obligations and build equities in the other property. The home may be sold or traded, alone or with other property, to the advantage of the estate. The home may be sold for the benefit of junior lienors, who therefore will not satisfy their claims from other property or the general fund; this leaves a proportionately larger equity for unsecured creditors and for debtors. On this analysis, the home is necessary to an effective reorganization, and notwithstanding the absence of equity, and leaving undecided the prospect of rehabilitation, relief from the stay is denied.

NOTE ON *KOOPMANS*

Central to the decision in *Koopmans* is the resolution of the question of what "necessary for an effective reorganization" should mean. Does it only apply to cases where a debtor is attempting to reorganize? Or should it also apply to any bankruptcy case, including one in liquidation, where the debtor can show that the assets are worth more if kept together than separate? Consider the following. Debtor is a computer firm. Among its assets, it has a number of government securities, with a market value of $80,000. These securities have been pledged to Finance Company, as security for a $100,000 loan that Finance Company has made to Debtor. Should Finance Company be able to gain relief from the automatic stay so as to exercise its default rights against these securities, on the ground that Debtor has no equity in the securities and they are not necessary for an effective reorganization? And can Finance Company make that argument whether Debtor is liquidating its business or attempting to reorganize? In a case such as this, isn't it the case that the government securities are worth no more in the hands of Debtor than they are in the hands of Finance Company? Given that, and assuming that Debtor has to provide Finance Company with $80,000 of present value adequate protection under §362(d)(1), which we will examine in connection with *American Mariner*, infra page 418, is there any reason even to get in a debate over what is and what is not adequate protection? Is there any reason not to let Finance Company sell the securities now? If so, what does this imply about how "necessary for an effective reorganization" should be construed? Is it consistent with the way Judge Mabey construed it in *Koopmans?* If not, should Debtor be able to require turnover of these securities under §542? We will consider §542 in connection with *Whiting Pools,* infra page 436. In *Whiting Pools,* as you will see, Justice Blackmun expressly reserves the question of whether his analysis would apply to a secured party in possession of marketable securities.

Consider, next, the case where Debtor has five sophisticated machines used in manufacturing. While the operations of these machines are related to one another, Debtor has granted a security interest in three of them to Commercial Credit and a security interest in two of them to Bank. Both of them move for relief from the automatic stay, and show convincingly that they are undersecured. Assuming that Debtor enjoys some going concern surplus with all five machines in place — that is to say that their value to Debtor together and working for Debtor exceeds their piecemeal liquidation value — this appears to be the classic case to which §362(d)(2) seems directed. But should it be applicable only if Debtor is seeking to reorganize itself? If the machines are indeed worth more together than apart, then it may be the case that, even if Debtor is liquidating itself, it would be best for Debtor to try to sell the five machines as a package to a new buyer, rather than piecemeal. If so, can Debtor argue that the machines are "necessary for an effective reorganization," in the sense that Debtor's other creditors are better off if Debtor sells the machines as a unit than if Bank and Commercial Credit are allowed to foreclose on the machines and sell them piecemeal? What is the implication of *Koopmans* on this issue?

In considering this issue, is there any reason Bank and Commercial Credit would want to seek relief from the automatic stay if the machines could fetch more money if sold together by Debtor? There are two reasons to think that Bank and Commercial Credit would want relief from the automatic stay under these circumstances. First, as we will see in examining §362(d)(1), the measure of protection Bank and Commercial Credit will receive if they are not permitted to foreclose on the collateral is almost certainly based on the value of the collateral as if they had foreclosed. Thus, Bank and Commercial Credit will gain nothing if they wait, even if the collateral fetches more sold as a package than separately. Second, if they are not permitted to foreclose, and are given a package of rights as "adequate protection" instead, there is a possibility that they will be undercompensated.

Now, consider *Koopmans* again. Does Judge Mabey convince you that his use of §362(d)(2) in connection with the facts of that case is proper? Is this a case where the units are worth more together than separately? Or is Judge Mabey saying that the assets, one by one, are worth more in the hands of Debtor than in the hands of the secured party? If the latter, is he convincing under these facts? In connection with this last question, note that Judge Mabey states that the home "earns $226 net income per month." If so, does this mean that the debtors have equity in the property? In footnote 3, however, the net income is calculated deducting only the mortgage to Empire, not to the junior debt that we are told also encumbers this property. Is that proper? In addition, in calculating that $226 net income, Judge Mabey has set aside a deduction of $30 for maintenance. Given that the time period is 1981-82, at least some skepticism should be evidenced as to the realism of a figure that sets aside only $30 a month for maintenance, although more would, of course, have to be known about the location and condition of the property—neither of which may be too good, given that the apartments apparently rent for less than $150 a month.

2.   Lack of Adequate Protection

Although, as we have just seen, it is not the exclusive way by which relief from the stay may be granted, "lack of adequate protection" under §362(d)(1) has been the focal point of most litigation under §362, and principally involves secured creditors trying to remove collateral from the bankruptcy proceeding so as to realize on it. The grounds a secured party may assert in seeking relief from the automatic stay are explored in §361 and the following legislative report.

S. REP. NO. 95-989
95th Cong., 2d Sess. 49, 53-54 (1978)

Sections 362, 363, and 364 require, in certain circumstances, that the court determine in noticed hearings whether the interest of a secured creditor or co-owner of property with the debtor is adequately protected in connection with the sale or use of property. The interests of which the court may provide protection in the ways described in this section include equitable as well as legal interests. For example, a right to enforce a pledge and a right to recover property delivered to a debtor under a consignment agreement or an agreement of sale or return are interests that may be entitled to protection. This section specifies means by which adequate protection may be provided but, to avoid placing the court in an administrative role, does not require the court to provide it. Instead, the trustee or debtor in possession or the creditor will provide or propose a protection method. If the party that is affected by the proposed action objects, the court will determine whether the protection provided is adequate. The purpose of this section is to illustrate means by which it may be provided and to define the limits of the concept.

The concept of adequate protection is derived from the fifth amendment protection of property interests as enunciated by the Supreme Court. See Wright v. Union Central Life Ins. Co., 311 U.S. 273 (1940); Louisville Joint Stock Land Bank v. Radford, 295 U.S. 555 (1935). . . .

. . . It is not, however, intended to be confined strictly to the constitutional requirement. This section and the concept of adequate protection are based as much on policy grounds as on constitutional grounds. Secured creditors should not be deprived of the benefit of their bargain. There may be situations in bankruptcy where giving a secured creditor an absolute right to his bargain may be impossible or seriously detrimental to the policy of the bankruptcy laws. Thus, this section recognizes the availability of alternate means of protecting a secured creditor's interest where such steps are a necessary part of the rehabilitative process. Though the creditor might not be able to retain his lien upon the specific collateral held at the time of filing, the purpose of the section is to insure that the secured creditor receives the value for which he bargained.

The section specifies two [three, as enacted] exclusive [sic] means of providing adequate protection, both of which may require an approximate determination of the value of the protected entity's interest in the property involved. The section does not specify how value is to be determined, nor does it specify when it is to be determined. These matters are left to case-by-case interpretation and development. In light of the restrictive approach of the section to the availability of means of providing adequate protection, this flexibility is important to permit the courts to adapt to varying circumstances and changing modes of financing.

Neither is it expected that the courts will construe the term value to mean, in every case, forced sale liquidation value or full going concern value. There is wide latitude between those two extremes although forced sale liquidation value will be a minimum.

In any particular case, especially a reorganization case, the determination of which entity should be entitled to the difference between the going concern value and the liquidation value must be based on equitable considerations arising from the facts of the case. Finally, the determination of value is binding only for the purposes of the specific hearing and is not to have a res judicata effect.

The first method of adequate protection outlined is the making of cash payments to compensate for the expected decrease in value of the opposing entity's interest. This provision is derived from In re Bermec Corporation, 445 F.2d 367 (2d Cir. 1971), though in that case it is not clear whether the payments offered were adequate to compensate the secured creditors for their loss. The use of periodic payments may be appropriate where, for example, the property in question is depreciating at a relatively fixed rate. The periodic payments would be to compensate for the depreciation and might, but need not necessarily, be in the same amount as payments due on the secured obligation.

The second method is the fixing of an additional or replacement lien on other property of the debtor to the extent of the decrease in value or actual consumption of the property involved. The purpose of this method is to provide the protected entity with an alternative means of realizing the value of the original property, if it should decline during the case, by granting an interest in additional property from whose value the entity may realize its loss. This is consistent with the view expressed in Wright v. Union Central Life Ins. Co., 311 U.S. 273 (1940), where the Court suggested that it was the value of the secured creditor's collateral, and not necessarily his rights in specific collateral, that was entitled to protection.

The section makes no provision for the granting of an administrative priority as a method of providing adequate protection to an entity as was suggested in In re Yale Express System, Inc., 384 F.2d 990 (2d Cir. 1967), because such protection is too uncertain to be meaningful.

The phrase "indubitable equivalent" in §361(d) is derived from an opinion by Judge Learned Hand. His opinion is worth examining in order to understand the concept of "adequate protection."

IN RE MUREL HOLDING CORP.
75 F.2d 941 (2d Cir. 1935)

L. HAND, Circuit Judge.

This appeal is from an order in bankruptcy denying a motion to vacate a stay of the prosecution of a suit in foreclosure in the state court; it arises upon the following facts: The Metropolitan Life Insurance Company held a mortgage upon an apartment house in the borough of Manhattan amounting to $400,500, owned as cotenants by the two corporations which are the petitioners herein. There was a second mortgage upon the same property, but for the purposes of this case it may be disregarded, for it was executed between the present co-owners and a company which holds all their stock. The mortgage being in default, the mortgagee filed a bill of foreclosure in the Supreme Court of New York on December 8th, 1934, and Leighton was appointed receiver of the rents. Immediately thereafter the owners filed petitions under section 77B of the Bankruptcy Act (11 USCA §207), and procured an ex parte stay against the foreclosure. The mortgagee and the receiver moved to vacate this on December 19th, 1934, and the judge denied their motion on January 16th, 1935. They appeal from this order. When the bill was filed the defaults on the mortgage amounted to nearly $100,000; about $20,000 of taxes and assessments, $43,000 of interest and $36,000 of amortization payments. The properties were assessed at $540,000, and the rentals came to $3,600 a month. On December 26, 1934, the debtors filed with the court a "plan of reorganization" . . . by which the second mortgagee was to provide $11,000, to be used by the debtors to alter the "line C" apartments in the building; this advance to have priority over all liens but the arrears of taxes and such new taxes as fell due during the nine months that the alterations were in progress. The debtors estimated that during this period there would be a slight deficit in interest and taxes, but that thereafter the "line C" apartments would be much more readily leasable. The expected rentals should then come to $59,346 and the expenses would be only $20,400, leaving a yearly surplus of $38,946. Against this there would be taxes of $14,280 and interest of $22,027.50, leaving a surplus of $2,638.50; enough to discharge existing arrears of taxes and leave about $3,000 at the end of ten years. In consideration of these expected benefits the mortgagee was to release the amortization payments ($9,000 per annum) and extend the due date; it was to receive its interest, 5½ percent, and all taxes were to be paid, both those in arrears and those to accrue. The mortgagee refused to consider this plan.

. . . The debtors' assumption is that under section 77B not only may a company effect a reorganization among its creditors, when two-thirds of each class consent, but that it may compel its unwilling creditors to accept a moratorium, though some of the classes refuse in toto. That was perhaps intended in subdivision (b)(5), 11 USCA §207(b)(5), but the power if it exists at all, is much hedged about. Normally it was expected that consents should be obtained. If they were not, the plan must "provide adequate protection for the realization by them," the dissenting class, "of the full value of their interest, claims, or liens". This may be done in four ways: (a) The liens may be merely kept in statu quo, the reorganization not going so deep down into the title, so to say, but being confined to the equity. That is not this case. (b) The property may be sold free and clear and the liens attach to the proceeds. This was a not uncommon course in bankruptcy when the court was in possession. Regardless of whether it may now apply to a case where it is not, nothing of the sort is here proposed. (c) The value of the liens may be appraised and paid, or, if the objectors prefer, the same

course might be taken with any new securities which shall be offered to them in reorganization. This again was not adopted here. (d) The last is not, properly speaking, a "method" at all; it merely gives power generally to the judge "equitably and fairly" to "provide such protection," that is, "adequate protection," when the other methods are not chosen. It is this alone which the debtors here invoke. In construing so vague a grant, we are to remember not only the underlying purposes of the section, but the constitutional limitations to which it must conform. It is plain that "adequate protection" must be completely compensatory; and that payment ten years hence is not generally the equivalent of payment now. Interest is indeed the common measure of the difference, but a creditor who fears the safety of his principal will scarcely be content with that; he wishes to get his money or at least the property. We see no reason to suppose that the statute was intended to deprive him of that in the interest of junior holders, unless by a substitute of the most indubitable equivalence.

[P]rima facie the creditor may go on to collect; if his hand is to be held up, the debtor must make a clear showing. The liens of the taxes and the first mortgage now are nearly $500,000 and the property is assessed for only $540,000; it has not been able to pay its way for several years. The amount to be advanced is a mere trifle compared with the debts; its effect is wholly speculative, based upon the expectations of those who have everything to gain and nothing to lose. The mortgagee is to be compelled to forego all amortization payments for ten years and take its chances as to the fate of its lien at the end of that period, though it is now secured by a margin of only ten per cent. It does not seem to us that this setting authorized any stay; it should appear that the plan proposed has better hope of success; full details may not be necessary, but there must be some reasonable assurance that a suitable substitute will be offered. No doubt less will be required to hold up the suit for a short time until the debtor shall have a chance to prepare; much depends upon how long he has had already, and upon how much more he demands. But a stay should never be the automatic result of the petition itself, and we cannot see that there was here anything else of substance.

Order reversed.

NOTE

Murel Holding did not involve a secured creditor's rights during the time the debtor was being reorganized, but his rights in the reorganized debtor after the bankruptcy proceeding. Does this make a difference?

In the following case, the Ninth Circuit concludes that the drafters of the Bankruptcy Code intended to protect the "opportunity cost" incurred

by senior creditors as a result of delays in the debtor's reorganization. Is it persuasive as a matter of statutory interpretation? As a matter of first principles?

IN RE AMERICAN MARINER INDUSTRIES
734 F.2d 426 (9th Cir. 1984)

JAMESON, Senior District Judge. . . .

The sole issue is whether an undersecured creditor who is stayed by a bankruptcy petition from repossessing its collateral is entitled, under the concept of "adequate protection", 11 U.S.C. §§361, 362, to compensation for the delay in enforcing its rights against the collateral. . . .

The facts are not disputed. In 1978 Crocker made a loan to American Mariner secured by a perfected security interest in "basically all of the American Mariner's assets." On December 12, 1980, American Mariner filed a petition for reorganization under Chapter 11 of the Bankruptcy Code. . . . At that time American Mariner's debt to Crocker, including accrued interest, was approximately $370,000, secured by collateral worth $110,000. Crocker filed a complaint for relief from or modification of the automatic stay under 11 U.S.C. §362(d)(1) on February 23, 1981. In its complaint, Crocker claimed inter alia that it was entitled to adequate protection under 11 U.S.C. §§361 and 362(d)(1) in the form of monthly payments equal to Crocker's prospective return from reinvestment of the liquidation value of the collateral. Crocker argues that state law grants the secured creditor the right, on the debtor's default, to take possession of the collateral, sell it, and loan the money out at interest. To the extent that the automatic stay delays or prohibits the creditor from exercising these rights, Crocker contends, the creditor is denied the present value of its interest in the collateral. Since section 361(3) requires such "adequate protection" as will provide the secured creditor with the "indubitable equivalent" of its interest in the collateral, Crocker concludes that it was entitled to monthly payment as compensation for what it might have earned on the reinvestment of its liquidated interest in the collateral.

The bankruptcy court rejected Crocker's contention that the value of its interest in the collateral was not adequately protected. For the purposes of section 362(d)(2), the court found: (1) the liquidation value of the collateral was $110,000; (2) the collateral was not depreciating[1]; and (3)

---

1. The bankruptcy court ordered American Mariner to pay Crocker $1,770 each month to protect against possible depreciation of the collateral. If it is later determined that the payments exceeded depreciation, the excess is to be applied to the principal of Crocker's allowed claim. The court arrived at the $1,770 figure by taking judicial notice that 18 percent, then the current prime interest rate, on $110,000, the collateral's liquidation value, yielded monthly payments of $1,770.

the collateral was "necessary for an effective reorganization." 10 B.R. at 712. In this appeal, Crocker does not contest the bankruptcy court's appraisal of the collateral nor its findings that the collateral is necessary for effective reorganization. . . .

Crocker appealed the adequate protection determination to the Bankruptcy Appellate Panel of the Ninth Circuit. The appellate panel majority similarly rejected Crocker's contentions. The majority recognized, however, that "[i]t is difficult to determine what Congress intended should constitute adequate protection in the context of the stay. . . . Apart from inferences to be sought from the use of the indubitable equivalent language, there is no expression of an intent to compensate the secured party for the delay. . . ." 27 Bankr. at 1009. While Crocker argued that the focus of protection was the value of *its interest* in the collateral, the majority concluded that "[a] construction more consistent with the language and policy to be served would recognize that it is the value of the collateral which is the focus of protection." 27 B.R. at 1010. Since the trial court had protected the collateral against depreciation, the majority affirmed the trial court's judgment as "consistent with the policy and language of §361(1)." . . .

Crocker's contention that the concept of adequate protection entitles it to interest on the present value of its collateral is principally founded on two sections of the Bankruptcy Code, 11 U.S.C. §§361, 362(d). Section 362(d) authorizes "a party in interest" to request relief from the automatic stay "for cause, including lack of adequate protection of an interest in property." Section 361 merely illustrates several means of providing adequate protection, and the methods illustrated are not exclusive. . . . Neither section, apparently by design, defines "adequate protection" or prescribes precisely what is to be protected. . . . Our inquiry begins with these threshold issues and requires us to construe sections 361 and 362. . . .

The central issue in this case is not how to provide adequate protection but what is to be protected. The bankruptcy court and bankruptcy panel concluded "that it is the value of the collateral which is the focus of protection." 27 B.R. at 1010. Crocker insists that section 361 protects the present value of *its interest* in collateral. . . . Contrary to the conclusion of the bankruptcy court, [§361] provides for adequate protection of "*an interest of an entity* in property . . . to the extent that the stay . . . results in a decrease in *the value of such entity's interest* in such property." (emphasis added). The plain meaning of this language must control unless we can point to convincing evidence that Congress intended something different by the words it chose. . . .

We find the legislative history of section 361 conflicting but not without significant support for the plain meaning of the statute. Both the House and Senate Reports clearly express the congressional intention to provide protection for the secured creditor's interest and not merely the value of the collateral:[4]

> The interests of which the court may provide protection in the ways described in this section [361] include equitable as well as legal interests. For example a right to redeem under a pledge or a right to recover property under a consignment are both interests that are entitled to protection.

H.R. Rep. No. 595 at 338; 1978 U.S. Code Cong. & Ad. News at 6294, 6295. Arguably the foregoing examples demonstrate some congressional concern for the safety of the property itself, but that concern does not diminish the general intention to protect a broad range of secured creditors' interests. As the appellate panel observed, the reports do not specifically mention the secured creditor's legal right to take possession of and sell the collateral; nor do the reports mention the creditor's equitable right to reinvest the proceeds of the sale. Unquestionably, however, these are valuable rights of secured creditors, and nothing in the reports suggests they are not among those equitable and legal interests entitled to protection.

The House Report emphasizes the breadth of adequate protection.

> It is not intended to be confined strictly to the constitutional protection required, however. The section, and the concept of adequate protection, is based as much on policy grounds as on constitutional grounds. Secured creditors should not be deprived of the benefit of their bargain. There may be situations in bankruptcy where giving a secured creditor an absolute right to his bargain may be impossible or seriously detrimental to the bankruptcy laws. Thus, this section recognizes the availability of alternate means of protecting a secured creditor's interest. Though the creditor might not receive his bargain in kind, the purpose of the section is to insure that the secured creditor receives in value essentially what he bargained for.

H.R. Rep. No. 595 at 339, 1978 U.S. Code Cong. & Ad. News at 6295. In this case it is clear that Crocker is *not* entitled to the "absolute right to his

---

4. Although the Senate version of section 361 proposed to protect "the value of such entity's interest in such property," the section was considerably more restrictive than the House version. . . . As a gloss on one of the two methods permitted by the Senate version for providing adequate protection, the Senate Report notes that the method was "consistent with the view expressed in Wright v. Union Central Life Ins. Co., 311 U.S. 273, 61 S. Ct. 196, 85 L. Ed. 184 (1940), where the Court suggested that it was the value of the secured creditor's collateral, and not necessarily his rights in specific collateral, that was entitled to protection." Id. Read in the context of the broad scope attributed to the term "value" in section 361 and the wide range of interests to be protected, we think the citation to *Wright* cannot be construed to limit adequate protection to the value of the collateral. Nonetheless, no such gloss appears in the House Report on its version of section 361, and its expansive approach to adequate protection was ultimately adopted by Congress. The only reference to *Wright* in the House Report is the observation that adequate protection under section 361 is not confined to the constitutional protection required in *Wright*. H.R. Rep. No. 595 at 339, 1978 U.S. Code Cong. & Ad. News at 6295. . . .

bargain," which is the right to take possession of and sell the collateral. The bankruptcy court's finding that the collateral is "necessary to an effective reorganization" made this impossible. Nonetheless, Congress seems to have recognized that the secured creditor's rights of repossession and sale are part of its "bargain," which section 361 insures it will receive at least "in value" if not "in kind".[5]

Value is another term intended to have broad scope in the context of providing adequate protection to secured creditors.

> The House Report stresses that the language of section 361 is directed toward "the value of the protected entity's interest in the property involved."
>
> The section does not specify how value is to be determined nor does it specify when it is to be determined. These matters are left to case-by-case interpretation and development. It is expected that the courts will apply the concept in light of facts of each case and general equitable principles.

H.R. Rep. No. 595 at 339, 1978 U.S. Code Cong. & Ad. News at 6295. In this case we are engaged in precisely the sort of case-by-case interpretation and development intended by Congress.

We recognize that a congressional directive for "case-by-case interpretation and development" must not be abused. Such judicial interpretation must not overlook the overriding purpose of the automatic stay, namely to give the debtor "a breathing spell from his creditors [to permit] the debtor to attempt a repayment or reorganization plan, or simply to be relieved of the financial pressures that drove him into bankruptcy." H.R. Rep. No. 595 at 340, 1978 U.S. Code Cong. & Ad. News at 6296-97. Nor can we ignore the purposes of business reorganization under Chapter 11 to initially relieve the debtor of its prepetition debts, to free cash flow to meet current operating expenses, and ultimately to permit the debtor "to restructure a business's finances so that it may continue to operate, provide its employees with jobs, pay its creditors, and produce a return for its stockholders." Id. at 220, 1978 U.S. Code Cong. & Ad. News at 6179.

At the same time, it seems clear that sections 361 and 362 include exceptional provisions specifically intended by Congress to benefit secured creditors at the expense of the debtor.[6] In addition to the substan-

---

5. "The Bankruptcy Code provides secured creditors various rights, including the right to adequate protection, and these rights replace the protection afforded by possession." United States v. Whiting Pools, Inc., 462 U.S. 198, 103 S. Ct. 2309, 2314-2315, 76 L. Ed. 2d 515 (1983).

6. Representative Edwards of California, a principal architect of the Bankruptcy Reform Act of 1978, observed that a major problem with the former bankruptcy process and an impetus to reform was "that creditors were not getting enough money out of bankruptcy proceedings to make it worth their while to participate in attempting to recover their money." Edwards admitted that

> [t]here is little we can do to make creditors participate when they do not want to, but we can protect their interests by more careful supervision of bankruptcy administra-

tive requirement of adequate protection, three procedural provisions of section 362 openly favor the interests of secured creditors over those of the debtor: (1) under 362(e) the stay terminates automatically (leaving the creditor free to proceed against the collateral) if a hearing is not held within 30 days; (2) 362(f) provides creditors with ex parte relief under limited circumstances; and (3) in all proceedings the debtor bears the burden of proving that the creditor's interest is adequately protected. We are convinced, therefore, that the case-by-case development, guided by equitable principles as Congress envisioned, must recognize and protect the *value* of a creditor's interest when, as here, that value is demonstrated to exist and is measurably threatened. . . .

The bankruptcy appellate panel concluded that adequate protection "is intended to provide a measure of protection against, rather than compensate for, risk." 27 B.R. at 1012. We disagree. Whether protection is adequate depends directly on how effectively it compensates the secured creditor for loss of value. Sections 361(1) and (2) by their own terms compensate for "a decrease in the value" of the secured creditor's interest. The compensatory nature of adequate protection is even more apparent from the catch-all alternative of section 361(3) authorizing "such other relief . . . as will result in the realization by such entity of the indubitable equivalent of such entity's interest in such property."

The history of 361(3) with the phrase "indubitable equivalent" lends significant support to the contention that section 361 protects the present value of the secured creditor's interest. Subsection (3) was the product of a compromise between the more restrictive Senate version of 361 and the expansive House version. . . . The Senate bill had specified two exclusive methods for providing adequate protection, . . . while the House bill contained four methods including a provision for an administrative expense priority and a general provision similar to the present subsection (3), but without the indubitable equivalent language. The compromise removed the administrative expense priority[7] and added the novel requirement of indubitable equivalence.

Since the original House language provided for "such other relief as will result in the realization by such entity of the value of such entity's interest in such property," we must determine whether Congress intended to change the meaning of the subsection by adding the phrase "indubitable

---

tion than exists today. That is part of the reason that we have proposed the United States trustee system . . . to supervise the people employed by the bankruptcy system to insure that it operates for the benefit of those whose money is involved — the creditors.

123 Cong. Rec. H. 11698 (daily ed. Oct. 27, 1977). To the extent that it provides the creditor with the benefit of his bargain, section 361 addresses what Congress perceived as one of the most serious shortcomings of the bankruptcy system.

7. Congress shifted the administrative expenses priority provision to 11 U.S.C. §507(b) as postfactum protection in the event adequate protection fails.

equivalent". After examining the origins of the phrase and its use else-where in the Bankruptcy Code, we conclude that it at least encourages if not requires a present value analysis under section 361.

As the bankruptcy court recognized, Congress derived the term "in-dubitable equivalent" from Judge Learned Hand's opinion in In re Murel Holding Corp., 75 F.2d 941 (2d Cir. 1935). . . .

In its context, Judge Hand's interpretation of adequate protection emphasizes two factors. First, it suggests that to be "completely compensa-tory" adequate protection must compensate for present value, "that pay-ment ten years hence is not generally the equivalent of payment now." This protection the owners of the apartment house provided in the form of interest. Second, adequate protection must insure the safety of the princi-pal. This the owners failed to do. Judge Hand concluded that the creditor's right "to get his money or at least the property" may be denied under a plan for reorganization only if the debtor provides "a substitute of the most indubitable equivalence." Such a substitute clearly must both com-pensate for present value and insure the safety of the principal. Signifi-cantly, however, Judge Hand added that "[n]o doubt less will be required to hold up the suit for a short time until the debtor shall have a chance to prepare." Id. at 943. This qualification, of course, reflects the absence under the former Bankruptcy Code of a statutory requirement for ade-quate protection during the stay, not to mention the absence of a require-ment for an automatic stay.

In the Bankruptcy Reform Act of 1978, "indubitable equivalent" first appeared in the Senate's version of section 1129(b), as part of the so-called cram down provisions similar to those encountered by Judge Hand. But for the use of "indubitable equivalent," it was not clear whether the section required present value compensation. In its final form, how-ever, 11 U.S.C. §1129(b)(2)(A)(i)(II) clearly requires deferred cash pay-ments under a reorganization plan to equal the present value of the allowed claim. The "indubitable equivalent" requirement appears in sec-tion 1129(b)(2)(A)(iii) as an alternative to deferred payments and carries with it, from its original context in *Murel*, the requirement of compensa-tion for present value. See 124 Cong. Rec. H. 1104 (daily ed. Sept. 28, 1978) (statement of Representative Edwards approving present value analysis at H.R. Rep. No. 595 at 414-415, 1978 U.S. Code Cong. & Ad. News at 6370-6371); S. Rep. No. 989 at 127, 1978 U.S. Code Cong. & Ad. News at 5913 ("The indubitable equivalent language is intended to follow the strict approach taken by Judge Learned Hand in In re Murel Holding Corp., 75 F.2d 941 (2d Cir. 1935)").

Against the foregoing background, we conclude that the use of the term "indubitable equivalent" in section 361 is significant of congres-sional intent. When the term was first employed by Judge Hand, the Bankruptcy Code did not require adequate protection during a temporary stay. Congress understood the term to represent a "strict approach" to adequate protection in the context of the cram down provisions. Use of the term in section 1129 plainly illustrates that Congress well understood the meaning of the term in its original context and intended to adopt the strict approach that the term represents. That Congress in 1978 should require adequate protection during the automatic stay and then add to that requirement language representing a strict approach to adequate protection convinces us that Congress intended to adopt or at least encourage the same approach to adequate protection in sections 361 and 362. . . .

The secured creditor's right to take possession of and sell collateral on the debtor's default has substantial, measurable value. The secured creditor bargains for this right when it agrees to extend credit to the debtor and both parties consider the right part of the creditor's bargain. The right constitutes an "interest in property" that is "created and defined by state law," and we are aware of no federal interest that requires this right of the secured creditor to go unprotected "simply because an interested party is involved in a bankruptcy proceeding." See Butner v. United States, 440 U.S. 48, 54-55, 99 S. Ct. 914, 917-918, 59 L. Ed. 2d 136 (1979). The Court in *Butner* observed that "[u]niform treatment of property interests by both state and federal courts within a State serves . . . to prevent a party from receiving 'a windfall merely by reason of the happenstance of bankruptcy.' " 440 U.S. at 55, 99 S. Ct. at 918 (quoting Lewis v. Manufacturers National Bank, 364 U.S. 603, 609, 81 S. Ct. 347, 350, 5 L. Ed. 2d 323 (1961)). To the extent that the debtor in bankruptcy can prevent the secured creditor from enforcing its rights against collateral while the debtor benefits from the creditor's money, the debtor and his unsecured creditors receive a windfall at the expense of the secured creditor.

We conclude that sections 361 and 362(d) were drafted to preclude such a windfall and to insure that the secured creditor receives the benefit of its bargain. We are satisfied that our holding in this case will not inhibit successful reorganization but rather will promote among other things the ready availability of affordable credit.

We hold that Crocker National Bank is entitled to compensation for the delay in enforcing its rights during the interim between the petition and confirmation of the plan. Crocker contended that such compensation should take the form of monthly interest payments at the market rate on the liquidation value of the collateral. We agree that this is one method of providing adequate protection but by no means the only method available to the debtor. Consistent with the policies behind sections 361 and 362, the debtor should be permitted maximum flexibility in structuring a proposal for adequate protection. The result, however, should as nearly as possible under the circumstances of the case provide the creditor with the value of his bargained for rights.[12]

12. There are a few general guidelines that the trial court and debtor should consider. First, to avoid overcompensating the secured creditor, the timing of adequate protection should take account of the usual time and expense involved in repossession and sale of

Remanded for further findings by the bankruptcy court consistent with this opinion.

NOTES

1. Consider the impact of footnote 12. Is it consistent with the general thrust of the opinion?

2. In In re South Village Inc., 25 Bankr. 987 (Bankr. D. Utah 1982), Judge Mabey reached the opposite result of that reached in *American Mariner,* and most bankruptcy judges have followed his lead. He observed that "the basis for opportunity cost, tied as it is to the method and outcome of valuation, may be either incalculable or evanescent." He concluded:

> Adequate protection is the fulcrum upon which the rights of debtors and creditors are balanced in a reorganization case. Congress knew that the payment of interest would be an impossible burden for debtors, many of whom file because of cash shortages. Congress allowed "periodic cash payments" in Section 361(1), but these are keyed to depreciation, not interest, and they are optional, not mandatory. If interest were required, it would run afoul of the nonprescriptive character of Section 361, as well as other provisions of the Code.

Is Judge Mabey correct in assuming that compensation for opportunity cost requires payments of cash? Couldn't the debtor offer a lien on other collateral or something else that was the "indubitable equivalent" of cash? Will valuing the property be difficult? (In many cases, including *South Village,* the collateral is a parcel of real property.) Even if it would be, does it follow that valuation should not be attempted? What exactly are the debtor's rights to which Judge Mabey refers, when the debtor, as in *South Village,* is an insolvent corporation?

3. In determining the value of the secured creditor's property interest that needs adequate protection, should one use the liquidation value or the reorganization value? Can one argue that the liquidation value is appropriate, because the only right being protected is one of repossessing and reselling the collateral, and its value is simply the property's sale price on the open market? Ultimately, there may be little difference between liquidation and reorganization value, because third parties who buy on the open market will, in valuing the property, take account of the opportunity

collateral. See In re South Village, Inc., 25 B.R. 987, 996 n.14 (Bkrtcy. Utah 1982). Second, the market rate of interest is not the only rate that may be applicable under the facts of each case. For example, noting that section 506(b) allows interest to *oversecured* creditors at the *contract* rate, see 3 Collier on Bankruptcy ¶506.05 (L. King 15th ed. 1983), an undersecured creditor would receive a windfall if the market rate of interest exceeds the contract rate. Compensating the creditor at the contract rate, as noted above, is one method approved in the Senate Report. S. Rep. No. 989 at 54, 1978 U.S. Code Cong. & Ad. News at 5840.

to sell it back to the debtor. But isn't this problem quite distinct from that of whether bankruptcy law should protect the time value of the secured creditor's interest? Cf. In re Phoenix Steel Corp., 39 Bankr. 218 (D. Del. 1984).

4. Should adequate protection turn out to be inadequate, §507(b) provides that a claim arising from such shortfall "shall have priority over every other claim allowable under" §507(a)(1). Section 507(a)(1) recognizes the right of some to be paid in full before the claims of the unsecured creditors are satisfied, including those whose claims arise out of the administration of the bankruptcy estate, such as the trustee (who is entitled to a fee) and post-petition lenders. Hence §507(a)(1) claims are typically called "administrative" claims. See In re Callister, 15 Bankr. 521 (Bankr. D. Utah 1981). We explore priorities in detail in Chapter 8.

PROBLEMS

7.13 Debtor borrows $10,000 from Bank on March 1, at 8 percent interest, to be repaid in two years. At the same time, Bank takes and properly perfects a security interest in Debtor's machine. The security agreement provides that filing a petition in bankruptcy constitutes a default. Debtor files a bankruptcy petition on January 1, when the machine had a market value of $7,500. All the parties agree that the reorganization will take six months and that Debtor will provide adequate protection to Bank by making monthly cash payments. On January 1, the risk-free rate of interest for a six-month loan (the interest rate charged the United States government for a six-month loan) is 10 percent. How large should the cash payments be if the machine depreciates at a rate of $100 a month?

7.14 Debtor has borrowed $100,000 from Bank to buy a machine. Bank negotiates to acquire a security interest in not only that machine, but also two other machines Debtor owns. At the time the loan is made, the three machines have a market value of $200,000. Two months later, when Debtor has repaid $10,000, and the machines are worth $170,000, Debtor files for bankruptcy. The machines will continue to depreciate in value. Is Bank entitled to "adequate protection" on the ground that it had bargained for, and is entitled to, an "equity cushion" of approximately twice the loan value, and this cushion is depreciating? What would such protection look like? See In re Mellor, 734 F.2d 1396 (9th Cir. 1984); In re Alyucan Interstate Corp., 12 Bankr. 803 (Bankr. D. Utah 1981); In re Pitts, 2 Bankr. 476 (Bankr. C.D. Cal. 1979).

7.15 Bank has loaned Debtor $100,000, to be repaid after ten years, bearing interest at 5 percent. This loan is secured by a machine worth $150,000. Debtor files a petition in bankruptcy. If Bank seeks adequate protection, what, if anything, must Bank be given? See §506(b). (Ignore, for now, the provisions of §1124, which apply to a Chapter 11 reorganization.) What if the machine is worth $70,000? See *American Mariner,* supra; In re Anchorage Boat Sales, 4 Bankr. 635 (Bankr. E.D.N.Y. 1980). Would your analysis change if the terms of the loan were that it was payable in six months, and bore an 18 percent interest rate?

NOTE ON VALUING THE STATE LAW RIGHTS OF A SECURED CREDITOR

Under state law, a secured creditor who specifies filing a bankruptcy petition as an event of default has a right to take possession of its collateral (say, a machine) and to sell it to satisfy the debt at the moment that the debtor files its bankruptcy petition. Bankruptcy law, as we have seen, provides for acceleration of debts upon the filing of a bankruptcy petition, even if the contract is silent. See §502(b); H.R. Rep. No. 95-595, 95th Cong., 1st Sess. 352 (1977). Apart from bankruptcy, converting that *right* into *reality* may take some time. See footnote 12 of the *American Mariner* opinion. Despite the secured party's right to repossess, it may take time to exercise that right, especially if the debtor resists and it is necessary to call upon the assistance of a court. In the discussion that follows, how should one account for this factor?

It is not enough to say that the secured creditor has a right to its collateral. One has to establish *when* it has that right. A right to a machine *now* is not the same as a right to the identical machine in six months. This becomes clear when one looks at a right to money instead of at a particular piece of property. Few are indifferent to having $1 million in cash today and a promise of receiving $1 million in cash one year hence.

There are three reasons one would prefer $1 million in cash immediately. See R. Brealey & S. Myers, Principles of Corporate Finance 10-22 (1981). First, one always has to discount the value of the promise by the possibility that the person making it will not keep it. How large the discount will be depends upon the person making the promise. Some debtors are more reliable than others. Most of us would rather have the United States government's promise to pay us a year from now than Braniff's. There is some chance that the United States government will not keep its promise, but this chance is very small, because unlike every other debtor, the federal government can honor its promises simply by using a printing press to make more money.

Let us assume that we have the United States government's promise to pay us a year from now. Are we still indifferent whether we have the cash now or a year from now? If recent history is any measure of the future, we would prefer to have the money now because we would expect inflation in the coming year, so that a dollar a year from now will buy less than a dollar today.

But assume that we can take inflation into account. (Note that this will be very difficult because there are several different measures of inflation and it will be hard to find one that captures the concept perfectly from our point of view.) Would we still be indifferent? Take an extreme example: Would you prefer to have $1 million today or the binding promise of the United States government to pay you the equivalent of $1 million one hundred years from now? If nothing affected the value of the promise other than the possibility of its being broken and the threat of inflation, you might think we should be indifferent between the two. But interest rates on risk-free investments (such as United States government obligations) have typically run one or two percent ahead of the inflation rate over the last forty years or so. This difference is known as the real rate of interest.

Consider in this respect Problem 7.13 — that of a lender with a security interest in a $7,500 machine. Merely compensating the lender for the machine's expected depreciation may not be sufficient to give it the economic equivalent of its security interest. The debtor is essentially promising to give the secured lender its machine six months in the future. What more must the debtor pay in order to put the lender in the same position the lender would be in if it had a right to the machine now? Besides the expected depreciation, the debtor would have to pay for the possibility that it will break its promise — that it will not give the creditor the machine in six months. The debtor may sell the machine to a third party, abuse it, or fail to maintain it. All of these things may be more likely to happen when the debtor is insolvent. Even if the debtor's promise were good as gold and the machine would not depreciate over the six months, the creditor would want to be compensated for the fact that having a machine in six months is not the same as having it now. If the creditor had the machine today, the creditor could sell it, buy six-month treasury bills, and, in six months, have more than $7,500. If the creditor waits for six months, then gets the machine and sells it, it will have only $7,500, even assuming there is no depreciation.

Why can't a creditor with a security interest in a machine argue that when the automatic stay prevents it from exercising its right to take possession of the machine tool and sell it for $7,500, it is in effect being forced to lease the machine to the debtor? If we accept this view, doesn't it follow that adequate protection means that the creditor should get the same amount that a third party owning the machine would charge the debtor for using the machine for six months?

Consider the following reasoning: We cannot simply let the secured party repossess the machine and then have the debtor bargain with it over a six-month lease, because the machine is probably not perfectly fungible. This machine is properly adjusted for debtor's plant and debtor's needs. The debtor has become used to its idiosyncrasies. If the secured party could dicker with the debtor over the lease terms, it would have an incentive to hold up the debtor for the value of all the specialized knowledge that the debtor has gained about using this particular machine. The value of this information may be larger than what the secured party bargained for — the right to repossess the machine and resell it in the market to a third party. (The debtor has a right, not waivable before default, to *require* the secured party to resell collateral it repossesses. UCC §§9-501; 9-504; 9-505.)

To surmount this problem, we need to hypothesize the bargain a debtor would reach if it were leasing the machine from a third party who did not take advantage of any investment the debtor had already made in this particular machine. Alternatively (and economically it amounts to the same thing), we can calculate how much a third-party lender would charge for a secured loan equal to the present value of the collateral. See In re Scovill, 18 Bankr. 633 (Bankr. D. Neb. 1982).

NOTE ON ADEQUATE PROTECTION AND THE RIGHTS OF THE SECURED CREDITOR IN BANKRUPTCY

The argument in the previous section assumed that the secured creditor must receive the economic equivalent of its state-law rights. Is it correct to assume that this is what the secured creditor must receive in order to be "adequately protected" within the meaning of §361? This inquiry, as *American Mariner* noted, is a statutory one. See Comment, Compensation for Time Value as Part of Adequate Protection During the Automatic Stay in Bankruptcy, 50 U. Chi. L. Rev. 305 (1983). Can one argue that the "indubitable equivalent" of a secured creditor's interest is less than its actual economic equivalent? Consider the following analysis of the problem, derived from Baird and Jackson, Corporate Reorganizations and the Treatment of Diverse Ownership Interests: A Comment on Adequate Protection of Secured Creditors in Bankruptcy, 51 U. Chi. L. Rev. 97 (1984).

When a firm files a petition in bankruptcy, two questions arise. First, one must decide what to do with the firm's assets, and, second, one must decide who gets them. Answering the second question should, ideally, not interfere with the answer to the first. As a first approximation, the law governing bankruptcy in general, and corporate reorganizations in particular, should ensure that the choice of what to do with the firm's assets is in everyone's interest, even though the vision of both senior and junior stakeholders is clouded. How a firm's assets are used should not turn on whether one, ten, or ten thousand people have rights to them. Bankruptcy law should work to allow the ten thousand to act as if they were one. It should, in short, work to keep the asset deployment question separate from the distributional question, and to have the deployment question analyzed as a single owner would. The best way to approximate this is to ensure that the parties who make the decision about how to deploy the assets enjoy all the benefits and incur all the costs.

As long as the classes of investors that stand to gain from any upswing in the firm's fortunes do not bear the full costs of an attempt to keep the assets together, they will tend to make the attempt, even if it is not worthwhile for the investors as a group. That is, they will try to reorganize even when an individual who had complete ownership of the assets would liquidate them immediately. Imposing the risks of keeping a firm intact on junior parties removes a powerful incentive from them because it forces them to recognize that keeping a firm together has costs as well as benefits. They become like a sole owner in the sense that they suffer the consequences of making the wrong decision and enjoy the benefits of making the right one. This imposition of costs might not make the junior parties behave exactly like a sole owner. But unless we impose these burdens on them, junior parties generally will tend to underestimate real costs.

We need to ask if respecting the full *value* of a secured creditor's rights will interfere with any bankruptcy policies. Isn't the relevant bankruptcy goal not that the firm stay in business, but rather that the assets are deployed in a way that advances the interests of those who have rights in them? Unless there is a "going-concern surplus," a reorganization would seem inappropriate because the firm's assets are worth more (and hence the owners recover more of what they advanced the debtor) if the assets are sold than they are if kept together.

Conversely, when a firm's assets *are* worth more as a going concern, the owners as a group, are probably better off if the assets are kept together. This is true even though the firm may have defaulted on some of its obligations or may be insolvent. Protecting the benefits that come from keeping the assets together is one of the fundamental goals of the bankruptcy process and the reason for a collective proceeding. The crucial question becomes whether giving the secured creditor the benefit of its bargain is inconsistent with the policy of ensuring that the firm's assets are deployed in a way that brings the most benefits to the owners as a group. The rights of a creditor with a security interest in a drill press are fixed by seeing how much the drill press would bring if it were sold to some third party on the open market. If the firm is in fact worth more as a going concern than if sold piecemeal, there must be enough to pay a secured creditor the machine's full liquidation value. One follows from the other. Both going-concern and liquidation values represent future income streams discounted to present value, and the concept of a going-concern surplus means that the stream represented by the going-concern value is larger than the stream represented by the liquidation value.

Let us assume that a drill press is a firm's sole tangible asset, and that a third party would pay $10,000 for it on the day the bankruptcy petition is filed. If the firm is worth preserving as a going concern (because of the good will it has generated among its customers and its expertise in running the machine), it must be worth more than $10,000 as of that time. If it is worth less, the drill press is being used ineffectively, and the firm is probably not worth preserving as a going concern.

A firm worth more than $10,000 when the bankruptcy petition is filed can give at least that much to a creditor with a security interest in the drill press. It can pay the creditor out of cash reserves, or it can obtain the money (on a secured, unsecured, or equity basis) from a new investor. In principle, moreover, the secured creditor does not need to be given cash at the time of the petition in order to receive the benefit of its bargain. It could change its investor status to another category. For example, the secured creditor could be given the benefit of its bargain if it were given rights to all the firm's assets, subject to an option of the general creditors to repurchase the firm from it at some later time for a fixed amount. (That amount will be more than $10,000, to account both for the time value of $10,000 between the date of the petition and the date the option is exercised, and for the possibility that the assets will turn out to be worth less than $10,000.) As long as the package of rights the secured creditor receives are worth $10,000 — i.e., can be sold by the secured creditor for that amount — it has received the benefit of its bargain.

Any firm that is worth more as a going concern than chopped up will be able to give the secured creditor the benefit of its bargain. To be sure, other creditors, such as general creditors or shareholders, will receive less or perhaps nothing. But how rights to the assets are divided among the investors is a question distinct from how the assets are deployed. Only the latter is a bankruptcy question. It is the difference between the size of the slices and the size of the pie. Giving the secured creditor the benefit of its bargain should not prevent a firm from staying together when a sole owner would keep it together. Indeed, a failure to recognize the secured creditors' rights in full will *undercut* the bankruptcy goal of ensuring that assets are put to the use that best advances everyone's interests, because it will keep junior parties, who stand to benefit from delay, from bearing its full cost, and they will tend to keep firms together even when a sole owner would not.

Assuming this point is true in the abstract, is it true in our world? Reorganizations take time. In the world as we actually find it, valuations are hard to come by. It may be unclear whether a firm is worth keeping intact. One may need time to decide whether liquidation piece by piece is the only available course. Whether the firm has a going-concern surplus may depend on whether there is an as yet undiscovered third party that needs such assets in their present form (perhaps for no other reason than the tax loss they bring). It may depend upon whether the market for the firm's goods or services changes or the eonomy as a whole turns around. Determining the optimal capital structure of a reorganized firm, moreover, may take time.

But does it follow that protecting the secured creditor's bargain promotes liquidations when the appropriate course is patience? Waiting for changed conditions or even for more information imposes a cost. If a firm's assets are worth $10,000 in a liquidation today, an investor who owned them outright would have to weigh the value of obtaining $10,000 immediately against the more uncertain value that waiting will bring. Even if delay were certain to bring some benefit in the abstract, it may not be worthwhile to wait. A sole owner would not delay simply because he thought that a year later the assets would be worth (in nominal dollars) $11,000. Assuming his goal was to enjoy the highest return on his investment, he would not keep the firm's assets together if one-year treasury bills offered a risk-free return of more than 10 percent. By investing his $10,000 today in treasury bills instead of the firm, he would be certain to receive more than $11,000 in a year's time. The analysis is exactly the same when the firm's ownership is dispersed. A reorganization would not be in the interests of the investors as a group.

When one is dealing with firms rather than treasury bills, moreover, one must also account for uncertainty. The firm's assets may be worth $11,000 in a year's time, but only if things go well. As best anyone can tell today, there might be a 50-50 chance that the firm can stay in business beyond a year and, if it fails after a year, a liquidation would then realize (again in nominal dollars) only $10,000. In this case, even if the risk-free rate of return were only 6 percent, instead of 10 percent, our sole owner would decide that the firm should be liquidated now. Assuming that the owner is risk-neutral, liquidating the firm today and investing its proceeds in treasury bills would generate $10,600 in a year's time, while waiting and attempting a reorganization would be expected to realize only $10,500. The possible benefits of a successful reorganization ($11,000) must be adjusted to account for the equally probable costs of failure ($10,000).

In our world, chances of success or failure over time can never be calculated with certainty. But that is not to say that they cannot be calculated at all. Everyone in day-to-day life weighs the benefits of certain sums in the present against uncertain sums in the future. Wrong decisions are made (indeed, that is part of the valuation process), but we generally believe that, at least when businesses rather than consumers are involved, the best means of ensuring the correct decision is to allow the businesses and their investors to make it.

Unlike a sole owner, dispersed investors, because their relative rights differ, have an incentive to make the *wrong* decision, if unchecked. The secured creditors will rush to liquidate, while the general creditors and shareholders (who often have more to gain than to lose from delay) will be too optimistic. Should bankruptcy law assume that the decision of one of these groups reflects the best decision about the assets for the investors as a whole, unless that group must pay for its choice? The best way of ensuring the correct decision — one that is not distorted by the self-interest of individuals at the expense of the interests of the group — is to create a legal rule that provides that the person who makes the decision receives all the benefits for a correct decision and incurs all the costs for a wrong one. A rule that forces general creditors and shareholders to give secured creditors the benefit of their bargain does precisely this.

To this point, the argument has been both abstract and normative. Does it square with the law as it currently exists? *American Mariner* says yes, but has it canvassed all the relevant provisions? For example, the Bankruptcy Code provides that, during the reorganization process, the secured creditor cannot be forced to accept a first claim upon the firm's unsecured assets at the conclusion of the bankruptcy proceeding in exchange for its matured state-law right to repossess the firm's property. §361(3). The bankruptcy judge must give the secured creditor who insists upon it a right in the here and now (such as a lien on specific assets, cash, or its "indubitable equivalent"), not pie in the sky (including administrative expense priority). What is the consequence of such a provision? What is its justification?

The effect of this requirement is that a firm must reach a deal by consent, or provide specific protection. A firm without unencumbered assets, a ready source of cash, or anything else beyond a vision of a brighter future, must persuade either the secured creditor or a third-party lender that the firm has value as a going concern. Two things about this requirement, however, should be noted. First, an inability to persuade someone (other than a bankruptcy judge) that the firm should stay alive may be good evidence that it should not. Of course, conveying the information necessary to make out a case for keeping the assets intact may be very difficult. But it should be just as easy in principle to persuade one of many potential third-party lenders as it is to persuade any other *neutral* third party, judicial or otherwise.

Second, Congress imposed this restriction on bankruptcy judges because it believed that they systematically deprived secured creditors of the benefit of their bargain. Any kind of interest in the reorganized debtor was deemed "too uncertain to be meaningful" (Sen. Rep. No. 95-989 at 54) because "in every case there is uncertainty that the estate will have sufficient property to pay administrative expenses in full." 124 Cong. Rec. H11,092 (daily ed. Sept. 28, 1978). Congress specified this for the purpose of ensuring that the secured creditor was paid in full in a "meaningful" way. Cf. In re Callister, 15 Bankr. 521 (Bankr. D. Utah 1981); Murphy, Use of Collateral in Business Rehabilitation: A Suggested Redrafting of Section 7-203 of the Bankruptcy Reform Act, 63 Cal. L. Rev. 1483, 1505 (1975). If this is the case rationale behind §361(3), how can one point to it as a justification for giving the secured creditor *less* than full compensation? See generally In re New York, New Haven & Hartford R. Co., 147 F.2d 40 (2d Cir. 1945).

Overvaluations by bankruptcy judges cause undercompensation of secured creditors. But the degree of undercompensation depends on the relative priority of the compensation received. Congress's restriction requires relatively senior forms of compensation to be used before a secured creditor can be involuntarily kept in the picture. The restriction directly eliminates the most egregious forms of undercompensation. Even if the effect of limiting the bankruptcy judge's ability to choose the form of protection given to secured creditors is to prevent some desirable reorganizations from taking place, this should not be pointed to as a justification for giving secured creditors less than the benefit of their bargain. It would be disingenuous to rely on a provision designed to protect secured creditors from undercompensation as a justification for a policy — such as not protecting the time value of money — that must undercompensate them, both in theory and in practice.

PROBLEM

7.16 Debtor buys Blackacre, a piece of undeveloped real estate, for $150,000. Over the course of several years, Debtor borrows $200,000 from Bank and grants Bank a security interest in Blackacre. At the time Debtor files its bankruptcy petition, everyone agrees that Blackacre is worth $150,000. Everyone also agrees that Bank must be compensated for the opportunity cost associated with its secured loan and that Bank must be paid $1500 a month, granted a lien for that amount, or otherwise given the indubitable equivalent of $1500 a month. Debtor argues that because a new highway is being built near Blackacre, its value will rise over the next year by at least 20 percent and that Bank's security claim of $150,000 can be adequately protected by granting it a security interest in the amount that Blackacre increases in value each month. Is Debtor's argument sound? If the asset is properly valued, shouldn't the benefits of the new highway already be discounted in the present value?

Assume that Debtor agrees to give Bank cash payments of $1500 a month. A year later, the bankruptcy proceeding is wrapped up and Blackacre has increased in value unexpectedly. It is sold to a third party for $200,000. Can Bank take the $200,000 (less perhaps the cash payments it has received)? Is Bank entitled to increases in the collateral's value after the filing of the petition? Or is the Bank's position frozen at that time so it neither faces the risk of a decrease in the property's value nor enjoys the benefits of any increase? Note that in valuing a creditor's rights, one must not only take account of what is necessary for purposes of adequate protection, but also square what is offered as adequate protection (in the form of cash, liens, or something else) with the payout that the secured creditor eventually receives. In this problem, for example, it would not seem to make sense to provide Bank with additional liens of $1,500 a month, if Bank's payout at the end of the bankruptcy proceeding would only be $150,000.

C. PROBLEMS RELATED TO THE AUTOMATIC STAY

1. *Turnover of Property*

A secured creditor who repossesses its collateral before the filing of the petition does not thereby receive a preferential transfer. Because in principle a secured creditor has a right in bankruptcy to the property's value, taking the property does not make it better off. Does it follow, however, that bankruptcy law should treat a secured creditor who has repossessed, but not yet sold, property as a third party unaffected by the automatic stay, or should the property be pulled into the bankruptcy proceeding?

Section 541 assembles an "estate," and §362 is designed to keep that estate together for purposes of the bankruptcy proceeding. But sometimes the property is in the hands of someone other than the debtor. Sections 542 and 543 are two rules governing the assembly and preservation of the estate and they deal with situations in which the party in possession must turn over the property to the debtor. What kinds of interests might a debtor have that would support a turnover order under either section?

If, for example, a general assignment for the benefit of creditors took place before the date of bankruptcy, may the trustee in bankruptcy require the assignee to turn over the property? See §§101(10), 543. See also §§303(h) and 547. Section 543(d)(2) was added to the Bankruptcy Code in 1984. A House Report, commenting on language similar to the 1984 Bankruptcy Amendments in an earlier bill, sought to justify the provision:

> This amendment is intended to except from the requirements of Section 543 certain proceedings from the state insolvency laws, i.e., general assignments for the benefit of all of the debtor's creditors, which have been in effect for more than four months before the filing of a petition under title 11, to assure that the transactions consummated within the context of such a proceeding not otherwise defective under applicable law will not be prejudiced because of the succeeding title 11 proceeding. It is recognized that within the context of such state insolvency proceedings many debtor-creditor matters can be dealt with expeditiously, efficiently, and at a lesser expense to all interested parties than might be the case on a formal bankruptcy proceeding.

H.R. Rep. No. 1195, 96th Cong., 2d Sess. 83-84 (1980). Is this revision necessary? After an assignment, what is the status of property?

Apart from assignments for the benefit of creditors and the like, the turnover issue can come up in a number of different contexts. For example, what about the secured party who has repossessed collateral following default? Can the debtor require that property to be turned over under either §§542 or 543? What about other rights, such as a special property right under UCC §2-501? How well does the following case focus on the relevant concerns?

UNITED STATES v. WHITING POOLS
462 U.S. 198 (1983)

Justice BLACKMUN delivered the opinion of the Court.

Promptly after the Internal Revenue Service (IRS or Service) seized respondent's property to satisfy a tax lien, respondent filed a petition for reorganization under the Bankruptcy Reform Act of 1978, hereinafter referred to as the "Bankruptcy Code." The issue before us is whether §542(a) of that Code authorized the Bankruptcy Court to subject the IRS to a turnover order with respect to the seized property.

I

A

Respondent Whiting Pools, Inc., a corporation, sells, installs, and services swimming pools and related equipment and supplies. As of January 1981, Whiting owed approximately $92,000 in Federal Insurance Contribution Act taxes and federal taxes withheld from its employees, but had failed to respond to assessments and demands for payment by the IRS. As a consequence, a tax lien in that amount attached to all of Whiting's property.[1]

On January 14, 1981, the Service seized Whiting's tangible personal property — equipment, vehicles, inventory, and office supplies — pursuant to the levy and distraint provision of the Internal Revenue Code of 1954.[2] According to uncontroverted findings, the estimated liquidation

---

1. Section 6321 of the Internal Revenue Code of 1954, 26 U.S.C. §6321, provides:

   If any person liable to pay any tax neglects or refuses to pay the same after demand, the amount . . . shall be a lien in favor of the United States upon all property and rights to property, whether real or personal, belonging to such person.

2. Section 6331 of that Code, 26 U.S.C. §6331 provides:

   (a) Authority of Secretary
   If any person liable to pay any tax neglects or refuses to pay the same within 10 days after notice and demand, it shall be lawful for the Secretary to collect such tax (and such further sum as shall be sufficient to cover the expenses of the levy) by levy upon all property and rights to property . . . belonging to such person or on which there is a lien provided in this chapter for the payment of such tax. . . .
   (b) Seizure and sale of property
   The term "levy" as used in this title includes the power of distraint and seizure by any means. . . . In any case in which the Secretary may levy upon property or rights to property, he may seize and sell such property or rights to property (whether real or personal, tangible or intangible).

value of the property seized was, at most, $35,000, but its estimated going-concern value in Whiting's hands was $162,876. The very next day, January 15, Whiting filed a petition for reorganization, under the Bankruptcy Code's Chapter 11, 11 U.S.C. §§1101 et seq. (1976 ed., Supp. V), in the United States Bankruptcy Court for the Western District of New York. Whiting was continued as debtor-in-possession.

The United States, intending to proceed with a tax sale of the property,[4] moved in the Bankruptcy Court for a declaration that the automatic stay provision of the Bankruptcy Code, §362(a), is inapplicable to the IRS or, in the alternative, for relief from the stay. Whiting counterclaimed for an order requiring the Service to turn the seized property over to the bankruptcy estate pursuant to §542(a) of the Bankruptcy Code. Whiting intended to use the property in its reorganized business.

B

The Bankruptcy Court determined that the IRS was bound by the automatic stay provision. In re Whiting Pools, Inc., 10 B.R. 755 (Bkrtcy. 1981). Because it found that the seized property was essential to Whiting's reorganization effort, it refused to lift the stay. Acting under §543(b)(1) of the Bankruptcy Code, rather than under §542(a), the court directed the IRS to turn the property over to Whiting on the condition that Whiting provide the Service with specified protection for its interests. 10 B.R. at 760-761.[7]

The United States District Court reversed, holding that a turnover order against the Service was not authorized by either §542(a) or §543(b)(1). . . . The United States Court of Appeals for the Second Circuit, in turn, reversed the District Court. 674 F.2d 144 (1982). It held that a turnover order could issue against the Service under §542(a), and it remanded the case for reconsideration of the adequacy of the Bankruptcy Court's protection conditions. The Court of Appeals acknowledged that

---

4. Section 6335, as amended, of the 1954 Code, 26 U.S.C. §6335, provides for the sale of seized property after notice. The taxpayer is entitled to any surplus of the proceeds of the sale. §6342(b).

7. Section 363(e) of the Bankruptcy Code provides:

> Notwithstanding any other provision of this section, at any time, on request of an entity that has an interest in property used, sold, or leased, or proposed to be used, sold, or leased by the trustee, the court shall prohibit or condition such use, sale, or lease as is necessary to provide adequate protection of such interest. In any hearing under this section, the trustee has the burden of proof on the issue of adequate protection. 11 U.S.C. §363(e) (1976 ed., Supp. V).

Pursuant to this section, the Bankruptcy Court set the following conditions to protect the tax lien: Whiting was to pay the Service $20,000 before the turnover occurred; Whiting also was to pay $1,000 a month until the taxes were satisfied; the IRS was to retain its lien during this period; and if Whiting failed to make the payments, the stay was to be lifted. 10 B.R. at 761. [11 U.S.C. §363(e) was reworded slightly in 1984 and a portion of it was moved to §363(o). — EDS.]

its ruling was contrary to that reached by the United States Court of
Appeals for the Fourth Circuit in Cross Electric Co. v. United States, 664
F.2d 1218 (1981), and noted confusion on the issue among bankruptcy
and district courts. 674 F.2d at 145 and n.1. We granted certiorari to
resolve this conflict in an important area of the law under the new Bankruptcy Code. . . .

II

By virtue of its tax lien, the Service holds a secured interest in Whiting's
property. We first examine whether §542(a) of the Bankruptcy Code
generally authorizes the turnover of a debtor's property seized by a secured creditor prior to the commencement of reorganization proceedings. Section 542(a) requires an entity in possession of "property that the
trustee may use, sell, or lease under §363" to deliver that property to the
trustee. Subsections (b) and (c) of §363 authorize the trustee to use, sell, or
lease any "property of the estate," subject to certain conditions for the
protection of creditors with an interest in the property. Section 541(a)(1)
defines the "estate" as "comprised of all the following property, wherever
located: (1) . . . all legal or equitable interests of the debtor in property as
of the commencement of the case." Although these statutes could be read
to limit the estate to those "interests of the debtor in property" at the time
of the filing of the petition, we view them as a definition of what is included
in the estate, rather than as a limitation.

A

In proceedings under the reorganization provisions of the Bankruptcy Code, a troubled enterprise may be restructured to enable it to
operate successfully in the future. Until the business can be reorganized
pursuant to a plan under 11 U.S.C. §§1121-1129 (1976 ed., Supp. V), the
trustee or debtor-in-possession is authorized to manage the property of the
estate and to continue the operation of the business. See §1108. By permitting reorganization, Congress anticipated that the business would continue to provide jobs, to satisfy creditors' claims, and to produce a return
for its owners. H.R. Rep. No. 95-595, p. 220 (1977), U.S. Code Cong. &
Admin. News 1978, p. 5787. Congress presumed that the assets of the
debtor would be more valuable if used in a rehabilitated business than if
"sold for scrap." Ibid. The reorganization effort would have small chance
of success, however, if property essential to running the business were
excluded from the estate. . . . Thus, to facilitate the rehabilitation of the
debtor's business, all the debtor's property must be included in the reorganization estate.

This authorization extends even to property of the estate in which a creditor has a secured interest. §363(b) and (c); see H.R. Rep. No. 95-595, p. 182 (1977). Although Congress might have safeguarded the interests of secured creditors outright by excluding from the estate any property subject to a secured interest, it chose instead to include such property in the estate and to provide secured creditors with "adequate protection" for their interests. §363(e), quoted in n.7, supra. At the secured creditor's insistence, the bankruptcy court must place such limits or conditions on the trustee's power to sell, use, or lease property as are necessary to protect the creditor. The creditor with a secured interest in property included in the estate must look to this provision for protection, rather than to the nonbankruptcy remedy of possession.

Both the congressional goal of encouraging reorganizations and Congress' choice of methods to protect secured creditors suggest that Congress intended a broad range of property to be included in the estate.

B

The statutory language reflects this view of the scope of the estate. As noted above, §541(a) provides that the "estate is comprised of all the following property, wherever located: . . . all legal or equitable interests of the debtor in property as of the commencement of the case." 11 U.S.C. §541(a)(1).[8] The House and Senate Reports on the Bankruptcy Code indicate that §541(a)(1)'s scope is broad.[9] Most important, in the context of this case, §541(a)(1) is intended to include in the estate any property made available to the estate by other provisions of the Bankruptcy

---

8. Section 541(a)(1) speaks in terms of the debtor's "interests . . . in property," rather than property in which the debtor has an interest, but this choice of language was not meant to limit the expansive scope of the section. The legislative history indicates that Congress intended to exclude from the estate property of others in which the debtor had some minor interest such as a lien or bare legal title. See 124 Cong. Rec. 32399, 32417 (1978) (remarks of Rep. Edwards); id., at 33999, 34016-34017 (remarks of Sen. DeConcini); cf. §541(d) (property in which debtor holds legal but not equitable title, such as a mortgage in which debtor retained legal title to service or to supervise servicing of mortgage, becomes part of estate only to extent of legal title); 124 Cong. Rec. 33999 (1978) (remarks of Sen. DeConcini) (§541(d) "reiterates the general principle that where the debtor holds bare legal title without any equitable interest, . . . the estate acquires bare legal title without any equitable interest in the property"). Similar statements to the effect that §541(a)(1) does not expand the rights of the debtor in the hands of the estate were made in the context of describing the principle that the estate succeeds to no more or greater causes of action against third parties than those held by the debtor. See H.R. Rep. No. 95-595, pp. 367-368 (1977). These statements do not limit the ability of a trustee to regain possession of property in which the debtor had equitable as well as legal title.

9. "The scope of this paragraph [§541(a)(1)] is broad. It includes all kinds of property, including tangible or intangible property, causes of action (see Bankruptcy Act §70a(6)), and all other forms of property currently specified in section 70a of the Bankruptcy Act." H.R. Rep. No. 95-595, p. 367 (1977); S. Rep. No. 95-989, p. 82 (1978), U.S. Code Cong. & Admin. News 1978, pp. 5868, 6323.

Code. . . . Several of these provisions bring into the estate property in which the debtor did not have a possessory interest at the time the bankruptcy proceedings commenced.[10]

Section 542(a) is such a provision. It requires an entity (other than a custodian) holding any property of the debtor that the trustee can use under §363 to turn that property over to the trustee.[11] Given the broad scope of the reorganization estate, property of the debtor repossessed by a secured creditor falls within this rule, and therefore may be drawn into the estate. While there are explicit limitations on the reach of §542(a),[12] none requires that the debtor hold a possessory interest in the property at the commencement of the reorganization proceedings.

As does all bankruptcy law, §542(a) modifies the procedural rights available to creditors to protect and satisfy their liens.[14] . . . In effect, §542(a) grants to the estate a possessory interest in certain property of the debtor that was not held by the debtor at the commencement of reorganization proceedings.[15] The Bankruptcy Code provides secured creditors various rights, including the right to adequate protection, and these rights replace the protection afforded by possession.

10. See, e.g., §§543, 547, and 548. These sections permit the trustee to demand the turnover of property that is in the possession of others if that possession is due to a custodial arrangement, §543, to a preferential transfer, §547, or to a fraudulent transfer, §548.

We do not now decide the outer boundaries of the bankruptcy estate. We note only that Congress plainly excluded property of others held by the debtor in trust at the time of the filing of the petition. See §541(b); H.R. Rep. No. 95-595, p. 368 (1977); S. Rep. No. 95-989, p. 82 (1978). Although it may well be that funds that the IRS can demonstrate were withheld for its benefit pursuant to 26 U.S.C. §7501 (employee withholding taxes), are excludable from the estate, see 124 Cong. Rec. 32417 (1978) (remarks of Rep. Edwards) (Service may exclude funds it can trace), the IRS did not attempt to trace the withheld taxes in this case. . . .

11. The House Report expressly includes property of the debtor recovered under §542(a) in the estate: the estate includes "property recovered by the trustee under section 542 . . . , if the property recovered was merely out of the possession of the debtor, yet remained 'property of the debtor.'" H.R. Rep. No. 95-595, p. 367 (1977), U.S. Code Cong. & Admin. News 1978, p. 6323. . . .

12. Section 542 provides that the property be usable under §363, and that turnover is not required in three situations: when the property is of inconsequential value or benefit to the estate, §542(a), when the holder of the property has transferred it in good faith without knowledge of the petition, §542(c), or when the transfer of the property is automatic to pay a life insurance premium, §542(d).

14. One of the procedural rights the law of secured transactions grants a secured creditor to enforce its lien is the right to take possession of the secured property upon the debtor's default. Uniform Commercial Code §9-503, 3A U.L.A. 211 (1981). A creditor's possessory interest resulting from the exercise of this right is subject to certain restrictions on the creditor's use of the property. See §9-504, 3A U.L.A. 256-257. Here, we address the abrogation of the Service's possessory interest obtained pursuant to its tax lien, a secured interest. We do not decide whether any property of the debtor in which a third party holds a possessory interest independent of a creditor's remedies is subject to turnover under §542(a). For example, if property is pledged to the secured creditor so that the creditor has possession prior to any default, 542(a) may not require turnover. . . .

15. Indeed, if this were not the effect, §542(a) would be largely superfluous in light of §541(a)(1). Interests in the seized property that could have been exercised by the debtor—in this case, the rights to notice and the surplus from a tax sale, see n.4, supra—are already part

c

This interpretation of §542(a) is supported by the section's legislative history. Although the legislative reports are silent on the precise issue before us, the House and Senate hearings from which §542(a) emerged provide guidance. Several witnesses at those hearings noted, without contradiction, the need for a provision authorizing the turnover of property of the debtor in the possession of secured creditors. Section 512(a) first appeared in the proposed legislation shortly after these hearings. . . . The section remained unchanged through subsequent versions of the legislation.

Moreover, this interpretation of §542 in the reorganization context is consistent with judicial precedent predating the Bankruptcy Code. Under Chapter X, the reorganization chapter of the Bankruptcy Act of 1878, as amended, §§101-276, 52 Stat. 883 (1938) (formerly codified as 11 U.S.C. §§501-676 (1976 ed.)), the bankruptcy court could order the turnover of collateral in the hands of a secured creditor. Reconstruction Finance Corp. v. Kaplan, 185 F.2d 791, 796 (C.A.1 1950). . . . Nothing in the legislative history evinces a congressional intent to depart from that practice. Any other interpretation of §542(a) would deprive the bankruptcy estate of the assets and property essential to its rehabilitation effort and thereby would frustrate the congressional purpose behind the reorganization provisions.[17]

We conclude that the reorganization estate includes property of the debtor that has been seized by a creditor prior to the filing of a petition for reorganization.

III

A

We see no reason why a different result should obtain when the IRS is the creditor. The service is bound by §542(a) to the same extent as any other secured creditor. The Bankruptcy Code expressly states that the term "entity," used in §542(a), includes a governmental unit. §101(14). . . . Moreover, Congress carefully considered the effect of the new Bank-

---

of the estate by virtue of §541(a)(1). No coercive power is needed for this inclusion. The fact that §542(a) grants the trustee greater rights than those held by the debtor prior to the filing of the petition is consistent with other provisions of the Bankruptcy Code that address the scope of the estate. See, e.g., §544 (trustee has rights of lien creditor); §545 (trustee has power to avoid statutory liens); §549 (trustee has power to avoid certain post-petition transactions).

17. Section 542(a) also governs turnovers in liquidation and individual adjustment of debt proceedings under Chapters 7 and 13 of the Bankruptcy Code, 11 U.S.C. §§701-766, 1301-1330 (1976 ed., Supp. V). See §103(a). Our analysis in this case depends in part on the reorganization context in which the turnover order is sought. We express no view on the issue whether §542(a) has the same broad effect in liquidation or adjustment of debt proceedings.

ruptcy Code on tax collection, see generally S. Rep. No. 95-1106 (1978) (report of Senate Finance Committee), and decided to provide protection to tax collectors, such as the IRS, through grants of enhanced priorities for unsecured tax claims, §507(a)(6),* and by the nondischarge of tax liabilities, §523(a)(1). S. Rep. No. 95-989, pp. 14-15 (1978). Tax collectors also enjoy the generally applicable right under §363(e) to adequate protection for property subject to their liens. Nothing in the Bankruptcy Code or its legislative history indicates that Congress intended a special exception for the tax collector in the form of an exclusion from the estate of property seized to satisfy a tax lien.

B

Of course, if a tax levy or seizure transfers to the IRS ownership of the property seized, §542(a) may not apply. The enforcement provisions of the Internal Revenue Code of 1954, 26 U.S.C. §§6321-6326 (1976 ed. and Supp. V), do grant to the Service powers to enforce its tax liens that are greater than those possessed by private secured creditors under state law. . . . But those provisions do not transfer ownership of the property to the IRS.

The Service's interest in seized property is its lien on that property. The Internal Revenue Code's levy and seizure provisions, 26 U.S.C. §§6331 and 6332, are special procedural devices available to the IRS to protect and satisfy its liens, . . . and are analogous to the remedies available to private secured creditors. . . . They are provisional remedies that do not determine the Service's rights to the seized property, but merely bring the property into the Service's legal custody. . . . At no point does the Service's interest in the property exceed the value of the lien. . . . The IRS is obligated to return to the debtor any surplus from a sale. 26 U.S.C. §6342(b). Ownership of the property is transferred only when the property is sold to a bona fide purchaser at a tax sale. . . . In fact, the tax sale provision itself refers to the debtor as the owner of the property after the seizure but prior to the sale. Until such a sale takes place, the property remains the debtor's and thus is subject to the turnover requirement of §542(a).

IV

When property seized prior to the filing of a petition is drawn into the Chapter 11 reorganization estate, the Service's tax lien is not dissolved; nor is its status as a secured creditor destroyed. The IRS, under §363(e), remains entitled to adequate protection for its interests, to other rights enjoyed by secured creditors, and to the specific privileges accorded tax

_____

* Renumbered as §507(a)(7) in 1984. — EDS.

collectors. Section 542(a) simply requires the Service to seek protection of its interest according to the congressionally established bankruptcy procedures, rather than by withholding the seized property from the debtor's efforts to reorganize.

The judgment of the Court of Appeals is affirmed.

It is so ordered.

NOTE ON THE RIGHTS OF SECURED PARTIES AFTER REPOSSESSION

Does Justice Blackmun persuade you that this case is appropriately governed by §542? That section requires the turnover of property "that the trustee may use, sell, or lease under section 363." But the definition of "property of the estate" in §541, which §363 uses, refers to "interests" in property, not the property itself. Aren't the debtor's only "interests" remaining in repossessed property those of redemption and surplus? Why, then, must the IRS turn over the property? Justice Blackmun avoids this point (which was made in Cross Electric Co. v. United States, 664 F.2d 1218 (4th Cir. 1981)), by stating that "[a]lthough these statutes could be read to limit the estate to those 'interests of the debtor in property' at the time of the filing of the petition, we view them as a definition of what is included in the estate, rather than as a limitation." But don't definitions function as limitations? What persuades the Court to construe §542 as reaching such repossessed goods?

This problem might be approached from a slightly different angle. Consider, first, a *fully* secured creditor who, following the debtor's default, repossesses the collateral. Following repossession, but before final disposition, one of the debtor's state-law rights is that of redeeming the collateral "by tendering fulfillment of all obligations secured by the collateral." UCC §9-506. If the collateral is worth more in the debtor's hands than in those of a third party, and if the third-party value of the collateral is greater than the debt owed the creditor, it follows that redemption is in the best interest of the debtor (and its creditors). Indeed, as long as the debtor is obliged to give adequate protection that fully compensates the secured creditor for its state-law rights, the debtor has no incentive to redeem the collateral unless it is worth more to the debtor than to a third party.

When the collateral is more valuable to the debtor than to a third party, it may appear odd that the debtor defaulted in the first place. When a debtor is insolvent, however, at least part of the reason may be that it simply had insufficient incentives to keep the assets together. Only the debtor's other creditors might benefit from preventing one creditor's right to repossess from being triggered. And the other creditors are likely to be too dispersed to come up with an effective consensual solution. Notwithstanding that the creditor's repossession may not reflect opt out behavior, therefore, it may well result from debtor passivity and may compromise the interests of the creditors as a group. Should other creditors in a bankruptcy proceeding be bound when one creditor has repossessed before the petition was filed only because of debtor passivity? Should creditors in bankruptcy be able to return to the status quo ante (have the collateral returned and the debt accelerated)?

Viewed another way, requiring turnover upon the receipt of adequate protection is, in effect, redeeming the collateral, at least when the debt was fully collateralized. Whereas redemption usually requires repayment of the debt, here can't it be argued that as is normal in adequate protection cases, the *value* of that return performance is preserved, instead of the actual *right* itself? Phrased this way, isn't this problem merely a variant of the automatic stay problems discussed in the previous section, in which the secured creditor's right to repossess and sell the collateral is taken away, in the name of bankruptcy policy, but in exchange for adequate protection of the *value* of that right? See Jackson, Avoiding Powers in Bankruptcy, 36 Stan. L. Rev. 725 (1984).

There is another facet to *Whiting Pools* that can be analyzed by focusing on repossession by the *under*secured creditor. Such a repossession may in fact reflect "opt out" behavior of the preferential type in two ways. First, an undersecured creditor who repossesses collateral may be attempting to "skim" off a portion of the difference between the collateral's value to the debtor and its value to a third party. Assuming a secured creditor with a security interest has a legitimate right only to sell the collateral to a third party, this attempt to gain more, by virtue of the collateral's "extra" value to the debtor, may be a species of misbehavior against the debtor (and, in bankruptcy, the other creditors).

Alternatively, the undersecured creditor may be trying to improve its position in bankruptcy through redemption. After repossession, the only way a debtor can reacquire the collateral directly is through redemption. Under Article 9, however, redemption requires paying the *entire* debt. UCC §9-506. To the extent the debt is undercollateralized, any such payment before bankruptcy would be preferential. To make redemption, in bankruptcy, a condition for the return of the collateral would likewise reward opt out behavior. It would allow the undersecured creditor to receive indirectly what it could not obtain directly — payment in full of that part of the debt that was unsecured. Because an undersecured creditor can improve its position only by inducing the debtor to exercise that right of redemption, the creditor's ability to improve its position lasts only as long as it holds the property. Once it is sold to a third party, the redemption right disappears.

The result in *Whiting Pools*, accordingly, may appropriately resolve the two problems that a secured creditor's repossession may present: When the debtor is solvent, payment of the whole debt is not detrimental to the interests of any other group. But when the debtor is insolvent, it may not care sufficiently to stop the repossession, because the loss falls on the other creditors. Second, an undersecured creditor may obtain payment in full and opt out of an impending bankruptcy proceeding by repossessing property and forcing the debtor, who values the property more than third parties who might buy it from the creditor, to exercise its redemption right. But so viewed, *Whiting Pools* does not seem to be a "property of the estate" problem. This line of analysis may be both formalistic and troublesome. See Jackson, Avoiding Powers in Bankruptcy, 36 Stan. L. Rev. 725 (1984).

2. Set-off Rights and the Freezing of Accounts

A set-off right in theory is simply a creditor's right to offset a debt it owes against a debt that the other person owes the creditor. See supra page 343. When an entity deposits money in a bank account, it creates an obligation running from the bank to it, just as when the entity borrows money from a bank it creates an obligation running from itself to the bank. Nevertheless, we usually think of the relationship between a bank and a depositor in quite different terms. We imagine that a separate earmarked account exists, and that disputes between a bank and a depositor are over a particular piece of property, even though a bank account has no tangible existence. In reading the next case and the excerpts following it, consider whether there is an unstated assumption that a bank account is a tangible thing over which either the bank or the depositor can exercise dominion.

In the ordinary case of mutual off-setting debts, an entity that files a bankruptcy petition has no power to compel repayments from the creditor, and a creditor hence cannot violate the automatic stay if it does not make them. See §542(b). To what extent should a bank be treated any differently? To what extent is a "freeze" on a bank account any more than the bank's refusal to do what it has no obligation to do in any event? If the bank cannot freeze the account, what can the debtor do? Can the debtor withdraw the money? See §363(a), (c)(2). When do you think the issue arises? What harm is likely to befall the debtor if the bank freezes the account? What harm is likely to befall the bank if debtor withdraws cash and uses it in violation of §363? Does this give you any indication as to how it should be resolved? Should it make a difference if the debtor is an individual or a corporation, given an individual debtor's possible right to keep some cash under §522 for a fresh start?

IN RE EDGINS
36 Bankr. 480 (9th Cir. Bankr. App. 1984)

VOLINN, Bankruptcy Judge.

The Bank of America appeals from an order holding the bank in contempt for violation of the automatic stay. The question presented is, may the bank, a creditor of the debtor, defer withdrawal of funds from debtor's account without violating the 11 U.S.C. Section 362 stay? We hold that the bank may defer access to the account and accordingly reverse. . . .

On July 9, 1982, the debtor, William F. Edgins, filed a bankruptcy petition pursuant to 11 U.S.C. Chapter 13. At the time of filing, the debtor owed $12,500 to the appellant, Bank of America National Trust and Savings Association where he also maintained a checking account. Between July 9, 1982 and the date that the bank received notice of the filing, July 14, 1982, the lowest balance in the debtor's checking account was $7,101.11. The bank placed an "administrative freeze" on the debtor's checking account, precluding him from withdrawing $7,101.11 from said account. . . .

On August 5, 1982, the debtor's Chapter 13 plan was confirmed by the bankruptcy court. On August 9, 1982, the bank filed a proof of claim as an unsecured creditor. The bank amended its proof of claim on August 18, 1982, to assert that $7,101.11 of its claim against the debtor was secured pursuant to 11 U.S.C. Section 506(a).

On August 10, 1982, the debtor filed an application with the bankruptcy court for an order to show cause why the bank should not be held in contempt for violating the automatic stay of 11 U.S.C. Section 362 by withholding from the debtor the funds under the "administrative freeze". The debtor also filed a complaint for turnover of the funds, damages, sanctions and attorneys fees. The bankruptcy court issued an order to show cause on the same date. A contempt hearing was held on August 23, 1982.

On September 7, 1982, the bankruptcy court entered Findings of Fact and Conclusions of Law holding the bank "guilty of contempt for violating the restraining order in the above entitled case"; that a hearing would be held in the future to determine sanctions, damages, costs and attorneys' fees; and that the bank was to release the funds subject to the "administrative freeze", for the debtor's use. . . .

This case, despite its simple facts, involves interaction of the automatic stay of 11 U.S.C. Section 362, setoffs under 11 U.S.C. Sections 553, turnover of property of the estate under 11 U.S.C. Section 542(b), determination of secured status under 11 U.S.C. Section 506(a), and use of cash collateral under 11 U.S.C. Section 363.

Upon the filing of a bankruptcy petition, 11 U.S.C. Section 362(a)(7) operates as a stay of "the setoff of any debt owing to the debtor that arose before the commencement of the case under this title against any claim against the debtor". 11 U.S.C. Section 362(a)(4) operates as a stay of "any act to create, perfect, or enforce any lien against property of the estate", assuming that the secured creditor contemplated by 11 U.S.C. Section 506(a), has a lien.

The elements of a setoff are principally defined in 11 U.S.C. Section 553 which, with certain exceptions apparently not applicable here, allows:

a creditor to offset a mutual debt owing by such creditor to the debtor that arose before the commencement of the case under this title against the debtor that arose before the commencement of the case. . . .

The wording of the statute would indicate that the creditor need not have consummated nor even have asserted the existence of a setoff prior to the filing of the bankruptcy petition.

11 U.S.C. Section 542(b), dealing with the obligation to turnover property of the estate, provides:

. . . [A]n entity that owes a debt that is property of the estate . . . , shall pay such debt to, or on the order of, the trustee, except to the extent that such debt *may* be an offset under Section 553 of this title against a claim against the debtor. (emphasis supplied)

11 U.S.C. Section 542(b) would appear, then, to allow a creditor of the estate who may have a right to setoff funds owing to the debtor or the estate, to defer payment pending a hearing on the right to setoff.

When a creditor defers payment pursuant to an asserted right to setoff, the creditor is not entitled to actually setoff the deferred funds, which would be a violation of 11 U.S.C. Section 362. In turn, the debtor is not permitted to use cash collateral without first obtaining court authority and after notice and hearing.

This stalemate may be alleviated by either party initiating a number of alternative proceedings in the bankruptcy court. Either party might make application for a declaratory determination of whether the frozen account is security by virtue of Section 506(a) and thus subject to a right of setoff under Section 553. The creditor might bring an action for relief from the automatic stay for the purpose of asserting and exercising its security interest and right to setoff. The debtor might bring a motion for use of the security as cash collateral under 11 U.S.C. Section 363. Any of these methods could be pursued by motion and in a shortened time frame, given an emergency. The bankruptcy code does not specify which should be used nor whether the creditor or the debtor should initiate action to break what appears to be a statutory logjam. . . .

The court below concluded that by freezing the subject bank account, the bank has violated 11 U.S.C. Sections 362(a)(7) and (a)(4). The court indicated that the bank should have turned the account funds over to the debtor when demanded and immediately have moved for a freeze of the debtor's use of the funds pursuant to 11 U.S.C. Section 363, until adequate protection could be determined. The court also stated in its findings and conclusions that ". . . the bank is listed as one of the three unsecured creditors, but by its bit of legerdemain it has apparently turned an unsecured claim into a secured claim to allow itself to be preferred over its fellow unsecured creditors."

The bank account represents funds which the bank owes to the debtor. The bank states that it has deferred payment of such funds in which it claims a security interest under 11 U.S.C. Section 506(a) and an eventual right of setoff under 11 U.S.C. Section 553. 11 U.S.C. Section 362(a)(7) enjoins the bank from setting off the funds or applying the funds in the subject account against the debtor's unsecured loan. . . . In re Davis, 29 B.R. 652 (Bkrtcy. W.D.N.Y. 1983). During the hearing on contempt, counsel for the debtor stated that it was his understanding that the subject funds had not been setoff. . . . By deferring payment of the account pending a decision of the bankruptcy court, the bank was not acting to create, perfect, or enforce a lien as prohibited by 11 U.S.C. Section 362(a)(4). The bank held the account open but precluded the debtor's use of the funds pending a determination of its right to setoff. Such an action is recognized and countenanced by 11 U.S.C. Section 542(b), a section of the bankruptcy code which the court below did not consider.

As to the court's characterization of the bank's action as an attempt to prefer itself, the right of a creditor of the debtor's estate to utilize the right to setoff is expressly extended to creditors entitled thereto under 11 U.S.C. Sections 553, 506(a) and 542(b). Given this right, the bank's action was proper.

There is no requirement that the bank bring an action under 11 U.S.C. Section 363 to defer payment of the account funds. The debtor could have moved expeditiously for a determination of the secured status of the funds or a right to setoff, or for use of the account funds as cash collateral under 11 U.S.C. Section 363. The debtor apparently chose not to do so. Since the debtor initiated the problem and had, through his knowledge of the prospect of bankruptcy, control of subsequent events, it should have been his obligation to initiate proceedings to determine a proper disposition of the account funds. Had he done so, the respective claims of interest in the funds would probably have come to a timely disposition, without the ensuing confusion and cost. . . .

Our analysis, is in accord with the decision in Kenney's Franchise Corp. v. Central Fidelity Bank NA, Lynchburg, 22 B.R. 747 (W.D. Va. 1982). See also, In re Davis, supra; In re Gazelle, Inc., 17 B.R. 617 (Bkrtcy. W.D. Wis. 1982).

Certain decisions have come to a different conclusion. Illustrative of these cases is Cusanno v. Fidelity Bank, 29 B.R. 810 (E.D. Pa. 1983).[1] In *Cusanno,* the court stated that 11 U.S.C. Section 553 provides that creditors retain the right to setoff except as provided in 11 U.S.C. Section 362. The court was of the view that a bank's administrative freeze constituted a setoff or was so tantamount to a setoff as to violate Section 362. In addition, it stated that such a freeze was an "act to obtain possession of prop-

---

1. The reasoning of *Cusanno* as to the effect of 11 U.S.C. Section 362 is dicta, the case being decided on the basis that the property was exempt and not subject to setoff.

erty" of the debtor's estate, as prohibited by 11 U.S.C. Section 362(a)(3), and was by the appellant bank's admission, an "act to collect, . . . or recover a claim against the debtor"* as prohibited by 11 U.S.C. Section 362(a)(6). *Cusanno* criticizes the holdings in *Kenney's Franchise,* supra, and *Gazelle,* supra, by observing that such rulings would allow banks to make a determination as to which funds are property of the estate and which funds are cash collateral.

Assuming that the debtor-creditor relationship of bank and depositor allows of positing an argument regarding possession, it is not clear to us how an administrative freeze is an attempt to obtain possession of property of the debtor's estate. The debtor parted with possession or ownership of the funds in question when he made the deposit prior to bankruptcy. The bank in the case at bar has maintained the status quo without taking action to collect or recover a claim against the debtor. It has simply deferred payment of the funds pending the outcome of any proceedings brought by it or the debtor to determine their use and ownership. The debtor does not deny this, stating that it is his understanding, that the funds have not been setoff.

The criticisms of *Kenney's Franchise* and *Gazelle,* supra, seem to be made with little foundation. In this type of situation, banks are not so much making a determination of ownership as giving notice to the debtor that they claim an interest in the funds and intend to prevent dissipation of the bank's claimed interest pending the court's determination of ownership. The *Cusanno* line of cases are not persuasive. They put the burden on the wrong party. Creditors with a valid right of setoff under 11 U.S.C. Section 553 would be required to turnover to the debtor funds subject to setoff and thereafter attempt to obtain an order from the court to preclude the debtor from improvidently dissipating the funds. This will, all too often, be an attempt to lock the barn door after the horse has been stolen. The shield of 11 U.S.C. Section 362, which is procedural and vests no intrinsic interest in property to the estate, should not be used as a sword to divest other parties of legitimate interests in property particularly where the debtor has the knowledge and means to bring whatever claim he may have for use of the funds on for prompt hearing. . . .

The bank's reaction to the complex legal problem brought about by the bankruptcy petition was not improper and does not warrant a finding of contempt. The bank's action to maintain the status quo was a proper and responsible action necessary to create a balance pending prompt action, presumably by the debtor, or ultimately by the bank to resolve the rights of the parties to the funds.

We hold that the bankruptcy court erred in finding the bank guilty of contempt for violating the automatic stay of 11 U.S.C. Section 362. We,

---

* Expanded in 1984 to extend to any act "to exercise control over property of the estate." — EDS.

therefore, reverse the Order Re Contempt entered by the bankruptcy court and remand for proceedings consistent herewith.

ASHLAND, Bankruptcy Judge, dissenting.

I respectfully dissent.

The issue before us is whether the conduct of the bank supports a finding of contempt. I cannot say that the trial court's determination is clearly erroneous.

Under §542(b) an entity is required to turnover property of the debtor except to the extent it is subject to being offset in §553. The setoff in §553 is subject to the automatic stay of §362(a)(7). The administrative freeze is tantamount to a setoff. The bank should have asked for relief from the stay.

I would affirm.

NOTES

1. This issue has been the subject of much litigation. In addition to the cases cited in *Edgins,* similar results have also been reached by In re Stann, 39 Bankr. 246 (D. Kan. 1984); In re Owens-Peterson, 39 Bankr. 186 (Bankr. N.D. Ga. 1984). But a number of other courts have reached the opposite result. See, e.g., In re Lee, 35 Bankr. 452 (Bankr. N.D. Ga. 1983); In re LHG Resources, 34 Bankr. 202 (Bankr. W.D. Tex. 1983). As noted in *Edgins,* Cusanno v. Fidelity Bank, 29 Bankr. 810 (E.D. Pa. 1983), vacated and remanded, 734 F.2d 3 (3d Cir. 1984), also reached the opposite result. Its reasoning was as follows:

> The principal issue in this case is whether the administrative hold placed upon the Cusannos' account by Fidelity constituted a set-off as the term is used in Section 362. However, the Court wishes to note that Section 362 also expressly places a stay upon "any act to obtain possession of property" of the debtor's estate. The freeze on their bank account deprived Mr. and Mrs. Cusanno of the use of those funds. The bank's action was thus tantamount to removing the funds from the possession of the Cusannos and placing the funds in the bank's possession until resolution of the distribution of the estate. Fidelity's action thus appears to have violated 11 U.S.C. §362(a)(3) even if the administrative hold was not a "setoff" within the meaning of §362(a)(7).
>
> Furthermore, §362(a)(6) places a stay upon "any act to collect, assess, or recover a claim against the debtor." By Fidelity's own admission, it froze the assets of the Cusanno account so that Fidelity might eventually collect a greater share of the loan obligation owed to it by the Cusannos. Fidelity's action was thus one to help it collect a claim or recover a claim. Therefore, for the reasons previously noted, the bank's actions violated the automatic stay regardless of whether the freezing of the bank account constituted a setoff.

. . . In [the cases reaching the opposite result], the courts determined that the banks involved had not violated the automatic stay because the funds frozen were "cash collateral" used to secure loans by the debtors within the meaning of 11 U.S.C. §363(c)(2). It should be pointed out, however, that Section 363 prohibits a debtor operating a business from using cash collateral without first obtaining approval of the bankruptcy court or the consent of the bank holding the cash collateral.

[These other] courts seem to assume that the bank has the right to make the initial determination of which bank accounts are cash collateral which the debtor may not use. . . . However, this determination is conclusive only when made by the courts, not when unilaterally decided by interested parties. When there exists a dispute as to the classification of a bank account, neither party has the authority to take action affecting the funds. Instead, the party seeking to take action concerning the funds should first approach the bankruptcy court and file a motion for a declaration of the account's status . . . and a partial lifting of the automatic stay.

2. A similar issue has arisen in connection with the IRS's attempts to "retain" an accrued tax refund of the debtor because of other prepetition tax liabilities of the debtor. United States on Behalf of IRS v. Norton, 717 F.2d 767 (3d Cir. 1983), concluded that such actions violated the automatic stay. While the IRS contended that it had simply "frozen" the refund, and had not engaged in a set off proscribed by §362(a)(7), the Third Circuit concluded that a court must look "to state law to determine when a setoff has occurred." And, under applicable state law, "the retention of a debtor's funds by a creditor provides sufficient evidence of an intent to setoff."

D. EXECUTORY CONTRACTS

With §365, we examine one of the most important provisions of the Bankruptcy Code. Section 365 deals with the trustee's relations to a particular type of asset: "executory contracts and unexpired leases." In one sense, §365 deals with a special class of cases that are generally covered by §541. It tries to implement the bankruptcy principle that a debtor's relationship with the rest of the world should not change simply because the debtor is in bankruptcy. This should mean both that the trustee's rights under an executory contract should be no greater inside of bankruptcy than outside, and that parties contracting with the debtor cannot treat the debtor differently simply because it has filed a bankruptcy petition. But §365, as we shall see, changes nonbankruptcy rights in a number of ways.

In some respects, the provisions of §365 reflect many of the concerns that underlie §362, for §365, in part, allows the estate to keep advantageous contracts and leases the debtor has made, and "stays" at least some

efforts to cancel them while the trustee decides what he wants to do. The
debtor's contracting opposite, however, does not receive the same protection as the holder of rights in other assets. For example, as we have seen,
§362 protects the value of the secured creditor's right to repossess and sell
collateral to pay itself off. In the case of an executory contract or lease,
however, the trustee can often override attempts to cancel and he enjoys
certain rights to assign contracts that the estate cannot itself use.

It is commonly thought that §365 grew out of the trustee's power to
abandon burdensome property. See §554; Brown v. O'Keefe, 300 U.S.
598 (1937); Sparhawk v. Yerkes, 142 U.S. 1 (1891). And §365 does authorize the trustee to reject executory contracts and unexpired leases under
some (perhaps most) circumstances. See In re Minges, infra page 409. But
in a number of respects, the trustee's power under §365 to *assume* and
assign contracts may be the more significant powers granted by that section.

1.   General Nature of Executory Contracts

Section 365 defines neither "executory contract" nor "unexpired lease."
While the latter term may present few interpretive difficulties, the exact
meaning of the phrase "executory contract" in §365 is not self-evident.
The legislative history suggests only that "it generally includes contracts
on which performance remains due to some extent on both sides. A note is
not usually an executory contract if the only performance that remains is
repayment. Performance on one side of the contract would have been
completed and the contract is no longer executory." This statement appears to be based on Professor Countryman's analysis, which follows, and
which is generally considered to be the classic definition of an executory
contract for purposes of bankruptcy law. See, e.g., In re Alexander, 670
F.2d 885 (9th Cir. 1982); Jenson v. Continental Finance Corp., 591 F.2d
477 (8th Cir. 1979); In re J.M. Fields, Inc., 22 Bankr. 861 (Bankr.
S.D.N.Y. 1982). Other suggestions, however, are occasionally made by the
courts, as in the next case, In re Booth. How would these definitions
handle the following problems? How *should* these problems be handled?

PROBLEMS

7.17 Manufacturer has a contract to ship to Debtor 1,000 pairs of
jeans on January 1, with Debtor to pay for them at the rate of $1,000 a
month for seven months. After Manufacturer ships the jeans, but before
Debtor pays for them, Debtor files a bankruptcy petition. Is this an executory contract that the Debtor may assume or reject under §365? What
would be the effect of an assumption of the contract? See Countryman,
Executory Contracts in Bankruptcy, infra.

7.18 Manufacturer contracts in January to ship to Debtor 200 pairs of jeans each month from February through August. In return, to finance the manufacture of the jeans, Debtor prepays the contract price of $10,000. On February 1, before any jeans have been shipped, Debtor files for bankruptcy. Is this an executory contract that the Debtor may assume or reject under §365?

7.19 Consider the facts of Problem 7.17. What happens if on February 1, before any jeans are shipped, Manufacturer rather than Debtor, files a petition in bankruptcy? Is this an executory contract that Manufacturer may assume or reject under §365? Why might Manufacturer might *want* to assume the contract? What if Manufacturer hopes to rehabilitate itself, and needs Debtor as a customer?

7.20 Consider the facts of Problem 7.18, except assume that Debtor only advanced $9,000 of the $10,000. Is this an executory contract that Debtor may assume or reject under $365?

7.21 Debtor orders a drill press from Manufacturer on January 1. The contract specifies that title will pass when the drill press has been identified to the contract and Debtor will pick up the drill press from Manufacturer on January 10. On January 5, Debtor files a petition in bankruptcy. Is this an executory contract?

7.22 Same facts as Problem 7.21, except the contract states that Manufacturer retains title until paid in full. See UCC §§2-401; 1-201(37). Is this an executory contract?

7.23 Business enters into a lease of office space from Debtor in December 1983 for a period of two years. Concurrently, Business leases office furniture from Debtor for the same period at a rental of $5,000 per month. The furniture lease grants Business an option to purchase the furniture at any time before the lease expires at its fair market value at that time, less amounts previously paid under the lease. Debtor files a bankruptcy petition in May 1985. Business wishes to exercise the option to purchase. May Business do so? May Debtor reject the lease and with it Business's ability to exercise the option? Does it matter how large the furniture's fair market value is relative to the rental amounts paid? Cf. UCC §1-201(37).

COUNTRYMAN, EXECUTORY CONTRACTS IN BANKRUPTCY, PART I
57 Minn. L. Rev. 439, 450-452, 458-461 (1973)

II. What Is an Executory Contract?

As Professor Williston has said, "All contracts to a greater or less extent are executory. When they cease to be so, they cease to be contracts." But that expansive meaning can hardly be given to the term as used in the Bankruptcy Act or even to the Act's occasional alternative reference to contracts "executory in whole or in part." The concept of the "executory contract" in bankruptcy should be defined in the light of the purpose for which the trustee is given the option to assume or reject. Similar to his general power to abandon or accept other property, this is an option to be exercised when it will benefit the estate. A fortiori, it should not extend to situations where the only effect of its exercise would be to prejudice other creditors of the estate.

A.   CONTRACTS PERFORMED BY THE NONBANKRUPT

Executory contracts, in the sense in which Professor Williston spoke, abound in a bankruptcy proceeding. One example is the contract under which the nonbankrupt party has fully rendered the performance to which the bankrupt is entitled, but which the bankrupt has performed only partially or not at all. Such a contract will give the nonbankrupt party a provable claim in the bankruptcy proceeding, whether it is liquidated or unliquidated and whether it is absolute or contingent as to liability. The trustee's option to assume or reject should not extend to such contracts. The estate has whatever benefit it can obtain from the other party's performance and the trustee's rejection would neither add to nor detract from the creditor's claim or the estate's liability. His assumption, on the other hand, would in no way benefit the estate and would only have the effect of converting the claim into a first priority expense of administration and thus of preferring it over all claims not assumed — a prerogative which the Bankruptcy Act has never been supposed to have vested in either the trustee or the court. . . .

B.   CONTRACTS PERFORMED BY THE BANKRUPT

Another example of a contract executory in the Willistonian sense which should not be treated as an executory contract within the meaning of the Bankruptcy Act is a contract which the bankrupt has fully performed, but which the nonbankrupt party has performed only partially or not at all. The bankrupt's claim to further performance under such a contract obviously is an asset which in most instances will pass to the trustee under §70a(5) or (6). It is fairly obvious from the terms of the Act alone that such claims in favor of the bankrupt were not viewed as executory contracts. Obviously, the trustee's assumption of the underlying contract would add nothing to his title to the claim. And it would make no sense to say, as §63c does of executory contracts, that the trustee's rejection of a contract fully performed by the bankrupt "shall constitute a breach of such contract." Nor could the other contracting party, who has received full performance from the debtor, have much of a claim under provisions in the chapters providing that upon rejection of an executory contract any person injured by the rejection shall be deemed a creditor.

Since the bankrupt's claim against the other party is an asset which will pass to the trustee, it is one which the trustee can accept or abandon just as he can accept or abandon noncontractual claims. But his acceptance of the asset merely leaves the other party's liability where §70a of the Act has already transferred it, while his abandonment of it merely leaves the other party liable to the bankrupt as he was before bankruptcy. . . .

C. CONTRACTS UNPERFORMED ON BOTH SIDES

Thus, by a process similar to one method of sculpting an elephant,[85] we approach a definition of executory contract within the meaning of the Bankruptcy Act: a contract under which the obligation of both the bankrupt and the other party to the contract are so far unperformed that the failure of either to complete performance would constitute a material breach excusing the performance of the other.[86]

Such a contract, similar to the contract under which the other party has fully performed but the bankrupt has not, represents a claim against the estate. But here that claim may be reduced or totally eliminated if the trustee rejects the contract, because the other party is required to mitigate damages by an amount approximating the value of the performance he is spared by the trustee's rejection. In addition, such a contract, like the one under which the bankrupt has fully performed but the other party has not, represents an asset of the estate to the extent that it carries the unperformed obligation of the other party. But if the trustee elects to assume the contract, as when he accepts other assets to which he takes the title of the bankrupt under §70a, he takes it *cum onere* and must render that performance which the bankrupt had contracted to perform as a condition to receiving the benefits of the contract. Whether in a given case the trustee will assume or reject depends, presumably, on his comparative appraisal of the value of the remaining performance by the other party and the cost to the estate of the unperformed obligation of the bankrupt, although the Act is silent on that point.

———————

The next case finds Professor Countryman's definition too rigid to achieve the purposes the court finds embodied in the Bankruptcy Code.

———————

85. Obtain a large piece of stone. Take hammer and chisel and knock off everything that doesn't look like an elephant.

86. To avoid further complication of an already complex subject, this article speaks generally of two-party contracts. But its analysis will apply to multiparty contracts as well, so long as the "other party to the contract" is limited to one from whom some performance is owing to the bankrupt. Thus, if A and B in a single contract each undertakes to sell a given quantity of goods to C and at C's bankruptcy A has performed but B has not, and C has paid neither, the contract is not executory as to A, but is executory as to B. If C is joined in bankruptcy by D, who had guaranteed payment of the purchase price, D's contract is also not executory as to A, but is executory as to B.

But is the court doing anything more than redefining a state property right? If a state wants to treat land sellers better than general (or even secured) creditors, does §365 necessarily upset that determination? What harm exactly would have been caused had Professor Countryman's definition been used?

IN RE BOOTH
19 Bankr. 53 (Bankr. D. Utah 1982)

Ralph R. MABEY, Bankruptcy Judge.

INTRODUCTION AND FACTUAL BACKGROUND

This case asks whether debtor, who is vendee under a contract for deed, has rights in an "executory contract" within the meaning of 11 U.S.C. Section 365.

Debtor is a debtor in possession under Chapter 11.[1] He is a broker and dealer in real property. His schedules show land worth $2,641,550, most of which has been bought or sold on contracts for deed.

Lewis and Edris Calvert (sellers) made a contract to sell land to debtor at a price of $97,200, with $1,100 down, and the balance payable over time with interest. Sellers must convey title when debtor completes performance. They may forfeit his interest if he defaults. Debtor has resold the property, again using a contract, to a third party, John Collett.

Sellers moved for an order, pursuant to Section 365(d)(2),* directing debtor to assume or reject their contract. Debtor demurred, arguing that the contract is not executory and therefore Section 365 is inapplicable. After denying the motion orally on the record, the court files this explanatory memorandum.

EXECUTORY CONTRACTS AND BANKRUPTCY POLICY

Sellers point to the definition of executory contract formulated by Professor Countryman: "a contract under which the obligations of both the bankrupt and the other party to the contract are so far unperformed that the failure of either to complete performance would constitute a material breach excusing the performance of the other." Countryman, "Executory Contracts in Bankruptcy: Part I," 57 Minn. L. Rev. 439, 460 (1973). This

---

1. He therefore has the powers of a trustee, 11 U.S.C. Section 1107(a), and may assume or reject executory contracts under Section 365(a). "Debtor" is used as a synonym for "trustee."

* Section 365(d) was extensively amended in 1984. Before the amendments (d)(2) applied to nonresidential real property. — EDS.

definition embraces the contract for deed, they maintain, because both sides have unperformed obligations, viz. payment by debtor and delivery of title by sellers. Failure of either to complete performance would constitute a material breach excusing the performance of the other.[3]

Countryman propounded a definition of executory contract which was "functional," that is, "defined in the light of the purpose for which the trustee is given the option to assume or reject. Similar to his general power to abandon or accept other property, this is an option to be exercised when it will benefit the estate." Countryman, supra at 450. From this premise, he framed his test of performance due on both sides. If the creditor has performed, rejection would be meaningless, since "the estate has whatever benefit it can obtain . . . and . . . rejection would neither add to nor detract from the creditor's claim or the estate's liability." Id. at 451. Assumption likewise would be meaningless, and further, would transform the obligation of debtor into a cost of administration, "a prerogative which the Bankruptcy Act has never been supposed to have vested in either the trustee or the court." Id. at 452. If the debtor has performed, assumption adds nothing to his right to performance. Rejection, on the other hand, would not constitute a breach. In short, the Countryman test is an index to when assumption or rejection of a contract will "benefit the estate" and therefore of when a contract is executory.

Section 365, however, reflects a number of policies, including not only benefit to the estate but also protection of creditors. The Countryman test may often define the benefit to the estate, but does it always? And does it speak to the protection of creditors? . . . These questions underlie the refusal of the Commission to define executory contract, Report of the Commission on the Bankruptcy Laws of the United States, H. Doc. No. 93-137, Part I, at 199 (1973) ("any succinct statutory language risks an unintended omission or inclusion"), especially in relation to the contract for deed.

Sections 365(i) and 365(j), for example, give special treatment to nondebtor vendees of land sale contracts. They were passed in response to the plight of nondebtor vendees under former law. In In re New York Investors Mutual Group, 143 F. Supp. 51 (S.D.N.Y. 1956), the debtor had contracted to sell land to a buyer for $105,000. There was a down payment of $15,000 with the balance due at closing in 18 months. Prior to closing, debtor was adjudicated bankrupt. The trustee sought and the referee ordered rejection of the contract with buyer. This order was affirmed on appeal. The court ruled that the interest of buyer was subject to rejection by the trustee and that the remedy of buyer "is a claim for damages for breach of the agreement." Id. at 54. Thus buyer, who under state law may have owned the land, was relegated to the status of an unsecured creditor. . . .

3. Most, if not all, authorities have assumed, often without analysis, and at least where debtor is vendor, that contracts for deed are executory contracts. . . .

Meanwhile, reformers sought change. The Commission spearheaded this movement and Sections 365(i) and 365(j) evolved from its report, see Report of the Commission on the Bankruptcy Laws of the United States, supra at Sections 4-602(d) and 4-602(f)(1), which in turn, was derived from a working paper, . . . later published as Lacy, "Land Sale Contracts in Bankruptcy," 21 U.C.L.A. L. Rev. 477 (1973).

The method for apportioning the benefits and burdens of insolvency, Lacy wrote, cannot be found through "definitions of 'executory.' . . . Instead, the search should be for a policy which defines those interests of present or potential value which may properly be taken from others for the benefit of the bankrupt or his estate." Id. at 482. Nondebtor vendees deserve special treatment, not because their contract is executory in the sense that performance remains due on both sides, but because "the purchaser in this kind of contract is likely to be the buyer of a home or farm or small business who has adjusted to a new location. Very often, especially in the case of a residential buyer, he will be poor. Certainly, modern American bankruptcy policy places as high a value on relieving the poor from the consequences of their own and others' improvidence as in doing perfect justice between creditors." Id. at 484.

He criticized the assumption that "the purchaser whose contract is rejected after he has paid a part of the price will have only an unsecured claim" but that "he may get the land if he has paid the entire price on the ground that the contract is no longer 'executory.' . . . The suggested distinction between paid-in-part and paid-in-full seems utterly capricious. Instead, one should not speculate about the meaning of 'executory' but rather should consider what ought to be thrown into the pot for general creditors and when it is fair to recognize special claims to certain assets." Lacy, supra at 487. . . .

Thus, Sections 365(i) and 365(j), far from representing the Countryman test, are a tonic for the consequence of its application. This suggests that, in the final analysis, executory contracts are measured not by a mutuality of commitments but by the nature of the parties and the goals of reorganization. A debtor as vendee is free from the constraints of Section 365, and is thereby afforded flexibility in proposing a plan, but meanwhile must provide, upon request, adequate protection to vendors. A debtor as vendor may use Section 365 as a springboard to rehabilitation but not at the expense of vendees. . . . Thus, it is the consequences of applying Section 365 to a party, especially in terms of benefit to the estate and the protection of creditors, not the form of contract between vendor and vendee, which controls. This conclusion is supported by many statutory provisions and much judicial gloss.[6]

6. There are many examples of the use of "policy," rather than a rule like the Countryman test, in determining what is an "executory contract" within the scope of Section 365 under the Code and Section 70(b) under the Act. . . .

This approach may be criticized for being result oriented. Result-orientation, however, is endemic to the policymaking which has determined what is an executory contract and when

EXECUTORY CONTRACTS AND THE POLICIES OF BENEFIT TO
THE ESTATE AND THE PROTECTION OF CREDITORS

The contract for deed, where debtor is vendee, benefits the estate more
when viewed as a lien than as an executory contract. This is because
treatment of the contract for deed as a lien enlarges the value of the estate
and furthers the rehabilitation of the debtor. This treatment likewise
makes adequate protection available to creditors.

1. *Enlarging The Value of The Estate.* The assumption or rejection of
executory contracts, like the strong-arm and other avoiding powers, "is a
valuable weapon . . . in the armory of the trustee," meant to free "his
estate to pay a larger dividend to general creditors." Silverstein, "Rejection of Executory Contracts In Bankruptcy and Reorganization," 31 U.
Chi. L. Rev. 467, 468 (1964). If the contract for deed is viewed as an
executory contract, it may be assumed or rejected, but if assumed, it must
be taken *cum onere*, that is, debtor must take the contract as written, with its
benefits and burdens.

In practical terms this means that, absent assumption of the contract,
vendor may enforce his remedy of forfeiture. Vendor, although in substance a mortgagee, may receive an advantage over other lienors, and the
estate may be deprived of whatever equity exists in the property. The
bankruptcy court, as a court of equity, regards substance over form, demands equality of treatment among creditors, and loathes a forfeiture.
The contract should be treated as a lien; the vendor is thereby placed on a
par with other lienors; forfeiture and the loss of equity are prevented. . . .

2. *Furthering the Rehabilitation of the Debtor.* Executory contracts
should be handled to "assist in the debtor's rehabilitation." H.R. Rep. No.
95-595, 95th Cong., 1st Sess. 348 (1977), U.S. Code Cong. & Admin.
News, p. 6304. If the contract is executory, and if it is assumed during the
interim between petition and plan, defaults must be cured, damages must
be paid, and adequate assurance of performance must be given, all as costs
of administration. If the contract is assumed in a plan, the same conditions
must be satisfied with the accumulated costs of administration payable on
the effective date of the plan. The same burdens are imposed if the contract is assigned, in or without a plan. . . .

If the contract is a lien, assumption is irrelevant, and no administrative
costs are incurred. Instead of taking the contract *cum onere*, the lien may be
"dealt with" in a plan, viz., by scaling down the debt, reducing the interest

---

it is rejectable within the scope of Sections 365 and 70(b). Indeed, the Countryman test,
which is predicated on the policy of benefit to the estate, is result oriented. Some commentators and courts have frankly admitted as much. See, e.g., . . . In re Jolly, 574 F.2d 349, 351
(6th Cir. 1978) ("such definitions [as the Countryman test] are helpful, but do not resolve this
problem. The key, it seems, to deciphering the meaning of the executory contract rejection
provisions, is to work backward, proceeding from an examination of the purposes rejection is
expected to accomplish. If those objectives have already been accomplished, or if they can't
be accomplished through rejection, then the contract is not executory within the meaning of
the Bankruptcy Act").

rate, and extending maturities. With or without a plan, the property may be sold free of the lien.

Debtor, like most dealers in the contract for deed, uses that instrument because other financing is unavailable. He can afford little down, and hopes to subdivide and resell in order to meet payments. Chapter 11 has not improved his cash flow. . . . Treating the contract as a lien thus allows more latitude in proposing a plan and thereby furthers the rehabilitation of the debtor.[17]

3. *Adequate Protection of Creditors.* Vendors have two rights under a contract for deed: the right to payment, which is not adequately protected,[18] and the right to hold title as security, which is adequately protected. While the right to payment is suspended, the interest in property is adequately protected. This strikes a balance between vendors, other creditors, and the estate. Vendors are not preferred, for example, in terms of administrative claims, but are treated on a par with other mortgagees, . . . who are protected against any decrease in the value of their liens. . . .

The Basis for Distinguishing between Debtors as Vendors and as Vendees

Sellers contend that Sections 365(i) and 365(j) mean that contracts for deed are executory contracts. They argue that because Sections 365(i) and 365(j) treat some contracts for deed as executory contracts, all contracts for deed must be executory contracts. Put differently, it would be anomalous if contracts where the debtor *sells* realty are executory but contracts where the debtor *buys* realty are not. This would result in the contract between debtor and Collett being executory and the contract between debtor and sellers being nonexecutory although both are identical in form. Consistency in the treatment of contracts for deed, whether debtor is vendor or vendee, is necessary for a sensible construction of the Code.

Seller's argument founders, however, on at least two shoals. First, treatment of the contract for deed as an executory contract, where debtor

---

17. The debtor may still "reject" the contract, if it is "burdensome." Instead of relying upon Section 365, however, he may use the procedure for abandonment in 11 U.S.C. Section 554. Abandonment may save administrative expense since, unlike Section 365(a), it may not require court approval. . . .

18. The right to payment may not be an "interest in property" for purposes of obtaining adequate protection. 11 U.S.C. Section 361 protects against any decrease in value of the lien, it does not guarantee performance of the contract. If Section 361 guaranteed the benefit of the bargain as distinct from the bargain in value, it would be duplicative of Section 365. There would be no breathing spell for debtor to elect whether to assume or reject a contract. This election, in effect, would be made for him by Section 361. Moreover, upon assumption of a contract, "adequate assurance" of performance, unlike adequate protection, may be accomplished by promising an administrative priority. . . .

is vendee, ignores the reasons for enacting Sections 365(i) and 365(j). They were passed to give nondebtor vendees the protection of mortgagors. Viewing the contract for deed as a lien, where debtor is vendee, therefore is consistent with the spirit of these provisions. Second, consistency in terminology, that is treating contracts for deed as executory contracts under Section 365 in every instance, favors nondebtor vendees over debtor vendees and debtor vendors over debtor vendees in bankruptcy. Particularized treatment of the contract for deed is necessary to avoid these consequences.

First. Sections 365(i) and 365(j), as discussed above, were enacted to prevent harm which had occurred under prior law to nondebtor vendees. They accomplish this purpose, where the vendee is in possession, by allowing him to stay, continue payments, and receive title. In short, he is treated as a mortgagor, an analogy frequently drawn by proponents of Sections 365(i) and 365(j). . . .

Countryman notes that mortgages are not executory contracts and "where the vendor of land is himself the purchase money mortgagee, including those cases where applicable nonbankruptcy law will treat the land sale contract as a mortgage, the situation seems no different." Countryman, supra at 472. Then what of a debtor as vendor in California where contracts for deed are deemed mortgages? Under the Countryman test this would not be an executory contract. But this interpretation would deprive homeowners of the protection of Section 365(i). We afford them protection either by sacrificing the symmetry of sellers' argument or by recognizing that vendees are seen as mortgagors under Section 365(i). What about the debtor as vendee? We can take Countryman at face value and call the contract a lien, bypassing Section 365, but it will still be the same piece of paper, which under different circumstances, mandates special treatment to nondebtor vendees under Section 365(i).

Second. Consistency in the characterization of the contract leads to disparity in the treatment of the parties for other reasons. Where debtor is vendor, vendees are protected at least with a lien for the amount paid on the contract under Section 365(j). But where debtor is vendee, he has no protection under Section 365(j). Absent cure and adequate assurance of performance, he stands to lose, through forfeiture, his equity in the property. Likewise, debtor as vendor, under some circumstances, may sell the property free of liens. Thus, unencumbered proceeds, or encumbered proceeds for which adequate protection is provided, may underwrite operations pending workout of a plan, or fund a plan. But debtor as vendee may have no similar option. He must find cash to cure and supply adequate assurance of performance before he may assume the contract. And assumption is a condition to assignment of the contract.

The upshot is that nondebtor vendees, by virtue of Sections 365(i) and 365(j), may receive more favorable treatment in bankruptcy than debtor vendees. And debtor vendors, because of other policies and provisions in the Code, may fare better than debtor vendees. It may be argued that this disparity in treatment is warranted because of the risk of default when debtor is vendor, or because the nondebtor, in each instance, is an innocent victim. But this argument admits that the reasons for calling a contract "executory" may have less to do with the terms of the "paper" than with the status of the parties and their interests in light of bankruptcy policies.

Conclusion

The court is reluctant to depart from a rule as workable as the Countryman test. But application of the rule in this case contradicts the reason for its existence. Classifying the contract for deed, where debtor is vendee, as a lien rather than an executory contract benefits the estate by enlarging the value of the estate and furthering the rehabilitation of the debtor. Sellers, as lienors, enjoy adequate protection. This is in harmony with the rationale for Section 365(i) and 365(j). The blessings and burdens of reorganization are fairly distributed between creditors and the estate.

NOTES

1. In re Gladding Corp., 22 Bankr. 632 (Bankr. D. Mass. 1982), in adopting the approach of *Booth*, stated:

> In so choosing, I do not think there is effected any repudiation of the Countryman rule, but merely a recognition of its function and its limitations. I am fairly certain that no contract which could not pass Countryman muster could ever be called "executory," within the meaning of the Act. On the other hand, Countryman sets out only the threshold inquiry, and leaves for the courts further considerations to determine whether a contract is "truly executory." On that basis, Countryman serves more as an "exclusionary" rule rather than as the ultimate test of an executory contract.

See also In re Adolphsen, 38 Bankr. 780 (D. Minn. 1983).

2. In re Alexander, 670 F.2d 885 (9th Cir. 1982), held a deposit receipt sales contract to sell a house to be executory. Debtor had entered into the contract to sell her house to Buyer for $73,000, under certain conditions to be met in 60 days. On the date for closing, Buyer tendered the $73,000, but Debtor refused to convey title or surrender possession. After Buyer sued, Debtor filed a petition in bankruptcy. The court held that the contract did not cease to be executory when Buyer tendered performance, for "[p]erformance or the rendering of performance, not just tender of performance, is required." Applying the Countryman test, the court noted that:

the deposit receipt sales agreement remained executory. The agreement remained substantially unperformed: plaintiff still had to pay the remainder of the purchase price, and defendant had to give up possession and convey title. Undoubtedly, the contract remained so far unperformed that failure of either side to complete performance by conveying title or paying the purchase price would have constituted a material breach.

2. Grounds for Assumption or Rejection

IN RE MINGES
602 F.2d 38 (2d Cir. 1979)

FEINBERG, Circuit Judge.

Control Data Corporation, lessee of space in an office building owned by James Minges, the debtor in a Chapter XII proceeding, appeals from an order . . . permitting appellee Steven Zelman, the debtor's Chapter XII trustee, to reject certain covenants in the lease. . . . For reasons set forth below, we remand the case for further findings.

I

So far as we can tell from the somewhat sketchy record before us, the following facts appear to be undisputed. Control Data Corporation, which we shall refer to as the lessee, is the successor in interest of Service Bureau Corporation, the original signatory to the lease with Minges for second floor office space in an office complex called Pro Park in Farmington, Connecticut. The lease provided for a 10-year term, commencing December 1, 1967, with an option in the tenant to extend in successive two-year terms for up to 10 more years. Under the lease, the landlord is obligated to furnish hot and cold water, heat, air-conditioning (including the necessary electricity) and janitorial services. The tenant pays utility charges only for lighting its office premises and for the office machines. These charges are separately metered and billed directly to the tenant by the utility company. The lease also gives the tenant a right of first refusal of all other space in the same building and the right to require the landlord to provide up to 16,000 square feet of additional space. The lessee uses the premises 24 hours a day, every day of the year, as a computer facility and service bureau operation. The lease also provides that it is subordinate to any mortgage but that the mortgage shall contain provisions that the mortgagee, in the event of foreclosure "will not attempt to terminate this lease . . . nor interfere with the rights of" the lessee, if the latter is not in default.

In October 1972, Capital for Technology Corporation (CTC) made a loan to Minges, which was secured by a second mortgage on Pro Park.

CTC's parent, Hartford National Bank, also obtained a third mortgage on the property. A year later, CTC paid the arrearages on the first mortgage and exercised its right to take possession of Pro Park. CTC then began a foreclosure action in the state courts and obtained a judgment. Execution of that judgment, however, was stayed after Minges filed his Chapter XII petition in October 1974. The bankruptcy court has allowed CTC to remain as mortgagee in possession of Pro Park, managing the property and collecting the rents.

In September 1976, the Chapter XII trustee petitioned the bankruptcy court to allow him to reject certain portions of the lease as burdensome pursuant to section 413(1) of the Bankruptcy Act. These are the provisions that require the landlord to provide utilities and janitorial service, that grant the tenant the right of first refusal on space in the building that becomes vacant, and that allow the tenant to extend the lease on the original space for five additional two-year terms. According to the bankruptcy judge, there was evidence at the hearing that the value of the space rented under the lease has increased considerably since 1967 from $4.30 per square foot, the lease rate, to "$7.00 per foot or more." The bankruptcy judge also found that in 1967 a reasonably prudent landlord would have expected to spend each year about $7,000 on electricity and $3,000-$4,000 on janitorial service. In contrast, the landlord's annual cost of supplying these services to the lessee in 1975 was approximately $19,000 and $15,250 a year respectively.

After the hearing, the bankruptcy judge in a lengthy opinion granted the trustee's petition to reject the landlord's covenants to supply utilities and janitorial service as well as the tenant's right to additional space, but denied the petition with regard to the tenant's options to extend the term of the lease. Judge Blumenfeld, in a brief opinion, affirmed the decision of the bankruptcy judge. The trustee has not appealed from the portion of the ruling that was adverse to him, and the lessee apparently does not contest in this court the trustee's rejection of the lessee's right to first refusal on additional space. This appeal, therefore, concerns the trustee's rejection of the landlord's covenants to supply utilities and janitorial service.

II

Appellant lessee argues to us that the bankruptcy judge applied the wrong legal standards in deciding whether to grant the relief sought by the trustee. Thus, appellant argues that to justify rejection of the lease, or any part of it, the trustee had to show that the lease caused a net loss to the estate rather than merely insufficient profits, that rejection will serve the purpose of Chapter XII, and that rejection will benefit creditors other than CTC and its parent, which are secured by mortgages. None of these conditions, appellant says, was met.

Before assessing these arguments, the statutory scheme must be briefly reviewed. In proceedings initiated under various chapters of the Bankruptcy Act, the bankruptcy court may allow the trustee or debtor in possession to reject executory contracts of the debtor. Thus, the trustee or debtor, in the proper circumstances, may cancel pre-bankruptcy executory contracts of the debtor that are burdensome. See Countryman, Executory Contracts in Bankruptcy: Part I, 57 Minn. L. Rev. 439, 447-450 (1973). When such rejection occurs, the other party to the rejected contract becomes a general creditor of the estate for any damages flowing from the rejection. See section 63a(9), c. . . .[1]

Turning specifically to Chapter XII provisions, section 413(1) of the Act provides:

> Upon the filing of a petition, the court may, in addition to the jurisdiction, powers, and duties hereinabove and elsewhere in this chapter conferred and imposed upon it—
>
> (1) permit the rejection of executory contracts of the debtor, upon notice to the parties to such contracts and to such other parties in interest as the court may designate;

Section 406(4) of the Act defines "executory contracts" as including "unexpired leases of real property." . . . Therefore, there is no doubt that a Chapter XII trustee has the power, with the permission of the court, to reject a lease as an executory contract. . . .

Although leases are generally treated as executory contracts in the bankruptcy context, they raise some unique considerations, particularly in the relatively rare instance where it is a debtor landlord who seeks to reject the lease. A lease is partly the conveyance of an estate, which is deemed fully executed once the tenant takes possession. Therefore, the weight of authority is that the conveyance aspect of a lease may not ordinarily be unilaterally disturbed by a debtor landlord or his trustee. . . . In this case, the Chapter XII trustee is not seeking to disturb the lessee's possession.

Another nice question that arises with respect to unexpired leases is whether under the Bankruptcy Act they may be rejected in part, i.e., on a clause by clause basis, or only as a whole. Collier states generally that executory contracts must be either rejected or assumed as a whole. See, e.g., 4A Collier on Bankruptcy ¶70.42[1] at 500 (1978). But leases may be an exception, as the bankruptcy judge held in this case, since section 70b

---

1. The recent revision of the Bankruptcy Act, effective October 1, 1979, retains the power of a debtor-lessor, or its trustee, to reject executory contracts including unexpired leases. 11 U.S.C.A. §365(a) (Supp. 1979). However, under that revision, if the lessee remains in possession, as is contemplated here, the lessee may offset damages flowing from the rejection "against the rent reserved under such lease," and the lessee has no further rights against the lessor's estate. Id. §365(h)(2). Our opinion today is predicated solely on the trustee's rejection power under the present Bankruptcy Act, and we intimate no views on what would happen on these facts under the revision.

speaks of "rejection of the lease *or of any covenant therein.* . . ." (Emphasis added). But see 8 Collier on Bankruptcy ¶3.15[7] n.28 (1978), where it is argued that the quoted language merely underscores that a lessee's estate may not be rejected, and that it does not provide support for rejection of only some of the executory portions of a lease. In any event, we need not decide the question whether rejection of only a few of the executory covenants of a lease is permissible since appellant does not challenge the rejection on that basis. On these facts, it is apparent that to the extent the lease is not rejected appellant is benefitted. With these special problems in mind, we turn to the general doctrines in bankruptcy concerning rejection of executory contracts, the framework within which we must work.

The Bankruptcy Act does not list any criteria for authorizing the rejection of an executory contract. As indicated above, section 419(1) of the Act merely provides that "the court may . . . permit" the trustee to do so. However, it is accepted that to justify rejecting an executory contract, it must at least be shown to be "burdensome," since the power to reject derives from the long held doctrine that the bankrupt estate may abandon burdensome property. . . . Appellant argues that this condition is not met here because, as the bankruptcy judge pointed out:

> In the instant case, the debtor is not showing an actual net loss. It is rather showing a net return substantially less than it could obtain without the burden of providing services under the lease covenants.

According to appellant, citing American Brake Shoe & Foundry Co. v. New York Rys. Co., 278 F. 842, 844 (S.D.N.Y. 1922), for the proposition, an executory contract cannot be deemed "burdensome" so long as it produces a profit, and the possibility of greater profit is irrelevant. The bankruptcy judge rejected this view so that the issue is squarely posed on appeal.

In Group of Institutional Investors v. Chicago, Milwaukee, St. Paul & Pacific R.R. Co., 318 U.S. 523, 63 S. Ct. 727, 87 L. Ed. 959 (1943), relied on by the bankruptcy judge, the Court was faced with the same argument also based on the *American Brake Shoe* case. While not explicitly rejecting the contention, the Court did approve rejection of a lease under which the debtor "received a net financial benefit," and concluded that

> the question whether a lease should be rejected and if not on what terms it should be assumed is one of business judgment.

318 U.S. at 549-550, 63 S. Ct. at 743. Appellant stresses that *Institutional Investors* was a railroad reorganization and that the implications of the decision should be confined to bankruptcy proceedings of comparable public interest.

We disagree. Even though the "business judgment" test has been most frequently applied in railroad reorganization cases, . . . the test has not been confined to that context. . . . Moreover, without explicitly using the "business judgment" terminology, a number of courts have employed the substance of that test in emphasizing potential greater profit for the debtor's estate in deciding whether to permit rejection of a particular contract. . . . We believe that such a flexible test for determining when an executory contract may be rejected, however termed (and "business judgment" is as good a label as any), is most appropriate. For in bankruptcy proceedings, the trustee, and ultimately the court, must exercise their discretion fairly in the interest of all who have had the misfortune of dealing with the debtor. A rigid test, permitting rejection only where the executory contract will cause a net loss to the debtor's estate if performed, might work a substantial injustice in cases where it can be shown that the non-debtor contracting party will reap substantial benefits under the contract while the debtor's creditors are forced to make substantial compromises of their claims.

In this case, there is support in the record for a finding that the lease is burdensome. The lessor's covenants to provide utilities and janitorial service consume what has come to be a very large portion of the rental income. Further, there is evidence in the record that the market rental value of the premises has almost doubled, although as indicated above, the trustee does not seek to reject the entire lease, including the relatively low rental figure. Thus, based on that evidence alone, it is not clearly erroneous to find the specific lease covenants at issue here burdensome, since the property is clearly capable of producing more income without them.

Appellant argues that to justify rejection of an executory contract, the trustee must show that doing so will "serve th[e] rehabilitative function of Chapter XII." . . . This position is incorrect. To require that a trustee show that rejection of a particular contract will aid in the rehabilitation of the debtor would substantially undermine the rejection power under section 413(1). Under that section, the power may be exercised at any time, whether or not a plan has been prepared. . . . It may be too early to predict whether the Chapter XII proceeding will ultimately be successful in rehabilitating the debtor when the trustee is faced with the decision of which executory contracts will be assumed and which rejected. It is enough, if, as a matter of business judgment, rejection of the burdensome contract may benefit the estate. Appellant rejoins that even that test was not met, and to that issue we now turn.

The bankruptcy judge found that:

> It is obvious that relieving the debtor of the burdensome executive covenants re utilities and janitorial service will automatically enhance the value of the premises to the benefit of the ultimate beneficiaries, the creditors in Class 3 [the general creditors].

Appellant argues that there is no evidence in the record to support this statement, and that enhancement of the value of the premises would benefit only the secured creditors, CTC and its parent, and not the general creditors. To buttress its claim, appellant points out that the trustee's motion to reject the lease is being prosecuted solely by counsel for CTC, who purports to speak for both CTC and the trustee. And, finally, appellant urges the inequity of permitting the secured creditors to utilize the Chapter XII powers to improve their position over what it would be had they continued their foreclosure action in the state courts, where presumably they would be bound by the provisions in the lease not to "attempt to terminate" it and not to "interfere with the rights of" the lessee. See Butner v. United States, 440 U.S. 48, 99 S. Ct. 914, 59 L. Ed. 2d 136 (1979). The trustee rejoins that the issue remains only one of sound business judgment and that it does not "matter who, secured or unsecured creditors, ultimately benefits from the rejection." . . .

The parties thus lock horns on whether benefit to the secured creditors is enough, on these facts, to justify rejection of the lease covenants under the business judgment test. The disagreement, however, is irrelevant if there was a sound basis for the finding of the bankruptcy judge, quoted above, that the general creditors would benefit from the "enhance[d] . . . value of the premises." We are not satisfied that the record before us on the issue is adequate to decide this issue. We find only the most general estimate of increase in market value if the covenants involved here are rejected and no detailed support, by appraisal or otherwise, for this statement. Nor do we know the amount of the secured debt. Further relevant facts are whether the estate is likely to be adequate to cover administrative expenses and other priority claims, whether there are other properties beside Pro Park in the estate, and if there are, the extent of encumbrances on them. In short, we do not know whether a sound basis exists for a finding that there is a reasonable likelihood that general creditors will derive substantial or significant benefit from the proposed lease rejection. We therefore believe that the proceedings should be returned to the bankruptcy judge to make specific findings after giving the parties an opportunity to present further evidence. While we regret the further delay in the proceedings that a remand for this limited purpose will require, we believe that in the long run it will assist in a proper disposition of the remaining issues raised by the appeal.

Case remanded for further proceedings consistent with this opinion.

MANSFIELD, Circuit Judge (concurring).

I concur in Judge Feinberg's carefully considered opinion.

Where rehabilitation of the debtor is contemplated, I agree that a Chapter XII trustee should be governed by the "business judgment" standard in determining whether burdensome executory lease provisions should be rejected. At the same time, as Judge Feinberg indicates, the standard governing the trustee should be whether there is a reasonable likelihood that general creditors will derive any substantial or significant benefit. If, for instance, the rejection would probably result in no benefit to general creditors or in recovery of only a few dollars for distribution to general creditors holding claims of many thousands of dollars and would result in the mortgagees gaining a windfall at the expense of the lessee, the trustee should not have the power to reject. In the latter case he would in effect be acting as a pawn for the mortgagees, benefiting them at the expense of the lessee, even though the mortgagees took their security with notice of the burdens involved (including the risk of higher utility costs), without any substantial resulting benefit to creditors generally.

As a representative of the bankruptcy court, which is a court of equity, the trustee should not play favorites between the lessee and secured creditors by manipulating the obligations affecting them, absent some significant benefit to the creditors generally. To do so would be inequitable. Although rejection of onerous lease obligations would increase the value of the mortgagees' security, thereby reducing the size of any portion of their claims that could not be satisfied out of the security, it would simultaneously generate claims by the lessee against the estate for loss of his rejected executory rights.

In the present case all parties, including Bankruptcy Judge Saul Seidman, agree that the debtor is in liquidation, having long since lost any hope of rehabilitation. Counsel for the Trustee and the second mortgagee, Capital for Technology Corp., estimated that rejection of the Professional Park lease might increase the value of the property "by approximately $200,000.00," and that "[a]s a result, there might be sufficient equity in the Professional Park property to pay the second mortgage indebtedness held by Capital for Technology Corp. in full and to provide additional funds to satisfy the third mortgage indebtedness to Hartford National Bank and Trust Company." See "Appellees Supplementary Memorandum in Support of Bankruptcy Court's Order Re: Rejection of Executory Lease Covenants as to Control Data Corporation" dated January 17, 1978. However, they refuse to give any opinion as to whether rejection would result in any overage at all for general creditors other than to say it would "enhance the possibility of recovery." I do not think this is enough to justify rejection.

Accordingly, although I agree that a remand for the limited purposes of obtaining more specific findings on the issue of whether the general creditors would benefit from the rejection is appropriate, I would not favor rejection except upon a showing that it would result in some substantial or significant benefit to the creditors generally.

NOTE

On the court's statement that "the weight of authority is that the conveyance aspect of a lease may not ordinarily be unilaterally disturbed by a debtor landlord or his trustee," see §365(h).

NOTE ON THE REASONS FOR REJECTION

The basic and obvious reason for rejecting instead of assuming an executory contract or unexpired lease is that, by reducing what would otherwise be the estate's out-of-pocket expense (or at least administrative expense) to a claim for damages, the estate as a whole is benefitted. Thus, for example, if Debtor has a contract with Seller to buy 1,000 bushels of wheat for $4 a bushel, and the price of wheat falls to $3 a bushel, Debtor can reject the contract and purchase wheat elsewhere for $3 a bushel, saving $1,000.

Upon rejection, Seller will have a claim for damages of $1,000, for rejection is fundamentally equivalent to a breach. Had Debtor's breach occurred before bankruptcy, Seller would be an unsecured claimant in bankruptcy. Section 502(g) provides the same treatment for Seller:

> A claim arising from the rejection . . . of an executory contract or unexpired lease of the debtor that has not been assumed shall be determined, and shall be allowed . . . the same as if such claim had arisen before the date of the filing of the petition.

Seller's claim, therefore, will be unsecured. If, before the rejection, Debtor had $11,000 of assets and $20,000 of creditors' claims, then completion of its contract with Seller would require Debtor to spend $4,000 to get wheat worth $3,000. Debtor's assets would decline to $10,000 total. Each of Debtor's creditors would then be paid 50 cents on the dollar. But if Debtor rejects the contract, Debtor keeps $11,000 of assets, and Seller must be added to the list of Debtor's creditors, so Debtor now has $21,000 of claims against it. But now each creditor (including Seller) gets slightly more than 50 cents on the dollar — about 52 cents. So, the creditors as a group benefit by about 2 cents per dollar of claim; Seller, as a general creditor, receives 52 cents on the dollar as well, and recovers $520. It would have enjoyed a $1,000 benefit had Debtor performed.

Under *Minges,* this is viewed as beneficial to the creditors as a whole, so Debtor may reject. But isn't this just a transfer of wealth — or a transfer of economic misery — from Debtor's creditors as a group to Seller? Is there any reason for this transfer? Treating damages arising from rejected contracts as pre-petition obligations may reflect a judgment that the beneficiary of a favorable contract typically has nonbankruptcy rights identical to those of general creditors (an action for money damages if the debtor reneges on its promises), so it is appropriate in bankruptcy to treat it like a general creditor. Assuming that is so, note that the right §365 gives the trustee to reject executory contracts is unexceptional. Even without that right, and indeed without bankruptcy, the debtor could breach a contract and convert the other party's entitlement into an unsecured obligation. So viewed, rejection is just a fancy word for breach.

But is this always the case? Consider, for example, what the result should be if the beneficiary of a favorable contract has a right to specific performance outside of bankruptcy. Section 365 also appears to permit rejection here, where the claim would be converted into one for damages. Should this right not be recognized in full in bankruptcy? In considering that, recall that the justification for refusing to recognize a party's right to specific performance outside of bankruptcy generally is that specific performance is less a property right than a surrogate measure of damages under circumstances in which ascertaining actual damages is difficult. See supra page 168. Though crude, using a damage measure for land and other kinds of unique property in bankruptcy ensures that all such parties share the misery more or less equally with general creditors. (Whether this rationale would also apply to special forms of specific performance rights, such as exist in labor law contracts, is examined in the Note on Labor Law Contracts in Bankruptcy, infra page 474.) What if the contract in issue is a licensing agreement in which the nonbankrupt party is the licensee and has invested substantial money in developing the product? Outside of bankruptcy these, too, are protected by a specific performance right. Is such a licensing agreement an executory contract, capable of rejection? See In re Richmond Metal Finishers, 38 Bankr. 341 (E.D. Va. 1984); cf. In re Rovine Corp., 6 Bankr. 661 (Bankr. W.D. Tenn. 1980) (franchise agreement with covenant not to compete). Would it matter, in deciding whether to permit rejection, whether one could show that harm to the licensee would be substantial (such as costs in developing a product that, without use of the license, would be useless)? See In re Petur U.S.A. Instrument Co., 35 Bankr. 561 (Bankr. W.D. Wash. 1983). Would it be proper for the debtor to argue that rejection was intended simply to coerce the licensee into paying a new, higher royalty for the product, and thus should be permitted? Is this a proper purpose of §365? Cf. *Richmond Metal Finishers,* supra. Should it be enough for the licensee to show that creditors of the licensor would have no way to set aside the licensing agreement outside of bankruptcy?

Would anything change if a secured creditor were in the picture (or a buyer or someone else)? Who is getting the benefit of any rejection in *Minges?* Does that matter?

PROBLEM

7.24 Debtor owns a plot of land on Rodeo Drive. In 1982, Debtor leased the land to *A* Corp. on a 99-year lease, at $100,000 a year, giving rights to *A* Corp. to improve the land. *A* Corp. built a two-story retail complex in 1983, at a cost of $15 million. *A* Corp. then leased out the stores to various businesses. In 1985, Debtor files a petition in bankruptcy. May Debtor reject the lease? Should there be any limits on its right to do so? Will

§365(h) be of any relevance? Cf. In re Unishops, Inc., 543 F.2d 1017 (2d Cir. 1976); In re Petur U.S.A. Instrument Co., 35 Bankr. 561 (Bankr. W.D. Wash. 1983).

JACKSON, TRANSLATING ASSETS AND LIABILITIES TO THE BANKRUPTCY FORUM
14 J. Legal Studies 73, 104-107 (1985)

Much of the difficulty caused by executory contracts arises out of the failure to perceive the relationship between assets and liabilities in bankruptcy. Fundamentally, executory contracts are "mixed" assets and liabilities arising out of the same transaction. If the nonbankrupt party has fully performed, then the contract is not executory because the issue is only one of a liability of the debtor — a claim. Bankruptcy treats such contracts as automatically rejected in the sense that the claimant must share according to nonbankruptcy priorities. These claims are, at that time, analytically no different from claims arising out of simple loan transactions where the debtor has not repaid borrowed money. If, on the other hand, the debtor has performed fully, then the contract is not executory for precisely the opposite reason. Since the debtor only has to await a return performance by the other party, the contract is an asset of the estate that, like all assets, is automatically assumed.

Contracts, however, that remain to be performed to a substantial extent by both parties bear attributes both of assets and of liabilities. The debtor's unperformed obligations are liabilities from the perspective of the debtor's other claimants, while the nonbankrupt party's unperformed obligations are an asset from their perspective. The question how to treat these mixed contracts in bankruptcy would have been aided if bankruptcy law just traced out the consequences of recognizing any such contract as *both* an asset and a liability. This analysis would really not be different from that raised by cases such as *Chicago Board of Trade* or *TMC Industries,* where an asset was coupled to a particular liability. In those cases, one determines relative values concurrently with establishing the residual value of the asset. That valuation is done by netting out the difference between the asset and the liability and giving the holder of the liability a superior "claim" to the extent of the value of the asset. There is conceptually no reason to treat executory contracts any differently.

In *Chicago Board of Trade,* for example, the debtor held an asset (membership in the Board of Trade) that could be sold for, say, $10,000. But because of the rules of the Board of Trade, it could not be sold without first paying off membership debts. If there were $5,000 of such debts, the net value of the asset would have been $5,000 to the debtor's other claimants. If, however, there were $15,000 of such debts, the membership liabilities would exceed the value of the asset, and there would be no residual value to the other claimants (beyond getting rid of $10,000 of competing claims). There is no normative reason to reach a different result simply because one characterizes the membership as an executory contract.

This principle, of course, may be extended. For example, a lease that has one year to run at a rental of $10,000 may or may not be valuable to the other claimants, depending on the value of the leased space to the debtor. If, however, the lessor has the right to terminate the lease under nonbankruptcy law, then *Chicago Board of Trade* would suggest that the value of the lease to the debtor's other claimants would be net of the liability to the landlord — which, in this case, may be a residual of zero.

Understanding this simple relation between assets and liabilities would remove much of the current obscurity in bankruptcy law respecting executory contracts. Much case law and existing analysis asking whether a contract is executory, for example, create unnecessary work on the question of rejection. Rejection occurs when the debtor is trying to affect the liability. Apart from contracts that effectively give the holder a right of specific performance . . . , rejection is simply tantamount to a breach of the contract permitted under nonbankruptcy law. Under applicable nonbankruptcy law, a breach gives rise to a monetary claim for damages. For that reason, when the issue is one of rejection of an "ordinary" contract, it makes no difference whether the contract is executory (in which case rejection gives rise to a claim for damages) or nonexecutory (in which case the filing of bankruptcy itself is viewed as a breach of the debtor's obligations — such as loan repayment — also giving rise to a claim for damages). That much ink has been spilled on the question, however, comes from the failure to appreciate the nature of both claims and property in bankruptcy.

Recognizing that all executory contracts really raise the same type of inquiry as other "claims" or "property" cases — having mixed attributes of both assets and liabilities, subject to the special feature that the asset is coupled to the liability — would have a number of implications for the shape and direction of the Bankruptcy Code. Like secured creditors and other property claimants, parties to an executory contract would, for example, be prohibited by the automatic stay from removing the "asset" represented by the contract from the bankruptcy estate. Nonetheless, the price for that protection would be that the debtor "adequately protect" the liability represented by the contract to the extent of its value in the hands of the other party. Prebankruptcy terminations of executory contracts, moreover, would be reachable by the trustee using his avoiding powers, just as prebankruptcy grabs by other creditors are. But again, once the trustee recovered the asset represented by the contract, the condition of keeping it would be that the asset's value to the non-bankruptcy party be adequately protected.

The failure to see the components of asset and liability in each executory contract and, accordingly, to see the close kinship between executory contracts and other forms of claims and property rights has introduced complex and unnecessary structures in the Bankruptcy Code that, in turn, lead to undesirable incentives to resort to bankruptcy for reasons that do not spring from the justification for bankruptcy's existence. Section 365 permits the trustee to cure defaults and assume executory contracts if, on balance, the asset represented by the contract is worth more to the debtor than its corresponding liability. But the level of protection that the other party receives under the section is that specified in the contract, not the market rate (which is the level of protection received by secured creditors and other holders of property rights when the debtor wishes to retain use of an asset). The preference section, conversely, is not construed to reach prebankruptcy terminations of executory contracts and unexpired leases, notwithstanding that these terminations also remove assets from the bankruptcy estate.

NOTE

"Were it not for §365, all contracts and leases in which the debtor had a legal or equitable pre-petition interest would become property of the estate under §541(a)(1). Perhaps §365 should be viewed as a limitation on §541(a)(1) giving the debtor . . . an option to decide whether executory contracts and unexpired leases should become property of the estate." Bordewieck and Countryman, The Rejection of Collective Bargaining Agreements by Chapter 11 Debtors, 57 Am. Bankr. L.J. 293, 303 (1983).

NOTE ON LABOR LAW CONTRACTS IN BANKRUPTCY

Outside of bankruptcy, an entity's right to refuse to perform a contract and pay damages is limited. We have already seen how this limitation is largely ignored in bankruptcy when a right to specific performance exists, in order to insure parity between those having actions for debt and those having actions for breach of contract, supra page 168. But what of labor law contracts? Section 8(d) of the National Labor Relations Act requires an employer to engage in an elaborate ritual before it may unilaterally reject a contract. A failure to follow it is an unfair labor practice that, in theory, subjects the employer to an injunction requiring it to comply with the collective bargaining agreement.

This part of labor law is presumably justified by more than that specific performance measures the injury suffered by an innocent party more accurately than a money damages award. Should the trustee have any power to disaffirm a collective bargaining agreement? Has an employer who enters a collective bargaining agreement fundamentally restructured its enterprise both with respect to its workers and all third parties in a way that someone who enters into a simple contract has not? Do employees under a collective bargaining agreement have something akin to a lien on their employer's assets? For purposes of bankruptcy law, do we ever need to ask if giving employees such rights is a good idea? Is this a *bankruptcy* question?

Under traditional labor law doctrine, the owners of a firm are always free to liquidate its assets and to invest the proceeds in a different kind of enterprise. Hence, labor law may skew the owners' decision about the proper use of their firm's assets toward liquidation. Even if the assets under their current configuration are worth more to the owners than if liquidated or sold as a unit to another manager, the owners may liquidate the firm or sell the assets because it allows them to escape from a collective bargaining agreement. Arguably, we would be better off if workers had the same claims on the assets regardless of whether they remained in their current configuration, were broken up, or were sold to a third party. But other policies of labor law may outweigh the undesirable deployment of assets that may result from this rule. More to the point, whether this labor law policy is good or bad is not a concern of bankruptcy law. Shouldn't bankruptcy law take labor law as it finds it, and respect the distinction drawn between continuing the firm and liquidating it or selling it to third parties?

In NLRB v. Bildisco and Bildisco, 104 S. Ct. 1188 (1984), the Supreme Court addressed the questions of whether a collective bargaining agreement was an executory contract subject to rejection under §365(a) and, if it were, what standard should govern the rejection. Justice Rehnquist, writing for the Court, rejected arguments that, in assessing how a bankruptcy petition changed the firm's rights and obligations, it was bound to follow one of the two labels that nonbankruptcy law would apply to a change in ownership, 104 S. Ct. at 1197-1198:

> Much effort has been expended by the parties on the question of whether the debtor is more properly characterized as an "alter ego" or a "successor employer" of the prebankruptcy debtor, as those terms have been used in our labor decisions. . . . We see no profit in an exhaustive effort to identify which, if either, of these terms represents the closest analogy to the debtor-in-possession. Obviously if the latter were wholly a "new entity," it would be unnecessary for the Bankruptcy Code to allow it to reject executory contracts, since it would not be bound by such contracts in the first place. For our purposes, it is sensible to view the debtor-in-possession as the same "entity" which existed before the filing of the bankruptcy petition, but empowered by virtue of the Bankruptcy Code to deal with its contracts and property in a manner it could not have done absent the bankruptcy filing.
>
> The fundamental purpose of reorganization is to prevent a debtor from going into liquidation, with an attendant loss of jobs and possible misuse of

economic resources. . . . [T]he authority to reject an executory contract is
vital to the basic purpose of a Chapter 11 reorganization, because rejection
can release the debtor's estate from burdensome obligations that can impede
a successful reorganization.

As it rejects the use of nonbankruptcy labels, does the Court properly
identify the purpose of reorganization law in particular and bankruptcy in
general? Does it recognize that economic resources can be misused either
by liquidating a firm *or* by trying to reorganize it? Does it recognize that the
total number of jobs in a society does not necessarily fall if one firm is
closed down and the assets are sold to another firm? In *Bildisco,* the Court,
adopting a standard generally used by the courts of appeal, unanimously
held

> that the Bankruptcy Court should permit rejection of a collective bargaining
> agreement if the debtor can show that the collective bargaining agreement
> burdens the estate, and that after careful scrutiny, the equities balance in
> favor of rejecting the labor contract. . . .
>   Before acting on a petition to modify or reject a collective bargaining
> agreement, however, the Bankruptcy Court should be persuaded that rea-
> sonable efforts to negotiate a voluntary modification have been made and
> are not likely to produce a prompt and satisfactory solution.
>   Since the policy of Chapter 11 is to permit successful rehabilitation of
> debtors, rejection should not be permitted without a finding that that policy
> would be served by such action. The Bankruptcy Court must make a rea-
> soned finding on the record why it has determined that rejection should be
> permitted. Determining what would constitute a successful rehabilitation
> involves balancing the interests of the affected parties — the debtor, credi-
> tors, and employees. The Bankruptcy Court must consider the likelihood
> and consequences of liquidation for the debtor absent rejection, the reduced
> value of the creditors' claims that would follow from affirmance and the
> hardship that would impose on them and the impact of rejection on the
> employees. In striking the balance, the Bankruptcy Court must consider not
> only the degree of hardship faced by each party, but also any qualitative
> difference between the types of hardship each may face.
>   The Bankruptcy Court is a court of equity, and in making this determi-
> nation it is in a very real sense balancing the equities. . . . Nevertheless, the
> Bankruptcy Court must focus on the ultimate goal of Chapter 11 when
> considering these equities. The Bankruptcy Code does not authorize free-
> wheeling consideration of every conceivable equity, but rather only how the
> equities relate to the success of the reorganization. The Bankruptcy Court's
> inquiry is of necessity speculative and it must have great latitude to consider
> any type of evidence relevant to this issue.

The Court also held, although on a 5-4 vote, that unilateral rejection of the
collective bargaining agreement did not violate the National Labor Relations Act.

A collective bargaining agreement is different from an ordinary contract in that it governs the relations between an employer and its workers, present and future. For example, in *Bildisco*, the employer had only three employees at the time of the lower court hearing on rejection, even though it once had 18 and hoped in the future to expand its work force to 10. The greatest savings a debtor's creditors enjoy from the rejection of a collective bargaining agreement may come from being able to pay lower wages to new workers who never had contractual dealings with the employer. The definition of "claim" under the Bankruptcy Code is broad enough to encompass all the losses existing workers incur from the breach of the collective bargaining agreement. Does it also include the reduction in wages future workers would otherwise have received?

In *Bildisco*, the Court also asserted that the bankruptcy court must consider the hardships both creditors and workers would experience following assumption or rejection. But don't the two considerations necessarily balance each other out? If the collective bargaining agreement is favorable to the workers and is affirmed, the creditors are worse off. If it is rejected, the workers are worse off to the same extent. If these concerns disappear, why doesn't the Court's "balance of the equities" test simply reduce to the conventional test we saw in *Minges* of whether affirming the contract benefits or harms the debtor? What are the "qualitative differences between the types of hardship" workers and creditors may face? Do workers face greater hardships because they have only a single debtor, while most creditors have many and are protected through diversification? Or might the Court argue that creditors face greater hardships because they stand to lose cash, while workers may lose more intangible things such as favorable work rules?

If one concedes that collective bargaining agreements can be rejected in bankruptcy (as all the parties in *Bildisco* were willing to do), can one find a principled justification for a standard different from the one we ordinarily use for executory contracts? How can one justify a test allowing a rejection only if it makes a successful reorganization more likely than not? Note that under such a test, the trustee would have to assume a collective bargaining agreement even if assumption would increase the chances of liquidation from 5 percent to 45 percent, but could reject if assumption would increase the chances of a successful reorganization from 49 percent to 51 percent. Determining how assumption or rejection would affect the chances of liquidation or reorganization, however, may be so difficult that the party with the burden of proof might usually lose.

Bildisco was viewed in the popular press as a defeat for organized labor. While one can question that assessment, in light of the union's ability to strike (see Briggs Transportation Co. v. International Brotherhood of Teamsters, 739 F.2d 341 (8th Cir. 1984); see also *Crowe*, supra page 397), and the need of the debtor to pay damages for breach of the collective bargaining agreement, the issue immediately returned to Congress. One

of the most important changes made by the 1984 Bankruptcy Amendments was a new section, §1113, designed to deal explicitly with the issues
raised in *Bildisco*. Labor contracts are different from ordinary contracts.
Parties are usually free to choose whether to perform or pay money damages, but not with respect to labor contracts. There are procedural hoops
management must jump through if it wants to renegotiate labor law contracts. Section 1113 arguably mimics these procedures. Nevertheless, one
might ask if a new section were necessary. As a practical matter, the most
important issue is whether a debtor can unilaterally repudiate a collective
bargaining agreement. Section 365 arguably can be read as allowing a
debtor to reject a contract or its terms only after receiving court approval.
This question was never put before the Court in *Bildisco*, which discussed
only whether unilateral rejection was an unfair labor practice.

One might also note that the new labor law provisions are misplaced.
They form a new section added to Chapter 11, which governs reorganizations. But they should apply to Chapter 7 liquidations as well. (One can
have a liquidation under Chapter 7 in which the assets are sold as a unit so
that the firm stays intact as a going concern under new ownership.)

Playing out the new procedures in §1113 is very difficult. It is hard to
know where they will all lead. The popular press reported these provisions
as a victory for organized labor and an overruling of *Bildisco*. But one can
read §1113 as saying that the *Bildisco* standard remains. The only change is
that unions get greater (or at least more definite) procedural rights than
the Court guaranteed in *Bildisco*. Yet the new procedures under §1113
may also be interpreted as working a fundamental change in the substantive rights of labor and management that effectively overrules *Bildisco*.
This ambiguity may not be due to careless drafting. Sometimes compromises are possible and legislative deadlocks are broken precisely because
crucial details are left uncertain.

Debtor files a Chapter 11 petition. Assume Debtor is insolvent and all
agree it belongs in Chapter 11. As in *Bildisco* itself, there is no abuse of the
bankruptcy process. Debtor pays its workers $20 an hour under a collec-
tive bargaining agreement. The prevailing wage for these workers in the
open market is $10 an hour. (The discrepancy is due in large part to the
fact that Debtor's industry was recently deregulated, and Debtor's labor
contract was signed back in the days of regulated prices for Debtor's
product or service.) Debtor would like to get rid of the collective bargaining agreement. It has a much better chance of surviving in the market if its
labor costs are the same as its competitors'. What does Debtor (or its
trustee) have to do?

Under *Bildisco*, Debtor could unilaterally reject without violating the
National Labor Relations Act. In approving the rejection, a bankruptcy
court was supposed to balance the equities, but in what manner was not
clear. Giving the workers more means giving everyone else less and vice
versa. It is hard to find a baseline. But Debtor didn't have to show that the

business would fold and the workers lose their jobs anyway if the contract were rejected. Debtor arguably had to do little more than show that rejecting the agreement made the firm marginally more competitive. Courts largely neglected the tricky damages issue that ought to arise whenever a collective bargaining agreement is rejected, although some recognized that it was there. See, e.g., In re Bildisco, 682 F.2d 72, 80 (3d Cir. 1982), aff'd, 104 S. Ct. 1188 (1984).

What happens now under §1113? After it files a petition, Debtor must make a proposal of contract modifications to the union that are necessary to permit the reorganization and that treat all affected parties (including, presumably, nonunion workers) fairly and equitably. Debtor also has to provide the information that shows its financial condition, although it can obtain protective orders to prevent disclosure to competitors of confidential information. Debtor then can file an application for rejection of the collective bargaining agreement. The court must have a hearing within 14 days, unless the interests of justice require an extension, but the hearing must be within 21 days unless Debtor consents to a longer delay. The court then must rule within 30 days. If it does not, Debtor can terminate or alter any provision of the collective bargaining agreement pending the court's ruling. Before the hearing, Debtor and the union representatives have to meet and discuss Debtor's proposal. The court will approve the rejection if it finds that Debtor made a proposal for modification, the union refused to accept it, and the balance of equities favors a rejection.

What should be made of this? One can argue that management won a nearly complete victory. It is true that unilateral rejections are not possible, but the bankruptcy court has to decide within seven weeks, which is faster than many other decisions it makes, and an employer can obtain interim modifications if it needs them. The standard for rejection is the "balance of the equities" test, which is exactly what existed in *Bildisco*.

But there may be a catch here. One may never get to balancing the equities. Before Debtor can reject, it has to propose modifications, and Debtor can advance only those necessary to permit the reorganization. Only after these proposals are made in good faith and rejected by the union, does one reach the balance of the equities test. To satisfy the procedure (negotiate with the union), management may have to propose modifications that are much less attractive than simply insisting that workers take the market wage.

NOTE ON LIMITATIONS ON REJECTIONS

Minges discusses the general constraints on the trustee's powers to reject an executory contract or unexpired lease, while the issue of collective bargaining agreements raises a special case. Section 365 contains other effective limitations on the trustee's powers to reject, not by restricting the *right* to reject, but by restricting the *effect* of any rejection. *Booth,* supra, discussed those restrictions in §365(i) and (j). In addition, you should review §365(h). All of these deal with persons buying or leasing real property. Are the reasons for carving out these exceptions, and limiting them to real estate, persuasive? Consider the following, from a working paper prepared for the Commission on Bankruptcy Laws, Report of the Commission on Bankruptcy Laws, part I, at 199 (1973):

> an installment contract purchaser . . . has made his payments in reliance on a particular asset belonging to the vendor and this, taken with his right of possession and substantial protection against loss of rights through the default, justifies full preservation of his right to the property in the vendor's bankruptcy. If further reason is needed for distinguishing installment contracts from "really executory" ones it may be found in the consideration that the purchaser in this kind of contract is likely to be the buyer of a home or farm or small business who has adjusted to a new location. Very often, especially in the case of a residential buyer, he will be poor. Modern American bankruptcy policy certainly places as high a value on relieving the poor from the consequences of their own and others' improvidence as in doing perfect justice between creditors.

Even if some right of possession is being recognized in these cases, do those reasons also justify §365(j)? Why should a prepayment by a purchaser be treated any differently on a real estate transaction than on a chattel transaction? Is §365(j) justifiable *because* of the relation to §365(i)?

3.   *Limitations on the Power to Assume*

Section 365 contains a number of restrictions on the power to assume an executory contract or unexpired lease. Section 365(b) provides that if defaults have occurred in the contract or lease, the trustee must cure such defaults, or provide adequate assurance of prompt cure (unless such defaults are of the kind specified in §365(b)(2), which we will explore below) and must provide "adequate assurance of future performance under such contract or lease." Note that this provision applies only to contracts that are assumed *after* breach. Why shouldn't the trustee be required to provide such assurance of future performance in all cases?

If there has been a default, particular types of assurances must be given in the case of a shopping center (§365(b)(3)) regarding tenant mix, percentage leases, and so forth, before such a lease may be assumed. As originally enacted, this subsection required the trustee to give adequate assurance that provisions on tenant mix and other conditions would not be breached "substantially." This qualification was dropped in 1984. The legislative history states that "[p]rotection for tenant mix will not be required in the office building situation." Why are shopping centers treated differently than office buildings? What *is* a shopping center?

The timetable for assuming or rejecting executory contracts or unexpired leases is set forth in §365(d). Is the distinction between residential and personal property, on the one hand, and nonresidential real property, on the other hand, sound? Does §365(d)(3) as drafted ensure that the debtor cannot use nonresidential real property at the lessor's expense? But does §365(d) implicitly allow the debtor to take advantage of lessors of other kinds of property?

PROBLEMS

7.25 Contractor, the general contractor on a highrise office building, engages Subcontractor to perform the electrical work. During the construction of the building, Subcontractor files for bankruptcy. What does Contractor do? May Contractor hire a new subcontractor? Does it matter whether Subcontractor is yet in default?

7.26 Seller enters into a contract with Debtor on July 1, to sell 100,000 pairs of jeans to Debtor at a price of $800,000. The jeans are scheduled to be delivered on December 1, and payment is to be made in $100,000 installments for the eight months thereafter. You represent Seller, and discover on November 1 that Debtor has filed a petition in bankruptcy. You call Debtor (as debtor in possession) to see whether it will assume the contract, but receive noncommittal answers. What do you advise Seller to do? Is Seller required to continue making the jeans and to deliver them on December 1? See §362(d); see also UCC §2-609. What role does §365(e)(1) play in your advice? Could Seller refuse to deliver on December 1, except for cash? Is the contract one to "extend . . . financial accommodations," §365(c)(2)? See legislative history to §365. How much is Seller harmed if it performs under the terms of the contract? If Debtor then accepts? If Debtor then rejects?

7.27 Debtor has a contract with Lessor to rent a computer for three years, cancellable at any time on ten days' notice. Debtor has filed a bankruptcy petition. May Debtor keep the lease in force? May Lessor cancel the contract by giving the ten-day notice, or is that barred by the automatic stay? Cf. In re Cahokia Downs, supra page 364. If Debtor refuses to disclose whether it will affirm or reject, what should Lessor do? See §365(d).

IN RE R. S. PINELLAS MOTEL PARTNERSHIP
2 Bankr. 113 (Bankr. M.D. Fla. 1979)

Alexander L. PASKAY, Bankruptcy Judge. . . .
This is a business reorganization case filed by R. S. Pinellas Motel Partnership (the Debtor) who seeks relief under Chapter 11 of the Bankruptcy Code, 11 U.S.C. 1101 et seq. The matter under consideration is an application for temporary restraining order sought by the Debtor pending

the resolution of its claim for an injunction against Ramada Inns, Inc., the Defendant named in this adversary proceeding (Licensor). . . .

The Debtor-Licensee is the owner and operator of a motor hotel facility located in St. Petersburg, Florida. The facility which opened for business in 1971 contains 177 guest rooms, together with a restaurant and a cocktail lounge and banquet facilities and other facilities such as a swimming pool. The facility is operated as Ramada Inn pursuant to a License Agreement entered into on the 31st of December, 1969 by Ramada Inns, Inc. (Licensor) and the Debtor (Licensee). Pursuant to the terms of the Agreement, the Licensee is entitled to all benefits offered by the Licensor, such as national advertising, use of the distinctive sign (logo), use of the system's central computerized nationwide and international reservation system, and access to a toll free number where the public may make advance reservations in all facilities operated as part of the Ramada System. In addition, the Licensee has the benefit of the good will and the favorable name recognition established by the Ramada System. The Licensee under the agreement is required, in addition, to pay a royalty to the Licensor, and to maintain the facility in conformity with the standard of the quality established by the Licensor. In order to assure a compliance with this provision of the License Agreement, the Licensor conducts periodic on site inspections of the premises of its Licensees. The Agreement authorizes the Licensor to cancel and terminate the License Agreement if the Licensee fails to maintain the premises in conformity with the standard of operation set forth in detail in the License Agreement. The License Agreement further provides that in the event the Licensee shall violate any terms, provisions [or] covenants of the License Agreement and such violation continues for a period of 30 days after a written notice from the Licensor, the Licensor may at its option, immediately declare the License Agreement cancelled and terminated.

The License Agreement further provides that whenever under the Agreement a notice is required, the same shall be in writing and any notice so mailed shall, for all purposes, be deemed to have been given to and received by the party for whom the notice was intended 48 hours from the date said notice was mailed. The record further reveals that the Debtor prior to August, 1979 was delinquent in its royalty payment obligations under the License Agreement and it was indebted to the Licensor in the amount of $57,212.68. It further appears that in August, 1979, the Debtor negotiated for and obtained a loan from Florida Federal Savings and Loan (Savings & Loan). As part of this transaction, the Licensor assured the Lender that if the delinquency is cured, and all past due royalty payments are made and brought current, it will consider the License Agreement to be in good standing, in full force and effect and all previous monetary defaults will be disregarded and forgiven. There is no dispute that the Debtor satisfied the outstanding obligation mentioned above and paid to the Licensor all past due sums under the License Agreement.

It is further without dispute that the periodic inspection conducted by the Licensor found the Licensee to be in violation in several respects of the standard of operations set forth in the License Agreement . . . and these violations continued to exist at least for a year. . . . These violations are recognized and admitted by the Debtor itself as it appears from an internal inspection report prepared by an employee of the Debtor. . . . The last inspection conducted by the Licensor was on October 30, 1979 and indicated that while the restaurant operation lived up to the standard of operation, the hotel operation did not. The Debtor concedes that substantial deficiencies exist but claims that they could be cured within 60 days at an expenditure of $120,000. There is no evidence in this record that the Debtor has sufficient funds at this time to cure these deficiencies. According to the Debtor, it is not renting now the 50 rooms which are currently substandard and the rooms which are rented do meet the standard of operation required by the Licensor.

The record further reveals that on October 13, 1979, the Licensor mailed through certified mail, "Return Receipt Requested," a Final Termination Notice to the Debtor from Phoenix, Arizona where the headquarters of its System is located. . . . The notice stated that the License Agreement is cancelled and terminated due to the Debtor's failure to maintain the quality standards required by the Licensor. The notice also informed the Debtor that the Licensor issued the necessary instructions to have the Debtor's facility disassociated from the Ramada System; to remove the listing of the Debtor's facility from the Directory issued by the Licensor and from the Ramada Reservation System; and that it notified all credit card companies of the termination of the License Agreement and that it intends to cause a removal of the neon signs bearing the registered name and the logo of the Licensor. On the same date when this Final Termination Notice was mailed from Phoenix, the Debtor filed its petition for an Order for Relief under Chapter 11 of the Code; U.S.C. 1101 et seq. The petition was filed at 1:45 PM and there is no doubt that while the final termination notice may have been mailed prior to the filing of the Debtor's petition, it is without dispute that the same was not received by the Debtor until after the commencement of the reorganization proceeding. The record further reveals that the Licensor did immediately refuse to honor any reservation attempts by prospective guests through its central reservation system and prohibited any further use of the computer and its toll free number, both of which are essential to the use of the central reservation system which provided in the past 70 percent of the total business of the Debtor. The evidence further reveals that as the result of the loss of the use of the central reservation system of the Licensor, the Debtor has already received several cancellations and its business is heading for a serious downturn on the eve of its prime season which, of course, provides the lifeblood of the motor hotel business in Florida.

It further appears that as the result of the Termination Notice, the credit card companies increased their service charges to the Debtor from 2 percent to 4 percent placing an additional financial burden on the Debtor. It further appears from the record that as the result of the Termination Notice, the Savings & Loan filed a complaint and now seeks a modification of the automatic stay imposed by §362 of the Code; 11 U.S.C. §362 in order to institute a foreclosure proceeding because it considers the loss of the Ramada Inn franchise a significant impairment of the value of its collateral.

These are the facts germane to the matter under consideration which is the basis for the preliminary relief sought by the Debtor, who seeks to preserve the status quo through an order directing the Licensor to maintain the availability of its Reservation System and to furnish to the Debtor, pending final determination of this controversy, all the other services which are otherwise available under the License Agreement to Licensees of the Ramada System.

In support of its claim for relief, the Debtor contends, first, that the final termination notice did not become effective until it was received and since it was admittedly received after the institution of the reorganization proceeding, the automatic stay of the Code, Sec. 362; and 11 U.S.C. §362 prevented termination without leave of court and since none was sought and obtained by the Licensor, the termination notice has no legal force or effect. In addition, it is the contention of the Debtor that unless this Court grants the preliminary injunctive relief sought, it will suffer irreparable harm and its chances to obtain rehabilitation under the provision of Chapter 11 will be destroyed. The Debtor further urges that if the injunction is issued, the detriment to the Licensor is nominal and in any event the Licensor is estopped to assert the claimed defaults by virtue of its admission in August that if the delinquent payments are made it considers the License Agreement in good standing and in full force and effect, and since the payments were made, it is now bound by this admission and is estopped to claim defaults.

In response, to these contentions, the Licensor responds that the Final Termination Notice was mailed prior to the institution of the reorganization proceeding; it became effective upon mailing, thus, the automatic stay of the Code, Sec. 362; 11 U.S.C. §362, had no effect on the validity of the notice of termination. This being the case, so contends the Licensor, the License Agreement was cancelled and terminated by the time the Debtor filed its petition for relief and under the holding of the Fifth Circuit Court of Appeals, in Schokbeton Industries Inc. v. Schokbeton Products Corp., 466 F.2d 171 (1972), since the rights under a License Agreement were terminated prior to the commencement of the reorganization case, they can no longer be resuscitated by the institution of the reorganization proceeding. In that case the Court, speaking through Chief Judge Brown stated that contractual termination provisions are unaffected by filing of a petition in bankruptcy or a petition for arrangement and may be enforced against the trustee or a debtor in possession. The Court concluded that since the Debtor's rights under the licensing agreement evaporated *upon the receipt of the written notice of termination* (emphasis supplied), neither the mere filing of the petition for arrangement nor the referee's order purporting to extend the grace period for curing the default nor a "mystical combination of both could effect their recondensation." Thus, it is apparent from the foregoing that the effective date of the cancellation is crucial and represents a threshold question to the resolution of this controversy. This is so because, if the Termination Notice became effective upon mailing, *Schokbeton,* supra would control. On the other hand, if it became effective only upon receipt, *Schokbeton,* supra is inapposite and distinguishable. This is so because the holding of *Schokbeton,* supra was based on the undisputed fact that at the time the Debtor sought the injunctive relief against cancellation of the Franchise Agreement, the agreement was already effectively cancelled and the grace period expired and there was nothing left to be preserved since all rights under the franchise agreement evaporated.

In the case under consideration, the notice of cancellation and termination of the License Agreement did not become effective until it was received, that is, after the institution of the reorganization proceeding. This is so because the Court in *Schokbeton,* supra itself concluded that the rights of the Debtor under the license agreement evaporated upon *receipt of the written notice of termination* (emphasis supplied) and not upon the mailing of the notice. However, one need not rely on *Schokbeton,* supra to accept this conclusion because the effectiveness of the notice of cancellation is determined by the specific terms of the contract itself. . . . and the License Agreement involved in this controversy specifically provides in clause 9 that "any notice . . . shall for all purposes, be deemed to have been given to and received by the party for whom intended 48 hours from the date said notice was mailed." Thus, it is clear that the cancellation was not effective until the Termination Notice was received by the Debtor. . . . This is supported by the undisputed fact that the Termination Notice mailed on October 31, 1979 was not received by the Debtor until November 2, 1979 or two days after the commencement of the reorganization proceeding.

This leaves for consideration the next question, i. e. the impact of the automatic stay provision of the Code, Sec. 362; 11 U.S.C. §362, on the validity and effectiveness of the Notice of Termination. . . .

The automatic stay is one of the most fundamental debtor protection devices provided by the Code. There is no doubt that the scope of the protection is broad and was designed to reach all proceedings, including license revocations, arbitrations, administrative and judicial proceedings and its operation is no longer limited to civil action, but includes proceedings even if they are not before governmental tribunals. . . . It should be noted at the outset that an attempt to cancel the License Agreement is neither the commencement nor the continuation of a judicial, administrative proceeding against the debtor. It is equally clear that the attempted action by the Licensor is not an "employment of process" or an "attempt to enforce a judgment," "an attempt to create, perfect or to enforce a lien against property of the estate," actions expressly stayed by Sec. 362(1)(2)(4)(5); 11 U.S.C. §362(1)(2)(4)(5). Neither is it an attempt to cancel the License Agreement an act to collect a debt, recover a claim, exercise the right of set-off or to commence or continue a proceeding before the U.S. Tax Court, all of which are obviously within the reach of the automatic stay of the Code. Sec. 362(6)(7)(8); 11 U.S.C. §362(6)(7)(8).

Thus, unless the attempt to cancel the License Agreement falls within the reach of the terms "or other proceedings" used in subclause (1) or within subclause (3) of the automatic stay, Sec. 362(a) of the Code, it furnishes no assistance or support to the debtor.* The term "or other proceedings" when read in conjunction with the type of proceeding specifically enumerated in subclause (a)(1) leaves no doubt that it does refer only to proceedings before quasi governmental units, such as administrative agencies or licensing boards, created to police certain professions, i.e. contractors, barbers, attorneys, doctors and the like. While the Court is not unmindful that the legislative history might call for a different conclusion, . . . this Court is of the opinion that the attempt to cancel the License Agreement by the Licensor is not the type of "proceeding" which was intended by Congress to be stayed by the filing of a petition for order for relief under the Code.

The only remaining provision of the Sec. 362 of the Code; 11 U.S.C. §362 which may assist the debtor is subclause (a)(3) which stays any acts instituted for the purpose of obtaining "possession of property of the estate or of property from the estate." This subclause was designed to prevent dismemberment of the estate. Intangible property rights, e.g. rights acquired under a license agreement are properties of the estate and are capable of possession. . . . Thus, an attempt to cancel such rights, after the commencement of the case may come within the protective provisions of the Code under subclause (a)(3) of Sec. 362; 11 U.S.C. §362. This is so because the cancellation of the License Agreement may be deemed to be an attempt to obtain possession of "property" of the estate.

. . . It is clear from the legislative history of §362 that Congress intended the automatic protection to be afforded by the automatic stay to be far reaching and to eliminate the previously existing limited perimeters of the pre-Code automatic stay. This conclusion is further supported by an overriding policy aim of Chapter 11 of the Code which is to provide the broadest protection to debtors in general. . . .

Having concluded that the notice of termination of the License

---

* The words "action or" were added to §362(a)(1) in 1984. §362(a)(3) was amended to include "exercise control over property of the estate."— EDS.

Agreement did not become effective until after the commencement of the reorganization case; this Court is satisfied that the Notice of Termination was an act designed to obtain possession of "property" from the estate, an act within the reach of the automatic stay of the Code, Sec. 362(1)(3); 11 U.S.C. §362(1)(3), and that it has no force and effect, since it was not authorized by the Court.

However, even assuming that this conclusion is an overly broad application of the automatic stay, there is an additional reason why this debtor is entitled to the temporary relief it seeks under the overall equity power granted by the Code. Sec. 105 of the Bankruptcy Code, 11 U.S.C. §105 provides that the bankruptcy court "may issue any order, process or judgment that is necessary or appropriate to carry out the provisions of this title." . . .

The License Agreement involved in this controversy is without a doubt an executory contract. The Code expressly authorizes the Debtor to assume or reject executory contracts, Sec. 365 of the Code; 11 U.S.C. §365, and permits a debtor to assume an executory contract even if the contract is in default at the time of the commencement of the case under certain conditions; Sec. 365b(1)(A)(B)(C); 11 U.S.C. §365b(1)(A)(B)(C). These sections provide several alternative methods to cure defaults compliance with one of which is a condition precedent to the assumption of an executory contract which is in default.

The evidence presented established, without the shadow of a doubt, that the rights and benefits flowing from the License Agreement in favor of the debtor are extremely valuable, and as a fact of the matter, well-nigh indispensable to the economic survival of the debtor and its chances to obtain rehabilitation under the Code will be destroyed if the License to operate its facilities as a Ramada Inn is lost. Thus, even if this right is not protected by the automatic stay of the Code, this Court certainly has the power under Sec. 105; 11 U.S.C. §105 to "issue the necessary and appropriate order" to protect these valuable property rights at least temporarily. In addition while there are, no doubt, deficiencies in the current operation of the hotel, the Debtor should be given an opportunity to cure the defects by providing adequate protection to the Licensor pursuant to Sec. 361; 11 U.S.C. §361. In addition, this record is not sufficient to permit the conclusion that the harm inflicted upon the Licensor if the injunction is issued is sufficiently significant as to tip the balance of hurt in its favor. . . .

This does not mean, of course, that the Licensor is helpless and is at the mercy of the debtor indefinitely. On the contrary, the licensor may move forthwith to seek relief from the automatic stay pursuant to Sec. 362(a)(1); 11 U.S.C. §362(a)(1) or may seek an order to compel the debtor to assume this executory contract on or before the time fixed by the Court and, of course compel before the debtor is permitted to assume his contract to comply with the requirements of the Code, Sec. 365b(1)(A)(B)(C);

11 U.S.C. §365b(1)(A)(B)(C), and cure all defaults as they relate to the standard of operation required by the License Agreement.

In sum, this Court is satisfied that the plaintiff's claim for relief is well-founded and for the reasons stated, should be granted. . . .

NOTE

Does §365 have any room to operate in a case where a warrant of removal has been issued ordering Debtor to vacate a store it has leased, but Debtor files a bankruptcy petition two hours before the execution of warrant? Assume that, under applicable state law, the issuance of a warrant of removal cancels the agreement under which the tenant held the premises, but the tenant is still in possession and may have a right of redemption. In re GSVC Restaurant Corp., 10 Bankr. 300 (S.D.N.Y. 1980), analyzed such a situation as follows:

> Upon this appeal the debtor argues that the court below did not consider the possible rights of redemption which a tenant might have. . . . It is true that a tenant may have such rights, but at this moment they are no more than a chose in action. Undoubtedly a trustee or a debtor in possession under the bankruptcy laws may assume and protect whatever rights the debtor had as of the time of the filing. If the termination of a lease has not been completed, or if it can be reversed by application of state procedures (so that the matter is still *sub judice*), the trustee or debtor in possession may still assume such rights and pursue them. . . . However, a more difficult problem arises where the lease has already been terminated according to its terms under the applicable state law and final state process has been issued evicting the tenant. . . . In this instance, the trustee has nothing to assume. . . . It would be chaotic if every eviction proceeding could ultimately be frustrated by the last minute filing of a Chapter 11 proceeding in federal court.

Has the court dealt adequately with the effect of the right of redemption? Is its discussion of that issue affected by the Supreme Court's opinion in *Whiting Pools*? Should the court have discussed §108? See In re Santa Fe Development, infra; Problem 7.4 supra.

NOTE ON *PINELLAS* AND THE POWER TO ASSUME

R.S. Pinellas Motel Partnership introduces a number of related issues. As the case suggests, questions involving the automatic stay are highly intertwined with §§361 and 365. Section 365, in particular, deals with the trustee's ability to take over a valuable contract of the debtor. Absent

§365, extending the automatic stay to executory contracts and leases would be hard to justify unless Ramada Inns were thought to be a *creditor* taking some action to "opt out" of the collective proceeding, as might have occurred, for example, in *Cahokia Downs*. Should people be prevented from terminating relationships with debtors on the eve of bankruptcy? When we looked at the preference section in Chapter 6, we saw that under certain circumstances *creditors* paid on the eve of bankruptcy will find that such payment is not recognized. People in other relationships with a debtor, however, are not subject to the preference section, and can pull out of a relationship as long as they do so before bankruptcy. The trustee may assume a contract under §365 only if it was in existence on the date of bankruptcy. See Moody v. Amoco Oil Co., 734 F.2d 1200 (7th Cir. 1984). Is there a reason for this different treatment of creditors and other people? Does *R.S. Pinellas Motel Partnership* have anything to say about that?

More technically, in *R.S. Pinellas Motel Partnership*, what "act" is found to violate §362(a)(3)? Assume that the notice had not only been sent, but received, before the filing of the bankruptcy petition by R.S. Pinellas Motel Partnership. Would §362 then have any force? Can you answer that without first looking at whether §365 could still be used to assume the contract? The court uses §105 as an alternative ground for its decision. But if §362 does not stay the termination of the motel franchise, what is left for the §105 injunction to work on?

The court notes that the "rights and benefits flowing from the License Agreement . . . are extremely valuable." If the debtor had been negotiating with Ramada Inns for a license, but had not yet obtained it, could the court order Ramada Inns to grant the license because it would be "important" to the debtor? We will consider this question again when we look at In re Ike Kempner & Bros., infra page 531, but consider now the comment of the court in White Motor Corp. v. Nashville White Truck, Inc., 5 Bankr. 112, 117 (Bankr. M.D. Tenn. 1980):

> The Code does not, however, grant the debtor in bankruptcy greater rights and powers under the contract than he had outside of bankruptcy. The court finds nothing in the Code which enlarges the rights of [the debtor] under the contract or which prevents the termination of the contract on its own terms on [the expiration date].

To what extent is *R.S. Pinellas Motel Partnership* consistent with that?

In considering *R.S. Pinellas Motel Partnership* and its relation to cases such as *Cahokia Downs*, you might also want to consider an issue mentioned, but not decided, in *Cahokia Downs*: Can the debtor require an insurance company (or other contracting party) to renew a contract? In In re Garnas, 38 Bankr. 221 (Bankr. D.N.D. 1984), the court found that a refusal to renew an insurance policy simply because the insured had filed a bankruptcy petition was tantamount to terminating an executory contract. The bankruptcy court was therefore entitled to order the insurance company to renew the policy and keep it in force as long as the premiums were current:

> Although a policy may state a termination date, that date in most circumstances is simply ignored and the policy continues on and on with the relationship between the insurance company and the policyholder continuing over the term without any interaction between the two except for payment of premium. Under such circumstances, this Court is persuaded that an executory contract within the [purview] of the Bankruptcy Code does indeed exist between an insurance company and a policyholder despite the fact that an individual policy may provide for one-year coverage. . . . [T]he policy . . . would have [been] automatically renewed had it not been for the fact that they filed for relief under the Bankruptcy Code. This is the sole reason that American Family elected not to renew the policy, and it is precisely that reason which is prohibited by section 365(e)(1) of the Code. This Court is persuaded that an injunction preventing nonrenewal of the Debtors' insurance policy is warranted. Nonrenewal would seriously impair the reorganization because the Debtors, if they are to continue in their farming operation, must have insurance and without it they would be subjected to a great risk of loss that would seriously jeopardize their reorganization.

Sometime after this case was decided, §541(b) was amended to provide that property of the estate does not include the interest of a debtor in nonresidential real property that has terminated at the end of the stated term before the commencement of the case and ceases to include such property that terminates at the end of the stated term during the case. Assuming this provision were in force, would the court's analysis in *Garnas* have been different if Debtors were leasing a store and the court concluded that the lease was not renewed simply because a bankruptcy petition had been filed? Does this principle apply by analogy here? Or does the existence of §541(b) suggest the opposite result whenever one is concerned with an interest in something other than nonresidential real estate?

Why does it follow from the Debtors' need for insurance that American Family ought to provide it? As long as there are other insurance companies, and as long as debtors will have to pay in full for insurance, why would "[n]onrenewal . . . seriously impair the reorganization"? In denying a similar request, the court in In re Heaven Sent, Ltd., 37 Bankr. 597 (Bankr. E.D. Pa. 1984), stated that it was "unaware of any provision in the Code which authorizes [the court] to direct [an insurance company] to renew the subject policies and thereby to create new contractual rights between it and the debtor where none heretofore existed." Does this adequately respond to the concern in *Garnas?* Or can one argue that this isn't simply a case where the debtor is being given greater rights than it enjoyed outside of bankruptcy? We will see the problem of sorting out a pre-petition creditor in examining *Ike Kempner*, infra page 531. Also, recall the facts of *Cahokia Downs*. But American Family does not seem to be a pre-petition creditor. Why, then, is American Family refusing to renew its policy? If Debtors owe it no money on account of prior insurance and are willing to pay cash for the renewal, would American Family terminate for any reason other than a belief that Debtor were now a higher insurance risk? Assume that Debtors are a higher insurance risk. If Debtors could not prevent a new third party insurer from taking this into account in setting its rate or in deciding whether to provide insurance at all, why should they be able to stop American Family from considering it? Should an entity that is not a pre-petition creditor, and who is a fortiori not trying to coerce payment on account of a pre-petition debt, be forced to subsidize a debtor who has filed a bankruptcy petition? Is that the situation of American Family? How can we tell if there has been a change in risk? One can argue that insurance companies and other contracting parties mistakenly think that debtors that file bankruptcy petitions are greater insurance risks, when in fact they are not, and that §365(e) is desirable because it prevents these parties from acting on a misimpression. But how likely is it that these companies would be systematically prejudiced in their calculation of things such as fire insurance risks by something like a bankruptcy filing?

This case may be made more difficult if the concept of renewal between Debtors and American Family was more than a general practice. If the concept of renewal was considered a "contract right" under state law, giving Debtors a *right* of renewal at, say, "standard" rates, so long as the insurance company could not prove that their risk level had changed, then shouldn't it also be the case that this contract should be enforceable in bankruptcy? Say, for example, that Debtors had a "right" to renew the insurance policy for $100 a year, while another person (quite apart from bankruptcy) would have to pay $200 a year for the same coverage. Isn't the purpose of §365(e) to ensure that this asset of Debtors (the right to obtain insurance at less than market value) is not lost simply because a bankruptcy petition has been filed? Does this purpose apply to these facts? Can one find a contractual obligation to renew that would be enforceable under state law?

PROBLEMS

7.28 Ramada Inns delivers to R.S. Pinellas Motel Partnership, on October 10, a notice stating "your franchise with us is terminated, effective the last day of this month. We have programmed our computer to remove you from our reservation system as of that day." The partnership files for bankruptcy on October 13. Will cancelling the franchise on October 31 violate the automatic stay? See Moody v. Amoco Oil Co., 734 F.2d 1200 (7th Cir. 1984).

7.29 Lessor rents a computer to Debtor on a five-year lease. After one year, Debtor defaults, and Lessor repossesses the computer. Two weeks after Lessor repossesses the computer, Debtor files a petition in bankruptcy. May Lessor lease the computer to another without first getting relief from the automatic stay?

7.30 Lessor rents a computer to Debtor on a five-year lease. Debtor fails to make both the March and April payments during the second year of the lease. On April 5, pursuant to a term of the lease, Lessor sends a cancellation notice. Debtor receives the cancellation notice on April 6. On April 10, Debtor files a petition in bankruptcy. May Lessor repossess the computer? See §362(a)(3).

7.31 Farmer has a contract with Debtor to sell Debtor 50,000 bushels of wheat during the course of the year. Debtor files for bankruptcy. Farmer wants to breach the contract, because the price of wheat has risen. If Farmer breaches, does he violate the automatic stay? Does §525 have anything to say about this issue?

NOTE ON ADEQUATE ASSURANCE OF FUTURE PERFORMANCE

Section 365(b)(1) requires the trustee, under certain circumstances, to give adequate assurance of future performance before it can assume a contract. What sorts of limitations does this place on its right to assume contracts? Consider, in this respect, In re General Oil Distributors, 20 Bankr. 873 (Bankr. E.D.N.Y. 1982). In that case, General, the debtor, sought bankruptcy court authorization to assume its executory contract for the sale of oil to New York City. Its contract called for it to deliver 5.7 million gallons of fuel oil to city facilities (including the Staten Island Ferry) at a fixed price. A drop in oil prices had made the contract a valuable asset of the debtor. General had failed to make a scheduled delivery of oil needed to run the ferry before its bankruptcy. The city, however, had suffered no damages, in part because of the drop in oil prices.

The court refused to allow General to assume the contract, on the ground that General was unable to give adequate assurance of future performance:

> [I]nasmuch as this default engendered no monetary damages, it follows that there is nothing to cure. Accordingly, General could assume the contract provided it could provide adequate assurance of future performance. . . .
>
> The concept of adequate assurance of future performance is one borrowed from section 2-609 of the Uniform Commercial Code. . . . Accordingly, the case law under UCC section 2-609 has been held applicable to section 365(b)(1)(C). . . .
>
> In general section 365(b)(1) attempts to strike a balance between the interest of the estate in preserving (or disposing of at a profit) a valuable asset

and the interest of the nondebtor party to the contract in receiving its bargained for performance. . . .

Applying the foregoing to the case at bar, the Court cannot ignore the reality of who the nondebtor party to this contract is. It is the City of New York; and the oil is needed that the Staten Island Ferry might run and that several waste treatment plants might be able to process refuse prior to its disposal at sea. Nor can this Court ignore the precarious financial position that General has been shown to be in; nor the fact that General has defaulted on past deliveries; nor the fact that General is presently out of oil and out of money. . . .

Would it have made any difference if General had managed to survive the pre-bankruptcy period without any uncured defaults? Would the bankruptcy court then have had the authority to deny approval of General's assumption of the contract? Even assuming adequate assurance of future performance is necessary, what should that mean in this context? What happens if General assumes the contract and then defaults? See §§502(g), 503(b), 507(a)(1). Does it matter what the status of New York City's oil supply is?

PROBLEMS

7.32 Debtor ran a beauty salon in a J.C. Penney store pursuant to a license agreement. The license agreement stated that it "shall continue in effect until terminated by either party hereto by giving at least 60 days prior written notice of the effective date of such termination to the other party." On March 28, 1980, Penney notified Debtor that the license agreement would be terminated effective June 14, 1980. On May 16, 1980, Debtor filed a petition in bankruptcy. May the trustee assume the license agreement? See In re Beck, 6 B.C.D. 1119 (D. Hawaii 1980); In re R.S. Pinellas Motel Partnership, supra.

7.33 Debtor is a lessee under a five-year lease. During the second year, Debtor falls behind in her payments on the lease. The Debtor is three months behind in payments when she files a petition in bankruptcy. The lease provides that it may be terminated whenever Debtor is more than two months behind in her rental obligations. The lease is a favorable lease, and the trustee wants to assume it. May he?

IN RE SANTA FE DEVELOPMENT
16 Bankr. 165 (9th Cir. Bankr. App. 1981)

KATZ, Bankruptcy Judge.

Prior to the filing of the within bankruptcy the debtor, Santa Fe Development and Mortgage Corporation, was involved in extensive state court litigation with the appellees, James L. and Loretta J. McCormack (hereinafter McCormack). As a result of that litigation the parties entered into a stipulated settlement which became effective on July 11, 1979.

The settlement provided the basis for the sale of three parcels of property located in Roseville, California. The purchase price for the property was $485,000. The escrow provided that the sale would be consummated upon Santa Fe Development paying $285,000 in cash and executing a note for $200,000. The escrow further provided that the payment must be made on or before June 16, 1980. Santa Fe Development failed to close escrow on June 16, 1980.

The settlement agreement allowed Santa Fe Development to extend the final day to close escrow by paying a non-refundable sum of $25,000. Under the agreement the escrow could be extended for three thirty day periods, however, the escrow could not be extended past September 16, 1980.

In accordance with the agreement Santa Fe Development extended the close of escrow until August 16, 1980 by making payments on June 15, 1980 and July 15, 1980. The agreement also provided that in the event escrow did not close, then Santa Fe Development would lose all rights in and to the subject property.

On August 5, 1980 the debtor filed a petition under Chapter 11 of the Code. The debtor failed to extend the escrow beyond August 16, 1980. However, on August 20, 1980, the debtor-in-possession filed a complaint for declaratory relief. The complaint sought a determination as to the respective rights of the parties including a determination as to whether the subject parcels were property of the estate.

On November 20, 1980 the trial court held a hearing on the appellees' motion for summary judgment.

On February 12, 1981 the trial court granted summary judgment in favor of McCormacks and terminated all rights that the debtor may have had in the subject property. In rendering the decision the trial judge held that 11 U.S.C. §362 does not stay the time in which to perform an act under a contract.

On appeal appellant claims that the trial court erred in holding that the running of the escrow period terminated any rights that the debtor-in-possession acceded to under 11 U.S.C. §541. Appellant argues that at a minimum the court should have set a date upon which the debtor-in-possession would need to perform after it accepted the executory contract.

The appellee claims that under California law the failure to exercise an option by the last day to do so terminates the option. . . . Citing Good Hope Refineries, Inc. v. Benavides, 602 F.2d 998 (1st Cir. 1979)), cert. denied, 444 U.S. 992, 100 S. Ct. 523, 62 L. Ed. 2d 421 (1979)[, a]ppellee states that the filing of the within bankruptcy did not act to stay the running of the escrow period.

It is undisputed, between the parties, that on the date the bankruptcy was filed the debtor-in-possession had the right to assume the executory sales contract and either consummate the sale or extend the closing date of escrow through the appropriate payment. The sole question before the Panel is whether the above stated options terminated on August 16, 1980 or whether they were preserved for the estate through the operation of the Bankruptcy Code.

Were this case to be decided strictly under California law it is clear that the debtor would have lost all rights in the contract when the escrow period was not extended on August 16, 1980. . . . However, the Bankruptcy Code and its inherent purposes are of paramount concern in deciding cases which come under its jurisdiction. We must therefore turn to the Code in order to determine whether the law of the state is altered by the application of the Code. U.S. Const., art. VI, cl. 2.

Section 108 (11 U.S.C. §108) provides for extensions of time to perform various acts. Subsection (a) (11 U.S.C. §108(a)) provides a minimum period of two years in which the trustee may commence an action. Subsection (c) (11 U.S.C. §108(c)) extends the time in which a creditor may bring an action against a debtor for a minimum of 30 days after the expiration of the stay under sections 362, 922 or 1301. Subsection (b) (11 U.S.C. §108(b)) gives the trustee 60 days to take other actions not covered under subsection (a). House Report No. 95-595, 95th Cong. 1st Sess. (1977) 318, U.S. Code Cong. & Admin. News 1978, p. 5787. The purpose of section 108 is to permit the trustee, when he steps into the shoes of the debtor, an extension of time for filing an action or *doing some other act that is required to preserve the debtor's rights.* House Report No. 95-595, supra. (emphasis added).

Section 108(b) was derived in part from section 11(e) of the Act. (11 U.S.C. §29(e)). Under the Act several courts held that section 11(e) did not toll the period in which an option must be exercised. See In re Good Hope Refineries, Inc. v. Benavides, 602 F.2d 998 (1st Cir. 1979); cert. denied, 444 U.S. 992, 100 S. Ct. 523, 62 L. Ed. 2d 421 (1979); Schokbeton Industries, Inc. v. Schokbeton Products Corp., 466 F.2d 171 (5th Cir. 1972).

The court in *Good Hope Refineries* found that the wording of 11(e) limited its broader application to "proceedings." The "option to drill" in that case was construed as a limitation created by agreement and therefore not a proceeding. The court further held that 11(e) only expanded consensual limitations if they involved the "like" of presenting a proof of claim, proof of loss, demand, or notice. The court opined that a payment to extend or exercise an option is not akin to making a claim against an insurance company or surety bond.

Even though the *Good Hope Refineries* case was decided under the Act the court also analyzed section 108(b) of the Code. The court held that the only change brought about by section 108 from existing law was to give the trustee an extension of time to "cure defaults." The court rationalized that once an option has run there is no contractual default to cure.

We think that the *Good Hope Refineries* case overlooks basic differences in syntax between section 11(e) and the current section 108. While the syntax of 11(e) may have limited a broader application of the extension of time to actions in "proceedings" we believe that section 108 does not contain such a limitation. As applied to this case we read section 108(b) to state:

> [I]f . . . an agreement fixes a period within which the debtor . . . may file a pleading, demand, notice, or proof of claim or loss, cure a default, or perform any other similar act, and such period has not expired before the date of the filing of the petition, the trustee may only file, cure, or *perform*, as the case may be, before the later of—(1) the end of such period, including any suspension of such period occurring on or after the commencement of the case; and* (2) 60 days after the order for relief. (emphasis added)

Under such a reading we view the act of making a payment to extend an escrow or consummate an executory contract of sale as the performance of any other act similar to filing a demand, notice or curing a default. Therefore, under section 108(b) the debtor-in-possession has a minimum of 60 days in which to accept an executory contract and make the appropriate payment necessary to preserve the contract for the benefit of the estate. We find that a broad reading of section 108(b) better serves the purposes of bankruptcy by preserving the maximum amount of property and business opportunities to be used for the rehabilitation of the debtor. . . .

The courts in the *Good Hope Refineries* and *Schokbeton* cases were worried about the inequitable results which might occur where the debtor's obligations under an executory contract are suspended while simultaneously the other party is held to the bargain. For example, the seller of a ten day option to purchase securities could find his expectations and economic position radically altered if the option were automatically extended 60 days. While we hold that the effect of section 108(b) is to at a minimum extend the limitation period by 60 days, we find that the Code provides adequate procedures for shortening this time such that gross inequities will not result. See 11 U.S.C. §365(d)(1)(2);† 11 U.S.C. §105(a). Under the Act periods of limitation could be extended by an order of the court where the equities of the case demanded. . . . Our reading of section 108(b) merely switches the burden to the creditor to reduce the extension of time during the 60 day period under the statute.

Having held that debtor-in-possession had a continuing right to perform the executory contract for a 60 day period following the filing of the

---

* Changed to "or" in 1984. — EDs.
† §365(d) was extensively amended in 1984. — EDs.

petition under 11 U.S.C. §108(b) (unless reduced by the court), we hold that the trial court erred in holding that the debtor's rights to the property terminated on August 16, 1980.

We therefore reverse on this issue alone and remand the case to the trial court for further proceedings in conformance herewith.

VOLINN, Bankruptcy Judge, concurring.

I concur with the result but differ with the majority in their application of 11 U.S.C. §108(b) to the facts in this case. Rather than viewing Santa Fe's rights as those of an optionee, I would characterize its rights as those arising from an executory contract.[1]

In attempting to avoid the impact and reasoning of Good Hope Refineries, Inc. v. Benavides, 602 F.2d 998 (1st Cir. 1979) cert. denied, 444 U.S. 992, 100 S. Ct. 523, 62 L. Ed. 2d 421 (1979), the majority tries to distinguish §108(b) of the Code from §11(e) of the prior Bankruptcy Act. The *Good Hope* court, while considering §11(e), had occasion to also consider its successor, §108(b). The court reasoned that basically, as with §11(e), the term "or perform any other similar act" related to the preceding language, particularly as to curing a default. Since lapse of an option does not involve default, the time for cure is not extended by §108(b).

The wording of §108(b), emphasized by the majority, that an extension is provided for the trustee "to cure default, or perform any other similar act" is still subject to the logic of *Good Hope*. There is a significant qualitative difference between default and allowing an option to lapse. The essential characteristic of an option is that it purchases a specific calendar period during which the optionee has the discretion to make a choice. Non-exercise of the option does not involve a default, but, rather, exercise of discretion not to proceed with the option. Default, on the other hand, implies failure to meet a binding commitment. In this regard, the logic in *Good Hope* is persuasive. . . .

The fundamental legal relationship between Santa Fe and the McCormacks was based on their contract for purchase and sale of real estate. Disagreements arose and litigation ensued. Consequently, in July, 1979, the parties entered into a settlement agreement which provided that:

> In the event Santa Fe does not close escrow on or before June 16, 1980, then in such event, Santa Fe shall, upon payment to McCormacks of the sum of $25,000 cash on or before June 17, 1980, have an additional 30 days to close said escrow until July 15, 1980. . . .

The agreement provided for three extensions to September 15, 1980, further providing that:

1. In their brief, appellants argue that the contract between the parties is executory which may be assumed or rejected under 11 U.S.C. §365. Ironically, reference to §108(b) surfaced tangentially in appellee's brief with a quote from *Good Hope*, infra.

> In the event said escrow does not close on or before September 15, 1980, then, in such event, Santa Fe shall have no further right or interest in and to the subject real property . . .

The agreement made it clear that the foregoing provisions were ancillary to, and in settlement of, the original contract and litigation thereon. The litigation was not to be concluded until the alternatives incident to settlement had occurred. It states:

> It is the intent of this agreement to eliminate any further disputes or litigation between the parties hereto. If Santa Fe does not close escrow on or before September 15, 1980, the dismissal with prejudice of all parties shall be filed in the above entitled action. If Santa Fe closes escrow on or before September 15, 1980, the dismissal with prejudice shall likewise be filed by the escrow in the above entitled action concurrently with the recording of the deed.

No option to purchase was involved in the settlement agreement. The agreement focuses upon September 15, 1980, more or less as a deadline replacing that stated in the original contract.

The question presented in this light is whether §§365 and 362 apply. The automatic stay of §362 came into effect on August 5, 1981, when Santa Fe filed bankruptcy. This suspended the rights of the parties under the settlement. Bankruptcy intercepted the conclusion of the litigation insofar as it could effect dismissal of appellant's claim. Although the two $25,000 payments to extend the date escrow was to be closed did not apply to the purchase price and did not create an equity in the property, they may be considered from an equitable standpoint. Since the time within which to close escrow was extended by operation of §365 of the Code, if the trustee decides to adopt the contract, it will have to make the $25,000 payment it missed, with interest. . . . In the event that the trustee rejects the contract, appellees will have a claim against the estate for damages. . . .

In conclusion, I would hold that the legal relationship between the parties originated in an executory contract subject to a settlement which was not concluded prior to bankruptcy. Consequently, the filing of bankruptcy gave the debtor-in-possession or the trustee, the right to accept or reject the contract as provided for by §365. In effect the date on which escrow had to be closed, was suspended.

NOTES

1. The court disagrees with Good Hope Refineries v. Benavides, 602 F.2d 998 (1st Cir. 1979), a case arising under the 1898 Act, but discussing as well the effect of §108. *Good Hope* dealt with what is called an "unless"

lease, which has the effect of terminating a lease after a period of time (say, one year) unless before that time, drilling has begun or a delay rental has been paid. The parties agreed that the act required to extend the lease "may be fairly analogized to exercising an option to extend an option to purchase property." The court held that §11(e), the predecessor to §108, did not provide an automatic extension of 60 days from the date of adjudication:

> Although not a model of clarity, we think the statute can only be read as affecting two separate types of limitations derived from two different sources, both types being extended for 60 days upon filing. First, there are "period[s] of limitation" created "by an agreement." Such periods are extended only if they set a limit on the time available "for instituting a suit or proceeding upon any claim, or for presenting or filing any claim, proof of claim, proof of loss, demand, notice, *or the like*. . . ." (Emphasis added.) Second, there is a broader category of types of limitations, giving the trustee an extra 60 days "for taking any action, filing any claim or pleading, or doing any act. . . ." This broader category of limitations extended by section 11(e) only comes into play, however, "where in any *proceeding*, judicial or otherwise, a period of limitations is fixed. . . ." The instant case does not involve any "proceeding." Rather, if the time limit on appellant's option to drill can be viewed as a "period of limitation" at all, it is a limitation created by agreement.
>
> By its language section 11(e) only expands consensual limitations if they involve "the like" of presenting proof of claim, proof of loss, demand, or notice. We do not think that making a payment to extend or exercise an option is akin to making a claim against an insurance policy or surety bond. . . . In the case of a payment to extend an option, the debtor is obliged to tender a certain performance, which performance is the consideration for the extension, by a certain time, and time is expressly of the essence. . . .
>
> . . . If the debtor has committed, or the trustee commits, an incurable breach, the trustee has no continuing rights under the contract. . . . It would be anomalous indeed if section 11(e), a provision dealing mainly with suits and claims by the trustee, could be used to alter contractual rights substantially where time is of the essence and the debtor or the trustee has defaulted. It would be even more anomalous if, in the case of an option contract, section 11(e) allowed the trustee to procure a right that never existed and for which no consideration has ever been paid, i.e., the right to exercise an option long after its termination date.

The court stated that §108 of the Bankruptcy Code did not reflect any different policy: "When a debtor or a trustee fails to exercise or renew an option by paying the agreed price, there is no contractual 'default' to be cured." Are the court's policy reasons for interpreting §11(e) (and §108) in this way persuasive? Does *Santa Fe Development* adequately respond to these concerns?

2. Johnson v. First Natl. Bank of Montevideo, 719 F.2d 270 (8th Cir. 1983), held that neither §362 nor §105 stayed the running of a statutory redemption period following a real estate foreclosure sale, and the only relief that was available was provided by §108(b). Does this decision involve the same concerns?

4.   The Power to Assume and Assign and Exceptions Thereto

NOTE ON THE POWER TO ASSUME AND IPSO FACTO CLAUSES

Section 365(a) allows the trustee, with court approval, to "assume or reject *any* executory contract or unexpired lease of the debtor." While the word "any" is cut back by §365(c), it is suggestive of the trustee's powers in one respect. Section 365(e)(1) — echoed in subsection (b)(2) — provides that the trustee may assume a contract notwithstanding a clause in the contract, or in applicable law, that attempts to terminate or modify the contract based on

(A)   the insolvency or financial condition of the debtor at any time before the closing of the case;

(B)   the commencement of a case under this title; or

(C)   the appointment of or taking possession by a trustee in a case under this title or a custodian before such commencement.

We shall look at exceptions to this section, but for the moment consider its impact. In many respects, this may be one of the most important changes made by the new Bankruptcy Code, for under the old Act, so-called bankruptcy clauses or ipso facto clauses were generally recognized in bankruptcy (see §70d of the 1898 Bankruptcy Act), although case law had watered down this protection a bit. See, e.g., Queens Blvd. Wine & Liquor Store v. Blum, 503 F.2d 202 (2d Cir. 1974). The scope of §365(e)(1), however, is not limited to traditional bankruptcy clauses, such as, "the filing of a petition in bankruptcy shall be an event of default under this contract." Instead, it also applies to clauses permitting termination based on "financial condition" (such as net worth clauses). Moreover, §365(f)(3) empowers the trustee to assign contracts he assumes, notwithstanding an anti-assignment clause. These are dramatically different powers than exist with respect to loans and nonexecutory contracts, which, as we have seen, are automatically accelerated upon bankruptcy.

Is §365(e)(1) justified? Does it create, in conjunction with the trustee's power to assume or reject, an unsound asymmetry among those who contract with those who might file bankruptcy petitions? If the contract is favorable to the bankrupt, the trustee assumes it and the nonbankrupt party suffers the burden of its bad deal notwithstanding an ipso facto clause. If the contract is favorable to the nonbankrupt party, the trustee rejects it and the nonbankrupt party is left with a claim for breach of contract against a bankrupt debtor. Should this asymmetry be eliminated? Or should it be limited by a rule allowing the trustee to reject only contracts that seriously burden the estate? Does the existing rule sensibly allocate the risk of bankruptcy among the different parties? Why should we not rely on the risks the parties accepted when they contract? See Jackson, Bankruptcy, Non-Bankruptcy Entitlements, and the Creditors' Bargain, 91 Yale L.J. 857, 885-892 (1982). Consider these questions as you look at the following problems.

PROBLEMS

7.34 Lessor has a long-term lease with Debtor. One of its terms states that Lessor will have the power to terminate the lease at any time if Debtor is insolvent. May the trustee assume the lease notwithstanding this provision? See §365(b). What if the lease provides that it will terminate automatically at any time Debtor becomes insolvent? Would it make any difference if the provisions were couched in terms of something other than insolvency, such as the ratio of assets to liabilities (say 2 to 1) or minimum net working capital? What about a ratio of current assets to current liabilities?

7.35 Debtor has two principal assets, Asset 1 and Asset 2, each with a fair market value of $100,000. Debtor also has two major lenders, Creditor 1 and Creditor 2, each of whom has an outstanding loan to Debtor of $100,000, at 10 percent interest, maturing in 1990. When the loans were made, the prime rate of interest on loans of a similar duration was 8 percent; that rate is now 14 percent. Debtor also has various trade creditors, with claims currently due amounting to $100,000. What are the claims of Creditor 1, Creditor 2, and the trade creditors in Debtor's bankruptcy? See §502. Assuming Debtor has no other assets, what will each of them get in Debtor's liquidation? What would the result be if Creditor 1 and Creditor 2 each had a security interest in Asset 1 and Asset 2, respectively?

7.36 Debtor has two principal assets, Asset 1 and Asset 2, under long-term leases from Creditor 1 and Creditor 2, respectively. The rental rate for these leases is below market, so that the difference, in present value terms, between the value of each leasehold at the current market rate ($150,000) and the cost of that leasehold at the contract rate ($100,000) is $50,000. Debtor has various trade creditors, with claims currently due amounting to $100,000. If Creditor 1 and Creditor 2 have an enforceable right to terminate the leases, what will each of Creditor 1, Creditor 2, and the trade creditors get in Debtor's bankruptcy? Assume Debtor has no other assets. What do each of Creditor 1, Creditor 2, and the trade creditors get if the Debtor exercises its right to assume and assign the leases under §365(a) and (f)?

The Commission on Bankruptcy Laws made the following proposal in 1973, Report of the Commission on the Bankruptcy Laws of the United States, H.R. Doc. 93-137, 93rd Cong., 1st Sess., pt. 1, at 198. The proposal suggests changes from the treatment of executory contracts under the 1898 Act, but draws a distinction, as §365 does not, between liquidation and reorganization cases. Are the proposal and distinction it draws sound?

> The Commission recommends that both executory contracts . . . and unexpired leases be enforceable in business reorganization cases, notwithstanding such a "bankruptcy clause" or anti-assignment clause, if the debtor or his trustee cures past defaults and, for contracts but not leases, gives adequate assurance of future performance. The rule should not apply in liquidation cases, however, where the provisions in the agreement between the parties should prevail. In addition, any nondebtor party should be permitted to exercise termination rights under nonbankruptcy law otherwise applicable, such as Uniform Commercial Code section 2-702. . . .
>
> The difference in policy is justified on the ground that in reorganization cases the purpose of assumption is the continuation of the business. In liquidation cases the purpose is typically for the assignment of the agreement to a purchaser from the trustee. In the former situation the reorganization of the debtor should be paramount, provided that the nondebtor party is protected. In the case of a supply or manufacturing contract, in which the nondebtor party may be called upon to incur substantial costs in anticipation of future performance, the protection should include adequate assurance of the debtor's future performance. In the liquidation situation, however, the right of the nondebtor party to choose to deal only with the debtor, as provided by an anti-assignment or similar contractual clause, should be preserved.

Section 365(c) provides some exceptions to the trustee's power to assume and assign executory contracts and unexpired leases. Think about these limitations in light of the following cases and problems.

IN RE SWIFT AIRE LINES
30 Bankr. 490 (9th Cir. Bankr. App. 1983)

VOLINN, Bankruptcy Judge.
[For the facts of this case, see supra page 184.]

EXECUTORY CONTRACT/FINANCIAL ACCOMMODATION

11 U.S.C. §365(c)(2) provides:

> The trustee may not assume or assign an executory contract . . . of the debtor . . . if . . . such contract is a contract to make a loan, or extend other debt financing or financial accommodation, to or for the benefit of the debtor. . . .

Crocker argues that the court below erred by rejecting the argument that the letter of credit was an executory contract to make a financial accommodation to and for the benefit of the Swift estate. We agree.

While, the terms "executory contract" and "financial accommodation" are not defined in the Bankruptcy Code, the legislative history of 11 U.S.C. §365(c) is pertinent. It states that:

> [T]he section permits the trustee to continue to use and pay for property already advanced, but is not designed to permit the trustee to demand new loans or additional transfers of property under lease commitments.
> *Thus, under the provision, contracts such as* loan commitments and *letters of credit are* non-assignable, and *may not be assumed by the trustee.* House Report No. 95-595, 95th Cong., 1st Sess. 348 (1977), Senate Report No. 95-989, 95th Cong., 2nd Sess. 59 (1978), U.S. Code Cong. & Admin. News 1978, pp. 5787, 6304 (emphasis added).

The drafters of the Bankruptcy Code considered that letters of credit were executory contracts to make a financial accommodation to or for the benefit of the debtor. This would appear to be dispositive unless there are countervailing reasons to hold otherwise. We have examined appellee's arguments and conclude, in view of the specificity of the legislative history and the statement of policy against enforcing financial loans or accommodations, that §365(c)(2) precludes enforcement of this letter of credit.[6]

The trustee argues that the letter agreement dated January 20, 1981, whereby Colin agreed in favor of Wells Fargo that the "letter of credit may be drawn upon by Swift notwithstanding that Swift may be in any type of proceeding under Title 11 of the United States Code — Bankruptcy; . . ." precludes Crocker from objecting to the documents tendered by the trustee. We disagree. The issuing party under a letter of credit is not concerned with or bound by any underlying contract. This January 20, 1981 letter agreement appears to be an underlying contract which does not bind Crocker. Crocker's only obligation was to determine whether the tendered documents strictly complied with the letter of credit. . . .

---

6. It should be noted that if Crocker was required to pay the trustee on the letter of credit, Colin would have been entitled to a loan from or stock of the debtor which would have been of questionable value. 11 U.S.C. §365(c)(2) would appear to be available to prevent this.

IV. Conclusion

Pursuant to the doctrine of strict compliance and the inability of the trustee to assume the letter of credit, we reverse the decisions of the court below denying Crocker's motion for summary judgment and granting the trustee's motion for partial summary judgment. The case is remanded to the trial court to enter judgment consistent with this Opinion.

PROBLEM

7.37 Debtor needed to borrow $100,000 from Creditor. As a condition of making the loan, Creditor required Debtor to find a guarantor. Surety agreed to guarantee Debtor's repayment obligation. Before the loan was repaid, Creditor filed for bankruptcy. Is Surety off the hook on its guarantee because of §365(c)?

NOTE ON LETTERS OF CREDIT AND §365(c)(2)

Section 365(c)(2) appears to have been added to the Bankruptcy Code at the urging of bankers, who feared that the general language in §365(c)(1) would not be clear enough to cover contracts to make loans. It is useful to examine the prototype case that concerned the bankers: a commitment to make a loan in the future. Traditionally, such contracts are considered nonassignable without the bank's consent.

But does that type of loan commitment cover a case such as *Swift Aire*? To answer that question, consider first Problem 7.37. In that problem, where a guarantee was issued prior to bankruptcy to support a loan made earlier, should there be any question that this type of obligation continues notwithstanding §365(c)(2)? But can you articulate why? Is this a contract to extend a "financial accommodation"? If so, is it also *executory*? Can Creditor breach the contract with Surety? Debtor can fail to repay the loan, but is that a breach?

Is *Swift Aire* any different? Banks issue letters of credit instead of guarantees. Should an issued letter of credit be considered to fall within the scope of §365(c)(2)? Under letter of credit law, the obligations between the issuing bank and the beneficiary are not considered "contractual" rights under state law. But does that preclude this from being an "executory contract" within the meaning of the Bankruptcy Code? Considering the attributes of the transaction, rather than labels nonbankruptcy law might attach to it, is this letter of credit obligation executory? How could Swift Aire breach any obligation to Crocker Bank? If you conclude that this obligation is not executory, then what do you make of the legislative history, which refers to letters of credit? Might those references address contractual obligations between the issuing bank and its customer, so that, like a guarantee, they should be read to apply only to obligations to *issue* a letter of credit, not to obligations under an existing letter of credit? Is there any policy reason for giving §365(c)(2) any other reading?

Having puzzled over the scope of §365(c)(2), what do you make of the more general test in §365(c)(1)? What does it mean to say that "applicable law excuses a party"? Consider that question in connection with the following case.

IN RE PIONEER FORD SALES
729 F.2d 27 (1st Cir. 1984)

BREYER, Circuit Judge.

The Ford Motor Company appeals a federal district court decision, 30 B.R. 458, allowing a bankrupt Ford dealer (Pioneer Ford Sales, Inc.) to assign its Ford franchise over Ford's objection to a Toyota dealer (Toyota Village, Inc.). The district court decided the case on the basis of a record developed in bankruptcy court. The bankruptcy court, 26 B.R. 116, had approved the transfer, which ran from Pioneer to Fleet National Bank (Pioneer's principal secured creditor) and then to Toyota Village. Fleet sought authorization for the assignment because Toyota Village will pay $10,000 for the franchise and buy all parts and accessories in Pioneer's inventory at fair market value (about $75,000); if the franchise is not assigned, Ford will buy only some of the parts for between $45,000 and $55,000. Thus, the assignment will increase the value of the estate. Fleet is the appellee here.

The issue that the case raises is the proper application of 11 U.S.C. §365(c)(1)(A), an exception to a more general provision, 11 U.S.C. §365(f)(1), that allows a trustee in bankruptcy (or a debtor in possession) to assign many of the debtor's executory contracts even if the contract itself says that it forbids assignment. . . .

The words "applicable law" in this section mean "applicable non-bankruptcy law." . . . Evidently, the theory of this section is to prevent the trustee from assigning (over objection) contracts of the sort that contract law ordinarily makes nonassignable, i.e. contracts that cannot be assigned when the contract itself is silent about assignment. At the same time, by using the words in (1)(A) 'whether *or not* the contract prohibits assignment,' the section prevents parties from using contractual language to prevent the trustee from assigning contracts that (when the contract is silent) contract law typically makes assignable. Id. Thus, we must look to see whether relevant nonbankruptcy law would allow Ford to veto the assignment of its basic franchise contract "whether or not" that basic franchise contract itself specifically "prohibits assignment."

The nonbankruptcy law to which both sides point us is contained in

Rhode Island's "Regulation of Business Practices Among Motor Vehicle Manufacturers, Distributors and Dealers" Act, R.I. Gen. Laws §31-5.1-4(C)(7). It states that

> [N]o dealer . . . shall have the right to . . . assign the franchise . . . without the consent of the manufacturer, except that such consent shall not be unreasonably withheld.

The statute by its terms, allows a manufacturer to veto an assignment where the veto is reasonable but not otherwise. The statute's language also indicates that it applies "whether or not" the franchise contract itself restricts assignment. Thus, the basic question that the case presents is whether Ford's veto was reasonable in terms of the Rhode Island law.

Neither the district court nor the bankruptcy court specifically addressed this question. Their failure apparently arose out of their belief that 11 U.S.C. §365(c)(1)(A) refers only to traditional personal service contracts. But in our view they were mistaken. The language of the section does not limit its effect to personal service contracts. It refers *generally* to contracts that are not assignable under nonbankruptcy law. State laws typically make contracts for personal services nonassignable (where the contract itself is silent); but they make other sorts of contracts nonassignable as well. . . . The legislative history of §365(c) says nothing about "personal services." To the contrary, it speaks of letters of credit, personal loans, and leases — instances in which assigning a contract may place the other party at a significant disadvantage. The history thereby suggests that (c)(1)(A) has a broader reach.

The source of the "personal services" limitation apparently is a bankruptcy court case, In re Taylor Manufacturing, Inc., 6 B.R. 370 (Bkrtcy. N.D. Ga. 1980), which other bankruptcy courts have followed. The *Taylor* court wrote that (c)(1)(A) should be interpreted narrowly, in part because it believed that (c)(1)(A) conflicted with another section, (f)(1), which states in relevant part:

> Except as provided in subsection (c) . . . , notwithstanding a provision . . . in applicable law that prohibits . . . the assignment of [an executory] contract . . . the trustee may assign [it].

As a matter of logic, however, we see no conflict, for (c)(1)(A) refers to state laws that prohibit assignment "whether or not" the contract is silent, while (f)(1) contains no such limitation. Apparently (f)(1) includes state laws that prohibit assignment only when the contract is *not* silent about assignment; that is to say, state laws that enforce contract provisions prohibiting assignment. . . . The section specifically excepts (c)(1)(A)'s state laws that forbid assignment even when the contract *is* silent; they are to be heeded. Regardless, we fail to see why a "conflict" suggests that (c)(1)(A) is limited to "personal services."

. . . [S]ince it often is difficult to decide whether or not a particular duty can be characterized by the label "personal service," it makes sense to avoid this question and simply look to see whether state law would, or would not, make the duty assignable where the contract is silent. . . .

Although the district court did not explicitly decide whether Ford's veto was reasonable, it decided a closely related question. Under other provisions of §365 a bankruptcy court cannot authorize assignment of an executory contract if 1) the debtor is in default, unless 2) there is "adequate assurance of future performance." §365(b)(1)(C). Pioneer is in default, but the bankruptcy and district courts found "adequate assurance." For the sake of argument, we shall assume that this finding is equivalent to a finding that Ford's veto of the assignment was unreasonable. And, we shall apply a "clearly erroneous" standard in reviewing the factual element in this lower court finding. . . . On these assumptions, favorable to Fleet, we nonetheless must reverse the district court, for, in our view, any finding of unreasonableness, based on this record, is clearly erroneous.

Our review of the record reveals the following critical facts. First, in accordance with its ordinary business practice and dealer guidelines incorporated into the franchise agreement, Ford would have required Toyota Village, as a dealer, to have a working capital of at least $172,000, of which no more than half could be debt. Toyota Village, however, had a working capital at the end of 1981 of $37,610; and its net worth was $31,747. Although the attorney for Fleet at one point in the bankruptcy proceedings said Toyota Village could borrow some of the necessary capital from a bank, he made no later reference to the point, nor did he ever specifically state how much Toyota Village could borrow. Since the tax returns of Toyota Village's owner showed gross income of $27,500 for 1981, there is no reason to believe that the owner could readily find the necessary equity capital.

Second, at a time when Japanese cars have sold well throughout the United States, Toyota Village has consistently lost money. The financial statements in the record show the following operating losses:

	1977	1978	1979	1980	1981
Loss	($7,522)	($7,552)	($13,938)	($12,684)	($21,317)

At the same time, the record contains no significant evidence tending to refute the natural inference arising from these facts. The bankruptcy court mentioned five factors that it said showed that Toyota Village gave "adequate assurance" that it could do the job.

1) Toyota Village was an established dealership.
2) Toyota Village was "located within 500 yards of the present Ford dealership."
3) Toyota Village had a proven track record for selling cars.

4) Toyota Village was willing and able to pay $15,000 that Pioneer
    still owed Ford.
5) The owner and sole stockholder of Toyota Village testified that
    he was willing and able to fulfill the franchise agreement.

The first of these factors (dealer experience), while favoring Toyota Village, is weak, given the record of continuous dealership losses. The second
(location) proves little, considering that Pioneer went bankrupt at the very
spot. The third (track record) cuts against Toyota Village, not in its favor,
for its track record is one of financial loss. The fourth (willingness to pay a
$15,000 debt that Pioneer owed Ford) is relevant, but it shows, at most,
that Toyota Village *believed* it could make a success of the franchise. The
fifth (ability to act as franchisee) is supported by no more than a simple
statement by the owner of Toyota Village that he could do the job.
    We do not see how the few positive features about Toyota Village that
the record reveals can overcome the problem of a history of losses and
failure to meet Ford's capital requirements. In these circumstances, Ford
would seem perfectly reasonable in withholding its consent to the transfer.
Thus, Rhode Island law would make the franchise unassignable.
    The Rhode Island authority we have found supports this conclusion.
In Dunne Leases Cars & Trucks v. Kenworth Truck Co., 466 A.2d 1153
(R.I. 1983) the Supreme Court of Rhode Island held that failure to meet a
condition in the franchise agreement requiring a leasing business to be
removed from the dealership site, provided due cause for the manufacturer's decision to *terminate* the dealership agreement. In Scuncio Motors,
Inc. v. Subaru of New England, Inc., 555 F. Supp. 1121 (D.R.I. 1982),
aff'd, 715 F.2d 10 (1st Cir. 1983), the federal district court for the District
of Rhode Island wrote that failure to meet a franchise requirement to
provide additional selling space provided cause to terminate a dealer contract. Inability to meet capital requirements, as revealed here, would seem
to provide reasonable grounds for objecting to a franchise transfer a fortiori. If not, a manufacturer would have to allow the transfer of its franchise to virtually any auto dealer.
    One might still argue that under Rhode Island law the only "reason-
able" course of action for Ford is to allow the transfer and then simply
terminate Toyota Village if it fails to perform adequately. This suggestion,
however, overlooks the legal difficulties that Ford would have in proving
cause for termination under the Rhode Island "Regulation of Business
Practices Among Motor Vehicle Manufacturers, Distributors and
Dealers" Act. R.I. Gen. Laws §31-5.1-4(D)(2). The very purpose of the
statute — protecting dealer reliance — suggests that it ought to be more
difficult for a manufacturer to terminate a dealer who has invested in a
franchise than to oppose the grant of a franchise to one who has not. In any
event, the law does not suggest a manufacturer is "unreasonable" in objecting to a transfer unless he would have "good cause" to terminate the

transferee. And, to equate the two standards would tend to make the "unreasonable" provision superfluous. Thus, we conclude that the Rhode Island law would make the franchise unassignable on the facts here revealed. Therefore, neither the bankruptcy court not the district court had the power to authorize the transfer. . . .

Reversed.

NOTES

1. In re Braniff Airways, Inc., 700 F.2d 935, 943 (5th Cir. 1983), in denying Braniff's attempt to assign its lease with the United States for the use of facilities at Washington National Airport, also rejected the reading of §365(c) given in cases such as *Taylor Manufacturing:*

> Nothing in the statute authorized the district court to depart from the express language of §365(c), which provides for its application to unexpired leases and belies any limitation to personal service contracts. . . . Surely if Congress had intended to limit §365(c) specifically to personal service contracts, its members could have conceived of a more precise term than "applicable law" to convey that meaning.

This argument, in turn, was criticized by the bankruptcy court in In re Fulton Air Service, 34 Bankr. 568, 572 (Bankr. N.D. Ga. 1983):

> Under the *Braniff* holding, *any* executory contract or unexpired lease would be unassignable if "applicable law" excused acceptance of performance. The question then becomes what does the language "notwithstanding a provision in . . . applicable law, that prohibits, restricts, or conditions the assignment of such contract or lease, the trustee may assign such contract or lease under paragraph (2) of this subsection," which appears in §365(f), mean? The Fifth Circuit's interpretation renders this portion of §365(f) meaningless.
>
> . . . While the Court agrees with the Fifth Circuit that Congress could have chosen words which would have made the meaning of §365(c) more readily apparent, the Court cannot ignore the distinct use of "prohibits" and "excuses." It is evident that the drafters intended subsection (c) to apply to a different group of executory contracts and leases than that to which (f) applies. The Court agrees with the . . . point of view that subsection (f) must be read as the general rule and that subsection (c) must be limited to executory contracts and unexpired leases in which applicable law excuses acceptance of performance such as nondelegable personal service contracts.

2. See In re Harms, 10 Bankr. 817, 821 (Bankr. D. Colo. 1981):

> A partnership agreement creates a fiduciary relationship among the members of the partnership. . . . Under applicable nonbankruptcy law, the

limited partners in a limited partnership do not have to accept substituted
performance from a general partner other than the one with whom they
have contracted. . . .

It is obvious that the Trustee cannot assume the position of general
partner of these limited partnerships. . . . Thus, the partnerships dissolved
when the Trustee was appointed.

The court continued by concluding that, since the debtor-in-possession
was a "different entity" than the debtor, the partnership terminated upon
the commencement of the bankruptcy case. *Bildisco*, however, cast doubt
on this reasoning, see supra page 474.

3. Why does §365(c)(2) except contracts to make loans? Why should
lenders be in a better position than suppliers and others that enter into
contracts with a debtor? If the loan were made to the debtor in bankruptcy,
wouldn't the debtor be required to repay it? Isn't that the consequence of
assumption?

4. Can it be argued that the principal problem with §365(c) is that
Congress should not have drawn the line where it did? In other words,
even if there is something special about personal service contracts (or
similar agreements), does the special attribute grow out of concern over
having someone *other* than the debtor perform the services? If so, should
the line have been drawn at assumption, instead of at assignment?
Shouldn't a debtor be able to assume every contract, even personal service
contracts, but should not be able to assign all of them? Consider this in
connection with the following excerpt. (Note that a change in §365(c)
made in 1984 apparently does not move the line. That amendment added
the following italicized language of §365(c)(1)(A): "The trustee may not
assume or assign . . . if (1)(A) applicable law excuses a party, other than
the debtor, to such contract or lease from accepting performance from or
rendering performance to an entity other than the debtor *or the debtor in
possession.*" If applicable law does not permit nonconsensual assignments
to a third party, then the trustee (which includes the debtor in possession,
§1107) is precluded from assuming the contract or lease, even if applicable
law would permit performance by the debtor in possession.)

JACKSON, TRANSLATING ASSETS AND LIABILITIES TO THE BANKRUPTCY FORUM
14 J. Legal Studies 73, 108-109 (1985)

Even if we accept the basic premise of section 365 (that executory contracts
can be assumed by reinstating the terms of the contract), the section muffs
the relationship between bankruptcy law and nonbankruptcy law in dealing with personal service contracts. Sections 365(c) and (f) prohibit the
assumption or assignment of so-called personal service contracts, explicitly

including within their ambit contracts to make loans or extend financial accommodations.

The relationship between the bankruptcy debtor and the pre-bankruptcy debtor remove, however, any reason to distinguish between personal service contracts and other types of executory contracts, based on the ability of the debtor to assume such contracts. Instead, the relevant nonbankruptcy law governing these two types of contracts suggests that any relevant distinction takes hold at the point of assignment, not assumption. This . . . requires one to focus on the nature of the debtor in bankruptcy as evaluated by nonbankruptcy norms. If, as a matter of nonbankruptcy law, the contract in question would have been performable by the debtor notwithstanding a change in management or a change in ownership (such as would occur when the majority of the shareholders sold their stock to another), then that result is best mirrored in bankruptcy by allowing the debtor to assume, and thereby to perform, the contract. In those cases, there simply is no conflict to be resolved between bankruptcy goals and the policies that underlie personal service contracts. Section 365(c), perceiving there to be such a conflict, wrongly distinguishes these contracts from others at the prior stage of assumption.

NOTE ON COMMON LAW ASSIGNMENT RULES

The law of assignments places two general obstacles in the way of an attempted delegation of duties without prior consent: It prohibits the delegation of certain duties entirely, and it does not allow a party to free itself of an obligation if its assignee fails to perform. Consider, first, the general question of delegation. Contract law generally distinguishes the delegation of "fungible" duties from the delegation of "nonfungible" duties. See 4 A. Corbin, Corbin on Contracts 865 (1951); see also Taylor v. Palmer, 31 Cal. 240 (1866). Certain kinds of contracts, often called "personal service contracts," are nondelegable at common law because they are based on particular skills or other unique features of the contracting party. See Restatement (Second) of Contracts §318 comment c (1981) ("Delegation of performance is a normal and permissible incident of many types of contracts. . . . The principal exceptions relate to contracts for personal services and to contracts for the exercise of personal skill or discretion"). In essence, holders of these contracts are protected by a property rule: They do not have to deal with any assignees of their contracting counterpart unless they consent. This protects the expectations of a party that contracted with a particular entity in much the same way as the specific performance rule does in other circumstances. Section 365(c) and (f) can be seen as protecting these expectations, by refusing to permit assignment of personal service contracts.

But there is another common law restriction on assignments without consent. Even when duties may be delegated without prior consent, the original contracting party remains ultimately responsible for the performance of its contractual obligations. See Restatement (Second) of Contracts §318(3) (1981) ("delegation of performance . . . [does not] discharge any duty or liability of the delegating obligor"). That is to say, a party subject to a contractually created obligation ordinarily cannot divest itself of liability by substituting another in its place without the consent of the party owed the duty. While the assignee may be entitled to perform for the original obligor, the original obligor nonetheless remains ultimately liable until discharged by performance (or otherwise).

Section 365(k) does not respect this rule. Is there a reason for treating the two common law rules on assignment differently? Does this justify the distinction the Commission on Bankruptcy Laws suggested between cases of reorganization and liquidation in the excerpt quoted supra page 502.

IN RE U.L. RADIO CORP.
19 Bankr. 537 (Bankr. S.D.N.Y. 1982)

MEMORANDUM & ORDER

John J. GALGAY, Bankruptcy Judge.
Debtor, U.L. Radio Corp., has moved for an order, pursuant to Bankruptcy Code section 365(f), authorizing it to assume its lease ("Lease") with Jemrock Realty Company ("Jemrock"), the landlord, and authorizing U.L. Radio to assign the Lease to Just Heaven Restaurant, Ltd. ("Just Heaven"). U.L. Radio operates the leasehold as a television sales and service store. Just Heaven, the prospective assignee, will operate the premises as a small bistro. Jemrock opposes such an assignment, citing a use clause in the Lease which provides that the lessee shall use the premises only for television service and sale of electrical appliances. Jemrock asserts that the assignment of the Lease to Just Heaven would unlawfully modify the Lease by violating the use clause. Such modification, Jemrock avers, is not permitted under section 365 without the landlord's consent, which consent Jemrock withholds. . . .

I. BACKGROUND

On September 17, 1979, the debtor entered into the Lease with Jemrock for a store located at 2656 Broadway, New York, New York. The store is located in a building which is also occupied by a grocery store, a Chinese restaurant, a liquor store, and 170 apartments. The term of the Lease is for ten years. The rent required to be paid is as follows: $9600 per year from November 1, 1979, to October 31, 1982; $10,800 from November 1, 1982, to October 31, 1985; and $12,000 from November 1,

1985 to October 31, 1989. Paragraph 43 of the Rider to the Lease provides that the tenant may assign the Lease with written consent of the Landlord, which consent is not to be unreasonably withheld.

On May 20, 1981, the debtor filed an original petition under Chapter 11 of the Bankruptcy Code and continues to operate its business as debtor in possession. No creditors' committee has been formed. The debtor intends to propose a liquidation plan of reorganization. The debtor is current in the payment of rent and related charges required by the terms of the Lease and is not in default of any of the Lease terms.

In furtherance of its intention to liquidate all of its assets and to propose a plan of reorganization, the debtor, subject to the approval of this Court, entered into an assignment of the Lease to Just Heaven. The proposed assignment provides, inter alia, that Just Heaven will pay to the Debtor as consideration for the assignment as follows: for the period commencing three months after this Court's approval of the assignment to October 31, 1988, the sum of $2000 per month. Such payments will fund a plan paying unsecured creditors 100 percent of their claims. Rockwell International, the largest creditor, recommends the assignment.

The president of Just Heaven has executed a personal guarantee for the payment of rent in favor of the landlord for the first two years of the assignment, together with a statement that her net worth exceeds $50,000.

The Lease provides in paragraph 45 of the rider to the Lease that "any noise emanating from said premises shall be deemed a breach of the terms and conditions of this Lease." Just Heaven has allocated $20,000 for construction, including soundproofing. David Humpal St. James, Vice President and Secretary as well as a director and a shareholder of Just Heaven, is a noted interior designer including the design of commercial restaurants. His design work has involved soundproofing. . . .

II.   ISSUES

Two issues confront this Court:

(1) Have the provisions of section 365, regarding assumption and assignment of leases, been satisfied?

(2) Can deviation from a use clause prevent the assignment of a lease, when the assumption and assignment otherwise comport with the requirements of section 365?

III.   ASSUMPTION AND ASSIGNMENT UNDER SECTION 365

Code section 365 governs the assumption and assignment of executory contracts, providing broad authority to a trustee or debtor in possession to assume and assign an unexpired lease. . . . The aim of this statutory authority to assume a lease is to "assist in the debtor's rehabilitation or liquidation." House Report at 348, U.S. Code Cong. & Admin. News 1978, p. 6304; Senate Report at 59, U.S. Code Cong. & Admin. News 1978, p. 5845.

Assignment of a lease, which is at issue here, must comply with section 365(f). . . .

Subsection (f)(1) "partially invalidates restrictions on assignment of contracts or leases by the trustee to a third party." House Report at 349, U.S. Code Cong. & Admin. News 1978, p. 6305; Senate Report at 59, U.S. Code Cong. & Admin. News, p. 5845; see Fogel, Executory Contracts and Unexpired Leases in the Bankruptcy Code, 64 Minn. L. Rev. 341, 360 (1980) [hereinafter "Executory Contracts"]. Subsection (f)(2) "imposes two restrictions on assignment by the trustee: (1) he must first assume the contract or lease, subject to all the restrictions found in the section; and (2) adequate assurance of future performance must be provided to the other contracting party." House Report at 349, U.S. Code Cong. & Admin. News 1978, p. 6305; Senate Report at 59, U.S. Code Cong. & Admin. News 1978, p. 5845.[2] Finally, subsection (f)(3) "invalidates contractual provisions that permit termination or modification in the event of an assignment, as contrary to the policy of this subsection." House Report at 349, U.S. Code Cong. & Admin. News 1978, p. 6305; Senate Report at 59, U.S. Code Cong. & Admin. News 1978, p. 5845.

A.   Requirements of Assumption

The first requirement of assignment under section 365(f)(2) is proper assumption under section 365. . . . The broad authority of a trustee or debtor in possession to assume is limited in Code section 365 by subsections (b), (c), and (d). . . .

Sections 365(b)(1) and (2) prescribe conditions to assumption of a lease if a default has occurred. "Subsection (b) requires the [debtor] to cure any default in the . . . lease and to provide adequate assurance of future performance . . . before he may assume." House Report at 347, U.S. Code Cong. & Admin. News 1978, p. 6304; Senate Report at 58, U.S. Code Cong. & Admin. News 1978, p. 5844. . . . (15th ed. 1981). No default exists under the Lease before this Court; therefore, the subsection (b) requirements for assignment are not applicable.

Section 365(c) prohibits a debtor from assuming a lease if applicable nonbankruptcy law "independent of any language in the contract or Lease itself" excuses the other party from giving performances to or receiving performance from someone other than the debtor. . . . Such "nondelegable" and, therefore, non-assumable contracts and leases include those for unique personal services, as well as those to extend credit, to make

---

2. Code section 365(f) does not state which party must provide assurance. However, since Code section 365(k) relieves the debtor-assignor of liability under the lease after assignment, it is sensible that the assignee must provide the assurance of performance.

loans, and to issue securities. The Lease before this Court does not fall under the prohibition of section 365(c). See In re Taylor Manufacturing, Inc., 6 B.R. 370 (Bkrtcy. N.D. Ga. 1980).

Section 365(d) sets time limits on the assumption of unexpired leases. The time requirements of subsection (d) have been met and are not at issue.

B. Adequate Assurance of Future Performance

The second requirement of assignment under section 365(f)(2) is adequate assurance of future performance ("adequate assurance"). . . . Adequate assurance also appears in section 365(b) as a requirement of assumption if an executory contract is in default. 11 U.S.C. §365(b)(1)(C). The phrase "adequate assurance of future performance" is not found in the Bankruptcy Act.

. . . In the legislative history of section 365(b), Congress while discussing assumption under section 365(b) and the bankruptcy clause under section 365(f), provided this explanation of adequate assurance:

> If a trustee is to assume a contract or lease, the courts will have to insure that the trustee's performance under the contract or lease gives the other contracting party the full benefit of the bargain.

House Report at 348, U.S. Code Cong. & Admin. News 1978, pp. 6304-6305; Senate Report at 59, U.S. Code Cong. & Admin. News 1978, p. 5845.

Beyond equating adequate assurance with the full benefit of the bargain, Congress offers no definition of adequate assurance except in the case of real property leases in shopping centers.[4] The Lease at issue here is not located in a shopping center. Congress described a shopping center as "often a carefully planned enterprise, and though it consists of numerous individual tenants, the center is planned as a single unit, often subject to a master lease or financing agreement." House Report at 348, U.S. Code Cong. & Admin. News 1978, p. 6305. The building in which U.L. Radio is located is primarily a residential apartment building, with a liquor store, a grocery store, a restaurant, and U.L. Radio on the first floor. Thus the

---

4. Regarding real property leases in shopping centers, Congress expressly defined adequate assurance in Code section 365(b)(3), including adequate assurance:

(A) of the source of rent . . .
(B) that any percent rent due under such lease will not decline substantially;
(C) that assumption or assignment of such lease will not breach substantially any provision such as radius, use, or exclusivity provision, in any other lease, financing agreement, or master agreement relating to such shopping center; and
(D) that assumption or assignment of such lease will not disrupt substantially any tenant mix or balance in such shopping center.

11 U.S.C. §365(b)(3)(A)-(D). [Reworded in 1984.—EDS.]

specific provisions of adequate assurance in the shopping center case do not apply to the assignment at issue here. . . .

Apart from shopping center leases, Congress "entrusted the courts with the definition of adequate assurance of the performance of contracts and other leases." . . . Adequate assurance of future performance are not words of art, but are to be given practical, pragmatic construction. What constitutes "adequate assurance" is to be determined by factual conditions. . . . The broad authorization of the trustee or debtor to assume or assign unexpired leases, notwithstanding anti-assignment or bankruptcy clauses, prompted the admonition from Congress that the courts must "be sensitive to the rights of the nondebtor party to . . . unexpired leases." House Report at 348, U.S. Code Cong. & Admin. News 1978, p. 6304; Senate Report at 59, U.S. Code Cong. & Admin. News 1978, p. 5845.

The phrase "adequate assurance of future performance" was adopted from Uniform Commercial Code section 2-609. . . . UCC section 2-609 provides that a party with reasonable grounds for insecurity regarding another party's performance may demand "adequate assurance." Official Comment 4 to section 2-609 . . . indicates that "adequate assurance" focuses on the financial condition of a contracting party and his ability to meet his financial obligations. Regarding adequate assurance under an assignment pursuant to section 365(f)(2), the Court in In re Lafayette Radio Electronics [9 B.R. 993 (Bankr. E.D.N.Y. 1981)] stated, "[T]he Court's primary focus will be on the ability of [the assignee] to comply with the financial obligations under the agreement." 9 B.R. at 998.[6]

In In re Pin Oaks Apartments, 7 B.R. 364, 6 B.C.D. 1396 (Bkrtcy. S.D. Tex. 1980), the Court found that changes in financial provisions of a lease, a percentage rental clause and a sublease provision which protected that rental clause, precluded a finding that adequate assurance had been provided because of the drastic effect the changes would have on rentals received.

Thus, the primary focus of adequate assurance is the assignee's ability to satisfy financial obligations under the lease. In this case, the president of the assignee has executed a personal guarantee of the payment of rent in favor of the landlord for the first two years of the assignment, together with a statement that her net worth exceeds $50,000. The assignee has budgeted $20,000 for construction, enhancing the chances of success of the assignee's enterprise. The assignee will have operating capital of an additional $30,000. . . . Upon these facts, the Court rules that adequate

---

6. The *Lafayette Radio* Court found that the agreement in that case was a sublease not an assignment. Thus, the Court's inquiry was the debtor's ability to fulfill the financial obligations of the lease. 9 B.R. at 998. Nonetheless, *financial* wherewithal is the key component of adequate assurance.

assurance of future financial performance has been provided by the assignee.

IV. USE CLAUSE

However, adequate assurance of future financial performance is not the complete statutory requirement; adequate assurance of future performance is. The financial capability of an assignee may be sufficient for a finding of adequate assurance under an executory sales contract or a similar commercial transaction. In a landlord-tenant relationship, more than an assignee's ability to comply with the financial provisions of a lease may be required. More particularly, will compliance with a use clause be required in order to provide adequate assurance?

Congress indicates that adequate assurance will give the landlord the full benefit of his bargain. . . . In its case-by-case determination of those factors, beyond financial assurance, which constitute the landlord's bargain, the Court will generally consider the provisions of the lease to be assigned. See In re Lafayette Radio Electronics, 9 B.R. at 998 (a "landlord cannot be granted any greater rights than what the lease provides"); In re Pin Oaks Apartments, 7 B.R. at 369, 6 BCD at 1400 (citing Hurley v. Atcheson, Topeka & Santa Fe Ry., 213 U.S. 126, 29 S. Ct. 466, 53 L. Ed. 729 (1909), for the proposition that assumption and assignment of a lease entails acceptance by the assignee of the burdens as well as the benefits of the lease).

However, it is equally clear that, by requiring provision of adequate assurance under section 365, i.e., "the lessor's receipt of the 'full benefit of his bargain'," Congress did not require the Court to assure "literal fulfillment by the lessee of each and every term of the bargain." . . . Section 365, by its own terms, empowers the court to render unenforceable bankruptcy clauses and anti-assignment clauses which permit modification or termination of a lease for filing in bankruptcy or assignment of the lease. 11 U.S.C. §365(e), (f)(3). Section 365(k) relieves the estate of liability for future breaches of a lease after assignment, notwithstanding lease provisions to the contrary. 11 U.S.C. §365(k). . . .

The Court in In re Pin Oaks Apartments argued that court authority to abrogate lease provisions extends only to those provisions expressly stated by Congress:

If Congress intended to give this Court or the trustee the power to abrogate any contractual rights between a debtor and non-debtor contracting party other than anti-assignment and "ipso facto" [i.e. bankruptcy] clauses, it would have expressly done so.

7 B.R. at 367, 6 B.C.D. at 1398.

Such a narrow view of court authority is not supported by the statute or the legislative history. First, such a narrow view would frustrate the express policy of Congress favoring assignment. Under the *Pin Oaks* reasoning, lessors could employ very specific use clauses to prevent assignment and thus circumvent the Code. Section 365(f), in broad language, empowers the Court to authorize assignment of an unexpired lease and invalidate any lease provision which would terminate or modify the lease because of the assignment of that lease. 11 U.S.C. §365(f)(1), (3). Any lease provision, not merely one entitled "anti-assignment clause," would be subject to the court's scrutiny regarding its anti-assignment effect. The court could render unenforceable any provision whose sole effect is to restrict assignment, "as contrary to the policy of [subsection (f)(3)]." House Report at 349; Senate Report at 59.

Further, when Congress intended that all terms and provisions of an agreement remain unaltered, it expressly stated such an intent. Section 1124 sets down stringent requirements to define unimpaired claims, requiring the cure of defaults and the unaltered maintenance of legal, equitable, and contractual rights. 11 U.S.C. §1124(2)(D). . . . Under both sections 1124 and 365, Congress expressly stated the requirements. Under section 365, literal compliance with all lease terms was not required. Even under the tightly drawn definition of adequate assurance in the shopping center case, Congress did not envision literal compliance with all lease provisions; insubstantial disruptions in, inter alia, tenant mix and insubstantial breaches in other leases or agreements were contemplated and allowed. 11 U.S.C. §365(b)(3)(C), (D). . . . [Changed in 1984.]

Thus, provision of adequate assurance of future performance does not require an assignee's literal compliance with each and every term of the lease. The court may permit deviations from strict enforcement of any provision including a use clause. . . .

One commentator suggested that the court render completely invalid any use clause in a non-shopping center lease because: (1) "the lessor is seeking to protect his tenant mix with the lease provision, and the Code does not require the court to provide such protection"; and (2) a use clause "invalidly conditions assignment." Fogel, Executory Contracts at 364 (footnote omitted); see Simpson, Leases at 37 n.45. The Court rejects this "per se unenforceable" reading of a use clause.

However, the Court will not go to the other extreme and adopt the "insubstantial" breach or disruption standard for non-shopping center cases that is applicable only to shopping center leases. . . . The Court's authority to waive strict enforcement of lease provisions in the non-shopping center cases will permit deviations which would exceed those permitted in the shopping center cases. . . .

Within the range between unenforceability of a use clause and insubstantial breaches of a use clause, the Code provides no specific standard by which to measure permissible deviations in use. Whatever standard is applied must serve the policy aims of Congress.

Section 365 expresses a clear Congressional policy favoring assumption and assignment. Such a policy will insure that potential valuable assets will not be lost by a debtor who is reorganizing his affairs or liquidating assets for distribution to creditors. This policy parallels case law which disfavors forfeiture. . . . To prevent an assignment of an unexpired lease by demanding strict enforcement of a use clause, and thereby contradict clear Congressional policy, a landlord or lessor must show that actual and substantial detriment would be incurred by him if the deviation in use was permitted.

In this case, the contemplated deviation in use is from an appliance store to a small bistro. The building in which the unexpired leasehold is located already contains a restaurant, a laundry, and a liquor store. The landlord has failed to demonstrate any actual and substantial detriment which he would incur if the proposed deviation in use is permitted. The Court also notes that the contemplated use, along with the planned sound-proofing, will have no adverse effect on other tenants in the building. Thus, this Court rules that the use clause may not be enforced so as to block assignment of this lease to Just Heaven. The fact that Jemrock withholds its consent to the proposed assignment will not prevent the assignment. Consent is required only in leases governed by section 365(c). The lease here is not subject to section 365(c). . . .

Congress, in section 365, has stated a general policy favoring assignment. Balanced against this general policy is the requirement that the non-debtor contracting party receive the full benefit of his bargain. Jemrock Realty will receive the full benefit of its bargain under the proposed assignment of the leasehold from U.L. Radio to Just Heaven. No defaults exist under the lease. The lease has properly been assumed and Just Heaven has provided adequate assurance of future performance. The landlord has shown no actual or substantial detriment to him from the proposed assignment. The statutory requirements have been satisfied. The assignment is authorized.

It is so ordered.

NOTES

1. See also In re TSW Stores of Nanuet, 34 Bankr. 299 (Bankr. S.D.N.Y. 1983); In re Evelyn Byrnes, Inc., 32 Bankr. 825 (Bankr. S.D. N.Y. 1983); In re Fifth Avenue Originals, 32 Bankr. 648 (Bankr. S.D.N.Y. 1983).

2. Note that had *U.L. Radio* involved a lease in a shopping center, the case almost surely would have come out differently, because of special

provisions in §365(b) regarding shopping center leases. Is there any reason, however, to have those rules for shopping centers or limit their reach to them?

PROBLEMS

7.38 Lessor has a lease with Debtor that contains, as one of its terms, a requirement that Debtor maintain a net worth of at least $1,000,000. Debtor wishes to assume and assign the lease to Acme Corp. Must the trustee satisfy the court that Acme Corp. can maintain that net worth?

7.39 Lessor has a lease with Debtor that contains, as one of its terms, a requirement that the leasehold premises be used as an office. Debtor wishes to assume and assign the lease to Acme Corp. Must the trustee satisfy the court that Acme Corp. will use the premises as an office?

7.40 Same facts as Problem 7.39, except that the lease provides that the leasehold premises be used as a law office.

7.41 Same facts as Problem 7.39, except that the lease provides that the leasehold premises be used as a law office with not less than 20 partners.

7.42 Debtor operates an electronics store in a large surburban shopping center, leasing space from the center. The lease contains a number of restrictions on use, minimum percentage rent, and so forth. Debtor stayed current in all of its payments up until the time it went into bankruptcy. Debtor now wishes to assume the lease. May it? See §365(b)(3). May Debtor assign the lease to Acme Corp., who wants to open a pizza parlor on that site? See §365(f)(2). May Debtor sublease the premises to Acme Corp. for the duration of the lease, minus one day? See In re Lafayette Radio Electronics, 12 Bankr. 302 (Bankr. E.D.N.Y. 1981).

7.43 Recall the facts of R.S. Pinellas Motel Partnership, supra page 481. May the trustee assume the franchise agreement? Does it matter what the franchise agreement says about why the franchisee was chosen in the first place?

7.44 Debtor is a famous opera singer. Like most major opera singers, he has long-term contracts to sing at great opera houses throughout the country. After a series of financial reverses, he files a Chapter 11 bankruptcy petition. Should he, as a debtor in possession, be able to assume the contracts that he signed before he filed the petition? If he could assume these contracts, does §365 allow him to assign them to other singers upon a showing that their performances would be adequate? Should a sharper distinction be drawn between the ability of the trustee (or debtor in possession) to assume a contract, and his ability to assign it? See supra, pages 510-511. How would the problem be analyzed if §365 did not exist, and contract rights were treated as property rights under §541?

E. POST-PETITION BARGAINS WITH PRE-PETITION CREDITORS

NOTE ON THE TRUSTEE'S POWER TO RUN THE BUSINESS

Section 1108 empowers the trustee (or debtor in possession) to continue to run a business in Chapter 11, unless the court orders otherwise; the trustee in Chapter 7 first needs permission. §721. The trustee, however, needs court permission in any event to engage in a number of transactions. Section 363, which we touched on in *Edgins*, supra page 445, mirrors §362 in some respects. Whereas §362 stops a creditor from taking property away from the estate, §363 allows the trustee to *use* that property under some circumstances. It also permits the trustee to sell or lease the property under many of the same circumstances.

To examine §363, you need to become accustomed to making two distinctions. The first is between transactions made in the ordinary course of business and those that are not. The second is between "cash collateral" and all other property of the estate. Cash collateral is defined in §363(a). In examining §363, pay particular attention to subsections (b) through (f) and (k) through (m).

Adequate protection here, as in §362, is the linchpin of the system. §363(e). When the trustee both resists relief from the automatic stay and seeks to use collateral, do §§362(d) and 363(e), taken together, impose any greater protective burdens than does §362(d) standing alone? What interest does §363(e) seek to protect?

Does the following provide "adequate protection" to a party with an interest in cash collateral, In re Xinde International, 13 Bankr. 212 (Bankr. D. Mass. 1981)?

> While it is true that use of cash collateral in an ongoing business to maintain its business activity may enhance the estate, and that the collateral would ordinarily be replenished as the business continues, a particular creditor can have realistic fears that replenishment of the cash collateral will not occur. The court in a reorganization case must balance the needs of the creditor's protection against the debtor's likelihood of a successful rehabilitation. . . . In this case, the debtor has equity in its equipment and fixtures sufficient to secure the entire debt, and maintain at least a 50 percent equity cushion, yet it is unable to generate sufficient cash to purchase raw materials to make its product. Without a manufactured product, the debtor will not be able to rehabilitate itself.
>
> Because Xinde is showing a marginal profit in reduced operations, the court believes that at this time this debtor is operating at a break-even point or at a small profit, and the cash collateral will be replenished so as to maintain the creditor's secured position. Furthermore, the debtor has shown that it has a substantial equity cushion available to its creditors.

> Pursuant to 11 U.S.C. §363(e), this court is going to allow the debtor to use the cash collateral without court-ordered payments to the creditor for a period of 90 days. During this time, the court is instructing the debtor to move toward the formation of a plan. . . . If a plan cannot be arranged and confirmed by that time, the court is cognizant that a more concrete form of assurance of adequate protection may be needed by this creditor.

Why does Xinde need cash to purchase raw materials? Should Xinde first be required to see if it can purchase them on credit? As for the prospects of doing that, we need to look at §364, which we turn to next.

The extent to which a business may be sold as a unit using §363 may depend on whether the business is in Chapter 11, where plans of reorganization are subject to disclosure and voting requirements. We examine this question in Chapter 9 of this book.

NOTE ON §364 AND POST-PETITION BORROWING

Section 364 may be thought of as the flip side of *both* §§362 and 363. While §§362 and 363 deal with keeping an estate together and using property to keep it together (or otherwise advance the goals of a bankruptcy proceeding), §364 (in conjunction with §503(b)(1)(A)) enables the trustee to persuade others to deal with the bankrupt estate. A trustee running a business may need to buy supplies, hire services, or borrow money. Section 363 may allow the trustee to run the business on a "cash and carry" basis, but this may be unduly restrictive. Under what conditions can the trustee buy on credit, borrow money, and so forth? How can he persuade third parties that their new extensions of credit will be repaid?

PROBLEMS

7.45 Debtor needs to borrow $50,000 to operate its business. May it do so, giving Lender administrative expense priority without court permission? See §364(a).

7.46 Debtor needs to borrow $50,000 to operate its business. Lender wants more than an administrative expense priority. Debtor offers Lender a security interest on some previously unencumbered assets. May Debtor do so, without court permission? See §364(c). Compare this problem with the prior one. Is there any reason to have a different standard? Whose rights are affected as a result of the different treatment? What should Debtor have to show under §364(c)?

7.47 Debtor owes Manufacturer $300,000. This debt is secured by a security interest in Debtor's equipment. Debtor files a Chapter 11 petition.

After notice and hearing, the bankruptcy court authorizes Debtor to borrow $100,000 from Bank and to give Bank a security interest on the equipment with priority over Manufacturer's security interest. The bankruptcy court finds that Manufacturer is adequately protected, because the value of the equipment is $500,000. Can Manufacturer have this authorization reviewed? What effect would it have? Cf. §§364(e) and 507(b).

NOTE ON BARGAINING WITH PRE-PETITION CREDITORS

The problems we have addressed in this chapter arise largely from the amount of time a bankruptcy proceeding consumes. Although a bankruptcy judge can force all the creditors to stand still, the judge is largely powerless to make the rest of the world stand still. The bankruptcy process must ensure not merely that rights to the debtor's assets are sorted out according to the creditors' entitlements under state law, but also that the value of the assets is preserved or enhanced while these rights are being sorted out. Preserving the value of these assets, however, is not always possible. A bankruptcy proceeding is designed to bring all the creditors together and to enable them to work as one. It generally does not (and should not) limit the rights of noncreditors. If it did, it would give the creditors as a group greater powers than a sole owner of the debtor's business would have. For example, a bankruptcy judge generally cannot (and in any event should not) force consumers to buy cars they do not want, even if the consequence is that an auto manufacturer will fail and its value as a going concern will be lost. Similarly, a bankruptcy judge generally cannot force banks to lend the debtor money or suppliers to give it parts, simply on the ground that the loans or supplies would preserve the value of the debtor as a going concern.

This limitation on the power of the bankruptcy judge — the ability to stay the actions of creditors, but not those of third parties — leads to a difficult problem. It is not always easy to distinguish between the action of creditors and those of third parties. The next case raises this problem in the context of post-petition financing.

IN RE TEXLON CORP.
596 F.2d 1092 (2d Cir. 1979)

FRIENDLY, Circuit Judge.
This appeal from an order of the District Court for the Southern District of New York concerns a controversy between Manufacturers Hanover Commercial Corporation (MHCC) and the trustee in bankruptcy of Texlon Corporation (Texlon), formerly a debtor in possession in a

Chapter XI proceeding, which began early in 1975. It concerns a practice, euphemistically called "cross-collateralization," which, we are told, has been authorized not infrequently by bankruptcy judges in the Southern District of New York. What this term means is that in return for making new loans to a debtor in possession under Chapter XI, a financing institution obtains a security interest on all assets of the debtor, both those existing at the date of the order and those created in the course of the Chapter XI proceeding, not only for the new loans, the propriety of which is not contested, but for existing indebtedness to it. We must determine whether the bankruptcy court properly authorized such "cross-collateralization" in this case, and, if not, whether the trustee's challenge came too late. We uphold Judge Brieant in answering both questions in the negative.

I

The facts can be briefly stated: On November 1, 1974, Texlon filed a petition for an arrangement under Chapter XI of the Bankruptcy Act. The bankruptcy judge signed on the same day *ex parte* an order continuing the debtor in possession, other orders routinely entered at the commencement of such proceedings and the order giving rise to this litigation (hereafter referred to as the financing order). This authorized Texlon to enter into a number of agreements with MHCC for the factoring of accounts on a nonrecourse basis and for advances in connection therewith and, in MHCC's discretion, additional advances up to $100,000 to be evidenced by certificates of indebtedness issued pursuant to §344 of the Bankruptcy Act. Texlon gave MHCC a security interest in all of its inventory and equipment and in the equity in the accounts, not merely for amounts paid under the factoring agreement and for certificates of indebtedness, but also for preexisting debt held by MHCC.[1] The application represented that any delay in authorizing these arrangements would be prejudicial to Texlon's continued viability, that only immediate approval would enable it to continue in business, and that the need for the relief was urgent and could not await a creditors' committee meeting. On November 6 MHCC began purchasing the accounts receivable. On the same day counsel for the debtor sent a copy of all the November 1 orders to the firm of Otterbourg, Steindler, Houston & Rosen, P.C. which had represented an informal creditors' committee prior to Texlon's decision to file under Chapter XI.

---

1. Prior to November 1, 1974, MHCC, in addition to factoring Texlon's accounts, had lent Texlon $1,000,000 for the purchase of equipment, of which a large balance remained unpaid. MHCC had received, as security for this loan, a lien on Texlon's machinery, fixtures, and equipment. The financing order provided that the Chapter XI collateral (the inventory and the equity in new accounts receivable) would stand as additional security for MHCC's outstanding indebtedness, and further provided that Texlon could continue to make payments to MHCC on account of its pre-Chapter XI equipment loan in the same amounts as before.

A week later MHCC made a $40,000 advance against a certificate on indebtedness.

A creditors' committee meeting was held on November 19, on notice to the 100 largest creditors. The meeting elected an unofficial creditors' committee for which Mr. Otte, the present trustee, acted as secretary. Counsel for Texlon informed the creditors of the terms of the financing order. The committee retained the Otterbourg firm as counsel, and elected Mr. Otte as "stand-by" trustee. Thereafter MHCC advanced a further $60,000 against a certificate of indebtedness and factored new receivables. On December 10 the unofficial committee was elected as the official committee and was later authorized to retain the Otterbourg firm as counsel.

Texlon continued to suffer heavy losses. On January 10, 1975, it was adjudicated a bankrupt under §376(2) of the Bankruptcy Act, and Mr. Otte was appointed Trustee. By this time MHCC had made factoring advances of $567,000 in addition to the loan of $100,000. Texlon's assets were sufficient to repay these and leave a surplus of $267,000, which MHCC contends to be applicable to pre-petition indebtedness, variously stated as $660,000 or $695,000. According to appellee, allowance of MHCC's claims would denude the estate of substantially all its assets.

The Trustee moved on January 16, 1975 to modify the financing order "so as to provide that any equity in the collateral held by MHCC after satisfaction of the indebtedness due it under its Chapter XI factoring and other agreements, shall be applied for the benefit of all creditors pro rata, rather than in satisfaction of the unsecured portion of the pre-Chapter XI due MHCC from TEXLON." After proceedings unnecessary to detail and countless adjournments, Bankruptcy Judge Babitt denied the motion on November 11, 1977. He held that the financing order was "interdicted by the Act" and similar orders should not be entered in the future, both because the order gave pre-petition debt priority over that accorded post-petition Chapter XI creditors under §64a(1), and also because it preferred the position of a pre-petition creditor over that of others in violation of §70d(5). However, he declined to vacate the order because "[t]he elements of reliance on the order by MHCC, and the rights which vested because of such reliance, support this court's judgment that the order should be left in repose."

The trustee appealed to the district court. Agreeing with the bankruptcy judge that the "cross-collateralization" provision should not have been included in the financing order, although not clearly on the same grounds, Judge Brieant held that this was not the sort of case "where supervening equities attach in favor of a lender relying on a facially void order" since MHCC would be fully paid for all post-petition advances. Accordingly he reversed the order of the bankruptcy judge and directed that the Trustee's application be granted. On appeal MHCC argues that both the bankruptcy judge and the district judge were in error in holding that the Bankruptcy Act forbids "cross-collateralization" and that in any event the district judge erred by failing to recognize that the financing order had become final and non-appealable prior to the trustee's application.

II

We begin our discussion of the merits by agreeing with MHCC that the financing order did not run afoul of §64a. Although, by virtue of §302, §64a applies in Chapter XI proceedings insofar as it is "not inconsistent with or in conflict with the provisions of" that Chapter, §344 empowers the court to authorize a debtor in possession to issue:

> certificates of indebtedness for cash, property, or other consideration approved by the court, upon such terms and conditions and with such security and priority in payment over existing obligations as in the particular case may be equitable.

It has long been the practice, both in equity receiverships and in reorganization proceedings under §77, former §77B, and Chapter X, for courts to authorize the issuance of certificates priming claims that would otherwise be entitled to prior payment. Moreover the point at issue here is the creation not of a super-priority but of a secured interest. . . . Indeed, it is common ground that, despite §64a, the financing order is valid insofar as it created a new lien to secure the $100,000 of advances and any unpaid balance under the factoring agreement, even if enforcement of such a lien would deplete the funds from which priority claims could be paid. . . .

The bankruptcy judge and the district judge were nevertheless correct in concluding that the ex parte financing order was unauthorized insofar as it granted MHCC additional security for the pre-petition debt in consideration for its entering into the factoring agreement and making $100,000 in advances. Any such arrangement made by the bankrupt while insolvent and within four months before the filing of a petition would have constituted a voidable preference. . . . We have been pointed to no appellate decisions in the long history of reorganization under §77, former §77B, Chapter X and Chapter XI of the Bankruptcy Act, that has sustained an order authorizing action by a receiver, trustee or a person with equivalent powers which, if done by the debtor, "would be a fraud on the act, as it would work an unequal distribution of the bankrupt's property." Tiffany v. Boatmen's Institution, 18 Wall. (85 U.S.) 375, 388, 21 L. Ed. 868 (1873). While §357(6) permits a Chapter XI arrangement to contain "provisions for payment of debts incurred after the filing of the petition and during the pendency of the arrangement, in priority over the debts affected by such arrangement," nothing in that section suggests that dif-

ferent treatment for pre-petition debts of the same class is permissible. Yet
the financing order allows MHCC, by entering into the factoring agreement and making fresh advances, to obtain security for its pre-petition
debt commensurate with that of a post-petition debt.

MHCC argues that to forbid "cross-collateralization," more accurately a post-adjudication preference, in the absence of any express prohibition in the Bankruptcy Act would ignore the breadth of the language of
§344, as well as of §2(a)(15) which empowers the bankruptcy court to:

> Make such orders, issue such process, and enter such judgments, in addition
> to those specifically provided for, as may be necessary for the enforcement of
> the provisions of this title. . . .

and would run counter to the general policy of Chapter XI to promote
rehabilitation. It claims these considerations to be supported by In re
Applied Logic Corp., 576 F.2d 952, 959-960 (2 Cir. 1978), where we
quoted with approval an extract from Judge Pope's dissent in First Natl.
Bank of Portland v. Dudley, 231 F.2d 396, 403-404 (9 Cir. 1956), and by
§364 of the Bankruptcy Reform Act of 1978. We do not find these arguments persuasive. In *Applied Logic* we were dealing with a bank's statutory
right of setoff under §68a, a provision which by its very nature produces
inequality, see 576 F.2d at 957. Judge Pope's statement was simply to the
effect that a bank participating in a rescue effort should not lightly be
found to have waived a right to preferred treatment derived from a specific provision of the Bankruptcy Act. And we expressly recognized that
§68a could not be utilized to effect a preference under §60a, 576 F.2d at
962-963. To such limited extent as it is proper to consider the new Bankruptcy Act, which takes effect on October 1, 1979, in considering the
validity of an order made in 1974 . . . we see nothing in §364(c) or in
other provisions of that section that advances the case in favor of "cross-
collateralization."

In order to decide this case we are not obliged, however, to say that
under no conceivable circumstances could "cross-collateralization" be authorized. Here it suffices to hold that . . . a financing scheme so contrary
to the spirit of the Bankruptcy Act should not have been granted by an *ex
parte* order, where the bankruptcy court relies solely on representations by
a debtor in possession that credit essential to the maintenance of operations is not otherwise obtainable. The debtor in possession is hardly neutral. Its interest is in its own survival, even at the expense of equal
treatment of creditors, and close relations with a lending institution tend
to prevent the exploration of other available courses in which a more
objective receiver or trustee would engage. A hearing might determine
that other sources of financing are available; that other creditors would
like to share in the financing if similarly favorable terms are accorded
them; or that the creditors do not want the business continued at the price

of preferring a particular lender. We recognize that even so limited a holding means that, in cases originating under §322 (or under §321 where no creditors' committee had yet been appointed under §44(b)), an order like the one here at issue perhaps could not be made until the first meeting of the creditors which, under §334, shall be held "[n]ot less than twenty-five nor more than forty days after the petition is filed," or possibly even later, and that some possibly resuscitable debtors might sink in the interval. The risk of this, occurring only when the debtor has no unmortgaged assets adequate, in addition to those created by the advances, to induce existing creditors or new sources of financing to make them, is not too high a price to pay in order to protect the basic aim of the Bankruptcy Act to avoid inequality in the treatment of pre-petition debt. We note in this connection that under §364 of the new Bankruptcy Act, to which MHCC has invited our attention, all orders authorizing a trustee to obtain unsecured or secured credit (except unsecured credit in the ordinary course of business allowable as an administrative expense) can be made only after notice and hearing. Although §102(1)(B)(ii) construes this language as dispensing with "an actual hearing" if "there is insufficient time for a hearing to be commenced before such act must be done, and the court authorizes such act," such notice "as is appropriate in the particular circumstances" seemingly must be given in all cases where the Act requires notice and hearing.

III

MHCC contends that, however all this may be, the trustee's attack on the financing order came too late. Bankruptcy Rule 803 provides that:

> Unless a notice of appeal is filed as prescribed by Rules 801 and 802, the judgment or order of the referee shall become final.

Rules 801 and 802 require that a notice of appeal be filed with the bankruptcy judge within 10 days of the date of the entry or judgment appealed from except that he may extend the time for not more than 20 days. Since no such motion was made, MHCC contends that the financing order became final on November 11, 1974. . . .

    . . . In Wayne United Gas Co. v. Owens-Illinois Glass Co., 300 U.S. 131, 137-138, 57 S. Ct. 382, 386, 81 L. Ed. 557 (1937), the Supreme Court held that a district court sitting in bankruptcy could in its discretion rehear a cause even after the expiration of the period allowed for appeal "if no intervening rights will be prejudiced by its action" and that if the court rehears the petition "upon the merits," the time to appeal would run from its grant or denial. Pfister v. Northern Illinois Finance Corp., 317 U.S. 144, 63 S. Ct. 133, 87 L. Ed. 146 (1942), applied the same rule to orders of a conciliation commissioner under §75 of the Bankruptcy Act, the functional equivalent of the bankruptcy judge here.

We cannot believe that Bankruptcy Rule 803 or Rule 924 making F.R. Civ. P. 60 generally applicable in bankruptcy proceedings intended to diminish the force of these two well-known decisions. . . .

If *Wayne* and *Pfister* have survived, as MHCC seemingly concedes, we have no difficulty in finding that the trustee's application was encompassed by them. Although the bankruptcy judge characterized his opinion as merely "advisory," it is clear that he reconsidered the financing order, concluded he had erred in signing it, but thought he was precluded from amending it. This is all that is needed to constitute "reexamination." . . . The trustee's application also fulfilled the requirement stated in *Wayne,* supra, 300 U.S. at 137, 57 S. Ct. at 385, that it be made "before rights have vested on the faith of [the] action" and that "no intervening rights will be prejudiced by its action." MHCC has not suffered any actual loss from reliance on the financing order as the factored accounts more than sufficed to reimburse MHCC for the Chapter XI advances against them as well as for all interest charges, factoring commissions and other expenses. Additionally there are ample funds to repay the $100,000 certificates of indebtedness.

While it may be that MHCC would not have engaged in these transactions but for its hope of securing a preferred position for the pre-petition debt, this is not the kind of prejudice that bars reconsideration. The test is whether, upon granting the motion to reconsider, the court will be able to reestablish the rights of the opposing party as they stood when the original judgment was rendered. . . . Almost by definition it cannot be necessary for reconsideration that the court should be able to place a losing party in the same position as if there had been none.

The order of the district court is affirmed.

NOTE

Would §364(e) have changed the outcome in this case? We consider the scope of §364(e) in conjunction with In re EDC Holding Co., infra page 536.

NOTE ON CROSS-COLLATERALIZATION CLAUSES

Businesses often depend on revolving credit lines. In many industries, it is common to ship goods in return for the buyer's promise to pay in 30 days. Thus, in effect many businesses always have large numbers of short-term loans outstanding to their customers. They often must borrow money themselves in order to provide these extensions of credit. A debtor that files a petition in bankruptcy but continues to operate its business has this same need to borrow money as anyone else in the industry. It may not be able to compete if it does business on a cash-only basis. In a frictionless world, such a debtor would be able to borrow money from a third-party lender who had never made any previous loans to it. Section 364 of the Bankruptcy Code, as we have seen, allows the debtor in possession to incur debt in the ordinary course of business and give the new lender a claim against the debtor's assets superior to those of all existing general creditors. Under the Bankruptcy Code, the bankruptcy judge may also authorize the debtor to borrow outside the ordinary course of business after a notice and a hearing and, if necessary, give the new lender a lien on the debtor's assets. §364.

The requirement of a notice and hearing ensures that every creditor who might be adversely affected can monitor the debtor in possession and ensure that the loan is both necessary and given on competitive terms. Sometimes, however, the party willing to make the new loan is a preexisting creditor, and the terms it offers may affect both the old loan and the new one. For example, a creditor may offer to lend only if the debtor is willing to give it an interest in its property securing both the new loan and the old one. The provision in the new loan imposing this condition is a cross-collateralization clause.

Such clauses are hard for a court to analyze because when a party wears the hats of both a new lender and a preexisting creditor, there are two competing explanations for that party's insistence upon the clause. It could be a disguised effort on the part of a preexisting creditor to improve its position at the expense of other creditors. By making a new loan at a competitive rate, it also obtains a higher priority for its earlier loan. Alternatively, the clause might be part of a package of terms that were in fact fair and promoted everyone's interest. A lender, for example, may be willing to offer a lower rate of interest on the new loan or to give up rights it would otherwise have against the debtor in return for a cross-collateralization clause. The package of terms it offered might be more attractive to the debtor, even with the cross-collateralization clause, than the package anyone else was offering.

When the debtor in possession accepts a post-petition loan, one cannot assume that it will invariably act in the interests of all the creditors as a group. As Judge Friendly notes, "[t]he debtor in possession is hardly neutral." The managers of a closely held corporation, for example, may have guaranteed pre-petition loans made to the debtor by the prospective post-petition lender. In any event, the managers are apt to be more concerned about keeping the debtor in business (thus keeping their own jobs) than about striking a deal that best promotes the creditors' interests. Ultimately this problem is not conceptually difficult. One can limit the debtor's freedom to borrow and require an adversary hearing, at least for some kinds of borrowing. In limiting the debtor's freedom of action, one has a fairly clear benchmark upon which to rely, because whether a particular post-petition loan is in the debtor's interests can always be measured by the cost of obtaining such loans in the marketplace.

The simpler solution—banning cross-collateralization clauses outright—would avoid the valuation errors that always arise, but would bring its own costs, because such clauses may have advantages, at least in situations in which the pre-petition creditor has a pre-petition security interest in property that turns over rapidly, such as accounts receivable. In re General Oil Distributors, Inc., 20 Bankr. 873 (Bankr. S.D.N.Y. 1982), may have been a case in which a cross-collateralization clause provided such advantages. In that case, Bank had a perfected security interest in General Oil's accounts receivable and was, at the time of the bankruptcy petition, fully secured. It agreed to advance further funds to the debtor on the condition that it be granted a security interest in all of the debtor's unencumbered property. The cross-collateralization clause did not improve Bank's position if its pre-petition loan was in fact already fully secured. Moreover, given that Bank already had a security interest in General's accounts, General would be forced by §363 to provide it with adequate protection before General could use any of the cash acquired when account debtors paid their bills. The cross-collateralization clause gave Bank only powers that it could have insisted on in any event, and the clause may not have placed any general creditor in a worse position than if the loan had not been made.

IN RE IKE KEMPER & BROS., INC.
4 Bankr. 31 (Bankr. E.D. Ark. 1980)

Arnold M. ADAMS, Bankruptcy Judge.

On December 7, 1979, the debtor filed this Chapter 11 case under the new Code. 11 U.S.C. §§301 et seq. On December 20, 1979, the debtor-plaintiff filed adversary complaint against U.S. Shoe Corporation, the defendant herein. Simultaneously, the Court entered a temporary order requiring defendant to ship shoes previously ordered with requirement that orders be paid on delivery; and ordered defendant to appear before the Court on January 3, 1980, to show cause why said temporary order should not be made permanent. . . .

This case exposes a paper war between plaintiff and defendant. From the preponderance of the testimony, the Court finds that there was no effective cancellation of the sundry orders for shoes, each of which is a separate executory contract which the debtor in possession has the authority to assume or reject.

The debtor has been a retail outlet for men and ladies' shoes and apparel in central Arkansas for more than 80 years; it has had business relations with the defendant for at least 50 years; and for a considerable number of years it has been the sole retail store for defendant's Selby line of goods on which defendant has trade-mark rights.

In recent times, the debtor has experienced cash flow problems as a result of managerial problems. To correct this situation, the plaintiff engaged Mr. Norwood Jones on November 20, 1979, an expert in aiding companies with financial difficulties, who has made substantial and positive changes in the debtor's operation and has arranged an accord with practically all of plaintiff's trade creditors except the defendant herein.

A substantial portion of plaintiff's profit is from shoes sold to it by the defendant from its Selby Division.

The Court specifically finds that without the goods of the defendant, a successful reorganization will be scuttled, resulting in liquidation proceedings under Chapter 7 of the Code, to the substantial prejudice of more than 200 trade creditors of the plaintiff who are owed approximately $1,271,025.43.

The Court further finds that from the case as a whole, a reasonable inference may be drawn that the defendant refused to complete orders of plaintiff unless debts incurred prior to filing of the Chapter 11 case be paid in full, which is tantamount to harassment prohibited by Chapter 11.

The defendant should be ordered to fill orders for shoes applied for prior to filing of this case, conditioned that plaintiff issue its debtor in possession check prior to shipment unless the parties agree otherwise, conditioned further that plaintiff be given the usual trade discounts.

The Court further finds that under the unique circumstances of this case, the defendant should be required to fill future orders upon assurances of payment and that defendant will be required to accept a debtor in possession check prior to the shipment of said orders as adequate assurance of payment unless the parties agree otherwise. . . .

The temporary order will be made permanent. . . .

NOTES

1. Why aren't U.S. Shoe's actions simply a breach of contract? What authority is there to require someone to complete a contract? Cf. §525. Is this a case for specific performance?

2. Apart from the breach issue, what about future orders? Can a bankruptcy judge tell a supplier the terms on which it must do business? Require the extension of credit? Set the price of the shoes? Would U.S. Shoe be allowed to breach and refuse to deliver more shoes if U.S. Shoe had been paid in full up through the time of filing the bankruptcy petition? If so, why should orders such as Judge Adams's turn on whether or not the debtor is in default?

3. In re Blackwelder Furniture Co., 7 Bankr. 328 (Bankr. W.D.N.C. 1980), involved the following theory:

Blackwelder claims that the defendants should be permanently enjoined from terminating their business relationships with Blackwelder because of the actions of said defendants in allegedly illegally refusing to ship furniture to Blackwelder. Blackwelder claims and alleges that the defendants have refused to deal with it because of its filing under Chapter 11 of the Bankruptcy Code, and that said refusals on said grounds are illegal and unlawful. It urges this Court to find that the defendants have unlawfully discriminated against the debtor . . . and that they have therefore violated the letter and spirit of the Bankruptcy Code and should be enjoined [under §105] from further violation.

In deciding to issue a preliminary injunction, requiring the defendants "to deal with Blackwelder according to the business relationship that existed" immediately before the filing of Blackwelder's petition under Chapter 11, the court stated:

The cause of action put forward does not directly rely on the Sherman Act, the Clayton Act, or any other specific antitrust law. Instead, the plaintiff contends that the actions of the defendants are unlawful and illegal in that they discriminate against the plaintiff because it took advantage of the provisions of the [Bankruptcy Code]. The plaintiff contends that such actions are unlawful and illegal because they frustrate the purposes of the Bankruptcy Code. The plaintiff contends that such actions are unlawful and illegal because many of the creditors who helped formulate and voted for the plaintiff's plan of reorganization are now attempting to frustrate that plan and drive the plaintiff out of business. . . . [T]he Court finds that the plaintiff "has raised questions going to the merits so serious, substantial, difficult and doubtful, as to make them fair ground for litigation and thus for more deliberative investigation."

NOTE ON *IKE KEMPNER* AND POST-PETITION PAYMENTS TO PRE-PETITION SELLERS

Would the case have been the same if Ike Kempner was not indebted to U.S. Shoe on the date of bankruptcy? In that case U.S. Shoe would not be a pre-petition creditor. As such, it would appear indistinguishable, from the perspective of bankruptcy policy, from any number of other shoe suppliers that might never have dealt with Ike Kempner in the past but with which Ike Kempner would now like to do business. In other words, apart from U.S. Shoe's status as a pre-petition creditor, would there be any basis (assuming no executory contract for the continued delivery of shoes existed that §365 could work on) for ordering U.S. Shoe to supply Ike Kempner with shoes? Is it enough that Ike Kempner had sold U.S. Shoe brand shoes in the past?

Assuming U.S. Shoe's status as a pre-petition creditor may make the analysis slightly different, what weight should be given to that factor? U.S. Shoe argued that its position as a creditor of Ike Kempner should not change its right to stop doing business with it: It should no more be required to supply the debtor with new shoes than any of the banks that were owed money were required to extend new credit. Ike Kempner in turn argued that U.S. Shoe had no reason to refuse to do business with it other than as a means for collecting a pre-petition debt. Before one can analyze either claim, however, one should ask whether U.S. Shoe was in fact unwilling to supply shoes at the competitive rate or whether Ike Kempner was trying to impose upon U.S. Shoe terms it could not have received from a third party. There is, after all, no bankruptcy reason to force U.S. Shoe to provide supplies to Ike Kempner for less than a third party would be willing to provide the same goods. Forcing U.S. Shoe to provide goods at a bargain price compromises the rights it had outside of bankruptcy and hence rights it should also have inside bankruptcy.

In the case, Ike Kempner was willing to pay U.S. Shoe by check before shipment and was not asking to be given any terms that were not ordinarily offered shoe stores that were similarly situated. These terms may not have compensated U.S. Shoe, however, for the additional risks it was taking by virtue of Ike Kempner being in reorganization. U.S. Shoe, for example, may have feared that Ike Kempner would not provide adequate service to its customers or that U.S. Shoe's reputation might be tarnished if its shoes were sold by someone who was in financial distress. Ike Kempner had been buying shoes from U.S. Shoes for 50 years and for a long time had been the sole retail outlet in the area for U.S. Shoe's Selby line of shoes. Even though other suppliers of similar shoes existed, switching to them might have entailed significant costs. Ike Kempner probably had many of the Selby shoes in its store, and it may have depended upon U.S. Shoe to fill gaps in its inventory. Another competitor would not be able to supply Ike Kempner with Selby shoes in size 9E. Moreover, Ike Kempner's advertising may have relied on its being a source of Selby shoes.

That Ike Kempner was dependent upon U.S. Shoe supplying it, however, does not resolve the inquiry in its favor. If Ike Kempner had chosen to, it could have entered into a contract with U.S. Shoe to supply it. As it was, it subjected itself to being cut off by U.S. Shoe at any time. If U.S. Shoe wanted to rely on another shoe store in the area or raise its prices dramatically, Ike Kempner, in the absence of any bargain to the contrary, would be powerless to stop it. U.S. Shoe can argue that even though it in fact used the market power it had over Ike Kempner to obtain payment on a pre-petition indebtedness, it could have simply used it to exact a higher price for its goods. Its ability to make Ike Kempner pay more for its shoes is ultimately independent of its being a preexisting creditor, so this ability should not be compromised simply because it happened to be a preexisting creditor.

Ike Kempner had been doing business for a half a century with U.S. Shoe and it was not until the bankruptcy petition was filed that U.S. Shoe decided to take advantage of the opportunity to exploit all the costs Ike

Kempner had sunk into selling U.S. Shoe's goods. Perhaps Ike Kempner had no exclusive dealing arrangement with U.S. Shoe because U.S. Shoe's interest in maintaining its reputation among shoe stores as a reliable and trustworthy supplier kept it in check. This reputation may not have been compromised by exercising whatever power it had to take advantage of the investment Ike Kempner had sunk into selling U.S. Shoes' Selby line. The other creditors of Ike Kempner, rather than the owners of the shoe store, are the ones who bear the burden of this exercise of power, and U.S. Shoe may not have to worry about its reputation among the creditors of its customers.

This observation, however, says little more than that suppliers such as U.S. Shoe can take advantage of firms in bankruptcy in a way they cannot take advantage of firms outside of bankruptcy. It does not account for U.S. Shoe's status as a pre-petition creditor. One should ask if a supplier would behave differently because it was also a preexisting creditor. A new supplier would be indifferent to whether it sold shoes to Ike Kempner or to someone else. U.S. Shoe, once it is a pre-petition creditor, can never be indifferent. If U.S. Shoe cuts off supplies and Ike Kempner goes out of business, U.S. Shoe will lose the chance to collect the debts that are owed it. If U.S. Shoe continues shipment of new inventory and Ike Kempner remains in business, U.S. Shoe will receive some, but probably not all, of what it is owed. Finally, if it is allowed to threaten to cut off supplies unless it is paid before other creditors, and Ike Kempner succumbs to the threat, U.S. Shoe will receive everything that is owed. That is, however, the thrust of §365(b); can U.S. Shoe be viewed as simply trying to get the same treatment as if it had a long-term supply contract? Should suppliers who are pre-petition creditors but not under contract be treated the same as those that are? Are the provisions for cure appropriate in either case?

Is it possible that U.S. Shoe's behavior threatens to cut off supplies not merely because it may be able to obtain payment in this case, but also because it wants to send a message to its other buyers? In other words, might U.S. Shoe be signalling other buyers that it will not deal with anyone who files a bankruptcy petition who does not first pay all pre-petition debts owed U.S. Shoe in full (and presumably then wait 90 days)?

What should the outcome be, if one can show that U.S. Shoe is behaving the way it is only because it is a pre-petition creditor who is seeking payment? Can one argue that a bankruptcy judge should be able to enjoin it to continue to supply shoes using the authority of §105 of the Bankruptcy Code to issue any order necessary or appropriate to carry out the provisions of the Bankruptcy Code? If a creditor has a credible threat against the debtor and uses it as an effort to obtain repayment, shouldn't a bankruptcy judge, as a general matter, be able to enjoin it? For example, if the creditor states that it is withholding future services "based on your failure to pay for the [previous services]," isn't that clearly a violation of §362(a)? See In re Olson, 38 Bankr. 515 (Bankr. N.D. Iowa 1984). But absent such a declaration of intent, can a bankruptcy judge identify when a firm such as U.S. Shoe is acting as a pre-petition creditor, attempting to collect a debt, and when it is acting as a post-petition supplier? What if it is acting out of both motives? Should the test be a "but-for" one — that is to say, would the supplies have been withheld but for the pre-petition debt? Or should the test be one of absolute prohibition any time a mixed motive appears to be present? Cf. In re Sportfame of Ohio, 40 Bankr. 47 (Bankr. N.D. Ohio 1984) (evidence supported finding "that defendant's sole animus in refusing to ship goods to debtor for cash was its desire to coerce debtor's repayment of its prepetition indebtedness," and that this violated §362(a)(6)).

In the case that follows, the pre-petition creditors are workers who have the right under the labor laws to engage in acts (such as picketing) for the purpose of obtaining payment of pre-petition debts. Other things being equal, the workers would be enjoined by the automatic stay, but the policies in our labor law are thought in this instance to trump the policies of our bankruptcy laws. Recall *Crowe*, supra page 397. Once this issue is settled, however, one must decide how to deal with exercise of power by the workers. How well does the court in the case that follows come to grips with this problem?

IN RE EDC HOLDING CO.
676 F.2d 945 (7th Cir. 1982)

POSNER, Circuit Judge.
Section 364 of the Bankruptcy Code empowers the bankruptcy judge to authorize the bankrupt to borrow money and give the lender priority over certain other creditors. Subsequent reversal, by the district court or the court of appeals, of the grant of priority does not affect the validity of the priority if it was granted "to an entity that extended such credit in good faith, whether or not such entity knew of the pendency of the appeal," unless the transaction was stayed pending appeal. 11 U.S.C. §364(e). We are required in this case to interpret and apply the term "in good faith."

Before Wisconsin Steel (as we shall refer jointly to the affiliated corporations that are the bankrupts in this case) went bankrupt, the Chase Manhattan Bank had loaned it money secured by a lien on inventory and by a bank account that the company maintained with Chase. Wisconsin Steel defaulted, and Chase set off against these defaults the funds in the account. Wisconsin Steel was accustomed to paying its employees with checks drawn on this account. Chase's set-off caused those checks to bounce, which induced Wisconsin Steel to petition for protection under Chapter 11 of the Bankruptcy Code.

The union representing Wisconsin Steel's workers filed a complaint in the bankruptcy court seeking payment to its members of their unpaid wages. Chase was named as a defendant along with Wisconsin Steel. The union claimed that it had a lien on the same inventory on which Chase claimed a lien. Although the bankruptcy court authorized Chase to take possession of the inventory, the union, by picketing Wisconsin Steel, prevented Chase from doing so. Eventually a settlement was reached by which Chase agreed to lend Wisconsin Steel some $1.7 million in exchange for the union's dropping its suit and allowing the inventory to be removed. The agreement stated that Wisconsin Steel would pay out of the proceeds of the loan $77,000 to the union to reimburse it for attorneys' fees and other legal expenses incurred in its suit, and the rest (except for some small amounts for various taxes) to the company's employees in settlement of their claims. The agreement further provided that the entire loan was to receive the priority that 11 U.S.C. §507(a)(3) gives wage claims.

Since the proposed loan involved the grant of a special priority to the lender, the bankruptcy judge's approval was required by section 364. He gave it, over the objection of the Official Creditors' Committee of WSC Sales Company, representing the general creditors of Wisconsin Steel, that the priority should not extend to the $77,000 earmarked for the union's lawyers. The Committee appealed to the district court from this part of the bankruptcy judge's order but the district court dismissed the appeal as moot. The Committee appeals that dismissal to this court.

The bankruptcy judge's order was never stayed. Therefore, if in lending Wisconsin Steel $77,000 to pay the union's legal expenses Chase was acting in good faith, its priority could not be affected by the validity of the order and the issue of validity is therefore moot as the district court held. . . . But if Chase was not acting in good faith, the Committee was entitled to have the merits of its objection to the grant of priority adjudicated.

Section 364(e) is explicit that knowledge of the pendency of an appeal from a bankruptcy judge's order granting a lender special priority does not forfeit the protections that the statute gives to a lender who is in good faith, even though such knowledge implies the further knowledge that there are objections to the order. Therefore the mere fact that Chase knew the Committee objected to its receiving a special priority with regard to that portion of the loan that was to pay the union's legal expenses does not show bad faith. . . . These provisions seek to overcome people's natural reluctance to deal with a bankrupt firm whether as purchaser or lender by assuring them that so long as they are relying in good faith on a bankruptcy judge's approval of the transaction they need not worry about their priority merely because some creditor is objecting to the transaction and is trying to get the district court or the court of appeals to reverse the bankruptcy judge. The proper recourse for the objecting creditor is to get the transaction stayed pending appeal. . . .

But all this presupposes good faith. . . . And while it is clear as we have said that knowledge that there are objections to the transaction is not enough to constitute bad faith, we can find neither cases nor legislative history, pertaining either to good faith lenders to bankrupts or to good faith purchasers from bankrupts, that tell us what is enough. Chase argues that so long as the terms of the transaction are not misrepresented to the bankruptcy judge, as they were not here, the creditor may rely on the bankruptcy judge's order unless it is stayed, no matter how obviously erroneous the order is. But if this is what Congress intended, the words "in good faith" could have been deleted, as it would be perfectly clear even without them that an order obtained from a bankruptcy judge by fraud was ineffective to put the lender who procured the order ahead of other creditors. We assume the statute was intended to protect not the lender who seeks to take advantage of a lapse in oversight by the bankruptcy judge but the lender who believes his priority is valid but cannot be certain that it is, because of objections that might be upheld on appeal. If the lender *knows* his priority is invalid but proceeds anyway in the hope that a stay will not be sought or if sought will not be granted, we cannot see how he can be thought to be acting in good faith.

The loan agreement here stated that $77,000 of the proceeds would be used to pay the union for attorneys' fees and other legal expenses incurred in the prosecution of the union's action for the unpaid wages of its members. The agreement thus gave the union a claim against the bankrupt for $77,000 and simultaneously paid it in full, and Chase's priority meant that the burden would be borne by the bankrupt estate, in effect the general creditors, rather than by Chase itself.

Viewed realistically, as a claim by the union's attorneys for time and expenses incurred in prosecuting the union members' claims for unpaid wages, the union's claim not only was not entitled to priority over the claims of the general creditors but could not be paid out of the bankrupt's estate at all. Subject to exceptions that Chase does not claim the union's attorneys come within, the rule is that no allowance will be made to a creditor's attorney for proving his client's claim. . . . We cannot think it makes a difference that the nominal recipient of the payment was the union rather than its lawyers. The payment is denominated for legal fees and expenses and we have no doubt that the lawyers actually received it. At oral argument Chase's counsel was not quite willing to concede this but he allowed that he "suspected" it was so, which will do.

Where it is evident from the loan agreement itself that the transaction has an intended effect that is improper under the Bankruptcy Code, the lender is not in good faith, and it is irrelevant what the improper purpose is. If the loan agreement had stated that Wisconsin Steel would use the proceeds to buy one-way airplane tickets to Brazil for its officers, we do not think Chase would be arguing to us that it had extended credit to the company in good faith and therefore had an untouchable priority. Of course in such a case the general creditors should be able to obtain a stay but we do not think their failure to do so would place Chase's priority beyond the power of judicial correction; otherwise the good faith requirement would be read out of the statute. The present case is less extreme but no different in principle. Just as Chase would not have been a purchaser in good faith if it had bought from Wisconsin Steel property to which it knew the company did not have good title, so it could not be a lender in good faith in extending credit in exchange for a priority that it knew the company could not properly give it since the transaction amounted to taking money out of the pockets of the general creditors to pay lawyers whose claims were not allowable under bankruptcy law at all.

But we must consider whether it may make a difference that the agreement to pay the lawyers was part of a settlement of the three-cornered litigation among the union, the bankrupt, and Chase. Normally if someone was willing to settle his suit against a bankrupt for $77,000, there would be no impropriety in a bank's lending money (and receiving a special priority) to finance the settlement and thereby enable the bankrupt to disentangle itself from potentially costly litigation, provided that the settlement was a reasonable one. But the origin of the litigation in this case has to be borne in mind. The union was trying to collect its members' wage claims. Those claims were valid creditors' claims but the cases cited earlier forbid the creditors' attorney to collect his fee from the bankrupt. It can make no difference that the attorney has actually filed suit to enforce his client's claim. If an employee sued his bankrupt employer for $1000 in unpaid wages and the bankrupt settled the suit by paying the employee $900 and the lawyer $100, the $100 for the lawyer would be disallowed. This is not just a fuss over labels. A claim, to be allowed, must be proved. The employee could split his claim with his lawyer if he wanted to but he could not first prove his own claim and then add on the lawyer's. Unless we are to ignore the explicit recital in the loan agreement, that is this case. Again it is more than a matter of labels. Wisconsin Steel could not grant Chase a special priority without showing that the proceeds of the loan would be used for a proper purpose. The stated purpose of $77,000 of those proceeds was improper. It is immaterial that the expenditure might, for all we know, have been justifiable on some other ground.

As all this must have been as obvious to Chase as it is to us — probably more so — we do not think that the context (settlement of litigation) in which the loan was made and the special priority received casts enough doubt on the forbidden nature of the transaction to rebut an inference of bad faith — that is, knowledge of improper purpose. Nor, finally, are we persuaded by Chase's argument that the priority it received on the $77,000 was a *sine qua non* of the entire loan transaction — a transaction beneficial to the bankrupt and hence to the general creditors of the bankrupt as well as to Chase — because the union would not have called off its pickets unless it was given its legal fees and unless the union did call off its pickets and thereby allowed Chase to remove the inventory on which it had a lien Chase would not have made the loan to cover the unpaid wage claims. Chase could have paid the union's legal fees out of its own pocket if that was what was required to get the inventory out. Instead it claims a right to force the company's general creditors to pay the union's legal expenses out of their pockets. That is an improper use of the bankrupt's estate, to which the general creditors are the residual claimants. The fact that Chase was a defendant in the suit by the union actually strengthens the inference of bad faith. Chase was not a disinterested lender but a settling litigant that saw an opportunity to reduce the cost of the settlement by putting the union's lawyers ahead of the general creditors of Wisconsin Steel. An extension of credit having such an ulterior purpose is not in good faith within the meaning of section 364(e).

The judgment of the district court is reversed, and the case is remanded with instructions to reverse the order of the bankruptcy judge approving the grant to Chase of a special priority with respect to the $77,000 that it loaned Wisconsin Steel to pay the union for its legal expenses.

So ordered.

NOTE

Under UCC §1-201(19), "good faith" means "honesty in fact in the conduct or transaction concerned." Is Judge Posner applying this definition of good faith, or does he find that the Bankruptcy Code imposes a different definition of good faith? Exactly what did the lender know? If the order was so clearly improper as to deny the lender the protection of §364(e), why did the bankruptcy judge issue it? Why did the district court not strike it down? Doesn't §364(e) express a policy that the burden is on those who oppose the order to get a stay?

NOTE ON *EDC HOLDING* AND BARGAINING AFTER THE FALL

The opinion in *EDC Holding* does not make it clear why Chase found it so important to repossess the steel. The record in the case reveals some additional facts. Chase had made large loans to Wisconsin Steel but it thought it was well protected in the event of default. Moreover, Chase had a security interest in its debtor's inventory, 100 million pounds of steel, and the option to sell it to a third party for $50 million. Under the applicable law, Chase had the right to take possession of the collateral, because Wisconsin Steel had no equity in the property and it did not need the inventory to reorganize. Indeed, the firm planned to liquidate all of its assets in any event. The now unemployed workers were general creditors.

Under bankruptcy law, they would take their share of the debtor's assets behind the secured creditors and post-petition lenders, but before most other general creditors. They would have no right to be paid before the bankruptcy proceeding was wrapped up, which would typically not be for many months.

The price of steel fell dramatically. Chase stood to lose over $20 million if it were unable to take possession of the steel and deliver it to the third party that agreed to buy it for $50 million. The former workers established a picket line, which they insisted they would not lift unless they were paid the $5 million in back wages. Because of the Norris-LaGuardia Act, a bankruptcy judge, like any federal judge, probably does not have the power to enjoin the picketing, even though it is nothing more than the effort of creditors to obtain immediate payment of a pre-petition debt. *Crowe,* supra page 397. Chase was either unwilling or unable to cross the picket line.

The dispute was not simply one between Chase and the workers. (If it were, one could simply demand that Chase strike a deal with the workers. Chase could pay the workers $5 million (or some lesser sum) and the workers could assign their claims to Bank.) But to the extent that Chase's collateral was worth less than the amount of its loan ($50 million), it would have had an unsecured claim for the difference against Wisconsin Steel's other assets. To the extent that it had an unsecured claim where it had none before, all the other creditors were made worse off. It was in the interest of all the creditors as a group (including the former workers) that Chase exercise its option to resell the steel. The exercise of the option would have had the effect of increasing the value of the debtor's assets by $20 million.

One strategy of dealing with threats that pre-petition creditors are able to exercise is simply to have a flat bankruptcy rule that forbids a debtor from paying a pre-petition creditor under any circumstances. It is analogous to a policy of never negotiating with terrorists. If, in *EDC Holding,* for example, the workers had known that Wisconsin Steel would never give in to their demands, they might not have set up a picket line that would destroy one of Wisconsin Steel's assets and reduce the union's recovery. This strategy, however, is unlikely to work effectively. Moreover, it may not be easy to identify when bargains that creditors try to strike are efforts to collect pre-petition debts or agreements to provide new credit, goods, or services. Many times, creditors will be moved by both.

In *EDC Holding,* there was the further problem that Wisconsin Steel's refusal to deal with the picketing workers did not eliminate the incentive to picket, because the workers, in addition to trying to strike a deal with the debtor, could also strike a deal with creditors individually. Chase would have preferred that Wisconsin Steel get rid of the picket line, but it would have paid the workers itself if that were the only way that would allow it to exercise a $20 million option. Creditors have always been able to assign claims and reach other agreements inter se, at least in cases in which their agreement did not diminish the assets which the other creditors could draw upon. To make a no-negotiation strategy effective, one would have to have a bankruptcy rule that sharply limited the ability of creditors to negotiate among themselves. Such a rule would have significant costs. One would, for example, lose the efficiencies that arise from consolidating claims, and one would keep some who needed cash immediately, and had no expertise in pursuing claims in bankruptcy (such as an unpaid worker) from assigning a claim to someone who did not need money immediately and who did have the expertise.

In addition, there are practical limitations that prevent adopting such a strategy. It is hard to maintain a posture of ignoring threats from pre-petition creditors in order to establish a general principle. Judges resist invoking per se rules, and even if they could always identify threats with precision and could prevent any response to them, they are unlikely to do so if the immediate consequence appears to be to impose large economic losses on all the parties that are actually in court. Even apart from these problems, the no-deal strategy might not be effective. Many of the players in a bankruptcy proceeding are not experienced. It is one thing to have a no-deal strategy, and it is another to convince people that there is a no-deal strategy, particularly when the parties bargain with each other only once. Finally, even apart from the strategic games that everyone plays, one cannot rely on the players being perfectly rational. Picket lines might remain in place, even if keeping them in place is in fact in no one's interest.

As a practical matter then, bargaining with creditors after the filing of the petition is going to be necessary, and, unlike much of the bargaining with third parties in bankruptcy, the firm may not have the opportunity to turn elsewhere if an agreement cannot be reached. Two problems make monitoring the bargaining the firm engages in under these circumstances (and by extrapolation the bargaining it engages in after bankruptcy generally) difficult. Any bargaining that the debtor engages in should be done with a view to advancing the interests of the creditors as a group. Under the facts of any individual case, however, a bargain may benefit both a particular creditor and the group generally, or it may benefit only a particular creditor. Determining in a particular case whether a particular deal that has been reached makes the creditors as a group better off may be quite difficult. The second problem arises even if a deal is in the interests of the creditors as a group. Even assuming a particular deal makes the creditors as a group better off than they would have been had there been no deal at all, it may not be easy to tell whether a better deal could have been reached if the debtor had kept in mind the interests of the creditors generally, rather than the interests of a particular creditor. These problems are presented in cases such as *Texlon*, but there the market may provide some guidance. *EDC Holding* illustrates both problems in a context where less market-based assistance can be expected. In the following discussion, we shall simplify matters by assuming that the workers are not entitled to a special priority as to any of their claims.

Bank, Wisconsin Steel, and the workers negotiate and reach the following agreement: Bank will lend Wisconsin Steel $2 million. Wisconsin Steel will give it the administrative priority most post-petition lenders receive. Wisconsin Steel will pay $1.9 million to the workers, and $100,000 to the worker's union, which, we will assume, spent that much in its negotiations. Such a loan must be approved after an adversary hearing in which all the other creditors have an opportunity to voice their objections. Assuming any other creditors object, the bankruptcy judge must then decide whether to approve the deal.

Whether Wisconsin Steel can borrow this money on the proposed terms and use it to pay off the workers turns on whether such a payment is in the interests of the creditors as a whole. This is not an easy question. The debtor could not spend $2 million so that its managers could go to Rio de Janeiro, and, as Judge Posner suggests, it could not borrow money for this purpose either because spending the money for such a purpose does not promote the interests of anyone with rights to the debtor's assets. But to show that does not carry the day. There is no question but that Wisconsin Steel could borrow money to pay its employees for work they had done after the filing of the petition, when it was in the interest of the creditors as a group to keep the firm running.

The workers have no right to be paid before the end of the bankruptcy case for pre-petition work, and their union has no right to be paid at all, because a creditor's expenses in pursuing its claim in a bankruptcy proceeding are not cognizable at all. On the other hand, from the point of view of the creditors what seems to matter is the existence of a credible threat. It was a matter of indifference to the creditors whether the money would go to the workers, their union, or their favorite charity. What mattered was that in the absence of reaching an agreement with the workers and their union, the picket line would remain and the creditors would be $20 million poorer. The creditors could not prevent the picketing and they could not, for reasons already discussed, adopt the strategy that they would not bargain with the workers and count on that strategy being sufficient for the workers to stop of their own accord.

But to say that the creditors as a group would want to strike some deal with the workers is not to say that *any* deal that was struck would make them better off than they would have been had there been no deal at all or that the deal that was struck was the best from their standpoint. Bank is not a neutral stakeholder. It is always better off if Wisconsin Steel pays the workers. Under our assumptions, Bank is fully secured (and hence will be paid in full) only if it can exercise its option. If Bank cannot exercise its option, part of its claim will be unsecured and as to that part, it will recover less than 100 cents on the dollar. The general creditors other than the workers, however, are not similarly indifferent. Let us assume that they have claims of $10 million, and that the debtor's unencumbered assets also equal $10 million. (Often these creditors will be unpaid suppliers of raw materials, but they can also be financial institutions who choose to lend on an unsecured basis.) We shall continue to assume that the unpaid workers have a prepetition claim for $5 million.

If there were no picket line at all, Bank would be paid in full and the general creditors (including the workers) would have claims of $15 million against assets worth $10 million, and they would recover 67 cents on the dollar. If the debtor pays off the workers so that Bank can exercise its option, then the general creditors would have $10 million of claims (the $5 million claim of the workers having been met) against $5 million in assets ($5 million having already been given to the workers). If we continue to assume, however, that Bank's option to resell the steel is worth $20 million, the other general creditors are better off if the debtor pays the workers in full than if it does not and Bank cannot exercise its option. The unencumbered assets would continue to be $10 million, but to the $10 million claim of the trade creditors, one would have to add the $5 million claim of the workers and the $20 million unsecured claim of the Bank that arose because of its inability to exercise its option. The general creditors would receive less than 30 cents on the dollar. Thus, if the choice were between the picket line remaining and the workers being paid their claim in full, they would prefer that the workers be paid.

The general creditors, however, would not always want the workers to be paid off. For example, if the Bank's option was worth only $4 million, the creditors as a group would be unwilling to pay the workers any more than that. It is only in their interest to pay the workers in full if the amount of money they have to give up is less than what they would have to give up because of the new unsecured claim that would come into being. If Bank could not exercise its option, it would have an unsecured claim of $4 million, the workers would have a claim for $5 million and the other general creditors would have a claim for $10 million. Because there would be $19 million in claims and $10 million in assets, each creditor would receive 53 cents on the dollar. By contrast, if the workers were paid off in full, neither they nor Bank would have a claim against the assets, but the others would have $10 million in claims against $5 million in assets, and they would receive only 50 cents on the dollar.

In the world as we find it, however, things are never cut and dried. Valuations are never easy to make. Moreover, someone who was bargaining with the interests of the creditors as a group in mind would not face simply the choice of paying the workers in full or suffering the consequences of losing the value of the option. The person doing the bargaining could offer to pay the workers less than the full value of their claim, or could pay them for a portion of their claim and allow them to recover the remainder along with the other general creditors. All the general creditors, including the workers, suffer if Bank cannot exercise its option.

Assuming again that the option is worth $20 million, the workers face the possibility of recovering in full if their threat brings the expected response, but their threat promises to bring them only 30 cents on the dollar if it backfires and Bank refuses to pay them off and does not exercise its option. If their threat does not have its intended effect, they are much worse off than they would have been if there had been no picket line at all. In that case they would receive 67 cents on the dollar. (Their claims and those of the other general creditors would total $15 million, and there would be $10 million in assets to satisfy them.) Therefore, the workers, like the creditors as a group, also have an incentive to bargain.

One cannot create a set of rules that responds adequately to the problem a case like *EDC Holding Co.* presents. One cannot look to the market or any other ascertainable standard to determine what the bargain that is in the interests of all the creditors would look like. One would expect that the parties would be sensitive to their own self-interest and compromise, but the exact shape of this hypothetical compromise is hard to determine. We know only that the bargain that Bank would reach if left to negotiate on behalf of the debtor would tend to give the workers too much, because Bank has nothing to lose from paying the workers in full and it has a lot to gain. On the other hand, if the general creditors were left to do the negotiating, they would tend to give the workers too little, because they would rely on the incentive Bank would have to make a side-deal with the workers and use its own money to buy the workers off.

The problem is compounded by the fact that it is not simply a question of bargaining between Bank and the workers or between the other general creditors and the workers. There is also bargaining between Bank and the general creditors. If the legal rule (or the realities of the situation) put Bank in the position of being able to negotiate the deal with the workers, the other creditors would bargain with Bank to ensure it was not too generous. If the general creditors were in charge, Bank would bargain with them to ensure they were not too tight fisted.

Whenever a debtor has to negotiate a particular deal, one needs to scrutinize it to ensure that it is in the interests of the creditors as a group. That is the lesson of *Texlon* as well as *EDC Holding*. When the result of the ideal bargain is indeterminate, it is, however, impossible to judge the appropriateness of any particular bargain that may have been struck. Sometimes it is possible to create a set of incentives that promotes the bargains that a single owner would have struck. One can, for example, create bankruptcy rules that impose the costs of any bargain on those parties who stand to benefit from it. This approach, however, is not possible when the bargaining is among creditors, and the outcome of the bargain affects not only the value of the debtor's assets, but also who gets what.

One could have a rule that allowed Bank to strike any deal it wanted with the workers, but only after it paid the general creditors what they would have received had there been no buy-out of the workers and no picketing. In this case, Bank would have the incentive to ensure that the workers received the same kind of bargain they would have received if Bank's interests and the interests of the general creditors were consolidated. But such a rule ensures a proper incentive in the distributional issue at stake between Bank and the general creditors on the one hand and the workers on the other only by dictating the outcome of the distributional question as between Bank and the general creditors.

The central goal of bankruptcy law — the goal of keeping the creditors in the positions they are in at the time that the petition in bankruptcy is filed — is usually pointed to as the appropriate baseline from which to judge the rights of each creditor. A problem arises, however, when we choose, for whatever reason, to depart from that standard and to allow a particular pre-petition creditor a means (a picket line) to coerce repayment while everyone else must stand still. Once one decides that one creditor is not bound by the automatic stay, there is no easy means of deciding which of the other creditors should bear the consequences.

Chapter 8
CONCLUDING THE CASE:
PAYOUT (PRIORITIES)

A. PRIORITIES IN DISTRIBUTION

NOTE ON THE BASIC SYSTEM

The preceding chapters have traced most of the life cycle of a bankruptcy proceeding. A bankruptcy case is commenced (either voluntarily or involuntarily), the assets are assembled (either from the debtor, §541; or from third parties, through §§542 and 543; or through exercise of the trustee's avoiding powers), and the claims of those entitled to participate in the bankruptcy proceeding are determined pursuant to §§502 and 506. In order to wind up the bankruptcy proceeding, however, the assets have to be distributed to the claimants. In these materials we have already studied, at least in rough contours, the basic order in which claimants are "paid." Implicit in previous discussions of property rights in bankruptcy has been the concept that, as a general matter, if such rights are recognized, the claimant holding them normally will be able to assert them fully in bankruptcy. Thus, holders of unavoided security interests, and other property claimants, are entitled, when the assets are distributed at the end of a bankruptcy case, to have their claims satisfied first, up to the extent of the value of that property right. This notion — that holders of nonavoided property rights take precedence over general claimants — is central to much of what we have already looked at in bankruptcy law, yet it has existed in bankruptcy law largely as an acknowledged premise. Under the current Bankruptcy Code, this principle is embodied, albeit incompletely, in §725. The force of §725 is explained in somewhat greater detail in the accompanying legislative reports:

> The purpose of this section is to give the court appropriate authority to ensure that collateral or its proceeds is returned to the proper secured creditor, that consigned or bailed goods are returned to the consignor or bailor,

and so on. Current law is curiously silent on this point, though case law has grown to fill the void. The section is in lieu of a section that would direct a certain distribution to secured creditors. It gives the court greater flexibility to meet the circumstances, and it is broader, permitting disposition of property subject to a co-ownership interest.

After claimants holding nonavoided property interests have had those interests satisfied under §725, the question then becomes one of how to divide up the remaining assets among the remaining claims. In considering this question, it is useful to keep in mind what these remaining claims are. Many of them are pre-petition claims held by unsecured creditors. Some of them are likely to be claims against the estate that came into existence *after* the filing of the bankruptcy petition, such as unsecured claims that arose under §364 out of the conduct of business in bankruptcy, and are not deemed to be pre-petition claims under §502. Not all such claims, whether pre- or post-bankruptcy, are treated equally, even though they are all held by unsecured creditors. The bankruptcy concept of "priorities" specifies, among unsecured creditors, who gets paid in what order. The basic section is §507, although it should be read in conjunction with §§502, 503, 725, and 726, in order to get the full picture. It is important, at the outset, to remember that the subject of "priorities," as the Bankruptcy Code uses that term, is a subject of rankings among creditors who do not hold property interests. Nonavoided property claims come first under §725. Section 507 sets forth a detailed list of priority claimants, and expresses a variety of policies at work that suggest (or at least suggested to Congress) that one group or another of claimants should be favored, in bankruptcy payout, over the unsecured creditors generally. After the §507 priority claimants have been satisfied, in order, §726 provides the order in which other claimants are satisfied.

Generally speaking, therefore, the order of distribution in a piecemeal liquidation under Chapter 7 will be, after unavoided property interests have been satisfied under §725: (1) the payment of §507(a) priorities in order, with each category of such claimants entitled to be paid in full before the next lower category is reached; (2) then the general unsecured claims that have been allowed under §502 (which will include any portion of a claim that remains after its §507 priority has been exhausted); (3) followed, finally, by the various other claims specified in §726, if the property of the estate holds out (such as tardily filed claims, etc.). If there is anything left over after all this is done — that is, if, at the time of distributing assets, it turns out that the debtor was not insolvent — §726(a)(6) provides that the remainder will be returned to the debtor.

The first — highest level — priority in §507 is for administrative expenses — expenses of running the estate. These administrative expense priorities are defined at greater length in §503(b), which you should examine in conjunction with §507. Among this category of claimants are normal post-bankruptcy business creditors, and you should relate this priority to the discussion in Chapter 7 of this book concerning §364 and getting suppliers (and others) to deal with a debtor who is in bankruptcy. We will examine in somewhat greater detail the rationale of this priority in conjunction with Reading Co. v. Brown, the next case. In addition, when examining administrative expenses, you should be aware of the provision of §507(b). Section 507(b) refers back to the granting of adequate protection under §§362 and 363 that we also discussed in the last chapter. If the trustee is allowed to keep or use property under those sections on the ground that the creditor is "adequately protected," and if, despite that assurance of adequate protection, the creditor in fact turns out not to have been adequately protected, §507(b) provides that the creditor gets a kind of "super-priority" over all other administrative expense claimants. This provision creates a ranking *within* the category of administrative expense claimants by creating a category of claims that is first among firsts. (A loophole in the §507(b) protection, however, exists as a result of §364(c)(1). The relationship between §507(b) and §503(b) is explored in In re Callister, 15 Bankr. 521 (Bankr. D. Utah 1981).)

The remaining priority provisions of §507(a) are reasonably straight forward, and can be learned in conjunction with Problems 8.1 through 8.6 below. They become complicated principally in trying to sort out the priority of various kinds of employment taxes. The following excerpt, from the floor statements made immediately prior to the passage of the Bankruptcy Code, should provide some guidance in sorting those provisions out as they relate to employment taxes:

> The priority rules . . . governing employment taxes can thus be summarized as follows: Claims for the employees' shares of employment taxes attributable to wages both earned and paid before the filing of the petition are to receive sixth priority. In the case of employee wages earned, but not paid, before the filing of the bankruptcy petition, claims for the employees' share of employment taxes receive third priority to the extent the wages themselves receive third priority. Claims which relate to wages earned before the petition, but not paid before the petition (and which are not entitled to the third priority under the rule set out above), will be paid as general claims. Since the related wages will receive no priority, the related employment taxes would also be paid as nonpriority general claims.
>
> The employer's share of the employment taxes on wages earned and paid before the bankruptcy petition will receive sixth priority to the extent the return for these taxes was last due . . . within 3 years before the filing of the petition, or was due after the petition was filed. Older tax claims of this nature will be payable as general claims. In the case of wages earned by employees before the petition, but actually paid by the trustee (as claims against the estate) after the title 11 case commenced, the employer's share of

the employment taxes on third priority wages will be payable as sixth priority claims and the employer's taxes on prepetition wages which are treated only as general claims will be payable only as general claims. In calculating the amounts payable as general wage claims, the trustee must pay the employer's share of employment taxes on such wages. . . .

In the case of employment taxes relating to wages earned and paid after the petition, both the employees' shares and the employer's share will receive first priority as administration expenses of the estate.

See also United States v. Friendship College, 737 F.2d 430 (4th Cir. 1984).

PROBLEMS

8.1 Debtor is a corporation that runs a foreign language school. After setting up business, Debtor has received $1,200 from each of 20 students as tuition for a course. Before classes start, however, Debtor files for bankruptcy, and its assets are gathered and liquidated. Debtor has a computer, worth $10,000, subject to a perfected security interest in favor of Bank securing a $5,000 loan. Debtor also has other assets (furniture and so forth) worth $30,000. Debtor, in addition to the loan from Bank, has the following obligations: (1) a claim by the landlord for $1,000 rent for use of the property while Debtor was in bankruptcy; (2) a claim by Debtor's employees for $5,000 of wages accrued by them while Debtor was in bankruptcy; (3) $1,500 of withholding taxes due for those wages; (4) a wage claim by Debtor's secretary for $3,000 for wages earned during the last month before Debtor filed for bankruptcy; (5) a withholding tax claim by the United States government for $1,000 based on the wages earned by the secretary under (4); (6) a claim for $200 for each of Debtor's 15 employees—aggregating $3,000—based on Debtor's failure to make a contribution to the employee benefit plan for their last month's services; (7) a claim by the 20 students for a refund of their money, aggregating $24,000; (8) $10,000 of other unsecured, pre-bankruptcy claims. How will Debtor's property be distributed? (On category (3), see §503(b)(1)(B)(i) and United States v. Redmond, 36 Bankr. 932 (D. Kan. 1984).)

8.2 You have filed a voluntary bankruptcy petition for your client, Debtor. Debtor owns an apartment in a high rise condominium complex. It is unclear whether a condominium qualifies as a homestead under applicable state law. If you litigate this question, will your fees and expenses be treated as administrative expenses under §§330 and 503? Should you have obtained a retainer from Debtor for such litigation before filing a Chapter 7 petition for Debtor? See §329.

8.3 Schatz Federal Bearings Co. filed a bankruptcy petition on March 5. Under a collective bargaining agreement, which has been assumed by

Schatz, "[a]ny employee on the active payroll of the Company on July 15 of any year in the contract period . . . shall be entitled to vacation pay based on years of service." Schatz and the union assert that because the vacation pay clause makes no provision for payment on an accrual basis, it is another form of compensation that should be treated as coming due during the post-petition period, and hence should be classified as an administrative expense for all employees on Schatz's payroll on July 15. The creditors' committee asserts that vacation pay, if it is allowed at all, should be based, for purposes of administrative expense priority, on the period of actual services rendered to the debtor after the commencement of the case. How should the issue be decided? See In re Schatz Federal Bearings Co., 5 Bankr. 549 (Bankr. S.D.N.Y. 1980). Does §365(b) bear on this issue?

8.4 Same facts as in Problem 8.3, except the claim involved is a claim for severance pay by an employee discharged during the bankruptcy proceeding, and the severence pay provision is based on years served. Compare In re Health Maintenance Foundation, 680 F.2d 619 (9th Cir. 1982); In re Mammoth Mart, 536 F.2d 950 (1st. Cir. 1976), with Straus-Duparquet, Inc. v. Local 3, International Brotherhood of Electrical Workers, 386 F.2d 649 (2d Cir. 1967).

8.5 Debtor is a shipping line that has a collective bargaining agreement with Union. Under the terms of that agreement, Debtor contributes to an employee benefit plan based on the number of days worked by employees during the prior month. (Debtor is required to make such payments on behalf of a particular employee even though that employee may not yet be eligible for benefits.) The payments are due by the twentieth of the next month. Debtor files for bankruptcy under Chapter 11 on June 1. Debtor owes $550,000 in such contributions for April (not having made the payment on May 20) and $600,000 for May (which payment, under the agreement, is due on June 20). Are either or both of these payments entitled to administrative expense priority? In considering this, can these payments be distinguished from severence pay payments, considered in Problem 8.4? See In re Pacific Far East Line, 713 F.2d 476 (9th Cir. 1983) (old Act case distinguishing severance pay cases).

8.6 Kessler, a manufacturer of clothing, files a petition in bankruptcy on November 21, and proceeds to liquidate its business. Kessler, under collective bargaining agreements previously entered into, participated in a Multi-employer Pension Plan established under the Multi-employer Pension Plan Amendments Act of 1980. Under this Plan, Kessler had to make contributions to the union, thereby providing the union with funds for distribution as pensions to each employee of each participating employer. The collective bargaining agreement also provides that upon cessation of an employer's operations, and the termination of its employees, the employer incurs a "withdrawal liability." The union claims that the withdrawal liability is entitled to administrative expense priority. Evaluate that claim. In re Kessler, 23 Bankr. 722 (Bankr. S.D.N.Y. 1982), rejected the claim, by contrasting it to severance pay (see Problem 8.4), as follows:

> Severance pay is direct compensation to an employee who works post petition and whose employment is nevertheless terminated. Such an employee has contributed to the preservation of the estate by working post petition. He is therefore entitled to the full benefits flowing directly from his employment. One such direct benefit which comes due upon termination of employment is severance pay.
>
> Withdrawal liability, however, is not direct compensation to an employee for termination of his post-petition employment relationship with the debtor in possession. Rather, the withdrawal liability is an obligation of the debtor to the Multi-employer Pension Fund pursuant to the MPPA. Although the employee and other union employees might benefit from the contribution, the liability is not a direct payment to an employee for his post-petition services.

NOTE ON PRIORITY FOR ADMINISTRATIVE EXPENSES

The first priority is for "administrative expense claims" allowed under §503(b). In part, this priority takes us back to Chapter 7 of this book, where we examined the scope of §364 and the problem of getting people to continue to do business with a debtor in bankruptcy. The administrative expense priority seems to be an integral part of bankruptcy's solution to that problem, and the ability of those whose claims arise during the bankruptcy proceeding to be paid before the general, unsecured creditors holding pre-petition claims seems consistent with the notion that bankruptcy's collective proceeding is in the collective interest of the general creditors in existence at the time of bankruptcy. If keeping the business operating is in the collective interest of those creditors (because the size of the asset pie is larger than if the assets are pulled apart in a piecemeal liquidation—as might occur if a collective proceeding were not commenced) those creditors should be willing to allow "newcomers" to be paid ahead of them, so as to ensure that the suppliers (of materials, labor, office space, and so on) that enable the business to keep running do not stop supplying the debtor.

Is this explanation, however, sufficient? Does it extend to nonconsensual creditors as well as consensual creditors. Reading Co. v. Brown, the next case, raises that issue in looking at whether post-petition tort claimants are entitled to administrative expense priority. The case, which arose under the old Bankruptcy Act, contains an important dispute between Justice Harlan, writing for the majority, and Chief Justice Warren, writing for the minority. Chief Justice Warren, you will discover in reading the opinion, sees the principal purpose of the bankruptcy process—initiated, as he sees it, by the debtor for its benefit and not for the benefit of its creditors—as one of achieving equality of treatment among those similarly situated. Accordingly, Chief Justice Warren thinks that there should be no better treatment for post-petition tort claimants based on the "fortuity" of their being post-petition. Justice Harlan, on the other hand, sees such post-petition torts as a cost of running the bankrupt's business. As such, the costs of those torts, he believes, should be borne by the pre-petition creditors (including pre-petition tort creditors), on whose behalf, in his view, the bankrupt's business is being run.

READING CO. v BROWN
391 U.S. 471 (1968)

Justice HARLAN delivered the opinion of the Court.

On November 16, 1962, I. J. Knight Realty Corporation filed a petition for an arrangement under Chapter XI of the Bankruptcy Act, 11 U.S.C. §§701-799. The same day, the District Court appointed a receiver, Francis Shunk Brown, a respondent here. The receiver was authorized to conduct the debtor's business, which consisted principally of leasing the debtor's only significant asset, an eight-story industrial structure located in Philadelphia.

On January 1, 1963, the building was totally destroyed by a fire which spread to adjoining premises and destroyed real and personal property of petitioner Reading Company and others. On April 3, 1963, petitioner filed a claim for $559,730.83 in the arrangement, based on the asserted negligence of the receiver. It was styled a claim for "administrative expenses" of the arrangement. Other fire loss claimants filed 146 additional claims of a similar nature. The total of all such claims was in excess of $3,500,000, substantially more than the total assets of the debtor.

On May 14, 1963, Knight Realty was voluntarily adjudicated a bankrupt and respondent receiver was subsequently elected trustee in bankruptcy. The claims of petitioner and others thus became claims for administration expenses in bankruptcy which are given first priority under §64a(1) of the Bankruptcy Act, 11 U.S.C. §104(a)(1). The trustee moved to expunge the claims on the ground that they were not for expenses of administration. It was agreed that the decision whether petitioner's claim is provable as an expense of administration would establish the status of the other 146 claims. It was further agreed that, for purposes of deciding whether the claim is provable, it would be assumed that the damage to petitioner's property resulted from the negligence of the receiver and a workman he employed. The United States, holding a claim for unpaid prearrangement taxes admittedly superior to the claims of general creditors and inferior to claims for administration expenses, entered the case on the side of the trustee.

The referee disallowed the claim for administration expenses. He also ruled that petitioner's claim was not provable as a general claim against the estate, a ruling challenged by neither side. On petition for review, the referee was upheld by the District Court. On appeal, the Court of Appeals for the Third Circuit, sitting en banc, affirmed the decision of the District Court by a 4-3 vote. We granted certiorari, 389 U.S. 895, because the issue is important in the administration of the bankruptcy laws and is one of first impression in this Court. For reasons to follow, we reverse.

Section 64a of the Bankruptcy Act provides in part as follows:

> The debts to have priority, in advance of the payment of dividends to creditors, and to be paid in full out of bankrupt estates, and the order of payment, shall be (1) the costs and expenses of administration, including the actual and necessary costs and expenses of preserving the estate subsequent to filing the petition . . .

It is agreed that this section, applicable by its terms to straight bankruptcies, governs payment of administration expenses of Chapter XI arrangements. Furthermore, it is agreed that for the purpose of applying this section to arrangements, . . . the words "preserving the estate" include the larger objective, common to arrangements, of operating the debtor's business with a view to rehabilitating it.

The question in this case is whether the negligence of a receiver administering an estate under a Chapter XI arrangement gives rise to an "actual and necessary" cost of operating the debtor's business. The Act does not define "actual and necessary," nor has any case directly in point been brought to our attention. We must, therefore, look to the general purposes of §64a, Chapter XI, and the Bankruptcy Act as a whole.

The trustee contends that the relevant statutory objectives are (1) to facilitate rehabilitation of insolvent businesses and (2) to preserve a maximum of assets for distribution among the general creditors should the arrangement fail. He therefore argues that first priority as "necessary" expenses should be given only to those expenditures without which the insolvent business could not be carried on. For example, the trustee would allow first priority to contracts entered into by the receiver because suppliers, employees, landlords, and the like would not enter into dealings with a debtor in possession or a receiver of an insolvent business unless priority is allowed. The trustee would exclude all negligence claims, on the theory that first priority for them is not necessary to encourage third parties to deal with an insolvent business, that first priority would reduce the amount available for the general creditors, and that first priority would discourage general creditors from accepting arrangements.

In our view the trustee has overlooked one important, and here decisive, statutory objective: fairness to all persons having claims against an insolvent. Petitioner suffered grave financial injury from what is here agreed to have been the negligence of the receiver and a workman. It is conceded that, in principle, petitioner has a right to recover for that injury from their "employer," the business under arrangement, upon the rule of respondeat superior. Respondents contend, however, that petitioner is in no different position from anyone else injured by a person with scant assets: its right to recover exists in theory but is not enforceable in practice.

That, however, is not an adequate description of petitioner's position. At the moment when an arrangement is sought, the debtor is insolvent. Its existing creditors hope that by partial or complete postponement of their claims they will, through successful rehabilitation, eventually recover from the debtor either in full or in larger proportion than they would in immediate bankruptcy. Hence the present petitioner did not merely suffer injury at the hands of an insolvent business: it had an insolvent business thrust upon it by operation of law. That business will, in any event, be unable to pay its fire debts in full. But the question is whether the fire claimants should be subordinated to, should share equally with, or should collect ahead of those creditors for whose benefit the continued operation of the business (which unfortunately led to a fire instead of the hoped-for rehabilitation) was allowed.

Recognizing that petitioner ought to have some means of asserting its claim against the business whose operation resulted in the fire, respondents have suggested various theories as alternatives to "administration expense" treatment. None of these has case support, and all seem to us unsatisfactory.

Several need not be pursued in detail. The trustee contends that if the present claims are not provable in bankruptcy they would survive as claims against the shell. He also suggests that petitioner may be able to recover from the receiver personally, or out of such bond as he posted. Without deciding whether these possible avenues are indeed open, we merely note that they do not serve the present purpose. . . .

The United States, as a respondent, suggests instead that tort claims arising during an arrangement are, if properly preserved, provable general claims in any subsequent bankruptcy under §63a of the Act, 11 U.S.C. §103(a). [Discussion omitted.]

In any event, we see no reason to indulge in a strained construction of the relevant provisions, for we are persuaded that it is theoretically sounder, as well as linguistically more comfortable, to treat tort claims arising during an arrangement as actual and necessary expenses of the arrangement rather than debts of the bankrupt. In the first place, in considering whether those injured by the operation of the business during an arrangement should share equally with, or recover ahead of, those for whose benefit the business is carried on, the latter seems more natural and just. Existing creditors are, to be sure, in a dilemma not of their own making, but there is no obvious reason why they should be allowed to attempt to escape that dilemma at the risk of imposing it on others equally innocent.

More directly in point is the possibility of insurance. An arrangement may provide for suitable coverage, and the court below recognized that the cost of insurance against tort claims arising during an arrangement is an administrative expense payable in full under §64a(1) before dividends to general creditors. It is of course obvious that proper insurance premiums must be given priority, else insurance could not be obtained; and if a receiver or debtor in possession is to be encouraged to obtain insurance in adequate amounts, the claims against which insurance is obtained should be potentially payable in full. In the present case, it is argued, the fire was of such incredible magnitude that adequate insurance probably could not have been obtained and in any event would have been foolish; this may be true, as it is also true that allowance of a first priority to the fire claimants here will still only mean recovery by them of a fraction of their damages. In the usual case where damages are within insurable limits, however, the rule of full recovery for torts is demonstrably sounder.

Although there appear to be no cases dealing with tort claims arising during Chapter XI proceedings, decisions in analogous cases suggest that "actual and necessary costs" should include costs ordinarily incident to operation of a business, and not be limited to costs without which rehabilitation would be impossible. It has long been the rule of equity receiverships that torts of the receivership create claims against the receivership itself; in those cases the statutory limitation to "actual and necessary costs" is not involved, but the explicit recognition extended to tort claims in those cases weighs heavily in favor of considering them within the general category of costs and expenses.

In some cases arising under Chapter XI it has been recognized that "actual and necessary costs" are not limited to those claims which the business must be able to pay in full if it is to be able to deal at all. For example, state and federal taxes accruing during a receivership have been held to be actual and necessary costs of an arrangement. The United States, recognizing and supporting these holdings, agrees with petitioner that costs that form "an integral and essential element of the continuation of the business" are necessary expenses even though priority is not necessary *to* the continuation of the business. Thus the Government suggests that "an injury to a member of the public — a business invitee — who was injured while on the business premises during an arrangement would present a completely different problem [i.e., could qualify for first priority]" although it is not suggested that priority is needed to encourage invitees to enter the premises.

The United States argues, however, that each tort claim "must be analyzed in its own context." Apart from the fact that it has been assumed throughout this case that all 147 claimants were on an equal footing and it is not very helpful to suggest here for the first time a rule by which lessees, invitees, and neighbors have different rights, we perceive no distinction: No principle of tort law of which we are aware offers guidance for distinguishing, within the class of torts committed by receivers while acting in furtherance of the business, between those "integral" to the business and those that are not.

We hold that damages resulting from the negligence of a receiver acting within the scope of his authority as receiver give rise to "actual and necessary costs" of a Chapter XI arrangement.

The judgment of the Court of Appeals is reversed, and the case remanded for further proceedings consistent with this opinion.

It is so ordered.

Chief Justice WARREN, with whom Justice DOUGLAS joins, dissenting.

In my opinion, the Court has misinterpreted the term "costs and expenses of administration" as intended by §64a(1) of the Bankruptcy Act and, by deviating from the natural meaning of those words, has given the administrative cost priority an unwarranted application. The effect of the holding in this case is that the negligence of a workman may completely wipe out the claims of all other classes of public and private creditors. I do not believe Congress intended to accord tort claimants such a preference. Accordingly, I would affirm the judgment below.

On other occasions, this Court has observed that "[t]he theme of the Bankruptcy Act is 'equality of distribution' . . . ; and if one claimant is to be preferred over others, the purpose should be clear from the statute." Nathanson v. NLRB, 344 U.S. 25, 29 (1952). . . . More particularly, the Act expressly directs that eligible negligence claims are to share *equally* with the unsecured claims in a pro rata distribution of the debtor's nonexempt assets. Bankruptcy Act §§63a(7), 65a, 11 U.S.C. §§103(a)(7), 105(a). Departing from this statutory scheme, the Court today singles out one class of tort claims for special treatment. After today's decision, the status of a tort claimant depends entirely upon whether he is fortunate enough to have been injured after rather than before a receiver has been appointed. And if the claimant is in the select class, he may be permitted to exhaust the estate to the exclusion of the general creditors as well as of the wage claims and government tax claims for which Congress has shown an unmistakable preference. In my view, this result frustrates rather than serves the underlying purposes of a Chapter XI proceeding, and I would not reach it without a clear indication that Congress so intended.

Congress enacted Chapter XI as an alternative to straight bankruptcy for individuals and small businesses which might be successfully rehabilitated instead of being subjected to economically wasteful liquidation. The success of a Chapter XI proceeding depends largely on two factors: first, whether creditors will take the chance of permitting an arrangement; second, whether other businesses will continue to deal with the distressed business. With respect to the first of these considerations, today's decision will undoubtedly discourage creditors from permitting arrangements, because it subjects them to unpredictable and probably uninsurable tort liability. I do not believe the statutory language requires such an interpretation. I would construe §64a(1) with reference to the second consideration mentioned above. In my opinion, the Court would reach a result more in line with congressional intent and the Bankruptcy Act generally by regarding as administrative costs only those costs required for a smooth and successful arrangement. Accordingly, the administrative cost priority should be viewed as a guaranty to the receiver and those who deal with or are employed by him that they will be paid for their goods and services. Any broader interpretation will discourage creditors from permitting use of the rehabilitative machinery of Chapter XI and tend to force distressed businesses into straight bankruptcy.

It is equitable, the Court believes, that the general creditors (and wage and tax claimants) bear the loss in this case because they have "thrust" an insolvent business upon petitioner for their own benefit. I respectfully submit that this is a most unfair characterization of arrangements. An economically distressed businessman seeks an arrangement for his own and not for his creditors' benefit.[2] Of course the creditors will benefit if the arrangement is successful, just as they would have benefited if the businessman had been successful without resorting to an arrangement. But a business in arrangement is no more thrust on the public than is any other business enterprise which is conducted for the mutual prosperity of the owners, the wage earners and the creditors. Realistically, the only difference is that a business administered under Chapter XI has not been prosperous. If the arrangement is successful, the owners, wage earners and creditors will all benefit; if it is not, they will all be injured. Thus, I would not distinguish in this case between petitioner and the other general creditors, none of whom was responsible for the catastrophe for which all of them must sustain some loss. Instead, in deciding this case, I would adhere to the Act's basic theme of equality of distribution.

The Court states that its decision will encourage Chapter XI receivers to obtain "adequate" insurance. The Court fairly well concedes, however, that in this case "adequate" insurance "probably could not have been obtained and in any event would have been foolish." In other words, so far as this Court knows, the insurance taken out by the receiver in this case was in fact "adequate," in the sense that no reasonable receiver could or should obtain fire insurance in the amount of $3,500,000 on the assumption that his workman might accidentally cause a fire of the proportions which occurred here. Moreover, quite apart from the case at bar, there is absolutely no indication that today's decision is needed to encourage receivers to obtain insurance. I see no basis in the Act or in sound policy for a ruling that the creditors of an estate under a Chapter XI arrangement become involuntary insurers against a liability which probably would not and should not be insurable by more traditional means.

2. Unlike straight bankruptcy, only the debtor himself may file a petition for an arrangement under Chapter XI. . . .

The Court also relies, in my opinion mistakenly, upon analogies to equity receiverships. In reorganizations under Chapter X and §77, Congress has directed the courts to apply the rules of priority developed in equity. However, arrangements under Chapter XI are governed strictly by the statutory priorities fixed by §64a. These statutory priorities differ in many respects from those applicable to equity receiverships, and they have been amended repeatedly to narrow the class of claimants which may participate ahead of the general creditors. . . .

I see no basis in equity or in the statutory language or purpose for subjecting every class of creditors except petitioner's to a loss caused by the negligence of a workman. Consequently, I would construe "actual and necessary costs" as limited to those costs actually and necessarily incurred in preserving the debtor's estate and administering it for the benefit of the creditors. I would not include ordinary negligence claims within this class.

PROBLEM

8.7 Creditor is a firm that arranges for the publication of advertisements in various "Yellow Pages" of telephone directories. Debtor arranged with Creditor to have a number of such advertisements placed in directories to be published during 1985 (each directory, and hence each advertisement, to be in force for 12 months). When Debtor filed for bankruptcy in January 1985, the closing date had passed on arranging advertisement for many such directories, committing Creditor to pay for the advertisements, and for Debtor to reimburse Creditor for such payments. Debtor owes Creditor $300,000 for such advertisements. Creditor seeks administrative expense priority for that amount, claiming that the advertisements were effective post-bankruptcy, and hence are an administrative expense. Evaluate that contention. See In re Jartran, 732 F.2d 584 (7th Cir. 1984).

NOTE ON POST-PETITION TORT CLAIMS

In considering the opinions in Reading Co. v. Brown, isn't it clear that Justice Harlan is correct *if* one assumes that the principal beneficiaries of the bankruptcy proceeding are the creditors? In deciding to undertake a collective proceeding, and in deciding to keep the assets together as a going concern, one needs to value the alternatives to see if, indeed, the enterprise is worth more kept together than split apart. But valuations do not exist in the abstract. The value of a firm to its owners is based on a determination of the income stream that can be generated off of its assets in the future, *net* of the costs of running the business. Isn't it fair to say that one of the costs that should be netted out is that represented by tort suits?

After the bankruptcy case is over, those tort suits will be reflected as a cost of doing business; is there any reason not to treat them as such a cost (and hence as entitled to administrative expense priority) *during* the bankruptcy proceeding?

In fact, isn't it *necessary* to treat tort claims that arise during the bankruptcy proceeding as expenses of administration in order to give the existing creditors the proper incentive to make the right choice between piecemeal liquidation of the business and its continuation as a going concern? They are the ones who, presumptively, gain the benefit of a collective proceeding if the debtor is insolvent. Putting aside strategic bargaining rules that we will examine in Chapter 9, isn't Chief Justice Warren clearly wrong in asserting that a bankruptcy proceeding is designed to benefit the debtor, and not its creditors?

If post-filing tort claims should come ahead of pre-bankruptcy unsecured claims, because of the need to give the pre-bankruptcy claimants the proper incentive to choose the path that makes the most of the debtor's assets, what do we do with Chief Justice Warren's point that these post-petition tort claimants are tort claimants just like the pre-petition ones, and the difference in treatment stems from the "fortuity" of which side of the line the tort was committed on? Can one approach this by focusing on the pre-petition creditors (including pre-petition tort creditors) *not* as creditors but, for purposes of the bankruptcy proceeding at least, as the new "owners" of the business? If the business were sold as a going concern to a buyer, that buyer would pay based on the buyer's estimate of the income stream to be generated by the assets, net of the possibility of liabilities such as tort suits in the future. When those tort suits arose, the new owners would then bear their costs, in the sense that their equity ownership would decrease.

Aren't the pre-bankruptcy creditors, in effect, the "purchasers" of the debtor's assets in bankruptcy? Although this issue is explored in greater detail in Chapter 9 of this book, it isn't too early to consider whether it makes sense to view the reorganization process as one in which the assets are "sold" to the pre-bankruptcy creditors, instead of to a third party.

If you focus on the pre-bankruptcy creditors as *owners* of the new business, following a sale (that occurs at the time the petition is filed), doesn't the policy behind Justice Harlan's result come into sharper focus? Then it is just as if the reorganization was completed (the sale having taken place) and *then* the fire occurred. Isn't that the result Justice Harlan reaches? To the extent this is obscure in the case, it is because those creditors seem to exist in both capacities. If they had in fact sold the business for cash, and then the tort unexpectedly occurred, they still would have gotten the whole cash value of the enterprise, and they would have been unaffected by what actually happened. But isn't the relevant point that they *did not* sell the business for cash? It is as if they sold the business to people who agreed to pay them for the business out of its profits, but with no personal liability. As for the apparent disparity in treatment of a tort claimant whose claim arose one minute *before* the filing of a bankruptcy petition and a tort claimant whose claim arose the moment *after,* isn't this just simply the consequence of the need to have a line that separates groups? The same line would exist if the business were sold for cash. And the same line would exist, under Chief Justice Warren's approach, at the *end* of the bankruptcy case when the assets actually were sold.

The following problem focuses on whether it makes any difference if the debtor were an individual instead of a corporation. In considering that distinction, moreover, you might want to go back to the concept of "property of the estate" in §541, and the policy expressed there to exclude "future" assets from the bankruptcy proceeding in the case of individuals.

PROBLEM

8.8 Reconsider the facts of Problem 3.1, supra page 133. Is Bystander's claim entitled to administrative expense priority under §503(b)? Does it matter, in answering that question, if Debtor is an individual or a corporation? What if Debtor is an individual in Chapter 7, but the accident is caused by the trustee driving to a meeting with Debtor's creditors?

NOTE ON THE POLICIES BEHIND PRIORITIES

Having looked at §507 and having worked through Problems 8.1 through 8.6, can you articulate any *bankruptcy*-related justifications for the classes of claims that appear on the priority list in §507? Or does the list just reflect the sort of political compromises that are perhaps inevitable in any statute of importance? If the latter, do these priorities conflict with any bankruptcy policies?

1. **Post-Petition Claims.** The priority of §507(a)(1) (and (a)(2)) is, in one respect at least, fundamentally different from the remainder of the priorities in §507(a). Section 507(a)(1) deals with claims that arise during the course of the bankruptcy proceeding itself. These claims would not fit into §502(b) because they were not in existence (and accordingly had no value) "as of the date of the filing of the petition." People who provide a business in bankruptcy with supplies on credit or people against whom the debtor commits torts during the bankruptcy proceeding are in a position quite different from pre-petition creditors, even those with unliquidated, contingent, or unmatured claims. Reading Co. v. Brown, which we just examined, discusses some of the justifications for giving priority to even nonconsensual claims that arise during the bankruptcy proceeding itself;

the principal justification being that those people that bankruptcy's collective proceeding is designed to benefit (the pre-petition claimants) must bear the costs of that proceeding if they are to be given the proper incentive to make the right decision as to what to do with the debtor's assets — or, indeed, to make the correct decision between a collective proceeding and pursuit of individual remedies.

Is this analysis complete, however? Can one argue that giving trade creditors (and other consensual creditors) priority for goods and services provided to a debtor after a bankruptcy petition is filed may itself induce premature filings of bankruptcy petitions? Consider the position of an unsecured, recurrent, trade creditor (such as a company that supplies baked goods to a restaurant). This company, when faced with a restaurant that appears to be in a shaky financial condition, is confronted with several choices to increase its security with respect to its future deliveries. It can raise its price or demand collateral. It can sell for cash only. It can cease doing business with the restaurant. Or it can persuade the restaurant to file for bankruptcy or, subject to the constraints of §303, it can put the restaurant into bankruptcy involuntarily. If it pursues the voluntary or involuntary petition route, once a bankruptcy case is commenced, the company's further debts based on the delivery of new supplies will receive administrative expense priority under §503 and §507(a)(1).

Does this last option — which results from the different priority status accorded credit deliveries made the day before the filing of the bankruptcy petition (a pre-petition unsecured claim entitled to no particular priority status) and deliveries made the day after the filing of a bankruptcy petition (administrative expense claims under §503 and §507(a)(1) in the case of voluntary petitions; second priority claims under §502(f) and §507(a)(2) in the case of an involuntary petition before the order for relief or the appointment of a trustee) — create an undesirable incentive to cause bankruptcies to be filed prematurely?

Isn't it correct to say that this difference in priority creates an incentive on the part of such continuous suppliers to cause a bankruptcy case to be commenced whenever there is a perception that the debtor may be insolvent? Isn't, then, the question one of whether such an incentive is undesirable, when it is limited to a category of people (such as suppliers) whose claims (such as for future services) have not yet arisen? This, in a number of respects, is the inquiry of Chapter 3, where we examined the limits on the commencement of bankruptcy cases. The question here is whether those limitations are sufficient, or if additional ones are needed peculiar to this category of claimants. And the answer to that may turn, in part, on whether there is anything undesirable, in general, about creating incentives to commence a collective proceeding when a debtor is thought to be insolvent, or in lodging that decision in people such as suppliers.

2. The Six-Months Rule of Railroad Reorganizations. The question we just explored may be lurking in a judge-made rule that grew up in conjunction with railroad receivership law and eventually was codified in Section 77B of the old Bankruptcy Act, known as the "six-months rule." The six-months rule evolved out of a practice of initiating railroad receiverships with an order appointing a receiver and authorizing him to pay, from operating receipts, certain expenses incurred in the period immediately preceding the receivership. (These payments came out of funds that usually were to be rounded up for the mortgagees.) The principle was first recognized by the Supreme Court in Fosdick v. Schall, 99 U.S. 235, 25 L. Ed. 339 (1879), which seemed to place the rule on correcting a "diversion of funds" to the mortgagee in the pre-receivership period. But as the six-months rule evolved in railroad receivership cases, its rationale became that the rule was a good thing because it kept the railroads running longer, for the benefit of the public *and* the creditors. See, e.g., Gregg v. Metropolitan Trust Co., 197 U.S. 183 (1905) (dissent); In re New York, N.H. & H.R.R., 278 F. Supp. 592 (D. Conn. 1967), aff'd, 405 F.2d 50 (2d Cir. 1968), cert. denied, 394 U.S. 999 (1969); FitzGibbon, The Present Status of the Six Months' Rule, 34 Colum. L. Rev. 230 (1934).

By 1980, the First Circuit was explicitly justifying the rule on the indistinguishability of administrative expenses and those incurred in the immediate pre-bankruptcy period, In re Boston & Maine Corp., 634 F.2d 1359, 1378-1379 (1st Cir. 1980):

> The criterion of priority to have intrinsic validity must be found in the nature of the claim and in the nature of the reorganization. If the claim is for a service or supply indispensable to the maintenance and operation of the railroad, and if the railroad continues to operate while in reorganization, the real difficulty is in finding a ground on which a court can fairly deny payment of a pre-reorganization expense claim indistinguishable from current administration expenses that are being paid and indistinguishable from kindred operating expenses that were incurred in the ordinary course of business by the railroad company in the months preceding reorganization and were paid by the railroad before reorganization or were paid thereafter by the trustees as liabilities arising out of the operation of the railroad. If a claim has the generally accepted characteristics of a six months claim, . . . that is, (1) it represents a current operating expense necessarily incurred, (2) was incurred within six months before the reorganization petition was filed, and (3) the goods or services were delivered in the expectation that they would be paid for out of current operating revenues of the railroad, and not in reliance on the road's general credit, it will inevitably be for an expense indistinguishable from and essentially contemporaneous with expenses paid by the railroad before reorganization, and will be indistinguishable from currently paid administration expenses. . . . The desideratum is equality of treatment for the current operating expenses of a railroad enterprise the operations of which have continued without interruption of service, revenues and expenses. That equality is readily achieved by recognizing administration expenses as extending backward to the period preceding reorganization to the extent necessary to assure that there is

continuity in the payment of indispensable operating expenses without reference to the date the petition is filed so long as the current expenses of the
pre-reorganization period that are brought forward for payment conform to
the strict standard established for administration expenses of the current
operating class, and are not so dated as to forbid the conclusion that they are
in fact current. The inequity in treatment arising out of the accidental circumstance of non-payment before the filing of the petition is eliminated.

A rationale such as this echoes Chief Justice Warren's opinion in
Reading Co. v. Brown, except here the equality is achieved by elevating
the pre-petition claims to the status of administrative expense priority
(instead of vice versa). Is the explanation any more satisfactory here? Does
the six-months rule provide a sensible priority rule, justifiable either on
incentive grounds or on equity grounds? The rule has been continued in
the subsection of Chapter 11 dealing with railroad reorganizations,
§1171(b) (although the language of that section will be impenetrable to
anyone unfamiliar with the history of the six-months rule and its similar
statutory codification in Section 77B of the old Bankruptcy Act). See also
§9-503(d) of the Proposed Bankruptcy Act of 1973 (confirm railroad
reorganization plan if, inter alia, it "provides for payment of all allowed
claims for current operating expenses incurred by the debtor during the
six months immediately preceding the filing of the petition"); S. Rep. No.
989, 95th Cong., 2d Sess. 135–136 (1978).

Should the rationale of the six-months rule be applied to debtors
other than railroads, as it has been on a few occasions? See, e.g., Dudley v.
Mealey, 147 F.2d 268 (2d Cir.), cert. denied, 325 U.S. 873 (1945) (hotel).
In a case arising under the Bankruptcy Code, the Ninth Circuit has declined to extend the six-months rule to nonrailroad reorganizations. In re
B & W Enterprises, 713 F.2d 534 (9th Cir. 1983). The court concluded
that Congress "intended to continue limiting its applicability to railroad
reorganizations," and that the courts did not possess general equitable
powers to apply the six-months rule "where appropriate":

> What appellants seek is not subordination of a certain claim, but rather
> elevation of their claims over those of other creditors of the same class, the
> class of unsecured creditors. This is not a power given the courts by the 1978
> Act . . . Section 507 establishes the priorities of creditors intended
> by Congress. . . . There is no indication that Congress intended the courts
> to fashion their own rules of super-priorities within any given priority
> class.

3. Pre-petition Claims and §507 Priority. Return, now, to the remaining categories of priority claims under §507(a). Certain categories of
these may have justifications similar to those of the six-months rule. Con

sider, for example, the priority given by §507(a)(3) for certain wages earned within 90 days of bankruptcy. (While §507(a)(3) contains dollar limits on pre-petition employee claims entitled to priority (see In re Columbia Packing Co., 35 Bankr. 447 (Bankr. D. Mass. 1983)), what should a debtor do who owes its employees more, and whose employees may strike if not paid? Recall *Crowe*, supra page 397 and *EDC Holding*, supra page 536. In practice, workers are frequently paid pre-petition wages immediately, despite any statutory authorization. As *EDC Holding* might suggest, making payments to workers may be in the interests of the creditors if the creditors want to keep the business operating and the workers insist upon being paid as a condition of continuing.) Others may attempt to protect groups otherwise considered disadvantaged, such as consumers who make down payments. §507(a)(6). (On this issue, see Schrag and Ratner, Caveat Emptor — Empty Coffer: The Bankruptcy Law Has Nothing to Offer, 72 Colum. L. Rev. 1147 (1972), which argues that consumer claims should have priority even over administrative claims, primarily because most consumers are unaware that they become creditors when they make down payments.) Other categories, such as the priority of §507(a)(7) for certain tax claims, seem justified on neither rationale, but represent instead a policy decision that these claimants should do better than general unsecured creditors for some other, unarticulated, reason. (Some categories, of course, may involve a bit of each of these rationales, such as, perhaps, §507(a)(5).)

Notwithstanding the merits of a particular justification, is there a reason for extending the priority only in bankruptcy? If not, isn't the problem really the same as that created by state created priorities and bankruptcy statutory liens, that we examined in Chapter 4? The priorities of §507 apply only in bankruptcy. Don't they, too, create an undesirable "bankruptcy" incentive on the part of the holder of them that is unrelated to a collective need for a bankruptcy proceeding? Doesn't that, in turn, suggest that the appropriate solution (at least for priorities that are not justified on a bankruptcy related ground) is to establish these priorities generally, and not just in bankruptcy? *Could* that have been done? How?

Is the priority list of §507 sufficiently broad to account for the categories of claimants one might desire? There have been some suggestions, for example, that the nature of certain consumer oriented businesses (such as Chrysler or perhaps International Harvester, to pick two that experienced severe financial problems in the early 1980s) supports a priority for the holder of warranty claims. The following solution was offered in Note, Consumer Warranty Claims Against Companies in Chapter 11 Reorganizations, 14 U. Mich. J.L. Ref. 347, 363 (1981):

> Warranty creditors are more than just creditors; they are also the debtor's customers. While preferential treatment of any creditor's claim has a beneficial effect on the goodwill of the business, it is *customer* goodwill which

determines how successfully a business competes for consumers' attention and money on a day-to-day basis. Accordingly, the court should consider the payment of warranty claims an administrative expense.

Is this persuasive? In analyzing this suggestion, note that it is only dealing with warranty claims arising out of sales (of automobiles, for example) that occurred *pre*-petition and that would be considered to be pre-petition claims under normal analysis (a matter that, as we saw in Note on Unmanifested Tort Injuries in Bankruptcy, supra page 134, is not wholly free from doubt). Warranty claims arising out of post-petition sales of automobiles are, almost certainly, entitled to administrative expense priority under §364. Isn't it sufficient for people who purchase automobiles *after* the manufacturer files for bankruptcy to know they will be taken care of? Is anything else gained by extending that protection to pre-bankruptcy purchasers? The Note just cited offers the following hypothesis: "This position [that claims arising out of pre-petition sales do not need special protection to ensure consumer confidence] may underestimate consumer reaction to knowledge that *some* warranty claims are not being paid—a reaction which may not be overcome by promises from the trustee that post-petition sale warranties will be honored." Id. Thus formulated, the rationale for administrative expense priority for warranty claims appears to be based on incomplete information. See also Schrag and Ratner, Caveat Emptor—Empty Coffer: The Bankruptcy Law Has Nothing to Offer, 72 Colum. L. Rev. 1147 (1972). But is the problem faced by such companies in bankruptcy really caused by *this* sort of informational problem? Isn't it much more likely to be caused by another sort of informational problem: that the filing of a bankruptcy petition increases the consumer's information about the financial problems of the company, causing them to increase their doubt over the company's continued viability? In that case, isn't the problem not so much one of priority of warranty claims but, simply, a worry that the company may not be around for the life of the car? Is that a perception that juggling the priority of claims can do much to change?

Should involuntary claimants (such as tort victims) have a higher priority than others? Or can one argue that there is no *bankruptcy* reason for treating them differently from other creditors? See Note, Tort Claimants in the Secured Credit System: Asbestos Times, the Worst of Times, 36 Stan. L. Rev. 1045 (1984); Schwartz, Products Liability, Corporate Structure and Bankruptcy: The Unknowable Risk Relationship, 14 J. Legal Studies—(1985).

Whatever the *scope* of the various categories of priority claims, should such claims—along with their priority—be transferable? That question is raised by §507(d) and the next case.

IN RE MISSIONARY BAPTIST FOUNDATION
OF AMERICA
667 F.2d 1244 (5th Cir. 1982)

TATE, Circuit Judge.

The debtor, Missionary Baptist Foundation of America, Inc. ("Missionary"), issued payroll checks to its employees on October 10, 1980. The claimant, Brooks Supermarket, Inc. ("Brooks"), cashed several of these checks for Missionary employees, in a total amount of $7,231.48. On October 15, 1980, Missionary filed a bankruptcy petition for relief under Chapter 11 of Title 11 of the United States Code. The checks cashed by Brooks were dishonored for lack of sufficient funds.

Brooks filed a claim for the $7,231.48 in the Missionary proceedings in bankruptcy court. Brooks sought priority treatment for its claim under 11 U.S.C. §507(a)(3), which grants priority to the extent of $2,000 to wages earned by an individual within ninety days of the filing of the petition. (None of the payroll checks cashed by Brooks for Missionary employees exceeded the $2,000 priority limit.)

The trustee objected, but the court nevertheless allowed priority on the Brooks claim. 12 B.R. 570 (Bkrtcy. N.D. Tex. 1981). The trustee appeals.[1] Finding that the assignments are entitled to the same priority as were the initial wage claims, we affirm.

The facts, which are undisputed, are recited in greater detail in the bankruptcy court's opinion. Both sides agree that the question whether the Brooks claim is entitled to priority turns on the interpretation given to section 507(d) of the Bankruptcy Reform Act of 1978 ("1978 Act"), 11 U.S.C. §507(d), which states:

> An entity that is *subrogated* to the rights of a holder of a claim of a kind specified in subsection (a)(3), (a)4, (a)5, or (a)6 of this section is *not* subrogated to the right of the holder of such claim to priority under such subsection. (Emphasis added)

The trustee asserts that Brooks is "subrogated" to the employees' wage claims and that §507(d) therefore precludes priority treatment, even though the underlying claims themselves undisputedly would have been entitled to priority under §507(a)(3) had they been made by the employees themselves. Brooks, in contrast, argues that §507(d) does not prevent priority treatment of its claims, on the theory that it is an "assignee," rather than a "subrogee," of the employees' claim, and entitled to the same priority treatment.

Under the pre-1978 bankruptcy law, in the absence of special circumstances, both assignees and, at least in some instances, subrogees were entitled to the same priority as that to which their assignors or subrogors

---

1. The 1978 Act, 28 U.S.C. §1293(b), permits a direct appeal to a circuit court of appeals, if the parties so agree. . . .

would have been entitled. . . . However, at least with respect to subrogees, §507(d) of the 1978 Act clearly changes the previous law.

Section 507(d) is a rather curious provision. It was not included in the House version of the bill that became the 1978 Act (H.R. 8200, 95th Cong., 1st Sess.), nor was it included in the substitute bill passed by the Senate (S. 2266, 95th Cong., 2d Sess.). After the Senate sent its version of the bill back to the House, the floor managers from both Houses met and agreed upon a compromise bill, which was enacted into law. §507(d) was included in the compromise bill. The floor managers who drafted this bill offered no explanation for the addition of §507(d),[2] and commentators have been unable to identify any policy reasons that might have prompted the inclusion of this provision.

Noting that in many instances courts have treated the terms "assignment" and "subrogation" as synonymous, the trustee in the present case forcefully contends that the two concepts have become merged, and that Congress must have intended §507(d) to preclude claims to priority by both assignees and subrogees. The bankruptcy court rejected this contention, and offered the following rationale:

> Some indication as to Congressional intent can be gleaned from an analysis of the provisions of the only other sections in the Code which use the term "subrogation."
> 11 U.S.C. §509(a),* entitled "Claims of Codebtors," provides:
>> Except as provided in subsection (b) and (c) of this section, an entity that is liable with the debtor on, or that has secured, a claim of a creditor, and that pays such claim is *subrogated* to the rights of such creditor to the extent of such payment.
>
> §502(e)(1)(C) disallows any claim for reimbursement or contribution of an entity that is liable with the debtor on or has secured the claim of a creditor to the extent that such entity requests subrogation under §509 to the rights of the creditor. It appears that the term "subrogation" as contained in those sections is used in restrictive sense. It refers to sureties, co-debtors, or other entities which are liable with the debtor or which have secured a claim of a creditor. This states the general rule of subrogation. 3 Collier 15th ed. ¶509.02 at 509-4 (1980).
>
> There are two presumptions of statutory construction which enure to the benefit of Brooks.
> First, there is a presumption that where the same words are used in different parts of an act, and where the meaning in one instance is clear, other uses of the word in the act have the same meaning as that where the

---

2. The joint explanatory statement of the managers refers to §507(d) in only two sentences: "Section 507(d) of the House amendment prevents subrogation with respect to priority for certain priority claims. Subrogation with respect to priority is intended to be permitted for administrative claims and claims arising during the gap period." 124 Cong. Rec. S17411 (daily ed. Oct. 6, 1978) (remarks of Sen. DeConcini); id. H11095 (daily ed. Sept. 28, 1978) (remarks of Rep. Edwards).
    * Reworded in 1984. — EDS.

definition is clear. . . . The presumption can be overcome only by a show-ing that the term "subrogation" was intended to be used in a more expansive sense in §507(d) or by demonstrating that the more restrictive definition of "subrogation" would be plainly at variance with the policy of the legislation. It is apparent in this case that Brooks is not liable with Missionary as a co-debtor nor has it secured a claim of a creditor. Brooks was not "subro-gated" within the meaning of §509(a) or §502(e)(1)(C) and, therefore, it does not appear to be "subrogated" within the meaning of §507(d).

There is another presumption which operates in favor of Brooks. It is presumed that Congress is aware of the existing constructions of a statute when it re-enacts a statute. . . . The repeal of the prior constructions by re-enactment of a statute must be clear and manifest. . . . The construction of the priority provisions under the Bankruptcy Act permitted one, like Brooks, who cashed a payroll check of an employee of a debtor to retain the same priority enjoyed by that employee. . . .

I conclude, therefore, that Congress did not intend to prevent one who cashed a payroll check for an employee of a debtor from enjoying the same priority for the claim which the employee possesses.

12 B.R. at 572-73.

Under the lower court's rationale, §507(d) would bar only sureties and co-debtors from claiming priority. This approach has appeal—it would deny priority treatment only to those who have knowingly accepted the risk of a debtor's insolvency. Cf. In re Transamerican Freight Lines, Inc., 16 Collier Bankruptcy Cases 422, 425-426, 4 Bankruptcy Court Decisions 82 (E.D. Mich. 1978) (surety receives fee to accept risk of debtor's bankruptcy; therefore, no equitable justification for according priority to surety's claim). However, one problem with this view is that §509(a) cannot logically be considered a "definition" of the term "subro-gee." §509(a) establishes that co-debtors and sureties *are* subrogees, but it does not necessarily follow from this that others are *not* subrogees.

As the bankruptcy court noted, repeals of judicial constructions of legislation are usually required to be clear and manifest. Once again, however, this does not conclusively prove that Brooks is entitled to priority treatment on its claim. §507(d) *does* clearly and manifestly mandate a change of law, at least with respect to subrogees. The only question is as to the extent of the change, i.e., whether Congress intended to change the law with respect to those formerly characterized as assignees as well as to subrogees.

In this regard, we find of persuasive force the Congressional inaction in light of Judge Augustus Hand's decision in In re Stultz Brothers, 226 F. 989 (S.D.N.Y. 1915). In that case, which is factually similar to the present one, Judge Hand held that a person who cashed paychecks for the em-ployees of the bankrupt 1) was *not* subrogated to the employees' claims; 2) *was* an assignee of the employees' claims; and 3) *was* therefore entitled, as an assignee, to assert the employees' wage priority.

Under the above-noted presumption that is often used in statutory interpretation, Congress was presumptively aware of *Stultz Brothers* when it passed the 1978 Act, and further presumptively aware: 1) that the courts had treated subrogation and assignment as distinct concepts in the priority context, when concerned with a claim by a creditor based upon his cashing later-dishonored checks of the bankrupt for wages, and 2) that persons such as Brooks were considered assignees, *not* subrogees, of the wage earners for purposes of priority distinctions. Since §507(d) makes no reference to assignees, and because the legislative history reflects no congressional disapproval of these characterizations reflected by the *Stultz Brothers* decision, we are unwilling to interpret §507(d) (denying by its terms priority only to "subrogees") as depriving wage claim "assignees" of their former priority. Accordingly, the bankruptcy judge properly allowed Brooks priority treatment on its assigned wage claim.

Under the former Bankruptcy Act of 1898, the judicial policy to allow priority to assigned wage claims was designed for the protection of the worker, who is thereby enabled to liquidate his claim against the bankrupt more advantageously. Otherwise, simply to make ends meet, the employees might be forced to assign at ruinous discounts their claims for unpaid wages. In fact situations such as the present one, wage earners, who are subject to liability as endorsers of their worthless payroll checks, might (if similar priority treatment were not accorded those who cashed their wage checks) be required to reimburse the holder, possibly after the funds received by them have been depleted for basic necessities.

. . . At least in the absence of indicia of a legislative intent to overrule the sound policy reflected by these decisions, we adhere to the rationale of the pre-1978 decisional law that accorded the same priority to claims based on assignments by the wage earner as to claims for wages made by the wage earner himself.

Accordingly, we hold that Brooks is entitled to wage priority treatment on its claim. The judgment of the bankruptcy court is therefore affirmed.

NOTES

1. As a condition of receiving a liquor license, Debtor was required to find a surety that would stand behind any of Debtor's state tax obligations. After Debtor filed for bankruptcy, at a time when he owed $2,500 in back taxes, the surety paid the taxes. Is the surety entitled to the taxing authority's priority under §507(a)(7)? In re Walsey, 29 Bankr. 328 (Bankr. N.D. Ga. 1983), held no. *Walsey,* looking to state law, held that there was no assignment of the tax claim by the taxing authority, and that the surety's right to assert the claim of the taxing authority derived from its state-law subrogation right — the right to "step into the shoes" of the person the surety compensated. And, as the holder of a subrogation right, *Walsey* held

that the surety was blocked from priority by the provision of §507(d). (In looking at this, you should know that the priority for taxes was renumbered from (a)(6) to (a)(7) in connection with the 1984 amendments (which added §507(a)(5)), but that Congress failed to amend §507(d) as well. As §507(d) read, it did not apply to §507(a)(7) at all. In 1985, Congress considered amending §507(d) to include §507(a)(7).) See also In re P.J. Nee Co., 36 Bankr. 609 (Bankr. D. Md. 1983) (credit card issuer a subrogee, not assignee, and therefore not entitled to assert the §507(a)(6) priority.)

2. Both *Missionary Baptist Foundation* and *Walsey* depend, ultimately, on a classification of a claim as one arising by subrogation or assignment. What law defines the difference between a subrogee and an assignee? Is the definition controlled by state law? Does §507(d) mean simply to incorporate state law here, with whatever foibles might exist under that law? Or does §507(d) intend to substitute a federal definition of assignee? Can you advance a policy argument for why §507(d) exists? Does any such argument (assuming you can find one) justify leaving the definition of assignee — as opposed to subrogee — to state law?

NOTE ON §726

After exhausting the priorities of §507 (and, a fortiori, after nonavoided property claimants have had their property claims satisfied under §725), distribution is made according to the rules of §726. Two issues of some interest are raised by the structure of §726. This note will examine them in turn.

1. **Section 726(a)(4).** The first issue is the extent of §726(a)(4)'s coverage of payments "of any allowed claim, whether secured or unsecured, for any fine, penalty, or forfeiture, or for multiple, exemplary, or punitive damages . . . to the extent that [it or they] are not compensation for actual pecuniary loss suffered by the holder of such claim." It is important, first, to understand that this provision is, in effect, a *subordination* provision. The holders of such claims get paid only if the general, unsecured claimants have been paid in full, notwithstanding that nonbankruptcy law treats the two categories of claims as equal (or even as superior in the case of secured penalty claims). Can you articulate a justification for this provision? If so, is it a justification that is limited to bankruptcy? Does the existence of §726(a)(4) create an incentive, among the holders of general, unsecured claims to file for bankruptcy for the sole purpose of subordinating such penalty claims?

For example, consider the facts of In re American Federation of Television & Radio Artists, 32 Bankr. 672 (Bankr. S.D.N.Y. 1983). In that case, the debtor (AFTRA) filed for bankruptcy "as a result of an antitrust verdict rendered . . . against AFTRA in favor of Tuesday Productions, Inc." The damages were in excess of $3 million, increased to $9 million as a result of the treble damage provision of 15 U.S.C. §15. AFTRA sought to have the treble damage award declared unenforceable as a penalty, on the grounds that as a court of equity, a bankruptcy court should not enforce a penalty and that "where innocent third parties would suffer, punitive damages may not be collected from an estate." The bankruptcy court rejected this contention, relying on §726(a)(4). But doesn't the subordination, itself, create untoward effects? To be sure, AFTRA still has to pay the penalty before any assets are returned to it under §726(a)(6). But has the full effect of the treble damage provision been diluted in the process? To the extent that the treble damage award is designed to deter otherwise undetected antitrust violations, it is possible that some of the monitoring is expected to come from a debtor's creditors, instead of from the government or some other third party policeman. Does §726(a)(4) dilute this monitoring incentive by providing that, in bankruptcy at least, the creditors need not worry about the trebling of damages? Even if the provision does have that effect, is there an offsetting bankruptcy policy that has been advanced? In re GAC Corp., 681 F.2d 1295 (11th Cir. 1982), a case arising under the Bankruptcy Act, asserted that "the effect of allowing a punitive damages claim would be to force innocent creditors to pay for the bankrupt's wrongdoing," and that such a "result would be inequitable." The Eleventh Circuit further asserted that to the extent punitive damages are designed to deter future conduct, "future wrongful conduct will not be deterred when the punitive damages are paid from the wrongdoer's estate rather than from his own pocket." Do you agree? Is this the rationale behind §726(a)(4)?

2. Section 726(a)(5). Section 726(a)(5) provides for the paying of interest "at the legal rate from the date of the filing of the petition" on any claim paid under the four preceding paragraphs of §726. What accounts for this rule? Consider the following explanation. Normally, claims are accelerated and interest stops at the commencement of a bankruptcy case. §502. But, as we have seen, secured creditors may be entitled to interest, either as a result of §506(b) or as a result of "adequate protection" under §§361 and 362. We earlier suggested (supra page 429) that this result was correct, on the ground that those who gain the benefit of bankruptcy's collective proceeding should pay for it. Why, then, don't the unsecured creditors also accrue interest during bankruptcy? The answer given by §726(a)(5), at least in rough approximation, is that they do, in cases in which there is a "lower" class (equity interests or the debtor himself) who ultimately gains the benefits, if any, of the bankruptcy proceeding. In those cases, that class should pay the unsecured creditors for *their* lost time value. But, if there is nothing to be returned to the debtor (or its equity owners), accruing interest among the unsecured creditors is a pointless exercise. To see why, assume a simple example where the debtor's assets are worth $100,000, and that value does not change in bankruptcy. (This last assumption is perhaps unrealistic, but it does not really matter — the example would be the same if it were omitted.) The unsecured creditors have $200,000 of claims at the start of the bankruptcy proceeding, held by A ($50,000), B ($50,000), and C ($100,000). If interest accrues on these claims at a rate, say, of 20 percent a year, after one year, A's claim would be for $60,000, B's claim would be for $60,000, and C's claim would be for $120,000. While their claims have all increased, this simply shuffles paper numbers, for their relative slice of the asset pie has *not* changed: A would get $25,000 both before and after the adjustment; B would get $25,000; and C would get $50,000. Therefore, accounting for the time value of money among unsecured creditors is unnecessary *unless* there is enough to pay their basic claims in full. Section 726(a)(5), as a first approximation at least, simply tracks that result. Cf. John W. Cooney Co. v. Arlington Hotel Co., 101 A. 879, 892 (Del. Chanc. 1917) (receivership case, notes denial of interest is "an administrative measure, because if there is not enough of assets to pay all the principal the addition of interest does not increase the dividend").

Even under this analysis, however, §726(a)(5) has several troublesome edges. The first is its limit on compensation to "legal rate of interest." Doesn't the analysis of the secured creditor's claim to "adequate protection" (supra, page 429) suggest that the appropriate rate should be the market rate, not the "legal rate"? The second question is the apparent pro rata treatment by §726(a)(5) of each of §726(a)(1) through (a)(4). Assuming one can justify the hierarchy of claims set forth by (a)(1) through (a)(4), shouldn't (for example) the class of (a)(2) claims be entitled to interest on account of their claims *before* the members of the (a)(3) class receive *anything*? That is to say, §726(a)(5) may enunciate the correct policy as between *creditors* and the *debtor,* but should it also have differentiated among *classes* of general creditors? Or is that a needless complexity without any clear cut gain?

NOTE ON SUBORDINATION UNDER §509

Section 509, together with §502(e), deals with the status of people such as sureties and guarantors — people liable with the debtor on a claim. Sections 509 and 502(e) allow a guarantor (for example) who has paid a claim to a creditor to choose between subrogation and reimbursement. If the guarantor chooses subrogation, the guarantor steps into the shoes of the creditor it pays. So, if the creditor was secured, the guarantor will also be secured. But if the *guarantor* was secured in the first instance, and the creditor is not, the guarantor might want to enter a claim in its own right, for reimbursement, since that claim will be allowed as a secured claim. Section 509 allows the guarantor to choose, and, indeed, insists that it make a choice. That section, moreover, imposes a limitation on the guarantor. Whether its claim against the debtor is by way of subrogation or by way of reimbursement, the claim will be subordinated in payment until the principal creditor's claim is paid in full.

Consider this in light of the following hypothetical. Creditor loans Debtor $10,000. Debtor's debt is guaranteed by Guarantor. Debtor subsequently defaults and files a petition in bankruptcy. Guarantor pays Creditor $5,000. Section 509 states that, in Debtor's bankruptcy, Guarantor's claim for $5,000, whether by subrogation or reimbursement, is subordinated to Creditor's claim (for the remaining $5,000) *until* Creditor has been paid a total of $10,000. How does this work? Don't Creditor and Guarantor both file a claim for $5,000? But, because of the subordination provision, any payments that Guarantor would otherwise be entitled to receive, in bankruptcy, on its claim, will flow to Creditor until Creditor receives payments of $5,000. This means that unless unsecured creditors receive more than 50 cents on the dollar, Guarantor will get nothing.

Before leaving this hypothetical, look at §502(e). Pursuant to §502(e)(1)(C), Guarantor cannot submit a claim for reimbursement if Guarantor is seeking subrogation under §509. And, if Guarantor is seeking reimbursement, its claim is disallowed *until* Guarantor pays on the guarantee to Creditor (§502(e)(1)(B)) at which time the claim becomes allowed (§502(e)(2)) but it is then subordinated (§509) until Creditor is paid in full.

All of this is done, according to the legislative history, to prevent "competition between a creditor and his guarantor for the limited proceeds in the estate." It places the risk of nonpayment on the guarantor. Is this result sensible? It may be if, as in the example above, the guarantor has guaranteed the entire obligation. Is it as clearly right if, to modify the above example, Guarantor's guarantee was limited to $5,000? In looking at these questions, does it matter how these claims would be treated outside of bankruptcy? For example, consider the facts of American Surety Co. v. Sampsell, 327 U.S. 269 (1946). American Surety issued a bond that, in effect, guaranteed laborers on Debtor's construction project that they would be paid. (The bond was required by California law.) After Debtor failed to pay the laborers, American Surety stepped in and paid those laborers who notified it within the required statutory period. The other laborers were not paid by American Surety, as they did not comply with the statutory notification procedures. Debtor then filed for bankruptcy. In Debtor's bankruptcy proceeding, may American Surety get paid on its claim alongside the claims of those laborers who remained unpaid, and were no longer entitled to claim against American Surety on its bond? The Supreme Court held no:

> The bond was intended to protect materialmen and laborers who worked on the job so that they would not have to bear the risk of [Debtor's] insolvency. But for his insolvency and bankruptcy these laborers and materialmen

would have been able to recover from him the money due them, no matter what their rights against the surety might have been. Consequently, the surety should not, by claiming under subrogation or indemnity for money paid to some of the creditors for whose benefit the bond was intended, be allowed to reduce the share of the bankrupt's assets due to other creditors whom the bond also was intended to protect from insolvency. For this would tend to defeat the very purpose for which the bond was given and therefore cannot be permitted under the equitable principles governing distribution of a bankrupt's assets.

Does this analysis convince you? It is true that the California statute was designed to protect laborers; in this sense, it is a bit like the priority given to wage claims by §507. But what is the scope of the protection? Doesn't the notice requirement indicate a view that the protection of these workers only extended so far? Is the problem that of seeing a surety compete with the principal creditors for the remaining limited assets? But isn't that a consequence of state law? American Surety was entitled to pursue Debtor under state law for the amounts paid the laborers. That claim would compete with the claims of the yet unpaid laborers who had lost their right to be paid by American Surety. Why should anything in bankruptcy law change that result? How would the case come out if it were to arise under the Bankruptcy Code?

B.   EQUITABLE SUBORDINATION

NOTE ON THE POLICIES BEHIND
EQUITABLE SUBORDINATION

The doctrine of "equitable subordination" in bankruptcy originated with Pepper v. Litton, 308 U.S. 295 (1939). In that case, the dominant shareholder of a corporation had caused the corporation, before bankruptcy, to confess judgment to long-dormant wage claims held by the shareholder, and obtained a lien enforcing the judgment that was perfected outside the preference period. Recognition of those claims would have consumed the remaining assets of the corporation, to the detriment of a corporate creditor. Justice Douglas, for the Court, noted that the case did not "turn on the existence or non-existence of the debt. Rather [it involved] simply the question of order of payment. At times equity has ordered disallowance or subordination by disregarding the corporate entity." The context, however, suggested that the *bona fides* of the debt were, in fact, in question. Justice Douglas started his opinion by noting that "[t]he findings . . . reveal a scheme to defraud creditors reminiscent of some of the evils with which 13 Eliz. c. 5 was designed to cope." The opinion, moreover, contained an extensive discussion of the need to look with care at the "claims presented by an officer director, or stockholder in the bankruptcy proceedings of his corporation." A showing that the dominant shareholder had manipulated the corporation's affairs so that an unsecured creditor would receive nothing, failed the test of "whether or not under all the circumstances the transaction carries the earmarks of an arm's length bargain." The Court therefore concluded "that the District Court properly disallowed or subordinated" the claim. What was peculiar about the case, therefore, was its holding that the validity of the debt would not be contested per se, but its ranking would be affected by the associated conduct and inferences.

This standard for subordination was enunciated in a bit more detail in a companion case, Taylor v. Standard Gas & Electric Co., 306 U.S. 307 (1939), which is often called the "Deep Rock" case:

> Deep Rock finds itself bankrupt not only because of the enormous sums it owes Standard but because of the abuses in management due to the paramount interest of interlocking officers and directors in the preservation of Standard's position, as at once proprietor and creditor of Deep Rock. It is impossible to recast Deep Rock's history and experience so as even to approximate what would be its financial condition at this day had it been adequately capitalized and independently managed and had its fiscal affairs been conducted with an eye single to its own interests. In order to remain in undisturbed possession and to prevent the preferred stockholders having a vote and a voice in the management, Standard has caused Deep Rock to pay preferred dividends in large amounts. Whatever may be the fact as to the legality of such dividends judged by the balance sheets and earnings statements of Deep Rock, it is evident that they would not have been paid over a long course of years by a company on the precipice of bankruptcy and in dire need of cash working capital. This is only one of the aspects in which Standard's management and control has operated to the detriment of Deep Rock's financial condition and ability to function. . . .
>
> If a reorganization is effected the amount at which Standard's claim is allowed is not important if it is to be represented by stock in the new company, provided the stock to be awarded it is subordinated to that awarded preferred stockholders. No plan ought to be approved which does not accord the preferred stockholders a right of participation in the equity in the Company's assets prior to that of Standard, and at least equal voice with Standard in the management. Anything less would be to remand them to precisely the status which has inflicted serious detriment on them in the past.

These cases suggest that the foundation of equitable subordination lies in fraudulent conveyance law. The principal twist is that the activity is punished by subordination, not disallowance of the claim. Do the standards also vary from fraudulent conveyance law? See Clark, The Interdisciplinary Study of Legal Evolution, quoted infra. What should be the conditions for equitable subordination? If sufficient "wrongdoing" is found to warrant invocation of the doctrine of equitable subordination, should the corporate veil also be pierced with respect to that person, making his assets available for the debtor's creditors? Are the tests, in fact, different? To what extent should equitable subordination be limited to the harm caused? Professor Clark suggested three plausible interpretations of equitable subordination doctrine, Clark, The Duties of the Corporate Debtor to Its Creditors, 90 Harv. L. Rev. 505, 519-520 (1977):

> Under the Full Subordination Rule, invocation of the doctrine automatically and invariably implies full subordination of all creditor claims of the controlling party. . . . As a result, the insider may in some cases be penalized in an amount greater than the unjust advantage he reaped from his controlling position. The second and third interpretations are supposed to be corrective but not punitive — the controlling party is subordinated only to the extent of the unfair advantage taken of the corporation. Under the Offset Rule, the nonpunitive objective is construed to mean that the amount of the unjust benefit will be deducted from the insider's legitimate creditor claim and then the estate will be distributed pro rata. Finally, under the Constructive Distribution Rule the pro rata shares would be computed as if the tainted transaction had not occurred and the controlling party is then considered to have already received an anticipatory distribution in the amount of his unjust benefit.

In re Westgate-California Corp., 642 F.2d 1174 (9th Cir. 1981), suggested that generalized, and essentially unascertainable, harm must first be shown:

> the claims of the debtor's fiduciaries may not be subordinated simply by virtue of the fact that the claimants are fiduciaries; it must be shown that they have acted inequitably toward the debtor to its detriment or to their own benefit. . . .
>
> . . . Bankruptcy courts must take care not to subordinate claims where doing so will operate only to penalize the claimant. . . . As a general matter, the import of this restriction will be that the court ought not to subordinate where the value of the claim greatly exceeds the amount of damage that the claimant has inflicted by his inequitable conduct. . . . Moreover, where the claimant has provided full restitution or adequate assurances thereof, subordination of his claims will operate only to punish his wrongdoing and will therefore be inappropriate. . . .
>
> This does not mean, however, that before subordination will be appropriate a court must conduct extensive litigation to determine the extent of damage that the claimant has caused. Where it has been shown that the claimant acted inequitably in his relationship with the debtor, and that the debtor has suffered harm thereby, it is incumbent upon that claimant to come forward, with reasonable dispatch and certainty, with evidence indicating that the harm caused by the challenged conduct was discrete in nature and did not result in general prejudice to the bankruptcy proceedings, and that the court can without undue complication determine the amount and depth of harm done. . . . Even where the claimant succeeds and the damage

caused has been ascertained, restitution to the estate should be a condition of avoiding subordination.

See also In re Missionary Baptist Foundation of America, 712 F.2d 206 (5th Cir. 1983) (need to show three things: (1) claimant has engaged in inequitable conduct; (2) misconduct resulted in injury to creditors or an unfair advantage to claimant; (3) no inconsistency with Bankruptcy Code provisions). Is equitable subordination needed as a doctrine? Should fraudulent conveyance law do the work in place thereof? Should equitable subordination be turned into automatic subordination? That latter approach was adopted by the Proposed Bankruptcy Act of 1973, Section 4-406, which read in part:

> (a) *Subordinated Classes of Claims.* The following claims are subordinated in payment to all other non-subordinated but allowable claims: . . .
>> (3) any claim, whether secured or unsecured, of any principal officer, director, or affiliate of a debtor, or of any member of the immediate family of such officer, director, or affiliate.

The Bankruptcy Code did not adopt this proposal, but instead essentially codified case law developments of equitable subordination. §510(c). Consider the question of equitable subordination in light of the following materials.

CLARK, THE INTERDISCIPLINARY STUDY
OF LEGAL EVOLUTION
90 Yale L.J. 1238, 1249-1250 (1981)

The law of fraudulent conveyances, which has existed for thousands of years, creates a kind of universal minimum-security agreement between debtors and creditors. It embodies a presumption that most rational debtors and creditors would, if the issues were squarely presented to them, expressly contract for the minimal creditor-protection rules it lays down. It thus lowers transaction costs by freeing parties from continually having to negotiate and contract about very basic rules of a common commercial relationship. Yet, beginning in the late nineteenth century, new bodies of law arose to provide minimal rules for the protection of creditors of *corporate* debtors: the bankruptcy doctrines of equitable subordination, cases allowing the piercing of the corporate veil, and statutes imposing restraints on dividends and other corporate distributions.[18] These developments give rise to a puzzle, for analysis has made it clear that the established principles of fraudulent-conveyance law could be applied to the factual

---

18. Technically, the first of these three bodies of law can be invoked in bankruptcies of debtors that are not corporations. But its main use is in the corporate context.

situations dealt with by these new rules, and that the policies and principles behind the new rules are identical or very similar to those underlying fraudulent-conveyance law. Why, then, did the new rules arise when they did?

The general answer is that the rise of *large* modern corporate enterprises created new opportunities for cost reduction that could be realized only by new specific rules implementing the old creditor-protection principles. For example, the managers of a large corporation with numerous subsidiaries could cause thousands of transactions to occur among the members of a corporate family. In an insolvency proceeding involving this corporate family, the facts about a fair *sample* of particular transactions, in addition to evidence that top management of the parent corporation had de facto power to direct most of the transactions and an incentive to insist on terms that were biased in certain ways, may justify inferring the existence of a general pattern of transactions that were fraudulent or unfair to creditors of specified members of the corporate family. In situations of this kind, the doctrine of equitable subordination offers a feasible remedy. Traditional fraudulent-conveyance rules, because of their insistence on proving each unfair transaction and measuring the amount of unfairness, do not. Before the rise of large corporate enterprises, equitable-subordination doctrine, which allows courts to look at an entire situation rather than at minutiae when defining a wrong and to substitute a shotgun for a rifle as the remedy, was less needed and less justified. The paradigmatic case of a fraudulent conveyance was simply that of the individual owner of a failing business who conveys title to his business and personal assets to his wife or to a friend just a short time before his creditors take him to court — or even, as in the deservedly famous *Tywne's Case*, while the sheriff is riding over to attach his goods. In these small-numbers situations, a sampling procedure is inapposite.

NOTE ON THE SUBORDINATION OF CLAIMS

The following represents the culmination of an exchange between Professor Landers (now in private practice) and Professor Posner (now on the federal bench). The exchange is pieced together from Landers, A Unified Approach to Parent, Subsidiary, and Affiliate Questions in Bankruptcy, 42 U. Chi. L. Rev. 589, 597-599 (1975); Posner, The Rights of Creditors of Affiliated Corporations, 43 U. Chi. L. Rev. 499, 518, 523-524 (1976); and Landers, Another Word on Parents, Subsidiaries and Affiliates in Bankruptcy, 43 U. Chi. L. Rev. 527, 536-538 (1976).

LANDERS:

The present doctrine governing the subordination of claims of parent and affiliated corporations in the bankruptcy of a subsidiary or affiliate is based on two essential premises. First, there is the rule that the claim of the parent or affiliate will generally be allowed. The rationale for this rule is that the relationship between the claimant and the bankrupt is not enough, by itself, to overturn the normal consequences of separate corporate status. Second, the exception to this rule is that where the parent or the affiliate has somehow abused its dominant position, its claim will be subordinated or disallowed. To date, most of the learning has been addressed to this second issue, namely, the question of what constitutes a sufficient abuse of control to warrant subordination. . . .

Rarely, if ever, does a court question the major premise of the subordination doctrine that, absent one or more of these subordinating factors, the claims of parent and affiliated corporations must be allowed to compete with claims of outside creditors for the assets of the bankrupt. The premise is vulnerable to two separate attacks. First, since the owners of the enterprise are concerned with maximizing return on their investment commensurate with the desired risk, any loan to the subsidiary or affiliate must be designed to maximize overall profits and thus is inherently more like risk capital than ordinary debt. Given that it is essentially risk capital, the "debt" owed to the related corporation should not be permitted to share *pari passu* with the true debts owed to other creditors. Second, since the enterprise owner is concerned with maximizing return on his entire investment, decisions regarding the operation of the subsidiary or affiliate will be made with that goal in mind — not with a view to ensuring that the subsidiary will function as a viable corporate entity. Thus, in terms of the traditional test outlined above, the economic reality of the situation gives rise to a presumption that the parent has not used its control in the best interests of the subsidiary. To ensure that the creditors are treated fairly, the claim of the parent or affiliate must be subordinated.

POSNER:

In effect, Landers is proposing that the only kind of investment that a corporation may make in an affiliated corporation is an equity investment. This is less objectionable than the piercing rule from the standpoint of burdening creditors of the parent, but it is independently objectionable as undermining the overall efficiency of the investment process. Parent corporations are sometimes the most efficient lenders to their affiliates because the enterprise relationship may enable the parent to evaluate the risk of a default at a lower cost than an outsider would have to incur. A rule that placed heavier liabilities on a parent lender than on an outside lender might thus distort the comparative advantages of these two sources of credit.

The proposed rule is a dubious one even from the excessively narrow standpoint of protecting creditors of the affiliate receiving the loan. The parent may extend credit to its subsidiary on terms more advantageous to the latter than an independent creditor would offer because the parent fears that its own creditworthiness would suffer if the subsidiary became insolvent. The availability of such loans thus reduces the risk that the subsidiary will in fact default. If the parent is not allowed to make a "real" loan to a subsidiary — if in effect the only permitted method of rescue is a contribution of equity capital — the added risks of this method of rescue may deter the parent from trying to salvage the subsidiary. If so, the creditors of the subsidiary will be hurt. There is, to be sure, another side to the coin. The parent may make the loan merely to conceal the subsidiary's precarious state and thereby attract new creditors who, but for the loan, would have been warned away by slow payment or other symptoms of financial distress that the loan may mask. But this possibility indicates only that parent-subsidiary lending is susceptible of abuse, and not that creditors in general would be benefited by a rule of automatic subordination of the parent's loan to the rights of independent creditors. . . .

. . . Although a rule of automatic subordination would be inappropriate, a creditor should be permitted to show that the parent's loan misled him regarding the amount of assets the corporation had available for repayment of his loan. He may have reasonably believed that the corporation had the usual equity capitalization for a corporation of its size and line of business. If these reasonable expectations were defeated because the parent supplied capital to the corporation in the form of a loan rather than equity, the parent should be estopped to deny that the loan is actually a part of the subsidiary's equity capital. . . .

In all cases in which estoppel is successfully invoked some competing group of creditors will be disadvantaged whose expectations may have been just as reasonable as those of the creditors invoking estoppel. But to the extent that enforcing the estoppel or misrepresentation principle will discourage borrowers from using the corporate form to mislead creditors, creditors in general will benefit — as will society since the costs of credit transactions will be lower, and hence interest rates will be lower for any given level of risk.

LANDERS:

My point was that debts of a parent should be subordinated not only because of the usual enterprise factors, but also because such debts are more inherently risk capital than debts of other creditors. Professor Posner does not really deny that this is the case, but simply suggests that the parent is sometimes the most efficient lender because of its lower information costs. This argument cannot be taken seriously. In fact, virtually all the cases involve loans or advances that an outside lender would not make at all or, at least, would not make on equally favorable terms. A better explanation is that the parent has an additional incentive to make the loan insofar as it seeks to preserve its investment in the subsidiary. Also, owners may be more optimistic than outsiders because their judgment is based on impaired vision or wishful thinking. One can make a strong argument — as does Professor Posner — that the outside lender is in a better position to make a realistic appraisal of the risk since he is free of emotional factors such as a reluctance to see a unit of the enterprise go under or a desire to preserve a shaky investment. Advances from the parent sometimes benefit existing creditors by infusing new resources and staving off bankruptcy. But such advances obviously harm subsequent creditors, who would otherwise never have become creditors, and often harm existing creditors, for whom a postponed bankruptcy may mean a lower realization. . . .

Professor Posner's test, by requiring voluntary creditors seeking subordination to show either that their information costs were too high or that they were misled, would require individualized proof by each creditor of facts unique to its transaction. While Professor Posner does suggest treating groups of creditors as a class, misrepresentation is not the kind of claim that lends itself readily to class adjudication. Indeed, the pressures of class adjudication have been largely responsible for the elimination of the need to prove reliance in securities fraud class actions. Insofar as other creditors are concerned, the duty to investigate will presumably vary in part according to the amount of the transaction and the creditor's prior dealings with the bankrupt. Professor Posner proposes no effective mechanism for proving such matters. . . . As a practical matter, Professor Posner's proposal would deter all but the largest creditors from seeking subordination because of disproportionate costs. And, ironically, it is these largest creditors who, because they were in the best position to investigate the facts, are least likely to warrant subordination.

Before leaving this debate, can you articulate its contours? Is the debate one over what nonbankruptcy law should be or is it over what bankruptcy law should be? If the latter, what bankruptcy policies suggest changing the nonbankruptcy rule? Or should equitable subordination — whether as a rule or a standard — be applied across the board? Isn't that essentially Professor Clark's argument?

NOTE ON THE SUBORDINATION OF SECURITIES LAW CLAIMS

Section 510(b) requires the subordination of any claim for either recission of the purchase or sale of a security of the debtor or for a damage claim arising from the purchase or sale of such a security. Such claims are to be subordinated "to all claims or interests that are senior or equal the claim or interest represented by such security, except that if such security is common stock, such claim has the same priority as common stock." The section, which has a very scant legislative history, first made its appearance in the Proposed Bankruptcy Act of 1973, as §4-406(a)(1). The intellectual drive for the section, however, seems to be an article that appeared in 1973 by Professors Kripke and Slain, in which they asserted (and we dramatically simplify their argument) that allowing a person to assert a claim as an unsecured creditor based on the purchase of an equity interest impermissibly permits a person purchasing a risky security to bootstrap himself into a less risky class. See In re Flight Transportation Corp. Securities Litigation, 730 F.2d 1128 (8th Cir. 1984). The essence of the article appears in the following excerpt, Slain and Kripke, The Interface Between Securities Regulation and Bankruptcy — Allocating the Risk of Illegal Securities Issuance Between Securityholders and the Issuer's Creditors, 48 N.Y.U. L. Rev. 260, 286-288 (1973):

> We suggest that it would advance analysis if the problem were reconceptualized as one of risk allocation. The situation with which we are concerned involves two risks: (1) the risk of business insolvency from whatever cause; and (2) the risk of illegality in securities issuance.
>
> By their separate contracts with the issuer, both the general creditor and the stockholder accept the risk of enterprise failure. However, the law provides that in the event of insolvency the creditor's claim can be given priority over the stockholder's and this is implicit in their contracts. The stockholder's greater risk is merely the downside of the phenomenon of leverage. . . . The absolute priority rule reflects the different degree to which each party assumes a risk of enterprise insolvency; no obvious reason exists for reallocating that risk. . . .
>
> The second risk is that the enterprise with which the general creditor and the shareholder are dealing has made an illegal stock offering to the shareholder. When the recission right is enforced in bankruptcy or reorganization . . . , the effect is to allocate that risk to general creditors. It is difficult to conceive of any reason for shifting even a small portion of the risk of illegality from the stockholder, since it is to the stockholder, and not to the creditor, that the stock is offered.

Do you agree with this analysis? A decade later, another article took issue with it, Davis, The Status of Defrauded Securityholders in Corporate Bankruptcy, 1983 Duke L.J. 1. Professor Davis argues that it is difficult to distinguish the risk to creditors caused by fraud in the issuance of securities from other risks (such as antitrust violations by the debtor) that they also bear, and that, moreover, there is little reason to have a policy that calls for subordination of securities law claims against the issuer but not against others (such as the underwriter). Id., at 22-23. Professor Davis asserts that, instead, it is necessary to separate out the loss in value of the security caused by business risks (where the purchaser of equity securities takes greater risk in return for the possibility of greater return) and the loss in value of the security caused by fraud (or the like) in issuance (where the purchaser of equity securities, Professor Davis asserts, does not agree to that risk). "[S]ecurities law claims," he suggests, "should be accorded parity, with their participation limited to an amount consistent with investors' out-of-pocket damages and the balance of the claim, if any, subordinated." Id., at 41. The article concludes with an extended discussion of the proposition that "permitting securities law claimants to participate on a par with general creditors to the extent of out-of-pocket fraud losses produces the fairest allocation of the overall fraud loss among the various claimants of the bankrupt."

In analyzing this debate, it may be helpful to keep two issues distinct. The first issue is what the general status of securities law claims should be relative to other claims against a debtor. This issue is one of nonbankruptcy law, and asks what the general resolution should be. The second issue is whether there is any bankruptcy policy that calls for changing that nonbankruptcy rule (whatever it may be). Isn't it fair to say that, whatever the merits of the debate between Professors Kripke and Slain on the one hand, and Professor Davis on the other hand, they really are exploring which rule would be preferable as a question of nonbankruptcy law? Once that rule is chosen (whatever it may be), isn't it fair to say that creditors and security purchasers take whatever package of risks state law has assigned, so that it does not advance *bankruptcy* analysis to assert that a creditor (or securityholder) has or has not assumed a particular risk? If this is so, is there also a bankruptcy related reason to change the rule in bankruptcy, either by providing total subordination of the claim (Professors Kripke's and Slain's proposal and that adopted by §510(b)) or partial subordination (Professor Davis's proposal)? Does §510(b) apply if the purchasers of securities can assert a constructive trust on funds of the debtor derived from the sale of securities? See In re Flight Transportation Corp. Securities Litigation, 730 F.2d 1128 (8th Cir. 1984) (raising, but not deciding, the issue); In re U.S. Financial Inc., 648 F.2d 515 (9th Cir. 1980), cert. denied, 451 U.S. 970 (1981) (old Act case).

C.   SUBSTANTIVE CONSOLIDATION

Section 302 provides for the "consolidation" of estates in the case of husbands and wives. The legislative history states that, in deciding whether to consolidate — to combine the assets and the liabilities of a husband and wife into a single pool — the relevant factors to consider

include the extent of jointly held property and the amount of jointly-owned debts. The section, of course, is not [a] license to consolidate in order to avoid other provisions of the title to the detriment of either the debtors or their creditors. It is designed mainly for ease of administration.

Despite the fact that §302 is the only provision in the Bankruptcy Code expressly authorizing consolidation, most of the case law on consolidation has arisen in the area of related corporations, under the judge-made doctrine known as "substantive consolidation." The issue arises when two related corporations file for bankruptcy, and the two corporations have some degree of cross-claims, either because the corporations have loaned money to each other, or because the corporations have guaranteed each other's debts, or because the books and records of the two corporations are not kept sufficiently separate, so it is difficult, if not impossible, to sort out the assets and liabilities of the respective companies.

In those cases, creditors of one corporation or another may push for "substantive consolidation." Conceptually, it is an issue similar in a number of respects to "veil piercing" between affiliated corporations. (Veil piercing may arise when there is a perceived abuse of the corporate form and two separate corporations exist where only one business is being conducted. Veil piercing — which is sparingly used — is traditionally studied in a basic corporations course.) The recurrent issue raised by substantive consolidation is: Under what circumstances should the assets and liabilities of two related entities, both in bankruptcy, be combined for substantive (and not just procedural) purposes in bankruptcy? Are these issues the same as §302 consolidation, or should the tests differ? The next case represents the general approach taken by courts in deciding the issue in the context of corporations; the materials following the case pursue the issue in a bit more detail, and resurrect, in a slightly different garb, the Landers-Posner debate we have already seen in connection with equitable subordination.

IN RE COMMERCIAL ENVELOPE MANUFACTURING CO.
3 B.C.D. 647 (Bankr. S.D.N.Y. 1977)

Roy Babitt, Bankruptcy Judge.

The movants are four related corporations, each of which filed its own separate petition seeking the relief contemplated by Chapter XI of the Bankruptcy Act, Sections 301 et seq., 11 U.S.C. Secs. 701 et seq., on October 20, 1976. Pursuant to the order of this court of October 27, 1976, these cases are being jointly administered. Bankruptcy Rules 117(b) and (c), 411 U.S. 1015, authorize joint or procedural administration in the interest of economy of judicial and clerical time. It affects no substantive rights. . . .

The relief sought by the motion now before the court is for a substantive consolidation which does deal with the rights of the debtors' creditors.

Substantive consolidation, as will be seen, is now part of the warp and woof of the fabric of the bankruptcy process involving related debtors, though to be used sparingly. It has no statutory or rule basis; rather it is the product of judicial gloss in the face of changes in the makeup of companies involved with the country's insolvency laws.

Although each of the debtors is a separate corporation, all four are related by virtue of common stock ownership, in that the common stock of Commercial Envelope Manufacturing Co., Inc. is owned by Mr. and Mrs. Ira B. Kristel; Commercial Envelope Manufacturing Co., Inc., in turn, owns the common stock of Business Envelope Manufacturers, Inc.; and Business Envelope Manufacturers, Inc. owns the common stock of the remaining debtors, Business Envelope Manufacturers of Tennessee, Inc. and Business Envelope Manufacturers of California, Inc. All of the directors of these debtors are the same individuals — members of the Kristel family.

The debtors are convinced, and hope to convince the court, that the only way [a] meaningful Chapter XI plan can be presented to creditors is for that plan to be a single, unitary one affecting all of the debtors and all of their creditors. To achieve this result, the debtors have moved for a multi-faceted order authorizing and directing the consolidation of all four cases into a single one with a concomitant merger of all of the assets and liabilities of the four corporations into the consolidated entity. As a necessary corollary of such relief the debtors ask that all claims filed in each of the individual cases be treated as having been filed in the consolidated case; that all duplicate claims for the same indebtedness filed in more than one case be expunged; that all inter-company claims be eliminated and disallowed; that all cross-corporate guarantees of these debtors be eliminated and disallowed; and finally, that all the consolidated debtors be authorized to file a single set of schedules and a single plan in the consolidated proceeding. In a matter as pregnant with consequence to all concerned as is substantive consolidation and alert to the frequent reminders that the grant is to be given only a proper showing of the criteria the courts have engrafted on the power, the court is to scrutinize the evidence offered. The evidence in support should satisfy the court and should be more than a pro forma exercise. This is particularly so here where as a creditor claims he would be prejudiced by the favorable exercise of this court's power to achieve what the debtor seeks.

The facts underlying the relationship between the parties, as gleaned from the pleadings, may be briefly summarized as follows. In 1971, the Industrial Development Board of Anderson County ("Industrial Board"), State of Tennessee, purchased a building to be used by the now debtor, Business Envelope Manufacturers of Tennessee, Inc. To fund the purchase, the Industrial Board issued first mortgage revenue bonds in the aggregate principal amount of $1,350,000 pursuant to an indenture of mortgage and deed of trust dated October 1, 1971. Simultaneously, the

Tennessee Company entered into a lease for the property with the Industrial Board which lease was guaranteed by Commercial Envelope Manufacturing Co., Inc. Both the lease and the guarantee were security for the payment of the bonds. When the motion to consolidate was filed the Industrial Board interposed objection insisting that the Tennessee plant and the operation there were profitable and that a consolidation and concomitant merger of assets and liabilities would jeopardize its claim in these proceedings. Subsequently, the Security Bank and Trust Company of Ponca City, Oklahoma ("Bank"), an Indenture Trustee, also filed its objection to the motion to consolidate alleging that consolidation would or could adversely affect the substantive rights of the holders of the first mortgage revenue bonds, since such consolidation would render assets of the debtors, Commercial Envelope Manufacturing Co., Inc. and Business Envelope Manufacturers of Tennessee, Inc. subject to claims of creditors of the other debtors, a result which would reduce the amounts available to satisfy the bonded indebtedness.

At the trial, the debtors elicited testimony from an accountant, one Abraham Nowick, a member of the firm of accountants authorized in these proceedings to conduct an audit of the debtors' books and records. . . . Mr. Nowick testified as to the difficulty of isolating and ascertaining the individual assets and liabilities of each of the debtors. This was due to the arbitrary and inaccurate system of bookkeeping maintained by the companies. No separate accounting was had nor were separate records kept. Financial statements were issued on a consolidated basis. Each debtor had cross-guaranteed obligation of the others. Mr. Nowick went on to describe the astronomical cost of performing such audit as might be necessary to permit one to distinguish between the assets and liabilities of the debtors. However, this witness continued, because of the complexity and length of time over which the inter-corporate transactions had taken place, he could give no guarantee that such an audit would be successful. He also testified that it was impossible to determine whether or not the individual operations of each of the debtors were even profitable. He expressed his opinion that physical consolidation into a single location would probably improve the profitability of the entire operation.

As noted earlier, the Bankruptcy Court has jurisdiction to consolidate proceedings and to merge the assets and the liabilites of the debtors. Soviero v. The Franklin National Bank of Long Island, 328 F.2d 446, (2d Cir. 1964); Stone v. Eacho, 127 F.2d 284 (4th Cir. 1942). This jurisdiction is based on considerations of equity, one of the touchstones of that jurisdiction, Bank of Marin v. England, 385 U.S. 99 (1966), and on the broad statutory grant of Section 2a(15) of the Act, 11 U.S.C Sec. 11a(15), to enter such appropriate orders in addition to those specifically provided for by statute, as might be necessary to enforce the provisions of the Bankruptcy Act.

When balancing the equities of each individual case when consolidation is sought, the court must be mindful that "while the term has a disarmingly innocent sound, consolidation in bankruptcy . . . is no mere instrument of procedural convenience . . . but a measure vitally affecting substantive rights." In the Matter of Flora Mir Candy Corporation, 432 F.2d 1060, 1062 (2d Cir. 1970). The same court in Chemical Bank New York Trust Company v. Kheel, 369 F.2d 845, 847 (1966) was aware earlier that if under certain circumstances there existed the possibility of unfair treatment to creditors of a corporate debtor, then the power to consolidate was to be used sparingly.

There are numerous cases emanating from this circuit which have dealt with consolidation. Although none of these cases has described conclusively the criteria that must exist before a case for consolidation is established, the cases do describe the common ingredients that seem to be present in all instances where consolidation was permitted. It is the opinion of this court that those elements exist in the present context and that therefore consolidation should proceed.

I turn to the cases. In Soviero v. Franklin National Bank of Long Island, supra, the court authorized consolidation upon the finding of extensive commingling of assets and business functions and the existence of a unity of interest and ownership common to all the debtor companies. All the debtors in Soviero had been engaged in the same business, and gratuitous transfers of assets were made from one debtor to another. Guarantees to purchasers had been given in the parent's name.

In Matter of Seatrade Corporation, 255 F. Supp 696 (S.D.N.Y. 1966), the debtors, almost entirely owned by one family, operated with frequent disregard of the corporate formalities usually observed in independent corporation[s]. The court found that it would have been unreasonable in terms of time and cost to attempt to separate the assets and liabilities of this corporation, and even if audit steps were to be taken, there was no assurance that the true situation of the debtors would fairly be reflected. The court also found that there was no evidence that particular creditors would be unfairly dealt with on a consolidated basis. There also existed intercorporate guarantees and frequent transfers of assets without formal observance of accounting proprieties. Again, that court authorized consolidation of the debtors.

In Chemical Bank N.Y. Trust v. Kheel, supra, the Court of Appeals for this Circuit, for the first time relying on Soviero, set forth an additional criterion to justify consolidation. That criterion turned on the findings that the interrelationship of the group of debtors was hopelessly obscured and that the time and expense necessary to even attempt to unscramble them was so substantial that it would threaten the realization of any net assets for all creditors. The court felt that if such findings could be made, an equitable base existed for the invocation of the court's broad equity powers to consolidate even in the absence of a showing that the creditor dealt with the bankrupt and its affiliates as one.

The Court of Appeals for this circuit faced the issue again in Continental Vending Machine Corp. v. Wharton, 517 F.2d 997 (2d Cir. 1975). There the court approved a plan of reorganization which called for consolidation of the pending Chapter X cases involving a debtor parent and its subsidiary corporations, finding that such consolidation was fair and equitable, and stating that the power to consolidate to reach assets for the satisfaction of debts of a related corporation does not require that creditors knowingly dealt with the debtors as a unit. The court again reminded that such power should be "used sparingly, because of the possibility of unfair treatment of creditors who have dealt solely with the companies having a surplus as opposed to those who have dealt with the related entities with deficiencies." 517 F.2d at 1001.

Yet, the court observed that when the inequities involved are heavily outweighed by practical considerations such as accounting difficulties and expense which may occur where the inter-relationships of the corporate group are highly complex or perhaps untraceable, then the consolidation should be favored. . . . The facts in those cases which are bases for their teachings are strikingly similar to the facts at bar. Indeed, they seem to be ever present in this day of access to Bankruptcy Court by parent companies and their multi-tiered subsidiaries.

As in *Soviero*, supra, all the debtors here are engaged in the same business; they share the same officers and directors; they made gratuitous transfers of assets from one corporation to another; they issued a consolidated financial statement for all four corporations; and they gave inter-corporate guarantees in the name of the parent corporation.

It is true that unlike the fact in *Soviero*, supra, there is no evidence that Commercial Envelope Manufacturing Co., Inc. paid monies to finance and fund organization and operation of its affiliates. Nevertheless, the pleadings here indicate that the debtors collectively financed their accounts receivable through A.J. Armstrong Co. and borrowed additional monies from Prudential Insurance Co. of America. These funds were used as a common fund by and for all four companies as the need for the funds arose. Furthermore, the above lenders received cross-corporate guarantees from each of the four companies so that in effect all the assets of all of the debtors stand as security for the total indebtedness due. This illustrates how inter-related and dependent the debtors really are.

As in *Chemical Bank*, supra, the inter-relationships are complex and in many instances obscured. Many of the day to day operations have occurred as though the debtors were one consolidated and integrated entity. The effusion of time and money would be almost prohibitive were any sophisticated effort to make sense out of the complex of cross lines undertaken. The expense and difficulty of reconstructing the financial records of the debtors to determine the inter-corporate claims, liabilities, and ownership of assets, have been testified to by Mr. Nowick. Furthermore, Mr. Nowick testified that due to the immense internal confusion, even if the expense of an audit were undertaken, there could be no assurance that it would be successful in unscrambling the relationships.

Another element in *Chemical Bank* also exists here. There, the court, upon the authority of *Soviero*, stated that "while the record in the *Soviero* case indicates that there was evidence that the Bank had dealt with the bankrupt and its affiliates as one, the opinion does not make this a necessary foundation for the result." 369 F.2d at 847. The court seemed reluctant to place the burden of making such a showing on the party moving for consolidation, preferring that the objecting creditor establish that it relied on [a] particular separate entity. While the objectant here has not claimed that it relied on the separate identity of a particular debtor, it insists that there is no evidence in the record showing that creditors of Business Envelope Manufacturers of Tennessee, Inc. or Commercial Envelope Manufacturing Co., Inc. dealt with those two debtors with knowledge of the existence of affiliated corporations. But even a cursory glance at the record would seem to indicate otherwise. The Industrial Board received guarantees from Commercial Envelope Manufacturers, Inc. and presumably relied on its credit. . . . While it is true, as the court in In re Continental Vending Machine Corp., supra at 1005, observed, that a creditor might have dealt separately with each debtor and relied on the assets of each for its protection without knowledge that the debtors were in fact operating as a hopelessly intertwined single entity, still it is not unreasonable to assume that because guarantees were given by the parent corporation, the creditors were aware of the complex corporate structure and were put on notice that some sort of inter-relationship, in fact, existed. Furthermore, the court in *Chemical Bank*, supra, held that once the proponent of consolidation makes out a prima facie case, the burden shifts to the objectant to show that there was a reliance on separateness. Here, the objecting creditor has furnished no proof that it relied on the existence of solely one or two of the four debtors seeking to consolidate.

These principles were affirmed in *Continental Vending Machine Corp.*, supra, where the court stated that

> because consolidation in bankruptcy is a "measure vitally affecting substantive rights," the inequities it involves must be heavily outweighed by practical considerations such as the accounting difficulties (and expense) which may occur where the inter-relationships of the corporate group are highly complex or perhaps untraceable.

The court also stated that

> The power to consolidate is one arising out of equity, enabling a bankruptcy court to disregard separate corporate entities to pierce their corporate veils in the usual metaphor, in order to reach assets for the satisfaction of debts of a related corporation. . . . While it does not require that the creditors knowingly deal with the corporations as a unit, *Chemical Bank*, it

should nevertheless be used sparingly because of the possibility of unfair treatment of creditors who have dealt solely with the corporation having surplus as opposed to those who have dealt with the related entities with deficiencies.

Here the objecting creditor has made no showing that it dealt solely with the Tennessee Corporation. On the contrary, it received an inter-corporate guarantee from the parent corporation. Likewise, the objectant has alleged only very generally that the consolidation of the debtors *will* or may adversely affect the substantive rights of the holders of the bonds. While such an allegation by itself might be sufficient to state a claim, it is obviously outweighed by the exigencies of the situation. Furthermore, it does not appear from the record that the objectant has established the factual basis upon which this argument would be predicated. The cost of an audit would consume a large share of the assets. Mr. Nowick has testified that the companies are operating profitably on a consolidated basis, in fact, and consolidation, in law, would probably increase continued profitability. Such continued business success would enure to the benefit of all creditors by a successful Chapter XI. While this court should not ignore the objectant's rights, still its showing that consolidation would be the reverse of equity is simply not enough. In short, mindful of Judge Friendly's wise teaching in his separate opinion in *Chemical Bank*, supra, at 848, that consolidation could yield "not equity but its opposite," I conclude that consolidation here is appropriate.

The essence of the objecting creditor's resistance to consolidation is that it could adversely affect the substantive rights of the holders of the First Mortgage Revenue Bonds, since such consolidation will render assets of the debtors, Commercial Envelope Manufacturing Co., Inc. and Business Envelope Manufacturers Inc. of Tennessee, subject to the claims of creditors of the other debtors, thereby reducing the amounts available to satisfy the bonded indebtedness. Support is claimed for this assertion in the decision by the Court of Appeals for this Circuit in In re Flora Mir Candy Corporation, supra. There, the court, while upholding consolidation of twelve of the thirteen debtors involved, refused such relief in the fact of the objection by the creditors of one of the thirteen debtor companies. The court concluded that under the circumstances surrounding the *Flora Mir* corporate complex, the inequities of consolidation were overwhelming and insurmountable. However, *Flora Mir* must be limited to its own facts, for it emerges as the "rare case" rather than the common one. An analysis of the facts there is in order.

Debentures had been issued more than six years before the debtor, Meadors, had been acquired by the parent, *Flora Mir*. Prior to its association with this parent, Meadors had existed as a separate, independent, corporate entity with its own history and its own creditors. Almost immediately upon its acquisition, it ceased all operations and eventually became defunct. The court, convinced of the "near certainty of unfair treatment," commented on the adverse impact that consolidation would have on Meadors' creditors, observing that

> Consolidation not only would wipe out Meadors' claim against Flora Mir for the misappropriation of its assets but also would permit the creditors of Flora Mir and the other corporations to share in any recovery . . . for transactions antedating Meadors joining the Flora Mir group-transactions in which these creditors had not the slightest legitimate interest. We doubt that any showing of accounting difficulties would warrant consolidation under such circumstances, at least if the Meadors creditors were willing to confine themselves to assets that were obviously theirs. But here there was no evidence such as in the *Chemical Bank* case cited, that the inter-relationships of the group are hopelessly obscured and the time and expense necessary even to attempt to unscramble them so substantial as to threaten the realization of any net assets for all the creditors, 369 F.2d 847. To the contrary, the accountants in relatively short order had managed to come up with financial statements of each of the debtors. Whatever problems there might be with respect to inter-company accounts among other debtors, those with respect to Meadors were few for the reasons stated. Id, at 1063.

The above lengthy excerpt highlights the numerous differences between the plight of the creditors here and those victimized in the "Flora Mir plot," for in *Flora Mir,* Meadors' creditors "clearly bargained on a different basis than the creditors of the other Flora Mir companies," and "were indeed being ripped off." . . . But that is not this case. The state of the record in *Flora Mir* bears reflection. For one thing, the accountant's testimony had little, if any, bearing on the operations of Meadors. He principally relied on the period from December 31, 1968 through May 11, 1969, a time frame within which Meadors was largely defunct. Thus, there was no evidence pointing to any intercompany transactions that left matters so hopelessly intertwined as to discourage any attempt to unravel them. Indeed, the evidence was decidedly otherwise, not the case here, supra. In the instant case, it is clear that inter-corporate transactions existed which involved all the debtors and predated the 1971 lease entered into with the Industrial Board. The undisputed evidence on that score brings this case squarely into the *Chemical Bank* case, supra, where the court observed that the "inter-relationship of the group was hopelessly obscured" at 847.

In *Flora Mir,* unlike the evidence here, there was no evidence that the consolidation of Meadors with the related debtors would improve the financial positions of all the debtors. Indeed, there was evidence that Meadors was a defunct company, implying that its inclusion of Meadors would have no positive effect on the continuing operations of the other debtors. Here, testimony of an expert witness showed that consolidation of operations would improve profitability, a relevant factor in the unfolding of the rehabilitative scheme of Chapter XI.

In *Flora Mir,* the debentures which underlay the claimants' position, had been issued when Meadors was an independent company, and its future acquisition by *Flora Mir* unpredicted. On the other hand, the lease presently before the court was entered into after all the debtors·had already commenced their incestuous relationship. While creditors involved in this corporate structure may not have dealt with more than any one corporation at a time, the knowledge that there existed an inter-corporate relationship could have bolstered these creditors' confidence in dealing with any individual corporation. This is particularly true by reason of the existence of inter-corporate guarantees. The instant case is, in this respect, not *Flora Mir,* but closer to *Chemical Bank,* supra and *Continental Vending Machine Co.,* supra, also.

It should also be observed that the debentures here were not issued by any of the debtors. They were issued by the Industrial Board. One of the debtors merely entered into a lease with the Industrial Board and another debtor guaranteed the lease. It was the Industrial Board which assigned the lease and guarantee as security for the bonds. The debentures were not the subject of any direct relationship between the debtors and the debenture holders. No showing has been made that the debenture holders in any way relied on the assets of the debtors. On the other hand, in *Flora Mir* there existed a direct relationship between the debenture holders and Meadors, and consolidation would have been prejudicial to those bond holders.

Finally, in *Flora Mir,* in addition to the claim that Meadors' creditors had bargained for different rights than the other creditors of the Flora Mir complex, there was also a claim by Meadors' stockholders against Flora Mir for the misappropriation of its assets by Flora Mir. The granting of the motion to consolidate would have had the effect of wiping out a legitimate claim for the misappropriation of Meadors' assets. While the *Flora Mir* court did not indicate that this was a primary concern in denying the motion to consolidate, such a factor must be given its due weight. Here, on the other hand, no such additional claim exists. Mere disregard of corporate formalities and a lack of awareness of the necessity of having appropriate inter-corporate record keeping is not evidence of deliberate fraud.

When all is said and done, there is a practicability to authorizing consolidation here. In effect, by this consolidation, all of the assets of all of the debtors are to be treated as common assets, and claims of all creditors against any of the debtors are to be treated as claims against this created common fund. This would eliminate duplicated claims filed against several of the debtors by creditors uncertain as to where the liability should be allocated. There appears to be no feasible alternative to consolidation from a practical standpoint, particularly where, as here, all of the companies are already before the court. . . .

This court cannot read *Flora Mir* as a mandate that consolidation must inevitably be refused where some creditor might be marginally injured.

All conflicting interests must be balanced. Here the balance is decidedly in favor of all of the creditors of all of the debtor companies and in favor of achieving that debtor rehabilitation which Chapter XI contemplates and which cannot be achieved unless consolidation is granted. So much is implicit in the words of the *Chemical Bank* case that consolidation may be had in order "to reach a rough approximation of justice to some rather than deny any to all." 369 F.2d at 847.

It is, therefore, the judgment of this court that in order that a meaningful plan might be proposed and accepted and found to be in the best interests of creditors, Section 366 of the Act, 11 U.S.C. Sec. 766, consolidation is warranted. The motion is granted and the objection overruled. . . .

NOTES

1. Why do creditors ever seek substantive consolidation? Why did the Industrial Board oppose substantive consolidation? How would Bankruptcy Judge Babitt have ruled if the objecting creditor had made a showing that it had "dealt solely" with the Tennessee corporation?

2. What would have happened had only one of the entities filed for bankruptcy? Compare In re Alpha & Omega Realty, 36 Bankr. 416 (Bankr. D. Idaho 1984) with In re 1438 Meridian Place. N.W., 15 Bankr. 89 (Bankr. D.D.C. 1981).

PROBLEM

8.9 Creditor *C1* loans $100,000 to *A* Corp. That loan is guaranteed by *B* Corp., a sister corporation to *A* Corp. The guarantee requires *C1* to exhaust its rights against *A* Corp. first; *C1* can then sue *B* Corp. for the deficiency. *A* Corp. has $500,000 assets, and $900,000 in debts apart from its obligation to *C1*. *B* Corp. also has $500,000 in assets, and it also has $900,000 in debts, apart from the obligation arising from its guarantee of *A* Corp.'s debt to *C1*. Apart from the guarantee, none of the creditors of *A* Corp. and *B* Corp. overlap. *A* Corp. and *B* Corp. simultaneously file for bankruptcy. Assume no fraudulent conveyance issues of the sort discussed supra page 270.

a. If *A* Corp. and *B* Corp. remain "unconsolidated" in bankruptcy, what will the various creditors of *A* Corp. and *B* Corp. receive in bankruptcy?

b. If *A* Corp. and *B* Corp. are substantively consolidated in bankruptcy, what will the creditors of *A* Corp. and *B* Corp. receive?

c. Compare (a) to (b). Who has done better? Who has done worse? Can you make any generalization about when, under these facts, substantive consolidation should be allowed?

NOTE ON THE NEED FOR SUBSTANTIVE CONSOLIDATION

In considering a problem such as Problem 8.9 or, indeed, in considering the general question of substantive consolidation, perhaps it is useful to start with a "clean" case (that is, assume no fraud or other overt misbehavior). In those cases, can't we extract several general comments about incentives? If one corporation, Y Corp., is relatively asset rich (comparatively more assets relative to liabilities) than another, related corporation, Z Corp., isn't it likely that the creditors of Z Corp. will seek consolidation, while those of Y Corp. will oppose it? Moreover, if there are inter-company guarantees, can't we also make a general prediction that consolidation will favor general unsecured creditors of only one corporation as opposed to those who have (because of guarantees) claims against both? (To test these statements, examine Problem 8.9 again.)

Given these incentives, is substantive consolidation ever warranted on a "greater good" theory, or does it simply represent a "grab" by one set of creditors that is made at the expense of another set? Is the approach of *Commercial Envelope* persuasive? Judge Babitt relies on knowledge of affiliation, but does such knowledge tell you anything about whether the corporate form is being respected? What about a test based on whether the entity "deceived" its creditors about the extent of its separateness? Isn't there a problem, at least some of the time, with this test? Even if creditors of one of the corporations have been deceived, is consolidation nonetheless fair to the creditors of the other corporation unless they, too, have been deceived?

Wholly apart from issues of fraud, however, there does appear to be one case in which substantive consolidation is desirable. It is possible that sometimes the assets and liabilities of two enterprises will be so entwined that the benefits from sorting them out are simply not worth the costs of doing so, and that *all* creditors would be better off with a consolidation, where that cost doesn't have to be incurred. Does that explain *Commercial Envelope*? Even if it does, how would you decide, as a practical matter, whether substantive consolidation were necessary in a particular case? How would you decide between the costs and the benefits? Could the relevant creditor groups (creditors of A Corp.; creditors of B Corp; creditors of both) vote as separate groups on the need for consolidation?

Are there other justifications for substantive consolidation? You might reconsider the Landers-Posner debate in looking at the following excerpt.

NOTE, SUBSTANTIVE CONSOLIDATIONS IN
BANKRUPTCY: A FLOW-OF-ASSETS APPROACH
65 Calif. L. Rev. 720, 723-728, 730-737 (1977)

With today's complex forms of business organization, the scope of a
business enterprise often extends beyond a distinct corporation to include
its nominally independent affiliates. Such enterprises are often controlled
by a single management, and, accordingly, the affiliates comprising them
will often engage in interrelated activities. Not uncommonly, the profitability of any given affiliate might be sacrificed for the good of the whole
enterprise.

From the creditor's standpoint, a transaction that names its debtor
can be detrimental because it almost necessarily impairs the prospects for
repayment. Aside from foresighted contracting, however, a creditor can
do little to protect itself against the risk that the profitability of its debtor
will be sacrificed in favor of affiliated corporations. As long as each affiliate
can pay its debts, there is no effective legal constraint on the fragmentation
of a single enterprise into many smaller corporations and the possible
abuses that might follow. Only after both the privilege to incorporate is
abused and the affiliate becomes insolvent does the corporate law provide
significant protection. At that time, if abuse is evident, the courts will
"pierce the corporate veil" to hold the shareholder liable for the corporation's debt.

In this "standard" alter ego case only shareholder limited liability is at
stake; thus the decision to pierce turns on whether the individual shareholders deserve limited liability. Substantive consolidations are significantly different. Conceptually, the shareholders are not involved; their
corporation's remaining assets belong entirely to its creditors. The only
issue is whether the bankrupt affiliates will be administered as separate
corporations, or whether the veil between them will be pierced to create
one large bankrupt entity. The parties in interest will be the creditors of
the affiliates, who are intimately concerned with how the enterprise assets
are distributed.[24] Thus, a simple examination of shareholder/creditor
equities creates a misleading picture. A creditor's reliance on even fraudulent representations by the bankrupt's shareholders or management
should not be used to grant or deny a consolidation, because such an action
would affect the rights of other creditors not parties to the transaction.
Instead, in substantive consolidation the relative equities of both sets of

24. Substantive consolidation litigation essentially is a dispute between the creditors of
two affiliated corporations over how the assets of the corporations should be distributed. As a
practical matter, a request for consolidation will arise only when representatives of an affiliate
will gain by having the estates of both bankrupts consolidated. Accordingly, the petitioner,
always associated with an affiliate with a relatively low asset/debt ratio, seeks to improve its
situation through consolidation with an affiliate possessing a higher asset/debt ratio. Of
course, parties associated with the relatively healthier affiliate will oppose the motion. . . .

creditor/litigants must be examined to determine whether piercing the veil will be equitable.

Since the creditors of the various affiliates have probably had no prior transactions with one another, when determining whether a motion for consolidation is meritorious it is necessary to look for factors that bear indirectly on the relative equities of the two sets of creditor/litigants. In most substantive consolidation cases such a factor is readily available. When related corporations engage in intra-enterprise transactions, each affiliate tends to strike friendlier bargains with the others than it would with outside parties. As long as all the affiliates benefit equally from the transactions over the long run, no creditor has cause to complain. If the benefits tend to flow in one direction, however, the transactions strengthen one affiliate at the expense of another, with the net effect of a gratuitous transfer. The assets reachable by one affiliate's creditor are diminished while those of the other are increased. Recognition of this fact provides the key for determining the relative equities of the opposing sets of creditors in a substantive consolidation case. If one set of creditors was harmed by the intra-enterprise transactions, the other set invariably must have benefited to a corresponding degree. . . .

Despite the confusion in the current law of substantive consolidation, two distinct themes run throughout the cases and commentary: (1) the reliance norm (the notion that a decision whether to consolidate should be based on some analysis of creditor reliance); and (2) administrative impracticality (the notion that affiliated bankrupts should be consolidated whenever it is impractical to separate their past affairs). . . .

In the vast majority of cases the decision whether to consolidate is based on some analysis of creditor reliance. Since, however, the principled use of reliance in a substantive consolidation requires an evaluation of the reliance of two independent groups of creditors, a dilemma is created when the reliance-based equities of the opposing creditors are equally compelling. For example, one set of creditors may move for consolidation by claiming reliance on the assets of the entire enterprise, while another group of creditors opposes the motion on the ground that they relied on the separate assets of their debtor. The courts and commentators invariably have dealt with this dilemma simply by finding the requisite reliance for the creditor they favor and by overlooking the equities on the other side. Consequently, the equities in virtually all substantive consolidation cases are presented in a one-sided fashion, regardless of whether reliance is used in support of or in opposition to consolidation. . . .

Reliance is essentially an estoppel argument. In the substantive consolidation context it is based on equities that arise out of the transactions between the creditor and the debtor enterprise. Hence it is said that the creditor relied on the enterprise assets or an affiliate's separate status. In substantive consolidation, however, the controversy is between creditors of the various affiliates who typically have had no prior contact with one another. The past reliance of one creditor should not be used to bind another creditor who was not party to the primary transaction. Nevertheless, the courts have permitted sets of opposing creditors to assert against each other equities derived from transactions with third parties. . . .

Two proposals have recently been advanced that would have the effect of avoiding the dilemma of conflicting reliance by focusing analysis on just one set of creditors. Professor Jonathan M. Landers of the University of Illinois has recently proposed what he terms a "unified approach" to substantive consolidation problems. He contends that since affiliated corporations are managed to maximize enterprise profitability, strong incentives exist to commingle funds, to undercapitalize, and in general to subordinate the interests of each individual affiliate for the betterment of the enterprise. Given this thesis, he recommends that when both parent and subsidiary are bankrupt, the estates should always be consolidated and all creditors should share equally unless there has been "specific reliance" on a debtor's separateness by a creditor.

The simplicity of the proposal is disarming. By focusing only on reliance on separateness, however, it fails to provide a reasoned solution whenever there is reliance by opposing sets of creditors. Such a situation could typically occur in a parent/subsidiary enterprise in which the subsidiary obtains financing from creditors who rely on its separate assets. If the parent subsequently loots the subsidiary so that the parent is relatively more healthy, and the entire enterprise eventually goes bankrupt, the creditors of the "harmed" subsidiary would naturally seek to consolidate. Professor Landers, however, totally ignores their equities. His "unified approach" would base the decision whether to consolidate entirely on the equities of the creditors of the "benefited" parent. If they had "specifically relied" on separateness, he would refuse the motion to consolidate, regardless of whether the creditors had in fact benefited from the alter ego. Thus, Professor Landers' approach to substantive consolidation does not result in a principled solution to the dilemma of conflicting reliance. At best, it arbitrarily prefers one set of relying creditors over the other.

In response to the Landers article, Professor Richard A. Posner of the University of Chicago has proposed an essentially opposite approach to substantive consolidation. He would apply a "misrepresentation test" to allow consolidation only "where the creditor of one of the affiliates reasonably relied on an appearance of greater capitalization than in fact existed." This offensive use of creditor reliance to obtain consolidation contrasts with Professor Landers' recognition of defensive reliance to oppose consolidation. His proposal, however, is no improvement over Landers'. It still entails ignoring the reliance of an entire, albeit different, set of creditors, and for that reason is but an arbitrary solution to the dilemmas posed by substantive consolidations.

The lesson to be learned from both the Landers and Posner modifications is that a principled approach to substantive consolidation must reject reliance entirely. Mere modification of the old norm cannot equitably resolve the dilemmas that the use of reliance creates. . . .

An alternative theme of some recent case law is that the bankruptcy proceedings of affiliated corporations should be consolidated whenever it is impractical to separate their financial affairs. The outstanding example of this proposition is the majority opinion in Chemical Bank New York Trust Co. v. Kheel, which involved the disposition of the assets of an insolvent shipping empire. The enterprise consisted of eight affiliates, which the referee found were "operated as a single unit with little or no attention paid to the formalities usually observed in independent corporations. . . ." Upon motion by a major creditor the assets and liabilities of the corporations were consolidated. Chemical Bank, a creditor of one of the stronger affiliates, appealed. It opposed consolidation, contending that its ability to satisfy its claim should not be diminished "absent a showing that it knowingly dealt with the group as a unit and relied on the group for payment."

Although there was ample precedent to place this burden of proof on the proponents of consolidation, the court chose to depart from precedent by affirming the consolidation without resort to reliance arguments. It distinguished the present case on the basis of "the expense and difficulty amounting to practical impossibility of reconstructing the financial records of the debtors to determine intercorporate claims, liabilities, and ownership of assets."

The majority opinion in *Kheel* undoubtedly states a correct proposition of law. If the relationships between affiliates are so obscured that it is impossible to disentangle their affairs, of course their bankruptcy proceedings should be consolidated. In such a situation even a simplistic reliance argument could not seriously be advanced. If a court could not determine the assets of each affiliate, neither could a "relying" creditor.

The difficulty with *Kheel* is that its holding is a virtual truism, and consequently of little use in resolving the tough problems that arise in substantive consolidation litigation. Rarely, if ever, do consolidation cases arise in which the affairs of the affiliates are so obscured that some estimate of each affiliate's assets cannot be made. Indeed, Judge Friendly in his concurring opinion states that even *Kheel* was not such a case. The opinion thus begs the hard question: if the intra-enterprise relationships are only *partially* obscured, when is it equitable to consolidate? . . .

Most cases decided in terms of reliance or administrative impracticality would have been resolved identically had a flow-of-assets approach been adopted. Since judges can manipulate reliance but have no power over the past flow of assets, it appears as if the flow constitutes a common denominator unifying what otherwise would appear to be an ad hoc use of reliance. . . .

Stated generally, the equitable remedy of substantive consolidation should be used only upon a showing that the corporate form has been abused to such an extent that creditors are unable to reach the transferred assets of the debtor affiliate through methods of creditor protection available under traditional corporate law. If the affiliated corporations have in fact operated as separate entities, the creditors need not be protected through consolidation. Any net deficit from the interaffiliate transfers will probably result in provable debts reachable by the trustee in bankruptcy. Moreover, to order consolidation simply because there has been a net flow of assets between the affiliated corporations would be to disregard the legislative directive allowing affiliates to incorporate separately.

If, however, the intra-enterprise relationship is complex and results in transfers between affiliates that are difficult to appraise, substantive consolidation may be the sole remedy realistically available to the harmed creditor. Any claim against the bankrupt intra-enterprise debtor would probably be subordinated under the *Deep Rock* doctrine. In addition, any attempt to use the fraudulent conveyance law to protect against uncompensated transfers would probably fail owing to difficult problems of proof.

Recognition of a need to prove a threshold level of disregard of affiliate separateness before piercing the veil is simply an extension of the *Kheel* holding that affiliates should be consolidated whenever their affairs cannot be disentangled. Defining the threshold in terms of alternative methods of creditor protection, however, may incline the courts to assess the appropriateness of substantive consolidation in a manner more meaningful to the parties involved in the litigation.

Chapter 9
BANKRUPTCY ALTERNATIVES TO LIQUIDATION: REORGANIZATIONS UNDER CHAPTER 11

A. INTRODUCTION

NOTE ON THE RATIONALE UNDERLYING CORPORATE REORGANIZATIONS

A bankruptcy proceeding is a day of reckoning for those with ownership interests in an insolvent firm. In a Chapter 7 proceeding, as we have seen, all the ownership interests (whether held by secured or unsecured creditors, or various classes of equity interests) are valued, the assets are sold, and the proceeds are divided among the owners. But the "sale" may be hypothetical rather than real, as might occur when the existing owners decide to continue the business (as the firm's best course of action), but are convinced that its fixed obligations must be reduced. This may occasion a collective reassessment of ownership rights, on the ground that the original allocation has become inappropriate in light of the firm's financial condition. Some creditors, for example, may become shareholders in this restructuring. Both these forms of dealing with a business in trouble are reflected in the bankruptcy laws. Bankruptcy proceedings take one of two forms, depending on whether ownership rights to the assets are sold on the open market to one or more third parties, or transferred to the old owners in return for the cancellation of their pre-bankruptcy entitlements. The first kind of bankruptcy proceedings are typically called liquidations and are governed by Chapter 7 of the Bankruptcy Code; the second kind are called reorganizations and are governed by Chapter 11 of the Bankruptcy Code.

In a Chapter 11 proceeding, the managers of the debtor firm usually continue to operate the business as a "debtor in possession." They have six months (presumptively) in which to propose a "plan of reorganization."

Typically this plan will propose that pre-petition creditors give up their claims against the debtor in exchange for claims against and interests (such as stock) in a reorganized firm that has been stripped of all pre-petition liabilities. There is a complicated set of rules giving individual creditors and groups of creditors the power to block a plan that the debtor in possession proposes, as well as giving, under certain circumstances, the debtor in possession the power to override these objections. In the process of formulating a plan of reorganization, the membership of these groups also depends both on the debtor's wishes and on a set of statutory constraints. After the debtor has had six months to propose a plan, but has failed to do so, others — again presumptively — are free to propose plans of their own. The same set of rules again protects the interests of individual creditors and groups of creditors from plans that undervalue their rights or overvalue the interests they are given in the reorganized firm.

One of the key distinctions, then, between reorganizations under Chapter 11 and liquidations under Chapter 7, is the *process* itself. (The results may not be so different: It is possible to sell assets as a going concern in Chapter 7, as well as to wind up a business and liquidate it under Chapter 11. See §1141(d)(3)(A).) In Chapter 7, what various claimants are entitled to receive is relatively fixed. If a firm is sold for cash, substantive nonbankruptcy entitlements largely determine who gets what cash in what order. There is often little to argue over, because rights are fixed and payments are made in cash. In Chapter 11, on the other hand, many more issues are open — not merely which creditors get stock and which get bonds, and not even how much of each, but also questions such as who should be in a particular group for voting purposes, and who should be barred from voting in the first place. As a consequence, Chapter 11 encourages negotiations that are largely absent in Chapter 7; these negotiations, in turn, are constrained by the statutory requirements. See In re Barrington Oaks General Partnership, 15 Bankr. 952 (Bankr. D. Utah 1981).

A threshold question is whether the complications of Chapter 11's rules on reorganizations and the opportunities they provide for undercompensation and strategic game playing by creditors, shareholders, and managers, are worth the benefits they bring. The justification for Chapter 11 of the Bankruptcy Code begins with the observation that many firms are worth more if kept intact (or largely intact) than if sold piecemeal. It is important to note that there is no necessary connection between insolvency and failure. A firm that has assets that can generate income with a present value of $8 million will be insolvent if it has fixed liabilities of $10 million. Yet the next best use of the assets may bring an income stream with a present value of only $5 million. In that case, the assets should continue to be used to do what they are presently doing, which will require scaling down the fixed obligations. The creditors and everyone else with rights to the firm's assets would be made worse off if the firm's assets were put on the chopping block and sold separately. Yet nothing in Chapter 7 requires assets to be sold separately. Indeed, the trustee is probably obliged to try to sell the firm's assets as a single unit if that approach promises the most for the creditors as a group. See Roe, Bankruptcy and Debt: A New Model for Corporate Reorganization, 83 Colum. L. Rev. 527 (1983). A sale of the assets as a going concern in Chapter 7, accordingly, differs from a Chapter 11 reorganization principally in who ends up as the owner of the assets after bankruptcy.

The rationale for Chapter 11, therefore, must not be simply that some firms are worth more as "going concerns" than if liquidated. A crucial question we must ask is what advantages a Chapter 11 reorganization has over a going-concern sale in Chapter 7. The place to start is to identify the differences between the two. A Chapter 11 reorganization can be seen as a sale of the firm to its former creditors in exchange for their claims (as opposed to a going-concern sale of the assets in Chapter 7, made to third parties in exchange for cash). See Clark, The Interdisciplinary Study of Legal Evolution, 90 Yale L.J. 1238, 1250-1254 (1981). But what are the advantages of a sale of the firm to its former creditors that warrants Chapter 11's more cumbersome procedures? Does the reason the old creditors become the new owners stem from difficulties in finding anyone willing to buy the firm as a unit? But how difficult is it to find third-party buyers for firms *that are worth preserving as going concerns?* Do the rules presently existing in Chapter 7 give the trustee enough time and flexibility to find a third party willing to buy the firm intact? The trustee in Chapter 7 largely displaces the firm's management during the pendency of the bankruptcy proceeding, but if the firm is sold to a third party, the new owner is free to retain the old management if it chooses. During the bankruptcy itself, moreover, the trustee, with court permission, could continue to run the business and continue to employ the old management (see §721) at least for such time as is "consistent with the orderly liquidation of the estate."

One might first look at the disadvantages of selling assets to a third party (or third parties) for cash. A sale of the firm's assets may be difficult to monitor and orchestrate. The sale should be conducted by the residual claimants to the firm's assets, because they have an incentive to obtain the best price. If Firm can be sold for about $100,000 (for more than $50,000, but less than $150,000), and if secured creditors are owed $50,000, general creditors $100,000, and subordinated debenture holders $100,000, the general creditors should conduct the sale. They stand to gain if they make the right choice, but they suffer all the costs if they make the wrong one about whether to sell the firm in pieces or as a unit, if they devote insufficient resources to finding a buyer or buyers, or if they waste time and money trying to sell the assets for more than anyone is willing to pay.

But ensuring that the residual claimants conduct the sale is not easy. For example, the identity of the residual claimants may be uncertain. If the assets may or may not be worth more than is necessary to satisfy the claims of general creditors and those senior to them, a choice must be made between allowing the general creditors (or the trustee, as their representative) to conduct the sale alone and allowing those junior to them to participate. Either decision brings difficulties. If the general creditors act alone, they have no incentive to invest resources to sell assets for more than the amount of their claims. On the other hand, if owners junior to the general creditors participate, they will tend to favor any tactic that might bring a higher price — such as costly searching or endless delay — even if it were not justified from the perspective of all claimants. These junior claimants would have the correct set of incentives only if they bore the additional costs of searching for a buyer who would pay more than the total amount of claims senior to their own. See Baird and Jackson, Corporate Reorganizations and the Treatment of Diverse Ownership Interests: A Comment on Adequate Protection of Secured Creditors in Bankruptcy, 51 U. Chi. L. Rev. 97 (1984).

In addition, there may be more than one residual claimant. A firm, for example, may have dozens or hundreds of general creditors. Even if they can be identified easily, it may be difficult to fashion a set of rules that enables them to work together or to appoint someone to act on their behalf. See Internal Procedures upon Commencement, infra page 989. Under current law, the bankruptcy trustee is charged with acting on behalf of the general creditors, but in practice it is hard for general creditors to monitor the trustee and ensure that he heeds his obligations to them. Problems of monitoring arise whenever one person acts as the agent of others. See Kraakman, Corporate Liability Strategies and the Costs of Legal Controls, 93 Yale L.J. 857 (1984). The problem is exacerbated in bankruptcy. Unlike the directors of a corporation, a trustee's reputation is not closely tied to the fortunes of any particular firm. The trustee's relationship with those whom he represents is transitory. Concern for his reputation may be insufficient to check the temptation to place his own interests above those of the creditors he represents. Perhaps for this reason, the costs of assembling a debtor's assets and conducting the bankruptcy proceeding (many of which are incurred by the trustee) consume, in practice, a large part of the proceeds of many sales of assets.

Yet a sale of assets for cash may actually be free from the defects generally attributed to it. The most common complaint about this procedure is that third parties undervalue firms in distress and are not willing to pay what the firm is really worth. But one must ask why buyers would be unwilling to pay what a firm was worth. Of course, valuing the firm's assets is a tricky business. One must project how much income can be derived from the assets in their current use and alternative uses and discount all these to present value. The value of assets may depend upon much that is uncertain (such as whether and upon what terms the old managers will (or should) continue to run the firm). As a result, third parties may underestimate a firm's chances for success. On the other hand, they may overestimate them. The question is not how likely third parties are to offer too much or too little for a collection of assets, but whether they are more likely than others to be too low rather than too high. Third-party buyers may not value firms accurately, but before rejecting a sale of assets to a third party (or third parties) as the best means of ending a particular ownership arrangement, one must explain why anyone else would appraise them more accurately.

If assembling information on the firm's value is hard for third parties, why would it be easier for anyone else? Third party buyers have an advantage over all others in the sense that they bear all the consequences of guessing right or wrong. If they overvalue a firm, they will not enjoy the same return on their investment as other buyers in the marketplace. If they undervalue assets, they will lose in the bidding to other, more astute buyers. Perhaps third party purchasers are not willing to pay as much for these firms as the old shareholders and bankruptcy judges think they are worth, but how likely is it as a general matter that shareholders and bankruptcy judges rather than buyers will value the firm correctly? Unlike competing third party buyers, the shareholders have nothing to gain (and something to lose) from undervaluing the firm. Unlike competing third party buyers, a bankruptcy judge enjoys no benefits and suffers no costs if he under- or overvalues a firm. A bankruptcy judge may be less able to cast a cold eye on an enterprise and make rough decisions than someone who has put his own money on the line. The judge may have no effective constraint on processes that lead him naturally to underestimate risks. See Note on Alternative Ways to Think About Discharge, infra page 736.

Suppose that, instead of selling the assets to one or more third parties, one allocates shares in the assets following the bankruptcy according to the priorities the "owners" (creditors as well as shareholders) originally negotiated. Opportunities then arise for game playing and manipulation by all claimants. Is a process that allows these contending forces to invoke various procedures and argue competing claims before a largely unaccountable arbitrator a particularly good method of valuing an insolvent firm? Experience has shown that many bankruptcy judges tend to overvalue firms, a result that recent work on cognitive psychology suggests is quite normal even for conscientious judges. See Note on Alternative Ways to Think About Discharge, infra page 736. Asserting that marketplace valuations are too low, they may blame the messenger for the message. A low marketplace valuation of assets may reflect the consensus judgment of those who are placing their money on the line that a firm's assets are ineffectively deployed and the firm should not survive as a going concern.

The current legal regime encourages existing owners of firms to accept readjusted interests in the firm in exchange for their non-bankruptcy entitlements. If one assumes that sales of a firm's assets on the market are possible and indeed desirable, why would the firm's owners as a group prefer a forced sale of assets to themselves (which is what reorganization is, in effect)? Ownership interests in publicly held corporations are largely fungible. Ownership and management of assets are usually quite separate. The value of such a firm is largely independent of who owns its bonds or shares of stock. If a rearrangement of ownership interests in a publicly held firm is necessary, why should we think that the firm's present owners (rather than some other group of investors) would place a higher value on the assets or that the future owners of the assets should be the former owners in a different configuration? Holders of stocks, bonds, and debentures probably have no special expertise or knowledge with respect to this firm that would give them an advantage over others. They are typically indifferent whether they hold an interest in this firm or one in another firm offering similar risks and returns.

If an existing owner of a firm has special expertise, nothing prevents the owner from bidding at the sale for an interest in the firm or reacquiring one from the successful third party purchaser. The ability investment bankers have shown to take very large firms public (such as Ford Motor Company or Apple Computer), and the willingness of others to acquire firms for huge sums (such as General Motors' purchase of EDS for several billion dollars), suggests that it is possible to sell the assets of even very large firms that need to readjust ownership interests.

A common justification for corporate reorganizations of closely held corporations is that the firm's survival as a going concern crucially depends upon continued participation of the existing managers, who are also the present shareholders. Does a sale of the firm to a third party, however, prevent the firm from surviving intact? Because the creditors have no claim to the managers' expertise, they are entitled only to the value of the firm without it. The third party acquiring the assets can bargain with the managers and obtain their services by striking a separate deal with them. If the managers will work only if given an equity interest in the firm, the new owners will offer it to them. This, of course, may engender negotiations of the same sort that take place within a Chapter 11 proceeding: One needs to reach a deal with the current management.

But the desirability of continued participation may not be limited to former stockholders. Other owners may also have special knowledge and expertise. Just as the managers might bargain successfully for an equity interest in the new firm, a finance company that has monitored the firm for years and knows its operations might be best able to buy the new firm's accounts and take a floating lien on its inventory. The bank that lent the firm money initially might be more confident that the firm's business would improve than a lender who had not dealt with the firm before. The bank, therefore, might also come to terms with the purchaser so that it could participate in the credit extended to the new enterprise.

Bargaining between several diverse former owners and the purchaser is likely to be difficult and costly. The more diverse owners there are, the less likely it is that bargains can be reached with all of them. If enough of the owners of an insolvent enterprise have expertise or other advantages that potential third party purchasers do not possess, the assets of the firm may in fact have their highest value in the hands of the existing owners, albeit with a different allocation of ownership interests (to solve the problem of existing fixed obligations probably exceeding income streams or asset values). If these diverse owners cannot cooperate, however, a sale of the firm may separate the assets from the existing owners, making them worse off because the assets will not be put to their best use. Therefore, a reorganization may be justified in those cases in which it provides a forum in which existing owners can bargain for new ownership interests more effectively than elsewhere.

In the abstract, it is very difficult to determine how important it will be for existing owners to continue participating in an enterprise and how much more a reorganization ensures their participation than the alternatives. Because a corporate reorganization introduces so many costs that a Chapter 7 liquidation or nonbankruptcy workout does not, the uncertain benefits it may provide in some cases (such as those involving closely held corporations) may be dwarfed by the costs it seems to impose on so many others (such as large, publicly held companies run by professional managers).

A reorganization brings two major sorts of costs that do not arise when assets are sold to one or more third parties. First, reorganizations take more time. Parties need to bargain and dicker with one another; there must be proposals and counterproposals. If a party holds out, a court proceeding may be necessary to determine whether it is trying to take advantage of the problems large groups face in reaching agreement, or simply insisting upon the priority and procedural rights it bargained for or would have bargained for when it became an owner.

Second, monitoring the bargaining among owners requires a valuation of their rights. Valuing assets without the discipline of a market is inherently difficult. While it might be easy enough to determine that the market value of the firm's used drill press is $10,000 and its real estate $100,000, it is not easy to project the value of the firm as a whole, which might well be greater than that of the assets piece by piece. If the firm is using the assets to market a new product, the assets may be worth considerably more if the new product becomes a huge success. But predicting the future of a firm is a formidable job, and one for which a judge is not well trained. See Roe, Bankruptcy and Debt: A New Model for Corporate Reorganization, 83 Colum. L. Rev. 527 (1983) (noting problem and suggesting a "float" of 10 percent of common stock on market, to set value, followed by an all-common stock distribution to claimants, as one method of reducing these valuation problems and concomitant negotiations).

But there is another — and more intractable — valuation problem. If the corporate reorganization is justified because many of the owners bring significant expertise to the enterprise, part of the valuation process should, if possible, put a value on that expertise. If the presence of the existing shareholders increases the firm's value by $10,000, then in theory the shareholders should receive at least this amount, because the owners senior to them never bargained for their future participation after a day of reckoning, and these senior owners may be unable to bargain for it once the reorganization proceeding is over. But allocating the gains resulting from keeping the same group of owners in the picture will not be easy. By hypothesis, all (or at least many) of the parties are adding value. Thus, simply knowing how much more the firm is worth in the hands of its present owners (which is virtually impossible to determine) than in the hands of third parties is not nearly enough. Ideally, we need to know how much each of the participants is adding. The question is not simply a distributional one. If those who have the expertise are not compensated for it in a corporate reorganization, they will, at the margin, have less incentive to invest resources in becoming experts in the first instance, and it will be harder to use their expertise after the reorganization.

The following case — a classic in the field of corporate reorganizations, and one that establishes what has become known as the "absolute priority rule" — explores to what extent the expertise the former owners bring to the new enterprise should be taken into account in distributing shares in the reorganized corporation. Its solution to the problem, however, has been modified in the changes made by the Bankruptcy Code, as we will explore later in this chapter.

CASE v. LOS ANGELES LUMBER PRODUCTS CO.
308 U.S. 106 (1939)

Justice DOUGLAS delivered the opinion of the Court. . . .

The debtor is a holding company owning all of the outstanding shares of the capital stock (except for certain qualifying shares held by directors) of six subsidiaries. Three of these have no assets of value to the debtor. Two have assets of little value. The debtor's principal asset consists of the stock of Los Angeles Shipbuilding and Drydock Corporation which is engaged in shipbuilding and ship repair work in California. This subsidiary has fixed assets of $430,000 and current assets of approximately $400,000. This subsidiary has only current debts of a small amount, not affected by the plan. The debtor's assets other than the stock of its subsidiaries aggregate less than $10,000.

The debtor's liabilities[2] consist of principal and interest of $3,807,071.88 on first lien mortgage bonds issued in 1924 and maturing

---

2. Other liabilities, not material here, are $6,075.94 of current accounts payable and $496,899.76 due the Los Angeles Shipbuilding and Drydock Corporation.

in 1944, secured by a trust indenture covering the fixed assets of Los Angeles Shipbuilding and Drydock Corporation (one of the subsidiaries) and the capital stock of all of the subsidiaries. No interest has been paid on these bonds since February 1, 1929. In 1930, as a consequence of the financial embarrassment of the debtor, a so-called voluntary reorganization was effected. To that end, a supplement to this trust indenture was executed, pursuant to a provision therein, with the consent of about 97 percent of the face value of all the outstanding bonds, which reduced the interest from $7\frac{1}{2}$ percent to 6 percent and made the interest payable only if earned. At the same time the old stock of the debtor was wiped out by assessment and new stock issued, divided into Class A and Class B, with equal voting rights. Class A stock was issued to some of the old stockholders who contributed $400,000 new money which was turned over to the Los Angeles Shipbuilding and Drydock Corporation and used by it as working capital. In consideration of this contribution the bondholders who agreed to the modification of the indenture likewise released the stockholders' liability under California law in favor of these contributors. Some Class B stock was issued to bondholders in payment of unpaid interest coupons. At present there are outstanding 57,788 shares of Class A stock and 5,112 shares of Class B stock.

In 1937 the management prepared a plan of reorganization to which over 80 percent of the bondholders and over 90 percent of the stock assented. This plan of reorganization, as we shall discuss hereafter, provided for its consummation either on the basis of contract or in a §77B proceeding, such election to be made by the board of directors. In January 1938 the directors chose the latter course and the debtor corporation filed a petition for reorganization under §77B of the Bankruptcy Act, with the plan attached and reciting, inter alia, that the required percentage of security holders had consented to it. This plan as filed was later modified by the debtor, as we point out later, in a manner not deemed by us material to the issues here involved. That plan as modified provides for the formation of a new corporation, which will acquire the assets of Los Angeles Shipbuilding and Drydock Corporation, and which will have a capital structure of 1,000,000 shares of authorized $1 par value voting stock. This stock is divided into 811,375 shares of preferred and 188,625 shares of common. The preferred stock will be entitled to a 5 percent non-cumulative dividend, after which the common stock will be entitled to a similar dividend. Thereafter all shares of both classes will participate equally in dividends. The preferred stock will receive on liquidation a preference to the amount of its par value. Thereupon the common will receive a similar preference. Thereafter all shares of both classes participate equally.

170,000 shares of preferred are reserved for sale to raise money for rehabilitation of the yards. 641,375 shares of the preferred are to be issued to the bondholders, 250 shares to be exchanged for each $1000 bond. The Class A stockholders will receive the 188,625 shares of common stock, without the payment of any subscription or assessment. No provision is made for the old Class B stock. The aggregate par value of the total preferred and common stock to be issued to existing security holders is $830,000 — an amount which equals the going concern value of the assets of the enterprise.

The plan was assented to by approximately 92.81 percent of the face amount of the bonds, 99.75 percent of the Class A stock, and 90 percent of the Class B stock. Petitioners own $18,500 face amount of the bonds. They did not consent to the so-called voluntary reorganization in 1930 whereby the trust indenture was amended. And throughout the present §77B proceedings they appropriately objected that the plan was not fair and equitable to bondholders.

The District Court found that the debtor was insolvent both in the equity sense and in the bankruptcy sense. The latter finding was based upon "appraisal and audit reports." In this connection the court found that the total value of all assets of Los Angeles Shipbuilding and Drydock Corporation was $830,000, those assets constituting practically all of the assets of the debtor and of its various subsidiaries of any value to the estate. Yet in spite of this finding, the court, in the orders now under review, confirmed the plan. And the court approved it despite the fact that the old stockholders, who have no equity in the assets of the enterprise, are given 23 percent of the assets and voting power in the new company without making any fresh contribution by way of subscription or assessment. The court, however, justified inclusion of the stockholders in the plan (1) because it apparently felt that the relative priorities of the bondholders and stockholders were maintained by virtue of the preferences accorded the stock which the bondholders were to receive and the fact that the stock going to the bondholders carried 77 percent of the voting power of all the stock presently to be issued under the plan; and (2) because it was able to find that they had furnished the bondholders certain "compensating advantages" or "consideration." This so-called consideration was stated by the District Court in substance as follows:

1. It will be an asset of value to the new company to retain the old stockholders in the business because of "their familiarity with the operation" of the business and their "financial standing and influence in the community"; and because they can provide a "continuity of management."

2. If the bondholders were able to foreclose now and liquidate the debtor's assets, they would receive "substantially less than the present appraised value" of the assets.

3. By reason of the so-called voluntary reorganization in 1930, the bondholders cannot foreclose until 1944, the old stockholders having the right to manage and control the debtor until that time. At least the bondholders cannot now foreclose without "long and protracted litigation" which would be "expensive and of great injury" to the debtor. Hence, the

virtual abrogation of the agreement deferring foreclosure until 1944 was "the principal valuable consideration" passing to the bondholders from the old stockholders.

4. Bonding companies are unwilling to assume the risk of becoming surety for the debtor or its principal subsidiary "because of the outstanding bond issue." The government's construction program will provide "valuable opportunities" to the debtor if it is prepared to handle the business. Hence, the value to the bondholders of maintaining the debtor "as a going concern, and of avoiding litigation, is in excess of the value of the stock being issued" to the old stockholders.

The Circuit Court of Appeals in affirming the decree confirming the plan stated that it was not possible for it to do other than accept these findings because of a stipulation and the state of the record thereunder. That stipulation provided for an abbreviated record and stated that the dissenting bondholders intended "to raise questions of substantive law only." But it also specified as errors, inter alia, the inclusion of stockholders in a plan where they have no equity and the finding that the plan was "fair" and "equitable." Thereby the stipulation adequately reserved the question of law as to whether on these facts the plan was fair and equitable within the meaning of §77B. But in any event a stipulation does not foreclose legal questions. . . .

On that question of law we think that the District Court erred in confirming the plan and that the Circuit Court of Appeals erred in affirming that decree. We think that as a matter of law the plan was not fair and equitable.

At the outset it should be stated that where a plan is not fair and equitable as a matter of law it cannot be approved by the court even though the percentage of the various classes of security holders required by §77B(f) for confirmation of the plan has consented. It is clear from a reading of §77B(f)[6] that the Congress has required both that the required percentages of each class of security holders approve the plan and that the plan be found to be "fair and equitable." The former is not a substitute for the latter. . . .

The words "fair and equitable" as used in §77B(f) are words of art which prior to the advent of §77B had acquired a fixed meaning through judicial interpretations in the field of equity receivership reorganizations. . . .

. . . In Louisville Trust Co. v. Louisville, N.A. & C. Ry. Co., [174 U.S. 674], this Court reaffirmed the "familiar rule" that "the stockholder's interest in the property is subordinate to the rights of creditors;

6. It provides in part: "After hearing such objections as may be made to the plan, the judge shall confirm the plan if satisfied that (1) it is fair and equitable and does not discriminate unfairly in favor of any class of creditors or stockholders, and is feasible; (2) it complies with the provisions of subdivision (b) of this section; (3) it has been accepted as required by the provisions of subdivision (e), clause (1) of this section; . . ."

first of secured and then of unsecured creditors." And it went on to say that "any arrangement of the parties by which the subordinate rights and interests of stockholders are attempted to be secured at the expense of the prior rights of either class of creditors comes within judicial denunciation" (p. 684). This doctrine is the "fixed principle" according to which Northern Pacific Ry. Co. v. Boyd, [228 U.S. 482], decided that the character of reorganization plans was to be evaluated. And in the latter case this Court added, "If the value of the road justified the issuance of stock in exchange for old shares, the creditors were entitled to the benefit of that value, whether it was present or prospective, for dividends or only for purposes of control. In either event it was a right of property out of which the creditors were entitled to be paid before the stockholders could retain it for any purpose whatever." (p. 508.) . . . In application of this rule of full or absolute priority this Court recognized certain practical considerations and made it clear that such rule did not "require the impossible and make it necessary to pay an unsecured creditor in cash as a condition of stockholders retaining an interest in the reorganized company. His interest can be preserved by the issuance, on equitable terms, of income bonds or preferred stock." Northern Pacific Ry. Co. v. Boyd, supra, p. 508. And this practical aspect of the problem was further amplified in Kansas City Terminal Ry. Co. v. Central Union Trust Co., [271 U.S. 445], by the statement that "when necessary, they (creditors) may be protected through other arrangements which distinctly recognize their equitable right to be preferred to stockholders against the full value of all property belonging to the debtor corporation, and afford each of them fair opportunity, measured by the existing circumstances, to avail himself of this right" (pp. 454-455). And it also recognized the necessity at times of permitting the inclusion of stockholders on payment of contributions, even though the debtor company was insolvent. As stated in Kansas City Terminal Ry. Co. v. Central Union Trust Co., supra, p. 455: "Generally, additional funds will be essential to the success of the undertaking, and it may be impossible to obtain them unless stockholders are permitted to contribute and retain an interest sufficiently valuable to move them. In such or similar cases the chancellor may exercise an informed discretion concerning the practical adjustment of the several rights." But even so, payment of cash by the stockholders for new stock did not itself save the plan from the rigors of the "fixed principle" of the *Boyd* case, for in that case the decree was struck down where provision was not made for the unsecured creditor and even though the stockholders paid cash for their new stock. Sales pursuant to such plans were void, even though there was no fraud in the decree. Northern Pacific Ry. Co. v. Boyd, supra, p. 504. As this Court there stated, p. 502, "There is no difference in principle if the contract of reorganization, instead of being effectuated by private sale, is consummated by a master's deed under a consent decree."

Throughout the history of equity reorganizations this familiar rule was properly applied in passing on objections made by various classes of creditors that junior interests were improperly permitted to participate in a plan or were too liberally treated therein. In such adjudications the doctrine of Northern Pacific Ry. Co. v. Boyd, supra, and related cases, was commonly included in the phrase "fair and equitable" or its equivalent. As we have said, the phrase became a term of art used to indicate that a plan of reorganization fulfilled the necessary standards of fairness. . . .

In view of these considerations we believe that to accord "the creditor his full right of priority against the corporate assets" where the debtor is insolvent, the stockholder's participation must be based on a contribution in money or in money's worth, reasonably equivalent in view of all the circumstances to the participation of the stockholder.

The alleged consideration furnished by the stockholders in this case falls far short of meeting those requirements.

1. The findings below that participation by the old Class A stockholders will be beneficial to the bondholders because those stockholders have "financial standing and influence in the community" and can provide a "continuity of management" constitute no legal justification for issuance of new stock to them. Such items are illustrative of a host of intangibles which, if recognized as adequate consideration for issuance of stock to valueless junior interests, would serve as easy evasions of the principle of full or absolute priority of Northern Pacific Ry. Co. v. Boyd, supra, and related cases. Such items, on facts present here, are not adequate consideration for issuance of the stock in question. On the facts of this case they cannot possibly be translated into money's worth reasonably equivalent to the participation accorded the old stockholders. They have no place in the asset column of the balance sheet of the new company. They reflect merely vague hopes or possibilities. As such, they cannot be the basis for issuance of stock to otherwise valueless interests. The rigorous standards of the absolute or full priority doctrine of the *Boyd* case will not permit valueless junior interests to perpetuate their position in an enterprise on such ephemeral grounds.

2. The District Court's further finding that if the bondholders were to foreclose now they would receive "substantially less than the present appraised value" of the assets of the debtor corporation is no support for inclusion of the old stockholders in the plan. The fact that bondholders might fare worse as a result of a foreclosure and liquidation than they would by taking a debtor's plan under §77B can have no relevant bearing on whether a proposed plan is "fair and equitable" under that section. Submission to coercion is not the application of "fair and equitable" standards. Such a proposition would not only drastically impair the standards of "fair and equitable" as used in §77B; it would pervert the function of that Act. One of the purposes of §77B was to avoid the consequences to debtors and creditors of foreclosures, liquidations, and forced sales with their drastic deflationary effects. To hold that in a §77B reorganization creditors of a hopelessly insolvent debtor may be forced to share the already insufficient assets with stockholders because apart from rehabilita-

tion under that section they would suffer a worse fate, would disregard the standards of "fair and equitable"; and would result in impairment of the Act to the extent that it restored some of the conditions which the Congress sought to ameliorate by that remedial legislation.

3. The conclusion of the District Court that the virtual abrogation of the agreement deferring foreclosure until 1944 ("the principal valuable consideration" given to the bondholders by the stockholders) justified participation by the stockholders in the plan is likewise erroneous. [Discussion of this issue is omitted.]

4. The holding of the District Court that the value to the bondholders of maintaining the debtor as a going concern and of avoiding litigation with the old stockholders justifies the inclusion of the latter in the plan is likewise erroneous. The conclusion of the District Court that avoidance of litigation with the stockholders gave validity to their claim for recognition in the plan involves a misconception of the duties and responsibilities of the court in these proceedings. Whatever might be the strategic or nuisance value of such parties outside of §77B is irrelevant to the duties of the court in confirming or disapproving a plan under that section. In these proceedings there is no occasion for the court to yield to such pressures. If the priorities of creditors which the law protects are not to be diluted, it is the clear duty of the court to resist all such assertions. Of course, this is not to intimate that compromise of claims is not allowable under §77B. There frequently will be situations involving conflicting claims to specific assets which may, in the discretion of the court, be more wisely settled by compromise rather than by litigation. Thus, ambiguities in the wording of two indentures may make plausible the claim of one class of creditors to an exclusive or prior right to certain assets as against the other class in spite of the fact that the latter's claim flows from a first mortgage. Close questions of interpretations of after-acquired property clauses in mortgages, preferences in stock certificates, divisional mortgages and the like will give rise to honest doubts as to which security holders have first claim to certain assets. Settlement of such conflicting claims to the res in the possession of the court is a normal part of the process of reorganization. In sanctioning such settlements the court is not bowing to nuisance claims; it is administering the proceedings in an economical and practical manner. But that is not the situation here. As a result of the filing of the petition in this case, the court, not the stockholders, acquired exclusive dominion and control over the estate. Hence, any strategic position occupied by the stockholders prior to these proceedings vanished once the court invoked its jurisdiction. Threats by stockholders of the kind here in question are merely threats to the jurisdiction of the court, which jurisdiction these selfsame stockholders invoked for their benefit when they caused the debtor's petition to be filed. Consequently, these claims of the stockholders are, as we have said, entitled to no more dignity than any claim based upon sheer nuisance value.

In this connection it should be observed that the finding of the court that it was important to admit the stockholders to participation in the plan so as to maintain the debtor as a going concern and thus protect the bondholders was based upon a misconception of its legal powers and duties. For the court assumed that the only alternative to acceptance of this debtor's plan was a dismissal of the proceeding or a liquidation. But this is not true. In the first place, no special perquisites (of consequence here) flow to stockholders by virtue of the fact that the proceedings are instituted by a voluntary rather than an involuntary petition. The criteria for exclusion or inclusion of stockholders in a plan are precisely the same in both situations. In practice it is not infrequent to find proceedings which start with a debtor's petition ending up with plans of reorganization which exclude stockholders. Reading Hotel Corp. v. Protective Committee, 89 F.2d 53. In the second place failure to accept this plan does not force dismissal or liquidation. Section 77B(c)(8) gives the court explicit powers where "a plan of reorganization is not proposed or accepted within such reasonable period as the judge may fix" either to "extend such period" or to "dismiss the proceeding" or, with exceptions not relevant here, to cause liquidation, such choice to be made "as the interests of the creditors and stockholders may equitably require." Accordingly, dismissal has not infrequently been properly denied. In re Bush Terminal Co., 84 F.2d 984. And in this case there has been no showing that a plan which is not only fair and equitable but also meets the other requirements of the Act cannot be adopted nor that all reasonable time for proposal of such alternative plans has expired.

We therefore hold that the plan is not fair and equitable and that the judgment below must be and is reversed.

NOTE

Case v. Los Angeles Lumber Products Co. is still, at bottom, good law. As a matter of substantive right, the rights of individual owners are set by the "absolute priority rule" enunciated in this case: Senior owners are entitled to be paid in full before junior claimants are paid anything. As we will see later, however, under the Bankruptcy Code this protection can be waived by a class-wide vote of the senior owners.

NOTE ON BARGAINING IN REORGANIZATIONS

A bankruptcy reorganization proceeding often does not entail an actual appraisal of the value of the firm's rights and the rights of each individual (according to the absolute priority rule). The reorganization rules of Chapter 11 encourage claimants and groups of claimants to waive their procedural rights. A bankruptcy statute must devise rules that protect some owners from overreaching by other owners. The owners as a group are worse off if there is too much or too little procedure. If they could have bargained together before they became owners, each would have been willing to pay for additional procedures to protect its interest until the cost of the uncertainty eliminated by additional procedure was less than the cost of the procedures designed to eliminate it. Determining either the kind or the amount of procedure is difficult.

These procedures form the background against which the parties negotiate. Parties always negotiate against a background of legal rules, in bankruptcy or out. See Mnookin and Kornhauser, Bargaining in the Shadow of the Law: The Case of Divorce, 88 Yale L.J. 950 (1979). The major premise of the reorganization provisions is that the bargain owners can reach in a corporate reorganization proceeding, against its procedures, is closer to the bargain they would reach in the absence of transaction costs than the bargain they could reach outside of bankruptcy (where creditors can invoke individual debt collection procedures), or in a liquidation (where the new owner must bargain separately for the expertise of the diverse owners). But the correctness of the premise is difficult to determine and the premise may be stronger in some categories of cases than others. The bargain that owners strike among themselves in a reorganization is hard to evaluate, because it takes account of a number of different elements. If, for example, the general creditors agree to a plan of reorganization that allows shareholder participation, they are recognizing more than that the value of the firm's assets may exceed its liabilities. They are also taking account of the value of the shareholders' participation (usually as managers) in the reorganized company, and the dollar value of procedures (such as an appraisal of the firm's assets) the shareholders are waiving. Only the value of the shareholders' substantive rights can be assessed according to a market standard, but this element is often the least important. Most corporations in bankruptcy have liabilities in excess of assets, so that on a day of reckoning the shareholders' substantive nonbankruptcy rights are worthless.

Bargaining over shareholder expertise (or rather, bargaining among owners for the expertise they all have to one degree or another) is a bilateral (or, more precisely, multilateral) monopoly problem. Its existence may justify the reorganization proceeding, not on the theory that it makes the problem disappear, but that it makes it less intractable. Bargaining over procedural rights may be less troublesome because it is easier to see what is at stake. If the shareholders have the right to insist upon a valuation that would consume $10,000 of the firm's assets, it is in the interests of the other owners as a group to offer the shareholders something less than $10,000 to waive this right. But bargaining over the waiver of procedural rights is itself costly and brings with it hold-out and freerider problems. If one knew what procedural rights each of the owners would have bargained for (and have been willing to pay for) before becoming an owner, one would want to provide each such owner with these rights and no more. Offering more procedural rights would either create valuation procedures that were not cost-effective or costly bargaining over the waiver of those procedures.

A corporate reorganization is designed to capture the diverse expertise of individual owners that could not be effectively captured by a new owner through conventional bargaining. Does expertise that would vanish in the absence of a reorganization really exist? Is its value larger than the costs and uncertainty that accompany a corporate reorganization? Even if it does exist and its value is sometimes significant, can one identify cases in which it is unlikely to exist at all and exclude them from Chapter 11 entirely? Arguably, all publicly held firms fall into this category. After all, these are cases in which the costs of the reorganization mechanism and the uncertainties it introduces are enormous, and diverse expertise among owners seems almost nonexistent. Managerial expertise is still present, but in a publicly held company, it is often the case that the managers hold a trivial portion of the common stock of the company. In those cases, arguments for compensating the common shareholders because of the need to preserve management expertise seem wide of the mark.

In the case of closely held corporations, diverse owners (from the shareholder managers to the secured creditors to the trade creditors) may have special knowledge that is very hard to transfer to someone else. We still face a second inquiry, however, even if we assume that the existing owners should continue as the owners, not because giving them ownership rights is cheaper than going through the mechanics of a sale, but because they are better suited to being the owners than other people are. If the existing owners should be the future owners, is Chapter 11 a particularly good means of ensuring that it happens, bearing in mind that a bankruptcy judge is not even allowed to consider the special expertise that an owner contributes to the firm in determining the size of his interest in the reorganized company?

Chapter 11 is supposed to promote bargaining, and, as a practical matter, few firms go through the full route in which a bankruptcy judge actually does a full scale valuation. It is (and was intended) to be a forum in which parties would be able to reach some kind of deal without involving all the procedures. The whole structure of Chapter 11 is designed to ensure that parties bargain with one another and that there is not a full-blown valuation. Yet bargaining is always going to take place among creditors and shareholders. The way that bargain is structured is going to be influenced in large part by the legal rules. When ownership interests in a firm need to be readjusted, creditors will meet. Like any other bargain, it takes the tone of "Give me X or else." The big problem with Chapter 11 may be what is often promoted as its big strength—that it permits bargaining among creditors and other owners of an insolvent firm. Can we ever say bargaining is good until we know what the bargaining is about? We may want the existing owners to bargain over the unique contribution they make to the firm. We want them to be able to say, "Compensate me for what I contribute to the firm or I won't participate in the enterprise." But couldn't this happen in a Chapter 7 going-concern liquidation? In Chapter 11, the bargaining is over the procedures of Chapter 11. The "or else" is the threat of invoking a complicated, cumbersome, and unreliable valuation mechanism. To the extent Chapter 11 promotes bargaining, it may be promoting bargaining about the wrong thing.

Is there a fundamental inconsistency in Chapter 11? It has a forced sale and elaborate procedures to capture diverse expertise, but these same rules are structured around the notion that this expertise is best captured in private bargaining. But even if one wants to capture this expertise through private bargaining, wouldn't one want private bargaining about it, rather than about the procedures of Chapter 11?

Should the present set of legal rules, which make it easy for a firm's managers to file a Chapter 11 petition, be changed so that firms could enter Chapter 11 only if it were in fact likely that it would provide the best means of preserving or enhancing the value of the assets for the owners (creditors and shareholders) as a group? You should keep these questions in mind as you read the materials in the rest of this chapter.

1. Overview of the Chapter 11 Process

NOTE ON THE STRUCTURE OF CHAPTER 11

Chapter 11 is necessarily more complex than Chapter 7. Virtually all of the issues explored in previous chapters of these materials exist in Chapter 11 proceedings as well as Chapter 7 proceedings. Indeed, many of them (such as the provisions designed to get people to deal with a debtor in bankruptcy, which we examined in Chapter 7 of this book) are more likely to arise in a Chapter 11 reorganization than a Chapter 7 liquidation. But Chapter 11 also has additional issues that simply do not arise in Chapter 7 cases. Because the business is being "sold" to the creditors themselves, instead of to third parties (as it would be in Chapter 7), the method of payment is substantially different. The creditors under Chapter 11 will "buy" the enterprise by turning in their old claims against the corporation. They will receive as payment new claims against the corporation (bonds, common stock, or whatever). This, as we have noted, substantially increases the valuation problems over a system (such as Chapter 7) where assets are sold for cash or marketable securities, and the claimants are then paid, in the order of their priority, with this cash or cash equivalent. Moreover, because the reorganization involves not only the "sale" of the business, but also a decision as to what type of new capital structure it should have, the possible approaches one could take are multiplied. See Jackson, Bankruptcy, Non-Bankruptcy Entitlements, and the Creditors'

Bargain, 91 Yale L.J. 857, 892-895 (1982). In addition, there are inherently "class" conflicts about the size of the pie and which approach should be taken in dividing it. Though one might look to the market to test valuations of the debtor's assets and interests in the reorganized companies (See Roe, Bankruptcy and Debt: A New Model for Corporate Reorganization, 83 Colum. L. Rev. 527 (1983)), bankruptcy judges typically do not do so. In the absence of such a mechanism to test valuations, anyone with a junior interest has an incentive to urge the bankruptcy judge to adopt an overly generous assessment of the value of the assets and of interests in the reorganized company. Similarly, anyone with a senior interest has an incentive to urge the bankruptcy judge to be very cautious in valuing the enterprise. Historically, bankruptcy valuations have been quite optimistic — which works to the advantage of lower priority classes, such as equity interests. See Blum, The Law and Language of Corporate Reorganization, 17 U. Chi. L. Rev. 565 (1950); Brudney, The Investment-Value Doctrine and Corporate Readjustments, 72 Harv. L. Rev. 645, 679 (1959).

These considerations suggest that a Chapter 11 proceeding is substantially more open-ended, and the subject of substantially more discretion, than a sale of assets to third parties. Consequently, in Chapter 11, much more than in Chapter 7, bargaining strategies are important, and may be influenced by the legal rules set forth in the Bankruptcy Code. Who gets to set the agenda — who, that is, may propose the "plan" of reorganization? How is the voting conducted, and who shapes the categories of creditors who are grouped together to vote on the plan? What restrictions are there on these bargaining strategies? This tension can be seen in the issue presented by *Lionel*, the next case, and it pervades the Chapter 11 process and, accordingly, efforts to restructure a business without using bankruptcy. See generally The Business in Trouble — A Workout Without Bankruptcy, 39 Bus. Lawyer 1041 (1984).

Much of Chapter 11 can be viewed as channeling this bargaining process by setting forth rules as to who can propose plans of reorganization and how they become effective. These rules form the core of Chapter 11. We have already encountered, in Chapter 7 of these materials, the rules governing how the business is run during the bankruptcy proceeding and how claims are determined. The questions raised by §§361-365 are likely to be of greater importance in the context of a reorganization than a liquidation — at least a piecemeal liquidation — for the concept of a going concern means that there is value in keeping the assets together and running the business during the pendency of the bankruptcy process, but they can arise in either kind of bankruptcy proceeding.

Before turning to a detailed examination of Chapter 11, the following excerpt is designed to give you a flavor of where Chapter 11 came from, and a brief overview of its salient provisions.

COOGAN, CONFIRMATION OF A PLAN UNDER
THE BANKRUPTCY CODE
32 Case W. Res. L. Rev. 301, 309-326 (1982)

It is helpful, and perhaps necessary, to understand the elements of the two principal direct predecessors of chapter 11 — chapters X and XI of the Bankruptcy Act. These two chapters, which differed drastically between themselves in philosophy and method, became part of the Bankruptcy Act in 1938 when the Chandler Act became law. Chapter X throughout shows the influence of the staff of the Securities and Exchange Commission (SEC); chapter XI does not. . . .

Partisans of former chapter XI are wont to say that new chapter 11 discards too much of old chapter XI. Some authorities, particularly aca demic experts, may think that chapter X has been weakened too much. A case can be made for either position. In any event, it is necessary to have some understanding of what these two chapters were like. While a confirmation under section 1129(a) in many ways resembles the confirmation of a plan of arrangement under old chapter XI, parts of old chapter X show themselves even in this section 1129(a) confirmation by consent of each impaired class. Chapter X is more fully revived, though again with modifications, in a confirmation where one class does not consent and the debtor, with or without cooperation of a majority of the other classes, forces it to accept something which the judge finds is the fair equivalent of what they now hold in rights.

A.   FORMER CHAPTER X

The principal objective of chapter X, when it was drafted in the later 1930's, was to correct the ostensible deficiencies in section 77B — a section which in the earlier 1930's had been created to remedy the real or alleged deficiencies of the federal equity receivership system. The staff of the Securities and Exchange Commission played a significant role in establishing the philosophy of chapter X. William O. Douglas was an influential participant. The SEC staff was critical of the part which the old management played in equity receiverships. Management usually represented stock interests. The SEC staff was also critical of the part played by the corporation's investment bankers. The staff thought that stockholders had too much influence, while creditors, especially senior creditors, had too little influence in formulating a reorganization plan. It apparently was assumed that bonds were likely to be held largely by holders who were both scattered and unsophisticated, while stocks tended to be held by insiders. Furthermore, the SEC staff thought that the equity receiver, often a former officer of the debtor, would be reluctant to investigate responsibility for the corporation's financial problems since he was once associated with its management. A plan devised by the receiver would likely favor the class the receiver was thought to have represented. Equity receivership law was entirely case law and necessarily left many problems unresolved.

To remedy these and other defects, chapter X was devised as a complete reorganization vehicle. A plan under chapter X could modify all kinds of claims — secured and unsecured, fixed and contingent. Changes in rights of stockholders as well as creditors could be affected to meet the real or imagined management control problem and the necessary shifts of equity ownership. Chapter X relieved management not only of major responsibilities for formulation of the plan, but also for the current operations of the debtor,[50] except that the independent trustee might engage services of some officers. Not only the debtor's management, but also its counsel were replaced by the judge's appointees. The chapter X reorganization process became the responsibility of the federal district judge who would designate a "disinterested" trustee who, in turn, would receive advice from "disinterested" counsel. In keeping with the philosophy of the times, therefore, crucial decisions were shifted away from the then unpopular business managers and entrepreneurs. In short, the trustee had the responsibility of discovering any management wrongdoing, supervising the operations of business, and eventually formulating a plan. The trustee might listen to some creditors, but subject to control by the judge, supervision was his responsibility.

The disinterested trustee, by definition, initially was ignorant of the corporation's affairs and was required, therefore, to learn on the job. Creditors were fearful that too much of this stranger's time would be spent looking for the devil who caused the financial crisis rather than thinking about changes in the firm's production or marketing decisions, its financial structure, or remedies designed to alleviate its financial difficulties. After their investigation of past management's sins, however, much time of the trustee and his counsel was devoted to an involved process of determining the future earnings and, therefore, the present value of the firm. From this determination, these individuals hoped a plan of reorganization would emerge. Only after the judge's tentative approval of the plan could it be submitted to creditors and stockholders for their acceptance or rejection.

Even if holders of two-thirds in amount and number of each class affected by the plan accepted it, under old chapter X, a judge could not confirm a plan until he made an independent determination that the plan was "fair and equitable, and feasible." Finding that the plan was "feasible" required the creation of a capital structure which would not crumble from the weight of its own fixed charges in a future financial storm. Finding a plan fair and equitable usually meant that every holder of a claim or equity interest would have received full compensation in the order of his contract priorities before any member of the class below his class was allowed any

---

50. Chapter X required the appointment of a disinterested trustee when indebtedness was greater than $250,000. Fed. R. Bankr. P. 10-202.

participation in the reorganized corporation. Approval of the statutory two-thirds of the class did not excuse the judge from making a fair and equitable finding. The words "fair and equitable" were so interpreted by Justice Douglas, writing for the Court in Case v. Los Angeles Lumber Products Co.[57] Two years later, in Consolidated Rock Products Co. v. DuBois,[58] the Supreme Court required a valuation of the reorganized corporation based primarily on its probable estimated future earnings in a typical year to make the fair and equitable determination. That earnings estimate was then multiplied by a suitable times earnings multiple to produce an entity valuation.

. . . A present valuation based on estimated future earnings necessarily involves crystal ball gazing into the future, with limited help from past earnings performance and modifications of those earnings hopefully influenced by the debtor's cure from its financial ills, predictable changes in the industry, and changes in the reorganized entity's operations. The desired result was, according to Justice Douglas in *Consolidated Rock Products,* an educated guess. The valuation was not necessarily a statement of the entity's present earnings or present market value, but rather, what its earnings and values would be should it recover from the trauma of reorganization, perhaps two or three years hence.

Although abstractly this two-step method may have been and still is the best method available, it does have make-believe characteristics. Estimating earnings of a healthy company for several years in the future is difficult enough; adding the cost of recovery by a business almost sure to have had losses for perhaps several years back complicates the practice. Under this method, for example, various creditor and equity classes would argue for a result that favored the interests of their class. . . .

. . . Ultimately, the decision as to which earnings estimates and which multiple to use would be made by the judge and not by the interested parties. . . . The valuation, and the determination of which classes could participate in the reorganized entity, would follow. . . .

The judge's valuation set a ceiling on the amount of securities which the reorganized corporation could issue. The absolute priority rule of chapter X required that each class be compensated fully before any junior class could participate. If the senior class prevailed in establishing its future earnings estimate and/or a low earnings multiple, the absolute priority rule would reduce or eliminate junior interests, beginning with stockholders and continuing in inverse order according to the priority of the different classes of investors. . . .

---

57. 308 U.S. 106 (1939). It is not easy to trace the history of the "fair and equitable" phrase. The Court cites railroad receivership cases as authority for the meaning of the phrase. Although none of the cited cases used that exact phrase, the Court concluded that "the phrase became a term of art used to indicate that a plan of reorganization fulfilled the necessary standards of fairness." Id. at 118.

58. 312 U.S. 510 (1941).

The requirement that the judge find the plan to be feasible would prevent an all secured debt structure or, for that matter, an all senior capital structure. To avoid too much debt, senior classes might be given some or all of their compensation in junior securities. It often was necessary, therefore, to downgrade the quality of the securities issued to old prior classes to prevent the capital structure from becoming an economic monstrosity. Since a thousand-dollar par value of common stock is not the equivalent of a thousand-dollar bond, the decrease in the quality demanded an increase in the quantity of a lower grade security to be given to the higher priority class.

This adjustment further reduced what was left for junior classes. Often the reorganization values would have been exhausted before the junior class was reached. The new capital structure must be kept within the feasibility aspect of the "fair, equitable and feasible" requirement. . . .

For good reasons or bad, neither creditors nor debtors made great use of chapter X. The Commission on the Bankruptcy Laws of the United States observed in its 1973 Report "that Chapter XI has evolved into the dominant reorganization vehicle." The draftsmen of chapter 11 were influenced, no doubt, by the preference of the market for the simpler, if theoretically less accurate, procedures of chapter XI.

B. FORMER CHAPTER XI

While chapter X was being drafted by one group of members of the National Bankruptcy Conference (largely reflecting the practice under the old equity receivership and section 77B as well as the influence of Justice Douglas and the SEC staff), another group of members, whose experience and outlook were quite different, drafted a dissimilar piece of legislation — chapter XI. This latter group of draftsmen typically represented trade creditors or their small and medium sized debtors. These lawyers were familiar, therefore, with common law compositions and Sections 12 and 74 of the Bankruptcy Act. The draftsmen of Chapter XI did not purport to cover the entire corporate reorganization area. Not every kind of debt was affected — some kinds of debt were not dischargeable. Chapter XI made no provision for altering secured claims or equity interests. Who would decide whether the debtor's plan was satisfactory better than the parties concerned? Since each secured party was likely to be in a class by himself, approval by a majority in amount and number often was not meaningful.

Draftsmen with a background of nonstatutory or statutory workouts could not be expected to be enthusiastic about at least two features which became part of chapter X. The first feature was the appointment of a disinterested trustee to operate the business. This arrangement, for example, made no sense for a small to medium sized retail entity — a "mom and pop" store, more common in the late 1930's than now. Creditors depended on the relationships between management and its customers for continuing operations, and without continued operations, the debtor could not pay. Replacement of management often would end the business. Who other than an owner, hoping to revive the business, would "keep store" nights and Sundays? There was also probably no money to pay for an independent trustee, even if the old customers would accept one.

Another feature which must have been objectionable to the draftsmen of chapter XI was the stipulation that the stockholders could retain their equity interest only if the creditors first were compensated fully. In many rearrangements, some class of creditors, and sometimes every class, will be less than fully compensated. If a class with payment due now is to be paid in the future, some rights are taken away from the class, and under chapter X, this loss would require compensation at the expense of the stockholder. This requirement of chapter X — that each creditor be compensated fully before shareholders could participate in the reorganized entity — often would have entailed the transfer of part, and sometimes all, of the stockholders' equity interest to the creditors. Was it realistic for creditors to expect the debtor to pull the entity out of its financial hole for the prime benefit of his creditors and retain little or no equity for himself? Trade creditors were generally philosophical about giving up something to the debtor. Without owner-management, there was no equity for the creditors to take over. And if, as was not too infrequent, the situation was such that the creditors were entitled to a share of the equity in return for the sacrifices which they were asked to make, who could decide better than the parties themselves what the division would be? Creditors could refuse to vote for a plan which did not compensate them for their sacrifice.

The chapter XI draftsmen began, therefore, with quite different premises than did the chapter X draftsmen. Under the draftsmen's "plan of arrangement," the debtor remained in control of the enterprise, management was not ousted, and a trustee was not appointed. The debtor began with the assumption that he could retain all or much of his equity; he entered into a composition, which if approved by a majority of unsecured creditors, would either reduce the amount of unsecured debt or postpone the time of payment, or both. The share of equity ownership to be transferred to the creditors was a bargaining point between the debtor and his creditors. If a majority in amount and number of unsecured creditors approved an arrangement, regardless of whether the creditors were compensated fully, the judge would have been required to confirm the arrangement if satisfied as to two major conditions: the arrangement had to be both feasible and "in the best interest of creditors." Basically, the test largely meant that the creditors had to receive at least as much as they would have received if the enterprise had been liquidated.

. . . Chapter XI's relative simplicity and creditor-debtor direct bargaining may explain its popularity with both creditors and debtors. The time-consuming adversary process was considerably shortened and often eliminated under chapter XI. In contrast, the complex procedures of chapter X, almost necessitating the adversary process, deterred both debtors and creditors because its mechanics consumed too much of the time that was critical to the life of the corporation. Even a good plan may fail if its help is delayed too long.

The necessity for the appointment of a trustee in almost all chapter X cases and its absence in chapter XI further increased the desirability of chapter XI. It is too much to expect that corporate executives and directors would rush to file under chapter X where filing almost certainly would result in their replacement by a trustee not of their choosing. . . . Similarly, creditors seemingly preferred to negotiate with interested parties directly instead of entrusting their fate to an unknown trustee. Creditors also might have preferred to negotiate directly with equity owners for an interest in the new entity, rather than leaving it to the judge to determine, under a fair and equitable analysis of the plan, that junior classes should or should not be allowed to continue to participate in the enterprise.

Chapter XI, however, had serious shortcomings, particularly when used for cases for which it was not designed — the debtor with substantial assets and many security holders. Chapter XI had no provisions by which a minority of any class other than unsecured creditors could be bound by a majority and no provisions to bind a class which had not accepted the plan; furthermore, certain debts were not dischargeable. The terms of secured debt could be changed only by contract with each holder. Chapter XI gave no power to alter rights of shareholders. . . .

IV. CHAPTER 11: PRINCIPAL CHANGES IN REORGANIZATION

Today, reorganization of almost any business, regardless of size, can be conducted under chapter 11 if the entity is not entirely excluded from any form of relief under the Bankruptcy Code. . . .

A review of some of the principal changes in the law will illustrate how chapter 11 follows parts of chapters X, where it follows chapter XI, and where it breaks new ground. Unlike old chapters X and XI, the relief available under new chapter 11 generally is not influenced by the character of the debtor unless it is in a class entirely excluded from the Bankruptcy Code. While only a corporation could be a debtor under chapter X, a chapter 11 petition may be filed by or against an individual, partnership, corporation, or almost any other entity.[82] Almost any person who qualifies for a chapter 7 liquidation can become a debtor under chapter 11.[83]

---

82. 11 U.S.C. §109(b), (d) (Supp. III 1979).

83. Id. §109(a) provides: "Notwithstanding any other provision of this section, only a person that resides in the United States, or has a domicile, a place of business, or property in the United States, or a municipality, may be a debtor under this title." Id. §109(d), relating to chapter 11, provides: "Only a person that may be a debtor under chapter 7 of this title, except

Another principal change resulting from chapter 11's enactment concerns the nature of the debt, including limits on its dischargeability. In this area, chapter 11 is patterned after chapter X rather than chapter XI. While chapter XI could affect only unsecured debt and contained limits on dischargeability, chapter X could affect any type of debt or equity interest. . . .

Under chapter 11, however, debt and equity interests may be altered and all debts may be discharged except those listed in section 1141[87] or in the actual plan. Failure to file a claim, therefore, does not prevent discharge.

New chapter 11 also follows in the footsteps of chapter X regarding who may file a petition for relief. Chapter 11, somewhat like chapter X, allows either the debtor or the debtor's creditors (ordinarily three or more) to file a petition for relief.[89] Only the debtor, however, has a period of exclusivity.[90] In contrast, chapter XI permitted voluntary filings by the debtor and permitted no filings by the creditors. Thus, there were situations under the act where the creditors, who would have preferred another plan under chapter XI, had to choose among the available alternatives: they could convince the debtor that he should change the plan; they could file for an involuntary liquidation under the act; they could make (as to a corporation only) an involuntary filing under chapter X; they could convince enough unsecured creditors to reject the plan; or they could simply let the debtor drift. Often, none of these alternatives were satisfactory.

Chapter 11 also varies from its predecessors with respect to the appointment of a trustee.[92] Under chapter X of the Bankruptcy Act, the appointment of a disinterested trustee was mandatory for any case of significant size.[93] This trustee operated the business and was responsible for the formulation of a plan. Under chapter XI, however, the debtor was

---

a stockbroker or a commodity broker, and a railroad may be a debtor under chapter 11 of this title."

87. 11 U.S.C. §1141(d)(2), (3) (Supp. III 1979). Section 1141(d)(2) provides that the confirmation of a plan does not discharge an individual debtor from any debt excepted from discharge under §523. Section 1141(d)(3) states:

The confirmation of a plan does not discharge a debtor if — (A) the plan provides for the liquidation of all or substantially all the property of the estate; (B) the debtor does not engage in business after the consummation of the plan; and (C) the debtor would be denied a discharge under section 727(a) of this title if the case were a case under chapter 7 of this title.

89. 11 U.S.C. §§301, 303(a), (b), 1121 (Supp. III 1979).
90. Id. §1121(b). Only the debtor may file a plan until 120 days after the date of the order for relief.
92. See 11 U.S.C. §1104 (Supp. III 1979).
93. Fed. R. Bankr. P. 10-202. This rule raised the statutory amount in regard to trustee appointment to $250,000; few chapter X cases involved less than this amount.

the only person who could file a plan and ordinarily he was left in possession; occasionally, a receiver was appointed. Under new chapter 11, as was
true under old chapter XI, the debtor is ordinarily left in possession.[95] A
trustee's appointment occurs only at the request of a "party in interest,"
and only where there has been fraud, incompetence, or like cause; or,
where such appointment is "in the interest of creditors or equity
holders."[96] Under section 1106, an examiner may be appointed to perform the investigatory function similar to that of a chapter X trustee.

It is fair to assume that the parties in interest usually will not request a
trustee under chapter 11. Their preference for a debtor in possession is
indicated by their preference for chapter 11. Thus, in this regard, chapter
11 more closely parallels chapter XI. And, in the case where a trustee is
appointed at the request of a party, the appointment may be terminated,
restoring the debtor to possession.[97]

The administrative role of the judge in what is expected to be the
normal chapter 11 case — one in which confirmation of a plan is based on
approval of the statutory majority of each impaired class — may be limited
indeed. The judge appoints a creditor's committee at an early stage; he
need only satisfy himself on a limited number of points before confirmation. In any case where the parties fail to agree, a party in interest may ask
the judge to decide any number of issues. Where acceptance by a majority
of each class cannot be obtained, the role of the judge is increased, but even
then his responsibility with respect to the accepting classes is limited. . . .

The new chapter 11 accords the debtor or creditors the right to
convert a chapter 11 reorganization into a chapter 7 liquidation.[100] The
debtor's power is subject to limitations; he can convert only if he is a debtor
in possession.[101] If an involuntary petition is filed by creditors under chapter 11, or they convert their chapter 7 proceeding to a chapter 11 proceeding, the debtor has no power to convert to chapter 7.[102] Either the debtor
or the creditors, however, may move to transfer from a chapter 7 proceeding to a proceeding under chapter 11.[103]

In situations where the debtor is not in possession and initially could
have been subjected to an involuntary chapter 7 liquidation, creditors may
request the court either to convert a chapter 11 reorganization into a

95. See 11 U.S.C. §§1104-1108 (Supp. III 1979).
96. Id. §1104(a).
97. Id. §1105.
100. Id. §1112(a).
101. Id. §1112(a)(1).
102. Id. §1112(a)(2), (3).
103. See id. §§1112(a)-(b), 706. Under §1112(a), the debtor may convert unless the
debtor does not have possession, the case is an involuntary case originally commenced under
chapter 11, or the case was converted previously to a chapter 11 case by someone other than a
debtor. Id.

chapter 7 liquidation or dismiss the case.[104] Section 1112(b) enumerates the reasons for dismissal which include the unlikelihood of any reorganization being accomplished, continued loss to the estate, and undue delay in effectuating a plan.[105]

Under chapter X, the trustee initially had the duty of formulating a plan, though others could make suggestions. Eventually, a creditor could file his own plan. Under chapter XI, however, only the debtor could file a plan. Creditors could influence the debtor's plan by making it plain to the debtor that a plan with certain features would not obtain the necessary majority vote for confirmation, but the debtor had the sole right to present a plan of arrangement.

There are other ways in which chapter 11 follows and modifies parts of chapter XI, and sometimes, chapter X. Under section 1121, the debtor has an exclusive right to file a plan, but unlike his perpetual exclusivity under chapter XI, this right exists only for a limited period of time. If a trustee has not been appointed, the debtor has the exclusive right to file a plan within 120 days of the relief order. If the debtor files a plan within the 120-day period, another 60 days remain to obtain acceptances.

The judge may extend or shorten the 120-day or 180-day periods at the request of a party in interest after notice and hearing. In a situation where the debtor does not meet the 120-day or 180-day limit or where a trustee has been appointed, a party in interest (including creditors, the trustee, the debtor, and the security holders' committee) may file a plan.

Under chapter XI, only the debtor could file a plan of arrangement. Since a plan under chapter XI could "affect" only unsecured claims, secured creditors had no vote; any secured creditor could agree or not agree as to a change in his rights but not the rights of his class (if there were other members). Under the code, a statutory majority may control any class, secured or unsecured creditors, or equity owners, if each other class is somehow to be bound, subject to compliance with certain general provisions of chapter 11. Assuming, for simplicity, one class of unsecured claims, the chapter XI plan could be approved under former section 362(1) by holders of a majority in number and amount of unsecured claims.

Under chapter 11, secured creditors and equity holders also can be impaired, and if so, they also would vote. Instead of a majority in number and amount, chapter 11, in section 1129(a)(8), requires a "statutory majority" (as herein defined) of each class for approval. Sections 1126(c) and (d) require holders of two-thirds in amount and more than half in number (except that for equity interests the numbers test does not apply). At least one class of claims must accept under section 1129(a)(10). The plan propo-

---

104. Id.
105. Id. §1112(b).

nent under new chapter 11 has a higher hurdle to jump to obtain confirmation through class acceptance, and contrariwise, an opposing group can more readily prevent approval. A nonassenter may defeat the plan if he can prevent the proponent from obtaining the required two-thirds in amount or more than one half in number vote. Unlike a creditor under chapter XI, any holder of a claim or interest under chapter 11 can file his own plan (after a period of exclusivity for the debtor) and can have the plan approved over the debtor's opposition if he can muster the needed statutory majority. The debtor or other plan proponent who has failed to obtain the requisite majority may be able, under the fairly stringent provisions of section 1129(b), to obtain confirmation if the judge can make certain findings. . . .

Chapter 11's most significant aspect is the provision contained within section 1129(a) which reduces the role of the judge in the proceeding where the statutory majority of each impaired class approves under section 1129(a)(8). This provision is not in keeping with the standards of chapter X. It is more like chapter XI which did not require a judge to determine whether the plan is fair and equitable as to a member of any class when the statutory majority of each unsecured class had consented to the plan.

Chapter 11 almost reversed Case v. Los Angeles Lumber Products Co.,[118] a landmark decision which held that chapter X's predecessor, section 77B, imposed a two-fold requirement on the confirmation of a plan: First, the plan must be approved by the requisite majority; and second, the judge must find independently that the plan was "fair and equitable, and feasible." *Case*, however, was not reversed completely; the fair and equitable requirement survives in section 1129(b), but that situation applies only where consent of at least one impaired class has not been obtained. The feasible requirement survives as to every plan in section 1129(a)(11).

The *Case* doctrine survives only as to the dissenting class. Section 1129(a) of chapter 11, however, requires compliance only with the first test of *Case* — acceptance by the statutory majority of each class whose rights have been impaired. In addition to finding that this requirement has been met, the judge must find that the plan is feasible — another test of that case. Under section 1129(a)(11), the judge must find that the plan is "feasible," as therein defined. This last requirement is aimed at insuring that the contemplated reorganization cures the debtor's problems — that the debtor will not be back for further relief in the foreseeable future.

If, however, the plan proponent cannot meet the test of 1129(a)(8) and a party asks the judge to confirm under section 1129(b)(2), other aspects of *Case* return to life, but in a limited manner — only as to reach rejecting class. As to that class, the judge must be satisfied that the plan is fair and equitable under the revised standards of 1129(b).

118. 308 U.S. 106 (1939).

NOTE

The decline in the relative use of Chapter X can be seen from the following:

Year	Chapter XI filings	Chapter X filings
1940	990	320
1950	583	134
1960	622	90
1970	1,262	115
1979	3,042	63

U.S. Dept. of Commerce, Bureau of the Census, Statistical Abstract of the United States 539 (102d ed. 1981).

2. Reorganization Rules and Conflicts Among Creditors

NOTE ON SALES OF ASSETS UNDER §363

The trustee (or debtor in possession) has to have freedom to run the business after the filing of the petition in order to ensure that the value of the firm's assets does not go down. §1108. This includes, obviously, the ability to sell assets of the firm from time to time, both in and out of the ordinary course of business. §363. This section, however, has been used on occasion to sell substantially all of the debtor's assets. See, e.g., In re Brookfield Clothes, 31 Bankr. 978 (S.D.N.Y. 1983). The conversion of the assets to cash makes the rest of the Chapter 11 proceeding quite simple, because the value of the debtor's assets is firmly established by the sale, as well as the value of the senior creditors' claims against those assets. The rules under §1129 for dividing the assets — at least where the senior creditors insist on it — is clear: The senior creditors are entitled to be paid in full before the junior creditors get anything. Moreover, because the assets have been converted to cash (or marketable securities), there is no longer any argument for postponing the day of reckoning. The case begins to look much more like a Chapter 7 case. This often works to the advantage of senior creditors, who have nothing to gain from delay, and to the detriment of junior creditors (or equity interests), who may have little or nothing to lose by delay, and accordingly seek delay hoping for a miraculous recovery.

The underlying question is whether it is proper to use §363 to simplify the Chapter 11 process — and thereby to circumvent some of the procedural advantages and/or protections junior interests enjoy in the Chapter 11 process. A case that illustrates this tension between Chapter 11 and §363 might take the following form. Imagine that Debtor is a badly managed firm. Bank has lent $10 million to Debtor and has taken (and properly perfected) a security interest in all of Debtor's assets. Debtor owes $20 million to a variety of other creditors, all of which have interests inferior to Bank's. Bank decides that the best way for it to cut its losses is to replace the current set of managers and otherwise have a complete housecleaning. Bank finds Buyer, which is willing to purchase and operate Debtor. Buyer will pay $9 million for the firm's assets and take over its operations, but only if three conditions are met: (1) Bank must lend it most of the purchase price; (2) Buyer must obtain the firm's assets free and clear of all prior liens and encumbrances; and (3) the whole deal must be completed within a month.

Bank is willing to finance Buyer's efforts (because it thinks well of Buyer's managerial skills), but it has trouble meeting the second condition. Bank goes to firm's managers who are also its principal shareholders. They initially refuse to abandon the firm and give up all hope of ever turning it around, but they change their minds when Bank threatens to call on the personal guarantees that the managers signed when the loan was made. Bank has no similar pressure, however, to bring to bear on the junior creditors. Because Debtor's managers might eventually turn the firm around, the junior creditors have nothing to lose by waiting and nothing to gain by abandoning all their claims against Debtor. Even if Bank were willing to pay the junior creditors some token amount to abandon their claims, there are so many of them that Bank cannot hope to strike deals with all of them during the next 30 days.

Bank therefore encourages Debtor to file a Chapter 11 petition. The day after it files the petition, Debtor, as the debtor in possession with the powers of the trustee, goes to the bankruptcy judge and asks the judge to approve a sale of all the firm's assets to Buyer for $9 million cash, their fair market value. (Buyer has borrowed $8.5 million from Bank.) The bankruptcy judge approves the sale. The following day Debtor submits a plan of reorganization that provides that the entire $9 million goes back to Bank. Because, as we will examine in detail soon, Bank is entitled to be paid $10 million before anyone else is paid under §1129, the bankruptcy judge approves the plan. Now Buyer owes Bank $8.5 million. Buyer has the firm it wanted, and Bank, the only creditor whose rights in Debtor had a positive value, has replaced a $10 million loan to a very risky debtor with an $8.5 million loan to a very safe debtor and $500,000 in cash. Everyone else is out of the picture.

Is such a transaction an abuse of the bankruptcy process? Can one justify short-circuiting the procedures laid down in Chapter 11? Keep these questions in mind in reading the following case. Note that in this case, we reencounter the familiar tension between senior and junior claimants. Senior claimants often have nothing to lose by an immediate sale. By contrast, junior creditors frequently get nothing from an immediate sale. But if the sale is delayed, the value of the assets is as likely to rise as to fall. If the value falls, the junior creditors (who were getting nothing anyway) are no worse off, but if it rises, the firm might be worth enough to pay off the senior creditors and leave something for the junior creditors. The junior creditors also have a chance to gain if they can prevent a cash sale of the firm to a third party and instead force a traditional reorganization in which all creditors trade in their claims for an interest in the reorganized firm. Not only are firms often systematically overvalued by bankruptcy judges, but if the junior creditors can prevent a transaction in which the firm's value is unambiguous, they can induce the senior creditors to compensate them for their waiving their right to insist on a full-scale valuation of the firm that would be both time-consuming and expensive.

IN RE LIONEL CORP.
722 F.2d 1063 (2d Cir. 1983)

CARDAMONE, Circuit Judge.

This expedited appeal is from an order of United States District Judge Dudley B. Bonsal dated September 7, 1983, approving an order entered earlier that day by the United States Bankruptcy Court for the Southern District of New York (Ryan, J.). The order authorized the sale by Lionel Corporation, a Chapter 11 debtor in possession, of its 82 percent common stock holding in Dale Electronics, Inc. to Peabody International Corporation for $50 million.[1]

I.   FACTS

On February 19, 1982 the Lionel Corporation — toy train manufacturer of childhood memory — and two of its subsidiaries, Lionel Leisure, Inc. and Consolidated Toy Company, filed joint petitions for reorganization under Chapter 11 of the Bankruptcy Code. Resort to Chapter 11 was precipitated by losses totalling $22.5 million that Lionel incurred in its toy retailing operation during the two year period ending December 1982.

There are 7.1 million shares of common stock of Lionel held by 10,000 investors. Its consolidated assets and liabilities as of March 31, 1983 were $168.7 million and $191.5 million, respectively, reflecting a negative net worth of nearly $23 million. Total sales for 1981 and 1982

---

1. The agreement between Lionel and Peabody provides that the parties will be relieved of their respective obligations to purchase and sell the Dale shares unless the closing takes place on or before November 30, 1983. In section 1.03 of the contract, the parties specifically contemplated the possibility of "a stay pending disposition of any appeal from the bankruptcy court's order." On November 22, 1983 Peabody made a motion under Fed. R. App. P. 27 requesting in part that this court extend the November 30 deadline. In view of the contract language, Peabody bargained for this provision. Accordingly, we deny its motion.

were $295.1 million and $338.6 million. Lionel's creditors hold approximately $135.6 million in pre-petition claims, and they are represented in the ongoing bankruptcy proceedings by an Official Creditors' Committee whose 13 members hold $80 million of those claims. The remaining $55 million is scattered among thousands of small creditors.

Lionel continues to operate its businesses and manage its properties pursuant to 11 U.S.C. §§1107-1108, primarily through its wholly-owned subsidiary, Leisure. Leisure operates Lionel's presently owned 56 specialty retail stores, which include a number of stores formerly managed by Lionel's other subsidiary, Consolidated Toy. In addition to the stock of Leisure and Consolidated Toy, Lionel has other assets such as the right to receive royalty payments relating to the manufacture of toy trains.

Lionel's most important asset and the subject of this proceeding is its ownership of 82 percent of the common stock of Dale, a corporation engaged in the manufacture of electronic components. Dale is not a party to the Lionel bankruptcy proceeding. Public investors own the remaining 18 percent of Dale's common stock, which is listed on the American Stock Exchange. Its balance sheet reflects assets and liabilities as of March 31, 1983 of $57.8 million and $29.8 million, respectively, resulting in shareholders equity of approximately $28.0 million. Lionel's stock investment in Dale represents approximately 34 percent of Lionel's consolidated assets, and its interest in Dale is Lionel's most valuable single asset. Unlike Lionel's toy retailing operation, Dale is profitable. For the same two-year period ending in December 1982 during which Lionel had incurred its substantial losses, Dale had an aggregate operating profit of $18.8 million.

On June 14, 1983 Lionel filed an application under section 363(b) seeking bankruptcy court authorization to sell its 82 percent interest in Dale to Acme-Cleveland Corporation for $43 million in cash. Four days later the debtor filed a plan of reorganization conditioned upon a sale of Dale with the proceeds to be distributed to creditors. Certain issues of the reorganization remain unresolved, and negotiations are continuing; however, a solicitation of votes on the plan has not yet begun. On September 7, 1983, following the Securities and Exchange Commission's July 15 filing of objections to the sale, Bankruptcy Judge Ryan held a hearing on Lionel's application. At the hearing, Peabody emerged as the successful of three bidders with an offer of $50 million for Lionel's interest in Dale.

The Chief Executive Officer of Lionel and a Vice-President of Salomon Brothers were the only witnesses produced and both testified in support of the application. Their testimony established that while the price paid for the stock was "fair," Dale is not an asset "that is wasting away in any sense." Lionel's Chief Executive Officer stated that there was no reason why the sale of Dale stock could not be accomplished as part of the reorganization plan, and that the sole reason for Lionel's application to sell was the Creditors' Committee's insistence upon it. The creditors wanted to turn this asset of Lionel into a "pot of cash," to provide the bulk of the $70 million required to repay creditors under the proposed plan of reorganization.

In confirming the sale, Judge Ryan made no formal findings of fact. He simply noted that cause to sell was sufficiently shown by the Creditors' Committee's insistence upon it. Judge Ryan further found cause — presumably from long experience — based upon his own opinion that a present failure to confirm would set the entire reorganization process back a year or longer while the parties attempted to restructure it.

The Committee of Equity Security Holders, statutory representatives of the 10,000 public shareholders of Lionel, appealed this order claiming that the sale, prior to approval of a reorganization plan, deprives the equity holders of the Bankruptcy Code's safeguards of disclosure, solicitation and acceptance and divests the debtor of a dominant and profitable asset which could serve as a cornerstone for a sound plan. The SEC also appeared and objected to the sale in the bankruptcy court and supports the Equity Committee's appeal, claiming that approval of the sale side-steps the Code's requirement for informed suffrage which is at the heart of Chapter 11.

The Creditors' Committee favors the sale because it believes it is in the best interests of Lionel and because the sale is expressly authorized by §363(b) of the Code. Lionel tells us that its ownership of Dale, a nonoperating asset, is held for investment purposes only and that its sale will provide the estate with the large block of the cash needed to fund its plan of reorganization.

From the oral arguments and briefs we gather that the Equity Committee believes that Chapter 11 has cleared the reorganization field of major pre-plan sales — somewhat like the way Minerva routed Mars — relegating §363(b) to be used only in emergencies. The Creditors' Committee counters that a bankruptcy judge should have absolute freedom under §363(b) to do as he thinks best. Neither of these arguments is wholly persuasive. Here, as in so many similar cases, we must avoid the extremes, for the policies underlying the Bankruptcy Reform Act of 1978 support a middle ground — one which gives the bankruptcy judge considerable discretion yet requires him to articulate sound business justifications for his decisions.

II.   DISCUSSION

The issue now before this Court is to what extent Chapter 11 permits a bankruptcy judge to authorize the sale of an important asset of the bankrupt's estate, out of the ordinary course of business and prior to acceptance and outside of any plan of reorganization. Section 363(b), the focal point of our analysis, provides that "[t]he trustee, after notice and a hearing, may use, sell, or lease, other than in the ordinary course of business, property of the estate." 11 U.S.C. §363(b) (Supp. V 1981).

On its face, section 363(b) appears to permit disposition of any property of the estate of a corporate debtor without resort to the statutory safeguards embodied in Chapter 11 of the Bankruptcy Code, 11 U.S.C. §1101 et seq. (Supp. V 1981). Yet, analysis of the statute's history and over seven decades of case law convinces us that such a literal reading of section 363(b) would unnecessarily violate the congressional scheme for corporate reorganizations. . . .

Section 116(3) of the 1938 Act, which was the immediate predecessor of §363(b), was originally enacted as section 77B(c) in 1937. Section 116(3) provided:

> Upon the approval of a petition, the judge may, in addition to the jurisdiction, powers and duties hereinabove and elsewhere in this chapter conferred and imposed upon him and the court . . . (3) authorize a receiver or a trustee or a debtor in possession, upon such notice as the judge may prescribe and upon cause shown, to lease or sell any property of the debtor, whether real or personal, upon such terms and conditions as the judge may approve.

This section applied in Chapter X proceedings, and a similar provision, §313(2), pertained to Chapter XI cases. Thus, when reorganization became part of the bankruptcy law, the long established administrative powers of the court to sell a debtor's property prior to adjudication were extended to cover reorganizations with a debtor in possession under Chapter XI pursuant to §313(2), 11 U.S.C. §§701 et seq., as well as a trustee in control under Chapter X pursuant to §116(3), 11 U.S.C. §§501 et seq. These sections, as their predecessors, were designed to handle leases or sales required during the time lag between the filing of a petition for reorganization and the date when the plan was approved.

The Rules of Bankruptcy Procedure applicable in Chapters X and XI, the Act's reorganization procedures, provided for a sale of all or part of a bankrupt's property after application to the court and "upon cause shown." Rules 10-607(b), 11-54. Despite the provisions of this Rule, the "perishable" concept, expressed in the view that a pre-confirmation or pre-adjudication sale was the exception and not the rule, persisted. As one commentator stated, "[o]rdinarily, in the absence of perishable goods, or depreciation of assets, or actual jeopardy of the estate, a sale will not be ordered, particularly prior to adjudication." 1 Collier on Bankruptcy ¶2.28(3) (14th ed. 1978) (footnotes omitted). . . .

[Courts have recently] upheld sales prior to plan approval under the Bankruptcy Act where the bankruptcy court outlined the circumstances in its findings of fact indicating why the sale was in the best interest of the estate. E.g., In re Equity Funding Corporation of America, 492 F.2d 793, 794 (9th Cir. 1974), cert. denied, 419 U.S. 964, 95 S. Ct. 224, 42 L. Ed.2d 178 (1974) (finding of fact that because market value of asset was likely to deteriorate substantially in the near future, sale was in the estate's best interests); In re Dania Corporation, 400 F.2d 833, 835-837 (5th Cir. 1968), cert. denied, 393 U.S. 1118, 89 S. Ct. 994, 22 L. Ed.2d 122 (1969) (upholding sale of stock representing debtor's major asset where its value was rapidly deteriorating causing the reorganizing estate to diminish); In re Marathon Foundry and Machine Co., 228 F.2d 594 (7th Cir. 1955) (heavy interest charges justified sale of stock which had been pledged to secure loan). In essence, these cases evidence the continuing vitality under the old law of an "emergency" or "perishability" standard. As we shall see, the new Bankruptcy Code no longer requires such strict limitations on a bankruptcy judge's authority to order disposition of the estate's property; nevertheless, it does not go so far as to eliminate all constraints on that judge's discretion. . . .

Section 363(b) of the Code seems on its face to confer upon the bankruptcy judge virtually unfettered discretion to authorize the use, sale or lease, other than in the ordinary course of business, of property of the estate. Of course, the statute requires that notice be given and a hearing conducted, but [no] reference is made to an "emergency" or "perishability" requirement nor is there an indication that a debtor in possession or trustee contemplating sale must show "cause." Thus, the language of §363(b) clearly is different from the terms of its statutory predecessors. And, while Congress never expressly stated why it abandoned the "upon cause shown" terminology of §116(3), arguably that omission permits easier access to §363(b). See In re Brookfield Clothes, Inc., 31 B.R. 978, 984 (S.D.N.Y. 1983). Various policy considerations lend some support to this view.

First and foremost is the notion that a bankruptcy judge must not be shackled with unnecessarily rigid rules when exercising the undoubtedly broad administrative power granted him under the Code. As Justice Holmes once said in a different context, "[s]ome play must be allowed for the joints of the machine. . . ." Missouri, Kansas & Texas Ry. Co. v. May, 194 U.S. 267, 270, 24 S. Ct. 638, 639, 48 L. Ed. 971 (1904). To further the purposes of Chapter 11 reorganization, a bankruptcy judge must have substantial freedom to tailor his orders to meet differing circumstances. This is exactly the result a liberal reading of §363(b) will achieve.

Support for this policy is found in the rationale underlying a number of earlier cases that had applied §116(3) of the Act. In particular, this Court's decision in [In re Sire Plan, Inc., 332 F.2d 497 (2d Cir. 1964)] was not hinged on an "emergency" or "perishability" concept. Lip service was paid to the argument that a partially constructed building is a "wasting asset"; but the real justification for authorizing the sale was the belief that the property's value depended on whether a hotel could be built in time for the World's Fair and that an advantageous sale after the opening of the World's Fair seemed unlikely. Thus, the reason was not solely that a steel skeleton was deteriorating, but rather that a good business opportunity was presently available, so long as the parties could act quickly. In such cases therefore the bankruptcy machinery should not straightjacket the bankruptcy judge so as to prevent him from doing what is best for the estate.

Just as we reject the requirement that only an emergency permits the use of §363(b), we also reject the view that §363(b) grants the bankruptcy judge carte blanche. Several reasons lead us to this conclusion: the statute requires notice and a hearing, and these procedural safeguards would be meaningless absent a further requirement that reasons be given for whatever determination is made; similarly, appellate review would effectively be precluded by an irreversible order; and, finally, such construction of §363(b) swallows up Chapter 11's safeguards. In fact, the legislative history surrounding the enactment of Chapter 11 makes evident Congress' concern with rights of equity interests as well as those of creditors.[3]

Chapter 5 of the House bill dealing with reorganizations states that the purpose of a business reorganization is to restructure a business' finances to enable it to operate productively, provide jobs for its employees, pay its creditors and produce a return for its stockholders. The automatic stay upon filing a petition prevents creditors from acting unilaterally or pressuring the debtor. Report of the Committee on the Judiciary, House of Representatives, to accompany H.R. 8200, H.R. Rep. No. 95-595, 95th Cong. 1st Sess. (1977) at 16, U.S. Code Cong. & Admin. News, 1978, p. 5787, reprinted in 2 Collier on Bankruptcy (appendix) (15th ed. 1983) (hereinafter H.R. Rep. No. 95-595). The plan of reorganization determines how much and in what form creditors will be paid, whether stockholders will continue to retain any interests, and in what form the business will continue. Requiring acceptance by a percentage of creditors and stockholders for confirmation forces negotiation among the debtor, its creditors and its stockholders. Id. at 221. A fair analysis of the House bill reveals that reorganization under the 1938 Chandler Act, though designed to protect creditors had, over the years, often worked to their detriment and to the detriment of shareholders as well. Id. at 221. The primary reason reorganization under the Act had not served well was that disclosure was minimal and reorganization under the Act was designed to deal with trade debt, not secured or public debt or equity. The present bill, it was believed, provides some form of investor protection to make it a "fairer reorganization vehicle." Id. at 226. The key to the reorganization Chapter, therefore, is disclosure. Id. To make disclosure effective, a provision was included that there be a disclosure statement and a hearing on

---

3. The Commission on the Bankruptcy Laws of the United States submitted a draft provision that would have permitted resort to section 363(b) in the absence of an emergency, even in the case of "all or substantially all the property of the estate." See Report of the Commission on the Bankruptcy Laws of the United States, H.R. Doc. No. 93-137, 93rd Cong., 1st Sess. (1973) at 239 (proposed §7-205 and accompanying explanatory note). Congress eventually deleted this provision without explanation, an action which we hardly consider dispositive of the issue before us here.

the adequacy of the information it contains. Id. at 227. The essential purpose served by disclosure is to ensure that public investors are not left entirely at the mercy of the debtor and its creditors. For that reason the Securities and Exchange Commission, for example, has an absolute right to appear and be heard on behalf of the public interest in an orderly securities market. Id. at 228.

The Senate hearings similarly reflect a concern as to how losses are to be apportioned between creditors and stockholders in the reorganization of a public company. S. Rep. No. 95-989, 95th Cong. 2d Sess. 9 (1978), reprinted in 3 Collier on Bankruptcy (appendix) (15th ed. 1983) (hereinafter S. Rep. No. 95-989). Noting that "the most vulnerable today are public investors," the Senate Judiciary Committee Report states that the bill is designed to counteract "the natural tendency of a debtor in distress to pacify large creditors with whom the debtor would expect to do business, at the expense of small and scattered public investors." S. Rep. No. 95-989 at 10, U.S. Code Cong. & Admin. News p. 5796. The Committee believed that investor protection is most critical when the public company is in such financial distress as to cause it to seek aid under the bankruptcy laws. Id. The need for this protection was plain. Reorganization under the 1938 Act was often unfair to public investors who lacked bargaining power, and these conditions continued. Echoing the conclusion of the House Committee, the Senate Committee believed that the bill would promote fairer and more equitable reorganizations granting to public investors the last chance to conserve values that corporate insolvency has jeopardized. Id. at 10-11.

III.   CONCLUSION

History surrounding the enactment in 1978 of current Chapter 11 and the logic underlying it buttress our conclusion that there must be some articulated business justification, other than appeasement of major creditors, for using, selling or leasing property out of the ordinary course of business before the bankruptcy judge may order such disposition under section 363(b).

The case law under section 363's statutory predecessors used terms like "perishable," "deteriorating," and "emergency" as guides in deciding whether a debtor's property could be sold outside the ordinary course of business. The use of such words persisted long after their omission from newer statutes and rules. The administrative power to sell or lease property in a reorganization continued to be the exception, not the rule. Collier on Bankruptcy ¶2.28(b) (supra). In enacting the 1978 Code Congress was aware of existing case law and clearly indicated as one of its purposes that equity interests have a greater voice in reorganization plans — hence, the safeguards of disclosure, voting, acceptance and confirmation in present Chapter 11.

Resolving the apparent conflict between Chapter 11 and §363(b) does not require an all or nothing approach. Every sale under §363(b) does not automatically short-circuit or side-step Chapter 11; nor are these two statutory provisions to be read as mutually exclusive. Instead, if a bankruptcy judge is to administer a business reorganization successfully under the Code, then—like the related yet independent tasks performed in modern production techniques to ensure good results—some play for the operation of both §363(b) and Chapter 11 must be allowed for.

The rule we adopt requires that a judge determining a §363(b) application expressly find from the evidence presented before him at the hearing a good business reason to grant such an application. In this case the only reason advanced for granting the request to sell Lionel's 82 percent stock interest in Dale was the Creditors' Committee's insistence on it. Such is insufficient as a matter of fact because it is not a sound business reason and insufficient as a matter of law because it ignores the equity interests required to be weighed and considered under Chapter 11. The court also expressed its concern that a present failure to approve the sale would result in a long delay. As the Supreme Court has noted, it is easy to sympathize with the desire of a bankruptcy court to expedite bankruptcy reorganization proceedings for they are frequently protracted. "The need for expedition, however, is not a justification for abandoning proper standards." Protective Committee for Independent Stockholders of TMT Trailer Ferry, Inc. v. Anderson, 390 U.S. 414, 450, 88 S. Ct. 1157, 1176, 20 L. Ed. 2d 1(1968). Thus, the approval of the sale of Lionel's 82 percent interest in Dale was an abuse of the trial court's discretion.

In fashioning its findings, a bankruptcy judge must not blindly follow the hue and cry of the most vocal special interest groups; rather, he should consider all salient factors pertaining to the proceeding and, accordingly, act to further the diverse interests of the debtor, creditors and equity holders, alike. He might, for example, look to such relevant factors as the proportionate value of the asset to the estate as a whole, the amount of elapsed time since the filing, the likelihood that a plan of reorganization will be proposed and confirmed in the near future, the effect of the proposed disposition on future plans of reorganization, the proceeds to be obtained from the disposition vis-a-vis any appraisals of the property, which of the alternatives of use, sale or lease the proposal envisions and, most importantly perhaps, whether the asset is increasing or decreasing in value. This list is not intended to be exclusive, but merely to provide guidance to the bankruptcy judge.

Finally, we must consider whether appellants opposing the sale produced evidence before the bankruptcy court that such sale was not justified. While a debtor applying under §363(b) carries the burden of demonstrating that a use, sale or lease out of the ordinary course of business will aid the debtor's reorganization, an objectant, such as the Equity Committee here, is required to produce some evidence respecting its objections. Appellants made three objections below: First, the sale was premature because Dale is not a wasting asset and there is no emergency; second, there was no justifiable cause present since Dale, if anything, is improving; and third, the price was inadequate. No proof was required as to the first objection because it was stipulated as conceded. The second and third objections are interrelated. Following Judge Ryan's suggestion that objections could as a practical matter be developed on cross-examination, Equity's counsel elicited testimony from the financial expert produced by Lionel that Dale is less subject than other companies to wide market fluctuations. The same witness also conceded that he knew of no reason why those interested in Dale's stock at the September 7, 1983 hearing would not be just as interested six months from then.[4] The only other witness who testified was the Chief Executive Officer of Lionel, who stated that it was only at the insistence of the Creditors' Committee that Dale stock was being sold and that Lionel "would very much like to retain its interest in Dale." These uncontroverted statements of the two witnesses elicited by the Equity Committee on cross-examination were sufficient proof to support its objections to the present sale of Dale because this evidence demonstrated that there was no good business reason for the present sale. Hence, appellants satisfied their burden.

Accordingly, the order appealed from is reversed and the matter remanded to the district court with directions to remand to the bankruptcy court for further proceedings consistent with this opinion.

WINTER, Circuit Judge, dissenting:
In order to expedite the decision in this matter, I set forth my dissenting views in summary fashion.

The following facts are undisputed as the record presently stands: (i) Lionel sought a buyer for the Dale stock willing to condition its purchase upon confirmation of a reorganization plan. It was unsuccessful since, in the words of the bankruptcy judge "the confirmation of any plan is usually somewhat iffy," and few purchasers are willing to commit upwards of $50 million for an extended period without a contract binding on the other party; (ii) every feasible reorganization plan contemplates the sale of the Dale stock for cash; (iii) a reorganization plan may be approved fairly soon if the Dale stock is sold now. If the sale is prohibited, renewed negotiations between the creditors and the equity holders will be necessary, and the submission of a plan, if any, will be put off well into the future; and (iv) the Dale stock can be sold now at or near the same price as it can be sold later.

The effect of the present decision is thus to leave the debtor in possession powerless as a legal matter to sell the Dale stock outside a reorganization plan and unable as an economic matter to sell it within one. This, of course, pleases the equity holders who, having introduced no evidence

---

4. As noted, the bidding for Dale started with a $43 million offer from Acme-Cleveland and has since jumped to $50 million. There is no indication that this trend will reverse itself.

demonstrating a disadvantage to the bankrupt estate from the sale of the Dale stock, are now given a veto over it to be used as leverage in negotiating a better deal for themselves in a reorganization.

The likely results of today's decision are twofold: (i) The creditors will at some point during the renewed protracted negotiations refuse to extend more credit to Lionel, thus thwarting a reorganization entirely; and (ii) notwithstanding the majority decision, the Dale stock will be sold under Section 363(b) for exactly the same reasons offered in support of the present proposed sale. However, the ultimate reorganization plan will be more favorable to the equity holders, and they will not veto the sale.

It seems reasonably obvious that result (i) is something that the statutory provisions governing reorganizations, including Section 363(b), are designed to avoid. Result (ii) not only is contrary to the purpose of the reorganization provisions in causing delay and further economic risk but also suffers from the legal infirmity which led the majority to reject the proposed sale, the only difference between the two sales being the agreement of the equity holders.

The equity holders offered no evidence whatsoever that the sale of Dale now will harm Lionel or that Dale can in fact be sold at a reasonable price as part of a reorganization plan. The courts below were quite right in not treating their arguments seriously for they are the legal equivalent of the "Hail Mary pass" in football.[1]

NOTE ON *LIONEL*

The Second Circuit decided that the equityholders should be able to prevent the sale of the Dale stock outside of a formal reorganization plan unless there was a business reason for selling it sooner. But it could have reached the opposite conclusion — reached by Judge Winter in dissent — just as easily: The equityholders should be able to prevent a sale of assets

---

1. With due respect to my colleagues, the problem of statutory interpretation is entirely straightforward and not deserving of a lengthy exegesis into legal history. The language of Section 363(b) is about as plain as it could be and surely does not permit a judicial grafting of stringent conditions on the power of trustees. As for its legislative history, the words "upon cause shown" were dropped by the Congress from the predecessor to Section 363(b) in 1978, a signal clearly dictating that Congress meant what it said.

The equity holders argue that Chapter 11's provisions for disclosure, hearing and a vote before confirmation of a reorganization plan stringently limit the authority of trustees under 11 U.S.C. §363(b). However, a reorganization plan affects the rights of the parties as well as the disposition of assets, and there is no inconsistency in allowing the disposition of property outside the confirmation proceedings. Arguably, some transactions proposed under Section 363(b) would, if carried out, eliminate a number of options available for reorganization plans and thereby pre-ordain a particular kind of plan or preclude a reorganization entirely. In such a case, a colorable claim can be made for a limitation on a trustee's power under Section 363(b) narrowly tailored to prevent such a result in order to effectuate the core purposes of Chapter 11. However, it is not disputed that in the present case the final reorganization plan will include a sale of Dale stock. A sale now thus does not preclude any feasible reorganization plan.

only if there was a reason for selling it later. The tension in the case is between the senior owners' right to sell assets without engaging in costly procedures and the junior owners' right to insist upon procedures that protect their interests.

In principle, one can resolve the kind of dispute in *Lionel* by positing what the parties would have bargained for before the fact. When owners are diverse, every owner receives a package of procedural and substantive rights. The shareholders bargain for whatever is left after all others are paid off, but if transaction costs were low enough, they also would insist upon procedures to protect their rights and prevent senior owners from taking more than they bargained for. The crucial question in *Lionel* is whether, in principle, shareholders and senior creditors would prefer the costs of additional procedures (such as the notification and valuation rules embodied in Chapter 11) to the uncertainty of less orchestrated sale of assets.

In his dissent, Judge Winter implies that the shareholders in *Lionel* were simply holding the senior claimants up for more money, even though the debtor was insolvent and their residual claims on the day of reckoning were worthless. But the general resolution of this conflict between owners should not turn on the facts of a particular case. Moreover, the shareholders' willingness to exchange their procedural rights for cash may mean simply that elaborate procedures are unnecessary in this particular case, not that they are always superfluous or would not be bargained for if explicit bargaining among owners had taken place.

Deciding whether senior claimants should be able to conduct a sale such as was proposed in this case requires a resolution of many antecedent issues as well. For example, the procedures the shareholders insist upon in this case may seem unnecessary in *Lionel,* not because shareholders are given too many rights in cases that properly belong in Chapter 11, but because Lionel itself does not belong in Chapter 11. Given the facts of this case, would it be more appropriate to have a bankruptcy rule requiring publicly held corporations whose primary assets were marketable securities to file under Chapter 7 if they were to use bankruptcy at all? Note also that the senior claimants' desire to dispose of a large asset of a debtor by using §363 may reflect the ineffectiveness of creditor remedies outside of bankruptcy. For example, the ability of junior creditors to subject senior creditors' remedies outside of bankruptcy to a fraudulent conveyance attack inside of bankruptcy makes it more likely that such creditors will resort to bankruptcy to avoid the attack, even if there is no other reason to have a collective proceeding.

In this case Lionel later received an offer of $55 million for Dale. Does this fact change your analysis of the problem? Do the shareholders want to prevent a sale now simply because the stock price might go up? Would Lionel be able to use the proceeds of the sale in its operations? Would Lionel have to provide adequate protection?

B. ARRIVING AT A PLAN OF REORGANIZATION

1. Parties in the Process

NOTE ON TRUSTEES AND CREDITORS' COMMITTEES

Creditors' Committees. As soon as practicable after the commencement of a Chapter 11 case, the bankruptcy court must appoint a creditors' committee. §1102(a)(1). This committee, which represents all creditors holding unsecured claims, is "ordinarily" composed of the seven largest unsecured creditors willing to serve on the committee. If a committee organized by such creditors outside of bankruptcy was "fairly chosen and is representative of the different kinds of claims to be represented," the court may appoint the members of that committee. §1102(b)(1). The committee's composition or size can be changed "if the membership of such committee is not representative of the different kinds of claims or interests to be represented." §1102(c). See In re Schatz Federal Bearings Co., 5 Bankr. 543 (Bankr. S.D.N.Y. 1980) (allowing a union representing employees to serve on creditors' committee, where employees had unfunded pension benefit claims). Additional committees, representing equity interests or other kinds of creditors, may be appointed "if necessary to assure adequate representation of creditors or of equity security holders." §1102(a)(2).

The committee's powers and duties are set forth in §1103, although their real "power" comes less from §1103 than from the fact that the creditors' committee is well positioned to negotiate with the debtor over the shape of a plan of reorganization. For that reason, many important issues in a Chapter 11 case will be reviewed by the creditors' committee. It normally will make the initial decision whether to ask the court to order liquidation or appointment of a trustee (although it is not the only entity that can do so). The committee may hire professionals who may be compensated out of the estate's assets, §§1103(a); 328; 503. (Members of the creditors' committee, however, may not obtain reimbursement of *their* costs from the assets of the estate. In re Major Dynamics, 16 Bankr. 279 (Bankr. S.D. Calif. 1981).) The committee may conduct its own investigation of the debtor. Under §1121(c), it may propose its own plan of reorganization (although, again, it is not the only entity that can). Various decisions authorize creditors' committees to initiate proceedings to recover preferences (Committee of Unsecured Creditors v. Monsour Medical Center, 5 Bankr. 715 (Bankr. W.D. Pa. 1980)), to prosecute antitrust claims (Liberal Market, Inc. v. Malone & Hyde, Inc., 14 Bankr. 685 (Bankr. S.D. Ohio 1981)), and to intervene in adversary proceedings (Official Unsecured Creditors' Committee v. Michaels, 689 F.2d 445 (3rd Cir.

1982)). See generally Meir and Brown, Representing Creditors' Committees Under Chapter 11 of the Bankruptcy Code, 56 Am. Bankr. L.J. 217 (1982).

Trustees. Unlike Chapter X of the old Bankruptcy Act, where appointment of a trustee was mandatory if the debtor's liquidated and non-contingent indebtedness exceeded $250,000, Chapter 11 contains a flexible standard for determining when a trustee should be appointed. §1104. If a trustee is appointed, his duties are set forth in §1106. If no trustee is appointed, the debtor, as "debtor in possession," has most of the substantive powers of a trustee. §1107. If the bankruptcy court decides not to appoint a trustee, it must, on request of a party in interest, appoint an examiner (§1104(b)) if (a) "such appointment is in the interests of creditors, any equity security holders, and other interests of the estate" or (b) "the debtor's fixed, liquidated, unsecured debts, other than debts for goods, services, or taxes, or owing to an insider, exceed $5,000,000." The powers of an examiner are those of a trustee under §1106(a)(3) and (4), plus whatever other duties of a trustee the court orders the debtor in possession not to perform. §1106(b).

When should the court order the appointment of a trustee? Section 1104(a) specifies it should be done either "for cause," such as "fraud, dishonesty, incompetence, or gross mismanagement," or if it is "in the interests of creditors, any equity security holders, and other interests of the estate." How should this be interpreted? In re Anchorage Boat Sales, 4 Bankr. 635 (Bankr. E.D.N.Y. 1980), drew the following conclusion:

> As enacted, subsection (a)(2) provides a flexible standard for the appointment of a trustee. . . . The appointment of a trustee in a chapter 11 case is an extraordinary remedy, and one which may impose a substantial financial burden on a hard pressed debtor seeking relief under the Bankruptcy Code. . . . In many cases, the appointment of a trustee may preclude an effective reorganization because of the substantial administrative expenses which must be paid by the debtor's estate. Accordingly, under subsection (a)(2), the Court may utilize its broad equity powers to engage in a cost-benefit analysis in order to determine whether the appointment of a trustee would be in the interests of creditors, equity security holders, and other interests of the estate. . . .
>
> Under subsection (a)(1), the Court's discretionary powers are more circumscribed. Here, the Court's discretion is limited to a determination of whether "cause" exists for such appointment, and such "cause" must be in the nature of "fraud, dishonesty, incompetence, or gross mismanagement" of the debtor by current management, either before or after the commencement of the case. Since one would expect to find some degree of incompetence or mismanagement in most businesses which have been forced to seek the protections of chapter 11, the Court must find something more aggravated than simple mismanagement in order to appoint a trustee.

See generally In re L.S. Good & Co., 8 Bankr. 312 (Bankr. N.D.W.Va. 1980); In re Liberal Market, 11 Bankr. 742 (Bankr. S.D. Ohio 1981).

2.   Formulating a Plan of Reorganization

The main business of a reorganization under Chapter 11 is the process of *formulating* a plan and then getting it *accepted* by the various groups "interested" in the debtor's business. Section 1121 places the first strategic chip of the Chapter 11 bargaining process in the hands of the debtor, for it specifies who can propose a plan of reorganization. While §1121 allows any "party in interest" to file a plan of reorganization, it is important to note that only the debtor may file a plan for the first 120 days *unless* a trustee has been appointed under §1104 or the court, for cause, has reduced that period under §1121(c). Moreover, if the debtor in fact proposes a plan within that 120 days, the exclusive period during which other parties cannot file plans is extended to 180 days, to give the debtor time to see if it can garner acceptances for its plan. These timetables are subject to extension or reduction under §1121(c), and extensions are frequently granted in larger corporate reorganizations. The rationale for the exclusive period — and for the limitation on it — is explained in the legislative history, H.R. Rep. No. 95-595, at 231-232:

> Chapter XI gives the debtor the exclusive right to propose a plan. Creditors are excluded. The exclusive right gives the debtor undue bargaining leverage, because by delay he can force a settlement out of otherwise unwilling creditors, and they have little recourse except to move for conversion of the case to Chapter X. That is contrary to their interests, as it is to the debtor's, and thus is rarely done. The debtor is in full control, often to the unfair disadvantage of the creditors.
>
> Proposed Chapter 11 recognizes the need for the debtor to remain in control to some degree, or else debtors will avoid the reorganization provisions in the bill until it would be too late for them to be an effective remedy. At the same time, the bill recognizes the legitimate interests of creditors, whose money is in the enterprise as much as the debtor's, to have a say in the future of the company. The bill gives the debtor an exclusive right to propose a plan for 120 days. In most cases, 120 days will give the debtor adequate time to negotiate a settlement, without unduly delaying creditors. The court is given the power, though, to increase or reduce the 120-day period depending on the circumstances of the case. For example, if an unusually large company were to seek reorganization under Chapter 11, the court would probably need to extend the time in order to allow the debtor to reach an agreement. If, on the other hand, a debtor delayed in arriving at an agreement, the court could shorten the period and permit creditors to formulate and propose a reorganization plan.

See In re Tony Downs Foods Co., 34 Bankr. 405 (Bankr. D. Minn. 1983) ("Congress attempted to strike a careful balance in this section which was intended to put a certain amount of pressure on the debtor"); In re Lake in the Woods, 10 Bankr. 338 (E.D. Mich. 1981) ("extensions are impermissible if they are for the purpose of allowing the debtor to prolong reorganization while pressuring a creditor to accede to its point of view on an issue in dispute").

The following represents a fairly typical plan of reorganization.

INFOREX, INC. PLAN OF REORGANIZATION

UNITED STATES BANKRUPTCY COURT
FOR THE DISTRICT OF MASSACHUSETTS

In re: INFOREX, INC. INFOREX INTERNATIONAL SALES CORP. *Debtors*	Chapter 11 Cases Nos. 79-01966-L 79-01965-L

SECOND AMENDED PLAN OF REORGANIZATION

Inforex, Inc. ("Inforex") and its wholly-owned subsidiary, Inforex International Sales Corp. ("DISC"), the above-named Debtors, whose estates have been consolidated pursuant to an order of the Bankruptcy Court dated April 2, 1980 (the "Consolidation Order") for the purpose of proposing this second amended plan, propose, in complete substitution for, and amendment of, their plan filed on February 20, 1980, and their amended plan filed on June 26, 1980, the following consolidated Second Amended Plan of Reorganization (the "Plan") to their creditors and to the equity security holders of Inforex, pursuant to Section 1121(a) of Chapter 11 of the Bankruptcy Code (11 U.S.C. §§101 et seq.) (the "Bankruptcy Code"). This Plan is based upon and subject to a Stock Exchange Agreement among Inforex, Inc. ("Inforex"), Datapoint Corporation ("Datapoint") and Flex, Incorporated ("Flex"), all of which are Delaware corporations, dated as of June 10, 1980 (the "Acquisition Agreement"), (a copy of which has been filed with the Bankruptcy Court and is available upon written request to Inforex), whereby, subject to certain conditions precedent set forth in the Acquisition Agreement, Flex will acquire all of the outstanding stock of Inforex.

ARTICLE I. ADMINISTRATIVE EXPENSES AND PRIORITY CLAIMS

All claims for administrative expenses (including, without limitation, attorneys', accounting, printing, examiner and trustees' fees) and claims entitled to priority in accordance with Section 507(a) of the Bankruptcy Code (11 U.S.C. §507(a)), as scheduled or filed and allowed, shall be paid in full in cash on the first business day following the last day on which an appeal from an order of the Bankruptcy Court confirming this Plan may be taken under applicable law, provided that no stay of the confirmation order is then in effect (the "Plan Distribution Date"), or upon entry of an order by the Bankruptcy Court allowing such claim, whichever shall be later, or in accordance with such terms as may be agreed upon by the Debtors and each administration or priority creditor. All trade and service debts and obligations incurred in the normal course of business by the Debtors during these proceedings shall be paid when due in the ordinary course of business.

ARTICLE II. DESIGNATION OF CLASSES OF CLAIMS AND INTERESTS

All claims, as defined in Section 101(4) of the Bankruptcy Code (11 U.S.C. §101(4)), against the Debtors, of whatever nature, whether or not scheduled, liquidated or unliquidated, absolute or contingent, including all claims arising from the rejection of executory contracts and unexercised warrants and options to purchase shares of common stock, $.25 par value, of Inforex (the "Inforex Common Stock") (collectively, the "Claim(s)"), and all interests arising from the ownership of Inforex Common Stock, shall be bound by the provisions of this Plan and are hereby classified as follows:

Class One: All Claims of The First National Bank of Chicago ("Chicago").

Class Two: All Claims of the Industrial National Bank of Rhode Island ("Industrial").

Class Three: All Claims of Manufacturers Hanover Leasing Corporation ("Manufacturers Hanover").

Class Four: All Claims of Wells Fargo Leasing Corporation ("Wells Fargo").

Class Five: All Claims of New England Merchants Funding Corporation ("New England Merchants").

Class Six: All Claims of Citytrust ("Citytrust").

Class Seven: All Claims of Knox Leasing Corporation and its parent Lease Financing Corporation ("Knox").

Class Eight: All Claims of Citibank, N.A. ("Citibank").

(The Claims of Classes One through Eight are secured by various security and/or ownership interests in assets of, or claimed by, the Debtors.)

Class Nine: All Claims of United States Portfolio Leasing Corp. ("U.S. Leasing").

Class Ten: All Claims of the two District of Columbia limited partnerships, Spence Associates ("Spence") and Warwick Associates ("Warwick").

Class Eleven: All Claims arising from the $20,000,000 in principal amount of Inforex' 10⅝% Subordinated Debentures due May 1, 1998, and the $80,000 in principal amount of Inforex' 10½% Subordinated Debentures due January 2, 1982 (the "Debenture Claims").

Class Twelve: All other Claims (including Claims based upon the rejection of executory contracts, and based upon termination of all unexercised warrants and options to purchase Inforex Common Stock) not included in one of the other classes, including Class Thirteen (the "Unsecured Claims").

Class Thirteen: All holders of shares of Inforex Common Stock at 5:00 P.M., Eastern Time, on the day immediately preceding the Plan Distribution Date (the "Equity Security Interests").

Any holder of a claim or interest in Classes One through Thirteen who fails to object in writing to the classifications provided in this Plan, filed with the Bankruptcy Court and served upon the Debtors' counsel at least forty-eight (48) hours prior to the hearing on confirmation of the Plan, shall be deemed to have accepted such classifications and to be bound thereby.

ARTICLE III.   PROVISIONS FOR ALTERATION AND
                MODIFICATION OF THE RIGHTS OF
                THE SECURED CLAIMS IN CLASSES
                ONE THROUGH SEVEN

All Claims in Classes One through Seven (including any administrative Claim arising from Inforex' note to the claimants in Classes One through Nine in the principal amount of $6,182,000 dated December 3, 1979, issued pursuant to an order of the Bankruptcy Court dated December 3, 1979) shall be fully satisfied and discharged by the execution and delivery of an unsecured note or notes of Inforex aggregating $34,300,000 in principal amount (the "Financing Group Notes"). The Financing Group Notes will be guaranteed by Datapoint, will not bear interest, and will be payable in twenty-one quarterly installments beginning on September 30, 1980. The aggregate quarterly installment under all Financing

Group Notes will be in the amount of $1,633,333.33 and will be divided among the holders of Claims in Classes One through Seven on a non pro rata basis in accordance with an allocation agreement among such classes which will be filed with the Bankruptcy Court prior to confirmation of this Plan.

If and to the extent that, on the Plan Distribution Date, all Claims for administrative expenses and Claims entitled to priority, as described in ARTICLE 1 of this Plan, aggregate less than $1,500,000, the difference between such Claims and $1,500,000 will be distributed to the holders of Claims in Classes One through Seven. Any such amount will be distributed on the Plan Distribution Date, in addition to delivery of the Financing Group Notes, and will be allocated among the claimants in Classes One through Seven in accordance with the allocation agreement referred to above. Inforex believes that such administrative and priority Claims will exceed $1,500,000, and that therefore no additional amounts will be distributed to the holders of Claims in Classes One through Seven.

Upon delivery of the Financing Group Notes to the Class One through Seven claimants, all security and/or ownership interests claimed by Classes One through Seven in the assets of, or claimed by, the Debtors will be terminated and/or conveyed to the Debtors.

ARTICLE IV. PROVISIONS FOR ALTERATION AND MODIFICATION OF THE RIGHTS OF CLASS ELEVEN DEBENTURE CLAIMS

Each holder of a Class Eleven Debenture Claim shall receive in full settlement and satisfaction of his Debenture Claim the following consideration for each $1,000 in principal amount of Debenture Claim:

a) Inforex' unsecured note in a principal amount equal to 100% of the principal amount of the Debenture (all claims for accrued but unpaid interest shall be deemed waived by each Debenture holder); the note will not bear interest, will be due and payable in one installment eight and one-half ($8\frac{1}{2}$) years after the Plan Distribution Date and will not be guaranteed by Datapoint (but see ARTICLE IX, paragraph 7 below) (the "Debenture Notes"); and

b) One share of Datapoint Common Stock, $.25 par value ("Datapoint Common Stock") for every $1,000 in principal amount of the Debenture Notes delivered to a Class Eleven claimant; *provided* that if the market value (as defined below) of Datapoint Common Stock is less than $45 or more than $55 per share, each Class Eleven claimant will receive Datapoint Common Stock with a market value of $45 or $55, as the case may be, per $1,000 of Debenture Notes delivered to a Class Eleven claimant. "Market value" will be based on the average closing sales price of Datapoint Common Stock as reported in The Wall Street Journal (S.W. Edition) during the ten consecutive trading days beginning with the twentieth trading day preceding the Plan Distribution Date. For administrative convenience, claimants who would receive a fractional share or less than ten shares of Datapoint Common Stock will be paid in cash the market value thereof.

The Debenture Notes will be issued under an Indenture qualified under the Trust Indenture Act of 1939, as amended.

On the Plan Distribution Date, the Indenture dated as of May 1, 1978, between Inforex and State Street Bank and Trust Company, as trustee, relating to the 10⅜% Subordinated Debentures Due 1998 of Inforex shall be cancelled.

ARTICLE V.   PROVISIONS FOR ALTERATION AND MODIFICATION OF THE RIGHTS OF CLASS TWELVE UNSECURED CLAIMS

Each holder of a Class Twelve Unsecured Claim shall be paid in full satisfaction thereof in accordance with his election of one of the following options:

Option A:

For administrative convenience, each holder of Unsecured Claims aggregating $1,000 or less shall receive, and each holder of Unsecured Claims aggregating more than $1,000 who in writing reduces such Claims to $1,000 prior to confirmation may elect to receive, a cash payment equal to 30% of its allowed Unsecured Claims on the Plan Distribution Date or within 30 days of the allowance of its Claims, whichever is later.

Option B:

All other holders of Unsecured Claims aggregating more than $1,000 may make any one of the following elections:

Election 1:

26% of its allowed Unsecured Claims payable in cash on the Plan Distribution Date or upon the allowance of its Claims, whichever is later.

Election 2:

35% of its allowed Unsecured Claims payable 15% in cash on the Plan Distribution Date or upon the allowance of its Claims, whichever is later, and the balance thereafter in ten semi-annual installments of 2% each, payable by Inforex commencing six (6) months after the Plan Distribution Date (see also ARTICLE IX, paragraph 7 below). In the event that Inforex defaults in the payment, when due, of any of the ten semi-annual installments, the unpaid balance shall be accelerated and shall become due and payable immediately. Inforex shall pay all costs of collection (including reasonable attorneys' fees) incurred by the holder of any Claim electing treatment hereunder in connection with enforcement of such holder's right to payment.

Election 3:

Payment of its allowed Unsecured Claims in accordance with the treatment of the Class Eleven Debenture Claims described in ARTICLE IV above. The aggregate amount of all such Claims held by any Class Twelve claimant electing Debenture Claim treatment shall be deemed rounded down to the nearest $1,000, and the right to receive any distribution with respect to any amount in excess of such $1,000 shall be deemed to be waived.

In the event that no option or election is made in writing prior to confirmation, each holder of a Class Twelve Unsecured Claim will be deemed to have elected the cash option. Thus, all Unsecured Claims aggregating $1,000 or less will be paid in accordance with Option A and all Unsecured Claims aggregating more than $1,000 will be paid in accordance with Option B, Election 1.

ARTICLE VI. PROVISIONS FOR ALTERATION AND MODIFICATION OF THE RIGHTS OF CLASS THIRTEEN EQUITY SECURITY INTERESTS

Class Thirteen Equity Security Interest holders shall receive for each share of Inforex Common Stock held (which shall be deemed to be cancelled and exchanged on and as of the Plan Distribution Date for the following):

(a) $.50 in market value (determined as set forth in ARTICLE IV, paragraph (b) above) of Datapoint Common Stock on the Plan Distribution Date; and

(b) the contingent right to receive an amount equal to $4,789,977.50 divided by the aggregate number of shares of Inforex Common Stock held by Class Thirteen interests (approximately $1.43 per share), payable in cash or Datapoint Common Stock (determined as set forth below) one year from the Plan Distribution Date or within forty-five (45) days after the month in which Inforex has post-Plan Distribution Date cumulative consolidated gross revenue in excess of $50,000,000, whichever is later.

For purposes of the foregoing, the post-Plan Distribution Date cumulative consolidated gross revenue of Inforex will be determined by the management of Inforex based on the generally accepted accounting principles utilized by Datapoint on the Plan Distribution Date (including the assumptions and methods used by Datapoint to account for leases).

The additional payment to the Class Thirteen Equity Security Interests may be made either in cash or in Datapoint Common Stock, at the sole option of Datapoint. If such payment is made in Datapoint Common Stock, the market value of Datapoint Common Stock used to compute the number of shares payable will be the average closing sales price as reported in The Wall Street Journal (S.W. Edition) during the last ten trading days of the month in which the $50,000,000 cumulative consolidated revenue condition is met.

For administrative convenience, payments in cash (at market value determined in accordance with the preceding paragraph) will be made for any fractional share of Datapoint Common Stock and to persons who would receive less than ten shares of Datapoint Common Stock at the time of either payment to Class Thirteen claimants.

After confirmation of the Plan, holders of Class Thirteen Equity Security Interests will receive instructions regarding surrender of their certificates representing Inforex Common Stock and the issuance to them of certificates for Datapoint Common Stock.

ARTICLE VII.   PROVISIONS RESPECTING UNIMPAIRED CLASS EIGHT

Class Eight claimant, Citibank, which holds a secured guaranty of the Debtors, will retain the guaranty of the Debtors and will be granted a security interest in certain or all of the post-reorganization assets of the Debtors, but in no event will Citibank be impaired.

ARTICLE VIII.   PROVISIONS FOR ALTERATION AND MODIFICATION OF THE RIGHTS OF CLASSES NINE AND TEN

Class Nine claimant, U.S. Leasing, which has an ownership interest in certain Inforex equipment, will amend its agreements with Inforex to provide for terms for sharing the residual value of equipment (including subsequent rental of such equipment) and to convey title in such equipment to Inforex when a certain level of residual sharing derived from such equipment is reached.

Class Ten claimants, Spence and Warwick, which have ownership interests in certain Inforex equipment, resulting from sale and leaseback transactions, will amend their agreements with Inforex to reaffirm certain mutual obligations with respect to note payments to and lease payments by Inforex and to provide greater flexibility to Inforex to lease such equipment to its customers.

ARTICLE IX.   PROVISIONS FOR THE EXECUTION
OF THE PLAN WHICH MAY AFFECT,
ALTER OR MODIFY THE RIGHTS
OF ALL CLASSES

1. The Debtor shall retain all of its property.

2. Each holder of a Claim in Classes One through Seven shall terminate any security interest and reconvey any ownership interest which it may have in any assets of, or claimed by, the Debtors or any assets of Spence and Warwick.

3. Confirmation of this Plan shall constitute a settlement and release of all claims of the Debtors against the holders of Class One through Eight claims including without limitation any claim with respect to the $2,600,000 paid to such holders during the proceedings.

4. Confirmation of this Plan or any modification thereof shall constitute an order for substantive consolidation of Inforex and the DISC pursuant to the Consolidation Order.

5. The rights and benefits of subordination of the Debenture Claims held by the claimants in Classes One through Eight will be deemed waived and extinguished with respect to any Claim which is satisfied under this Plan.

6. In accordance with section 1123(a)(6) of the Bankruptcy Code (11 U.S.C. §1123(a)(6)), Inforex' Certificate of Incorporation, as amended to date, shall be deemed to prohibit the issuance of nonvoting equity securities. No provision is made with respect to distribution of power among other classes of securities because Inforex has only one class of equity securities.

7. Pursuant to the Acquisition Agreement, Datapoint will be secondarily liable for payment of the Debenture Notes and the semi-annual payments under ARTICLE V, Option B, Election 2 if and to the extent that, prior to payment in full by Inforex of such obligations, assets of Inforex (net of liabilities) are transferred or otherwise distributed by Inforex to Datapoint or to a subsidiary of Datapoint upon the dissolution or liquidation of Inforex, as a dividend by Inforex on its Common Stock or upon a similar distribution. In addition to the foregoing, Datapoint and Flex have informed Inforex that they will enter into an agreement prior to the Plan Distribution Date, pursuant to which Datapoint will agree to cause sufficient funds to be

made available to Inforex to pay all of the debts of Inforex, both
secured and unsecured, in a timely manner from the Plan Distribution Date until distribution of all amounts payable by Inforex under
this Plan.

8. In the event that the Acquisition Agreement is terminated by
any party thereto prior to the Plan Distribution Date, this Plan shall
be deemed to be withdrawn and rescinded.

ARTICLE X.   EXECUTORY CONTRACTS

A. The Debtors have rejected or hereby reject the executory
contracts and terminate the warrants and options listed in Exhibit A
hereto. Any person or entity injured by such rejection or termination
shall be deemed to hold an Unsecured Claim against the Debtor and,
within ten days following confirmation of the Plan, shall file a proof
of claim for any damages resulting therefrom or be forever barred
from asserting any Claim.

B. The Debtors reserve the right to apply to the Bankruptcy
Court at any time prior to confirmation of the Plan to reject any and
all contracts which are executory in whole or in part as provided in
Sections 365 and 1123 of the Bankruptcy Code (11 U.S.C. §§365
and 1123).

ARTICLE XI.   RETENTION OF JURISDICTION

The Court shall retain jurisdiction of these cases pursuant to the
provisions of Chapter 11 of the Bankruptcy Code, until the final
allowance or disallowance of all Claims affected by the Plan, and with
respect to the following matters:

A. To enable Inforex to consummate the Acquisition
Agreement and to resolve any disputes arising with respect
thereto;

B. To enable the Debtors to consummate any and all proceedings which they may bring prior to entry of the order of
confirmation to set aside liens or encumbrances, and to recover
any preferences, transfers, assets or damages to which they may
be entitled under applicable provisions of the Bankruptcy Code
or other federal, state or local law;

C. To adjudicate all controversies concerning the classification or allowance of any Claim or Equity Security Interest;

D. To enforce the payment of the Financing Group Notes,
the Debenture Notes and the installments under ARTICLE V,
Option B, Election 2;

E. To hear and determine all Claims arising from the rejection of any executory contracts, including leases, and from the

termination of warrants and options, and to consummate the rejection and termination thereof or with respect to any executory contracts, warrants or options as to which an application for rejection or termination is filed prior to entry of the order of confirmation;

F. To liquidate damages in connection with any disputed, contingent or unliquidated Claims;

G. To adjudicate all Claims to a security or ownership interest in any property of the Debtors or in any proceeds thereof;

H. To adjudicate all Claims or controversies arising out of any purchases, sales or contracts made or undertaken by the Debtors during the pendency of the proceedings;

I. To recover all assets and properties of the Debtors, wherever located; and

J. To make such orders as are necessary or appropriate to carry out the provisions of this Plan.

INFOREX, INC.
Inforex International Sales Corp.
by their attorneys

Frederick G. Fisher, Jr.
Paul P. Daley
Ellen B. Corenswet
HALE AND DORR
60 State Street
Boston, Massachusetts 02109

John T. Manaras
INFOREX, INC.
Burlington, Massachusetts 01803

NOTE ON CLASSIFICATION OF CLAIMS AND INTERESTS

The contents of a plan or reorganization are set forth in §1123 under two groups: *Mandatory* ("shall") provisions and *permissive* ("may") provisions. Section 1123 starts off with a mandatory requirement of a designation of classes. This is centrally important to the structure of Chapter 11, as most things in Chapter 11 are done by "classes." What is a class, accordingly, will be crucial. On a substantive level, it is significant because although individual creditors receive a certain degree of protection, a class of creditors receives more. Moreover, §1126 does not require that all members of the class approve a plan. Only a certain percentage are required for approval. In that case, some individually contracted-for rights can be overridden by class approval. Section 1123(a)(1) requires the division of claims and interests (other than as specified in the section) into classes, because voting is done by classes.

Manipulating classes for purposes of voting is inherent in the concept of classification. The Bankruptcy Code imposes limitations on that classification process in §1122 and §1123(a)(4). Section 1122's basic provision is that claims or interests may be placed in the same class *only* if they are "substantially similar" to the rest of the class. This raises two questions. First, what limits are there on who *can* be lumped together into the same class? Second, can similarly situated people be placed into *separate* classes? (Chapter 13 has a requirement, as a matter of classification, that one cannot discriminate unfairly among classes (see §1322(b)); does Chapter 11 call for any different result? Cf. §1129(b).) Read §1122 in light of the cases and materials that follow.

IN RE U.S. TRUCK CO.
42 Bankr. 790 (Bankr. E.D. Mich. 1984)

Stanley B. Bernstein, Bankruptcy Judge.

May the Debtor include as members of a single class of unsecured creditors under its plan of reorganization persons entitled to workers' compensation benefits?

The Debtor, U.S. Truck Company, Inc., filed an amended plan of reorganization with the Court on September 7, 1983. The plan provides for a payment of 55 percent of the allowed unsecured claims — 5 percent upon confirmation and the balance in ten semi-annual installments of 5 percent. All of the unsecured creditors with claims above $200 are included in a single class under the Debtor's plan.

The Michigan Self-Insurers' Association (MSIA) filed its written objections to confirmation of the Debtor's plan. The basic objections of MSIA are that (1) the plan [has] improperly classified all claims for workers' compensation benefits as prepetition claims; (2) the plan has radically underestimated the amount of workers' compensation claims and is, therefore, not feasible. The Attorney General of Michigan has joined in MSIA's objections on behalf of Michigan Self-Insurers' Security Fund. . . .

I. The Position of the Parties

At bottom, the dispute between the Debtor and the objecting parties is based upon radically different conceptions of how workers' compensation benefits may be treated as claims under the Bankruptcy Code and under a plan of reorganization. The Debtor treats all claims for benefits as arising from the date of a work-related injury, and if the injury occurred on a date prior to the petition, as a pre-petition unsecured claim. As such, the Debtor proposed to treat those claims like all other pre-petition claims and pay them at the rate of 55 percent of the claim dollar.

Consistent with that view, the Debtor stopped paying all disability benefits after it filed its petition. Under state law, benefits are payable weekly to disabled employees. The practical consequence of this decision was to deprive disabled employees of all benefits—a business decision so fundamentally lacking in human decency as to be morally reprehensible. In the history of Chapter 11 cases filed in this district, no Debtor ever provided for impairment of workers' compensation disability claims in any proposed plan or reorganization. . . . Fortunately, for the affected employees, the Administrator of the Michigan Self-Insurers' Trust Fund advanced disability payments on the magnitude of $500,000.00 directly to these employees. The Fund will be submitting a request for payment of administrative expenses to recover these advances. . . .

The Debtor changed its initial position during the continued hearings on the scope and treatment of claims for unpaid disability benefits. The Debtor, however, continues to assert that all payments due to holders of these claims are to holders of unsecured, pre-petition claims.

The objecting parties took a much more sophisticated, perhaps too sophisticated, view of worker's compensation benefits. They argued that under the Workers' Disability Compensation Act of 1969 in Michigan, M.C.L.A. §§418.101, et seq., (Compensation Act), an employee who suffers a wage loss attributable to a disability arising from a work-related injury is entitled to be paid *weekly benefits,* and that the right to payment of those weekly benefits *accrues each week.* In a word, there is no single pre-petition claim, but instead a series of discrete claims, arising each week, so long as the disability continues. The objecting parties stressed that the weekly amount of benefits may be increased, decreased, terminated, or reinstituted depending on the changing character of the disability as it directly affects the worker's ability to perform his or her original job.

Applying the Bankruptcy Code to workers' compensation benefits, the MSIA argued that a disabled worker could, in one formulation, have a successive series of different types of unpaid claims over time: a pre-petition general unsecured claim, a priority unsecured claim, and an administrative claim. . . .

III. CLASSIFICATION OF CLAIMS REVISITED

The Debtor conceded during the evidentiary hearing on the objections that it was now prepared to pay 55 percent of the weekly disability benefits arising from pre-petition injuries throughout the period of the open award. Once the Debtor has made that concession, it follows that the Debtor had improperly classified pre-petition trade claims and "pre-petition" disability claims as comprising one class. For under the plan, a trade creditor with a $100,000 allowed claim would receive a total of $55,000 in eleven semi-annual installments of $5,000, and a partially disabled employee with an open award of $100 a week would receive $55.00 each week for the duration of his or her award. Quite clearly, the terms of payment to these two types of pre-petition creditors are substantially dissimilar. The trade creditor has a claim for unpaid goods or services supplied during the pre-petition period—the transaction is closed; the disabled employee may have suffered an injury during the pre-petition period, but there the similarity between the two creditors stops abruptly —the disabled employee's transaction is not closed; it may continue for the duration of his or her lifetime.

Nor may the Debtor treat the disabled employee as analogous to a tort victim who suffered an injury at the workplace. There is no lump sum judgment for damages possible under the workers' compensation system of "open awards." Only in the limiting circumstances of a "redemption" of a claim is there ever a lump sum payment, and that requires an informed consent of the disabled employee, the employer, and a finding by an administrative law judge that such a "redemption" is, among the several statutory criteria, in the best interest of the employee. Absent a redemption, the administrative law judge can only enter an open award to an employee with a continuing disability. To be sure, one could resort to complex actuarial assumptions and discount an open award to a present value, but that is inconsistent with the law of workers' compensation in Michigan; moreover, there is nothing contingent about an open award— the liability and amount is fixed, undisputed, and liquidated. So estimation under 11 U.S.C. §502(c) would be improper. And the Debtor has conceded as much—it is now prepared to pay 55 percent of the weekly benefit amount as each payment becomes due.

In light of the foregoing, the Debtor's plan cannot be confirmed because it has violated the provisions of 11 U.S.C. §1122(a). That section requires that "a plan may place a claim or an interest is substantially similar to the other claims or interest of such class." The Debtor has included substantially dissimilar claims—trade claims and workers' compensation claims—in the same class. Because the classification is improper, the provisions of 11 U.S.C. §1129(a)(1) is violated—the plan cannot be confirmed because the plan does not comply with an applicable provision of Chapter 11 of the Code, to-wit: 11 U.S.C. §1122(a). The objecting creditors' other objections as to feasibility do not have to be considered.

IV.   CLASSIFICATION

The statutory criterion under review is that each claim be included in a class of claims such that each claim in the class is "substantially similar." The working assumption held by most bankruptcy practitioners, judges, and commentators is that all unsecured claims must be included in a single class with the limited exception under 11 U.S.C. §1122(b) for claims in modest amounts which for "administrative convenience" may be separately classified for more favorable treatment. The rationale supporting this working assumption is that ultimately an unsecured claim is defined by its relative priority position in a liquidation scheme. . . .

This line of analysis was explicitly adopted by the court in In re Pine Lake Village Apartment Co., 19 Bankr. Rptr. 819 (Bankr. S.D.N.Y. 1982). . . . In the *Pine Lake* case, the bankruptcy court stated its opposition to the designation of two separate classes of unsecured claims, one class consisting of a single claim based upon a deficiency on an undersecured mortgage indebtedness in excess of $4,000,000 and a second class of unsecured trade creditors whose claims in the aggregate totalled $44,952.06. Creditors in the second class were to be paid in full upon confirmation; the first class was to be paid substantially less than the allowable amount of its claim. The second class would not be impaired under 11 U.S.C. §1124 and as such would be deemed to have accepted the plan under 11 U.S.C. §1126(f). By virtue of the acceptance, the plan would satisfy a critical element for confirmation, namely, 11 U.S.C. §1129(a)(10) which requires that at least one class accepts the plan.

The *Pine Lake* court took the initial position that the designation of the second class was wholly manipulative — had there been one class, and the deficiency claim were included, 11 U.S.C. §1129(a)(10) would not have been satisfied because the undersecured creditor would have voted against acceptance and the required dollar amount of voting claims needed for acceptance could not be obtained. By this manipulation, the debtor sought to neutralize the voting power of the under-secured creditor.

The *Pine Lake* court did not have to, and did not ultimately, rely upon this analysis. The classification argument proved to be a red herring because the court relied upon 11 U.S.C. §1129(b)(2)(B)(ii), the cram-down section as it pertains to a non-accepting class of impaired creditors. The debtor could not retain its interest in the mortgaged premises in the face of rejection of the plan by the mortgagee. That rejection would occur whether the deficiency claim occupied its own separate class or dominated the class of all unsecured creditors. At bottom, the mortgagee could not be crammed-down.

This Court would follow the thrust of the *Pine Lake* court's opinion on the cram-down issue, and would also concur on the specific application of the classification objection to the deficiency claim. But that court asserts too broad a position on classification. The statute does not say that all unsecured claims are of the same nature. Nor is an analysis based upon a distribution scheme in Chapter 7 controlling in Chapter 11 proceedings. It is not necessarily the case that a classification of claims must be developed solely with a Chapter 7 distribution scheme as the source of specifying the relevant criteria. The Aristotelian exercise in determining the *nature* of claims and the criteria of "substantial similarity" is far more difficult and elusive.

The *Pine Lake* court is properly concerned with preventing abusive manipulations of the voting rules in acceptance. But there are all sorts of other abuses which the *Pine Lake* court ignores. It is just as easy to hypothesize a Chapter 11 case in which a discrete sub-class of unsecured claims was intentionally included within a more inclusive class to deny that sub-class any vote on a plan. Must we forget majority tyranny of an "insular minority?" In a word, an analysis that "all unsecured claims are equal" is simplistic and mischievous. There is surely no satisfactory a priori rule that some types of unsecured claims may not be "substantially similar." Yes, one has to be concerned that one does not unleash the proliferation of nuclear weapons in the world of bankruptcy. There have to be meaningful controls against unleashing myriad separate classes of unsecured claims. But it is too early in the history of the Code to lock all non-nuisance unsecured claims in a single cell. The Code does not require such a lock-up. . . .

. . . Ultimately the control against abuse is to deny confirmation because the plan is not propounded in good faith, but short of that a plan may be struck when the classification is improper. Generally, courts have struck plans or denied confirmation when the debtor has formed more than one class of unsecured creditors. In this case, the Court has determined to strike a plan because the Debtor has failed to form separate classes.

At this juncture this Court is reasonably satisfied that the claims for unpaid weekly workers' compensation disability benefits are materially *dissimilar* in *nature* to justify a separate classification. There are salient *legal* characteristics of these claims that justify different classification and treatment under a plan. In the most important respect, these claims are "open ended" in character. The language of the state law is illuminating — the awards are *open* as opposed to closed. Pre-petition claims arising out of ordinary contractual relationships are closed — they have occurred and the damages are measurable (or estimatable). The workers' compensation claims share the important characteristics under the state act that the date of injury, a pre-petition event, is controlling for most purposes — establishing the average weekly wage, the number of dependents, the identity of the employer, and the adversely affected type of work. But the administrative treatment of these claims is also different in other critical respects, and therein lies the rub.

The Debtor's plan of reorganization is struck as nonconfirmable. . . .

NOTE ON CLASSIFICATION AND THE *MICRO-ACOUSTICS* CASE

Many classification issues may be almost intractable. For example, when you get to Problem 9.18, consider whether you could devise *any* classification scheme that will adequately deal with the problem of contractually subordinated classes without introducing strategic distortions. But sometimes classification issues may obscure the underlying question of relative ranking in the first place. Consider a case such as In re Micro-Acoustics Corp., 34 Bankr. 279 (Bankr. S.D.N.Y. 1983). In that case, Drelinger, one of the principal shareholders of Micro-Acoustics, filed a proceeding in state court in 1980 to dissolve the corporation under the provisions of the New York Business Corporation Law. That proceeding was effectively ended in 1981 by Micro-Acoustics' election to repurchase Drelinger's stock at its face value, under court supervision — a procedure also authorized by the Business Corporation Law. Drelinger thereupon asserted, in a 1982 court proceeding, that the fair value of his shares was $700,000. Before the state court reached any decision, Micro-Acoustics filed for bankruptcy. The plan of reorganization placed Drelinger's $700,000 claim (still disputed) in a separate class, subordinate to the class of general unsecured creditors, but ahead of the common stockholder class. The court held that the classification was proper "because there is a difference in the nature of their claims. . . ."

Is this satisfying? After the election is made, what if state law treated Drelinger as a *creditor,* rather than a shareholder? In that event, isn't he entitled to be treated in the same way as other general, unsecured creditors? There are two reasons to think that he might not be. The first involves the provisions of §510(b) *if* Drelinger's underlying claim could be viewed as a "rescission." Apart from that, however, is there something troubling about a shareholder of an arguably insolvent company converting his equity interest into a creditor's claim? He has effectively "opted out" into a higher class. Had the corporation *paid* Drelinger the money upon the election, it would have been reachable — assuming insolvency — as a fraudulent conveyance for one year (using §548) or for the applicable state limitations period (using §544(b) and state fraudulent conveyance law). Is it any less a fraudulent conveyance to give Drelinger the *right* to be treated as a creditor instead of a shareholder? Can you find a "transfer" in that case?

Assume fraudulent conveyance law is the appropriate tool to reach what happened here. If reachable by fraudulent conveyance law, shouldn't Drelinger's claim be classified with the equity interests, *not* ahead of them? And if the reachback period of fraudulent conveyance law has passed, why should Drelinger be classified behind the other unsecured creditors?

Before leaving *Micro-Acoustics,* consider one last puzzle as you examine the provisions of §1129. What do you think the proponents of the plan hoped to accomplish by Drelinger's classification? Assuming the proponents were the other equity interests, do they gain anything by placing Drelinger in a separate class, if that class is still senior to their own?

IN RE MARTIN'S POINT LTD. PARTNERSHIP
12 Bankr. 721 (Bankr. N.D. Ga. 1981)

William L. NORTON, Jr., Bankruptcy Judge.

FINDINGS OF FACT

The Plan of Reorganization (hereinafter referred to as the "Plan") under discussion in this opinion was filed by Martin's Point Limited Partnership (hereinafter referred to as "Debtor") on July 29, 1980. . . . The Plan provides for the reorganization of the affairs of the Debtor and, toward that end, provides for reconveyance to the holders of purchase money secured indebtedness of certain real property on Wadmalaw Island, South Carolina (sometimes hereinafter referred to as Martin's Point Plantation) which, for all practical purposes, constitutes the sole asset of the debtor. The Plan also provides for the payment of all other undisputed obligations of the Debtor.

The Partners of the Partnership, i.e., its equity security holders, who, since 1973, have contributed over $391,900.00 towards the purchase of Martin's Point Plantation, have, without dissent, voted to approve the Plan. With only one exception, every creditor of the Partnership who voted on the Plan, voted to accept the Plan. The only objection filed to the Plan was by C. Stuart Dawson, Jr.

THE PLAN

The Plan of Reorganization filed by the Debtor divides the Debtor's creditors into five classes as set forth below:

(A) The Class of First Priority Secured Creditors, which consists of one creditor — The Federal Land Bank — which has a first priority security interest in Martin's Point Plantation.

(B) The Class of Second Priority Secured Creditors, which consists of three creditors — C. Stuart Dawson, Jr., Harold E. Igoe, Jr., and Wadmalaw Island Land Company, Inc. — who have security interests in Martin's Point Plantation equal in priority with each other, but which are subordinate to The Federal Land Bank's security interest in the property.

There are four other classes of creditors which are unimpaired and not in dispute as to this Confirmation of Plan. The Plan provides that the Partnership shall convey all of its right, title and interest in Martin's Point Plantation and all of its interest in 13,000 shares of the stock of The Federal Land Bank Association of Walterboro to Wadmalaw Island Land Company, Inc. and Messrs, Igoe and Dawson, in full and complete satisfaction of the indebtedness owing by the Partnership and any of its partners to each of the transferees. Conveyance to these parties is to be made in the following percentages of undivided interest:

C. Stuart Dawson, Jr.	31.68%
Harold E. Igoe, Jr.	34.16%
Wadmalaw Island Land Company, Inc.	34.16%

The conveyance of Martin's Point Plantation will be made subject to the first mortgage of The Federal Land Bank.

The Plan further provides that M.E. Ellinger, Jr., as general partner of Martin's Point Limited Partnership, shall contribute to the Partnership in an amount of money which, when added to the funds presently held by the Partnership, will be sufficient to enable the Partnership to pay the claims of all the creditors in the Class of Tax Creditors, the Class of Unsecured Creditors Whose Claims Are Not In Dispute, and the Class of Post-Filing Creditors.

Alternatively, Mr. Dawson may elect, within the first 10 days following confirmation of the Plan and in lieu of receiving a conveyance of the aforesaid property, to receive either cash in the amount of $160,000.00 or a note in the amount of $190,000.00, in full and complete satisfaction of his claims against the Partnership and any of its partners. The cash and note will be received from the Wadmalaw Island Land Company, Inc. and Harold E. Igoe.

ACCEPTANCE OF THE PLAN

Every creditor and every equity security holder who voted on the Plan voted to accept the Plan, with the sole exception of Mr. Dawson. The voting was as follows:

Class	No. accepting	No. rejecting
A. The Class of First Priority Secured Creditors	1	0 (unanimous)
B. The Class of Second Priority Secured Creditors	2	1

The only class in which any dissenting vote was cast concerning the Plan was the Class of Second Priority Secured Creditors, which consisted of C. Stuart Dawson, Harold E. Igoe, Jr., and Wadmalaw Island Land Company, Inc. Mr. Igoe and Wadmalaw Island Land Company, Inc., as of the date of the Debtor's Petition, each had claims against the debtor in the amount of $258,290. Mr. Igoe and Wadmalaw Island Land Company, Inc. both voted to accept the Plan. Mr. Dawson, as of the date of the filing of the Debtor's Petition, had claims against the Debtor in the amount of $239,480.00. Mr. Dawson voted to reject the Plan. Because Mr. Igoe and the Wadmalaw Island Land Company, Inc. amount to more than one-half of the creditors of the class, and since their claims collectively amount to more than two thirds in amount of all claims of the creditors of their class, the class in which they are members are deemed, pursuant to Section 1126 of the Bankruptcy Reform Act of 1978 [11 U.S.C. §1126(c)] (hereinafter sometimes referred to as the Bankruptcy "Code"), to have accepted the Plan — along with the other classes of creditors and equity security holders who voted unanimously to accept the Plan.

Mr. Dawson has appeared at the hearing on Confirmation of the Plan and stated an objection to the Plan. He has also filed a written objection to his classification under the Plan, contending that the classifications set forth in the Plan are improper in that he should be placed in a class by himself rather than in a class with Mr. Igoe and the Wadmalaw Island Land Company, Inc. Should the claim of Mr. Dawson be required to be placed in a separate class, that class would constitute an objecting class and the claim would have to be dealt with separately. The court will first discuss the classification issue.

CLASSIFICATION

Three creditors, i.e., Mr. Igoe, Mr. Dawson, and the Wadmalaw Island Land Company, Inc., each hold purchase money promissory notes executed by the Debtor in connection with its purchase of Martin's Point Plantation. While there are three separate promissory notes, all three of those notes are secured by a single, second-priority, purchase money mortgage security interest in Martin's Point Plantation.

The purchase money notes held by Messrs. Igoe and Dawson represent the unpaid portion of their shares of the purchase price for Martin's Point Plantation by the Partnership in December of 1973. The note held by Wadmalaw Island Land Company, Inc. was originally issued to Mr. Albert Fuchs to evidence the unpaid portion of the purchase price due him, and was subsequently assigned by Mr. Fuchs to Wadmalaw Island Land Company, Inc.

In 1978, Mr. Dawson instituted suit for the collection of his note by the foreclosure of the mortgage security interest held jointly by Dawson, Igoe, and Wadmalaw Island Land Company, Inc. Mr. Dawson joined Mr. Igoe and Mr. Fuchs as defendants in that action, and obtained a judgment ordering foreclosure of the owner's equity in Martin's Point Plantation. That judgment also sets forth the relationship of Messrs. Dawson and Igoe and the Wadmalaw Island Land Company, Inc., inter se, with respect to the proceeds of any such foreclosure. Under that judgment, the creditors are to share the proceeds of any such foreclosure. Under that judgment, the creditors are to share the proceeds of any foreclosure pro rata, according to the outstanding principal amounts of their various creditor claims.

Mr. Igoe and Mr. Fuchs (the transferor to Wadmalaw Island Land Company, Inc. of the purchase money notes) are limited partners in the Debtor.

Mr. Dawson has objected to his claim being classified in the Class of Second Priority Secured Creditors, asserting that the other members of that class are also equity security holders and, therefore, the holders of claims which are not substantially similar to his claim.

Section 1122(a) of the Bankruptcy Reform Act of 1978 [11 U.S.C. §1122(a)] provides:

> (a) Except as provided in subsection (b) of this section, a plan may place a claim or an interest in a particular class only if such claim or interest is substantially similar to the other claims or interests of such class.

The court, in In re Iacovoni, 2 B.R. 256, 260 (Bkrtcy. D. Utah 1980), in interpreting the above section, recently held that:

> 11 U.S.C. §1122 provides that claims and interests may be classified in a particular class only if such claim or interest are "substantially similar." Reference to the legislative history makes clear that this section is a codification of current case law which requires "classification based on the nature of the claims or interests classified." H.R. Rep. No. 95-595, supra at 406. S. Rep. No. 95-989, supra at 118, U.S. Code Cong. & Admin. News, p. 5904.

Case law concerning classification of creditors prior to the enactment of Section 1122 was summarized by the court in In re Los Angeles Land and Investments, Ltd., 282 F. Supp. 448, 453 (D. Hawaii 1968) aff'd., 447 F.2d 1366 (9th Cir. 1971), wherein it was stated:

> The Act requires the classification be in accordance with the 'nature' of the claim and in this determination it is necessary that the judge have discretionary powers. 'It is obvious from this language [of the statute] that Congress intended to give the court a broad latitude in the classification of debtors. Such classification, of course, should not do substantial violence to any claimant's interest, nor should it uselessly increase the number of classifications unless there be substantial differences in the nature of the claims.' In the Matter of Palisades-on-the-Desplaines, C.A. 7th (1937) 89 F.2d 214, 217.
>
> The test to be applied appears to be one directed toward a determination of the 'nature' of the claim. This would encompass an analysis of the legal character or the quality of the claim as it relates to the assets of the debtor. . . . 'All creditors of equal rank with claims against the same property should be placed in the same class.' In re Scherk v. Newton, C.A. 10th (1945) 152 F.2d 747.

An examination of the claims of Mr. Dawson, Mr. Igoe, and the Wadmalaw Island Land Company, Inc., which are not substantially different in nature, indeed, of equal rank with each other, against the same property, indicates that under the above tests, these claims may be classified together. Prior to Martin's Point Plantation being sold to the Partnership, the property was owned by Messrs. Igoe, Dawson, and Fuchs (who later assigned his interest to Wadmalaw Island Land Company, Inc.), as joint tenants. Each had an undivided interest in the property as a whole. Together, the three men sold the property to the Partnership, each taking a note for the deferred portion of the purchase price, which notes were secured by one mortgage. The security interest of each of the creditors in the property was, and remains, equal in priority and subordinate to the security interest which The Federal Land Bank had in the property.

A reasonable description concerning the relationship between the interests of Messrs. Igoe and Dawson, and the Wadmalaw Island Land Company, Inc. as transferee of Mr. Fuchs, is that set forth in the Special Master's Report which was prepared in conjunction with the foreclosure proceedings instituted by Mr. Dawson in Charleston, South Carolina. In that report, the Special Master stated:

> I find that said individual notes to [Dawson] and to the defendants, Igoe and Fuchs, were made, executed and delivered by the Defendant Partnership as part of a *single transaction* involving the sale of certain real estate jointly owned by [Dawson] and by the defendants Igoe and Fuchs to the Defendant Partnership and that the Defendant Partnership executed and [Dawson] and the defendants Igoe and Fuchs accepted several notes as part of the consideration for said land as part of a *common arrangement*. . . . [Emphasis supplied.]

The Special Master further found that the mortgage on the property was part of a "common scheme or plan by which the single mortgage secured the three several notes payable to [Dawson] and . . . Igoe and Fuchs." . . . That court awarded one single judgment of foreclosure, in effect merging the claims of the three creditors.

The apparent reasons of Mr. Dawson for objecting to the classification set forth in the Plan are that (1) Mr. Igoe and Mr. Fuchs are both creditors and limited partners of the Debtor, and (2) Mr. Dawson is entitled to seek a deficiency after a foreclosure. Each of these contentions will be discussed below.

A.   PARTNERSHIP INTEREST

Mr. Dawson claims that because Messrs. Igoe and Fuchs each own limited partnership units in the Debtor, the interests of Igoe and Wadmalaw Island Land Company, Inc. conflict with his, and should not be put in the same class. Yet, it is Wadmalaw Island Land Company, Inc., and not

Mr. Fuchs, which is the creditor that has been placed in the same class as Mr. Dawson. Also, Wadmalaw Island Land Company, Inc. owns no partnership units in the Debtor. In addition, the one unit Mr. Igoe owns was obtained by him when it was taken in lieu of an interest payment in 1977, at a point in time when he could have legitimately refused to take such unit and demanded that the partnership pay him his interest. However, even if Wadmalaw Island Land Company, Inc. and Mr. Igoe had been partners from the very beginning, this fact still would not require that they be classified separately from Mr. Dawson.

Mr. Dawson argues that the limited partners of the Debtor may, under certain circumstances, be required to make certain contributions to the Partnership to pay creditors and that, as a result, Wadmalaw Island Land Company, Inc. (since Mr. Fuchs has a controlling interest in the company) and Mr. Igoe would want to resist a plan which called for this.

First, it appears that both Igoe and Fuchs stand to gain more than they would lose if the limited partners were required to contribute to the partnership; second, a limited partner cannot be held accountable for the general debts of the partnership, and, therefore, Igoe and Fuchs have no personal exposure for the general debts of the partnership; third, the law does not require that creditors of a class be homogeneous in all of their claims or interest in the debtor, but just that claims within a class be substantially similar; and fourth, it is well settled that, absent inequitable conduct, holders of an ownership interest in a debtor are not to be subordinated or treated differently from other creditors. . . .

Even if the interest of Igoe and Fuchs, because of their equity security interest in the Debtor, diverged from Mr. Dawson's, this would still not require that their claims be classified differently. It is the "nature" of their claims being classified together that is significant, not the nature of other claims or interests a creditor might have. The Code merely requires that an equity interest which a party may have in a Debtor is to be placed in a class separate from a claim that that party may have against the Debtor. The Court has been cited to no authority to support the proposition that individuals or corporations having claims against a debtor are to be treated differently from other creditors simply because that person or corporation also has an equity interest in the Debtor. . . .

B. DEFICIENCY

Mr. Dawson also contends that he should be classified separately because he is allegedly entitled to seek a deficiency under the judgment authorizing foreclosure if the property in question after sale does not provide sufficient funds to retire Mr. Dawson's debt in full. Mr. Dawson has not shown the Court that his claim is unique or different from the claims of Igoe and Wadmalaw Island Land Company, Inc. in this respect. While the Debtor does not admit that any of the three creditors classified in the Class of Second Priority Secured Creditors is entitled to a deficiency, the notes of the three creditors do not differ in this respect, and in the foreclosure collection proceeding instituted by Mr. Dawson, the Court in South Carolina made no such distinction. However, even if Mr. Dawson were entitled to a deficiency and the other two creditors were not, this fact would not in itself require that Dawson be classified separately from Mr. Igoe or the Wadmalaw Island Land Company, Inc. The Code provides that in order for creditors to be classified together, their interest need be only substantially similar and not identical. Hence, creditors who have security interest in the same property and whose interests are equal in priority, even though their interests arise out of different loan instruments containing different terms and conditions, including deficiency provisions, are normally classified together. . . .

THE OBJECTION TO CONFIRMATION OF THE PLAN OF REORGANIZATION

The Plan of Reorganization filed with the Court on July 29, 1980, meets each of the requirements set forth in Section 1123 of the Code (11 U.S.C. §1123) in that:

1. The claims of the creditors have been classified in accordance with Section 1122 of the Code;

2. The claims which have not been impaired have been specified;

3. The treatment of any class of claims or interest that is impaired under the Plan, has been specified;

4. The same treatment has been provided for each claim or interest of a particular class, unless the holder of a particular claim or interest agrees to a less favorable treatment of such particular claim or interest; and

5. Adequate means for the Plan's execution have been provided, in that the Plan calls for the transfer of all of the property of the estate to various entities pursuant to Section 1123(a)(5) of the Code.

In addition to fulfilling the requirements of Section 1123 of the Code concerning the contents of the Plan, the Debtor has also obtained the requisite number of acceptances under Section 1126 of the Code. Section 1126(c) provides in pertinent part that:

> (c) A class of claims has accepted a plan if such plan has been accepted by creditors . . . that hold at least ⅔ in amount and more than ½ in number of the allowed claims of such class held by creditors, . . . that have accepted or rejected such plan.

This test was met for each class of claims. In fact, except for Mr. Dawson, the voting creditors and equity security holders voted unanimously to accept the Plan. Because the Class of Second Priority Secured Creditors is composed of only three creditors — Mr. Igoe, Mr. Dawson, and the Wadmalaw Island Land Company, Inc. — and because Mr. Igoe and the Wadmalaw Island Land Company, Inc., who represent more than ⅔ in amount and ½ in number of the creditors of the class, voted to accept the Plan, the class, pursuant to Section 1126(c), is deemed to have accepted the Plan. As a result, the Debtor has obtained acceptances from all the classes set forth in the Plan.

The Plan having been accepted by all classes, the only remaining issue before the Court is whether the Plan should be confirmed pursuant to Section 1129 of the Code.

The only provision of Section 1129 concerning confirmation in controversy is subsection (a)(7) which provides:

> (a) The court shall confirm a plan only if all of the following requirements are met: . . .
> (7) With respect to each class —
> (A) each holder of a claim or interest of such class —
> (i) has accepted the plan; or
> (ii) will receive or retain under the plan on account of such claim or interest, property of a value, as of the effective date of the plan, that is not less than the amount that such holder would so receive or retain if the debtor were liquidated under chapter 7 of this title on such date . . .*

The undisputed testimony at the hearings held on July 21, 1980, and September 11, 1980, indicates that that requirement has clearly been satisfied under the Plan.

The Plan of Reorganization provides that the Debtor will convey all of its right, title and interest in Martin's Point Plantation and all of its interest in 13,000 shares of stock in The Federal Land Bank Association of Walterboro to Harold E. Igoe, C. Stuart Dawson, Jr., and the Wadmalaw Island Land Company, Inc., in full and complete satisfaction of the indebtedness owing by Martin's Point Limited Partnership and any of its partners to each of the transferees. Conveyance to such parties is to be in the following percentages of undivided interests:

C. Stuart Dawson, Jr.	31.68%
Harold E. Igoe, Jr.	34.16%
Wadmalaw Island Land Company, Inc.	34.16%

Conveyance of the property is to be made subject to the first mortgage of The Federal Land Bank.

As regards the objection interposed at the hearing on confirmation, held on September 11, 1980, Mr. Dawson has contended that, by receiving a 31.68 percent interest in Martin's Point Plantation, he is receiving less than he would receive in a liquidation under Chapter 7 of the Bankruptcy Code. Mr. Dawson's assertion ignores the value of Martin's Point

---

* This section was reworded slightly in 1984. — Eds.

Plantation, which appears to presently exceed the debt. Mr. Dawson has failed to prove that a deficiency is likely should a Chapter 7 case ensue, or that the value under the Plan would be less than the value which might be received under Chapter 7.

The claims of Messrs. Dawson and Igoe, and the claim of Wadmalaw Island Land Company, Inc., are secured by a single, second-priority mortgage on Martin's Point Plantation. Accordingly, except to the extent that the mortgage secures a penalty avoidable under Sections 724(a) and 726(a)(4), the proceeds of liquidation of the property would be paid to the holders of secured claims in order of their priority, i.e., to The Federal Land Bank the extent of its claim, with any excess being paid pro rata to Dawson, Igoe, and Wadmalaw Island Land Company, Inc. If the value of the property exceeded the amount of the secured debt and Mr. Dawson received his pro rata share of such proceeds, his claim would be discharged in full. The Plan would provide Mr. Dawson with a 31.68% interest in the land, as opposed to the proceeds of the sale of the land. Accordingly, the initial step in the analysis should be a determination of the fair market value of the land.

Mr. Frank Parker Hudson, Jr., an expert called on behalf of the Partnership, testified:

> My opinion of the value today is between — and I like to speak in ranges — I would say on the low side of at least $2,200 an acre, which equates to a little over $1,200,000, and I would feel comfortable with the possibility of a sale of around $2,400 an acre, which would be, say, $1,350,000. . . .

Mr. C.O. Thompson, a second expert called on behalf of the Partnership, concurred with Mr. Hudson when he testified that the subject property was worth One Million Two Hundred Thousand Dollars ($1,200,000.00). . . . He also added, however, that "I think that it's a reasonable possibility that there exists in the market place a buyer who would pay substantially more for that, for the property. . . ." . . .

The testimony of Messrs. Thompson and Hudson indicates that Martin's Point Plantation has a fair market value in the range of $1,200,000.00 to $1,350,000.00. As of the date of the hearing on confirmation, the total amount of the secured claims held by the Class of First Priority Secured Creditors and the Class of Second Priority Secured Creditors was $1,103,799.00. When the fair market value of Martin's Point Plantation is compared with that amount, there is a minimum equity in the property of some $96,201.00. True, the interest debt is rising, but the testimony is that the monthly inflation value of the property equals or exceeds such increase in the debt.

Mr. Dawson will receive under the Plan a value no less than he would receive in liquidation under Chapter 7. Thus, Section 1129(a)(7)(A)(ii) is satisfied.

Each of the standards of confirmation of Section 1129(a) having been satisfied, the Plan of Reorganization is confirmed.

NOTES

1. In re Sullivan, 26 Bankr. 677, 678 (Bankr. W.D.N.Y. 1982):

> Class 2 does not meet the requirement of section 1122. It contains four separate and distinct claims. The claim of Lockport Savings Bank is secured by a mortgage on real property at 90 Erie Street. The claim of James R. Hutchinson is secured by a mortgage on realty at 291 Caledonia Street. The claim of General Motors Acceptance Corporation is secured by a 1976 Oldsmobile and that of the Manufacturers and Traders Trust by a 1975 Ford truck. These can hardly be held to be substantially similar.

2. 2 Gerdes, Corporate Reorganization 682 (1936):

> All creditors of equal rank with claims against the same property should be placed in the same class. This is natural, logical, and a simple basis of division.
>
> Conversely, creditors of different ranks, or creditors of the same rank but with claims against different properties, should be placed in different classes. The owners of a mortgage which is a first lien on certain property should be in a class other than the one containing the owners of a mortgage which is a second lien on the same property. So, also, the holders of a mortgage, which is first lien on certain property should be in a class other than the one containing the holders of a mortgage which is a first lien on other property.

See also Trost, Business Reorganizations Under Chapter 11 of the New Bankruptcy Code, 34 Bus. Law. 1309, 1327 (1979) ("[e]ach secured creditor is normally in a class by itself"). Is *Martin's Point* consistent with the thrust of these statements?

PROBLEMS

9.1 Debtor has filed a plan of reorganization. The plan divides unsecured creditors into three classes. The first class is comprised of attorneys and accountants. The second class contains Bank, which holds an unsecured claim against Debtor that is guaranteed by Debtor's president. The third class is made up of all other unsecured creditors. The plan of reorganization proposes to pay the first two classes 25 percent of their claims, in cash, and proposes to give the third class common stock equal to 10 percent of their claims. As a matter of classification, is the plan proper?

9.2 Debtor has proposed a plan in its Chapter 11 proceeding that provides for a "Class 4" as follows: "All unsecured allowed claims of $10,000 or less will be paid in full, in cash, upon consummation of the plan." Under the plan, "Class 5" creditors, consisting of all other unsecured creditors, will be given five year notes, at 10 percent interest, in an amount equal to 20 percent of each such claim. Creditor holds an allowed unsecured claim against Debtor in the amount of $11,000. Creditor wants advice as to whether this plan meets the requirements of §§1122 and 1123. Advise Creditor.

9.3 Debtor's plan of reorganization specifies three classes of unsecured claims: those under $20,000; those over $20,000; and disputed claims. The plan proposes to treat the over- and under-$20,000 classes identically. The plan fails to state what treatment is afforded to the disputed claims class. As a matter of classification, what objections can be made to this plan? If you were the proponent of the plan, what defenses could be made to your classification? See In re Mastercraft Record Plating, 32 Bankr. 106 (Bankr. S.D.N.Y. 1983), rev'd on other grounds, 39 Bankr. 654 (S.D.N.Y. 1984).

9.4 Look at Class 12 of Inforex's Plan of Reorganization, supra. Is it proper?

NOTE ON VOTING ON A PLAN OF REORGANIZATION

Section 1126 specifies how plans of reorganization are accepted or rejected by each class. Section 1126(f), however, calls off the requirement of a vote by a particular class and its members, if that class "is not impaired under a plan," for it, and each of its members, is "conclusively presumed to have accepted the plan, and solicitation of acceptances with respect to such class from the holders of claims or interests of such class is not required." The critical concept of "impairment" is set forth in §1124, and you should examine that section with care in conjunction with the problems below. You should also attempt to relate §1124 to §1129 when these materials reach the latter section. See also Trost, Business Reorganizations Under Chapter 11 of the New Bankruptcy Code, 34 Bus. Law. 1309, 1330-1333 (1979). In addition, §1126(g) provides that a class that will receive nothing under the plan of reorganization is deemed *not* to have accepted the plan.

Before a vote on a plan, votes must be solicited according to the requirements of §1125. Many Chapter 11 plans may be viewed as involving the issuance of securities: Instead of selling securities and receiving cash, a Chapter 11 debtor is selling securities and receiving a release from debts. And because Chapter 11 contemplates voting on a plan as part of the confirmation process, creditors (and interest-holders) are being asked to make an informed decision about a particular plan. Section 1145(a) of the

Bankruptcy Code generally exempts Chapter 11 securities transactions from the registration requirements of federal and state securities laws. Section 1145(b) then sets forth the circumstances under which a creditor who receives securities in a Chapter 11 reorganization may resell them without being deemed an "underwriter." See Orlanski, The Resale of Securities Issued in Reorganization Proceedings and The Bankruptcy Reform Act of 1978, 53 Am. Bankr. L.J. 327 (1979); see also Corotto, Debtor Relief Proceedings Under the Bankruptcy Act and the Securities Act of 1933: The Registration Requirement and Its Implications, 47 Am. Bankr. L.J. 183 (1973).

Although §1145 generally provides an exemption from securities law registration requirements, the transactions are still subject to the antifraud provisions of federal securities laws. Sections 12 and 17 of the Securities Act of 1933 and Rule 10b-5, promulgated under the Securities Exchange Act of 1934, apply to a securities transaction even if it is exempt from registration. Section 1125 sets out the types of disclosure that must be made in soliciting acceptances of a Chapter 11 plan; §1125(e) provides a "safe harbor" from these antifraud securities provisions. See also Epling and Thompson, Securities Disclosure in Bankruptcy, 39 Bus. Lawyer 855 (1984); Note, Disclosure of Adequate Information in a Chapter 11 Reorganization, 94 Harv. L. Rev. 1808 (1981); In re Metrocraft Publishing Services, 39 Bankr. 567 (Bankr. N.D. Ga. 1984); In re Brandon Mill Farms, 37 Bankr. 190 (Bankr. N.D. Ga. 1984); In re Egan, 33 Bankr. 672 (Bankr. N.D. Ill. 1983); In re The Stanley Hotel, 13 Bankr. 926 (Bankr. D. Colo. 1981); In re Northwest Recreational Activities, Inc., 8 Bankr. 10 (Bankr. N.D. Ga. 1980); In re D.M. Christian Co., 7 Bankr. 561 (Bankr. N.D.W. Va. 1980). It is possible to obtain acceptances of a Chapter 11 plan before the Chapter 11 petition is filed. Section 1126(b) provides that acceptances solicited before filing may be counted, in deciding whether a class of claims or interests has accepted a plan, if (a) they were solicited in compliance with any "applicable nonbankruptcy law, rule, or regulation governing the adequacy of disclosure" (such as?) or (b) if there is no applicable law, rule, or regulation, the acceptances were solicited after disclosure of "adequate information," as defined in §1125(a)(1).

PROBLEMS

9.5 Citibank holds a mortgage lien on the property of Antilles Yachting, Inc., a Chapter 11 debtor, which secures a loan of $106,000, bearing interest at the prime rate from time to time plus 3 percent. In late 1978, Citibank brought a foreclosure proceeding on the property against Antilles Yachting; in late 1979, Antilles Yachting consented to a judgment of foreclosure in return for Citibank's agreement to refrain from seeking a judicial sale for 60 days. Before Citibank sought such a sale, Antilles Yachting filed a Chapter 11 petition. Under a plan of reorganization filed in May of 1980, Antilles Yachting proposed a cash payment of $30,000 to Citibank and a payout of the remainder of the loan from future cash flow at the prime rate from time to time plus 3 percent. Is Citibank impaired under §1124?

9.6 Creditor files a plan of reorganization in which the existing shareholders of Debtor will retain all their present shares of common stock. The plan also provides that enough new shares of common stock will be issued to the unsecured creditors so that, after the reorganization, the existing shareholders of Debtor will own 25 percent of its common stock and the unsecured creditors will own 75 percent. Are the existing common stockholders impaired?

9.7 Debtor, who is in Chapter 11, proposes to sell one of its operating divisions as a part of its plan of reorganization. Before the sales, that operating division accounted for 40 percent of Debtor's assets, income, expenditures, and net profit (or loss). Debtor's plan proposes to leave the common stockholders' securities untouched. Are those common stockholders impaired?

9.8 Class 5 consists of unsecured creditors. One hundred creditors holding allowed claims of $400,000 are in Class 5. Seventy creditors, holding $250,000 of claims, vote on the plan. Of those voting, 40 creditors, holding $200,000 of claims, vote to approve the plan; the remainder vote against the plan. Has Class 5 approved the plan? See §1126(c).

9.9 Class 6 consists of preferred stockholders. One hundred stockholders are in this class, holding 200,000 shares of preferred stock. Seventy of these stockholders vote. Of those voting, 25 stockholders, holding 140,000 shares of preferred stock, approve the plan; the remainder vote against the plan. Has Class 6 approved the plan? See §1126(d).

9.10 Debtor has filed a plan of reorganization. In this plan, Class 5 consists of unsecured creditors. Twenty creditors holding allowed claims of $100,000 are in this class. All of them vote. Fifteen of them, holding allowed claims of $50,000, vote to approve the plan. Five of them, holding allowed claims of $50,000, vote against the plan. One of the five voting against the plan is Reynolds, who holds an allowed claim of $25,000. Debtor asserts that Reynolds' rejection was not in good faith — and hence can be struck under §1126(c) — for the following two reasons:

> One is that the Plan proposes a payment of 10 percent on each unsecured claim, liquidation would give the unsecured creditors nothing and rejection of the Plan, therefore, makes no economic sense. The other is that debtor and Reynolds are engaged in litigation, including an anti-trust claim made by debtor. If debtor were proceeding in liquidation rather than reorganization, this litigation would be directed by the trustee in bankruptcy rather than debtor's officers. Debtor argues that the trustee would have less incentive to pursue the litigation than would debtor's officers.

Should Reynolds' vote be disregarded? See In re Landau Boat Co., 8 Bankr. 432 (Bankr. W.D. Mo. 1980).

9.11 Debtor has proposed a plan of reorganization. Class 1 consists of the bondholders. There are 30 bondholders, holding bonds with a face amount of $1,000,000. The plan proposes to extend the maturity date of the bonds by ten years. Ten of the bondholders, holding $300,000 of the bonds, vote against the plan. Twenty of the bondholders, holding $700,000 of the bonds vote in favor of the plan. Of these 20, five, holding $500,000 of bonds, are also majority stockholders of Debtor. May their votes bc disregarded under §1126(c)? Cf. Aladdin Hotel Co. v. Bloom, 200 F.2d 627 (8th Cir. 1953).

9.12 Debtor has filed a plan that describes "Class 4" as follows: "All allowed unsecured claims; each holder of a claim will receive, upon election of such holder, either (a) the amount of the claim, up to $1,000 in cash at confirmation, or (b) 50 percent of the allowed amount of the claim in a one year promissory note, bearing interest at 7 percent per annum." Creditor, a member of the class holding a $10,000 claim, votes against the plan, but is outvoted by reason of the presence of 95 creditors holding claims of between $500 and $1,000, all of whom (not surprisingly) accept the plan. Does Creditor have any basis for objecting? See §§1122, 1126; cf. Inforex's Plan of Reorganization, supra.

C. CONFIRMATION OF THE PLAN OF REORGANIZATION

NOTE ON THE BASIC ELEMENTS

The mechanics for confirming a plan are summarized in the following excerpt from In re Polytherm Industries, 33 Bankr. 823 (W.D. Wisc. 1983):

> A bankruptcy court can confirm a plan that has the voluntary acceptance of all creditors, including "deemed" acceptances by unimpaired classes of creditors, provided the plan meets the eleven conditions precedent set forth in 11 U.S.C. §1129(a). . . .
>
> If the reorganization plan meets all the requirements set forth in §1129(a) except for §1129(a)(8), the bankruptcy court may still confirm the plan under the cramdown provisions in §1129(b), that is, provisions which permit confirmation over objection. The cramdown provisions require a determination that adequate protection is afforded the dissenting impaired classes under the reorganization plan. 11 U.S.C. §1129(b). In this case, I will first review the amended plan to determine if it meets the §1129(a) requirements. Only if the amended plan passes muster under these conditions precedent excluding §1129(a)(8) will I apply the §1129(b) cramdown provisons.

The requirements for confirmation of a plan, set forth in §1129 (which, by virtue of §1129(a)(1), incorporates the other "applicable provisions of this title"), are numerous, and, as the excerpt from *Polytherm* suggests, the court should review those requirements sua sponte. But the heart of the requirements goes to the nature of the "creditors' bargain." When, if ever, may a *class* of claims or interests approve a plan over the objection of *individual* members of the class? And when, if ever, may a plan be approved over the objection of an entire *class* of claims or interests? Outside of bankruptcy, bond and trust indentures generally do not purport to authorize a majority, however large, to surrender other bondholders' rights to a cash payment in a specified amount or to maturity on a specified date, even though other contract provisions may be modified by majority vote. See Billyou, Corporate Mortgage Bonds and Majority Clauses, 57 Yale L. J. 595 (1948). Should this matter? On the other hand, should it matter that, in reorganizations, debt security holders often continue in the enterprise instead of being cashed out as in liquidations? Does this require some other means of measuring rights, instead of by liquidation values? Should rules applicable to a class of claimants under a single indenture apply as well to a class of discrete claimants (such as trade creditors) who have no contractual ties to one another?

Throughout the history of reorganizations, this question of rights of individuals in classes, and the rights of classes inter se, has been warmly debated. The two most commonly articulated standards of protection are called the "absolute priority rule" and the "relative priority rule," first named in Bonbright and Bergerman, Two Rival Theories of Priority Rights of Security Holders in a Corporate Reorganization, 28 Colum. L. Rev. 127 (1928). See also Blum, Full Priority and Full Compensation in Corporate Reorganizations: A Reappraisal, 25 U. Chi. L. Rev. 417 (1958); Blum, The Law and Language of Corporate Reorganization, 17 U. Chi. L. Rev. 565 (1950); Guthmann, Absolute Priority in Reorganization: Some Defects in a Supreme Court Doctrine, 45 Colum. L. Rev. 739 (1945); Foster, Conflicting Ideals for Reorganization, 44 Yale L.J. 923 (1935). The absolute priority rule, which Case v. Los Angeles Lumber Products Co., supra page 608, held controlled the procedures under Chapter X of the Bankruptcy Act of 1898, is embodied in §1129(b) of the Bankruptcy Code. Unlike old Chapter X, however, the absolute priority rule now comes into play only if a *class* of claims or interests has rejected the plan of reorganization, and the proponent of the plan nonetheless is attempting to achieve its confirmation. As a result, §1129(b)'s procedure is often called "cram down." Protection to the dissenting individual is provided in §1129(a)(7), which expresses a "not less than liquidation" standard.

PROBLEMS

9.13 Debtor is a closely held corporation whose sole asset is an apartment building. Debtor has 10 trade creditors to whom it owes a total of $12,000. Bank, which has a mortgage on the apartment building, is owed

$100,000. Bank's loan was made several years ago when interest rates were much lower. Debtor has filed for reorganization under Chapter 11, and Debtor's plan proposes paying all trade creditors in full and curing the defaults on the loan from Bank. Can the bankruptcy judge confirm this plan over Bank's objection? Would it make any difference if Debtor also owed Finance Company $10,000 on a loan that matures next year and Finance Company had a second lien on the apartment building? Assume that the plan proposes to pay Finance Company $1,400 a year for the next ten years, that Finance Company objects to the plan, but that the plan satisfies both the fair and equitable test and the best interests of the creditors test. See §§1124; 1129(a)(10).

9.14 Debtor has three unsecured creditors. Creditors A and B have claims under $1,000 each; Bank's claim, however, was for $200,000. Debtor's plan or reorganization placed Creditors A's and B's claims in an "administrative convenience" class (see §1122) and proposed to pay them with a cash payment of 95 percent of the claims on confirmation. The plan, however, proposed to pay Bank's claim with a five-year note at 20 percent of the value of the claim. Bank rejects the plan; Creditors A and B approve it. May Debtor use the acceptance of the administrative convenience class to satisfy §1129(a)(10)? See In re S & W Enterprises, 37 Bankr. 153 (Bankr. N.D. Ill. 1984).

9.15 Debtor has filed for reorganization under Chapter 11. At that time, Debtor owed $300,000 in back taxes to the federal government. May this tax claim be included in the same class with all the other unsecured claims? §507(a)(7). May Debtor's Chapter 11 plan propose payment of the $300,000 tax claim in installments? See §1129(a)(9)(C); cf. §1129(d). If so, may the plan propose payment of the $300,000 federal tax claim in six installments of $50,000 each? See In re Southern States Motor Inns, 709 F.2d 647 (11th Cir. 1983).

9.16 Debtor filed for reorganization under Chapter 11 on January 1. On February 1, Creditor sold supplies to Debtor "in the ordinary course of business" (§364(a)) with credit terms calling for payment of the amount due in 12 equal monthly installments, plus interest of 10 percent on the unpaid amount. On March 1, Debtor proposes a plan that schedules payment to Creditor under the terms provided in the February 1 contract. May Creditor insist on payment of the remainder of the amount due, in cash, on the effective date of the plan? See §§507(a)(1), 1129(a)(9); Inforex's Plan of Reorganization, supra.

IN RE JONES
32 Bankr. 951 (Bankr. D. Utah 1983)

Glen E. CLARK, Bankruptcy Judge.
The issue in this case is whether cure and compensation payments under 11 U.S.C. §1124(2) may be made in deferred cash payments com-

mencing after the effective date of a chapter 11 plan. The ruling is that they may not.

INTRODUCTION

Debtors' chapter 11 plan places two allowed secured claims into separate classes, designated B-2 and B-3. The obligation underlying each claim is in default. The plan intends to cure the defaults and leave these two classes unimpaired by complying with Section 1124(2).

Section 1124(2) provides for curing defaults and leaving classes unimpaired under a chapter 11 plan. A class of claims or interests is not impaired even though there has been a default which, under a contract or applicable law, triggers the right to demand or receive accelerated payment if, with respect to each holder of a claim or interest of that class, the plan

> (A) cures any such default, other than a default of a kind specified in section 365(b)(2) of this title,[1] that occurred before or after the commencement of the case under [title 11];
> (B) reinstates the maturity of such claim or interest as such maturity date existed before such default;
> (C) compensates the holder of such claim or interest for any damages incurred as a result of any reasonable reliance by such holder on such contractual provision or applicable law; and
> (D) does not otherwise alter the legal, equitable, or contractual rights to which such claim or interest entitles the holder of such claim or interest.*

Debtors plan to pay the money required to cure and compensate for defaults under subsections (A) and (C) by making monthly cash installment payments commencing thirty days after the effective date of the plan.[2]

---

1. Section 365(b)(2) specifies three types of defaults: defaults that are breaches of a provision relating to (1) the insolvency or financial condition of the debtor at any time before the closing of the case; (2) the commencement of a bankruptcy case; or (3) the appointment of or taking possession by a trustee in a bankruptcy case or a custodian before the commencement of a case. These defaults need not be cured under Section 1124(2)(A). It is by no means clear that the right to demand or receive accelerated payment must arise under a contract or a statute. Section 1124(2) uses the term "law" not the term "statute." In re Madison Hotel Associates, 29 B.R. 1003 (D.C.W.D. Wis. 1983), for example, reads Section 1124(2) too narrowly when it refers to "a right to accelerated payments arising under a contractual provision or statute." 29 B.R. at 1006. See also 29 B.R. at 1008: "[C]laims that reflect an automatic statutory or contractual right to acceleration."

* This section was reworded slightly in 1984. — EDS.

2. The plan defines "effective date" as "the date 30 days after the date upon which the order of confirmation is no longer subject to appeal or certiorari proceedings, on which date no such appeal or certiorari proceeding is then pending, and on which date all of the conditions to the effectiveness of the plan expressly set forth in the plan have been satisfied fully or effectively waived." The propriety of such a definition has been questioned. See note 13.

Class B-2 will receive about $1,436.00 in approximately eighteen and one-half monthly payments of $85.00. Class B-3 will receive approximately $7,000.00 in one $5,500.00 payment on the effective date of the plan and the balance in monthly payments of $50.00. Debtors propose to add 12 percent annual interest to the unpaid cure and compensation amounts.

At the confirmation hearing, the court questioned whether the cure and compensation payments specified by Section 1124(2) may be made over time after the effective date of the plan even if sufficient interest is added to give present value as of the effective date, or whether those payments must be made on or before the effective date. That issue was taken under advisement and is decided by this memorandum opinion.

DISCUSSION

Debtors advance two arguments. First, debtors claim entitlement to make their cure and compensation payments over time after the effective date of their plan because the language of Section 1124(2) fixes no time limits for cure or compensation, unlike Section 1322(b)(5) which requires cure of defaults "within a reasonable time," unlike Section 365(b)(1)(A) which requires cure or adequate assurance of prompt cure of defaults "at the time of assumption" of a contract or lease, and unlike Section 1124(3) which requires payment of cash "on the effective date of the plan." See also Section 1110(a)(2) (requiring cure of certain defaults under contracts relating to aircraft equipment and vessels within 60 days after the date of the order for relief) and Section 1168(a)(2) (similar provision for contracts relating to rolling stock).

Second, debtors contend that classes designated to receive installment payments for cure and compensation of defaults do not need the protections given by Section 1129(b) because, in debtors' view, the only Section 1129(b) issues raised by this plan are the interest rate necessary to give present value and the feasibility of the plan. Debtors say these issues can be determined at confirmation just as easily under Section 1124(2) as under Section 1129(b). This contention is made in view of the second approach to impairment described in In re Barrington Oaks General Partnership, 15 B.R. 952, 963-964 (Bkrtcy. D. Utah 1981), viz., a class is impaired "where necessary to prevent wrongs which are redressable under Section 1129(b)."

In my judgment, debtors' proposal for installment payments after the effective date of their plan, though well-intentioned and arguably not forbidden by the words of Section 1124(2), impairs classes B-2 and B-3. This conclusion is based on an analysis of the plan under the two approaches to impairment explained in *Barrington Oaks*.

The bankruptcy code adopts the concept of "private control [of the reorganization process] with a minimum of judicial intrusion." *Barrington Oaks,* supra at 958. Chapter 11 is "a vehicle to channel negotiation among the parties." Aaron, "The Bankruptcy Reform Act of 1978: The Full-Employment-For-Lawyers Bill Part V: Business Reorganization," 1982 Utah L. Rev. 1, 16. . . .

Courts, debtors, and creditors should approach reorganization in ways that discourage litigation and promote negotiation. Chapter 11 supplies useful tools which, in the hands of enlightened debtors and creditors willing to substitute bargaining for brawling, can remedy otherwise irreparable financial disasters. Two provisions of chapter 11 which were designed to limit litigation are Sections 1124 and 1129.

If all classes of claims and interests accept a chapter 11 plan, the plan's proponent need only satisfy the requirements of Section 1129(a) to secure confirmation of the plan. But if any class is impaired under and has not accepted the plan, the plan's proponent must also prove that the plan meets the specifications of Section 1129(b). Section 1129(b) bars confirmation of a plan impairing a class that has not accepted the plan unless "the plan does not discriminate unfairly, and is fair and equitable."

Deciding whether a chapter 11 plan does not discriminate unfairly and is fair and equitable is complicated. Kenneth N. Klee, one of the drafters of Section 1129(b), has stated that to understand when a plan may be confirmed over the dissent of a class "involves a tortuous journey through the statute and legislative history that is fraught with complex concepts, terms of art, and innuendoes." Klee, "All You Ever Wanted to Know About Cram Down Under the New Bankruptcy Code," 53 Am. Bank. L.J. 133, 136 (1979). Although an intellectual grasp of the statute can be gained by study, applying the statute to particular cases is arduous. Litigation under Section 1129(b) is expensive, time consuming, and unpredictable. In many cases the cost and delay can be fatal to the reorganization. "[T]he patient may die on the operating table while the lawyers are diagnosing." H.R. Rep. No. 95-595, 95th Cong., 1st Sess. 229 (1977), U.S. Code and Admin. News 1978, pp. 5787, 6189.

For these reasons, the threat of forcing a hearing under Section 1129(b) is a potent source of creditor power in chapter 11. On the other hand, the power to confirm a plan over the dissent of a class of claims or interests gives the proponent of a chapter 11 plan a significant advantage in negotiating a plan. Thus, "[t]he threat of cramdown . . . overshadows the bargaining." Miller, [Bankruptcy Code Cramdown Under Chapter 11, 62 B.U.L. Rev. 1059 (1982)], at 1076. "Perhaps the principal use of Section 1129(b) will be as a bargaining club which dissidents on the one hand or plan proponents on the other may employ to reach agreement rather than face the trials and tribulations of a section 1129(b) proceeding." Coogan, [Confirmation of a Plan Under the Bankruptcy Code, 32 Case W. Res. L. Rev. 301 (1982)], at 362. . . .

Congress interposed the unfair discrimination and fair and equitable tests as safeguards for dissenting impaired classes. At the same time, however, Congress determined that those protections are not needed and that the burdens and risks of a hearing under Section 1129(b) may be avoided for a class not impaired under the plan. Thus, classes left unimpaired by a plan are deemed by Section 1126(f) to have accepted the plan and solicitation of acceptances from holders of claims or interests of those classes is not required.

Debtors, anxious to avoid the perils of a Section 1129(b) hearing, may wish to use Section 1124 to leave unimpaired as many classes as possible. Classes of claims or interests, hoping to have the protection and leverage given by Section 1129(b), may desire to be found impaired under Section 1124.

Debtors may also wish to create unimpaired classes under Section 1124(2) because it enables reversal of contractual or legal acceleration and retention of advantageous contract terms. "Curing of the default and the assumption of the debt in accordance with its terms is an important reorganization technique for dealing with a particular class of claims, especially secured claims." S. Rep. No. 95-989, 95th Cong., 2d Sess. 120 (1978) U.S. Code Cong. & Admin. News 1978, p. 5906. But see In re Taddeo, [685 F.2d 24, 29 (2d Cir. 1982)] (The authority to cure is found in Section 1123(a)(5)(G) not in Section 1124(2)). . . . But creditors who are parties to agreements a debtor wishes to reinstate under Section 1124(2) may argue they are impaired in order to escape a contract with terms favorable to the debtor. Section 1124 and its interpretation therefore occupy a pivotal position.

Barrington Oaks, supra, offers two approaches to impairment. The first examines the plan in light of the language and purpose of Section 1124 and strictly construes Sections 1124(1) and (2) to find impairment whenever the plan alters rights in any way not expressly permitted by Sections 1124(1) and (2). The second scrutinizes the plan's treatment of the affected classes in light of the protections provided by Section 1129(b) and finds impairment "where necessary to prevent wrongs which are redressable under Section 1129(b)." 15 B.R. at 964. Debtors' plan impairs the two classes designated to receive installment payments of cure and compensation money under either approach.

IMPAIRMENT UNDER THE FIRST APPROACH

Classes B-2 and B-3 are impaired under the first approach to impairment of *Barrington Oaks* because the imposition of installment payments to cure and compensate for defaults is an expansion of the permissible alterations intended under Section 1124(2). Debtors' proposal collides, in several particulars, with the intended use and effect of Section 1124. Senate Report 95-989, U.S. Code Cong. & Admin. News 1978, p. 5906, supra, explains Section 1124(2) as follows:

[A] claim or interest is unimpaired by curing the effect of a default and reinstating the original terms of an obligation when maturity was brought on or accelerated by the default. The intervention of bankruptcy and the defaults represent a temporary crisis which the plan of reorganization is intended to clear away. The holder of a claim or interest who under the plan is restored to his original position, when others receive less or get nothing at all, is fortunate indeed and has no cause to complain.[10]

While it may be argued that Section 1124(2) does not expressly require claim or interest holders to be restored to their original positions by the effective date of the plan, a better interpretation is that "Section 1124(2) requires that the curing of the default occur as of the effective date of the plan because the creditor is impaired until the time the default is cured." In re Otero Mills, Inc., [31 Bankr. 185 (Bankr. D.N. Mex. 1983)], at 1042. Several reasons recommend this interpretation.

Debtors' proposal encourages wasteful litigation over the timing, methods, and effects of cure and compensation under Section 1124(2). The absence of guidelines for the timing of post-effective date payments would multiply litigation. For example, if debtors' proposal for cure and compensation over approximately eighteen months with respect to class B-2 were permissible, what of cure and compensation over twenty-four, thirty-six, or forty-eight months? The court would have no standards by which to decide the issue, causing the proper cure period under Section 1124 to expand and contract without a controlling statutory rationale. Section 1124 is supposed to be a measuring rod for impairment. *Barrington Oaks*, supra at 959 n.19. A measuring rod with inconstant increments, changing between measurements, is useless. Thus, Section 1124 should be strictly construed.

Methods for leaving a class unimpaired under Section 1124 should be exclusive. The non-limiting terms "includes" and "including" do not precede Section 1124's list of options. A class is impaired unless the plan provides one of the three specified alternative treatments. From the outset, parties know that any plan specifying a class as unimpaired must give one of only three treatments. No creativity, with resulting unpredictability, is permitted. Debtors' proposal, if accepted, would broaden the terms "cures" and "compensates" under Sections 1124(2)(A) and (C) and thus create ambiguity and invite disputes.

Section 1124 is meant to be definitive. A class is either impaired or not. There is no middle ground. The uncertainties of former law, with its reference to "material" and "adverse" effects, are abolished. The change from "material" and "adverse" effect to Section 1124's three options avoids disputes over degree and direction of the workings of a plan. Sec-

---

10. This justification of Section 1124 may not be wholly comforting to creditors in some cases. A class may be impaired in fact and yet not be impaired in law under Section 1124. See In re Rolling Green Country Club, 26 B.R. 729, 735 (Bkrtcy. D. Minn. 1982). Nonimpairment under Section 1124 may not mean that a class receives all of its legal rights. . . .

tion 1124 should establish, as nearly as possible, a bright line test for impairment. . . .

Debtors' proposal would cloud the certainty of Section 1124 by requiring the court to inquire into the effects of delay of cure and compensation.

Finally, debtors' proposal encourages litigation over the value of the deferred payments. Section 1124 is designed to be free, for the most part, of disputes over valuation. As explained in *Barrington Oaks,* supra at 962-963, "Value . . . is irrelevant under Section 1124; 'any alteration of rights constitutes impairment even if the value of the rights is enhanced.'" [Citing 5 Collier on Bankruptcy, supra at ¶1124.03(1) at 1124-12 and 1124-14 and Klee, supra at 140 n.55]. "Indeed, the purpose of Section 1124 to avoid cramdown would be defeated by requiring valuation of claims to determine impairment. By driving a wedge between the concept of impairment and the vagaries of value, parties may know with greater certainty whether or not they are impaired. This certainty should reduce litigation and aid negotiation toward a plan, the goals which Section 1124 was established to further." The history of the congressional development of Section 1124 illustrates the drafters' "aversion to valuation hearings." Id. at 963 n.24. Thus, courts should, where possible, construe Section 1124 to eliminate the obscurities of valuation. Debtors' proposal would require the court to value the deferred cash payments. This would necessitate a determination of the appropriate interest rate, a concept which, like value in bankruptcy cases, has proven itself to be "an elusive Pimpernel." In re Jones, 5 B.R. 736, 738 (Bkrtcy. E.D. Va. 1980).[12]

For these reasons Section 1124(2) should be construed to require completion of cure and compensation by the effective date of the plan. While the term "effective date" is subject to interpretation,[13] requiring

---

12. Few other issues under the bankruptcy code have produced so many opinions with such varied results as has the issue of the appropriate interest rate for determining present value. . . .

13. The phrase "effective date of the plan" is not defined by the code. Thus, the outside limits on the effective date of a plan are somewhat hazy. A rule of reason is probably the best rule. . . . The entry of an order confirming a chapter 11 plan has far-reaching statutory effects independent of the effective date of the plan. See §§347(b) and 1143, 362(c), 365(b)(2), 524, 1104, 1105, 1106(a)(7) and Rule 2015(a)(5), 1112(b)(7) and (8), 1112(d), 1129(c), 1141, 1142, and 1144. See also Bankruptcy Rules 2015(a)(5), 3020(c), 3021, 4008, and 8002(a); Hopper, "Confirmation of a Plan Under Chapter 11 of the Bankruptcy Code and the Effect of Confirmation on Creditors' Rights," 15 Ind. L. Rev. 501 (1982). This fact supports placing the effective date on or close to the date of the entry of the order confirming the plan. "The effective date of the plan" is expressly designated as the critical point for the major financial standards for confirmation. See §§1129(a)(7), 1129(a)(9), 1129(b). The valuations required by these sections are likely to be less accurate if the effective date is not close to the date of the hearing on confirmation. As a practical matter, it may not be possible in some cases to make the effective date the same date as the date of the hearing on confirmation because some claims may not have been allowed by then. For example, administrative claims covered by Section 1129(a)(9)(A) may remain unallowed or objections to claims may be unresolved. See Hopper, supra at 517. It is difficult to combine these considerations into a rule more precise than that the effective date of the plan should be reasonably close to the date of the confirmation hearing.

cure and compensation by the effective date of the plan would minimize litigation over timing, method, and effect of cure and compensation, conform Section 1124(2) to Section 1124(3) which requires payment on the effective date of the plan, and shift litigation over present value to Section 1129(b) where it belongs.

IMPAIRMENT UNDER THE SECOND APPROACH

Debtors' plan impairs classes B-2 and B-3 under the second approach to impairment of *Barrington Oaks*. Because the plan proposes deferred cash payments, both classes need the protection of Section 1129(b). Section 1129(b) was intended to test deferred cash payments. Debtors' plan would permit Section 1124(2)'s use as a cram down device without shielding the affected classes from unfair or inequitable treatment, a use of Section 1124 which was both anticipated and disapproved by the drafters of Section 1124.

Section 1124 was not intended for use as a tool for cram down. An illustration is Section 1124(3)'s requirement of payment in cash. One early version of Section 1124(3) would have permitted payment in cash or property having a present value equalling cash. H.R. 8200, 95th Cong., 1st Sess. §1124(3) (1977); S. 2266, 95th Cong., §1124(3), as introduced (Oct. 29, 1977). Payments over time were permitted if they had a value as of the plan's effective date equal to the allowed amount of the claim or interest. See H.R. Rep. No. 95-595, supra at 408.

At hearings held before a Senate subcommittee, witnesses criticized proposed Section 1124(3) for not requiring prompt cash payment. . . . After these hearings, the Senate Judiciary Committee favorably reported S. 2266 with amendments to Section 1124(3) requiring "cash payments." According to Collier,

> [T]he language of the Senate amendment was intended to prevent Section 1124(3) from being used as a form of cram down. This was possible because the House bill [H.R. 8200] did not require payment of claims in cash, but rather permitted a claim to be unimpaired if the holder of the claim received 'full' payment in property, other than securities of the debtor. Since 'property' as used in the House Bill included all forms of property including evidence of debt, and since commercial notes were excluded from the definition of security, it could be argued that a secured creditor receiving an unsecured commercial note of a value, as of the effective date of the plan, equal to the allowed amount of its secured claim, would be unimpaired and thus not entitled to vote against the plan or to the protection afforded under Section 1129(b).

Collier supra. . . . ¶1124.01 at 1124-3. See also S. Rep. No. 95-989, supra at 120, U.S. Code Cong. & Admin. News 1978, p. 5906. ("Section 1124 does not include payment 'in property' other than cash. Except for a rare case, claims or interests are not by their terms payable in property, but a plan may so provide and those affected thereby may accept or reject the proposed plan. They may not be forced to accept a plan declaring the holders' claims or interests to be 'unimpaired.' "). Section 1124(3) was amended again before its enactment. One amendment underscored the requirement of cash in full on the effective date of the plan by changing the words "cash payments" to "cash."

These amendments manifest congressional intent to prohibit deferred cash payments under Section 1124(3) and thus to prevent dissenting classes from being forced to accept deferred cash payments, even if of a present value equal to their claims or interests, without being given sanctuary against unfair discrimination or unfair or inequitable treatment. Section 1124(2) should be construed to prevent its use as a cram down device by permitting forced non-contractual time payments. Section 1124(2), like Section 1124(3), does not protect against unfair discrimination or require fair and equitable treatment. Surely Congress did not intend to permit under Section 1124(2) the same injury it prevented when it narrowed Section 1124(3).

Although debtors propose, in effect, to amend Section 1124(2) to permit the affected classes to litigate feasibility and present value under Section 1124(2), that power is reserved to Congress.[14] Accord, In re Otero Mills, Inc., supra at 1042.

CONCLUSION

Classes B-2 and B-3 are impaired under debtors' plan. Cure and compensation required by Section 1124(2) must be completed by the effective date of the plan if impairment is to be avoided. Debtors may treat classes B-2 and B-3 in the same manner proposed in the plan but, if they desire to do so, must amend the plan to specify that classes B-2 and B-3 are impaired and permit them to vote.

14. Moreover, even if these proposals were judicially grafted onto Section 1124(2), the full protection afforded by Section 1129(b) would still be lacking. The fair and equitable standard includes more elements than those listed in Sections 1129(b)(2)(A), 1129(b)(2)(B), and 1129(b)(2)(C). Because Section 1129(b)(2) uses the non-limiting term "includes," the alternatives listed in subsections (A), (B), and (C) of Section 1129(b)(2) are not safe harbors for meeting the fair and equitable test. "Fair and equitable" is a term of art which carries with it decades of judicial interpretation. . . . Congress clearly intended to transfer some of the judicial gloss placed on the fair and equitable test under former law into the fair and equitable test under Section 1129(b). An example of an uncodified element of the fair and equitable test is that "a dissenting class should be assured that no senior class receives more than 100 percent of the amount of its claims." 124 Cong. Rec. H.11,103 (Sept. 28, 1978); S.17,420 (Oct. 6, 1978). Other requirements may apply. See, e.g., In re Lloyd Hendricks, Bankr. No. 82M-00590, unpublished transcript of ruling at 29 (Bk. D. Utah May 17, 1983). (The requirement under former law that classes required to take a lower grade of interest are entitled to receive some compensation or bonus for that reduction in rights is part of the fair and equitable test.) . . .

NOTE ON JUDGMENTS OF FORECLOSURE
AND §1124

Section 1124(2) provides that a class of interests is not impaired if, inter alia, the plan cures defaults and "reinstates the maturity of such claim or interest. . . . " One consequence of this is specified in §1126(f): "a class that is not impaired under a plan, and each holder of a claim or interest of such class, are conclusively presumed to have accepted the plan. . . . " One troublesome question concerning §1124 is *when* it can be used. More specifically, can §1124(2) be used if, in addition to a default, there has also been a judgment of foreclosure? A negative answer to that question was given by the District Court in In re Madison Hotel Associates, 29 Bankr. 1003 (W.D. Wisc. 1983), rev'd, 749 F.2d 410 (7th Cir. 1984). The core of Judge Crabb's reasoning follows; is it persuasive?

In the bankruptcy court's opinion [in In re Hewitt, 16 Bankr. 973 (Bankr. D. Alaska 1982)], §1124 read with 11 U.S.C. §101(4), evinces "a Congressional intent *to apply the remedy of §1124(2)* to obligations regardless of whether or not they have been reduced to judgment." (Emphasis added.) In this last statement, the bankruptcy court reveals its misconception of §1124. This statute has nothing to do with "remedies" of cure and default; it is concerned only with identification of those classes entitled to vote on the acceptance of a plan. . . .

. . . §1124(2) is not a provision to be interpreted broadly; rather, it is a narrow exception to the general concept of impairment.

The bankruptcy court erred again in *Hewitt* when it stated that §1124 "declares that 'no class of claims' is impaired by reversal of acceleration, and 'claim' is defined in §101(4) to include any 'right to payment, whether or not such right is reduced to judgment. . . . '" In re Hewitt, 16 Bankr. at 977. This is not what §1124 "declares." Section 1124 does not say anywhere that "no class of claims is impaired by reversal of acceleration"; it says that any class of claims is impaired except those claims that reflect an automatic statutory or contractual right to acceleration and that are to be cured in the plan.

In my opinion, the bankruptcy court was also wrong in holding that the formal entry of judgment is nothing more than the application of a contractual provision or statute requiring acceleration of payments upon default. A judicially-recognized right to foreclosure is something different from a right to accelerated payments that arises by operation of a contractual provision or of applicable law. It is a right that arises only at the conclusion of a judicial proceeding and only after a court has determined the rights and obligations of the parties. To say that a court order is nothing more than the application of "applicable law" to "contractual provision," and therefore within the exception set out in §1124(2) is to misread the language of the statute and the intention of Congress. . . .

It is consistent with its expressed concern for *temporary* crises "which the plan of reorganization is intended to clear away," . . . that in §1124, Congress excluded only those creditors who had *automatic* acceleration rights from voting on the acceptance of a plan. By its very nature, a court order of foreclosure is a different kind of claim, reflecting a longer lasting financial crisis, extending at least as long as the period of time necessary for the lender to seek and obtain relief from a court.

It is not only the derivation of Prudential's right to foreclosure that distinguishes from the class of claims considered unimpaired under §1124(2), it is the fact that through the judicial proceeding Prudential has acquired a right that is separate from, and additional to, the right to accelerated payments. By virtue of the decision determining its right to foreclosure, Prudential is not limited to recovery of accelerated payments from the debtor; it has the right to begin proceedings to seek recovery of its investment from some source other than the financially-troubled mortgagor.

In footnote 1 of *Jones,* Judge Clark criticizes a portion of *Madison Hotel* as reading §1124(2) "too narrowly." Do you agree? A more sustained disagreement surfaced in Valente v. Savings Bank of Rockville, 34 Bankr. 362 (D. Conn. 1983), which focuses on §1123(a)(5)(G) as well. In *Valente,* the bankruptcy judge held that, under the state-law doctrine of "merger," "once a foreclosure has gone to judgment, the mortgage is merged into the judgment, leaving the mortgagor with only the right to redeem by payment of the entire debt." The bankruptcy judge then held that the merger doctrine should not be upset by bankruptcy without explicit Congressional authorization. In reversing, Judge Clarie first held that the judgment of foreclosure was not final, and there could be no merger until that time. The court, however, did not rest its decision entirely on that state-law point:

> Because the opportunity to cure a default, secured by federal bankruptcy law and designed to protect "the estates of debtors for their rehabilitation," is "paramount" to state law, no actual conflict exists with "state court jurisdiction." . . . Thus, where cure is allowed by the Bankruptcy Code, any debtor who maintains a viable interest in property comprehended by the Code should have the opportunity to present a plan of cure before the equitable powers of the Bankruptcy Court.
>
> The Valentes are just such debtors. Under Connecticut law, they own an equity of redemption, unless and until a sale takes place and is confirmed. . . . Equities of redemption are "equitable interests of the debtor in property," 11 U.S.C. §541, and are thus part of the estate over which the Bankruptcy Court has jurisdiction. . . . Thus, the Bankruptcy Code, specifically the curative provisions of Chapter 11, may be exercised by the debtors in this case, even after a final state court judgment, to attempt to de-accelerate their debt and reinstate their mortgage. . . .
>
> Chapter 11 authorizes cure of a default in 11 U.S.C. §1123(a)(5)(G). . . . The Court finds that the authority to cure granted by §1123(a)(5)(G) encompasses the "power to de-accelerate."
>
> The Court further finds that the power to cure . . . reaches even to state courts' final judgments. Nothing in the language of this sub-section restricts its "power to deaccelerate" from reaching such judgments. Rather,

the express language of the subsection provides for the cure of "any default" without limitation. This conclusion is buttressed by the context in which the curing authorization arises. This provision is part and parcel of subsection (a)(5), which provides the means by which a debtor executes his proposed plan. The latter's plan, as evidenced by §1123(a)(1-4), reorganizes and disposes of "claims." "Claims," according to 11 U.S.C. §101(4), include any rights to payment, whether or not they have been "reduced to judgment." If the plan, and by necessary implication, its executing section, §(a)(5), were meant to dispose of judgments, as well as claims not yet reduced to judgment, so, too, must the curing provision, one of the several means listed in §(a)(5) for said disposition, reach judgments. . . .

. . . Deciding whether a plan cures a defaulted-upon claim is therefore a necessary precondition to determining whether or not that claim is impaired. Thus, if the Bankruptcy Court on remand finds that the debtors' plan cures the default at issue, the bank's claim may be deemed "not impaired" under §1124(2).

This Court is aware that In re Madison Hotel, 29 Bankr. 1003 (D.C. Wis. 1983) holds otherwise regarding impairment, but this Court declines to follow the holding of that case. Although *Madison Hotel* conducted a thorough investigation of the statutory language of §1124, it did so outside of the context of §1123(a)(5)(G). In so doing, *Madison Hotel* failed to consider the impact of the latter sub-section, the provision authorizing cure, upon §1124(2). . . .

The Seventh Circuit reversed Judge Crabb, relying on its reading of the legislative history and the reasoning in *Hewitt.* How broadly is §1123(a)(5)(G) to be read? Could the debtor cure a default after an eviction pursuant to a judgment of foreclosure? If not, is it so obvious that the line should be drawn where *Valente* draws it? This issue will also arise, albeit in a slightly different statutory context, in considering Chapter 13 plans, which we will examine in conjunction with *Taddeo,* infra page 922, in Chapter 12.

IN RE MERRIMACK VALLEY OIL CO.
32 Bankr. 485 (Bankr. D. Mass. 1983)

James N. GABRIEL, Bankruptcy Judge.

This matter arises out of the application for confirmation of the Chapter 11 plans proposed by these five jointly administered debtors. . . .

FINDINGS OF FACT

The five debtors in these cases are: Thomas F. Fay, Jr., Oil Sales, Inc. ("Fay Oil"), Merrimack Valley Oil Co., Inc. ("Merrimack"), The Fay Group, Inc. ("Fay Group"), and Thomas F. Fay, Jr. and Mary B. Fay, husband and wife ("The Fays"). The three corporations filed voluntary Chapter 11 petitions on November 18, 1981. The Fays filed on December 30, 1981.

Fay Oil, the parent company, is engaged in the wholesale purchase and sale of industrial and home heating oil in North Andover, Massachusetts. Merrimack, a wholly-owned subsidiary, is a retailer of home heating fuel in North Andover. The other wholly-owned subsidiary, the Fay Group, buys, sells, raises and races standard-bred horses. The Fays, husband and wife, reside in Windham, New Hampshire.

Since the commencement of these cases, the debtors have operated their businesses as debtors-in-possession. They have incurred substantial losses and approximately $400,000 in post-petition debt that is entitled to priority pursuant to 11 U.S.C. Section 503. Approximately $390,000 of the post-petition indebtedness represents new purchases of oil from Global Petroleum Corporation ("Global") which has extended the oil company debtors a line of credit of $500,000. The indebtedness to Global is secured by a security interest in all assets of the debtors.

The debtors' major unsecured creditor is Belcher New England, Inc. ("Belcher"), a former supplier, which alleges it is owed approximately two million dollars for goods sold and delivered and opposes confirmation of the debtors' plan.

The debtors' consolidated First Amended Plan of Reorganization ("Plan"), filed on October 5, 1982, provides for a thirty-five per cent (35 percent) dividend to unsecured creditors, to be paid over three years, and an extra five per cent (5 percent) to Belcher. Administrative expenses ($157,000) are to be paid on confirmation together with a five per cent (5 percent) dividend to unsecured creditors ($159,700) and a partial tax dividend ($20,875) for a total $447,575. For the next two years the debtors must pay $339,400 each year in cash on the anniversary of confirmation. The third deferred payment is to be combined with a bonus of $136,350 to Belcher for a required fourth payment of $475,750 on the third anniversary of confirmation. Total payments required under the plan are $1,492,125 assuming that all claims are allowed in full.

The debtors' disclosure statement and plan and ballots were sent to creditors and a hearing on acceptances and confirmation was scheduled for December 16, 1982. At this time the debtors objected to the claims of Belcher and sought to disqualify Belcher from voting because its three proofs of claims totalling two million three hundred thousand dollars ($2,300,000) were undocumented, and because Belcher's votes rejecting the plan were in bad faith. After an examination of the proofs of claims, argument of counsel for both parties, and review of the applicable Rules of Bankruptcy Procedure, the Court disallowed Belcher's claims for voting purposes only.

Having disqualified the votes of Belcher, it appeared that the requisite number of acceptances was present, and the Court conducted the hearing on confirmation.

BEST INTEREST OF CREDITORS TEST

One prerequisite of confirmation is that creditors receive as much under the plan as they would under a Chapter 7 liquidation. Unless there is unanimous acceptance of the plan by each member of each class, the Court must find that each creditor:

> will receive or retain under the plan on account of such claim or interest property of a value, as of the effective date of the plan, that is not less than the amount that such holder would so receive or retain if the debtor were liquidated under Chapter 7 of this title on such date;

11 U.S.C. Section 1129(a)(7).

The liquidation values are found to be as follows:

Cash	$ 310,900
Inventories	63,600
Real Estate — Business	100,000
Real Estate — Residential	340,000
Transportation Equipment	294,000
Furniture and Fixtures	10,000
Race Horses	173,000
Accounts Receivable	282,400
Other Assets	14,000
TOTAL NET REALIZABLE VALUE	$1,587,900

The value of goodwill and customer list is found to be highly speculative in the light of the restrictions and covenants required for their sale to be of any consequence.

The secured and priority claims are as follows:

Notes and mortgages	$ 126,100
Chapter 11 fees and expenses	157,500
Priority claims under Chapter 11	113,100
Post-filing debt	394,900
Estimated Chapter 7 expenses	160,000
TOTAL	$ 951,600

The net amount available on liquidation is therefore $636,000 or approximately twenty per cent (20 percent) of unsecured debt of $3,193,975.

The plan provides for thirty-five per cent (35 percent) to unsecured creditors and forty per cent (40 percent) to Belcher for its allowed claim. The present value of said payments is twenty-nine per cent (29 percent) (32 percent to Belcher). In liquidation, payment would not be made for at least six months of conversion to Chapter 7 because creditors have six months to file proofs of claims pursuant to Bankruptcy Rule 302(e). Secured creditors and administrative claimants are not impaired under the plan. Accordingly, I find that the debtors' plan which offers creditors 35 percent to 40 percent over three years, which amounts to a present value of 29 percent to 32 percent, is in the best interests of creditors, and complies with the requirements of 11 U.S.C. Section 1129(a)(7).

FEASIBILITY

The next issue is the debtors' compliance with U.S.C. Section 1129(a)(11) which obliges a Court to find that:

> confirmation of the plan is not likely to be followed by the liquidation, or the need for further financial reorganization, of the debtor or any successor to the debtor under the plan, unless such liquidation is proposed in the plan.

The purpose of this requirement, which was adopted from the 1898 Bankruptcy Act's requirement of feasibility, is to ensure that the plan offers a reasonably workable prospect of success and is not a visionary scheme. . . . In determining whether a plan passes the feasibility test, the Court should consider (1) the adequacy of the capital structure; (2) the earning power of the business; (3) economic conditions; and (4) the ability of management. . . .

Where a debtor proposes to fund a plan out of operating revenue, its financial record during the pendency of the Chapter 11 is probative of feasibility. . . . Income projections indicating financial progress must be based on concrete evidence of financial progress, and must not be speculative, conjectural or unrealistic predictions. . . .

In the present case the debtors intend to make their payments from the income of the three companies and if they fall short on any payment, they will liquidate the amount of assets necessary to make any payment. The plan proposes the following repayment schedule:

On confirmation	$ 337,575
First anniversary	339,400
Second anniversary	339,400
Third Anniversary	475,750
Total	$1,492,125

It is undisputed that the debtors have no commitment for financing except the line of credit of $500,000 for purchases of oil. The reorganized debtors will have only horses — worth $173,000 — and the oil company's fixed assets — vehicles and equipment worth $300,000 — to serve as collateral. The debtors intend to grant a $250,000 mortgage on their home to the creditors' committee. Both accountants attested to the difficulties the reorganized debtors would have in obtaining financing. In addition, the lack of any present commitment precludes reasonable reliance on financing as a method of funding the plan. In addition, to the extent additional financing is necessary, even if available, the debt service required would be an additional drain on cash flow.

There is no doubt that the debtors can meet the first payment on confirmation from the cash on hand which was raised by the simple expedient of creating post-filing secured debt from the principal supplier, Global, which is, in effect, a funder, rather than a source of working capital. However, I am unable to accept that the debtors' projections are reliable.

Historically, the previous five years of operation of the debtors amounted to losses totalling $325,000 as follows:

Fiscal year ended	Sales	Net income or (loss)
September 30, 1978	$12,071,000	$ 9,000
September 30, 1979	17,088,000	9,000
September 30, 1980	23,907,000	64,000
September 30, 1981	36,763,000	(226,000)
September 30, 1982	8,757,000	(181,000)

The debtor's projections seek to establish that there will be a profit for the fiscal year ended September 30, 1983, of $79,150 plus an additional profit for the quarter ended December 31, 1983 of $28,700 or a total profit of $107,800 for the fifteen-month period. To this amount the debtors seek to add all of the depreciation expense of $277,200 for this fifteen-month period as a source of funds to meet the payment schedule of the plan.

The depreciation during this period is as follows:

Race Horses	$110,400
Motor Vehicles, etc.	111,900
Total	$222,300

While the debtors point to the depreciation as a source of funds to meet the payments due, the total of net profit plus depreciation or gross cash flow of $301,450 is still $37,950 short of the $339,400 due in each of the next two years and $174,300 short of the final payment of $475,750. Thus, there is an initial shortfall of $250,200 before taking into account the cash requirements for replacement of race horses and motor vehicles, increases in accounts receivable and inventories (especially at peak season), and the servicing of mortgage debt on the personal assets as well as the other advances to the principal officer. Although the debtors' various assets have a limited life, the debtors project no expenditures for any purchases of trucks, horses or equipment which must be replaced. The projections do not provide a cushion for contingencies or extraordinary expenses which will necessarily be required by virtue of the wasting nature of the assets. Furthermore, the debtors' failure to include costs for replacement of assets is inconsistent with Thomas Fay's testimony that he took withdrawals of $69,000 in 1982 to purchase horses for the Fay Group. Expenditures for replacement of fixed assets must be contemplated, but no such expenditures are included in any of the projections. Without expenditures for such purchases the projections cannot be considered reliable.

A critical flaw in the debtors' projections is their blanket extension of their projections for the period for September 1982 to December 1983. Forgetting that this period covers fifteen months, debtors use the fifteen month figures to cover each subsequent year of operations without any basis. Moreover, using the first fifteen months projections for the subsequent years ignores any inflation factor, which should be included. While on the subject of the economy, it should be noted that any projections in the businesses of these debtors must be suspect in view of the unstable nature of the oil market, both in terms of cost and consumption, and in view of the unpredictability of profit in the horse racing business.

The debtors inappropriately intend to use all of their accumulated operating surplus to pay the extra five percent to Belcher at the time of the final plan payment. Even assuming that each year the debtor will have $60,000 remaining working capital surplus, the debtors will likely have to use the surplus to fund their operations, and cannot totally rely on the existence of the surplus to pay Belcher.

A further defect in the debtors' projections is that the projected cost of sales are at variance with the debtors' historical costs. The debtors use 92 percent of gross as the cost of sales, asserting that they have cut costs by $175,000 during the Chapter 11, which approximates two per cent. Historically, debtors' costs of sales have been 97 percent of gross. Thus, according to their own evidence, a more accurate percentage of cost of sales is 95 percent. The costs of sales substantially affect the projections because a one percent increase in costs of sales means a $100,000 decrease in annual net income. Thus assuming the accuracy of debtors' projections in all other respects, but using a 95 percent cost factor the debtors' projections would not show $64,000 in net income, but rather would show a $250,000 loss. In view of the debtors' own evidence that costs of sales have been historically 97 percent, and have been reduced by one and three quarters per cent, I find that the use of 92 percent, as cost of sales is improper, and that the projections based on this cost percentage are inaccurate.

Belcher's main objection to debtors' projections of profitability is that the projections conflict with debtors' losses during the pendency of this case. The debtors do not dispute that they have not operated profitably during this period. Mr. Fay admitted that on a consolidated basis debtors have sustained losses during their tenure as debtors in possession, the extent of which is unknown. In my view, a debtor's financial progress or lack thereof, while under the protection of Chapter 11, is an indicator of the debtors' fate. Unfortunately, for an unknown reason, the debtors neglected to produce actual profit and loss figures for the period from June through December 1982. For the eight months ending May 1982 we do know that the consolidated debtors had net losses of $138,000. Belcher's accountant demonstrated that from June to September 1982 the debtors lost $33,000, whereas they had projected $16,000 in net income for this period. Therefore it is not unreasonable to conclude that debtors' have lost over $100,000 during this Chapter 11. Moreover, debtors' projected gross sales figures for June to September 1982 do not comport with actual sales for the same period. Sales were $185,000 less than projected.

The net profit figures projected for the three months ended September 30, 1982 of $18,650 are to be compared to the loss of $42,456 for the four month period from June 1, 1982 through September 30, 1982. No sales or actual figures were submitted to compare with the projected profit of $6,800 for the subsequent quarter ended December 31, 1982. The debtors chose not to produce any actual net income figures for the fourth quarter 1982 simply relying on the fourth quarter projection. Although the confirmation hearing was held in early January 1983, and debtors' counsel asserted that the actual figures for the fourth quarter were not available, I must draw a negative inference from the failure to produce the third quarter figures and at least some of the financial information for the fourth quarter 1982. The debtors have been unable to show a positive cash flow during this Chapter 11 bearing any resemblance to the projections, despite the claims of decreased expenses. In contrast, nothing in the debtors' recent financial progress during reorganization, and in view of the unreliability of the projections, it is impossible to find that the debtors will be able to execute their plan with operating revenues.

As an alternative, the debtors propose to sell certain assets to satisfy any shortage should revenues be insufficient. I am not convinced of the adequacy of this proposal. The debtors' total liquidation value at present is $636,000. This does not even consider the blanket security interest of Global in all assets of the debtor to secure the $500,000 line of credit for business operations. Borrowings to date are in the amount of $380,000, and the companies intend to use the full line of credit. Thus, realistically, we must decrease the liquidation value by a figure ranging from $300,000 to $500,000, leaving a true liquidation value of somewhere from $136,000 to $336,000. The plan's payment requirements are over $1,100,000. Even assuming the first payment can be made from cash on hand, there still must be paid over $800,000 over the next two years.

In view of these facts, the debtors' reliance on In re Nite Lite Inns, 17 B.R. 367 (Bkrtcy. S.D. Cal. 1982) is misplaced. Although the Court in *Nite Lites* found the plan feasible because it was supplemented by a liquidation proposal, the value of the debtors' assets exceeded the amount to be paid under the plan. In re Nite Lite Inns, 17 B.R. at 370. In the present case the alternative of liquidation is not comparable to that approved by the Court in *Nite Lite* because here the value of assets is far less than the deferred payments promised over the duration of the plan.

The success of the liquidation alternative is unpredictable as the amount of the shortfall on each deferred payment is unknown. Neither party's projections reliably estimated the shortfall. Debtors predicted no shortfall, but a review of their accountant's testimony supports the conclusion that based on the projections the shortfall could be $200,000 per deferred payment. Belcher's projections were defective in that they contained duplicate expenses for hauling. Thus, the amount of the shortfall is not known. The Court can only look to the debtors' estimated $100,000 loss during the Chapter 11 which compels the conclusion that the shortfall could easily range in the vicinity of $300,000. Clearly assets capable of being liquidated do not approach this amount in view of the Global Security interest.

In response to the assertion that assets could be liquidated to effectuate the plan, it must be noted that all assets are fully pledged and there can be no assurance that the proceeds would be available to unsecured creditors. With the sole exception of the residences, a disposition of race horses or motor vehicles would certainly have an adverse effect on the operating results as projected and unduly restrict future operations and profitability.

Moreover, the evidence supports the conclusion that the assets debtors intend to liquidate are not readily saleable. Mr. Fay has been attempting to sell the oil company trucks, which have a value of somewhere between $259,000 and $279,000 for over a year without success. Moreover, there was evidence that the horses' value had decreased and will continue to decrease with age. It is unreasonable for debtors to rely so heavily on liquidation of these assets.

In summary, this Court is of the opinion that the debtors' plan in its present form puts creditors at considerable risk. The projections are not reliable, and do not form a basis for finding feasibility. The liquidation alternative does not guarantee creditors what the debtors have promised. The Court has serious concerns that these debtors will require further reorganization if this plan is confirmed. Accordingly, it is my conclusion that the plan fails to meet the requirement of confirmation set forth in 11 U.S.C. Section 1129(a)(11) and confirmation of the debtors' plan is hereby denied.

NOTE ON *MERRIMACK VALLEY OIL*

A case such as *Merrimack Valley Oil* provides you an opportunity to witness the reasoning of the participants and the bankruptcy judge in reaching a decision whether to accept (and confirm) a plan of reorganization. In this case, the bankruptcy judge denies confirmation based on feasibility. In itself, that determination is interesting. Do you find the reasoning convincing? For example, the court relies in part on a perceived flaw in the debtor's figures: "using the first fifteen months projections for the subsequent years ignores any inflation factor." Do you agree? If a firm earns $100,000 in 1984, is it impermissible to use that as a base figure, without discounting? Even if inflation is at 20 percent wouldn't it be proper also to increase the expected earnings for 1985 to $120,000, still giving a present value of $100,000? How many of the judge's assumptions could be questioned in a similar fashion? Do any of them, however, really affect his ultimate conclusion?

This opinion is instructive for another reason. Although principally an opinion on feasibility, a number of other issues are decided along the way, either sub silentio, or without drafting a formal opinion. Do you agree with these decisions?

Let's examine some of them. First, the plan of reorganization provided for an extra 5 percent dividend to Belcher. Is this treatment proper? What issues does it raise? Do you think it complies with the classification requirements of §1122? Notwithstanding this 5 percent "kicker," Belcher votes against the plan. (As a matter of plan drafting and negotiation, it is odd — even assuming it is permitted — to see a "bonus" given to a particular creditor without some assurance that the creditor will then support the plan.) We are told that Belcher's claim is subsequently "disallowed . . . for voting purposes only." What does that mean? Is the court applying the test of §1126(e) or some other test? Assuming the action is taken under §1126(e), is it proper?

One final point to note about *Merrimack Valley Oil*. The court, before reaching feasibility, addresses the "best interest of creditors test" of §1129(a)(7), and finds it is met. The court concludes that nominal payments of 35 percent over time have a present value of 29 percent. What discount rate did the court use? Do you think the discount rate was proper in light of the court's subsequent treatment of the feasibility issue? Even assuming that valuation procedures outside of §1129(b) are intended by Congress to be less rigorous than those within §1129(b), what kind of valuation hearing should have been held for §1129(a)(7)? What kind of evidence would you want to see?

NOTE ON THE RELATION BETWEEN §1129(a)(7) AND §1129(b)

A bankruptcy court cannot approve a plan of reorganization without the consent of a majority in number and two-thirds in dollar amount of the creditors in a given class actually voting on the plan, unless everyone in the class is paid in full or unless no one in a junior class gets anything. A plan may be "crammed down" (as the process is usually referred to) a class of objecting creditors only if the bankruptcy court decides those conditions have been met. Section 1129(b) defines what being paid in full means. (Note that such valuation problems typically do not arise in straight Chapter 7 proceedings because one can value assets by the price the trustee is able to sell them for on the market.)

The drafters of the Bankruptcy Code believed that the difference between §1129(a)(7)'s "best interests of creditors" test and §1129(b)'s "absolute priority rule" test, was a question of allocation of the "going-concern surplus." See J. Trost et al., Resource Materials: The New Federal Bankruptcy Code 335-339 (1979). But because there is nothing prohibiting the sale of an enterprise as a going concern in Chapter 7, the correct comparison between distributions made under Chapter 7 and those under Chapter 11 may be between *two* going-concern values (one to third parties and one to the creditors themselves). This suggests that the "going-concern surplus" to be allocated by "avoiding" §1129(b) may often be small indeed. See Jackson, Bankruptcy, Non-Bankruptcy Entitlements, and the Creditors' Bargain, 91 Yale L.J. 857 (1982).

A related consideration should also be noted. It is generally assumed that §1129(b)'s absolute priority rule valuation procedures are cumbersome and expensive, and that senior creditors will be "stimulated" to pass some portion of the going-concern bonus on to junior classes "in return for elimination of the full valuation hearing," J. Trost et al., supra. And H.R. Rep. No. 596, 95th Cong., 1st Sess. 414 (1978), states that "[w]hile section 1129(a) does not contemplate a valuation of the debtor's business, such valuation will almost always be required under section 1129(b) to determine the value of the consideration to be distributed." Is this correct? If an individual creditor dissents from a plan of reorganization, it is entitled to the protections of §1129(a)(7), even if its class accepts the plan by requisite vote. How does one value how well a creditor would have done in Chapter 7, assuming that the business may have been sold as a going concern in Chapter 7? And, how does one decide how well a dissenting creditor does in Chapter 11 without valuing the consideration it will receive? If the consideration consists of claims against the debtor (such as bonds, preferred stock, or common stock), won't valuing that consideration necessarily involve valuing the debtor's business? If that is so, what has been saved by avoiding §1129(b)? See Broude, Cramdown and Chapter 11 of the Bankruptcy Code: The Settlement Imperative, 39 Bus. Lawyer 441 (1984) (suggesting §1129(a)(7) valuation procedures are more informal than those under §1129(b)).

The next case raises, in the context of §1129(b), an issue that we first saw raised in Case v. Los Angeles Lumber Products Co., supra page 608.

IN RE LANDAU BOAT COMPANY
8 Bankr. 436 (Bankr. W.D. Mo. 1981)

Joel PELOFSKY, Bankruptcy Judge.

In this Chapter 11 proceeding, the debtor has proposed a plan with four classes of creditors. Administrative costs constitute Class One; Secured claims constitute Class Two. Both of these classes are to be paid in full. Class Three is composed of unsecured creditors. This class is to be paid 10 percent of their allowed claims. Class Four is composed of stockholders who are to receive no distribution under the plan but will retain their interest in the corporation.

The plan did not receive the votes necessary to be confirmed. . . . At the time debtor filed its plan, it moved the Court to confirm the plan under §1129(b) of the Code, Title 11, U.S.C. Premature at that time, the Motion is now timely and will be considered.

Section 1129(b) provides, in part, that

> Notwithstanding section 510(a) of this title, if all of the applicable requirements of subsection (a) of this section other than paragraph (8) are met with respect to a plan, the court, on request of the proponent of the plan, shall confirm the plan notwithstanding the requirements of such paragraph if the plan does not discriminate unfairly, and is fair and equitable, with respect to each class of claims or interests that is impaired under, and has not accepted the plan.

Paragraph 8 refers to classes which have accepted or are not impaired under the plan. In this plan, the unsecured class is impaired and has not accepted the plan. Section 1129(b)(2) sets out criteria for "cram down" as it affects unsecured creditors.

> (2) For the purpose of this subsection, the condition that a plan be fair and equitable with respect to a class includes the following requirements: . . .
>   (B) With respect to a class of unsecured claims—
>   (i) the plan provides that each holder of a claim of such class receive or retain on account of such claim property of a value, as of the effective date of the plan, equal to the allowed amount of such claim; or
>   (ii) the holder of any claim or interest that is junior to the claims of such class will not receive or retain on account of such junior claim or interest any property.*

The issue of priority in corporate reorganization has a long history, originating in the railroad reorganizations of the turn of the century. In Louisville Trust Co. v. Louisville, N.A. & C. Ry. Co., et al, 174 U.S. 674, 19 S. Ct. 827, 43 L. Ed. 1130 (1899), the bondholders and the mortgage

---

* Reworded slightly in 1984. — EDS.

holders arranged a foreclosure of the railroad property. The Supreme Court condemned the transaction in no uncertain terms.

> a foreclosure which attempts to preserve any interest or right of mortgagor in the property after the sale must necessarily secure and preserve the prior rights of general creditors thereof. This is based upon the familiar rule that the stockholders interest in the property is subordinate to the rights of creditors. And any arrangement of the parties by which the subordinate rights and interests of the stockholders are attempted to be secured at the expense of the prior rights of either class of creditors comes within judicial denunciation. 174 U.S. at 684, 19 S. Ct. at 830.

This statement of principle was broadened to reach reorganization foreclosures in Northern P.R. Co. v. Boyd, 228 U.S. 482, 33 S. Ct. 554, 57 L. Ed. 931 (1913). Here again the bondholders and stockholders agreed to create a new company, eliminating the claims of general creditors.

> As between the parties . . . the sale was valid. As against creditors, it was a mere form. . . .
> The invalidity of the sale flowed from the character of the reorganization agreement regardless of the value of the property, for in cases like this the question must be decided according to a fixed principle, not leaving the rights of the creditors to depend upon the balancing of evidence as to whether, on the day of sale, the property was insufficient to pay prior encumbrances. . . . If the value of the road justified the issuance of stock in exchange for old shares, the creditors were entitled to the benefit of that value, whether it was present or prospective, for dividends or only for purposes of control. In either event it was a right of property out of which the creditors were entitled to be paid before the stockholders could retain it for any purpose whatever. 228 U.S. at 506-508, 33 S. Ct. at 561.

The fixed principle, set out in *Louisville Trust Co.* and restated in *Boyd*, was further explicated in Case v. Los Angeles Lumber Products Co. Ltd., 308 U.S. 106, 60 S. Ct. 1, 84 L. Ed. 110 (1939). The Court noted that creditors were entitled to priority over stockholders to the extent of their debt and that the continued participation of stockholders in a reorganization would depend upon new equity contributions. The Court went on to comment upon the notion that benefit under the plan to creditors was immaterial. "The fact that bondholders might fare worse as a result of a foreclosure and liquidation than they would by taking a debtor's plan under Section 77B can have no relevant bearing on whether a proposed plan is 'fair and equitable' under that section." 308 U.S. at 123, 60 S. Ct. at 11.

The Eighth Circuit follows the reasoning of these cases.

> Stockholders may not better their position at the cost of bondholders or other creditors and to justify a retention of stock interest by stockholders of a

debtor it must appear that they have furnished some compensatory additional consideration or have an equity in the estate of the debtor after the
rights of creditors are fully provided for. Sophian v. Congress Realty Co.,
98 F.2d 499, 502 (8th Cir. 1938).

Here the plan proposes to compromise the unsecured debts at 10
percent. The fund to pay this amount is to be received from outside
investors, otherwise unidentified. There is nothing in the plan to suggest
that the existing stockholders will provide new equity as a condition of
retaining their interest. It is apparent from the schedules that the assets of
the debtor are insufficient to pay the unsecured creditors in full and,
therefore, the stockholders have no equity in the debtor.

The absolute priority rule of *Boyd*, as embodied in Section 1129(b),
requires that a senior class of debt is to be paid in full if a junior class is to
receive any property. Here, the unsecured debt is not being paid in full,
while the stockholders, a class junior to the unsecured, retains its equity
interest. Does the retention of an equity interest constitute the receiving of
property if the interest, as here, has no value? The answer seems to be
clearly yes.

In *Boyd*, the Court suggested that the value of the property received by
the junior class need not be cash but could also be "prospective, for dividends or only for purposes of control." Quite clearly, retention of the
stockholders interest in this case is for prospective earnings and for control. But also, although this is more speculative, if the debts of the unsecured creditors are compromised, the stockholders may realize some
immediate equity value. The statute prohibits such a result. . . .

Under the pending plan, the unsecured creditors are not paid an
amount equal to the allowed amount of their claims and a junior class (the
stockholders) receives property. The plan is not fair and equitable and
cannot be confirmed under the provisions of Section 1129(b). Debtor's
Motion is denied.

NOTES

1. After this decision, Landau Boat Co. filed an amended plan that
proposed canceling the existing common stock and issuing a new class of
common stock to be made available to purchasers, including creditors, at
par of $1.00 per share. The plan also required subscribers to "offer an
irrevocable loan commitment in the sum of" $3.00 for each $1.00 of stock
purchased. The plan stated that the existing shareholders had offered to
purchase the issue in its entirety, but that the court had the right to allocate
the stock if some creditors subscribed. This plan was again rejected by the
unsecured creditors, who were being paid 10 percent of their allowed
claims. The court approved this plan, over their objection, on the ground

that the stockholders had justified the retention of their stock by the new investment and the irrevocable commitment to loan operating funds. In re Landau Boat Co., 13 Bankr. 788 (Bankr. W.D. Mo. 1981). See also Buffalo Savings Bank v. Marston Enterprises, 13 Bankr. 514 (Bankr. E.D.N.Y. 1981).

2. What if the shareholders who are being left out complain? How much solace can they gain from §1129(b)? Consider the following objection and the court's response, In re Toy & Sports Warehouse, 37 Bankr. 141, 147-148 (Bankr. S.D.N.Y. 1984):

> The minority shareholders state in their objections to confirmation:
>
> > The cancellation of their stock and the issuance of all the stock of the corporation to the funder for $300,000 is neither fair nor equitable as the company has upon confirmation, a net worth of $1,955,000.
>
> This objection eludes the fact that the debtors' liabilities of $5,108,000 presently exceed its assets of $4,224,000 and that there is no equity for any of the debtors' current shareholders. The unsecured creditors will not be paid in full. Their consent to accept a 35 percent deferred payment for their allowed claims is premised on the fact that the debtors' present shareholders will not receive anything for their interests. Had the unsecured creditors not consented to this arrangement, they could not be required to accept less than full payment of their allowed claims as long as a holder of a junior interest, such as a shareholder, retained any equity interest in the debtors. . . .
>
> That a pro forma net worth of approximately $1,900,000 is produced after confirmation as a result of giving effect to the reduced indebtedness of the debtors under the plan, does not mean that the new investor thereby receives a windfall. This balance sheet equity is subject to the payments required by the plan, the risks of the toy market and the debtors' ability to continue to operate successfully following confirmation. Indeed, even existing shareholders are entitled to receive equity interests in exchange for new investments after the cancellation of their former equity shares. . . . Here, the outside funder is taking a calculated risk and is entitled to receive, with the consent of the unsecured creditors, 100 percent of the common stock of the post-confirmation debtors. That is what reorganization is all about.

In considering this, should it matter that the funding of $300,000 is from the cousin of the majority shareholder (who is also receiving nothing from the plan of reorganization, which he has proposed)? The court apparently saw no relevance, as it did not discuss this point.

PROBLEMS

9.17 Debtor has a piecemeal liquidation value of $500,000 and a going-concern value of $1,000,000. The creditors have $700,000 of allowed claims. The creditors (after waiting the required 120 days), have proposed a plan whereby they will receive, in exchange for their claims, all of the equity in Debtor; the current stockholders will receive nothing. Is there any ground on which the current stockholders can object to the plan? See §§1123, 1126, 1128, 1129. What if, instead, the plan left the equity-holders with their equity, but allocated $900,000 worth of notes to the creditors? Cf. Consolidated Rock Products Co. v. DuBois, 312 U.S. 510 (1941); Note on the Quality of the Securities Received, infra page 710.

9.18 Debtor has proposed a plan providing that members of "Class 4," consisting of all unsecured claimants, will be paid 50 percent of their claims, in cash, on the effective date of the plan. "Class 5" consists of stockholders of Debtor who, under the plan, would retain all stock owner-ship in the company. In Class 4 are Bank, which has a claim for $100,000, and Finance Company, which also has a claim for $100,000. By contract, Finance Company's claim is subordinated to that of Bank, so that Finance Company is not entitled to anything until Bank has been paid in full. May Finance Company object to this classification? Is Finance Company other-wise protected? See §§510, 1122, 1126, 1129(a)(2) and (b).

IN RE LANDMARK AT PLAZA PARK
7 Bankr. 653 (Bankr. D.N.J. 1980)

Richard W. HILL, Bankruptcy Judge. . . .

Debtor, Landmark at Plaza Park, Ltd., is a limited partnership whose only substantial asset is a 200-unit garden apartment complex located in Morrisville, Pennsylvania. City Federal (hereafter City) holds a first mort-gage on this property in the face amount of $2,250,000. The mortgage bears an interest rate of 9.5 percent and is due and payable on October 1, 1986. On October 2, 1980, this Court issued a written decision denying City's request for relief from the automatic stay provisions of Section 362 of the Bankruptcy Code, 11 U.S.C. Section 362, and continuing the stay until the conclusion of the hearing on confirmation of the debtor's plan. This opinion deals with debtor's plan as it affects City, the only objecting class of creditors. As to all other classes of creditors, there is no dispute and the Court is satisfied that the confirmation standards specified in 11 U.S.C. Section 1129 have been met.

Before discussing the merits of debtor's plan three things should be noted. First, the parties have stipulated that the record from the Section 362 hearing is part of the record herein. Second, the parties have stipu-lated that for the purpose of the confirmation hearing $2,260,000 is the fair market value of the property. This value was fixed by the Court after lengthy testimony was presented at the Section 362 hearing. And third, City has made an election pursuant to Section 1111(b)(2) of the Code.

Thus, its claim in the amount of $2,512,457 will be treated as fully secured.[3]

I. THE PLAN AS MODIFIED

Crucial to an understanding of the Court's decision is a discussion of the plan and how it affects City. Contractually, City is a first mortgagee without recourse. It has possession of the property and is collecting the rents pursuant to a rent assignment agreement. The mortgage has been in default since at least December, 1979. City is undersecured and wants to complete its foreclosure action.

The debtor has proposed in substance the following plan:

1. City is to redeliver possession of the property to the debtor.
2. On the 16th month after the effective date of the plan and through the 36th month debtor will commence monthly interest payments at the rate of 12.5 percent computed on the value of the property — $2,260,000.
3. Debtor will deliver to City a non-recourse note, payable in three years in the face amount of $2,705,820.31, in substitution of all existing liabilities.
4. The existing mortgage will secure the note set forth in paragraph 3, except to the extent that it is inconsistent with or modified by the plan.
5. City is the only member of the class of creditors to which it has been assigned.

The face amount of the note is derived as follows:

a.	Current value of collateral	$2,260,000.00
b.	Unpaid interest: months 1-15 @ 12.5%	353,125.00
c.	Interest on unpaid interest: 21 months @ 15%	92,695.31
	Face amount of note	$2,705,820.31

The debtor's principal theory is that the note will be paid off at the end of 36 months by a combination of refinancing and accumulation of cash from the project, all of which will subsequently be discussed at length. The key

---

3. . . . Reading [§506] alone, City would have a secured claim for $2,260,000 and an unsecured claim for $252,457. Section 1111(b)(2), however, provides that, notwithstanding Section 506(a), a creditor in the position of City may elect to be treated as fully secured. Since City has made the election, for purposes of this hearing its claim of $2,512,457 is fully secured. . . .

to the debtor's plan is a proposal to obtain a new first mortgage in three years in the face amount of $2,400,000.

It is undisputed that pursuant to this plan City is impaired within the meaning of Section 1124 of the Code. City has rejected the plan.

II.   The Issues

Confirmation standards under the Code are set forth in Section 1129. Clearly, the debtor has complied with all provisions of that section except for the following subsections: (a)(7)(B); (a)(8); (a)(11); (b)(1); and (b)(2)(A). Actually the list is much shorter. The requirements of (a)(7)(B) are, in effect, carried forward in (b)(1) and (b)(2). Thus if the requirement of subsections (b)(1) and (b)(2) are met (a)(7)(B) will also have been met. Similarly, the requirements of (a)(8) are waived by the specific language of (b)(1) if other requirements of (b)(1) and (b)(2) are met. That leaves at issue the debtor's compliance with subsections (a)(11), (b)(1) and (b)(2). Subsection (a)(11) of Section 1129 is the feasibility requirement and, in a general sense, deals with whether the debtor can and will accomplish what it has proposed. Subsection (b) of Section 1129 is the "cram-down" provision of the Code. It describes those circumstances in which a class of creditors or interests may over its objection be involuntarily subjected to the provisions of a plan. Each of these sections will be discussed at length. The provisions of subsection (b) will be discussed first because certain determinations made there bear on the feasibility determination required by subsection (a)(11).

III.   The Requirements of Section 1129(b)(1) and (2)

The provisions of Section 1129(b) specify the circumstances under which a class of creditors or interests may be involuntarily subjected to a plan of reorganization. . . .

The concept that a plan is fair and equitable is not fully defined in the Code. Section 1129(b)(2)(A), (B) and (C) states several factors which are included in that requirement but the legislative history accompanying that section makes clear that other factors fundamental to fair and equitable treatment of a dissenting class were omitted to "avoid complexity." . . . Given the present posture of this case the Court is satisfied that the factors set forth in Section 1129(b)(2)(A)(i), dealing with the cram down of a secured creditor, adequately deal with the question of whether the plan, as to City, is fair and equitable, and the Court will limit its consideration to those factors.

To meet the requirements of Section 1129(b)(2)(A)(i) the debtor's plan must do three things. First, it must provide for retention by the creditor of its lien. Second, the total stream of deferred cash payments proposed by the plan must at least total the amount of the secured claim. Third, the total stream of payments must have a value equal to the value of the property. The plan before the Court satisfies the first two requirements, but may not satisfy the third.[5]

The third requirement is found in that portion of Section 1129(b) (2)(A)(i)(II) stating that "each holder of a claim . . . receive . . . deferred cash payments . . . of a value . . . of at least the value of such holder's interest in the estate's interest in such property." This provision requires the Court to determine the present value of the payments to be made under the plan. Here the total stream of payments under the plan is $3,200,195.17. The discounted value of these payments must equal $2,260,000, the value of the value of the property.

The debtor's construct for meeting subsection (b)(2)(A)(i)(II) is simple. It assumes that the value of the property constitutes the principal amount of a loan and purports to repay to City that principal amount together with interest at 12.5 percent per annum.[7] Thus, the debtor argues that if the interest rate fixed is adequate the discounted value of the principal plus interest must equal the present value of the property. To support the fixing of a 12.5 percent interest rate debtor presented evidence that at the time of the confirmation hearing certain institutional investors would provide first mortgage loans on similar property at that rate. The testimony also revealed, however, that 12.5 percent is at the low end of the interest range.

City strongly rejects the present value approach asserted by the debtor. It focuses on the question of whether the stream of payments offered by the debtor could be sold as of the effective date of the plan for a price at least equal to $2,260,000. City presented expert testimony that attempted to establish two facts: (1) that even assuming that the property was in good condition and under capable management, the only market for debtor's proposed payment stream would be the secondary mortgage market with the purchase price being 50 to 60 percent of the value of the collateral. It is City's contention that regardless of the interest rate offered the value of the payment stream will be less than the value of the property; (2) that with income producing property, a non-recourse note in excess of the value of the property would always be worth less than the value of the property because an investor would always prefer the property to the note. City's expert grudgingly conceded that his opinion of the value of the note would change if he had confidence in management and believed that

---

5. For purposes of this opinion the allowed amount of the secured claim is $2,512,457. The total stream of payments is $3,200,195.17 consisting of the face amount of the note, $2,705,820.31, plus 21 months interest totaling $494,374.86. Requirement (2) is thus satisfied.

7. The plan is somewhat oversimplified by this statement because 15 months interest is deferred and the deferred interest itself bears interest at a 15 percent rate.

future income projections would in fact be sufficient to pay off the note. The expert, however, then backtracked and concluded that mortgage loans could not be made in reliance on future income projections.

In the Court's view, City's expert so overstated his position that his opinion on saleability and value cannot be considered. Succinctly stated, the Court is satisfied that a non-recourse note in excess of the value of the property can be worth at least the value of the property if sufficient interest is paid on the note and repayment is sufficiently certain. The question in the present case becomes whether the 12.5 percent interest rate offered by the debtor is adequate and whether repayment is sufficiently certain.

Conceptually, the modified plan seeks to force City to make a $2,260,000 loan, repayable in three years, with the first 15 months of interest deferred. There is no amortization over the term of the loan. Since there is currently no equity in the property the debtor is asking City to make a 100 percent loan. The rate of interest on a loan of this type should correspond to the rate of interest which would be charged or obtained by a creditor making a loan to a third party with similar terms, duration, collateral and risk. . . . Although the rate of interest may be identical to the market rate of interest, this will often not be the case because of the particular risk involved.[8]

It appears clear to the Court that the forced loan proposed by the debtor includes terms less favorable to City than would typically be found in the market and that any confirmable plan must compensate City for this deficiency. Testimony presented at the confirmation hearing revealed that institutions such as thrifts, life insurance companies and pension funds would make first mortgage loans on garden apartments with an interest rate ranging from 12.5 to 14 percent. The typical first mortgage loan would have a term of three to ten years, with amortization calculated on a 25 year payout and a 75 percent maximum loan to value ratio. Secondary mortgage financing would be available for additional borrowing requirements at five points over the prime rate (which was 14 percent at the time of the confirmation hearing). For interest rate purposes, therefore, it appears appropriate to treat City as the forced holder of two mortgages: a first mortgage to the extent of 75 percent of the loan and a second mortgage to the extent of 25 percent of the loan. The Court believes that the first 75 percent of the loan should bear an interest rate between 13.5 percent and 14 percent, the high end of the range for a typical garden apartment loan. Although the three year term is consistent with that in the marketplace, the deferral of interest and the lack of amortization requires a higher interest rate. The remaining 25 percent of the loan should bear an

---

8. Although risk is a factor in determining rates of interest, its importance must not be overstated. We must assume when fixing an interest rate that the plan will be confirmed. If risk of repayment is too great the plan will not be confirmed because the debtor has not met the requirements of Section 1129(a)(11). The question of an interest rate would therefore become irrelevant.

interest rate at least consistent with that charged in the commercial secondary mortgage market. Testimony at trial indicated that interest on such mortgages is generally five points over prime. With the prime rate approximately 14 percent at the time of confirmation, the Court believes that 19 percent is the minimum interest rate on this portion of the loan.[11] A composite loan rate of 15 percent is then arrived at, computed as follows:

$$
\begin{array}{rcl}
.75(.135) & = & .1013 \\
.25(.19) & = & \underline{.0475} \\
& & .1488 \\
\\
.75(.14) & = & .1050 \\
.25(.19) & = & \underline{.0475} \\
& & .1525
\end{array}
$$

Say 15%

Thus, if a note and interest payments were offered to City by debtor at a 15 percent rate debtor would appear to meet the requirement that the discounted stream of payments equal the value of the property. Because the 12.5 percent rate proposed by debtor is below the 15 percent minimum rate established by the Court the plan as presented does not comply with Section 1129(b)(2)(A)(i)(II) and, therefore, cannot be confirmed. Since the plan could be readily modified, however, the Court must determine whether the plan is feasible if funded at a 15 percent rate. . . .

IV.   THE REQUIREMENTS OF SECTION 1129(a)(11)

Debtors seeking to confirm plans under Chapters 10, 11 and 12 of the 1898 Bankruptcy Act, as amended, were required to demonstrate that the plan was feasible. . . . Section 1129(a)(11) of the Code, which for the most part incorporates the policy of the Act, requires the Court to scrutinize the plan proposed by a debtor to determine whether it offers a reasonable prospect of success and whether it is workable. Specifically Section 1129(a)(11) requires the Court to find that:

> Confirmation of the plan is not likely to be followed by the liquidation, or the need for further financial reorganization, of the debtor or any successor to the debtor under the plan, unless such liquidation or reorganization is proposed in the plan. 11 U.S.C. Section 1129(a)(11).

---

11. Five points over prime is, of course, a floating rate. Since the Court cannot predict where prime will be during the next three years, for the purpose of testing feasibility it has utilized a fixed rate of 19 percent based on the prime in existence at the time of the confirmation hearing.

Collier states that the purpose of Section 1129(a)(11) is to prevent confirmation of visionary schemes that promise creditors and equity security holders more under a proposed plan than the debtor could possibly attain after confirmation. 5 Collier on Bankruptcy, para. 1129.02 (15th ed. 1980). Thus, if the facts indicate that the plan will ultimately lead to liquidation, it is not feasible and cannot be confirmed even if the debtor is sincere and has made a best effort to perform according to the terms of the plan. . . . The factors courts should generally consider in making the above determination are (1) the adequacy of the capital structure; (2) the earning power of the business; (3) economic conditions; (4) the ability of management; (5) the probability of the continuation of the same management; and (6) any other related matters which determine the prospects of a sufficiently successful operation to enable performance of the provisions of the plan. . . .

In the instant case feasibility depends on debtor being able to pay off in three years a note to City in the amount of $2,794,984.38 and pay to City interest of $28,250 per month for 21 consecutive months beginning in the 16th month. The cornerstone of debtor's scheme is to refinance the project in three years with a new first mortgage in the amount of $2,400,000. The balance of the needed cash, an additional $394,984.38, would come from secondary mortgage financing, cash accumulated from the project over the next three years, and equity contributions of some $60,000. The key to debtor's goals is the net income that the project will generate, for it is the amount of the net income that will determine the size of the first and second mortgages that will be obtainable and the amount of cash available from the project to apply to the note at the end of three years. The net income will also determine whether debtor can pay its debt service beginning in the 16th month. Finally, the amount of net income will determine debtor's financial ability to cure certain deferred maintenance items, a step necessary to attract and retain tenants and to secure financing. The debtor and City have serious disputes as to all these matters. . . .

FULFILLMENT OF THE PLAN

As stated earlier, fulfillment of the plan contemplates the ability of the debtor to cure certain deferred maintenance items, to make certain interest payments to City, and to pay off a note to City in three years. All of this requires substantial amounts of cash, which is potentially available from the following sources: (1) income from the project itself; (2) primary and secondary mortgage financing; (3) sale of the project; and (4) capital contributions. As noted at the outset of this opinion debtor's primary option is to remortgage the project for $2,400,000 at the end of the three-year period. The Court is convinced that the plan cannot be fulfilled. . . .

In the Court's judgment, the net income of this project after three years will be $292,570.20. . . . Utilizing a coverage factor in the 1.25 to 1.33 range would justify debt service maximums of $234,056.16 and $219,977.59, respectively. The debt service on a $2,400,000 mortgage would vary with a particular interest rate, . . . but even at a 10.5 percent rate, the low range of the scale, the annual debt service of $272,160 substantially exceeds what would be available from income. With first mortgage financing unavailable to debtor, it is unnecessary to consider the possibility of second mortgage financing. Even debtor's proposed equity infusion of $60,000 by debtor's limited partners would be of little help.

Debtor's alternative suggestion, also unconvincing, is that the property could be sold to satisfy the $2,794,984.33 note. Although it is impossible to accurately predict the value of this property three years in the future, if the Court were to consider the net income after three years of $292,570.20 as a stabilized net income figure and apply to that a capitalization rate of .12 (the figure utilized at the Section 362 hearing) a value of only $2,438,085 would be derived. This value is clearly insufficient to pay off the note.

If the Court assumes a 10 percent income increase, debtor's ability to meet its plan obligations becomes better, but, nevertheless, unconvincing. Cure costs and current debt service could be met but with a $2,400,000 mortgage there would still be a cash shortfall of $239,715.26. It is clear that debtor's $60,000 proposed equity infusion would not dent this. Debtor suggests the possibility of secondary mortgage financing to meet the shortfall but, realistically speaking, first mortgage financing would first have to be secured. If the coverage ratios used above are kept constant, but income is increased by 10 percent to $370,097.96, it is easily seen that the maximum income available for debt services ranges from $296,078.37 to $278,269.14. A 1.25 coverage ratio justifies a mortgage at 11.5 percent and a 1.33 factor justifies a mortgage at only 10.5 percent. Since the availability of a particular mortgage rate three years hence is entirely speculative, however, debtor is left with a problem. If it is forced to pay a 12.5 percent interest rate, a rate thought low at the confirmation hearing, income will be insufficient to cover the $314,160 debt service. Given the testimony at trial the Court can only conclude that debtor's ability to refinance is dubious at best. Similarly, the Court is convinced that a sale, even with a 10 percent income increase, is purely speculative. Assuming that the third year income figure of $370,097.96 is a stabilized figure, and again applying a .12 capitalization rate, the value of the premises would compute to $3,084,149.67 — a price sufficient to pay off the note. Two questions arise, however: (1) would the debtor be able to find a purchaser at the end of the three year period at that price, and (2) would the sale be for cash. The answer to question (1) is not known and question (2) probably must be answered in the negative because any new purchaser would have the same difficulty obtaining mortgage financing as the debtor. Since a cash sale is improbable, a pay off of the mortgage note is, at best, unlikely.

The Court has discussed the cost of curing deferred maintenance and the income and expenses of the project over the next three years. In the Court's opinion fulfillment of the plan by the debtor is not possible if its "best judgment" figures are utilized. Furthermore, even assuming a 10 percent income increase, fulfillment of the plan's conditions is highly doubtful. In the Court's judgment it is more probable than not that confirmation of a plan would likely be followed either by a liquidation or further reorganization proceedings. Thus, the debtor has not fulfilled the requirements of Section 1129(a)(11) and confirmation of the debtor's plan, as modified, must be denied.

RELIEF FROM STAY

At the hearing on City's complaint for relief from the automatic stay the stay was continued only to allow the debtor a hearing on confirmation of its plan. Since confirmation has been denied, the stay must be vacated.

NOTE

Note that City Federal made an election under §1111(b). We will explore the reasons for, and effect of, the §1111(b) election below.

NOTE ON THE QUALITY OF THE SECURITIES RECEIVED

In Consolidated Rock Products Co. v. DuBois, 312 U.S. 510 (1941), Justice Douglas, in discussing the absolute priority rule, stated:

> Thus it is plain that while creditors may be given inferior grades of securities their "superior rights" must be recognized. Clearly, those prior rights are not recognized, in cases where stockholders are participating in the plan, if creditors are given only a face amount of inferior securities equal to the face amount of their claims. They must receive, in addition, compensation for the senior rights which they are to surrender.

This has become known as the "bonus rule," which requires a deterioration in the type of claim held by a creditor to be compensated by a "bonus" in the amount of the compensation. See Citibank, N.A. v. Baer, 651 F.2d 1341 (10th Cir. 1980).

Is the need for this bonus, in fact, so "clear"? Or has Justice Douglas fallen into the error of assuming that a ton of feathers weighs less than a ton of lead? Professor Blum has asserted:

> If that valuation [placed on the entire enterprise] is approved, then, logically, the value attributed to the new common stock — computed by deducting the principal or par amount of all higher ranking securities from the total enterprise value — must also be accepted as correct. Doubt about the value of the common necessarily translates into doubt about the valuation of the firm itself. The very acknowledgment of need for a quantitative bonus to creditors receiving the common is an admission that the firm has been overvalued.

Blum, Corporate Reorganization Doctrine as Recently Applied by the Securities and Exchange Commission, 40 U. Chi. L. Rev. 96, 110 (1972). Do you agree? See Note, Giving Substance to the Bonus Rule in Corporate Reorganizations: The Investment Value Doctrine Analogy, 84 Yale L.J. 932 (1975).

Does the absolute priority rule require that senior creditors receive "better quality" securities than their junior counterparts before a "cram down" may be urged? Compare In re Central Railroad Co., 579 F.2d 804, 812 (3d Cir. 1978) (rejecting, as inconsistent with the absolute priority rule, the use of Conrail securities to pay some administrative claimants when lower priority administrative claimants were receiving cash: "That Conrail's current valuation is speculative and uncertain is enough to indicate that cash is plainly a superior consideration which, if it is to be distributed, must be distributed to claimants with the highest priorities") with In re The Duplan Corp., 9 Bankr. 921 (S.D.N.Y. 1980) (rejecting argument of noteholders that the absolute priority rule entitled them to receive the cash that was going to junior debenture-holders under the plan).

NOTE ON CONTINGENT PARTICIPATION FOR EXCLUDED CLASSES

Many of the questions involved in Chapter 11 raise the uncertainty of valuations. Can lower priority classes rely on this uncertainty to argue that they should not be frozen completely out of a reorganization based on a projected valuation of the business showing that too little value exists to allow them to participate? This issue was raised in Spitzer v. Stichman, 278 F.2d 402 (2d Cir. 1960), which involved the Hudson Rapid Tubes Corporation, which ran what is now known as "PATH" between New York and New Jersey. The corporation's plan of reorganization excluded the equity from participation, based on the conclusion that the enterprise's present value, "after giving full effect to assets, earnings, and prospects of sale of the railroad property to a public authority," was insufficient to pay the creditors in full. The common stockholders appealed, in part on the ground that some or all of the debtor's commuter railroad plant might be purchased or condemned by a public authority at some unknown time in the future, at a price "many times its present value, when such value is considered apart from the prospect of such a public takeover." The common stockholders proposed that they be given "contingent interest certificates" that would entitle them to any excess proceeds on such a sale or condemnation. Should the court grant them such a contingent participation?

Section 7-303(3) of the proposed Bankruptcy Act of 1973 provided that a plan of reorganization

> may include, if the plan is based on an estimated valuation which would preclude other participation by any class of creditors, the partners of a partnership debtor, an individual debtor, or equity security holders of the debtor, provisions for delayed participation rights for such a class or classes, holders, partners, or individuals conditioned on the court's determination within a period specified in the plan but not later than five years from the date of confirmation that the reorganized debtor or the successor under the plan has attained a financial status that warrants such participation.

Should this proposal have been included in the Bankruptcy Code? Does it recognize that the value of a firm can decline as well as rise and the ability of senior claimants to enjoy possible increases compensates them for possible decreases? Compare Rochelle and Balzersen, Recommendations for Amendments to Chapter X, 46 Am. Bankr. L.J. 93, 99-102 (1972) with Brudney, The Bankruptcy Commission's Proposed "Modifications" of the Absolute Priority Rule, 48 Am. Bankr. L.J. 305 (1974); Note, The Proposed Bankruptcy Act: Changes in the Absolute Priority Rule for Corporate Reorganizations, 87 Harv. L. Rev. 1786 (1974).

NOTE ON THE §1111(b) ELECTION

Generally, under §506(a), a claim is secured only to the extent of the value of the collateral; the remainder is unsecured. Under §1111(b), however, a creditor may elect to have a claim secured for its entire amount, irrespective of the collateral's value. Moreover, §1111(b) states that, if a creditor makes no such election, the claim will be treated as a recourse claim regardless of whether it would be one under applicable nonbankruptcy law or contractual provision. Section 1111(b) cannot be understood without reference to §1129(b), which you should read (again).

The impetus for §1111(b) is generally considered to be the decision in In re Pine Gate Associates, Ltd., CCH Bankr. ¶66,325 (Bankr. N.D. Ga. 1976). In that case, Pine Gate, a limited partnership, filed a petition for a real property arrangement under Chapter XII of the Bankruptcy Act of

1898. Pine Gate owned and operated an apartment project. Secured creditors held a mortgage on the project, and the promissory notes evidencing the underlying debts stated that the debtor would not be liable on the notes beyond the value of the property and improvements constituting the apartment project. In other words, neither Pine Gate nor any of the partners were personally liable on the debts owed to the secured creditors: It was a "nonrecourse" loan. The secured creditors disapproved of Pine Gate's plan of arrangement. Pine Gate thereupon proposed that the apartment project be appraised and the creditors be paid the appraised value so the plan could be confirmed. The secured creditors objected and insisted that Chapter XII required their debts to be paid in full or the mortgaged property surrendered to them. The bankruptcy court rejected the creditors' argument:

> [I]f the creditor in lieu of the return of the property receives cash in the appraised value of that property, the creditor receives the "value of the debt" and the creditor is adequately protected . . . and the plan can be confirmed without the consent of said creditor.

The court also held that the nonrecourse secured creditors were not entitled to vote on Pine Gate's plan as unsecured creditors because they had limited their claims to the value of the security.

What exactly seems to be the objection to *Pine Gate*? Isn't *Pine Gate* simply giving secured creditors what they bargained for? Is this a fight over who gets the future appreciation in the property's value? 5 Collier on Bankruptcy ¶1111.02 (5th ed. 1981). Why should that be at issue? Isn't the possibility of appreciation captured in the value of the property and, on foreclosure, wouldn't the creditor be required to sell the asset, cutting it off from appreciation in any case? At heart, we may again have a *valuation* issue, the principal objection to which is the possibility that the bankruptcy court will undervalue the property. Is §1111(b) essentially addressing that issue? If so, what of the bankruptcy judge whose valuations are, on the whole, accurate? Doesn't the nonrecourse creditor then get *more* than it is entitled to? Can a debtor and a creditor agree, in a nonrecourse loan agreement, to waive the protection of §1111(b)?

IN RE SOUTHERN MISSOURI TOWING SERVICE
35 Bankr. 313 (Bankr. W.D. Mo. 1983)

Joel PELOFSKY, Bankruptcy Judge.

In this Chapter 11 case an undersecured creditor, the SBA, has made a timely Section 1111(b) election. The debtor disputes the impact of the election. The plan cannot be confirmed until the Court determines whether the claim is treated properly. Except for valuation of the collateral, there are no disputed issues of material fact. The parties have filed briefs and the Court has taken the matter under advisement. . . .

The SBA is classified separately in the plan. The value of the collateral is not inconsequential and is not to be sold under the plan. SBA, therefore, is eligible to make the Section 1111(b) election and has done so. . . . The question which must be resolved is the amount of money to be paid SBA.

Under the provisions of Section 506(a) of the Code a claim may be divided into secured and unsecured parts. As to the secured part, the creditor must be paid the present value. Section 1129(a)(7) of the Code. . . . The unsecured part may be paid in the same manner as other unsecured debt. If payment of the part allowed as secured is deferred, those deferred payments must include interest so that the total of the payments equal the present value. There is no such requirement as to the unsecured part.

When the creditor makes the Section 1111(b) election, the whole amount of the debt is allowed as secured. The right to have an unsecured claim is given up. By making this election the creditor prevents the debtor from "cashing him out." . . . But the debtor does not have to pay the whole secured claim in the same manner as if it were fully collateralized. If that were not so, every holder of an undersecured claim would make the election.

The real value of a Section 1111(b) election is where the collateral appreciates and the debtor defaults. The creditor could then recover the value of his claim and not just the part that was collateralized at the time the case was administered. . . .

The effect of a Section 1111(b) election was discussed during the House debate on the Code.

[I]f a creditor loaned $15,000,000 to a debtor secured by real property worth $18,000,000 and the value of the real property had dropped to $12,000,000 by the date when the debtor commenced a proceeding under chapter 11, the plan could be confirmed notwithstanding the dissent of the creditor as long as the lien remains on the collateral to secure a $15,000,000 debt, the face amount of present or extended payments to be made to the creditor under the plan is at least $15,000,000 and the present value of the present or deferred payment is not less than $12,000,000. . . . Congressional Record, September 28, 1978, at H11104 reprinted in App 2 Collier on Bankruptcy IX-117 (15th ed.).

The value of the collateral has not been determined in this case. Debtor schedules it at $190,000. The SBA claim is $226,993.34. In light of the election, assuming the collateral has a value of $190,000, the debtor must pay to SBA an amount equal to the entire debt but it need pay interest only on the amount of $190,000. Debtor must, therefore, design a plan treatment which pays the $190,000 at present value, which means with interest if payments are deferred, but need not pay SBA more than

$226,993.34. It may not be possible to do both. To accommodate debtor's cash flow, it may be necessary to stretch the payments so that principal and interest paid will exceed the amount of the allowed claim. That is not objectionable. Alternatively if debtor would design a plan treatment where principal and interest payments totalled only the amount of the claim, thus paying nothing on the unsecured part, that would not be objectionable either.

The parties are granted to January 6, 1984, to agree on a value of the collateral or to request a hearing on that issue. In the event of agreement, debtor is granted twenty (20) days thereafter to file an amended plan treating the SBA in accordance with this opinion in light of the agreed value of the collateral. For guidance to the parties, the Court notes that the contract rate of interest, prime and the IRS rate are considered in determining the rate to be paid by a debtor to maintain present value. . . .

IN RE GRIFFITHS
27 Bankr. 873 (Bankr. D. Kan. 1983)

James A. PUSATERI, Bankruptcy Judge.

In this chapter 11 proceeding, the parties have asked the Court, in a declaratory action, to determine if 11 U.S.C. §1129(b)(2)(A)(iii) allows the debtors to cram down their plan of reorganization when an electing secured creditor intends to vote to reject the plan.

The issues presented for determination are:

1. If a recourse, undersecured creditor, in its own class, has made an election under 11 U.S.C. §1111(b)(2), and rejects the debtor's plan of reorganization, is the creditor receiving the "indubitable equivalent" of its claim, under 11 U.S.C. §1129(b)(2)(A)(iii) when the debtors propose to surrender to the creditor a portion of the collateral, and pay the creditor a lump sum equal to the highest value of the collateral retained by the debtor.

2. Is the creditor equitably estopped from opposing the proposed treatment. . . .

FINDINGS OF FACT

The debtors are farmers and filed a chapter 11 petition in bankruptcy on August 6, 1982.

The creditor, Union State Bank (USB), has a security interest in personal property of the debtors including machinery, equipment, livestock and stored grain. USB filed an "election" under 11 U.S.C. §1111(b)(2) in September, 1982.

The debtors intend to treat USB in the plan as follows:

The debtors will return a portion of USB's collateral and pay a lump sum equal to the value of the remaining collateral in total satisfaction of USB's claim. As the disclosure statement indicates:

> It is debtors position that this combination of property turnover and payment in lump sum of the fair market value of said property is the "indubitable equivalent" of the creditor's allowed secured claim. This treatment will effectively satisfy Union State Bank's claim and no further payments are contemplated under the Plan.

(First Amended Disclosure Statement, pg. 20).

USB has filed a claim in the amount of $570,670.94. . . . The total value of the security pledged to USB is less than the amount of the debt and thus, USB is "undersecured."

The debtors also allege the following facts in their reply memorandum which the Court accepts as correct for the purpose of this opinion:

> On November 1, 1982, Debtors turned over their commercial cowherd to U.S.B. On November 23, 1982, an adequate protection order was entered whereby Debtors were to pay U.S.B. $500.00 per month for the depreciation to the personal property being retained by Debtors. On December 8, 1982, Debtors turned over to U.S.B. and to Massey Ferguson, certain machinery and equipment and subsequently turned over the Registered Cowherd owned by Debtors. On that date, U.S.B. accepted the payment of $2,000.000, the fair market value of two cows, and Debtors retained two registered cows, which are being used in rebuilding Debtors' herd and in the reorganization efforts. Debtors have determined that the personal property still in their possession in which U.S.B. claims an interest, will be beneficial to the rehabilitative efforts they are undergoing and to their Plan of Reorganization. Debtors subsequently proposed to pay U.S.B. more than they would receive if Debtors were to turn over the property. On the notification of U.S.B. that it would not accept such a proposal, its Motion and this Response ensued.

CONCLUSIONS OF LAW

Section 1111(b)(2) states:

> If . . . an election is made, then notwithstanding section 506(a) of this title, such claim is a secured claim to the extent that such claim is allowed.

11 U.S.C. §1111(b)(2). An undersecured creditor, a creditor whose security is worth less than the total amount owed to the creditor, may choose to have its claim treated in two manners. First, it can have a bifurcated claim, with a secured claim to the extent of the value of the collateral, and an unsecured claim for the remainder of the debt owed. 11 U.S.C. §506(a).

Second, the secured creditor can waive its unsecured claim and elect to have its total claim treated as secured. 11 U.S.C. §1111(b)(2). . . .

There are two situations in which the election cannot be made. First, if the creditor's interest in the collateral "is of inconsequential value . . . ," the election cannot be made. 11 U.S.C. §1111(b)(1)(B)(i). Second, if the creditor has recourse against the debtor, such as under K.S.A. §84-9-504(2) (Supp. 1981), and the debtor intends to sell the collateral, such as under 11 U.S.C. §363(k), the election cannot be made. In the instant case, the collateral has significant value, no sale is in the offing, and therefore the election is not prohibited.

USB is in a class of its own and intends to reject the debtors' plan. The parties agree USB's claim is being impaired. Thus, in order to confirm the plan the debtors will have to seek a cram down on USB. 11 U.S.C. §1129(b)(1). There are three alternatives to cramming down a class of secured claims. Although not applicable herein, property can be sold, a lien granted on the sale proceeds, and the lien satisfied under one of the remaining two cram down alternatives. 11 U.S.C. §1129(b)(2)(A)(ii). There can be a cash payment cram down, requiring the debtor to make cash payments of at least the allowed amount of the claim, and the discounted value of these payments must equal at least the value of the collateral. 11 U.S.C. §1129(b)(2)(A)(i)(II). The debtor does not propose to cram down under this provision.

The debtors choose the third option of giving USB "the indubitable equivalent of such claim. . . ." 11 U.S.C. §1129(b)(2)(A)(iii). The phrase "indubitable equivalent" is derived from Judge Learned Hand's opinion in In Re Murel Holding Corp., 75 F.2d 941 (2nd Cir. 1935). It includes "abandonment of the collateral" to the secured creditor. . . . Indubitable equivalent cash payments must equal at least the secured claim. Payments less than the secured claim are not the indubitable equivalent of the secured claim. . . .

The Court believes there are several reasons the debtors cannot return a portion of the collateral and pay the value of the remaining collateral as the indubitable equivalent of USB's section 1111(b)(2) claim.

First, USB's post-election secured claim is the total amount owed to it, $570,670.94, reduced by the value of any property returned. The debtors must pay the indubitable equivalent of the remaining amount owed, and not simply the indubitable equivalent of the value of the remaining property. The indubitable equivalent of the claim must be realized. The post-election claim is something more than the value of the remaining property.

Second, often a creditor will not elect under §1111(b)(2) because it will

> be reluctant to give up the distribution to unsecured creditors under the plan in exchange for a lien for the full amount of their secured and unsecured claims. . . . The election to relinquish an unsecured recourse deficiency

claim for a larger secured claim will normally be used to prevent a "cash out." Absent the election, a plan could free the collateral by paying the secured creditor the value of the collateral as this would not "impair" the secured creditor.

3 Norton, Bankruptcy Law and Practice §57.02 at 14-15 (Supp. 1982). Thus, creditors may choose to elect in cases where the debtor's plan proposes a minimal or zero payment to unsecured claims. In such a plan, the debtor is proposing to "cash out" the secured creditor by paying the value of the collateral. As Judge Norton indicated, §1111(b)(2) allows the creditor to decide if it will be cashed out for the value of the collateral. The creditor elects to "prevent a 'cash out.'" . . . In the instant case, the debtor is essentially proposing to "cash out" USB for the value of the remaining collateral. Section 1111(b)(2) gives USB the ability to prevent the cash out. The Court cannot agree that a cash out payment is the indubitable equivalent of a post election claim that prevented a cash out.

Third, under §1129(b)(2)(A)(i)(II), payments to the dissenting electing creditor must pass two tests. Under the first test, the total payments must be at least the total allowed claim. When the election has been made, the total amount owed is the allowed claim. Under the second test, those payments must have a present value equal to the value of the collateral. In the instant case, the debtors do not propose to pay the total remaining allowed claim of USB (after credit for returned collateral), but rather only propose to pay the value of the collateral. Thus, under §1129(b)(2)(A)(i)(II), the first requirement of cash payment cram down would not be satisfied. The Court does not believe §1129(b)(2)(A)(iii) was intended as an alternative to the cash payment requirements of §1129(b)(2)(A)(i)(II).

. . . If all the collateral is not returned, indubitable equivalent in the form proposed by the instant debtors is not available. . . . "Nothing less than the value assured to an electing creditor by section 1129(b)(2)(A)(i) . . . could be crammed down as an "indubitable equivalent." Stein, Section 1111(b): Providing Undersecured Creditors with Postconfirmation Appreciation in the Value of the Collateral, 56 Am. Bankr. L.J. 195, 210 (1982).

Finally, the debtors point out that they could return all the collateral in satisfaction of the post election secured claim. USB agrees. The Court agrees. The debtors argue that there is equitably no difference between returning collateral that could be sold by USB for $x, or just giving USB $x. The argument is alluring, but it has the effect of shifting the power granted under §1111(b)(2) from the creditor to the debtor. Section 1111(b)(2) gives the creditor the power to decide how it will be treated, and an ability to seek greater payments under a plan calling for zero percent payments to unsecured creditors. Under the debtors' argument, in a cash out plan, the power is always shifted back to the debtor. A debtor could propose zero payments to unsecured creditors under a cash out plan paying nothing to undersecured creditors. If the creditor elects to prevent cash out, the debtor could return anywhere from a small amount of property to a substantial amount of property and pay the value of the remaining property as the indubitable equivalent of returning all the property. The creditor would still be cashed out by receiving only the value of the collateral, and would be powerless to prevent the cash out. . . . A lump sum cash out payment, that removes the impaired electing creditor's power to prevent cash out is not the indubitable equivalent of the electing creditor's claim.

Therefore, the Court holds that the debtor's proposal will not satisfy the provisions of 11 U.S.C. §1129(b)(2)(A)(iii).

The debtors also argue that USB is equitably estopped from opposing the proposed treatment. The way USB would oppose the treatment under the plan is, of course, to vote not to accept the plan. At that point, the Court, not USB, must determine if the plan can be crammed down under §1129(b)(2)(A). The Court is not aware, and the debtors do not argue that USB would be estopped from voting on the plan. In fact, 11 U.S.C. §1126(a) allows impaired holders of claims to vote and does not mention a situation in which a creditor would lose its right to vote. Furthermore, equitable estoppel prohibits an assertion of rights inconsistent with past conduct if the result would be unconscionable . . . and if there was affirmative inducement. . . . The Court does not believe USB's election, rejection and opposition to treatment under §1129(b)(2)(A)(iii) is inconsistent with the acceptance of some collateral in satisfaction of some of the debt. USB is merely utilizing the leverage granted to creditors by Congress. USB does not appear opposed to the surrender of all the collateral by the debtor. Thus, the acceptance of some collateral is not inconsistent with a desire that the debtor either surrender all the collateral or make cash payments under §1129(b)(2)(A)(i). Moreover, there is nothing inequitable or unconscionable in USB's actions and the Court sees no inducement. The debtors' estoppel argument is therefore rejected.

In summary, the Court holds the debtors' proposal will not satisfy the provisions of §1129(b)(2)(A)(iii), and the debtors are given 15 days to modify the plan. . . .

NOTE ON THE CONSEQUENCES OF THE §1111(b) ELECTION

Creditor has loaned Debtor $1 million, secured by a security interest on Debtor's machinery. Debtor has filed for bankruptcy. Debtor needs to keep this machinery in order to continue running its business. (Even if it could find other machinery, Debtor could not run it as easily or as cheaply as machinery that it is already familiar with.) With the machinery in place,

Debtor alleges that the business is worth $2 million; without it, the business is worth only $1 million. Debtor also alleges that the machinery can be sold to a third party for only $600,000, because it is more suited to Debtor's business than to anyone else's.

Assume for the moment that §1111(b) does not exist. What would Creditor receive in Chapter 11? Debtor might use §1124 to reinstate the loan if Creditor's interest rate were favorable and the loan had long enough to run. Alternatively, using §1124(3), Creditor could be deemed unimpaired if given cash equal to the "allowed amount of such claim" on the effective date of the plan.

Section 506(b) bifurcates claims into secured and unsecured portions. The allowed amount subject to §1124 treatment will be the secured claim. What is that amount? Is it $1 million (the difference in the value of Debtor with and without the machinery)? Is Creditor entitled to that amount? Can one justify using a going-concern valuation of the collateral? Creditor is entitled only to the amount it would realize if it could repossess the collateral. But can't Creditor argue that a third party might pay more than $600,000 (but less than $1,000,000) because of the possibility that it could sell the machinery back to the Debtor?

Who resolves this controversy? Remember, Debtor wants to keep the property. The bankruptcy court values the property. Is this preferable to selling the property to a third party with an option by Debtor to buy it back then at the sale price? Is such a rule practical?

Assume that the bankruptcy court agrees that liquidation value should be used and the liquidation value here is $600,000. That means Creditor's secured claim can be paid with $600,000 cash and satisfy §1124(3). What, however, if Debtor does not want to pay cash on the effective date of the plan? Section 1129 allows plans to be confirmed even if Creditor is "impaired" within the meaning of §1124. The relevant subsection is (b)(2)(A), because we are dealing with a secured creditor. That provision requires that the holder of the claim retain its lien, as well as that it receive "on account of such claim deferred cash payments totaling at least the allowed amount of such claim, of a value, as of the effective date of the plan, of at least the value of such holder's interest in the estate's interest in such property." Debtor, for example, could provide Creditor with deferred payments — instead of paying Creditor cash on the effective date of the plan — as long as Creditor retained a lien on the property securing the claim. Presumably the lien, like the claim, would be for $600,000. In addition, the stream of payments would have to total at least $600,000 and have a present value of $600,000. See *Griffiths*.

If Creditor were a recourse creditor, Creditor would also have an unsecured claim for $400,000, and would be put in the pool of unsecured creditors. If Creditor has a large enough unsecured claim, it may be able to block any attempt by Debtor to keep any property for the shareholders.

Creditor's vote may be enough for the class to reject any plan, and a dissenting class is protected by the "absolute priority rule" of §1129(b). But Creditor may be only one of many in the unsecured class, and might be outvoted by the others. (In that case, Creditor receives the same pro rata share of the assets for its unsecured claim as others in its class.) The amount of leverage Creditor has will depend largely on what the rest of Debtor's situation looks like. If Creditor's loan were nonrecourse, there would be no remaining claim — that's the point of a nonrecourse loan.

Is anything conceptually wrong with these rules? A basic premise of bankruptcy is that creditors may have to allow the debtor to retain property because it is in everyone's interest. When Debtor keeps the property and Creditor gets cashed out, Creditor seems to receive just what it is entitled to, assuming that the bankruptcy judge makes accurate valuations. Can legal rules correct for the possible tendency of bankruptcy judges to undervalue property (and hence undervalue the secured creditor's rights)? Section 1111(b) tries to do precisely this, but whether it succeeds is an open question. Section 1111(b) provides that if the class (and a class often consists of only one secured creditor) fails to make the election, its claim is recourse, whether or not it would be recourse under applicable non-bankruptcy law. That means, with respect to our example, an unsecured deficiency claim of $400,000 would exist even if the claim were nonrecourse under nonbankruptcy law.

How does this help the valuation problem? It helps the *nonrecourse creditor* by giving it an unsecured claim. This may increase that creditor's leverage in bargaining with Debtor and, if the claim is large enough, it may have substantial leverage (because it can block an unfavorable plan). But note that this increased leverage is costly. If the bankruptcy judge's valuation is accurate, so the property is in fact worth only $600,000, §1111(b) gives the creditor something it isn't entitled to outside of bankruptcy — a deficiency claim — and this means less for the other claimants. This rule brings costs, like any other substantive rule that applies only in bankruptcy.

Assume that Creditor makes the §1111(b) election. Section 1111(b)(2) states that "such claim is a secured claim to the extent that such claim is allowed." This means that the claim is secured to the tune of $1 million. If Creditor makes the election and Debtor wants Creditor's claim to be unimpaired, §1124(3) now requires a cash payment on the effective date of the plan of "the allowed amount of such claim," or $1 million. The effect of §1124(2) is, of course, unchanged.

What are the consequences if Debtor intends to make a stream of cash payments and must satisfy the absolute priority rule of §1129? One of its requirements is that Creditor receive a lien securing the claim. §1129(b)(2)(A). Creditor must be given a $1 million lien on the equipment. But the bankruptcy court has said that the equipment is worth only

$600,000. (Could one argue that, under the language of §1129(b)(2)(A), the relevant amount should be the going-concern value to the debtor, or $1 million?)

Creditor must also receive deferred cash payments totalling at least the allowed amount of the claim, which is $1 million. And these payments must total "at least the value of such holder's interest in the estate's interest in such property." What is "the value of [Creditor's] interest in the estate's interest"? Isn't that *value* $600,000? The bankruptcy court has ruled that the estate's interest in the property is worth $600,000. Creditor therefore should receive deferred cash payments that total at least $1 million, with a present value of $600,000. See *Southern Missouri Towing Service*, supra.

The plan is deemed to be fair and equitable, therefore, if Creditor retains a lien on the property for $1 million and receives deferred payments of $1 million with a present value of at least $600,000. If Creditor makes the election, there is no unsecured portion of the claim. Therefore, Creditor loses any right (a) to vote on the plan with the general creditors and (b) to receive any distribution as an unsecured creditor. So, if there is an election, one must have a $1 million lien after the bankruptcy proceeding is over. But the payments need only have a present value of $600,000. That's the same present value as what Creditor would have received if it had not made the election.

Why, then, would Creditor make the election? *If* Creditor believes that the bankruptcy judge is wrong and the property is really worth more than $600,000, by making the election Creditor would have a $1 million lien, whereas before Creditor only had a $600,000 lien. But a lien is of no value to Creditor unless it can also reach this property. A lien is only a contingent right to property.

Creditor will (subject to the complications still to be discussed) make the election only if it believes *both* that the property has been undervalued *and* that Debtor will default (or sell the property, assuming the loan agreement has a due-on-sale clause) in the near future, so that Creditor can get its hands on the property. Thus, in our example, *if* the property is worth more than $600,000 *and if* Debtor is likely to default in the near future or otherwise accelerate its obligation, Creditor has a shot at getting more than $600,000. In other words, it allows a creditor to "opt out" of the bankruptcy judge's valuation. This is stated by Judge Pelofsky in *Southern Missouri Towing Service*, supra:

> The real value of a Section 1111(b) election is where the collateral appreciates and the debtor defaults. The creditor could then recover the value of his claim and not just the part that was collateralized at the time the case was administered.

See also Stein, Section 1111(b): Providing Undersecured Creditors with Postconfirmation Appreciation in the Value of the Collateral, 56 Am.

Bankr. L.J. 195 (1982). Even if such a default is not likely, an election may nonetheless place some additional constraints on the debtor (consider a case such as *Griffiths*). It may, for example, restrict the use of §1124(3). See In re Hallum, 29 Bankr. 343 (Bankr. E.D. Tenn. 1983). If so, this may be another reason for making the election.

The advantages of making the election must be weighed against what has to be given up — the strategic and monetary value of the unsecured claim. Perhaps giving up that claim will cost Creditor little — having a vote as an unsecured creditor and the pro rata share of a general creditor may not be worth much. The gain and the cost must be weighed on a case by case basis.

Several additional factors must be added to the analysis. Remember what Creditor gets in both cases. If Creditor doesn't make the election, its secured status would be as follows:

Lien	$600,000
Aggregate Payments	$600,000
Present Value	$600,000

If the election is made, Creditor's secured status is as follows:

Lien	$1,000,000
Aggregate Payments	$1,000,000
Present Value	$ 600,000

Try to imagine what a note that satisfied each would look like. Look first at the nonelection note. It is a note secured for $600,000. Isn't the *principal*, almost by necessity, $600,000? And the interest must be at a proper rate (which we'll look at soon). Assume it is 20 percent (to make calculation easy). What we might have, then, is six annual principal payments of $100,000, plus interest. That looks like this:

Year 1	$220,000	($100,000 + 120,000)
Year 2	$200,000	($100,000 + 100,000)
Year 3	$180,000	($100,000 + 80,000)
Year 4	$160,000	($100,000 + 60,000)
Year 5	$140,000	($100,000 + 40,000)
Year 6	$120,000	($100,000 + 20,000)

The total payments to Creditor are $1,020,000. What about the note given if an election is made? It is a note secured for $1,000,000. Does the principal need to be $1,000,000? Note that nothing in the statute explicitly requires this — only that the deferred payments must *total* $1 million. How this is interpreted is going to make a big difference. For if the principal need not be $1,000,000, Debtor could give Creditor the same note as above – $600,000 principal, with interest payments — with one change: The lien would be for $1 million. In that case, Debtor might be able to make the same six annual payments of $100,000, plus interest of 20 percent. (See above.) The total payments are $1,020,000, which complies with §1111(b).

Even here we need to ask whether the same interest rate should be used. If Creditor made the election and there was a default at the time of the first payment, Creditor would have a claim for $720,000: $600,000 principal plus $120,000 of accrued but unpaid interest. This entire claim would be secured, whereas, if Creditor did not make the election, Creditor's $720,000 claim would only be secured to $600,000, because the nonelecting creditor's lien is only $600,000. This might support a slightly *lower* interest rate if Creditor makes the election, because Creditor might be better secured if the property is worth more than $600,000. (Put another way: ask which note you would rather have *if* the interest rate were the same, and if both had the same rights (an issue discussed next). You almost certainly would rather have the note with the $1 million lien.) Does that mean, to equalize the two notes, the interest rate should be adjusted downward on the "election" note relative to the "nonelection" note? If so, that cost must also be considered in deciding whether or not to make the election.

But it may not be appropriate to pay the electing secured creditor with a note having a principal of only $600,000. The rationale behind §1111(b) may be to allow Creditor to recover $1 million if there is a default (and if Creditor were right that the court undervalued the property). If this is the rationale, shouldn't Creditor receive something like a zero coupon note with a $1 million principal, paid off over five years at $200,000 a year? But how do we know whether the implicit discount rate of 20 percent in this pay out schedule is the appropriate one? Should it be even *lower* than under either of the other two alternatives, because, if a default occurs, Creditor is even *better* off (because its accelerated principal would be $1 million)?

Or should the 20 percent interest rate used for the *nonelecting* creditor be used for *any* note given the electing creditor? In other words, is this interest rate a benefit Creditor traded for in giving up its unsecured claim? Indeed, should we consider a *higher* interest rate? See Blum, The "Fair and Equitable" Standard for Confirming Reorganizations Under the New Bankruptcy Code, 54 Am. Bankr. L.J. 165 (1980).

Section 1111(b) contains other ambiguities. Consider the case of the nonelecting creditor. If its claim were nonrecourse before bankruptcy, is the note the creditor gets in bankruptcy also nonrecourse? If so, Creditor, in our example, would only be entitled in the event of a subsequent default to the lesser of: (a) the value of the property or (b) $600,000. Similarly, what if Creditor makes the election? Is *its* claim still nonrecourse? If it is, then if the court correctly valued the property and Debtor subsequently defaults, Creditor receives only $600,000, with no right to get a deficiency. What if Creditor was *recourse* before making the election? The answers to all these questions, to which the statute provides no guidance, may be important in deciding whether to make the election in the first place.

One other factor should be considered. *When* is the election to be made? On the one hand, should the creditor have a right to see how it will be treated in any plan of reorganization before it makes the election? On the other hand, how can a reorganization plan be drawn up if Debtor does not know who will make election? What if a creditor sees a plan of reorganization, and then makes the election? See, e.g., In re Hallum, 29 Bankr. 343 (Bankr. E.D. Tenn. 1983). The plan is then blocked. If a new plan is proposed, can the creditor now decide not to make the election? (This is answered in Bankruptcy Rule 3014 — the election may be made at any time before the conclusion of the hearing on the disclosure statement — but was it drafted with these strategic difficulties in mind?)

Note that all this uncertainty will feed into the negotiation process. It isn't at all clear that anyone *knows* what the consequences will be of making an election in a particular case. That may encourage both parties to be a little more flexible in their negotiations, because of the fear that the section will be construed according to their worst nightmares.

Other difficulties still remain. What would you do if the loan were $1 million and the collateral was valued at only $50,000? In this context, does the §1111(b) election give the creditor too much leverage? Would the debtor effectively be required to give it a package with a present value in excess of $50,000? In considering that, think of the tests of §1129(b). How could you arrange payments of $1 million to have a present value of only $50,000? Would payments spread over 50 or 100 years be permitted by a court? In re White, 36 Bankr. 199 (Bankr. D. Kan. 1983), suggests no. Such a situation, should it occur, may encourage the use of §1124(3).

For an analysis of the §1111(b) election and other issues, see Eisenberg, The Undersecured Creditor in Chapter 11 Reorganizations and the Nature of Security, 38 Vand. L. Rev.— (1985).

NOTE ON THE EFFECT OF CONFIRMATION

Section 1141 states the general effects of confirmation of a plan of reorganization. Central to this are the provisions of §1141(c) and (d), which effectively discharge all the debtor's pre-petition debts, other than as specified in the plan of reorganization itself. While some of the subtler effects of discharge are examined in the next chapter, in connection with the individual's "fresh start" policy, one distinct question arises here.

Section 727(a)(1) provides, in effect, that *only* debtors who are individuals can receive discharges in Chapter 7 proceedings. A corporation cannot obtain a discharge. This is not particularly troublesome, however, because following a Chapter 7 liquidation, a corporation can always dissolve under state law, giving those who care (shareholders) their effective "discharge."

Should a corporation decide to liquidate in Chapter 11 — a procedure permissible under the Bankruptcy Code and known as a "liquidating plan of reorganization" — the corporation will likewise be denied a discharge. §1141(d)(3). But why do continuing corporations get a discharge in Chapter 11? It is unlikely to have anything to do with the "fresh start" policy that exists for individuals. Corporations, after all, are creatures of the state. Instead, the reason may stem from a desire to allow the corporation's owners to make an unbiased decision whether to continue or liquidate, by permitting the same treatment of claims under either path. Seen in this way, since a corporation dissolving under state law effectively "discharges" its obligations, an insolvent corporation that continues may need the same treatment so assets may continue to be used in their "optimal" way (from the perspective of all the owners). Section 1141(c) and (d) provide that mechanism. It may be viewed as a sale of assets to a new corporation, coupled with an effective disappearance of the old corporation.

What is the scope of §1141(c) and (d)? The language of (d)(1)(A) suggests that confirmation of the plan will discharge all pre-petition debts, whether a proof of claim was filed or whether the claim was allowed. In re Safeguard Co., 35 Bankr. 44 (Bankr. W.D. Pa. 1983) construed this as binding "unscheduled creditors . . . even if those creditors have no knowledge of the bankruptcy proceeding." Is this scope justified? In re Kuempel Co., 14 Bankr. 324 (Bankr. S.D. Ohio 1981), quoting statements by Senator DeConcini and Representative Edwards on the floor of Congress, reasoned:

> It is necessary for a corporation or partnership undergoing reorganization to be able to present its creditors with a fixed list of liabilities upon which the creditors or third parties can make intelligent decisions.

Is this persuasive? Should creditors who never received notice of a pending bankruptcy proceeding likewise have their debts discharged in a corporate reorganization under Chapter 11? If §1141(d) is construed that way, is it constitutional? Reliable Electric Co. v. Olson Constr. Co., 726 F.2d 620 (10th Cir. 1984), concluded that such debts are not dischargeable, despite §1141(d)(1), because "notwithstanding the language of section 1141, the discharge of a claim without reasonable notice . . . is violative of the fifth amendment to the United States Constitution." It continues:

> A fundamental right guaranteed by the Constitution is the opportunity to be heard when a property interest is at stake. Specifically, the reorganization process depends upon all creditors and interested parties being properly notified of all vital steps in the proceeding so they may have the opportunity

to protect their interests. . . . We will not require Olson to subject its claim to a confirmed reorganization plan that it had no opportunity to dispute.

See also In re Sullivan Ford Sales, 25 Bankr. 400 (Bankr. D. Me. 1982). Is this persuasive? Would it matter if the trustees had no knowledge of the creditors' claim? What would happen to such claims if the corporation was liquidating under Chapter 7? Dissolving under state law? Does the answer to these questions matter?

Chapter 10
BANKRUPTCY'S "FRESH START" POLICY FOR INDIVIDUALS

A. INTRODUCTION

In theory, a bankruptcy process for individuals does not need to culminate in the discharge of debts. Indeed, as we discussed in Chapter 1, the concept of discharge emerged in the eighteenth century more than a century after bankruptcy law itself was well established and even then began principally as a device to ensure that the debtor cooperated with his creditors. Much of the complexity of bankruptcy law stems from the difficulty of establishing a collective proceeding that works out conflicts among creditors. The vast majority of the bankruptcy provisions are concerned with issues such as gathering the estate and parceling it out among creditors. These provisions would be necessary regardless of whether there were a discharge at the end of the bankruptcy proceeding. They have formed the focus of our examination to this point, and those rules are largely unaffected by the presence of the discharge issues we now turn to.

In the case of corporations and other business entities, indeed, it is fair to say that the bankruptcy process is *only* concerned with these creditor-oriented rules. Liquidating corporations do not need the bankruptcy process in order to gain a discharge of debts, for they can accomplish that end through dissolution under state law. The Bankruptcy Code emphasizes this point by explicitly providing that there shall be no discharge in any bankruptcy liquidation of corporate and partnership debtors. §§727(a)(1), 1141(d)(3). Congress thought that discharges in these cases would serve no valid purpose and encourage fraudulent practices. See H.R. Rep. No. 595, 95th Cong., 1st Sess. 384 (1977). (The shareholders, moreover, never need to be "discharged" from the debts of their corporation because of the state law doctrine of limited liability of shareholders for the debts of their corporations.)

Reorganizing corporations, as we have seen, are a different matter, and Chapter 11 provides for their discharge. The justification for discharge in Chapter 11, however, has nothing to do with a "fresh start" policy. Instead, it is still a part of the creditor-oriented nature of bankruptcy. As we explored in Note on the Effect of Confirmation, supra page 725, given the possibility of discharge through dissolution under state law, claimants will not make the correct choice between piecemeal liquidation (followed by dissolution) and continuation *unless* a reorganizing corporation can wipe the slate clean and begin again. Unless it can, there will always be an incentive to discharge obligations by dissolving under state law after a piecemeal liquidation.

Nonetheless, in the case of individuals, federal bankruptcy law also reflects, in its discharge provisions, a separate policy that is unquestionably debtor-oriented in its focus. This has not always been the case. Discharge has not always been a feature of this nation's bankruptcy laws and, as the Supreme Court has noted, discharge "is a legislatively created benefit, not a constitutional one," United States v. Kras, 409 U.S. 434 (1973). Originally, discharge depended upon a favorable vote of a majority of creditors (and also on the size of the dividend paid to the creditors). This requirement has been whittled away over time and, since the Bankruptcy Act of 1898, the right of individuals to have their debts discharged in bankruptcy (whether in voluntary or involuntary proceedings) has not been conditioned on creditor consent.

The ability of individuals to discharge existing debts probably also explains why there are so many bankruptcy cases each year. Most bankruptcy cases are brought by individuals, possessing few or no nonexempt assets, principally for the purpose of getting a discharge from debts. In these "no asset" cases, the creditors get little or nothing and the bankruptcy case itself tends to be relatively simple. Some form of a discharge for individuals has become a central and, one can safely assume, virtually permanent feature of bankruptcy law, although the debate over the proper scope of that discharge continues. In 1984, for example, Congress added §707(b), which provides that a bankruptcy judge can dismiss a case filed by (and hence deny a discharge to) an individual debtor whose debts are primarily consumer debts if the judge finds that granting relief would be a "substantial abuse" of the provisions of Chapter 7. (To understand the actual effects of this provision, it will be necessary to understand the principal alternative for such a debtor (Chapter 13 of the Bankruptcy Code), an examination we undertake in Chapter 12 of this book.)

In examining the scope of bankruptcy's discharge policy, it is helpful to keep separate what are essentially several different inquiries. First, one must identify exactly the scope of relief bankruptcy provides individuals. In the case of corporations, no distinction is drawn between present and future assets. The value of a corporation today is the discounted present value of all its future earnings. Moreover, all of a corporation's assets are reachable by its creditors. As we noted in the previous chapter, even in a reorganization, creditors are entitled to be paid in full before the shareholders receive any of the firm's assets. §1129(b). In the case of individuals, however, the picture is quite different. As we discussed in Chapter 4, an individual's future earnings can be seen as a present asset, supra page 175. Someone with a law degree generally has a greater net worth (and is able to borrow more money) than someone of comparable age with only a high school diploma, even if they otherwise have the same assets and liabilities. Nevertheless, bankruptcy law draws a distinction between this "future" asset — the kind of asset that would lose all its value if we knew the debtor would die tomorrow — and other assets. Under current law an individual who obtains a discharge is able to free this asset, oftentimes called "human capital," from the claims of present creditors. One can ask whether a debtor should be able to free all future earnings from the claims of creditors. Whether present law should be changed depends upon the justifications for having a fresh start policy in the first instance.

The scope of the bankruptcy discharge raises a further question as well: What does it mean to say an individual has been "discharged" from pre-bankruptcy debts? At a minimum, it must mean that the person discharged has an affirmative defense to a suit brought by a creditor on the debt. To what extent does it — or should it — mean more? Can the creditor harass or threaten the debtor to collect despite the discharge? Can a creditor whose debt was discharged refuse to confer some collateral benefit on the debtor on the ground, in whole or in part, that the debt that was discharged in bankruptcy remains unpaid? Can someone other than such a creditor (such as an employer, a landlord, or a government agency) refuse to confer some benefit on the debtor, or otherwise discriminate against the debtor, on the same grounds? These questions are addressed in §§524 and 525.

In addition to the scope of the discharge right, discharge raises two more issues. There are some situations in which the debtor will be denied a discharge altogether — for all his debts — if he has done something that is thought to be basically inconsistent with the purpose or spirit of the bankruptcy laws. The various grounds for denying a debtor a discharge in its entirety are set out in §727. Moreover, even if the debtor gets a general discharge, certain debts may nonetheless be excepted from this general discharge by being made nondischargeable. The rules govering these nondischargeable debts are set forth in §523.

Nondischarge of particular debts might be justified on either of two grounds. At one extreme, the debtor's conduct may be exemplary, but the type of debt involved is thought to be of a kind that, for policy reasons, should be nondischargeable. At the other extreme, the denial of a discharge for a particular debt may reflect a view that the debtor's behavior was wrongful and does not deserve discharge. There is, not suprisingly, some overlap in the type of behavior that may fit in §§523 and 727, and we will explore this in connection with *McCloud,* infra page 793. All these questions are the focus of this chapter.

Merely allowing a debtor to shield future income from the claims of creditors may not go far enough. One may want to allow the debtor to keep some existing assets as well. Under current law a bankruptcy discharge gives a debtor a right to enjoy future income. In addition, a debtor may also keep some existing assets. To a large extent these assets, such as Keogh retirement plans or tools of trade, cannot be reached by creditors outside of bankruptcy either, and hence are not part of a "fresh start" that is unique to bankruptcy law. The details of the provisions governing exempt property (§541 and §522) and the policies underlying them are explored in Chapter 11 of this book.

B.   THE SOCIAL POLICY OF DISCHARGE

Bankruptcy, at least during this century, has implied a "fresh start" when the debtor is an individual. Why do individuals enjoy a right of discharge in bankruptcy? What are the costs of providing such a right? Are there reasons for the right of discharge being (as you will see) nonwaivable?

In thinking about discharge, there are two separate baseline questions to keep in mind. First, why does there exist a right to a discharge at all? And, second, why is a debtor not able to waive this right of discharge? For example, if a creditor is willing to make a debtor a loan at a lower interest rate if the debtor waives his right to have that debt discharged in bankruptcy, why doesn't this represent the sort of trade off that the legal system encourages us to make all the time? Individuals are free to waive many other things, including, apparently, the right to legal process. D.H. Overmyer Co. v. Frick Co., 405 U.S. 174 (1972). Yet, in the case of a bankruptcy discharge, such a before the fact waiver is not possible. We start by examining why this should be so, and the trade-offs involved. The case that follows is the seminal discussion by the Supreme Court of the policy behind giving individuals a discharge right.

LOCAL LOAN CO. v. HUNT
292 U.S. 234 (1934)

Justice SUTHERLAND delivered the opinion of the Court.

On September 17, 1930, respondent borrowed from petitioner the sum of $300, and as security for its payment executed an assignment of a portion of his wages thereafter to be earned. On March 3, 1931, respondent filed a voluntary petition in bankruptcy in a federal district court in Illinois, including in his schedule of liabilities the foregoing loan, which constituted a provable claim against the estate. Respondent was adjudicated a bankrupt; and, on October 10, 1932, an order was entered discharging him from all provable debts and claims. On October 18, 1932, petitioner brought an action in the municipal court of Chicago against respondent's employer to enforce the assignment in respect of wages earned after the adjudication. Thereupon, respondent commenced this proceeding in the court which had adjudicated his bankruptcy and ordered his discharge, praying that petitioner be enjoined from further prosecuting said action or attempting to enforce its claim therein made against respondent under the wage assignment. The bankruptcy court, upon consideration, entered a decree in accordance with the prayer; and this decree on appeal was affirmed by the court below. . . .

Challenging this decree, petitioner contends: . . . the rule is that an assignment of future wages constitutes an enforceable lien. . . .

. . . Whether an assignment of future earned wages constitutes a lien within the meaning of §67(d) of the bankruptcy act,[2] is a matter upon which the decisions of the state and federal courts are not in complete accord; although by far the larger number of cases and the greater weight of authority are in the negative. We do not stop to review the state decisions. . . . The lower federal courts which have had occasion to consider the question concur in the view that the lien has no existence or is ineffective as against an adjudication and discharge in bankruptcy. Judge Bellinger, in In re West, 128 Fed. 205, succinctly stated the ground of his ruling in accordance with that view as follows:

"The discharge in bankruptcy operated to discharge these obligations as of the date of the adjudication, so that the obligations were discharged before the wages intended as security were in existence. The law does not continue an obligation in order that there may be a lien, but only does so because there is one. The effect of the discharge upon the prospective liens was the same as though the debts had been paid before the assigned wages were earned. The wages earned after the adjudication became the property of the bankrupt clear of the claims of all creditors." . . .

The earning power of an individual is the power to create property; but it is not translated into property within the meaning of the bankruptcy act until it has brought earnings into existence. An adjudication of bankruptcy, followed by a discharge, releases a debtor from all previously incurred debts, with certain exceptions not pertinent here; and it logically cannot be supposed that the act nevertheless intended to keep such debts alive for the purpose of permitting the creation of an enforceable lien upon a subject not existent when the bankruptcy became effective or even arising from, or connected with, preëxisting property, but brought into being solely as the fruit of the subsequent labor of the bankrupt. . . . To the

2. "Liens given or accepted in good faith and not in contemplation of or in fraud upon this Act, and for a present consideration, which have been recorded according to law, if record thereof was necessary in order to impart notice, shall, to the extent of such present consideration only, not be affected by this Act." U.S.C. Title 11, §107(d).

foregoing array of authority petitioner opposes the decisions of the Supreme Court of Illinois in Mallin v. Wenham, 209 Ill. 252; 70 N.E. 564, and Monarch Discount Co. v. C. & O. Ry. Co., 285 Ill. 233; 120 N.E. 743. Undoubtedly, these cases hold, as petitioner asserts, that in Illinois an assignment of future wages creates a lien effective from the date of the assignment which is not invalidated by the assignor's discharge in bankruptcy. The contention is that even if the general rule be otherwise, this court is bound to follow the Illinois decisions, since the question of the existence of a lien depends upon Illinois law.

. . . It is important to bear in mind that the present case is one not within the jurisdiction of a state court, but is a dependent suit brought to vindicate decrees of a federal court of bankruptcy entered in the exercise of a jurisdiction essentially federal and exclusive in character. And it is that situation to which we address ourselves, and to which our decision is confined.

One of the primary purposes of the bankruptcy act is to "relieve the honest debtor from the weight of oppressive indebtedness and permit him to start afresh free from the obligations and responsibilities consequent upon business misfortunes." Williams v. U.S. Fidelity & G. Co., 236 U.S. 549, 554-555. This purpose of the act has been again and again emphasized by the courts as being of public as well as private interest, in that it gives to the honest but unfortunate debtor who surrenders for distribution the property which he owns *at the time of bankruptcy*, a new opportunity in life and a clear field for future effort, unhampered by the pressure and discouragement of preëxisting debt. . . . The various provisions of the bankruptcy act were adopted in the light of that view and are to be construed when reasonably possible in harmony with it so as to effectuate the general purpose and policy of the act. Local rules subversive of that result cannot be accepted as controlling the action of a federal court.

When a person assigns future wages, he, in effect, pledges his future earning power. The power of the individual to earn a living for himself and those dependent upon him is in the nature of a personal liberty quite as much as, if not more than, it is a property right. To preserve its free exercise is of the utmost importance, not only because it is a fundamental private necessity, but because it is a matter of great public concern. From the viewpoint of the wage earner there is little difference between not earning at all and earning wholly for a creditor. Pauperism may be the necessary result of either. The amount of the indebtedness, or the proportion of wages assigned, may here be small, but the principle, once established, will equally apply where both are very great. The new opportunity in life and the clear field for future effort, which it is the purpose of the bankruptcy act to afford the emancipated debtor, would be of little value to the wage earner if he were obliged to face the necessity of devoting the whole or a considerable portion of his earnings for an indefinite time in the future to the payment of indebtedness incurred prior to his bankruptcy.

Confining our determination to the case in hand, and leaving prospective liens upon other forms of acquisitions to be dealt with as they may arise, we reject the Illinois decisions as to the effect of an assignment of wages earned after bankruptcy as being destructive of the purpose and spirit of the bankruptcy act.

Decree affirmed.

NOTES

1. The narrow issue in Local Loan Co. v. Hunt is whether a pre-bankruptcy assignment or garnishment of wages (recall *Riddervold*, supra page 336) survives bankruptcy discharge. As we shall see later in the chapter, the general rule under a doctrine first enunciated in Long v. Bullard, 117 U.S. 617 (1886), is that unavoided interests in property survive even if the debt itself is discharged. *Local Loan* held that an assignment or garnishment, however, could not survive bankruptcy, even if it were labeled a "lien" under state law. Does this policy survive enactment of the Bankruptcy Code? Although nothing in the Bankruptcy Code speaks to the point, courts assume that the policy continues. See In re Miranda Soto, 667 F.2d 235 (1st Cir. 1981) (payroll deductions made to repay "loan" from employees' association cannot survive bankruptcy; distinguishes *Villaire*, supra page 128, on the ground that this constituted a lender-borrower relationship, not an "advance"); see also §552 (similar policy with respect to consensual security interests).

2. Eisenberg, Bankruptcy Law in Perspective, 28 U.C.L.A. L. Rev. 953, 981-983 (1981):

> Limiting the availability of discharges focuses only on one of the actors in a credit transaction. By focusing on the creditor, one might encourage prudent lending by a generous system of discharge. . . . If a lenient discharge rule is in effect, one expects creditors to charge higher interest rates that offset any increased demand for funds by debtors who seek to avail themselves of a too liberal discharge rule. [These considerations] raise the possibility that the rule of discharge does not really matter.
>
> Upon deeper analysis, economic considerations may support a more conditional system of discharge. If enforcement of contracts is to foster efficient allocation of resources, one economic theory argues, the contracting party more able to protect himself against loss resulting from an event should bear the risk of such loss. A discharge system provides a technique for allocating the risk of financial distress between a debtor and his creditors. . . .
>
> This basic analysis [of risk allocation based on contract notions of impossibility] needs some refinement. As an empirical matter, debtors neither are always superior insurers nor are always better able than creditors to assess the likelihood of bankruptcy and to factor that possibility into the terms of

the contract. Some sophisticated commercial lenders probably are better than many of their borrowers about protecting the borrowers' future financial status, and some undoubtedly purchase reasonably priced bad-debt insurance. Yet other lenders, like the corner hardware store selling on credit, are likely to be at an informational disadvantage relative to the debtor. . . .

But even assuming that some lenders are better placed than some debtors to assess the likelihood and effect of bankruptcy, it is implausible that all or even most lenders could be so situated. In general, borrowers know more about themselves and have greater control of their affairs than lenders do. If bankruptcy law is going to reach a single conclusion with respect to discharge, the single economic answer would most likely be to limit the discharge.

3. Does the corporate law doctrine of limited liability for the shareholders of an incorporated firm provide an analogy of sorts? The shareholders invest in the firm, but can lose only their investment; the remainder of their wealth cannot be touched. What are the justifications for this doctrine of limited liability? Richard Posner identifies two reasons for limited liability for corporations. First, Judge Posner asserts that creditors of an enterprise are in a better position to appraise the risks and hence are superior risk bearers. Second, Judge Posner asserts that limited liability — at least in the case of publicly held corporations with widely dispersed ownership — may be advantageous because the shareholders are likely to be more risk averse than the creditors. See Posner, The Rights of Creditors of Affiliated Corporations, 43 U. Chi. L. Rev. 499 (1976).

Both these reasons may apply to individuals. To the extent the first does, it seems to be inconsistent with Professor Eisenberg's analysis quoted in Note 2 above. Judge Posner's second justification for limited liability may be more powerful. The ability to earn money in the future may be a large part of the assets of (younger) individuals. Moreover, there may be no way that individuals can successfully diversify by investing in other assets with different risk characteristics. But does this analogy explain why individuals should not be able to waive their discharge right? In the corporate setting, limited liability can be waived either generally, by setting up a business in another form, or in a particular case, as where principal shareholders guarantee a corporation's obligations.

NOTE ON JUSTIFYING THE NONWAIVABILITY OF THE RIGHT OF DISCHARGE

Might it be useful to think of the discharge right as a form of an insurance policy — a policy that insures that things can only get so bad and no worse? A discharge right, in some sense, provides a form of a guarantee that downside losses will be limited. But does the analogy to insurance explain why individuals should not be able to waive their discharge right? Is it like social security? If so, are there alternative arrangements that could provide the same kind of benefits as a nonwaivable discharge right? For example, suppose that the federal government just guarantees that no one — regardless of his debts — will be permitted to fall below a certain lifestyle: Food, clothing, and shelter will be provided. As such, it appears to have at least two attractive features: Debtors (and those who depend on them for support) will be protected *and* creditors may eventually get paid in full. The tax system could provide the mechanism through which this arrangement would be financed and the costs spread. Would this system have advantages over the current system in that it would be more selective as to who is "protected"? But wouldn't there also be disadvantages to such a system? For example, isn't there (as with many insurance schemes) a "moral hazard" problem here? The debtor "buys" a policy by paying his taxes. He then has an incentive to incur large debts or undertake riskier activities, because he knows he can never fall below the threshold. His creditors, moreover, because they have a somewhat greater chance of being paid, may watch over the debtor less carefully.

Does this suggest that discharge may be a *more* effective system in some respects, particularly in increasing the creditors' incentives to prevent the debtor from misbehaving? Might the nonwaivabilty of discharge spur monitoring that will minimize, through greater limits on — higher costs of — credit, an individual's incentive to rationally underestimate, because of society's safety nets, the costs of current investments? Creditors may be better able to monitor an individual debtor than the government, and the existence of the right to discharge and the concomitant reduction in their expected recovery may give them the incentive to engage in such monitoring.

Such an explanation, however, only explains why we might want to have a right of discharge given the presence of other social insurance programs. Is there a need for any of these systems — at least a need to which discharge is a very satisfactory response? Does society have a reason to prohibit waivers of a right of discharge because individuals do not account for the costs of their waiver? But what kinds of costs might a fully rational individual not take into account in deciding whether to waive a right to discharge? First, there are the costs imposed on dependents — people the debtor supports — and perhaps more broadly on family and friends. Are there reasons to think that a debtor rationally underestimates the costs his behavior may impose on these people and that, accordingly, the nonwaivable nature of discharge is designed, in part at least, to protect such people? Second (and even more broadly), might discharge (and its nonwaivable feature) be designed to protect society at large? But a justification based on the costs an individual without a discharge right would impose on others also needs to explain why an individual would not take account of family and friends in making the decision about whether to waive the right (or, alternatively, not to bargain for the right). Further, it would need to explain why the gain to society from having this individual work was not directly commensurate with the wage he earned. For an examination of the circumstances under which an "externality" of this sort might exist, see Jackson, The Fresh Start Policy in Bankruptcy Law, 98 Harv. L. Rev. — (1985).

The discussion to this point has assumed that individuals are perfectly rational and fully capable of determining their own self-interest (or at least as capable as anyone else). But is this assumption correct? In the case of firms acting in the marketplace, it may well be. Firms that systematically act impulsively or underestimate risks in investments will (in theory at least) be weeded out and replaced by firms that are more careful calculators of risks. But what is true about firms in the marketplace may not necessarily be true about individuals, for two closely related reasons. First, individuals may act impulsively. Few of us have not succumbed to temptation that we later regret. The point is not that we value pleasures of the moment more intensely than more distant ones. Rather, it is that some of us might prefer to never be placed in a position that we must confront a temptation that we cannot resist, but which we will later regret. A simple case is of the compulsive gambler who instructs a casino not to extend him credit after he loses his initial stake. See J. Elster, Ulysses and the Sirens: Studies in Rationality and Irrationality (1979). The psychologists call this the problem of "impulse control." A summary of studies involving this problem is found in Crain, Deaton, Holcombe and Tollison, Rational Choice and the Taxation of Sin, 8 J. Public Econ. 239, 244 (1977), which describes an experiment with pigeons from Pachlin and Green, Commitment, Choice and Self-Control (mimeo, SUNY at Stony Brook):

> When offered a choice between small immediate reward and a large delayed reward, pigeons invariably chose the small immediate reward. However, if pigeons are offered the choice now to restrict their future choices so that they can only select the large delayed reward, they will do so. In other words, they will choose now to eliminate the small immediate reward from their future opportunity sets.

A bankruptcy discharge can be justified because it provides a means of controlling impulse. Everyone might be better off if they were foreclosed from giving up their right to a "fresh start." Although a small immediate reward is given up (the opportunity to borrow more or to borrow on more favorable terms), a larger later reward is preserved (the fresh start). Individuals, if given the choice *in advance*, might prefer to have their choices limited at some later time to protect themselves from impulsive decisions that are not ultimately in their self-interest.

Individuals must constantly make decisions in the face of uncertainty.

Right and wrong decisions will be made, but do individuals acting under conditions of uncertainty systematically underestimate the costs of their activities? Firms are disciplined by the marketplace, but are individuals? We have seen that some bankruptcy judges overestimate the likelihood of a rejuvenated firm's success and systematically underestimate the risks at stake. Do individuals share this characteristic? Consider the following excerpt from Tversky and Kahneman, Judgment Under Uncertainty: Heuristics and Biases, 185 Science 1124, 1129 (1974):

> Biases in the evaluation of compound events are particularly significant in the context of planning. The successful completion of an undertaking, such as the developments of a new product, typically has a conjunctive character: for the undertaking to succeed, each of a series of events must occur. Even when each of these events is very likely, the overall probability of success can be quite low if the number of events is large. The general tendency to overestimate the probability of conjunctive events leads to unwarranted optimism in the evaluation of the likelihood that a plan will succeed or that a project will be completed on time. Conversely, disjunctive structures are typically encountered in the evaluation of risks. A complex system, such as a nuclear reactor or a human body, will malfunction if any of its essential components fails. Even when the likelihood of failure in each component is slight, the probability of an overall failure can be high if many components are involved. Because of anchoring [use of the stated probability of the elementary event as the starting point for the estimation of the probabilities of multiple events], people will tend to underestimate the probabilities of failure in complex systems.

This phenomenon is not well understood by people in their decision making process. As Professors Tversky and Kahneman also observe, at 1130:

> What is perhaps surprising is the failure of people to infer from lifelong experience such fundamental statistical rules as regression toward the mean, or the effect of sample size on sampling variability. Although everyone is exposed, in the normal course of life, to numerous examples from which these rules could have been induced, very few people discover the principles of sampling and regression on their own. Statistical principles are not learned from everyday experience because the relevant instances are not coded appropriately.

A bankruptcy discharge may be justified on the grounds that it corrects for a systematic bias that individuals might have. We might systematically underestimate the chances of encountering financial reverses and hence our ability to repay loans, while we overestimate our chances of financial success (through, for example, promotions at work or rises in the housing market).

Both of these justifications for bankruptcy discharge (controlling our impulses and correcting for biases we generally have in estimating probabilities) may prove too much. There are many other activities (from hang-gliding to cigarette smoking) for which we do not use legal rules to curb biases and impulses, even though in the abstract it might seem a good idea. (People who hang glide or smoke cannot resist the opportunity it puts before them and people systematically underestimate the hazards of both activities.) If we do not interfere with freedom of action with respect to either of these activities, why do we do it with respect to obtaining credit? How does one ever draw the line between activities that should be regulated and those that shouldn't? How confident does one have to be that the regulation will bring more benefits than costs? (In the case of discharge, the cost may be in the form of increased costs and reduced availability of credit.) Even if one thinks that these justifications (or justifications based on the costs that insolvency imposes on others) are sound, how does one tailor a fresh start policy? For a general discussion of these issues, see Jackson, The Fresh Start Policy in Bankruptcy Law, 98 Harv. L. Rev. — (1985).

NOTE ON ACCOMMODATING A RIGHT OF DISCHARGE TO A CREDIT ECONOMY

The availability of discharge to a debtor is a cost as well as a benefit. Whatever the justifications for a nonwaivable right of discharge, the likelihood of its exercise will be reflected in the terms on which credit (at least consensual credit) is extended. Assuming that creditors adjust to the aggregate possibility of discharge, if the right of discharge were otherwise costless to a debtor, one would expect that such an adjustment by creditors would be quite large.

Discharge, however, is not "otherwise costless." In a Chapter 7 liquidation proceeding, a debtor must turn over all nonexempt assets as the "price" for obtaining a discharge. This limits the extent of the discharge, and may also cause a debtor to lose assets which the debtor values highly. Undoubtedly, a part of the phenomenal recent popularity of Chapter 13 plans is that (as we will see in a later chapter) Chapter 13, like Chapter 11 but unlike Chapter 7, does not impose any "asset-loss" costs on the debtor, although the extent of the discharge is measured by the value of those assets. The remaining economic cost of using discharge is reputational in origin: A person who uses bankruptcy and obtains a discharge may find, apart from the "protections" of §727(a)(8), that it is more difficult to obtain credit in the future, as he has given a signal to creditors that he will, in fact, use discharge. These costs limit the likelihood of a debtor using discharge. They also limit the "before the fact" adjustments that creditors would otherwise make in contemplation of potential discharge.

How substantial these limits are affects the magnitude of the creditors' adjustments. The Bankruptcy Code, in §525, in effect provides that governmental agencies and employers may not take into account the use of the bankruptcy process or any discharge obtained thereunder. While no comparable provision presently restricts other private parties, the proposed Bankruptcy Act of 1973 provided, in §4-508, that

> A person shall not be subjected to discriminatory treatment because he, or any person to whom he is or has been associated, is or has been a debtor or has failed to pay a debt discharged in a case under the Act.

If a provision such as this (assuming it could be effectively enforced) were coupled with an ability to obtain a discharge without giving up current assets, few legal or economic restrictions would exist to inhibit the incentives to obtain a discharge. While this world might look attractive to debtors who have already obtained credit, it may appear far less attractive from the "before the fact" position of those needing to obtain credit. The credit world may well adjust for the costs of a particular bankruptcy rule. In such a world, one would expect that the presence of such a discharge right would substantially affect the cost and existence of credit in the first instance.

From that perspective, debtors might be less happy with the nonwaivable nature of the "right" to a discharge. However they might feel on balance, the relevant point is that discharge policy should be analyzed in these terms. Freely available, nonwaivable, "costless" discharge rights are not costless at all, once adjustments to the legal rules are considered.

Student loans illustrate the predicted effects of freely available discharge rules. As a general matter, college and graduate students have few current assets but a large future income stream. A liquidation is relatively painless to them, in a lost-asset sense, while a discharge has a substantial benefit in "freeing up" that future income stream from the existing obligation of repaying a student loan. It should come as no surprise that a number of students, before the fall of 1977 (when the first restriction, the predecessor to existing §523(a)(8), became effective), enthusiastically discharged their student loans shortly after completing their education. Had the private market been providing funds, isn't it fair to suggest that student loans would have been substantially more expensive than many other loans, because of the increased risk of nonpayment represented by freely available discharge? If students had been provided with the opportunity to "opt out" of their discharge right with respect to such loans in return for a significantly lower cost of such loans, undoubtedly many would have sensibly elected such an option. The exemption from discharge in bankruptcy for certain student loans (§523(a)(8)) makes that election for students (and effectively lowers the extent of the government subsidies). It illustrates the type of response that may selectively be considered, even if one concluded that the right to a discharge should be, in general, nonwaivable.

But while there are certain benefits to restricting discharge, one must remember that the effects may not be entirely beneficial. One has to try to take account of the whole picture. Creditor practices have changed dramatically during the past several decades. Creditors from Visa to Macys rely more upon an individual's future earnings than their counterparts did several decades ago. The less creditors can rely on future earnings, the harder it will be for all individuals (including the vast majority who will never file bankruptcy petitions) to obtain credit. Credit may not be simply more expensive. Those without assets might find themselves unable to obtain loans or even credit cards. Moreover, the creditors who discover that they will not be paid will not always be large financial institutions with deep pockets. Those who become creditors involuntarily (because state law gives them claims against someone who ran over them with a car or sold them asbestos) will find themselves without recourse, even though the debtor might make enough in the future to pay some of the debt back.

Like any dramatic change in the legal order, however, the effects of abolishing or restricting greatly the right to discharge are not easy to predict. We have seen that there may in fact be plausible reasons why a right of discharge should exist. Although that does not tell us exactly what its contours would be, there are reasons to be cautious about restricting discharge's provisions unduly. It is difficult to know how many people who file petitions in bankruptcy would in fact repay money lent them if they were denied a discharge right. Under existing law, through a Chapter 13 plan, debtors can try to repay part of what they owe. Yet these court approved efforts to reschedule debts frequently end in failure, even though the debtors who succeed prevent creditors from taking any of their existing assets. Repayment schedules imposed involuntarily might be even less successful.

If an individual had a predictable and consistent record of past earnings and steady fortunes, he probably would not be in bankruptcy. Individuals in bankruptcy may have a hard time keeping their jobs even with a discharge. Moreover, keeping track of the hundreds of thousands who file petitions in bankruptcy, finding out how much they make and how much they should keep, and establishing some mechanism to account for changed circumstances are the ingredients of a procedural nightmare. Debtors, too, might simply stop working so hard, and enjoy more leisure, because the creditors cannot seize their leisure. Finally, the ability that debtors have shown over the years to rearrange their affairs so as to keep assets from creditors (either legitimately, such as by ensuring that wills are rewritten in favor of someone else, or illegitimately, such as by transferring assets to people or places where they cannot be found) compounds all these problems.

It is also useful to remember that none of this matters very much for those who present the least sympathetic cases for discharge. Someone with an income of $15,000 who has gambled and snorted $500,000 away is never going to be able to repay his creditors if the real rate of interest is above 3 percent. Docking his pay for years might lead him to lose his job, and it might turn him into a public charge. It might also lead him to gamble even more desperately, in a last ditch chance to get out from under these obligations. In all likelihood, however, it will not result in his creditors' being paid much of what they are owed.

The balance between ensuring that individuals can enjoy a fresh start and that they can obtain credit is a subtle and delicate one. Restriking it (perhaps by tying the ability of the debtor to exempt property even more closely to his willingness to repay past obligations out of future earnings) may be in order. But the trade offs of doing so are not necessarily clear and one sided. Limiting a debtor's right to future earnings may well not bring benefits worth its costs.

C. THE EFFECT OF DISCHARGE

1. *Effect on Liens*

In United States National Bank v. Chase National Bank, 331 U.S. 28, 33-34 (1947), the Supreme Court summarized:

> several avenues of action open to a secured creditor of a bankrupt. . . . (1) He may disregard the bankruptcy proceeding, decline to file a claim and rely solely upon his security if that security is properly and solely in his possession. . . . (2) He must file a secured claim, however, if the security is within the jurisdiction of the bankruptcy court and if he wishes to retain his secured status, inasmuch as that court has exclusive jurisdiction over the liquidation of the security. . . . (3) He may surrender or waive his security and prove his entire claim as an unsecured one. . . . (4) He may avail himself of his security and share in the general assets as to the unsecured balance.

The statement in this quotation respecting the second option open to the secured creditor is perhaps misleading. Proof of a secured claim under the old Bankruptcy Act related to the creditor's desire to share in the general assets to the extent of the unsecured balance over and above the value of the security. Under old Act §57e, if the creditor were fully secured, its claim would not even be allowed. See In re Jack Kardow Plumbing Co., 451 F.2d 123, 134 and n.43 (5th Cir. 1971).

Under the doctrine of Long v. Bullard, 117 U.S. 617 (1886), security interests and other liens survive discharge in bankruptcy. The reasoning of that opinion, however, was not in the abstract, but focused on the fact that the bankruptcy statute in existence at that time "release[d] the bankrupt only from debts which were or might have been proved," and secured debts could "only be proved for the balance remaining due after deducting the value of the security." The Bankruptcy Code has, of course, dropped the concept of "provable" debts, and secured creditors now participate in the bankruptcy process along with other creditors. The legislative history to §522 nonetheless states that "[t]he bankruptcy discharge will not prevent enforcement of valid liens. The rule of Long v. Bullard . . . is accepted with respect to the enforcement of valid liens on nonexempt property as well as on exempt property."

If a creditor has a security interest on exempt property that is not avoided pursuant to §522, or if a creditor with a security interest in other property is not paid in bankruptcy (see In re Honaker, 4 Bankr. 415 (Bankr. E.D. Mich. 1980), may that creditor continue to assert the security interest after the debtor's discharge? While the legislative history just quoted suggests yes, what does one do with §524(a)(2)? That section as originally enacted stated that a discharge

> operates as an injunction against the commencement or continuation of an action, the employment of process, or any act, to collect, recover or offset any such debt as a personal liability of the debtor, or from property of the debtor, whether or not discharge of such debt is waived.

In 1984, §524(a)(2) was amended and the phrase "or property of the debtor" was deleted. Before the amendment, Judge Pusateri held that §524(a)(2) had the effect of overruling Long v. Bullard in In re Ray, 26 Bankr. 534, 541 (Bankr. D. Kan. 1983). Virtually all bankruptcy judges disagreed with Judge Pusateri even before the 1984 Amendments. See, e.g., In re Weathers, 15 Bankr. 945 (Bankr. D. Kan. 1981).

The next case addresses the question of exactly what sorts of obligations are discharged in bankruptcy, by addressing the question of what is a "claim." §101(4).

OHIO v. KOVACS
105 S. Ct. 705 (1985)

Justice WHITE delivered the opinion of the Court.

Petitioner State of Ohio obtained an injunction ordering respondent William Kovacs to clean up a hazardous waste site. A receiver was subsequently appointed. Still later, Kovacs filed a petition for bankruptcy. The question before us is whether, in the circumstances present here, Kovacs' obligation under the injunction is a "debt" or "liability on a claim" subject to discharge under the Bankruptcy Code. . . .

Kovacs was the chief executive officer and stockholder of Chem-Dyne Corp., which with other business entities operated an industrial and hazardous waste disposal site in Hamilton, Ohio. In 1976, the State sued Kovacs and the business entities in state court for polluting public waters, maintaining a nuisance, and causing fish kills, all in violation of state environmental laws. In 1979, both in his individual capacity and on behalf of Chem-Dyne, Kovacs signed a stipulation and judgment entry settling the lawsuit. Among other things, the stipulation enjoined the defendants from causing further pollution of the air or public waters, forbade bringing additional industrial wastes onto the site, required the defendants to remove specified wastes from the property, and ordered the payment of $75,000 to compensate the State for injury to wildlife.

Kovacs and the other defendants failed to comply with their obligations under the injunction. The State then obtained the appointment in state court of a receiver, who was directed to take possession of all property and other assets of Kovacs and the corporate defendants and to implement the judgment entry by cleaning up the Chem-Dyne site. The receiver took possession of the site but had not completed his tasks when Kovacs filed a personal bankruptcy petition.[1]

Seeking to develop a basis for requiring part of Kovacs' post-bankruptcy income to be applied to the unfinished task of the receivership, the State then filed a motion in state court to discover Kovacs' current income and assets. Kovacs requested that the Bankruptcy Court stay those proceedings, which it did. The State also filed a complaint in the Bankruptcy Court seeking a declaration that Kovacs' obligation under the stipulation and judgment order to clean up the Chem-Dyne site was not dischargeable in bankruptcy because it was not a "debt," a liability on a "claim," within the meaning of the Bankruptcy Code. In addition, the complaint sought an injunction against the bankruptcy trustee to restrain him from pursuing any action to recover assets of Kovacs in the hands of the receiver. The Bankruptcy Court ruled against Ohio, In re Kovacs, 29 B.R. 816 (S.D. Ohio 1982), as did the District Court. The Court of Appeals for the sixth circuit affirmed, holding that Ohio essentially sought from Kovacs only a monetary payment and that such a required payment was a liability on a claim that was dischargeable under the bankruptcy statute. In re Kovacs, 717 F.2d 984 (1983). We granted certiorari to determine the dischargeability of Kovacs' obligation under the affirmative injunction entered against him. 465 U.S. (1983). . . .

Except for the nine kinds of debts saved from discharge by 11 U.S.C. §523(a), a discharge in bankruptcy discharges the debtor from all debts that arose before bankruptcy. §727(b). It is not claimed here that Kovacs' obligation under the injunction fell within any of the categories of debts excepted from discharge by §523. Rather, the State submits that the obligation to clean up the Chem-Dyne site is not a debt at all within the meaning of the bankruptcy law.

. . . The provision at issue here is §101(4)(B). For the purposes of that section, there is little doubt that the State had the right to an equitable remedy under state law and that the right has been reduced to judgment in the form of an injunction ordering the cleanup. The State argues, how-

---

1. Kovacs originally filed a reorganization petition under Chapter 11 of the Bankruptcy Code, 11 U.S.C. §1101 et seq., but converted the petition to a liquidation bankruptcy under Chapter 7. See 11 U.S.C. §1112.

ever, that the injunction it has secured is not a claim against Kovacs for bankruptcy purposes because (1) Kovacs' default was a breach of the statute, not a breach of an ordinary commercial contract which concededly would give rise to a claim; and (2) Kovacs' breach of his obligation under the injunction did not give rise to a right to payment within the meaning of §101(4)(B). We are not persuaded by either submission.

There is no indication in the language of the statute that the right to performance cannot be a claim unless it arises from a contractual arrangement. The State resorted to the courts to enforce its environmental laws against Kovacs and secured a negative order to cease polluting, an affirmative order to clean up the site, and an order to pay a sum of money to recompense the State for damage done to the fish population. Each order was one to remedy an alleged breach of Ohio law; and if Kovacs' obligation to pay $75,000 to the State is a debt dischargeable in bankruptcy, which the State freely concedes, it makes little sense to assert that because the cleanup order was entered to remedy a statutory violation, it cannot likewise constitute a claim for bankruptcy purposes. Furthermore, it is apparent that Congress desired a broad definition of a "claim"[3] and knew how to limit the application of a provision to contracts when it desired to do so.[4] Other provisions cited by Ohio refute, rather than support, its strained interpretation.[5]

The courts below also found little substance in the submission that the cleanup obligation did not give rise to a right to payment that renders the order dischargeable under §727. The definition of "claim" in H.R. 8200 as originally drafted would have deemed a right to an equitable remedy for breach of performance a claim even if it did not give rise to a right to payment.[6] The initial Senate definition of claim was narrower,[7] and a compromise version, §101(4), was finally adopted. In that version, the key phrases "equitable remedy," "breach of performance," and "right to payment" are not defined. See 11 U.S.C. §101. Nor are the differences between the successive versions explained. The legislative history offers only a statement by the sponsors of the Bankruptcy Reform Act with respect to the scope of the provision:

Section 101(4)(B) . . . is intended to cause the liquidation or estimation of contingent rights of payment for which there may be an alternative equitable remedy with the result that the equitable remedy will be susceptible to being

3. H.R. Rep. No. 95-595, p. 309 (1977); S. Rep. No. 95-989, p. 21 (1978). . . .

4. See 11 U.S.C. §365 (assumption or rejection of executory contracts and leases).

5. Congress created exemptions from discharge for claims involving penalties and forfeitures owed to a governmental unit, 11 U.S.C. §523(a)(7), and for claims involving embezzlement and larceny. §523(a)(4). If a bankruptcy debtor has committed larceny or embezzlement, giving rise to a remedy of either damages or equitable restitution under state law, the resulting liability for breach of an obligation created by law is clearly a claim which is nondischargeable in bankruptcy.

6. H.R. 8200, 95th Cong., 1st Sess., 309-310 (House Committee print 1977), as reported September 8, 1977.

7. See S. 2266, 95th Cong., 1st Sess., 299 (1977), as introduced October 31, 1977.

discharged in bankruptcy. For example, in some States, a judgment for specific performance may be satisfied by an alternative right to payment in the event performance is refused; in that event, the creditor entitled to specific performance would have a "claim" for purposes of a proceeding under title 11.[8]

We think the rulings of the courts below were wholly consistent with the statute and its legislative history, sparse as it is. The Bankruptcy Court ruled as follows, In re Kovacs, 29 B.R., at 816:

> There is no suggestion by plaintiff that defendant can render performance under the affirmative obligation other than by the payment of money. We therefore conclude that plaintiff has a claim against defendant within the meaning of 11 U.S.C. §101(4), and that defendant owes plaintiff a debt within the meaning of 11 U.S.C. §101(11). Furthermore, we have concluded that that debt is dischargeable.[9]

The District Court affirmed, primarily because it was bound by and saw no error in the Court of Appeals' prior opinion holding that the State was seeking no more than a money judgment as an alternative to requiring Kovacs personally to perform the obligations imposed by the injunction. To hold otherwise, the District Court explained, "would subvert Congress' clear intention to give debtors a fresh start." . . . The Court of Appeals also affirmed, rejecting the State's insistence that it had no right to, and was not attempting to enforce, an alternative right to payment:

> Ohio does not suggest that Kovacs is capable of personally cleaning up the environmental damage he may have caused. Ohio claims there is no

----

8. 124 Cong. Rec. 32393 (1978) (remarks of Rep. Edwards); see also id., at 33992 (remarks of Sen. DeConcini).

9. More fully stated, the Bankruptcy Court's observations were:

> What is at stake in the present motion is whether defendant's bankruptcy will discharge the affirmative obligation imposed upon him by the Judgment Entry, that he remove and dispose of all industrial and/or other wastes at the subject premises. If plaintiff is successful here, it would be able to levy on defendant's wages, the action prevented by our Prior Decision, after defendant's bankruptcy case is closed and/or the stay of 11 U.S.C. §362 as interpreted by our Prior Decision is no longer in force. The parties have crystallized the issue here in simple fashion, plaintiff stoutly insisting that the just identified affirmative obligation is not a monetary obligation, while defendant says that it is. The problem arises, of course, because it is not stated as a monetary obligation. Essentially for this reason plaintiff argues that it is not a monetary obligation. Yet plaintiff in discussing the background for the Judgment Entry says that it expected that defendant would generate sufficient funds in his ongoing business to pay for the clean-up. Moreover, we take judicial notice that plaintiff sought discovery with respect to defendant's earnings, the matter dealt with in our Prior Decision, for the purpose of levying upon his wages, a technique which has no application other than in the enforcement of a money judgment. There is no suggestion by plaintiff that defendant can render performance under the affirmative obligation other than by the payment of money. We therefore conclude that plaintiff has a claim against defendant within the meaning of 11 U.S.C. §101(4), and that defendant owes plaintiff a debt within the meaning of 11 U.S.C. §101(11). Furthermore, we have concluded that that debt is dischargeable. 29 B.R., at 818.

alternative right to payment, but when Kovacs failed to perform, state law gave a state receiver total control over all Kovacs' assets. Ohio later used state law to try and discover Kovacs' post-petition income and employment status in an apparent attempt to levy on his future earnings. In reality, the only type of performance in which Ohio is now interested is a money payment to effectuate the Chem-Dyne cleanup. . . .

The impact of its attempt to realize upon Kovacs' income or property cannot be concealed by legerdemain or linguistic gymnastics. Kovacs cannot personally clean up the waste he wrongfully released into Ohio waters. He cannot perform the affirmative obligations properly imposed upon him by the State court except by paying money or transferring over his own financial resources. The State of Ohio has acknowledged this by its steadfast pursuit of payment as an alternative to personal performance. 717 F.2d, at 987-988.

As we understand it, the Court of Appeals held that, in the circumstances, the cleanup duty had been reduced to a monetary obligation.

We do not disturb this judgment. The injunction surely obliged Kovacs to clean up the site. But when he failed to do so, rather than prosecute Kovacs under the environmental laws or bring civil or criminal contempt proceedings, the State secured the appointment of a receiver, who was ordered to take possession of all of Kovacs' nonexempt assets as well as the assets of the corporate defendants and to comply with the injunction entered against Kovacs. As wise as this course may have been, it dispossessed Kovacs, removed his authority over the site, and divested him of assets that might have been used by him to clean up the property. Furthermore, when the bankruptcy trustee sought to recover Kovacs' assets from the receiver, the latter sought an injunction against such action. Although Kovacs had been ordered to "cooperate" with the receiver, he was disabled by the receivership from personally taking charge of and carrying out the removal of wastes from the property. What the receiver wanted for Kovacs after bankruptcy was the money to defray cleanup costs. At oral argument in this Court, the State's counsel conceded that after the receiver was appointed, the only performance sought from Kovacs was the payment of money. . . . Had Kovacs furnished the necessary funds, either before or after bankruptcy, there seems little doubt that the receiver and the State would have been satisfied. On the facts before it, and with the receiver in control of the site, we cannot fault the Court of Appeals for concluding that the cleanup order had been converted into an obligation to pay money, an obligation that was dischargeable in bankruptcy.[11] . . .

It is well to emphasize what we have not decided. First, we do not

11. The State relies on Penn Terra, Ltd. v. Department of Environmental Resources, 733 F.2d 267 (C.A.3 1984). There, the Court of Appeals for the Third Circuit held that the automatic stay provision of 11 U.S.C. §362 did not apply to the State's seeking an injunction against a bankrupt to require compliance with the environmental laws. This was held to be an effort to enforce the police power statutes of the State, not a suit to enforce a money

suggest that Kovacs' discharge will shield him from prosecution for having violated the environmental laws of Ohio or for criminal contempt for not performing his obligations under the injunction prior to bankruptcy. Second, had a fine or monetary penalty for violation of state law been imposed on Kovacs prior to bankruptcy, §523(a)(7) forecloses any suggestion that his obligation to pay the fine or penalty would be discharged in bankruptcy. Third, we do not address what the legal consequences would have been had Kovacs taken bankruptcy before a receiver had been appointed and a trustee had been designated with the usual duties of a bankruptcy trustee.[12] Fourth, we do not hold that the injunction against bringing further toxic wastes on the premises or against any conduct that will contribute to the pollution of the site or the State's waters is dischargeable in bankruptcy; we here address, as did the Court of Appeals, only the affirmative duty to clean up the site and the duty to pay money to that end. Finally, we do not question that anyone in possession of the site — whether it is Kovacs or another in the event the receivership is liquidated and the trustee abandons the property, or a vendee from the receiver or the bankruptcy trustee — must comply with the environmental laws of the State of Ohio. Plainly, that person or firm may not maintain a nuisance, pollute the waters of the State, or refuse to remove the source of such conditions. As the case comes to us, however, Kovacs has been dispossessed and the State seeks to enforce his cleanup obligation by a money judgment.

The judgment of the Court of Appeals is affirmed.

Justice O'CONNOR, concurring.

I join the Court's opinion and agree with its holding that the cleanup

---

judgment. But in that case, there had been no appointment of a receiver who had the duty to comply with the state law and who was seeking money from the bankrupt. The automatic stay provision does not apply to suits to enforce the regulatory statutes of the State, but the enforcement of such a judgment by seeking money from the bankrupt — what the Court of Appeals for the Sixth Circuit concluded was involved in this case — is another matter.

12. The commencement of a case under the Bankruptcy Act creates an estate which, with limited exceptions, consists of all of the debtor's property wherever located. 11 U.S.C. §541. The trustee, who is to be appointed promptly in Chapter 7 cases, is charged with the duty of collecting and reducing the property of the estate and is to be accountable for all of such property. 11 U.S.C. §704. A custodian of the debtor's property appointed before commencement of the case is required to deliver the debtor's property in his custody to the trustee, unless the bankruptcy court concludes that the interest of creditors would be better served by permitting the custodian to continue in possession and control of the property. 11 U.S.C. §543. After notice and hearing, the trustee may abandon any property of the estate that is burdensome to the estate or that is of inconsequential value to the estate. 11 U.S.C. §554. Such abandonment is to the person having the possessory interest in the property. S. Rep. No. 95-989, p. 92 (1978). Property that is scheduled but not administered is deemed abandoned. 11 U.S.C. §554(c). Had no receiver been appointed prior to Kovacs' bankruptcy, the trustee would have been charged with the duty of collecting Kovacs' nonexempt property and administering it. If the site at issue were Kovacs' property, the trustee would shortly determine whether it was of value to the estate. If the property was worth more than the costs of bringing it into compliance with state law, the trustee would undoubtedly sell it for its net value, and the buyer would clean up the property, in which event whatever obligation Kovacs might have had to clean up the property would have been satisfied. If the property were worth less than the cost of cleanup, the trustee would likely abandon it to its prior owner, who would have to comply with the state environmental law to the extent of his or its ability.

order has been reduced to a monetary obligation dischargeable as a "claim" under §727 of the Bankruptcy Code. I write separately to address the petitioner's concern that the Court's action will impede States in enforcing their environmental laws.

To say that Kovacs' obligation in these circumstances is a claim dischargeable in bankruptcy does not wholly excuse the obligation or leave the State without any recourse against Kovacs' assets to enforce the order. Because "Congress has generally left the determination of property rights in the assets of a bankrupt's estate to state law," Butner v. United States, 440 U.S. 48, 54 (1979), the classification of Ohio's interests as either a lien on the property itself, a perfected security interest, or merely an unsecured claim depends on Ohio law. That classification — a question not before us — generally determines the priority of the State's claim to the assets of the estate relative to other creditors. Cf. 11 U.S.C. §545 (trustee may avoid statutory liens only in specified circumstances). Thus, a State may protect its interest in the enforcement of its environmental laws by giving cleanup judgments the status of statutory liens or secured claims.

The Court's holding that the cleanup order was a "claim" within the meaning of §101(4) also avoids potentially adverse consequences for a State's enforcement of its order when the debtor is a corporation, rather than an individual. In a Chapter 7 proceeding under the Bankruptcy Code, a corporate debtor transfers its property to a trustee for distribution among the creditors who hold cognizable claims, and then generally dissolves under state law. Because the corporation usually ceases to exist, it has no postbankruptcy earnings that could be utilized by the State to fulfill the cleanup order. The State's only recourse in such a situation may well be its "claim" to the prebankruptcy assets.

For both these reasons, the Court's holding today cannot be viewed as hostile to state enforcement of environmental laws.

NOTE ON *KOVACS* AND TOXIC WASTES IN BANKRUPTCY

A number of businesses that have dumped toxic wastes and violated state and federal antipollution statutes have filed bankruptcy petitions. We saw several examples in Chapter 7 of this book, such as Penn Terra and Quanta Resources. *Kovacs,* however, is unusual because the debtor is an individual, rather than a corporation. *Kovacs* presents two distinct questions, the first of which applies to every debtor in bankruptcy that has dumped toxic wastes and the second of which applies only to individuals such as Kovacs. The first question focuses on the rights the state or federal government have against a debtor's assets to enforce environmental cleanup orders. The second question asks whether an individual's right to a discharge of prebankruptcy obligations includes a right to be free of a duty to clean up toxic wastes.

The question in the *Kovacs* case was not whether Kovacs — or Chem-Dyne — must comply with the environmental laws of Ohio with respect to future operations. They, like anyone else in Ohio, must comply with those environmental laws as long as they stay in business. Debtors in bankruptcy have no license to pollute in violation of state and federal laws. At issue in *Kovacs* was the obligation of Kovacs and Chem-Dyne to pay for the clean-up of *prebankruptcy* violations of Ohio's environmental laws. Because the obligation arises out of Kovacs's past, Ohio is entitled to use Kovacs's existing assets to satisfy that obligation and, accordingly, it bears the attributes that make it a "claim" for purposes of bankruptcy. The more difficult question, and one that will arise in cases involving both individuals and corporations, is the nature of the rights associated with enforcing that obligation against the debtor's assets relative to the rights of other claimants.

How would the case have come out if no receiver had been appointed? Is Justice O'Connor correct to emphasize the need to bear in mind both the case of the individual and the corporate debtor? Is she also correct to address the question of the priority of the government's rights against a debtor's assets? Consider the following analysis in light of both opinions.

The simple case of a corporate debtor illustrates the point. Before we even look at bankruptcy law, we should understand the state-law consequences of having an obligation owed by a corporation. Assume that Debtor, a corporation, owns land on which it has dumped toxic wastes in violation of state law. In addition to the land, which is worthless, Debtor has $500,000 in assets. At the request of State, a court has previously enjoined Debtor from dumping any more wastes on its land and has required it to file regular reports on the toxic materials it handles each month. The court has also ordered Debtor to clean up the wastes already there. The clean-up will cost $400,000. Debtor also owes $600,000 to a number of general creditors.

The obligation Debtor owes to State to clean up toxic wastes is "dischargeable," not because of anything bankruptcy law says or does — and, indeed, independently of whether the corporation ever resorts to bankruptcy. Liquidating corporations do not even receive a discharge in bankruptcy. But corporations always have the privilege of dissolving under state law. State law permits individuals to create corporations with limited liability. When the obligations of a corporation exceed its ability to meet them, some of those obligations obviously will not be met. Once the assets of a corporation are exhausted and the corporation is dissolved, those with otherwise enforceable obligations will have no place they can turn unless they have the right to pursue those assets into the hands of the buyers. That includes State with its judgment requiring Debtor to clean up toxic wastes.

To counter Kovacs's argument that his obligation was a "claim" that is discharged in bankruptcy, Ohio argued that Kovacs's obligation was not a "claim" within the meaning of the Bankruptcy Code at all and hence could not be extinguished. The definition of "claim" in the Bankruptcy Code, however, does not depend on whether the debtor is an individual or a corporation. If Kovacs's obligation to clean up wastes was not a claim for purposes of bankruptcy, neither is Debtor's. But if that is so, then State will not share in Debtor's assets when they are distributed in bankruptcy. In a Chapter 7 liquidation proceeding, after the assets are sold, the proceeds are distributed first to recognized property claimants and then as specified in §726. Section 726, however, speaks only of payments on "claims." If Kovacs's obligation to Ohio were not a claim, then only the general creditors who are owed $600,000 will share in the proceeds. They will receive the entire $500,000 fetched by the sale of Debtor's assets on account of those claims and State will receive nothing in bankruptcy.

To be sure, liquidating corporations do not receive a discharge in bankruptcy, but that will not help State. After this bankruptcy distribution, Debtor has no remaining assets. The obligation of Debtor to clean up the toxic wastes will continue only until Debtor dissolves under state law. When Debtor dissolves under state law, State will have nothing. Debtor's assets will all have been sold and the proceeds paid out to holders of claims. Bankruptcy discharge is never even involved. Had Debtor dissolved under state law without resorting to bankruptcy, State surely would have received some of Debtor's assets on account of Debtor's obligation to clean-up the toxic waste site. Should bankruptcy law be interpreted to upset such state entitlements?

Of course one can argue, as Ohio did, that an obligation to clean up toxic wastes is neither "a right to payment" nor "an equitable remedy for breach of performance," breach of which gives rise to a right to payment. But isn't there a distinction that the drafters of the Bankruptcy Code were trying to capture (albeit somewhat awkwardly) in their definition of "claim"? Wasn't the purpose of excluding some equitable relief from the definition of "claim" to distinguish two kinds of obligations: those obligations of a debtor that arise before the filing of the petition and that exist even if the debtor goes out of business or dies the moment the bankruptcy petition is filed, and those that arise because of the debtor's continued existence and that would disappear if the debtor were to cease operations or die?

An order to clean up toxic wastes already deposited is a "claim" because the equitable remedy arises out of a pre-petition obligation and does not depend upon Debtor's continued existence. By contrast, an injunction to cease polluting is not a claim within the meaning of the Bankruptcy Code because it is directed at Debtor's future operations. An order that Debtor provide regular reports on its operations every month would not be a claim in bankruptcy either. Even though the order exists only because of past conduct, and can be converted into money (one can calculate the costs of compliance), it is not a "claim" because it is tied to Debtor's future operations.

Having gotten this far, however, doesn't Justice O'Connor's opinion suggest that this is really only a partial examination of the issue in *Kovacs*? What is the *status* of the obligation Debtor owes State to clean up the toxic waste site? Doesn't that depend in the first instance on how nonbankruptcy law would treat the right of State to use Debtor's assets to enforce that obligation compared with the rights of other claimants to use those assets to enforce obligations owed them? Holders of claims do not always share equally under nonbankruptcy law, and bankruptcy law, which is largely procedural, generally respects, as we have seen, the different attributes of state-law claims.

For example, if a "claim" is secured or the subject of a statutory lien or a statutory trust, that claim is entitled to be paid first out of the associated assets. Equally, if such a claim is not paid in bankruptcy, the "lien" given by statute or the secured contract will, as we saw earlier in this chapter, "pass through" bankruptcy and be enforceable against the debtor's pre-bankruptcy property, notwithstanding that the underlying debt itself was discharged.

Isn't the key issue in a case such as *Kovacs,* then, the priority of the government's claim against a debtor's property? A priority claim can result not only from consensual security interests, statutory liens, or statutory trusts — all cases that are, or should be, uncontroversial — but also from simply observing the entitlements of a particular claimant under state law to the asset against others. The priority right of a particular claimant, in other words, may be inherent in the restrictions placed by the state on the use of property in the first instance. Recall *Chicago Board of Trade,* supra page 192, and *Anchorage International Inn,* supra page 209.

If the obligation Kovacs owes to Ohio is tantamount to a restriction on the value of the property to its owner or to entities that assert claims through that owner, Ohio would be entitled to be paid from the property before Kovacs's other creditors receive anything. And if the property were not used first to satisfy the obligation to Ohio, wouldn't it also follow from the analysis of *Chicago Board of Trade* that the "lien" of Ohio would pass through bankruptcy under the doctrine of Long v. Bullard notwithstanding that the debt was discharged?

Does anything in this discussion change when the debtor is an individual? Individuals, like corporations, have a discharge right. While corporations get their discharge right under state law, individuals enjoy this right because of bankruptcy law's "fresh start" policy. A corporation gives up all its assets in dissolving, whereas bankruptcy's discharge for individuals generally permits them to keep an important asset: future earnings. Because individuals keep an asset, it is also possible to talk about nondischargeable debts. And, unlike corporations, individuals are not freed of all pre-petition debts as a result of that discharge. Some obligations, such as tax obligations, federally backed student loans, and alimony payments, as we will soon see, are specifically excepted from discharge. What distinguishes the scope of obligations against individuals, then, is *not* the question of whether something is a claim (which determines whether the obligee can pursue the debtor's existing property) but, rather, whether the claim fits in §523 (which determines whether the obligee can also pursue the debtor's future assets). If a claim does not fall into any of the exemptions from discharge, it does not ultimately matter whether the debtor is an individual or a corporation.

As Justice O'Connor notes, if Ohio wanted to give greater recognition to its environmental laws, it could give (and may already have given) clean-up judgments the status of statutory liens. If Kovacs did not have enough assets to pay for that clean-up in full, the obligation to Ohio would then be discharged, just as it would if the obligation were owed by a corporation. Because the obligation was owed by an individual, Ohio has a second chance — to have the obligation declared nondischargeable. But whether Kovacs's obligation was dischargeable under existing law should have been a narrow question of whether that obligation falls within one of the exceptions in §523.

Does §523 apply to *Kovacs*? Is a change in §523 necessary to reach the result desired by Ohio in this case? Kovacs's dumping of hazardous wastes may have been in deliberate and flagrant disregard of state and federal law, at least with respect to wastes deposited after the state court injunction. Did Kovacs's actions amount to "willful and malicious injury by the debtor to another entity or to the property of another entity"? The court has left that question open. Isn't it fair to say that this issue, not whether Ohio has a "claim," should have been the focus of the bankruptcy litigation? See Baird and Jackson, *Kovacs* and Toxic Wastes in Bankruptcy, 36 Stan. L. Rev. 1199 (1984).

2. Operative Consequences of Discharge

Once a discharge has been granted, how far does it reach? The issue of *creditor* conduct is addressed in §524(a). Commencing with Perez v. Campbell, 402 U.S. 637 (1971), however, the issue was cast broader: To what extent could a debtor's "fresh start" be impeded by people or entities — not just creditors with discharged claims — categorizing debtors because they had used bankruptcy or because they had not paid back, in full, debts that were discharged in bankruptcy? Section 525 codifies a part of this development; the contours of that section — and of §524(a) — are explored in the following materials.

PROBLEM

10.1 Creditor has a claim against Debtor for $5,000. Debtor files for bankruptcy in a "no asset" case and receives a discharge. Following that discharge, Debtor sues Creditor based on a pre-bankruptcy event. May

Creditor use the $5,000 claim as a set-off to any recovery Debtor might obtain? See §§524(a)(2), 553; compare In re Ford, 35 Bankr. 277 (Bankr. N.D. Ga. 1983); In re Slaw Construction Corp., 17 Bankr. 744 (Bankr. E.D. Penn. 1982) with In re Johnson, 13 Bankr. 185 (Bankr. M.D. Tenn. 1981).

HENRY v. HEYISON
4 Bankr. 437 (E.D. Pa. 1980)

NEWCOMER, District Judge.

This action was instituted by plaintiff, on behalf of herself and all others similarly situated, to challenge certain provisions of Pennsylvania's Financial Responsibility Law, 75 Pa. C.S.A. §1701 et seq. (hereinafter the "Act") as they are applied to persons who have had tort judgments discharged in bankruptcy. The issue before this Court is whether certain provisions of the Act are unconstitutional because they conflict with the purposes of the Bankruptcy Code 11 U.S.C. §525 and therefore run afoul of the Supremacy Clause of the United States Constitution. . . . Specifically, does the Act by its provisions, subvert the Bankruptcy Code's policy of giving a debtor a "fresh start" after the debtor has had a motor vehicle tort judgment discharged in bankruptcy. . . .

FACTUAL BACKGROUND

As a result of an automobile accident in 1969, a default judgment was entered in the Court of Common Pleas of Philadelphia County against the named plaintiff, Mrs. Ellen Henry, and her husband. The default judgment, entered on March 11, 1971, was never satisfied. Pursuant to the financial responsibility provision of "The Vehicle Code" of 1959, Act of April 29, 1959 (P.L. 58, No. 32), plaintiff Henry's operating privileges were suspended because she failed to satisfy the judgment.

On August 18, 1975 Mrs. Henry's judgment was discharged in a bankruptcy proceeding. Despite the discharge, defendants refused to restore plaintiff's operating privileges until she provided proof of financial responsibility in the form of special "nonowners" insurance.[3] Proof of financial responsibility was not required of other license applicants. Plaintiff never furnished such proof to the State and, as a result, was never permitted to drive. Plaintiff indicates in her belief [sic], that she has been handicapped in finding work because of her inability to drive. She alleges that because of the State's financial responsibility requirement she has been denied the "fresh start" which she believes bankruptcy should have given her.

3. Proof of financial responsibility is required under 75 Pa. C.S.A. §1747.

DISCUSSION

Plaintiffs contend that defendants' financial responsibility requirement impinges on the policies of the Bankruptcy Code, and is therefore invalid under the Supremacy Clause.[4] The landmark case in this area is Perez v. Campbell, 402 U.S. 637, 91 S. Ct. 1704, 29 L. Ed. 2d 233 (1971) in which the Supreme Court considered a challenge to the Arizona Financial Responsibility Act. The issue before the Court was "whether Ariz. Rev. Stat. Ann. §28-1163(B) (1956), . . . [was] invalid under [the Supremacy Clause] as being in conflict with the mandate of §17 of the Bankruptcy Act, 11 U.S.C. §35, providing that receipt of a discharge in bankruptcy fully discharges all but certain specified judgments." 402 U.S. at 638, 91 S. Ct. at 1705. The Court noted that under the Arizona Act a judgment debtor in an automobile accident who failed to satisfy such judgment within 60 days after entry could not regain his license unless he overcame two hurdles. He was required both to satisfy the amount of the debt and to supply the state with proof of financial responsibility. The statute specifically provided that a driver's license and registration "shall remain suspended and shall not be renewed, nor shall any license or registration be thereafter issued in the name of the person . . . until the person gives proof of financial responsibility. . . ." Ariz. Rev. Stat. Ann. §28-1163(A). Under the statute, "a discharge in bankruptcy following the rendering of any such judgment, [as a result of an automobile accident did not] relieve the judgment debtor from any of the requirements of [the Act]." Ariz. Rev. Stat. Ann. §28-1163(B).

The Court in Perez indicated that "[w]hat is at issue here is the power of a state to include as part of this comprehensive enactment designed to secure compensation for automobile accident victims a section providing that a discharge in bankruptcy of the automobile accident tort judgment shall have no effect on the judgment debtor's obligation to repay the judgment creditor, at least insofar as such repayment may be enforced by the withholding of driving privileges by the State." 402 U.S. at 643, 91 S. Ct. at 1708. Thus the constitutional question faced by the Court was whether a state statute that protects judgment creditors from financially irresponsible persons "is in conflict with a federal statute that gives discharged debtors a new start 'unhampered by the pressure and discouragement of pre-existing debt'." 402 U.S. at 649, 91 S. Ct. at 1711. The Court

---

4. The parties have stipulated to the following facts regarding the overall operation of the financial responsibility requirement:

1. In the period of one year preceding the date of this stipulation, twelve thousand (12,000) licensed drivers in Pennsylvania have had an unsatisfied motor vehicle tort judgment against them and as a result have had their driver's license suspended.

2. In a period of one year preceding the date of this stipulation, of those persons whose licenses have been so suspended, three hundred (300) have reported to defendants that their motor vehicle tort judgments were discharged in a bankruptcy proceeding. Approximately one hundred fifty (150) of these persons do not own motor vehicles.

declared the Arizona Act constitutionally invalid, and in so holding recognized the primary importance of the fresh start doctrine. "One of the primary purposes of the Bankruptcy Act is to give debtors a new opportunity in life and a clear field for future effort, unhampered by the pressure and discouragement of preexisting debt". 402 U.S. at 648, 91 S. Ct. at 1710 citing Local Loan Co. v. Hunt, 292 U.S. 234, 244, 54 S. Ct. 695, 699, 78 L. Ed. 1230 (1934).

Although the requirements of the Pennsylvania law are less burdensome than those in the Arizona law, this Court finds the Supreme Court's emphasis on the fresh start doctrine equally applicable. The Pennsylvania law does not require an individual with a debt discharged in bankruptcy to repay the debt itself; instead a driver must only purchase the financial responsibility insurance. Under the Arizona law, a driver had to both repay the debt and provide proof of financial responsibility. Thus, the Court, in *Perez*, did not specifically address the issue of whether a state could require a bankrupt to insure himself against future motor vehicle tort indebtedness. It is, however, difficult to imagine a fresh start for a bankrupt individual, if the individual remains saddled with the incidents of prior debts. The Court specifically indicated that one of the primary purposes of the Bankruptcy Act was "to give debtors a clear field for future effort, unhampered by the pressure and discouragement of preexisting debt." 402 U.S. 648, 91 S. Ct. 1710 [citations omitted.] Similarly, in the present case, members of plaintiff's class are denied a fresh start. They are required to purchase financial responsibility insurance following bankruptcy proceedings solely because of a debt incurred prior to such proceedings.

Since the *Perez* decision several cases have discussed the fresh start concept in the context of challenges to state statutes. . . .

The . . . cases demonstrate that courts have defined the fresh start concept to include matters incidental to the discharge of debts. The contractors license, the job security of a police officer, and the obtaining of a transcript are all matters incidental to the debt discharged. In the present case, the debtor is faced with an analogous situation. If the debtor chooses to declare bankruptcy, he or she may lose an important benefit — that of the ability to drive. Thus, instead of a fresh start, debtors who wish to drive are burdened by the consequences of prior discharged debts and are forced to purchase financial responsibility insurance.

In the instant case, the specific sections of the Pennsylvania Financial Responsibility law at issue are Sections 1743 and 1747.

Section 1743 of the new "Vehicle Code" of 1976 provides, in pertinent part, that:

> A person's operating privilege . . . shall remain suspended and shall not be renewed . . . until every such judgment is stayed, satisfied in full or to the extent provided in this subchapter, *and until the person furnishes proof of financial responsibility as required.* 75 Pa.C.S. Section 1743 (emphasis supplied).

Section 1747 of the new "Vehicle Code" of 1976, provides, in pertinent part, that:

> Proof of financial responsibility may be furnished by filing evidence satisfactory to the department . . . , if the person has no motor vehicle, that the person is covered by a nonowner's policy having the same limits of liability as are required. Section 104 of (the "Pennsylvania No-Fault Motor Vehicle Insurance Act"). 75 Pa.C.S. Section 1747.

Under the Pennsylvania Act the State will not renew operating privileges if an individual fails to satisfy a judgment arising out of a motor vehicle accident, unless the operator furnishes proof of future financial responsibility. Thus under §1743, bankrupt drivers cannot obtain a license unless they purchase insurance to prove their financial responsibility. By requiring the bankrupt to purchase such proof, the State insures that bankrupts are not freed of the consequences of their past obligations.

The *Perez* case requires this Court to look beyond the stated purpose of the Pennsylvania statute and consider the effect of the statute on the federal act. The statute discourages the use of bankruptcy by someone in debt. A debtor is forced to buy special liability insurance, despite the discharge. A bankrupt debtor is faced with the choice of either doing without a license or accepting the burden of paying for special liability insurance. Controlling case law mandates that neither of these alternatives is acceptable.

The fresh start doctrine discussed in *Perez* and its progeny, has been codified in the Bankruptcy Code. In particular, 11 U.S.C. §525 discusses the rights of bankrupts with respect to governmental actions based upon discharged debts. That Section includes in pertinent part:

> a governmental unit may not deny, revoke, suspend, or refuse to renew a license, permit, charter, franchise, or other similar grant to, condition such a grant to, *discriminate with respect to such a grant against,* deny employment to, terminate the employment of, or discriminate with respect to employment against, a person that is or has been a debtor under this title or a bankrupt or a debtor under the Bankruptcy Act, or another person with whom such bankrupt or debtor has been associated, solely because such bankrupt or debtor is or has been a debtor under this title or a bankrupt or debtor under the Bankruptcy Act, has been insolvent before the commencement of the case but before the debtor is granted or denied a discharge, or *has not paid a debt that is dischargeable in the case under this title or that was discharged under the Bankruptcy Act* . . . (emphasis added).* . . .

The language of the Bankruptcy Code and the supporting House and Senate reports makes Congress' intent clear. Once a debt has been dis-

---

* Section 525 was amended in 1984.— Eds.

charged under the Code a state may not treat a debtor differently than a person who never incurred a debt. Thus, although, a state could legitimately require financial responsibility insurance for all its non-owner drivers, the Code prohibits it from treating those with judgments discharged in bankruptcy differently from those who never had such debts. The House Report specifically indicates that while Section 525 prohibits discrimination based solely on the basis of bankruptcy "it does not prohibit consideration of other factors such as future financial responsibility or ability, and does not prohibit imposition of requirements as net capital rules, *if applied nondiscriminatorily.*" House Report at 367, U.S. Code Cong. & Admin. News 1978, pp. 179, 538 (emphasis added). Thus, the Court is compelled to decide that the Pennsylvania Act, by its financial responsibility requirement, makes such a discriminatory distinction.

Defendants contend that the discharged bankrupt is not discriminated against by Pennsylvania's financial responsibility requirement since every person who fails to satisfy a motor vehicle accident must provide proof of future financial responsibility. In their brief, defendants focus exclusively on the language in Section 525 which prohibits discrimination because of the bankruptcy itself. They therefore contend that bankruptcy has nothing to do with the requirement.

Defendants, however, fail to consider the language in Section 525 which prohibits discrimination based upon a debt which was discharged under the Bankruptcy Act or Code. By focusing exclusively upon the language prohibiting discrimination because of the bankruptcy itself, defendants ignore that part of the statute which is directly applicable to this case. Plaintiffs have never argued that the financial responsibility requirement discriminates against persons because of their bankruptcy. Thus to say that the financial responsibility requirement does not discriminate against persons because of their bankruptcy misses the point. The financial responsibility requirement clearly does discriminate on the basis of debts which have been discharged in bankruptcy and therein lies the conflict with Section 525 of the Bankruptcy Code.

The Court must therefore hold that by establishing an eligibility requirement not required of the general public for operating privileges, based solely on a debt which has been discharged, defendants directly contravene the statutory language of 11 U.S.C. §525. The financial responsibility requirement is not one which is applied indiscriminately to all non-owner drivers; instead a person with a discharged debt is treated differently than a person who never had the debt. This difference effectively impairs a fresh start and is precisely what Section 525 was designed to prevent. . . .

NOTE

Section 4-508 of the proposed Bankruptcy Act of 1973 stated:

A person shall not be subjected to discriminatory treatment because he, or any person with whom he is or has been associated, is or has been a debtor or has failed to pay a debt discharged in a case under the Act. This section does not preclude consideration, where relevant, of factors other than those specified in the preceding sentence, such as present and prospective financial condition or managerial ability.

This proposed section is somewhat different than §525 in that it is not limited to acts of discrimination by governments or employers. Should this section have been incorporated into the Bankruptcy Code?

NOTE ON *HENRY* AND LIMITS ON THE PRINCIPLE OF NONDISCRIMINATION

Has the court focused on the right issue in *Henry?* The state is not requiring Mrs. Henry to pay the discharged debt as a condition of getting her license back; such activity would almost certainly violate §524, and attempts by a governmental unit to attach collateral consequences to nonpayment would probably also run afoul of §525. But is that what the *Henry* case is about? The state is requiring proof of financial responsibility. But is it based on the nonpayment of a debt discharged in bankruptcy? If not, isn't it outside of §525?

Test the reasoning of the opinion by varying the facts somewhat. Assume that Mrs. Henry had incurred an obligation arising out of an automobile accident and then failed to pay it after a judgment was entered. After a delay of more than 60 days, Mrs. Henry finally paid the debt. One hundred days later (after the preference period has run), Mrs. Henry files for bankruptcy. Doesn't Mrs. Henry still fall within the ambit of the Pennsylvania statute in that she failed to satisfy a judgment arising out of an automobile accident within 60 days of the judgment? Accordingly, to get her license back, the statute required her to pay the debt (which she had done) *and* provide the state with proof of financial responsibility. Does §525 have anything to say about this case? If not, can the result in *Henry* be supported?

Is *Henry* a persuasive reading of §525, even considered on its own terms? May a state attach any adverse consequences to the prior financial activities of someone who uses bankruptcy, even if the state is willing to attach the same consequences to prior financial difficulties of those who did not use bankruptcy? Should it matter in *Henry* what percentage of those to whom the financial responsibility requirement applies in fact went through bankruptcy? Footnote 4 of *Henry* indicates very few did.

Is there a problem reconciling the doctrine of Long v. Bullard, supra page 743, with §525? Can one interpret a statute that prevents renewal of a license when a tort judgment remains unpaid as a law that imposes a lien on the license that survives the bankruptcy proceeding and the discharge? How does an automobile license differ from a liquor license? In light of cases such as In re Anchorage International Inn, supra page 209, would such restrictions on liquor licenses survive a bankruptcy discharge under the doctrine of Long v. Bullard? In re Aegean Fare, Inc., 35 Bankr. 923 (Bankr. D. Mass. 1983), held that a state statute requiring a licensee to pay pre-petition taxes as a condition precedent to renewal of a liquor license violated the supremacy clause, because of §§362 and 525. But why should that be so, if *Anchorage International Inn* and *Long* are both good law?

At least some of these issues are addressed in the next case. Does it satisfactorily respond to *Henry*? Or is the opinion flawed because it focuses on discrimination against debtors who use bankruptcy — a focus that *Henry* found too narrow?

DUFFEY v. DOLLISON
734 F.2d 265 (6th Cir. 1984)

ENGEL, Circuit Judge.

The precise issue presented by this appeal is whether Ohio's Motor Vehicle Financial Responsibility Act, Ohio Revised Code §§4509.01-.99 (Baldwin 1975), as it has been applied to the Duffeys, conflicts with section 525 of the Bankruptcy Act of 1978, 11 U.S.C. §525 (1982), thereby violating the Supremacy Clause of the United States Constitution. U.S. Const. art. VI, cl. 2.

Motor vehicle financial responsibility laws, which require motorists to maintain some type of automobile insurance or otherwise to furnish proof of financial responsibility, have been enacted in nearly all states. Some states compel all drivers to furnish proof that they are adequately insured as a precondition to the issuance of driver's or automobile licenses. . . . Other states, such as Ohio, have enacted less comprehensive laws which require proof of financial responsibility only when a driver has failed, within a reasonable time, to satisfy a judgment for damages arising from an automobile accident or has been convicted of certain serious traffic offenses. . . .

[T]he present controversy is significant because it involves a potential conflict between important state and federal interests: state concern for public safety and federal concern for establishing uniform bankruptcy laws. Clearly if these competing interests are incompatible, the Supremacy Clause dictates that we resolve the conflict in favor of federal law. Good policy and good sense, however, suggest the desirability of accommodating both interests if this can reasonably be achieved.

I

The facts here are stipulated. On June 18, 1979, a judgment of $912.76, arising from an auto accident, was entered against George Duffey in the Municipal Court of Franklin County, Ohio. This judgment was not satisfied within 30 days and, consequently, Mr. Duffey's operator's license and vehicle registration were suspended on July 28, 1980, by the Registrar of Motor Vehicles, Dean Dollison, pursuant to Ohio Revised Code section 4509.37. On May 23, 1980, a judgment of $1,131.90, arising from an auto accident, was entered against Shari Duffey in the Franklin County Municipal Court. This judgment also was not satisfied within 30 days, resulting in the suspension of Mrs. Duffey's driving privileges on October 28, 1980.

The Duffeys, on January 27, 1981, filed a voluntary joint bankruptcy petition under Chapter 7 of the Bankruptcy Act. A copy of their bankruptcy petition, which listed the unsatisfied accident-related judgments in the schedule of debts, was sent by the Duffeys to Registrar Dollison with the request that he reinstate their driving privileges. Dollison, while recognizing that the judgment debts were subject to discharge and that the Duffeys could not be required to satisfy or reaffirm the debt as a condition to reobtaining their licenses, nevertheless refused to vacate the order of suspension until the Duffeys had filed evidence of financial responsibility as required under Ohio Revised Code section 4509.40.

On February 24, 1981, the Duffeys brought suit in bankruptcy court in the Southern District of Ohio for reinstatement of their driving privileges. In that action the Duffeys argued that Ohio's requirement of proof of financial responsibility, as it applies to individuals whose unsatisfied tort judgments have been stayed or discharged by bankruptcy, unconstitutionally conflicts with the federal bankruptcy provision prohibiting the discriminatory treatment of bankrupts, 11 U.S.C. §525 (1982). . . .

II

The Supreme Court, in Perez v. Campbell, 402 U.S. 637, 91 S. Ct. 1704, 29 L. Ed. 2d 233 (1971), stated that "[d]eciding whether a state statute is in conflict with a federal statute and hence invalid under the Supremacy Clause is essentially a two-step process of first ascertaining the construction of the two statutes and then determining the constitutional question whether they are in conflict." Id. at 644, 91 S. Ct. at 1708. In making this decision a reviewing court must "determine whether a challenged state statute 'stands as an obstacle to the accomplishment and execution of the full purposes and objectives of Congress.'" Id. at 649, 91 S. Ct. at 1711 (quoting Hines v. Davidowitz, 312 U.S. 52, 67, 61 S. Ct. 399, 404, 85 L. Ed. 581 (1941)). . . .

A

The Ohio Motor Vehicle Financial Responsibility Act provides that "[w]henever any person fails within thirty days to satisfy a judgment rendered within this state, upon written request of the judgment creditor or his attorney," the court must forward a certified copy of the judgment to the registrar of motor vehicles. Ohio Rev. Code Ann. §4509.35 (Baldwin 1975). Upon receipt of a certified copy of the unsatisfied judgment, the registrar shall "suspend the license and registration and nonresident's operating privilege of any person against whom such judgment was rendered, except as provided in sections 4509.01 to 4509.78 of the Revised Code." Ohio Rev. Code Ann. §4509.37 (Baldwin 1975). Driving privileges must remain suspended for seven years; however, "[t]he registrar shall vacate the order of suspension *upon proof that such judgment is stayed,* or satisfied in full . . . *and upon such person's filing with the registrar of motor vehicles evidence of financial responsibility* in accordance with section 4509.45 of the Revised Code." Ohio Rev. Code Ann. §4509.40 (Baldwin 1975) (emphasis added). Proof of financial responsibility must be maintained for three years and may be given by filing a certificate of insurance, a surety bond, a certificate of deposit, or a certificate of self-insurance. Ohio Rev. Code Ann. §4509.45 (Baldwin 1975).

. . . Following the United States Supreme Court's decision in Perez v. Campbell, 402 U.S. 637, 91 S. Ct. 1704, 29 L. Ed. 2d 233 (1971), the former version of Ohio's Motor Vehicle Financial Responsibility Act was declared unconstitutional to the extent that it required payment of a tort judgment as a condition to restoration of driving privileges, even though the underlying judgment was stayed, or discharged in bankruptcy. . . . The Act as it is now written cures that defect. . . . However, bankruptcy does not relieve the judgment debtor of the requirement of posting proof of future financial responsibility. . . .

The Ohio Act has as its object the protection of the public from financially irresponsible motorists who have proved unwilling or unable to satisfy a judgment arising from an automobile accident. The statute embodies a "one-bite" approach to achieving this purpose by permitting motorists the privilege of driving without any proof of financial responsibility until they incur an accident-related judgment and fail to satisfy it within 30 days.

B

[Section 525] has yet to be authoritatively construed by the United States Supreme Court. However, the legislative history indicates that section 525, "codifies the result of Perez v. Campbell, 402 U.S. 637, 91 S. Ct. 1704, 29 L. Ed. 2d 233 (1971), which held that a State would frustrate the

Congressional policy of a fresh start for a debtor if it were permitted to refuse to renew a drivers license because a tort judgment resulting from an automobile accident had been unpaid as a result of a discharge in bankruptcy." S. Rep. No. 989, 95th Cong., 2d Sess. 81, reprinted in 1978 U.S. Code Cong. & Ad. News 5787, 5867. Therefore when construing section 525, it is helpful to examine the *Perez* holding.

In *Perez,* the petitioners filed a voluntary bankruptcy petition two days before judgment was entered against them for personal injuries and property damages which arose from an automobile collision. The judgment was discharged in bankruptcy by order of the district court. Nevertheless, the State of Arizona suspended the Perezes' driving privileges pursuant to a statute which provided for such suspension when an accident-related judgment went unsatisfied for 60 days. In order to regain their privileges, the Perezes were required to satisfy the judgment and give proof of future financial responsibility. Unlike the Ohio Act, the Arizona statute required satisfaction of the judgment even though it was discharged in bankruptcy or its collection stayed. Id. at 638-642, 91 S. Ct. at 1705-1707.

In considering whether the Arizona law unconstitutionally conflicted with the Bankruptcy Act, the Court noted that "the validity of [the] limited requirement that some drivers post evidence of financial responsibility for the future in order to regain driving privileges is not questioned here." Id. at 642, 91 S. Ct. at 1707. The only issue the Court examined was whether a State may enact a statute "providing that a discharge in bankruptcy of [an] automobile accident tort judgment shall have no effect on the judgment debtor's obligation to repay the judgment creditor, at least insofar as such repayment may be enforced by the withholding of driving privileges by the State." Id. at 643, 91 S. Ct. at 1708. The majority determined that the statute jeopardized the "fresh start" objectives of the Bankruptcy Act by providing creditors leverage for collection of judgments which had been discharged in bankruptcy. Id. at 646-648, 91 S. Ct. at 1710-1711. In the majority's view, one of the primary purposes of the Bankruptcy Act "is to give debtors 'a new opportunity in life and a clear field for future effort, unhampered by the pressure and discouragement of preexisting debt.'" Id. at 648, 91 S. Ct. at 1710 (quoting Local Loan Co. v. Hunt, 292 U.S. 234, 244, 54 S. Ct. 695, 699, 78 L. Ed. 1230 (1934)). Because the Arizona law obstructed these objectives, it was found to be invalid under the Supremacy Clause. Id., 402 U.S. at 656, 91 S. Ct. at 1714.

Thus the *Perez* decision, which section 525 of the Bankruptcy Act codifies, specifically left open the issue we now consider: whether bankrupts who have discharged an accident-related judgment can be required, as a condition to the restoration of driving privileges suspended prior to the bankruptcy, to post evidence of financial responsibility. The legislative history indicates that section 525 was intended by Congress to incorporate further refinements of the *Perez* doctrine:

[T]he enumeration of various forms of discrimination against former bankrupts is not intended to permit other forms of discrimination. The courts have been developing the *Perez* rule. This section permits further development to prohibit actions by governmental or quasi-governmental organizations that perform licensing functions, such as a State bar association or a medical society, or by other organizations that can seriously affect the debtors' livelihood or fresh start. . . .

S. Rep. No. 989, supra, at 81, 1978 U.S. Code & Ad. News at 5867. It appears that section 525 is intended to ensure that bankrupts are not deprived of a "fresh start" because of governmental discrimination against them, based "solely" on the bankruptcy. Senate Report 989 specifies that "the effect of . . . section [525], and of further interpretations of the *Perez* rule, is to strengthen the anti-reaffirmation policy found in section 524(b). Discrimination based solely on nonpayment could encourage reaffirmations, contrary to the expressed policy." Id. The House further noted regarding Section 525:

[T]he purpose of the section is to prevent an automatic reaction against an individual for availing himself of the protection of the bankruptcy laws. Most bankruptcies are caused by circumstances beyond the debtor's control. To penalize a debtor by discriminatory treatment as a result is unfair and undoes the beneficial effects of the bankruptcy laws. However, in those cases where the causes of a bankruptcy are intimately connected with the license, grant, or employment in question, an examination into the circumstances surrounding the bankruptcy will permit governmental units to pursue appropriate regulatory policies and take appropriate action without running afoul of bankruptcy policy.

H.R. Rep. No. 595, 95th Cong., 1st Sess. 165 reprinted in 1978 U.S. Code Cong. & Ad. News 5963, 6126 (footnote omitted). Therefore, we agree with the district court's conclusion that "the primary purpose of section 525 of the Bankruptcy Code is to prevent the government either from denying privileges to individuals solely as a reaction to their filing bankruptcy or from conditioning the grant of privileges on the bankrupt's reaffirmation of certain debts." . . . It is thus necessary to determine whether the Ohio Financial Responsibility Act impedes the accomplishment of, or frustrates, these Congressional objectives. . . .

III . . .

The Duffeys contend that Ohio law requires them to post proof of financial responsibility "solely" because they have not paid a debt that is dischargeable in bankruptcy. Therefore in the Duffeys' view, the Ohio Act violates section 525 of the Bankruptcy Act because section 525 specifically prohibits states from using the failure to pay a debt as the basis for denying a driver's license.

We agree with the district court that the Duffeys misinterpret both section 525 and the Ohio Act. Of course, the former Ohio statute, by requiring payment of the judgment notwithstanding bankruptcy, would indeed violate section 525; as the legislative history of section 525 indicates, this would be "the *Perez* situation." . . . However, since the present Ohio Act provides that a judgment stayed or discharged in bankruptcy need not be satisfied by the judgment debtor as a condition to the restoration of driving privileges, it clearly is consistent with the immediate holding in *Perez*: the Act neither provides creditors "leverage for the collection of damages," nor under the facts here does it coerce bankrupts into reaffirming discharged debts. Perez v. Campbell, 402 U.S. 637, 646-647, 91 S. Ct. 1704, 1710. 29 L. Ed. 2d 233 (1971).

We recognize that the portion of the Ohio Act which suspends motorists' driving privileges for failure to satisfy a judgment is not triggered unless a judgment creditor requests in writing that a certified copy of the unsatisfied judgment be forwarded to the Registrar. Ohio Rev. Code Ann. §4509.35 (Baldwin 1975). It is conceivable that under certain circumstances not present here, a creditor might attempt to use this ability to initiate license suspension proceedings to coerce a debtor into reaffirming all or part of a judgment that is stayed by the Bankruptcy Act.

However under the facts of this case, the Duffeys could not have been coerced into reaffirming the stayed judgments because the judgments had been certified to the Registrar and the requirement of furnishing proof of financial responsibility had been fixed *before* the Duffeys filed in bankruptcy. Once the judgments were certified, the Duffeys could not have regained their driving privileges without furnishing proof of financial responsibility even by paying the judgments. Thus, at that juncture, the judgment creditors could do nothing further to benefit or inconvenience the Duffeys; there was no leverage which could have induced the Duffeys to reaffirm their debts. As applied here the Ohio Act, which depends on judgment creditors to initiate license suspension proceedings, employs a reasonable method for relieving the state of the burden of policing every accident-related judgment. Ohio simply has chosen in civil cases to place the responsibility for reporting unsatisfied tort judgments on the party in the best position to know whether a judgment has been satisfied, and with the greatest incentive to notify the Registrar of nonpayment.

The Duffeys would have us hold that the Ohio Motor Vehicle Financial Responsibility Act violates section 525 because the Act fails to treat a bankrupt as though he or she had never incurred a dischargeable, accident-related tort judgment. Under such an interpretation, once a judgment is discharged or stayed, states would be absolutely prohibited from imposing or continuing any burden, whether a reaffirmation of liability or the imposition of financial responsibility requirements. We believe that this reads more into section 525 than Congress intended.

. . . This conclusion is amply supported by the legislative history. Senate Report 989 specifically observes that section 525 "does not prohibit consideration of other factors, *such as future financial responsibility or ability*, and does not prohibit imposition of requirements such as net capital rules, if applied nondiscriminatorily." S. Rep. No. 989, supra, at 81, 1978 U.S. Code Cong. & Ad. News at 5867 (emphasis added). House Report No. 595 makes this point even more emphatically:

> [T]he prohibition [of section 525] *does not extend so far as to prohibit examination of the factors surrounding bankruptcy, the imposition of financial responsibility rules if they are not imposed only on former bankrupts*, or the examination of prospective financial condition or managerial ability. . . . [I]n those cases where the causes of a bankruptcy are intimately connected with the license, grant, or employment in question, an examination into the circumstances surrounding the bankruptcy will permit governmental units to pursue appropriate regulatory policies and take appropriate action without running afoul of bankruptcy policy.

H.R. Rep. No. 595, 95th Cong. 1st Sess. 165 reprinted in 1978 U.S. Code Cong. & Ad. News 5963, 6126 (emphasis added). Thus, Congress has evinced a clear intent to permit the imposition of financial responsibility requirements, so long as they are not discriminatorily applied to bankrupts.

The Ohio Financial Responsibility Act in no way discriminates against bankrupts, or penalizes them for filing in bankruptcy. The Act provides that "any person" who fails to satisfy an accident-related judgment within 30 days shall have his or her driving privileges suspended by the Registrar. Ohio Rev. Code Ann. §§4509.35, .37 (Baldwin 1975). The statute applies without exception to *any* person who fails to satisfy a judgment for whatever reason, whether because of unwillingness, inadvertence, or inability to pay. Once a judgment has been certified to the Registrar for nonpayment, the debtor's obligation to furnish proof of financial responsibility becomes fixed. Thereafter, neither payment of the debt, reaffirmation, nor bankruptcy can relieve the debtor of this requirement. Judgment debtors such as the Duffeys who seek relief under the bankruptcy laws are therefore treated no differently from any other judgment debtor. Indeed it is this lack of discrimination to which the Duffeys take exception. By arguing that bankrupts who have proved to be irresponsible drivers should be excused from the requirement of posting proof of financial responsibility, the Duffeys in effect ask this court "to go beyond the fresh start policy of *Perez* and . . . give a debtor a head start over persons who are able to satisfy their unpaid judgment debts without resort to a discharge in bankruptcy." In re Cerny, 17 B.R. 221, 224 (Bkrtcy. N.D. Ohio 1982). We do not believe that section 525 was intended by Congress to afford debtors in bankruptcy such preferential treatment.

We therefore hold that Ohio's "one-bite" approach to the imposition of financial responsibility requirements, as applied to the Duffeys, violates neither the *Perez* holding nor its statutory codification, section 525 of the Bankruptcy Act. As Judge Holschuh persuasively reasoned,

> [i]t is undisputed that Ohio may require all motorists to carry liability insurance or post security before they are issued operator's licenses. Bell v. Burson, 402 U.S. 535, 91 S. Ct. 1586, 29 L. Ed. 2d 90 (1971). If the State may legitimately establish such a prerequisite to the grant of driving privileges, a less stringent requirement should *a fortiori* be valid. The challenged Ohio statutes afford individuals the opportunity of driving without any showing of financial responsibility until they incur a judgment which they are unable to pay. This "one-bite" approach undoubtedly makes it possible for many individuals who otherwise could not afford insurance to obtain driving privileges. [The Duffeys] argue that because Ohio has used this more lenient approach, it is forbidden to suspend their driving privileges, despite the fact that they have demonstrated irresponsibility as a driver coupled with an inability to satisfy a resulting judgment. [This] argument, however, ignores the potential consequences to the victims of an accident caused by an individual who is an irresponsible driver.

Duffey v. Dollison, C-2-81-1154, slip op. at 12 (S.D. Ohio Aug. 13, 1982).

Our ruling here is a relatively narrow one. We uphold the Ohio Act where the requirement to furnish proof of financial responsibility has become fixed, through certification to the Registrar, prior to bankruptcy. Where the obligation has thus become fixed, neither payment of the judgment, nor arrangement with the creditor, nor bankruptcy can relieve the debtor of the requirement of furnishing proof of financial responsibility. In this respect the Ohio Act does not have the effect of discriminating between those who are bankrupt and those who are not. It cannot induce the bankrupt to reaffirm a discharged debt, or to pay thereafter, for neither action can affect the legal requirement to post proof of financial responsibility.

The judgment of the district court is affirmed.

NOTE ON STUDENT LOANS AND TRANSCRIPTS

In re Heath, 3 Bankr. 351 (Bankr. N.D. Ill. 1980), involved a recurring problem of discharged student loans and transcripts. Heath borrowed money from the University of Illinois to finance his education. Subsequently, Heath filed for bankruptcy and proposed a plan, in Chapter 13, whereby the university would be paid ten cents on the dollar. Heath then requested a transcript from the university. The university refused. The court held that this violated §§525 and 362(a)(6) (see also §524 for post-bankruptcy discharge "continuation" of the policy behind §362(a)(6)). As for §525, the court noted that "Heath's transcript, as such, has no intrinsic value to the University. Thus, the Court finds that the University is withholding Heath's transcript for the sole purpose of compelling Heath to pay a pre-petition debt." The court rejected the university's argument that for §525 to apply the "discriminatory actions must impair a debtor's fresh start." As for the automatic stay, the court noted that §362(a)(6) reached, as the old Bankruptcy Act did not, "informal means of inducing Heath to pay the pre-petition debt," thereby distinguishing old Act cases, such as *Girardier*, discussed next. Compare Johnson v. Edinboro State College, 728 F.2d 163 (3d Cir. 1984) (distinguishes *Heath*, on ground that the debt "owed by *Heath* . . . [was] dischargeable and, in fact, had been discharged; the debt Johnson owes Edinboro College is not dischargeable [because of the application of §523(a)(8) to Chapter 7 cases]. Consequently, we can find no basis in the Bankruptcy Code to nullify Edinboro State's policy of withholding transcripts from those students who have made no payments on their educational loans").

In Girardier v. Webster College, 563 F.2d 1267 (8th Cir. 1977), a similar issue was raised under the old Bankruptcy Act: whether a student whose student loans were discharged in bankruptcy was later entitled to a transcript. The Eighth Circuit held no, noting that *Perez* was based on state action, and the action involved in the case before the Eighth Circuit involved a private university. Judge Bright concurred, but was unwilling to follow the private/public distinction:

> A college transcript differs radically from the essential driver's license at stake in *Perez*. A student who obtains a degree from a college acquires not only the present benefit of that education, but also a fund of knowledge of lifelong value. In other words, it is not like purchasing an article of consumable goods that immediately is consumed or even durable goods with more lasting usefulness. Instead, an education yields ever-continuing benefits.
>
> Webster College, which has conferred upon now-bankrupt, former students an education represented by a degree, has taken no steps to penalize appellants in their use of knowledge gained in college, nor has it sought to prevent them from exhibiting a degree to the world at large. Rather, Webster College refuses further to enhance the benefit of those degrees by certification of the transcripts. That transcript represents far more in intangible worth than its mere two dollar cost of reproduction, for it embodies an additional certification of the debtors' already-received, but unpaid for, degrees, and provides the bankrupts with entry into graduate studies. Indeed, issuance of the transcripts affords these debtors a recommendation by the college of their intellectual worth. . . .
>
> [I]n my view, neither the statute nor the fresh start principle applies here.

First, Webster College merely declined to confer any additional benefits upon the debtors by furnishing transcripts of their grades for the unpaid educational courses. Otherwise, it in no way coerced the debtors to pay the discharged debts. Second, appellants have obtained far more than the fresh start contemplated by the Bankruptcy Act — they have obtained a head start because each has secured something of value that cannot be lost or taken away and which will give each appellant a continuing, lifelong economic benefit. No college, public or private, should be required to enhance such a benefit by issuing a transcript when it has not been paid for its services. The equities here lie with the college.

How would Judge Bright decide a case such as *Girardier* or *Heath* under the Bankruptcy Code? Although we look at exemptions from discharge later in this chapter, you should take note of §523(a)(8) at this point, which exempts from discharge certain educational loans. Is this exception wise?

Section 525 prohibits certain actions if they are taken "solely" because a debtor was in bankruptcy, or was discharged, or did not pay a dischargeable debt. The legislative history states "[i]t does not prohibit consideration of other factors, such as future financial responsibility or ability, and does not prohibit imposition of requirements such as net capital rules, if applied nondiscriminatorily." How does one decide how the line is drawn? The next case, and the problems that follow it, address that question.

IN RE RICHARDSON
27 Bankr. 560 (E.D. Pa. 1982)

HANNUM, District Judge.

The appellants, Pennsylvania Higher Education Assistance Agency (PHEAA) and two of its officials, Kenneth R. Reeher, and Jay Evans, herein appeal an order of the Bankruptcy Court which determined that PHEAA Regulation 121.4(b),[1] 22 Pa. Code §121.4(b) is unconstitutional pursuant to §525 of the Bankruptcy Code as applied to the appellee. The

---

1. Currently, PHEAA Regulation 121.4(b) provides:

Eligibility for a loan guaranty will be denied to any person who has allowed a loan to mature through purchase from the lender by the Agency under the guaranty of a previous loan in the Loan Guaranty Program, or has a current loan default record with the Agency as a result of a claim on the loan having been submitted to the Agency by the lender unless the applicant has repaid the loan in whole or in part, and in the judgment of the Agency, did not make such repayment merely to gain loan eligibility or unless the applicant otherwise shows good cause why loan eligibility should be reinstated. . . .

22 Pa. Code §121.4(b). This regulation was effective June 20, 1981 and is substantially similar to the version of the same regulation considered by the Bankruptcy Court. . . .

Bankruptcy Court's order also enjoined appellants from applying PHEAA Regulation 121.4(b) to deny the application of Reginald Richardson for a guaranteed student loan, and the order directed PHEAA to approve the application of Richardson for a guaranteed student loan.

The facts, as found by the Bankruptcy Court are as follows: Reginald Richardson attended undergraduate school at the University of Pennsylvania between 1972 and 1976. During that time the plaintiff applied for and received student loans guaranteed by PHEAA totaling $5,800.00. After leaving school prior to graduation, Richardson failed to contact the lending institution and establish a repayment schedule or to repay any of his student loans as required by his loan agreements. As a result, PHEAA was obliged to purchase Richardson's loans from the lending institution.

Thereafter, on March 12, 1979, Richardson filed a voluntary petition in bankruptcy under the Bankruptcy Act. On June 29, 1979, Richardson obtained a discharge from all of his dischargeable debts including the debt owed to PHEAA for his student loans.[3]

In the spring of 1980, Richardson returned to the University of Pennsylvania to complete his undergraduate degree. At that time he applied for a PHEAA-guaranteed grant which application was denied by PHEAA because of the fact that Richardson had defaulted on his prior PHEAA-guaranteed student loans. At the same time, he applied for a PHEAA-guaranteed loan which application was not processed by the University of Pennsylvania. Because Richardson was able to obtain other loans and grants through the school, he failed to appeal PHEAA's denial of his grant application or to take any other steps to obtain relief from that decision.

In May of 1981, Richardson graduated from the University of Pennsylvania. He had applied to several law schools and had decided in May to attend Temple Law School. On June 21, 1981, Richardson filed an application for a PHEAA-guaranteed student loan through Girard Bank. That application was initially denied by Girard Bank but, after discussions with Richardson's lawyer, the Bank approved the application and sent it on to PHEAA for approval.

On June 22, 1981, Richardson filed a complaint in Bankruptcy Court seeking declaratory and injunctive relief against PHEAA to prevent it from denying his guaranteed loan application. On August 10, 1981, PHEAA filed a motion to dismiss that complaint. Thereafter the appellee was admitted to the University of Virginia Law School and filed a new guaranteed loan application which was processed through the Bank. A hearing was held on the complaint and motion to dismiss on August 20, 1981, at which time the plaintiff also filed a motion for a temporary restraining order or for a preliminary injunction to require PHEAA to process his loan application immediately and to enjoin PHEAA from de-

---

3. Section 523(a)(8) of the current Bankruptcy Code now provides that guaranteed student loans are not dischargeable.

nying that application for discriminatory reasons. Following an evidentiary hearing, the Bankruptcy Court granted the relief sought by issuance of an order dated October 9, 1981. . . .

. . . In enacting Section 525, Congress intended to codify the result of Perez v. Campbell, 402 U.S. 637, 91 S. Ct. 1704, 29 L. Ed. 2d 233 (1971). H. Rep. No. 95-595, 95th Cong., 1st Sess., 366-367 (1977). . . . In *Perez*, the Supreme Court found that Arizona's policy of denying a driver's license to bankrupts with discharged tort judgments was in conflict with Congress' intent to provide bankrupts with a fresh start unhampered by preexisting debt. 402 U.S. at 643, 91 S. Ct. at 1708. Subsequently, many cases followed and expanded upon *Perez*. For instance, in Grimes v. Hoschler, 12 Cal. 3d 305, 115 Cal. Rptr. 625, 525 P.2d 65 (1974), the Supreme Court of California held that the revocation of a building contractor's license by a state licensing board was invalid in light of *Perez*. In Handsome v. Rutgers University, 445 F. Supp. 1362 (D.N.J. 1978), the Court invalidated the State University's practice of withholding student transcripts based on *Perez*. See also, Matter of Heath, 3 B.R. 351, 1 C.B.C.2d 736 (Bkrtcy. N.D. Ill. 1980) (section 525 was violated when a state university refused to furnish a Chapter 13 debtor his transcript until the debtor's prepetition loan was paid in full). In Henry v. Heyison, 4 B.R. 437 (E.D. Pa. 1980), the District Court held that the Pennsylvania Financial Responsibility Law conflicted with Section 525 in its imposition of special eligibility requirements to operate a vehicle for persons with unsatisfied motor vehicle tort judgments discharged in bankruptcy.

In the case at hand, appellee instituted the adversary proceeding below during the pendency of his PHEAA loan application by the agency. The Bankruptcy Court nonetheless concluded that the matter was ripe by reason of the clear language of the then applicable PHEAA regulation:

(b) Eligibility for a loan guaranty shall be denied to any person who has allowed his loan to mature through purchase from the lender by the Agency under the guaranty of a previous loan in the Loan Guaranty Program, unless in the judgment of Agency staff such loan should be guaranteed and one of the following has occurred:

(1) The defaulted loan has been repaid in full.

(2) An approved lending institution has purchased the outstanding balance of the defaulted loan.

(3) The student has taken positive steps toward repayment of the loan or toward supplying reasons in justification of the failure to repay. . . .

22 Pa. Code §121.4(b) (1981) (superseded June 21, 1981).[6] Finding Section 525 applicable to the case at hand, the Bankruptcy Court concluded:

6. See note 1 supra.

In the instant case it is clear that PHEAA's regulations treat a person who has had his student loan obligation discharged in bankruptcy different from a person who has never incurred a student loan debt. PHEAA admits that a person who has never had a student loan guarantee before is automatically approved for a student loan guarantee as long as he is a resident of Pennsylvania. Therefore, PHEAA's regulation 22 Pa. Code §121.4(b) which provides that the plaintiff's application must be denied initially is an unlawful discrimination under §525 of the Bankruptcy Code.

Thus, the Bankruptcy Court granted appellee immediate injunctive relief.

Among those cases applying the principles of *Perez*, supra, and its codification in Section 525, the most similar to the case at hand are those decisions addressing the withholding of transcripts to a debtor whose student loans have been discharged in bankruptcy. Handsome v. Rutgers University, supra, In Re Heath, supra; Lee v. Board of Higher Education, 1 B.R. 781 (S.D.N.Y. 1979). While these decisions have uniformly held that a state university may not withhold transcripts under such circumstances, the Court in Handsome v. Rutgers University, supra, was careful to note, "This is not to say that defendant [Rutgers University] may not in the future validly decline to extend credit to one who has previously discharged his debts in bankruptcy. . . ." 445 F. Supp. at 1362. Similarly, it has been noted that "[t]he prohibition against discriminatory treatment does not affect decisions to grant credit to the debtor because of the fact that future financial responsibility may be taken into account by a creditor." 3 Collier On Bankruptcy §525.02 at 525-3, 4 (15th ed. 1982). . . .

Unquestionably, Section 525 of the Bankruptcy Code can not be interpreted so as to preclude PHEAA from making reasonable inquiry into the future financial responsibility of a loan applicant such as appellee, prior to the extension of additional credit in the form of a guaranteed student loan. This is particularly so where, as here, there exists legitimate basis for denial of the application quite apart from the appellee's bankruptcy, or the simple fact of his failure to pay a debt dischargeable in bankruptcy. Following appellee's leaving college in 1976, he not only failed to make any payments on his PHEAA loan, but he failed to contact the lender relative to a repayment schedule. Under applicable PHEAA regulations, had appellee given notice to the lending institution, he could have been afforded an additional twelve months or more grace period prior to making any payments, on grounds of hardship. Thus, the maturation of appellee's loan through purchase by the agency could have been avoided without the need to start making payments on the loan. See 22 Pa. Code §121.67(f).[8]

---

8. "A borrower may defer repayment of his loans for a period not to exceed 12 months during which the borrower is seeking and unable to find full-time employment, upon proper notice to the lender holding the lien." 22 Pa. Code §121.67(f). Moreover, such a borrower is entitled "to an additional six-month post deferment grace period before resuming payment on loans disbursed by the lender before October 1, 1981." 22 Pa. Code §121.67(h). More-

Under these circumstances, it is appropriate to conclude that PHEAA had reason independent of appellee's bankruptcy or the discharge of a previous loan, to warrant investigation of the appellee's future financial responsibility. In any event, the Bankruptcy Court's decision having been rendered prior to a loan eligibility determination by PHEAA, the agency was precluded from any inquiry into the future financial responsibility of appellee. In sum, we view PHEAA Regulation 121.4(b) as was considered by the Bankruptcy Court, to be capable of application without violating 11 U.S.C. §525 and therefore, we do not deem it appropriate to invalidate the Commonwealth agency's regulation or practice. Accordingly, that portion of the Bankruptcy Court's order finding 22 Pa. Code §121.4(b) unconstitutional as applied to appellee will be vacated. . . .

NOTES

1. If Richardson had filed under the Bankruptcy Code, would §524 have affected the outcome in the case?
2. Florida Board of Bar Examiners, 364 So. 2d 454 (Fla. 1978), involved the question of the denial of bar admission following bankruptcy and, more particularly, "the effect of a bankruptcy petition on a Bar applicant's fitness to practice law." The applicant filed for bankruptcy three days before graduating from law school, at a time when he had received approximately $10,000 in student loans, repayment to begin nine months after graduation. The court noted that "[w]ith the exception of one debt in the amount of $8.01, none of his debts listed in his petition were due at the time of filing." The Florida Supreme Court upheld his denial of bar admission, stating:

> We find that the Board had ample record evidence from which it could conclude that the principal motive of the petitioner in filing his petition for bankruptcy was to defeat creditors who had substantially funded seven years of educational training. Whether that motive was present as the debts were incurred or was formed toward the end of his law school training, the Board could fairly conclude from the petitioner's own testimony and prior behavior that he exercised his legal right to be freed of debt by bankruptcy well before the first installments on his debt became due, with absolutely no regard for his moral responsibility to his creditors. The petitioner's admittedly legal but unjustifiably precipitous action, initiated before he had ob-

---

over, these deferment provisions could *follow* the nine month period after leaving school, which is when repayments become due. 22 Pa. Code §121.67(a). Besides not utilizing any of the non-payment procedures to avoid default, evidence was presented that appellee did not get in touch with PHEAA officials, although PHEAA officials had placed several telephone calls to his family's residence. Hearing Transcript at 73-75.

tained the results of the July bar examination, exhausted the job market, or given his creditors an opportunity to adjust repayment schedules, indicates a lack of the moral values upon which we have a right to insist for members of the legal profession in Florida. . . .

The record before us reflects that the petitioner suffered no unusual misfortune or financial catastrophe prior to his filing the bankruptcy petition. . . . In our view, his filing of the bankruptcy petition showed a disregard not only for the rights of his creditors but also for future student loan applicants. The filing of the bankruptcy petition was not illegal, but in our view it was done in such a morally reprehensible fashion that it directly affects his fitness to practice law.

Is this opinion consistent with *Perez* (which the Florida Supreme Court did not cite)? Would it be consistent with §525 if the issue were to arise under the Bankruptcy Code?

PROBLEMS

10.2 The federal government imposes a $12,000 limit on federally guaranteed student loans, 20 U.S.C. §1087dd(a)(2). Debtor had received $3,000 of such loans by the time Debtor filed for bankruptcy. If those loans are discharged in bankruptcy, will Debtor be entitled to receive $9,000 or $12,000 more in federally guaranteed student loans?

10.3 Debtor works for Company. Debtor files a petition in bankruptcy. Company fires Debtor, explaining that Company will not continue its employment of anyone who files a petition in bankruptcy. Do Company's actions violate the automatic stay? After Debtor is discharged do Company's actions violate §525? What if Debtor were a loan officer for Bank, and Bank fires Debtor after he files a bankruptcy petition, on the ground that the filing sets a bad example, given the nature of Debtor's job? Cf. McLellan v. Mississippi Power & Light Co., 545 F.2d 919 (5th Cir. en banc 1977) (old Act case).

10.4 Ike Kempner runs a shoe store as a sole proprietorship. Kempner files a bankruptcy petition and receives a discharge. U.S. Shoe, which has been supplying shoes to Kempner for 30 years, refuses to sell any more shoes to Kempner on the grounds that it does not do business with anyone who files a bankruptcy petition. Does Supplier violate any provision of the Bankruptcy Code? Would it make a difference if U.S. Shoe had not been paid $5,000 for goods it shipped before the filing of the petition?

10.5 Debtor borrows $5,000 from Bank, and this debt is discharged in bankruptcy. Debtor subsequently seeks to borrow $10,000 from Bank. May Bank refuse on the ground that Debtor had discharged its previous debt in bankruptcy? How would you advise Bank to proceed in such a case? Cf. In re Rose, 23 Bankr. 662 (Bankr. D. Conn. 1982).

10.6 Alessi had been racing horses under a temporary license. At his hearing for a final license, the Illinois Racing Board investigated allegations that Alessi had negotiated a number of checks that had been returned to the payees marked NSF as well as allegations that Alessi owed debts to several other entities that had not been paid. On January 7, after the hearing, but before the decision on the license, Alessi files for bankruptcy. On February 10, the Illinois Racing Board denies Alessi's petition for a permanent license on the ground that Alessi fails to meet the financial responsibility requirements of its rules. May Alessi be denied his license on that ground? See In re Alessi, 12 Bankr. 96 (Bankr. N.D. Ill. 1981).

10.7 Hillcrest Foods, Inc. was a "self-insurer" under Maine's Workers' Compensation law. Hillcrest Foods files a voluntary petition in bankruptcy. May the Maine Department of Business Regulation send the following notice to Hillcrest Foods?

> The authority of Hillcrest Foods to self-insure workers' compensation benefits in this state is hereby suspended indefinitely, for the reason that the filing of a petition for voluntary bankruptcy constitutes failure to satisfactorily establish solvency and financial ability to pay the compensation and benefits required under the Workers' Compensation Act.

See In re Rath Packing Co., 35 Bankr. 615 (Bankr. N.D. Iowa 1983); In re Hillcrest Foods, Inc., 10 Bankr. 579 (Bankr. D. Me. 1981).

3.   Reaffirmation and Redemption

NOTE ON REAFFIRMATION

Longstanding contract law doctrine provides that a discharge in bankruptcy does not make a subsequent promise to pay the discharged debt unenforceable for lack of consideration. Restatement (Second) of Contracts §83. Prior bankruptcy law was silent on reaffirmation, and, accordingly, placed no limit on the ability of debtors to enter into reaffirmation agreements. Such limits as existed came from nonbankruptcy law. A binding reaffirmation agreement, in effect, waives the debtor's right to a discharge of the reaffirmed debt. In light of that, why was reaffirmation even allowed, when a debtor is unable to waive his right to a discharge in advance of bankruptcy?

Section 524(c) and (d) changes the rules governing reaffirmation. It sets forth a two-step inquiry. First, the reaffirmation must be effective under nonbankruptcy law. Second, if it is, it must also be effective under the tests of §524(c) and (d). The provisions of §524(c) and (d) should be studied in conjunction with the following problems.

PROBLEMS

10.8 Corporation has gone through a Chapter 11 proceeding and has been discharged from all of its debts. May Corporation reaffirm a debt to Supplier? Would it matter if Corporation felt that Supplier would not treat it as well (in miscellaneous and largely unprovable ways) unless the debt were reaffirmed? See §524(c)(1). Can Corporation seek revocation of its discharge under §1144? See In re McQuality, 5 Bankr. 302 (Bankr. S.D. Ohio 1980). Can Corporation voluntarily pay the debt without reaffirming it? See In re LaFave, 9 Bankr. 859 (Bankr. E.D. Mich. 1981).

10.9 Same facts as Problem 10.8, except that Corporation reaffirms the debt the day before filing its petition in bankruptcy. Is this reaffirmation enforceable? As of when?

10.10 Individual wishes to reaffirm a debt to Credit Union. She comes to you for advice as to how to proceed. What do you tell her? Does it matter if: (1) The debt is guaranteed by Relative? (2) The debt is secured by Individual's automobile? (3) The debt is secured by Individual's house?

IN RE AVIS
3 Bankr. 205 (Bankr. S.D. Ohio 1980)

•

Charles A. ANDERSON, Bankruptcy Judge.

This matter is before the court upon a motion filed on 20 February 1980 by International Harvester Employee Credit Union, later joined by Debtors approving a reaffirmation agreement, pursuant to 11 U.S.C. §524(c).

FINDINGS OF FACT

On November 2, 1979, the debtors filed their petition and schedules listing assets totalling $10,950.00 all of which were claimed as exempt.

The only income that Donald L. Avis receives is disability retirement from International Harvester, Springfield, Ohio. At present, that disability income amounts to approximately $710.00 per month.

Ada M. Avis had been a part time employee of J. C. Penney Company, Upper Valley Mall, Springfield, Ohio, although at present, she is not regularly employed.

The schedules of creditors listed the following claims against the debtors, to-wit:

One secured claim (homestead), totalling $24,700.00.
Thirteen unsecured claims without priority, totalling $11,813.35.

Among the unsecured claims scheduled were two loans; one by the Springfield Bank with a balance due of approximately $5,000.00 and one by the International Harvester Employee Credit Union with approximately a $4,300.00 balance due. Both loans were made with co-signors.

On December 27, 1979, the debtors amended their schedule of creditors by adding two debts that totaled $6,600.00, for which they were obligated as co-signors.

On February 20, 1980, International Harvester Employee Credit Union filed a motion for court approval of a reaffirmation agreement, pursuant to Title 11, United States Code §524(c) regarding the debtors' loan for $5,486.82 (which then had a $4,342.26 balance due).

During the discharge hearing held on February 22, 1980, the debtors stated that their sole reason for agreeing to the reaffirmation of the credit union loan was because they had caused friends to be obligated as co-signors for the debt.

CONCLUSION OF LAW AND FACT

The single issue in this case is whether the debtors' reaffirmation agreement with the credit union should be approved as being in the debtors' "best interests." Title 11 U.S.C. §524(c)* governs court approval of the submitted agreement, as follows:

> (c) An agreement between a holder of a claim and the debtor, the consideration for which, in whole or in part, is based on a debt that is dischargeable in a case under this title is enforceable . . . , only if— . . .
> (4) in a case concerning an individual, to the extent that such a debt is a consumer debt that is not secured by real property of the debtor, *the court approves such agreement as—*
> (A)(i) not imposing an undue hardship on the debtor or a dependent of the debtor; and
> (ii) *in the best interest of the debtor.* . . .

The pivotal question presented by §524(c)(4)(A) is the meaning of a debtor's "best interests," as a matter of law. No specific interpretation of the term is provided by the Code and no direct reference was found in the legislative history. However, the history of the development of the present §524 and the wording of other Code Sections do provide strong guidance and do support the interpretation that financial or economic concerns of the bankrupt should be paramount, if not exclusive.

Enforceability of a claim is the basic issue controlled by §524(c) and (d). The present wording of these subsections is the result of compromise

---

* This section was substantially revised in 1984. The current version is now §524(c)(6). — EDS.

reached between the Senate and the House of Representatives just prior to passage of the Bankruptcy Act of 1978. . . . In its original Bills the House disallowed reaffirmation or renewal of any extinguished debts (H.R. 31 §4-507 and H.R. 32 §4-507). On October 28, 1977, the House approved H.R. 8200 with §524(c) allowing only two exceptions to that ban, namely:

1. In settlement of litigation under §523, and
2. An agreement providing for redemption under §722.

Arguing in opposition to that strict limitation, the consumer finance industry proposed allowance of any *voluntary* repayment by the bankrupt. . . . However, since enforceability of an agreement was at issue, and should any subsequent default occur on an approved claim, the courts would be required to force repayment and voluntariness would disappear. With this possible result in mind, the Senate proposed an amendment to §524 that was designed to make possible a truly voluntary reaffirmation without eroding the effectiveness of bankruptcy relief. That effectiveness was dependent on compliance with three basic principles, namely:

1. to give the bankrupt a "fresh start,"
2. to discourage bankrupts from immediately seeking credit, and
3. to treat all creditors substantially alike (Cong. Rec. S. 14,743, Sept. 7, 1978).

The apparent intent of the Senate then was that the easing of the ban on reaffirmations was to be viewed collectively with the stated principles underlying bankruptcy relief. Hence the inescapable conclusion is that the intended meaning of a debtor's "best interests" are strictly financial or economic.

The proposed Senate amendment to §524 was the final compromise adopted into the Bankruptcy Code of 1978. No other consideration was found in the legislative history which would support any other interpretation.

Probably the strongest non-financial interest that possibly deserves consideration is presented in this case. Pressure to reaffirm an agreement is exerted on the bankrupt by the existence of co-debtors on the claim. That pressure will necessarily influence any decisions by the bankrupt, and the character of the relationship between the co-debtors and the bankrupt.

This may appear to be valid and acceptable, until the principles underlying bankruptcy relief stated in Congress are applied. Court approval of an agreement because of the existence of a co-debtor would weaken the "fresh start" for the bankrupt. Also, any other unsecured creditors would not be treated substantially the same. Court disapproval on the other hand, would secure the effectiveness of discharge relief while not denying the bankrupt an opportunity voluntarily to pay the debt to either the creditor or to a co-debtor. The claim would just not be enforceable against debtors if or when future circumstances might change, such as the death or insolvency of the co-debtor.

Indirectly, other Sections of the Code address the problem of pressure on the bankrupt resulting from the existence of a co-debtor. §524(e) states that the discharge of a debtor does not affect the liability of any co-debtor. §362 imposes an automatic stay of action against a debtor upon the filing of a petition under Chapter 7, 9, 11, or 13, but not against co-debtors. §1301(a) does impose a stay against co-debtors but lifts the stay when the case is closed, dismissed, or converted to a Chapter 7, or a Chapter 11 case.

All these ancillary sections of the Code show some slight congressional concern for the co-debtors. Only in Chapter 13 cases is the co-debtor insulated by a stay of action by a creditor, and the protection is incidental and temporary. The stay is designed to protect the debtor from creditor and co-debtor pressures while financial affairs are being rearranged. No intent is shown to deprive creditors of any rights, other than to delay enforcement of a claim against co-debtors.

In this case, the debtors have stated that their sole reason for agreeing to the reaffirmation was the existence of co-debtors. The amount of the proposed reaffirmation is more than one third of the total listed unsecured claims against them. Another claim with co-debtors obligated ($5,000.00), is not proposed for reaffirmation. Approval of the submitted reaffirmation would violate the basic principles guiding bankruptcy relief, the effectiveness of discharge would be weakened; and all creditors would not be treated substantially alike. No sufficient reasons have been presented to justify approval or to override the debtors' financial consideration. Therefore the court will not render the credit union claim enforceable.

Obviously, the debtors may, nevertheless, voluntarily pay the debt to either the creditor or to the co-debtors, although not legally obligated and subject to future legal actions. . . .

NOTES

1. See also In re Bertich, 7 Bankr. 483 (Bankr. E.D. Pa. 1980) (debt guaranteed by mother and secured by lien on mother's real estate. Held: Debtor's desire not to have creditor move against mother to collect debt is understandable, but does not consitute "sufficient basis for finding that the reaffirmation is in the *debtor's* best interests"). In light of *Avis* and *Bertich*, when would a reaffirmation be in the debtor's best interest? Is it sensible to have procedures on reaffirmation turn on whether the debtor is represented by a lawyer? See §524(c)(6).

2. Discharge, as we have noted, is not waivable in advance, at the time of the extension of credit. Assume that a creditor is willing to charge a

lower interest rate in exchange for the debtor's waiver of discharge with respect to that debt. Should a waiver be allowed under such circumstances, if coupled with a mechanism such as that in §524? Is there a reason to distinguish the two cases?

NOTE ON REDEMPTION

Under §722, an individual debtor may "redeem tangible personal property intended primarily for personal, family, or household use, from a lien securing a dischargeable consumer debt" if the property is exempt under §522 or has been abandoned under §554. Redemption is effected "by paying the holder of such lien the amount of the allowed secured claim of such holder that is secured by such lien." The section is derived from UCC §9-506, and to understand the scope and impact of §722, it is necessary to be able to relate it to UCC §9-506, as well as to the earlier discussion, supra page 743, of lien "pass through." For example, in In re Bell, 700 F.2d 1053 (6th Cir. 1983), the question was whether §722 permitted redemption of property that was subject to a security interest by means of installment payments. Debtor owned a van that was subject to a $6,000 purchase money security interest in favor of GMAC. The fair market value of the van exceeded the amount due GMAC by about $1,000. Debtor exempted that equity interest (see §522, discussed in the next chapter) and the trustee abandoned the estate's interest under §554. Debtor sought to retain possession of the van upon continuing the monthly installment payments. No monetary default had yet occurred. *Bell*, however, concluded that §722 precluded such a redemption. *Bell* asserted, first, that nothing in the history of §722 suggested that Congress "contemplated anything other than an intent to incorporate the fundamental requirement of 'lump sum' redemption as suggested in the underlying UCC provision upon which §722 was predicated." Moreover, the court in *Bell* thought that the existence of the reaffirmation provision in §524 precluded the Debtor's proposed method of redemption under §722:

> Simply, a debtor incapable or unwilling to tender a lump-sum redemption and redeem the secured collateral for its fair market value may reaffirm with the creditor; contrawise, a debtor confronted with a creditor unwilling to execute a renegotiation may retain the secured collateral by redeeming it for its fair market value, which value may be substantially less that the contractual indebtedness. However, §524(c) facially contemplates that the creditor, for whatever reason, may reject any and all tendered reaffirmation offers; §524(c) envisions execution of an "agreement" which, by definition, is a voluntary undertaking. . . . Accordingly, if a debtor is authorized by the bankruptcy court to redeem by installments over the objection of the creditor, such practice would render the voluntary framework of §524(c) an exercise in legislative futility.

Finally, *Bell* concluded that installment redemption was a procedure ill-suited to Chapter 7's structure, which contemplated that the bankruptcy proceeding would be over before the end of the installment payments.

Note that a construction of §722 — such as *Bell's* — that does not permit installment redemption cuts down substantially on the use of that section in Chapter 7. Chapter 7 strips the debtor of all nonexempt assets (if the debtor is insolvent); unless the debtor converts some exempt assets to cash, lump-sum redemption might seem to be virtually impossible. *Bell* noted that problem, but suggested its solution was for the debtor to use Chapter 13, which "is designed to provide a debtor with a fresh start through rehabilitation, unlike Chapter 7 which provides a fresh start through liquidation. As such, Chapter 13 authorizes redemption by installment over an objection of the creditor. . . . 11 U.S.C. §1325(a)(5)." In Chapter 7, a debtor's future earnings are "freed up" of debts arising out of the debtor's past. *Bell's* reading of §722 may require the debtor to borrow money against that income from a third party, so as to gain the money necessary to cash out the secured creditor under §722. Seen that way, is *Bell's* reading of §722 anything more than a conclusion that the debtor must find a *willing* lender, instead of subjecting the existing secured creditor to an involuntary loan? Is that policy supportable?

One final point should be noted about §722. The section is limited to property exempted under §522 (which we examine in detail in the next chapter) or to property abandoned under §554 (as occurred in *Bell*). This limitation seems designed to ensure that the trustee (and, hence, the estate) claims no interest in the asset for the benefit of the general creditors; that point, however, should be related to the following statement from the House Report:

> The right to redeem extends to the whole of the property, not just the debtor's exempt interest in it. Thus, for example, if a debtor owned a $2,000 car, subject to a $1,200 lien, the debtor could exempt his $800 interest in the car. The debtor is permitted a $1,500 [now $1,200] exemption in a car [pursuant to §522(d)(2)]. This section permits him to pay the holder of the lien $1,200 and redeem the entire car, not just the remaining $700 of his exemption. The redemption is accomplished by paying the holder of the lien the amount of the allowed claim secured by the lien. The provision amounts to a right of first refusal for the debtor in consumer goods that might otherwise be repossessed.

PROBLEMS

10.11 Debtor owns an automobile with a fair market value of $5,000. It is subject to a security interest of $2,000 held by Bank. Debtor will elect her bankruptcy exemptions, and hence have access to the $1,200 exemption of §522(d)(2). May debtor use §722? How? Will the trustee be able to claim any portion of the automobile?

   10.12 Debtor owns a computer with a fair market value of $5,000. It is subject to a security interest of $8,000 held by Bank. The trustee has abandoned the computer pursuant to §554. In order to redeem the computer, how much must Debtor pay? Compare UCC §9-506 with §§506(b); 722.

4. Denial of Discharge; Nondischargeable Debts

Given the importance of discharge in the decision of individuals to use bankruptcy, its denial, in whole or with respect to particular claims, is likely to be a matter of substantial concern to the debtor — a concern that should be addressed by the debtor and his attorney before filing a voluntary petition. (From the perspective of many debtors, using bankruptcy without obtaining a discharge may be a waste of time or worse.)
   Congressional solicitude, measured by the discharge, stops, it is commonly explained, at the "honest but unfortunate debtor" (Local Loan Co. v. Hunt, 292 U.S. 234, 244 (1933)), determined in various ways over the years. Why should this be so? As a matter of history, limiting discharge to the honest (and cooperative) debtor is easy to explain. As we explored in Chapter 1, the Statute of 4 Anne, passed in 1705, offered debtors a discharge as a carrot to gain their cooperation. The death penalty for uncooperative debtors was the stick. But the discharge is now offered for radically different reasons. Isn't it therefore necessary to address limitations on a right of discharge in light of the present justifications for the discharge right itself? Don't we return, then, to the question of what the social policy behind discharge is? Is it to protect *debtors* only? What if it is also to protect (a) those who depend on the debtor or (b) society itself? See Note on Justifying the Nonwaivability of the Right of Discharge, supra page 736.
   The activities listed in §727 — in common with those in bankruptcy statutes of the last 100 years or so — have one attribute in common: They all have to do with what may be considered to be forms of fraud or related egregious misbehavior directed against creditors or their collection efforts. Many forms of behavior that we might consider more egregious do not deny the debtor a discharge. There is, for example, no exception in §727 for individuals who have committed arson or murder. The fact that society wants to deter the types of activities listed in §727 does not itself suggest that the proper way to achieve such deterrence is through denial of discharge. Fines, prison terms, and other such criminal or quasi-criminal sanctions are alternatives (sometimes used in conjunction with denial of discharge). In considering the appropriate remedy for certain behavior, we should not automatically assume that misbehavior towards creditors must have a punishment that is tied to discharge. Because the behavior reached by §727 is directed at creditor collection efforts while the individual debtor is insolvent, however, it represents behavior that is likely to arise in connection with a bankruptcy proceeding. Unlike murder, the occur-

rence of which is unlikely to be connected to the advent of a bankrupt proceeding, these actions may be best deterred through a mechanism that defeats much of the usefulness of doing them in the first place. But is the denial of the "fresh start" too severe a penalty for the offense? To say that the activity should be prevented is quite different from determining that a penalty is either too lenient or too severe.

Section 727(b) is the principal section (apart from §§524 and 525) governing discharge. It provides that, save for the exceptions specified in §523, a discharge under §727 discharges the debtor (if an individual) from all debts that arose before the order for relief under Chapter 7, and from any debt that is determined under §502 as a pre-petition claim. The debts covered by a discharge are unenforceable, whether or not a proof of claim is filed in respect of them or whether or not they are allowed. This represents a substantially broader class of dischargeable debts than under the old Bankruptcy Act, which discharged only provable debts (recall Kuehner v. Irving Trust Co., supra page 160). Note that §727 will apparently discharge contingent or unliquidated claims, estimated under §502(c) "for purposes of allowance under this section." Recall, too, that discharge apparently affects only personal liabilities, not liens securing them (which, however, may be limited in scope by §552).

The present grounds for objection to discharge found in §727 evolved over a long period and have been, in the past, in rather continual flux. Section 14 of the old Bankruptcy Act, the predecessor to §727, was amended many times, writing and rewriting categories of specific conduct that would prevent a discharge. Moreover, while certain other actions will not bar discharge in toto, they will exempt from such discharge certain enumerated debts. §523. A discharge, once entered, is subject to revocation for the reasons and within the limitations of §727(d) and (e).

IN RE REED
700 F.2d 986 (5th Cir. 1983)

Alvin B. Rubin, Circuit Judge.

We hold that a debtor who converts nonexempt assets to an exempt homestead immediately before bankruptcy, with intent to defraud his creditors, must be denied a discharge in bankruptcy because of the provisions of Section 727 of the Bankruptcy Code, 11 U.S.C.A. §727 (West 1979), and, therefore, we affirm the decision of the district court.

I

Hugh D. Reed, as sole proprietor, opened a shop using the trade name, Reed's Men's Wear, in Lubbock, Texas. He financed the venture in part by obtaining from the Texas Bank & Trust Company a $150,000 loan which was guaranteed by the Small Business Administration (SBA). Three months later, the bank gave Reed a $50,000 line of credit, and the SBA agreed that the original loan would be subordinated to the line of credit. The store showed a profit for the first nine months of operation in 1977, but began to lose money in 1978. By February 1979, Reed knew that his business was insolvent. After meeting with the bank, the SBA, and his major trade creditors, he signed an agreement to turn over management of the store to a consulting firm for the year 1979. In turn, Reed's trade creditors agreed to postpone collection efforts and Reed promised to resume payments in January 1980. Despite management by the consultant, the business continued to fail, and on December 15, 1979, Reed and his wife, Sharon Marcus Reed, signed a foreclosure agreement surrendering the store to the bank. Six days later, the Reeds filed voluntary petitions for bankruptcy.

From 1977 to 1979, in addition to operating Reed's Men's Wear, Reed traveled extensively as a sales representative for Scully Leather, Inc. (Scully). In 1977, he worked in Reed's Men's Wear about 75 percent of the time and traveled for Scully about 25 percent of the time. In 1978, he divided his time evenly between the store and sales for Scully. By 1979, he worked in the store only 40 percent of the time, and traveled for Scully 60 percent of the time. On the advice of his accountant, in December 1978 and January 1979 Reed set up Reyata Corporation (Reyata), wholly owned by himself, to receive the sales commissions paid by Scully for his services. Reyata in turn paid some of the commissions to Reed as salary. This arrangement allowed the corporation to retain part of Reed's earnings and reduced the tax paid by Reed on his commissions. In 1979, Scully paid Reyata $15,000 in commissions each month, including an advance commission for December, sent at Reed's request, that would not otherwise have been paid until January 1980. The bankruptcy judge found that Reyata was simply Reed's alter ego.

Reed had catholic interests and much energy. He found time to collect antiques, gold coins, and guns, and to make other investments. In a financial statement provided to the bank and to the SBA on April 1, 1979, Reed valued his gun collection at $20,000 and his antiques collection at $3,000. In the four months prior to bankruptcy, Reed augmented each of his collections. He caused Reyata to borrow $11,000, which he used to purchase more antiques. In three separate transactions during October and November, Reed accumulated, at a cost of $22,115, a collection of Krugerrands and Mexican fifty-peso pieces. One month before filing for bankruptcy, Reed purchased, for $15,000, a one-third interest in a business known as Triple BS Corporation.[1]

Two months before bankruptcy, Reed opened an account at the Bank

---

1. The significance of the initials is not elucidated in the record.

of the West without the knowledge of his creditors. From that time until the store closed in mid-December, he deposited the daily receipts from Reed's Men's Wear in this separate account. From this account, in late November Reed repaid the loan Reyata made to purchase the antiques.

Reed began selling his personal assets in late November. He first sold three items from his antiques collection to an acquaintance, Charles Tharpe, for $3,500. He sold the remainder of his antiques on December 11 to a friend, Steve Gallagher, for $5,000. Whether this represented their fair market value was not established, but the total realized on the antiques was $8,500, while the original value plus the cost of recent purchases was $14,000. On December 10, he sold his gold coins through a broker for $19,500 cash, their approximate market value. The next day, on December 11, Reed sold to Gallagher for $5,000 each both his gun collection and his Triple BS stock. Whether or not Gallagher paid fair market value for the items was not established, but the stock had been purchased only one month earlier for $15,000.

Reed applied all of the proceeds to reduce the mortgages on his family residence, which was exempt from creditor's claims under Texas law, with the objective, the bankruptcy court found, of reducing the value of his nonexempt assets and increasing the value of his homestead exemption prior to bankruptcy. Thus he raised about $35,000, applying about $30,000 to wipe out a second mortgage home improvement loan and applying the balance of approximately $15,000 to reduce the first mortgage on his home to about $28,000.

Reed cavalierly justified his sale of assets for what appeared to be less than their fair market value. This was of no concern to his creditors, he testified, because, if he had received more for the assets, he would have simply applied the additional sum to reduce the mortgage on his homestead. No matter how much he got, there would be nothing for his creditors.

Reed also failed to account for the disposition of $19,586.83 in cash during the year preceding filing. Reed attempted to explain the "unaccounted for" cash by testifying that he habitually carried huge sums of money in cash on his person and frequently made purchases and payments in cash without obtaining receipts. He argued that the amount of "unaccounted for" cash represents only a small percentage of the amount of money which went through his hands in 1979.

The bankruptcy judge found that Reed had effected transfers designed to convert nonexempt property into exempt property less than two weeks before bankruptcy with the intent to hinder, delay, or defraud creditors. 11 U.S.C.A. §727(a)(2) (West 1979). He found that, regardless of the amount of money that might have passed through Reed's accounts, $19,586.83 is a significant sum, and that Reed had failed satisfactorily to explain its loss. This constituted an additional basis for denying discharge. 11 U.S.C.A. §727(a)(5) (West 1979).

The district court affirmed the judgment.

II

The Bankruptcy Code provides that a debtor may be denied discharge if he has transferred property "with intent to hinder, delay, or defraud a creditor," 11 U.S.C.A. §727(a)(2) (West 1979), or has "failed to explain satisfactorily . . . any loss of assets. . . ." 11 U.S.C.A. §727(a)(5) (West 1979). Reed was denied discharge on both bases. Though either would suffice, we review the grounds seriatim.

In considering the effect of Reed's transfers of assets, we distinguish, as did the careful opinion of the bankruptcy court, the debtor's entitlement to the exemption of property from the claims of his creditors and his right to a discharge from his debts. The Bankruptcy Code allows a debtor to retain property exempt either (1) under the provisions of the Bankruptcy Code, if not forbidden by state law, 11 U.S.C.A. §522(b) and (d) (West 1979), or (2) under the provisions of state law and federal law other than the minimum allowances in the Bankruptcy Code, 11 U.S.C.A. §522(b)(2) (West 1979).

Under the Bankruptcy Act of 1898, most courts, applying state exemption laws, had held property that would otherwise have been exempt to be deprived of its immunity if there was evidence other than the simple act of conversion showing that the debtor had acquired it with the intention of defrauding his creditors. . . . If intent to defraud was not proved, however, and it was shown only that granting the exemption would defeat the creditor's claim, the exemption was granted. . . . As stated in 3 Collier on Bankruptcy, ¶522.08[4] (15th ed. 1982): "Under the Act, the mere conversion of nonexempt property into exempt property on the eve of bankruptcy was not of itself such fraud as will [sic] deprive the bankrupt *of his right to exemptions.*" (Emphasis supplied.)

Before the Bankruptcy Code was adopted in 1978, it had been urged that property obtained in such last-minute conversions be ineligible for exemption. . . . The Code, however, adopts the position that the conversion of nonexempt to exempt property, without more, will not deprive the debtor of the exemption to which he would otherwise be entitled. . . . Thus, both the House and Senate Reports state:

> As under current law, the debtor will be permitted to convert nonexempt property into exempt property before filing a bankruptcy petition. The practice *is not* fraudulent as to creditors, and permits the debtor to make full use of the exemptions to which he is entitled under the law.

H.R. Rep. No. 595, 95th Cong., 1st Sess. 361 (1977), reprinted in 1978 U.S. Code Cong. & Ad. News 5963, 6317; S. Rep. No. 989, 95th Cong., 2d Sess. 76, reprinted in 1978 U.S. Code Cong. & Ad. News 5787, 5862 (emphasis supplied). The rationale behind this congressional decision is summed up at 3 Collier, supra, ¶522.08[4]: "The result which would obtain if debtors were not allowed to convert property into allowable exempt property would be extremely harsh, especially in those jurisdictions where the exemption allowance is minimal." Nonetheless, the phrase, "[a]s under current law," qualifies the apparently blanket approval of conversion, since as noted above, courts denied exemptions under the Act if there was extrinsic evidence of actual intent to defraud (and if the state law permitted disallowance of the exemption for fraud).

Reed elected to claim his exemptions under state law. The bankruptcy judge, therefore, referred to Texas law to determine both what property was exempt and whether the exemption was defeated by the eleventh-hour conversion. Texas constitutional and statutory protection of the homestead is absolute, and the bankruptcy judge interpreted Texas law to allow the exemption in full regardless of Reed's intent. . . .

While the Code requires that, when the debtor claims a state-created exemption, the scope of the claim is determined by state law, it sets separate standards for determining whether the debtor shall be denied a discharge. The debtor's entitlement to a discharge must, therefore, be determined by federal, not state, law. In this respect, 11 U.S.C. §727(a)(2) is absolute: the discharge shall be denied a debtor who has transferred property with intent to defraud his creditors. The legislative history of the exemption section, as noted above, does not mean that conversion is never fraudulent as to creditors, but simply that, as under prior law, mere conversion is not to be considered fraudulent unless other evidence proves actual intent to defraud creditors. While pre-bankruptcy conversion of nonexempt into exempt assets is frequently motivated by the intent to put those assets beyond the reach of creditors, which is, after all, the function of an exemption, evidence of actual intent to defraud creditors is required to support a finding sufficient to deny a discharge. For example, evidence that the debtor, on the eve of bankruptcy, borrowed money that was then converted into exempt assets would suffice to support a finding of actual intent to defraud. Only if such a finding is made may a discharge be denied.

The evidence amply supports the bankruptcy court's finding that Reed had an actual intent to defraud. Reed's whole pattern of conduct evinces that intent. Cf. Farmers Co-op. Assn. v. Strunk, 671 F.2d 391, 395 (10th Cir. 1982) ("Fraudulent intent of course may be established by circumstantial evidence, or by inferences drawn from a course of conduct.") His rapid conversion of nonexempt assets to extinguish one home mortgage before bankruptcy, after arranging with his creditors to be free of payment obligations until the following year, speaks for itself as a transfer of property in fraud of creditors. His diversion of the daily receipts of Reed's Men's Wear into an account unknown to his creditors and management consultant and his subsequent use of the receipts to repay a loan that had been a vehicle for this conversion confirm his fraudulent motivation. . . .

. . . The denial of a discharge on this ground alone was appropriate. It would constitute a perversion of the purposes of the Bankruptcy Code to permit a debtor earning $180,000 a year to convert every one of his major nonexempt assets into sheltered property on the eve of bankruptcy with actual intent to defraud his creditors and then emerge washed clean of future obligation by carefully concocted immersion in bankruptcy waters.

Reed asserts that denial of a discharge makes the exemption meaningless. This is but fulmination. Reed may retain his home, mortgages substantially reduced, free of claims by his creditors. In light of the ample evidence, aside from the conversion itself, that Reed had an actual intent to defraud his creditors, he simply is not entitled to a dischage despite the fact that a generous state law may protect his exemption.

The argument that we should reject the other ground for denying discharge gets but the short shrift it deserves. We must affirm the fact findings of the bankruptcy court unless they are clearly erroneous. See Northern Pipeline Construction Co. v. Marathon Pipeline Co., — U.S. at — n.5, 102 S. Ct. at 2863 n. 5, 73 L. Ed. 2d at 605 n.5. The fact findings concerning unaccounted-for cash, which we have already summarized, are amply supported by the record. . . .

III

The district court found that Sharon Marcus Reed benefitted from the "prohibited activities" and possibly had knowledge of them but that she did not participate in them. Accordingly, he granted her discharge. The evidence showed that Sharon Reed made out the daily reports of the sales receipts of Reed's Men's Wear during the time that Reed was surreptitiously diverting those receipts to a bank account unknown to his creditors and management consultant. From this, it would have been possible to infer that Sharon Reed shared her husband's fraudulent intent, but the bankruptcy judge's findings to the contrary are not clearly erroneous. . . . That dictates affirmance of the result.

While the trustee and creditors contend the ruling was based on an incorrect standard, their major attack is on the sufficiency of the evidence to support the conclusion by pointing out all that Mrs. Reed did in the men's wear business and in connection with her husband's activities. The one legal issue raised by the trustee and creditors is whether the intent to defraud requisite under 11 U.S.C. §727 must be shown for each debtor. The bankruptcy court correctly concluded that the Code does not allow attribution of intent from spouse to spouse. . . .

NOTE

See also Mickelson v. Anderson, 31 Bankr. 635 (Bankr. D. Minn. 1982); In re Wallace, CCH Bankr. ¶ 69,237 (Bankr. C.D. Ill. 1983); In re White, 28 Bankr. 240 (Bankr. E.D. Va. 1983).

NOTE ON *REED* AND DENIAL OF DISCHARGE

Whether *Reed* is correct turns, in large part, on whether the question of fraudulent conversion to exempt assets is one that should be determined by state law or by bankruptcy law. The answer to this question requires you to explore the tension between having bankruptcy exemptions and permitting (as we will soon examine systematically) states to "opt out" of that exemption scheme. If the question of exemptions is one that is left to state law, then it may be appropriate for the state law to deem fraudulent efforts to convert assets to exempt assets, if done with an intent to "hinder, delay, or defraud" creditors. If, on the other hand, bankruptcy law has, as an element of its fresh start policy, a notion that individuals should be left with an irreducible minimum of assets, then isn't reliance on state law to determine whether the conversion of assets to an exempt status should deny discharge substantially more dubious? On the other hand, whatever the reasons behind deeming certain assets to be exempt, is it likely those reasons encompass people who deliberately acquire those assets on the eve of bankruptcy? Is that normatively any different than simply declaring that a debtor may keep so many dollars from the clutches of bankruptcy? We discuss exempt property in greater detail in the next chapter.

Consider, in this context, the statement in the House and Senate reports (quoted in *Reed*) to the effect that:

> As under current law, the debtor will be permitted to convert nonexempt property into exempt property before filing a bankruptcy petition. The practice is not fraudulent as to creditors, and permits the debtor to make full use of the exemptions to which he is entitled under the law.

This statement was written *before* the compromise that allowed states to opt out of the bankruptcy exemption system. Is it, therefore, proper to ignore the statement in the House and Senate reports on the ground that it was written with the idea of an irreducible minimum in mind, and the statute as enacted was not? What if *Reed* involved a debtor who converted nonexempt assets to assets that would be exempt under the bankruptcy exemptions of §522(b), but would not have been exempt under state exemption law? (Assume also that the state has not opted out of the set of bankruptcy exemptions.) If the debtor then filed for bankruptcy and selected the set of bankruptcy exemptions, should state law still be resorted to in determining whether discharge should be denied under §727? If not, should the outcome be any different if the debtor elected the set of state exemptions? Is the answer to this question "yes" because state fraudulent conveyance rules are part and parcel of the warp and woof of state exemption law, which the Bankruptcy Code because of the last minute compromise, respects? Or is the answer to the question "no" because what actions should deny a debtor a bankruptcy discharge ultimately must be a federal bankruptcy question? Under *Reed*, similar activity may or may not result in a denial of discharge, depending on which state the debtor resides in. Should the answer to that question vary from state to state? *Mustn't it*, because of the presence of §727 and its requirements? (This tension between what states can do and arguable bankruptcy policy will be seen again in connection with our examination of §522(f) and *McManus*, infra page 874.)

In *Reed*, the court permits the debtor to claim the exemption, but upholds the denial of a discharge. Is this the proper resolution? Under §727? As a normative matter? Put another way, does the punishment in *Reed* fit the crime? What if Reed's only "sin" was the eve of bankruptcy conversion of nonexempt assets into exempt assets? Is it anything more than a fraudulent conveyance? How would a fraudulent conveyance have been treated under §727? Isn't the asset, in the first instance, recovered (unless in the hands of a bona fide purchaser)? Why should *Reed* be any different? Moreover, consider the consequences of the debtor making an intentional fraudulent conveyance. Should that deny the debtor a discharge in bankruptcy entirely? Or only vis-a-vis certain debts or certain creditors? Is it possible to *identify* any such category of debts or creditors? If not, is denial of discharge in toto (as opposed to up to the value of the converted assets) justifiable either as a prophylactic rule *or* as a rule that eliminates troublesome valuation questions? Doesn't the answer to that question turn on how undesirable such conversion is? And doesn't that question inevitably implicate bankruptcy's fresh start policy? Again, how should that policy relate to a variety of state law policies? What guidance does §727 provide? Is that guidance correct?

Consider, in this respect, the following analysis of the issue, Eisenberg, Bankruptcy Law in Perspective, 28 U.C.L.A. L. Rev. 953, 993-995 (1981):

> Creditors who take action on the eve of bankruptcy run a gauntlet of rules that threaten to undo that action. The new act contains important limitations on creditors' ability to insulate themselves by contract from the risk of a debtor's bankruptcy. The preference rules . . . threaten to undo creditor actions that occur while the debtor is in financial difficulty. Yet debtors may plan in contemplation of their own bankruptcy by eve-of-bankruptcy behavior. With startling brevity, the act's legislative history recites, "As under current law, the debtor will be permitted to convert nonexempt property into exempt property before filing a bankruptcy petition."
>
>   . . . There are extreme cases of successful bankruptcy planning by debtors. Debtors have successfully transferred assets from nonexempt to exempt investments weeks or even days before bankruptcy. A debtor may preserve extraordinary amounts . . . through judicious planning. In one case, an individual converted over $50,000 to exempt status prior to bankruptcy. . . . Courts ought to be able to treat more conversions to exempt assets as what they are: efforts to crowd into exempt categories as much value

as possible without regard to what the debtor needs for survival and a fresh start.

Some courts do impose limits on prebankruptcy efforts to convert property to exempt status. But they require a finding of something called actual fraud, which may designate cases in which the proceeds of assets sold on credit are used to purchase exempt property. Actual fraud does not include most simple purchases of exempt assets made in contemplation of bankruptcy.

Accepting that there is a minimal core of assets that debtors should keep notwithstanding bankruptcy, the conversion question in important respects is similar to that addressed by the preference provisions. In each case the law is concerned with preserving a pool of assets for distribution in bankruptcy. In the case of preferences, this is needed to prevent rapid and unjust accumulation of the debtor's assets in one or more creditors on the eve of bankruptcy. In the case of conversion to exempt assets, the problem is to avoid an unfair accumulation in the debtor's hands. Furthermore, in both cases state law blesses dissipation of the debtor's assets.

There are two peculiarities to the new act's unquestioning continuation of the old state-law system. First, there is an inconsistency between bankruptcy law's traditional treatment of preferences, where state law is not followed, and exemptions, where state law is followed. In the case of eve-of-bankruptcy conversions considerations analogous to those underlying the preference provisions suggest that a federal rule is appropriate. Regardless of state law, if the bankruptcy proceeding is going to have any assets to distribute, one needs rules to limit eve-of-bankruptcy dissipation. Preference rules prevent dissipation to creditors. Exemption rules should limit dissipation to the debtor.

Is this convincing? Is the analogy to preference law correct? Is this a case, such as preference law is, where state law should not be followed in bankruptcy? Can one assert that, unlike preference law, exemption law sets forth a presumptive minimum of property required for a "fresh start" that is not to be whittled away by a case-by-case analysis of whether the property is actually needed for a fresh start? Professor Eisenberg's proposal is criticized in Harris, A Reply to Theodore Eisenberg's Bankruptcy Law in Perspective, 30 U.C.L.A. L. Rev. 327 (1982), and defended in Eisenberg, Bankruptcy Law in Perspective: A Rejoinder, 30 U.C.L.A. L. Rev. 617 (1983).

PROBLEMS

10.13 Debtor is a real estate developer. Creditor, a judgment creditor, is seeking to levy on the debtor's property. Debtor owned four lots that were under construction and were under contract to various purchasers. Construction mortgages covered the lots. On April 18, Debtor transferred the four lots to his attorney for one dollar. The deeds were properly recorded. On May 15, the attorney reconveyed the lots to Debtor, who immediately conveyed them to other purchasers in fulfillment of the various purchase contracts. On October 24, Debtor filed for bankruptcy under Chapter 7. Should discharge be denied under §727(a)(2)(A)? See In re Steinberg, 4 Bankr. 593 (Bankr. D. Mass. 1980).

10.14 Consider the facts of *Kindom Uranium Corp.*, supra page 260. If this case arose under the Bankruptcy Code, would Cole be denied a discharge under §727 on the ground that she made a fraudulent conveyance?

10.15 Bartolotta was a refrigerator mechanic who sold Christmas trees in an otherwise empty lot as a parttime business during the Christmas season. Bartolotta's business was cash-and-carry. Bartolotta never maintained any books and records. Bartolotta files for bankruptcy. Creditor, who had sold Bartolotta Christmas trees, objected to Bartolotta's discharge under §727(a)(3). Should Bartolotta be denied a discharge? See Bartolotta v. Lutz, 485 F.2d 227 (5th Cir. 1973); In re Kirst, 37 Bankr. 275 (Bankr. E.D. Wisc. 1983).

10.16 Debtor filed a petition under Chapter 7 on January 1. Debtor has few assets, and a number of debts. Principal among the debts are medical expenses resulting from a serious medical condition. On May 1, before a discharge had been granted, Debtor files a motion to dismiss his petition under §707 on the ground that it had been filed by mistake, the mistake being that Debtor had believed his medical condition had stabilized. It had not, and Debtor had accumulated $3,700 more in medical debts since the filing of the petition. Debtor wishes to have the bankruptcy petition dismissed, so he can refile, and include these new debts in the debts that will be discharged. Should Debtor be permitted to do this? Does §727(a)(8) have anything to say about this? Does §727(a)(10)? See In re Reynolds, 4 Bankr. 703 (Bankr. D. Me. 1980).

The next case explores the relationship between §727 and §523. Given the nature of the penalty imposed by finding an action to be within §727, there may be, not surprisingly, some attempt to fit activity within the less painful alternative of §523. To what extent does that tendency explain *McCloud*?

IN RE McCLOUD
7 Bankr. 819 (Bankr. M.D. Tenn. 1980)

Russell H. HIPPE, Jr., Bankruptcy Judge.

This matter is before the court upon a complaint filed by a secured creditor seeking to deny the debtor's discharge under §727 of the Bankruptcy Reform Act of 1978 or, in the alternative, to except a state-court judgment from the debtor's discharge under §523 of the Act.

On June 6, 1978, the debtor executed a promissory note payable to the plaintiff [hereinafter cited as the Bank] in the principal amount of $2,006. The debtor contemporaneously with the execution of the note granted the Bank a security interst in ten Holstein cows. The terms of the security agreement and of each of the other two security agreements to which reference is made below provided that the collateral was not to be moved from the location described in the agreement without the Bank's prior written consent. The agreement also prohibited the debtor from selling or offering to sell or otherwise transferring the collateral or any interest therein without the Bank's prior written consent. Finally, the agreement provided that such an unauthorized disposition of the Bank's security would constitute an event of default that entitled the Bank to immediate possession of its security.

On August 11, 1978, the debtor executed a note payable to the Bank in the principal amount of $1,246.53. The debtor also granted the Bank a security interest in six additional Holstein cows, which was evidenced by a security agreement that in form was identical to the first.

In November and December of 1978, the debtor sold the livestock in which the Bank held security interests without notifying the Bank and without securing its prior consent.

On January 12, 1979, the debtor obtained an additional loan from the Bank in the principal amount of $1,000. As evidence of the loan, the debtor executed a note payable to the Bank. The debtor also granted the Bank a security interest in nine calves, which was evidenced by a security agreement that in form was identical to the first two.

In February, the debtor sold the nine calves that secured the January loan without notifying the Bank and without obtaining its prior consent.

When the debtor defaulted on the notes, the Bank brought an action against the debtor in General Sessions Court for Sumner County, Tennessee. That court subsequently awarded the Bank a judgment in the principal amount of $4,242.53 plus fifteen percent interest and attorney fees.

The Bank now seeks to deny the debtor's discharge or, in the alternative, to except its judgment from the discharge.

Section 727(a)(4)(A) as a Ground for Relief

The court initially disposes of the Bank's assertion that the debtor's listing of the Bank in his schedules as an unsecured rather than as a secured creditor constituted a false oath warranting a denial of the debtor's discharge under §727(a)(4)(A).

There is some authority for the proposition that the listing of a secured creditor in a bankruptcy petition as an unsecured creditor may be a ground for denying discharge under §14(c)(1) of the Bankruptcy Act of 1898, as amended. . . . It was clear under §14(c)(1), however, that, in order to warrant a denial of discharge, the debtor's false oath must have been made "knowingly and fraudulently." E.g., Willoughby v. Jamison, 103 F.2d 821 (8th Cir. 1939). . . . As articulated by the court in Willoughby v. Jamison, supra.

> The false oath to justify a denial of a discharge must be "knowingly and fraudulently" made, that is, it "must contain all the elements involved in perjury at common law, namely, an intentional untruth in a matter material to an issue which is itself material."

103 F.2d at 823.

Section 727(a)(4)(A) continues the requirement that a false oath warranting a denial of discharge must have been knowingly and fraudulently made. There is no evidence before the court that would warrant a finding that the debtor's scheduling of the Bank as an unsecured rather than as a secured creditor was intentional. The court, therefore, denies the relief sought by the Bank under §727(a)(4)(A).

SECTION 727(a)(2)(A) AS A GROUND FOR RELIEF

Section 727(a)(2)(A) provides for the denial of the debtor's discharge if the debtor, with intent to hinder, delay, or defraud a creditor or an officer of the estate, has transferred property of the debtor's within one year before the date of the filing of the petition.

This court's recent decision in Murfreesboro Production Credit Assn. v. Harris, Adv. Proc. No. 380-0097, 8 B.R. 88 (Bkrtcy. M.D. Tenn. 1980), is dispositive of the Bank's theory that the debtor's sale of its collateral warrants a denial of the debtor's discharge. In *Harris* the court held that a transfer of property that is subject to a security interest and in which the debtor has no equity does not constitute a transfer of the debtor's property with intent to hinder, delay, or defraud a creditor under §727(a)(2)(A). The debtor testified that he had received "about $5,000" from the sale of the cattle, a sum that is only slightly in excess of the principal balance due the Bank. It is apparent, therefore, that the debtor had little, if any, equity in the Bank's collateral and that the debtor's transfer of this property does not constitute a transfer warranting a denial of the debtor's discharge under §727(a)(2)(A).

SECTION 523(a)(4) AS A GROUND FOR RELIEF

Section 523(a)(4) excepts from the discharge any debt for fraud or defalcation while acting in a fiduciary capacity. The Bank's assertion that the debtor's sale of collateral in contravention of the terms of the security agreements violated the Tennessee breach-of-trust statute and thus brings the Bank's debt within the scope of §523(a)(4) is without merit in the light of this court's recent holding in Borg-Warner Acceptance Corp. v. Binkley, BK No. 79-30291 (Bankr. Ct. M.D. Tenn. June 4, 1980), that a violation of Tennessee Code Annotated §39-4237 (1975), which characterizes the wrongful disposition of collateral as a "fraudulent breach of trust," did not constitute a breach of the express or technical trust that was required under §17(a)(4) of the Bankruptcy Act of 1898, as amended.

Section 523(a)(6) as a Ground for Relief

Section 523(a)(6) excepts from the discharge any debt for willful and malicious injury by the debtor to the property of another.[1] The phrase "willful and malicious injury" as used in §523(a)(6) is intended to include a willful and malicious conversion of the property of another. . . .

It was well established under §17(a)(2) of the prior Act that an improper disposition of collateral was a ground for excepting a debt from the discharge if such disposition was willful and malicious. . . . This court held under §17(a)(2), however, that, under the controlling Tennessee decision relative to the conversion of collateral, in order for a secured creditor to maintain a cause of action for conversion under the present status of the law in this state, it must show that the disposition of the collateral was unauthorized and that the creditor had a right to immediate possession at the time of the unauthorized disposition. . . . This court also cited with approval the holding . . . that a debt will be discharged when a secured creditor fails to take reasonable steps to protect its security interest in cattle after learning that the bankrupt is likely to sell the livestock. . . .

The facts in this proceeding differ from those that were before the court in [other cases]. In each of these prior cases, the court found that there had been no showing of a conversion because the disposition had been authorized and because the creditor had no right to immediate possession at the time of the disposition. The court's conclusions in these cases resulted from proof demonstrating that disposition of the collateral and unrestricted use of the proceeds therefrom had been permitted by the creditors either under the terms of their security agreements or as a result of a course of dealings between the parties. Neither factual showing is

---

1. The debtor is his post-trial brief asserts that res judicata prohibits the relitigation in this court of the nature of his debt to the Bank on the ground that the Bank's state-court judgment was based upon an action ex contractu in which the Bank did not raise as an issue the debtor's alleged willful and malicious conversion of its security. Such an assertion is ill founded in the light of the United States Supreme Court's decision in Brown v. Felsen, 442 U.S. 127, 99 S. Ct. 2205, 60 L. Ed. 2d 767 (1979), that bankruptcy courts may consider evidence extrinsic to the judgment and record in a prior state-court action when determining whether a debt represented by the judgment is dischargeable under §17 of the Bankruptcy Act of 1898, as amended.

present in this case. Each of the three security agreements herein at issue specifically forbade the removal of the collateral from the locations specified therein without the Bank's prior written consent and prohibited the debtor from selling or offering to sell or otherwise transferring the collateral or any interest therein without the Bank's prior written consent. In addition, each of the security agreements defined default to include any unauthorized disposition of the collateral and thus granted to the Bank a right to immediate possession upon the debtor's unauthorized disposition. Moreover, the debtor was unable to prove any prior course of dealings with the Bank that would have permitted his disposition of the livestock without the Bank's consent and the unrestricted use of the proceeds therefrom. . . .

Having found that the debtor's disposition of the Bank's collateral was unauthorized, that the Bank was entitled to immediate possession at the time of the disposition, and that the Bank was unaware of any likelihood that its collateral would be sold and was unaware that the debtor had in fact sold its security without complying with the terms of the security agreement, the court concludes that the debtor's disposition of the livestock constituted a conversion of the property of another for the purpose of §523(a)(6).

A conversion within the scope of §523(a)(6) must be shown to have been both willful and malicious. The term "willful" means deliberate or intentional. . . . The proof in this proceeding clearly establishes that the debtor's disposition of the Bank's collateral was a willful act. The debtor testified that he had read the terms of the security agreements and that he fully had understood that he was obligated not to dispose of the Bank's security without prior written consent. The debtor's deliberate and intentional sale of the Bank's security thus plainly falls within the scope of the willful act required by §523(a)(6).

In order to come within the exception provided by §523(a)(6), a creditor must show that the debtor's conduct was malicious as well as willful. . . . In order to apply the proper definition of the term "malicious," the court initially must determine whether the Congress, by adopting §523(a)(6), intended to effect a change in the definition of the same term that had been applicable under the prior Act.

In Tinker v. Colwell, 193 U.S. 473, 24 S. Ct. 505, 48 L. Ed. 754 (1904), the United States Supreme Court concluded that a state-court judgment against the bankrupt for damages arising from a criminal conversation with the plaintiff's wife had been based upon a willful and malicious injury to the plaintiff's property rights and thus was not dischargeable in bankruptcy under §17(a)(2) of the Bankruptcy Act of 1898. At issue in *Tinker* was not whether the bankrupt's conduct had been willful; the Court stated that the act had been intentional and voluntary and thus clearly had been willful for the purpose of §17(a)(2). 193 U.S. at 485, 24 S. Ct. at 508. At issue in *Tinker* was whether the bankrupt's conduct had been malicious for the purpose of §17(a)(2). The Court initially examined the common-law definition of the term "malice." The English and American courts, the Court found, had not defined malice in terms of hatred or ill will toward an injured party but had implied malice from a showing of an unlawful, wrongful, and tortious act, done intentionally, and without justification or excuse. Id. at 485-487, 24 S. Ct. at 508-509. The Court also considered the construction of the term under statutes prohibiting the malicious destruction of property that required proof of special malice toward the injured party for conviction. Id. at 487, 24 S. Ct. at 509. Reasoning that the purpose of the Bankruptcy Act was to provide relief for the honest debtor, the Court rejected the latter construction and concluded that the term "malicious" as used in §17(a)(2) was to be construed using the common-law definition of malice. In order to bring a judgment like the one before it within the scope of §17(a)(2), the Court declared, it was not necessary that the original cause of action have been based upon special malice. Neither a malignant spirit nor a "specific intention to hurt a particular person" was an essential element of the term "malicious" for the purpose of §17(a)(2):

> [W]e think a wilful disregard of what one knows to be his duty, an act which is against good morals, and wrongful in and of itself, and which necessarily causes injury and is done intentionally, may be said to be done wilfully and maliciously, so as to come within the exception.

Id. at 487, 24 S. Ct. at 509. The Court attempted to qualify its holding, however, by further declaring:

> It is not necessary in the construction we give to the language of the exception in the statute to hold that every wilful act which is wrong implies malice. One who negligently drives through a crowded thoroughfare and negligently runs over an individual would not, as we suppose, be within the exception. True, he drives negligently, and that is a wrongful act, but he does not intentionally drive over the individual. If he intentionally did drive over him, it would certainly be malicious. It might be conceded that the language of the exception could be so construed as to make the exception refer only to those injuries to person or property which were accompanied by particular malice, or, in other words, a malevolent purpose towards the injured person, and where the action could only be maintained upon proof of the existence of such malice. But we do not think the fair meaning of the statute would thereby be carried out. The judgment here mentioned comes, as we think, within the language of the statute, reasonably construed. The injury for which it was recovered is one of the grossest which can be inflicted upon the husband, and the person who perpetrates it knows it is an offense of the most aggravated character; that it is a wrong for which no adequate compensation can be made, and hence personal and particular malice towards the husband as an individual need not be shown, for the law implies that there must be malice in the very act itself, and we think Congress did not intend to permit such an injury to be released by a discharge in bankruptcy.
> An action to redress a wrong of this character should not be taken out of

the exception on any narrow and technical construction of the language of such exception.

Id. at 489-490, 24 S. Ct. at 509-510.

Although the Court in *Tinker* addressed only the definition of the term "malicious" as used in §17(a)(2) and was clear in requiring that a malicious act under §17(a)(2) also must have been an intentional act, some courts subsequently interpreted *Tinker* to imply that a willful act need not necessarily have been an intentional act. Such courts, in cases involving drunk driving or auto injuries but not drunk drivers, construed *Tinker* to permit conduct in "reckless disregard" or with "reckless indifference" to the rights of another and even "gross negligence" to come within the definition of a willful act under §17(a)(2) and under the parallel exception provided by §17(a)(8). . . .

The legislative history of §523(a)(6) indicates that, under this exception,

> "willful" means deliberate or intentional. To the extent that Tinker v. Colwell, 193 U.S. 473 [24 S. Ct. 505, 48 L. Ed. 754 (1904)], held that a looser standard is intended, and to the extent that other cases have relied on *Tinker* to apply a "reckless disregard" standard, they are overruled.

S. Rep. No.95-989, 95th Cong., 2d Sess. 79 (1978); H.R. Rep. No.95-595, 95th Cong., 1st Sess. 365 (1977), U.S. Code Cong. & Admin. News 1978, p. 6320. It is clear, therefore, that the Congress intended to overrule those decisions that had construed *Tinker* to permit conduct in "reckless disregard" or with "reckless indifference" to the rights of another and even "gross negligence" to come within the definition of a willful act under the prior Act. Nothing in the legislative history of §523(a)(6), however, suggests that the Congress intended to overrule the *Tinker* Court's interpretation of the term "malicious" as it appeared in the prior statute, and this court declines to imply such an intention. It is this court's opinion, therefore, that the proper definition of the term "malicious" for the purpose of §523(a)(6) is the common-law definition that was approved and adopted by the Court in *Tinker*.

If an act of conversion is done deliberately and intentionally in knowing disregard of the rights of another, it falls within the statutory exclusion even though there may be an absence of special malice. . . .

Although the cattle sold by the debtor continued to be impressed with the Bank's security interest, the debtor intentionally concealed his disposition of the cattle from the Bank and knowingly disregarded the fact that, because the livestock were not identified in any way, the sale effectively deprived the Bank of its security by precluding the creditor's ability to pursue it in the hands of an unknown purchaser.

It is the court's opinion, therefore, that, because the debtor's conversion of the Bank's security was both willful and malicious in nature, the debt herein at issue comes within the exception provided by §523(a)(6) and accordingly is not dischargeable. . . .

NOTES

1. United Bank of Southgate v. Nelson, 35 Bankr. 766 (N.D. Ill. 1983), discussed the divergence of interpretive views regarding §523(a)(6) as follows:

> One line of cases . . . read the legislative record to entirely obviate *Tinker.* Consequently, these courts interpret the requirements of §523(a)(6) to be: (1) *willful,* meaning intentional or deliberate (i.e., not reckless); and (2) *malicious,* to require an "intent to do harm," (i.e., something more than implied malice). . . .
>
> A second . . . line of cases, places much less emphasis on the legislative record in interpreting §523(a)(6) and continues to allow malice to be established through implied or constructive malice. These courts interpret the exceptions to require: (1) *willful* to mean deliberate or intentional; and (2) *malicious* to be implied or constructive malice similar to the holding in *Tinker.*

2. Do you agree that the transfer of fully secured property is not a "transfer of the debtor's property"? Is this conclusion consistent with the cases discussing whether foreclosure sales are fraudulent conveyances, supra page 275? With *Whiting Pools,* supra page 436? Would §727(a)(2)(A) have been applicable if debtor had sold the cattle for $6,000? $10,000? Note the consequence of using §727(a)(2)(A) instead of §523(a)(6).

3. The scope of the "false oath" exception, now in §727(a)(4)(A), is considered in detail in In re Robinson, 506 F.2d 1184 (2d Cir. 1974), which concludes that "materiality does not require a showing that the creditors were prejudiced by the false statement. . . ." See also In re Mascolo, 505 F.2d 274 (1st Cir. 1974) (dealing with revocation of discharge due to a false oath).

NOTE ON "LOADING UP"

Section §523(a)(2)(C) was added in 1984. The legislative report accompanying an earlier version of this subsection (that applied not to debts for luxury goods, but to debts that were not incurred for expenses that were reasonably necessary for the support of the debtor or the debtor's dependents) explained the purpose of this modification in the following manner:

> Excessive debts incurred within a short period prior to the filing of the petition present a special problem: that of "loading up" in contemplation of

bankruptcy. A debtor planning to file a petition with the bankruptcy court has a strong economic incentive to incur dischargeable debts for either consumable goods or exempt property. In many instances, the debtor will go on a credit buying spree in contemplation of bankruptcy at a time when the debtor is, in fact, insolvent. Not only does this result in direct losses for the creditors that are the victims of the spree, but it also creates a higher absolute level of debt so that all creditors receive less in liquidation.

During this period of insolvency preceding the filing of the petition, creditors would not extend credit if they knew the true facts. Nevertheless, it is often difficult to prove that such debts are fraudulent.

Is this proposal sensible? Does it properly belong under §523 instead of under §727? Consider several possible objections to its location under §523. First, the harm is not just imposed on the creditor who lends the money on the eve of bankruptcy; as the report notes, the consequence of this activity might be the creation of "a higher absolute level of debt so that all creditors receive less in liquidation." (Whether it does result in that creation depends on what the debtor does with the money that is borrowed.) In those cases, the solution represented by §523(a)(2)(C) is to allow the "new" creditor to participate in the liquidation of the assets (thus lowering the assets received by the remaining creditors) *and* to have a second bite at the apple, because only its debt is not discharged. Isn't this the wrong solution, at least from the perspective of the other creditors? Second, is it possible to argue that the people in the best position to monitor a debtor who is about to go into bankruptcy are the potential extenders of credit, and that this solution simply reduces the care with which they will monitor the debtor?

On the other hand, if you feel that the solution represented by §523(a)(2)(C) is proper, and is properly located in §523, should it be broadened to include (for example) the purchase of exempt assets within a fixed period before bankruptcy by, for example, holding that the assets purchased within that time are not exempt? Would that be a preferable way of dealing with the *Reed* problem?

The next case, in addition to showing the popularity of the exception used in *McCloud*, also tries to give substance to §523(a)(2)—perhaps the prototype of the exceptions specified in §523.

IN RE SIMPSON
29 Bankr. 202 (Bankr. N.D. Iowa 1983)

William W. THINNES, Bankruptcy Judge. . . .

The Creditor, Webster City Production Credit Association (hereinafter, PCA), is seeking to have the debt owed to it by the debtor, Leslie G.

Simpson (hereinafter, Simpson), declared nondischargeable. In support of its dischargeability complaint, the PCA alleges that the debtor, Simpson, violated three different subdivisions of 11 U.S.C. §523.

The Plaintiff's complaint places three issues before the Court: (1) did the debtor's promise to deliver certificate of title to the PCA constitute a violation of 11 U.S.C. §523(a)(2)(A)? (2) Did the debtor's false financial statement constitute a violation of 11 U.S.C. §523(a)(2)(B)? (3) Did the debtor's sale of certain encumbered property constitute a violation of 11 U.S.C. §523(a)(6)? . . .

Section 523(a)(2) divides all statements into two mutually exclusive categories. 124 Cong. Rec. H11,096 (1978); 124 Cong. Rec. S17,412 (1978). Statements concerning the debtor's financial condition are governed by subsection (B). Representations not concerning the debtor's financial condition must be considered under subsection (A). . . .

Section 523(a)(6) declares nondischargeable any debt "for willful and malicious injury by the debtor to another entity or the property of another entity." The phrase "willful and malicious injury" includes willful and malicious *conversions*. . . .

For the reasons analyzed in more detail below, the Court concludes that all debts owed by Defendant/Simpson to Plaintiff/PCA are dischargeable except for $1,200.00. That amount represents the value of the grain sold by Defendant in November, 1980. The Court believes that the Plaintiff has produced clear and convincing evidence to show that the Defendant converted the grain willfully and with the malicious intent of injuring the Plaintiff. As regards the other acts of conversion, the Plaintiff did not produce clear or convincing evidence of the Defendant's intent or of the extent of the harm, if any, suffered by the Plaintiff. Therefore, those acts cannot support a claim under §523(a)(6).

Plaintiff's claim based on false representations cannot stand because the alleged false representations are mere promises. Plaintiff's claim based on false financial statements also cannot stand. Many financial status documents were submitted by the Defendant, but only the July Balance Sheet and Loan Application were given before the Plaintiff, by its own admissions, was aware of possible errors in the Defendant's reporting of assets and his failure to pay over proceeds. Because of that awareness, it would have been unreasonable for the Plaintiff to have relied upon documents submitted by the Defendant after that time. Therefore, only the July Balance Sheet will be considered for analysis under §523(a)(2)(B). None of the other documents add any relevant facts to the issues involved. In addition, the July balance sheet is the strongest evidence for Plaintiff's position. If it cannot support Plaintiff's claim, none of the others would be able to do so. Further, the Defendant has cast considerable doubt upon the claim that the Defendant intended to deceive the Plaintiff by use of false financial statements.

The Plaintiff had the burden of proving by clear and convincing evidence each element of its claim under §523(a)(2)(B). That standard is somewhat greater than a mere preponderance of the evidence, but the testimony and other evidence present leaves the credibility question in equilibrium. The Court has no reason to place greater weight with the Plaintiff than with the Defendant. Because there is no basis for believing one party more than another, the Plaintiff may not prevail.

I. FAILURE TO DELIVER TRUCK TITLE

The Plaintiff's first claim for non-dischargeability is that Simpson violated 11 U.S.C. §523(a)(2)(A). Plaintiff alleges that certain monies were advanced to Defendant partly upon the Defendant's oral promise to secure clear title to his 1979 Ford ¾-ton truck and deliver that title to Plaintiff as partial security for Plaintiff's loan. Defendant contends the promise was not made.

It is undisputed that the promise, if made, was not performed. A failure to perform some promised action, however, is not a violation of 11 U.S.C. §523(a)(2)(A). There is a three-pronged test for violation of §523(a)(2)(A): (1) Does the alleged violation constitute a false representation? (2) Does the alleged violation constitute false pretenses? or (3) Does the alleged violation constitute actual fraud?

To constitute a false representation[1] under §523(a)(2)(A), a statement must falsely purport to depict current or past facts. . . . Defendant did not state that he had clear title to the truck. In fact, Plaintiff's own allegations show that Defendant merely promised to obtain clear title. Any utterance that promises future action certainly does not purport to depict current or past facts. A similar analysis applies to whether the Defendant's statement was a false pretense.[2] Therefore, the Defendant's statement, if made at all, cannot be a false representation or false pretense for purposes of §523(a)(2)(A).

To prevent discharge for fraud under §523(a)(2)(A), Plaintiff must prove actual fraud and not merely fraud implied in law. . . . The elements of actual fraud, also known as common law deceit, have been described by numerous courts. Those elements are:

1.   That the debtor made the representations;
2.   That at the time made, the debtor knew the representations to be false;
3.   That the representations were made with the intention and purpose of deceiving the creditor;
4.   That the creditor relied on such representations; and

---

1. This Court has exclusive jurisdiction to determine the meaning of "false representations" without referring to state law. Matter of Pappas, 661 F.2d 82, 86 (7th Cir. 1981).

2. False pretenses are generally defined as ". . . a false representation of a material *present* or *past fact*. . . ." (emphasis added) Black's Law Dictionary 541 (rev. 5th ed. 1979).

5.   That the creditor sustained the alleged loss and damage as the proximate result of the representations having been made. . . .

The plaintiff bears the burden of proving each element by clear and convincing evidence. . . .

Actual fraud encompasses any "deceit, artifice, trick or design . . . used to cheat another — something said, done or omitted with the design of perpetrating . . . a cheat or deception." Black's Law Dictionary 595 (rev. 5th ed. 1979). Defendant's promise, technically, could be fraud as defined above, but the legislative history of the Bankruptcy Act[3] and case law indicate that proof of actual fraud requires a showing of moral turpitude or intentional wrong. . . . It is also a well-established principle that statements purporting to depict a future factual situation cannot be the basis for fraud; similarly, "mere promises, though false and intended to deceive" cannot support a finding of actual fraud. In re Boese, 8 B.R. 660, 662 (Bkrtcy. D.S.D. 1981). . . .

If the foregoing analysis had determined that Defendant's statement were false pretenses, false statements, or actual fraud, the Plaintiff still could not prevail because Plaintiff has failed to show by clear and convincing evidence that, by uttering the alleged false statements, the Defendant obtained any property, money, or services. Plaintiff's own witness testified that the loan possibly would have been made even if Plaintiff had known that Defendant would not deliver title to the truck as security. Although the creditor need not prove it relied solely on a particular misrepresentation, the creditor must show that the alleged misrepresentation would have made a difference. . . . Plaintiff failed to make that showing. Consequently, Plaintiff's objection to discharge cannot be sustained under §523(a)(2)(A).

II.   False Financial Statement

The Plaintiff's next objection to dischargeability is that Defendant violated the provisions of 11 U.S.C. §523(a)(2)(B). Plaintiff alleges that a balance sheet purporting to show Defendant's financial condition as of July 3, 1979, was submitted to the Plaintiff by the Defendant; that the balance sheet was materially false; that the Defendant knew it was false; that the Plaintiff relied upon that statement in granting Defendant a loan; and that the Defendant submitted the false balance sheet with the intention of deceiving the Plaintiff. Plaintiff specifically alleges that the Defendant listed 60 sows as assets, only 20 were owned, and 40 were leased. Plaintiff also alleges that certain machinery and equipment was listed as

---

3. Section 523(a)(2) of the Bankruptcy Code superseded §17a(2) of the Bankruptcy Act, but case law applying §17a(2) may be used in interpreting the scope of §523(a)(2). . . .

owned when, in fact, it was owned by another person. Plaintiff alleges that Defendant's assets were overstated by at least $30,000. Defendant doesn't deny that the balance sheet was incorrect in that regard, but he claims that Plaintiff's agent knew the true factual situation when that agent prepared the balance sheet for Defendant's signature.

Section 523(a)(2)(B) first requires that the statement be in writing and that it be a statement of the Debtor's financial condition. Next, it must be shown: (1) that the statement was materially false, (2) that the creditor reasonably relied upon the false statement, and (3) that the debtor caused the statement "to be made or published with intent to deceive." The concept of publication is the same as in the tort area and generally means to make known to another. . . . The first requirement is clearly met in this case, inasmuch as a balance sheet is a statement of financial position at any given time, and it was in writing and was signed by the Defendant. What must now be determined is whether the other three requirements of §523(a)(2)(B) were also present.

1. MATERIALITY

There appears to be no question that a $30,000 overstatement of assets is material in this case because that amount represents approximately 20 percent of the total loan. There should be a point at which a misstated sum would be considered de minimis, but relatively small amounts have been held to be material. . . . In the case of the July 3, 1979, balance sheet, Plaintiff has clearly shown the materiality of the false statements.

2. RELIANCE

While having shown the material falsity of the balance sheet, Plaintiff now must show that it relied on the false statements in the balance sheet and that such reliance was reasonable. . . .

An inference of reliance is created when a financial statement is executed by a debtor in support of a loan application. . . . That inference may be rebutted, however, by the defendant's testimony, and plaintiff then has the burden of going forward with other evidence and bears the risk of nonpersuasion. . . . Since the policy of the Bankruptcy Code is to give debtors a fresh start, the various provisions will be construed strictly against the creditor and liberally in favor of the debtor. . . .

The testimony of Plaintiff's agent regarding preparation of the balance sheet and his reliance on information supplied by the Defendant was controverted by the Defendant. In addition, Plaintiff's own evidence showed that the financial statement of a loan applicant is only one of five factors used in making the lending decision. Consequently, Plaintiff's evidence did not clearly establish that the balance sheet signed by the

Defendant was a significant factor in its decision to grant the loan. It is possible, for example, that the other four factors were such that the financial statement became irrelevant to the lending decision. Plaintiff's evidence simply did not address this point.

The reasonableness of Plaintiff's reliance is also questionable. Although the dollar amount of the false statement is not very significant for purposes of determining materiality, it can be important for deciding if reliance was reasonable. One court has held that a $9,000 overstatement of net worth was not significant for a bank's reliance when the loan amount was $400,000. In re Schade, 10 B.R. 115, 117 (Bkrtcy. N.D. Ill. 1981). In another case, reliance was found to be reasonable when a large portion of total debts was not disclosed and the bank would not have made the loan if all had been listed. In re LaRocca, 12 B.R. 56, 59 (Bkrtcy. W.D. La. 1981). If the Plaintiff's figures are accepted at face value, Defendant/Simpson, overstated his net worth by approximately $30,000 in obtaining a loan for approximately $145,000. If considered alone, that amount would tend to support a finding of reasonable reliance. The Defendant, however, has claimed that he told Plaintiff's agent, at the time the balance sheet was prepared, that he did not own the assets which Plaintiff now claims were falsely listed by Defendant. If that claim is true, then the PCA's reliance was unreasonable because it knew that the financial statement was not accurate. Such a "red flag" would make further investigation the only prudent course. . . . Plaintiff's agent, however, denied that Defendant ever informed him of the true ownership situation.

If the standard of proof in these matters was a preponderance of the evidence, this Court would have to decide whose testimony was more credible. The Plaintiff's burden, however, is to prove each element by clear and convincing evidence. . . . Given that standard, the Plaintiff has failed to prove reasonable reliance. The Plaintiff did make a prima facie case for reliance by showing that the financial statement is one of five factors normally considered in the decision whether to grant a loan. The Defendant, however, rebutted any presumption of reliance that may have arisen from Plaintiff's evidence by alleging that Plaintiff's agent was aware of the errors in the balance sheet. . . . When the Plaintiff's agent denied any such awareness, the Court was faced with the task of weighing the credibility of the two witnesses. The evidence is in equilibrium with the Court having no basis for placing greater weight on the testimony of either party.

An additional factor weighing against the reasonableness of Plaintiff's reliance is that the Plaintiff made disbursements and additional loans after it became obvious that Defendant's original balance sheet had been in error, and after the Defendant had proved to be less than totally co-operative in his dealings with Plaintiff. This factor alone is certainly not determinative of the issue of reasonable reliance, but it is a strong factor to be considered.

Because the Court finds that the parties have presented equally weighted evidence for and against the reasonableness of Plaintiff's reliance, it cannot be said that Plaintiff has proven reliance by clear and convincing evidence.

3. INTENT TO DECEIVE

As with the issue of reliance, intent to deceive may be presumed from the use of a false statement to procure credit. . . . Here again, however, the Defendant/Debtor may rebut the presumption by denying the alleged intent. The Plaintiff then has the burden of going forward and ultimately bears the risk of non-persuasion. . . .

Because direct proof of intent (i.e., debtor's state of mind) is nearly impossible to obtain, the creditor may present evidence of the surrounding circumstances from which intent may be inferred. . . . The debtor cannot overcome such an inference with an unsupported assertion of honest intent. . . .

In the present case, the Plaintiff did present sufficient evidence of the surrounding circumstances to raise an inference of intent to deceive. The Defendant, however, made certain allegations that, if true, would vitiate the inference.

The Plaintiff's evidence was that Defendant failed to honor his agreement with the Plaintiff, that he continuously failed to apply the proceeds of the sale of crops and livestock to the loan, that he continued to overstate his assets, and that he incurred other debts that hampered his ability to repay the Plaintiff. The Defendant contends that he made the Plaintiff aware of the true status of his assets, thus making the Plaintiff's reliance on the balance sheet unreasonable and the Plaintiff's assertion of intent to deceive spurious. In addition, the Defendant alleges that the Plaintiff did not initially require that he refrain from selling secured property or that he pay over the proceeds to the Plaintiff. Defendant also alleges that it was necessary for him to retain those proceeds because the Plaintiff was not providing the promised funds for him to meet his expenses.

Whether intent to deceive was present is mostly a factual issue. The court has no basis to place more credibility with the Plaintiff's evidence than with the Defendant's. The evidence presented by each party, though perhaps understandably self-serving, was of equal credibility on this issue. The Plaintiff had the burden of proving intent by clear and convincing evidence, and did not meet that standard. Therefore, the requisite intent has not been established.

The Plaintiff has neither established that its reliance was reasonable, nor shown that Defendant intended to deceive Plaintiff when applying for the loan. Since each element of §523(a)(2)(B) must be proven before a debt will be excepted from discharge, the Plaintiff's dischargeability complaint cannot be sustained under §523(a)(2)(B).

Plaintiff's final objection to dischargeability is based on 11 U.S.C. §523(a)(6). That section exempts from discharge any debt "for willful and malicious injury by the debtor to another entity or to the property of another entity."

Hatred, spite or ill-will is not required to support a finding of willful and malicious, Tinker v. Colwell, 193 U.S. 473, 24 S. Ct. 505, 48 L. Ed. 754 (1904), but the legislative history of the Bankruptcy Code makes it clear that "willful" means deliberate or intentional, and that reckless disregard cannot be the standard. . . . To be willful and malicious, an act must be wrongful, done intentionally, necessarily produce harm, and without just cause or excuse. . . .

The basis for Plaintiff's Complaint under §523(a)(6) is that the Defendant sold hogs and corn on which the Plaintiff had a security interest without paying-over the proceeds to the Plaintiff. That action, Plaintiff alleged, was a conversion of Plaintiff's property and the Defendant effected the conversion with the intent to harm the Plaintiff.

In general, a mere technical conversion is not enough to establish a willful and malicious injury. This liberal rule regarding conversion is deemed necessary to effect the intention of Congress: to afford the honest debtor a fresh start. . . . Standing alone, the failure to pay-over money received from the sale of secured property is not sufficient to show willful and malicious injury. . . . Therefore, to be a violation of §523(a)(6), a conversion must be willful and malicious.

The Plaintiff points to two types of conversion by the Defendant, sale of grain and sale of hogs, and alleges that those acts were willful and malicious. The Defendant denies that he had any intent to harm the Plaintiff. In addition, the Defendant alleges that the Plaintiff was aware of the sales, and that he was forced to sell the property to meet living expenses. The sale of encumbered property to generate living expenses does not, in itself, establish the intent to harm necessary for a finding of willful and malicious injury. In re Hodges, 4 B.R. 513, (Bkrtcy. W.D. Va.1980). In Hodges, the debtor sold a stereo, which was subject to the creditor's security interest, to make house payments and purchase food. The Court held that the conversion, although willful, was not malicious because the debtor intended to repay the creditor if possible. Most of Simpson's acts of conversion are similar to that of Hodges. His uncontroverted testimony was that he used the money from the sale of hogs to pay living expenses. Further, he continued to make payments on the loan balance. The PCA did introduce some evidence that would tend to rebut Simpson's claims, but neither party has clearly established its claims. Congress not only made the requirements of §523(a)(6) conjunctive, so that both willful and malicious must be found, but also expressly overruled the Tinker v. Colwell standard: that "willful and malicious" can mean "reckless disregard." See H.R. Rep. No. 595, supra. Given such clear Congressional intent to limit the applicability of §523(a)(6), the Court must have clear proof before finding the debt nondischargeable.

In one respect, however, the Plaintiff has provided clear and convincing evidence that the [Defendant] willfully and maliciously converted grain on which Plaintiff had a security interest. In November of 1980, the Defendant sold some grain for $1,200. This sale apparently took place less than 24 hours after Defendant had been informed that one of Plaintiff's officers had been appointed receiver for Defendant's property, and that all harvested grain should be turned over to the receiver. The Defendant offered as excuse for the sale only that he had used the money for expenses.

Clearly the Defendant knew he had no right to sell this grain. Also the Defendant must have known that the use of the $1,200 in proceeds would deprive the Plaintiff of those funds. It appears that the Defendant knew he was about to lose control of his assets, and he took the opportunity to salvage some of those assets for his own use. This sale differs from others on which the Plaintiff relies in at least two important aspects. It has been clearly established that it occurred over the express warning of the Plaintiff not to dispose of assets, and the amount of the sale is not in dispute. More importantly, the Defendant surely knew at this point that he would no longer be paying Plaintiff for the outstanding loan. Therefore, Plaintiff has shown by clear and convincing evidence that this act of conversion gave rise to a debt of $1,200 that should not be dischargeable.

For all other alleged acts of conversion, however, the Plaintiff has not produced direct evidence to show willful and malicious intent. Further, the Plaintiff has neither provided any clear evidence regarding the circumstances surrounding the alleged conversions nor any clear evidence regarding the value of property that was converted.

The court has serious doubts that the alleged acts of conversion rise to the level of willful and malicious injury.

The Plaintiff has failed to establish its claims under §523(a)(2) and all but one claim under §523(a)(6). Therefore, Plaintiff's complaint should be dismissed and Defendant's debt declared dischargeable except for the $1,200.00 debt for which Plaintiff did establish its claim under §523(a)(6).

The following problems explore a number of the issues that arise in connection with the various provisions of §523(a).

PROBLEMS

10.17 Debtor owned and operated a fast food store with self-service gasoline pumps. Creditor, an oil company, provided Debtor with gasoline and motor fuel products. The contract between Debtor and Creditor provided that title to the gasoline and motor fuel products remained with Creditor until Debtor sold it to retail customers. The contract also provided that Debtor will "hold in trust for the use and benefit of [Creditor] all money, checks, and other things of value received by him from the sale of [Creditor's] gasoline and/or motor fuel products," and that Debtor deposit all such checks and money in a bank account designated by Creditor. Debtor files for bankruptcy under Chapter 7. Creditor moves for a holding that its debt is nondischargeable under §523(a)(4). Evaluate that contention. See In re Adkisson, 26 Bankr. 879 (Bankr. E.D. Tenn. 1983).

10.18 Angelle was a building contractor. He had entered into contracts with five customers to build homes for each of them. Each of the five advanced funds to Angelle to be used for the construction of his particular home. Angelle deposited all of this money in his own bank account, and used substantial sums of it for general business debts. Angelle files for bankruptcy without having completed the houses. Under state law, it is a criminal offense for a contractor to use funds advanced by a contracting party for any purpose other than material and labor for the advancing party's project. The customers move for a holding that their debts are nondischargeable under §523(a)(4). Evaluate that contention. See In re Angelle, 610 F.2d 1335 (5th Cir. 1980). Would a statute such as that existing in Selby v. Ford Motor Co., discussed in the Note on Statutory Trusts, supra page 203, have made any difference?

10.19 Petrini had a bank card issued by Bank. She used the card, on average, twice a month, for credit purchases. On September 21, Bank notified Petrini that her charge account had reached its credit limit. In November and December, 37 purchases were made on the card, totalling $750; all the purchases were under the $50 amount at which stores are required to obtain phone authorization. Can Bank avoid discharge of this debt under §523(a)(2)(A)? What would it have to show? Would it help Bank's case if it could show that Petrini had consulted a bankruptcy attorney in October? See In re Petrini, 23 Bankr. 981 (Bankr. E.D. Pa. 1982); In re Turner, 23 Bankr. 681 (Bankr. D. Mass. 1982).

10.20 Debtor buys a sofa bed from Seller, and pays for it with a check. The check is returned for insufficient funds. Is Seller's debt nondischargeable under §523(a)(2)(A)? Would it matter if the state had a statute making an "NSF" check prima facie evidence of an intent to defraud? See In re Anderson, 10 Bankr. 296 (Bankr. W.D. Wisc. 1981).

10.21 Debtor maliciously backs his van into a bar. In so doing, Debtor causes $10,000 worth of damage to the bar, and injures two patrons, who incur medical bills of $8,000 and $15,000. Debtor is indicted by Arizona on three criminal counts, and plea bargains to one offense. Among the court approved terms and conditions of probation, Debtor agreed to make restitution in the amount of $5,000 (total) to the three people. After making one payment, Debtor files a petition in bankruptcy listing the unliquidated tort obligations to the three people as debts, as well as listing the "Clerk of the Superior Court" for restitution in the criminal case in the amount of $5,000. Are the debts to the individuals dischargeable? Is the restitution requirement dischargeable? See §§101(4), (9), (11); compare In re Brown, 39 Bankr. 820 (Bankr. M.D. Tenn. 1984) with In re Magnifico, 21 Bankr. 800 (Bankr. D. Ariz. 1982); In re Button, 8 Bankr. 692 (Bankr. W.D.N.Y. 1981); cf. *Kovacs*, supra page 744.

10.22 Debtor left work at 5:00. He went to his favorite bar and drank five martinis. At 6:00 he began his drive home. He ran over Pedestrian on his way. Pedestrian spent six weeks in the hospital. Debtor was charged with drunk driving, and he pleaded guilty. Shortly thereafter Debtor filed a bankruptcy petition. Can Pedestrian assert a claim against Debtor in bankruptcy? Is Debtor's obligation to Pedestrian discharged? Would it make any difference if Pedestrian had filed a lawsuit against Debtor, but had not reduced it to judgment? See §523(a)(9).

10.23 Debtor spent an evening on the town, where Debtor proceeded to get quite drunk. Debtor then got in his car, and proceeded to drive into Plaintiff's car (causing little damage). Following an argument with Plaintiff, Debtor stepped on his accelerator. Noting he was about to hit a crowd of people, Debtor swerved, and his car hit Plaintiff's a second time, causing $1,500 in damage. Is that debt dischargeable in Debtor's subsequent bankruptcy? See §523(a)(6), (9); In re Cloutier, CCH Bankr. ¶69,389 (Bankr. D. Me. 1983); In re Wooten, 30 Bankr. 357 (Bankr. N.D. Ala. 1983).

10.24 Debtor, in 1977, engaged in coal mining without obtaining a required permit from the state. This mining activity, which was not carried on in conformity with the requirements of the state Mineral Surface Mining Law, caused environmental damage and was conducted in a manner that made reclamation highly difficult. The state, after a trial, ordered Debtor to reclaim the land and to pay a civil penalty of $60,000. In 1981, without having done either, Debtor filed a petition in bankruptcy. Is the $60,000 award dischargeable? See §523(a)(7); In re Daugherty, 25 Bankr. 158 (Bankr. E.D. Tenn. 1982). What about the order to reclaim the land? Recall *Kovacs*, supra page 744.

10.25 Debtor had borrowed $1,000 from Bank. Rather than repay the loan when due, Debtor obtained from Bank a consolidation loan in the amount of $2,000, with $1,000 of the new loan being applied to repay the old loans. In obtaining the consolidation loan, and at the request of Bank, Debtor prepared a financial statement on which he indicated a positive net worth by omitting a $7,000 debt to another financial institution. Is the debt to Bank dischargeable? If so, to what extent? See §523(a)(2); In re Carter, 11 Bankr. 992 (Bankr. M.D. Tenn. 1981).

10.26 Debtor had borrowed $1,000 from Bank. Before the $1,000 was due, Debtor wanted to borrow another $1,000 from Bank. Bank agreed to loan the new money in a consolidation loan of $2,000, with

$1,000 of the new loan being applied to repay the old, and not yet due, loan. Everything else is the same as Problem 10.25. Is the outcome necessarily the same? Why or why not?

10.27 In a state court action against the debtor and a guarantor, the guarantor had alleged that the debtor induced him to sign the guarantee "by misrepresentations and non-disclosures of material facts." The action against the debtor and the guarantor was settled by a stipulation that led to the entry of a judgment. May the bankruptcy court grant the debtor a discharge on this debt? See Brown v. Felsen, 442 U.S. 127 (1979) (issue of res judicata; concludes yes; explicitly does not reach collateral estoppel effect of a prior state judgment).

10.28 Husband and Wife, before their marriage, entered into an antenuptial agreement providing for "a decent support [for Wife] during [Husband's] natural life." Nothing in the agreement spoke of divorce. In 1978, they were divorced, and the divorce court interpreted the "decent support" language to require Husband to pay Wife $300 a month for the remainder of his or her life. Husband subsequently filed a petition in bankruptcy. Is the support decree dischargeable? See §523(a)(5); In re Jackson, 27 Bankr. 892 (Bankr. W.D. Ken. 1983).

10.29 Debtor was adjudged to be the father of an illegitimate son. In the paternity suit, the court ordered Debtor to pay $85 a month for the support of his son. Debtor subsequently filed a petition in bankruptcy. Is the support order dischargeable? See §523(a)(5); In re Fenstermacher, CCH Bankr. ¶69,366 (Bankr. D. Neb. 1983).

5.   *Proposals to Limit the Scope of Discharge*

Congress has been considering various bills to change current law in certain respects, particularly with respect to individuals. We have seen already a number of these changes. Perhaps the most sweeping of the proposed changes are those relating to the present law concerning access to discharge. The following excerpt is from S. Rep. No. 97-446, which accompanied S.2000, the proposed "Bankruptcy Improvements Act of 1982." The proposal contained in the following excerpt did not survive in its proposed form in the 1984 Amendments, which provided only an amendment to §707 that gave a bankruptcy judge discretion to deny discharges to consumer debtors when it would be a "substantial abuse" of the bankruptcy process. Nevertheless, this proposal is an example of perhaps the most dramatic proposals for change in the current system. Undoubtedly, as the process unfolds, further proposals will emerge in the future. Still, the following warrants study, as it has a substantially different vision of the role of bankruptcy in the case of debtors that are individuals than does the current system.

The methods of gathering data and the resulting empirical study on which this Senate Report relies in large part, are attacked in Sullivan, Warren and Westbrook, Limiting Access to Bankruptcy Discharge: An Analysis of the Creditors' Data, 1983 Wisc. L. Rev. 1091.

S. REP. NO. 97-446
2-3, 6-7, 10-11, 14, 19-23 (1982)

[T]he changes wrought by the 1978 law in certain areas have disrupted the delicate balance of equity between debtors and creditors, particularly with respect to consumer credit transactions. It is the committee's view that these imbalances are already having serious economic and social repercussions that call for remedial legislation.

One event of great concern since passage of Public Law 95-598 has been the dramatic, unparalleled, and constant increase in the number of consumer bankruptcy cases filed each year, and the substantial pressure on the consumer credit industry which has resulted. Data from the Administrative Office of the U.S. Courts reveals [the results in Table 1].

There is no doubt that part of the 103-percent increase in nonbusiness

TABLE 1
Individual Bankruptcies Filed[1] (excluding business filings)
Fiscal Years 1966-81[2]

Year	Number of estates	Percent change (rounded)
1966 (to June 30)	175,924	—
1967	191,729	+9
1968	181,266	−5
1969	169,500	−7
1970	178,202	+5
1971	182,249	+2
1972	164,737	−10
1973	155,707	−6
1974	168,767	+8
1975	224,354	+28
1976	211,348	−6
1977	182,210	−14
1978	172,423	−6
1979	196,976	+12
1980	314,856	+60
1981 (to June 30)	452,145	+43

[1] Statistics reflect total number of individuals seeking relief under the bankruptcy laws from collection of personal debts.
[2] July 1 to June 30.
Source: Administrative Office, U.S. Courts.

cases since the end of fiscal year 1979 results from factors other than the Bankruptcy Code. . . .

These factors, however, simply do not explain the unprecedented increase in bankruptcy cases. Instead, it is apparent that provisions of the code have played a substantial role in stimulating the number of bankruptcy filings. . . .

The ever-increasing number of bankruptcies, and the resultant financial losses, constitutes a general burden on the economy of billions of dollars annually. In the short term, these costs are shifted from debtor to lender (and stockholders and owners of the institutions providing credit). In the long run, however, creditors will not continue to bear the losses; instead, the realities of the marketplace will force them to seek greater protection by increasing the cost of obtaining credit, requiring additional collateral or cosignors, and/or reducing their financial risks by eliminating some transactions completely. . . . As a consequence of such creditor responses, credit will become more difficult to obtain, and the general cost of doing business will escalate. Such a result is directly at odds with congressional efforts to make credit more widely available — for example, by statutes such as the Equal Credit Opportunity Act, and the Fair Credit Reporting Act.

The overall social and economic cost of such trends is that the people most in need of credit may be driven to illegal lenders, and those individuals who pay their debts end up subsidizing those who do not to a greater extent than would be the case under normal circumstances. This result is not fair and not acceptable.

The above facts suggest an unprecedented number of consumer bankruptcy filings and a concomitantly high level of bankruptcy losses. These trends would not warrant any change in the bankruptcy laws if the evidence showed that the bulk of persons filing bankruptcy simply had no choice — that they were financially "driven to the wall." The purpose of bankruptcy relief is to enable the honest but unfortunate debtor to obtain relief from burdensome debt. Excessive debt is a serious social problem which may result in a number of interrelated personal, economic, and family difficulties, and can cause the debtor to withdraw from the productive segment of the economy; thus, it is in the public interest to discharge persons who have incurred unmanageable financial burdens.

At the same time, it is essential to public acceptance of the Bankruptcy Reform Act that the law be seen to fairly balance the legitimate interests of all parties to bankruptcy proceedings, so as to insure that the structure of the law itself does not encourage the filing of petitions which are not justified by economic necessity. . . .

Extensive testimony was offered at committee hearings held on October 29, 1981, concerning the question of whether or not the future earnings capabilities of individual debtors should be taken into account in determining eligibility for chapter 7 relief. In general, bankruptcy practitioners, representatives of the judiciary, and representatives of the credit industry agreed that a percentage of individuals filing in chapter 7 had a substantial repayment capability when anticipated future earnings were taken into account in evaluating the total financial position of the debtor. There was sharp disagreement, of course, on the size of that group. . . .

In examining the financial status of persons filing under chapter 7, it is obvious that most debtors have little prospect of paying any reasonable portion of their debts out of future income. The debtor's continuing obligation to provide support for himself and his family frequently exhausts the debtor's available income, and the debtor will often not have any substantial discretionary income left after satisfying these basic living expenses; or, the debtor may have suffered such serious financial reverses from illness, income reductions, or family difficulties, that any possibility of repayment is ephemeral. No purpose is served by continuing to burden such debtors with legal obligations which they simply cannot satisfy. At the other extreme, however, lie a substantial percentage of debtors who are not financially incapacitated at the time of filing bankruptcy, and for whom a discharge in bankruptcy constitutes a "head start" rather than a "fresh start" when their expectation of substantial future earnings is taken into account. . . .

Who are the chapter 7 debtors? Professor Johnson testified that the Credit Research Center study revealed that 72 percent of all debtors surveyed were employed full time, and almost all expected to have the same, or higher income 6 months after the interviews (which were conducted immediately following the first meeting of creditors). Moreover, the mean annual pretax income of the persons who could repay 100 percent, or between 75 and 100 percent of their debts, was $17,058 and $15,335, respectively. In short, most of these persons are not living at or near the poverty level. . . .

The Brimmer survey further demonstrated that almost 18 percent of the bankrupts had annual family income above $20,000; 13 percent of the respondents held assets valued at over $20,000; and 23 percent had debt in excess of $20,000. These statistics, coupled with the response that "using too much credit" and "overspending" were the two reasons most cited for filing bankruptcy (ahead of "loss of job," "marital difficulties," "medical expenses," and "business failures"), imply that the debtor's difficulties are quite often of his or her own making.

As reflected by the Brimmer survey, attitudes of many debtors further indicate a certain irresponsibility and nonchalance toward the entire concept of bankruptcy. When asked what social impact bankruptcy had on debtors and their families, an amazingly high 65 percent responded that there was none. Moreover, 12 percent of the respondents believed that bankruptcy had no financial effect on them or their families. . . .

The present Bankruptcy Code looks only to the debtor's ability to pay debts out of present assets, and requires the debtor to surrender his nonexempt assets as a condition of bankruptcy relief. In contrast, consumer credit is not extended against the liquidation value of present assets, but rather, on the assumption that the debts will be paid out of future income. As presently structured, then, the Bankruptcy Code is at odds with the modern trends in the consumer finance industry.

Judge Conrad Cyr, speaking of the need to clarify the standards for confirming chapter 13 plans, has given the most eloquent statement of this inconsistency:

> Consumer credit is seldom extended in reliance upon the debtor's present net worth, this is, the present value of unencumbered assets, but on basis of future income. [The Code permits the] debtor, unilaterally, on a demand and without demonstrated need, to alter or nullify the entire credit transaction, notwithstanding the fact that the ability of the debtor to pay has not deteriorated and may even have improved.
>
> A legal procedure at such cross purposes with the economy it regulates runs the risk of falling into disuse due to its own irrelevance, or, more importantly, threatens actual deflection of powerful economic forces at work in the consumer credit marketplace. The devastating social and economic impact of a return to pre-World War II net worth consumer credit extension policies needs no elaboration. It would seem a sound policy to conform the insolvency system to the economic system, especially since the reality is that consumer credit represents a primary driving force in American society.
>
> Additionally, there is little, if any, quarrel with the view that the law should encourage debtors voluntarily to repay their just obligations to the extent reasonably able to do so. The ethical premise upon which this near-universal view is based is the core of our consumer credit system.

In consideration of this evidence, the committee has concluded that the present bankruptcy laws, by failing to take future earnings capabilities into account in determining eligibility for chapter 7, have contributed to abuse of the bankruptcy system by individuals who are not actually in need of straight liquidation relief.

Chapter 11
PROPERTY OF THE ESTATE, EXEMPTIONS, AND THE FRESH START

An individual debtor, after discharge in bankruptcy, is left with assets in addition to his ability to earn in the future. These are the assets that are "exempt" from the claims of creditors. Unlike discharge policy, the subject of exemptions is not unique to bankruptcy law. Historically, exemptions have been the subject of nonbankruptcy law (state and federal), the provisions of which were applicable regardless of whether a bankruptcy proceeding was started. Bankruptcy always has recognized nonbankruptcy exemptions. Moreover, the influence of bankruptcy's "fresh start" policy has led to a set of independent "bankruptcy" exemptions being written into the Bankruptcy Code.

The scope of the "fresh start" in bankruptcy requires us to return to questions involving property of the estate that we first encountered in Chapter 4. We know that future wages are not included within the scope of §541, but what about other kinds of rights, such as retirement benefits that may seem similar in some respects (they may depend upon the debtor's continued existence), but are like ordinary assets in other respects (the debtor acquired them by virtue of past labor)? One of the questions we should ask is whether the right of creditors to reach such property under nonbankruptcy law is a necessary condition to their ability to reach it in bankruptcy. If it is, then it may be possible to avoid difficult questions about the policies underlying the fresh start. It may be sufficient to note that unless some feature of a collective proceeding calls for it, creditors should have no greater substantive rights in bankruptcy than outside. These questions are the focus of the first half of this chapter.

As we emphasized in the last chapter, the contours of the fresh start policy are not clear-cut. We have grown used to equating a fresh start with a right to keep future earnings (and inheritances and gifts) free of liabilities that arose out of a debtor's past. But the distinction between present and future assets is not inevitable. As with any other asset, an individual's future earnings can be given a present value. It by no means follows that an individual needs to keep all future earnings in order to be given a fresh start or that future earnings alone ensure a fresh start. A blacksmith without tools may be less able to start over than a blacksmith who kept his tools, but had to give creditors 10 percent of his future earnings. The debate is usually cast in terms of whether a particular scheme provides a "fresh start" or a "head start," but, without a baseline, these characterizations do not take us very far. Moreover, existing law is an amalgam of legislative compromises and out-dated state legislation.

The component of the fresh start that involves assets other than future income is largely a feature of nonbankruptcy law. State law, and various provisions in federal law, have generally allowed individuals to keep certain property from the clutches of their nonconsensual creditors. That is to say, under so-called exemption laws, certain property of a debtor cannot be reached by a creditor with an execution lien. See, e.g., N.Y. C.P.L.R. §5205. It is important, however, not to overstate the status of exemptions. State law generally allows exempt property to be alienated consensually, including through the granting of security interests. See State v. Avco Financial Service of New York, 50 N.Y.2d 383, 429 N.Y.S.2d 181, 406 N.E.2d 1075 (1980).

For this reason, *most* forms of property that are exempt under state law are exempt only from involuntary creditor attachment. Here, as always, however, one must examine the particular exemption scheme. This is particularly true with respect to nonbankruptcy federal exemptions, as federal law often does not permit consensual transfers of property it deems exempt. See, e.g., 42 U.S.C. §407 (social security benefits). Also, nonbankruptcy law uses different labels to describe somewhat similar attributes. Some property is explicitly called exempt, as in N.Y. C.P.L.R. §5205. Other property, that is not labeled exempt, is nonetheless not subject to creditor process, because it cannot be assigned or transferred, either (depending on the statutory scheme) at all, or involuntarily, see N.Y. Gen. Obligations Law §13-101 (assignment or transfer of a claim for personal injury prohibited); N.Y. C.P.L.R. §5201(b). This is true of some forms of retirement funds, by state or federal statute, as we will see in this chapter. A recurrent question in this chapter is how to relate these various kinds of property to the scheme enacted by the Bankruptcy Code.

A.   INDIVIDUAL BANKRUPTCIES AND PROPERTY OF THE ESTATE

In light of the policies behind §541 and the notion of the fresh start, consider the following case.

IN RE GOFF
706 F.2d 574 (5th Cir. 1983)

Jerre S. WILLIAMS, Circuit Judge.

This appeal is from a final order of the Bankruptcy Court for the Western District of Texas. It presents a new facet of the question whether, and under what circumstances, a bankrupt's pension trust may be exempt from the "property of the estate" subject to the reach of the trustee in bankruptcy on behalf of the bankrupt's creditors. Debtors, Elbert Wayne Goff and Gloria Jane Schadoer Goff, seek refuge for their self-employed retirement (Keogh) plans[2] under Section 541(c)(2) of the new Bankruptcy Code,[3] which exempts property subject to restrictions on alienation which are enforceable "under applicable nonbankruptcy law." The Goffs argue that this reference to "applicable nonbankruptcy law" was intended to reach broadly by encompassing restrictions on transfer recognized in other federal statutory law as well as traditional state trust law. Their argument presents a question of first impression to this Court. The contention is that Section 541(c)(2) exempts all pension trusts which are qualified under the Employee Retirement Income Security Act of 1974 (ERISA),[4] because of ERISA's restrictions on assignment and alienation of qualified trusts. 26 U.S.C. §401(a)(13); 29 U.S.C. §1056(d)(1). For the reasons set out below, we conclude that Congress did not intend Section 541(c)(2) to have the extensive reach urged by appellant-debtors and that ERISA's anti-alienation provisions do not operate by their own force to shelter pension funds in bankruptcy.

Debtors, husband and wife, filed a voluntary joint petition in bankruptcy, under Chapter 7 of the Code, on March 20, 1980. Pursuant to Section 522(b)(2)(A), 11 U.S.C. §522(b)(2)(A), they elected to avail themselves of the state rather than the federal (11 U.S.C. §522(d)) bankruptcy exemptions, presumably because of the high equity value of their homestead which could be retained under Texas law but not the federal law. . . .

The subjects of this appeal are the Goffs' self-employed retirement trusts (Keogh Plan), administered by City National Bank pursuant to an ERISA-qualified pension plan. At the time of the proceedings below, the Keogh trusts were valued at over $90,000, including a $2,878 contribution made by the Goffs only three days prior to declaration of bankruptcy.

---

2. These plans are established pursuant to the Keogh-Smathers Act, Pub.L. No. 87-792, 76 Stat. 809 (1962) (codified in scattered sections of the I.R.C.).

3. 11 U.S.C. §541(c)(2) provides:

(2) A restriction on the transfer of a beneficial interest of the debtor in a trust that is enforceable under applicable nonbankruptcy law is enforceable in a case under this title.

4. Pub. L. No. 93-406, 88 Stat. 898 (codified in 29 U.S.C. §§1001-1144, and in scattered sections of the I.R.C.).

The trust agreement provided:

> Section XIII — Miscellaneous
> Neither the assets nor the benefits provided hereunder shall be subject to alienation, anticipation, assignment, garnishment, attachment, execution or levy of any kind, and any attempt to cause such benefits to be so subjected shall not be recognized, except to such extent as may be required by law.

No withdrawals were ever made although the trust agreement arguably granted Dr. Goff the right to withdraw funds prematurely, i.e., prior to either retirement, sale or termination of his business, or death, subject only to the ten percent tax penalty exacted by the Internal Revenue Code, 26 U.S.C. §72(m)(5). . . .

. . . Our examination of the Bankruptcy Code's provisions and of discernible congressional intent reveals that applicable nonbankruptcy law was intended as a narrow reference to state "spendthrift trust" law and not as a broad reference to all other law, both federal and state, including ERISA.

I

A.   "PROPERTY OF THE ESTATE"

The Bankruptcy Code was intended to create a more uniform and comprehensive scope to "property of the estate" which is subject to the reach of debtors' creditors than had previously existed under the old Bankruptcy Act. Under Section 70(a) of the earlier Act,[9] the inclusion of an asset within the estate varied in accordance with (1) an individual examination of the legal nature of the asset (2) in light of the purposes of the Bankruptcy Act. This two part test reflected the dual and often conflicting policies woven into the Act. These policies were to secure for the benefit of creditors everything of value the bankrupt might possess in alienable or leviable form, but to permit a bankrupt to accumulate new wealth after the date of his petition and to allow him an unencumbered fresh start. Relying upon these competing considerations, the Supreme Court developed a rule that where property "is sufficiently rooted in pre-bankruptcy past and so little entangled with the bankrupts' ability to make an unencumbered

---

9. Section 70(a)(5) of the Bankruptcy Act formerly provided that

(a) The trustee of the estate of a Bankrupt . . . shall . . . be vested by operation of law with the title of the bankrupt as of the date of the filing of the petition [to] . . . (5) property, including rights of action, which prior to the filing of the petition he could by any means have transferred or which might have been levied upon and sold under judicial process against him, or otherwise seized, impounded or sequestered. . . .

fresh start . . . it should be regarded as 'property' [of the estate]." Segal
v. Rochelle, 382 U.S. 375, 380, 86 S. Ct. 511, 515, 15 L. Ed. 2d 428
(1966). . . .

The enactment of the Bankruptcy Code undertook to obviate this
analytical conundrum. Under Section 541 of the Code, all property in
which a debtor has a "legal or equitable interest" at the time of bankruptcy
comes into the estate, 11 U.S.C. §541(a)(1). This is so "notwithstanding
any provision [except as recognized in subsection (2)] that restricts or
conditions transfer of such interest by the debtor." Id. §541(c)(1)(A). The
sweeping scope of this automatic inclusion was intended to remedy much
of the old Act's perceived deficiencies: "[The Act was] a complicated
melange of references to State law, and [did] little to further the bankruptcy policy of distribution of the debtor's property to his creditors in
satisfaction of his debts." H.R. Rep. No. 95-595, 95th Cong., 2d Sess. 175
(1977), reprinted in 1978 U.S. Code Cong. & Ad. News 5963, 6136. See S.
Rep. No. 95-989, 95th Cong., 2d Sess. 82, reprinted in 1978 U.S. Code
Cong. & Ad. News 5787, 5868.[10]

B. EXEMPTION AND EXCLUSIONS

Of relevance to the question posed herein, two sections of the Code
— Sections 522 and 541(c)(2) — permit a debtor to retain certain assets
which would otherwise remain subject to the reach of his creditors. The
property exempted pursuant to Section 522 initially enters the estate, and
is subsequently excluded pursuant to the section's provisions. By contrast,
Section 541(c)(2) property never enters the estate.

1. Section 522: Exemptions

Section 522(b) permits a bankrupt a choice between a "federal" or
"state" exemption system. The debtor may elect to exempt either as the
"federal" exemption the property set out in subsection (d) of Section 522
of the Code, or as the "state" exemptions the property specified as exempted under the law of his domicile, plus property exempted by "Federal
law, other than subsection (d)." The election choice of federal versus state

---

10. The Senate Report, in explanation of the broadened scope of §541 of the Code,
over §70 of the Act, explained that the subsequently enacted Code provision "has the effect
of overruling Lockwood v. Exchange Bank, 190 U.S. 294, 23 S. Ct. 751, 47 L. Ed. 1061
(1903), because it includes as property of the estate all property of the debtor, even that
needed for a fresh start. After the property comes into the estate, then the debtor is permitted
to exempt it. . . ." S. Rep. No. 95-989, 95th Cong., 2d Sess. 82, reprinted in 1978 U.S. Code
Cong. & Ad. News 5787, 5868 (footnote omitted). The Report also concludes that the
provision overrules Lines v. Frederick, 400 U.S. 18, 91 S. Ct. 113, 27 L. Ed. 2d 124 (1970).
Id. . . .

While the existence of a "legal or equitable interest" may turn upon state nonbankruptcy law, once it is determined that such an interest exists, it automatically becomes
property of the estate under §541 of the Code.

exemptions is the debtor's to make.[13] The choice, obviously, will hinge upon the debtor's individual assessment of which exemption system would permit him to retain a larger share of his assets. This decision, in turn, will often depend upon the type of property held by the debtor, as state exemptions may vary in kind as well as degree from the federal bankruptcy exemptions.

In the immediate case, debtors selected the state exemption option, which does not provide in terms at least a partial exemption for Keogh plans as does the federal exemption. Under Section 522(d)(10)(E), 11 U.S.C. §522(d)(10)(E), a debtor who elects the federal exemption may exempt his "right to receive a payment under a . . . pension . . . plan . . . to the extent reasonably necessary for the support of the debtor and any dependent of the debtor," unless the plan demonstrates three disqualifying characteristics.[14] The Goffs' plans did not contain the disqualifying characteristics and would have been covered by Section 522(d)(10)(E) to the extent "reasonably necessary" for the Goffs' support.

2.   Section 541(c)(2): Exclusion

The second relevant code provision, Section 541(c)(2), is the focus of the immediate dispute. The claim of the Goffs is raised solely under this provision. Section 541(c)(1)(A) provides, with one caveat, that "any provision" "that restricts or conditions transfer" of property by the debtor is ineffective in bankruptcy to keep the property from becoming part of the estate. 11 U.S.C. §541(c)(1)(A). The caveat situation, in which a restriction will keep property free from the estate, is set out in subsection (2):

(2) A restriction on the transfer of a beneficial interest of the debtor in a trust that is enforceable *under applicable nonbankruptcy law* is enforceable in a case under this title.

13. Two caveats to this general proposition should be noted. First, a state may prohibit a federal §522(d) election for its domiciliaries, leaving its debtors with only the state exemption option. 11 U.S.C. §522(b)(1). . . . Texas, the state of debtors' domicile, has not enacted such legislation. . . . Second, the Bankruptcy Code envisions the possibility that a bankrupt, having made an improvident election, may petition to obtain relief, or have his election choice changed for him by the courts on their own motion, in the interest of justice. . . .

14. Section 522(d)(10)(E) provides that a debtor may exempt (emphasis added):

(E) *a payment under*, a stock bonus, *pension*, profitsharing, annuity, or similar *plan* or contract on account of illness, disability, death, age, or length of service, *to the extent reasonably necessary for the support of the debtor and any dependent of the debtor, unless* —
(i) such plan or contract was established by or under the auspices of an insider that employed the debtor at the time the debtor's rights under such plan or contract arose;
(ii) such payment is on account of age or length of service; *and*
(iii) such plan or contract does not qualify under section 401(a), 403(a), 403(b), 408, or 409 of the Internal Revenue Code of 1954 (26 U.S.C. 401(a), 403(a), 403(b), 408, or 409).

Since a plan must exhibit all three of the above traits to be ineligible for §522(d)(10)(E) exemption, the exemption provision has a broad reach. Provided that the plan does not fall within both subsections (i) and (ii), the plan would be subject to exemption whether or not it was (iii) an ERISA and Internal Revenue Code "qualified" plan. . . .

11 U.S.C. §541(c)(2) (emphasis added). The Goffs claim that their ERISA-qualified Keogh plans are excluded from the property of the estate by operation of this provision. The Goffs argue that the restrictions against assignment or alienation in their plans, included pursuant to ERISA, 26 U.S.C. §401(a)(13)[17] and 29 U.S.C. §1056(d)(1),[18] are "enforceable under applicable nonbankruptcy law," as that latter term was intended. We find, however, that Congress did not evidence an intent, by reference to "applicable nonbankruptcy law" to include an ERISA plan exemption. Rather, we find that Congress intended to exclude only trust funds in the nature of "spendthrift trusts" from the property of the estate.

In general terms, a spendthrift trust is a trust created to provide a fund for the maintenance of a beneficiary, with only a certain portion of the total amount to be distributed at any one time. The settlor places "spendthrift" restrictions on the trust, which operate in most states to place the fund beyond the reach of the beneficiary's creditors, as well as to secure the fund against the beneficiary's own improvidence. Although a given state's nonbankruptcy law of spendthrift trusts might afford protection to a particular pension trust, it is clear in the immediate case that appellant's self-settled trust did not constitute a spendthrift trust entitled to exclusion under relevant state law.

Our conclusion is reached through a three step analysis. First, we examine the explicitly narrow legislative intent behind the facially broad reference in Section 541(c)(2) to "applicable nonbankruptcy law." Second, we consider the overall congressional scheme embodied in the Bankruptcy Code, particularly the exemption system election provision, Section 522, which directly addresses the degree to which pensions may therein be exempted and also explicitly references "Federal law" and ERISA. Third, we assess the relationship and effect upon ERISA of the intent of the Bankruptcy Code. The indicia of legislative intent, along with existing case law, lead to the inexorable conclusion that Section 541(c)(2)'s reference to "applicable nonbankruptcy law" was an acknowledgement of traditional state spendthrift trust law, and not of ERISA.

II

A. "APPLICABLE NONBANKRUPTCY LAW": STATUTORY INTENT

The legislative history of Section 541(c)(2) indicates that Congress had something very specific in mind with its facially broad reference to "applicable nonbankruptcy law" as the benchmark for assessing the en-

17. 26 U.S.C. §401(a)(13) requires, in relevant part, that in order to be tax-qualified, a pension trust must "provide[ ] that benefits provided under the plan may not be assigned or alienated."

18. 29 U.S.C. §1056(d)(1) provides: "Each pension plan shall provide that benefits provided under the plan may not be assigned or alienated."

forceability of trust restraints on alienation in bankruptcy. In its section-by-section analysis, the House Report accompanying their bill, H.R. 8200, explained:

> Subsection (c) [of Section 541] invalidates restrictions on the transfer of property of the debtor, in order that all of the interests of the debtor in property will become property of the estate. . . . *Paragraph (2) of subsection (c), however, preserves restrictions on transfer of a spendthrift trust to the extent that the restriction is enforceable under applicable nonbankruptcy law.*

H.R. Rep. No. 95-595, 95th Cong., 2d Sess. 369 (1977), reprinted in 1978 U.S. Code Cong. & Ad. News 5963, 6325 (emphasis added). Even more significant, in providing an overview comparison of the proposed Code to the old Act, the House Report said:

> The bill also continues over the exclusion from property of the estate of the debtor's interest in a *spendthrift trust to the extent the trust is protected from creditors under applicable State law. The bankruptcy of the beneficiary should not be permitted to defeat the legitimate expectations of the settlor of the trust.*

Id. at 176, 1978 U.S. Code Cong. & Ad. News at 6136 (emphasis added).

The Senate Report, accompanying S. 2266, similarly explained that Section 541(c)(2) "preserves restrictions on a transfer of a *spendthrift trust* . . . enforceable [under] nonbankruptcy law." S. Rep. No. 95-989, 95th Cong., 2d Sess. 83, reprinted in 1978 U.S. Code Cong. & Ad. News 5787, 5869 (emphasis added). The Senate version of the Code, however, was dissimilar to that proposed by the House, in that it limited the extent to which Section 541(c)(2) property would be insulated from the estate, to that "reasonably necessary for the support of a debtor and his dependents." Id. This even narrower Senate version was rejected in the final enacted version, which followed the position taken in the House bill.

In summary, from the legislative history of Section 541(c)(2), it is clear that Congress intended by its reference to "applicable nonbankruptcy law" to exempt from the estate only those "spendthrift trusts" traditionally beyond the reach of creditors under state law. This provision carries over from the old Act the previously recognized exemption for spendthrift trusts. . . .

B.   THE OVERALL SCHEME AND THE FEDERAL-STATE EXEMPTION ELECTION

The specific legislative intent behind Section 541(c)(2) is reinforced by a consideration of the overall congressional scheme embodied in the Bankruptcy Code. Appellant debtors argue for an expansive definition of "nonbankruptcy law" in Section 541(c)(2) to include federal laws which prohibit alienation. We find that the other provisions of the Code negate this intent because the Code explicitly makes reference to "federal law" or pension laws, including ERISA, when federal as opposed to state law is the subject of the reference.

The most telling example lies with Section 522 and its legislative history. As summarized above, Section 522 provides debtors a choice between the "state" or the "federal" exemption systems. If the "state" system is selected, a debtor may also exempt property pursuant to "Federal law other than subsection (d)." 11 U.S.C. §522(b)(2)(A). The Goffs, who made the state election, did not attempt to claim exemption of their ERISA-qualified Keogh plans under this other "Federal law" exemption. The applicability of this exemption, therefore, is not directly involved in this appeal. Yet we do find a consideration of this provision helpful in understanding this case because we find that Congress did not intend to do ambiguously in Section 541 that which it clearly did not do directly in Section 522, although Section 522 explicitly addresses the extent to which other "Federal law" and retirement benefit exemptions would be recognized.

The House and Senate Reports, in explanation of the other "Federal law" provision which was subsequently enacted in Code §522(b)(2)(A), provide a list of illustrative property which might be exempted under federal laws other than the Bankruptcy Code:

Foreign Service Retirement and Disability payments, 22 U.S.C. 1104;
Social security payments, 42 U.S.C. 407;
Injury or death compensation payments from war risk hazards, 42 U.S.C. 1717;
Wages of fishermen, seamen, and apprentices, 46 U.S.C. 601;
Civil service retirement benefits, 5 U.S.C. 729, 2265;
Longshoremen's and Harbor Workers' Compensation Act death and disability benefits, 33 U.S.C. 916;
Railroad Retirement Act annuities and pensions, 45 U.S.C. 228(L);
Veterans benefits, 45 U.S.C. 352(E);
Special pensions paid to winners of the Congressional Medal of Honor, 38 U.S.C. 3101; and
Federal homestead lands on debts contracted before issuance of the patent, 43 U.S.C. 175.

S. Rep. No. 95-989, 95th Cong., 2d Sess. 75, reprinted in 1978 U.S. Code Cong. & Ad. News 5787, 5861; H. Rep. No. 95-595, 95th Cong. 2d Sess. 360 (1977), reprinted in 1978 U.S. Code Cong. & Ad. News 5963, 6316. The reports provide no further insight into which other, if any, federal laws were intended to be brought within this provision's scope.

The restrictive nature of the exemption listed is marked. . . .

. . . We find that Congress did not intend to include ERISA-qualified plans among those "exempt under Federal law," pursuant to 11 U.S.C. §522(b)(2)(A).

The failure of Congress to include ERISA in its listing of illustrative federal statutes is highly probative of congressional intent that ERISA was not within the group of "federal law" based exemptions. ERISA, a comprehensive and much-debated statute with sweeping coverage was enacted in 1974; the House and Senate reports on the subsequently enacted Bankruptcy Code Section 522(b)(2)(A) were issued in 1977 and 1978, respectively. Congress knew of the previously-enacted ERISA when drafting Section 522(b)(2)(A), yet neither the House nor the Senate deemed fit to include it within their respective illustrative lists. Congress did refer to ERISA where it wanted to do so in other provisions of the Code. Of similar relevance is the specific reference in another subsection of Section 522 itself to the very ERISA provision relied upon by appellants as constituting a "Federal law" exemption. 11 U.S.C. §522(d)(10)(E)(iii) (reference to pension benefit exemption when the federal exemptions are elected by the debtor). . . .

Further, we stress that ERISA's anti-assignment and alienation provisions are different in kind from those contained in the statutes listed in the Code's legislative history. We do not see across-the-board differences in the explicitness of the restraints against alienation in the listed statutes and in ERISA. But we do find that the contingent nature of ERISA's restraints on alienation differs markedly from the absolute prohibitions contained in the listed statutes. ERISA merely provides that *as a condition of obtaining qualified status* — with its attendant tax and other benefits — a pension plan must preclude alienation or assignment of its benefits. It does not prohibit pension funds from permitting alienation or assignment; rather, while it encourages and favors qualified plans, it envisions that "disqualified" plans may be formed which are still subject to ERISA's regulatory scheme but which do not restrict alienation or assignment. By contrast, the listed statutes which establish or guarantee certain benefits *directly preclude all* such benefits from alienation or assignment.

As additional reenforcement of our view of the Section 522 exemptions, we find that "property" covered by ERISA differs in nature from that covered under the enumerated statutes. While it is true that ERISA and the cited statutes share the common denominator of "pension and welfare" benefits, the *private pension and welfare benefits sweepingly regulated* by ERISA differ considerably from the *public funded and/or created pension and welfare systems,* or the *few exceptional, traditionally guarded industries* covered by the illustrative listings. We believe that these latter, narrow characteristics of the cited statutes, rather than the broad, common trait of private pension and welfare legislation, was intended as the operative thread by which other federal statutes — overlooked or yet to be enacted — might be included. Thus, we conclude that Congress did not intend to include ERISA-qualified plans within the other "Federal law" exemption of the Section 522 election provision.

C. "APPLICABLE NONBANKRUPTCY LAW"
UNDER SECTION 541 AND ERISA

Flowing out of this discussion is clear indication of a congressional intent that Section 541(c)(2) — the exemption relied upon by the Goffs' on appeal — was never intended to include ERISA in its reference to "applicable nonbankruptcy law." Congress made reference to federal law and pension benefits when such a characterization was intended; yet it did not do so in Section 541(c)(2). As we have pointed out above, Congress while well aware of ERISA, specifically considered the role of pension benefits in bankruptcy proceedings in Section 522, and did not grant a broad exemption. The only reasonable inference to draw is that Congress intended that pensions provided for by federal law be insulated from bankruptcy only to the extent recognized in Section 522. While pensions might be excludable from the property of the estate pursuant to Section 541(c)(2), the state law exemption, their exclusion under that section is provided solely by state spendthrift trust law and not by the operation of ERISA.

It is well to make a final telling observation on the relationship between ERISA and the Bankruptcy Code. While ERISA preempts state law, 29 U.S.C. §1144(a), it clearly was not intended to affect the operation of other federal law. It provides: "Nothing in this [Act] shall be construed to alter, amend, modify, invalidate, impair, or supersede any law of the United States [except pre-existing federal pension law] or any rule or regulation issued under such law." 29 U.S.C. §1144(d). As we have already discussed, the Bankruptcy Code was, generally, intended to broaden the "property of the estate" available to creditors in bankruptcy and, specifically, intended to limit any exemption of pension funds. These policy-based provisions of the Code would be frustrated were ERISA's anti-alienation and assignment provisions applied with a sweeping brush. Thus, ERISA's specific provision precluding interference with the operation of federal law renders the Bankruptcy Code effective over any ERISA provisions to the contrary.

Having reached this conclusion we must nevertheless stop short of an arbitrary interpretation urged by the trustee in bankruptcy. The trustee argues that the inclusion in Section 522(d) of a pension benefit exemption, 11 U.S.C. §522(d)(10)(E), for those making a federal election, negatives any congressional intent to include any ERISA pensions at all within the ambit of Section 541. The trustee reasons that the Section 522(d)(10)(E) exemption would be surplusage if Section 541 had the effect of keeping all possible ERISA-qualified plans from ever entering the estate. While, as set out above, we find the wording and breadth of Section 522 enlightening of congressional intent for other reasons, we cannot agree with appellees' proffered construction. Section 522(d)(10)(E) reaches a broad array of employment benefits, and exempts both qualified and unqualified pension plans, to the extent such benefits are reasonably necessary for the support of debtor and his dependents. Given this much broader exemption of benefits available only to those making a federal election, we find no reason to doubt that ERISA-qualified pension funds are included in Section 541 if they qualify as spendthrift trust plans under state law.

. . . We thus conclude that Section 522(d)(10)(E) does not preclude consideration of qualified pension plans under the Section 541 exclusion provision so long as they qualify as a "spendthrift trust" under the applicable state law.

III

We have now concluded that Section 541(c)(2) was intended to exempt only "spendthrift trust" assets from the bankruptcy estate. We now consider whether the Goffs' Keogh plans can fall within the spendthrift trust definition. The general rule is well established that if a settlor creates a trust for his own benefit and inserts a "spendthrift" clause, restraining alienation or assignment, it is void as far as creditors are concerned and they can reach the settlor's interest in the trust. In re Witlin, 640 F.2d 661, 663 (5th Cir. 1981). . . . This general proposition is the law in Texas, which in this case provided the "applicable nonbankruptcy law." . . .

Our reasoning in the *Witlin* case is persuasive. There we held that self-settled Keogh plans were not exempt under the spendthrift trust provision of the old Bankruptcy Act. We said: "There is . . . a strong policy that will prevent any person from placing his property in what amounts to a revocable trust for his own benefit which would be exempt from the claims of his creditors." 640 F.2d at 662. . . . Here, as in *Witlin,* appellant-debtors attempted such a revocable trust for their own benefit. They retained the freedom to withdraw their Keogh plan assets, yet purported to insulate those assets from their creditors. If this dichotomous treatment were to be recognized, the strong common law policy of spendthrift trusts, as well as the Bankruptcy Code's intent, would be subverted. Debtors could shelter funds in Keogh plans immediately before declaring bankruptcy—as did the Goffs with at least some of their funds—and immediately after discharge of all debts withdraw such funds for their own benefit.[37] Whatever might be the rule in a nonbankruptcy setting involving ERISA's provisions we hold that neither law nor equity would afford self-settled Keogh plans "spendthrift trust" exemption in bankruptcy.

Finally, appellants argue that reliance upon traditional spendthrift trust law results in disparate treatment of self-employed and employer-created pension trusts which, in turn, offends both law and reason. Appellants contend that since ERISA requires that all qualified plans include re-

37. Exercise of this right is subject only to a ten percent tax penalty under the Internal Revenue Code.

straints on alienation, and its provisions extend equally to guarantee all workers the benefits of their contributions in retirement years, distinctions in bankruptcy exemption status according to employment status would conflict with ERISA's statutory intention to treat all retirement plans the same way. Further, the Goffs argue, since employees may quit their employment postbankruptcy and thus be entitled to withdraw their pension contributions under ERISA, any bankruptcy distinction made on the basis of the revocable, self-settled nature of self-employed pension plans is arbitrary.

We are not persuaded by appellants' arguments. In analyzing the effectiveness in bankruptcy of spendthrift provisions in pension plans, the courts have generally concluded that those contained in employer-created plans were effective [while] similar provisions in self-settled plans were not. The latter conclusion is inescapable since, as discussed earlier, the traditional law of spendthrift trusts has rejected the notion of effective spendthrift provisions in self-settled trusts. As to the former, without passing upon the exact limits of plans which could properly be characterized "spendthrift trusts," the employer-created-and-controlled nature of those plans may well make them analogus to a spendthrift trust.

We find that this difference is contrary to neither law nor logic. First, whether or not *ERISA* bestows equal treatment upon both types of plans is not at issue. As discussed previously, ERISA was not intended to affect the operation of other federal laws including federal bankruptcy laws. If a distinction is created by operation of bankruptcy law, which might conflict with ERISA, bankruptcy law prevails. Even assuming *arguendo* that the court-drawn distinction conflicts with federal pension law, it is nonetheless enforceable if valid under federal bankruptcy law.

Second, we disagree with appellants' characterization that the degree of beneficiary control over both types of pension plans is indistinguishable, thus rendering their separate treatment unreasonable. Under appellants' self-employed Keogh plans considerable control, including withdrawal authority, was retained. The only limitation upon withdrawal was a ten percent tax penalty. We find this to be significantly different from the usual case of employer-created funds in which the beneficiary employee has little or no control during the term of his employment, and may only withdraw funds upon termination of employment. He must quit his job in order to gain premature access to his retirement funds. We cannot equate a "tax penalty" with "employment termination" as equal restraints upon withdrawal of pension funds.[42] We thus find the court-drawn distinction a reasonable one, and appropriately made under the Bankruptcy Code.

---

42. We leave open the question of whether an appropriate case might be presented in which the restrictions upon a settlor-beneficiary's control and withdrawal of funds in a self-settled trust would ever render effective a spendthrift clause under applicable state law. Consider, for example, a restriction that would condition premature withdrawal upon a self-employed individual's sale of his business or career change.

IN CONCLUSION

After considering the legislative history of Section 541(c)(2) specifically, and of the Bankruptcy Code generally, as well as the statutory framework within which Section 541(c)(2) appears, it is apparent that Congress did not intend by reference to "applicable nonbankruptcy law" to exempt ERISA-qualified pension plans from the bankruptcy estate by virtue of ERISA's provisions precluding assignment or alienation. Rather, it is clear that Congress intended a limited exemption for "spendthrift trusts," as defined by reference to state law. Since we find that the self-settled Keogh plans at issue do not qualify as "spendthrift trusts" under state law, we affirm the bankruptcy court's inclusion of the pension trusts in the bankrupts' estate.

Affirmed.

NOTES

1. Did the court pay sufficient attention to §541(c)(1)? Does the *presence* of this provision itself suggest a narrower role for §541(c)(2) than the Goffs were asserting? Or is §541(c)(1) speaking only to contractual provisions, not provisions that arise "under applicable law"? See In re Graham, 726 F.2d 1268 (8th Cir. 1984) (agrees with *Goff* that "[t]he change in the scope of property of the estate effected by the new Bankruptcy Code, the legislative history of §541(c)(2), the exemption provision of the Code and the preemption provisions of ERISA all convince us that Congress did not intend 'applicable nonbankruptcy law' to include ERISA. Rather, Congress only intended by §541(c)(2) to preserve the status of traditional spendthrift trusts, as recognized by state law"); In re Ross, 18 Bankr. 364 (N.D.N.Y. 1982) (limits on assignment and attachment of proceeds of retirement funds in New York Retirement and Social Security Law not effective in keeping property out of estate in bankruptcy, because of §541(c)(1)(A)). How clearly, in any event, can you define the line between §541(c)(1) and (c)(2)?

2. See In re Howerton, 21 Bankr. 621 (Bankr. N.D. Tex. 1982) (Individual Retirement Annuity (IRA) contracts are property of the estate, notwithstanding restrictions on transfer imposed by 26 U.S.C. §408(b); court cannot ignore "the real nature of the Debtors' IRAs. They are basically tax deferment plans over which the Debtors exercise a great deal of control. They may withdraw the cash value of the annuity subject to a tax assessment at anytime. . . . If the Debtors have the unlimited capacity to reach these funds, so does the Trustee"); In re Johnson, 724 F.2d 1138 (5th Cir. 1984) (annuity with anti-alienation clause not a spendthrift trust; would be against public policy to allow a debtor to voluntarily place property in a "revocable trust for his own benefit and claim it as exempt

from the claims of his creditors"); but cf. In re Wright, 39 Bankr. 623 (D.S.C. 1983).

NOTE ON *GOFF* AND ATTRIBUTES OF PROPERTY UNDER STATE LAW

Goff looks at property of the estate in the context of a Keogh plan. The structure of §541 is generally that it excludes one kind of property ("future" assets) and includes everything else. If it is "present" property that is necessary for the fresh start, §522 provides that this property of the estate goes to the debtor rather than his creditors. An exception to this scheme, however, is §541(c)(2). Even if we assume that the Keogh plan is not a "future" asset, does the (c)(2) exception nevertheless apply? The court in *Goff* focuses on the debtor's ability to cash out. But why is this relevant? It is one thing to say that a debtor could cash out, but isn't it quite another to say that his creditors can reach it? Isn't it relevant that outside of bankruptcy creditors had no way to reach this asset?

Goff asks whether state law would consider this a "spendthrift trust." But isn't the relationship between federal and state law clear in this respect: We don't care what the state law calls it, but rather we care what *attributes* it enjoys under state law. Or should our presumption that creditors in bankruptcy should get no more than they could outside change in the case of individuals? Should bankruptcy's fresh start have a ratchet effect: Creditors inside of bankruptcy can be denied assets they would have been able to reach outside of it, but they cannot touch any assets inside of bankruptcy that would have been beyond their grasp outside? Or does the readjustment of rights between debtor and creditor in individual bankruptcies fundamentally alter the essentially procedural nature of the bankruptcy process? But if it does, what are landmarks by which one judges how the new balance should be struck?

Does the Bankruptcy Code compel a different result? The drafters of the Bankruptcy Code thought that Keogh plans should be exempt property. They placed them in §522(d)(10)(E). Section 522(d) contains bankruptcy exemptions, a set of exempt property that the drafters will allow debtors to have. But §522 exempts property that would otherwise be property of the estate. Does the existence of §522(d)(10)(E), therefore, evidence Congress's intent to deem the property to be property of the estate under §541 in the first instance? If so, note the consequence. Debtors get to exempt the property listed in §522(d) only by electing to claim the exemptions provided by the Bankruptcy Code, as opposed to other state and federal exemptions. §522(b). Someone who elects nonbankruptcy exemptions will not be able to keep the funds in a Keogh plan from creditors if they are not exempt under state (or nonbankruptcy federal) law, which *Goff* states they are not. Moreover, in a last-minute compromise, Congress allowed states to opt out of the federal exemptions scheme by passing statutes prohibiting their residents from electing the §522(d) exemptions. In more than half the states now, Mr. Goff could not get to §522(d)(10). We will return to the question of whether Keogh plans are exempt property under nonbankruptcy law, and hence under §522(b), in connection with *Clark,* infra page 857.

The following case raises similar issues involving property of the estate in the context of military retirement benefits.

IN RE HARTER
10 Bankr. 272 (Bankr. N.D. Ind. 1981)

Robert K. RODIBAUGH, Bankruptcy Judge.
At South Bend, Indiana, on April 13, 1981.
This matter is before the Court on the trustee's application for turnover order pursuant to Section 542(a) of the Bankruptcy Code. . . .

The debtor, James Edward Harter, after retiring from the United States Army in September 1975, has been receiving a pension of approximately $6,000.00 a year. The trustee contends that future Army retirement benefits are a property right of the debtor which pass to the estate for the benefit of the debtor's creditors. Although the $100.00 exemption for intangibles contained in Indiana Code Section 34-2-28-1 may be applicable, the debtor has claimed that exemption for other property.[3]

Initially, trustee's application requested this Court's assistance in commuting the pension to a lump sum distribution. However, the trustee has broadened relief sought to include a request that this Court enter an order requiring the debtor to turn over to the trustee all Army pension payments received since the date of filing of the petition until the claims of the creditors are satisfied.

The debtor maintains that he has no present interest in the future benefits which are contingent upon his survival. Thus, he has no interest which could become property of the estate. Additionally, the debtor asserts that unlike annuities and private pensions, the benefits are necessary to his obtaining a fresh start. Finally, debtor argues that his creditors will not be deprived of any pre-bankruptcy asset since no money from his pre-bankruptcy estate was expended to purchase this future income stream.

---

3. Although federal legislation specifically exempts from attachment, levy or seizure benefits administered by the Veterans Administration [38 U.S.C.A. §3101], the special pensions of Congressional Medal of Honor winners [38 U.S.C.A. §562(c)], railroad retirement benefits [45 U.S.C. §231m], social security payments [42 U.S.C.A. §407], military pay annuities [10 U.S.C.A. §1440], and others, Congress has failed to provide that Army retirement pensions are free from levy and attachment.

To determine what constitutes property of the estate, initially we turn to Section 541 of the Bankruptcy Code which states in pertinent part:

Section 541.   Property of the estate.
(a) The commencement of a case under section 301, 302, or 303 of this title creates an estate. Such estate is comprised of all the following property, wherever located:
    (1) Except as provided in subsections (b) and (c)(2) of this section, all legal or equitable interests of the debtor in property as of the commencement of the case.

Thus, the question becomes whether the retirement benefits are a legal or equitable interest of the debtor in property. The Code, however, neither defines "property" nor "interest in property."

Under the Bankruptcy Act of 1898, the question of what is property under Section 70(a) was a federal question[5] and we find no reason to believe that it is not a federal question under the Bankruptcy Code. In addressing this question, the United States Supreme Court has determined in cases arising under the Bankruptcy Act that the purposes of the Bankruptcy Act itself ultimately determines the scope and limitations of the term "property."[7] To this end, the Supreme Court explained that there is a twofold purpose to be balanced: first, the purpose of converting the estate into cash for distribution among creditors, and second, the purpose of providing the debtor with a fresh start by leaving him free after the date of the filing of his petition to accumulate new wealth in the future.

Considering these purposes in determining whether inchoate claims for loss-carry-back refunds are property, in dicta in Segal v. Rochelle, the Court stated:

However, limitations on the term [property] do grow out of other purposes of the Act; one purpose which is highly prominent and is relevant in this case is to leave the bankrupt free after the date of his petition to accumulate new wealth in the future. Accordingly, future wages of the bankrupt do not constitute "property" at the time of bankruptcy nor, analogously, does an intended bequest to him or a promised gift — even though state law might permit all of these to be alienated in advance. [Citations omitted.]

However, the advent of the Bankruptcy Code of 1978 diminishes the relevance of this analysis due to the broadened scope of paragraph (1) of subsection (a) of Section 541. The Senate Judiciary Committee reporting on Section 541 of Senate Bill 2266 stated:[9]

---

    5. Segal v. Rochelle, 382 U.S. 375, 86 S. Ct. 511, 15 L. Ed. 2d 428 (1966).
    7. Kokoszka v. Belford, 417 U.S. 642, 94 S. Ct. 2431, 41 L. Ed. 2d 374 (1974); *Segal,* supra.
    9. S. Rep. No. 95-989, 95th Cong., 2nd Sess. 82 (1978) U.S. Code Cong. & Admin. News 1978, 5787.

> Paragraph (1) has the effect of overruling Lockwood v. Exchange Bank, 190 U.S. 294, 23 S. Ct. 751, 47 L. Ed. 1061 (1903), because it includes as property of the estate all property of the debtor, even that needed for a fresh start. After the property comes into the estate, then the debtor is permitted to exempt it. . . .

The House Report on Section 541 of House Bill 8200 recites the above language verbatim.[10] Accordingly, the legislative history indicates Congress' intent that the purposes of the Bankruptcy Code would not control what constitutes property in the same manner that the purposes were controlling under the repealed Bankruptcy Act. However, the principle that future wages do not constitute property at the time of the filing of the debtor's petition remains sound.

The military retirement benefits in the case at bar are paid monthly on the contingency that the debtor is alive on the first day of each month. The military plan differs from other pension plans in that it is non-contributory, is entirely taxable, and is subject to garnishment and attachment. These qualities liken the payments to wages.

Section 1315 of title 10 of the United States Code states that a member of the armed forces retired for length of service "is entitled to retired pay" to make explicit the entitlement. First, noteworthy is the word choice of this provision as the word "pay" connotes "wages." Second, the right to payment must be distinguished from the payment itself. Although the statute grants an entitlement, the entitlement is the only interest which the debtor has at the commencement of his bankruptcy case, not the payments themselves. The debtor does not have the ability to proceed to a court of law to enforce his interest in receiving future payments by demanding the future payments at the present time. Rather, the debtor may proceed to court to protect his right to the future payments, the right to payment being the only "property" in which the debtor has an interest at the commencement of the case. The right to future payment is of no value to the debtor's estate due to the fact that the Army will not make a lump sum distribution or any distribution in advance.[12]

The very nature of a proceeding under Chapter 7 of the Bankruptcy Code militates against trustee's approach. The debtor chose to file his request for an order for relief under Chapter 7 of the Bankruptcy Code, initiating a liquidation. This demonstrates the debtor's willingness to lose his assets in return for a speedy fresh start. The liquidation avenue sharply contrasts with a Chapter 13 case where the debtor develops and performs under a plan for repayment of his debts over an extended period of three years, or, for cause, up to five years. The opportunity for a prompt fresh

10. H.R. Rep. No. 95-595, 95th Cong., 1st Sess. 368 (1977), U.S. Code Cong. & Admin. News 1978, 5963.

12. Because the debtor does not have a present right to withdraw benefits, his entitlement would also fall outside the definition of property found in Indiana Code §31-1-11.5-2 for purposes of dissolution of marriage. . . .

start cannot be deprived the debtor; the Code specifically provides that the Court may not convert a case to a Chapter 13 unless so requested by the debtor. The trustee herein would effectively force the debtor into a quasi-Chapter 13 by taking his monthly retirement checks and applying them to achieve full payment of his debts.

Further, under Chapter 7, when a debtor's assets are applied to his debts, it is rare that all creditors receive full payment. Obviously, if a debtor was capable of payment in full to all his creditors generally he would not seek assistance from the bankruptcy courts. However, the trustee herein proposes to take the debtor's retirement checks monthly until full payment is achieved. Thus, the trustee proposes a hybrid liquidation with forced 100 percent repayment while the debtor suffers all the disadvantages of Chapter 7 (loss of one's property with the attendant stigma attached) and forgoes the advantages of Chapter 13 (comparatively liberal discharge provisions, and the ability to retain one's possessions). Even if this Court would view the future retirement benefits as present property, it could not find that the trustee's proposed procedure is consistent with the bankruptcy laws enacted by Congress.

Viewing the Army retirement benefits as future wages, the Court finds that the future payments are not property in which the debtor has an interest under Section 541 of the Bankruptcy Code. Accordingly, the trustee's application for turnover is hereby denied.

So ordered.

NOTE

In re Haynes, 679 F.2d 718 (7th Cir. 1982), dealt with the same issue that confronted the court in *Harter* — whether Navy retirement pay constituted "property of the estate." The court in deciding *Haynes,* also concluded that such pay did not constitute property of the estate, although its reasoning was substantially different than that of the court in *Harter.* The court in *Haynes* first commented that, after retirement from the Navy, the debtor received "retainer pay" for serving in the fleet reserve, and discussed the responsibilities of the debtor while receiving such pay. Because the debtor had transferred in 1981 to the retired list of the Navy, however, his retainer pay had ceased, and he had commenced receiving "retirement pay." The court noted that the debtor remained subject to the Uniform Code of Military Justice and could be recalled to active duty in time of war or national emergency. The court concluded that this meant his retirement pay was compensation for future services, and, because of §541(a)(6), not property of the estate, reasoning:

> Under most pension plans, the retiree is not required to perform any services for his former employer. The military retiree, however, remains obligated to the federal government to perform certain duties. . . . If the

retiree fails to perform these duties, his retirement benefits may be terminated. . . . In light of the obligations imposed on a military retiree as conditions of receipt of retirement pay, military retirement pay is actually reduced compensation for reduced current services.

Do you agree? Why did the court, en route to its decision, refer to "retainer pay," and discuss its attributes, when what was at issue, as the only pay relevant to the post-bankruptcy period, was "retirement pay"?

NOTE ON *HARTER* AND PENSION RIGHTS IN BANKRUPTCY

The court in *Harter* states that "the legislative history indicates Congress's intent that the purposes of the Bankruptcy Code would not control what constitutes property in the same manner that the purposes were controlling under the repealed Bankruptcy Act." Do you agree? How, then, does the court conclude that the principle regarding future wages "remains sound"? That such a principle should govern military retirement benefits?

Does the court do an adequate job of assessing whether Mr. Harter's pension is property of the estate? Putting aside the approach of *Haynes*, aren't these retirement benefits a product of Mr. Harter's *past* efforts? Could the court actuarially estimate the amount of military retirement benefits to be received by Mr. Harter, discount that to present value, and require the Army to pay that amount over? Does the answer to this question matter? Should it matter? See §542. The court states that "[t]he right to future payment is of no value to the debtor's estate due to the fact that the Army will not make a lump sum distribution or any distribution in advance." This argument is fleshed out in In re Sheridan, 38 Bankr. 52 (Bankr. D. Vt. 1983):

> The principle that an interest in a retirement plan does not become part of the debtor's estate is sound where, as here, the plan member may not, short of truncating his employment, force present distribution of any sum. At the time of the filing of his petition for relief, the debtor held only an entitlement to future payments, not a right of present access to the funds. A right of future payments that are non-transferable, non-assignable and non-attachable, is of no value to the estate, for the reason that the entitlement may not be prematurely liquidated into a lump sum or other current distribution.

Even assuming that the Army could not be forced by a bankruptcy court to give a lump sum distribution to the trustee, do you agree with the conclusion — that the value is therefore zero? Would you pay anything — say $100 — for an assignment of the right to receive Mr. Harter's pension payments when and if those payments were actually due and made? If you would, doesn't that mean the contingent future payments have *some* present value? If so, isn't the right to receive those pension payments "property of the estate" unless *Goff* is wrong and §541(c)(2) does in fact apply?

But *Harter* does not rely on §541(c)(2). Isn't it fair to say that *Harter* is trying to fit this pension into a category that is like future wages, which are explicitly excluded, §541(a)(6)? (See, in this respect, *Haynes.*) But if §541, as the legislative history states, "includes as property of the estate all property of the debtor, even that needed for a fresh start," should not the wage analogy be limited? What if Mr. Harter, instead of getting an Army pension, had been self-employed, and each year took a couple of thousand dollars and placed it into a private annuity plan? Would that, under *Goff,* be property of the estate? Why should Mr. Harter be treated any more favorably?

Is *Harter* perhaps justifiable from a different approach? Can one argue that what §541 is attempting to do, conceptually, is take a "snapshot" of the debtor's assets that his creditors would be entitled to get, as of the date of the filing of the petition, if the debtor were to die on that date? More precisely, does it help to approach §541, in the case of individuals, by asking the following question: If the debtor knew he was going to die tomorrow, and gathered together all assets that he could gather together before he died, what assets would his estate have when he died? Does this, subject to some wrinkles such as §541(a)(5), essentially capture the line that §541 is attempting to draw?

If one were to follow this approach, future wages would not be an asset of the debtor at death, and accordingly would not be available to his creditors upon his death. Therefore (to reach the conclusion suggested by this analogy), future wages should not be "property" for purposes of bankruptcy law. Is *Harter* much the same because Mr. Harter cannot get at his pension, except by living, and his creditors cannot either? If Mr. Harter were to die, the pension apparently would lapse. Does this support the conclusion in *Harter?* What if Harter had opted for a pension plan where the pension would last as long as either he *or* his wife were alive? Should determining what is property of the estate turn on distinctions such as this? Can the analogy just suggested accommodate this? See Jackson, Translating Assets and Liabilities to the Bankruptcy Forum, 14 J. Legal Studies 73 (1985).

What are the consequences of reaching the opposite conclusion in *Harter?* Assume that the pension is considered to be property of the estate. Doesn't §522(d)(10)(E) suggest that this pension would be exempt? If so, why doesn't *Harter* just rely on that provision to reach the same result? That subsection, as *Goff* notes, is a part of the set of exemptions provided by the Bankruptcy Code. In *Harter,* the issue is important, for Mr. Harter apparently has elected his state exemptions (which today would be required in Indiana by virtue of Indiana having enacted an opt-out statute).

Given that, Mr. Harter (without withdrawing his election) cannot rely on §522(d)(10)(E), as it is located in the set of *bankruptcy* exemptions and Mr. Harter has not chosen to take the set of bankruptcy exemptions. Nonetheless, doesn't the *presence* of §522(d)(10)(E), and its clear applicability to the type of pension that Mr. Harter is claiming, suggest that his pension *is* property of the estate under §541? After all, §522(d) only exempts things that are property of the estate in the first place. See §522(b). Isn't the problem that confronts Mr. Harter created by the fact that §522(d) doesn't apply to all debtors but only those that elect the bankruptcy set of exemptions? But even so, should Mr. Harter's army pension be considered to be "exempt" property for purposes of §522(b)? These questions are pursued in connection with *Clark*, infra page 857.

PROBLEMS

11.1 Debtor was a district manager for Company. His employment agreement, which he entered into in 1979, provided for a termination payment, should he leave his employment with Company for any reason. This termination payment would be based on years of service and on commissions earned. In February 1983, Debtor filed a petition in bankruptcy. In November 1983, Debtor terminated his position with Company. Under the termination agreement, the Company owes Debtor $20,000. Does the $20,000 go to Debtor, or does it go to the trustee, as property of the estate? See In re Ryerson, 30 Bankr. 541 (9th Cir. Bankr. App. 1983). Would it make any difference if, by its terms, the termination payment did not vest until Debtor had been with Company four years, a milestone that was passed in June 1983?

11.2 Debtor was an insurance salesman. Before Debtor filed for bankruptcy, Debtor sold a health insurance policy to an automobile dealers association. The monthly premiums on this policy vary depending on the number of employees covered in any given month, and Debtor receives a commission of 10 percent of these premium amounts. Debtor is entitled to continue to receive monthly commissions as long as the association maintains the policy and he is the agent of record for it. The association has the power to cancel the policy or change agents at any time. Are the insurance premiums payable after Debtor's petition in bankruptcy property of the estate under §541? See §541(a)(6) and In re Selner, 18 Bankr. 420 (Bankr. S.D. Fla. 1982). (In considering this question, do not try to take what might appear to be the easy way out, by using §541(a)(7). That subsection applies only to interests in property that the *estate* — not the debtor — acquires after the commencement of the case.)

11.3 Debtor is an attorney, who operates a law practice as a sole proprietorship. Several other attorneys and staff work for Debtor's business. Debtor files a petition in bankruptcy. Debtor claims that all the earnings generated by her law practice after she files for bankruptcy fall within §541(a)(6). Evaluate that contention. See In re Fitzsimmons, 725 F.2d 1208 (9th Cir. 1984).

11.4 Debtor's father died in 1970. In his will, Debtor's mother is given a life estate and the power of appointment, which enables her to direct the trustee of a residuary trust to turn over any of the corpus of the trust to any descendant of the testator, or to pay any income from the trust to any such descendant. Debtor's mother has not exercised this power of appointment. The residuary trust will go to the testator's children that are alive upon the death of Debtor's mother, the life tenant. Under state law, the children are contingent remaindermen during the life of the mother. If Debtor files a petition in bankruptcy, may the trustee reach any of the corpus or income of the trust? Assume that, under state law, contingent remainders are alienable by the beneficiary, but are not reachable by the creditors. See In re Hicks, 22 Bankr. 243 (Bankr. N.D. Ga. 1982); see also In re Arney, 35 Bankr. 668 (Bankr. N.D. Ill. 1983); cf. In re McCourt, the next case.

11.5 Debtor accepts a summer job for three months (June, July, and August) at $10,000, payable at the end of the three months. On August 1, Debtor files a petition in bankruptcy. On September 1, who should the employer pay the $10,000 to?

In the case that follows, the question turns not on a right that is similar to future wages, but rather on an individual right (the right to elect against a spouse's will) that does not seem like an asset in the usual sense.

IN RE McCOURT
12 Bankr. 587 (Bankr. S.D.N.Y. 1981)

Howard SCHWARTZBERG, Bankruptcy Judge.

Crucial to the resolution of the conflict in this case is whether or not a distinction should be drawn between property rights of a debtor that pass to a trustee in bankruptcy under Code §541 and personal rights of a debtor which may or may not be exercised by him as he sees fit. The trustee in bankruptcy seeks an order under Code §521(2)* directing the debtor to cooperate with the trustee and execute a right of election to which he is entitled under the New York State Estate Powers and Trust Law, Section 5-1.1 against the estate of the debtor's deceased wife so as to entitle the debtor to receive one-third of her estate.

* Renumbered as §521(3) in 1984. — EDS.

FACTS

1. The facts are not disputed. On May 20, 1981 the debtor filed a voluntary petition for relief under Chapter 7 of the Bankruptcy Reform Act of 1978. Pursuant to Code §301, the commencement of a voluntary case constitutes an order for relief under such Chapter. The interim trustee in bankruptcy, who was appointed by the United States Trustee in accordance with Code §15701(a), became the permanent trustee in this case.

2. On August 5, 1968 debtor and his wife, Margaret P. McCourt purchased jointly a real estate parcel located at 141 Lakeview Avenue, Hartsdale, New York. On June 24, 1972 the debtor conveyed the property at 141 Lakeview Avenue, Hartsdale, New York to his wife, Margaret P. McCourt, thus making her the sole owner. The debtor has lived at the premises from August 5, 1968 through the present time.

3. Margaret McCourt died on October 13, 1980. Under her will dated June 27, 1974, which was admitted to probate on February 9, 1981, she left all of her property to her father, one Vito Varlotta. No property was left to any members of her family including her husband, the debtor Joseph McCourt.

4. The debtor has not yet filed a Notice of Election against the estate as a surviving spouse.[2] Under EPTL 5-1.1 the election must be made within six months from the date of issuance of letters testamentary. Letters were issued to Joseph McCourt as Executor under decedent's will on February 9, 1981. Therefore the six-month period expires on August 9, 1981.

5. The trustee has been provided with an appraisal of the property located at 141 Lakeview Avenue, Hartsdale, New York, prepared by one Joseph R. Warren, a licensed real estate broker for the purpose of evaluating the premises for the Estate of Margaret McCourt. Mr. Warren values the property at $110,000.00 as of October 13, 1980. The property is presently encumbered by a mortgage held by Hastings-On-Hudson Federal Loan Association in the amount of $35,000.00 as of November 30, 1976.

6. The trustee asserts that based on the above figures, the equity in the property is at least $75,000, and that Mr. McCourt is entitled under EPTL 5-1.1(c)(1)(B) to exercise a right of election to one-third of the net estate left by his deceased spouse. . . . The trustee contends that the debtor's failure thus far to exercise his right of election against the will is a conscious and deliberate plan to place assets that the debtor would be entitled to under law beyond the reach of his creditors.

---

2. Pursuant to EPTL 5-1.1(c)(1) for wills executed after August 31, 1966 where the testator disposes of his entire estate in his will a personal right of election is given to the surviving spouse to take a share of the decedent's estate. An elective share of one-third the net estate is available if the deceased is survived by one or more issue. The trustee bases his claim on a one-third share, although it is unclear from the facts whether or not the deceased was survived by issue.

Discussion

The trustee in bankruptcy draws upon Code §521(2), which directs a debtor to "cooperate with the trustee as necessary to enable the trustee to perform the trustee's duties under . . . [Title 11 of the Act]." One of the most important duties imposed upon the trustee is to gather in for the estate and creditors all of the property of the estate, as encompassed under Code §541, which includes "all legal or equitable interests of the debtor in *property* as of the commencement of the case." [Emphasis added]. The emphasis throughout Code §541 is placed upon the debtor's interests in property. In the instant case, the trustee concedes that he is not seeking to reach an interest of the debtor in property, but rather the debtor's personal statutory right of election with respect to his deceased wife's estate. Indeed, the trustee ignores the distinction between property interests and personal interests when he states that "the debtor's estate . . . consists of all the legal and equitable interests of the debtor as of the commencement of the case" and that "the filing of the petition by the debtor creates an estate which is comprised of all interests of the debtor whatever the nature of the interest."

By deleting the words "in property" when describing the debtor's interests under Code §541, the trustee substantially changes the meaning of this section. Until the debtor exercises his personal statutory right to the election, no rights in his deceased wife's property are ascribable to the debtor. That the interest in question is solely of a personal nature and not a property right is made clear by the New York Surrogate's Court in In re Herter's Estate, 193 Misc. 602, 607, 83 N.Y.S.2d 36, 41, affirmed 274 App. Div. 979, 84 N.Y.S.2d 913, affirmed 300 N.Y. 532, 89 N.E.2d 252 (1948), where it said with respect to the statutory right of election:

> The act grants no property right in *esse*, but only a property right in *posse* which springs into existence only if the statutory right is exercised under the conditions which create the right only as of the time of the exercise of the election.

Manifestly, the debtor has no rights in the property in his deceased wife's estate unless and until he exercises his personal right of election. The trustee seeks to force the debtor to exercise his election. Moreover, the trustee also urges that he can exercise the right of election on behalf of the debtor on the theory that the right was assigned to him as a matter of law when the debtor filed his petition in bankruptcy. The trustee reasons that the filing of a petition in bankruptcy is tantamount to an assignment of the debtor's interest in the deceased wife's estate, in that the debtor should be deemed to have agreed to convey all of his rights with respect to his deceased wife's estate for the purpose of liquidating his estate in bankruptcy. The trustee's argument elides the fact that the debtor cannot assign an interest in property that he does not have. Having failed to exercise his personal right of election before the filing of his voluntary bankruptcy petition, the debtor has no property rights in his late wife's estate capable of being assigned to the trustee.

The personal nature of a surviving spouse's privilege to elect against a will has been uniformly stressed. . . .

Hence, the courts have recognized that a personal power conferred by statute, such as the surviving spouse's right to elect against a will, requires personal action by the benefitted individual for its exercise, . . . except in the two situations in which the surviving spouse is an infant or incompetent and personal action by the surviving spouse is impossible or extremely difficult. However, there have been a few cases which hold that a foreign consular officer may exercise the right of election on behalf of a surviving spouse, under principles of international law, as they are deemed international attorneys-in-fact for their nationals. . . .

The EPTL expressly provides that an election may be made by the guardian of property of an infant spouse (5-1.1(d)(4)(A)) or by the committee of an incompetent spouse (5-1.1(d)(4)(B)).

The absence of an express grant of authority allowing any other persons to exercise the election on behalf of the surviving spouse indicates a legislative intent, by application of the principle *inclusio unius est exclusio alterius,* to limit them to those enumerated. In re Zalewski's Estate, 177 Misc. 384, 387, 30 N.Y.S.2d 658, affirmed 265 App. Div. 878, 38 N.Y.S.2d 37, appeal denied 265 App. Div. 1002, 39 N.Y.S.2d 619 (1942). . . . "The choice of waiver or assertion of the right rests with the individual upon whom the right has been conferred by law," . . . "and where a question of personal choice is involved its exercise must rest upon the decision of the individual to whom such privilege of choice has been granted, in the absence of an express grant of authority to some other person to make the relevant decision on his behalf." *Zalewski,* 177 Misc. at 387, 30 N.Y.S.2d 658. . . .

The *Charkowsky* case [89 Misc. 2d 623, 392 N.Y.S.2d 368 (1977)], does state, however, that the personal nature of the right of election does not preclude the spouse from delegating his personal right to a third person "to make an election in a specified manner under the spouse's direction." The debtor's having the *choice* of delegating the right of election cannot be viewed in the same light as being *required* on demand of the trustee in bankruptcy to exercise this right for the benefit of creditors who may then reach assets in which the surviving spouse, by executing his election, then has a vested interest.

In Dalisa v. Dumoff, 206 Misc. 259, 132 N.Y.S.2d 550, affirmed, 286 App. Div. 856, 141 N.Y.S.2d 700, appeal denied, 286 App. Div. 967, 146 N.Y.S.2d 477 (1955), the plaintiff, a judgment creditor, brought an action to set aside defendant's waiver of his right of election against his deceased wife's will. If the waiver were set aside, the plaintiff could then reach the one-third interest in the deceased wife's estate to which the debtor would have been entitled, if he chose to exercise his right of election.

The Supreme Court dismissed the complaint, and the judgment creditor appealed. The Appellate Division held that the right of election is personal to the surviving spouse and that "[i]t cannot be exercised in his behalf by a party acting in hostility to the spouse, nor may he be compelled to exercise it for the benefit of his creditors." Dalisa v. Dumoff, 286 App. Div. 856, 141 N.Y.S.2d 700 (1955).

In sum, if the trustee, or a creditor, can neither compel the debtor to exercise the right of election, nor exercise it in his behalf, it necessarily follows that it is not an interest in property within the reach of Code §541. In the circumstances of this case, the mandate of Code §521(2) that the debtor should cooperate with the trustee does not extend to the involuntary exercise of a personal right that does not fall within the category of property interests comprising the debtor's estate as delineated under Code §541.

CONCLUSIONS OF LAW

1. The trustee in bankruptcy may not compel the debtor to exercise a statutory right of election with respect to the debtor's deceased wife's estate, nor may the trustee exercise such right of election for the debtor, because the unexercised statutory right is not a property interest.

2. The trustee's application is denied.

It is so ordered.

NOTES

1. What if McCourt had waived the right to elect against the will the day before he filed for bankruptcy? Should this election be upheld? In answering that, does it depend on whether or not the decision in *McCourt* is correct? Does the discussion of fraudulent conveyance law in Chapter 5 have any relevance to your answer?

2. What if McCourt filed for bankruptcy and, seven months later, his wife died? See §541(a)(5).

NOTE ON *McCOURT* AND
THE POWER OF ELECTION

In Problem 11.4, the property in question was in the hands of a third person — the debtor's mother — under a discretionary power of appointment. *McCourt* is substantially different: The power of a spouse to elect against a will from which he has been omitted is a power in the hands of the debtor himself, not in the hands of a third party. Given that the power is in the hands of the debtor, should we not ask whether there is any reason why this should not be treated as property of the estate?

The court in *McCourt* finds that the right to elect against the will is an interest solely of a personal nature and is not a property right. But should state law be followed here insofar as it tells us what is and what is not *property*? Isn't the right to elect itself a kind of property interest, no matter what state law says about it? As such, isn't it included as property of the estate *within the meaning of §541*? Has the court, in other words, focused on the wrong definition of property? Isn't the debtor "entitled" to acquire this property under §541(a)(5)? To look at this a slightly different way, consider the analogy that we raised before: the debtor who gathers together all possible assets today, in contemplation of dying tomorrow. Isn't the right to elect against the will a right that could be gathered by the debtor today? Shouldn't that make it property of the estate?

Before one concludes that this should be property of the estate, is there anything to be said on the other side of the issue? Is there, in other words, any reason why this power to elect against the will should *not* be considered property of the estate? Apart from bankruptcy, when would a spouse ever *not* elect against the will? Isn't there an estate planning function attributable to this? By failing to elect against the will, the benefits of the spouse's estate will pass to other (and presumably younger) generations. Thus, the power not to elect against the will may serve a form of estate planning.

But is that response sufficient? Is it enough to show that there are reasons, other than the avoidance of creditors, to waive the right to elect against the will? If the debtor is insolvent, shouldn't the creditors have rights against this property? Or is the answer to that inquiry that this is effectively a §541(c)(2) case — a form of spendthrift trust? Note the court's discussion of Dalisa v. Dumoff, which would not let a creditor set aside the waiver of election. Does this mean that this is a form of asset that the creditors could not reach under state law, and hence is a form of asset that they should not have access to in bankruptcy? Or should this right to elect be viewed as a §541(c)(1) case, and therefore one that the bankruptcy court is free to disregard? Just because the debtor cannot assign this right to elect (even voluntarily — it can only be done subject to the debtor's direction), does that say anything more than that this is a §541(c)(1) case?

In looking at this power as a form of property from the perspective of bankruptcy, perhaps one should examine the power as an estate planning tool in greater detail. How much would bringing in the power of appointment as property of the estate disrupt estate planning? Consider the following. Wife has constructed a trust, with a life estate to Husband, and the remainder to Children. The life estate portion is spendthrift. Husband also has a special power of appointment: He can designate who, among the children, get income if he does not want it. Note that the present value of this may be considerable from the standpoint of the Husband. But it does the Husband's creditors little good, whether in or out of bankruptcy. In bankruptcy, for example, the spendthrift portion keeps this out under §541(c)(2), and the special power of appointment is kept out under §541(b).

Wife dies, and Husband files for bankruptcy. Husband is not mentioned in Wife's will, and so has the power to elect against the will. Because of the presence of the trust, there may be very good estate planning reasons for Husband not to elect against the will. Should the trustee be able to require, in that case, an election against the will to be made by Husband? The present value of that election to the creditors is substantial, and much greater than what those creditors will get if the election is not made. But the present value to Husband is substantially less, and the whole estate planning scheme would be frustrated (although careful lawyering, in some circumstances, perhaps could have prevented it, by making the proper arrangements in Wife's will).

How should cases such as these be handled? Should we allow the election to be waived, as long as the debtor is willing to waive it? That is to say, *if* the debtor elects against the will, the resulting property becomes property of the estate, but if he does not, the trustee (and hence the creditors) cannot reach it? Do we *then* examine the debtor's decision not to elect against the will in light of fraudulent conveyance law? If there does not appear to be any estate planning, is it a fraudulent conveyance? Under those circumstances, waiver of the election *could* be seen as nothing more than an attempt by the debtor to keep assets out of the hands of his creditors, but should it? Under this approach, how would McCourt fare? Note that, in *McCourt,* the beneficiary of the wife's will was the *father.* Without knowing more about the particular facts of this case, having property pass to an older generation does not sound like it is an estate planning device. In that case, can one argue that the failure of McCourt to elect against the will could be viewed as a fraudulent conveyance from the perspective of his creditors? Consider the facts of In re Peery, 40 Bankr. 811 (Bankr. M.D. Tenn. 1984). Peery was a beneficiary under his grandfather's will. When his grandfather died, he became entitled to a one-eleventh share of property worth almost $200,000. Shortly after one of his creditors demanded repayment of a loan, Peery renounced his entitlement to the bulk of his share in his grandfather's estate. A few months later, Peery filed a bankruptcy petition. Bank argued that the debtor's renunciation was a fraudulent transfer justifying a denial of discharge under §727(a)(2)(A). The court accepted Bank's argument and denied debtor a discharge.

The facts of this case convincingly demonstrate the requisite intent. The renunciation was executed for no consideration. The debtor renounced a substantial interest in real property in which he held no exemptable interest; however, he retained an interest in exemptable personal property. The

transfer was to and substantially benefitted family members. The renunciation was made while the debtor was under pressure from creditors, was in
receipt of demand letters, and was the defendant in a state collection lawsuit.
The renunciation was not revealed on the debtor's statement and schedule
of financial affairs. At the meeting of creditors and again in his deposition,
the debtor admitted that the renunciation was executed to keep his family
from becoming embroiled in his financial problems. The debtor renounced
with intent to keep the property within his family and out of the reach of his
creditors. The totality of the circumstances demonstrates intent to hinder,
delay or defraud creditors.

Is this kind of inquiry either necessary or appropriate? Is this case distinguishable from *McCourt* other than that an affirmative act was required in
Peery? Is there any doubt that in *McCloud* the right of election, if not
property itself, "entitles" the debtor to something that definitely is property? If the debtor were put to the choice, he might not acquire the property even though he is entitled to, but is this relevant? If the debtor had not
filed the bankruptcy petition, he *could* exercise the right to take the nonbarrable share. Because the trustee succeeds to the debtor's rights, why
can't he exercise the right himself? But doesn't this extend the right
beyond its purpose? Should this case ultimately be treated any differently
than *Goff*? The threshold question is whether creditors can reach the property outside of bankruptcy, and because in this case they cannot, the court
in *McCourt* reached the correct result.

NOTE ON TENANCIES BY THE ENTIRETY

How does the Bankruptcy Code treat special kinds of "jointly" held
property? In dealing with one form of jointly held marital property —
community property — the Bankruptcy Code's solution is clear. The community property comes into the estate (§541(a)(2)) but then is effectively
set aside, and there is then a little "mini collective proceeding" for the
community creditors. §726(c). This is a procedure that recognizes the
special nature of community property and its state-law limitations as to
what sorts of creditor claims that property is subject. See generally Pedlar,
The Implication of the New Community Property Laws for Creditors'
Remedies and Bankruptcy, 63 Calif. L. Rev. 1610 (1975).

Because of §726(c), community property has generated little litigation in bankruptcy. Another form of "joint" marital property — tenancies
by the entirety — has generated a fair amount of litigation, because no
provision (such as §726(c)) applies to it. See generally Note, Estates by the
Entirety in Bankruptcy, 15 U. Mich. J.L. Ref. 399 (1983); Ackerly, Tenants by the Entirety Property and the Bankruptcy Reform Act, 21 Wm. &
Mary L. Rev. 701 (1980).

A tenancy by the entirety is a form of property ownership held by the marital unit that is recognized in approximately one-half the jurisdictions. As commonly stated, it has the four "unities" of a joint tenancy (time, title, interest, and possession) plus the additional unity of marriage. In its pure form, four characteristics follow: (1) the property is not subject to partition; (2) neither spouse may dispose of any part of the property without the consent of the other; (3) neither spouse may subject the property to the payment of his or her *individual* debts; and (4) upon the death of either spouse, the entire estate passes to the survivor. See In re Abdallah, 39 Bankr. 384 (Bankr. D. Mass. 1984) (post-bankruptcy death of debtor divested bankruptcy estate of any interest in property held in tenancy by the entirety). What is difficult for bankruptcy purposes is that creditors of an *individual* spouse cannot levy on it.

Discussing tenancies by the entirety in bankruptcy requires one to focus not only on §541, but also on §522(b)(2)(B), a provision that provides that an individual debtor may exempt (if and only if the debtor does not — or cannot — elect the bankruptcy exemptions of §522(d), see §522(b)(1) ("in the alternative")):

> any interest in property in which the debtor had, immediately before the commencement of the case, an interest as a tenant by the entirety or joint tenant to the extent that such interest as a tenant by the entirety or joint tenant is exempt from process under applicable nonbankruptcy law.

The problem is that there is no particular procedure in the Bankruptcy Code like the one that exists for community property — where the property comes into the estate, and then is set aside for a particular purpose. Outside of bankruptcy, as we have noted, individual creditors cannot levy on property held in a tenancy by the entirety. Bankruptcy law could ignore this, but such a solution would fundamentally rearrange, in bankruptcy, the ordering of claims outside of bankruptcy — for outside of bankruptcy, the claimants of the marital unit do not have to share that property with anyone else. The House Report suggests that the problem has been solved by a provision in §363(h), permitting sale of the tenancies property, and requiring a pay-over of the spouse's share:

> With respect to other co-ownership interests, such as tenancies by the entirety, joint tenancies, and tenancies in common, the bill does not invalidate the rights, but provides a method by which the estate may realize on the value of the debtor's interest in the property while protecting the other rights. The trustee is permitted to realize on the value of the property by being permitted to sell it without obtaining a consent or a waiver of rights by the spouse of the debtor or the co-owner, as may be required for a complete sale under applicable State law. The other interest is protected under H.R. 8200 by giving the spouse a right of first refusal at a sale of the property, and by requiring the trustee to pay over to the spouse the value of the spouse's

interest in the property if the trustee sells the property to someone other than the spouse.

This may fairly allocate the property as between the debtor and the debtor's spouse, but does it not upset the rights of the various creditors? One of the first cases to recognize this problem, In re Jeffers, 3 Bankr. 49 (Bankr. N.D. Ind. 1980), concluded that §541(a)(1) did not cover tenancies by the entirety property because including it would dramatically rearrange priorities:

> If this Court allows the entireties property in question to become part of the estate and allows exemptions thereon and sale pursuant to Section 363(h) of the Code . . . , the effect will be to change the law of Indiana regarding real estate held as tenants by the entirety. Exemptions are not allowed to tenants by the entirety of real estate in Indiana because no such tenant has a separate or individual interest in the real estate so held. The allocation of proceeds from a sale to the spouse of a debtor, envisioned in Section 363 (j), is not possible under current Indiana law, as such spouse has no independent interest which can be isolated.
>
>   . . . The words of the Code and its legislative history are not sufficient to convince us . . . that Congress intended to change Indiana law regarding tenancies by the entirety, and the legislative history actually evidences a contrary intent. . . . [S]tate created property rights, in a bankruptcy context, will not be destroyed by implication. Butner v. United States, 440 U.S. 48 (1979). We therefore find that the real estate held as tenants by the entirety in Indiana does not become property of the estate pursuant to Section 541 of the Code.

The court in *Jeffers*, however, went on to conclude that the trustee can nonetheless reach the property for the benefit of the spouses' *joint* creditors, at least in cases where both spouses had filed a petition in bankruptcy and the cases were being administered together (§302) as the trustee has the powers of joint creditors of the debtor under §544(a). The end result of *Jeffers*, therefore, is a remedy that is substantially similar to the one the Bankruptcy Code has fashioned for community property.

Jeffers, however, seems to reach its result by ignoring §541. See, for example, §522(b)(2)(B), and recall *Goff*, which discusses the relationship between §541 and §522. Moreover, the ultimate solution of *Jeffers*, using the trustee as a joint creditor of both spouses, works only when both spouses have filed for bankruptcy, and their estates are being administered jointly pursuant to §302. In a case where only one spouse filed for bankruptcy, the result in *Jeffers* seems to be that the property is simply outside of the estate, whether or not there are any community creditors.

At least two other approaches to the problem illustrated in *Jeffers* have been used by courts. In re Ford, 3 Bankr. 559 (Bankr. D. Md. 1980), aff'd, 638 F.2d 14 (4th Cir. 1981), for example, suggested that the debtor has several legal and equitable interests in such property. The debtor has an in futuro expectancy based upon his right of survivorship — an expectation of the ownership of the whole of the property. Although the event of survivorship may be contingent and uncertain, the *right* to that survivorship interest is itself a present interest and not a future contingent right. . . . In addition to the debtor's present right of survivorship, the court finds that the debtor has an undivided, indivisible present right to the use, possession, and income from his tenants by the entireties property.

Ford also noted that §541(a) "does not contain the transferability prerequisites present in §70a," and thereby "does not restrict interests in entireties property and other non-transferable interests from becoming assets of the estate." *Ford* concluded

that the debtor's undivided interest in property which he held immediately before the commencement of the case as a tenant by the entirety with his nonbankrupt spouse . . . is property of the estate in bankruptcy under the Code, that the interest is subject to administration under §541(a)(1), and that the tenancy by the entirety is not severed by the filing of a petition under the Code.

As for §522(b)(2)(B), the court held that because "it is not the tenancy by the entirety property itself which becomes a part of the estate, but only the interest which the debtor held in such property immediately before the commencement of the case," what passed to the estate was only the individual undivided interest, and "[t]his interest alone is not subject to the claim of either individual creditors . . . or joint creditors." Therefore, the interest was exempt under §522(b)(2)(B). Because it was exempt, the debtor kept it out of the bankruptcy estate. But according to *Ford,* joint creditors could reach it, at least if they (a) got a release from the automatic stay and (b) foreclosed on the property before the debtor got a discharge (thereby bringing into play the provisions of §524(a)(2)). (Query whether this conclusion that joint creditors can reach the property is consistent with §522(c).) See also In re Anderson, 12 Bankr. 483 (Bankr. W.D. Mo. 1981) (same result, but observes that this last portion resurrects the "grab" race feature of individual creditor remedies); D'Avignon v. Palmisano, 34 Bankr. 796 (D. Vt. 1982) (concluding under §522(b)(2)(B) that a "sole debtor may exempt all of his interest in property held by the entirety," but a different result follows if both spouses file).

Apart from the "grab" race aspects of it, *Ford* ultimately may not end up working too differently than *Jeffers,* at least if the debtor selects the nonbankruptcy exemptions and thereby has access to §522(b)(2)(B), and if the joint creditors can get their work done before the discharge. Napotnik v. Equibank & Parkvale Savings Assn., 679 F.2d 316 (3rd Cir. 1982) and In re Cipa, 11 Bankr. 968 (Bankr. W.D. Pa. 1981), suggest a somewhat different approach. Under these cases, tenancies property comes into the estate via §541(a)(1). It then can be exempted via §522(b)(2)(B) *to the extent* that applicable law exempts it. Thus, if applicable law states that entireties property is exempt from levy by creditors of one spouse, so, too, is it exempt in bankruptcy. But it is not exempt "to the extent" that joint creditors could levy on it. Therefore, the entireties property remains in the estate to the extent of that value.

Is there a problem with this approach? Consider the following objection. The value of the property that remains in the estate (i.e., that cannot be exempted) is determined by the value of the joint claims that could have been asserted against the property (or, at least the value of the claims of joint claimants that have already gotten liens). Yet, once in the estate, the property is an asset of the estate available for all unsecured creditors, not just the joint creditors. Under the solution of *Napotnik* and *Cipu*, therefore, some of the problems envisioned by the *Jeffers* court remain.

Is it fair to conclude from these various approaches that what is really needed for entireties property is a provision like §726(c) for community property? Until Congress enacts such a section, isn't it fair to say that none of the results discussed above can fairly take account of the special attributes — both among owners and creditors — of property held in a tenancy by the entirety?

B. SECTION 522 AND EXEMPT PROPERTY

Before the enactment of the Bankruptcy Code, bankruptcy law followed state (and nonbankruptcy federal) rules on exemptions. A number of commentators, however, criticized the state law system of exemptions, principally on the grounds of nonuniformity and of the archaic quality of the exemptions. See Countryman, For a New Exemption Policy in Bankruptcy, 14 Rutgers L. Rev. 678 (1960); Karlen, Exemptions from Execution, 22 Bus. Law. 1167 (1967); Vukowich, Debtors' Exemption Rights, 62 Ga. L.J. 779 (1974); Joslin, Debtors' Exemption Laws: Time for Modernization, 34 Ind. L.J. 355 (1959). In 1976, the National Conference on Uniform State Laws approved a Uniform Exemptions Act, derived in large part from the exemptions in the Proposed Bankruptcy Act of 1973. The Bankruptcy Code, in turn, derives its set of "bankruptcy" exemptions from the Uniform Exemptions Act. Following passage of the Bankruptcy Code, the Uniform Exemptions Act was amended in 1979 by the National Conference, to bring it in closer conformity with the Bankruptcy Code. See Prefatory Note to Uniform Exemptions Act, 13 U.L.A. 365 (1980).

Section 522 of the Bankruptcy Code makes a number of changes in the subject of individual exemptions in bankruptcy. As enacted, and as a result of several last minute changes, §522 is a compromise between those who wanted an exclusive set of federal exemptions, and those who favored the old regime. Section 522(b) gives a debtor a choice — that can be taken away by the state, as we explore in the next paragraph — of electing either the set of exemptions set forth in §522(d) (the "bankruptcy exemptions") or the exemptions set forth elsewhere in the legal world (either state exemptions or nonbankruptcy federal exemptions). The debtor must choose either one set or the other in their entirety; he cannot "pick and choose" among them.

Because of a last minute compromise in Congress, this choice between nonbankruptcy exemptions and bankruptcy exemptions may be precluded if the domiciliary state passes a statute after the effective date of the Bankruptcy Code that requires that "its" exemptions be used (along, of course, with the nonbankruptcy federal exemptions). Passage of such a statute will call off the ability of a debtor to elect the bankruptcy exemptions set forth in §522. This has been an unexpectedly popular path: To date, over 35 states have passed such a statute.

Section 522(l) specifies that the debtor "shall file a list of property that the debtor claims as exempt." Bankruptcy Rule 4003 states that this list should be filed on the schedule of assets to be filed pursuant to §521(1) and Bankruptcy Rule 1007 (that is, concurrently with the filing of a voluntary petition or within 15 days of the order for relief in an involuntary case). Creditors should object within 30 days. Bankruptcy Rule 4003. There is no required procedure for creditors to receive formal notice of this list of exemptions. See generally Vukowich, Debtors' Exemption Rights Under the Bankruptcy Reform Act, 58 N.C.L. Rev. 769 (1980).

The effect of exempting property is specified in §522(c), which is discussed in *Lanctot,* infra page 864. Section 522(c) suggests that exempt property is retained by the debtor, and that there are only three groups of pre-petition creditors who may have recourse to such property: (a) certain tax claimants; (b) creditors with claims for alimony and/or child support; and (c) creditors with liens on certain property. (The ability of liens to pass through bankruptcy even though the underlying debt is discharged, was discussed, supra page 743 and was, inferentially, at least, the basis of the discussion of redemption under §722, supra page 781.)

Before the passage of the Bankruptcy Code, exempt property never became property of the estate. See Lockwood v. Exchange Bank, 190 U.S. 294 (1903). The legislative history to §541 states that "Paragraph (1) has the effect of overruling Lockwood v. Exchange Bank . . . because it includes as property of the estate all property of the debtor, even that needed for a fresh start. After the property comes into the estate, then the debtor is permitted to exempt it under proposed 11 U.S.C. 522, and the court will have jurisdiction to determine what property may be exempted and what remains as property of the estate."

Section 522 also gives a debtor the power to "avoid" certain types of property interests (such as execution liens and some security interests) on exempt property. See §522(f)-(h). As a result, exemption law, as embodied in §522, currently covers what may conveniently be thought of as two disparate subjects. First, §522 reflects the power of an individual debtor to remove property from the estate—and hence from the pool of assets available to the unsecured creditors generally. In this respect, less property is available for distribution to creditors, but no specific lien or vested property right of a creditor is actually "avoided." Second, §522 reflects the power of the individual debtor to avoid some liens—property rights —that would otherwise impair exemptions, notwithstanding that such liens are permitted under nonbankruptcy law. This power allows the debtor not only to remove property from the bankruptcy proceeding, but also, to some extent, to remove competing claims to that property.

NOTE ON CONSTITUTIONAL CHALLENGES TO §522

Two provisions of §522 have been the subject of substantial constitutional litigation. The first is the provision of §522(f), allowing a debtor to avoid certain liens (including some security interests) on exempt property. Here, the constitutional challenge has focused on the retroactive nature of §522(f)—on the ground that if that section allows the avoidance of security interests that existed before the date of the passage (or, perhaps, effective date) of the Bankruptcy Code, application of that section would constitute an uncompensated "taking" of a property right in violation of the Fifth Amendment to the U.S. Constitution. The Supreme Court avoided this constitutional issue, by holding, in United States v. Security Industrial Bank, 459 U.S. 70 (1982), that, in light of the substantial constitutional problems a retroactive interpretation would raise, "[n]o bankruptcy law shall be construed to eliminate property rights which existed before the law was enacted in the absence of an explicit command from Congress." Despite this holding, both the majority opinion (authored by Justice Rehnquist) and the concurring opinion (authored by Justice Blackmun), engaged in extended dicta on the underlying constitutional question: The majority virtually stating that the statute, if retroactive, would be unconstitutional; the concurrence explicitly stating that, if the case were being decided on a clean slate, it would uphold the constitutionality of the statute if applied on a retroactive basis.

The other major constitutional challenge that has surfaced concerning §522, involves the power of states to "opt-out" of the federal exemptions system, on the ground that this violates the constitutional command that bankruptcy statutes be "uniform." This contention was rejected in In re Sullivan, 680 F.2d 1131 (7th Cir. 1982), which relied principally on Hanover National Bank v. Moyses, 186 U.S. 181 (1902). *Moyses* had rejected a "uniformity" challenge to the old Bankruptcy Act's practice of simply adopting state exemption systems, holding that "uniformity is geographical, and not personal, and we do not think that the provision of the Act of 1898 as to exemptions is incompatible with that rule." 186 U.S., at 188. In *Sullivan*, the Seventh Circuit in upholding the "opt-out" provision of §522, commented:

> Although the arguments posed by the debtors regarding the correctness of the *Moyses* decision are forceful, this court obviously lacks the authority to overrule a Supreme Court case. Further, we are not convinced that recent Supreme Court authority has indicated a retreat from the *Moyses* rule.

See Koffler, The Bankruptcy Clause and Exemption Law: A Reexamination of the Doctrine of Geographic Uniformity, 58 N.Y.U. L. Rev. 22 (1983).

IN RE EVANS
29 Bankr. 336 (Bankr. D.N.J. 1983)

William LIPKIN, Bankruptcy Judge.

The debtors, Robert and Kathleen Evans, filed a joint petition under Chapter 7 of the Bankruptcy Code on October 13, 1981. Thereafter, John Casarow, Jr. was appointed trustee of the estate. While attending the §341, first meeting of creditors, the trustee became aware of the husband debtor's pending worker's compensation claim resulting from a pre-petition injury. The trustee filed an adversary proceeding which objected to the exemption of the pending worker's compensation award and claimed that the award was property of the estate.

The worker's compensation award at issue is the result of an injury suffered by the husband debtor when a metal rack fell on him on March 21, 1980 while working at Owens Corning Fiberglass. As a result of his accident the husband was off work and recuperating for 20 months. During this period the husband collected $185.00 per week for 67 weeks for temporary disability. The husband's worker's compensation claim was filed prior to the filing of the Chapter 7 and was not settled until March 19, 1982. At that time the worker's compensation court determined that the debtor had 45% partial-permanent disability and awarded the debtor $29,970.00 payable over 270 weeks, in addition to the temporary disability payments.

The trustee argues that the temporary disability award, that was paid after the filing of the bankruptcy petition, is the same as a receivable due the debtor at the time of bankruptcy, and, therefore, property of the estate. The trustee further argues that the award for the permanent-partial disability is only exempt up to $7,500.00 under §522(d)(11)(D) as a payment for a bodily injury. The debtors argue that pursuant to §522(d)(10)(A) & (C), and in the alternative, §522(d)(11)(E), both the temporary award and the partial-permanent disability award are exempt in the entirety.

The Bankruptcy Code Sections that the parties rely on in support of their respective arguments read as follows:

§522(d): The following property may be exempted under subsection (b)(1) of this section: . . .
(10) The debtor's right to receive—
    (A) a social security benefit, unemployment compensation, or a local public assistance benefit; . . .
    (C) a disability, illness, or unemployment benefit; . . .
(11) The debtor's right to receive, or property that is traceable to— . . .
    (D) a payment, not to exceed $7,500, on account of personal bodily injury, not including pain and suffering or compensation for actual pecuniary loss, of the debtor or an individual of whom the debtor is a dependent; or
    (E) a payment in compensation of loss of future earnings of the debtor or an individual of whom the debtor is or was a dependent, to the extent reasonable necessary for the support of the debtor and any dependent of the debtor.

The legislative history of section 522(d) does not specifically state what Congress intended with regard to worker's compensation benefits. Congress used the following language in discussing section 522(d)(10):

Paragraph (10) exempts certain benefits that are <u>akin to future earnings</u> of the debtor. These include social security, unemployment compensation, or public assistance benefits, veterans benefits, disability, illness or unemployment <u>benefits</u>. . . . [underlining added]

In discussing section 522(d)(11), which also refers to a loss of future earnings, the following language is used:

Paragraph (11) allows the debtor to exempt certain <u>compensation for losses</u>. These include crime victim's reparation benefits, wrongful death benefits (with a reasonably necessary for support limitation), life insurance proceeds, . . . <u>compensation</u> for bodily injury, not including pain and suffering, . . . and loss of furture [sic] earnings payments (support limitation). [underlining added] [House Report No. 95-595, 95th Cong., 1st Sess. (1977) 361-62, U.S. Code Cong. & Admin. News 1978, p. 5787, 6318.]

Although both §§522(d)(10) and (11) were Congressionally intended to compensate for a loss of future income, Congress must have intended a distinction between them. Worker's compensation awards have been determined to be akin to future earnings and exempt without limit under section 522(d)(10)(C). In re Fernand J. LaBelle, 18 B.R. 922, 8 B.C.D.

1199 (Bkrtcy. D. Me. 1982). The court in *LaBelle* based its decision on both the legislative history cited above and the nature of worker's compensation claims. The court concluded that worker's compensation benefits are generally intended only to prevent the individual from becoming destitute, while compensation for loss of future earnings referred to in §522(d)(11) deals with compensation in the nature of tort liability.

The Bankruptcy Court in In re Lambert, 9 B.R. 799, 7 B.C.D. 508 (Bkrtcy. W.D. Mi. 1981) also decided that worker's compensation awards were exempt, but used an analysis rejected by the court in *LaBelle*. That court held that the part of the award pertaining to accrued disability would be " 'a disability . . . benefit' which the debtor had a right to receive as of the date of the filing of the petition," and therefore exempt under section 522(d)(10)(C). The balance of the award was found to be "a payment in 'compensation of loss of future earnings' ", and exempt with the support limitations imposed by section 522(d)(11)(E).

The husband, in the present case, was awarded temporary disability for 67 weeks at $185.00 per week. Additionally, he was awarded $29,970.00 for 45 percent partial-permanent disability. Under New Jersey law, temporary disability awards are made on the basis of 20 percent to 75 percent of the average weekly wages earned by the employee. N.J.S.A. 34:15-12(a). Temporary disability benefits represent a partial substitute for loss of current wages. . . . The temporary disability benefits received by the husband are, therefore, exempt in the entirety under section 522(d)(10)(C) of the Code as disability benefits that are "akin to future earnings" within the meaning set forth in the legislative history.

New Jersey law, however, does distinguish partial-permanent disability payments from both temporary and permanent disability payments. Partial permanent disability payments are viewed as disability payments as well as a substitution for future earnings. Katz v. Township of Howell, 67 N.J. 51, 63, 335 A.2d 14 (1975). . . . Compensation for partial permanent disability under N.J.S.A. 34:15-12, 22 is satisfied by a ". . . personal injury which detracts from the former efficiency of the workman's body or its members in the ordinary pursuits of life." Id. at 63, 335 A.2d 14. . . . This definition clearly comes within the meaning of a "disability" benefit under section 522(d)(10)(C) and within the legislative history to this section, which indicates an exemption for "benefits that are akin to future earnings of the debtor." [underlining added]

The statute awarding compensation for partial-permanent disability specifically refers to a "disability partial in character and permanent in quality." N.J.S.A. 34:15-12(c). The difference in legal definition between temporary and permanent partial disability benefits, under state law, does not require a different exemption treatment under the Bankruptcy Code; both awards come within the definition in §522(d)(10)(C). In addition, New Jersey law exempts all worker's compensation awards, including temporary and partial-permanent, from all claims of creditors and from levy, execution or attachment. N.J.S.A. 34:15-29. The same exemption from execution on funds realized from a "tort" recovery does not exist under New Jersey statutes. Although this exemption is not binding on this court for purposes of applying federal bankruptcy law, it is certainly indicative of the purpose of these payments to provide compensation for workers' disabilities.

The trustee's argument, that these partial-permanent disability payments are only exempt in the amount of $7500.00 under section 522(d)(11)(D) as a payment for a bodily injury, must fail. Section 522(d)(11)(D) has been interpreted to apply only to compensation in the nature of tort liability. . . .

The entire tenor of §522(d)(11) relates to tort compensation, i.e. crime victim's reparation, life insurance payments, bodily injury and loss of future earnings. Payments for loss of future earnings do not occur solely in the context of worker's compensation. See N.J.S.A. 39:6A-4(b), where there is compulsory insurance for lost future income as a result of a disability from an automobile accident. Therefore, section 522(d)(11) is most reasonably interpreted as applying to general tort-related awards, and not worker's compensation awards. Worker's compensation was legislatively defined outside the area of general tort law. This distinction logically appears to have been continued by Congress in specifying exemptions under the Bankruptcy Code.

Thus, the worker's compensation awards to the husband debtor, for temporary disability and permanent-partial disability, are exempt under Section 522(d)(10)(C) of the Code in their entirety. This section does not limit the exemption to an amount necessary for the debtor's support. Submit an order accordingly.

NOTES

1. Relying on the presence of §522(d)(11)(D), and its $7,500 limitation, the Fourth Circuit has held that a "debtor's claim for injuries to the person, whether unliquidated as when the petition was filed, or settled as occurred during the proceeding, are thus property of the estate as of the commencement of the case." Tignor v. Parkinson, 729 F.2d 977 (4th Cir. 1984).

2. *Evans* requires you to focus on the relationship between §522(d)(10) and §522(d)(11) and, in particular, the reasons for limiting the exemption in (d)(11)(D) to $7,500. Is it possible to make the distinction the court does — that (d)(11) "is most reasonably interpreted as applying to general tort-related awards, and not worker's compensation awards"? Isn't that distinction unsupportable? Historically, workers' compensation systems were designed to *replace* traditional tort recovery systems. Subsection (d)(11)(D)'s limitation to $7,500, moreover, only applies to payments

to compensate for personal injury, whereas (d)(11)(E) covers tort payments for loss of future income, and does not contain the dollar limit. Is there any reason why workers' compensation awards should not be bifurcated, as tort awards are, into (d)(11)(D) and (d)(11)(E) categories?

More generally, what supports the limitation of subsection (d)(11)(D)? Isn't a tort award for personal injury designed to compensate an individual for something his creditors couldn't get at in bankruptcy anyway? If Debtor loses an arm in a machine accident, tort payments to him would be designed to compensate him for his loss. That loss may be broken down into two rough categories: (a) loss of economic value (such as by reduced future wages) and (b) pain and suffering. But don't both of these awards compensate Debtor for the loss of something that creditors would not have been entitled to go after in bankruptcy anyway? If that is so, why should a tort compensation award for personal injury be treated differently than the underlying physical attribute would have been treated? Isn't the only limitation that needs to be made caused by the possibility that part of the tort award may compensate Debtor for lost wages in the *pre-petition* period that, but for the tort, would presumably have been available for the creditors? Or is this whole inquiry one of bankruptcy law only?

Having puzzled through *Evans,* we need to return to an issue raised in *Goff,* supra page 819: the treatment of retirement plans in bankruptcy. *Clark,* which follows, analyzes a Keogh plan under §522(d)(10)(E), and concludes it does not fit. Why?

IN RE CLARK
711 F.2d 21 (3rd Cir. 1983)

GIBBONS, Circuit Judge.

Robert H. Clark, a discharged bankrupt, appeals from a final order of the Bankruptcy Court for the District of New Jersey denying his claim for exemption under 11 U.S.C. §522(d)(10)(E) (Supp. V 1981) of $17,466 in his Keogh retirement plan. . . .

On September 18, 1981 Clark, a 43-year old licensed family therapist, filed a Chapter 7 petition in bankruptcy and claimed an exemption for his Keogh retirement plan. Contributions to such plan are tax-deductible, and income tax on the fund and its earnings is deferred until withdrawn. Funds may be withdrawn when a participant becomes 59½, dies, or is disabled. If funds are withdrawn before these events, the participant must pay a penalty tax of 10 percent in addition to regular income taxes, and is barred from making contributions to the plan for five years.

Thomas J. O'Neill, the interim trustee, filed an objection to the claimed exemption, and Clark filed a complaint against the trustee seeking a denial of the objection. The bankruptcy court noted that the case involved only the issue of exemption under section 522(d)(10)(E); not whether the fund was property of the bankruptcy estate, or whether it was exempt as a matter of state law. The court agreed with the trustee that because Clark had no present right to receive payments from the plan, his exemption claim did not fall within the literal terms of section 522(d)(10)(E).

The general purpose of the exemption provisions of the Bankruptcy Code is to give debtors a fresh start. As noted in the House Report on H.R. 8200:

> The historical purpose of [ ] exemption laws has been to protect a debtor from his creditors, to provide him with the basic necessities of life so that even if his creditors levy on all of his nonexempt property, the debtor will not be left destitute and a public charge. [This] purpose has not changed.

H.R. Rep. No. 595, 95th Cong., 1st Sess. 126 (1977), reprinted in 1978 U.S. Code Cong. & Ad. News, 5787, 5963, 6087. The exemption of present Keogh payments, to the extent they are necessary for the support of the debtor, is consistent with this goal. The exemption of *future* payments, however, demonstrates a concern for the debtor's long-term security which is absent from the statute.

The result of denying the exemption with respect to future payments is in accord with the case law. . . .[2] The court in Matter of Kochell, 26 B.R. 86 (Bkrtcy. W.D. Wis. 1982), . . . squarely faced the issue of whether section 522(d)(10)(E) exempts pension plans themselves rather than present payments. The *Kochell* court agreed that the underlying purpose of the section was to alleviate present rather than long-term need, a condition which the 44-year old debtor, a doctor in apparent good health, could not demonstrate. Cf. In re Donaghy, 11 B.R. 677 (Bkrtcy. S.D.N.Y. 1981) (lump sum disbursement under pension plan is exempt as equivalent to right to receive payment); Matter of Taff, 10 B.R. 101 (Bkrtcy. D. Conn. 1981) (retiree's pension is exempt only to extent necessary to meet basic needs).

Clark's alternative argument, that the income which accrued from the Keogh plan subsequent to the filing of the bankruptcy petition is exempt regardless of the nonexempt status of the plan, must also be rejected. As noted by the trustee, 11 U.S.C. §541(a)(6) requires the inclusion of such

---

2. Under the Bankruptcy Act of 1898, a trustee was vested with the title of bankrupt except to the extent that such property was exempt under section 6 which recognized both federal and state nonbankruptcy exemptions. . . . The exemption of pension plans turned to a large extent on questions such as whether the debtor had a choate, vested interest in the fund or whether the state frowned on the immunity of spendthrift trusts created by a settlor for his own benefit. . . . Thus the initial issue of title received more emphasis than the subsequent application of federal or state exemptions. Here, Clark concedes that the Keogh plan is property of the bankruptcy estate under the more expansive provisions of 11 U.S.C. §541 (Supp. V 1981).

income as property of the estate. Likewise, 11 U.S.C. §522(d)(11)(E) does not exempt future earnings but payments "in compensation for the loss of future earnings." Whatever the "equitable" considerations to which Clark refers, . . . we cannot ignore the fact that his right to an exemption is governed by statute, and that none of the statutory exemption provisions apply to the income from the plan.

The judgment appealed from will be affirmed.

BECKER, Circuit Judge, concurring.

I agree with the majority that Clark is not entitled to an exemption for his Keogh retirement plan, but I rely on grounds different from the majority's.

The majority concludes that "[t]he exemption of *future* payments . . . demonstrates a concern for the debtor's long-term security which is absent from the statute." I have substantial doubts that the majority has correctly assessed congressional intent, for the distinction required by the majority's reasoning effectively penalizes self-employed individuals for the form in which their retirement assets are held. The majority's holding will not affect employee pension and annuity plans created by employers, because the assets of such plans would not be included in the debtor's estate under section 541, and thus cannot be reached by the trustee. The assets of a Keogh plan, in contrast, are clearly assets of the estate.[1] Thus Congress' putative lack of concern for the long-term security of the debtor works to the detriment only of self-employed debtors—a result I find inconsistent with Congress' manifest solicitude for retirement benefits for self-employed individuals.

In light of this inconsistency, it seems to me equally plausible to infer a congressional intent to encompass all retirement plans of whatever form. Section 522(d)(10)(E) exempts the debtor's right to receive payments "under a stock bonus, pension, profit-sharing, annuity, or *similar* plan. . . ." (emphasis added) . . . under the relevant plans, Congress narrowed the language in section 522(d)(10)(E) to include only "[t]he right to receive payments" under the relevant plans.[2] The bankruptcy

---

1. As I read the majority's opinion, no retirement or disability plan whose assets are included in the debtor's estate under section 541 would be exempt if the right to payment thereunder was a future right. This would presumably preclude exemption of the assets of Individual Retirement Accounts (IRA's) as well.

2. The bankruptcy court noted as well that a second proposal before Congress, the Proposed Bankruptcy Act of the Commission on Bankruptcy Laws of the United States, also contained language that would have allowed exemption of Keogh assets. Section 4-503(c)(6) provided:

(c) The following property shall be allowed as exempt. . . .

(6) before or after retirement, such rights as the debtor may have under a profit-sharing, pension, stock bonus, annuity or similar plan which is established for the primary purpose of providing benefits upon retirement by reason of age, health, or length of service . . . to the extent . . . the debtor's interest therein is reasonably necessary for the support of the debtor and his dependents.

This proposal, too, was rejected.

court concluded that Congress intended this narrower language to preclude the exemption of assets held under Keogh retirement plans. Unfortunately, the bankruptcy court's analysis would seem to foreclose exemption of Keogh assets even if a debtor's right to receive payment had vested because he or she had reached retirement age. I would find that result even more troubling than the majority's.

Although the bankruptcy court's discussion provides some evidence of congressional intent, it is not the strongest of evidence — there is nothing but the fact of the difference in language to go on. The legislative history nowhere discusses the changes made or their intended impact. I would thus be reluctant to rely on this inference of intent, given the incongruity of the result for different retirement plans.

The appropriate resolution of these issues is thus far from clear. In my view, however, it is not necessary for this court to resolve them here, for there is a narrower and surer ground upon which we can decide this case.

Section 6.2 of appellant's Keogh plan, sponsored by Merrill, Lynch, Pierce, Fenner & Smith, provides that "[t]he Plan shall terminate . . . if the Employer judicially is declared insolvent." Section 6.5 provides that "[u]pon termination of the Plan for any of the reasons set forth in Article 6.2 . . . no further contributions shall be made . . . and the Custodian shall make distributions of all Benefits to the Participants." Thus, upon his adjudication as a bankrupt, Clark's Keogh plan terminated. The funds either have been or are to be distributed, and Clark palpably has no right to receive payment under any plan on account of illness, disability, death, age or length of service. Under these circumstances, Clark was not entitled to an exemption. I therefore concur in the judgment of the Court.

NOTES

1. A similar conclusion was reached in In re Graham, 726 F.2d 1268 (8th Cir. 1984), relying principally on the fact that ERISA was not listed in the legislative history as an example of federal exemptions, and on the assertion that "there is a conceptual distinction between the property exempted by the listed laws and the property covered by ERISA," in that ERISA "regulates private employer pension systems," and is not "peculiarly federal in nature." Why, however, should these distinctions matter? If creditors cannot levy on the property outside of bankruptcy, shouldn't it be considered exempt *in* bankruptcy, whatever its label might be? See Jackson, Translating Assets and Liabilities to the Bankruptcy Forum, 14 J. Legal Studies 73 (1985); cf. In re Wright, 39 Bankr. 623 (D.S.C. 1983).

2. In analyzing cases such as *Clark,* is the following of any relevance? Eisenberg, Bankruptcy Law in Perspective, 28 U.C.L.A. L. Rev. 953, 972-973 n.60 (1981):

In states where state law now precludes resort to federal exemptions, on the surface debtors appear to be no worse off than they were under the old bankruptcy act. . . . Under the old law [, however], exemptions did not provide the only legitimate route through which debtors could keep assets despite bankruptcy. Courts allowed debtors to keep additional nonexempt assets out of the estate by construing such assets not to be "property" within the meaning of §70a of the old act, see Lines v. Frederick . . . or by straining to read state law in a manner that would avoid satisfying one of §70's requirements for inclusion of an asset in the bankruptcy estate. . . . Under the new act, §541, which determines the assets to be included in the bankruptcy estate, was intended to be all inclusive. All of the debtor's assets are to be in the estate and the exemption provisions alone determine what the debtor is permitted to keep. . . . The Senate and House Reports expressly state that §541 is intended to overrule Lines v. Frederick. Thus, Congress meant to foreclose the method of keeping assets out of the bankruptcy estate through interpretation of the term "property." Debtors who may only avail themselves of state exemptions are at least in this respect in a worse theoretical position than under the old act.

Notwithstanding the Senate and House Reports, the Lines v. Frederick method . . . may, and perhaps should, survive enactment of the new law. . . . Courts that construed the term "property" in the old act to keep assets out of the bankruptcy estate will not find congressional disapproval of those results in §541's text. Only the legislative history reveals the plan in this area. And the legislative history can be viewed as more equivocal than it first seems. The statements in the House and Senate Reports about the all inclusive scope intended for §541 were made at a time when the House version of the bankruptcy reform bill contained a system of federal exemptions that was available in bankruptcy regardless of state law. A system of federal exemptions that could not be stripped away by the states may have been viewed as fair compensation to debtors for the all inclusive nature of §541. Once §522 was recast on the eve of passage . . . , the trade-off between federal exemptions and a broad view of §541 arguably should no longer govern. . . .

The problems and materials that follow explore, in some greater detail, the various provisions of §522.

PROBLEMS

11.6 A state exemption statute exempts "[n]ecessary . . . wearing apparel, ordinarily and reasonably necessary to, and personally used by, the debtor." Debtor has a four carat diamond engagement ring, purchased with the insurance proceeds received when Debtor's original 3.5 carat diamond engagement ring was stolen. Is it exempt under the statute? See In re Westhem, 459 F. Supp. 556 (C.D. Calif. 1978), aff'd, 642 F.2d 1139 (9th Cir. 1981). Is it exempt in bankruptcy if Debtor elects the nonbankruptcy exemptions? The bankruptcy exemptions? See §522(d)(4).

11.7 Debtor owns twelve, five-piece place settings of sterling silver flatware. After Debtor files for bankruptcy, Debtor elects the set of bankruptcy exemptions in §522(d). Debtor claims that the entire set of sterling silver is exempt under §522(d)(3), because each individual piece of the sterling silver is worth less than $200. Evaluate that claim. Would your answer change if the value of the entire set were $5,000? See In re Wahl, 14 Bankr. 153 (Bankr. E.D. Wisc. 1981).

11.8 Debtor owns a rifle that he keeps at home. After Debtor files for bankruptcy, Debtor elects the bankruptcy exemptions of §522(d). May Debtor exempt the rifle under §522(d)(3)? See In re Noggle, 30 Bankr. 303 (Bankr. E.D. Mich. 1983).

11.9 Debtor received $21,000 in a lump sum payment of accrued pension benefits on April 1. On April 20, Debtor files a petition in bankruptcy. Assume that, had the funds not been received by Debtor before he filed his petition in bankruptcy, he would have been able to claim the pension funds as exempt under §522(d)(10)(E) (a perhaps questionable assumption in light of *Clark*). The trustee asserts that the pension funds lost that protection upon receipt by Debtor, prior to bankruptcy, and that the money therefore constituted property of the estate under §541. Who gets the $21,000? See In re Donaghy, 11 Bankr. 677 (Bankr. S.D.N.Y. 1981).

11.10 Debtor, a resident of New York, has filed suit for a tort claim for personal injuries. Debtor subsequently files for bankruptcy. Under New York law, the assignment or transfer of a claim for personal injury is prohibited, N.Y. Gen. Obligations Law §13-101, and under C.P.L.R. §5201(b), a "money judgment may be enforced against any property which could be assigned or transferred. . . ." The proceeds of such a tort claim, however, are assignable. What, if anything, may Debtor exempt in bankruptcy if she elects the nonbankruptcy exemptions? See In re Mucelli, 21 Bankr. 601 (Bankr. S.D.N.Y. 1982). What, if anything, may the Debtor exempt in bankruptcy if she elects the bankruptcy exemptions of §522(d)?

11.11 Debtor has a claim against Company for violations of the Truth-in-Lending Act. If Debtor elects the bankruptcy exemptions, may Debtor apply the $4,150 exemption of §522(d)(5) (the so-called wild-card exemption) to that claim? See In re Smith, 640 F.2d 888 (7th Cir. 1981).

11.12 Debtor is an attorney. He has, in his office, a typewriter, a desk, and a chair. Debtor files a petition in bankruptcy, and elects the bankruptcy exemptions of §522(d). May Debtor exempt the typewriter, desk, and/or chair (up to the applicable maximum) under §522(d)(6)? In considering this, do these constitute "implements" or "tools"? Is Debtor engaged in a "trade"? See In re Guard, 26 Bankr. 2 (Bankr. M.D. Fla. 1982).

11.13 Debtor has a 1966 Mustang. At the time Debtor filed for bankruptcy, the car had a market value of $1,200. By the close of the bankruptcy case, however, the market value of 1966 Mustangs had risen to $3,000. To what extent may Debtor claim an exemption in the Mustang under §522(d)(2)? See In re Dvoroznak, 38 Bankr. 178 (Bankr. E.D.N.Y. 1984).

NOTE ON THE DEBTOR'S "AVOIDING POWERS" OVER EXEMPT ASSETS

Sections 522(f), (g), and (h) raise an issue of how a debtor can preserve exempt property, despite the existence of a lien or a security interest on that property and the existence of §522(c). State laws, notwithstanding the Bankruptcy Code, will allow a debtor to avoid certain liens and security interests on exempt property. In part, this may be a necessary consequence of the fact that some kinds of property that are exempt under §522(d) are not exempt under state law, and hence may have acquired liens and the like that property exempt under state law would not have. But that explanation is only partial. The "avoiding powers" of §522 apply to certain consensual security interests, despite the fact that few state law exemptions systems prohibit such interests. Moreover, the §522 avoiding powers apply as well to property that *is* exempt under state law irrespective of whether the debtor has elected bankruptcy or nonbankruptcy exemptions. *Lanctot*, which follows, explores the operation of §522(f), (g), and (h), and *McManus*, which follows *Lanctot*, raises the question, again, of the relationship between state law and bankruptcy law. The legislative history comments on these points as follows:

> the bill gives the debtor certain rights not available under current law with respect to exempt property. The debtor may void any judicial lien on exempt property, and any nonpurchase money security interest in certain exempt property such as household goods. The first right allows the debtor to undo the actions of creditors that bring legal action against the debtor shortly before bankruptcy. Bankruptcy exists to provide relief for an overburdened debtor. If a creditor beats the debtor into court, the debtor is nevertheless entitled to his exemptions. The second right will be of more significance for the average consumer debtor. Frequently, creditors lending money to a consumer debtor take a security interest in all of the debtor's belongings, and obtain a waiver by the debtor of his exemptions. In most of these cases, the debtor is unaware of the consequences of the forms he signs. The creditor's experience provides him with a substantial advantage. If the debtor encounters financial difficulty, creditors often use threats of repossession of all of the debtor's household goods as a means of obtaining payment.
>
> In fact, were the creditor to carry through on his threat and foreclose on the property, he would receive little, for household goods have little resale value. They are far more valuable to the creditor in the debtor's hands, for they provide a credible basis for the threat, because the replacement costs of the goods are generally high. Thus, creditors rarely repossess, and debtors, ignorant of the creditors' true intentions, are coerced into payments they simply cannot afford to make.
>
> The exemption provision allows the debtor, after bankruptcy has been filed, and creditor collection techniques have been stayed, to undo the consequences of a contract of adhesion, signed in ignorance, by permitting the invalidation of nonpurchase money security interests in household goods.

Such security interests have too often been used by over-reaching creditors. The bill eliminates any unfair advantage creditors have.

Is this persuasive? To what extent, if any, should debtors be able to waive such protections? Many of these issues, you will note, echo back to the discussion of discharge discussed in the previous chapter.

PROBLEM

11.14 Debtor has real estate worth $25,000. Bank has a nonpurchase money security interest on the real estate securing a $15,000 loan. Debtor elects her bankruptcy exemptions. Can she avoid Bank's security interest under §522(f)? Would the case be any different if Debtor had filed a list of property that she claimed as exempt, listed the real estate there as having a value of $15,000, and then waited beyond the period where creditors had an opportunity to object to such a schedule? See §522(l); In re Carswell, 13 Bankr. 337 (Bankr. E.D. Pa. 1981).

IN RE LANCTOT
6 Bankr. 576 (Bankr. D. Utah 1980)

Ralph R. MABEY, Bankruptcy Judge.

On June 13, 1979, Local Loan Financial Services (Local Loan) loaned money to the Lanctots for the purchase of two Suzuki motorcycles in accordance with the terms of a purchase money security agreement signed by the parties. The lien was never properly noted on the certificates of title covering the motorcycles as required by Utah Code Ann. §§41-1-80 et seq. (Supp. 1979), and thus, Local Loan's security interest was never perfected. The Lanctots encountered financial difficulty and on February 26, 1980, filed a Chapter 7 bankruptcy petition claiming the motorcycles as exempt. At the Section 341 meeting of creditors on March 24, 1980, the Lanctots delivered unencumbered titles to the motorcycles to the trustee. Some three days later, the trustee informed the Lanctots that she claimed an interest in the motorcycles superior to theirs. On April 12, 1980, the trustee filed an adversary proceeding pursuant to 11 U.S.C. §§544 and 551, alleging that Local Loan had failed to perfect its security interest in the motorcycles and, therefore, the trustee was entitled to set aside Local Loan's interest in the motorcycles and to preserve the lien for the benefit of the estate.

Local Loan stipulated that an order could be entered granting the trustee the relief sought in the complaint. On May 2, 1980, the Lanctots received copies of the proposed stipulation and order avoiding the claimed security interest of Local Loan and also a Notice to Sell and Receipt by

Auctioneer. On the same day, the Lanctots moved to intervene in the adversary proceeding, requesting the Court to stay the sale pending a determination by the Court that the exemptions claimed by the Lanctots were valid and superior to the interest asserted by the trustee. . . .

Under Utah law, a security agreement becomes enforceable once three basic requirements are met. First, the collateral must be in the possession of the secured party or the debtor must sign a security agreement which contains an adequate description of the collateral. Second, value must be given. Third, the debtor must acquire rights in the collateral. See Utah Code Ann. §70A-9-203 (Supp. 1979). As between the Lanctots and Local Loan, the security interest attached and became enforceable as soon as the Lanctots signed the loan agreement, Local Loan advanced the money to the Lanctots, and that money was used to purchase the motorcycles. As the money advanced was used to purchase the collateral, a purchase money security interest was created under Utah Code Ann. §70A-9-107 (1968).

In Utah, a security interest in a motor vehicle required to be licensed must be filed with the motor vehicle division of the state tax commission in order to be perfected. . . . Perfection of an interest is important only to insure priority of the lien over intervening third parties. The absence of perfection does not affect, however, the enforceability of the lien against the parties to the transaction. Thus, even without a subsequent filing to perfect the security interest, the security interest became valid and enforceable against the Lanctots, as parties to the transaction, from the date on which the last of the three requirements for attachment occurred.

The unperfected security interest is, however, vulnerable to attack by certain third parties. These parties are granted priority over an unperfected security interest even though their interests arise subsequent in time. See Utah Code Ann. §70A-9-301 (Supp. 1979). One such party designated in Utah Code Ann. §70A-9-301(1)(b) as taking priority over an unperfected security interest is "a person who becomes a lien creditor before the security interest is perfected." Section 70A-9-301(3) includes in its definition of a lien creditor, "a trustee in bankruptcy from the date of filing of the petition." Thus, under state law, the trustee is granted priority over the unperfected lien of Local Loan.

Under 11 U.S.C. §544(a)(1), the trustee is granted certain avoiding powers in addition to his or her rights under state law. . . . Thus, as a hypothetical judicial lienholder who obtains his lien as of the date of filing the petition in bankruptcy, the trustee may avoid the unperfected security interest of Local Loan. Under 11 U.S.C. §551, the lien is then automatically preserved for the benefit of the estate of the debtor. Thereafter, Local Loan has claim only as an unsecured creditor of the estate.

The Lanctots claim the motorcycles in question as exempt property under 11 U.S.C. §522(d)(5)*, which reads:

---

* This subsection was revised in 1984. — Eds.

(d) The following property may be exempted under subsection (b)(1) of this section:

(5) The debtor's aggregate interest, not to exceed in value $400 plus any unused amount of the exemption provided under paragraph (1) of this subsection in any property.

This provision preserves for the debtor his "aggregate interest" in property of up to $400 plus the unused portion of the $7500 exemption allowed in subsection (d)(1). To exempt property, however, the debtor must first have an "aggregate interest" in the property, which means he must have right to the property or a portion of the property which is prior to all others. As the lien of Local Loan exceeds the value of the motorcycles, unless the Lanctots can claim an interest prior to Local Loan and to the trustee, who may avoid and then preserve Local Loan's lien for the benefit of the estate, they have no interest to exempt.

It is clear that under state law, the Lanctots are still subject to the security interest of Local Loan despite its failure to perfect. Therefore, to claim the property as exempt, free and clear of that lien, they must either have some right under the Bankruptcy Code to avoid directly the creditor's lien on their property or they must be entitled to derive the benefit of the trustee's avoiding powers over an unperfected lien. The rights of the debtor to either avoid liens on property claimed as exempt or to claim the benefit of liens avoided by the trustee on their exempt property are found exclusively in 11 U.S.C. §522, which governs exemptions.

Under the exemption statute, 11 U.S.C. §522, the debtor may avoid certain liens on exempt property. Section 522(f) reads:

(f) Notwithstanding any waiver of exemptions, the debtor may avoid the fixing of a lien on an interest of the debtor in property to the extent that such lien impairs an exemption to which the debtor would have been entitled under subsection (h) of this section if such lien is—

(1) a judicial lien; or
(2) a nonpossessory, nonpurchase-money security interest in any—
(A) household furnishings, household goods, wearing apparel, appliances, books, animals, crops, musical instruments, or jewelry that are held primarily for the personal, family, or household use of the debtor or a dependent of the debtor;
(B) implements, professional books, or tools of the trade of the debtor or the trade of a dependent of the debtor; or
(C) professionally prescribed health aids for the debtor or a dependent of the debtor.

The purpose of subsection (f) is discussed in H.R. Rep. No. 95-595, 95th Cong., 1st Sess., at 362 (1977), U.S. Code Cong. & Admin. News 1978, pp. 5787, 6318.

Subsection (f) protects the debtor's exemptions, his discharge, and thus his fresh start by permitting him to avoid certain liens on exempt property. The debtor may avoid a judicial lien on any property to the extent that the property could have been exempted in the absence of the lien, and may similarly avoid a nonpurchase-money security interest in certain household and personal goods. The avoiding power is independent of any waiver of exemptions.

Paragraph one of subsection (f) permits the debtor to avoid a judicial lien which impairs exempt property. A judicial lien is defined at 11 U.S.C. §101(27)* as a "lien obtained by judgment, levy, sequestration, or other legal or equitable process or proceeding." The term "lien" is further defined in Section 101(28)* as a "charge against or interest in property to secure payment of a debt or performance of an obligation." The nature of this definition of "lien" is described in H.R. Rep. No. 95-595, supra at 312, U.S. Code Cong. & Admin. News 1978, p. 6269, as follows:

> The definition is new and is very broad . . . It includes inchoate liens. In general, the concept of lien is divided into three kinds of liens: judicial liens, security interests, and statutory liens. *Those three categories are mutually exclusive except for certain common law liens.* (Emphasis supplied)

Not only does Local Loan's lien fail to meet the plain definition of a judicial lien inasmuch as defendant had not commenced any process attempting to levy, sequester, or obtain a judgment, legal or equitable, against the motorcycles, from this legislative history, it is evident that as Local Loan holds a security interest as defined in 11 U.S.C. §101(37),* its lien cannot be a judicial lien. Therefore, the unperfected security interest of Local Loan in the motorcycles cannot be set aside by the Lanctots under Section 522(f)(1).

Likewise, Section 522(f)(2) is inapplicable on these facts. The opening clause of this paragraph permits the debtor to avoid liens which impair exempt property, if such lien is "a nonpossessory, nonpurchase-money security interest . . ." in certain personal property. As discussed above, the loan arrangement between the Lanctots and Local Loan constituted a purchase money security interest under Utah Code Ann. 70A-9-107 (1968). Furthermore, a motorcycle is not the type of personal property enumerated in Section 522(f)(2).

Subsection (g) of Section 522 permits the debtor, under certain conditions, to exempt property which the trustee recovers through the exercise of his or her avoiding powers. Subsection (g) reads:

> (g) Notwithstanding sections 550 and 551 of this title, the debtor may exempt under subsection (b) of this section property that the trustee recovers under section 510(c)(2), 542, 543, 550, 551, or 553 of this title, to the extent that the debtor could have exempted such property under subsection (b) of this section if such property had not been transferred, if—

---

* Renumbered in 1984. — EDS.

(1)(A) such transfer was not a voluntary transfer of such property by the debtor; and

(B) the debtor did not conceal such property; or

(2) the debtor could have avoided such transfer under subsection (f)(2) of this section.

In 3 Collier on Bankruptcy §522.08, at 522-31 (15th ed. 1979), a summary of Section 522(g) is given in these words:

> Where the trustee recovers property fraudulently conveyed or concealed, the debtor may not claim exemptions out of the recovered property. The transfer need not be fraudulent to defeat the debtor's right to claim an exemption in such property. Section 522(g) provides that such transfer need only be voluntary. This section lists the various sections of the Code upon which the trustee may recover transferred property. Thus, the trustee may recover property if a transfer is avoided, or if the property is held by a custodian. If the debtor may exempt property held by an entity other than a custodian, such property may be recovered by the trustee. Additionally, the trustee may order any subordinated lien returned to the estate. Ordinarily, under section 522(g), in such recoveries of property, a claim of exemption would attach. *This is not the case, however, when the transfer was voluntary by the debtor.* (Citations omitted.) (Emphasis supplied.)

Thus, in order for the Lanctots to make use of Section 522(g)(1), they must show that the transfer was not voluntary and that they did not conceal the property. Since the motorcycles were accurately listed on debtor's Schedules B-2 and B-4, there was no concealment. Likewise, the voluntary nature of the transaction is undisputed. That the transaction constituted a "transfer" is apparent from the statute.

Section 101(40)* defines transfer as meaning "every mode, direct or indirect, absolute or conditional, voluntary or involuntary, of disposing of or parting with property or with an interest in property, including retention of title as a security interest." Even though Local Loan did not retain title in this case, with the acquisition of its security interest in the property, a transfer was made. In which party title vests is not a consideration in finding a transfer. H.R. Rep. No. 95-595, supra at 314, U.S. Code Cong. & Admin. News 1978, p. 6271, states:

> Under this definition [Section 101(40)], any transfer of an interest in property is a transfer, including a transfer of possession, custody, or control *even if there is no transfer of title,* because possession, custody and control are interests in property. (Emphasis supplied.)

See Utah Code Ann. §70A-9-202 (1968). Thus, the Lanctots are not entitled to claim the benefit of section 522(g)(1) in this case.

The findings of this Court are supported in In re Saberman, 1 C.B.C.

---

* Renumbered as §101(48) in 1984. — EDS.

671, 676, 3 B.R. 316 (Bkrtcy. N.D. Ill. 1980), where the bankruptcy court stated that "a purchase money interest, albeit under an improper UCC filing, is nonetheless a voluntary transfer by the debtor who cannot, therefore, assert a trustee's power to avoid a statutory lien under sec. 522(g) and 522(h)." . . .

11 U.S.C. §522(g)(2) permits the debtor to exempt property recovered by the trustee to the extent that the debtor could have avoided the transfer himself under Section 522(f)(2). As previously discussed, on these facts, the avoiding powers of Section 522(f)(2) are unavailable to the Lanctots. Therefore, the Lanctots cannot claim the benefit of the trustee's avoiding powers under Section 522(g)(2).

11 U.S.C. §522(h) is likewise inapplicable. Subsection (h) empowers the debtor, on conditions, to "avoid transfer of property of the debtor or recover a setoff *to the extent that the debtor could have exempted such property under subsection (g)(1) of this section* if the trustee had avoided such transfer . . ." (Emphasis supplied.) Since subsection (g)(1) does not allow the Lanctots to avoid the voluntary transfer to Local Loan, they cannot proceed under subsection (h).

Finally, subsection (c)* provides no grounds for claiming an exemption free and clear of Local Loan's lien. It states:

(c) Unless the case is dismissed, property exempted under this section is not liable during or after the case for any debt of the debtor that arose or that is determined under section 502 of this title as if such claim had arisen before the commencement of the case, except
  (1) a debt of a kind specified in section 523(a)(1) or section 523(a)(5) of this title; or
  (2) a lien that is
    (A) not avoided under section 544, 545, 547, 548, 549 or 724(a) of this title;
    (B) not voided under section 506(d) of this title; or
    (C)(i) a tax lien notice of which is properly filed; and
      (ii) avoided under section 545(2) of this title.

The legislative history of section 522(c) as contained in both H.R. Rep. No. 95-595, supra at 361, U.S. Code Cong. & Admin. News 1978, p. 6317, and Sen. Rep. No. 95-989, 95th Cong., 2d Sess., at 76 (1978), U.S. Code Cong. & Admin. News 1978, p. 5862, clarifies this section's meaning as follows:

Subsection (c) insulates exempt property from prepetition claims, except tax and alimony maintenance or support claims that are excepted from discharge. The bankruptcy discharge will not prevent enforcement of valid liens.

A reading of this subsection and its legislative history reveals an intent not to provide additional powers of exemption to the debtor, but rather to

* Reworded in 1984. — EDS.

provide a statement of the law respecting the rights of a debtor in property which has been allowed as exempt. Under prior law, all exemptions were state exemptions which were protected from certain claims by state law. With the advent of federal exemptions under 11 U.S.C. §522(d), section 522(c) was presumably passed to provide a clear statement of the extent of federal protection given to the new federal exemptions. This understanding is consistent with the spirit of the new Code in providing additional control to the bankruptcy court of many matters formerly left entirely under the jurisdiction of state law. See, e.g., 11 U.S.C. §524(c). Thus, subsection (c) does not provide the debtor with an exemption power, but rather protects property which has already been exempted.

The wording of subsection (c) reinforces this position, for it states that *"property exempted"* is "not liable" for any prepetition debts except those enumerated. Therefore, to claim protection under this section, the debtor must first be entitled to exempt his property under one of the other subsections of 522. As the Court has previously concluded, the Lanctots have no interest to exempt nor have they any claim to avoiding powers under any subsections of 522 so as to allow them an interest to exempt. As such is the case, they cannot claim any further rights of avoidance under this subsection.

Confusion, however, arises from the wording of Section 522(c)(2). It allows for the preservation of liens which are *not* voided or avoided under various sections of the Code on exempt property. As explained in the legislative history, this was added to insure that the discharge "will not prevent the enforcement of valid liens". H.R. Rep. No. 95-595, supra at 361, U.S. Code Cong. & Admin. News 1978, p. 6317; Sen. Rep. No. 95-989, supra at 76, U.S. Code Cong. & Admin. News 1978, p. 5862. It would be illogical to construe a separate avoiding power resulting from the negative implication of the language used in subsection 522(c)(2). What purpose would be served by allowing the trustee broader avoiding powers than the debtor and allowing those powers to be used for the benefit of the general creditors if, when those powers were used, the debtor could step in and claim an exemption? In fact, under 11 U.S.C. §1551 [sic], liens avoided by the trustee under the sections mentioned in Section 522(c) are *automatically* preserved for the benefit of the estate. Legislative history makes it apparent that this section was meant to prevent other claimants to the property, in specific junior lienors, but equally applicable to the debtor, from "improving their position at the expense of the estate when a senior lien is avoided". H.R. Rep. No. 95-595, supra at 376, U.S. Code Cong. & Admin. News 1978, p. 6332; Sen. Rep. No. 95-989, supra at 91, U.S. Code Cong. & Admin. News 1978, p. 5877.

Adequate relief has already been given to the debtor under other provisions of Section 522 to be freed from involuntary and other coercive liens on his property. As stated in Colliers, the policy is continued under the new Code that "the debtor should not profit at the creditors' expense from the trustee's efforts in undoing the debtor's own acts." 3 Colliers on Bankruptcy §522.08, at 522-532 (15th ed. 1979). Thus, only those exceptions to this general policy as carefully laid out in subsection (f), (g), and (h) of 522 are allowed to the debtor and not a general dismemberment of previous policy in subsection (c). Although section 522(g) gives the debtor some power to claim the benefit of the trustee's avoiding powers, in all cases the debtor is also given those avoiding powers himself. See 11 U.S.C. §522(f) and 522(h). To construe subsection (c) providing a separate exemption power, then, would be inconsistent with the rest of Section 522 as well as with Section 551.

A review of the debtor's rights under Section 522 reveals no applicable avoiding power available to the Lanctots. Neither does the law allow the debtors to benefit from the trustee's broader avoiding powers in this situation. Accordingly,

It is ordered that the debtors' motion to stay this adversary proceeding be, and it is, denied.

NOTE

Does §522(f) apply to a judicial lien that attaches to property before the debtor acquires an interest in the property? In re McCormick, 18 Bankr. 911 (Bankr. W.D. Pa. 1982), aff'd, 22 Bankr. 997 (W.D. Pa. 1982), concluded no, reasoning that Congress's concern was "that when a Debtor becomes unable to meet his financial obligations, creditors will take quick action to reduce their claim to judgment. . . . The consequence being that the Debtor will not retain any unencumbered property." *McCormick* went on to state that this rationale "contains the implicit assumption that the Debtor must have acquired the property interest 'before' the creditor attached a lien to it," and that the contrary construction

would encourage collusive transfers. For example, an individual could convey encumbered property to an indigent person who would then file a bankruptcy petition, avoid the lien, and reconvey the property to the original owner. This Court does not believe that Congress intended §522(f) to be used as a device to defraud judicial lien holders.

Is the court's concept of the possibility of collusive transfers correct?

NOTE ON THE SCOPE OF §522(f)

Generally, as *Lanctot* notes, the debtor is given more limited "avoiding power" rights with respect to exempt property than is the trustee with respect to property of the estate. Is there a reason for this? In re Berry, 10 Bankr. 512, 517 n.3 (Bankr. D.S.C. 1980), offers the following rationale:

The reason for these limitations is that a debtor may have a greater incentive to use these powers abusively to promote his self interest vis-a-vis the interests of the creditors; whereas, the trustee, as a fiduciary, has a duty to represent, and preserve the interests of, several parties, including the creditors and the debtor. Limitations have, thus, been placed upon the debtor's powers of avoidance in areas where the potential risk of abuse is greatest. Because of such limitations, a debtor is prevented from using the trustee's powers of avoidance to benefit himself unjustly by concealing his property or arranging a preferential, or fraudulent, transfer.

Is this convincing? In *Riddervold*, supra page 336, Judge Friendly commented that "[i]n view of the accepted learning that '[a] preference is not an act evil in itself but one prohibited by the Bankruptcy Act in the interest of equality of division' . . . , it is not clear why the 1978 Code extended the power to avoid preferences to bankrupts." Do you agree? Note that §522(f) gives, under some circumstances, *broader* avoiding powers to the debtor than the trustee possesses. See In re Dubrock, 5 Bankr. 353 (Bankr. W.D. Kan. 1980). Section 11 of the Uniform Exemptions Act contains a limitation on the enforcement of nonpossessory, nonpurchase money security interests in certain property that would otherwise be exempt.

Exactly what sort of property does §522(f) apply to? For example, Missouri exempts from attachment "tools or other mechanical instruments or appliances necessary to the practice of any trade, business or profession." Mo. Ann. Stat. §513.435(7). Can a debtor, using this section, exempt a truck that he uses in his business, and then avoid a lien on that truck under §522(f)? Compare In re Seacord, 7 Bankr. 121 (Bankr. W.D. Mo. 1980) (yes), with In re O'Neal, 20 Bankr. 13 (Bankr. E.D. Mo. 1982) (no). In re Sweeney, 7 Bankr. 814 (Bankr. E.D. Wisc. 1980), aff'd on other issues, 688 F.2d 447 (7th Cir. en banc 1982), found the following tie between §522(f) and §522(d):

Congress specified that §522(f) should apply to certain limited categories of personal property which are necessities of family life and have little if any resale value from the creditor's standpoint, but have a relatively high replacement cost so far as the debtor is concerned. Experience had shown that creditors were able to use the threat of repossession of such goods, rarely carried out, in order to extract a reaffirmation of the debt from the debtor, thus impairing the fresh start. . . .

A close inspection of subsections (2)(A), (B) and (C) of §522(f) shows that the property described therein and subject to its terms is identical, word for word, to the property exemptions granted in §522(d)(3), (4), (6), and (9). Having in mind the congressional purpose as set out above, we believe that the impact of §522(f) should be limited to those particular categories of exempted property. . . . For example, in some cases, the section has been applied to a motor vehicle, which has been found to be a "tool of the trade" of the debtor. We would not apply it in that fashion. As Congress has specifically and separately exempted motor vehicles in §522(d)(2), we would not

include them in the property described in §522(d)(6).[4] Similarly, we do not
believe that Congress intended that the so-called wild card exemptions of
§522(d)(1) and (5) should be subject to the lien avoidance provisions of
§522(f). The well-known rule that exemptions statutes are to be liberally
construed has been mentioned in a number of decisions dealing with the
validity of §522(f), but it is important to remember that the direct thrust of
the section in question deals not with the granting of exemptions, but with
the *avoidance of liens.*

Even as to property clearly falling within the sections covered by
§522(f), we would tend toward a restrictive rather than a broad interpretation.

See also In re Middleton, 37 Bankr. 36 (Bankr. D. Minn. 1983). Most
courts have disagreed with this analysis, holding, instead, that if the property fits within the generic categories listed in §522(f)(2), security interests
on such property may be avoided if they impair an exemption, notwithstanding whether the property was exempt under §522(d)(3), (4), (6), or
(9). Thus, for example, if the "wild card" exemption of §522(d)(5) is used
on a computer that is deemed to be a "tool of the trade," nonpossessory,
nonpurchase money security interests on that computer may be avoided
under §522(f)(2) to the extent that the security interest impairs the
§522(d)(5) exemption, and not just to the extent of $750 under
§522(d)(6). See, e.g., In re DiPalma, 24 Bankr. 385 (Bankr. D. Mass.
1982); In re Dillon, 18 Bankr. 252 (Bankr. E.D. Cal. 1982); In re Eagan, 16
Bankr. 439 (Bankr. N.D.N.Y. 1982). The Third Circuit has adopted this
approach, Augustine v. United States, 675 F.2d 582 (3rd Cir. 1982),
reasoning that:

> The central issue . . . is . . . whether a debtor may aggregate ex-
> emptions authorized by Subsection (d)(5) with the relatively smaller exemp-
> tions as granted in Subsection (d)(6) for purposes of lien avoidance with
> respect to these same types of goods. Apart from the question of lien avoid-
> ance, it is undisputed that Congress intended in a nondiscriminatory fashion
> to grant nonhomeowners an exemption equal in value to that of
> homeowners—an exemption worth $7,500 to be applied to whatever prop-
> erty the nonhomeowner debtors might choose.
>
> The government argues that to permit these consequences of Subsec-
> tion (d)(5) to be carried over into the provisions of Subsection (f)(2) would
> actually work an unintended discrimination against homeowners, since that
> subsection does not permit avoidance of liens on homes. It is not the function
> of this court to question why Congress chose to permit debtors to avoid the

---

4. . . . If repairmen using panel trucks or truckers using over the road truck-tractors in
their work should have a breakdown necessitating costly repairs, it will be extremely difficult
if not impossible for them to obtain a loan to finance repairs, using the vehicle as collateral, if
such motor vehicles are permitted to be classified as tools of the trade under subsection (6),
exempted under the dollar limitations of ss. (1), (2), (5) and (6), and this entire amount then
subjected to the lien avoidance provisions of §522(f).

particular liens enumerated in Subsection (f). We must assume that Congress understood that the language of that subsection — that the debtor may avoid a lien on property "to the extent that such lien impairs an exemption to which the debtor would have been entitled under subsection (b) of this section" — compels the result that Subsection (d)(5) exemptions may be applied to the kinds of property subject to lien avoidance under Subsection (f). Nothing in Section 522 suggests a distinction that would prohibit aggregation for purposes of lien avoidance while permitting it for exemption purposes.

IN RE McMANUS
681 F.2d 353 (5th Cir. 1982)

JOHNSON, Circuit Judge.

I

Two bankruptcy cases, both arising out of Louisiana, have been consolidated for appeal. In the case of McManus v. Avco Financial Services of Louisiana, a husband and wife filed a joint petition for relief under Chapter 13 of the Bankruptcy Act, 11 U.S.C.A. §1301, et seq. In the couple's petition and proposed plan, Avco Financial Services of Louisiana (Avco) was listed as an unsecured creditor. Avco, however, in its proof of claim and in a formal rejection of the couple's proposed plan, established that it was a fully secured creditor. Avco held a promissory note secured by a nonpossessory, nonpurchase money security interest in the form of a chattel mortgage on certain household goods and furnishings belonging to the couple and the couple's dependents. . . . On July 28, 1980, the couple moved to avoid Avco's lien under 11 U.S.C.A. §522(f), in order to allow them to exempt their household goods and furnishings from the bankruptcy estate. The Motion for Avoidance was consolidated with Avco's formal rejection.

Subsequently, the bankruptcy court rendered judgment in favor of Avco and against the couple, upholding Avco's rejection of the proposed plan and denying the couple's Motion for Avoidance of Avco's nonpossessory, nonpurchase money security interest in their household goods and furnishings. The couple appealed this determination to the district court. The district court affirmed the decision of the bankruptcy court and this appeal followed. This Court affirms the judgment of the district court in *McManus.*

The case of Gipson v. Blazer Financial Services arose in basically the same way. . . . In *Gipson,* the bankruptcy court cancelled Blazer's nonpossessory, nonpurchase money security interest. Blazer appealed the determination of the bankruptcy court to the district court. The district court affirmed the bankruptcy court's judgment and this appeal followed. This Court reverses the judgment of the district court in *Gipson*.

II

Section 541 of the Bankruptcy Act dictates that, upon commencement of an action in bankruptcy, all property of the debtor becomes property of the bankruptcy estate. 11 U.S.C.A. §541. However, once the property becomes a part of the estate, the debtor then is allowed to exempt certain property. The debtors involved in the consolidated cases contend that, in Louisiana, a nonpossessory, nonpurchase money security interest in household goods and furnishings may be avoided pursuant to 11 U.S.C.A. §522(f). Such an avoidance would allow the debtors to exempt some of their property from the bankruptcy estate. The creditors involved in the cases sub judice argue that the State of Louisiana, by enacting certain legislation, has precluded such an avoidance.

The first step in resolution of the controversy is an examination of the federal avoidance mechanism the debtors wish to utilize. This mechanism, expressed in 11 U.S.C.A. §522(f), states in full:

> (f) Notwithstanding any waiver of exemptions, the debtor may avoid the fixing of a lien on an interest of the debtor in property to the extent that such lien impairs an exemption to which the debtor would have been entitled under subsection (b) of this section, if such lien is —
>
> (1) a judicial lien; or
> (2) a nonpossessory, nonpurchase-money security interest in any —
>   (A) household furnishings, household goods, wearing apparel, appliances, books, animals, crops, musical instruments, or jewelry that are held primarily for the personal, family, or household use of the debtor or a dependent of the debtor;
>   (B) implements, professional books, or tools, of the trade of the debtor or the trade of a dependent of the debtor; or
>   (C) professionally prescribed health aids for the debtor or a dependent of the debtor.

Significantly, the avoidance provisions of section 522(f) are available to debtors seeking to avoid a lien only "to the extent that such lien impairs an exemption to which the debtor would have been entitled under subsection (b)" of section 522. In other words, this federal avoidance section is not a separate exemption statute. It provides only a limited mechanism for avoiding liens, since the only liens that may be avoided are those impairing an exemption the debtor would have been entitled to receive under section 522(b). Since the invocation of section 522(f) is dependent upon whether a debtor may be legally entitled to an exemption under section 522(b), the second step in resolving the controversy is an examination of section 522(b).

Section 522(b) provides the individual states with a choice of allowing their debtors one of two methods of exempting property from the bankruptcy estate. First, depending upon state law, a debtor may be entitled to utilize the federal "laundry list" exemptions specified in section 522(d).[2] Use of the federal laundry list is precluded, however, if "the state law that is applicable to the debtor . . . specifically does not . . . authorize" its use. In those instances in which state law precludes use of the federal laundry list, a debtor may exempt from property of the bankruptcy estate any property that is legally exempt under either (1) federal law other than the previously described laundry list or (2) applicable state or local law.

Section 522(b) expressly grants the states broad discretion and an open-ended opportunity to determine what property may be exempt from the bankruptcy estate, as long as the state law does not conflict with property exempt under federal law other than the laundry list. Significantly, the section does not mandate that debtors be guaranteed a right to exempt particular types of property. The unambiguous language of section 522(b) implicitly indicates a state may exempt the same property included in the federal laundry list, more property than that included in the federal laundry list, or less property than that included in the federal laundry list. The states also may prescribe their own requirements for exemptions, which may either circumscribe or enlarge the list of exempt property.

This leads to the third step in the Court's analysis. Examination of the avoidance provision — 11 U.S.C.A. §522(f) — reveals it is tied to the exemption provision, 11 U.S.C.A. §522(b). In turn, examination of 11 U.S.C.A. §522(b) reveals it is tied to applicable state law. Accordingly, the third step in resolving the present dispute is an evaluation of applicable state law.

Louisiana is the applicable state in the cases sub judice, and the State of Louisiana precludes a debtor's use of the federal laundry list by expressly not authorizing its use. LSA-R.S. 13:3881 B states,

> In cases instituted under the provisions of Title 11 of the United States Code, entitled "Bankruptcy," there shall be exempt from the property of the estate of an individual debtor only that property and income which is exempt under the laws of the State of Louisiana and under federal laws *other than subsection (d) of Section 522 of said Title 11 of the United States Code.*

(emphasis added). By enacting section 13:3881 B, Louisiana, pursuant to its federal authority to do so, has "opted out" of the opportunity to allow its debtors to use the federal laundry list of exemptions contained in 11 U.S.C.A. §522(d). The only property a Louisiana debtor is entitled to exempt from the bankruptcy estate is property exempt under federal law other than the laundry list and property exempt under Louisiana state law.

---

2. The federal laundry list expressed in 11 U.S.C.A. §522(d) lists eleven separate types of property that may be exempted. Household goods and furnishings are included in the list.

The exemptions available under Louisiana law are found in LSA-R.S. 13:3881. Subsection 3881(A)(4) lists household goods and furnishings as property a debtor may exempt from the estate. This general list of exemptions only provides part of the answer, however. LSA-R.S. 13:3885 expressly states that household goods and furnishings subject to a chattel mortgage are not exempt. The section states:

> Notwithstanding the provisions of R.S. 13:3881(2) and (4) to the contrary, a person who has granted a chattel mortgage on his property described in R.S. 13:3881(2) or (4) *may not thereafter claim an exemption* from the seizure of such mortgaged property for the enforcement of that mortgage.

(emphasis added). Section 13:3885 modifies and limits the general list of property that may be exempt by providing further elaboration and explanation of what property Louisiana allows debtors to exempt.[6] At the outset, the section is entitled, "Chattel mortgage; exception to exemption from seizure." The title of the section reveals that it is meant to clarify the definition of what property is exempt by delineating a specific exception to the general list provided in section 13:3881. Indeed, the section begins with the language, "Notwithstanding the provisions of R.S. 13:3881(2) and (4) to the contrary . . . ."

The language of section 13:3885 indicates that household goods and furnishings may take two forms in Louisiana. Such property, of course, may be unencumbered. In such a case, a Louisiana debtor is entitled to exempt his household goods and furnishings from the bankruptcy estate pursuant to section 13:3881(A)(4). Household goods and furnishings also may be subject to a chattel mortgage. If this is the case, a Louisiana debtor is not entitled to claim an exemption, notwithstanding the provisions of section 13:3881(A)(4) to the contrary. The inability to claim an exemption occurs regardless of whether a debtor could have claimed an exemption had there been no mortgage. While Louisiana allows a general exemption for household goods and furnishings, if a person changes the character of those goods or furnishings by making them the subject of a chattel mortgage, he can claim no exemption, because Louisiana expressly defines goods of such a character out of the list of exempt property.

If Louisiana had not expressly defined mortgaged household goods and furnishings out of the list of exempt property, the result would be arguably different. In such a hypothetical instance, household goods and furnishings would be, as a general rule, exempt pursuant to section 13:3881(A)(4). Of course, an individual could waive his exemption by

---

6. The debtors in the cases sub judice contend that section 13:3885 is not a modification of or an exception to the exemptions granted by subsection 13:3881(A)(4). The debtors contend that the granting of a chattel mortgage is nothing more than a waiver of an exemption. As such, the debtors argue, they may avoid any chattel mortgages, since 11 U.S.C.A. §522(f) begins, "Notwithstanding any waiver of exemptions. . . ."

granting a chattel mortgage on the property. If the debtor subsequently filed a petition for relief under Chapter 13 of the Bankruptcy Act, 11 U.S.C.A. §522 (f) would be available to avoid the waiver because the lien would impair an exemption to which the debtor would have been entitled under section 522(b).

The difference between the hypothetical instance and the cases sub judice is that, in the hypothetical instance, the state would not have exercised its authority to deny exemptions for household goods and furnishings under certain circumstances. Household goods and furnishings, in any form, would be exempt, although perhaps the exemption could be waived.

However, the State of Louisiana, for whatever policy justification, has utilized its authority under 11 U.S.C.A. §522(b) to mandate that property of a certain character—household goods and furnishings subject to a chattel mortgage—is, by definition, not exempt under 11 U.S.C.A. §522(b). Consequently, the chattel mortgages the debtors in the cases sub judice wish to avoid do not impair an exemption to which they would have been entitled under section 522(b). To the contrary, the chattel mortgages are the characteristic determinative of whether household goods and furnishings are exempt in Louisiana. This feature gives rise to Louisiana's specific denial of an exemption under 11 U.S.C.A. §522(b).[7]

This Court determines that debtors in Louisiana are not entitled to exempt household goods and furnishings subject to a chattel mortgage from the bankruptcy estate. Consequently, a Louisiana debtor may not utilize 11 U.S.C.A. §522(f) to avoid the chattel mortgage. Accordingly, this Court affirms the district court's determination in the case of McManus v. Avco Financial Services of Louisiana. It reverses the determination of the district court in the case of Blazer Financial Services v. Gipson and remands the case for further proceedings consistent with this opinion.

---

7. The debtors in the cases sub judice also argue that, although the states may opt out of the federal laundry list of exemptions, the states may not change the federal avoidance mechanism. The debtors argue that 11 U.S.C.A. §522(f) is intended to give debtors a "fresh start" by allowing them to avoid liens that may have been improvidently granted to creditors. They contend that the rehabilitative policy of §522(f)'s avoidance mechanisms is a policy that overrides any individual state policies, and a state cannot control, either directly or indirectly, the content of the policy of §522(f).

As previously noted, however, §522(f) is not a separate exemption statute. It gives effect to the state's choice of exemptions, and is dependent upon the states for the definition of what liens may be avoided. Section 522(f) is not available if an individual state says a debtor is not entitled to a particular exemption. As the district court in McManus stated, "It just strikes [this Court] that it is a conclusion that is inescapable that Congress must have realized that the states may enact different exemptions which would possibly conflict with Congress' own exemption policy as it was reflected in §522(d). If Congress has intended subsection (f) to be an overriding policy decision, it would not have made subsection (f) clearly dependent on the policy determinations by the states under §522(b)."

Because this Court finds no ambiguity in the language of the statutes, there is no need to resort to a review of legislative history. . . .

DYER, Circuit Judge, dissenting.

I respectfully dissent. The narrow issue in these appeals is whether 11 U.S.C.A. §522(f) is available to a Louisiana debtor to avoid an otherwise valid nonpossessory, nonpurchase-money security interest in the form of a chattel mortgage on certain household goods owned by the debtor, in light of LSA-R.S. 13:3885. In my view §522(f) is available.

The opening phrase of §522(f), "[n]otwithstanding any waiver of exemptions," indicates that the subsection's import is to return the situation to the status quo ante, i.e., prior to any improvident waiver of an exemption by the debtor. When the debtors entered the creditors' office they enjoyed an exemption under Louisiana law from seizure and sale of their household goods; and when they left the office they could no longer claim an exemption for those goods solely because they had improvidently granted a security interest to the creditors covering such goods. I fail to see how this could be characterized as anything but a waiver of exemptions, subject to the avoiding power found in §522(f).

Moreover, since "waiver" is modified by "any" it includes waivers resulting from operation of law, and Louisiana courts have long held that a debtor's execution of a mortgage on exempt property operates as a waiver of exemption. "It is well settled that a debtor, in mortgaging his property, may waive statutory exemptions. . . . Indeed, our jurisprudence recognizes an implied waiver through conduct, i.e. the execution of the chattel mortgage itself." Aetna Finance Co. v. Antoine, 343 So. 2d 1195 (La. App. 1977).

If the majority opinion correctly states the law, any state can by statute preclude a debtor from availing himself of the loan avoidance provisions found in §522(f). I cannot conclude that Congress intended to allow states to do this. There is no provision of the Bankruptcy Code which grants the states authority to preempt any subsection of §522(f) other than subsection (b), which concerns the exemption. Congress intended that even if a state opts out of the federal exemptions, the debtor's lien avoidance power under subsection (f) is not thereby affected. And under the supremacy clause, United States Constitution, art. VI, cl. 2, any conflict between the state lien conservation provision and the federal lien avoidance provision must be constitutionally resolved in favor of federal law. A state's policy determination respecting the manner in which its exemptions may be waived should be given application in its own courts but when the forum is a federal bankruptcy court such state policy determinations are subject to congressional override. . . .

Congress recognized that exemptions, whether state or federal in origin, are an essential feature of the system of financial rehabilitation afforded the hapless debtor in bankruptcy proceedings. Congress reasoned that since exemptions are so essential to this goal of rehabilitation they should be made available to the debtor regardless of whether or not state law would permit their waiver or surrender. This is clearly indicated in S. Rep. No. 95-989, 95th Cong., 2d Sess. 76, U.S. Code Cong. & Admin. News 1978, pp. 5787, 5862:

> [To] protect the debtors' exemptions, his discharge, and thus his fresh start, . . . [t]he debtor may avoid . . . to the extent that the property could have been exempted in the absence of the lien . . . a nonpossessory, nonpurchase-money security interest in certain household and personal goods.

Thus it was Congress's clear intent that a debtor benefit to the fullest extent possible exemptions granted to him by applicable state laws, even when he may have improvidently waived such exemptions. It is equally clear that Congress was particularly concerned with eradicating certain unconscionable creditor practices in the consumer loan industry. These practices were deemed to frustrate the rehabilitative nature of the bankruptcy laws by effectively denying the debtor his "fresh start" by taking from him and his family certain property essential to their welfare — household goods and furnishings, tools of the debtor's trade, and medical and health aids. Congress found that since such property has little realizable market value to a creditor, and the replacement cost to the debtor, now without credit, is usually very high, the creditor was able "to use the threat of repossession, rarely carried out, to extract more than he would be able to if he did foreclose or repossess." H.R. Rep. No. 595, 95 Cong., 1st Sess. 127 (1977), U.S. Code Cong. & Admin. News 1978, pp. 5787, 6088. Congress intended to preclude the creditor from executing this nonconscionable pressure by allowing the debtor to avoid such security interests. . . .

I would affirm the district court in Blazer Financial Services v. Gipson and reverse the district court in McManus v. Avco Financial Services of Louisiana.

NOTE ON McMANUS

As a result of the compromise over use of the set of bankruptcy exemptions in §522(d), states retain considerable power over exemptions. As noted in In re Allen, 725 F.2d 292 (5th Cir. 1984), "[t]here are three possibilities available to a state under 522(b): (1) remain silent and allow the federal law to be the sole remedy, (2) draft an exemption schedule which partially or wholly precludes the 522(d) remedy, and (3) allow election between state and federal exemption provisions." The question raised by McManus is the nature of the limitations (if any) imposed on states by §522(f). It is important to note the tension between §522(b) and (f).

Subsection (f) — as is explored more fully in the Note on the Compromise of §522 and the Fresh Start Policy, infra page 905 — seems to be based on the premise that there is a certain irreducible minimum of property that an individual is entitled to have to begin a "fresh start." Subsection (f), however, only applies to exempt property and, due to the last minute compromise involving §522, states are free to specify what is exempt property. (The dissent's quotation from the legislative history relies on a passage written *before* that compromise, at a time when states could not opt out of the bankruptcy exemptions.) *McManus* seems to say that all Louisiana has done is exercise a power under §522(b) and, because of that power, it has not interfered with (f). But is *McManus* right? To explore that, it is necessary to explore the relationship between (b) and (f) a bit more.

To get a handle on this question, start with a simple hypothetical. Section 522(d)(3) exempts, up to $200 per item, property such as household furnishings held primarily for personal, family, or household use up to an aggregate value of $4,000. If a state decides that things such as sofas, chairs, and tables should *not* be exempt, what powers does it have? It has the power, as we have seen, to opt out of the bankruptcy exemptions (and hence out of §522(d)(3)). Moreover, under its state exemption law, it can exclude from the category of exempt property such things as sofas, chairs, and tables, and this decision will be respected in bankruptcy (assuming — as is the case here — that federal nonbankruptcy law does not declare these items to be exempt).

Having gone this far, note that the state has avoided the impact of §522(f). While §522(f) covers household furnishings (such as sofas, chairs, and tables), it avoids a lien only "to the extent that such lien impairs an exemption to which the debtor would have been entitled under subsection (b)." Accordingly, for debtors residing in that state, §522(f) is inapplicable to liens on sofas, chairs, and tables. The lien does not impair an exemption, because the state has held that there is no exemption on such property.

Does the state, however, have a more refined power? For example, what happens if the state passes a statute that declares that sofas, chairs, and tables *are* exempt from execution, but that consensual security interests may be taken in such furniture? If the state passes such a statute, doesn't §522(f) apply to enable the debtor to avoid any such security interests (if neither possessory nor purchase money)? Put another way, isn't the state statute exactly the same, in effect, as exemption law such as New York's, when combined with a case such as *Avco Financial Services*, discussed supra page 14? Can §522(f) have any lesser meaning, when speaking of consensual security interests?

What, then, is different about the Louisiana statute involved in *McManus*? Louisiana's statute says that, notwithstanding its exemption statute, "a person who has granted a chattel mortgage on his property . . . may not thereafter claim an exemption from the seizure of such mortgaged property for the enforcement of *that* mortgage" (emphasis supplied). Read that language carefully. Doesn't it just restate the provision of a law such as New York's? Hasn't the Fifth Circuit, however, read it to say "If a person grants a security interest in X property, that property is no longer exempt"? That reading, note, is quite different, for it is no longer limited to the status of the property vis-a-vis the holder of a consensual interest. If the Fifth Circuit is right in how it has read the statute, then isn't its opinion right? Isn't the problem with *McManus,* however, one of how the Fifth Circuit has read Louisiana's statute? (The Fifth Circuit reached the same result when considering a Texas statute which read "[p]ersonal property . . . is exempt from attachment, execution and every type of seizure for the satisfaction of liabilities, except for encumbrances properly fixed thereon, if included [on a specified list]," In re Allen, 725 F.2d 292 (5th Cir. 1984). The court held that there was "no material distinction" between the Texas statute and the Louisiana statute in *McManus.* Isn't the court simply misreading the statutes?)

Has *McManus* successfully come to grips with the implication of §522(e)? Does it make sense to allow states to opt out of the bankruptcy exemptions, and then to prohibit, as §522(e) does, states from limiting the exemptions they provide in any manner they choose? Does §522(e) make sense only in the context of a universally available system of bankruptcy exemptions? Has *McManus* effectively given that power back to the states? Or can one argue that it is sensible to allow states to choose exemptions (because of regional variations in "necessary" property), but to have a uniform national rule on waivers of exemptions (because of a uniform problem of excessive optimism, see Note on Justifying the Nonwaivability of the Right of Discharge, supra page 736)?

The Sixth Circuit has relied on *McManus* in deciding cases out of Georgia and Tennessee. In re Pine, 717 F.2d 281 (6th Cir. 1983). The statutes involved read as follows:

> any debtor . . . may exempt . . . for the purposes of bankruptcy . . . the debtor's interest, not to exceed $200 in value in any particular item, in household furnishing, household goods, wearing apparel, appliances . . . that are held for the personal, family or household use of the debtor or a dependent of the debtor. The exemption of the debtor's interest in the items contained in this subsection shall not exceed $3500 in total value. . . . [Georgia]

> Personal property to the aggregate value of four thousand dollars . . . debtor's equity interest shall be exempt from execution, seizure or attachment. . . . [The debtor] may select for exemption the items of the owned and possessed personal property . . . up to the aggregate value of four thousand dollars . . . debtor's equity interest. [Tennessee]

Pine focuses on the language of these statutes that referred to the "debtor's interest" as explaining why there was nothing to avoid under §522(f):

The two legislatures have specifically declined to exempt household goods to the extent that they are encumbered by a lien. The Georgia statute refers only to the "debtor's interest" in property and the Tennessee statute refers to the "debtor's equity interest" when delineating the exempt property. Rather than simply listing the type of possessions that are exempt (e.g., the debtor's car) without regard to legal interests or specifying generally that the "debtor's property" is exempt, these two states have said that only the debtor's legal *interest* is exempt. In other words, the debtor may exempt only that interest in property which is owned by him and unencumbered by third party liens. . . .

The narrow question before us is whether the word "property" in subsection (b)(2)(A) includes the subdivision of "property" into legal interests or means property in the layman's sense. We believe that the word "property" is used to denote legal interests since the Act throughout characterizes property in terms of various security and other interests. . . . We agree with the Fifth Circuit [in *McManus*] that section 522(f) cannot be utilized independently of §522(b); the debtors may avoid liens only on that property which the states have declared to be exempt.

Does *Pine*, however, follow from *McManus*? Both Georgia's and Tennessee's statutes are explicitly directed at bankruptcy. Indeed, the statutes have little force outside of bankruptcy, as "exemption" statutes that do not exclude liens are hardly exemption statutes at all. Even if states retain the ability to opt out of the bankruptcy exemptions, do they have the power to pass a statute that is effective in bankruptcy only? Is *Pine* nonetheless right, as long as these provisions are *in addition to* the state's other exemption provisions, so that the debtor is treated at least as well in bankruptcy as outside? In considering that, you might want to note a possible dissenting view to *McManus* and *Pine*. In re Maddox, 713 F.2d 1526 (11th Cir. 1983), rejected a similar argument based on a Georgia statute that referred to the "debtor's interest." Adopting as its own the opinion of the District Court, the Eleventh Circuit commented that

If the court were to adopt the interpretation urged by the appellant, 11 U.S.C. §522(f)(2)(A) would be a meaningless provision. The Georgia provision upon which the appellee bases his argument is identical in relevant part to the corresponding federal provision in 11 U.S.C. §522(d)(3). If the phrase "debtor's interest" in 11 U.S.C. §522(d)(1) means only the debtor's equity, then a debtor could, under the federal scheme, avoid liens on property to the extent the property was free of liens. . . .

. . . *McManus* is inapposite because Louisiana, unlike Georgia, enacted a specific provision to avoid the effects of subsection 522(f) *in addition to* "opting out" of 11 U.S.C. §522(d). . . . Even if the Georgia legislature had enacted such a provision this court might have chosen not to follow the *McManus* case. . . . This court finds persuasive Judge Dyer's argument that the federal statute does not permit a state to "opt out" of the lien avoidance provisions of §522(f).

PROBLEM

11.15 Ohio's exemption statute expressly provides that it "does not affect . . . any security interest." May a debtor who resides in Ohio use §522(f) in bankruptcy? See In re Foster, 16 Bankr. 467 (N.D. Ohio 1981). Does *McManus* have anything to say on this? Does it matter whether the debtor is using the bankruptcy exemptions of §522(d) instead of the non-bankruptcy exemptions?

DEEL RENT-A-CAR v. LEVINE
721 F.2d 750 (11th Cir. 1983)

GOLDBERG, Senior Circuit Judge.

In this case, a creditor executed a judicial lien on the debtor's property less than ninety days before the debtor's petition for bankruptcy. Between the date of execution and the date of the petition, the debtor was married, thereby exempting the property under state law from the claims of every creditor except the lienor. We are asked to decide whether the execution of the lien constitutes a preference voidable by the debtor pursuant to sections 522(h) and 547 of the Federal Bankruptcy Code. We hold that it does, and affirm the judgment below.

FACTS AND PROCEDURAL HISTORY

Howard Levine and others guaranteed a debt of National Vehicle Leasing, Inc. to Deel Rent-A-Car, Inc. ("Deel"). Deel subsequently obtained a judgment against Levine in Florida state court. On January 9, 1980, Deel perfected the judgment and executed a lien against all real property owned by Levine in Broward County, Florida. At the time, Levine owned a condominium in Broward County, but was not married. On March 13, 1980, Levine was married and brought his wife into his residence in the Broward condominium.

On March 31, 1980, within 90 days of Deel's execution of the lien, Levine filed a voluntary petition for bankruptcy under Chapter 7 of the Bankruptcy Code ("Code"). The case was heard on June 10, 1980, in the United States Bankruptcy Court for the Southern District of Florida. Deel filed an amended adversary complaint, seeking, inter alia, to prevent Levine's discharge. Levine counterclaimed, seeking to avoid the judgment lien as a preference, pursuant to sections 522(h) and 547(b) of the Code. In an amended counterclaim, Levine also sought to avoid the lien as an impairment of his homestead exemption pursuant to section 522(f) of the Code.[2]

The bankruptcy court ruled against Levine on the section 522(f) claim, holding that under Florida law[3] the property acquired homestead status when Levine was married, but that the homestead exemption was not effective against a judgment lien that had attached before that date.

Levine did prevail, however, on his section 547(b) claim. The court avoided the lien, holding that all of the elements of a preference were present and that Levine had standing to bring an action under section 522(h) of the Code.

On appeal, the United States District Court for the Southern District of Florida affirmed the judgment of the bankruptcy court. This appeal follows.

ISSUES ON APPEAL

Levine has not challenged the bankruptcy court's interpretation of section 522(f). Therefore we need only consider whether the lien was a voidable preference under sections 522(h) and 547(b).[8] . . .

2. 11 U.S.C. §522(f) (1982).
Section 522 provides a number of mechanisms by which the insolvent debtor can sue to recover or protect assets that should be exempt from creditor claims.
Pursuant to section 522(f), he can sue to avoid certain liens that impair his exemptions. The liens include (1) judicial liens and (2) nonpossessory, nonpurchase-money security interests in certain types of property. 11 U.S.C. §522(f) (1982).
Second, if the trustee in bankruptcy uses his own avoiding powers to bring assets back into the bankrupt estate, the debtor can act to exempt such assets. 11 U.S.C. §522(g) (1982). The debtor is permitted to do so if (1) he had neither voluntarily transferred the assets out of the estate nor concealed them, or (2) he could have avoided the "transfer" of a nonpurchase-money security interest under section 522(f)(2), supra.
Finally, if the trustee could have avoided a transfer of property but did not, and if the debtor could have exempted the property had the transfer been avoided, then the debtor is permitted to step into the trustee's shoes and avoid the transfer himself. 11 U.S.C. §522(h) (1982). This final power is involved in the case at bar.
3. Levine must claim his exemptions under Florida law, since Florida has specified that federal exemptions will not apply to Florida debtors. See 3 Collier on Bankruptcy §522.08 at 522-544 n. 8a. Section 522(b)(1) of the Bankruptcy Code gives states the power to opt out of federal exemptions. 11 U.S.C. section 522(b)(1) (1982).
8. Without deciding the issue, we note in passing that Levine might have been successful on his section 522(f) claim. The language of the provision is somewhat ambiguous; it is not clear whether Deel's judicial lien "impairs an exemption to which [Levine] would have been entitled."
Deel would argue that the lien does not "impair" an exemption, since under Florida law the homestead exemption was not effective against Deel. The Bankruptcy Court took this position. . . .
However, the legislative history to section 522(f) suggests that even under these circumstances Deel's judicial lien impairs Levine's exemption:

Subsection (f) protects the debtor's exemptions, his discharge, and then his fresh start by permitting him to avoid certain liens on exempt property. The debtor may

Deel raises one issue concerning each provision. First, it argues that Levine has no standing to avoid the preference under section 522(h). Standing depends upon the debtor's ability to exempt the property from all creditors' claims; and under Florida law Levine's homestead exemption does not apply to Deel's lien — Levine cannot exempt the property from Deel's claim.

Second, Deel argues that one element of a preference under section 547(b) does not exist in this case. Deel relies on a number of cases which applied a "diminution of estate" requirement to section 60 of the old Bankruptcy Act ("Act"), the predecessor to section 547(b) of the current Code.[11] According to that gloss, a preferential transfer could be avoided only if it had diminished the estate available to other creditor claims — i.e. if the property could be used to pay off the claims of other creditors in the bankruptcy proceeding. In this case, Deel argues, avoiding the lien would benefit no other creditors, since the property would be exempt from their claims. Therefore, there has been no diminution of the estate, and the requirements for a preference are not met.

We reject both of Deel's contentions. First, a clear reading of section 522(h) requires only that Levine be able to exempt his property "if the trustee [has] avoided" Deel's lien. Under that test, Levine's property would be exempt. Second, we hold that the "diminution of estate" doctrine is not applicable in the case of a debtor bringing an action under section 522(h) to avoid a preference.

DISCUSSION

I.   SECTION 522(h) AND LEVINE'S STANDING

A.   When Must a Homestead be Exempt?

Deel argues that Levine has no standing. Levine's condominium would not be exempt under Florida law from Deel's pre-marriage lien.

---

avoid a judicial lien on any property to the extent that the property could have been exempted in the absence of the lien.

H. Rep. No. 595, 95th Cong., 1st Sess. 362; S. Rep. No. 989, 95th Cong., 2d Sess. 76: reprinted at 1978 U.S. Code Cong. & Ad. News 5787, 5862, 6318. In the absence of Deel's lien, Levine could have exempted his homestead against the claims of *every* creditor.

11.   Deel agrees that the literal statutory elements of a preference exist. A judicial lien is a "transfer." . . . The transfer was made to a creditor, Deel, for an antecedent debt. Levine was insolvent at the time, and the transfer was made within 90 days before Levine filed his petition for bankruptcy. See 11 U.S.C. §547(b)(1)-(4) (1982). Deel even admits that the literal language of the final requirement, section 547(b)(5), is met in this case. The judicial lien has given Deel more than it would receive if it had no lien and received its share of Levine's assets in a liquidation proceeding. See 11 U.S.C. §547(b)(5) (1982). Deel claims, however, that in addition to the literal requirements of that provision, courts must read in the diminution of estate requirement.

Therefore, Deel claims that Levine could not "have exempted such property under subsection (g)(1)," and he does not have standing under subsection (h). . . .

We accept Deel's characterization of Florida law, but we disagree with his conclusions about the Bankruptcy Code. Subsection 522(h), by its terms, gives Levine standing. The subsection provides:

> The debtor may avoid a transfer of property of the debtor . . . to the extent that the debtor could have exempted such property under subsection (g)(1) of this section *if the trustee had avoided such transfer.*

11 U.S.C. §522(h) (1982) (emphasis added). Reading that literally, Levine would have been able to exempt the property. If the trustee had avoided the transfer, Deel would have had no judgment lien and, therefore, no ground for claiming that the homestead exemption was not effective against its claim.

Moreover, subsection (h) directs us to examine the debtor's power to exempt the property under subsection (g), assuming that the trustee had avoided the lien. Subsection (g) provides:

> . . . the debtor may exempt under subsection (b) of this section property that the trustee recovers . . . , to the extent that the debtor could have exempted such property under subsection (b) of this section *if such property had not been transferred,* if—
> (1)(A) such transfer was not a voluntary transfer of property by the debtor; and
> (B) the debtor did not conceal such property. . . .

11 U.S.C. §522(g) (1982) (emphasis added).

Again, if the property had not been transferred (i.e. if no lien had been executed), then the condominium would be exempt under subsection (b), which merely provides for the application of various exemptions (including state law exemptions). Deel does not claim that the transfer was voluntary on the part of Levine or that Levine concealed the property.

Therefore, we hold that a straight-forward reading of section 522 supports the lower court's conclusion that Levine has standing to avoid Deel's lien. Levine could have exempted his condo "if the trustee had avoided the lien" and "if such property had not been transferred." Since he could have exercised that exemption, he can stand in the trustee's shoes to avoid the lien himself.

B. Conflicting Policies

We note that the debtor's power to avoid transfers may, in cases like this one, have the effect of giving the debtor a broader exemption than state law would provide. However, we feel that our holding is mandated by the clear language of the statute.

Moreover, in the context of avoiding a preferential transfer, our holding serves a central policy of the preference statute: preventing a race to the courthouse by creditors during the last three months before the debtor files a bankruptcy petition.[13] The House Report to the Bankruptcy Code states:

> [B]y permitting the trustee to avoid prebankruptcy transfers that occur within a short period before bankruptcy, creditors are discouraged from racing to the courthouse to dismember the debtor during his slide into bankruptcy. The protection thus afforded the debtor often enables him to work his way out of a difficult financial situation through cooperation with all of his creditors.[14]

As the Report indicates, section 547 of the Code would normally prevent a race to the courthouse by giving the trustee the power to avoid any judicial lien (however valid under state law) during the preference period. In the circumstances of this case, however, the transfer would stand up if we held for Deel and prevented the debtor from recovering the property. Thus, there would again be an incentive for a creditor to receive a preference period transfer. With any luck, he would be able to keep the asset, to the exclusion of the debtor and other creditors. Moreover, he would benefit even if other creditors established liens later than his but before the debtor converted assets into exempt property. At best, the first lien would be considered prior to the others. At worst, it would be considered a preference relative to the others, and the lien creditors (or perhaps all of the creditors) would share the asset. In either event, the execution of the lien would prevent the debtor from converting his asset into exempt property.

In future cases, the astute creditor, anticipating a debtor's bankruptcy, would attempt to establish a lien on every non-exempt asset — ensuring at least that the assets would be preserved for the creditors. Such a strategy would produce a race to the courthouse (or the altar) between creditors and the debtor during the preference period. This result would be antithetical to the policies of sections 522 and 547.

II.   DIMINUTION OF ESTATE DOCTRINE

In addition to the requirement that the debtor be able to exempt his transferred property, section 522(h) requires in pertinent part that

> (1) such transfer be avoidable by the trustee under section. . . . 547 . . . of this title.

13. Our holding does not affect the other central purpose of the preference provisions: ensuring equal distribution of assets among the creditors. . . . We benefit no creditor at the expense of the others when we return the homestead to Levine.

14. H.R. Rep. No. 595, 95th Cong., 1st Sess., 177, reprinted at 1978 U.S. Code Cong. & Ad. News 6138.

Deel's second argument on appeal is that the trustee could not have avoided the lien under section 547 because of the diminution of estate doctrine. The doctrine prevents a trustee from avoiding a preferential transfer when he cannot bring the asset back into the estate to benefit creditors other than the transferee. See Continental and Commercial Trust and Savings Bank v. Chicago Title and Trust, 229 U.S. 435, 33 S. Ct. 829, 57 L. Ed. 1268 (1913). . . . In this case, Deel claims that no other creditor would benefit from the avoidance of the lien and, therefore, neither a trustee nor Levine can take advantage of section 547. Deel takes particular note of the language in one old case holding that the preference avoidance provisions were not meant for the benefit of the debtor. See In re Coddington, 126 F. 891, 893 (E.D. Wis. 1903). We conclude, however, that the availability of assets to satisfy other creditors' claims is not relevant when a debtor avoids a preference pursuant to sections 522(h) and 547 of the new Code. In reaching this result, we consider the purposes of the diminution of estate doctrine and the differences in policy between the old Act and the new Code.

A. Origins of the Doctrine

Neither the Code nor the old Act contains an explicit diminution of estate requirement. However, in cases decided under the Act, courts held that the trustee could not avoid preference period transfers that did not diminish the estate available to other creditors. To avoid such transfers did not serve the purposes of the bankruptcy law.

For example, in Continental and Commercial Trust and Savings Bank v. Chicago Title and Trust, supra, the debtor, a member of the Chicago Board of Trade, held certain margin certificates representing his right to security deposits that he had made with other traders. During the preference period, he gave up the certificates as part of an arrangement to pay off various debts. The trustee attempted to avoid the transfer as a preference, but the Supreme Court held that the requirements of section 60 were not met:

> What was done did not in fact diminish the estate of Prince, otherwise available to the creditors in the bankruptcy administration, for the traders holding them would have had the benefit of the deposits under the terms of the certificates and the rules of the Board of Trade. It therefore appears that the essential element of a preferential transfer within the meaning of the bankruptcy act — diminution of the bankrupt estate — is wanting. The fact that what was done worked to the benefit of the creditor, and in a sense gave him a preference, is not enough, unless the estate of the bankrupt was thereby diminished.

229 U.S. at 443-444, 33 S. Ct. at 831.

In Walker v. Wilkinson, 296 F. 850 (5th Cir. 1924), the Fifth Circuit stated the essential policy behind the doctrine:

The purpose of the law of preferences is to secure an equal distribution of the bankrupt's assets among his creditors of like class. If a transaction, in its entirety, does not interfere with this purpose of the law, it does not constitute a voidable preference. The fact that one creditor is paid in full from a source to which other creditors have no right to resort, does not entitle other creditors to complain or the trustee to recover the amount so secured.

Id. at 852.

The doctrine has been applied where the transfer to a creditor is accompanied by an equal and contemporaneous benefit to the estate, see, e.g., Bachner v. Robinson, 107 F.2d 513, 514 (2d Cir. 1939) (net benefit to debtor's estate where debtor was lessee, and lessor's consent to assignment of lease was obtained by lessee's payment of overdue rent); or where the preferential transfer is made by a third party, see Creditors of D'Angio v. D'Angio, 554 F.2d 863, 864 (8th Cir. 1977) (no diminution of debtor's estate because check drawn on the account of an outsider).

Generally, though, the courts have applied the doctrine in cases in which one creditor receives an asset that, for some reason, is protected from the claims of other creditors. See, e.g., Continental and Commercial Trust and Savings, supra, (creditors of estate having no claim on margin certificates); Azar v. Morgan, 301 F.2d 78 (5th Cir. 1962) (payment to a secured creditor not diminishing the assets available to general creditors).

It is important to keep in mind, however, that most of the diminution of estate cases involved actions by a creditor or a trustee acting on behalf of the creditors. Under those circumstances, it is appropriate to ask whether the transferred assets could actually be returned to creditors. It makes no sense to let the trustee recover if the creditors will not benefit. When the *debtor* himself is the plaintiff, it is less appropriate to inquire whether or not *creditors* will benefit. Deel argues that the preference provisions are not meant for the benefit of the debtor and that the focus should still be on the availability of the assets to meet creditor claims. However, a brief analysis of the historical differences between the Act and the Code convinces us that this argument is wrong.

B.   The Debtor under the Act: A Juridical Weakling

The preference provisions of the Act were designed primarily to protect creditors. The drafters were concerned that a debtor would favor one creditor over the others; and, therefore, the trustee was empowered to recover preferential transfers made during the four months preceding bankruptcy. Bankruptcy Act §60.

The Act did not give the same power to a debtor who wished to recover exempt assets. . . . The debtor was not authorized to avoid a preferential transfer; and, even if the trustee avoided such a transfer, the debtor could not take advantage of his exemptions. Bankruptcy Act §6.[17] . . .

Thus, the District Court in In re Coddington stated:

> So far as the bankrupt himself is concerned, a preferential transfer is absolute, and cannot be recovered back. . . . Manifestly, the provisions which lay ground for a recovery . . . are not intended for the benefit of the bankrupt, but his general creditors, in order to secure an equal division among all.

126 F. at 893.

C. The Debtor under the Code: New-found Strength

The Code of 1978 reflects a new policy of protection for the debtor in a bankruptcy proceeding. In order to ensure the availability of exemptions and provide the debtor with the assets necessary for a "fresh start" after bankruptcy, the drafters of the Code created a number of new substantive and procedural protections. . . . The Code provides new Federal exemptions to augment state laws, 11 U.S.C. §522(d) (1982),[18] and gives debtors a number of new procedural powers to protect their exemptions, including the power to avoid liens that impair exemptions, id. §522(f), and the power to avoid preferential transfers, id. §522(h).

Subsection 522(h) is an integral cog in the new fresh start mechanism embodied in the Code. The debtor is relieved from relying on a trustee who might have little incentive to recover assets which could not go to the creditors. . . . Most important, the debtor is given the avoidance powers solely to protect his own exemptions. . . .

Thus, the words of the District Court in In re Coddington, supra, are no longer true. The preference avoidance provisions are clearly intended for the benefit of the debtor to the extent that he comes within the requirements of section 522(h). An action by the debtor should be tested according to whether the assets would come to him, not whether they would go to the creditors.

Application of the diminution of estate test in this context would in fact contradict the explicit language of section 522(h). The provision, as discussed above, requires that the debtor be able to exempt the property

---

17. 11 U.S.C. §24(1976). The statute provided in pertinent part:

[N]o such allowance shall be made out of the property which a bankrupt transferred or concealed and which is recovered or the transfer of which is avoided under this Act for the benefit of the estate, except that, where the voided transfer was made by way of security only and the property recovered is in excess of the amount secured thereby, such allowance may be made out of such excess.

18. The Code does give a state the authority to expressly opt out of the Federal exemptions, however. 11 U.S.C. §522(b)(1) (1982).

recovered. Of course, any time he can do that, the property is by definition unavailable to satisfy the claims of other creditors. The diminution of estate doctrine must automatically fail. In effect, application of the doctrine would nullify section 522(h). Because we wish to give effect to the explicit words of Congress and further the fresh start policy of the Code, we hold that the diminution of estate doctrine[19] is not applicable when a debtor sues to avoid a preference under section 522(h).

Given this limited holding, we need not decide Levine's broader claim that the doctrine has been annulled with respect to *all* actions by the trustee as well as the debtor.[20]

19. In using the phrase "diminution of estate doctrine," we mean the consideration of whether the transferred assets would be available to meet *creditor* claims. There might be an analog to the diminution of estate doctrine in a section 522(h) action if the transfer had not impaired the value of the assets available to meet the debtor's claim—for example, if the transfer of exempt assets had been accompanied by an equal and contemporaneous increase in the assets which the debtor could claim from the estate. However, we need not face that problem in this case.

20. . . . Levine argues that the doctrine has been annulled by a change in the wording of §547(b)(5). Section 60 of the former Act defined a preference inter alia as a transfer

To or for the benefit of a creditor . . . the effect of which transfer will be to enable such creditor to obtain a greater percentage of his debt than some other creditor of the same class.

11 U.S.C. §60(a)(1) (1976).

That language has been altered slightly in §547(b), which refers to a transfer

(1) to or for the benefit of a creditor; . . .
(5) that enables such creditor to receive more than such creditor would receive if—
   (A) the case were a case under Chapter 7 of this title;
   (B) the transfer had not been made; and
   (C) the creditor received payment of such debt to the extent provided by the provisions of this title.

11 U.S.C. §547(b).

Levine argues that the new wording reflects a change in focus from the creditor class to the individual creditor. Since the focus is on the individual, the diminution of estate doctrine is inappropriate.

While we do not decide this issue, we do note that there is a good argument that the focus in section 547(b) is still on the "amount that will be received by members of the *class* of which the preferee is a member." H.R. Rep. No. 595, 95th Cong., 1st Sess., 372; S. Rep. No. 989, 95th Cong., 2d Sess., 87; reprinted at 1978 U.S. Code Cong. & Ad. News 5873, 6328 (emphasis added). Moreover, we note that any change in the provision may well be a response to a technical problem in the wording of old section 60. . . .

If future courts determine that the diminution of estate doctrine still has some vitality in actions brought by the trustee, the particular application of the doctrine may turn on the purpose of the trustee's exercise of the preference avoidance power. For example, if he is trying to retrieve assets that would be exempt and therefore available to the debtor, the doctrine should not be applicable. Section 522(g) suggests that the Code permits such actions by the trustee in order to protect the debtor's exemptions.

With regard to other assets that the trustee would be recovering for the benefit of creditors, however, the doctrine might be an appropriate test of his powers. . . .

A FINAL RECAPITULATION

Our decision in this case reflects not only the clear language and history but also the main protective thrust of the Bankruptcy Code. The preference avoidance provisions are designed not to punish the debtor but to defend him from the ravenous maw of creditors during the preference period. Thus, while the literal language of section 522(g) and (h) gives Levine standing to avoid Deel's lien, Levine's action is also supported by the policy against a preference-period race to the courthouse.

Similarly, the policy of protecting a debtor's exemptions informs our interpretation of the diminution of estate doctrine. The availability of assets to the creditors cannot be relevant to an action by the debtor to avoid a preference pursuant to sections 522(h) and 547. Section 522(h) is designed to protect the debtor alone.

We do not decide, however, whether the diminution of estate doctrine still applies to actions brought by the trustee. Any further limitations on the doctrine will be developed in future cases.

Affirmed.

The following case raises another difficulty in trying to mesh the provisions of the Bankruptcy Code (here, §544 as well as §522(f)) with state exemption law. The difficulty arises because of the nature of the particular exemption law involved, which is described most fully in the dissenting opinion. Is, however, the *effect* of such exemption law really all that different from more "traditional" exemptions, which last only as long as the property is owned by the debtor? Should those differences matter for purposes of bankruptcy? How much effect should be given to the ability to *have* a lien on the property that cannot be used *until* the property is sold? Is this a question that should be answered by state law or by bankruptcy policy?

IN RE WEIMAN
22 Bankr. 49 (9th Cir. Bankr. App. 1982)

HUGHES, Bankruptcy Judge.
The debtors have appealed an order holding that their home, although exempt from property of the estate, was subject to a continuing lien in favor of the trustee in bankruptcy.

The exemption claim was based on California Code of Civil Procedure §690.31. The claim of lien was based on 11 U.S.C. §544(a)(1). The order appealed provides that the trustee may enforce the lien if and when the debtors sell or refinance their exempt home.

Judge Volinn and I agree, but for different reasons, that the order should be reversed to the extent it recognizes a lien.

Accordingly, the order appealed is reversed.

My analysis, which considers only federal law, follows.

I

Unlike my brothers, I do not believe that 11 U.S.C. §544(a)(1) gives the trustee a continuing lien on property of the estate. As discussed in Part II, I read the statute as giving the trustee only the rights and powers, i.e., the status, of a judicial lien creditor and then only "as of the commencement of the case. . . ."

Furthermore, any lien created on exempt property by section 544(a)(1) would be nullified by 11 U.S.C. §522(f)(1), which permits the debtor to avoid any judicial lien on property that impairs the debtors' exemption. It is evident that the trustee seeks to impair Mr. and Mrs. Weiman's exemption by means of a judicial lien.

Section 544 gives the trustee the "rights and powers" of a creditor holding a judicial lien on property of the debtor "as of the commencement" of the case. But any actual judicial lien held by the Weimans' creditors on their otherwise exempt home could have been avoided under section 522(f)(1). . . . It would be anomalous if section 522(f)(1) could permit the debtor to avoid actual liens but not fictitious ones.

However, in my opinion, there is no need to invoke section 522(f)(1).

II

The trustee's case rests upon the proposition that 11 U.S.C. §544(a)(1) gives him a lien on property of the estate. (In the words of the dissent, the "trustee herein obtains a lien" and "his lien could be effective for more than 10 years"). Neither the statute nor the cases construing its predecessor under the former Bankruptcy Act justify that proposition, however. (This section and section 70(c) of the former Act read essentially the same; both are known as the strong arm clause).

In relevant part, 11 U.S.C. §544(a)(1) provides that the trustee shall have "as of the commencement of the case. . . . the rights and powers . . . of a creditor . . . that obtains a judicial lien . . ." Thus, by its terms the statute does not give the trustee a lien. It does, of course, give the trustee rights and powers of one obtaining such a lien. The important question is how the trustee exercises such rights and powers.

The purpose and operation of the strong arm rights and powers is described in Sampsell v. Straub, 194 F.2d 228 (9th Cir. 1951):

Section 70c . . . is employed primarily to protect general creditors of the bankrupt against secret liens. To this end the trustee is given all the rights which a creditor with a lien by legal or equitable proceedings would enjoy.

The court also noted that section 70c "arms the trustee" with these rights and powers "as to all property of the bankrupt on the date of bankruptcy. . . ."

The date of bankruptcy is critical under the Code, as it was under the former Act. That date (sometimes called the date of cleavage) determines property of the estate and claims that may be asserted against the estate. See, e.g., 11 U.S.C. §§541(a)(1) and 502(b)(1).

Armed with the rights and powers of a judicial lien holder as of the commencement of the case, the trustee is enabled to free property of the estate of certain liens. It is not necessary for purposes of the strong arm powers that they exist at any time after commencement of the case, although the trustee necessarily will assert them at a later date.

Accordingly, the trustee has cited no cases under the Act in which the concept of a continuing lien has been recognized, and I am aware of none.

The strong arm clause was not restricted to avoiding secret liens under the Act. It also was used to restrict the debtor's right to an exemption in those states, such as California, where a judgment lien is enforceable notwithstanding a subsequently recorded homestead. Sampsell v. Straub, supra.

Sampsell v. Straub held that because the California judgment lien overrides "a tardily recorded homestead exemption" and because "at the date of bankruptcy" the trustee had the powers of a judgment lien holder, the bankrupt's exemption could not be honored if the "declaration of homestead had not been recorded as required to become effective under California law until after bankruptcy adjudication." Thus, as to the trustee in bankruptcy, it was immaterial that the homestead be recorded at all; if it were not of record on the date of bankruptcy, the property was not exempt in bankruptcy.

Sampsell v. Straub does not, therefore, supply any authority for a continuing lien in favor of the trustee.

I would rest reversal on a reading of 11 U.S.C. §544(a)(1) that restricts the trustee to the rights and powers of a judicial lien holder and then only as of the commencement of the case.

VOLINN, Bankruptcy Judge, concurring.

While I agree with the result of Judge Hughes' opinion, I do not agree with its reasoning. Consequently, I feel constrained to set forth, in some detail, my views as they relate to the foregoing opinion and also to the dissent. The Conclusion states my basic point of view.

I

FACTS AND BACKGROUND

The debtor had initially claimed a homestead under the basic homestead statutes of California, Civ. Code §2130 et seq. The debtor's equity in the property did not exceed the statutory maximum. The trustee attacked this declaration for want of a proper legal description. The debtor then moved to amend his bankruptcy exemption schedule, contending that his residence was exempt pursuant to another homestead statute, the automatic "dwelling house" exemption provided by C.C.P. §690.31. The trustee opposed the amendment, pursuant to §690.31(b)(1), because the debtor "has an existing declared homestead." The trial court ruled, first, that this exception to availability applied to an existing "*valid* homestead" (emph. supp.). Therefore, the trial court held §690.31 was available to the debtor. However, it was further held that the trustee was vested, by virtue of 11 U.S.C. §544, with the judgment lien of C.C.P. §674(c) in the amount of the allowed claims in the estate.

In so holding, the trial judge felt he should defer to the precedent set by a colleague in a similar case, In re Gale, No. S.A. 80-0082AP. (B. Ct. C.D. Cal.1980). He stated that a ruling to the contrary in a similar case in the Northern District of California, In re Moore, No. 4-79-2441 H.S. (B. Ct. N.D. Cal. 1980) was preferable, and would have been followed but for the precedent in his own district. Both *Moore* and *Gale* dealt with California law and the basic question as to whether the lien provided for by §674 could attach to the dwelling house. Each decision focuses on interpretation of state law.

II

ISSUE

The essential issue is whether the trustee may, pursuant to 11 U.S.C. §544, invest himself with the right of a judgment lien creditor created by C.C.P. §674(c). The issue turns on interpretation of the United States Bankruptcy Code. This is a federal question governed by the Code, and not state law. . . .

III

THE PRINCIPAL OPINION

The principal opinion states that §544 confines the trustee's derivative lien to a "moment" in time which, in its statutory terms, exists at the commencement of the case. It appears to reason that the lien may not subsist or continue on so as to apply to property which is sought to be exempted from the estate. Such an argument disregards the nature of a lien. It is there to begin with and continues on to ripen upon the happening of events which bring about the need for its application. This is characteristic of security interests, generally, which lead a contingent existence with respect to collateral until needed. But the liens are existing and continuing interests until the debt is paid. While I do not agree that such a result obtains here, because of the reasons stated below, the lien of C.C.P. §674(c) is not any less viable because it was designed to enforce payment when conditions permitting exemption under C.C.P. §690 are inapplicable (e.g., excess equity), then a lien providing for recourse to collateral in the event the debt is not paid.

The opinion further states that not only are the trustee's rights and powers restricted to a moment in time, but further the trustee does not receive a judicial lien by virtue of 11 U.S.C. §544 but only the "rights and powers" of a judicial lien holder. This argument appears to give the trustee the power to avoid liens as if he were a judicial lien creditor but not the lien itself. The reasoning does not square with the language of §544 nor the reasoning of Sampsell v. Straub, 194 F.2d 228 (9th Cir.) cert. denied, 343 U.S. 927, 72 S. Ct. 761, 96 L. Ed. 1338 (1952). The effort to distinguish Sampsell demonstrates that there was an interception of the right to declare a homestead by the filing of the bankruptcy and the trustee's claim of precedence to the subject property. The court held that it was the trustee's status or character as a judgment lien creditor which provided the rationale for depriving the debtor of the homestead. Functionally, the trustee was a judgment lien creditor.

Finally, it is stated 11 U.S.C. §522(f) may be invoked to avoid the lien of C.C.P. §674(c). The problem which arises in applying §522(f) to C.C.P. §674(c) is that it is structurally or organically part of §690.31: "the very same act by which section 690.31 was enacted added subdivision (c) to Code of Civil Procedure section 674. . . ." Krause v. Superior Court, 78 Cal. App. 3d 499, 507, 144 Cal. Rptr. 194, 198 (1978). Section 674(c) provides that as to the dwelling house, judicially determined to be exempt from levy of execution under §690.31:

A judgment lien created pursuant to subdivision (a) of this section shall attach to such real property notwithstanding the exemption provided by Section 690.31.

It is contended that this is an impairment of the exemption and subject to avoidance under §522(f). However, it is clear that, with respect to exemption, the California legislature gave the lien effect only when conditions supporting the exemption are inapplicable. To put it otherwise, the legislation does not allow the lien to impair the exemption.

The legislative history to 11 U.S.C. §522(f) states:

[t]he debtor may avoid a judicial lien on any property to the extent that the property could have been exempted in the absence of the lien. H.R. No. 95-595, 95th Cong., 1st Sess. (1977) 362; S.R. No. 95-989, 95th Cong., 2d Sess. (1978) 76 (under subsection (e)), U.S. Code Cong. & Admin. News 1978, pp. 5787, 5862, 6318.

Since the lien of C.C.P. §674 does not intrude upon the exemption of C.C.P. §690, there is nothing to avoid.

IV

THE DISSENT

While there may be some question as to the nature and application of the C.C.P. §674(c) lien in a non-bankruptcy setting, the threshold question here is whether a trustee in bankruptcy may be invested with such a lien by virtue of 11 U.S.C. §544, the Bankruptcy Code descendant of §70(c), the strong-arm clause of the prior Bankruptcy Act.

The dissent discusses §70(c) in historical context stating that its purpose was to cut off "secret and undisclosed claims" against (the debtor's property) and to equalize "distribution of assets to all unsecured creditors." This is true. However, the fictional status of a judgment creditor with a lien or unsatisfied execution against the debtor's property was created as a test with respect to the validity of various transfers of the debtor's property as to particular creditors. In the event the transfer could be held invalid or inferior to the rights of the hypothetical creditor of §544, it would be voidable by the trustee and could be automatically preserved for the benefit of the estate, 11 U.S.C. §551.

It should be noted that the trustee does not seek to invoke his hypothetical status to test the validity of or set aside a pre-bankruptcy transfer to another creditor. He seeks instead to affect the debtor's homestead property by claiming hypothetical status under §544, with an inchoate lien which would lie dormant until the debtor's post-bankruptcy circumstances would cause it to come to life. Use of the rights and powers given the trustee by §544 for purposes other than avoiding transfers to creditors has been rare if not anomalous.[1] . . .

The dissent cites In re Martin, No. 80-1054 (BAP 9th Cir. 1982), and In re Sanford, 8 B.R. 761, 7 B.C.D. 729 (N.D. Cal. 1981) as supporting the vesting of the §674 lien in the trustee by virtue of 11 U.S.C. §544. Those cases held the trustee may not use 11 U.S.C. §544 to defeat the debtor's

---

1. Sampsell v. Straub, supra, permitted such a result. That case held that the trustee, standing as a judgment creditor under §70(c), defeated the debtor's homestead since the debtor filed his declaration of homestead after he filed his bankruptcy petition. The effect of *Sampsell* in California is considerably attenuated under the Bankruptcy Code since a claim, directly impairing the exemption, is subject to avoidance by virtue of 11 U.S.C. §522(f).

claim of homestead under C.C.P. §690. They provide no conceptual basis for the position of investing the trustee with the §674 lien.

A bankruptcy estate consists of the debtor's property acquired by him prior to the date he files a petition in bankruptcy. Thereafter, the fundamental premise is that the debtor should be free to make a fresh start without having to apply future earnings or acquisitions (with limited exceptions) to pre-bankruptcy debt, 11 U.S.C. §541(a)(6). The question is whether the trustee, by virtue of §544, coupled with the C.C.P. §674, can reach post-bankruptcy accruals of equity in property which the debtor has declared exempt under California's automatic dwelling house exemption.

There is an inherent contradiction in allowing discharged creditors, by virtue of invoking §544, to have access to the debtor's future earnings, as they become equity, or to the homestead itself should the debtor, years later, desire to leave it.[3] The stay provisions of §362, and the character of discharge as an injunction, 11 U.S.C. §524(a), in order to serve such a fresh start would be subverted. The debtor, instead of having a fresh start, would have a homestead subject to doubt and uncertainty during the lifetime of the C.C.P. §674(c) lien. Moreover, such a result would violate the spirit, if not the letter, of 11 U.S.C. §522(c) which provides that property exempted under §522 is not liable during or after the case for pre-bankruptcy debts.

V

CONCLUSION

Should the fiction of §544 endow the claims of general creditors with the quality of a non-dischargeable debt? While fictions may be useful, they should not be employed to bring about a result which is so contrary to the fundamental fresh start policy of the Bankruptcy Code. There should be limits to literal application of language bringing about results so much at odds with the purpose and policy of rehabilitative legislation. As stated in Bank of Marin v. England, 385 U.S. 99, 103, 87 S. Ct. 274, 277, 17 L. Ed. 2d 197 (1966)

> Yet we do not read these statutory words with the ease of a computer. There is an overriding consideration that equitable principles govern the exercise of bankruptcy jurisdiction.

---

3. The primary purpose of §674 was to provide creditors with automatic access to surplus equity (over the homestead) in contradistinction to Calif. Civ. Code, §1260, which does not allow such access. The unlikely availability of the entire homestead through abandonment or waiver would hardly warrant legislative concern since the most logical event which occurs over the ten year life of the lien would be equity build-up.

See also Lewis v. Manufacturer's Trust, 364 U.S. 603, 608, 81 S. Ct. 347, 350, 5 L. Ed. 2d 323 (1961) which refused to allow the application of §70(c) to a point anterior in time where no creditor could have existed, stating:

> The construction of §70c which petitioner urges would give the trustee the power to set aside transactions which no creditor could void and which injured no creditor. That construction would enrich unsecured creditors at the expense of secured creditors, creating a windfall merely by reason of the happenstance of bankruptcy.

The substance and spirit of this language should preclude the trustee from employing the fiction of 11 U.S.C. §544 to deny or limit the homestead, thereby creating a windfall for discharged general creditors.

For the foregoing reasons I would hold that the trustee may not invoke or clothe himself with the judgment lien of C.C.P. §674(c) and would therefore reverse.

KATZ, Bankruptcy Judge (dissenting).

As evidenced by the majority and concurring opinions, no two issues addressed in this case have received unanimous approval by the Panel. The reason for this is that the inter-relationship between California's peculiar dwelling-house exemption and the operation of several sections of the Code is hard to define. The ability to differentiate between operation of law and achievement of desired results is key to reaching a proper decision in this case. While I agree with the concurring opinion that §522(f) is ineffective as against a lien created under California Code of Civil Procedure §674(c), I part sides with the majority on the issue of whether or not the trustee receives a lien, which could eventually reach some if not all of the debtor's equity in his dwelling house after the bankruptcy is filed.

In my opinion the practical effect of the majority opinion is to elevate the California automatic homestead to a position far superior than was ever intended by the California Legislature. While I further agree that the fresh start of the debtor is particularly important to preserve, I believe the Code and the confines of due process limit our ability to grant exemptions beyond that which is embraced by the exemption chosen by the debtor.

The basis for my dissent is an acute understanding of the nature and purposes of both the limited nature of the California dwelling-house exemption and the operation of the Bankruptcy Code. This understanding for the most part is brought out by a historical and logical analysis of the provisions in question.

California Constitution, Article XX, Section 1.5 provides: "The legislature shall protect, by law, from *forced sale* a certain portion of the homestead and other property of all heads of families." [Emphasis added.] In 1872 California Civil Code §1237 et seq., was created to provide a strict scheme by which a homeowner could formally record a homestead on a residence and exempt his home from execution of a judgment and forced sale. . . .

In 1975, California Code of Civil Procedure §690.235, now Code of Civil Procedure §690.31, was enacted as an alternative method to protect a homeowner's homestead exemption. Code of Civil Procedure §690.31 provides in part:

> (a)(1) A dwelling house in which the debtor or the family of the debtor actually resides shall be exempt from execution, to the *same extent and in the same amount* except as otherwise provided in this section, as the debtor or the spouse of the debtor would be entitled to select as a homestead pursuant to Title 5 (commencing with Section 1237). [Emphasis added.]

The new dwelling-house exemption was automatic in that no formal declaration of homestead needs to be recorded to gain the protection of the homestead. . . . The legislative purpose behind the dwelling-house exemption was to ensure that a homestead exemption was not a mere formality available only to the knowledgeable, but to make sure that all who are entitled to it had an opportunity to secure the exemption. . . .

The net effect of the dwelling-house exemption is that every dwelling house in California in which the debtor or the debtor's family actually resides is exempt from execution by any creditor unless that creditor would have been entitled to execute his judgment against the property even if it had been properly homesteaded at the time the judgment became a lien. . . . This application, however, is tempered by the major difference between the two homestead laws in that a judgment lien will attach to a dwelling exempt under Code of Civil Procedure §690.31, but will not attach to a dwelling which has been formally homesteaded. Code of Civil Procedure §674(c). . . .

The major issue herein is where do the trustee and creditors stand in relationship to a dwelling-house exemption when bankruptcy law is superimposed on the operation of the exemption. The law has long been well settled that the trustee and creditors in bankruptcy stand junior to a property recorded homestead. The law with respect to the automatic dwelling-house exemption is in need of clarification.

In the recent case of In re Martin, (9th Cir. BAP 1982), this Panel held that 11 U.S.C. §544 cannot be invoked by the trustee to defeat the debtor's dwelling-house exemption. Unlike the adverse result under the Act, the dwelling-house exemption prevents the trustee from achieving outright ownership of the dwelling on the date of the bankruptcy is filed. . . . Notwithstanding this holding, I believe the trustee is vested with certain rights which preserve equity in the dwelling for the estate to be realized at a point in time when the equity in the dwelling is no longer protected. This result is reached through the interplay between 11 U.S.C. §544 and the limited nature of the California dwelling-house exemption.

In addition to the rights conferred on the trustee in §§541 and 363, the trustee also derives the right to proceed against property under §544 (11 U.S.C. 544). Section 544(a)(1) gives the trustee the rights and powers of a creditor who obtains a judicial lien on all property on which a creditor on a simple contract could have obtained a lien. . . . Similar to the dwelling-house exemption, the nature and purpose of the trustee's §544 powers are better defined by a historical review of the section's derivation.

Section 544 is the descendant of over eighty years of case law interpretation and statutory evolution. In 1910 Section 47, cl.2(a) [11 U.S.C. §75(a)(2)] was amended such as to vest in the trustee for the interest of all creditors the potential rights of creditors possessing or holding liens upon the property coming into his custody by legal or equitable proceedings. . . . The major purpose of this amendment was to allow the trustee to cut off secret and undisclosed claims against the property. By cutting off these secret interests the bankruptcy laws brought about uniformity in administration and equalized the distribution of assets to all unsecured creditors. . . . By placing the trustee in the status of a lien creditor, the 1910 amendment sought to vest the trustee with the rights of those creditors who had yet to obtain liens either by equitable or legal proceedings. . . .

Under the Act the trustee could exercise his rights as a lien creditor to reach any asset which an ideal lien creditor could reach. . . . Thus, the trustee could either bring into the estate, or preserve for the estate, any and all property available at the time the petition was filed, to which his lien rights attached. . . .

The enactment of §544 in effect broadened the rights which were available to the trustee under prior §§70(c), 70(e) and 60(a)(4) of the Act. [11 U.S.C. §§110(c)(e), 96(a)(4); 124 Cong. Rec. H. 11,097 (Sept. 28, 1978); S. 17, 413 (Oct. 6, 1978).] Under §544(a) the trustee not only may seek to avoid transfers of property, but is additionally vested with any rights available to a creditor holding a judicial lien obtained in an action on a simple contract, *whether or not such a creditor exists.*

When viewing the powers of the trustee under §544 along with prior case law discussions and other provisions of the Code, a clear pattern emerges. The §544 powers given to the trustee are a form of bankruptcy trade-off. In exchange for having their debts discharged, the unsecured creditors are given certain rights, albeit artificial rights, which have the effect of bringing into the estate all property which could have been available to them on the day bankruptcy was filed. The debtor, on the other hand, is given a discharge of his debts and receives a fresh start through the election of exemptions under §522.

Given the purposes of the trustee's rights under §544(a) and the trade-offs inherent in the bankruptcy laws, it makes good sense to apply these considerations in determining a value for the trustee's lien. Consistent with these considerations and purposes I would hold that the value of the lien obtained under §544(a) is the lesser of the total of all unsecured claims or the amount of equity in the property upon which the §544(a) lien could attach on the date the petition is filed. By limiting the value of the lien to the value of property available on the date the petition was filed, the rights of creditors to secure equality in distribution and the legislative priority of preserving to the debtor a fresh start are fully balanced.

Under a normal absolute exemption statute a lien valuation would not be necessary. The peculiar limited nature of the California dwelling-house exemption, however, requires that the lien of the trustee be valued currently such that it can be paid in the future when the exemption no longer prevents execution on the property.

Having reached this point the question arises as to the length of time the trustee should be able to exercise his rights in the equity preserved for the estate.

There is nothing in the Bankruptcy Code to indicate that the trustee's rights as a judicial lien creditor are confined to the point in time when the bankruptcy case is commenced. That is merely the time the trustee's rights are created. . . . The trustee herein obtains a lien which is measured by the rights that a judicial lien creditor would have under the laws of California. . . . Under California law a judicial lien exists a minimum of 10 years unless extended through supplemental proceedings. California Code of Civil Procedure §§674(a), 685. Therefore, I would hold that as long as the trustee remains in the case his lien could be effective for more than 10 years.

Having discussed the trustee's lien, its value, and effective life, we must now discern what effect California law would have on the trustee's lien. Under California law, a lien creditor can execute against the dwelling house of the debtor after application has been made and the court finds that the current value of the dwelling house, over and above all liens and encumbrances thereon, exceeds the amount of the allowable exemption. Code of Civil Procedure §690.31(c). Even though a judicial lien attaches to the property under Code of Civil Procedure §674(c), it is clear that this lien is junior to the exemption amount as long as the debtor does not voluntarily sell the dwelling and reinvests the proceeds from any execution sale within six months into another dwelling in which the debtor or his family actually resides. See Code of Civil Procedure §690.31(j), (k). . . . Therefore, if there is excess equity above liens and the homestead amount, or the debtors sell the dwelling or voluntarily move out, the lien would need to be paid to the extent the proceeds would no longer be exempt. See CCP §690.31(j)

The concurring opinion claims that there is an inherent contradiction in allowing discharged creditors, by virtue of invoking §544, to have access to the debtor's post bankruptcy accruals in equity and future earnings. This proposition ignores the basis upon which the value of the trustee's lien would be fixed. His rights would be set in an amount certain on the date of the filing of the petition. Thereafter, the creditors would only be entitled to the funds upon which the lien attached. Clearly, any post-bankruptcy accruals in equity or future earnings of the debtor would only inure to the benefit of the debtor and his fresh start.[3]

The majority claims that the result of imparting a lien to the trustee would bring about a result which is contrary to the fundamental fresh-start policy of the Bankruptcy Code. In rendering my opinion, I am mindful that it would open the door to the situation where a debtor moves from the dwelling house 10 years after bankruptcy, but finds the equity in his house suddenly levied upon by the trustee in bankruptcy. Surely a debtor's fresh start is not well fostered by this possibility. Yet on the other hand the result is consistent with both the purposes of the Bankruptcy Code and the purpose of the California automatic dwelling-house exemption. It is consistent with the Code because it provides creditors with every bit of property they are legally entitled to in exchange for having their claims discharged. It is consistent with the California exemption chosen because it fully protects the debtor from the *forced sale* of a certain part of the homestead without providing an alternative chance to start over. See CCP §690.31(j).

When the Bankruptcy Code was drafted, it did not have California particularly in mind. It was written as a universal document with the Code provisions exercised uniformly among the various states. If any result achieved under my view is contrary to a fresh-start policy, it is not because of the universal application of the Code, but instead caused by the peculiar nature of the state exemption relied upon. Any unfortunate result reached under the laws of California can be changed through consideration and action by the California Legislature. This Panel's apparent authority to fractionalize the uniform operation of the Code to obtain a more desired result in California is, in my opinion, not warranted in this case. I would affirm the judgment below, with certain reservations relative to refinancing, and therefore respectfully dissent.

NOTE

If the lien involved were a judicial lien held by an actual creditor, could the debtor avoid that lien by using §522(f)(1)?

3. The operation of the exemption can be demonstrated by analogy. The California dwelling-house exemption is much like a glass bottle with liquid in it. The bottle represents the expendable nature of the exemption and the liquid, the debtor's equity therein. On the date of bankruptcy a portion of the liquid equal to the trustee's lien is frozen. Thereafter, any post-bankruptcy accruals in equity or future earnings of the debtor fill the bottle with additional liquid. This tends to push the frozen part of the liquid out of the top of the bottle. If down the road the frozen liquid is pushed out of the bottle, or the bottle breaks, the trustee and hence the unsecured creditors are entitled to receive the frozen part of the liquid. The debtor keeps the rest.

NOTE ON THE COMPROMISE OF §522 AND THE FRESH START POLICY

Is §522(f) sound policy? If it is, is it sound *bankruptcy* policy, or should it have been enacted across the board? Congress's explanation for the section is quoted, supra page 863. The basis of that explanation is that liens and security interests may create an asymmetry between the threat of the creditor (which is based on the value of the property to the debtor) and the (presumably lower) value of the property to the creditor. Doesn't this, however, assume what leverage state laws give (or should give) to holders of security interests and other liens? Even if there are persuasive reasons to apply that policy to the bankruptcy exemptions of §522(d) (or at least that subset of such exemptions that do not overlap with state exemptions), is there likewise a reason to apply §522(f) to a debtor who elects state exemptions?

Does §522(f) reflect a view that debtors should be entitled to have a certain irreducible set of exemptions? If so, isn't it odd to have §522(f) (and §522(e)) in a statute that does not *specify* a minimum set of exemptions? That is to say, the freedom given to states under §522(b) seems to vitiate that rationale for the existence of §522(f). So viewed, cases such as *McManus* and *Pine* simply reflect a product of the inevitable inconsistency of the policies underlying §522(f) and the compromise reflected in §522(b). Or does §522(f) reflect another policy, such as that under *any* exemption scheme, debtors are too likely to waive the exemption (by granting a security interest) in order to get credit at a lower cost?

Assuming that the Bankruptcy Code should have a set of irreducible bankruptcy exemptions as a part of its fresh start policy, is it clear that the approach of §522(d), (e), and (f) is the best path to take? In addition to the problems of §522(f), we have seen classification issues under (d) and problems caused by conversion of nonexempt assets to exempt assets on the eve of bankruptcy.

Can these problems be avoided? To the extent that there should be a certain level of assets that a debtor is left with following discharge, why have it turn on the *form* of existing assets at the time of bankruptcy? What about a bankruptcy exemption system that gave the debtor $25,000 (to pick a number) in hypothetical money that a debtor could use in bidding for goods at a judicial bankruptcy court sale? See Countryman, For a New Exemption Policy in Bankruptcy, 14 Rutgers L. Rev. 678, 746-747 (1960). That way, a debtor could select which assets to keep, and there would be no need to avoid otherwise unavoidable liens or security interests. Would such as system work? What would be its principal disadvantages?

S.445, a bill passed by the Senate in 1983, proposed cutting back on the use of §522(f). These provisions, however, were dropped from the 1984 Bankruptcy Amendments. The accompanying report, Sen. Rep. 65, 98th Cong., 1st Sess. 7-8, 14-15 (1983), discussed those issues as follows:

The new Code introduced a list of Federal exemptions into the bankruptcy law for the first time. Under prior law, property exemptions in bankruptcy proceedings were generally determined under State law. In promulgating a system of Federal exemptions, Congress was concerned that many state exemption laws had not been substantially revised in recent years to adequately serve the needs of individuals and to provide the fresh start contemplated in the bankruptcy proceeding. The historical purpose of exemptions was to provide a debtor with the basic necessities of life so that, after bankruptcy, the debtor could begin, or continue to lead, a productive life. . . .

Section 522(f)(2) . . . invalidates nonpossessory, nonpurchase money security interests in property which is exempt and which consists of household goods and personal articles, tools of the trade, and professionally prescribed health aids. This provision was based on the view that such property often had a high replacement cost for the debtor and might aid his fresh start, while it also had a low resale value to the creditor. Thus, invalidating the creditor's security interest seemed to offer substantial benefits at little cost.

Experience under the Code has shown that the invalidation of nonpurchase money security interests in such property has had several significant and detrimental effects on both consumers and creditors. First, consumers who previously qualified for credit only because they could post security in the form of household goods or tools of the trade, now are being denied credit altogether. Moreover, creditors who previously extended credit to such persons have withdrawn from these segments of the consumer credit market, thus decreasing the availability of consumer credit. . . . This result contradicts the strong congressional policies in favor of making credit more widely available to all segments of the population. Second, creditors often have insisted on new forms of security or protection which would not be invalidated under section 522(f)(2): for example, creditors may seek second mortgages, cosigners, and security posted by cosigners. Finally, the committee's attention was directed to cases where the debtor borrowed against equity in items of property of this type having high market value (such as antique furniture). In such cases, the effect of the new Code is to impair the creditor's security in property which has significant economic value and which does not fall within the high replacement/low resale rationale of section 522(f)(2).

The Committee bill resolves these competing interests by eliminating the avoidance of non-possessory, non-purchase money liens on household goods. Non-possessory, non-purchase money liens on tools of the trade, implements, and professional books having a value of $1,000 or less may still be avoided. . . .

Complementing these changes are provisions allowing the debtor to redeem non-avoided liens over a period of five years. Where the Court finds that a debtor has no reasonable ability to redeem the property affected by a non-avoided lien, and that the requirement of redemption would impose undue hardship, it may exempt the property completely from the operation of the lien.

Chapter 12

BANKRUPTCY ALTERNATIVES TO LIQUIDATION: "WAGE-EARNER'S" PLANS UNDER CHAPTER 13

A. GENERAL PROVISIONS OF A CHAPTER 13 PLAN

In the typical Chapter 7 bankruptcy case, an individual will be granted, in exchange for existing nonexempt assets, a discharge from most monetary obligations. Chapter 13, however, allows a debtor to keep all of his assets, but to give up a portion of his earnings in excess of the value of those assets. The basic theory of Chapter 13 — although obsolete in part due to the 1984 Amendments — was summarized in In re Rimgale, 669 F.2d 426 (7th Cir. 1982):

> One of Congress' purposes in enacting the Bankruptcy Reform Act of 1978 was to make the old Chapter XIII provisions more accessible and attractive to individual debtors. Liberalized provisions, Congress reasoned, would benefit both debtors and creditors. Debtors would be given more latitude to work out debt composition plans, thus avoiding the stigma of straight bankruptcy. Creditors would receive total or substantial repayment under a Chapter 13 plan, but little or nothing in a Chapter 7 plan.
>
> To make Chapter 13 work, Congress altered the old Chapter XIII in three important ways. First, it expanded the class of debtors who could take advantage of Chapter 13. Formerly restricted to wage-earner debtors, Chapter 13 was made available to any individual with regular income, whether from wages or other sources. Second, Congress eliminated the requirement that a plan be approved by a majority of unsecured creditors. Concerned that in the past short-sighted and stubborn creditors had blocked feasible plans, Congress provided for creditors to be heard, 11 U.S.C. §1324, but gave the bankruptcy judge the sole authority to confirm or reject a plan. It also set out the criteria he was to use, 11 U.S.C. §1325. . . . Finally, Congress added an incentive for debtors to complete performance

under the confirmed plan. 11 U.S.C. §1328 provides that a debtor who has carried out his plan is entitled to a discharge of virtually all debts provided for in the plan or disallowed. Thus a Chapter 13 debtor may be discharged from a variety of debts that a Chapter 7 bankrupt remains obligated to pay at the conclusion of a liquidation.

The statutory modification of Chapter 13 has had both intended and unintended effects. The number of Chapter 13 cases has increased sharply. Many of them correspond closely to the idealized case Congress had in mind when it wrote the legislation: the debtor, given time and relief from harassment, is able to pay all or most of his debts. Increasingly, however, bankruptcy courts are seeing cases . . . in which debtors propose less substantial, or even nominal, payments under a Chapter 13 plan, in order eventually to take advantage of Chapter 13's generous discharge provisions.

A *Rimgale* indicates, a Chapter 13 case is designed to be a relatively expeditious and inexpensive procedure for individuals with "regular income." It is available to any individual, other than a stockbroker or a commodity broker, whose income is sufficiently stable and regular to enable him to make payments under a plan, and whose noncontingent, liquidated, unsecured debts are less than $100,000, and whose noncontingent, liquidated, secured debts are less than $350,000 on the date of filing of a Chapter 13 petition. §109(e). A Chapter 13 case may be commenced *only* by a voluntary petition of the debtor; there is no such thing as an involuntary Chapter 13 case.

The baseline protection for creditors is that they are to receive not less than they would receive in a Chapter 7 proceeding (§1325(a)(4)), although, as we will see, a 1984 amendment to §1325 substantially changed the tenor of this section. In exchange for the commitment pursuant to a Chapter 13 plan to pay some percentage of outstanding debts (at least the Chapter 7 amount) from current assets and from future income over time, the Chapter 13 debtor enjoys certain benefits not afforded under Chapter 7 or 11. The baseline definition of property of the estate under §541 is modified by §1306 to include earnings from services performed by the debtor during the duration of the plan. Under Chapter 13, the debtor can retain his property and can continue business ventures and even increase his estate by continuing to purchase property while subject to a plan. §§1306, 1307. Litigation and collection efforts against the debtor are stayed, and §1301 also enjoins (with certain exceptions) actions against an individual who is liable on a consumer debt with the debtor or that secured such a debt unless such individual became liable on or secured such debt in the ordinary course of his business.

Perhaps as striking for the individual in Chapter 13, most of the limitations on individual discharge that we have been examining are called off in Chapter 13. A Chapter 13 case leading to a discharge may be commenced within six years of a prior bankruptcy proceeding (In re Baker, 736 F.2d 481 (8th Cir. 1984)) and will not bar another bankruptcy case leading to a discharge commenced less than six years after a Chapter

13 discharge was granted upon at least a 70 percent pay-out plan, if the plan was the "debtor's best effort." §727(a)(9). Moreover, since §727(a)(9) does not apply to Chapter 13 (§103(b)), a debtor can, in theory at least, file successive Chapter 13 plans, without regard to timing. Compare In re Ciotta, 4 Bankr. 253 (Bankr. S.D.N.Y. 1980) (six-year bar to successive discharges does not apply in cases commenced under Chapter 13 of the Bankruptcy Code) with In re Hubbard, 11 Bankr. 176 (Bankr. D. Or. 1981) (plan not calling for full or substantial payment over the objection of creditors after a previous discharge within six years may not be confirmed).

After a debtor completes performance under a Chapter 13 plan, the court grants the debtor a discharge from all of the debts provided for under the plan. §1328. A discharge granted under §1328(a) is not subject to all of the exceptions to discharge set out in §523. The only debts excepted from discharge under §1328(a) are: (a) claims not provided for (unless disallowed under §502), §1328(a); (b) long-term obligations, secured or unsecured, that run beyond the term of the plan, §§1328(a)(1) and 1322(b)(5); and (c) alimony and child support under §523(a)(5), 1328(a)(2). If the debtor fails to complete the plan, he can still get a discharge, *if* (a) it is concluded that the reason for the failure was events beyond the control of the debtor, (b) the debtor has paid out, in present value terms, the liquidation amount, and (c) modification of the plan under §1329, which permits scale-downs, extensions, and temporary moratoriums, is not practicable. §1328(b). But, in this event, the discharge given the debtor is limited — *all* the §523(a) debts are nondischargeable. §1328(c).

The provisions of Chapter 13, in the main, are consistent with the notion that Chapter 13 is a procedure for the benefit of the *debtor*. Chapter 13 provides, for example, that only the debtor may file a plan. §1321. The only requirements of a plan are that the debtor pay all priority claims (mainly administrative expenses) in full, submit such portion of future earnings to the supervision of the trustee as is necessary for the execution of the plan, and provide the same treatment for each claim within a class. §1322(a). Plans, however, are limited in duration. The plan may provide for full or partial payment of creditors over any period up to three years and, with the court's approval, up to five years. §1322(c). A plan may provide for the payment of those claims only out of future income, or out of future income and through liquidation of some of the debtor's existing property. Of particular importance, the plan may "modify the rights of holders of secured claims, other than a claim secured only by a security interest in real property that is the debtor's principal residence, or of holders of unsecured claims." §1322(b)(2). There is also a provision providing for the deacceleration of claims (§1322(b)(5)) although it, unlike §1124(2), does not include the words "reinstate the maturity," which has lead to an interpretive problem that we will see in *Taddeo*, infra page 922.

Standards of confirmation of a Chapter 13 plan are quite different than the standards of confirmation of a Chapter 11 plan. There is no vote in Chapter 13, and no requirement of gaining the consent of unsecured creditors. Rather, §1325(a)(4) provides that each unsecured creditor must receive no less, in present value terms, than it would have received in a Chapter 7 liquidation—a standard similar to that of §1129(a)(7), and which protects the individual creditors as if they each dissented. A secured creditor may have a plan "crammed down" over its objection if the plan provides that (1) the secured creditor retain its lien, while receiving payments over the life of the plan, whose present value is not less than the value of the allowed secured amount of its claim, or (2) the secured creditor receive its collateral back, §1325(a)(5). (This may sound quite similar to the protections given a secured creditor under the absolute priority rule of §1129(b).) In addition, for a confirmation of a plan, the bankruptcy court must find that the debtor will be able to make payments under and comply with the plan. §1325(a)(6). This is like Chapter 11's "feasibility" requirement.

The bankruptcy judge must find that the plan has been proposed in "good faith." This has given rise to cases in which a Chapter 13 plan proposed to pay unsecured creditors nothing, or very little, or when the principal use of Chapter 13 seems to be to discharge a debt that would not be dischargeable under Chapter 7. In 1984, an additional requirement was added. If either the trustee or the holder of an allowed unsecured claim objects to the confirmation of a plan, then the court may not approve the plan unless the creditor who objects is being paid in full or unless the plan provides that all of the debtor's projected disposable income for three years is to be applied to payments under the plan. §1325(b). In commenting on a earlier version of this amendment, a Senate Report, S. Rep. No. 97-446, observed, at 31-32:

> Chapter 13 does not contain any standard which specifies how much of the debtor's future income should be devoted to the plan. The only provisions which bear on this issue are found in section 1325(a)(4), which requires that creditors receive at least as much in a chapter 13 case as they would receive in a chapter 7 liquidation, and section 1325(a)(3), which requires the plan to be "proposed in good faith."
>
> In both theory and practice, the requirement that creditors in a chapter 13 case receive at least as much as they would receive in a chapter 7 liquidation, is not a meaningful standard. In theory, the liquidation standard necessarily looks to present assets as a source for paying debts. The fact that debts cannot be paid out of assets has no bearing upon the extent to which they can be paid out of future income. . . .
>
> The good faith standard provides little further protection. The standard is unduly vague. . . .
>
> The Code does not provide any target for the portion of debt which should be repaid, nor does the Code even provide that repayment of debt should take precedence over expenses for non-necessity or luxury items.

Given such vague and uncertain standards, it is not surprising to find widely different approaches among bankruptcy courts. . . .

A chapter 13 proceeding involves substantial benefits to the debtor who is able to retain his property, avoid most nondischargeable debts, and cram down debts of secured creditors. The *quid pro quo* for such benefits would seem to be a substantial effort by the debtor to pay his debts. Of course, the first criterion in such cases must be the debtor's obligations to support himself and his family. But beyond that, it is necessary to have a definite standard delineating how much of the debtor's future income should be committed to the plan.

Chapter 13 relief is essentially equitable, and contemplates a substantial effort by the debtor to pay his debts. Such an effort, by definition, may require some sacrifices by the debtor, and some alteration in prepetition consumption levels. . . . This approach will also permit plans to be confirmed where the debtor does make a substantial effort to pay his debts, even though the payment itself is not substantial.

The same Senate bill also proposed to change the dischargeability provisions of Chapter 13, most notably by amending §1328(a)(2), to read "of a kind specified in section 523(a) of this title." (The year before, a Senate Report, in proposing a similar change in a bill called the "Bankruptcy Amendments Act of 1981," called the change "a minor substantive amendment.") That, and related changes, which were not included in the amendments actually enacted in 1984, were explained in the accompanying Senate Report, at 27:

[The "as much as in a liquidation" test of §1325(a)(4)] does not, of course, consider the fact that creditors with nondischargeable claims have access to postpetition earnings and property, and in the committee's view it is inadequate to encourage satisfaction of these important claims. As witnesses emphasized, the provisions quoted above, as presently written, effectively undermine section 523(a) in several important respects. First, they permit persons with nondischargeable claims effectively to avoid section 523(a) by filing a chapter 13 plan providing for small payments to creditors with nondischargeable claims. . . . Second, they encourage debtors to propose the smallest possible chapter 13 payout, for, under chapter 13, if a debtor proposes a 10 percent payout and completes the plan, most of the nondischargeable debts are fully discharged. Anomalously, if the debtor proposes a 75 percent plan payment of nondischargeable debts and receives a hardship discharge under section 1328(b) after paying 25 percent of the claim, the claim is not discharged. . . . Third, because nondischargeable claims are not allowed special treatment in chapter 13, section 1322(b) probably forbids the creditor with a nondischargeable claim from being treated differently from other unsecured creditors.

The committee bill corrects these problems by (1) statutorily encouraging satisfaction of §523(a) debts in chapter 13, (2) conforming the treatment of such debts provided for in chapter 13 to that accorded them in chapter 7, and (3) allowing the chapter 13 plan to discriminate between section 523(a) debts and other debts scheduled so as to facilitate their integration into a workable plan.

Why did the Senate Bill focus on nondischargeable debts under §523 and not on grounds for denial of discharge under §727? Cf. §1328(e).

As a practical matter, notwithstanding §1325(b), creditors oftentimes cannot insist that a debtor "pay until it hurts," because a debtor always has the option of filing under Chapter 7. How attractive that option is will vary with the circumstances of the debtor. Because a debtor loses nonexempt assets in Chapter 7, the attractiveness of that chapter may depend in part on how much personal value the debtor has in those assets that will be lost if they are taken away. The attractiveness of Chapter 7 will also vary depending on the extent of the debtor's nondischargeable debts because of the limited application of §523 to Chapter 13 cases.

Consumer lenders likewise are pulled in two directions. On the one hand, they want to ensure that once a debtor has elected Chapter 13, they receive as much as possible. On the other hand, they want to reach a debtor's future income and hence want to make Chapter 13 more attractive. Among the other 1984 Amendments to the Bankruptcy Code was a provision requiring the debtor to file with the bankruptcy petition a statement that he was aware that he could choose between Chapter 7 and Chapter 13. Bankruptcy Amendments and Federal Judgeship Act of 1984, §322; Bankruptcy Rule 1002, Official Form No. 1. The same provision also required the debtor's lawyer to file a statement that he had told his client about the relief available under both Chapter 7 and Chapter 13.

The cases and problems that follow raise some of the more recurrent issues in Chapter 13 litigation.

PROBLEMS

12.1 Debtor was employed through last year, but presently is on welfare, and receives welfare payments of $850 a month. Is Debtor an "individual with regular income" within the meaning of §101(27), and thus able to use Chapter 13? See In re McGowan, 24 Bankr. 73 (Bankr. N.D. Ohio 1982); In re Wilhelm, 6 Bankr. 905 (Bankr. E.D.N.Y. 1980); In re Iacovoni, 2 Bankr. 256 (Bankr. D. Utah, 1980).

12.2 Debtor files a Chapter 13 petition, listing unsecured claims totalling $394,000. Of these claims, however, Debtor disputes three claims, scheduled in the amount of $219,000, $60,000, and $70,000. Each of these three claims is based on a lawsuit against Debtor seeking compensatory and punitive damages based on alleged fraudulent conduct of Debtor. Is Debtor eligible for relief under §109(e)? Compare In re Sylvester, 19 Bankr. 671 (9th Cir. Bankr. App. 1982) with In re King, 9 Bankr. 376 (Bankr. D. Or. 1981).

12.3 Debtor files for Chapter 13. Debtor's plan, which is confirmed by the bankruptcy court, proposes to pay the holders of unsecured claims 75 percent of their claims over a three-year period. Six months after confirmation of the plan, Debtor's mother becomes seriously ill. Debtor's mother cannot pay her medical bills, and Debtor wants to help. Can Debtor reduce the payments to his creditors? See §1329; cf. §1323.

12.4 Debtor files for Chapter 13. At that time, Debtor has $100,000 of unsecured claims and $25,000 of nonexempt, nonencumbered assets. Debtor's plan, which is confirmed by the bankruptcy court, proposes to pay the holders of unsecured claims 25 percent over a three-year period. Four months after the filing for Chapter 13, Debtor receives an inheritance of $200,000. Can the creditors require the Debtor to increase the payments under the Chapter 13 plan? See §1329; cf. §§541(a)(5); 1306. Would anything change in the problem if the inheritance were received by Debtor eight months after filing for Chapter 13? See In re Fluharty, 23 Bankr. 426 (Bankr. N.D. Ohio 1982).

BARNES v. WHELAN
689 F.2d 193 (D.C. Cir. 1982)

ROBB, Senior Circuit Judge.

In these consolidated cases the District Court reversed in part decisions of the Bankruptcy Court refusing to confirm Chapter 13 debt adjustment plans filed by appellees Wavalene N. Barnes and Abel Montano. The trustees in bankruptcy appeal, urging us to reinstate the Bankruptcy Court's decisions. Both plans provide that secured creditors or creditors holding cosigned debts receive full payment of the amounts owed them, but that other creditors receive only nominal payments. The central issue on appeal, a controversial question of bankruptcy law undecided in this circuit, is whether the "good faith" requirement for confirmation of personal bankruptcy plans under 11 U.S.C. §1325(a)(3) bars approval of plans proposing only such nominal payments. We adhere to the traditional meaning of good faith and hold that section 1325(a)(3) does not require any particular level of repayment to unsecured creditors. We also consider the classification of claims, an issue raised by Montano as cross-appellant in No 81-1825, and hold that Chapter 13 plans may generally classify unsecured debts based on the presence of a codebtor, but that Montano's plan as presently drafted "unfairly discriminates" between cosigned and noncosigned debts under 11 U.S.C. §1322(b)(1). . . .

Chapter 13 of the Bankruptcy Code, 11 U.S.C. §1301 et seq. (Supp. IV 1980), permits certain debtors to repay all or a percentage of their debts out of future income according to a court-approved plan. Unlike liquidation or "straight" bankruptcy under Chapter 7, 11 U.S.C. §701 et seq., Chapter 13 does not require the debtor to surrender all non-exempt assets for distribution to creditors. Instead, the debtor makes continuing payments to creditors over a three-to-five year period. 11 U.S.C. §1322(c). Upon completion of the plan, the Chapter 13 debtor is entitled to a broad discharge of his obligations. 11 U.S.C. §1328(a).

Before the plan can become effective, however, it must be confirmed by the Bankruptcy Court. Section 1325(a) sets out six criteria for confirmation. . . . If all six requirements are satisfied, the bankruptcy court must confirm the plan. . . .

This appeal encompasses two distinct Chapter 13 plans filed by two debtors, Wavalene N. Barnes and Abel Montano. In February 1980 Montano filed a debt adjustment plan with the United States Bankruptcy Court for the District of Columbia. Montano is employed as a clerk at the World Bank in the District of Columbia and earns a net income of $948 per month. His plan listed expenses of $749 per month for himself, his wife, and one dependent child, leaving an excess of approximately $200 per month available for repayment of his debts. His unsecured indebtedness totalled $31,507, and there were no secured creditors. Montano's plan proposed monthly payments of $200, the full amount available, to be applied as follows: (1) one hundred percent payments to the unsecured creditors with claims guaranteed by cosigners, totalling approximately $7,000; and (2) one percent payments to the remaining unsecured creditors, with claims totalling $24,500.

. . . The court ruled that in order to satisfy the "good faith" requirement of 11 U.S.C. §1325(a)(3), the debtor must propose "a plan of meaningful repayment," adding "[t]he court, in determining 'meaningfulness,' will look at each plan on a case-by-case basis, weighing both the interests of creditors and the debtors in light of the rehabilitative goals of Chapter 13." *Montano*, 4 B.R. at 539. The court concluded that Montano's plan, offering one hundred percent repayment to creditors holding cosigned debts and only one percent to all others, "fails to propose meaningful repayment. . . ." Id. The Bankruptcy Court also rejected Montano's attempt to treat debts guaranteed by cosigners more favorably than non-cosigned debts, ruling "a plan may classify only on the basis of substantial similarity" between claims, and that the "mere existence of a co-debtor is not legally sufficient to justify separate classification." Id. at 537. The court denied confirmation on both the "good faith" and classification grounds.

Wavalene Barnes, the other debtor in these appeals, filed her debt adjustment plan in December 1979. She is employed as a government secretary and earns $749 per month net income. Her monthly expenses total $658, leaving $91 in disposable income. Her debts are as follows: $3500 owed to the Treasury Federal Credit Union, secured to the extent of $1750 by the debtor's automobile; a secured debt of $710 owed to the Marcy Avenue Homebuyers Association; and approximately $6250 in other unsecured debts, mostly credit card obligations. Under her plan, Barnes proposed to repay these debts at the rate of $91 per month, providing one hundred percent to the secured creditors but only one percent to the unsecured creditors.

. . . Relying on the earlier opinion in the *Montano* case, the court ruled that Barnes' one percent repayment to unsecured creditors was not in "good faith," even though Barnes was devoting her entire disposable income to the plan. The court also ruled that Barnes underestimated her expenses and would be unable to meet all the payments under the plan, thus failing the "feasibility" requirement of 11 U.S.C. §1325(a)(6). The court concluded that confirmation should be denied and the proceeding converted to a Chapter 7 liquidation. *Barnes,* 5 B.R. at 379.

Both cases were appealed to the District Court. On April 22, 1981 the District Court reversed on the issue of good faith, stating "nothing in the Bankruptcy Code suggests that 'good faith' as used in section 1325(a) was intended to depart from the term's traditional meaning of honesty in fact or honesty of intention." In re Wavalene Barnes, 13 B.R. 997, 999 (D.D.C.1981). The District Court concluded that Barnes' plan "offered repayment to the maximum extent she honestly believed she was capable [and therefore] met Chapter 13's good faith requirement." Id. at 1000. As for Montano's plan, however, the District Court agreed with the Bankruptcy Court that 11 U.S.C. §1122(a) did not allow separate treatment solely on the basis that certain debts were guaranteed by a cosigner. Id. The District Court ruled that Montano's classification also failed because it discriminated unfairly between unsecured creditors in contravention of 11 U.S.C. §1322(b)(1). Id. . . .

I.   "GOOD FAITH" UNDER 11 U.S.C. §1325(a)(3)

Chapter 13 was enacted in 1978 as part of a comprehensive revision of the Bankruptcy Act of 1898. It replaced the wage earner's provisions contained in Chapter XIII under the 1898 Act, as amended, and modified prior law in many respects. Most important for our purposes here, Chapter 13 changed the procedure for confirmation of the debtor's bankruptcy plan. Under Chapter XIII, a majority of unsecured creditors had to approve the debtor's plan before a court could confirm it. See 11 U.S.C. §1052 (1976) (repealed 1978). Chapter 13 eliminates unsecured creditor approval, and leaves the confirmation decision to the court pursuant to the six criteria in 11 U.S.C. §1325(a). . . .

Section 1325(a)(3) requires that the debtor's Chapter 13 plan must be "proposed in good faith and not by any means forbidden by law." Bankruptcy courts divide sharply over the meaning of this "good faith" requirement in the context of Chapter 13 plans which offer low-percentage repayments to unsecured creditors. Some courts, including the Bankruptcy Court here, interpret section 1325(a)(3) to require "meaningful repayment."[5] . . . Such an interpretation is generally based on the legislative history and broad purposes of Chapter 13. Other courts, including the District Court here, hold that nothing in the Bankruptcy Code expressly contemplates a minimum payment requirement, and that section 1325(a)(3) requires nothing more than honest intentions. . . . As of this writing three circuit courts of appeals have considered the issue. In two of the cases, In re Goeb, 675 F.2d 1386 (9th Cir. 1982) and In re Rimgale, 669 F.2d 426 (7th Cir. 1982), both courts held that good faith could not be defined solely in terms of meaningful repayment, but that the amount of repayment was one factor that could be considered. In the third, In re Terry, 630 F.2d 634 (8th Cir. 1980), the court ruled that a plan proposing no payment whatsoever to any creditor was not in good faith.

We conclude section 1325(a)(3) does not require any particular level of minimum repayment as a prerequisite to Chapter 13 plan confirmation. Our conclusion is based on the following reasons. First, looking to the structure of section 1325, only one provision, section 1325(a)(4), explicitly addresses amounts to be paid to unsecured creditors. Section 1325(a)(4) requires merely that unsecured creditors receive no less under the Chapter 13 plan than they would have in a liquidation under Chapter 7. The presence of an explicit standard in section 1325(a)(4) undercuts the idea that general "good faith" language in section 1325(a)(3) was intended to impose another, more rigorous standard governing the minimum amount payable to unsecured creditors.

Second, in drafting section 1325(a)(3), Congress used language virtually identical to that found in various sections of the 1898 Bankruptcy Act. Although the case law is sparse, the few reported decisions mentioning "good faith" under prior law do so in the context of alleged debtor misconduct such as fraudulent misrepresentation, . . . nondisclosure of an agent's financial interest in the proceeding, . . . improper solicitation of creditors to obtain their consent, . . . failure to provide adequate security and to set aside voidable transfers, . . . or use of the bankruptcy proceeding to avoid child support payments. . . . In short, "good faith" questions under pre-1978 law generally arose in cases of debtor misconduct in the implementation of approval of the plan, and did *not* relate to the contents of the plan. This is exactly what would be expected, since under Chapter XIII a majority of unsecured creditors were able to block approval of a plan that offered insufficient repayment, and most debtors proposed full repayment plans. . . . Notwithstanding the differences between Chapter 13 and prior law, to interpret "good faith" as meaningful repayment would be to impose a definition radically different from the term's meaning at the time Congress enacted section 1325(a)(3). We hesi-

---

5. Courts have developed a variety of tests under section 1325(a)(3), requiring inter alia that the debtor make "substantial payments," that the payments represent the debtor's "best effort," and others. . . . For convenience we refer to these tests collectively as requiring "meaningful repayment."

tate to create such a new definition without explicit instructions from Congress.

Third, we think the legislative history too inconclusive to say that Congress in 1978 intended a new standard of minimum repayment as a prerequisite to Chapter 13 confirmation. Isolated portions of the committee reports do support the policies behind a meaningful repayment standard,[9] but nothing in those excerpts connects meaningful repayment with the "good faith" requirement in section 1325(a)(3). Moreover, other portions of the legislative history negate a meaningful repayment standard as a general policy or purpose of Chapter 13.[10] At most, the legislative history suggests Congress *expected* Chapter 13 debtors to repay a substantial portion of their debts. We cannot conclude that Congress therefore intended to bar confirmation of Chapter 13 plans proposing less than "substantial" or "meaningful" repayment. If Chapter 13 as presently enacted does not achieve the results Congress anticipated, it is for Congress not the courts to correct the situation.

Finally, recent action in Congress supports adherence to the traditional definition of "good faith." In 1980 the 96th Congress debated the Technical Amendments Bill which, among other things, would have added a "bona fide effort" test to section 1325(a)(4). Similar versions of the bill passed both the House of Representatives and the Senate, but the legislation was never enacted in final form. The House and Senate disagreed on the precise meaning of "bona fide effort," but both chambers agreed that "good faith" under section 1325(a)(3) was not intended to require a minimum percentage of repayment to unsecured creditors. Sen-

9. The House Report, for example, often mentions "repayment" of debts under Chapter 13 plans. See, e.g., H.R. Rep.No. 595, 95th Cong., 1st Sess. 117-118 (1977). A possible inference is that Congress did not intend confirmation of low-percentage plans which offer essentially no "repayment." Another sentence in the House Report notes creditors' losses under Chapter 13 "will be significantly less than if their debtors opt for straight bankruptcy." House Report, supra, at 118, U.S. Code Cong. & Admin. News 1978, p. 6079. The implication here is that one percent plans should not be confirmed because they do not "significantly" reduce creditors' losses. Finally, part of the Senate Report states, "[i]t is also necessary to prevent chapter 13 plans from turning into mere offers of composition plans under which payments would equal only the non-exempt assets of the debtor." S.Rep.No. 989, 95th Cong., 2d Sess. 13 (1978), U.S.Code Cong. & Admin. News 1978, pp. 5787, 5799. A strong argument can be made that low-percentage Chapter 13 plans are extremely close to such "mere offers of composition."

10. The same House Report cited above as supporting "repayment" notes in the same paragraph, "[i]n some cases, the plan will call for full payment. In others, it may offer creditors a percentage of their claims in full settlement." H.R. Rep. No. 595, 95th Cong., 1st Sess. 118 (1977), U.S. Code Cong. & Admin. News 1978 p. 6079. Further statements emphasize that Chapter 13 plans are to be based on the debtor's "exact circumstances," S. Rep. No. 989, 95th Cong., 2d Sess. 13 (1978), U.S. Code Cong. & Admin. News 1978, 5779, and stress the need to proved effective relief for "consumers who have overburdened themselves with debts," House Report, supra, at 116 (1977), U.S. Code Cong. & Admin. News 1978, 6076. Another portion notes the only restriction on plan content is that creditors receive more than they would get in a liquidation under Chapter 7, implying that no other provision entitles creditors to more. Id. at 123-124.

ator DeConcini, a leading sponsor of both the Technical Amendments Bill
and the 1978 Bankruptcy Reform Act, noted:

> [J]udges have had to strain the provisions of Section 1325 by decision or
> informal rule to reach the right result vis-a-vis the level of payment of the
> debtor for the particular case.
>
> Many courts have construed the good-faith language, Section 1325
> (a)(3) to this end, which was not intended by Congress in the enactment of
> that requirement.

126 Cong. Rec. S. 15,175 (daily ed. Dec. 1, 1980) (remarks on Sen. De-
Concini). . . . Senator DeConcini further stated that the good faith requirement "is meant to bar the confirmation of a Chapter 13 plan where
the debtor either does not intend to effectuate the plan as proposed or
where the proposed plan is for a purpose not permitted under Title 11,"
citing as an example "any plan the principal purpose of which is to render
the debtor incapable of meeting legal obligations for the support and
maintenance of a former spouse or dependent child." 126 Cong. Rec. S.
15,175 (daily ed. Dec. 1, 1980).

Although we must be cautious when dealing with legislative statements not contemporaneous with the provision in question, an unequivo-
cal statement of intent by a prime sponsor of the original legislation is quite
persuasive here. Moreover, we must recognize that the Technical Amendments Bill represents an unsuccessful attempt by Congress to deal with the
problem of nominal payment plans under Chapter 13. It seems inappropriate for courts to create a "meaningful payment" standard by interpretation and inference when Congress has failed to do so explicitly. In light of
the Supreme Court's ruling that the assignment of broad jurisdiction to
bankruptcy judges is unconstitutional, Northern Pipeline Construction
Co. v. Marathon Pipe Line Co., — U.S. —, 102 S. Ct. 2858, 73 L. Ed. 2d
598 (1982), it seems likely that Congress will reexamine the Bankruptcy
Act once again. If Congress wishes to prohibit or restrict low-percentage
Chapter 13 plans, it will soon have the opportunity to do so.

For the reasons given above we adhere to the traditional meaning of
"good faith" as honesty of intention. It is not necessary that we provide a
comprehensive definition of "good faith" today. No one has suggested
that either Abel Montano or Wavalene Barnes has engaged in any specific
misconduct, did not intend to carry out the plan, proposed the plan for an
improper purpose, or did anything else to bring either case within the
ambit of bad faith as traditionally interpreted. The Bankruptcy Court
ruled that the plans were not in good faith under 11 U.S.C. §1325(a)(3)
solely on the ground that the plans offered a low level of repayment to
unsecured creditors. We hold that section 1325(a)(3) does not prohibit
such nominal payment plans and therefore affirm the District Court on the
issue of good faith.

II. CLASSIFICATION OF DEBTS

Montano's Chapter 13 plan distributes his available monthly income so that creditors holding cosigned debts guaranteed by third parties receive one hundred percent payment, while all other unsecured creditors receive only one percent of their claims. The trustee argues that this arrangement is an improper classification under 11 U.S.C. §1322(b)(1). That provision states:

> [T]he plan may . . . designate a class or classes of unsecured claims, as provided in section 1122 of this title, but may not discriminate unfairly against any class so designated. . . .

Section 1122, referred to in the language immediately above, reads in full as follows:

> (a) Except as provided in subsection (b) of this section, a plan may place a claim or an interest in a particular class only if such claim or interest is substantially similar to the other claims or interests of such class.
>
> (b) A plan may designate a separate class of claims consisting only of every unsecured claim that is less than or reduced to an amount that the court approves as reasonable and necessary for administrative convenience.

11 U.S.C. §1122.

The Bankruptcy Court relied on section 1122(a) in rejecting Montano's plan, holding that cosigned and non-cosigned debts are "substantially similar" and thus may not be separately classified. In re Montano, 4 B.R. at 537. The District Court agreed, adding that a plan which provides one hundred percent payment to creditors with cosigned debts but only one percent to other unsecured creditors unfairly discriminates between classes of creditors within the meaning of section 1322(b)(1). In re Wavalene Barnes, 13 B.R. at 1000.

We think the courts erred in holding that section 1122(a) prohibits classification based on the presence of a co-debtor. Section 1122(a) specifies that only claims which are "substantially similar" may be placed in the same class. It does not require that similar claims *must* be grouped together, but merely that any group created must be homogenous. . . . Although some courts have held that section 1122(a) prohibits classification based on any criterion other than legal right to the debtor's assets, see, e.g., In re Iacovoni, 2 B.R. 256, 260-261 (Bkrtcy. D. Utah), the plain language of the statute contradicts such a construction. Moreover, section 1122(a) so interpreted would conflict with section 1322(b)(1), which specifically authorizes designation of more than one class of unsecured creditor, each presumably with equal legal rights to the debtor's estate. We therefore hold that section 1122(a) does not prohibit Montano from grouping his unsecured obligations according to whether or not a codebtor is present.

This does not mean Montano's plan should be confirmed. Section 1322(b)(1) states that a plan may not "unfairly dicriminate against any class. . . ." The critical question is not whether Montano may group cosigned debts apart from non-cosigned, but whether his plan, to pay one hundred percent to the first group "unfairly discriminates" against the second, which is to be paid only one percent.

Bankruptcy courts have interpreted unfair discrimination under section 1322(b)(1) in many ways without reaching a consensus. . . . Clearly some difference in treatment between classes is permissible, or there would be little point in creating separate classes in the first place. The limits of permissible discrimination, however, are undefined. Montano argues that a plan does not violate section 1322(b)(1) so long as a rational basis exists for the classifications, and each class of unsecured creditor receives more than it would in a Chapter 7 liquidation. . . . Some bankruptcy courts have applied similar criteria. . . .

Nonetheless, we cannot agree with Montano's formulation. Section 1322(b)(1) prohibits unfair discrimination, and an inquiry into fairness plainly involves more than the rationality of the debtor's classifications or some minimum amount creditors must receive.

What constitutes fair discrimination will vary from case to case, and we cannot offer a generally applicable definition. The court must examine the amounts proposed for each class in light of the debtor's reasons for classification, and exercise sound discretion. . . .

Considering the circumstances presented here, we think a ninety-nine percent differential in the amounts paid on cosigned versus non-cosigned debts is unfair. Montano argues that unless cosigned obligations are completely repaid, creditors can proceed against the cosigners, who in turn will put indirect pressure on Montano and interfere with the "fresh start" the Bankruptcy Code is supposed to provide. Filing a Chapter 13 plan, however, does not guarantee unqualified freedom from the pressures of bankruptcy. Nothing in the record suggests Montano will be unable to continue with his plan if cosigned obligations are not paid in full, and Montano raises no other factor that might justify departure from the basic principle that all unsecured creditors should be treated alike. Insulation of Montano from worry does not justify the unequal treatment he proposes.

We hold that Montano's plan "unfairly discriminates" against unsecured creditors holding non-cosigned debts, and therefore violates section 1322(b)(1). As presently drafted the plan may not be confirmed pursuant to section 1325(a)(1), which requires that plans "comply with the provisions of this chapter and with other applicable provisions of this title. . . ." If Montano chooses to modify his plan, the Bankruptcy Court must determine whether any difference in treatment between unsecured creditors is fair considering the circumstances and the debtor's offered justifications. . . .

NOTES

1. In re Terry, 630 F.2d 634 (8th Cir. 1980), reasoned as follows:

> We think that §101(24) [renumbered as §101(27) in 1984. — EDs.] contemplates that a debtor make payments, and that the debtor's income sufficiently exceeds his expenses so that he can maintain a payment schedule. The key statutory language is "make payments." The debtors in this case have no excess income out of which to "make payments," and therefore, they are not eligible for Chapter 13 relief under §109(e).
>
> [W]e cannot agree that a Chapter 13 plan to pay nothing may be in good faith. Such a plan amounts to an abuse of §1328 (granting a more generous discharge than Chapter 7) and of the spirit of the chapter, that the debtor "make payments" under a plan.

Two years later, in In re Estus, 695 F.2d 311 (8th Cir. 1982), the Eighth Circuit, reviewing recent cases (including *Barnes*), concluded

> that subsection (a)(3) good faith does not impose a rigid and unyielding requirement of substantial payment to unsecured creditors. A per se minimum payment requirement would infringe on the desired flexibility of Chapter 13 and is unwarranted. Nor should the courts perfunctorily conclude that good faith is achieved whenever the minimum requirements of subsection (a)(4) have been met.

Estus concluded that an important factor "that the courts must weigh in their analysis," was the percentage of payments to unsecured creditors. *Terry* was cited as addressing "a related, but not identical issue." See also In re Deans, 692 F.2d 968 (4th Cir. 1982).

2. On the classification issue, see also In re Wolff, 22 Bankr. 510 (9th Cir. Bankr. App. 1982) (the test "is (1) whether the discrimination has a reasonable basis; (2) whether the debtor can carry out a plan without the discrimination; (3) whether the discrimination is proposed in good faith; and (4) whether the degree of discrimination is directly related to the basis or rationale for the discrimination").

3. To what extent is the "good faith" issue rendered moot by the 1984 Amendments to §1325 discussed supra?

PROBLEM

12.5 Debtor went through bankruptcy in 1974. At that time, he was denied a discharge of his debts for failure to satisfactorily explain losses of assets under §14(c)(7) of the old Bankruptcy Act. Bank and Greenstreet are creditors who were in existence at that time, and whose debts, accordingly, were not discharged. In 1980, Debtor files for Chapter 13, and proposes a plan listing four unsecured creditors, with a total of $73,500 of debts. Two of these creditors are Bank and Greenstreet, who are owed $70,000 between them on those old debts. The plan proposes that the unsecured creditors be paid pro rata as funds become available until ten percent of each claim has been paid. Bank and Greenstreet object to the confirmation of the plan, on the ground that the prior denial of discharge of their debts prevents the plan from passing the good faith test of §1325(a)(3). Evaluate that claim. See §523(a)(9); In re Sanders, 13 Bankr. 320 (Bankr. D. Kan. 1981); In re Meltzer, 11 Bankr. 024 (Bankr. E.D.N.Y. 1981). Does §1307(c) have anything to say about this problem? Can Bank and Greenstreet argue that, in any case, they are not getting paid as much as they would in Chapter 7 (because the debts would not be dischargeable in Chapter 7), and therefore the plan does not satisfy §1325(a)(4)? See In re Walsey, 7 Bankr. 779 (Bankr. N.D. Ga. 1980).

12.6 Debtor applied for and received an automobile loan of $5,700, which was to be paid over 42 months at $233 per month. Two months after incuring the debt, and having made no payments, Debtor files for relief under Chapter 13. Debtor files a plan proposing to reduce the monthly payment to $157 and extending the repayment time to 60 months. The bankruptcy judge found that Debtor "puffed" her income somewhat on the loan application, but refused to find that Debtor acted dishonestly. May the court use this pre-plan conduct in deciding if the plan is proposed in "good faith" under §1325(a)(4)? See Memphis Bank & Trust Co. v. Whitman, 692 F.2d 427 (6th Cir. 1982).

B.   THE TREATMENT OF SECURED CLAIMANTS IN CHAPTER 13 PLANS

IN RE TADDEO
685 F.2d 24 (2d Cir. 1982)

LUMBARD, Circuit Judge.

Joseph C. and Ellen A. Taddeo live at 6 Ort Court, Sayville, New York. Three years ago they defaulted on their mortgage to Elfriede Di Pierro. Di Pierro accelerated the mortgage, declared its balance due immediately, and inititated foreclosure proceedings. The Taddeos sought refuge under Chapter 13 of the new Bankruptcy Code, staying the foreclosure action under the automatic stay, 11 U.S.C. §365(a) (Supp. IV 1980), and proposing to cure the default and reinstate the mortgage under

11 U.S.C. §1322(b)(5). Di Pierro is listed as the Taddeos' only creditor. She rejected the plan to cure the default, and applied for relief from the automatic stay in order to foreclose. Di Pierro contended that once she accelerated her mortgage, the Taddeos had no way to cure the default under the Bankruptcy Code except to pay the full amount as required by state law. Bankruptcy Judge Parente held that the Taddeos could cure the default and reinstate their mortgage, and denied Di Pierro's motion for relief from the stay. In re Taddeo, 9 B.R. 299 (Bkrtcy. E.D.N.Y. 1981). Judge Pratt affirmed, 15 B.R. 273 (Bkrtcy. E.D.N.Y. 1981). We affirm. We do not believe that Congress labored for five years over this controversial question only to remit consumer debtors — intended to be primary beneficiaries of the new Code — to the harsher mercies of state law.

Di Pierro originally owned the house at 6 Ort Court. On June 14, 1979, she sold the house to the Taddeos, taking in return a "purchase money second mortgage" to secure a principal balance of $13,000. The property is subject to a first lien held by West Side Federal Savings & Loan Association, which is not involved in this case. Di Pierro's second mortgage was payable over 15 years at 8.5 percent in equal monthly installments of $128.05.

Upon taking occupancy, the Taddeos notified Di Pierro that they had discovered defects in the property. On advice of counsel, the Taddeos said that they would withhold mortgage payments, depositing the money instead with their attorney. The Taddeos and Di Pierro corresponded for several months without reaching an agreement. On October 5, 1979, Di Pierro wrote that she was accelerating the mortgage and declaring the entire balance due immediately. The mortgage contained the acceleration clause specifically approved in N.Y. Real Prop. §258 Schedule M (McKinney 1968), which gives the mortgagee the option to accelerate after a default in mortgage payments.

Di Pierro commenced foreclosure proceedings in state court on October 19, 1979. The Taddeos tendered full payment of their arrears by check on October 31, 1979, but Di Pierro refused to accept payment. The state court granted summary judgment to Di Pierro and ordered a referee to determine the amount owed. After a hearing on June 30, 1980, the referee found the Taddeos liable for $14,153.48 in principal and interest, plus interest subsequent to the award.

Before Di Pierro could obtain final judgment of foreclosure and sale, the Taddeos filed a Chapter 13 bankruptcy petition in the Eastern District on July 10, 1980. . . . The petition listed Di Pierro as the only creditor, and stayed Di Pierro's foreclosure action. The Taddeos filed a plan proposing to pay off arrears on the mortgage in installments of $100 per month. The plan further proposed to restore the mortgage and its original payment schedule, with payments through McCord as trustee to Di Pierro during the 3-year life of the plan and directly to Di Pierro after the plan ended. Di Pierro objected to the plan, and petitioned for relief from the automatic stay so that she could proceed with her foreclosure action. Di Pierro contended that her rights as mortgagee could not be affected by the Chapter 13 plan. Bankruptcy Judge Parente, however, held that the Taddeos could pay their arrearages and reinstate their mortgage under this section notwithstanding Di Pierro's acceleration, analogizing §1322(b) to 11 U.S.C. §1124(2), which nullifies acceleration clauses in Chapter 11 corporate reorganizations. Therefore Bankruptcy Judge Parente denied Di Pierro relief from the automatic stay. District Judge Pratt affirmed on similar reasoning.

Because Di Pierro is the Taddeos' only creditor, continuance of the stay is justified only if the Taddeos' plan can in fact provide for Di Pierro's mortgage. Otherwise, the stay would serve only to delay foreclosure for delay's sake, and would not be justified. . . . Therefore, although the Taddeos' Chapter 13 plan is not before us for approval, the question of whether under the plan the Taddeos can pay arrearages to Di Pierro and thereby cure the default and reinstate the mortgage is squarely presented for decision.

The relevant parts of §1322(b)* read as follows:

> (b) . . . the plan may— . . .
> (2) modify the rights of holder of secured claims other than a claim secured only by a security interest in real property that is the debtor's principal residence, or of holders of unsecured claims;
> (3) provide for the curing or waiving of any default; . . .
> (5) notwithstanding paragraph (2) of this subsection, provide for the curing of any default within a reasonable time and maintenance of payments while the case is pending on any unsecured claim or secured claim on which the last payment is due after the date on which the final payment under the plan is due;

When Congress empowered Chapter 13 debtors to "cure defaults," we think Congress intended to allow mortgagors to "deaccelerate" their mortgage and reinstate its original payment schedule. We so hold for two reasons. First, we think that the power to cure must comprehend the power to "de-accelerate." This follows from the concept of "curing a default." A default is an event in the debtor-creditor relationship which triggers certain consequences—here, acceleration. Curing a default commonly means taking care of the triggering event and returning to pre-default conditions. The consequences are thus nullified. This is the concept of "cure" used throughout the Bankruptcy Code. Under §365(b), the trustee may assume executory contracts and unexpired leases only if he cures defaults—but the cure need address only the individual event of default, thereby repealing the contractual consequences. . . . See also 11

---

* Amended in 1984. — Eds.

U.S.C §1110(a)(2); 124 Cong. Rec. H 11,102 (Sept. 28, 1978); S 17,419 (Oct. 6, 1978) (trustee may continue in possession of aircraft and ships by curing defaults and making payments in original lease or contract); 11 U.S.C. §1168(a)(2), H.R. Rept. 595, 95th Cong. 1st Sess. 423 (1977) (trustee may retain rolling stock if he cures default and agrees to make original payments). Such legislative history as there is supports a similar reading of §1322(b)(5). Both the Bankruptcy Commission's Bill, see §6-201(2) & (4) and accompanying commentary, and the Bankruptcy Judges' Bill, §6-301(2), plainly permitted the cure and de-acceleration of residential debt accelerated prior to petition. Although H.R. 6, 95th Cong. 1st Sess. §1322(b) (1977), which superseded these bills, omitted a proviso contained in §6-301(2) of the Judges' Bill that made this entirely clear, it is evident that this was done because the clause was regarded as surplusage. H.R. 6 adopted language almost identical to §6-301(2) of the Commission's Bill, which accomplished just what the Judges' Bill did, albeit in different language. In fact, H.R. 6 went beyond either of its predecessors and permitted the *modification* of debt secured by a debtor's residence. Although the Senate later adopted a prohibition against modification of the rights of holders of secured real estate debt, S. 2266, 95th Cong. 2nd Sess. §1322(b)(2), which the House accepted insofar as it related to debt secured by a debtor's principal residence, 124 Cong. Rec. H11106 (September 28, 1978), the cure and maintain powers of paragraph (b)(5) remained unchanged. This history and the policy discussed above compel the conclusion that §1322(b)(5) was intended to permit the cure and de-acceleration of secured long-term residential debt accelerated prior to the filing of a Chapter 13 petition.

Policy considerations strongly support this reading of the statute. Conditioning a debtor's right to cure on its having filed a Chapter 13 petition prior to acceleration would prompt unseemly and wasteful races to the courthouse. Worse, these would be races in which mortgagees possess an unwarranted and likely insurmountable advantage: wage earners seldom will possess the sophistication in bankruptcy matters that financial institutions do, and often will not have retained counsel in time for counsel to do much good. In contrast, permitting debtors in the Taddeos' position to de-accelerate by payment of the arrearages will encourage parties to negotiate in good faith rather than having to fear that the mortgagee will tip the balance irrevocably by accelerating or that the debtor may prevent or at least long postpone this by filing a Chapter 13 petition.

Secondly, we believe that the power to "cure any default" granted in §1322(b)(3) and (b)(5) is not limited by the ban against "modifying" home mortgages in §1322(b)(2) because we do not read "curing defaults" under (b)(3) or "curing defaults and maintaining payments" under (b)(5) to be *modifications* of claims.

It is true that §1322(b)(5)'s preface, "notwithstanding paragraph

(2)," seems to treat the power to cure in (b)(5) as a subset of the power to modify set forth in (b)(2), but that superficial reading of the statute must fall in the light of legislative history and legislative purpose. The "notwithstanding"clause was added to §1322(b)(5) to emphasize that defaults in mortgages could be cured notwithstanding §1322(b)(2). See 124 Cong. Rec. H 11,106 (Sept. 28, 1978); S17,423 (Oct. 6, 1978). But the clause was not necessary. The Senate protected home mortgages from *modification* in its last bill, S.2266, 95th Cong., 2d Sess.; it evinced no intent to protect these mortgages from *cure*. Cf. Hearings on S.2266 Before the Subcommitee on Improvements in Judicial Machinery of the Senate Committee on the Judiciary, 95th Cong., 1st Sess. 836 (1977) (Statement of Charles A. Horsky, Chairman, National Bankruptcy Conference (S. 2266 "is completely unclear as to whether the plan can provide for the curing of defaults and the making of current payments.") Indeed, earlier Senate bills along with House bills and the present statute listed the power to cure and the power to modify in different paragraphs, indicating that the power to cure is different from the power to modify. Testimony submitted on behalf of secured creditors distinguished between modifying a claim (by reducing payments due thereon) and curing a default (and maintaining those payments). . . . Finally, the few cases under Chapter XIII of the old Bankruptcy Act distinguished between modifying a claim and maintaining payments thereon, . . . and indicate that curing a default and maintaining payments on a claim did not modify that claim. . . .

Our reading of the statute disposes of Di Pierro's major contentions on appeal. Di Pierro argues that the Taddeos cannot use §1322(b)(5) to cure their default and maintain payments on her mortgage because (b)(5) applies only to claims whose last payment is due after the last payment under the plan is due. Di Pierro maintains her acceleration of the mortgage makes all payments due *now*. See In re Williams, 11 B.R. 504 (Bkrtcy. S.D. Texas 1981); In re Paglia, 8 B.R. 937 (Bkrtcy. E.D.N.Y. 1981). But we hold that the concept of "cure" in §1322(b)(5) contains the power to de-accelerate. Therefore the application of that section de-accelerates the mortgage and returns it to its 15-year maturity. Alternatively, we hold that the ban on "modification" in §1322(b)(2) does not limit the Taddeos' exercise of their curative powers under either §1322(b)(3) or (b)(5). Therefore the Taddeos may first cure their default under (b)(3) and then maintain payments under (b)(5). . . .

Di Pierro also argues that under New York law the Taddeos cannot "cure" an accelerated mortgage without paying the full amount of the claim, and further asserts that the Bankruptcy Code does not empower the Taddeos to override New York law. She asserts that Congress explicitly gave corporate debtors the power to cure defaults without regard to acceleration by passing 11 U.S.C. §1124(2), and concludes that the absence of similar language in §1322(b) indicates that Chapter 13 debtors cannot cure defaults unless they also cure acceleration. See In re Williams, 11 B.R.

504 (Bkrtcy. S.D. Tex.1981); In re Paglia, 8 B.R. 937 (Bkrtcy. E.D.N.Y. 1981). The bankruptcy court took the opposite tack, reasoning that Congress, having provided corporate debtors with curative powers under §1124(2), must have intended similar powers to be exercised by consumer debtors under §1322(b) as consumers are more favored by Chapter 13 than corporate debtors are by Chapter 11.

Both rationales mistake the import of §1124. That section determines who has the right to vote on a Chapter 11 plan. Those parties with "impaired" claims or interest can vote, and §1124(1) declares that *any* change in legal, equitable or contractual rights creates impairment. Having defined impairment in the broadest possible terms, Congress carved out a small exception to impairment in §1124(2) providing that curing a default, even though it inevitably changes a contractual acceleration clause, does not thereby "impair" a creditor's claim. "The holder of a claim or interest who under the plan is restored to his original position, when others receive less or get nothing at all, is fortunate indeed and has no cause to complain." S. Rep. No. 989, 95th Cong., 2d Sess. 120 (1978). Section 1124(2) merely takes away the creditor's right to vote in the event of cure; the authority to cure is found in §1123(a)(5)(G) in plain language similar to §1322(b). . . . In short, "curing a default" in Chapter 11 means the same thing as it does in Chapters 7 or 13: the event of default is remedied and the consequences are nullified. A state law to the contrary must fall before the Bankruptcy Code.

Di Pierro argues further that §1322(b)(5) requires the Taddeos to cure their default "within a reasonable time," and that under New York law that time has passed. But clearly the "reasonable time" requirement refers to time after a Chapter 13 petition is filed. Otherwise Chapter 13 debtors would forfeit their right to cure merely by negotiating with their creditors, or, as in this case, litigating the right of their creditor to declare a default. The bankruptcy courts which have allowed Chapter 13 debtors to cure defaults under §1322(b)(5) have assumed that "reasonable time" refers to time after the petition was filed. . . . We find no support for Di Pierro's contention that state law must govern what constitutes a reasonable time.

Di Pierro's argument reduces in the end to an assertion that because she can accelerate her mortgage under state law, the Taddeos can cure only as provided by state law. This interpretation of §1322(b) would leave the debtor with fewer rights under the new Bankruptcy Code than under the old Bankruptcy Act of 1898.[7] Defaulting mortgagees would forfeit their right to cure even before the start of foreclosure proceedings, before they have hired lawyers and therefore before they knew anything about their rights under Chapter 13. Such a result would render the remedy in

---

7. Under the old Bankruptcy Act, a bankruptcy court could enjoin a mortgagee from foreclosure so long as the injunction did not impair the value of the mortgagee's security and the mortgagee received no less than the payments provided for in the mortgage. . . .

§1322(b) unavailable to all but a select number of debtors. . . . Such a result would be totally at odds with the "overriding rehabilitative purpose of Chapter 13." In re Davis, 15 B.R. 22, 24 (Bkrtcy. D. Kan.), aff'd, 16 B.R. 473 (D. Kan. 1981).

Affirmed.

NOTE

See Grubbs v. Houston First American Savings Assn., 730 F.2d 236 (5th Cir. en banc 1984) (reversing a panel opinion at 718 F.2d 694, and agreeing with *Taddeo*). In re Gwinn, 34 Bankr. 936 (Bankr. S.D. Ohio 1983), described the various approaches taken by courts as follows:

> An examination of the reported cases indicates that five basic positions have emerged. A small minority of courts have held that deceleration/reinstitution is not available once the mortgagee has exercised his contractual right to accelerate, regardless of whether or not the mortgagee has obtained a judgment. . . .
>
> Another, more sizeable group of cases have held that while deceleration is possible prior to judgment, it is no longer available once the mortgagee has obtained a judgment on the mortgage note. . . . While this is a more widely held view than the *per se* prohibition espoused by the first group, it is still the minority view. . . .
>
> The third approach likewise allows deceleration and reinstitution, but does not speak to what impact, if any, a judgment would have on the availability of this option. . . . This view is supported by several District Courts and would seem to be the overwhelming majority view.
>
> The fourth view holds that deceleration and reinstitution are possible even after the mortgagee has obtained a judgment on the accelerated mortgage note. *In re Taddeo*. . . . This seems to be a rapidly growing view and has been adopted by more appellate level courts than have any of the other views.
>
> The fifth view is perhaps the most adventurous of all. It holds that deceleration and reinstitution are available even after the foreclosure sale, as long as the state redemption period has not expired by the time the debtor files his bankruptcy petition.

See also In re Smith, 43 Bankr. 313 (Bankr. N.D. Ill. 1984). Did *Gwinn* correctly classify *Taddeo*?

NOTE ON *TADDEO* AND THE
REINSTATEMENT OF MORTGAGES

In considering *Taddeo* and its interpretation of Chapter 13, it might perhaps help to compare Chapter 13 to Chapters 7 and 11. What differences are there? How should those bear on interpreting Chapter 13? It appears that the Taddeos only concern in using bankruptcy was to save their home. They had no other creditors and their Chapter 13 plan contained no other important terms. Is this an abuse of the bankruptcy process, or is this precisely the sort of relief that individuals are to be given, because of bankruptcy's fresh start policy? Assuming that this is not considered an abuse of the bankruptcy process, it appears that the Taddeos could have just as well used Chapter 7, except for the fact that Chapter 7 contains nothing like §1322(b)(5). Should it? If §1322(b)(5) represents sound policy, why should it only be available to Chapter 13 debtors? Is it so clear that §1322(b)(5) *is* sound policy?

What if the Taddeos had bought their house from Di Pierro with a "balloon" mortgage (one that has payments based on a 30-year term, but has the principal due and owing after, say, three years)? Would they have been able to affect that mortgage under Chapter 13? See In re Maloney, 36 Bankr. 876 (Bankr. D.N.H. 1984). Is there anything different about the actual mortgage from Di Pierro, considering that it had been accelerated pursuant to a contract term?

Do you agree with the court's discussion of the role of §1124 in Chapter 11? Does it adequately deal with the fact that §1124(2)(B) explicitly provides that the plan may reinstate the maturity of such claim or interest, whereas §1322(b)(5) does not? In re LaPaglia, 8 Bankr. 937 (Bankr. E.D.N.Y. 1981), in reaching the opposite conclusion, suggested

> Section 1322(b)(2) must be read in conjunction with Section 1322(b)(5). The latter paragraph, relating to long term debt such as that of a mortgage on real estate, permits a plan to provide for the curing of *any* default on such a secured claim *so long as the last payment on the debt is not due until after payments under the Chapter 13 are completed.* . . .
>
> It is evident, then, that Congress anticipated Chapter 13 plans would provide for the curing of defaults on mortgages as well as for the maintenance of current payments thereon. The exact language of Section 1322(b)(5), however, states that a default may be cured within a reasonable time on a secured claim "on which the *last payment is due after the date on which the final payment under the plan is due.*" (emphasis mine) Defaults on debts which come due *before* the last payment under a Chapter 13 plan are not susceptible to cure under this provision.
>
> In order to decide whether the debt owed . . . is one which is capable of cure, I must make reference to New York State law to determine when the last payment on the bond and mortgage is due. . . .
>
> Thus, [under New York law] the accelerated debt becomes similar to a debt under a demand note and the notice of acceleration acts in the same manner as the demand on a demand note. Once demand has been made (or notice of acceleration given) the entire principal sum is due and owing. . . .
>
> Thus Section 1322(b)(5) is not available to cure a default in what is tantamount to a demand note since the maturity date of the last payment (the entire balance remaining due) is the date of the demand and does not extend beyond the final payment under the Chapter 13 plan.

Would it matter, in considering the discussion in *Taddeo*, whether there was a judgment of foreclosure? In re Shelly, 38 Bankr. 1000 (D. Del. 1984), concluded that the presence of a judgment of foreclosure decisively changed the relevant factors, reasoning:

> The Court . . . has treated debtors' mortgage as not merged in the judgment. Cure of debtors' default and maintenance of payments under sections 1322(b)(3) and (b)(5) could thus theoretically operate to decelerate and reinstate the *mortgage*. This deceleration and reinstatement would, however, leave the debtors obligation under the *judgment* unaffected. The existence of this independent judgment is a crucial difference from *Taddeo* where no foreclosure judgment had been obtained. Creditor's judgment is a secured claim in the personal residence of the debtor under Delaware law. Payment is due immediately. The judgment is not, and never was, a claim in which "the last payment is due after the date on which the final payment under the plan is due." 11 U.S.C. §1322(b)(5). It follows section 1322(b)(5) is unavailable as a statutory basis upon which to decelerate and reinstate a mortgage following a judgment of foreclosure in Delaware state court.
>
> Nor can, as in *Taddeo*, section 1322(b)(3) serve as an independent basis to achieve deceleration. . . . This case does not involve simply an accelerated mortgage which can be reinstated to a prior condition; it involves an independently existing debt obligation which cannot, literally, be "cured."
>
> In light of this facial statutory obstacle, debtors could prevail only if general congressional interest in rehabilitating Chapter 13 debtors were translated into congressional authorization for a federal bankruptcy court to suspend, modify or set aside state court liens and judgments. Nothing in section 1322(b), or anywhere else in Chapter 13 or its legislative history, suggests that Congress intended such a result.

Is this distinction justified? Does it make policy sense because it cures the spectre of an unseemly race to the courthouse? Acceleration can oftentimes occur immediately upon the giving of notice, whereas notice must be given in advance of a court judgment. Is this distinction important? Even if it is, is it one Congress has adopted? In re Clark, 738 F.2d 869 (7th Cir. 1984), concluded that cure was still possible, at least where the judgment of foreclosure had the effect described in the following excerpt:

> Despite the judgment of foreclosure, the Clarks still had an interest in the property at the time they filed their petition in bankruptcy, such that the property was part of the estate under 11 U.S.C. §§541 and 1307. Under Wisconsin law, a mortgagee has only a lien on the mortgaged property, even after a judgment of foreclosure is entered. Neither equitable nor legal title passes until the foreclosure sale is held. A judgment of foreclosure "does little more than determine that the mortgagor is in default, the amount of principal and interest unpaid, the amounts due to plaintiff mortgagee for taxes, etc. . . . The judgment does not destroy the lien of the mortgage but rather judicially determines the amount thereof." Marshall & Ilsley Bank v. Greene, 227 Wis. 155, 164, 278 N.W. 425, 429 (1938). . . .

Acceleration of a debt is a standard consequence of a default in payments. Most notes are like the one the Clarks executed here and provide that the lender can accelerate the payments upon default. Since to cure means to restore matters to the way they were before the default, we think that the power to cure in §1322(b) necessarily includes the power to de-accelerate the payments on the note. De-acceleration, therefore, is not a form of modification banned by (b)(2) but rather is a permissible and necessary concomitant of the power to cure defaults. . . .

. . . And though the chapter 13 petitions in both *Grubbs* and *Taddeo* were filed before a judgment of foreclosure was entered, we are not persuaded that the existence of such a judgment in the present case alters the result of those cases. As we have noted, in Wisconsin a judgment of foreclosure does nothing but judicially confirm the acceleration. Though we do not reach the question whether the same result obtains in a state in which the effect of a judgment of foreclosure is different, in Wisconsin such a judgment adds nothing of consequence as far as §1322(b) is concerned.

PROBLEM

12.7 Bank loaned Debtor $25,000, which was secured by a security interest on Debtor's principal residence and on Debtor's automobile. Debtor files for Chapter 13. May Debtor propose, in his plan, that Bank's loan be extended from two to five years? See §§1322(b)(2); 1325(a)(5). What if, one month before Debtor filed for Chapter 13, Bank released its security interest on Debtor's automobile? See In re Ivey, 13 Bankr. 27 (Bankr. W.D.N.C. 1981).

The next two cases both raise issues of whether various provisions of the Bankruptcy Code remain applicable in Chapter 13. Both cases, require one to understand the basic differences between Chapter 13 and Chapter 7, and how those differences should apply in the consideration of particular issues.

IN RE BLAKE
38 Bankr. 604 (Bankr. E.D.N.Y. 1984)

Conrad B. DUBERSTEIN, Bankruptcy Judge

This is an adversary proceeding brought pursuant to 11 U.S.C. Section 522(f) by William C. Blake, a Chapter 13 debtor, seeking to avoid a judicial lien to the extent that it impairs a statutorily authorized right to an exemption in his home. . . .

On March 17, 1983 the debtor, William C. Blake, filed a voluntary petition under Chapter 13 of the Bankruptcy Code. He listed as an unsecured debt a judgment for $12,404.60 obtained on July 6, 1981 by Dominique V. Ledan and Gerard A. Erie in an action for breach of contract. Although the debtor characterized this judgment as an unsecured debt it is clear that upon its docketing on July 22, 1981, a secured lien arose on the debtor's home. Ledan and Erie filed a claim as secured creditors. Notwithstanding that a secured claim was filed the debtor treated it as unsecured and the plan which proposed to pay the creditors 16% of their claims was confirmed on May 17, 1983. Neither the creditors nor their attorney appeared at the confirmation hearing.

In determining the adequacy of the plan the property was valued at $3,800 by both the debtor and the trustee in bankruptcy and a homestead exemption of $10,000 was claimed by the debtor pursuant to N.Y. Debt. & Cred. Law Section 282 (McKinney) and N.Y.Civ.Pract.Law & Rules Section 5206(a) (McKinney).[1]

On July 11, 1983 the debtor commenced this adversary proceeding pursuant to 11 U.S.C. Section 522(f) to avoid the judicial lien held by Ledan and Erie on the ground that it impairs his homestead exemption.

In their September 29, 1983 answer to the debtor's complaint Ledan and Erie disputed the debtor's contention that the property subject to the lien was worth only $3,800. In order to resolve this dispute the court, on November 1, 1983, appointed an appraiser, Cornelius A. Heaney, who examined the debtor's residence and valued it at $7,000. The court accepts this appraisal as the fair market value of the property. Subsequent to the appraisal, counsel for Ledan and Erie offered, by letter, to pay the debtor $10,000 cash for the property.

The debtor claims that under Chapter 13 he has the same right as a debtor in a chapter 7 case to claim exemptions and to avoid, pursuant to Section 522(f), a judicial lien to the extent that it impairs his homestead exemption.

The creditors respond by stating Section 522(f) does not apply to a Chapter 13 proceeding. In addition, they contend that no exemption is "impaired" and that this adversary proceeding must fail since it was brought after the confirmation of the Chapter 13 plan.

Courts which have considered whether or not Section 522(f) applies to a Chapter 13 proceeding have expressed differing views. Some have held it inapplicable. . . . However, a clear majority have held that lien avoidance pursuant to Section 522(f) is permissible in a Chapter 13 case. . . . This Court shares the majority view and finds Section 522(f) applicable to Chapter 13 proceedings. This conclusion not only recognizes and gives effect to the policies underlying the Bankruptcy Reform Act in

---

1. New York has chosen to "opt out" of the specific federal exemptions provided for in 11 U.S.C. Section 522(b). Debtors in New York are limited to the exemptions provided for in Article 10-A Section 282 of the Debtor and Creditor Law of New York. While the federal exemption scheme in Section 522(b) is no longer in effect in New York, the remaining subsections of section 522, including the right of lien avoidance found in subsection (f) remain applicable. . . .

general, but specifically furthers the intent of Congress in enacting Chapter 13. . . .

The legislative history of Section 522 indicates that it was enacted to further one of the Code's primary goals—providing the debtor with a meaningful "fresh start." H.R. Rep. No. 595, 95th Cong., 2d Sess. 126-127 (1977), reprinted in 1978 U.S. Code Cong. & Ad. News 5787, 5963, 6087-6088 (hereinafter cited as House Report). Subsection (f), in particular, was adopted to curb creditor harassment and threats of seizure of exempt property that often resulted in a debtor's reaffirmation of what would otherwise have been a debt dischargeable in bankruptcy. Id.

Nothing in the language or legislative history of Section 522(f) expressly limits its application to Chapter 7 proceedings. On the contrary, there are affirmative indications that the section was meant to apply to a Chapter 13 proceeding. The legislative history of Chapter 13 states that "the [Chapter 13] debtor [should be] given adequate exemptions and other protections to ensure that bankruptcy will provide a fresh start." House Report, supra at 118, reprinted in 1978 U.S. Code Cong. & Ad. News at 6078. It would be inconsistent with the "fresh start" philosophy of the Code to provide debtor who chose liquidation under Chapter 7 with adequate exemptions and the right to avoid liens to the extent they impair these exemptions, while denying the same protections to a debtor utilizing a Chapter 13 rehabilitation plan. . . . In fact, if a Chapter 13 debtor is denied the use of Section 522(f) he would open to creditor harassment, which Congress obviously intended to alleviate for all debtors. . . .

Some courts have held that 11 U.S.C Section 103(a) simply demands a finding that Section 522(f) applies in Chapter 13. . . . However, Section 103(a) does not automatically make every provision of Chapters 1, 3 and 5 applicable to all bankruptcy proceedings. Where there is a conflict between the specific provisions of Chapter 13 and the general provisions of Chapters 1, 3 and 5, the specific provisions of Chapter 13 take precedence. . . . For example, Section 521(3) of the Code requires a debtor to surrender all of the property of his estate to the trustee. However, that requirement is eliminated for Chapter 13 debtors by Section 1306(b) of the Code which says that a debtor does not have to surrender that property unless required to by the plan.

Ledan and Erie claim that a specific provision of Chapter 13, Section 1325(a)(5), conflicts with the more general requirements of Section 522(f). They therefore conclude that Section 1325(a)(5) controls. Section 1325(a)(5)* provides:

(a) The court shall confirm a plan if—
    (5) with respect to each allowed secured claim provided for by the plan—(B)(i) the plan provides that the holder of such claim retain the lien securing such claim. . . .

* Section 1325(a) was made subject to §1325(b) in 1984.—Eds.

However, Sections 522(f) and 1325(a)(5) do not conflict. . . . Section 1325(a)(5) only applies to allowed secured claims. Once a lien has been avoided pursuant to Section 522(f), it is no longer an allowed secured claim. It becomes an unsecured claim to which Section 1325(a)(5) is no longer relevant. . . .

Some of the courts which have held Section 522(f) inapplicable to a Chapter 13 case focus on the differences between a case under Chapter 13 and one under Chapter 7. . . . In Chapter 7 a debtor turns over all property to a trustee for liquidation and a speedy discharge. In contrast, a Chapter 13 debtor proposes a plan in which he uses his future income to repay secured creditors in full and unsecured creditors in full or in part at regular intervals for a period of three to five years, or even nothing at all. He retains and continues to use his property, both exempt and non-exempt. . . .

Courts which have denied the Chapter 13 debtor the use of Section 522(f) to avoid liens have reasoned that since the debtor retains his property, he is not entitled to exemptions. They reason further that if there are no exemptions there is certainly no "impairment" of an exemption as required by Section 522(f). . . . The creditors, Ledan and Erie, have proffered just such an argument in this case. However, this reasoning is faulty. As previously noted, the exemption provisions of Section 522 are applicable to a Chapter 13 proceeding. Furthermore, liens "impair" upon attachment and perfection, not upon enforcement. . . .

It was the desire of Congress to make Chapter 13, and thus debtor repayments, attractive to debtors and thus avoid a straight Chapter 7 liquidation. . . . Congress envisioned Chapter 13 as the most effective means of improving not only debtor relief, but also creditor recoveries. . . . Debtors benefit because they receive a more comprehensive discharge than in a Chapter 7 case, (c.f. 11 U.S.C. Section 1328 with 11 U.S.C. Section 727), while retaining most of their property, both exempt and non-exempt. Creditors benefit because they receive a greater percentage of their debt than in the typical Chapter 7 proceeding. . . .

The value of lien avoidance in Chapter 13 to both debtors and creditors can be seen from the following illustration based on an example in McLaughlin, Lien Avoidance by Debtors in Chapter 13 of the Bankruptcy Reform Act of 1978, 58 Am. Bankr. L.J. 45, 64-67 (1984). Assume that a debtor (1) owns a house valued at $10,000 on which there is a $10,000 judgment lien; (2) there are no other assets in the estate, and (3) he has $75 per month to devote to a Chapter 13 plan. 11 U.S.C. Section 1325(a)(5)(B)(ii) requires that holders of secured claims, which include judicial liens, receive payment in full over the life of the plan. If the debtor were denied the right to avoid the lien and required to pay the $10,000 lien holder in full over the maximum allotted time of five years, his minimum payments would need to be $167 per month. Since the debtor cannot afford that large a monthly payment, the plan would not be confirmed. The debtor would then convert to a Chapter 7 proceeding and avoid the judicial lien on his residence pursuant to 11 U.S.C. Section 522(f). After taking his $10,000 homestead exemption no assets would be left for distribution to the creditor.

However, if the Chapter 13 debtor were permitted to avoid the judicial lien pursuant to 11 U.S.C. Section 522(f), the creditor becomes unsecured for the amount avoided. 11 U.S.C. Section 1325(a)(4) would then become applicable to the now unsecured creditor. That section requires that unsecured creditors in a Chapter 13 plan receive at least as much as they would in a Chapter 7 liquidation. To make the determination of that amount it would be necessary for the Chapter 13 debtor to file a schedule of exempt property. 11 U.S.C. Section 1325(a)(4). In our illustration, the amount an unsecured creditor would receive would be "zero". The debtor could now propose a plan offering to pay to his Chapter 13 trustee the $75 per month available over a period of 60 months, for a total of $4,500. . . . [T]he debtor's ability to propose a viable Chapter 13 plan is dependent upon his ability to utilize Section 522(f) to avoid a lien on exempt property. As one commentator has aptly stated:

> By refusing to apply Section 522(f) in Chapter 13 cases, courts are not only failing to follow a Congressional mandate for Chapter 13, they are also forcing debtors into Chapter 7 with the unavoidable result being harsher treatment of the very creditors they are seeking to protect.

McLaughlin, Lien Avoidance by Debtors in Chapter 13 of the Bankruptcy Reform Act of 1978, 58 Am. Bankr. L.J. 45, 66-67, (1984).

Applying the principles discussed above the debtor may avoid the judicial lien on his residence to the extent that it impairs his right to an exemption on that property. The debtor is entitled to a homestead exemption, not exceeding $10,000 in his principal residence. . . . Since the debtor's residence has been valued at $7,000, he is entitled to a homestead exemption for that amount. Accordingly, the debtor may avoid the judicial lien to the extent of $7,000, and the entire amount of the judicial lien of $12,404.60 is allowed as an unsecured claim.

Finally, as mentioned earlier, the lien creditors have offered to buy the debtor's property for $10,000. However, this is meaningless in the context of this case since the debtor may exempt the property up to $10,000 in value. In any case, the offer can only be deemed an indicia of the property's value; the debtor cannot be compelled to sell it merely because some party has offered to purchase it. . . .

There remains for consideration, the creditors' claim that the debtor may not avoid a lien after confirmation of a Chapter 13 plan. For unexplained reasons, the debtor, at the time of the filing of his Chapter 13 petition, listed the judicial lien held by Ledan and Erie as an unsecured debt. The debtor also failed to make any attempt to avoid the judicial lien at that time.

Under 11 U.S.C. Section 350(b) the court may reopen a case "to administer assets, to accord relief to the debtor, or for other cause." Lien avoidance constitutes sufficient cause to reopen a case. . . . The creditors make no showing that contrary equitable considerations such as laches or prejudice to parties in interest should preclude the debtor from avoiding the lien at this time. . . . Since this case is still being administered the court finds no basis for denying the debtor the opportunity to avoid the lien in question.

It is so ordered.

NOTE

See Peeples, Five Into Thirteen: Lien Avoidance in Chapter 13, 61 N.C.L. Rev. 849 (1983).

NOTE ON *BLAKE* AND §522(f)

The question raised in *Blake* is whether the lien avoidance provisions of §522(f) apply to a Chapter 13 case. *Blake* does not take the easy way out, which is to observe that §103(a) provides that "[e]xcept as provided in section 1161 of this title, chapters 1, 3, and 5 of this title apply in a case under chapter 7, 11, or 13 of this title." It avoids the impact of §103(a) in part by noting that there are certain provisions in Chapters 1, 3, or 5 that seem to directly conflict with a particular provision of one of Chapters 7, 11, or 13. Nonetheless, doesn't §103(a) express a starting presumption that should be followed unless there is a conflict with a particular provision or with a clear policy of one of the chapters governing types of bankruptcy? So viewed, it is hard to say that §522(f) conflicts with Chapter 13, in the sense that it either conflicts with a provision or undercuts a particular goal.

There is a broader policy question, however, addressed in *Blake*: whether the general thrust of Chapter 13 suggests that a provision such as §522(f) has lost its original justification, and is not needed in Chapter 13 cases. This question may be more one of what Congress should have done rather than what Congress has in fact done, but it is worth pursuing, insofar as it raises the question of the underlying rationale of Chapter 13. What is the justification for §522(f)? *Blake* deals with a judgment lien obtained by a creditor without the consent of the debtors. Such liens are fundamentally inconsistent with the concept of exempt property. In these cases, §522(f) may exist to protect property that is exempt because of what the Bankruptcy Code says instead of what nonbankruptcy law says. (In the latter case, if the property is exempt, there will be no enforceable judgment liens on the property.) In these cases, the only issue raised by the interplay of Chapter 13 and §522(f) would seem to be whether there is any need for a system of bankruptcy exemptions under a regime where the debtor gets to keep *all* assets, and the principal questions are (1) how much income the debtor has to turn over to his creditors, §1325(a)(4), and (2) which creditors will be treated as holders of unavoided property rights, and hence will do relatively better than general unsecured creditors.

Do these concerns suggest a need for §522(f), as it applies to involuntary liens and the like, in Chapter 13? (Indeed, at least one case has started even further back, and suggested that there are no exemptions in Chapter 13. In re Aycock, 15 Bankr. 728 (Bankr. E.D.N.C. 1981); but see Baldwin v. Avco Financial Services, 22 Bankr. 507 (D. Del. 1982).) Consider *Blake's* discussion of the example concerning a $10,000 lien on a $10,000 house. Does this do any more than show the obvious: that any time a property right can be avoided, the unsecured creditors do better? To be sure, under this example, the creditor with the lien does worse in Chapter 7 than in Chapter 13, but is it odd to make the use of §522(f) in Chapter 13 into a creditor protection device? Can't the creditor protect itself, by agreeing with the debtor to accept less than full payment in a Chapter 13 case? In any event, even if this example is persuasive, does it suggest that §522(f) should apply across the board in Chapter 13, even to the cases where the impact of its existence vel non would not be likely to lead a debtor to debate between Chapter 7 and Chapter 13 (because, for example, the debtor has a number of debts that cannot be discharged in Chapter 7, or simply because there are many assets that the debtor wishes to keep, instead of turning over to his creditors)?

Section 522(f) applies as well to a very different type of lien — consensual, nonpurchase money, nonpossessory security interests in exempt property. Here, as we noted in the last chapter, §522(f) is substantially different from most forms of nonbankruptcy exemption law, which permits voluntary alienation — including by way of security — of exempt property. Is the rationale for §522(f) in these cases substantially different? What is it? If the rationale is related to a worry about a debtor waiving exemptions too freely, with possible loss of the debtor's personal value in the property (or, conversely, undue creditor "coercion"), does this rationale apply to a Chapter 13 case as well? If you were asked to draft a provision governing whether, and to what extent, §522(f) would apply in Chapter 13, what would your solution look like?

As for the issue discussed in the last two paragraphs of the court's opinion, see also *Pettit,* the next case.

IN RE PETTIT
18 Bankr. 832 (Bankr. S.D. Ohio 1982)

R. J. SIDMAN, Bankruptcy Judge.

William and Bonnie Pettit, joint Chapter 13 debtors, have made an application to this Court for an order avoiding the lien asserted by Bank

One of Columbus, NA ("Bank One") against their residential real estate. The lien is in the form of a certificate of judgment filed against the residential real estate of the debtors on October 26, 1977, and according to the proof of claim filed by Bank One is in the amount of $7,696.66. The debtors originally premised their application upon the provisions of §522(f)(1) of the Bankruptcy Code. . . .

The debtors claim that the judicial lien of Bank One impairs their exemption in their residential real estate. However, in an additional memorandum in support of this application, the debtors have alternatively requested that the judicial lien of Bank One be cancelled by virtue of certain provisions of §1327(b) and (c) of the Bankruptcy Code which state:

> (b) Except as otherwise provided in the plan or the order confirming the plan, the confirmation of a plan vests all property of the estate in the debtor.
> (c) Except as otherwise provided in the plan or in the order confirming the plan, the property vesting in the debtor under subsection (b) of this section is *free and clear of any claim or interest of any creditor provided for by the plan.* 11 U.S.C. §1327(b) and (c) (Emphasis Added).

The debtor's application has been opposed by Bank One. Relevant facts in deciding the present application are found by the Court as follows. The debtors filed a joint petition requesting relief under the provisions of Chapter 13 of the Bankruptcy Code on March 4, 1981. Bank One was a duly listed creditor in the accompanying Chapter 13 statement . . . as was duly notified of the filing of the petition. A meeting of creditors under the provisions of §341 of the Bankruptcy Code was held on April 10, 1981, and the debtors' plan was confirmed by this Court on April 23, 1981. Bank One filed no claim in this case until April 17, 1981, and its subsequent request to be included in the confirmed plan as a secured creditor was denied by Court Order of May 7, 1981. . . .

The debtors now seek to take advantage of the fact that Bank One has only an allowed *unsecured* claim in this Chapter 13 case by invoking the provisions of §1327(c) and having this Court declare that the judicial lien of Bank One is now cancelled by operation of that section.

There is no doubt that the Bank One debt is provided for in the Chapter 13 plan of these debtors. . . . There is at least one court that appears to have held that the literal language of §1327(c) of the Bankruptcy Code was not meant by Congress. See Second National Bank of Saginaw v. Honaker (In re Honaker), 4 B.R. 415, 6 B.C.D. 474 (Bkrtcy. E.D. Mich.1980). Indeed, a respected bankruptcy treatise seems to also so indicate. 5 Collier on Bankruptcy, ¶1327.01, p. 1327-5.

However, at least two courts have held that the language of §1327 directly affects the status of a holder of a secured claim in a confirmed Chapter 13 plan. For instance, the Court in Associates Commercial Corp.

v. Brock (In re Brock), 6 B.R. 105, 6 B.C.D. 1065 (Bkrtcy. N.D. Ill.1980), held that:

> Section 1327, therefore, virtually renders a secured creditor provided for in a Confirmed Plan impotent. In re Brock, supra, 6 B.R. 105, 6 B.C.D. at 1066.

Also, a bankruptcy court has held that all matters relating to a creditor's interest in the debtor's property, if the debt is provided for by the confirmed plan, are finally determined by the confirmation order, and no subsequent judicial proceeding can reopen those same issues. See Ford Motor Credit Company v. Lewis (In re Lewis), 8 B.R. 132, 7 B.C.D. 105 (Bkrtcy. D. Idaho 1981). Thus, the creditor in the *Lewis* case was prevented from relitigating the question of whether or not the confirmed plan of the Chapter 13 debtor adequately provided for the protection of its interest. Section 1327 of the Bankruptcy Code was cited as support for that position.

This Court hereby finds that the provisions of §1327(c) as applied in this case operate to exchange the previously held obligation of the Pettits, which was secured by a judicial lien of Bank One on their residential real estate, for an unsecured claim to be paid through the terms of the confirmed Chapter 13 plan. Thus, if the debtors fully comply with the terms of their Chapter 13 plan, the Bank One debt, having been paid as an unsecured claim in the confirmed plan, will be discharged. The rehabilitative purpose of Chapter 13 would be directly frustrated if a creditor in Bank One's posture could, after having been paid in accordance with the provisions of the confirmed Chapter 13 plan, and in accordance with the manner in which its claim was allowed, assert the continued validity of its judicial lien after the conclusion of this case. Bank One could have protected itself in this proceeding by filing a timely proof of claim and insisting on retaining its lien rights. See 11 U.S.C. §1325(a)(5)(B)(i). It did not. Bank One's only protection at this point in time is the promise of the debtors to pay their creditors under the terms of their confirmed plan, and if such promise is fulfilled, Bank One will have received its proper dividend in this case. It can, under applicable law, expect no more. The Court makes no present finding as to whether the Bank One judicial lien would be subject to a different treatment should the debtors fail to complete their Chapter 13 plan and their case is either dismissed or converted to a Chapter 7 case. The finding that this Court does make is premised upon the debtors' fulfillment of the terms of their confirmed Chapter 13 plan.

Based upon the foregoing, this Court hereby determines that the provisions of §1327(c) of the Bankruptcy Code operate to avoid Bank One's judicial lien. This Court thus determines that the application of the Pettits is meritorious and it is hereby granted. For the purpose of this

Chapter 13 case, Bank One's judicial lien on the debtors' residential real estate is hereby avoided.

It is so ordered.

NOTES

1. After completion of a Chapter 13 plan (extending three to five years, at the outside), may a secured creditor with a long-term obligation (extending beyond completion of the Chapter 13 plan) repossess its collateral? Does this depend on whether the debtor continues to make timely payments? Does *Pettit* bear on that question? See §1325(a)(5)(B).

2. *Pettit* asks the question of whether the doctrine of Long v. Bullard, supra page 743, applies in a Chapter 13 case. As with *Blake*, we have the starting ground that §524, at least as interpreted in light of Long v. Bullard, seems to provide for "lien pass through," and the question of whether §524 applies to a Chapter 13 plan of reorganization. As with lien pass through in Chapters 7 or 11, moreover, the issue is often not of relevance, because §1325(a)(5) provides that holders of allowed secured claims, absent consent or actually getting the collateral, should "retain the lien securing such claim." Thus, the issue is likely to arise only if, for some reason, the creditor does not assert its security interest prior to confirmation of the Chapter 13 plan.

Under those circumstances, does the operation of lien pass through conflict with either the provisions or purposes of Chapter 13? Does §1327(c) clearly resolve this issue? Would you reach a similar conclusion regarding lien pass through in Chapter 11, given the presence of §1141(c)? Can you articulate a policy justification for treating secured creditors of a Chapter 7 debtor better than secured creditors of a debtor in Chapter 13 (and perhaps Chapter 11 as well)? In a Chapter 13 case, at least, it is the debtor, rather than the other creditors who is likely to feel the effects of a doctrine of lien pass through. Is this necessarily bad? Can it be argued that the effect of such a doctrine may be to have the debtor be more cautious about including such creditors in a Chapter 13 plan, and that this is good?

Chapter 13

JURISDICTION AND PROCEDURES OF BANKRUPTCY COURTS

A. INTRODUCTION TO BANKRUPTCY JURISDICTION

NOTE ON BANKRUPTCY JURISDICTION BEFORE *MARATHON*

The principal jurisdictional provisions of the Bankruptcy Code are in scattered sections of 28 U.S.C. These were completely overhauled in 1984 as a result of Northern Pipeline Construction Corp. v. Marathon Pipe Line Co., 458 U.S. 50 (1982). In that case, the Supreme Court found unconstitutional those provisions of the Bankruptcy Reform Act of 1978 that allowed bankruptcy judges to exercise "judicial power" within the meaning of Article III of the Constitution without having life tenure. The structure of the current jurisdiction rules (and their potential constitutional infirmities) requires an understanding of the jurisdictional provisions of the 1978 Bankruptcy Reform Act. The basic jurisdictional grant was in 28 U.S.C. §1471. It gave jurisdiction over cases under Title 11 and cases arising in or related to cases arising in Title 11 in subsection (a) to the district courts, but then subsection (c) gave that jurisdiction to the bankruptcy courts, which were made "adjuncts" to the district courts pursuant to 28 U.S.C. §151(a). This seemingly pointless "two-step" approach was done quite consciously. Although it may have compounded the constitutional problems by making bankruptcy judges less like Article I judges, Congress was aware of the possible constitutional challenges to a scheme that gave the jurisdiction directly to the bankruptcy courts, and it thought this approach might possibly alleviate the problem.

The Supreme Court's decision in *Marathon* will remain the leading case on the constitutional limits of the powers of bankruptcy judges, who still do not enjoy life tenure, and it will undoubtedly influence the decisions on the scope of the jurisdictional provisions that were passed in its wake. Before we look at that case, however, it is useful to review the jurisdictional provisions of the 1898 Bankruptcy Act, because they have returned, in a slightly different guise in the 1984 Amendments. The 1978 Bankruptcy Reform Act was designed to consolidate, in one forum, actions that under the old Act were disbursed jurisdictionally. The old bankruptcy court was considered to be a court of equity and, as such, was said to have in rem jurisdiction over the estate. See, e.g., Katchen v. Landy, 382 U.S. 323 (1966).

The nature of this jurisdiction had two separate components. First, the bankruptcy court had jurisdiction over all "proceedings" under the old Bankruptcy Act. This meant that it had jurisdiction to decide all matters that are, so to speak, "internal" to the bankruptcy process, such as appointment of the trustee, approval of claims filed by creditors, and the granting of the discharge. In addition, the bankruptcy court had jurisdiction to decide disputes between a trustee and adverse claimants involving rights to money or property sought to be recovered for the estate or in which the estate claimed an interest. This branch of the bankruptcy court's jurisdiction, which was generally, if oddly, referred to as "summary" jurisdiction, extended, however, only so far as the bankruptcy court had "possession" of the property in controversy.

The bankruptcy court obtained possession of the property of the estate through the trustee, who derived it, in turn, from the bankrupt. So, if the bankrupt had possession, the bankruptcy court had jurisdiction to decide any controversies regarding the property in question. What if the bankrupt did not have possession? Suppose, for example, the property was in the possession of a creditor. In that case, if the trustee sought to recover the property, perhaps on the ground that the creditor's receipt of it was a voidable preference, he would, under the old Bankruptcy Act, have had to bring what was called a "plenary" action against the creditor in some court other than the bankruptcy court.

While jurisdiction of such matters rested on possession, the possession could have been "actual" or "constructive." The recognition of constructive possession as a basis for jurisdiction expanded the cases that could be heard in bankruptcy court, but it also was a fruitful source of litigation on the issue of whether the action was being brought in the right court. One situation in which the bankruptcy court was said to have constructive possession was where the property was in the possession of an adverse party under a merely colorable claim, or a fraudulent claim. Resolution of these jurisdictional issues, however, often required a mini-trial on the merits.

A second type of constructive jurisdiction was jurisdiction conferred by consent. But it was not only actual consent that filled this requirement. A failure to make a timely objection to the bankruptcy court's jurisdiction was deemed to be consent. And, if the creditor filed a claim in the bankruptcy court, it could result in the creditor being deemed to have given implied consent to jurisdiction over a counterclaim (such as for a preference) asserted by the trustee.

One last thing should be added about jurisdiction under the old Bankruptcy Act. Whether the bankruptcy court had jurisdiction was said to involve a question of "summary" versus "plenary" jurisdiction. But "summary" did not define one type of bankruptcy court jurisdiction; rather, it was a label for bankruptcy court jurisdiction. "Summary" meant the bankruptcy court had jurisdiction; "plenary" meant it did not. Once *in* a bankruptcy court (and, hence, necessarily in its summary jurisdiction), the procedure was different from a regular federal civil action. For example, because the bankruptcy courts were considered to be courts of equity, there were no jury trials. The net result of these rules was that proceedings in bankruptcy courts were in fact more expeditious. But the litigation over *where* a suit should be brought was considered troublesome. See generally Treister, Bankruptcy Jurisdiction: Is it Too Summary?, 39 S. Cal. L. Rev. 78 (1966).

NORTHERN PIPELINE CONSTR. CO. v. MARATHON PIPE LINE CO.
458 U.S. 50 (1982)

Justice BRENNAN announced the judgment of the Court and delivered an opinion in which Justice MARSHALL, Justice BLACKMUN, and Justice STEVENS joined.

In 1978, after almost ten years of study and investigation, Congress enacted a comprehensive revision of the bankruptcy laws. The Bankruptcy Act of 1978 (Act) made significant changes in both the substantive and procedural law of bankruptcy. It is the changes in the latter that are at issue in this case.

Before the Act, federal district courts served as bankruptcy courts and employed a "referee" system. Bankruptcy proceedings were generally conducted before referees, except in those instances in which the district court elected to withdraw a case from a referee. . . . The referee's final order was appealable to the district court. . . . The bankruptcy courts were vested with "summary jurisdiction"—that is, with jurisdiction over controversies involving property in the actual or constructive possession of the court. And, with consent, the bankruptcy court also had jurisdiction over some "plenary" matters—such as disputes involving property in the possession of a third person.

The Act eliminates the referee system and establishes "in each judicial district, as an adjunct to the district court for such district, a bankruptcy court which shall be a court of record known as the United States Bankruptcy Court for the district." 28 U.S.C. §151(a) (1976 ed., Supp. III). The judges of these courts are appointed to office for 14-year terms by the

President, with the advice and consent of the Senate. . . . They are subject to removal by the "judicial council of the circuit" on account of "incompetence, misconduct, neglect of duty or physical or mental disability." §153(b). In addition, the salaries of the bankruptcy judges are set by statute and are subject to adjustment under the Federal Salary Act. . . .

The jurisdiction of the bankruptcy courts created by the Act is much broader than that exercised under the former referee system. . . . This jurisdictional grant empowers bankruptcy courts to entertain a wide variety of cases involving claims that may affect the property of the estate once a petition has been filed under title 11 of the Act. Included within the bankruptcy courts' jurisdiction are suits to recover accounts, controversies involving exempt property, actions to avoid transfers and payments as preferences or fraudulent conveyances, and causes of action owned by the debtor at the time of the petition for bankruptcy. The bankruptcy courts can hear claims based on state law as well as those based on federal law. . . .

The judges of the bankruptcy courts are vested with all of the "powers of a court of equity, law and admiralty," except that they "may not enjoin another court or punish a criminal contempt not committed in the presence of the judge of the court or warranting a punishment of imprisonment." 28 U.S.C. §1481. . . . In addition to this broad grant of power, Congress has allowed bankruptcy judges the power to hold jury trials, §1480; to issue declaratory judgments, §2201; to issue writs of habeas corpus under certain circumstances, §2256; to issue all writs necessary in aid of the bankruptcy court's expanded jurisdiction, §451 . . . ; and to issue any order, process or judgment that is necessary or appropriate to carry out the provisions of title 11, 11 U.S.C. §105(a). . . .

This case arises out of proceedings initiated in the United States Bankruptcy Court for the District of Minnesota after appellant Northern Pipeline Construction Co. (Northern) filed a petition for reorganization in January 1980. In March 1980 Northern, pursuant to the Act, filed in that court a suit against appellee Marathon Pipe Line Co. (Marathon). Appellant sought damages for alleged breaches of contract and warranty, as well as for alleged misrepresentation, coercion, and duress. Marathon sought dismissal of the suit, on the ground that the Act unconstitutionally conferred Art. III judicial power upon judges who lacked life tenure and protection against salary diminution. The United States intervened to defend the validity of the statute. . . .

It is undisputed that the bankruptcy judges whose offices were created by the Bankruptcy Act of 1978 do not enjoy the protections constitutionally afforded to Art. III judges. The bankruptcy judges do not serve for life subject to their continued "good Behaviour." Rather, they are appointed for 14-year terms, and can be removed by the judicial council of the circuit in which they serve on grounds of "incompetence, misconduct, neglect of duty or physical or mental disability." Second, the salaries of the bankruptcy judges are not immune from diminution by Congress. In short, there is no doubt that the bankruptcy judges created by the Act are not Art. III judges. . . .

Congress did not constitute the bankruptcy courts as legislative courts. Appellants contend, however, that the bankruptcy courts could have been so constituted, and that as a result the "adjunct" system in fact chosen by Congress does not impermissibly encroach upon the judicial power. In advancing this argument, appellants rely upon cases in which we have identified certain matters that "congress may or may not bring within the cognizance of [Art. III] courts, as it may deem proper." Murray's Lessee v. Hoboken Land and Improvement Co., 18 How. 272, 284, 15 L. Ed. 372 (1855). But when properly understood, these precedents represent no broad departure from the constitutional command that the judicial power of the United States must be vested in Art. III courts. Rather, they reduce to three narrow situations not subject to that command, each recognizing a circumstance in which the grant of power to the Legislative and Executive Branches was historically and constitutionally so exceptional that the congressional assertion of a power to create legislative courts was consistent with, rather than threatening to, the constitutional mandate of separation of powers. These precedents simply acknowledge that the literal command of Art. III, assigning the judicial power of the United States to courts insulated from Legislative or Executive interference, must be interpreted in light of the historical context in which the Constitution was written, and of the structural imperatives of the Constitution as a whole. . . .

[T]his Court has identified three situations in which Art. III does not bar the creation of legislative courts. In each of these situations, the Court has recognized certain exceptional powers bestowed upon Congress by the Constitution or by historical consensus. Only in the face of such an exceptional grant of power has the Court declined to hold the authority of Congress subject to the general prescriptions of Art. III.

We discern no such exceptional grant of power applicable in the case before us. The courts created by the Bankruptcy Act of 1978 do not lie exclusively outside the States of the Federal Union, like those in the District of Columbia and the territories. Nor do the bankruptcy courts bear any resemblance to courts martial, which are founded upon the Constitution's grant of plenary authority over the Nation's military forces to the Legislative and Executive Branches. Finally, the substantive legal rights at issue in the present action cannot be deemed "public rights." Appellants argue that a discharge in bankruptcy is indeed a "public right," similar to such congressionally created benefits as "radio station licenses, pilot licenses, and certificates for common carriers" granted by administrative agencies. . . . But the restructuring of debtor-creditor relations, which is at the core of the federal bankruptcy power, must be distinguished from the adjudication of state-created private rights, such as the right to recover contract damages that is at issue in this case. The former may well be a "public right," but the latter obviously is not. Appellant Northern's right to recover contract damages to augment its estate is "one of private right, that is, of the liability of one individual to another under the law as defined." Crowell v. Benson, 285 U.S., at 51, 52 S. Ct., at 292.[26]

Recognizing that the present case may not fall within the scope of any of our prior cases permitting the establishment of legislative courts, appellants argue that we should recognize an additional situation beyond the command of Art. III, sufficiently broad to sustain the Act. Appellants contend that Congress' constitutional authority to establish "uniform Laws on the subject of Bankruptcies throughout the United States," Art. I §8, cl. 4, carries with it an inherent power to establish legislative courts capable of adjudicating "bankruptcy related controversies." . . .

The flaw in appellants' analysis is that it provides no limiting principle. It thus threatens to supplant completely our system of adjudication in independent Art. III tribunals and replace it with a system of "specialized" legislative courts. True, appellants argue that under their analysis Congress could create legislative courts pursuant only to some "specific" Art. I power, and "only when there is a particularized need for distinctive treatment." . . . They therefore assert, that their analysis would not permit Congress to replace the independent Art. III judiciary through a "wholesale assignment of federal judicial business to legislative courts." . . . But these "limitations" are wholly illusory. For example, Art. I, §8, empowers Congress to enact laws, inter alia, regulating interstate commerce and punishing certain crimes. Art. I, §8, cls. 3, 6. On appellants' reasoning Congress could provide for the adjudication of these and "related" matters by judges and courts within Congress' exclusive control. The potential for encroachment upon powers reserved to the Judicial Branch through the device of "specialized" legislative courts is dramatically evidenced in the jurisdiction granted to the courts created by the Act before us. . . .

. . . Art. III bars Congress from establishing legislative courts to exercise jurisdiction over all matters related to those arising under the bankruptcy laws. The establishment of such courts does not fall within any of the historically recognized situations in which the general principle of independent adjudication commanded by Art. III does not apply. Nor can we discern any persuasive reason, in logic, history, or the Constitution, why the bankruptcy courts here established lie beyond the reach of Art. III. . . .

Appellants advance a second argument for upholding the constitu-

26. This claim may be adjudicated in federal court on the basis of its relationship to the petition for reorganization. . . . But this relationship does not transform the state-created right into a matter between the Government and the petitioner for reorganization. Even in the absence of the federal scheme, the plaintiff would be able to proceed against the defendant on the state-law contractual claims.

tionality of the Act: that "viewed within the entire judicial framework set up by Congress," the bankruptcy court is merely an "adjunct" to the district court, and that the delegation of certain adjudicative functions to the bankruptcy court is accordingly consistent with the principle that the judicial power of the United States must be vested in Art. III courts. . . . As support for their argument, appellants rely principally upon Crowell v. Benson, supra, and United States v. Raddatz, 447 U.S. 667, 100 S. Ct. 2406, 65 L. Ed. 2d 424 (1980), cases in which we approved the use of administrative agencies and magistrates as adjuncts to Art. III courts. . . . The question to which we turn, therefore, is whether the Act has retained "the essential attributes of the judicial power," Crowell v. Benson, supra, 285 U.S., at 51, 52 S. Ct., at 292, in Art. III tribunals.

The essential premise underlying appellants' argument is that even where the Constitution denies Congress the power to establish legislative courts, Congress possesses the authority to assign certain factfinding functions to adjunct tribunals. . . .

[Our] cases establish two principles that aid us in determining the extent to which Congress may constitutionally vest traditionally judicial functions in non-Art. III officers.[31] First, it is clear that when Congress creates a substantive federal right, it possesses substantial discretion to prescribe the manner in which that right may be adjudicated — including the assignment to an adjunct of some functions historically performed by

---

31. Appellants and Justice WHITE's dissent also rely on the broad powers exercised by the bankruptcy referees immediately before the Bankruptcy Act of 1978. . . . But those particular adjunct functions, which represent the culmination of years of gradual expansion of the power and authority of the bankruptcy referee, . . . have never been explicitly endorsed by this Court. In Katchen v. Landy, 382 U.S. 323, 86 S. Ct. 467, 15 L. Ed. 2d 391 (1966), on which the dissent relies, there was no discussion of the Art. III issue. Moreover, when *Katchen* was decided the 1973 Bankruptcy Rules had not yet been adopted, and the District Judge, after hearing the report of magistrate, was free to "modify it or . . . reject it in whole or in part or . . . receive further evidence or . . . recommit it with instructions." Gen. Order in Bankruptcy No. 47, 305 U.S. 679 (1935).

We note, moreover, that the 1978 Act made at least three significant changes from the bankruptcy practice that immediately preceded it. First, of course, the jurisdiction of the bankruptcy courts was "substantially expanded by the Act." H.R. Rep. No. 95–595, supra, p. 13 (1977). Before the act the referee had no jurisdiction, except with consent, over controversies beyond those involving property in the actual or constructive possession of the court. . . . It cannot be doubted that the new bankruptcy judges, unlike the referees, have jurisdiction far beyond that which can be even arguably characterized as merely incidental to the discharge in bankruptcy or a plan for reorganization. Second, the bankruptcy judges have broader powers than those exercised by the referees. . . . Finally, and perhaps most significantly, the relationship between the district court and the bankruptcy court was changed under the 1978 Act. Before the Act, bankruptcy referees were "subordinate adjuncts of the district courts." . . . In contrast, the new bankruptcy courts are "independent of the United States district courts." . . . Before the Act, bankruptcy referees were appointed and removable only by the district court. . . . And the district court retained control over the referee by his power to withdraw the case from the referee. . . . Thus even at the trial stage, the parties had access to an independent judicial officer. Although Congress could still lower the salary of referees, they were not dependent on the political branches of government for their appointment. . . . [Footnote relocated — EDS.]

judges. . . . Second, the functions of the adjunct must be limited in such a way that "the essential attributes" of judicial power are retained in the Art. III court. Thus in upholding the adjunct scheme challenged in *Crowell*, the Court emphasized that "the reservation of full authority to the court to deal with matters of law provides for the appropriate exercise of the judicial function in this class of cases." [285 U.S. at 51.] And in refusing to invalidate the Magistrates Act at issue in *Raddatz*, the Court stressed that under the congressional scheme " '[t]he authority—and the responsibility—to make an informed, final determination . . . remains with the judge,' " 447 U.S., at 682. . . .

These two principles assist us in evaluating the "adjunct" scheme presented in this case. Appellants assume that Congress' power to create "adjuncts" to consider all cases related to those arising under title 11 is as great as it was in the circumstances of *Crowell*. But while *Crowell* certainly endorsed the proposition that Congress possesses broad discretion to assign factfinding functions to an adjunct created to aid in the adjudication of congressionally created statutory rights, *Crowell* does not support the further proposition necessary to appellants' argument—that Congress possesses the same degree of discretion in assigning traditionally judicial power to adjuncts engaged in the adjudication of rights *not* created by Congress. . . .

Although *Crowell* and *Raddatz* do not explicity distinguish between rights created by Congress and other rights, such a distinction underlies in part *Crowell*'s and *Raddatz*'s recognition of a critical difference between rights created by federal statute and rights recognized by the Constitution. Moreover, such a distinction seems to us to be necessary in light of the delicate accommodations required by the principle of separation of powers reflected in Art. III. The constitutional system of checks and balances is designed to guard against "encroachment or aggrandizement" by Congress at the expense of the other branches of government. Buckley v. Valeo, 424 U.S., at 122, 96 S. Ct., at 683. But when Congress creates a statutory right, it clearly has the discretion, in defining that right, to create presumptions, or assign burdens of proof, or prescribe remedies; it may also provide that persons seeking to vindicate that right must do so before particularized tribunals created to perform the specialized adjudicative tasks related to that right. Such provisions do, in a sense, affect the exercise of judicial power, but they are also incidental to Congress' power to define the right that it has created. No comparable justification exists, however, when the right being adjudicated is not of congressional creation. In such a situation, substantial inroads into functions that have traditionally been performed by the judiciary cannot be characterized merely as incidental extensions of Congress' power to define rights that it has created. Rather, such inroads suggest unwarranted encroachments upon the judicial power of the United States, which our Constitution reserves for Art. III courts.

We hold that the Bankruptcy Act of 1978 carries the possibility of such an unwarranted encroachment. Many of the rights subject to adjudication by the Act's bankruptcy courts, like the rights implicated in *Raddatz,* are not of Congress' creation. Indeed, the case before us, which centers upon appellant Northern's claim for damages for breach of contract and misrepresentation, involves a right created by *state* law, a right independent of and antecedent to the reorganization petition that conferred jurisdiction upon the bankruptcy court.[36] Accordingly, Congress' authority to control the manner in which that right is adjudicated, through assignment of historically judicial functions to a non-Art. III "adjunct," plainly must be deemed at a minimum. Yet it is equally plain that Congress has vested the "adjunct" bankruptcy judges with powers over appellant's state-created right that far exceed the powers that it has vested in administrative agencies that adjudicate only rights of Congress' own creation.

Unlike the administrative scheme that we reviewed in *Crowell,* the Act vests all "essential attributes" of the judicial power of the United States in the "adjunct" bankruptcy court. . . . [T]he agency in *Crowell* was required by law to seek enforcement of its compensation orders in the district court. In contrast, the bankruptcy courts issue final judgments, which are binding and enforceable even in the absence of an appeal.[38] In short, the "adjunct" bankruptcy courts created by the Act exercise jurisdiction behind the facade of a grant to the district courts, and are exercising powers far greater than those lodged in the adjuncts approved in either *Crowell* or *Raddatz.*[39]

We conclude that §241(a) of the Bankruptcy Act of 1978 has impermissibly removed most, if not all, of "the essential attributes of the judicial power" from the Art. III district court, and has vested those attributes in a

36. Of course, bankruptcy adjudications themselves, as well as the manner in which the rights of debtors and creditors are adjusted, are matters of federal law. Appellant Northern's state-law contract claim is now in federal court because of its relationship to appellant's reorganization petition. See n.26, supra. But Congress has not purported to prescribe a rule of decision for the resolution of appellant's contractual claims.

38. Although the entry of an enforcement order is in some respects merely formal, it has long been recognized that

The award of execution . . . is a part, and an essential part of every judgment passed by a court exercising judicial power. It is no judgment in the legal sense of the term, without it. ICC v. Brimson, 154 U.S 447, 484, 14 S. Ct. 1125, 1136, 38 L. Ed. 1047 (1894), quoting Chief Justice Taney's memorandum in Gordon v. United States, 117 U.S. 697, 702 (1864).

39. Appellants suggest that *Crowell* and *Raddatz* stand for the proposition that Art. III is satisfied so long as some degree of appellate review is provided. But that suggestion is directly contrary to the text of our Constitution: "The Judges, *both* of the supreme and inferior Courts, shall hold their Offices during good Behaviour, and shall . . . receive [undiminished] Compensation." Art. III, §1 (emphasis added). Our precedents make it clear that the constitutional requirements for the exercise of the judicial power must be met at all stages of adjudication, and not only on appeal, where the court is restricted to considerations of law, as well as the nature of the case as it has been shaped at the trial level. . . .

non-Art. III adjunct. Such a grant of jurisdiction cannot be sustained as an exercise of Congress' power to create adjuncts to Art. III courts.[40] . . .

The judgment of the District Court is affirmed. However, we stay our judgment until October 4, 1982. This limited stay will afford Congress an opportunity to reconstitute the bankruptcy courts or to adopt other valid means of adjudication, without impairing the interim administration of the bankruptcy laws. . . .

Justice REHNQUIST, with whom Justice O'CONNOR joins, concurring in the judgment. . . .

Marathon has simply been named defendant in a lawsuit about a contract, a lawsuit initiated by appellant Northern after having previously filed a petition for reorganization under the Bankruptcy Act. Marathon may object to proceeding further with this lawsuit on the grounds that if it is to be resolved by an agency of the United States, it may be resolved only by an agency which exercises "the judicial power of the United States" described by Art. III of the Constitution. But resolution of any objections it may make on this ground to the exercise of a different authority conferred on Bankruptcy Courts by the 1978 Act, see ante, should await the exercise of such authority. Particularly in an area of constitutional law such as that of "Art. III Courts," with its frequently arcane distinctions and confusing precedents, rigorous adherence to the principle that this Court should decide no more of a constitutional question than is absolutely necessary accords with both our decided cases and with sound judicial policy.

From the record before us, the lawsuit in which Marathon was named defendant seeks damages for breach of contract, misrepresentation, and other counts which are the stuff of the traditional actions at common law tried by the courts at Westminster in 1789. There is apparently no federal rule of decision provided for any of the issues in the lawsuit; the claims of Northern arise entirely under state law. No method of adjudication is

---

40. It is clear that, at the least, the new bankruptcy judges cannot constitutionally be vested with jurisdiction to decide this state-law contract claim against Marathon. As part of a comprehensive restructuring of the bankruptcy laws, Congress has vested jurisdiction over this and all matters related to cases under title 11 in a single non-Art. III court, and has done so pursuant to a single statutory grant of jurisdiction. In these circumstances we cannot conclude that if Congress were aware that the grant of jurisdiction could not constitutionally encompass this and similar claims, it would simply remove the jurisdiction of the bankruptcy court over these matters, leaving the jurisdictional provision and adjudicatory structure intact with respect to other types of claims, and thus subject to Art. III constitutional challenge on a claim-by-claim basis. Indeed, we note that one of the express purposes of the Act was to ensure adjudication of all claims in a single forum and to avoid the delay and expense of jurisdictional disputes. . . . Nor can we assume, as the chief justice suggests, . . . that Congress' choice would be to have this case "routed to the United States district court of which the bankruptcy court is an adjunct." We think that it is for Congress to determine the proper manner of restructuring the Bankruptcy Act of 1978 to conform to the requirements of Art. III, in the way that will best effectuate the legislative purpose.

[Footnote relocated. — EDS.]

hinted, other than the traditional common law mode of judge and jury. The lawsuit is before the Bankruptcy Court only because the plaintiff has previously filed a petition for reorganization in that Court.

The cases dealing with the authority of Congress to create courts other than by use of its power under Art. III do not admit of easy synthesis. In the interval of nearly 150 years between American Insurance Co. v. Canter, 1 Pet. 511, 7 L. Ed. 242 (1828), and Palmore v. United States, 411 U.S. 389, 93 S. Ct. 1670, 36 L. Ed. 2d 342 (1973), the Court addressed the question infrequently. I need not decide whether these cases in fact support a general proposition and three tidy exceptions, as the plurality believes, or whether instead they are but landmarks on a judicial "darkling plain" where ignorant armies have clashed by night, as Justice White apparently believes them to be. None of the cases has gone so far as to sanction the type of adjudication to which Marathon will be subjected against its will under the provisions of the 1978 Act. To whatever extent different powers granted under that Act might be sustained under the "public rights" doctrine of Murray's Lessee v. Hoboken Land & Improvement Co., 18 How. 272, 15 L. Ed. 372 (1855), and succeeding cases, I am satisfied that the adjudication of Northern's lawsuit cannot be so sustained.

I am likewise of the opinion that the extent of review by Art. III courts provided on appeal from a decision of the Bankruptcy Court in a case such as Northern's does not save the grant of authority to the latter under the rule espoused in Crowell v. Benson, 285 U.S 22, 52 S. Ct. 285, 76 L. Ed. 598 (1932). All matters of fact and law in whatever domains of the law to which the parties' dispute may lead are to be resolved by the Bankruptcy Court in the first instance, with only traditional appellate review apparently contemplated by Art. III courts. Acting in this manner the Bankruptcy Court is not an "adjunct" of either the District Court or the Court of Appeals.

I would, therefore, hold so much of the Bankruptcy Act of 1978 as enables a Bankruptcy Court to entertain and decide Northern's lawsuit over Marathon's objection to be violative of Art. III of the United States Constitution. Because I agree with the plurality that this grant of authority is not readily severable from the remaining grant of authority to Bankruptcy Courts under §241(a), . . . I concur in the judgment. I also agree with the discussion in Part V of the plurality opinion respecting retroactivity and the staying of the judgment of this Court.

Chief Justice BURGER, dissenting.

I join Justice White's dissenting opinion, but I write separately to emphasize that, notwithstanding the plurality opinion, the Court does *not* hold today that Congress' broad grant of jurisdiction to the new bankruptcy courts is generally inconsistent with Article III of the Constitution. Rather, the Court's holding is limited to the proposition stated by Justice

Rehnquist in his concurrence in the judgment — that a "traditional" state common-law action, not made subject to a federal rule of decision, and related only peripherally to an adjudication of bankruptcy under federal law, must, absent the consent of the litigants, be heard by an "Article III court" if it is to be heard by any court or agency of the United States. This limited holding, of course, does not suggest that there is something inherently unconstitutional about the new bankruptcy courts; nor does it preclude such courts from adjudicating all but a relatively narrow category of claims "arising under" or "arising in or related to cases under" the Bankruptcy Act.

It will not be necessary for Congress, in order to meet the requirements of the Court's holding, to undertake a radical restructuring of the present system of bankruptcy adjudication. The problems arising from today's judgment can be resolved simply by providing that ancillary common-law actions, such as the one involved in this case, be routed to the United States district court of which the bankruptcy court is an adjunct.

Justice WHITE, with whom THE CHIEF JUSTICE and Justice POWELL join, dissenting.
[Omitted]

NOTE ON *MARATHON*

Article III requires that the "judicial power" be vested in courts whose judges enjoy life tenure and an undiminishable salary, and bankruptcy judges under the Bankruptcy Reform Act of 1978 enjoyed neither. Thus, if the question were approached on a blank slate, it might not seem to be difficult. Bankruptcy judges did seem to exercise a power that might fairly be called judicial. The differences between the powers of a district judge and those of a bankruptcy judge might not be thought of as relevant for purposes of Article III. Under the provisions of the 1978 Bankruptcy Reform Act, bankruptcy judges had jurisdiction over all civil proceedings arising in or related to bankruptcy proceedings. If a debtor in a bankruptcy proceeding was enmeshed in an antitrust dispute, the bankruptcy judge had jurisdiction over the case. See In re Repair & Maintenance Parts Corp., 19 Bankr. 575 (Bankr. N.D. Ill. 1982). A bankruptcy judge might also have had jurisdiction over a property dispute between spouses that turned on state divorce law. See In re Heslar, 16 Bankr. 329 (Bankr. W.D. Mich. 1981). There were few civil proceedings over which a bankruptcy judge did not have jurisdiction as long as a plausible connection between the civil proceeding and the Bankruptcy Code could be drawn. See *Brentano's,* infra page 966.

The Supreme Court, however, did not face a blank slate. Chief Justice Marshall recognized that Congress had the power to create tribunals that would act as courts in territories. American Ins. Co. v. Canter, 26 U.S (1 Pet.) 511 (1828). Subsequent interpretations by the Supreme Court of the mandates of Article III for the most part recognized Congress's power to carve out one exception after another. Congress has the power to create courts martial. Moreover, Congress can create Article I tribunals to adjudicate some rights between the government and individuals, provided that the rights are not inherently judicial. Finally, Congress can create administrative agencies that can decide disputes between private individuals, such as those between employer and employee, that concern "public rights." The Supreme Court summarizes these exceptions in Palmore v. United States, 411 U.S. 389, 407-408 (1973):

> [T]he requirements of Art. III, which are applicable where laws of national applicability and affairs of national concern are at stake, must in proper circumstances give way to accommodate plenary grants of power to Congress to legislate with respect to specialized areas having particularized needs and warranting distinctive treatment.

It was difficult, however, to place the bankruptcy courts into one of the exceptions. It was also difficult to argue that bankruptcy was a specialized area that fell within Congress's power to create Article I tribunals. The clause that gives Congress the power to enact laws on the subject of bankruptcies is no different from clauses in Article I and constitutional amendments that give Congress the power to enact laws on other subjects. Limiting the subject matter over which a tribunal could act should not enable Congress to escape the dictates of Article III.

Even if Congress could create Article I bankruptcy tribunals by restricting the jurisdiction of the tribunal, it did not do so in the Bankruptcy Reform Act of 1978. The jurisdiction of the bankruptcy courts was not "specialized" in the sense that only a narrow class of disputes could have come before them. Finally, the rights a bankruptcy judge adjudicated under that scheme did not seem to be "public rights" that an Article I administrative tribunal would be competent to decide. Many, such as the breach of contract action at issue in *Marathon*, arose under state common law. If such rights were "public," then so were all other rights that were subject to litigation.

In *Marathon*, the Court tried to reconcile its decision with as many earlier ones as possible. But no amount of historical exegesis could save the Court from deciding between two unpleasant alternatives: Either Article III does not apply to lower federal trial tribunals, or it does. The first alternative was unpalatable, because it would render illusory the apparent requirement that those exercising the judicial power have life tenure. Why would the Framers empower Congress to create inferior federal courts whose judges must have tenure for life and an undiminishable salary and also tribunals that do exactly the same thing but whose judges need to have neither tenure for life nor an undiminishable salary? The second alternative was unpalatable because of its costs. Finding that courts that hear over half a million cases — and many more disputes within those cases — a year lack jurisdiction has practical consequences.

The issue raised by *Marathon* — as well as by Congress's response to *Marathon* — is whether bankruptcy judges can be given little enough power so that they do not have to be Article III judges and yet enough power so that district courts do not become swamped and bankruptcy proceedings remain a useful forum in which creditors can sort out rights among themselves. The simplest course available to Congress would have been to make bankruptcy judges Article III judges, but, as a practical matter, Congress has been unwilling to take such a step either before or after *Marathon*, in part because of intensive lobbying by the Chief Justice and a concern over "cheapening the currency" of Article III judges. But once the line needs to be drawn, it runs up against the fact that distinctions between Article III courts, whose judges must have life tenure and Article I tribunals, whose judges need not, are difficult to find.

In his concurring opinion, Justice Rehnquist argued that the Court needed to decide only whether the bankruptcy courts could exercise jurisdiction over Marathon. He reasoned that because the dispute involved in *Marathon* had been regarded as judicial since time immemorial, it could only be heard by an Article III judge. Justice Rehnquist reasoned further that he need not (and indeed should not) say more. Justice Rehnquist's position would have been more understandable if he had stated simply that a bankruptcy judge could not hear a dispute like the one in *Marathon* and that determining the exact contours of a bankruptcy judge's powers should await further litigation. He also agreed, however, with the plurality that the provision of the Bankruptcy Reform Act of 1978 giving the bankruptcy judge jurisdiction over this dispute was hopelessly entwined with all the other provisions giving the bankruptcy judge jurisdiction. *Marathon* did not merely adjudicate a dispute between two private parties; it forced Congress to rethink the relationship between bankruptcy jurisdiction and Article III. Given that Congress had to begin this inquiry quickly (although it did not end it quickly), Justice Rehnquist might well have explained his decision at greater length. Because his vote and Justice O'Conner's were the crucial ones, Congress had to divine from Justice Rehnquist's opinion a sense of what would pass constitutional muster and what would not.

The first person to interpret Justice Rehnquist's concurrence and to advise Congress how to draft an appropriate statute was the Chief Justice. The Chief Justice's assertion that the constitutional problem could be resolved simply by providing that ancillary common law actions be routed to the district courts is somewhat puzzling. Nowhere in his opinion did Justice Rehnquist say that Marathon's state law claim must be heard by an Article III court because it is "ancillary" or "peripheral" to a bankruptcy proceeding. Nor did Justice Rehnquist suggest that, had the parties consented to the jurisdiction of the bankruptcy court, the bankruptcy court would have had the power to hear the case. The Chief Justice may have focused on the fact that the parties in *Marathon* did not consent and on the fact that the dispute was "ancillary" to the bankruptcy proceeding because these features made *Marathon* a case that a bankruptcy referee could not have heard under the 1898 Bankruptcy Act.

The jurisdictional provisions of the 1898 Act might seem to be a safe harbor. But the referee system grew gradually over time, and referees did not initially exercise the power that they ultimately exercised under the 1973 Bankruptcy Rules. Although the Supreme Court promulgated these Rules, the Court's work merely endorsed the efforts of an advisory committee that included referees and scholars. More important, none of the opinions explain how the 1898 Act could be upheld in the wake of *Marathon*. In his plurality opinion, Justice Brennan notes several distinctions between the old Act and the Bankruptcy Reform Act of 1978, emphasizing in particular the control of a district judge over the bankruptcy referee under the old Act. But Justice Brennan did not endorse the old Act, and explicitly noted that the Court had not done so either. In a dissent, Justice White, joined by Justice Powell and the Chief Justice, insisted that the plurality never explained why the differences between the old Act and the Bankruptcy Reform Act of 1978 were relevant for purposes of Article III.

As we saw at the beginning of this chapter, before the Bankruptcy Reform Act of 1978, bankruptcy law distinguished between bankruptcy proceedings proper and other legal disputes in which a debtor who had filed a bankruptcy petition could be a party. Bankruptcy proceedings over which the referee presided were in rem actions. The remainder of the referee's power was over "summary" proceedings. One can argue that the distinction between a summary bankruptcy proceeding and a plenary one is coincidentally one of constitutional dimension, because the summary proceedings involve a specialized area of the law "having particularized needs and warranting distinctive treatment," and that a plenary action is not. But the special characteristics of a summary proceeding arose largely from the need to coordinate the claims of many creditors. The procedural rules needed to resolve a dispute among many parties should not obscure the commonplace character of the rights being adjudicated.

One party to a bankruptcy proceeding may claim that it lent money and that the debtor never repaid it. Another may claim that the debtor committed a tort against it. Identifying such claims and the appropriate measure of damages is the stuff of which every lawsuit is made. In all of the previous cases in which Article I tribunals have been upheld as constitutional, something special about the claim itself or the place where it arose warranted a decision by an Article I tribunal. Disputes in a summary bankruptcy proceeding lacked this characteristic.

Justice Brennan suggested at one point that summary proceedings differed from the dispute at issue in *Marathon* because, in a summary proceeding, rights between creditors and a debtor are readjusted. But as we have seen, bankruptcy law at its core does not involve a restructuring of debtor-creditor relations, at least not when the debtor is a corporation. Even if it did, Justice Brennan did not explain why that should matter.

The requirements of Article III are best understood if the fundamentally procedural nature of federal bankruptcy law (at least apart from the individual debtor's right to a "fresh start") is kept in mind. Justice Rehnquist's opinion emphasizes this point. He noted that the action by Northern against Marathon was a traditional action at common law. In all likelihood, so too were most of the existing claims against Northern. The distinctions between bankruptcy disputes that Article I tribunals can hear and those that only Article III courts can hear are obscure.

Once one establishes that an Article III court must hear some kinds of disputes involving a debtor who has filed a petition in bankruptcy, one cannot draw a safe distinction between Article III issues and non-Article III issues. Article III does not necessarily require all issues of fact and law to be decided by an Article III judge. Such a proposition is inconsistent with the tradition of special masters in equity. District courts may have adjuncts to assist them in bankruptcy disputes, as long as they are adjuncts in fact as well as in name.

In United States v. Raddatz, 447 U.S. 667 (1980), the Court found the Federal Magistrates Act to be consistent with the mandates of Article III. That Act provided that magistrates could hear and decide suppression motions, but that district court had to make a de novo determination of any portion of the magistrate's report to which objection was made. The issue in *Raddatz* was whether the district judge was required to conduct an evidentiary hearing when the disputed issue was one of credibility. In other words, the Court decided whether the district judge could forgo an evidentiary hearing, even if the gist of the magistrate's report was "I deny the motion to suppress because, on the basis of their demeanor on the witness stand, I am more inclined to believe the policeman than the defendant," and the district court had no way of confirming the magistrate's judgment.

The Court found that because district courts retained ultimate authority over the case, Article III was not violated. That the district judge must rely on judgments the magistrate made did not alter the fact that he retained complete control over the magistrate's activities. The control the district judge exercises over magistrates is, in fact, similar to the control that district courts exercised over bankruptcy referees before the 1973 Bankruptcy Rules. The Bankruptcy Reform Act of 1978 was not consistent with *Raddatz*, because it attempted to accommodate the mandates of Article III with labels. Bankruptcy judges are not "adjuncts" of the district courts if they have complete control over their dockets and their factual findings are subject only to appellate review. See generally Baird, Bankruptcy Procedure and State-Created Rights: The Lessons of Gibbons and Marathon, 1982 Sup. Ct. Rev. 25.

NOTE ON THE INTERREGNUM

The stay of the Court's judgment was extended once by the Court, finally expiring in December 1982. For the next 18 months, bankruptcy judges operated under an emergency rule promulgated by the Judicial Conference and adopted by the various courts of appeals. That rule found that exceptional circumstances existed and that "the orderly conduct of the business of the court system" required referral of bankruptcy cases to the bankruptcy judges. The rules drew a distinction between cases under Title 11 and cases arising under Title 11 and proceedings "related to" cases under Title 11. Related proceedings were those civil proceedings that, in the absence of a petition in bankruptcy, could have been brought in another court. In its definition of related proceedings, the rule expressly included claims brought by the estate against parties who had not filed claims against the estate. It expressly excluded contested and uncontested matters concerning the administration of the estate, orders with respect to obtaining credit, proceedings to set aside preferences, and fraudulent conveyances.

In the case of related proceedings, the bankruptcy judge could not enter a judgment or a dispositive order, but had to submit findings, conclusions and a proposed judgment or order to the district judge, unless the parties consented to the entry of a judgment or order. All other orders could be appealed to district judges and a bankruptcy judge could certify that circumstances required that the order be approved by a district judge, whether or not the matter was controverted before the bankruptcy judge. The certification procedure was particularly important in practice when a pre-petition creditor wanted to lend additional funds to a debtor in possession and wanted to be confident that the priority of the loan would not be upset by a challenge from the trustee or other creditors at some later time. In conducting its review of all orders of the bankruptcy courts, the district court could conduct its own hearings and did not have to defer to the findings of the bankruptcy judge. As a practical matter, however, many district judges simply rubber stamped the orders of the bankruptcy courts.

The Emergency Rule was subject to attack and was frequently struck down by bankruptcy judges. The courts of appeals, however, uniformly upheld it, see, e.g., In re Braniff Airways, 700 F.2d 214 (5th Cir. 1983), and the Supreme Court refused to hear any of the cases. (Indeed, the Supreme Court during this period promulgated a new set of Bankruptcy Rules, some of which were premised on the continuing effectiveness of the jurisdictional provisions the Court had found wanting in Marathon.)

Arguments about the legality of the Emergency Rule revolved around three issues. The first issue was a dispute over the holding in *Marathon* itself. Justice Brennan's plurality opinion and Justice Rehnquist's concurring opinion agreed that the grant of jurisdiction to bankruptcy judges to hear cases such as *Marathon* was hopelessly entwined with other jurisdictional grants in the Bankruptcy Reform Act of 1978. They both agreed that a large part of the jurisdictional grant had to be struck down because they could not tell what kind of jurisdictional provision Congress would have created if it had known that it could not enact the provisions it did. But neither opinion states exactly which jurisdictional provisions were no longer effective. It was not clear whether only bankruptcy judges were stripped of jurisdiction or whether district courts were as well. Because of the "two-step" procedure of 28 U.S.C. §1471 (part of §241 of the Bankruptcy Reform Act of 1978) — passing cases through the district court en route to the bankruptcy court — it was possible to argue that *Marathon* only struck down the portion of 28 U.S.C. §1471 that passed the jurisdiction to the bankruptcy judges, leaving intact the jurisdictional grant to the district courts. The courts of appeals usually held this to be the case in deciding whether there was jurisdiction in *any* court to hear bankruptcy cases following *Marathon*. The conclusion about 28 U.S.C. §1471 and the opinion in *Marathon*, was not inexorable, however. The district courts were mentioned in the statute only as window dressing. Congress might not have chosen to give bankruptcy judges jurisdiction over other disputes if they could not hear cases like *Marathon*. But Congress might also not have chosen to give jurisdiction of all bankruptcy disputes to district judges, if they could not pass all of them along to bankruptcy judges.

If district courts did not have jurisdiction because of §241 of the Bankruptcy Reform Act, it was not clear what jurisdiction they would have, unless the dispute arose under federal law within the meaning of 28 U.S.C. §1331 or unless there was diversity between the parties. The old 28 U.S.C. §1334 had been consistently interpreted to give district courts jurisdiction over summary bankruptcy disputes under the old Act, but not to many other kinds of bankruptcy disputes, including most of those that arise in a reorganization. Moreover, the difficulties of transplanting the plenary-summary distinction from the old Act to the new Code would have been formidable. But, following *Marathon*, courts of appeals also relied on the existence of 28 U.S.C. §1334 as sustaining the full Emergency Rule.

The Emergency Rule raised another problem. Even if district courts had jurisdiction to hear bankruptcy disputes, they may have lacked the power to delegate all their power to bankruptcy judges. Even assuming that the division of authority between Article III district courts and non-Article III bankruptcy judges is constitutional if enacted by Congress, it does not necessarily follow that the federal courts could institute such a scheme on their own motion. The bankruptcy judges had no statutory power, but because of the transition provisions in effect, they remained employed, under the provisions of the Bankruptcy Reform Act of 1978, until April 1984. Congress, while attempting to work out its resolution to the jurisdictional problem, found it necessary to extend that date several additional times, and finally enacted the 1984 Amendments two days after the last such extension expired. It is not clear, however, that federal courts could delegate their work (even if it were subject to de novo review) to other federal employees who were willing to do the work and who had nothing else to do. The power to appoint a special master under Federal Rules of Civil Procedure 53 had always been done before on a case-by-case basis. One district court struck down the Emergency Rule on the ground that the delegation was too broad, but used his powers under Rule 53 to refer the matter before him to a bankruptcy judge in any event. In re Matlock Trailer Corp., 27 Bankr. 318 (M.D. Tenn. 1983).

The last question involving the Emergency Rule was whether the power that bankruptcy judges exercised, assuming that district courts otherwise had the power to delegate it to them, fell within the proscriptions of *Marathon*. This question is closely allied with the question of whether the jurisdictional provisions of the 1984 Bankruptcy Amendments are themselves constitutional, a subject to which we now turn.

B. JURISDICTION UNDER THE 1984 BANKRUPTCY AMENDMENTS

NOTE ON THE JURISDICTIONAL PROVISIONS OF THE 1984 AMENDMENTS

The 1984 Amendments purported to extend the terms of the bankruptcy judges who had been serving under the provisions of the Bankruptcy Reform Act of 1978 until new judges could be appointed for 14-year terms. As we previously noted, the legislation that had authorized such interim terms for the bankruptcy judges expired (as extended by Congress) two days before Congress passed the amendments and almost two weeks before the President signed them into law. The "extension" of the terms of the pre-existing bankruptcy judges may not itself be constitutional. Article II of the Constitution provides that the President has the power to appoint:

> Judges of the Supreme Court, and all other Officers of the United States . . . but the Congress may by Law vest the Appointment of such inferior Officers, as they think proper, in the President alone, in the Courts of Law, or in the Heads of Departments.

The Court has inferred from this provision that Congress itself does not have the power to appoint officers of the United States. See Buckley v. Valeo, 424 U.S. 1 (1976). One could argue that because the term of all bankruptcy judges had expired, what Congress did was not an extension of existing terms of federal officers, which might be within its power, but a de novo appointment of federal officers, which is not. The Department of Justice has taken this position, but to date the district courts have held that the statute is constitutional. See, e.g., In re Benny, 44 Bankr. 581 (N.D. Cal. 1984).

The actual jurisdictional provisions of the amendments present many additional problems. If bankruptcy judges do not have life tenure and if they make decisions that are subject only to appellate review, one has to make a distinction between affecting conventional causes of action that constitute the exercise of the judicial power and those that do not. Congress was not going to give Article III status to bankruptcy judges and it was not going to make district judges review all bankruptcy decisions de novo. Therefore it had to draw some kind of line, and the summary-plenary line of the 1898 Act, or something similar to it, may have been no worse than any other.

But before we look at the potential problems that lurk in the jurisdictional provisions, we should get an overview of how they work. The place to begin is the new 28 U.S.C. §1334. It provides that district courts shall have exclusive jurisdiction of all cases under Title 11 and original, but not exclusive jurisdiction of all cases arising under Title 11, or arising in, or related to cases under Title 11. In all cases in which a district court does not have exclusive jurisdiction, it may abstain "in the interest of justice or in the interest of comity with State courts or respect for state law."

Section 1334 further provides that in related proceedings district courts must abstain if there would be no federal jurisdiction in the absence of the bankruptcy petition provided that "an action is commenced, and can be timely adjudicated, in a State forum of appropriate jurisdiction." It is not clear whether abstention is required only in cases that have already been commenced in state court or in cases that can be brought in state court, but have not yet been. Nor is it clear what "timely adjudication" means. In many state courts, simple contract disputes may take several years to go to trial and appeals may take several additional years. But even if the trial and appeals can be exhausted in a single year, it is not necessarily a timely adjudication, if the bankruptcy proceeding otherwise could be wrapped up in several months. The legislative history suggests the abstention provisions were enacted because of the fear that Congress did not have the power under the Constitution to let federal courts adjudicate related proceedings that involved no federal issue. This concern, as a matter of constitutional law, is close to frivolous. It is in any event undercut by 28 U.S.C. §157(b)(2)(B) and (4) that provide that the mandatory abstention provisions do not apply to the liquidation or estimation of contingent or unliquidated personal injury tort or wrongful death claims against the estate. (Such actions, not being related proceedings, would not have been affected by the mandatory abstention provision in any event.)

The crucial jurisdictional provision is 28 U.S.C. §157. It provides that the district courts may refer all cases under Title 11 and any or all proceedings arising under Title 11 or arising in or related to a case under Title 11 to bankruptcy judges. It then draws a distinction between "core proceedings" and "noncore proceedings" based roughly along the summary-plenary line. (Some proceedings that were considered plenary, such as proceedings to set aside voidable preferences made to parties who did not themselves assert a claim against the debtor's assets, are nevertheless included in the definition of "core proceedings.") A core proceeding is subject only to appellate review. Bankruptcy judges may hear noncore proceedings, if otherwise related to a bankruptcy case, and may decide them with the consent of the parties. In other cases, if the bankruptcy judge hears a noncore proceeding, he is to prepare proposed findings of fact and conclusions of law for the district court. Any matter — including core proceedings — before a bankruptcy court can be withdrawn by the district court on its own motion or on motion of a party. Finally, the statute requires the district court to withdraw a proceeding from a bankruptcy court "if the court determines that resolution of the proceeding requires consideration of both Title 11 and other laws of the United States regulating organizations or activities affecting interstate commerce." 28 U.S.C. §157(d).

PROBLEMS

13.1 Northern and Marathon enter into a contract. Each accuses the other of breach and threatens to sue for damages. Before either sues, Northern files a bankruptcy petition. The district court with jurisdiction over the bankruptcy proceeding does not have to abstain and relegate the dispute between Northern and Marathon to a state court, because there is diversity between the parties and hence an independent basis for federal jurisdiction. In the bankruptcy proceeding, Marathon files a claim against Northern for the damages it asserts it suffered as a result of Northern's breach. The trustee for Northern seeks to have a bankruptcy judge determine whether and how much Marathon owes as a result of its breach of the same contract. Is this proceeding a core proceeding? See 28 U.S.C. §157(b)(2)(C). Can a non-Article III judge resolve this dispute and be subject only to appellate review? See *Marathon,* supra.

13.2 Debtor is owed $100,000 by a Fortune 500 company for services it has already performed and that the company has already acknowledged as satisfactory. Payment from the company is due in 90 days. To raise cash,

Debtor wants to assign its right to collect $100,000 from the company in 90 days to Bank. Is approval of this sale a core proceeding? See 28 U.S.C. § 157(b)(2)(N). Should it be?

13.3 Debtor sold asbestos for a number of years. It files a bankruptcy petition in January 1985 and among its creditors are thousands of victims of asbestosis. Where will their rights to a share of Debtor's assets be adjudicated? 28 U.S.C. § 157(b)(4) seems to call off the mandatory abstention provisions of 28 U.S.C. § 1334. 28 U.S.C. § 157(b)(5) provides that personal injury tort and wrongful death claims be tried in the district court in which the bankruptcy case is pending or in the district court in the district in which the claim arose. But what does this mean? Is it simply a venue provision that establishes in what district a case should be heard? Does it say anything about whether a district judge has to try the case himself? Does 28 U.S.C. § 157(c)(1) allow a district judge to refer it to a bankruptcy judge subject to de novo review?

Can the victims insist upon a jury trial? Note that 28 U.S.C. § 1411 provides that neither Title 28 nor Title 11 affect any right to trial by jury that an individual has under applicable nonbankruptcy law with regard to a personal injury or wrongful death claim. Assuming that bankruptcy judges can have proceedings involving these claims refered to them, can they conduct jury trials? Or is conducting a jury trial an exercise of the "judicial power" within the meaning of Article III? In conducting a de novo review, would the district court have to conduct another jury trial?

NOTE ON THE RIGHT TO A JURY TRIAL

Because 28 U.S.C. § 1411 deals only with certain issues, it is limited in its scope. What right to a jury trial is there otherwise? Any interpretation of the right to a jury trial in bankruptcy needs to start with a consideration of Katchen v. Landy, 382 U.S. 323 (1966). In *Katchen,* the petitioner was an accommodation maker on a debt of the corporate bankrupt (of which petitioner was an officer). Petitioner made payments on the debt out of a corporate trust fund that was in his control. These payments were alleged to be preferential as to the petitioner, on the "indirect preference" ground that we have seen in connection with *Church Buildings and Interiors,* supra page 297. Under the summary-plenary jurisdiction under the old Bankruptcy Act, petitioner had possession of the property in question, so, to recover the preference, the trustee would have to sue petitioner in state court, in a plenary suit. And in that suit petitioner would have a right to a jury trial.

But petitioner became trapped in the "implied consent" doctrine. He filed a claim in the bankruptcy proceeding for (a) past-due rent and (b) a payment he made on the note. The trustee responded with a petition alleging a voidable preference. Justice White, for the Court, concluded that there was summary jurisdiction. He then went on to say that, insofar as the Seventh Amendment was concerned, the fact that someone had a right to a jury trial of the preference issue *outside* of bankruptcy, did not necessarily mean that that person was entitled to a jury trial *in* bankruptcy. For, Justice White stated, bankruptcy courts "are essentially courts of equity." Therefore, "when the same issue arises as part of the process of allowance and disallowance of claims, it is triable in equity. The Bankruptcy Act . . . converts the creditor's legal claim into an equitable claim to a pro rata share of the res. . . ."

Does this mean that there is no Seventh Amendment right to try anything by jury once one concludes that there is bankruptcy court jurisdiction? That is one possible reading of *Katchen*. Another possible reading of it is to see it as talking only about things intimately and traditionally connected with the administration of bankruptcy estates, such as the allowance of claims — things that become, in Justice White's words, "an equitable claim to a pro rata share of the res. . . ." A problem with this, however, is that the determination of what the assets of the estate are seems as intimately connected with the bankruptcy process as does the determination of what the claims are.

Thus, the Seventh Amendment right to a jury trial in bankruptcy court seems uncertain. Any interpretation of the Constitution that provides for a right to a jury trial in bankruptcy introduces serious problems if bankruptcy judges are unable to conduct jury trials, because both core and noncore proceedings are conducted initially by bankruptcy judges. If de novo review by an Article III court required a jury trial, the caseload of the district judges would be increased dramatically. If bankruptcy judges can conduct jury trials, should a distinction be drawn between core and noncore proceedings? In considering this question, 28 U.S.C. §1411 is unhelpfully silent. The jury trial provision it replaced in 1984, however, was broader but even more cryptic. It read:

> (a) Except as provided in subsection (b) of this section, this chapter and title 11 do not affect any right to trial by jury, in a case under title 11 or in a proceeding arising under title 11 or arising in or related to a case under title 11, that is provided by any statute in effect on September 30, 1979.
>
> (b) The bankruptcy court may order the issues arising under section 303 of title 11 to be tried without a jury.

28 U.S.C. §1480 (repealed, 1984). In interpreting that provision, several courts concluded that the right to a jury trial should turn on whether the issue would have been decided in plenary jurisdiction under the old Bankruptcy Act (making that the relevant "statute"). If it would have been then a right to a jury trial exists under the Bankruptcy Code. See, e.g., In re Fidelity American Financial Corp., 20 Bankr. 115 (Bankr. E.D. Pa. 1982); In re Portage Associates, 16 Bankr. 445 (Bankr. N.D. Ohio 1982). Is this

interpretation still likely to be followed under 28 U.S.C. §1411? In any event, should either the core-noncore or the summary-plenary distinction be of constitutional dimension?

Another possibility suggested when 28 U.S.C. §1480 was in force (see In re First Financial Group of Texas, 11 Bankr. 67 (Bankr. S.D. Tex. 1981) was that bankruptcy courts should now be treated as other federal trial courts. Under this view, the court, following the Federal Rules of Civil Procedure, looks to the nature of the cause of action, not to the type of court. A third possibility considered at that time was that one looked to the essential *administrative* tasks of the bankruptcy court. As to those matters, there was no right to a jury trial. But as to disputes between a trustee and adverse claimants, one was to look to nonbankruptcy law to determine whether there was a jury trial right. Other possibilities abound, see, e.g., In re Professional Air Traffic Controllers Organization, 23 Bankr. 271 (D.D.C. 1982); In re Fleming, 8 Bankr. 746 (N.D. Ga. 1980) (because federal law governs, the "sole inquiry is whether the Seventh Amendment provides a right to jury trial"). What impact, if any, do these have on jury trials under the Bankruptcy Code, now that 28 U.S.C. §1411 is silent outside of its narrow category of cases?

PROBLEMS

13.4 Debtor promises to buy corn from Seller at $4 a bushel. The price of corn plummets, and the prevailing market price of corn is $2 a bushel when Debtor files a bankruptcy petition. Trustee wants to reject the contract and seeks court approval as §365(a) requires. Is the hearing on whether to reject an executory contract a "core proceeding"?

13.5 Debtor files a bankruptcy petition. After following the procedures that §1113 lays down, Debtor applies to the court for a rejection of its collective bargaining agreement with its employees. Is this hearing a "core proceeding"? In any event can it be heard by a bankruptcy judge if one of the parties objects? 28 U.S.C. §157(d) requires the district court to withdraw a proceeding if the resolution of the proceeding requires consideration of bankruptcy law and other laws of the United States regulating organizations or activities affecting interstate commerce. Could a district court find that federal labor law did not have to be considered and hence the entire matter could be resolved, at least initially, by the bankruptcy judge?

13.6 Debtor files a bankruptcy petition. Debtor's trustee alleges that Debtor was driven out of business by Predator Corporation, which sold its goods at unreasonably low prices in order to drive Debtor out of business. Trustee brings an antitrust action against Predator. Predator moves to withdraw the proceeding from the bankruptcy judge. Must the district court withdraw the case under 28 U.S.C. §157(d) or can it conclude it is under no such obligation, because the proceeding requires consideration only of laws of the United States affecting interstate commerce, not any issue under Title 11? Does it make sense to leave only those antitrust cases that have nothing to do with bankruptcy law with bankruptcy judges and require others that do involve bankruptcy questions to be heard by district judges? Are district judges likely to adopt this interpretation?

13.7 Debtor files a bankruptcy petition. Worker files a claim against Debtor. Worker alleges that Debtor refused to hire him because he was black and that Debtor violated his rights under Title VII of the 1964 Civil Rights Act. Worker argues that his claim must be heard before a district judge, because the proceeding requires consideration of Title 11 (whether he has a claim under §101(4)) and a federal law affecting interstate commerce (the Civil Rights Act was passed under the aegis of Congress' commerce power). Should he prevail? If he does not, is a determination of the size of his claim a core proceeding?

13.8 Debtor files a bankruptcy petition. Bank has a security interest in Debtor's airplane. Should the hearing on whether Bank's security interest is being adequately protected be before a district court? (Federal law requires that security interests in airplanes be recorded with the Federal Aviation Administration.) If the bankruptcy judge hears the case initially, is it a core proceeding? Would the district court have to hear it if the trustee asserted that Bank did not properly perfect its security interest?

13.9 Debtor files a bankruptcy petition. Workers have set up a picket line and threaten to keep it in place until they are paid pre-petition wages. Debtor tries to assert that the picket line violates the automatic stay (recall *Crowe*, supra page 397). The workers assert that no federal court can enjoin them from picketing because of the Norris-LaGuardia Act. If one of the parties seeks it, must this dispute be heard before a district judge? Assume that the court refuses to enjoin the picketing. In order to pay the workers (and reopen its plant), Debtor seeks the approval of the bankruptcy court to borrow from Bank and grant Bank a first priority claim to its unencumbered assets under §364(b). One of the general creditors objects on the ground that Bank is simply substituting itself for workers and hence is entitled only to a third priority claim under §507 (or, alternatively, that because of the antisubrogation provision of §507(d), Bank is entitled only to a general claim against Debtor's assets).

Bank is fearful that on appeal the district court will find that it acted in bad faith in making the loan and hence is not entitled to priority under §364(b) notwithstanding bankruptcy court approval. (Recall §364(e) and *EDC Holding Co.*, supra page 536.) Is there a way that Debtor can have the district court approve the extension of credit and the grant of the administrative priority before Bank lends the money? Should the Bankruptcy Code provide for a certification procedure such as existed under the Emergency Rule, which allowed the bankruptcy judge to certify that circumstances required immediate review by the district judge and required the district judge to review the matter and enter an order or judgment as soon as possible?

NOTE ON THE LIMITS OF 28 U.S.C. §1334

To this point, we have been examining problems concerning which court, as between the bankruptcy court and the district court, should hear a given dispute under 28 U.S.C. §157. There is, however, a somewhat different jurisdiction issue, raised by 28 U.S.C. §1334, which provides that district courts "shall have original and exclusive jurisdiction of all cases under title 11" as well as "original but not exclusive jurisdiction of all civil proceedings arising under title 11, or arising in or related to cases under title 11." Here, the question is whether 28 U.S.C. §1334 provides a jurisdictional basis for the district court (and, a fortiori, the bankruptcy court) to hear a particular dispute. The next case and the problems that follow examine the limits on the scope of disputes that can be resolved in a bankruptcy proceeding.

IN RE BRENTANO'S, INC.
27 Bankr. 90 (Bankr. S.D.N.Y. 1983), remanded, 36 Bankr. 90
(S.D.N.Y. 1984)

John J. GALGAY, Bankruptcy Judge.

MacMillan Inc. moved to stay Pine Realty, Inc., a California corporation, from proceeding in California state court, or any other forum other than this bankruptcy court, against MacMillan, upon or in connection with a lease entered into by Brentano's, Inc., the chapter 11 debtor in this Court, with Pine Realty. MacMillan is a guarantor for the lease. . . .

BACKGROUND

In December 1977, Brentano's entered into a lease with Pine Realty for premises located in Westwood, California for the period September 1, 1978 through August 31, 1983. In connection with this lease, MacMillan executed a guaranty agreement. Pine Realty asserts that the guaranty was accepted in lieu of a security deposit and that it guaranteed full performance of the lease. On May 21, 1982, Brentano's filed a petition under chapter 11 of the Bankruptcy Reform Act of 1978 ("Code"). Pine Realty has filed a claim for pre-petition rent due and an administrative claim for post-petition arrears. In July 1982, Pine Realty commenced a suit in California Superior Court against MacMillan based upon the guaranty.

Brentano's is obligated to indemnify MacMillan for liability incurred by MacMillan on the guaranty. MacMillan has executed similar guaranty agreements in connection with 11 Brentano's leases. Brentano's is also liable for indemnification of MacMillan on those guaranty agreements. Brentano's contingent liability on these indemnification obligations approaches $8 million (including trade debt, MacMillan's potential claims exceed $8 million). MacMillan is the largest unsecured creditor; the disposition of its claim is one of the most important aspects (if not the most important) of the debtor's efforts to reorganize.

ISSUE

The issue before this Court is whether the California suit is "related to" the Chapter 11 proceeding before this Court, thus conferring jurisdiction upon the Bankruptcy Court pursuant to section 1471 of title 28 of the United States Code. If such jurisdiction exists, the Court must determine whether an order staying the California suit is "necessary and appropriate to carry out the provisions of [title 11]." 11 U.S.C. §105(a).

JURISDICTION

Section 1471, 28 U.S.C. §1471, in pertinent part, states:

> (b) . . . The district courts shall have original but not exclusive jurisdiction of all civil proceedings arising under title 11 or arising in or related to cases under title 11.
> (c) The Bankruptcy court for the district in which a case under title 11 is commenced shall exercise all of the jurisdiction conferred by this section on the district courts.

In order to determine whether a proceeding is "related to" a reorganization case,

> [t]he fundamental question . . . is whether the determination of the claims against the Non-Debtor will or will not affect the Debtor's assets and/or liabilities as they existed at the date of the petition and its bankruptcy schedules. The criteria to be adopted in such a situation will undoubtedly be related to a determination of whether the outcome of the proceeding could conceivably have *any effect upon the estate* being administered in bankruptcy. 1 Collier on Bankruptcy [¶3.01] at 3-49 [(15th ed. 1979)].

In re U.S. Air Duct Corp., 8 B.R. 848, 851 (Bkrtcy. N.D.N.Y. 1981). It has been held that the bankruptcy court has jurisdiction over a non-debtor third party guarantor of a debt. In re Lucasa International, Ltd., 6 B.R. 717 (Bkrtcy. S.D.N.Y. 1980). In *Lucasa* the trustee of the debtor commenced an adversary proceeding to recover a preference from a creditor. The creditor commenced a third party action against an alleged guarantor. On a motion to dismiss the third party complaint, the Court held that it had jurisdiction over the third party guarantor. The Court found that the third party action was sufficiently related to the debtor's bankruptcy proceeding. The Court reasoned that since the trustee's preference action was a civil proceeding clearly arising under the bankruptcy case, "[i]t follows, therefore, that the defendant's third party suit against . . . [its guarantor] . . . , is also a civil proceeding arising in and related to the Lucasa bankruptcy. Manifestly, therefore, this court has jurisdiction for all of this within the pervasive jurisdiction given bankruptcy courts by new 28 U.S.C. §1471(b) read with subsection (c)." Id. at 719.

Further support for the pervasiveness of the bankruptcy court's jurisdiction may be found in In re Brothers Coal Company, Inc., 6 B.R. 567 (Bkrtcy. W.D. Va. 1980). In the *Brothers Coal* case the bankruptcy court held that it had jurisdiction over an action by a creditor against a non-debtor guarantor of the debtor's obligation. . . .

The California state court action is clearly "related to" the Brentano's reorganization case before this Court and falls within this Court's jurisdictional grant. Underlying the entire matter is Brentano's lease (which Brentano's has rejected). If Pine Realty prevails against MacMillan, MacMillan can recover from Brentano's under its indemnification agreement. The disposition of this claim and other similar claims involving Brentano's leases, MacMillan guaranties, and the Brentano's-MacMillan indemnification agreement will ultimately determine the fate of this reorganization effort. This Court has jurisdiction over the Pine Realty action against MacMillan which is based on the MacMillan guaranty agreement.

STAY

Code section 105 authorizes this Court to "issue any order . . . that is necessary or appropriate to carry out the provisions of this title." 11 U.S.C. §105(a). The order staying Pine Realty is clearly necessary and appropriate in the Brentano's bankruptcy case. As noted above, the claims of MacMillan arising from the guaranty and indemnification agreements amount to the largest unsecured debt in the Brentano's case. Only this Court has a global view of the Brentano's case and reorganization efforts. Disposition of the largest unsecured claims in this forum will facilitate Brentano's efforts to formulate a plan of reorganization. Indeed, in this Court, settlements have been reached with lessors on three Brentano's leases involving MacMillan guaranty agreements. Multiple and haphazard state court litigations will delay and deter ultimate resolution of the bankruptcy case. This comment is not a criticism of state court proceedings; however, each forum has a restricted view of the factors and parties involved. This Court has an overall view of the Brentano's case and all aspects of that case should be before this Court, particularly actions that may determine whether reorganization efforts succeed. . . .

NOTE

In re Brentano's Inc., 36 Bankr. 90 (S.D.N.Y. 1984), remanded the case to the bankruptcy court for reconsideration in light of changed circumstances. It also noted:

> While 11 U.S.C. §105(a) does grant the bankruptcy court broad powers to issue any order "necessary or appropriate to carry out the provisions of this title," it is an extraordinary exercise of discretion to use that power to stay a third party action not involving the debtor. . . . In this case, the Court is not convinced that the stay order was necessary to an orderly disposition of the debtor's estate. Brentano's was required to indemnify MacMillan for any liability incurred by MacMillan on the guarantee. Thus, the only effect on Brentano's estate of *not* staying the California action would have been to substitute MacMillan's claim for indemnification for Pine Realty's claim pursuant to the lease. This circumstance does not, in the Court's view, justify depriving Pine Realty of its contractually bargained for right to seek judicial redress directly against the guarantor.

NOTE ON *BRENTANO'S*

Although the issue in *Brentano's* is one of whether an action should be stayed, that in turn rests on jurisdiction. Does the bankruptcy court have jurisdiction under 28 U.S.C. §1334 to hear this suit by two parties, neither of which is in bankruptcy? Is this a proceeding that is "related to" Brentano's bankruptcy case? As noted by the district court in remanding the case, if MacMillan loses, it files a claim against Brentano's. The effect of that is that MacMillan's claim for indemnification takes the place of Pine Realty's claim. Does this mean that there is not jurisdiction pursuant to 28 U.S.C. §1334, because Brentano's is unconcerned about *who* is asserting the claim?

Before concluding that there should be no jurisdiction in this case, is the issue as clear-cut as it might first appear? When MacMillan files the claim, is Brentano's bound by the determination in the action by MacMillan against Pine Realty? If it is, then isn't the dispute between MacMillan and Pine Realty in essence fixing a claim against Brentano's, and isn't that related to the bankruptcy case? See §502. If Brentano's is not bound by that determination, on the other hand, then it may not seem to be related to Brentano's bankruptcy case, but what position does that leave MacMillan in? Isn't MacMillan then subject to a risk of inconsistent adjudication? If so, is this reason enough to conclude that this suit should be within the jurisdictional ambit of 28 U.S.C. §1334?

Because of 28 U.S.C. §157, there would now be a separate issue in this case. Even if it is within 28 U.S.C. §1334, there would still be a question of whether the bankruptcy court or the district court was to hear the dispute. Finally, there is a removal question lurking in this case. As we will see in examining the removal provisions, if this case is removed to bankruptcy court, it will be removed to the bankruptcy court for the Central District of California, 28 U.S.C. §1452(a). Brentano's bankruptcy case, however, has been filed in the Southern District of New York. Is it so clear that this case is going to make it to the Southern District of New York, as apparently Judge Galgay wants? Alternatively, can Judge Galgay just start estimating MacMillan's claim against Brentano's, under §502(c), irrespective of the proceeding going on in California?

PROBLEMS

13.10 Cross, as subcontractor, entered into a contract with Driggs, as main contractor, to perform certain contract duties in the construction of a rest stop on a public highway. The contract contained an arbitration clause covering all claims, disputes, and other matters arising out of or relating to the contract or breach thereof. A dispute arises concerning Cross's work. Cross files a petition in bankruptcy. May the bankruptcy court hear and decide the dispute, notwithstanding the arbitration clause? See In re Cross Electric Co., 9 Bankr. 408 (Bankr. W.D. Va. 1981).

13.11 On April 1, Debtor files a bankruptcy petition. Debtor's spouse, Husband, wants to obtain a divorce from Debtor. Debtor and Husband are unable to agree as to the grounds for divorce, custody of the children, or division of the property. Where should Husband file for divorce? Does the bankruptcy court have jurisdiction to try the divorce? Is it required to abstain under 28 U.S.C. §1334(c)(2)? What if Husband seeks alimony from Debtor? Is he a "creditor" within the meaning of a Bankruptcy Code? If he is, is the dispute between him and debtor one that arises under Title 11, rather than one related to a case arising under Title 11? For a discussion of this issue under the 1978 Bankruptcy Reform Act, see In re Cunningham, 9 Bankr. 70 (Bankr. D.N.M. 1981); cf. In re Heslar, 16 Bankr. 329 (Bankr. N.D. Mich. 1981). Will it be necessary in any event to obtain relief from the automatic stay before filing for divorce? See In re Pagitt, 3 Bankr. 588 (Bankr. W.D. La. 1980).

13.12 Benjamin sells to Jack all the stock of Company. Benjamin subsequently sues Jack to rescind the sale of the stock, on the ground that Jack defrauded Benjamin. Company files for bankruptcy. Would the bankruptcy court have jurisdiction to hear the dispute between Benjamin and Jack? See In re Hurt, 9 Bankr. 386 (Bankr. N.D. Ga 1980).

13.13 Parent owns all the stock of Subsidiary. Creditor sues Subsidiary for breach of a contract. Parent files for bankruptcy. Subsidiary is not in bankruptcy. Does the bankruptcy court have jurisdiction over the suit by Creditor against Subsidiary? Under the old Bankruptcy Act, several courts answered this question in the negative. See, e.g., In re Adolf Gobel,

Inc., 80 F.2d 849 (2d Cir. 1936) (suit against subsidiary does not become part of parent's bankruptcy proceeding merely because the suit may reduce the value of the stock in the subsidiary); cf. In re Bankers Trust Co., 566 F.2d 1281 (5th Cir. 1978). Does 28 U.S.C. §1334 change that result?

13.14 H & R Ice Co. is a debtor in a Chapter 11 proceeding. At the time it filed its bankruptcy petition, there existed accrued but unpaid withholding and FICA taxes due the United States of $16,000. A plan of reorganization is proposed whereby the United States will eventually be paid, without interest, its taxes. The United States then informs Bennett, the President of H & R Ice, that it intends to assess a 100 percent penalty against him pursuant to §§6672 of the Internal Revenue Code of 1954. This penalty liability is personal to Bennett and not derivative, but it arises from the failure of H & R Ice to pay its taxes. Does the bankruptcy court have jurisdiction over this assessment? May it enjoin the IRS from assessing this penalty? See §505(a)(1); In re H & R Ice Co., 24 Bankr. 28 (Bankr. W.D. Mo. 1982); In re Major Dynamics, Inc., 14 Bankr. 969 (Bankr. S.D. Cal. 1981).

NOTE ON IN PERSONAM JURISDICTION

Subject matter jurisdiction is the topic of 28 U.S.C. §1334. What about personal jurisdiction? May a bankruptcy court in New York exercise personal jurisdiction over a creditor in California? Would it matter if a New York court were not able to assert such jurisdiction, (under International Shoe Co. v. Washington, 326 U.S. 310 (1945)), if the dispute had been brought in a state court in New York? The bankruptcy courts have held that the concept of "minimum contacts" is not relevant, because the jurisdiction of a federal court when applying a federal statue is not limited by state law, nor by state law jurisdictional concepts such as "minimum contacts." Instead, bankruptcy court personal jurisdiction is nationwide. See In re American Aluminum Window Corp., 15 Bankr. 803 (Bankr. D. Mass. 1981); see also In re Coby Glass Products Co., 22 Bankr. 961 (Bankr. D.R.I. 1982); In re Nixon Machinery Co., 15 Bankr. 131 (Bankr. E.D. Tenn. 1981); In re G. Weeks Securities, 5 Bankr. 220 (Bankr. W.D. Tenn. 1980); cf. Hogue v. Milodon Engineering, 736 F.2d 989 (4th Cir. 1984) (old Act case holding nationwide service of process authorized by Congress and held, under the facts of that case, consistent with due process).

C. VENUE AND REMOVAL

NOTE ON VENUE

At first reading, the venue provisions of 28 U.S.C. §§1408 and 1409 seem quite narrow and precise. Section 1408 specifies where a bankruptcy case may be brought. Section 1409, by contrast, deals with proceedings "arising under or related to" such cases. The various subsections of that section can be classified into groups. Section 1409(a) and (e) are the only subsections dealing with claims or proceedings brought *against* the trustee. Subsection (a), which also applies, in general, to suits *by* a trustee, states that the suit is to be brought in the court where the bankruptcy case is "pending." Subsection (e) governs venue of proceedings based on a claim against the trustee that arose out of the post-petition operation of the debtor's business; there, the plaintiff may choose, in addition to the "home" bankruptcy court, the bankruptcy court for the district where the claim could have been brought, but for the intervention of bankruptcy.

Subsections (b), (c), and (d) all deal with where the trustee may bring suits. Subsections (b) and (c) deal with matters other than post-petition claims of the trustee, as these are dealt with in subsection (d). Subsection (b) states that suits by the trustee to recover money or property worth less than $1,000 ($5,000 in the case of a consumer debt) may be brought only in the bankruptcy court for the district where the defendant resides, calling off the general applicability of subsection (a). Subsection (c), which is an alternative to subsection (a) for the trustee who fits in (c), deals with proceedings by the trustee on causes of action belonging to him as the statutory successor to the debtor (§541) or the creditors (§544(b)). And these claims, in addition to the places listed in subsection (a), may also be brought in the bankruptcy court for the district where the suit could have been brought if bankruptcy had not intervened. Finally, suits by the trustee based on post-petition claims, under subsection (d), may be brought only in the bankruptcy court for the district where suit could have been brought if bankruptcy had not intervened, again calling off the general applicability of subsection (a).

PROBLEM

13.15 Debtor filed for bankruptcy in the bankruptcy court for the Eastern District of Pennsylvania. Debtor lived in New Jersey. Debtor contended that, having been employed in the Eastern District of Pennsylvania for more than six months, venue was properly located in the Eastern District of Pennsylvania. Do you agree? May the court keep the case even if venue was not properly located? See Barnes v. Whelan, 689 F.2d 193 (D.C. Cir. 1982); In re Vann, 3 Bankr. 192 (Bankr. E.D. Pa. 1980).

IN RE BURLEY
27 Bankr. 603 (9th Cir. Bankr. App. 1982), rev'd on other grounds,
738 F.2d 981 (9th Cir. 1984)

KATZ, Bankruptcy Judge.

Appellants appeal from an order of the bankruptcy court denying their motion to vacate the order of discharge entered in the bankruptcy proccedings filed by the Burleys.

The salient facts are that the Burleys filed a Petition for Relief Under Chapter 7 of the Bankruptcy Code in the Central District of California.

The Brineys are creditors of the debtors as a result of a judgment having been entered in their favor in the state courts of Colorado and are the debtors' only creditors.

Upon receiving notice of the filing of the bankruptcy, which advised them of the time within which to file complaints objecting to the discharge or to determine dischargeability of debt, the Brineys timely filed such a complaint in the bankruptcy court for the District of Colorado. The clerk of the bankruptcy court in the Central District of California was notified of the timely filing of the complaint.

Thereafter, the Burleys moved in the Colorado court to dismiss the complaint for improper venue or in the alternative to transfer the proceeding to the California court. The motions were denied and the matters were set for trial.

Subscquently the California bankruptcy court entered the discharge of the Burleys. A motion under F.R.C.P. 60(b) and Bankruptcy Rule 924 to vacate the order of discharge was made by appellants and denied. The court below denied the motion on the grounds that the Colorado court had no authority to retain the proceedings under applicable law.

In its decision, In re Burley, 11 B.R. 369, the court concluded that it was free to grant the debtors a discharge despite the timely filed complaints pending in Colorado. The court below recognized that the Colorado court had jurisdiction to accept, process and file the creditors' complaint, but that venue was improper and therefore the Colorado court could not have retained the proceedings for ultimate disposition.

We agree with the trial court on the determination that the Colorado court had jurisdiction over the Brineys' complaint. We disagree on the venue issue and therefore reverse and remand with instructions to grant the motion of appellants to vacate the Order of Discharge.

In determining the venue issue, one must look to 28 U.S.C. §§1473, 1475 and 1477, as well as legislative history.

28 U.S.C. §1473 provides, in subdivision (a) thereof:

> Except as provided in subsections (b) and (d) of this section, a proceeding arising in or related to a case under title 11 *may* be commenced in the bankruptcy court in which such case is pending. [Emphasis added.]

The word "may" is permissive, indicating that while a proceeding may be filed in the court wherein the case is pending it may also be filed in another court.

The term "proceeding" in the Code is used in its broadest terms to include anything that occurs in a case. H.R. Rep. No. 95-595, 95th Cong., 1st Sess. 445 (1977), U.S. Code Cong. & Admin. News 1978, p. 5787.

28 U.S.C. §1477(a) states:

> The bankruptcy court of a district in which is filed a case or proceeding laying venue in the wrong division or district may, in the interest of justice and for the convenience of the parties, retain such case or proceeding, or may transfer, under section 1475 of this title, such case or proceeding to any other district or division.

These matters, taken together, indicate that any proceeding which includes disputes relating to administrative matters may be heard in a bankruptcy court other than the court in which the case is pending if it is in the interest of justice and for the convenience of the parties to do so.

We do not have before us the record of the Colorado court of the hearing on the motion to dismiss filed by the Burleys. Hence, whether the Colorado court abused its discretion in not granting that motion, thereby retaining venue, is not before us.

What is before us is the question of whether the California court abused its discretion in refusing to set aside the discharge. In basing its ruling on its belief that venue was improper, we think the court below was in error.

Reversed and remanded with instructions.

HUGHES, Bankruptcy Judge, dissenting.

I respectfully dissent because I believe the trial court properly denied the creditors' motion to vacate the debtors' order of discharge.

I

The essential facts, which are few, bear reiteration. The Burleys filed a petition under Chapter 7 of the Bankruptcy Code in the Central District of California. Their only creditors, the Brineys, filed a two-count complaint (1) objecting to discharge and (2) seeking an order holding their judgment nondischargeable in bankruptcy. The Brineys' complaint was filed in the District of Colorado.

The Burleys appeared before the Colorado bankruptcy court on a motion to dismiss or to change venue to California. The motion was denied by the Colorado court and the Burleys answered the complaint.

Meanwhile, the California court fixed the last date for filing objections to discharge. Bankruptcy Rule 404(a). A copy of the complaint filed in Colorado was lodged with the California court before the bar date, and the Brineys' attorney wrote to the California court requesting that entry of discharge be delayed, but no objection to discharge was ever filed in California.

Orders of discharge were entered by the California court pursuant to 11 U.S.C. §727 on March 19, 1981 and the Brineys' moved that court to vacate those orders pursuant to Rule 60(b), Fed. R. Civ. P., on March 27, 1981. The trial court denied the motion and the Brineys appealed.

That part of the Colorado complaint seeking an order holding the Brineys' judgment to be nondischargeable pursuant to 11 U.S.C. §523 was not affected by the motion below and is not before us.

II

The trial court summarized its reasons for denying the motion to vacate the Burleys' discharge orders. I summarize the summary:

The Colorado Court (1) had jurisdiction over the complaint objecting to discharge, but (2) lacked proper venue. Therefore, the trial court concluded, the motion should be denied. It also held that the facts did not justify exercise of discretion "to permit continuation of the 'proceeding' in Colorado."

I would affirm the order appealed on the ground that appellants have failed to establish that the trial judge abused his discretion, the standard of review for orders made on Rule 60(b) motions. . . . I would affirm notwithstanding my conclusion that the premises for the order were erroneous. Unlike the trial court, I would hold that the Colorado court lacked jurisdiction over the Burleys' discharge in bankruptcy. Furthermore, I believe that the trial court was not competent to question the Colorado court's venue rulings. Unlike the majority of this panel, I believe that the appeal ultimately turns on jurisdiction rather than venue.

I attempt to show in Part III that the Brineys failed to justify the relief they sought, in Part IV that the conflicting venue analyses of the trial court and the panel are beside the point; and in Part V that, contrary to the assumptions of the trial court and the panel, the Colorado court did not acquire jurisdiction to deny discharge to the Burleys.

III

The Brineys did not articulate a legal theory that would justify any interference with the Burleys' order of discharge in California, whether before or after it was entered. The Brineys first sought delay of entry of the discharge order and then vacation of the order on the following grounds:
1. The objection to discharge was timely filed in Colorado and notice of

the Colorado filing was timely given to the California court. 2. The Colorado court had jurisdiction over the objection to discharge. 3. The Colorado court had denied a motion to dismiss or change venue. I am unable to determine why the foregoing factors, accepted as true, affect the Burleys' discharge in California.

It is arguable that a Colorado judgment denying discharge to the Burleys would preclude the California court from entering discharge on res judicata grounds. . . . There was no judgment, however, so res judicata does not apply.

It is also arguable that the doctrine of federal comity is applicable. . . . but rulings under that doctrine are reversed only for an abuse of discretion. . . .

I conclude that there is no showing that the trial court should have withheld entry of discharge or that it abused its discretion in denying the motion to vacate the order after entry.

Nevertheless, I address the issues of venue and jurisdiction because the panel majority rests its decision of reversal on them.

IV

The panel and the trial court both consider venue determinative and both assume that the judgment of a court of improper venue may be ignored. (They differ in their conclusions, the panel holding that the Colorado venue ruling was correct). Both analyses are flawed because they treat rulings on venue as subject to collateral attack. To the contrary, venue is of concern only to the court whose venue is challenged, and to an appellate court on direct appeal.

Judgments may be collaterally attacked only for want of jurisdiction. . . . As was stated in Yale v. National Indemnity Co., 602 F.2d 642 (4th Cir. 1979), at 644,

> . . . the traditional rule, Restatement of Judgments §11 comment b . . . [is] that only void judgments are subject to collateral attack, and that a void judgment is only one that is rendered by a court lacking jurisdiction over the defendant or over the subject matter, or in violation of a procedural requirement so substantial that it is deemed . . . to be void, i.e., to be "jurisdictional."

Venue and jurisdiction are distinct concepts. Wright, Miller and Cooper Fed. Practice & Procedure §3826, p. 166-167. Unlike jurisdiction, venue does not involve the power or authority to adjudicate a controversy. It is a "forum limitation for the convenience of the parties." United States ex rel. Rudick v. Laird, 412 F.2d 16, 20 (2nd Cir. 1969). Proper venue is not a prerequisite to the rendition of a valid judgment. . . .

Accordingly, whether the Colorado court committed error with respect to venue is the exclusive concern of that court and of courts in which appeal from its judgments lie. Neither the Central District of California trial court nor this panel are in that line of appeal. Thus, I agree with the panel majority that the trial court erroneously disregarded the Colorado rulings on venue, but for different reasons.

V

The trial court's jurisdiction analysis is also flawed, in my opinion, because it considered the power of the Colorado court to render a valid judgment only as an abstract question of subject matter jurisdiction. It failed to consider whether the Colorado court had in fact acquired jurisdiction to deny the Burleys' discharge. As I now seek to demonstrate, even though the Colorado bankruptcy court had subject matter jurisdiction to grant or deny discharge in bankruptcy, its jurisdiction to deny the Burleys' discharge was never invoked. Accordingly, any judgment of the Colorado court denying discharge would be void and would not have res judicata effect.

A

A court can render a valid judgment only if it has (1) jurisdiction of the subject matter and (2) jurisdiction of the parties and then only if (3) subject matter and personal jurisdiction have been invoked. . . . We are concerned here only with the third requisite, i.e., whether a court has acquired subject matter jurisdiction over the matter in which judgment issues. (I assume but find it unnecessary to decide that the Colorado court had personal jurisdiction over the parties).

Subject matter jurisdiction may be invoked in a particular case only by following prescribed statutory procedure. . . .

The filing of proper pleadings is one requisite to invoking the court's jurisdiction over a particular matter. "The exercise of jurisdiction [is] conferred by the filing of a petition containing all the requisites and in the manner prescribed by law." The United States v. Arredondo, 31 U.S (6 Pet.) 691, 709, 8 L. Ed. 547 (1832). "[A] court can acquire jurisdiction in the concrete in a particular instance only when it is presented to the court as prescribed by law." Zarges v. Zarges, 79 N.M. 494, 445 P.2d 97, 99 (1968) quoting Riggs v. Moise, 344 Mo. 177, 128 S.W.2d 632, 635 (1939). . . .

A pleading that fails to present a claim on which relief can be granted does not invoke the jurisdiction of the court and any judgment rendered thereon is void. . . . An answer to a petition will not invoke the jurisdiction of the court unless it is in the nature of a cross or counterclaim setting up some independent ground for relief. . . .

B

The right to a discharge in bankruptcy is a creature of the Bankruptcy Code (Title 11 United States Codes) and does not exist independent of a bankruptcy case. There is no cause of action for a bankruptcy discharge under state law, or under nonbankruptcy federal law. It is unknown at common law.

The Bankruptcy Code, then, prescribes how a court having subject matter bankruptcy to adjudicate rights created by the Code acquires those rights in a particular instance. Under section 727(a) of the Code, an individual Chapter 7 debtor is entitled to an order of discharge unless a party in interest files a timely objection. 11 U.S.C. §727(c)(1). In the absence of such timely objection, "the court shall forthwith grant the discharge. . . ." Bankruptcy Rule 404(d).

An individual becomes a debtor under Chapter 7 of the Code through compliance with sections 301 et seq., which govern voluntary and involuntary petitions in bankruptcy. These sections prescribe the only manner in which a case may be commenced under the various chapters of the Code and thus the only manner in which a court's subject matter jurisdiction over a bankruptcy case may be invoked.

Once invoked, jurisdiction over a case may be transferred to a bankruptcy court in another district. 28 U.S.C. §1475. Only a court in which jurisdiction over a case has been invoked has the power to order such transfer. Presumably, that court is authorized to transfer part of the case, such as the disposition of an objection to discharge.

In summary, a court's jurisdiction to grant or deny discharge in bankruptcy is invoked either by the commencement of a case under Chapter 7 in the manner prescribed by 11 U.S.C. §§301 et seq. or by order of transfer pursuant to 28 U.S.C. §1475.

C

Applying the foregoing principles to the facts of this appeal, it is apparent that the Brineys did not take those statutory steps necessary to invoke the Colorado bankruptcy court's subject matter jurisdiction to grant or deny a discharge in bankruptcy to the Burleys. Their complaint objecting to discharge filed in Colorado can hardly be construed as an involuntary petition in bankruptcy. 11 U.S.C. §303. None of their contacts with the California court can be construed as a motion to transfer. 28 U.S.C. §1475.

As to the part of the complaint filed in Colorado that raised an objection to discharge, then, the Colorado complaint was a legal nullity because it did not invoke that court's jurisdiction and any judgment affecting discharge would have been void. The California court properly ignored the objection to discharge because it was not filed with it and because the filing in Colorado had no legal effect.

VI

I believe the foregoing analysis disposes of the jurisdictional issue: the Colorado bankruptcy court did not acquire subject matter jurisdiction over the Burleys' right to a discharge in bankruptcy because none of the statutory steps for conferring such jurisdiction were taken. In this part, I attempt to dispose of what appear to me to be false issues that intrude upon the analysis.

The major stumbling block is the notion that a complaint objecting to discharge is a proceeding or a civil proceeding and thus somehow governed by different principles than those I have addressed. Thus in its venue discussion, the majority notes that " 'proceeding' in the Code is used in its broadest terms to include anything that occurs in a case." Likewise, the trial court noted that "Congress did not bifurcate the term 'proceedings' to distinguish between . . . matter[s] . . . inherent and integral to the administration of a 'case' . . . and . . . plenary suits."

However valid these statements may be for other purposes, they miss the mark for purposes of determining whether subject matter jurisdiction is invoked in a particular instance. The basic grants of subject matter jurisdiction to bankruptcy courts distinguishes between *cases*, 28 U.S.C. §1471(a), (c) and *civil proceedings*, 28 U.S.C. §1471(b), (c). The bankruptcy court's jurisdiction over *cases* is exclusive, by the express terms of that grant (as an adjunct of the district court), and is shared with no other court. On the other hand, the statute expressly makes the bankruptcy court's jurisdiction over *civil proceedings* non-exclusive, i.e., it shares jurisdiction over *civil proceedings* with state and other federal courts.

Nowhere in 28 U.S.C. §1471 — which is the source of the bankruptcy court's subject matter jurisdiction — is the word *proceeding* found. Thus for purposes of jurisdiction, the word *proceeding* alone has no meaning. A particular matter, such as an objection to discharge, must then be characterized as either a *case* (or part thereof) or a *civil proceeding*. There is nothing of a convincing nature to suggest that an objection to discharge is a *civil proceeding*.

As demonstrated earlier, the right to discharge does not exist independent of a bankruptcy *case*. The right to discharge flows from the original Chapter 7 petition and, although parties in interest may oppose discharge, there is no right to deny discharge in the abstract.

Discharge is one of the "primary purposes" of United States bankruptcy law, Local Loan Co. v. Hunt, 292 U.S 234, 244, 54 S. Ct. 695, 699, 78 L. Ed. 1230 (1934), and is integral to the bankruptcy process. It follows that the bankruptcy court's exclusive jurisdiction "has extended to . . . the granting or denial of discharge." Kennedy, The Bankruptcy Court Under the New Bankruptcy Law, 11 St. Mary's Law Journal 251 (1979). Discharge jurisdiction that is exclusive to bankruptcy courts, not shared with state and other federal courts, cannot by definition be a *civil proceeding*, jurisdiction over which is non-exclusive. 28 U.S.C. §1471(b).

Nor is an *adversary proceeding* as defined in Part VII of the Bankruptcy Rules to be equated with a *civil proceeding* as used in 28 U.S.C. §1471(b). The rules draftsmen decided in 1973 that objections to discharge should be governed by Part VII of the Rules. Bankruptcy Rule 701(4).

Until 1938, an order of discharge was not granted unless the bankrupt filed an application. Bankruptcy Act §14. One opposing discharge filed a "specification . . . of the grounds of . . . opposition to discharge." General Order XXXII. The specification thus functioned as an answer to the application for discharge. In 1938, the Act was amended to provide that adjudication of an individual bankrupt operated as an application for discharge, thus eliminating the need for a separate application. Act §14a.

Throughout the history of the 1898 act, therefore, the bankrupt initiated the request for an order of discharge, either expressly by separate application or implicitly by petition for adjudication as a bankrupt.

The 1973 Bankruptcy Rules addressed the form the opposition to the application for discharge should take. Those rules required that what was functionally an answer (opposition to the request for discharge) be called a complaint and that the bankrupt reply to the opposition by way of an answer.

The anomaly that an objection to discharge under the Bankruptcy Rules is called a complaint does not affect the jurisdictional analysis. That analysis is based on the substantive provisions of titles 11 and 28 United States Codes and the rules "cannot abridge, enlarge or modify any substantive rights." 28 U.S.C. §2075.

VII

In summary, I would affirm the order denying the Brineys' motion to set aside the Burleys' discharge because they have not shown that the court abused its discretion. I am unable to accept the trial court's venue or jurisdiction analyses, however.

NOTE

In re Burley, 738 F.2d 981 (9th Cir. 1984), reversed the opinion of the Bankruptcy Appellate Panel on the ground that the bankruptcy court's denial of the motion of the creditors, made under Fed. R. Civ. P. 60(b), was not an abuse of discretion. The Ninth Circuit, in light of that conclusion, noted it "need not address the meaning of the venue provisions of the bankruptcy code. . . . [T]he bankruptcy court did not err in denying the Rule 60(b) motion, whether or not Colorado was a proper venue for the objection."

NOTE ON *BURLEY*

A problem that was touched briefly on in *Brentano's,* occurs again in *Burley.* That problem is: How do we relate things among the various bankruptcy courts? To what extent can a bankruptcy court in California decide issues related to a bankruptcy case that was filed in New York? Outside of bankruptcy, this is rarely a problem, for there is a piece of litigation, and things are either "in" that litigation or not. But a bankruptcy proceeding is fundamentally different. It is not a discrete piece of litigation, but rather a *framework* in which a lot of things happen, some of which may themselves be discrete pieces of traditional litigation.

The issue raised by *Burley* is the following. A bankruptcy case is filed in the bankruptcy court in State *A.* An issue involving the debtor, one of his creditors, or his assets is then raised in the bankruptcy court in State *B.* Does the court in State *B* have the power and the right to hear that issue?

In some cases, it must have the power to at least take the case. Consider the facts in *Brentano's.* Assuming removal was proper, in the sense of 28 U.S.C. §1334 permitting it, we have some litigation that is already proceeding in state court in California. Under the removal provision of 28 U.S.C. §1452, that case can only be removed to the bankruptcy court for the Central District of California. Whether this bankruptcy court should keep the case, once removed, or transfer it to the bankruptcy court for the Southern District of New York, is a separate question, but we know the bankruptcy court for the Central District of California *must* have the jurisdiction to take the case. Otherwise, the removal section would make no sense.

But what about a case such as *Burley?* In this case, Debtor files for bankruptcy in the bankruptcy court for the Central District of California. Creditor files an objection to discharge in the bankruptcy court for the District of Colorado. Does that court have jurisdiction? Does that court have venue?

Consider the following. Debtor files for bankruptcy in California. Creditor, who wants to object to discharge, then (with two other creditors) files an involuntary bankruptcy petition in the bankruptcy court in Colorado against Debtor. (Assume venue is either proper in both cases, or waived.) Can Creditor now block Debtor's discharge? Here, we have the unseemly case of two courts with the same "case"— the same bankruptcy —before them. How do we decide which one continues? Don't we have a general principle that the first court that gets jurisdiction keeps it, to the exclusion of others? Consider this as if it were a piece of ordinary litigation, not involving bankruptcy at all. If plaintiff files an antitrust case against defendant in federal court in California, defendant will not be able to file a motion in connection with that case in a federal court in Colorado.

Why should *Burley* be any different? Can we articulate when a particular issue must be heard in the "home" bankruptcy court? Sometimes, the issue is integrally related to the bankruptcy case, in the sense that the issue would not exist but for the existence of the bankruptcy case. Motions for denial of discharge or motions for relief from the automatic stay would appear to fit in that category. Shouldn't these issues be decided by the "home" court? Compare In re Coleman American Cos., 6 Bankr. 251 (Bankr. D. Colo. 1980) (Colorado court had power to lift automatic stay issued upon filing of bankruptcy petition in Kansas), with In re Coleman American Cos., 8 Bankr. 384 (Bankr. D. Kan. 1981) ("[a]n action to lift the stay has no life of its own independent of the primary proceeding from which it flows"; holding creditor in contempt for filing the Colorado action). On the other hand, certain issues that are "related to" a bankruptcy case have a life of their own — such as a foreclosure action by a creditor, or a suit involving whether there was a breach of contract. These issues have a separate identity of their own — they would exist even if the bankruptcy case was never filed — and, accordingly, perhaps can be heard by bankruptcy courts other than the "home" court.

Note that these issues come up because of the unusual nature of a bankruptcy case. It is a framework in which motions can be heard and in which typical litigation may be conducted. It gives rise to possible intercourt disputes that are unlikely to arise elsewhere on the legal scene.

NOTE ON REMOVAL

Removal is set forth in 28 U.S.C. §1452. With the exception of tax court proceedings or civil actions by governmental units to enforce such unit's police or regulatory powers, 28 U.S.C. §1452 authorizes the removal of "any claim or cause of action in a civil action" to the bankruptcy court for the district where such action is pending. Subsection (b) gives the court to which the claim or cause of action has been removed the power to remand it "on any equitable ground." The subsection further specifies that an order "remanding a claim or cause of action, or a decision not so remanding, is not reviewable by appeal or otherwise." The following case addresses both the scope of removal jurisdiction and the scope of subsection (b). Although it uses the removal provision prior to the 1984 Bankruptcy Amendments, that provision — 28 U.S.C. §1478 — is substantially similar to the existing 28 U.S.C. §1452.

IN RE ADAMS DELIVERY SERVICE
24 Bankr. 589 (9th Cir. Bankr. App. 1982)

ELLIOTT, Bankruptcy Judge.

The debtor in possession, Adams Delivery Service purported to remove to the bankruptcy court a proceeding pending before the National Labor Relations Board under the authority of 28 U.S.C. §1478. The NLRB challenged the authority of the bankruptcy court to assume jurisdiction of the NLRB's proceeding under the removal statute. The bankruptcy court refused to remand the case and the NLRB appealed. We grant leave to appeal the court's interlocutory order, 28 U.S.C. §1482(b), and reverse.

I. FACTS

Adams, a pharmaceutical delivery service, was a party to a collective bargaining contract with the Teamsters Union. The subject of the present litigation is the discharge of an employee, Dennis Wilson.

On August 30, 1978 the NLRB found the firing was an unfair labor practice under §8(a) of the National Labor Relations Act (the "Labor Act"). The primary issue was whether Wilson had been fired for discussing an overtime pay dispute with his union representative. In accordance with the Labor Act, the NLRB sought judicial enforcement of its order before the Ninth Circuit. See Labor Act §§10(e), 10(f). The Ninth Circuit enforced the order by a decision dated August 26, 1980. NLRB v. Adams Delivery Service, Inc., 623 F.2d 96 (9th Cir. 1980). The case was then returned to the NLRB for determination of the amount of backpay to be awarded to Wilson in accordance with the Labor Act's bifurcated system of determination of liability and liquidation of claims.

The hearing began before an NLRB Administrative Law Judge ("ALJ") on July 9, 1981, but was continued until August 6, 1981 in order to allow Adams to obtain certain documents it had subpoenaed. On August 5, 1981, Adams filed its Chapter 11 petition under the Bankruptcy Code. On August 6, 1981, prior to the appointed time of the NLRB hearing, Adams filed an application for removal of the NLRB proceeding to the bankruptcy court and notified the NLRB that the proceeding was subject to the automatic stay provisions of the Bankruptcy Code. See 11 U.S.C. §362. At the reconvened hearing, Adam's bankruptcy and labor counsel both refused to formally participate on the grounds that the hearing was stayed. Notwithstanding this, the NLRB submitted its case to the ALJ.

The ALJ then ordered briefs to be filed by September 8, 1981. On September 10, 1982 Adams sought and obtained an injunction from the bankruptcy court in the removed proceeding. The injunction prohibited the NLRB from pursuing the proceeding. However, the injunction was directed only to the NLRB *qua* litigant and did not purport to enjoin the ALJ.

Meanwhile, the NLRB sought a remand order from the bankruptcy court on the grounds that the purported removal was ineffective. While the remand motion was pending, the ALJ issued findings unfavorable to Adams which were later adopted by the NLRB.

On November 10, 1981 the bankruptcy court refused to remand the action even though it refused to expressly find that the removal was properly effected. In part this was based upon the events that occurred after removal and after the exercise of its injunctive powers. The court concluded:

> If NLRB's contention that this court is without jurisdiction and the automatic stay and temporary restraining order are void is correct there is no need to remand as the NLRB proceedings have continued regardless of the removal. If this court has jurisdiction it concludes that it should not remand in light of the proceedings which have been taken adverse to debtor.

. . . It is that failure to remand that the NLRB now appeals. . . .

II.   Issues

The NLRB's appeal presents two issues to the panel:

(1) Does 28 U.S.C. §1478(b) preclude this panel from reviewing the bankruptcy court's refusal to remand the case?

(2) Is a NLRB backpay liquidation proceeding subject to removal under 28 U.S.C. §1478? We conclude that the answer to both questions is no.

III.   Jurisdiction to Review

Adams claims that the trial court's order is not reviewable under 11 U.S.C. §1478(b). That section precludes review of a bankruptcy court order granting or denying a request to remand a claim or cause of action. We hold that if the court *has jurisdiction* over a matter which has been removed pursuant to §1478(a), its ruling on such a request to remand is within its absolute discretion and not subject to appellate review. But where an action has been wrongfully removed to a court with no jurisdiction, a motion to remand is not directed to the discretion of the court but is a challenge to the court's power to entertain the matter at all. A court always has the power to determine whether it has jurisdiction. In effect, the NLRB is not seeking review of the court's decision denying its motion to remand, rather it is challenging the jurisdiction of the trial court.

Apparently the NLRB styled its jurisdictional challenge as a "request for remand" because that is the terminology historically used with respect to removals to the United States District Courts and is the terminology used by Interim Bankruptcy Rule 7004(j) (adopted in the Northern District of California as a local rule) regarding jurisdictional challenges to the removal of civil actions. This result is consistent with the legislative history of the Bankruptcy Reform Act of 1978 which enacted §1478. It is clear that the authors of the principal House committee report on the subject contemplated that jurisdictional challenges to the removal of an action or claim would be heard by the appellate courts as are such challenges in the case of actions removed to the district courts. See House Report 95-595, 95th Cong. 2d Sess. at 51, U.S. Code Cong. & Admin. News 1978, p. 5787. Although the clause which provides that decisions under §1478(b) not to remand are not reviewable was added later in the legislative process to the then proposed §1478, we are aware of nothing in the legislative history indicating an intention to prevent review of a decision to assume jurisdiction over a case beyond the scope of the bankruptcy court's powers. Neither are we aware of any judicial authority for such a proposition. The sole case cited by Adams, Harlow v. Sargent, 14 B.R. 267 (Bkrtcy. D. Vt. 1981), is distinguishable since it dealt with an attempt to appeal an order remanding a case to the state courts, not a decision, as is the case here, to assume jurisdiction over a controversy allegedly beyond the court's authority.

We construe the trial court's refusal to remand in the face of the NLRB's objection as a determination that the removal was proper. Notwithstanding the court's equivocal language, its manifested intention to proceed evidences a determination that the case was removed in accordance with the statute. Accordingly, we conclude that the question is properly before us for review.

IV. Removability of NLRB Proceedings

The question whether the NLRB proceedings are subject to removal to the bankruptcy courts has not been the subject of any reported court decision. Removal to the bankruptcy courts was authorized for the first time by the Bankruptcy Reform Act of 1978. The statute enacted at that time authorizes removal of a broad range of claims to the bankruptcy court:

A party may remove any claim or cause of action in a civil action, other than a proceeding before the United States Tax Court or a civil action by a Government unit to enforce such governmental unit's police or regulatory power, to the bankruptcy court for the district where such civil action is pending, if the bankruptcy courts have jurisdiction over such claim or cause of action.

28 U.S.C. §1478(a).
Two of the restrictions on removability are relevant. First, only "civil actions" may be removed. Second, actions by "governmental units to enforce their police or regulatory powers" are not removable. After considering these limitations, we conclude that NLRB backpay liquidation actions are not removable.

A.   REMOVAL LIMITED TO CIVIL ACTIONS

The bankruptcy removal statute is patterned on the district court removal statute, 28 U.S.C. §1441. We agree with the editors of Collier on Bankruptcy that the term "civil action" as used in the statute should be read in light of the history and context of §1441. 1 Collier on Bankruptcy (15th Ed.) ¶3.01 at 3-70, 3-71. The *Collier* editors concluded that in light of the historical use of "civil action" in connection with §1441, "It is unlikely, that a 'civil proceeding' encompasses, for example, a proceeding before the National Labor Relations Board or other administrative agency." Id. ¶3.01 at 3-71. We reach the same conclusion.

While resort to court proceedings is required for execution of the enforced order, see 29 C.F.R. §101.15 (NLRB Rules and Regulations), we find it significant that no private action arises under the Labor Act. . . . Thus the NLRB is not functionally a forum where private parties may present labor disputes. Rather the NLRB determines which complaints it will act upon in its own name in furthering the policies of the federal labor laws.

Adams suggests that the term "civil action" as used, in §1478 must be construed against the NLRB as being narrower in meaning than the term "civil proceeding." . . . While there may be significance in the distinction between "civil proceedings" used in the bankruptcy jurisdictional statute, §1471(a), and "civil action" as used by the bankruptcy removal statute, §1478, the location of the "narrower" term "civil action" in the removal provision suggests the opposite. If anything, this implies that the class of claims that are removable is less inclusive than those subject to the original jurisdiction of the bankruptcy court. Thus, it is unclear how this distinction can be construed "against" the NLRB's efforts to prevent removal.

Because, with respect to backpay liquidation proceedings the NLRB is not acting as a court, and because the concept of a civil action is inseparable from a court proceeding, the conclusion follows that such a proceeding is not a "civil action."

B. ACTIONS TO ENFORCE POLICE & REGULATORY POWERS NOT REMOVABLE

Our determination that NLRB backpay liquidation actions are not removable because they are not "civil actions" under §1478(a) is consistent with the other restrictions of §1478(a). A civil action by a "governmental unit to enforce such governmental unit's police or regulatory power" is not removable. The language of this restriction is similar to §362(b)(4) of the Bankruptcy Code which excepts from the bankruptcy automatic stay "the commencement or continuation of an action or proceeding by a governmental unit to enforce such unit's police or regulatory power." It is obvious some effort was made by Congress to coordinate §362(b) with §1478(a) to ensure that certain proceedings that continue unabated by the automatic stay cannot be disrupted by removal to the bankruptcy court by the debtor. But Congress clearly did not achieve complete congruency between §1478 and §362. For example, actions exempted from the automatic stay under §362(b)(7) are generally removable. Nevertheless, we believe it would be anomalous to interpret the "police and regulatory" provision contained in §1478 so as to permit removal of causes of action that are not subject to the automatic stay because of §362(b)(4). Thus, we turn to the interpretation of §362(b)(4).

The Ninth Circuit has not ruled whether §362(b)(4) exempts proceedings before the NLRB from the automatic stay. In In re Bel Air Chateau Hospital, 611 F.2d 1248 (9th Cir. 1979), decided under the prior Bankruptcy Act, the court ruled that the automatic stay provisions of Rule 11-44(a) did not apply to an action for unfair labor practices pending before the NLRB. While the court disclaimed any views on the application of §362(b)(4), it suggested that its decision regarding Rule 11-44 under the Act "appears harmonious" with the Bankruptcy Code and that "(s)ection 362 makes explicit the principles of the old bankruptcy law: stays of regulatory proceedings should not be automatic but are appropriate when it is likely that the court proceedings will threaten the estate's assets." Id. at 1251. . . . In reaching this result, the Bel Air court relied upon the policies enunciated in Nathanson v. NLRB, 344 U.S. 25, 30, 73 S. Ct. 80, 83, 97 L. Ed. 23 (1952):

The Supreme Court held that the Board, not the bankruptcy court, should liquidate the amount of the back pay award owed by the bankrupt to its employees under a Board order. According, to the Court, where the matter has been entrusted by Congress to an administrative agency, the bankruptcy court should normally stay its hand pending administrative decision because Congress entrusted to the agency the authority to determine appropriate remedies.

In re Bel Air Chateau Hospital, Inc., 611 F.2d at 1250.

Since the *Bel Air* decision, the Fifth Circuit has squarely held that §362(b)(4) exempts an unfair labor practice proceeding before the NLRB. NLRB v. Evans Plumbing Co., 639 F.2d 291 (5th Cir. 1981).

These holdings, that the automatic stay does not apply to NLRB proceedings because of the "police and regulatory" exception, are consistent with and bolster our conclusion that NLRB proceedings may not be removed to the bankruptcy court.

In its decision refusing to remand, the bankruptcy court relied upon In re Barber, Inc., 13 B.R. 962 (Bkrtcy. N.D. Tex. 1981) and In re Unit Parts Company, 9 B.R. 386 (Bkrtcy. D.W.D. Okl. 1981). Both deal with the power of the bankruptcy courts to determine questions regarding allowability, amount, and priority of unfair labor practice claims when presented against the estate. Our decision is not inconsistent with either case. Our decision does not address these questions.

In sum, we hold that if the court has jurisdiction over the matter removed to it, that the decision to remand or not to remand is not reviewable. However, if the court has no jurisdiction over the removed matter, the court refusal to remand is reviewable and should be reversed.

Reversed and remanded to the trial court with instructions to remand the proceeding to the NLRB.

NOTE

Can the bankruptcy court now estimate the claim under §502(c)? Cf. In re Unit Parts Co., 9 Bankr. 386 (W.D. Okla. 1981). If so, what has been accomplished?

PROBLEMS

13.16 Coleman files a bankruptcy petition in Kansas. At the time that petition is filed, LNB is proceeding with a foreclosure action in a Colorado state court against some real property of Coleman. Can this action be removed? To what court? Cf. In re Green Tie Realty Corp., 14 Bankr. 923 (Bankr. S.D.N.Y. 1981); In re Dew Mortgage Co., 10 Bankr. 242 (Bankr. M.D. Fla. 1981). Can it be removed without relief from the automatic stay? If not, where does one get relief from the automatic stay? See In re Rapco Foam, 16 Bankr. 765 (Bankr. W.D. Mo. 1982).

13.17 Ford has used Automobile Transit, Inc. (ATI) for the transport of automobiles. Two insurance companies, TICO and CNI, provided insurance coverage for ATI, each insurance company's policy covering a different period of time. ATI files for bankruptcy in January. In October, Ford sues TICO for $2 million and CNI for $1 million, based on claims arising out of damage caused to Ford's automobiles by ATI prior to ATI's bankruptcy. This suit is brought in the district court, and ATI is not named as a defendant. TICO files a notice of removal of Ford's suit against TICO and CNI in the bankruptcy court, and announces that it intends to file an adversary action against Ford and ATI in the bankruptcy court.

Ford moves in the district court for a determination (a) that TICO's removal application does not affect Ford's claim against CNI in the district court and (b) that Ford's claim against TICO is not within the jurisdiction of the bankruptcy court. How should the district court rule on the two issues? See Ford Motor Co. v. Transport Indemnity Co., 508 F. Supp. 1092 (E.D. Mich. 1981).

D. INTERNAL PROCEDURES UPON COMMENCEMENT

NOTE ON THE TRUSTEE

If the petition filed is for a Chapter 7 liquidation, the bankruptcy proceeding will take place under the "supervision" of a trustee. Sections 321 and 322 specify who can serve as a trustee. Section 701 provides for the appointment of an interim trustee by the court "[p]romptly after the order for relief under this chapter." (The order for relief, you may recall, occurs simultaneously with the filing of the petition in the case of a voluntary bankruptcy (§301) but requires an order of the court in the case of an involuntary petition (§303(h)). If it is "necessary to preserve the property of the estate or to prevent loss to the estate" in the case of an involuntary petition prior to the order for relief, a court may, on notice and hearing, appoint an interim trustee prior to the order for relief (§303(g)—a step requested but denied in *Win-Sum Sports,* supra page 108.)

The interim trustee appointed by the court under §701 remains as the trustee unless and until supplanted by a creditor vote for a new trustee. §701(b), (c). The requirements for replacing the interim trustee by creditor vote are set forth in §702, and those requirements underscore something very important about the trustee. The vote is by *creditors* holding *unsecured* claims. Equity holders do not vote. Secured creditors do not vote. This suggests that, as a practical matter, the trustee represents the unsecured creditors, not the other participants in the bankruptcy process. While the Bankruptcy Code gives the trustee a number of administrative powers and rights, it is probably a mistake to view the trustee as a dispassionate figure, particularly when challenging transfers to creditors or in battling a debtor over exemptions. The directive of §323(a)—"[t]he trustee in a case under this title is the representative of the estate"— should be read in light of these election procedures.

Note that the vote for a trustee under §702 is by the holders of "allowable, undisputed, fixed, liquidated, unsecured claims of a kind entitled to be paid" as normal unsecured claims under §726. This statutory requirement is different from the question of who can be a petitioning creditor for purposes of §303(b). Cf. In re National Sugar Refining Co., 39 Bankr. 578 (Bankr. S.D.N.Y. 1984).

Does this seem to give the debtor a tremendous leverage, at least in the first instance, over who may vote for a trustee to investigate the debtor? Does this, in turn, give the debtor some leverage over who will be a trustee? (Once elected, §324 provides that a trustee can be replaced only "for cause." If the trustee is elected with a subset of creditors, and then other creditors become eligible to vote, it may be too late.) Bankruptcy Rule 2003(b)(3) provides:

> In a chapter 7 liquidation case, a creditor is entitled to vote at a meeting if, at or before the meeting, he has filed a proof of claim or a writing setting forth facts evidencing a right to vote pursuant to §702(a) of the Code unless objection is made to the claim or the proof of claim is insufficient on its face. Notwithstanding objection to the amount or allowability of a claim, for the purpose of voting, the court may after such notice and hearing as it may direct, temporarily allow it for that purpose in an amount that seems proper to the court.

Does this rule sensibly balance the concerns as to who can vote for the trustee? Even if it does, is the rule consistent with the statutory directive of §702?

In re Tartan Construction Co., 4 Bankr. 655 (Bankr. D. Neb. 1980), suggests another power the debtor may have over the election of the trustee. Section 702 requires a vote not just of creditors who have already filed claims; instead, for it to be a proper vote 20 percent of all creditors holding *allowable* claims must vote. Allowable claims are set forth in §502, and we examined that requirement in Chapter 3. The House Report states that this requirement exists to make sure that there is sufficient creditor interest in a trustee and to make sure that one or a few creditors cannot get "their" trustee appointed:

> At the first meeting of creditors, creditors will continue to have the right to elect a trustee of their own choice to serve in the case, subject to certain limitations not imposed under current law. The bill permits creditor election of a trustee only in cases in which at least creditors holding 20 percent in amount of certain scheduled unsecured claims request the election of a trustee. The minimum percentage request requirement is designed to insure that a trustee is elected only in cases in which there is true creditor interest, and to discourage election of a trustee by attorneys for creditors, as is so often the practice under current law. If a significant percentage of

creditors do not wish to elect a trustee, it is unfair to impose the will of a few creditors' attorneys on the rest of the creditor body.

It will be more difficult under this procedure for a trustee to be elected unless there is actual creditor interest in the case. In any case where there are significant assets, there is often creditor interest. The problems under current law occur most often in cases where the return to creditors from the estate promises to be small. Thus, they are uninterested, and attorneys can move in to control the case. By adopting the 20 percent requirement, the bill discourages attorney control, but retains the idea of true creditor control, because the theory of creditor control remains valid.

The requirement of allowable claims, however, may still cause problems. At the time the vote occurs, what actually are allowable claims may not be known. In the first instance, therefore, allowable claims will be taken off the debtor's schedules, which will include a calculation of the unsecured portion of secured claims. In *Tartan Construction*, the interim trustee was opposing a vote on a permanent trustee. Some $19,000 of claims had been voted in favor of a permanent trustee. At that time, proofs of claims of some $53,000 had been filed. If the proper figure was proof of claims, the 20 percent requirement had been easily met. The interim trustee, however, asserted that if the proper denominator was determined by proof of claims, the evil of potential control of an election by a very small number of creditors would still exist, because the vote might be held before many proofs of claims had been filed. The court agreed with this conclusion, on the ground that limiting the pool of those eligible to vote to those who had filed proofs of claims would frustrate the purpose of the statute. It therefore concluded that Bankruptcy Rule 2003(b)(2) should not be followed. But the problem remained: What number to use instead? The court rested on the following:

> [T]he unsecured portion of claims listed as secured would be determined by subtracting the scheduled value of the secured property from the scheduled secured claims. To this figure would be added the scheduled, nonpriority unsecured claims. . . .
>
> [This] method allows undersecured claims to be voted without giving undersecured creditors who choose to vote an undue advantage. . . . In some cases, valuation of the secured property will be a problem, but that issue . . . may be reserved for future consideration.

Under this test, the vote was insufficient, so no permanent trustee was elected. The approach — of subtracting the gross value of the collateral from the gross value of all secured claims — may be too simple. It does not account for *which* creditors are entitled to vote. For example, Creditor A might have a claim of $100,000 and collateral worth $125,000. Creditor B might have a claim of $100,000 and collateral of $10,000. In gross, there is $135,000 of collateral and $200,000 of claims, so there is an unsecured excess, by simple subtraction, of $65,000. But that number is not really right. Creditor *A* is fully secured, and is not entitled to vote at all. Creditor *B* is undersecured by $90,000, and should have a $90,000 unsecured vote. So, not only does *Tartan Construction* possibly give the wrong number, but it provides no basis, for deciding, if it becomes necessary, whose vote counts, and for how much if Creditor *A* votes for a trustee and Creditor *B* votes against the trustee. For that, a more fine-tuned approach is necessary.

NOTE ON THE DUTIES OF A TRUSTEE AND HIS COMPENSATION

Section 704 sets forth the duties of a trustee in a Chapter 7 case. (Chapters 11 and 13, as we have seen, have special provisions governing the duties of a trustee in those chapters.) The principal duties are: (1) collecting and reducing to money the property of the estate and attempting to expeditiously close up the estate; (2) investigating the financial affairs of the debtor; and (3) reporting and rendering an accounting on the administration of the estate. A fair amount is packed away in these duties. For example, among the duties of a trustee to "collect" property of the estate are his "avoiding powers — the power to set aside certain pre-bankruptcy transfers of property that we examined in Chapters 5 and 6.

Sections 326 through 331 set forth a series of compensation provisions for the trustee and people who the trustee selects to assist him in his duties. Section 330 and 326 speak to the compensation of the trustee. Section 330 awards reasonable compensation plus reimbursement for actual and necessary expenses, but §326 puts a ceiling on this in the form of a declining percentage of the value of the assets distributed. (These, as we saw in Chapter 8, are ultimately paid from the "estate," as an "expense of adminstration," §503(b)(2), although prior payment may be made on application to the court under §331.) Given the role of the trustee, are these compensation provisions adequate? What about in the case of a debtor with essentially no assets?

The Bankruptcy Reform Act of 1978 also set in place a "pilot project," which established, in ten pilot districts, a "U.S. Trustee," who is an independent officer appointed by the attorney general. In these pilot districts, the U.S. Trustee replaces the interim trustee, and is compensated, in part, by the federal government. Chapter 15 of the Bankruptcy Code deals with the United States Trustee, as does Chapter 39 of Title 28. The pilot project was to run until 1984, at which time, if it worked, the whole system would be switched over to it. Congress decided in the 1984 Bankruptcy Amendments to continue the pilot project until September 30, 1986.

NOTE ON THE MEETING OF CREDITORS
AND EXAMINATION OF THE DEBTOR

Section 341(a) provides that within "a reasonable time after the order for relief . . . there shall be a meeting of creditors." Bankruptcy Rule 2003(a) interprets "reasonable time" to be not less than 20 and not more than 40 days. The bankruptcy judge may not attend this meeting. §341(c). The refusal to permit the bankruptcy judge to attend the meeting reflects a conscious shift in the role of the bankruptcy judge under the Bankruptcy Code. Under the 1898 Act, the bankruptcy "referee" (later called "judge") was intimately involved in the adminstrative side of the bank-ruptcy process. Under the Bankruptcy Code, the bankruptcy judge is supposed to be much more a judicial officer.

The Bankruptcy Code is silent as to what is to occur at this first meeting of creditors, except that §343 states that the debtor *shall* attend and submit to examination under oath. Who the "debtor" is, is not stated. If the debtor is a corporation, must the chief executive officer attend? The chief operating officer? The chief financial officer? Former officers? Cf. In re Bohack Corp., 464 F. Supp. 35 (E.D.N.Y. 1978). Bankruptcy Rule 2003(b) provides that "[t]he clerk shall preside at the meeting of creditors unless (1) the court designates a different person, or (2) the creditors who may vote for a trustee under §702(a) of the Code and who hold a majority in amount of claims that vote designate a presiding officer." That pro-posed rule also provides that the presiding officer "shall have the authority to administer oaths."

The scope of the examination of the debtor is not clear. The legisla-tive history to §343 states that "[t]he purpose of the examination is to enable creditors and the trustee to determine if assets have improperly been disposed of or concealed or if there are grounds for objection to discharge." Bankruptcy Rule 2004(b) provides:

> The examination of any person under this rule or of the debtor under §343 of the Code may relate only to the acts, conduct, or property or to the liabilities and financial condition of the debtor, or to any matter which may affect the administration of the debtor's estate, or to the debtor's right to a discharge. In an individual's debt adjustment case under chapter 13 or a reorganization case under chapter 11 of the Code, other than for the reorga-nization of a railroad, the examination may also relate to the operation of any business and the desirability of its continuance, the source of any money or property acquired or to be acquired by the debtor for purposes of consum-mating a plan and the consideration given or offered therefor, and any other matter relevant to the case or to the formulation of a plan.

Under §7a(10) of the 1898 Act, a debtor (then called a "bankrupt") gained "use immunity" for anything stated at that meeting: "no testimony, or any evidence which is directly or indirectly derived from such testimony, given by him shall be offered in evidence against him in any criminal proceeding." Section 344 has changed this automatic immunity. The witness now must take the Fifth Amendment, and immunity can then be granted only under the procedures of part V of Title 18, which are briefly set forth in the legislative history to §344. Should no immunity be forthcoming, the debtor (or other witness) may plead the Fifth Amendment, with no bankruptcy consequences. If the witness is granted immunity, but fails to testify, then §727(a)(6) will bar discharge. The effectiveness of this sanction may be open to question in cases where the debtor is not an individual, because only individuals receive a discharge under Chapter 7. As for other debtors, what are the remedies? Cf. §707.

NOTE ON THE POWERS OF THE TRUSTEE

Debtor Corporation's managers consult with Lawyer in January about allegations of fraudulent conduct that has been committed by Debtor and its managers. A month later, Debtor files a Chapter 7 bankruptcy petition. The trustee begins to study, among other things, the possibility of bringing an action against the managers. The U.S. Attorney begins a criminal investigation of Debtor's managers, and requests access to all the communications between Debtor and Lawyer. These communications are privileged and Lawyer refuses to disclose them unless Debtor waives the attorney-client privilege. Trustee asserts that he has the power to waive the privilege on behalf of the corporation. The managers assert that because they are still the managers of the corporation only they have the power to waive the privilege.

The Seventh Circuit offered the following analysis of this issue in Commodities Futures Trading Commission v. Weintraub, 722 F.2d 338 (7th Cir. 1983), cert. granted, 105 S. Ct. 321 (1984).

> First, although the trustee holds broad management powers for the corporate debtor, he does not replace the corporation as an entity. The corporation is capable of numerous functions even after the filing of the petition in bankruptcy. . . . Nor does the trustee succeed to the positions of the officers and directors of the corporation . . . In brief, the corporation exists, and will continue to exist, until formally dissolved by action of its shareholders or by the state where the firm is incorporated. . . . The trustee may hold the power to manage the bankrupt corporation's property and assets, but he does not thereby acquire absolute power over the corporation's legal rights.
>
> Second, to accept appellee's argument would be to condone an inequality of treatment between bankruptcy corporations and bankruptcy individuals with regard to the attorney-client privilege. . . . There is little authority to support the position that the individual debtor's attorney-client

privilege passes to the trustee in bankruptcy. Such a passing of the privilege could engender the absurd result of the trustee waiving the debtor's privilege as to information sought by the trustee. The attorney-client privilege would then vanish whenever the trustee, at his whim, determined that information from the debtor was necessary. . . . We perceive no reason to afford a corporate debtor less protection than that afforded an individual debtor in bankruptcy.

Third, allowing the trustee in bankruptcy to waive the attorney-client privilege of the corporate debtor discriminates against the corporate debtor solely on the basis of economic status. . . . While the trustee's interest in investigating the affairs of the corporate debtor on behalf of the creditors is certainly legitimate, it does not justify erosion of the corporation's attorney-client privilege simply on the basis of a change in economic circumstances.

Finally, and most importantly, we reject the Commission's argument because of its potential chilling effect on attorney-client communications. If the trustee in bankruptcy is permitted to waive the corporate debtor's privilege, the trust inherent in the attorney-client relationship will be jeopardized. Corporate clients will be wary of communicating fully with their attorneys for fear that sensitive information could subsequently be disclosed due to bankruptcy. Free interchange between attorney and client is the cornerstone of effective advocacy.

Is the court's assertion that there is no relevant difference between corporations and individuals in bankruptcy for purposes of the attorney-client privilege correct? Whose interests are being protected if the corporation asserts or waives the attorney-client privilege? Most courts that have addressed this issue have decided that the trustee can waive the attorney-client privilege of a corporate debtor. See, e.g., Citibank, N.A. v. Andros, 666 F.2d 1192 (8th Cir. 1981); In re O.P.M. Leasing Services, 670 F.2d 383 (2d Cir. 1982) (ability to waive limited to facts of case); cf. In re Bioleau, 736 F.2d 503 (9th Cir. 1984) (examiner can waive privilege).

In examining this problem, it may be useful to return to some of the basic principles we have developed in earlier chapters. A corporation has a right to protect the confidentiality of communications between it and its lawyers. There is no reason why this right, any more than a garden-variety property right, should be altered by happenstance of bankruptcy. Bankruptcy law should try to give the corporation the same kind of attorney-client privilege as it had outside of bankruptcy. The difficulty we encounter, however, is that it may be hard to filter out all the effects brought about because there is a collective proceeding. The problem in this case is who in bankruptcy should be able to assert the privilege. In our discussion of *Swift Aire, supra* page 184, we suggested that it was appropriate in asking whether a letter of credit could be drawn upon in bankruptcy to ask whether the letter could be drawn on if the same substantive changes had taken place outside of bankruptcy. Should we do the same in this case?

Can we argue that the appointment of a trustee is the bankruptcy analogue in all substantive respects to a change in management and that the nominal presence of the old management should not matter? Outside of bankruptcy, a new set of managers can waive the attorney-client privilege on behalf of the corporation over the objection of the former managers. Can one argue that as a matter of substance (rather than simply as a matter of labels), the trustee represents the new management? Outside of bankruptcy, the managers are charged with representing the interests of the shareholders, who enjoy whatever is left after all other obligations are paid off. Isn't the trustee in the same position? Doesn't the trustee have an obligation to those with residual claims against the property? (The residual claimants, however, are typically general creditors rather than shareholders. Should this matter?)

Does the Seventh Circuit confuse the interests of the former managers (and their attorney-client privilege) and the interests of the corporation (and its attorney-client privilege)? The difference between the corporation and its managers is underscored by the possibility that the one will bring a suit against the other. Isn't the chilling effect that might exist the same chilling effect that managers concededly have outside of bankruptcy because of the possibility that they will be replaced by new managers? Isn't there a relevant difference between individual and corporate debtors in that a corporation has no assets or rights that are outside the bankruptcy proceeding, while an individual does? See Comment, Waiver of the Attorney-Client Privilege by the Trustee in Bankruptcy, 52 U. Chi. L. Rev. 1230 (1985).

Chapter 14
STATE LAW COLLECTIVE
PROCEEDINGS

In Chapter 1, we looked at individual state law remedies. Those remedies share several traits: (1) all are creditor-initiated (at least in substantial
part) and (2) all benefit the specific creditor that uses the remedies. They
are part and parcel of the "grab" law of individual creditor remedies. We
now turn to look briefly at some collective creditor remedies that exist
outside of the bankruptcy system, but which may provide a collective
alternative to the bankruptcy process. These remedies — compositions/
extensions and assignments for the benefit of creditors — require the consent of the debtor, who, in theory, is the person initiating these remedies.
In looking at these remedies, you should consider what are their strengths
and weaknesses, and whether, and to what extent, they need to be supplemented by a federal bankruptcy process.

A. COMPOSITION AGREEMENTS

A composition (sometimes called a "settlement agreement") is really a
multiparty contract, whose validity has been long recognized at common
law. It is a contract between a debtor and two or more creditors in which
the creditors agree to take a specified partial payment in full satisfaction of
their claims against the debtor. (An extension agreement, by contrast, is
one in which the debtor and two or more creditors agree to extend the
time for the payment of their claims against the debtor. An agreement can
be both a composition and an extension.) The reason why these agreements have two or more creditors is because in this way the preexisting
duty rule problems of Foakes v. Beer, 9 App. Cas. 605 (House of Lords
1884), can be avoided by finding fresh consideration in the mutual prom-

ises of the creditors to forebear. As this suggests, a composition is essentially a species of contract law, and is generally controlled by general contract doctrines. Why would creditors ever agree to a composition? Is there any reason to think that they would not view their individual creditor remedies as sufficient? As you address the question as to why creditors would ever agree to a composition agreement, we return to the questions of Chapter 1, as to why creditors would ever agree to act collectively. Isn't it fair to say that a composition agreement is simply a form of explicit agreement among creditors to act collectively? Given that, are there any reasons to have any sorts of limits on these composition agreements? The materials that follow address those questions.

UNITED STATES PLYWOOD CORP. v. NEIDLINGER
41 N.J. 66, 194 A.2d 730 (1963)

Per curiam.

The defendant Neidlinger had for many years conducted a business which involved his purchase of plywood materials and their installation in buildings under construction. In 1959, he discovered that his trusted bookkeeper had embezzled about $200,000 and, as a result, the business was insolvent. He consulted his attorney, the late Alfred J. Peer, who scheduled a meeting for May 18, 1959. The notice of the meeting was addressed to each of the defendant's creditors and stated that cooperation "with respect to the settlement of the various claims" was required "in order to effect some orderly payment." The meeting was held as scheduled and was attended by 25 or 30 persons, including Kermit Green, an attorney at law, who appeared for the plaintiff United States Plywood Corporation.

A memorandum, prepared after the meeting by Mr. Peer and distributed to the creditors, set forth his general summary of what had transpired. He noted that a creditors' committee has been appointed and that it consisted of Roy E. Scheider (representing Macy-Fowler, $2,087.85), Kermit Green (representing the United States Plywood Corporation, $23,000) and Frank Pascerella (representing Wood-Art, Inc., $6,000). The obligations of the defendant were reported as approximating $100,000 and his sole assets were reported as $4,000 in furniture, fixtures and equipment, $10,000 in accounts receivable, and some contracts on which no work had commenced. An attorney representing a corporation formed by William Fay, who had been associated with the defendant, offered to take over and complete these contracts and to remit the net profits (estimated at $25,000) to the creditors of the defendant. After referring to miscellaneous matters, the memorandum concluded with the comment that all of the creditors present expressed their willingness to go along with the plan suggested by the attorney for Mr. Fay's corporation.

The memorandum was never intended to be an integration of everything that had transpired at the meeting and could not be viewed as precluding supplemental oral testimony. . . .

The creditor's committee took control of the defendant's reported assets and he heard nothing further from the plaintiff or any of the other creditors for about a year. In May 1960 his wife died leaving him a substantial inheritance and, in the following month, the plaintiff instituted an action in the Superior Court seeking recovery of the sum of $23,157.36, which represented its claim for merchandise delivered to the defendant. The defendant's answer set forth that the plaintiff, along with the other creditors, had entered into a settlement and composition agreement under which the plaintiff was to receive a proportionate amount of the assets transmitted by the defendant to the creditors. In the pretrial order, the defendant admitted the receipt of the merchandise and the reasonableness of its price and asserted that the oral understanding at the May 18th meeting was, in essence, a settlement and composition under which the plaintiff's claim was to be deemed fully satisfied by a proportionate amount of the assets turned over to the creditors' committee.

At the trial the plaintiff rested its case without introducing any oral testimony. It relied on the pretrial order and the opening statement by the defendant's counsel in which the receipt and reasonable price of the merchandise were acknowledged, though the affirmative defense of settlement and payment was reasserted. . . . In support of his defense the defendant presented testimony by Max Geller, along with his own testimony. Mr. Geller stated that he was a creditor of the defendant, that he had attended the May 18th meeting, that there was discussion as to the defendant's liabilities and assets, and that it was stated that something could be salvaged and "a percentage would be given to the creditors for the amounts due them." Counsel for the plaintiff did not cross-examine Mr. Geller.

The defendant testified that, at the meeting, a creditors' committee was appointed with authority to take control of his inventory and accounts receivable and receive the net profits which would result from the Fay arrangement. When asked what was to happen to him, he said, "I was going bankrupt one way or another, and the term that I used at the time and I guess the only term I could use is a secondary form of bankruptcy." In response to a further question as to what was said at the meeting, he testified that his attorney told the creditors that the defendant would "either go bankrupt or an arrangement could be made which I had discussed with him prior to that in which the creditors could give a clearance to proceed under a bankrupt condition, and yet draw these profits of these contracts to the benefit of the creditors."

At the conclusion of the testimony on the defendant's behalf, the plaintiff still presented no oral testimony but moved for the withdrawal of the case from the jury and the entry of judgment. It urged (1) that nothing had been introduced to establish that Kermit Green was authorized to make a binding settlement on its behalf, and (2) that there was no evidence that the plaintiff and the other creditors had agreed to accept the assets turned over to the committee in full settlement of the claims against the defendant. The trial judge granted the motion on the latter ground and his action was sustained by the Appellate Division. We certified on the request of the defendant. . . .

When the plaintiff moved for the entry of judgment, the defendant was, under settled principles, entitled to have the facts considered most favorably from his point of view. If reasonable men could find from the testimony, and the inferences which might legitimately be drawn therefrom, that the parties attending the May 18th meeting contemplated that the defendant would be released upon the turnover of his assets to the committee, then it was the trial judge's duty to deny the motion, and call upon the plaintiff for any rebuttal testimony. . . . The absence of an explicit release agreement in express terms would not preclude an implication in fact of such agreement.

We consider that the lower courts erred in their view that no jury could reasonably infer from the evidence that the parties contemplated a release upon the defendant's turnover of his assets at the May 18th meeting. Mr. Geller, who was the only creditor called as a witness, testified that the discussion at the meeting bore upon the creditors' obtaining a percentage "for the amounts due them." While slight, the inference from this testimony points toward compromise and settlement rather than toward payment on account. The defendant's own testimony gave evidence of the contemplation that the turnover of the defendant's assets and the Fay arrangement for completion of his contracts, though in no sense a formal bankruptcy, would have the substantial incidences of bankruptcy. Thus he testified that his attorney had stated at the meeting that an arrangement could be made under which the creditors would give him "clearance to proceed under a bankrupt condition." And the defendant also testified that he viewed and referred to the arrangement as a sort of "secondary bankruptcy."

There was a time when bankruptcy was designed solely for the protection of creditors. Thus English bankruptcy law at the time of the American Revolution simply afforded a method for seizing the debtor's assets in order that they might be fairly distributed among his creditors. The first American bankruptcy act was molded along the same lines and it was not until the Act of 1841 that Congress provided that an honest debtor could voluntarily surrender his assets and effectively obtain a discharge from future liability with respect to past debts. . . . Later bankruptcy acts strengthened the discharge aspect of bankruptcy and in Local Loan Co. v. Hunt, 292 U.S. 234, 244, 54 S. Ct. 695, 699, 78 L. Ed. 1230, 1235 (1934), the court noted that, now, a primary aspect of bankruptcy is "to 'relieve the honest debtor from the weight of oppressive indebtedness, and permit him to start afresh free from the obligations and responsibilities consequent upon business misfortunes.'" The *Hunt* case stresses, as do many others, that this purpose is of high public as well as private concern, since it gives the honest but unfortunate debtor, who surrenders the property which he owns at the time of the bankruptcy, "a new opportunity in life and a clear field for future effort, unhampered by the pressure and discouragement of pre-existing debt." . . .

In the light of the common understanding, a jury could reasonably infer that when the defendant, directly or through his attorney, spoke at the settlement meeting on May 18th, in terms of bankruptcy or clearance to proceed under a bankrupt condition, he contemplated discharge or release upon the turnover of his assets to the creditors' committee. Similarly it could reasonably infer from all of the evidence including Mr. Geller's testimony that such was also the contemplation of the creditors. A jury would have the undoubted right to draw inferences to the contrary; however, if it credited the testimony introduced on the defendant's behalf and drew the suggested inferences favorable to him, the manifested mutual assent necessary in law to support the asserted settlement agreement would clearly be present. . . . See Massey v. Del-Valley Corp., 46 N.J. Super. 400, 402, 134 A.2d 802, 803 (App. Div. 1957):

> The law is settled that where two or more creditors agree to accept a stated percentage of their claims in full satisfaction of them, the agreement is binding, not only as among the creditors but as between each of them and the debtor. . . .

The plaintiff urges that, even if it be assumed that there was a settlement agreement on May 18th, the defendant may not prevail because there was no affirmative evidence that Mr. Green was authorized by it to make such settlement. . . . The claim of lack of authority was not set forth in the pretrial order; it was belatedly asserted when the plaintiff moved for judgment. The trial court did not pass on the claim but, if it had, it would have been obliged to reject it for there clearly was enough evidence in the record to withstand the motion insofar as it was grounded on the issue of authority.

The plaintiff knew that the meeting of May 18th had been specifically called to consider the settlement of creditors' claims. It sent its attorney Mr. Green, who is also its attorney in the present litigation. Throughout the meeting Mr. Green acted on its behalf. He was appointed to the creditors' committee which took over the defendant's assets and he thereafter acted as a member of that committee. His connection with the committee was never questioned by the plaintiff. If Mr. Green approved a settlement agreement, he presumptively had his client's authority to take that action. . . .

The plaintiff is, of course, at liberty to rebut the presumption by testimony from Mr. Green and others indicating that no authority had been granted. But even upon the introduction of such testimony there may be a factual issue for the jury . . . not only as to whether there had been a grant of authority, but also as to whether the circumstances here gave rise to an apparent authority sufficient to protect the defendant. . . .

Reversed.

NOTE ON *NEIDLINGER*

The principal issue in this case is whether or not the arrangement provided for the discharge of debts against Neidlinger. (Why is that relevant, under the facts of the case?) Why is this even in issue? What would the point of this whole exercise be otherwise? From Neidlinger's perspective? From the creditors' perspective?

What is the proper focus in this case? Is it on what Neidlinger thought? On what was "the contemplation of the creditors"? Or on what U.S. Plywood (or at least its agent) thought? Which one does the court focus on?

If all the creditors of Neidlinger do not agree to the composition agreement, what are the consequences? Can such creditors still levy on Neidlinger's assets? Are there incentives available to get them to join? In drafting a composition agreement, would you want to include a clause such as the following? "This Agreement shall not be binding on Debtor or on any Creditor unless agreed to and signed by all Creditors." What drawbacks are there to such a clause? Would a clause requiring the signing of 90 percent of the creditors (in number? in dollar amount? both?) be preferable? How would you, as attorney for the debtor, handle creditors with debts that were unliquidated or the subject of a bona fide dispute? How would you try to resolve disputes over, say, the value of collateral?

PROBLEM

14.1 Creditor 1, Creditor 2, and Creditor 3 enter into a composition agreement with Debtor pursuant to which they agree to take 40 percent of their respective claims, to be paid in four installments of 10 percent each pursuant to notes endorsed by the shareholders of Debtor. The composition agreement specifies that it discharges the original indebtedness. Creditor 1, before agreeing to sign the composition agreement, gets President, the president of Debtor (but not one of its shareholders) to guarantee the payments of the notes. Creditor 2 and Creditor 3 enter into the composition agreement not knowing of Creditor 1's deal with President. Should this side deal be allowed to stand? Should it affect the composition agreement itself? See Hanover National Bank of City of New York v. Blake, 142 N.Y. 404, 37 N.E. 519 (1894).

B. ASSIGNMENTS FOR THE BENEFIT OF CREDITORS

In connection with the following discussion, you may want to examine the provisions of Article 2 of the New York Debtor and Creditor Law, a collection of 24 statutory sections governing "General Assignments for the Benefit of Creditors" (hereinafter, N.Y. Assignment Law).

Assignments for the benefit of creditors take place pursuant to an agreement, which generally involves the following. A debtor conveys his property (usually, all his nonexempt property), subject to a trust, to a third party — called a trustee or assignee — who then executes the terms of the trust. These terms usually call for the payment of the debtor's debts in a certain order out of the estate that has been transferred. The basic model for assignments for the benefit of creditors is that of trust law, and not contract law. One effect of this divergence in labels is that creditor consent is not necessary. So, an assignment is a way of forcing creditor "participation" and, in that respect, shares an attribute of federal bankruptcy law that composition agreements lack.

Once an assignment has been executed, the assignee takes possession of the assets; a meeting of creditors is called; the assignor is present to explain to creditors the reasons for the assignment; and the assignee reports on the status of the assets, the methods of liquidation, and the likelihood of a dividend. The assignee has standing to sue on behalf of the assignor in connection with any of the assignor's causes of action. See generally Greenfield, Alternatives to Bankruptcy for the Business Debtor, 51 L.A. Bar J. 135 (1975). The assignee often has, by statute, greater rights than the assignor, such as the power to invalidate unperfected security interests (see UCC §9-301(3)) and to set aside preferential transfers of property (including not only money, but also security interests and execution liens) of the assignor made on the eve of the assignment. See N.Y. Assignment Law §15(6-a); Cal. Code Civ. Pro. §1800. In cases where the assignment takes place pursuant to statute, the court may be given the power to determine claims or resolve other disputes. N.Y. Assignment Law §15. These assignments, moreover, may not cover all claims against the estate. N.Y. Assignment Law §13, for example, does not cover unliquidated tort injuries. It also contains a limitation (id.) on the claims of landlords, somewhat similar to that of §502(b)(6) of the Bankruptcy Code. Certain claims may also be given priority status. See, e.g., N.Y. Assignment Law §22 (wages and salaries, up to $1,000 per employee, for services rendered during the three months prior to the assignment; deposits, up to $300, for retail purchases of merchandise or services).

An assignment, however, does not discharge a debtor of debts. This is not particularly a problem in the case of a corporate debtor that wishes to go out of business. As we discussed in the Note on the Effect of Confirmation, supra page 725, corporations can dissolve under state law, and the state-law concept that shareholders of a corporation are not liable for the debts of the corporation effectively provides such a discharge for the relevant parties. Moreover, if the shareholders wish to continue the business, they may be able to form another corporation after the existing one has been discharged. Individuals, however, may be extremely interested in discharge, as might be corporations that need to continue in business under the same charter.

Given that an assignment for the benefit of creditors does not itself involve a discharge, its principal benefit may lie in its ability to stop the "grab" race inspired by individual creditor remedies — a feature it shares in common with bankruptcy. Consider what those benefits might be. Even though an assignment is "initiated" by the debtor, its principal beneficiaries are really the creditors. The next case explores a common issue that arises in conjunction with the assignment: When a debtor seeks a discharge along with the assignment, what sorts of pressures may the debtor put on the creditors to grant that discharge?

GESSLER v. MYCO CO.
29 Ill. App. 2d 227, 172 N.E.2d (1961)

SMITH, Presiding Justice.

This appeal involves the validity of a general assignment for the benefit of creditors. Plaintiff is a judgment creditor of the assignor-debtor, Myco Company, Inc. Plaintiff's judgment postdates the assignment to which he did not consent. Finding no property of his debtor around he commenced garnishment proceedings against the debtor's assignee, Robert W. Gosdick. The court below gave plaintiff judgment in the full amount of his claim holding the assignment void as to him. The correctness of this ruling is brought here for review by the assignee.

General assignments for the benefit of creditors are a convenient trust device by which a debtor at the end of his rope divests himself of his estate by conveying it to an assignee. The assignee then sells the property, and if the proceeds are insufficient, pro rates them among the creditors. Such payments, however, do not release the debtor from future liability on the unpaid balance unless a creditor agrees that such payment shall act as a full release. The law has always sanctioned honest settlements made by a debtor with his creditors, because settlements of this character, fairly made, obviate litigation, expedite settlement and minimize waste. They have long been recognized in Illinois and approved of for these reasons. For these reasons, too, validity is not dependent upon consent of the creditors. However, an assignment may be rendered invalid by a debtor annexing thereto conditions onerous to his creditors and favorable to himself. In such happenstance, the assignment is no longer for the benefit of *creditors.* It is rather an assignment for the benefit of the *debtor* and it is then void as to creditors who do not consent thereto.

One condition which will render an assignment invalid is when it puts creditors to a choice of taking a fraction of their claims in settlement of the whole. In other words, an assignment must not contain a condition requiring a full release in order for a creditor to secure partial payment. "Thus assignments purportedly for the benefit of creditors, which place such creditors upon the choice of taking nothing at all or a fraction of their claims in settlement of the whole, are invalid as to nonconsenting creditors." Tribune Co. v. Canger Floral Co., 312 Ill. App. 149 37 N.E.2d 906, 909. Therein, quoting from Conkling v. Carson, 11 Ill. 503, it is stated:

> The law does not allow a debtor to impose such harsh and onerous conditions upon his creditors. . . . he is not permitted to say to any of his creditors that they shall not participate in his present estate, unless they will release all right to satisfy the residue of their debts out of his future acquisitions.

Is there such a condition here? The assignment instrument itself does not disclose any. We thus direct our attention to such other documents as may be pertinent. The first of these is a letter sent by the assignee on the same day the assignment became effective to the creditors, entitled "Offer," which advised them of the fact that an assignment had been made, the reasons behind it, and the debtor's general financial picture. It concluded as follows:

> So that we may know we have your *cooperation* in connection with this matter, won't you please sign and return the enclosed consent form together with an itemized statement of your account.

The second pertinent instrument, the "enclosed consent form," we set forth in full:

Consent

> "The undersigned, a creditor of Myco Company, Inc., a Delaware corporation having its principal place of business in Illinois at 705 Pleasant Street, Belvidere, Illinois, does hereby consent to the assignment of all the assets of every kind and description of the said Myco Company, Inc., to Robert W. Gosdick as Trustee for the benefit of creditors and does hereby *agree to accept the pro-rata share paid* on the undersigned claim from the fund derived from the liquidation of the aforesaid assets *in full settlement* of all claims of every name and nature against the said Myco Company, Inc.
>
> The undersigned further *authorizes* the said Robert W. Gosdick to *execute a full release* of the annexed account of the said Myco Company, Inc., after distribution of the proceeds derived from the assets has been made. The undersigned agrees not to institute proceedings for the collection of the annexed account during the life of this Trusteeship.

This exact consent-form, when coupled with a restrictive endorsement releasing the debtor from further liability on a dividend check, voided an assignment as to a non-consenting creditor in the Tribune Co. case, above noted:

> To allow such prohibited releases to be obtained through indirection by the assignee by their inclusion in consent forms and indorsements on dividend checks would be to sanction the very thing which the courts of this state refuse to permit debtors themselves to do. . . . Surely conditions which, if contained in assignments for the benefit of creditors, would render same invalid, cannot be legally imposed on the creditors by the assignee in behalf and for the benefit of the debtor assignors. Tribune Co. v. Canger Floral Co., 312 Ill. App. 149, 37 N.E.2d 906, 910.

There is no restrictive indorsement involved here. We thus come to the heart of the problem. Does the consent-form with the letter place upon plaintiff the choice of taking a fraction of his claim in settlement of the whole? We think they do. Even though a signed consent-form may not be in fact a pre-condition to pro rata payment, as the assignee argues, it certainly sounds like one. To ask a creditor to "agree to accept the pro-rata share paid" on his claim, "in full settlement of all his claims" and to authorize the assignee "to execute a full release," looks to us like the assignee on behalf of his debtor is trying to impose a condition, that if contained in the assignment would render it invalid. We quote further from the Tribune Co. case (at page 909 of 37 N.E.2d):

> We are impelled to agree with plaintiff that the facts and circumstances in evidence disclose that an obvious attempt has been made here to circumvent the foregoing rules of law by omitting from the assignments themselves a provision for the discharge in full of the creditors' claims upon their acceptance of their pro rata share of the proceeds of the sale of the assets of the debtors and then inserting such a provision both in the consents and indorsements on the dividend checks mailed to the creditors by the garnishee trustee.

The debtor by a general assignment is relieved from the chore of composing his creditors. He avoids the stigma of bankruptcy, the harried pursuit by anxious creditors, and he more or less weathers the storm with reputation intact. Nobody blames a debtor for desiring to wipe the slate clean, but he should not communicate this desire to his creditors in the form chosen here. When he does so, he transforms what was a mere wish, into a not too subtle hint that if the creditors do not oblige they might not get paid. Creditors do not have to abide such coercion, and if the choice is put to them, the debtor or here, the assignee, take the chance that if any particular creditor does not accept the assignment is invalid at his election.

It may be true, as the assignee argues, that plaintiff will be treated on a par with others, but if this is so, why send out the consent-forms in the first instance? The assignment itself is valid without the need of anyone's consent. Quite obviously, the assignee, for his debtor, was hoping to obtain the much-sought-for total release. He was hopeful that the creditors would be induced into signing. But here the inducement was baited. The implication in the "Offer" is that a creditor will be better off if he signs the consent-form. He is thus placed in a dilemma. If he chooses not to consent, there is certainly every good reason for him to believe that he will suffer, at the very least, some disparagement of position. If he does consent, he then, willy-nilly, agrees to release his debtor for less than the full amount of his claim. A creditor can do so if he wants to, but it should not be put to him in the context that if he doesn't he will be left out in the cold.

The assignee suggests that with a corporation there could never be after-acquired property anyway, and therefore, a creditor doesn't really sacrifice anything when he agrees to take less, hence there is no coercion and no onerous condition. The short answer to this is that the preservation of the balance of his unpaid-debt is a matter peculiarly within the province of the creditor, and is of no concern to the debtor or his assignee or, indeed, anyone. A creditor's reasons may not appear reasonable, but in the final analysis, that is a matter strictly for him to decide.

A debtor caught in the rain of adversity and seeking an umbrella over his assets may do so by way of the general assignment, but he should not at the same time importune his creditors for total absolution, by suggesting through his assignee that their "co-operation" demands it, and that there will be no payments to them absent total absolution. This is putting creditors to a forbidden choice. The uses of adversity may be sweet, but they are not so sweet that a debtor can convert himself into a "dispenser of alms" to his very own creditors. . . . There is here an attempt to indirectly coerce plaintiff into a release of his debt for less than the full amount. The assignment is void as to plaintiff and it follows that plaintiff has the right to reach funds in the hands of the assignee by garnishment proceedings. The judgment below is therefore affirmed.

Affirmed.

NOTE ON GESSLER v. MYCO CO.

Although the trust that resulted from Myco Co.'s assignment was not completed, we are told that "plaintiff will be treated on a par with others." Given that, what is plaintiff's complaint? Even assuming that the consent form leaves the (erroneous) impression that, in order for a creditor to participate in the distribution from the trust, he must agree to release his claim against Myco Co., unless Gessler relied to his detriment on this statement, what is his ground for attacking the assignment? More to the point, if this assignment is allowed to stand, won't Gessler get a pro rata share from the trust? In addition, because he refused to sign the stipulation, won't Gessler continue to be able to assert his debt against any future assets of Myco Co.? Doesn't this leave him *better* off than other creditors who signed the consent form, and granted Myco Co. a discharge?

Myco Co. is a corporation. If no conditions at all had been attached to this assignment, wouldn't Myco Co. still have an effective means to discharge its debts? If Myco Co. dissolves according to state law, there will be no future assets to reach. Absent the existence of a third party guarantee or the like that would get released when the debt was discharged, would Gessler have been hurt even if participation in the assignment was conditioned on discharge?

Should it be permissible for an assignment to "coerce" creditors into a discharge of their claims against a debtor by having as a condition to participation in the distribution from the trust a discharge of claims? Would be it any different if the assignment simply provided that it would give a preference in payment to those who agreed to accept a discharge? Consider the following argument against allowing such conditions, A. Burrill, Voluntary Assignments §165 (6th ed. 1894):

> The objections to the allowance of these stipulations in assignments to trustees are, first that they operate by way of coercing the creditors into a relinquishment of part of their demands. "The debtor," observes Mr. Justice Story, "surrenders nothing, except upon his own terms. He attempts to coerce his creditors by withholding from them all his property unless they are willing to take what he pleases to give, or is able to give, in discharge of their debts. This is certainly a delay, and, if the assignment be valid, to some extent a defeating of their rights." . . . The force of this objection lies not in the mere circumstances of stipulating for terms with a creditor, but in so stipulating when the debtor's property is no longer accessible to the creditor's remedies. "If a debtor with his property in his own hands," observes Mr. Justice Sutherland, "and open to the legal pursuit of his creditors, can satisfy them that it is for their interest, or the interest of any of them, to accept 2s. 6d. in the pound, and give him an absolute discharge, there is no legal objection to it; they treat upon equal terms; the ordinary legal remedies of the creditor are not obstructed. But the case is materially changed when the debtor first places his property beyond the reach of his creditors, and then proposes to them terms of accommodation."

Both *Neidlinger* and *Gessler* involve creditors who apparently are trying to avoid the effect of a discharge. The debtor seems to be trying to gain such a discharge, perhaps by giving incentives to the creditors who agree to provide a discharge. In the case of an assignment, providing for priority in payment to those who agree to grant a discharge may appear to be a pretty strong incentive, but it still leaves creditors with a choice as to whether they will do better by participating in the assignment (coupled with a discharge) or by remaining outside of the assignment (with whatever is left over plus post-assignment assets).

POLSON v. MORTON
262 Minn. 356, 114 N.W.2d 685 (1962)

KNUTSON, Chief Justice.

This is an appeal from a judgment entered pursuant to findings of fact, conclusions of law, and order for judgment in favor of defendants after a trial by the court without a jury.

The facts may be briefly stated as follows: New England Furniture Company, referred to hereinafter as New England, was a corporation engaged in the furniture business in Minneapolis. It was also a lessee of some property within what is known as the Hub Shopping Center. In May 1956 it became apparent that New England was in financial difficulties. Charles Harris, its president, instructed its attorney to call a meeting of local creditors to discuss what could be done. The meeting was held in the office of the attorney in April or May 1956. Plans for liquidating New England were discussed. The corporate defendants in this action were creditors of New England. Among those attending the meeting were defendant C. W. Bronstein, representing United States Bedding Company; defendant J. H. Bramson, representing defendant Levin Bros., Inc.; and either defendant Dale W. Morton or some other representative of defendant Baker Properties, Inc. Bronstein also represented Charles Manufacturing Company, another creditor of New England. Attorney William Kronebusch was also present, representing a number of New England creditors, and other creditors were also present.

At the meeting, the creditors were informed that New England was the lessee of the Hub Shopping Center lease, which contained a provision permitting the lessor, American Shopping Centers, to cancel the lease if the lessee suffered bankruptcy or insolvency and that some value might be realized for the creditors if the lease could be resold to the lessor.

Within about a week after this first meeting, a second meeting of New England creditors was held in Minneapolis at the office of New England. This meeting was attended by Bronstein, Bramson, Morton, Kenneth Owen, who was New England's attorney, Kronebusch, Harris, and a Mr. Mason, secretary of New England. In addition, representatives of certain Chicago creditors were present, as well as representatives of other local creditors who had attended the first meeting. At this meeting, Harris reported that he and Owen had not been successful in reselling the lease of the Hub Shopping Center, and the creditors were requested to cooperate by not pressing their claims through litigation or bankruptcy proceedings in order that the surrender value of this lease would not be lost through termination. It was reported to them that an assignment for the benefit of creditors would result in termination of the lease.

During the meeting, Harris and Mason were asked to leave the room while the creditors conducted a discussion among themselves. At this time the creditors decided that Bronstein, Bramson, and Morton would comprise a committee to work with New England and to communicate with creditors. It is the claim of those three defendants that at all times they acted only as an advisory committee for the creditors. Plaintiff, on the other hand, contends that they were assignees for the benefit of creditors.

Following this meeting, letters were mailed to the creditors on letterheads of Levin Bros., Inc., informing them of a general plan of liquidation and requesting their indulgence while the Hub Shopping Center lease was disposed of. The first letter called their attention to the fact that an independent auditing concern had been retained by this advisory committee to audit the books of New England. There were approximately 230 creditors with claims totaling some $240,000. The inventory of New England was finally sold to Boutells. A downpayment of $100,000 was received, and, in order to avoid garnishment by creditors who would not abide by the agreement to refrain from commencing litigation, the money was deposited in a Rochester, Minnesota, bank. The money was to be withdrawn on the check of Charles Harris, countersigned by a member of the so-called advisory committee. The fixtures belonging to New England were later sold by auction sale. The resale of the Hub Shopping Center lease failed to materialize, and it was later assigned to a separate corporation consisting of a wholly-owned subsidiary of New England.

The names and addresses of the creditors of New England were procured by the committee from Harris or the New England officers. They were eventually paid a first dividend of 26 percent and a later dividend of 3.65 percent.

Plaintiff operated a jewelry outlet under arrangement with New England. Claiming that he had money coming on this arrangement, he filed suit on April 20, 1956. Upon learning of the transactions regarding the purported liquidation of New England, plaintiff through his attorney sent defendant Bramson a letter in August 1956 informing him of plaintiff's claim. A meeting was called at which Harris emphatically stated that New England owed plaintiff nothing; that his claim was being contested in court; and that nothing would be paid thereon. Plaintiff did nothing to protect his rights and took a default judgment in the sum of $18,586 on July 10, 1957, some 5 months and 10 days after payment of the last dividend. A few days thereafter, New England was declared a bankrupt, and out of the assets in the bankruptcy proceeding plaintiff would realize less than one percent of the amount of his claim.

After a trial, the court found that defendants Morton, Bronstein, and Bramson were at all times acting only in an advisory capacity to Harris and that there had been no assignment for the benefit of creditors. In addition to the claim that defendants were acting in a fiduciary capacity as assignees for the benefit of creditors, plaintiff claims that the assets of New England constituted a trust fund for the benefit of all creditors, including himself.

The only question involved here is whether the evidence sustains the court's findings that there was neither an assignment for the benefit of creditors nor a trust fund created for them out of the assets of New England.

1. At the outset, it is clear that there was no statutory assignment for the benefit of creditors under Minn. St. 577.01. We have, however, long recognized common-law assignments for the benefit of creditors independent of statute. . . .

Under either statutory or common-law assignment, it is elementary that title to the property passes to the assignee and that the assignor must part with his whole interest in the thing assigned. . . .

2. The evidence in this case amply sustains the court's findings that there was no assignment for the benefit of creditors. Not only did New England actively participate in all phases of the disposition of its property and the determination of the creditors to whom the proceeds were to be paid, but it retained control over the proceeds. Checks drawn on the fund deposited in the Rochester bank were signed by either Harris or Mason, officers of New England. It is true that New England did grant the advisory committee some control over these funds, but the committee at no time had authority to draw on the account without the signature of either Harris or Mason. It is also significant that the money was deposited in the Rochester bank in order to avoid garnishment or attachment by recalcitrant creditors. If there had been an assignment for the benefit of creditors, the funds would not be subject to attachment by creditors and there would have been no necessity for placing the money in a bank where creditors who were unwilling to cooperate could not find it.

Plaintiff's theory of a trust fund is equally untenable. The cases he cites involve the exercise of equity powers of the court to conserve the assets of an insolvent corporation for its creditors. The simple answer to this contention is that plaintiff took no action to invoke the equity powers of the court. He sat silently by while the corporation liquidated its assets and distributed the proceeds thereof to those whom it considered its creditors. He now seeks to hold defendants personally liable although they were in no way acting for him or in any fiduciary relationship to him.

The case involves only a question of fact, and the court's findings are amply sustained by the evidence.

Affirmed.

NOTE

A number of states, like New York, have codified assignments for the benefit of creditor law. In a number of these states, however, courts — as in Polson v. Morton — have held that the statutory codification did not displace the common law assignment. E.g., Bumb v. Bennett, 51 Cal. 2d 294, 333 P.2d 23 (1958). This is important for it may hold valid an assignment that does not comply with the statute. As we saw in examining the N.Y. Assignment Law, however, those statutory assignment laws contain a number of provisions that it may not be possible to replicate apart from such statutory authorization.

NOTE ON "PREFERENTIAL" ASSIGNMENTS FOR THE BENEFIT OF CREDITORS AND CONSTITUTIONAL CONSTRAINTS

Some state laws have attempted to allow debtors to do exactly what Myco Co. was trying to do: gain a discharge by means of an assignment for the benefit of creditors. In doing this, however, there are constitutional problems of two sorts. The first stems from the Constitutional prohibition against the impairment of the obligation of contracts by states (U.S. Constitution, Article 1, Section 10) but this constraint is limited by the interpretation that it is applicable only to contracts entered into before the law was passed. Denny v. Bennett, 128 U.S. 489 (1888).

The second stems from the bankruptcy power itself. Congress has the power to "establish . . . uniform Laws on the subject of Bankruptcies throughout the United States. . . ." This has been held not to prohibit states from acting when there is no national bankruptcy law (as there was not during most of the nineteenth century), Sturges v. Crowninshield, 17 U.S. 122 (1819). But what if, as now, there is a federal bankruptcy statute? Does the *existence* of such a statute prohibit states from enacting "bankruptcy" statutes of their own, complete with mandatory discharge? The Supreme Court learning on this implied pre-emption in the bankruptcy context stems principally from two cases: International Shoe Co. v. Pinkus and Johnson v. Star.

In International Shoe Co. v. Pinkus, 278 U.S. 261 (1929), the Supreme Court struck down an Arkansas statute providing for a court-supervised assignment, whereby property was handed over to a "receiver" and under the terms of the statute paid out, with payout first going to creditors who filed discharge stipulations. The *Pinkus* court, in an opinion by Justice Butler, concluded:

> In respect of bankruptcies the intention of Congress is plain. The national purpose to establish uniformity necessarily excludes state regulation. . . . Congress did not intend to give insolvent debtors seeking discharge, or their creditors seeking to collect claims, choice between the relief provided by the Bankruptcy Act and that specified in state insolvency laws. States may not pass or enforce laws to interfere with or complement the Bankruptcy Act or to provide additional or auxiliary regulations. . . . It is clear that the provisions of the Arkansas law governing the distribution of property of insolvents for the payment of their debts and providing for their discharge, or that otherwise relate to the subject of bankruptcies, are within the field entered by Congress when it passed the Bankruptcy Act, and therefore such provisions must be held to have been superseded.

In reaching this conclusion, the Court quoted from Boese v. King, 108 U.S. 379 (1883), which focused on the invalidity of a state law "in so far as it provided for the discharge of the debtor from future liability to creditors who came in under the assignment. . . ."

Three years after *Pinkus,* however, the Supreme Court, in another opinion by Justice Butler, decided Johnson v. Star, 287 U.S. 527 (1932). *Star* dealt with a situation in which a state court held that its *statutory* provisions providing for discharge of participating creditors in an assignment were invalid, but that the assignment it was dealing with, which provided for priority in payment to creditors agreeing to a discharge, was nonetheless valid as a *common law* assignment. The Supreme Court upheld this, noting that the state courts had "observed the differences between state insolvency laws and those merely regulating voluntary assignments for the benefit of creditors. . . ." See also Pobreslo v. Joseph M. Boyd Co., 287 U.S. 518 (1933).

Commentators oftentimes seem to derive from these cases the general proposition that whether or not a state statute is preempted as being in conflict with the federal bankruptcy power depends principally on whether or not a discharge is available. See, e.g., Eisenberg, Bankruptcy Law in Perspective, 28 U.C.L.A.L. Rev. 953, 956 n.7 (1981) ("Given the existence of a federal bankruptcy statute, states lack constitutional power to have a complete system of distribution and discharge"); D. Epstein, Debtor-Creditor Law in a Nutshell 124-125 (2d ed. 1980) ("Some statutes, however, expressly provide for the very relief sought by a preferential assignment at common law, i.e., a discharge. Such provisions are, at best, of questionable validity."); see also In re Wisconsin Builders Supply Co., 239 F.2d 649 (7th Cir. 1956), cert. denied, 353 U.S. 985 (1957); Note, 45 Marq. L. Rev. 403 (1962).

Even assuming that discharge is the key provision that separates out essentially *bankruptcy* statutes from other sorts of statutes, why should the presence of discharge in the state statute lead to constitutional infirmity? Assume that a state law provides for statutory assignments for the benefit of creditors, coupled with a mandatory discharge or a preferential payment to those agreeing to a discharge. Should that be constitutionally infirm? To be sure, this statute *overlaps* with the subject matter of the federal bankruptcy laws, but is that dispositive, at least in the absence of an explicit preemption provision? Isn't the relevant question: Does the existence of the statute *frustrate* federal law? And, doesn't the resolution of that turn on whether creditors who are dissatisfied with the state proceeding can force the debtor into federal bankruptcy proceedings? That is to say, isn't the "conflict" solved if the federal system can "trump" the state system? See Note, 42 Harv. L. Rev. 60 (1929); Note, 42 Yale L.J. 1140 (1933).

In Chapter 2, we examined the requirements for putting a debtor into federal bankruptcy proceedings. The "normal" test for involuntary petitions was one of showing that the debtor was not generally paying debts as they became due. §303(h)(1). But §303(h)(2) called off that requirement if there had been an assignment for the benefit of creditors within 120 days of the date the involuntary petition was filed. Is this sufficient? There are two constraints on the ability of allowing disgruntled creditors to override the assignment for the benefit of creditors with a federal bankruptcy proceeding. The first stems from the 120-day limitation in §303(h)(2). But isn't it fair to say that this represents an explicit choice by Congress *not* to allow the federal statute to override the state assignment beyond that period? Can it also be used to justify the preemption of discharge policy? In considering that question, can you be sure that Congress would have had such a 120-day limitation had there been no such preemption?

A second limitation stems from the requirements of §303(b): three creditors generally are needed to commence an involuntary bankruptcy case, and they can do so only if their relevant claims are neither contingent nor the subject of a bona fide dispute, and at least some of them must be partially unsecured. This leaves certain categories of creditors without the ability to override the state assignment for the benefit of creditors. Is preemption justified on this ground? Or does it suggest that, whatever the merits for the constraints of §303(b) when dealing with the "generally not paying" test of §303(h)(1), the constraints of §303(b) make less sense when a creditor seeks bankruptcy because of a state law assignment?

What is, or should, be clear from this, however, is the crucial role a preeminent (even if as a last resort) federal law of bankruptcy will have. As long as a dissenting creditor (or debtor) can supersede a contractural, common law, or state statutory proceeding providing for the pay out and discharge of debts, with a federal bankruptcy proceeding, inevitably, the presence of this federal system will closely shape the contours of the non-federal proceedings. Any creditor who feels it is not getting as much as it would in a federal bankruptcy proceeding can opt into the federal pro-ceeding (again assuming it can put the debtor into those proceedings). Because of that, we would expect nonbankruptcy results to be closely shaped by what the participants could get in the bankruptcy proceeding — with divergences principally attributable to the cost savings believed to be gained by remaining outside the formal federal bankruptcy process. The special rights and remedies available inside of bankruptcy, therefore, will be relevant not only to the bankruptcy proceedings, but also to the shape and probable success of proceedings under these nonbankruptcy forums.

C.   LIMITS OF BANKRUPTCY LAW

Given this symbiotic relationship between the rules of bankruptcy law and the rules of state law, should there be any constraints on federal bankruptcy rules? We have spent much of the time in this book discussing, as a policy matter, the relationship between bankruptcy rules and non-bankruptcy rules. We close by examining a possible constitutional constraint on the ability of federal bankruptcy rules to rely (or perhaps to override) applicable nonbankruptcy rules: the grant of the bankruptcy power in article I, section 8, clause 4 of the Constitution. Congress is granted the power to establish "uniform Laws on the subject of Bankruptcies throughout the United States."

The next case focuses on the question of what it means to say that Congress has the power to enact "uniform" laws on the subject of bankruptcy. Is the case convincing? Is it clear that the bankruptcy clause was designed to be a limitation on Congress's power under other clauses — such as the commerce clause? Could an equally persuasive counterargument be made that the Framers simply wanted to ensure that Congress would have the power to enact uniform laws on the subject of bankruptcies, regardless of how the commerce clause came to be construed? Is a grant of a power to pass "uniform" laws necessarily a limitation on the passage of "nonuniform" laws under another enunciated power? Moreover, what does "uniform" mean? Does it mean that acts passed to apply only to the affairs of an individual debtor are necessarily "nonuniform"? Or does it mean something else — for example, that "uniformity" simply refers to the providing of a federal forum for resolving debtor-creditor disputes, which oftentimes involve the conflicting laws of several jurisdictions? How far can "uniformity" be taken? Does it violate uniformity to pass a bankruptcy law that allows the question of exempt property to turn on state law? See Hanover National Bank v. Moyses, 186 U.S. 181 (1902) (upholding such a provision); In re Sullivan, 680 F.2d 1311 (7th Cir. 1982). Does it violate uniformity to have a bankruptcy statute that leaves the extent to which security interests are recognized to state law? See generally, Baird, Bankruptcy Procedure and State-Created Rights: The Lessons of Gibbons and Marathon, 1982 Sup. Ct. Rev. 25.

RAILWAY LABOR EXECUTIVES' ASSN. v. GIBBONS
455 U.S. 457 (1982)

Justice REHNQUIST delivered the opinion for the Court.

In March 1975, the Chicago, Rock Island and Pacific Railroad Company (Rock Island) petitioned the United States District Court for the Northern District of Illinois for reorganization under §77, of the Bankruptcy Act of 1898; 11 U.S.C. §205. Under the protection of §77, the Rock Island continued to operate for approximately four and one-half years until it ceased all operations in September 1979 as a result of a labor strike that had depleted its cash reserves. Pursuant to 49 U.S.C. §11125, the Interstate Commerce Commission (ICC) directed the Kansas City Terminal Railway Company to provide rail service over the Rock Island lines.

On January 25, 1980, the reorganization court concluded that reorganization was not possible. It then directed the Trustee of the Rock Island estate to prepare a plan for liquidation, and to continue planning for the cessation of rail operations upon the March 1980 expiration of the ICC's directed service order. . . . Since the entry of the January 25, 1980 order, the Trustee has been liquidating the assets of the Rock Island estate.

On March 4, 1980, various railroads and labor organizations representing Rock Island employees reached an agreement as to Rock Island employees hired by carriers acquiring the Rock Island's trackage. The agreement covered such matters as hiring preferences, monetary protection, and seniority, but it did not cover those Rock Island employees who are not employed by acquiring carriers.

On April 14, 1980, the Rock Island Trustee petitioned the reorganization court to confirm the Rock Island's abandonment of all rail lines and operations. The reorganization court referred the petition to the ICC for its recommendation. On May 23, the ICC concluded that the Rock Island's abandonment and dissolution as an operating railroad was necessary.

On June 2, the reorganization court ordered the total abandonment of the Rock Island system and the discontinuance of its service. The court found that to order the Rock Island to continue its operations indefinitely at a loss for the public's benefit would violate the "Fifth Amendment rights of those who have a security interest in the enterprise. Brooks-Scanlon Co. v. Railroad Commission, 251 U.S. 396 [40 S. Ct. 183, 64 L. Ed. 323] (1920)." . . . The reorganization court also concluded that "no claim or arrangement of any kind or nature for employee labor protection payable out of the assets of the Debtor's estate is allowed or required by this Court." . . .

Congress responded to the crisis resulting from this demise of the Rock Island by enacting the Rock Island Transition and Employee Assistance Act (RITA), Pub. L. 96-254, 94 Stat. 399, 45 U.S.C. §1001 et seq. The President signed the act into law on May 30, 1980, three days before the reorganization court's abandonment order. At issue in these cases are RITA's employee protections provisions. Sections 106 and 110 require the Rock Island Trustee to provide economic benefits of up to $75 million to those Rock Island employees who are not hired by other carriers. 45 U.S.C §§1005, 1008. Benefits must be paid from the estate's assets. The employee benefit obligations must be considered administrative expenses of the Rock Island estate for purposes of determining the priority of the employees's claims to the assets of the estate upon liquidation.

On June 5, 1980, appellees filed a complaint in the reorganization court seeking to declare RITA unconstitutional and to enjoin its enforcement. On June 9, the reorganization court issued a preliminary injunction prohibiting the enforcement of §§106 and 110 of RITA. Although it suggested that RITA might have other constitutional infirmities, the court concluded that RITA's employee protection provisions constituted an uncompensated taking of private property for a public purpose in violation of the Just Compensation Clause of the Fifth Amendment. . . .

Congress responded to the reorganization court's injunction by enacting §701 of the Staggers Rail Act of 1980, Pub. L. 96-448, 94 Stat. 1959. With certain modifications, §701 of the Staggers Act re-enacted RITA §§106 and 110. The Staggers Act also added §124 to RITA, 45 U.S.C. §1018, which sought to avoid any implication that it had deprived appellees of any Tucker Act remedy otherwise available for the Trustee and creditors to pursue their takings claim against the United States.[6] The Staggers Act was signed into law on October 14, 1980.

Six days previously, appellant and the United States had moved the reorganization court to vacate its June 9 injunction on the basis that the passage of the Staggers Act rendered the injunction moot. In addition, it was argued that no irreparable injury could be shown because the Staggers Act amendments provided that a remedy under the Tucker Act, 28 U.S.C. §1346, would be available if the labor protection provisions were found to constitute a taking. On October 15, the reorganization court denied the motion to vacate and issued a new order enjoining implementation of the labor protection provisions of the "Rock Island Act, as amended and re-enacted by the Staggers Rail Act." . . . Pursuant to §124(a)(1) of RITA, 45 U.S.C. §1018(a)(1), appellant and the United States appealed this order to the Court of Appeals for the Seventh Circuit. The Court of Appeals affirmed without opinion by an equally divided vote. In re Chicago, Rock Island and Pacific Railroad Co., 645 F.2d 74 (CA 7 1980) (en banc).

. . . We affirm . . . because we conclude that RITA, as amended by the Staggers act, is repugnant to Art. I, §8, cl. 4 of the Constitution, which empowers Congress to enact "uniform Laws on the subject of Bankruptcies throughout the United States." We therefore find it unnecessary to determine whether the employee protections provisions of RITA violate any other provision of the Constitution.

Art. I, §8, cl. 4 of the United States Constitution provides that Congress shall have power to "establish . . . uniform Laws on the subject of Bankruptcies throughout the United States." It is necessary first to determine whether the labor protection provisions of amended RITA are an exercise of Congress' power under the Bankruptcy Clause, as contended by appellees, or under the Commerce Clause, as contended by appellant and the United States. Distinguishing a Congressional exercise of power under the Commerce Clause from an exercise under the Bankruptcy Clause is admittedly not an easy task, for the two clauses are closely related.

---

6. Section 124(c) provides that "nothing in this Act or in the Milwaukee Railroad Restructuring Act shall limit the right of any person to commence an action in the United States Court of Claims under [the Tucker Act.]" 45 U.S.C. §1018(c).

As James Madison observed, "[t]he power of establishing uniform laws of bankruptcy is so intimately connected with the regulation of commerce, and will prevent so many frauds where the parties or their property may lie or be removed into different States that the expediency of it seems not likely to be drawn into question." The Federalist No. 42, p. 285 (N.Y. Heritage Press 1945). See Sturges v. Crowninshield, 4 Wheat. 122, 195, 17 U.S. 122, 195, 4 L.Ed. 529 (1819) (Marshall, C.J.) ("The bankrupt law is said to grow out of the exigencies of commerce.")

Although we have noted that "[t]he subject of bankruptcies is incapable of final definition," we have previously defined "bankruptcy" as the "subject of the relations between an insolvent or nonpaying or fraudulent debtor and his creditors, extending to his and their relief." Wright v. Union Central Ins. Co., 304 U.S. 502, 513-514, 58 S. Ct. 1025, 1031-1032, 82 L. Ed. 1490 (1938). See Continental Bank v. Rock Island Ry., 294 U.S. 648, 673, 55 S. Ct. 595, 605, 79 L. Ed. 1110 (1935). Congress' power under the Bankruptcy Clause "contemplate[s] an adjustment of a failing debtor's obligations." Continental Bank v. Rock Island Ry., supra, at 673, 55 S. Ct., at 605. This power "extends to all cases where the law causes to be distributed, the property of the debtor among his creditors." Hanover National Bank v. Moyses, 186 U.S. 181, 186, 22 S. Ct. 857, 860, 46 L. Ed. 1113 (1902). It "includes the power to discharge the debtor from his contracts and legal liabilities, as well as to distribute his property. The grant to Congress involves the power to impair the obligations of contract, and this the States were forbidden to do." Id., at 188, 22 S. Ct. at 860.

An examination of the employee protection provisions of RITA, we think, demonstrates that RITA is an exercise of Congress' power under the Bankruptcy Clause. Section 106 authorizes the ICC to impose upon the Rock Island estate "a fair and equitable" employee protection arrangement. After such an employee protection arrangement is imposed, "the bankruptcy court shall immediately authorize and direct the Rock Island trustee to . . . immediately implement such arrangement." Section 106(c), 45 U.S.C. §1005(c). Section 106(e)(2) provides that employee protection benefits shall be paid from Rock Island's assets and employee claims shall be treated as administrative expenses of the Rock Island estate. 45 U.S.C. §1005(e)(2). Section 108(a) provides that any employee who elects to receive benefits under §106 "shall be deemed to waive any employee protection benefits otherwise available to such employee" under the Bankruptcy Act, subtitle IV of Title 49 of the United States Code, or any applicable contract or agreement. 45 U.S.C. §1007(a). Claims for "otherwise available" benefits are not accorded priority as an administrative expense of the estate. 45 U.S.C. §1007(c). Under §110, the United States guarantees the Rock Island's employee protections obligations. 45 U.S.C. §1008(a). As with the employee protection obligation itself, the guaranty is treated as an administrative expense of the Rock Island estate. 45 U.S.C. §1008(b).

In sum, RITA imposes upon a bankrupt railroad the duty to pay large sums of money to its displaced employees, and then establishes a mechanism through which these "obligations" are to be satisfied. The Act provides that the claims of these employees are to be accorded priority over the claims of Rock Island's commercial creditors, bondholders, and shareholders. It follows that the subject matter of RITA is the relationship between a bankrupt railroad and its creditors. . . .

The Act goes as far as to alter the relationship among the claimants to the Rock Island estate's remaining assets. In enacting RITA, Congress did nothing less than to prescribe the manner in which the property of the Rock Island estate is to be distributed among its creditors.

The events surrounding the passage of RITA, as well as its legislative history, indicate that Congress was exercising its powers under the Bankruptcy Clause. . . .

We do not understand either appellants or the United States to argue that Congress may enact bankruptcy laws pursuant to its power under the Commerce Clause. Unlike the Commerce Clause, the Bankruptcy Clause itself contains an affirmative limitation or restriction upon Congress' power: Bankruptcy laws must be uniform throughout the United States. Such uniformity in the applicability of legislation is not required by the Commerce Clause. . . .

Thus, if we were to hold that Congress had the power to enact nonuniform bankruptcy laws pursuant to the Commerce Clause, we would eradicate from the Constitution a limitation on the power of Congress to enact bankruptcy laws. It is therefore necessary for us to determine the nature of the uniformity required by the Bankruptcy Clause.

Pursuant to Art. I, §8, cl. 4 of the Constitution, Congress has power to enact bankruptcy laws that are uniform throughout the United States. Prior to today, this Court has never invalidated a bankruptcy law for lack of uniformity. The uniformity requirement is not a straightjacket that forbids Congress from distinguishing among classes of debtors, nor does it prohibit Congress from recognizing that state laws do not treat commercial transactions in a uniform manner. A bankruptcy law may be uniform and yet "may recognize the laws of the State in certain particulars, although such recognition may lead to different results in different States." Stellwagen v. Clum, 245 U.S. 605, 613, 38 S. Ct. 215, 217, 62 L. Ed. 507 (1918). Thus, uniformity does not require the elimination of any differences among the States in their laws governing commercial transactions. Vanston Bondholders Protective Committee v. Green, 329 U.S. 156, 172, 67 S. Ct. 237, 244, 91 L. Ed. 162 (1946) (Frankfurter, J., concurring). In Hanover National Bank v. Moyses, 186 U.S., at 189-190, 22 S. Ct., at 861, this Court held that Congress can give effect to the allowance of exemptions prescribed by state law without violating the uniformity requirement. The uniformity requirement, moreover, permits Congress to treat "railroad bankruptcies as a distinctive and special problem" and "does not deny Congress power to take into account differences that exist between different parts of the country, and to fashion legislation to resolve geographically isolated problems." [Blanchette v. Connecticut General Ins. Corps.] Regional Railroad Reorganization Act Cases, 419 U.S. 102, 159, 95 S. Ct. 335, 366, 42 L. Ed. 2d 320 (1974) (3R Act Cases). In the 3R Act Cases, we upheld Congress' response to the existing rail transportation crisis in the Northeast. Since no railroad reorganization proceeding was then pending outside of the region defined by the Regional Railroad Reorganization Act (3R Act), 87 Stat. 985, 45 U.S.C. §701 et seq., the Act in fact operated uniformly upon all railroads then in bankruptcy proceedings.

But a quite different sort of "uniformity" question is present in this case. By its terms, RITA applies to only one regional bankrupt railroad. *Only* Rock Island's creditors are affected by RITA's employee protection provisions and *only* employees of the Rock Island may take benefit of the arrangement. Unlike the situation in the *3R Act Cases*, there are other railroads that are currently in reorganization proceedings,[11] but these railroads are not affected by the employee protection provisions of RITA. The conclusion is thus inevitable that RITA is not a response either to the particular problems of major railroad bankruptcies or to any geographically isolated problem: it is a response to the problems caused by the bankruptcy of *one* railroad. The employee protection provisions of RITA cover neither a defined class of debtors nor a particular type of problem, but a particular problem of one bankrupt railroad. Albeit on a rather grand scale, RITA is nothing more than a private bill such as those Congress frequently enacts under its authority to spend money.[12]

---

11. At the time RITA was enacted, the New York, Susquehanna and Western Railroad was in the process of liquidation under §77 of the Bankruptcy Act of 1898. In re New York, Susquehanna & Western R.R., 504 F. Supp. 851 (D.N.J. 1980), aff'd, 673 F.2d 1301 (CA3 1981). Another bankrupt railroad is undergoing liquidation proceedings under §§1161-1174 of the Bankruptcy Act of 1978, 92 Stat. 2641, 11 U.S.C. §1162-1174. In re Auto-Train Corp., 11 B.R. 418 (Bkrtcy. D.D.C. 1981). The Milwaukee Road is in an income-based reorganization. That railroad is subject to its own employee protection requirements under §§5 and 9 of the MRRA, 45 U.S.C. §§904, 908. As with the case of §§106 and 108 of RITA, these sections of the MRRA apply only to one railroad. We have occasion in this case to consider the constitutionality of these provisions of the MRRA. Nevertheless, it is no argument that RITA is uniform because another statute imposes similar obligations upon another railroad, as the United States appears to contend. The issue is not whether Congress has discriminated against the Rock Island estate, but whether RITA's employee protection provisions are uniform bankruptcy laws. The uniformity requirement of the Bankruptcy Clause is not an Equal Protection Clause for bankrupts.

12. By its very terms, RITA applies only to the Rock Island. 45 U.S.C. §§1001, 1005, 1007-1008. Thus, we have no occasion to review a bankruptcy law which defines by identifying characteristics a particular class of debtors. Cf. *3R Act Cases,* supra, at 156-160, 95 S. Ct., at 365-367.

The language of the Bankruptcy Clause itself compels us to hold that such a bankruptcy law is not within the power of Congress to enact. A law can hardly be said to be uniform throughout the country if it applies only to one debtor and can be enforced only by the one bankruptcy court having jurisdiction over that debtor. . . . As the legislative history to the Staggers Act indicates, . . . Congress might deem it sound policy to impose labor protection obligations in all bankruptcy proceedings involving major railroads. By its specific terms, however, RITA applies to only one regional bankrupt railroad, and cannot be said to apply uniformly even to major railroads in bankruptcy proceedings throughout the United States. The employee protection provisions of RITA therefore cannot be said to "apply equally to all creditors and all debtors." 3R Act Cases, supra, 419 U.S. at 160, 95 S. Ct., at 367.

Although the debate in the Constitutional Convention regarding the Bankruptcy Clause was meager, we think it lends some support to our conclusion that the uniformity requirement of the Clause prohibits Congress from enacting bankruptcy laws that specifically apply to the affairs of only one named debtor.

The subject of bankruptcy was first introduced on August 29, 1787, by Charles Pinckney during discussion of the Full-Faith and Credit Clause. Pinckney proposed the following grant of authority to Congress: "To establish uniform laws upon the subject of bankruptcies, and respecting the damages arising on the protest of foreign bills of exchange." 2 M. Farrand, The Records of the Federal Convention 447 (1911). Two days later, John Rutledge recommended that the following be added to Congress' powers: "To establish uniform laws on the subject of bankruptcies." Id., at 483. The Bankruptcy Clause was adopted on September 3, 1787, with only Roger Sherman of Connecticut voting against. Id., at 489.[13]

Prior to the drafting of the Constitution, at least four States followed the practice of passing private acts to relieve individual debtors. Nadelmann, On the Origin of the Bankruptcy Clause, 1 Am. J.L. Hist. 215, 221-223 (1957). Given the sovereign status of the States, questions were raised as to whether one State had to recognize the relief given to a debtor by another State. . . . Uniformity among state debtor insolvency laws was an impossibility and the practice of passing private bankruptcy laws was subject to abuse if the legislators were less than honest. Thus, it is not surprising that the Bankruptcy Clause was introduced during the discussion of the Full Faith and Credit Clause. The framers sought to provide Congress with the power to enact uniform laws on the subject enforceable among the States. . . . Similarly, the Bankruptcy Clause's uniformity requirement was drafted in order to prohibit Congress from enacting pri-

---

13. "Mr. Sherman observed that Bankruptcies were in some cases punishable with death by the laws of England—& He did not chuse to grant a power by which that might be done here." Ibid.

vate bankruptcy laws. . . . The States' practice of enacting private bills had rendered uniformity impossible.[14]

Our holding today does not impair Congress' ability under the Bankruptcy Clause to define classes of debtors and to structure relief accordingly. We have upheld bankruptcy laws that apply to a particular industry in a particular region. See *3R Act Cases,* supra. The uniformity requirement, however, prohibits Congress from enacting a bankruptcy law that, by definition, applies only to one regional debtor. To survive scrutiny under the Bankruptcy Clause, a law must at least apply uniformly to a defined class of debtors. A bankruptcy law, such as RITA, confined as it is to the affairs of one named debtor can hardly be considered uniform. To hold otherwise would allow Congress to repeal the uniformity requirement from Art. I, §8, cl. 4 of the Constitution. . . .

[Affirmed.]

Justice MARSHALL, with whom Justice BRENNAN joins, concurring in the judgment.

I agree with the Court that the Rock Island Transition and Employee Assistance Act (RITA) violates the uniformity requirement of the Bankruptcy Clause. I write separately, however, because the Court accords a broader scope to that requirement than the Clause's language, its history, and the Court's cases justify. In particular, I am concerned that the Court's rationale may unduly restrict Congress' power to legislate with respect to the distinctive needs of a particular railroad or its employees. I conclude that the Clause permits such legislation if Congress finds that the application of the law to a single debtor (or limited class of debtors) serves a national interest apart from the economic interests of that debtor or class, and if the identified national interest justifies Congress' failure to apply the law to other debtors. However, because RITA does not satisfy this more stringent test, I agree that RITA is unconstitutional.

The Court argues that the uniformity requirement forbids Congress from enacting any bankruptcy law affecting a single debtor. But I do not believe that uniformity invariably requires that a bankruptcy law apply to a multiplicity of debtors. The term "uniform" does not necessarily imply either that the law must avoid specifying the debtors to which it applies or that the law must affect more than a single debtor. As we have noted in different contexts, a named individual may constitute a "legitimate class of one". Nixon v. Administrator of General Services, 433 U.S. 425, 472, 97

14. The framers' intent to achieve uniformity among the nations's bankruptcy laws is also reflected in the Contracts Clause. Apart from and independently of the Supremacy Clause, the Contracts Clause forbids the States from enacting debtor relief laws which discharge the debtor from his obligations, Sturges v. Crowninshield, 4 Wheat., at 197-199, 17 U.S., at 197-199, 4 L. Ed. 529, unless the law operates prospectively. Ogden v. Saunders, 12 Wheat. 213, 25 U.S. 213, 6 L. Ed. 606 (1827).

S. Ct. 2777, 2805, 53 L. Ed. 2d 867 (1977) (rejecting claim that statute applying, and referring by name, only to a single former President is a Bill of Attainder). . . .

In reviewing the scanty history of the Clause, the Court notes that one principal purpose was to avoid conflict between state laws concerning debtor insolvency. That concern, of course, is satisfied simply by uniform interstate application of federal bankruptcy laws under the Supremacy Clause. Another purpose, according to the Court, may have been to prevent the passage of private acts to relieve individual debtors. However, the references to private acts contained in the debates may have been intended only as examples of the first problem, in that other states failed to give credit to such acts. To the extent that the Framers were concerned about the passage of private acts, the question remains whether they intended to prohibit all such acts, and thus to disable Congress from enacting legislation applying to a specified debtor but promoting more general national policies than the simple economic interests of the debtor.

Our cases do not support the Court's view that any bankruptcy law applying to a single named debtor is unconstitutional. In the most relevant case, Regional Rail Reorganization Act Cases, 419 U.S. 102, 95 S. Ct. 335, 42 L. Ed. 2d 320 (1974) (3R Act Cases), this Court held that the Regional Rail Reorganization Act did not violate the uniformity clause even though it applied only to eight railroads in a specified geographic region. The Court squarely rejected the argument that the geographic nonuniformity of the Rail Act violated the Bankruptcy Clause. "The argument has a certain surface appeal but is without merit because it overlooks the flexibility inherent in the constitutional provision." Id., at 158, 95 S. Ct., at 366. Reviewing earlier cases, the Court emphasized Congress' power to recognize geographic differences and "to fashion legislation to resolve geographically isolated problems." Id., at 159, 95 S. Ct. at 366. The Court also noted that no other railroad was in reorganization during the time that the Act applied. The Court concluded that the Act satisfies the uniformity requirement because it is "designed to solve 'the evil to be remedied.' " Id., at 161, 95 S. Ct., at 367, quoting Head Money Cases, [Edye v. Robertson] 112 U.S. 580, 595, 5 S. Ct. 247, 252, 28 L. Ed. 798 (1884).

The Court's analysis in this case, too, "has a certain surface appeal." If a law applies to one debtor, it is invalid; if it applies to more than one debtor, it is valid if it satisfies the 3R Act Cases test, i.e., if it was designed to solve an identified evil. But there is nothing magical about a law that specifies only one object. I discern no principled ground for refusing to apply the same test without regard to the number of businesses regulated by the law.[1]

---

1. The Court implies that a law which is general in its terms but in operation applies only to a single debtor might satisfy the uniformity requirement. Again, such a formalistic requirement is not a principled reason for striking down Congressional legislation.

I would apply the *3R Act Cases* test in every instance. Congress may specify what debtors, or (which is often the same thing) what portion of the country, will be subject to bankruptcy legislation. The constraint of uniformity, however, requires Congress to legislate uniformly with respect to an identified "evil." In the Regional Rail Reorganization Act, Congress imposed certain requirements on all railroads in reorganization; all were deemed to present the same "evil." If Congress has legislated pursuant to its bankruptcy power, furthering federal bankruptcy policies, and if the specificity of the legislation is defensible in terms of those policies, then, but only then, has Congress satisfied the uniformity requirement. Where, as here, the law subjects one named debtor to special treatment, I would require especially clear findings to justify the narrowness of the law.

Although the question is close, I conclude that Congress did not justify the specificity of RITA in terms of national policy. Rather, the legislative history indicates an attempt simply to protect employees of a single railroad from the consequences of bankruptcy. No explanation for the specificity of the law is given that would justify such narrow application. In its statutory findings, Congress stated that "uninterrupted continuation of services over Rock Island lines is dependent on adequate employee protection provisions," and that a cessation of services would seriously affect certain state economies and the shipping public. 45 U.S.C. §1001. The findings explicitly refer, however, only to the Rock Island railroad. To be sure, in the legislative history Congress did recite more general purposes. Congressional reports advert to the need for labor protection in "bankruptcy proceedings involving major rail carriers," H. Conf. Rep. No. 96-1430, p. 139 (1980), U.S. Code Cong. & Admin. News 1980, p. 4171, and the need "to avoid disruption of rail service and undue displacement of employees." H. Conf. Rep. No. 96-1041, p. 26 (1980), U.S. Code Cong. & Admin. News 1980, pp. 1156, 1187. See S. Rep. No. 96-614, p. 5 (1980). But recitation of a general purpose does not justify narrow application to a single debtor where, as here, that purpose does not explain the nonuniform treatment of other comparable railroads that are now, or may be, in reorganization. . . .

With respect to such railroads, reorganization will result in the same displacement of employees and disruption of service — the same "evil" — that Congress purported to address in RITA. Because Congress' findings fail to demonstrate that the narrowness of RITA is addressed to a particular kind of problem, the law does not satisfy the uniformity requirement.

I agree with the Court that "[t]he employee protection provisions of RITA cover neither a defined class of debtors nor a particular type of problem, but a particular problem of one bankrupt railroad." . . . I do not agree that Congress may not legislate with respect to a single debtor, even if only that debtor presents "a particular type of problem." If, for example, Conrail were to fail, I cannot believe that Congress would be prohibited from enacting legislation addressed to the peculiar problems created by the bankruptcy of one of the nation's principal freight carriers.[2]

For the foregoing reasons, I concur in the result reached by the Court.

NOTES

1. Note the Court's discussion of the *3R Act Cases*. Had Congress enacted RITA more generally (for example by having it apply to all railroads in bankruptcy on the date of the enactment with assets over a certain amount), would the statute have met the uniformity requirement? See footnotes 11 and 12.

2. One view of uniformity would require "that the bankruptcy law, including the permissible exemptions, be identical in the fifty states," In re Sullivan, 680 F.2d 1131, 1133 (7th Cir. 1982), referring to Note, Bankruptcy Exemptions: Whether Illinois's Use of the Federal 'Opt Out' Provision is Constitutional, 1981 S. Ill. U.L.J. 65, 72. Another view would require only "geographical uniformity," a concept that emerged in tax cases, where there was a demonstrated intent of the framers to avoid discrimination among the states. See, e.g., Fairbank v. United States, 181 U.S. 283, 298 (1901). Still another view of uniformity, at least in bankruptcy, is that it is designed to eliminate discrimination among debtors. Which view is more persuasive? Are there others? Which view does *Gibbons* adopt?

NOTE ON *GIBBONS* AND THE LIMITS OF BANKRUPTCY POLICY

Whatever the merits of the ultimate decision, there may be a deeper lesson to be learned from *Gibbons*. *Gibbons* was brought about because Congress, responding to special interests, used its power to enact bankruptcy laws to create new substantive rights. Although the creation of many substantive rights may be within the scope of Congress's power under the bankruptcy clause, they turn away from the central purpose of bankruptcy law, a purpose that is served, in the first instance, by creating procedural rules rather than substantive rights. Bankruptcy law will probably continue to undergo the dramatic changes it has seen in the last two

---

2. It is indeed ironic that under the Court's approach, bankruptcy legislation respecting Conrail might be invalid. Conrail was created by the 3R Act, which reorganized eight bankrupt railroads into a single viable system operated by a private, for profit corporation. It is difficult to understand why legislation affecting the eight railroads passed constitutional muster in the *3R Act Cases*, supra, 419 U.S. at 156-161, 95 S. Ct., at 365-367, yet legislation affecting their successor might not.

decades. As it increases in importance, the potential it has to do good or ill rises in the same proportion.

Bankruptcy law in the 1980s confronts two fundamental dangers. The first follows from the kind of special interest lobbying that brought about *Gibbons.* The 1984 Amendments contain provisions (such as special rights for United States fishermen) that are special interest legislation of the most naked kind. We can expect more as bankruptcy law grows in importance. But the greater danger may be one of good intentions gone awry. A bankruptcy proceeding typically begins only after a debtor comes upon economic misfortune. If it were possible, we would want a bankruptcy proceeding to cure all the problems that brought on the debtor's collapse. Legal rules, however, cannot cure nonlegal problems. Legal rules cannot make the imprudent and unlucky, wise and fortunate. Legal rules can determine who owns property, but they cannot ensure that the property is used effectively.

The goals of the bankruptcy process should be modest. Individuals should be given a fresh start. Ownership interests in corporations can be changed or readjusted. A bankruptcy proceeding should ensure that individuals can begin again and that firms that can and should survive do survive. But bankruptcy law cannot work miracles, and more harm than good comes from seeking that which cannot be had.

TABLE OF CASES

TABLE OF STATUTES

Bankruptcy Code		§303(b)	42, 72, 74, 75, 77,
			78, 79, 86, 88, 97,
§101(4)	72, 74, 76, 124, 133,		990, 1014
	135, 136, 144, 147,	§303(b)(1)	72, 73, 80
	302, 367, 379, 396,	§303(b)(2)	73
	686, 688, 744, 811	§303(b)(3)	67
§101(8)	54, 59	§303(c)	72
§101(9)	72, 76, 121, 124,	§303(d)	78
	133, 135, 144, 147,	§303(e)	79, 87
	284, 811	§303(g)	989
§101(10)	80, 435	§303(h)	43, 78, 79, 82, 86,
§101(11)	302, 811		87, 97, 435, 989
§101(12)	54, 59	§303(h)(1)	81, 83, 84, 85, 86,
§101(14)	60		88, 96, 1014
§101(17)	71	§303(h)(2)	80, 245, 1014
§101(18)	71	§303(i)	79, 87, 115
§101(27)	912, 921	§305	43, 87, 99, 115, 116,
§101(28)	266, 285, 286, 295,		117
	332	§305(a)	114
§101(29)	44, 81, 82, 284	§321	989
§101(33)	54, 59	§322	989
§101(36)	65	§323(a)	989
§101(48)	277, 284, 285, 335,	§323(b)	367
	368	§324	990
§102(1)	154	§326	992
§103(a)	936	§330	550, 992
§103(b)	909	§331	992
§104	74	§341(a)	127, 993
§105	362, 369, 391, 392,	§341(c)	993
	403, 482, 500, 533,	§343	993
	535	§344	994
§108	488, 498, 499	§361	43, 403, 413, 425,
§108(b)	367, 500		429, 488, 572
§108(c)	367	§361(1)	425
§109	60, 65, 67	§361(3)	433
§109(a)	59, 64	§362	43, 117, 133, 153,
§109(b)	65, 66		183, 217, 230, 343,
§109(b)(2)	66, 67		359, 362, 363, 367,
§109(d)	66		368, 392, 413, 435,
§109(e)	66, 908, 912, 921		450, 451, 452, 489,
			500, 521, 522, 549,
§301	42, 60, 67, 97, 989		572, 761
§302	585, 848	§362(a)	363, 367, 396, 403
§303	70, 72, 73, 80, 81,	§362(a)(1)	367, 389
	97, 114, 115, 117,	§362(a)(3)	367, 450, 489, 492
	562	§362(a)(4)	303, 367
§303(a)	12	§362(a)(5)	368

1035

INDEX